Pro Spring 6 with Kotlin

An In-depth Guide to Using Kotlin APIs
in Spring Framework 6

Peter Späth
Iuliana Cosmina
Rob Harrop
Chris Schaefer

Apress®

Pro Spring 6 with Kotlin: An In-depth Guide to Using Kotlin APIs in Spring Framework 6

Peter Späth
Leipzig, Sachsen, Germany

Iuliana Cosmina
Edinburgh, UK

Rob Harrop
Reddish, UK

Chris Schaefer
Venice, FL, USA

ISBN-13 (pbk): 978-1-4842-9556-4
https://doi.org/10.1007/978-1-4842-9557-1

ISBN-13 (electronic): 978-1-4842-9557-1

Managing Director, Apress Media LLC: Welmoed Spahr
Acquisitions Editor: Melissa Duffy
Development Editor: Laura Berendson
Coordinating Editor: Mark Powers
Copy Editor: Bill McManus

Cover designed by eStudioCalamar

Cover image by Jack Blueberry on Unsplash (https://unsplash.com)

Distributed to the book trade worldwide by Apress Media, LLC, 1 New York Plaza, New York, NY 10004, U.S.A. Phone 1-800-SPRINGER, fax (201) 348-4505, e-mail orders-ny@springer-sbm.com, or visit www.springeronline.com. Apress Media, LLC is a California LLC, and the sole member (owner) is Springer Science + Business Media Finance Inc. (SSBM Finance Inc.). SSBM Finance Inc. is a **Delaware** corporation.

For information on translations, please e-mail booktranslations@springernature.com; for reprint, paperback, or audio rights, please e-mail bookpermissions@springernature.com.

Apress titles may be purchased in bulk for academic, corporate, or promotional use. eBook versions and licenses are also available for most titles. For more information, reference our Print and eBook Bulk Sales web page at https://www.apress.com/bulk-sales.

Any source code or other supplementary material referenced by the authors in this book is available to readers on GitHub (https://github.com/Apress). For more detailed information, please visit https://www.apress.com/gp/services/source-code.

Paper in this product is recyclable

To Alina
—Peter

Table of Contents

About the Authors

Peter Späth graduated in 2002 as a physicist and soon afterward became an IT consultant, mainly for Java-related projects. In 2016, he decided to concentrate on writing books on various aspects, but with a main focus on software development. With two books about graphics and sound processing, three books on Android app development, and a couple of books about Java, Jakarta EE, and Kotlin, Späth continues his effort in writing software development–related literature.

Iuliana Cosmina is a Spring Certified Web Developer and a Spring Certified Core Spring Professional. She is a Spring certified expert, as defined by Pivotal, the makers of Spring Framework, Spring Boot, and other tools. Cosmina has authored books with Apress on Core Spring certification and Spring Certified web development. She is a Lead Engineer at Cloudsoft, located in Edinburgh, Scotland, and is an active coder and software contributor on Apache Brooklyn, GitHub, StackOverflow, and more.

Rob Harrop is a software consultant specializing in delivering high-performance, highly scalable enterprise applications. He is an experienced architect with a particular flair for understanding and solving complex design issues. With a thorough knowledge of both Java and .NET, Harrop has successfully deployed projects across both platforms. He also has extensive experience across a variety of sectors, retail and government in particular. Harrop is the author of five books, including the book you are currently reading, not at its sixth edition, a widely acclaimed, comprehensive resource on the Spring Framework.

Chris Schaefer is a principle software developer for Spring projects at Pivotal, the makers of Spring Framework, Boot, and other Spring tools.

About the Technical Reviewer

Massimo Nardone has more than 25 years of experience in security, web/mobile development, cloud, and IT architecture. His true IT passions are security and Android. He has been programming and teaching how to program with Android, Perl, PHP, Java, VB, Python, C/C++, and MySQL for more than 20 years. He holds a master of science degree in computing science from the University of Salerno, Italy. He has worked as a CISO, CSO, security executive, IoT executive, project manager, software engineer, research engineer, chief security architect, PCI/SCADA auditor, and senior lead IT security/cloud/SCADA architect for many years. His technical skills include security, Android, cloud, Java, MySQL, Drupal, Cobol, Perl, web and mobile development, MongoDB, D3, Joomla, Couchbase, C/C++, WebGL, Python, Pro Rails, Django CMS, Jekyll, Scratch, and more. He worked as visiting lecturer and supervisor for exercises at the Networking Laboratory of the Helsinki University of Technology (Aalto University). He holds four international patents (PKI, SIP, SAML, and Proxy areas). He is currently working for Cognizant as head of cyber security and CISO to help both internally and externally with clients in areas of information and cyber security, like strategy, planning, processes, policies, procedures, governance, awareness, and so forth. In June 2017 he became a permanent member of the ISACA Finland Board.

Massimo has reviewed more than 45 IT books for different publishing companies and is the co-author of *Pro Spring Security: Securing Spring Framework 5 and Boot 2-based Java Applications* (Apress, 2019), *Beginning EJB in Java EE 8* (Apress, 2018), *Pro JPA 2 in Java EE 8* (Apress, 2018), and *Pro Android Games* (Apress, 2015).

Introduction

Covering version 6 of the Spring Framework, this book is the most comprehensive Spring reference and practical guide available for harnessing the power of this leading enterprise Java application development framework.

This edition covers core Spring and its integration with other leading Java technologies, such as Hibernate, JPA 3, Thymeleaf, Kafka, GraphQL, and WebFlux, using Kotlin as a programming language. The focus of the book is on using Kotlin configuration classes, lambda expressions, Spring Boot, and reactive programming. We share our insights and real-world experiences with enterprise application development, including remoting, transactions, web and presentation tiers, and much more.

With *Pro Spring 6 with Kotlin*, you'll learn how to do the following:

- Use inversion of control (IoC) and dependency injection (DI)

- Discover what is new in Spring Framework 6

- Build Spring-based web applications using Spring MVC and WebSocket

- Build Spring web reactive applications with Spring WebFlux

- Test Spring applications using Junit 5

- Genuinely use Kotlin constructs

- Use Spring Boot to an advanced level to get any kind of Spring application up and running in no time

- Package your Spring Native application into a Docker image with Cloud Native Buildpacks

There is a multimodule project associated with this book, configured using Gradle 8. The project is available on the Apress official repository: `https://github.com/apress/pro-spring-6-kotlin`. The project can be built immediately after cloning according to the instructions in its README.adoc file. If you do not have Gradle installed locally, you can rely on IntelliJ IDEA to download it and use it to build your project by using the Gradle Wrapper (`https://docs.gradle.org/current/userguide/gradle_wrapper.html`).

As the book was being written, new versions of Spring 6 and Spring Boot 3 were released, a new version of IntelliJ IDEA was released, and new versions of Gradle and other technologies used in the book were updated. We upgraded to the new versions to provide the most recent information and keep this book synchronized with the official documentation. Several reviewers have checked the book for technical accuracy, but if you notice any inconsistencies, please send an email to editorial@apress.com and errata will be created.

You can access the example source code for this book at `https://github.com/apress/pro-spring-6-kotlin`. It will be maintained, synchronized with new versions of the technologies, and enriched based on the recommendations of the developers using it to learn Spring.

We truly hope you will enjoy using this book to learn Spring as much as we enjoyed writing it.

CHAPTER 1

Introducing Spring

Every year there are tweets and blog posts announcing that Java is no longer relevant and there is a shiny new technology taking its place. And every year these turn out to be just industry rumors. Java is an ever-evolving technology that has been in the top 10 of most used technologies by companies to build software solutions since its initial release in 1995. A lot of libraries and frameworks have been built on Java, some of them available to developers as open source projects, others safely locked away in a private cloud because of the sensitive information they manage(e.g., banking applications).

One of the most popular frameworks written in Java is the Spring Framework. The first version of Spring was released in October 2002 and consisted of a small core with an inversion of control container that was easy to configure and use. Over the years the Spring Framework has become the main replacement of Java Enterprise Edition (JEE) servers and has grown into a full-blown technology made up of many distinct projects, each with its own purpose. Whether you want to build microservices applications, build classical Enterprise Resource Planning (ERPs), or compile your app into a native image to run on GraalVM, Spring has a project for that.

Throughout this book, you will see many applications of different open source technologies, all of which are unified under the Spring Framework. When working with Spring, application developers can use a large variety of open source tools, without needing to write reams of code and without coupling their application too closely to any particular tool.

This is an introductory chapter that covers important details about this book, introduces you to the Spring Framework, explains why understanding Spring in depth is so useful for developers, and describes how powerful Spring can be when used correctly. If you are already familiar with Spring, you might want to skip this chapter and proceed straight to **Chapter 2**.

About This Book

Covering version 6 of the Spring Framework, this book is the most comprehensive Spring reference and practical guide available for harnessing the power of this leading enterprise Java application development framework when using Kotlin as a programming language.

This edition covers core Spring and its integration with other leading Java technologies, such as Hibernate, JPA 2, Thymeleaf, Apache Kafka, and others. The focus of the book is on using Kotlin as a programming language for Spring, Java/Kotlin configuration classes, Spring Boot, and reactive programming. We share our insights and real-world experiences with enterprise application development, including remoting, transactions, the web and presentation tiers, and much more.

With Pro Spring 6 with Kotlin, you'll learn how to do the following:

- Use and understand inversion of control (IoC) and dependency injection (DI)

- Discover what's new in Spring Framework 6

- Build Spring-based web applications using Spring MVC and WebSocket

© Peter Späth, Iuliana Cosmina, Rob Harrop, Chris Schaefer 2023
P. Späth et al., *Pro Spring 6 with Kotlin*, https://doi.org/10.1007/978-1-4842-9557-1_1

- Test Spring applications using Junit 5 and other Java/Kotlin testing libraries

- Utilize the capabilities of Kotlin 1.8

- Use Spring Boot to an advanced level, but learn how to do without it as well

- Secure Spring applications

- Monitor Spring applications

- Write reactive applications using Spring

- Build your Spring application and run it on a compact native image with Spring Native

To make sure the focus of the book is on Spring and Kotlin, instructions on how to install additional technologies mentioned in the book are provided in documentation files for each project in the book repository. This, of course, will be pointed out to you in the book when necessary.

What Is Spring?

Perhaps one the hardest parts of explaining Spring is classifying exactly what it is. **Spring** was described since the beginning as a *lightweight framework* for building Java applications, but that statement brings up two interesting points:

- You can use Spring to build any application in Java/Kotlin (for example, stand-alone, web, mobile, or JEE applications), unlike many other frameworks (such as Apache Struts, which is limited to web applications).

- The *lightweight* part of the description is not related to the number of classes or the size of the distribution but rather defines the principle of the Spring philosophy as a whole—that is, *minimal impact*. Spring is lightweight in the sense that you have to make few, if any, changes to your application code to gain the benefits of the Spring Core, and should you choose to stop using Spring at any point, you will find that doing so is quite simple.

Notice that we qualified that last statement to refer to the Spring Core only—many of the extra Spring components, such as data access, require a much closer coupling to the Spring Framework. However, the benefits of this coupling are quite clear, and throughout the book we present techniques for minimizing the impact this has on your application. Also, if coupling your code to a framework brings with it development speed and better dependency management, which reduces the number of build failures during upgrades, isn't the price worth it? Also, with Spring Native, Spring applications now can be run on native images(e.g., GraalVM) that provide various advantages, such as an instant startup and reduced memory consumption, so gone are the days when JavaScript or .NET developers could diss on Spring by saying it is *heavyweight*.

Evolution of the Spring Framework

The Spring Framework originated from the book *Expert One-on-One: J2EE Design and Development* by Rod Johnson (Wrox, 2002). In his book, Johnson presented his own framework, called the Interface 21 Framework, which he developed to use in his own applications. Released into the open source world, this framework formed the foundation of the Spring Framework as we know it today. Over the last decade, the Spring Framework has grown dramatically in core functionality, associated projects, and community support. Spring 0.9 started as a community project made of a few core modules and without an official documentation. VMware took it over and started its transition from XML to Java Config (using annotations) in version **2.5**.

In 2012, Pivotal Software split from VMware and took over Spring and grew it from a framework to a collection of projects. There were two major releases under Pivotal: **4.x**, which was the first version to fully support Java 8, and **5.x**, which dropped support for XML configurations completely.

Together with Spring 4.x, Spring Boot was released and became one of the most used Spring projects. Spring Boot takes an opinionated view of building Spring applications. Developers at Pivotal have identified a few types of applications being built and have created templates for them using a set of default component dependencies and automatic configuration of components. These application templates are modeled by a set of Spring Boot starter projects. For example, if you would want to create a Spring web application, just add the `spring-boot-starter-web` dependency to your project and you have a minimal, Spring web application with default configurations. This is possible because Spring Boot has some cool features such as embedded application server (Jetty/Tomcat), a command-line interface based on Groovy, and health/metrics monitoring.

Spring Boot provides the ability to develop applications quickly, based on a stable, curated set of dependencies with all the required Spring Framework components configured correctly. This is good because it reduces the developer setup effort. However, this also reduces the need for a deeper understanding of the Spring Framework, which might trick developers into a false sense of confidence in their knowledge and understanding of the Spring Framework.

■ **Note**   In the previous edition of this book, this chapter contained a list with all the Spring versions ever release and their most important features. Since that information is available publicly on the internet, a decision was made to skip that to reduce the book in size and also dedicate that space to something more interesting such as Project Reactor[1] and Spring Native[2].

At the end of 2019, VMware bought Pivotal Software and took over Spring again, so at the end of 2021, Spring **6.x** will be out, the first major Spring Release under VMware. At the time this chapter is being written, the first milestone has already been released and the most important thing about it is that the codebase has been upgraded to JDK 17. This version is considered the first JDK[3] produced by Oracle that provides enough performance and security improvements for a migration from 1.8 to be worth it for companies that are (still) reluctant to do so.

A lot of deprecated classes and packages that provided support for deprecated third-party technologies have been removed and existing classes have been updated to work with newer versions of certain technologies (for example: Tomcat 10, Jetty 11, or Undertow 2.2.14)

Spring Projects

The current Spring Projects are listed on the official Spring site[4], but for your convenience here is a list of them with a short summary of each.

- **Spring Boot** consists of a set of libraries (called *starters*) that provide default application templates that can be customized easily to quickly develop multiple types of stand-alone, production-grade Spring-based applications.

---

[1] https://projectreactor.io
[2] https://docs.spring.io/spring-native/docs/current/reference/htmlsingle
[3] https://blogs.oracle.com/javamagazine/post/its-time-to-move-your-applications-to-java-17-heres-why-and-heres-how
[4] https://spring.io/projects

- **Spring Framework** consists of a set of libraries that provide support for dependency injection, transaction management, data access, messaging, and other core functionalities for any type of application. The Spring Framework now includes the Spring WebFlux framework that represents the Spring reactive-stack designed to build fully non-blocking, with back-pressure support reactive applications on servers such as Netty, Undertow, and Servlet 3.1+ containers.

- **Spring Data** consists of a set of libraries that provide a consistent programming model for accessing various databases both relational (e.g., MySQL and Oracle) and nonrelational (e.g., MongoDB and CouchBase). Support for in-memory databases (e.g., H2 and MongoDB) is included, which is pretty useful for testing applications without the drag of a concrete database. Also, Spring Data R2DBC makes it easy to access reactive databases.

- **Spring Security** provides the ability to secure applications easily, with a simple model for authentication and authorization.

- **Spring Cloud** provides a set of common tools for writing microservices applications destined to run in distributed systems.

- **Spring Cloud Data Flow** provides a set of common tools for streaming and batch processing of data between microservices running in Cloud Foundry and Kubernetes.

- **Spring Integration** provides support for building Spring applications that make use of lightweight messaging and integrate with external systems via declarative adapters.

- **Spring Session** provides an API and implementations for managing a user's session information.

- **Spring HATEOAS** provides some APIs to ease creating REST representations that follow the HATEOAS principle when working with Spring and especially Spring MVC. Some developers/architects consider that the hypermedia[5] pollutes the REST data and a better solution is to use Swagger[6] to expose (and document) an application's API or Spring REST Docs.

- **Spring for GraphQL** provides the tools to build Spring applications on GraphQL Java. GraphQL[7] is a query language to retrieve data from a server.

- **Spring REST Docs** provides the tools to expose and document a Spring application's API.

- **Spring Batch** is a framework that provides the tools to build lightweight and robust Spring applications that handle immense volumes of data.

- **Spring AMQP** provides the tools to build AMQP-based messaging solutions using Spring.

- **Spring CredHub** is part of the Spring Cloud project family and provides client-side support for storing, retrieving, and deleting credentials from a CredHub server running in a CloudFoundry platform.

---

[5] https://en.wikipedia.org/wiki/HATEOAS
[6] https://swagger.io
[7] https://www.graphql-java.com

- **Spring Flo** is a JavaScript library that offers a basic embeddable HTML5 visual builder for pipelines and simple graphs. Spring Cloud Data Flow is an extension of this project.

- **Spring for Apache Kafka** provides tools for building Kafka-based messaging solutions using Spring.

- **Spring LDAP** is a library to simplify LDAP programming in Java, built on the same principles as Spring JDBC.

- **Spring Shell** provides the tools to build a full-featured shell (aka command line) application by depending on the Spring Shell jars and adding their own commands (which come as methods on Spring beans).

- **Spring Statemachine** is a framework for application developers to use state machine concepts with Spring applications.

- **Spring Vault** provides familiar Spring abstractions and client-side support for accessing, storing, and revoking secrets. It offers both low-level and high-level abstractions for interacting with HashiCorp's Vault[8], freeing the user from infrastructural concerns.

- **Spring Web Flow** extends Spring MVC to provide the tools for implementing the "flows" of a web application. A flow encapsulates a sequence of steps that guide a user through the execution of some business task. It spans multiple HTTP requests, has state, deals with transactional data, is reusable, and may be dynamic and long-running in nature.

- **Spring Web Services** (Spring-WS) is a product of the Spring community focused on creating document-driven web services. Spring Web Services aims to facilitate contract-first SOAP service development, allowing for the creation of flexible web services using one of the many ways to manipulate XML payloads.

- **Spring Native** (currently still considered experimental, but quicky being adopted in the industry) provides support for compiling Spring applications to native executables using the GraalVM native-image compiler.

- **Spring Initializr** (not actually a project, but good to know), available at `https://start.spring.io`, provides a quick start for creating custom Spring Boot projects completely configurable according to the developer's necessities: programming language, build tool, Spring Boot version, and project requirements (database access, web access, event messaging, security, etc.).

There are a few projects that over the years have lost the developer community's interest (e.g., Spring Scala) and are now in a state called *in the attic*. If developers' interest continues to drop, these projects will be archived and others will surely take their place. If you want to keep up to date with the Spring projects ecosystem, check `https://spring.io/projects` from time to time.

That's enough about Spring projects to pique your interest; let's talk more in depth about Spring.

---

[8] `https://www.vaultproject.io`

Inverting Control or Injecting Dependencies?

The core of the Spring Framework is based on the principle of **inversion of control (IoC)**. IoC is a technique that externalizes the creation and management of component dependencies. The action performed by any program (not only Java) is the result of interaction between its interdependent components, usually named objects. Explaining IoC also requires an explanation of **dependency injection (DI)**, a concept that describes how dependent objects are connected at runtime by an external party. Take a look at Figure 1-1, which depicts two types of relationships between objects and how those objects "meet" each other.

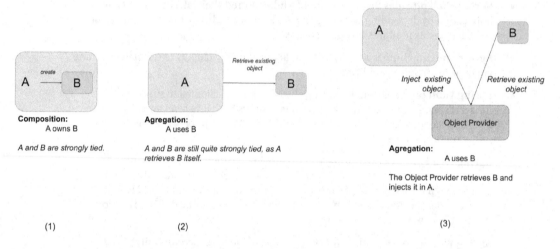

Figure 1-1. *Object relationships and how they "meet"*

Object A needs an object of type B to perform its functions, thus *A depends on B*. The ways these two objects get to interact shown in Figure 1-1 can be explained as follows:

- *Composition*: Object A directly creates object B. This ties them together, and basically object B exists as long as object A exists. This situation is depicted in section (1) in Figure 1-1.

- *Aggregation*: Object A itself retrieves object B that already exists. This ties them together as well, and object B must exist as long as object A needs it to. Also, object A must include the logic to be able to retrieve object B. This situation is depicted in section (2) in Figure 1-1.

Dependency injection allows severing that tie, as depicted in section (3) in Figure 1-1, by using an external party to provide object B to object A, which is still aggregation, but with no direct ties and a twist.

Inversion of control is a design principle in which generic reusable components are used to control the execution of problem-specific code, as in retrieving dependencies. Thus, you can say that Spring is a **dependency handler** used to perform dependency injection, and it was designed following the IoC principle, also known as the Hollywood Principle: *Don't call us, we'll call you.*

Spring's DI implementation is based on two core Java/Kotlin concepts: JavaBeans (also known as POJOs, plain old Java objects) and interfaces. When you use Spring as the DI provider, you gain the flexibility of defining dependency configuration within your applications in different ways. Up to Spring 2.5, XML was the only way to do it. Spring 2.5 introduced a few annotations to support configuration within the code. Spring 3 introduced Java/Kotlin configuration classes, which became the norm, although XML is still supported in case you really need it. Starting with version 4, Spring provides support for Groovy-based configurations. This means that Groovy classes can be legitimate Spring beans.

JavaBeans (POJOs) provide a standard mechanism for creating Java/Kotlin resources that are configurable in a number of ways, such as constructors and setter methods. In **Chapter 3**, you will see how Spring uses the JavaBean specification to form the core of its DI configuration model; in fact, any Spring-managed resource is referred to as a *bean*. If you are unfamiliar with JavaBeans, we present a quick primer at the beginning of **Chapter 3**.

Interfaces and DI are technologies that are mutually beneficial. Clearly designing and coding an application to interfaces makes for a flexible application, but the complexity of wiring together an application designed using interfaces is quite high and places an additional coding burden on developers. By using DI, you reduce to almost zero the amount of code you need to use an interface-based design in your application. Likewise, by using interfaces, you can get the most out of DI because your beans can utilize any interface implementation to satisfy their dependency. The use of interfaces also allows Spring to utilize JDK dynamic proxies (the Proxy pattern) to provide powerful concepts such as aspect-oriented programming (AOP) for crosscutting concerns.

In the context of DI, Spring acts more like a container than a framework—providing instances of your application classes with all the dependencies they need—but it does so in a much less intrusive way. Using Spring for DI relies on nothing more than following the JavaBeans naming conventions within your classes—there are no special classes from which to inherit or proprietary naming schemes to follow. If anything, the only change you make in an application that uses DI is to expose more properties on your JavaBeans, thus allowing more dependencies to be injected at runtime.

Evolution of Dependency Injection

In the past few years, thanks to the popularity gained by Spring and other DI frameworks, DI has gained wide acceptance among Java developer communities. At the same time, developers were convinced that using DI was a best practice in application development, and the benefits of using DI were also well understood. The popularity of DI was acknowledged when the Java Community Process (JCP) adopted JSR-330 ("Dependency Injection for Java") in 2009. JSR-330 had become a formal Java specification request, and as you might expect, one of the specification leads was Rod Johnson—the founder of the Spring Framework.

In JEE 6, JSR-330 became one of the included specifications of the entire technology stack. In the meantime, the EJB architecture (starting from version 3.0) was also revamped dramatically; it adopted the DI model in order to ease the development of various Enterprise JavaBeans apps.

Although we leave the full discussion of DI until Chapter 3, it is worth taking a look at the benefits of using DI rather than a more traditional approach.

- *Reduced glue code*: DI dramatically reduces the amount of code you have to write to glue the components of your application together. Code required to glue components together is often trivial, but repetitive, and a lot of it can increase the overall complexity of your solution. It gets trickier when you need to look up dependencies in a Java Naming and Directory Interface (JNDI) repository or when the dependencies cannot be invoked directly, as is the case with remote resources. In these cases, DI can really simplify the glue code by providing automatic JNDI lookup and automatic proxying of remote resources.

- *Simplified application configuration*: A variety of ways can be used to configure classes that are injectable to other classes. You can use the same technique to express the dependency requirements to the "injector" for injecting the appropriate bean instance or property. In addition, DI makes it much simpler to swap one implementation of a dependency for another. For example, using DI, a DAO component that performs data operations against a PostgreSQL database can easily be switched to perform the same operations on an Oracle database via configuration (as you will see in **Chapter 6**).

- *Ability to manage common dependencies in a single repository*: Using a traditional approach to dependency management of common services—for example, data source connection, transaction, and remote services—you create instances (or lookup from some factory classes) of your dependencies where they are needed (within the dependent class). This causes the dependencies to spread across the classes in your application, and changing them can prove problematic. When you use DI, all the information about those common dependencies is contained in a single repository, making the management of dependencies much simpler and less error-prone.

- *Improved testability*: Classes designed for DI are easily testable because dependencies can be replaced easily. For example, if you want to test a DAO component, you can replace the concrete database with an in-memory database via configuration. This has the benefit of your tests being executed faster but within an appropriate context that mimics as much as possible a production environment. This mechanism can be extended for testing any tier of your application and is especially useful for testing web components where you can create mock implementations of `HttpServletRequest` and `HttpServletResponse`.

- *Fostering of good application design*: A typical injection-oriented application is designed so that all major components are defined as interfaces, and then concrete implementations of these interfaces are created and hooked together using the DI container. This kind of design was possible in Java before the advent of DI and DI-based containers such as Spring, but by using Spring, you get a whole host of DI features for free, and you are able to concentrate on building your application logic, not a framework to support it.

As you can see from this list, DI provides a lot of benefits for your application, but it is not without its drawbacks. In particular, DI can make it difficult for someone not intimately familiar with the code to see just what implementation of a particular dependency is being hooked into which objects. Typically, this is a problem only when developers are inexperienced with DI. I've heard a lot of my colleagues in this situation mentioning that Spring *auto-magically* injects beans, or complaining that they don't understand where a bean is coming from, or, worst of all asking "Why is Spring is not finding my bean?" After becoming more experienced and following good DI coding practice (for example, putting all injectable classes within each application layer into the same package), developers will be able to discover the whole picture easily. For the most part, the massive benefits of DI far outweigh this small drawback, but you should consider this when planning your application.

Beyond Dependency Injection

Spring Core alone, with its advanced DI capabilities, is a worthy tool, but where Spring really excels is in its myriad of additional features, all elegantly designed and built using the principles of DI. Spring provides features for all layers of an application, from helper application programming interfaces (APIs) for data access right through to advanced Model-View-Controller (MVC) capabilities. What is great about these features in Spring is that, although Spring often provides its own approach, you can easily integrate them with other tools in Spring, making these tools first-class members of the Spring family.

The following list describes the most important Spring features and indicates the chapters in which they are covered in this book:

- *Aspect-oriented programming*: AOP provides the ability to implement crosscutting logic—that is, logic that applies to many parts of your application—in a single place and to have that logic applied across your application automatically. Spring's approach to AOP, covered in **Chapter 5**, is to create dynamic proxies to the target objects and weave the objects with the configured advice to execute the crosscutting logic. By the nature of JDK dynamic proxies, target objects must implement an interface declaring the method in which the AOP advice will be applied.

- *Spring Expression Language*: Expression Language (EL) is a technology to allow an application to manipulate Java/Kotlin objects at runtime. However, the problem with EL is that different technologies provide their own EL implementations and syntax. For example, Java Server Pages (JSP) and Java Server Faces (JSF) both have their own EL, and their syntax are different. To solve the problem, the Unified Expression Language (EL) was created. *Spring Expression Language (SpEL)* was introduced in Spring 3.0 and provides powerful features for evaluating expressions and for accessing Java/Kotlin objects and Spring beans at runtime.

- *Validation*: Data managed by an application must abide by specific validation rules. The ideal scenario is that the validation rules of the attributes within JavaBeans containing business data can be applied in a consistent way, regardless of whether the data manipulation request is initiated from the front end, a batch job, or remotely (for example, via web services, RESTful web services, or remote procedure calls [RPCs]). To address these concerns, Spring provides a built-in validation API by way of the Validator interface. This interface provides a simple yet concise mechanism that allows you to encapsulate your validation logic into a class responsible for validating the target object. In addition to the target object, the validation method takes an Errors object, which is used to collect any validation errors that may occur. The topic of validation and all aspects of it are covered in detail in **Chapter 11**.

- *Accessing data*: Data access and persistence seem to be the most discussed topics in the Java world. Spring provides excellent integration with a choice selection of data access tools. In addition, Spring makes plain-vanilla JDBC a viable option for many projects, with its simplified wrapper APIs around the standard API. Spring's data access module provides out-of-the-box support for JDBC (**Chapter 6**), Hibernate (**Chapter 7**), JDO the JPA (**Chapter 8**), and various NoSQL databases (**Chapter 10**). When using the Spring APIs to access data via any tool, you are able to take advantage of Spring's excellent transaction support. You'll find a full discussion of this in **Chapter 9**.

- *Managing transactions*: Spring provides an excellent abstraction layer for transaction management, allowing for programmatic and declarative transaction control. By using the Spring abstraction layer for transactions, you can make it simple to change the underlying transaction protocol and resource managers. You can start with simple, local, resource-specific transactions and move to global, multi-resource transactions without having to change your code. Transactions are covered in full detail in **Chapter 9**.

- *Object mapping*: Most applications need to integrate or provide services to other applications. One common requirement is to exchange data with other systems, either on a regular basis or in real time. In terms of data format, XML used to be the most commonly used, but nowadays JSON and YAML have taken over, mostly because the excellent support provided by the Jackson Project[9]. Starting with **Chapter 13**, in which we discuss remotely accessing a Spring application for business data in various formats, you will see how to use Spring's object mapping support in your application.

---

[9] https://github.com/FasterXML/jackson

- *Job scheduling support*: Most nontrivial applications require some kind of scheduling capability. Whether this is for sending updates to customers or performing housekeeping tasks, the ability to schedule code to run at a predefined time is an invaluable tool for developers. Spring provides scheduling support that can fulfill most common scenarios. A task can be scheduled either for a fixed interval or by using a Unix cron expression. On the other hand, for task execution and scheduling, Spring integrates with other scheduling libraries as well. For example, in the application server environment, Spring can delegate execution to the CommonJ library that is used by many application servers. For job scheduling, Spring also supports libraries including the JDK Timer API and Quartz, a commonly used open source scheduling library. The scheduling support in Spring is covered in full in **Chapter 12**.

- *MVC in the web tier*: Although Spring can be used in almost any setting, from the desktop to the Web, it provides a rich array of classes to support the creation of web-based applications. Using Spring, you have maximum flexibility when you are choosing how to implement your web front end. For developing web applications, the MVC pattern is the most popular practice. In recent versions, Spring has gradually evolved from a simple web framework into a full-blown MVC implementation. First, view support in Spring MVC is extensive. In addition to standard support for JSP and Java Standard Tag Library (JSTL), which is greatly bolstered by the Spring tag libraries, you can take advantage of fully integrated support for Apache Velocity, FreeMarker, Thymeleaf, XSLT, React, and Mustache templates. In addition, you will find a set of base view classes that make it simple to add Microsoft Excel, PDF, and JasperReports output to your applications. Starting with **Chapter 15**, we discuss developing web applications by using Spring MVC.

- *Remoting support*: Accessing or exposing remote components in Java, and later in Kotlin, has never been the simplest of jobs. Using Spring, you can take advantage of extensive support for a wide range of remoting techniques to quickly expose and access remote services: JMS, Advanced Message Queuing Protocol (AMQP), and REST. Accessing remote services nowadays more often than not involves real-time streaming data, and applications must adapt to the data streams; this is where Apache Kafka comes in handy. How Spring integrates with these technologies is covered in **Chapter 13**, except REST, which is covered in **Chapter 16**.

- *Simplified exception handling*: One area where Spring really helps reduce the amount of repetitive, boilerplate code you need to write is in exception handling. The core of the Spring philosophy in this respect is that checked exceptions are overused in Java and that a framework should not force you to catch any exception from which you are unlikely to be able to recover—a point of view that we agree with wholeheartedly. In reality, many frameworks are designed to reduce the impact of having to write code to handle checked exceptions. However, many of these frameworks take the approach of sticking with checked exceptions but artificially reducing the granularity of the exception class hierarchy. One thing you will notice with Spring is that because of the convenience afforded to the developer from using unchecked exceptions, the exception hierarchy is remarkably granular. Throughout the book, you will see examples in which the Spring exception-handling mechanisms can reduce the amount of code you have to write and, at the same time, improve your ability to identify, classify, and diagnose errors within your application.

- *WebSocket support*: Starting with Spring Framework 4.0, support for JSR-356 ("Java API for WebSocket") is available. WebSocket defines an API for creating a persistent connection between a client and server, typically implemented in web browsers and servers. WebSocket-style development opens the door for efficient, full-duplex communication enabling real-time message exchanges for highly responsive applications. Use of WebSocket support is detailed further in **Chapter 19**. The Spring Framework provides a reactive WebSocket API that you can use to write client and server-side applications that handle WebSocket messages, which is covered briefly in **Chapter 20**.

- *Reactive programming*: Reactive programming describes a design paradigm that relies on asynchronous programming logic to handle real-time updates to otherwise static content. It provides an efficient means — the use of automated data streams — to handle data updates to content whenever a user makes an inquiry. The Spring team created its own reactive streams implementation, Project Reactor, when the JDK Reactive support was delayed, so Spring could have a jump-start into providing support for building reactive applications with Spring. How to develop reactive Spring applications in covered in **Chapter 20**.

Kotlin has its own idea of reactive programming: Coroutines. In order to avoid confusion by mingling two different technologies, we present only the Spring way in this book.

- *Securing applications*: In a world where almost any business transaction is done over the Internet, securing data and ensuring access to it is no longer an option but a requirement. The Spring Security project[10], formerly known as the *Acegi Security System for Spring*, is another important project within the Spring portfolio. Spring Security provides comprehensive support for both web application and method-level security. It tightly integrates with the Spring Framework and other commonly used authentication mechanisms, such as HTTP basic authentication, form-based login, X.509 certificate, OAuth2 and single sign-on (SSO) products (for example, CA SiteMinder). It provides role-based access control (RBAC) to application resources, and in applications with more-complicated security requirements (for example, data segregations), it supports use of an access control list (ACL). Spring Security is mostly used in securing web applications, which is covered in **Chapter 17**. Reactive security is briefly touched upon in **Chapter 20**.

- *Monitoring applications*: An application made of multiple components should have a setup that, after being put into production, ensures the smooth functioning of the many components that make up the application. You need to monitor its performance—its resource usage, user traffic, request rates, response times, bottlenecks, memory issues, and so forth—to be able to overcome these limitations and ensure a good end-user experience. Spring Actuator is used to expose operational information about the running application—health, metrics, info, dump, env, and so on. It uses HTTP endpoints or JMX beans to enable you to interact with it. Actuator uses Micrometer, a dimensional-first metrics collection facade whose aim is

---

[10]https://projects.spring.io/spring-security

to allow you to time, count, and gauge your code with a vendor-neutral API. Despite its focus on dimensional metrics, Micrometer does map to hierarchical names to continue to serve older monitoring solutions like Ganglia or narrower scoped tools like JMX. The change to Micrometer arose out of a desire to better serve a wave of dimensional monitoring systems (think Prometheus, Datadog, Wavefront, SignalFx, Influx, etc.). This flexibility is an advantage of Spring being designed for DI, which allows easily swapping monitoring systems as well. Working with Actuator is covered in **Chapter 18**.

- *Run everywhere*: For a long time the technical evolution allow us to go big - we've found new ways of keeping CPUs cool while increasing their frequency, and we've managed to provide more memory with smaller chips, but recently a new trend has arisen. Deploying applications on privately owned clouds has made people worry about the cloud costs, so an emerging trend is to build compact applications that require smaller CPUs and less memory to run. Better performance with less resource consumption means less cloud costs, and this is why the age of compact native images is coming. The experimental (for now) Spring Native project provides support for compiling Spring applications to native executables using the GraalVM native-image compiler. GraalVM is a high-performance runtime that provides significant improvements in application performance and efficiency, which is ideal for microservices. This means applications start faster and need less resources while running. This makes them suitable to be deployed in a private cloud (Amazon, GCP, Hetzner, etc.) with decent costs. How to build a Spring project to be runnable using a GraalVM native image using Spring Native and other goodies is covered in **Chapter 14**.

The Spring Community

The Spring community is one of the best in any open source project we have encountered. The mailing lists and forums are always active, and progress on new features is usually rapid. The development team is truly dedicated to making Spring the most successful of all the Java application frameworks, and this shows in the quality of the code that is reproduced. As we mentioned already, Spring also benefits from excellent relationships with other open source projects, a fact that is extremely beneficial when you consider the large amount of dependency the full Spring distribution has. From a user's perspective, perhaps one of the best features of Spring is the excellent documentation and test suite that accompany the distribution.

Documentation is provided for almost all the features of Spring, making it easy for new users to pick up the framework. The test suite Spring provides is impressively comprehensive—the development team writes tests for everything. If they discover a bug, they fix that bug by first writing a test that highlights the bug and then getting the test to pass. Fixing bugs and creating new features is not limited just to the development team! You can contribute code through pull requests against any portfolio of Spring projects through the official GitHub repositories[11]. Or you can help experimental projects grow their wings by contributing though the official experimental GitHub repositories[12].

What does all this mean to you? Well, put simply, it means you can be confident in the quality of the Spring Framework and confident that, for the foreseeable future, the Spring development team will continue to improve what is already an excellent framework.

---

[11] https://github.com/spring-projects
[12] https://github.com/spring-projects-experimental

Alternatives to Spring

Going back to our previous comments on the number of open source projects, you should not be surprised to learn that Spring is not the only framework offering dependency injection features or full end-to-end solutions for building applications.

A popular DI framework is **Google Guice**[13]. Led by the search engine giant Google, Guice is a lightweight framework that focuses on providing DI for application configuration management. It was also the reference implementation of JSR-330 (Dependency Injection for Java).

Vaadin[14] is an open source web application development platform for Java. Vaadin includes a set of Web Components, a Java web framework, and a set of tools that enable developers to implement modern web graphical user interfaces using the Java programming language only, TypeScript only, or a combination of both. It's scope is limited to web applications, but for more complex applications it easily integrates with Spring and can harness the power of the Spring IoC container.

The now defunct **JBoss Seam Framework**[15] used to be a good alternative to Spring. When I took my first Spring training in 2012, I was pretty convinced the Spring annotation model for configuring its beans was inspired from it.

The now defunct **PicoContainer**[16] was an exceptionally small DI container that allowed you to use DI for your application without introducing any dependencies other than PicoContainer. Being nothing more than a DI container, writing a more complex application required adding of extra frameworks, such as Spring, in which case you would have been better off using Spring from the start. However, if all you needed was a tiny DI container, then PicoContainer was a good choice.

Summary

In this chapter, you were provided a 10,000-foot view of the Spring Framework and its evolution onto a collection of projects that can be used to build any type of application you might need, complete with discussions of all the important features. A guide to the relevant sections of the book where these features are discussed in detail was provided, together with references to the additional technologies that will be used throughout the book.

After reading this chapter, you should understand what Spring can do for you; all that remains is to see how it can do it. In the next chapter, you will be provided all the information you need to know to prepare your development environment to get up and running with a basic Spring application. **Chapter 2** introduces some basic Spring code and configuration, including a time-honored *Hello World* example in all its DI-based glory.

---

[13] https://github.com/google/guice
[14] https://vaadin.com
[15] https://www.seamframework.org
[16] http://picocontainer.com

Getting Started

The most difficult part when starting a new project is setting up a development process that involves selecting and optimizing the tooling, so that you can focus on writing the code. Fortunately, this book intends to make that easier. The project for this book is a Kotlin project that uses Spring components, which means there are quite a few choices when it comes to editors, build tools, and even JDKs.

This chapter provides all the basic knowledge you need to get off to a flying start, but first let's look at a few conventions.

Conventions

This book uses several formatting conventions that should make it easier to read. To that end, the following conventions are used within the book:

- Code or concept names in paragraphs appear as follows: `java.util.List`

- Code listings and configurations appear as follows:

```
fun main(args: Array<String>) {
    println("Hello World!")
}
```

- Logs in console outputs appear as follows:

```
01:24:07.809 [main] INFO c.a.Application - Starting Application
01:24:07.814 [main] DEBUG c.a.p.c.Application - Running in debug mode
```

- {xx} is a placeholder, where the xx value is a pseudo-value giving a hint about the real value that should be used in the command or statement. For example, {name_of_your_bean} means that in a concrete example, the whole construct should be replaced by the name of your bean.

- *Italic* font is used for humorous metaphors, expressions, and bits of text that need some kind of separation from the text around them. For example, in Chapter 1 the Hollywood Principle is introduced as *Don't call us, we'll call you.*

- **Bold** font is used for chapter references and important terms.

- (..) is used to replace sets of parameter declarations and arguments in methods and constructors, to avoid distracting you from the actual code.

© Peter Späth, Iuliana Cosmina, Rob Harrop, Chris Schaefer 2023
P. Späth et al., *Pro Spring 6 with Kotlin*, https://doi.org/10.1007/978-1-4842-9557-1_2

- … is used to replace code, configuration, and logs not relevant to the context.

- Package import statements are kept to a minimum, and only the ones relevant to the component being discussed are shown. This is to reduce the space taken up by code in the book, a better use of which is for more in-depth explanations. You have the full code in the project anyway!

- Each chapter has a few footnotes and links pointing you to documentation, tools, and blog articles. The book is readable without consulting them, so feel free to ignore them, but you might find them useful.

- Some paragraphs are shown in a rectangle and labeled with one of the icons in Table 2-1. The table also shows the meaning of each icon.

Table 2-1. *Special Paragraphs Icons and Meanings*

Label	Meaning
	You might find this useful.
	You will definitely find this useful.
	This is really useful.
	Be careful when using this.
	Whatever this is about, it is recommended not to do it.
	Whatever this is about, just don't do it.

As for my style of writing, I like to write my books in the same way I have technical conversations with colleagues and friends, sprinkling in jokes, giving production examples, and making analogies to non-programming situations. Because programming is nothing but just another way to model the real world.

Who This Book Is For

This book assumes you are somewhat familiar with Java, Kotlin, and tools involved in development of Java/Kotlin applications. If you are not, that might not be too much of a problem, because the project is neatly set up such that you could build it without having any knowledge about what Gradle does. Also, if you stick to the recommended editor, which is IntelliJ IDEA, you should be able to just clone the repository, build the project, and get right to business.

What You Need for This Book

You obviously need **a computer**, desktop or laptop, the choice of which doesn't really matter as long as it is up to date, running Windows, Linux, or macOS, and is connected to the **Internet**.

You need to have **JDK 17** (or OpenJDK 17) installed locally. Instructions on how to do so on any operating system are available on the Oracle official page[1,2].

 For any Unix-based system, SDKMAN![3] is very useful. SDKMAN! is a tool for managing parallel versions of multiple software development kits on most Unix-based systems. It provides a convenient command-line interface (CLI) and API for installing, switching, removing, and listing candidates. It works for JDK, Gradle, and many more.

As previously mentioned, the recommended **editor** is IntelliJ IDEA[4]; you can use the Enterprise version for free for 30 days, or you can help test Early Access versions. IntelliJ IDEA is a great editor for Spring applications because it comes with a great set of plug-ins that help you be very aware if your beans are properly configured. If you are more familiar with Eclipse IDE, you can try Spring Tools 4[5] to simplify developing for Spring.

There is also a community edition of IntelliJ IDEA, which is free to use (licensed under Apache 2.0). It lacks some extended support for Spring, but you still can use it for all the book's Kotlin sources.

You need the **sources** where all the code samples referenced in the book come from. Depending on how you are getting the project associated with this book, you might need **Git**[6] installed. You can use Git from the command line to clone the repository, or you can use the IDE, or you can download the sources as a zip from the repository page.

This is the project repository page: `https://github.com/Apress/pro-spring-6-kotlin`

Any project dependencies that are more complex than a Java/Kotlin library and need to run services that the Spring applications interact with are provided via Docker containers; thus, you need to install Docker[7] on your computer. Instructions on how to download images and start them are provided in `README.adoc` files for the respective chapters.

To summarize the requirements for you to become a Spring professional: this book, a computer, Internet, Java 17, `Git`, the sources, Docker, and a little bit of time and determination.

---

[1] `https://docs.oracle.com/en/java/javase/17/install/overview-jdk-installation.html`
[2] `https://openjdk.org/`, `https://jdk.java.net/archive/`, `https://jdk.java.net/19/`
[3] `https://sdkman.io`
[4] `https://www.jetbrains.com/idea`
[5] `https://spring.io/tools`
[6] `https://git-scm.com/`
[7] `https://www.docker.com/`

Prepare Your Development Environment

Here is the list of steps you have to go through to start running the code associated with the book:

- Sit comfortably in front of your computer.

- Install JDK 17 (or OpenJDK 17). Later versions might do as well.

If you have older versions installed, make sure JDK 17 is the default one used on your system by opening a terminal (Command Prompt or Power Shell on Windows systems) and running `java -version`. Expect the output to mention Java version 17, as depicted in Listing 2-1.

Listing 2-1. Output of Command `java -version` Showing JDK 17 Set As Default

```
> java -version
java version "17.0.1" 2021-10-19 LTS
Java(TM) SE Runtime Environment (build 17.0.1+12-LTS-39)
Java HotSpot(TM) 64-Bit Server VM (build 17.0.1+12-LTS-39, mixed mode, sharing)
```

- Clone the project repository or download the sources from the Apress official page and unzip them on your computer. Make sure you select the Kotlin variant of the sources. You should have a directory named `pro-spring-6` containing the modules as shown in Figure 2-1.

> 📁 build
> 📁 chapter02
> 📁 chapter03
> 📁 chapter04

...

> 📁 gradle
> 📁 .gradle
> 📁 .idea
  📄 gradle.properties
  📄 gradlew
  📄 gradlew.bat
  📄 settings.gradle

Figure 2-1. *The pro-spring-6 project and its modules*

- Open the IntelliJ IDEA editor, choose File ➤ Open in the main menu, and in the file selector window that opens, select the `pro-spring-6` directory. After a short while, on the left side (in a pane we'll call the *Project View* in this book), you should see the pro-spring-6 project and its modules listed. On the right side of the window, you should see a section showing you the Gradle configuration (we'll call this the *Gradle View* in this book). These views are shown in Figure 2-2.

For the Kotlin variant of the book, the build process concentrates on using Gradle as a build tool. Gradle setups are just a lot more concise compared to Maven setups. If you really need to use Maven, the Java variant of the sources plus the information provided at `https://kotlinlang.org/docs/maven.html` should help you.

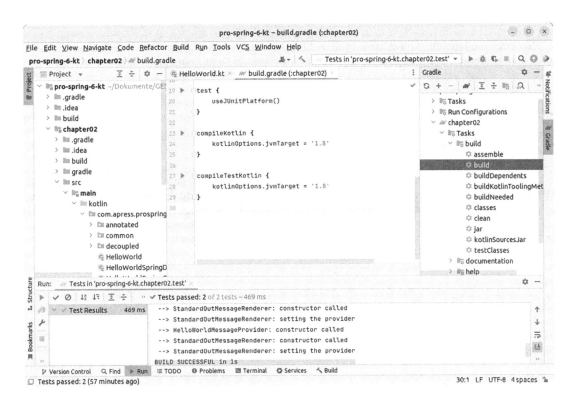

Figure 2-2. *The pro-spring-6 project, Gradle View*

The project is made up of a main Gradle project and multiple subprojects, each representing a Kotlin project. The name of each module includes the chapter number where its contents are referenced. Every project depends on a lot of libraries that will be automatically downloaded when your project is opened in an editor for the first time.

The project can be built right after cloning according to the instructions in its README.adoc file. The project does not need Gradle installed locally, since it is configured to use wrappers respectively IDE plugins.

The Gradle version used to build the project at the time this chapter is being written is 7.4. The version likely will change by the time the book is released, but the version will be mentioned in the main README. adoc file and in the Gradle wrapper configuration file: gradle/wrapper/gradle-wrapper.properties.

IntelliJ IDEA identifies the wrapper configurations and builds your project from them. If you want to explicitly trigger any of them from the interface, just click the ↻ symbol that you can see in the upper-left corner of Gradle View.

💡 IntelliJ IDEA keeps the state of your project internally and sometimes gets…*ahem*…confused. If your project shows class names in red and complains about missing dependencies, try building it from the command line as explained in the README.adoc file. If that works, you might to one of these options under the File menu: Invalidate Caches, Reload All from Disk, Restart IDE, Repair IDE.

Now that you have the project loaded and building successfully on your computer, we'll tell you more about Spring internals before explaining the pro-spring-6 project Gradle configurations.

Understanding Spring Packaging

Spring packaging is modular; it allows you to pick and choose which components you want to use in your application and to include only those components when you are distributing your application. Spring has many modules, but you need only a subset of these modules depending on your application's needs. Each module has its compiled binary code in a JAR file along with corresponding Javadoc and source JARs. IntelliJ IDEA scans the dependencies of your project and on request it can download the sources and Javadoc. This means that you can see the code and read about Spring classes in your editor.

The Javadoc for a class is shown in a rectangle when hovering over its name, as depicted in Figure 2-3 for the @SpringBootApplication annotation (the figure shows the Java variant; for Kotlin the view looks similar).

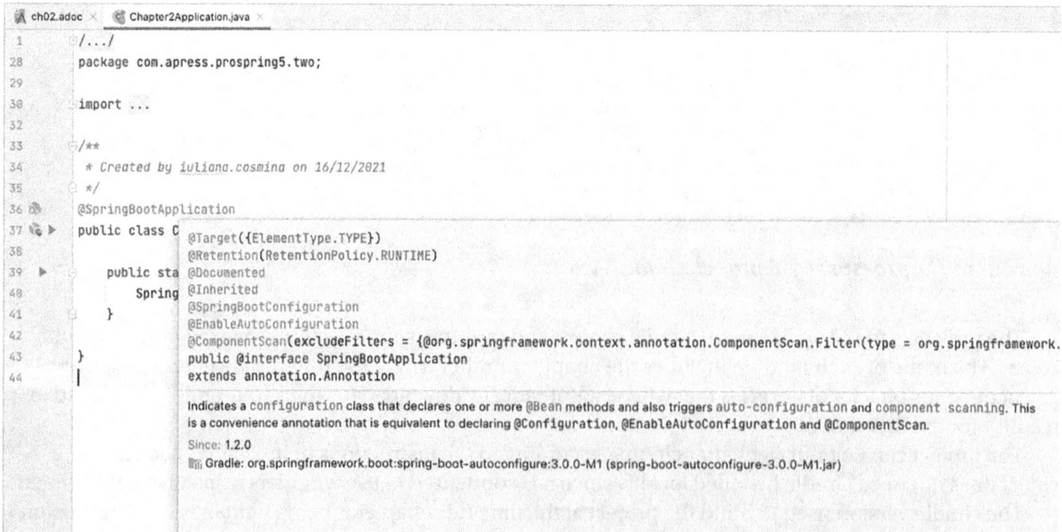

Figure 2-3. IntelliJ IDEA displaying the Javadoc for the @SpringBootApplication annotation

You can also choose to press the Ctrl (Command for macOS) key and click a class name, and IntelliJ IDEA will download the sources for it and open them in a new tab. In Figure 2-4 you can see on the right the source for the @SpringBootApplication annotation (again, the figure shows the Java variant, and the view looks similar for Kotlin).

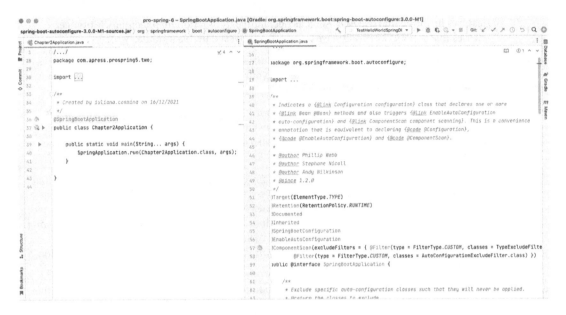

Figure 2-4. *IntelliJ IDEA displaying the source for the @SpringBootApplication annotation*

Back to the Spring modules. *Spring modules* are simply JAR files that package the required code for that module. The code base for the Spring Framework is publicly available on GitHub. If you are curious about what the code of the Spring Framework looks like and want and to be on the cutting edge of Spring development, check out the latest version of the source code from Spring's GitHub repository[8].

After you understand the purpose of each module, you can select the modules required in your project and include them in your code. As shown by the most recent tag on GitHub, it seems that Spring Framework version 6.0 comes with 22 modules. Table 2-2 describes these JAR files and their corresponding modules. The actual JAR file name is, for example, spring-aop-6.0.0.jar, though we have included only the specific module portion for simplicity (as in aop, for example).

---

[8] https://github.com/spring-projects/spring-framework

Table 2-2. *Spring Modules*

Module	Description
aop	This module contains all the classes you need to use Spring's AOP features within your application. You also need to include this JAR in your application if you plan to use other features in Spring that use AOP, such as declarative transaction management. Moreover, classes that support integration with AspectJ are packed in this module.
aspects	This module contains all the classes for advanced integration with the AspectJ AOP library. For example, if you are using Java classes for your Spring configuration and need AspectJ-style annotation-driven transaction management, you need this module.
beans	This module contains all the classes for supporting Spring's manipulation of Spring beans. Most of the classes here support Spring's bean factory implementation. For example, the classes required for processing the Spring XML configuration file and Java annotations are packed into this module.
context	This module contains classes that provide many extensions to Spring Core. You will find that all classes need to use Spring's ApplicationContext feature (covered in **Chapter 5**), along with classes for Enterprise JavaBeans (EJB), Java Naming and Directory Interface (JNDI), and Java Management Extensions (JMX) integration. Also contained in this module are the Spring remoting classes, classes for integration with dynamic scripting languages (for example, JRuby, Groovy, and BeanShell), JSR-303 ("Bean Validation"), scheduling and task execution, and so on.
context-indexer	This module contains an indexer implementation that provides access to the candidates that are defined in META-INF/spring.components. The core class CandidateComponentsIndex is not meant to be used externally.
context-support	This module contains further extensions to the spring-context module. On the user-interface side, there are classes for mail support and integration with templating engines such as Velocity, FreeMarker, and JasperReports. Also, integration with various task execution and scheduling libraries, including CommonJ and Quartz, are packaged here.
core	This is the main module that you will need for every Spring application. In this JAR file, you will find all the classes that are shared among all other Spring modules (for example, classes for accessing configuration files). Also, in this JAR, you will find selections of extremely useful utility classes that are used throughout the Spring codebase and that you can use in your own application.
expression	This module contains all support classes for Spring Expression Language (SpEL).
instrument	This module includes Spring's instrumentation agent for JVM bootstrapping. This JAR file is required for using load-time weaving with AspectJ in a Spring application.
jcl	This module is only present for binary compatibility with existing Apache Commons Logging usage, such as in Apache Commons Configuration.
jdbc	This module includes all classes for JDBC support. You will need this module for all applications that require database access. Classes for supporting data sources, JDBC data types, JDBC templates, native JDBC connections, and so on, are packed in this module.

(continued)

Table 2-2. (*continued*)

Module	Description
jms	This module includes all classes for Java Message Service (JMS) support.
messaging	This module contains key abstractions taken from the Spring Integration project to serve as a foundation for message-based applications and adds support for STOMP messages.
orm	This module extends Spring's standard JDBC feature set with support for popular ORM tools including Hibernate, JDO, and JPA. Many of the classes in this JAR depend on classes contained in the spring-jdbc JAR file, so you definitely need to include that in your application as well.
oxm	This module provides support for Object/XML Mapping (OXM). Classes for the abstraction of XML marshalling and unmarshalling and support for popular tools such as Castor, JAXB, XMLBeans, and XStream are packed into this module.
r2dbc	This module makes R2DBC easier to use and reduces the likelihood of common errors. It provides simple error handling and a family of unchecked concise exceptions agnostic of the underlying RDBM (Reactive Database Manager).
test	Spring provides a set of mock classes to aid in testing your applications, and many of these mock classes are used within the Spring test suite, so they are well tested and make testing your applications much simpler. Certainly we have found great use for the mock HttpServletRequest and HttpServletResponse classes in unit tests for our web applications. On the other hand, Spring provides a tight integration with the JUnit unit-testing framework, and many classes that support the development of JUnit test cases are provided in this module; for example, SpringExtension integrates the *Spring TestContext Framework* into JUnit 5's *Jupiter* programming model.
tx	This module provides all classes for supporting Spring's transaction infrastructure. You will find classes from the transaction abstraction layer to support the Java Transaction API (JTA) and integration with application servers from major vendors.
web	This module contains the core classes for using Spring in your web applications, including classes for loading an ApplicationContext feature automatically, file upload support classes, and a bunch of useful classes for performing repetitive tasks such as parsing integer values from the query string.
webflux	This module contains core interfaces and classes for the Spring Web Reactive model.
webmvc	This module contains all the classes for Spring's own MVC framework. If you are using a separate MVC framework for your application, you won't need any of the classes from this JAR file. Spring MVC is covered in more detail in **Chapter 15**.
websocket	This module provides support for JSR-356 ("Java API for WebSocket").

If you use Spring Boot, you don't have to select Spring modules to add as dependencies explicitly, because the appropriate set of Spring dependencies are configured depending on the Spring Boot starter dependencies used. The codebase for Spring Boot is also publicly available on GitHub. If you are curious about how the Spring Boot code looks like and want to be on the cutting edge of Spring Boot development, check out the latest version of the source code from Spring's GitHub repository[9]. Under `spring-boot-project/spring-boot-starters` there is a list of Spring Boot starter modules that can be used as dependencies for a Spring project to build a certain type of Spring application, with a default configuration and curated set of dependencies. The modules are nothing but dependency descriptors that can be added inside the `dependencies { }` section in `build.gradle`. There are currently more than 30 of them, and Table 2-3 lists the ones most often used and the dependencies they configure for your application.

Table 2-3. *Spring Boot Starter Modules*

Module	Description
`spring-boot-starter`	This is the simplest Spring Boot starter that adds the `spring-core` module as a dependency for your project. It can be used to create a very simple Spring application. It is used mostly for learning purposes and for creating base projects, that encapsulate common functionality shared among other modules in a project.
`spring-boot-starter-aop`	Adds the `spring-aop` as a dependency for your project.
`spring-boot-starter-data-*`	This type of starter adds various Spring dependencies for working with data in your project. The * replaces the technology from which data is coming. For example, `spring-boot-starter-data-jdbc` adds classes for creating Spring Repository beans for handling data from databases supporting a JDBC driver: MySQL, PostgreSQL, Oracle, etc.
`spring-boot-starter-web`	Configures minimal dependencies for creating a web application.
`spring-boot-starter-security`	Configures minimal dependencies for securing a Spring web application.
`spring-boot-starter-webflux`	Configures minimal dependencies for creating a reactive web application.
`spring-boot-starter-actuator`	Configures Spring Boot Actuator, which enables a set of endpoints for monitoring a Spring web application.
`spring-boot-starter-test`	Configures the following set of libraries: Spring Test, JUnit, Hamcrest, and Mockito.

Choosing Modules for Your Application

Without a dependency management tool such as Maven or Gradle, choosing which modules to use in your application may be a bit tricky. For example, if you require Spring's bean factory and DI support only, you still need several modules, including `spring-core`, `spring-beans`, `spring-context`, and `spring-aop`. If you need Spring's web application support, you then need to further add `spring-web` and so on. Thanks to build tools features such as Gradle's transitive dependencies support, all required third-party libraries would be included automatically.

---

[9] `https://github.com/spring-projects/spring-boot/`

Accessing Spring Modules on the Maven Repository

Founded by Apache Software Foundation, Maven[10] has become one of the most popular tools in managing the dependencies for Java applications, from open source to enterprise environments. Maven is a powerful application building, packaging, and dependency management tool. It manages the entire build cycle of an application, from resource processing and compiling to testing and packaging. There also exists a large number of Maven plug-ins for various tasks, such as updating databases and deploying a packaged application to a specific server (for example: Tomcat, WildFly, or WebLogic). As of this writing, the current Maven version is 3.8.4.

Almost all open source projects support distribution of libraries via the Maven repository. The most popular one is the Maven Central repository hosted on Apache, and you can access and search for the existence and related information of an artifact on the Maven Central website[11].

A detailed discussion of Maven is not in the scope of this book, and you can always refer to the online documentation or books that give you a detailed reference to Maven.

Accessing Spring Modules Using Gradle

The Maven project standard structure is depicted in Figure 2-5.

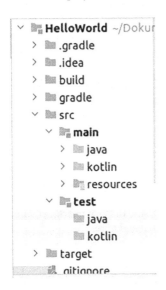

Figure 2-5. *Gradle typical project structure*

The `main` directory contains the application codebase in the `kotlin` directory and application configuration files in the `resources` directory. The `test` directory contains the application test code in the `kotlin` directory and the application test configuration files in the `resources` directory (not shown in the figure—you can easily add it).

---

[10] https://maven.apache.org
[11] https://mvnrepository.com/

Maven sources and other artifact categorization and organization is important because Gradle[12] respects the same rules and even uses the Maven Central repository to retrieve artifacts. Various other repositories can be configured as well. Gradle is a powerful build tool that has given up the bloated XML for configuration and switched to the simplicity and flexibility of Groovy. Which is very good and provides a lot of flexibility, up until a developer gets too creative with their configuration, that is. At the time of writing, the current version of Gradle is 7.3.3 Starting with version 4.x, the Spring team has switched to using Gradle for the configuration of every Spring product. That is why the source code for this book can be built and executed using Gradle. The default name of a Gradle configuration file for a project is build.gradle. An example of this file is shown in Listing 2-2.

Listing 2-2. build.gradle Snippet

```
plugins {
    id 'org.jetbrains.kotlin.jvm' version '1.8.10'
    id 'application' // make it runnable via Gradle
}
group 'com.apress.prospring6.ch02'
version '6.0-SNAPSHOT'
repositories {
    mavenCentral()
}
tasks.withType(JavaCompile) {
    options.encoding = "UTF-8"
}
dependencies {
    implementation group: 'org.apache.logging.log4j', name: 'log4j-core', version: '2.17.1'
}
application {
    // For running from Gradle. Note that the file name reads
    // HelloApplication.kt - the "Kt" gets added by the compiler.
    mainClass = 'book.spring6.helloworld.HelloApplicationKt'
}
```

That's quite readable, right? As you can observe, the artifacts are identified using the *group*, *artifact*, and *version*. Gradle itself is not in the scope of this book, so detailed coverage of it must end here.

Using Spring Boot Dependency Management

Since Gradle does not have a parent concept similar to Maven, dependency management is done using the io.spring.dependency-management plug-in. Listing 2-3 depicts a Gradle configuration.

---

[12] https://gradle.org/

Listing 2-3. Simple Spring Boot Project Gradle Configuration

```
plugins {
    id 'org.springframework.boot' version '3.0.0-SNAPSHOT'
    id 'io.spring.dependency-management' version '1.0.11.RELEASE'
    id 'org.jetbrains.kotlin.jvm' version '1.8.10'
}

group = 'com.apress.prospring6.ch02'
version = '6.0-SNAPSHOT'
sourceCompatibility = '17'

repositories {
    mavenCentral()
    maven { url 'https://repo.spring.io/milestone' }
    maven { url 'https://repo.spring.io/snapshot' }
}

dependencies {
    implementation 'org.springframework.boot:spring-boot-starter'
    testImplementation 'org.springframework.boot:spring-boot-starter-test'
}
...
```

Overriding Spring Boot managed dependency versions is possible by adjusting the `build.gradle` file. Figure 2-6 shows the IntelliJ IDEA's Gradle View showing the dependencies introduced by Spring Boot dependency management and the Gradle configuration syntax for overriding versions.

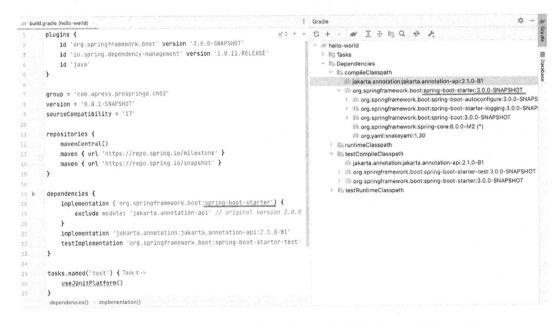

Figure 2-6. *Gradle Spring Boot Project with customized version for* `jakarta.annotation-api`

Since Spring Boot dependency management in Gradle is made using a plug-in, configuring Spring classic projects that make use of dependency management is possible without any additional change to the configurations, except removing starter dependencies and replacing them with the desired Spring dependencies.

Using Spring Documentation

One of the aspects of Spring that makes it such a useful framework for developers who are building real applications is its wealth of well-written, accurate documentation. In every release, the Spring Framework's documentation team works hard to ensure that all the documentation is finished and polished by the development team. This means that every feature of Spring is not only fully documented in the Javadoc but is also covered in the Spring reference manual included in every distribution. If you haven't yet familiarized yourself with the Spring Javadoc and the reference manual, do so now. This book is not a replacement for either of these resources; rather, it is a complementary reference, demonstrating how to build a Spring-based application from the ground up.

You can access the Spring Javadoc through the IntelliJ IDEA editor as mentioned previously, but if you prefer doing so in the browser, you can bookmark this URL: `https://docs.spring.io/spring-framework/docs/current/javadoc-api`.

For a more in-depth introduction to the Spring Framework, you can also bookmark the URL to the official reference documentation: `https://docs.spring.io/spring-framework/docs/current/reference/html`.

Putting a Spring into Hello World

At this point in the book, we are optimistic that you are convinced that Spring is a solid, well-supported project that has all the makings of a great tool for application development and that understanding it in depth will not only make you a better developer but boost your career as well. However, one thing is missing—we haven't shown you any Spring 6 code yet. We are sure you are dying to see Spring in action, and because we cannot go any longer without getting into the code, let's do just that. Do not worry if you do not fully understand all the code in this section; we go into much more detail on all the topics as we proceed through the book.

Building the Sample Hello World Application

Now, we are sure you are familiar with the traditional Hello World example, but just in case you have been living on the moon for the past 30 years, the code snippet in Listing 2-4 shows the Kotlin version in all its glory.

Listing 2-4. Classic Hello World Kotlin Application

```
package com.apress.prospring6.two

object HelloWorld {
    @JvmStatic
    fun main(args: Array<String>) {
        println("Hello World!")
    }
}
```

As examples go, this one is pretty simple—it does the job, but it is not very extensible. What if we want to change the message? What if we want to output the message differently, maybe to standard error instead of standard output or enclosed in HTML tags rather than as plain text? We are going to redefine the requirements for the sample application and say that it must support a simple, flexible mechanism for changing the message, and it must be easy to change the rendering behavior. In the basic *Hello World* example, you can make both of these changes quickly and easily by just changing the code as appropriate. However, in a bigger application, recompiling takes time, and it requires the application to be fully tested again. A better solution is to externalize the message content and read it in at runtime, perhaps from the command-line arguments, as shown in Listing 2-5.

Listing 2-5. Classic Hello World Kotlin Application with Arguments

```kotlin
package com.apress.prospring6.two

object HelloWorldWithCommandLine {
    @JvmStatic
    fun main(args: Array<String>) {
        if (args.size > 0) {
            println(args[0])
        } else {
            println("Hello World!")
        }
    }
}
```

This example accomplishes what we wanted—we can now change the message without changing the code. However, there is still a problem with this application: the component responsible for rendering the message is also responsible for obtaining the message. Changing how the message is obtained means changing the code in the renderer. Add to this the fact that we still cannot change the renderer easily; doing so means changing the class that launches the application.

If we take this application a step further (away from the basics of Hello World), a better solution is to refactor the rendering and message retrieval logic into separate components. Plus, if we really want to make your application flexible, we should have these components implement interfaces and define the interdependencies between the components and the launcher using these interfaces. By refactoring the message retrieval logic, we can define a simple MessageProvider interface with a single property, message, as shown in Listing 2-6.

Listing 2-6. MessageProvider Interface

```kotlin
package com.apress.prospring6.two.decoupled

interface MessageProvider {
    val message: String?
}
```

The MessageRenderer interface is implemented by all components that can render messages, and such a component is depicted in Listing 2-7.

Listing 2-7. MessageRenderer Interface

```
package com.apress.prospring6.two.decoupled

interface MessageRenderer {
    fun render()
    var messageProvider: MessageProvider?
}
```

As you can see, the MessageRenderer interface declares a method, render(), and also a JavaBean-style property, messageProvider. Any MessageRenderer implementations are decoupled from message retrieval and delegate that responsibility to the MessageProvider instance with which they are supplied.

Here, MessageProvider is a dependency of MessageRenderer. Creating simple implementations of these interfaces is easy, as shown in Listing 2-8.

Listing 2-8. MessageProvider Implementation

```
package com.apress.prospring6.two.decoupled

class HelloWorldMessageProvider : MessageProvider {
    init {
        println(" --> HelloWorldMessageProvider: constructor called")
    }

    override val message: String
        get() = "Hello World!"
}
```

You can see that we have created a simple MessageProvider that always returns "Hello World!" as the message. The StandardOutMessageRenderer class shown in Listing 2-9 is just as simple.

Listing 2-9. MessageRenderer Implementation

```
package com.apress.prospring6.two.decoupled

class StandardOutMessageRenderer() : MessageRenderer {
    override var messageProvider: MessageProvider? = null
        set(value) {
            field = value
            println(" --> StandardOutMessageRenderer: setting the provider")
        }

    init {
        println(" --> StandardOutMessageRenderer: constructor called")
    }

    override fun render() {
        println(messageProvider?.message?:throw RuntimeException(
            "You must set the property messageProvider of class:"
                + StandardOutMessageRenderer::class.java.name
        ) )
    }
}
```

Now all that remains is to rewrite the main(..) method of the entry class, as depicted in Listing 2-10.

Listing 2-10. New main(..) Method

```
package com.apress.prospring6.two.decoupled

object HelloWorldDecoupled {
    @JvmStatic
    fun main(args: Array<String>) {
        val mr: MessageRenderer = StandardOutMessageRenderer()
        val mp: MessageProvider = HelloWorldMessageProvider()
        mr.messageProvider = mp
        mr.render()
    }
}
```

Figure 2-7 depicts the abstract schema of the application built so far.

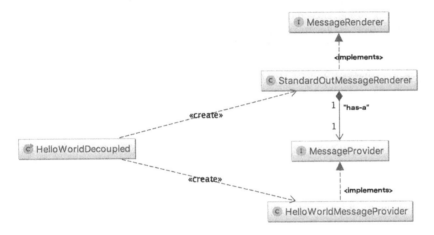

Figure 2-7. *A little more decoupled Hello World application*

The code here is fairly simple:

- We instantiate instances of HelloWorldMessageProvider and StandardOutMessageRenderer, although the declared types are MessageProvider and MessageRenderer, respectively. This is because we need to interact only with the methods provided by the interface in the programming logic, and HelloWorldMessageProvider and StandardOutMessageRenderer already implemented those interfaces, respectively.

- Then, we pass MessageProvider to MessageRenderer and invoke MessageRenderer#render().

If we compile and run this program, we get the expected "Hello World!" output. Now, this example is more like what we are looking for, but there is one small problem. Changing the implementation of either the MessageRenderer or MessageProvider interface means a change to the code.

To get around this we need to delegate the responsibility of retrieving the two implementation types and instantiating them to somebody else. The most *manual* one is to create a simple factory class that reads the implementation class names from a properties file and instantiates them on behalf of the application, as shown Listing 2-11.

Listing 2-11. Instance Factory Class Tasked with Retrieving the Two Implementation Types and Instantiating Them

```
package com.apress.prospring6.two.decoupled

import java.util.*

object MessageSupportFactory {
    var renderer: MessageRenderer? = null
    var provider: MessageProvider? = null

    init {
        val props = Properties()
        try {
            props.load(this.javaClass.getResourceAsStream("/msf.properties"))
            val rendererClass = props.getProperty("renderer.class")
            val providerClass = props.getProperty("provider.class")
            renderer = Class.forName(rendererClass).getDeclaredConstructor().newInstance() as
                MessageRenderer
            provider = Class.forName(providerClass).getDeclaredConstructor().newInstance() as
                MessageProvider
        } catch (ex: Exception) {
            ex.printStackTrace()
        }
    }
}
```

The implementation here is trivial and naive, the error handling is simplistic, and the name of the configuration file is hard-coded, but we already have a substantial amount of code. The configuration file for this class is quite simple and is depicted in Listing 2-12.

Listing 2-12. Configuration File Contents for the MessageSupportFactory Class, Ergo the Contents of the msf.properties File

```
renderer.class=com.apress.prospring5.ch2.decoupled.StandardOutMessageRenderer
provider.class=com.apress.prospring5.ch2.decoupled.HelloWorldMessageProvider
```

The configuration file must be on the project classpath. When running from IntelliJ IDEA, the file is located in the chapter02/src/main/resources directory and is added to the classpath when running the code.

To delegate the responsibilities of retrieving a MessageProvider and MessageRenderer instance to MessageSupportFactory, the main(..) method must be changed as shown in Listing 2-13.

Listing 2-13. HelloWorld Version Using MessageSupportFactory

```
package com.apress.prospring6.two.decoupled

object HelloWorldDecoupledWithFactory {
    @JvmStatic
    fun main(args: Array<String>) {
```

```
        val mr: MessageRenderer = MessageSupportFactory.renderer?:
            throw IllegalArgumentException(
                "Service of type 'MessageRenderer' was not found!")
        val mp: MessageProvider = MessageSupportFactory.provider?:
            throw IllegalArgumentException(
                "Service of type 'MessageProvider' was not found!")
        mr.messageProvider = mp
        mr.render()
    }
}
```

However, there is another way to do this with pure Kotlin, without creating the `MessageSupportFactory` class, because there is already a class named `ServiceLoader` in package `java.util` that does the exact thing. This class was introduced in Java 6 to facilitate discovering and loading implementations matching a given interface. The interfaces that this class retrieves implementations for are called *Service Provider Interface (SPI)*.

The approach is similar to the `MessageSupportFactory`, only the configuration file names have to respect three rules:

- Must be on the project classpath in a directory name `META-INF/services`.
- The file name is the fully qualified name of the SPI.
- Its content is the fully qualified name of the SPI implementation.

This means that in `src/main/resources` the directory and files structure shown in Listing 2-14 needs to be created.

Listing 2-14. Configuration Files Location for `ServiceLoader`

```
└─── resources
       └─── META-INF
              └─── services
                     ├─── com.apress.prospring6.two.decoupled.MessageProvider
                     └─── com.apress.prospring6.two.decoupled.MessageRenderer
```

The `com.apress.prospring6.two.decoupled.MessageProvider` file contains the fully qualified name of the SPI implementation, which in this case is `com.apress.prospring6.two.decoupled.HelloWorldMessageProvider`.

The `com.apress.prospring6.two.decoupled.MessageRenderer` file contains the fully qualified name of the SPI implementation, which in this case is `com.apress.prospring6.two.decoupled.StandardOutMessageRenderer`.

Listing 2-15 depicts the `main(..)` method that uses `ServiceLoader`.

Listing 2-15. `HelloWorld` Version Using `ServiceLoader`

```kotlin
package com.apress.prospring6.two.decoupled

import java.util.*

object HelloWorldWithServiceLoader {
    @JvmStatic
    fun main(args: Array<String>) {
        val slr: ServiceLoader<MessageRenderer> =
```

```kotlin
        ServiceLoader.load(MessageRenderer::class.java)
    val slp: ServiceLoader<MessageProvider> =
        ServiceLoader.load(MessageProvider::class.java)
    val mr: MessageRenderer = slr.findFirst().orElseThrow {
        IllegalArgumentException(
            "Service of type 'MessageRenderer' was not found!"
        )
    }
    val mp: MessageProvider = slp.findFirst().orElseThrow {
        IllegalArgumentException(
            "Service of type 'MessageProvider' was not found!"
        )
    }
    mr.messageProvider = mp
    mr.render()
    }
}
```

ServiceLoader is overkill for this example, and it shows its true power in multi-module projects, where Java modules are configured. The module providing the implementation declares the following in its `module.java` file: `provides {SPI} with {SPI-Implementation}`. The module using the service has no idea where the implementation is coming from, or its fully qualified name; it just declares in its `main.java` file `uses {SPI}` and the ServiceLoader picks whatever it finds on the classpath. You can find more details about this in *Java 17 for Absolute Beginners*, published by Apress in 2022.

Before we move on to see how we can introduce Spring into this application, let's quickly recap what we have done:

- We started with the simple Hello World application.

- We defined two additional requirements that the application must fulfill:

  - Changing the message should be simple.

  - Changing the rendering mechanism should also be simple.

- To meet these requirements, we used two interfaces: MessageProvider and MessageRenderer.

- The MessageRenderer interface depends on an implementation of the MessageProvider interface to be able to retrieve a message to render.

- Finally, we added a simple factory class to retrieve the names of the implementation classes and instantiate them as applicable. And this was just showing off, since ServiceLoader exists.

Refactoring with Spring

The `MessageSupportFactory` example shown earlier met the goals laid out for the sample application, but its main problem is the quantity of glue code needed to piece the application together, while at the same time keeping the components loosely coupled. Using `SpringLoader` is the Java way of using dependency injection in your application and removes the necessity of writing all that glue code. However, one problem remains: we still had to provide the implementation of `MessageRenderer` with an instance of `MessageProvider` manually and explicitly in the code of the `main(..)` method. This last problem can be solved by Spring.

Using Spring XML Configuration

Since we are using Spring for the full solution `SpringLoader` is no longer necessary and its place is taken by a Spring interface named `ApplicationContext`. Don't worry too much about this interface; for now, it is enough to know that this interface is used by Spring for storing all the environmental information with regard to an application being managed by Spring. This interface extends another interface, `ListableBeanFactory`, which acts as the provider for any Spring-managed bean instance. Take a look at the code snippet in Listing 2-16.

Listing 2-16. `HelloWorld` Version Using Spring

```
package com.apress.prospring6.two

import com.apress.prospring6.two.decoupled.MessageRenderer
import org.springframework.context.ApplicationContext
import org.springframework.context.support.ClassPathXmlApplicationContext

object HelloWorldSpringDI {
    @JvmStatic
    fun main(args: Array<String>) {
        val ctx: ApplicationContext =
            ClassPathXmlApplicationContext("spring/app-context.xml")
        val mr = ctx.getBean("renderer", MessageRenderer::class.java)
        mr.render()
    }
}
```

In the previous code snippet, you can see that the `main(..)` method obtains an instance of `ClassPathXmlApplicationContext` (the application configuration information is loaded from the file `spring/app-context.xml` in the project's classpath), typed as `ApplicationContext`, and from this, it obtains the `MessageRenderer` instances by using the `ApplicationContext#getBean()` method. Don't worry too much about the `getBean()` method for now; just know that this method reads the application configuration (in this case, an XML file), initializes Spring's `ApplicationContext` environment, and then returns the configured bean instance. This `app-context.xml` XML file serves the same purpose as the one used for `MessageSupportFactory` or the ones used for `ServiceLoader`. The contents of this file are shown in Listing 2-17.

Listing 2-17. Spring XML Configuration File

```
<?xml version="1.0" encoding="UTF-8"?>
<beans xmlns="http://www.springframework.org/schema/beans"
    xmlns:xsi="http://www.w3.org/2001/XMLSchema-instance"
```

```
xmlns:p="http://www.springframework.org/schema/p"
xsi:schemaLocation="http://www.springframework.org/schema/beans
    http://www.springframework.org/schema/beans/spring-beans.xsd">

<bean id="provider"
    class="com.apress.prospring6.two.decoupled.HelloWorldMessageProvider"/>

<bean id="renderer"
    class="com.apress.prospring6.two.decoupled.StandardOutMessageRenderer"
        p:messageProvider-ref="provider"/>
</beans>
```

Listing 2-17 shows a typical Spring ApplicationContext configuration. First, Spring's namespaces are declared, and the default namespace is beans. The beans namespace is used to declare the beans that need to be managed by Spring and to declare their dependency requirements (for the preceding example, the renderer bean's messageProvider property is referencing the provider bean). Spring will resolve and inject those dependencies.

Afterward, we declare the bean with the ID provider and the corresponding implementation class. When Spring sees this bean definition during the ApplicationContext initialization, it will instantiate the class and store it with the specified ID.

Then the renderer bean is declared, with the corresponding implementation class. Remember that this bean depends on the MessageProvider interface for getting the message to render. To inform Spring about the DI requirement, we use the p namespace attribute. The tag attribute p:messageProvider-ref="provider" tells Spring that the bean's property, messageProvider, should be injected with another bean. The bean to be injected into the property should reference a bean with the ID provider. When Spring sees this definition, it will instantiate the class, look up the bean's property named messageProvider, and inject it with the bean instance with the ID provider.

As you can see, upon the initialization of Spring's ApplicationContext, the main(..) method now just obtains the MessageRenderer bean by using its type-safe getBean() method (passing in the ID and the expected return type, which is the MessageRenderer interface) and calls render(). Spring has created the MessageProvider instance and injected it into the MessageRenderer instance. Notice that we didn't have to make any changes to the classes that are being wired together using Spring. In fact, these classes have no reference to Spring and are completely oblivious to its existence. However, this isn't always the case. Your classes can implement Spring-specified interfaces to interact in a variety of ways with the DI container.

With your new Spring configuration and modified main(..) method, let's see it in action. Using Gradle, build the full project by executing any of the commands in the pro-spring-6/README.adoc file.

The only required Spring module to be declared in your configuration file is spring-context. Gradle will automatically bring in any dependencies required for this module. In Figure 2-8 you can see the transitive dependencies of spring-context.jar in Gradle View.

```
description 'Chapter 02: Hello World!'

// we are using Spring Boot dependency management,
// but we configure Spring MVC in the classic manner
dependencyManagement {
    imports {
        mavenBom SpringBootPlugin.BOM_COORDINATES
    }
}

dependencies {
    implementation 'org.springframework:spring-context'
}

task copyDependencies(type: Copy) {
    from configurations.default
    into 'build/libs'
}
```

```
∨ ⚙ pro-spring-6
  › 🗂 Tasks
  › 📁 Dependencies
  › 🗂 Run Configurations
  ∨ ⚙ chapter02
    › 🗂 Tasks
    ∨ 📁 Dependencies
      ∨ 📁 compileClasspath
        › 📦 ch.qos.logback:logback-classic:1.2.10
          📦 com.google.code.findbugs:jsr305:3.0.2
          📦 org.apache.commons:commons-lang3:3.10
        ∨ 📦 org.springframework:spring-context:6.0.0-M2
          ∨ 📦 org.springframework:spring-aop:6.0.0-M2
            › 📦 org.springframework:spring-beans:6.0.0-M2
              📦 org.springframework:spring-core:6.0.0-M2 (*)
            📦 org.springframework:spring-beans:6.0.0-M2 (*)
            📦 org.springframework:spring-core:6.0.0-M2 (*)
          ∨ 📦 org.springframework:spring-expression:6.0.0-M2
            📦 org.springframework:spring-core:6.0.0-M2 (*)
      › 📁 runtimeClasspath
```

Figure 2-8. Gradle View showing `spring-context` and its dependencies

For module `chapter02` the build will result in an executable JAR file.

 Gradle stores artifacts produced by the build under `{module_name}/build/libs`.

You can run any of the executable JAR files using the commands in Listing 2-18, in a terminal.

Listing 2-18. Commands to Run Executable Jars Produced by Gradle for Module `chapter02`

```
cd pro-spring-6/chapter02/build/libs
java -jar  chapter02-6.0-SNAPSHOT.jar
```

Running any of the jars yields the output in Listing 2-19.

Listing 2-19. Output Produced by Running the Executable Jars Produced by Gradle for Module `chapter02`

```
--> HelloWorldMessageProvider: constructor called
--> StandardOutMessageRenderer: constructor called
--> StandardOutMessageRenderer: setting the provider
Hello World!
```

⚠ This section was kept in the book to show you how Spring configuration has evolved. Spring 5 has dropped support for XML configurations. This way of configuring Spring applications might still be used in legacy projects, so if you end up working on one, feel free to look for previous editions of this book.

Spring Configuration Using Annotations

Starting with Spring 3.0, XML configuration files are no longer necessary when developing a Spring application. They can be replaced with **annotations** and **Java/Kotlin configuration classes**. Configuration classes are Java/Kotlin classes annotated with @Configuration that contain bean definitions (methods annotated with @Bean) or are configured themselves to identify bean definitions in the application by annotating them with @ComponentScanning. The equivalent of the app-context.xml file presented earlier is shown in Listing 2-20.

Listing 2-20. Spring Java/Kotlin Configuration Class

```
package com.apress.prospring6.two.annotated

import com.apress.prospring6.two.decoupled.HelloWorldMessageProvider
import com.apress.prospring6.two.decoupled.MessageProvider
import com.apress.prospring6.two.decoupled.MessageRenderer
import com.apress.prospring6.two.decoupled.StandardOutMessageRenderer
import org.springframework.context.annotation.Bean
import org.springframework.context.annotation.Configuration

@Configuration
open class HelloWorldConfiguration {
    @Bean // equivalent to <bean id="provider" class=".."/>
    open fun provider(): MessageProvider {
        return HelloWorldMessageProvider()
    }

    @Bean // equivalent to <bean id="renderer" class=".."/>
    open fun renderer(): MessageRenderer {
        val renderer: MessageRenderer = StandardOutMessageRenderer()
        renderer.messageProvider = provider()
        return renderer
    }
}
```

The main(..) method has to be modified and must replace ClassPathXmlApplicationContext with another ApplicationContext implementation that knows how to read bean definitions from configuration classes. This class is AnnotationConfigApplicationContext. This version of the method is depicted in Listing 2-21.

Listing 2-21. main(..) Method to Start a Spring Application Configured Using Java Configuration

```
package com.apress.prospring6.two.annotated

import com.apress.prospring6.two.decoupled.MessageRenderer
import org.springframework.context.ApplicationContext
import org.springframework.context.annotation.AnnotationConfigApplicationContext

object HelloWorldSpringAnnotated {
    @JvmStatic
    fun main(args: Array<String>) {
        val ctx: ApplicationContext =
```

```
        AnnotationConfigApplicationContext(HelloWorldConfiguration::class.java)
    val mr: MessageRenderer = ctx.getBean("renderer", MessageRenderer::class.java)
    mr.render()
  }
}
```

This is just one version of configuration using annotations and configuration classes. Without XML, things get pretty flexible when it comes to Spring configuration. You'll learn more about that later in this book, but the focus when it comes to configuration is on Java/Kotlin configuration and annotations.

⚠️ Some interfaces and classes defined in the Hello World example may be used in later chapters. Although we showed the full source code in this example, future chapters may show condensed versions of code to avoid being verbose, especially in the case of incremental code modifications. The code has been organized to allow code reusability between modules. All classes that can be used in Spring future examples were placed under the `com.apress.prospring6.two.decoupled` and `com.apress.prospring6.two.annotated` packages.

Summary

In this chapter, we presented you with all the background information you need to get up and running with Spring. We showed you how to get started with Spring through dependency management systems and the current development version directly from GitHub. We described how Spring is packaged and the dependencies you need for each of Spring's features. Using this information, you can make informed decisions about which of the Spring JAR files your application needs and which dependencies you need to distribute with your application. Spring's documentation, guides, and test suite provide Spring users with an ideal base from which to start their Spring development, so we took some time to investigate what is made available by Spring.

Finally, we presented an example of how, using Spring DI, it is possible to make the traditional Hello World example a loosely coupled, extendable message-rendering application. The important thing to realize is that we only scratched the surface of Spring DI in this chapter, and we barely made a dent in Spring as a whole. In the next chapter, we take an in-depth look at IoC and DI in Spring.

■ ■ ■

## CHAPTER 3

Introducing IoC and DI in Spring

Chapters 1 and **2** have introduced you to the Spring world, explaining why this framework is necessary and why dependency injection is so cool and useful. In essence, Spring was built to make dependency injection easy. This software design pattern implies that dependent components delegate the dependency resolution to an external service that will take care of injecting the dependencies. The dependent component is not allowed to call the injector service and has very little to say when it comes to the dependencies that will be injected. This is why the behavior is also known as the *"Don't call us, we'll call you!"* principle, and it is technically known as *inversion of control (IoC)*. If you do a quick Google search, you will find a lot of conflicting opinions about dependency injection and inversion of control. You will find programming articles calling them *programming techniques*, *programming principles*, and *design patterns*. However, the best explanation comes from an article by Martin Fowler[1], which is recognized in the Java world as the highest authority when it comes to design patterns. If you do not have the time to read it, here is a summary: *Inversion of control is a common characteristic of frameworks that facilitate injection of dependencies. And the basic idea of the dependency injection pattern is to have a separate object that injects dependencies with the required behavior, based on an interface contract.*

In this chapter the following DI features are covered:

- *Inversion of control concepts*: In this section, we discuss the various kinds of IoC, including dependency injection and dependency lookup. This section presents the differences between the various IoC approaches as well as the pros and cons of each.

- *Inversion of control in Spring*: This section looks at IoC capabilities available in Spring and how they are implemented. In particular, you'll see the dependency injection services that Spring offers, including setter, constructor, and method injection.

- *Dependency injection in Spring*: This section covers Spring's implementation of the IoC container. For bean definition and DI requirements, BeanFactory is the main interface an application interacts with. However, other than the first few listings, the remainder of the sample code provided in this chapter focuses on using Spring's ApplicationContext interface, which is an extension of BeanFactory and provides much more powerful features. We cover the difference between BeanFactory and ApplicationContext in later sections.

- *Configuring the Spring application context*: The final part of this chapter focuses on the annotation approach for ApplicationContext configuration. Groovy and Java/Kotlin configuration are further discussed in **Chapter 4**. This section starts with a discussion of DI configuration and moves on to present additional services provided by BeanFactory, such as bean inheritance, life-cycle management, and autowiring.

---

[1] https://martinfowler.com/articles/injection.html#InversionOfControl

© Peter Späth, Iuliana Cosmina, Rob Harrop, Chris Schaefer 2023
P. Späth et al., *Pro Spring 6 with Kotlin*, https://doi.org/10.1007/978-1-4842-9557-1_3

Inversion of Control and Dependency Injection

At its core, IoC aims to offer a simpler mechanism for provisioning component dependencies (often referred to as an object's *collaborators*) and managing these dependencies throughout their life cycles. A component that requires certain dependencies is often referred to as the *dependent object* or, in the case of IoC, the *target*. In general, IoC can be decomposed into two subtypes: *dependency injection* and *dependency lookup*. These subtypes are further decomposed into concrete implementations of the IoC services. From this definition, you can clearly see that when we are talking about DI, we are always talking about IoC, but when we are talking about IoC, we are not always talking about DI (for example, dependency lookup is also a form of IoC).

Types of Inversion of Control

You may be wondering why there are two types of IoC and why these types are split further into different implementations. There seems to be no clear answer to this question; certainly, the different types provide a level of flexibility, but to us, it seems that IoC is more of a mixture of old and new ideas. The two types of IoC represent this. Dependency lookup is a much more traditional approach, and at first glance, it seems more familiar to Java programmers. Dependency injection, although it appears counterintuitive at first, is actually much more flexible and usable than dependency lookup. With dependency lookup-style IoC, a component must acquire a reference to a dependency, whereas with dependency injection, the dependencies are injected into the component by the IoC container. Dependency lookup comes in two types:

- Dependency pull
- Contextualized dependency lookup (CDL)

Dependency injection also has two common flavors:

- Constructor dependency injection
- Setter dependency injection

⚠️ For the discussions in this section, we are not concerned with how the fictional IoC container comes to know about all the different dependencies, just that at some point, it performs the actions described for each mechanism.

Dependency Pull

To a Java/Kotlin developer, dependency pull is the most familiar type of IoC. In dependency pull, dependencies are pulled from a registry as required. Anyone who has ever written code to access an EJB (2.1 or prior versions) has used dependency pull (that is, via the JNDI API to look up an EJB component). Figure 3-1 shows the scenario of dependency pull via the lookup mechanism.

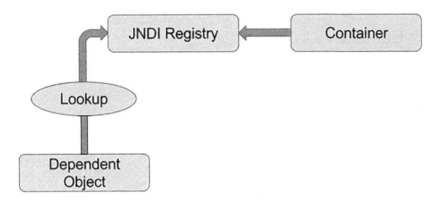

Figure 3-1. *Dependency pull via JNDI lookup*

Spring also offers dependency pull as a mechanism for retrieving the components that the framework manages; you saw this in action in **Chapter 2**. Listing 3-1 shows an example of a typical dependency pull lookup in a Spring-based application.

Listing 3-1. Spring Dependency Pull Example

```
package com.apress.prospring6.two.annotated

import com.apress.prospring6.two.decoupled.MessageRenderer
import org.springframework.context.ApplicationContext
import org.springframework.context.annotation.AnnotationConfigApplicationContext

object HelloWorldSpringAnnotated {
    @JvmStatic
    fun main(args: Array<String>) {
        val ctx: ApplicationContext =
            AnnotationConfigApplicationContext(HelloWorldConfiguration::class.java)
        val mr: MessageRenderer = ctx.getBean("renderer", MessageRenderer::class.java)
        mr.render()
    }
}
```

This code snippet and all classes referenced in it, was introduced at the end of Chapter 2 to show you how a Spring ApplicationContext is built. Notice that in the main(..) method the MessageRenderer bean is retrieved from the ApplicationContext that functions as a register of all beans in the application; this instance is therefore *pulled,* so its render() method can be invoked.

This kind of IoC is not only prevalent in JEE-based applications (using EJB 2.1 or prior versions), which make extensive use of JNDI lookups to obtain dependencies from a registry, but also pivotal to working with Spring in many environments.

Contextualized Dependency Lookup

Contextualized dependency lookup (CDL) is similar, in some respects, to dependency pull, but in CDL, lookup is performed against the container that is managing the resource, not from some central registry, and it is usually performed at some set point. Figure 3-2 shows the CDL mechanism.

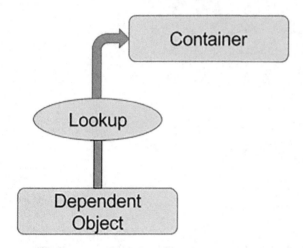

Figure 3-2. *Contextualized dependency lookup*

CDL works by having the component that requires a dependency implement an interface similar to the one in Listing 3-2.

Listing 3-2. Contextualized Dependency Lookup Interface

```
interface ManagedComponent {
    fun performLookup(container: Container)
}
```

By implementing this interface, a component is signaling to the container that it wants to obtain a dependency. The container is usually provided by the underlying application server or framework (for example, Tomcat or JBoss) or framework (for example, Spring). The code in Listing 3-3 shows a simple Container interface that provides a dependency lookup service.

Listing 3-3. Container Interface That Provides a Dependency Lookup Service

```
interface Container {
    fun getDependency(key: String): Any?
}
```

When the container is ready to pass dependencies to a component, it calls performLookup() on each component in turn. The component can then look up its dependencies by using the Container interface. To work with the already familiar example, the MessageRenderer interface is declared to extend the ManagedComponent interface, so that the StandardOutMessageRenderer class can look up its own dependency using the provided Container. The code for the MessageRenderer interface and StandardOutMessageRenderer class is displayed in Listing 3-4.

Listing 3-4. ManagedComponent Implementation Using the StandardOutMessageRenderer Class

```
interface MessageRenderer : ManagedComponent {
    fun render()
    var messageProvider: MessageProvider?
}
```

```kotlin
class StandardOutMessageRenderer : MessageRenderer {
    override var messageProvider:MessageProvider? = null

    override
    fun performLookup(container:Container) {
        this.messageProvider =
            container.getDependency("provider") as MessageProvider
    }

    // other code omitted, already listed in Chapter 2
}
```

❗ You might notice that many Kotlin files in this book contain more than one type, so there is no doubt where the bean definitions are coming from. We kept this approach wherever necessary in the project for this book.

Constructor Dependency Injection

In *constructor dependency injection* the IoC container injects a component's dependencies via its constructor (or constructors). The component declares a constructor or a set of constructors, taking as arguments its dependencies, and the IoC container passes the dependencies to the component when instantiation occurs. This means this version of the StandardOutMessageRenderer looks like the one depicted in Listing 3-5.

Listing 3-5. StandardOutMessageRenderer Modified for Constructor Injection

```kotlin
class StandardOutMessageRenderer(
            override var messageProvider:MessageProvider? = null) :
        MessageRenderer {

    // other code omitted, already listed in chapter 2
}
```

An obvious consequence of using constructor injection is that an object cannot be created without its dependencies; thus, they are mandatory.

Setter Dependency Injection

In *setter dependency injection*, the IoC container injects a component's dependencies via JavaBean-style setter methods. A component's setters expose the dependencies that the IoC container can manage. Listing 3-6 shows a typical setter dependency injection–based version of the StandardOutMessageRenderer.

Listing 3-6. StandardOutMessageRenderer Modified for Setter Injection

```
package com.apress.prospring6.three.di;

class StandardOutMessageRenderer : MessageRenderer {
    override var messageProvider:MessageProvider? = null

    // Kotlin provides this automatically, so don't add it:
    // fun setMessageProvider(messageProvider:MessageProvider) {
    //    this.messageProvider = messageProvider
    // }

    // other code omitted, already listed in Chapter 2
}
```

An obvious consequence of using setter injection is that an object can be created without its dependencies, and they can be provided later by calling the setter.

Within the container, the dependency requirement exposed by the setMessageProvider() method is referred to by the JavaBeans-style name, *dependency*. In practice, setter injection is the most widely used injection mechanism, and it is one of the simplest IoC mechanisms to implement.

ℹ️   There is another type of injection supported in Spring called *field injection*, but this will be covered later in the chapter, when you learn about autowiring using the @Autowire annotation.

Injection vs. Lookup

Choosing which style of IoC to use—injection or lookup—usually is not a difficult decision. In many cases, the type of IoC you choose is mandated by the container you are using. For instance, if you are using EJB 2.1 or prior versions, you must use lookup-style IoC (via JNDI) to obtain an EJB from the JEE container. In Spring, aside from initial bean lookups, your components and their dependencies are always wired together using injection-style IoC.

💡   When you are using Spring, you can access EJB resources without performing an explicit lookup. Spring can act as an adapter between lookup- and injection-style IoC systems, thus allowing you to manage all resources by using injection.

After reading thus far, what do you think? Would you use dependency injection or dependency lookup?

Using injection, you are free to use your classes completely decoupled from the IoC container that is supplying dependent objects with their collaborators manually, whereas with lookup your classes are always dependent on the classes and interfaces defined by the container. Another drawback with lookup is that testing your classes in isolation from the container becomes difficult. Using injection, testing your components is trivial because you can simply provide the dependencies yourself by using the appropriate constructor or setter, as you will see throughout this book.

The biggest reason to choose injection over lookup is that it makes your life easier. You write substantially less code when you are using injection, and the code that you do write is simple and can, in general, be automated by a good IDE. You will notice that all the code in the injection examples is passive, in that it doesn't actively try to accomplish a task. The most exciting thing you see in injection code is that objects get stored in a field only; no other code is involved in pulling the dependency from any registry or container. Therefore, the code is much simpler and less error prone. Passive code is much simpler to maintain than active code because there is very little that can go wrong. There are few things that could go wrong with the StandardOutMessageRenderer from Listing 3-4: the dependency key could change or the returned dependency might be the incorrect type. Using dependency lookup might decouple the components of your application, but it adds complexity in the additional code required to couple these components back together in order to perform any useful tasks.

Setter Injection vs. Constructor Injection

At this point in the book, it is clear that dependency injection is the way to go. *Constructor injection* is useful when dependency must be enforced, and the component requiring a dependency won't work without it. Many containers, Spring included, provide a mechanism for ensuring that all dependencies are defined when you use setter injection, but by using constructor injection, you assert the requirement for the dependency in a container-agnostic manner. Constructor injection also helps achieve the use of immutable objects—just use val instead of var for the constructor parameter.

Setter injection is useful in a variety of cases. If the component is exposing its dependencies to the container but is happy to provide its own defaults, setter injection is usually the best way to accomplish this. Another benefit of setter injection is that it allows dependencies to be declared on an interface, although this is not as useful as you might first think. Think about it, an interface can be implemented by multiple classes, that need to expose the same API, but need different dependencies. So, unless you are absolutely sure that all implementations of a particular business interface require a particular dependency, you should let each implementation class define its own dependencies and keep the business interface for business methods. Listing 3-7 depicts an interface for a newsletter sender service and it looks like a contraction to what was said so far.

Listing 3-7. NewsletterSender Interface

```
package com.apress.prospring6.three

interface NewsletterSender {
    var smtpServer: String?
    var fromAddress: String?

    fun send()
}
```

But here's the catch: the dependencies declared via this interface are configurations. Configuration parameters are a special case for dependencies. Certainly, your components depend on the configuration data, but configuration data is significantly different from the types of dependency you have seen so far. Thus, Kotlin automatically providing setters and getters for configuration parameters that way in the business interface helps a lot and makes setter injection a valuable tool.

Classes that send a set of newsletters via e-mail implement the NewsletterSender interface. The send() method is the only business method, but notice that we have defined two properties on the interface. Why are we doing this when we just said that you shouldn't define dependencies in the business interface? The reason is that these values, the SMTP server address and the address the e-mails are sent from, are not dependencies in the practical sense; rather, they are configuration details that affect how all implementations of the NewsletterSender interface function. The question then is this: what is the difference between a configuration parameter and any other kind of dependency? In most cases, you can clearly see whether a dependency should be classified as a configuration parameter, but if you are not sure, look for the following three characteristics that point to a configuration parameter:

- *Configuration parameters are passive*: In the NewsletterSender example depicted in Listing 3-7, the SMTP server parameter is an example of a passive dependency. Passive dependencies are not used directly to perform an action; instead, they are used internally or by another dependency to perform their actions. In the MessageRenderer example from Chapter 2, the MessageProvider dependency was not passive; it performed a function that was necessary for the MessageRenderer to complete its task.

- *Configuration parameters are usually information, not other components*: By this we mean that a configuration parameter is usually some piece of information that a component needs to complete its work. Clearly, the SMTP server is a piece of information required by the NewsletterSender, but the MessageProvider is really another component that the MessageRenderer needs to function correctly.

- *Configuration parameters are usually simple values or collections of simple values*: This is really a byproduct of the previous two points, but configuration parameters are usually simple values. In Java/Kotlin this means they are a (pseudo-) primitive (or the corresponding wrapper class) or a String or collections of these values. Simple values are generally passive. This means you can't do much with a String other than manipulate the data it represents; and you almost always use these values for information purposes—for example, an Int value that represents the port number that a network socket should listen on or a String that represents the SMTP server through which an e-mail program should send messages.

When considering whether to define configuration options in the business interface, also consider whether the configuration parameter is applicable to all implementations of the business interface or just one. For instance, in the case of implementations of NewsletterSender, it is obvious that all implementations need to know which SMTP server to use when sending e-mails. However, we would probably choose to leave the configuration option that flags whether to send secure e-mail off the business interface because not all e-mail APIs are capable of this, and it is correct to assume that many implementations will not take security into consideration at all.

ⓘ   Recall that in **Chapter 2** we chose to define the dependencies in the business interfaces. This was for illustration purposes only and should not be treated in any way as a best practice.

Setter injection also allows you to swap dependencies for a different implementation on the fly without creating a new instance of the parent component. Spring's JMX support makes this possible. Perhaps the biggest benefit of setter injection is that it is the least intrusive of the injection mechanisms.

In general, you should choose an injection type based on your use case. Setter-based injection allows dependencies to be swapped out without creating new objects and also lets your class choose appropriate defaults without the need to explicitly inject an object. Constructor injection is a good choice when you want to ensure that dependencies are being passed to a component and when designing for immutable objects. Do keep in mind that while constructor injection ensures that all dependencies are provided to a component, most containers provide a mechanism to ensure this as well but may incur a cost of coupling your code to the framework.

Inversion of Control in Spring

As mentioned earlier, inversion of control is a big part of what Spring does. The core of Spring's implementation is based on dependency injection, although dependency lookup features are provided as well. When Spring provides collaborators to a dependent object automatically, it does so using dependency injection. In a Spring-based application, it is always preferable to use dependency injection to pass collaborators to dependent objects rather than have the dependent objects obtain the collaborators via lookup. Figure 3-3 shows Spring's dependency injection mechanism.

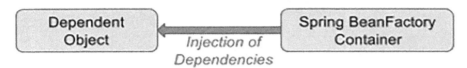

Figure 3-3. *Spring's dependency injection mechanism*

Although dependency injection is the preferred mechanism for wiring together collaborators and dependent objects, you need dependency lookup to access the dependent objects. In many environments, Spring cannot automatically wire up all of your application components by using dependency injection, and you must use dependency lookup to access the initial set of components. For example, in stand-alone Java/Kotlin applications, you need to bootstrap Spring's container in the main(..) method and obtain the dependencies (via the ApplicationContext interface) for processing programmatically. However, when you are building web applications by using Spring's MVC support, Spring can avoid this by gluing your entire application together automatically. Wherever it is possible to use dependency injection with Spring, you should do so; otherwise, you can fall back on the dependency lookup capabilities. You will see examples of both in action during the course of this chapter, and we will point them out when they first arise.

An interesting feature of Spring's IoC container is that it has the ability to act as an adapter between its own dependency injection container and external dependency lookup containers. We discuss this feature later in this chapter.

Spring supports both constructor and setter injection and bolsters the standard IoC feature set with a whole host of useful additions to make your life easier.

The rest of this chapter introduces the basics of Spring's DI container, complete with plenty of examples.

Dependency Injection in Spring

Spring's support for dependency injection is comprehensive and, as you will see in **Chapter 4**, goes beyond the standard IoC feature set we have discussed so far. The rest of this chapter addresses the basics of Spring's dependency injection container, looking at setter, constructor, and Method Injection, along with a detailed look at how dependency injection is configured in Spring.

Beans and BeanFactory

The org.springframework.beans and org.springframework.context packages are the basis for Spring Framework's IoC container. The central point of Spring's IoC container is the org.springframework.beans. factory.BeanFactory interface. Spring implementations of this interface are responsible for managing components, including their dependencies as well as their life cycles. Figure 3-4 shows the most commonly used BeanFactory implementations.

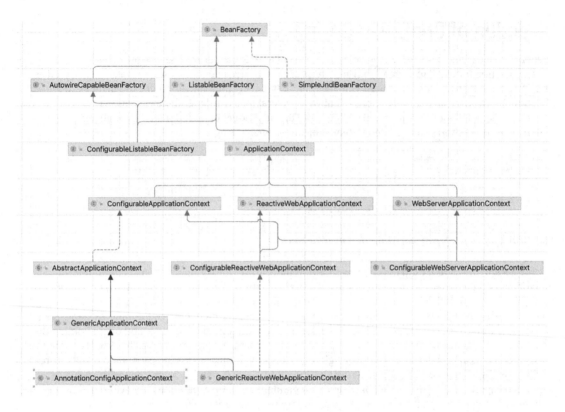

Figure 3-4. *BeanFactory most common implementations*

In Spring, the term bean is used to refer to any object managed by the Spring IoC container. The Spring IoC container creates, configures (assembles), and manages beans throughout their life cycle. Typically, your beans adhere, at some level, to the JavaBeans specification, but this is not required, especially if you plan to use constructor injection to wire your beans together.

If your application needs only DI support, you can interact with the Spring DI container via the BeanFactory interface. In this case, your application must create an instance of a class that implements the BeanFactory interface and configures it with bean and dependency information. This interface is implemented by objects that hold a number of bean definitions, each uniquely identified by a String name. After an instance of this type is created, your application can access the beans via BeanFactory and get on with its processing.

In some cases, all of this setup is handled automatically (for example, in a web application, Spring's ApplicationContext will be bootstrapped by the web container during application startup via a Spring-provided ContextLoaderListener class declared in the web.xml descriptor file). But in many cases, you need to code the setup yourself. Most examples in this chapter require manual setup of the BeanFactory implementation.

The ApplicationContext interface is an extension to BeanFactory. In addition to DI services, ApplicationContext provides other services:

- Integration with Spring's AOP features

- Message resource handling for internationalization (i18n)

- Application event handling

- Application-layer specific contexts (e.g., web, security, etc.)

In developing Spring-based applications, it's recommended that you interact with Spring via the `ApplicationContext` interface. Spring supports the bootstrapping of `ApplicationContext` by manual coding (instantiate it manually and load the appropriate configuration) or in a web container environment via `ContextLoaderListener`. From this point onward, all the sample code in this book uses `ApplicationContext` and its implementations.

Configuring ApplicationContext

In the first example in **Chapter 2**, the `org.springframework.context.ApplicationContext` was configured using an XML file. Although still possible, configuration using XML is limited to capabilities of Spring 4, since no technical investment in this area has been done from that version onward. During Spring's evolution there's been a long discussion about which way of configuring an application is better, XML or annotations. It really depends on developer preferences. Annotations are intertwined with the types of the configured beans and they provide a lot of context, which makes configurations more concise. XML configures a Spring application while being decoupled from the actual code(the Spring XML configuration files are resource files), although this is valid for Java configuration as well, which means the configuration can be externalized and modified without recompiling the code. One of the best things about Spring is that you can mix configuration styles easily.

To keep things simple and, Spring application are configured only through Java annotations and Java code, which provides enough flexibility to describe any type of Spring application.

Basic Configuration Overview

To configure a stand-alone Spring application, all that is needed is a class annotated with `@Configuration`. This annotation indicates that the class contains methods annotated with `@Bean`, which are bean declarations. This approach works for any type of object, especially types provided by third-party libraries— code that is not part of your project, and you cannot edit it to declare your beans. The same class can also be configured to enable looking for existing bean declarations by annotating it with `@ComponentScan`. The discoverable bean declarations are classes annotated with `@Component` and other stereotype annotations. The Spring container processes this type of class to generate bean definitions and service requests for those beans at runtime. All these annotations are basically used to describe what objects should be created, the order they should be created in, initialization operations, and even operations to be executed before being discarded by the Garbage Collector, most simply referred to as **configuration metadata**.

This is the most compact way in which Spring applications can be configured. However, slowly expanding the topic is more appropriate. Let's start with a Spring configuration class, shown in Listing 3-8 that declares two beans. You've already seen this class in **Chapter 2**, but now we are getting into details.

Listing 3-8. Simple Spring Configuration Class

```
package com.apress.prospring6.two.annotated
// other imports omitted
import org.springframework.context.annotation.Bean
import org.springframework.context.annotation.Configuration

@Configuration
open class HelloWorldConfiguration {
    @Bean // equivalent to <bean id="provider" class=".."/>
    open fun provider(): MessageProvider {
        return HelloWorldMessageProvider()
    }
```

```
@Bean // equivalent to <bean id="renderer" class=".."/>
open fun renderer(): MessageRenderer {
    val renderer: MessageRenderer = StandardOutMessageRenderer()
    renderer.messageProvider = provider()
    return renderer
}
}
```

Listing 3-8 declares two beans, one named provider and one named renderer; yes, the beans have the same name as the methods creating them. Naming beans is covered later in the chapter.

Spring configuration classes are typically bootstrapped using either AnnotationConfigApplicationContext or its web-capable variant, AnnotationConfigWebApplicationContext. Both classes implement ApplicationContext, and the code to bootstrap the application configured in Listing 3-8 can be written as shown in Listing 3-9.

Listing 3-9. Bootstrapping a Spring Application

```
package com.apress.prospring6.two.annotated

import org.springframework.context.ApplicationContext
import org.springframework.context.annotation.
       AnnotationConfigApplicationContext

object HelloWorldSpringAnnotated {
    @JvmStatic
    fun main(args: Array<String>) {
        val ctx: ApplicationContext = AnnotationConfigApplicationContext(
            HelloWorldConfiguration::class.java)
        val mr: MessageRenderer = ctx.getBean("renderer", MessageRenderer::class.java)
        mr.render()
    }
}
```

When running the HelloWorldSpringAnnotated class, a Spring application context is created that contains the beans configured by the HelloWorldConfiguration class. A reference to the renderer bean is obtained by calling the getBean("{name}", {type}.class) method and its render() method is called. Since Spring injects the MessageProvider dependency according to the configuration, the "Hello World!" message is printed in the console, as expected.

The bootstrapping process consists of instantiating the AnnotationConfigApplicationContext class and providing the configuration simple class name as a parameter. By instantiating this class, we are creating an instance of a Spring IoC container that will read the bean declarations, create the beans, add them to its registry, and manage them. Using a reference to the container, beans can be retrieved and used, exactly as shown in Listing 3-9.

Declaring Spring Components

Another way to declare beans is to annotate the classes directly with *stereotype* annotations. These annotations are called *stereotype* because they define the roles of types or methods in the overall architecture. They are part of a package named org.springframework.stereotype. This package groups together annotations used to define beans. These annotations are relevant to the role of a bean. For example,

@Service is used to define a service bean, which is a more complex functional bean that provides services that other beans may require, and @Repository is used to define a bean that is used to retrieve/save data from/to a database, etc. And @Component is the annotation that marks a class as a bean declaration. @Component is a meta-annotation, and all other annotations in this paragraph are annotated with it. This makes them candidates for auto-detection when using annotation-based configuration and classpath scanning.

To create bean definitions using annotations, the bean classes must be annotated with the appropriate stereotype annotation, and the setters or constructors used to inject dependencies must be annotated with @Autowired to tell the Spring IoC container to look for a bean of that type and use it as an argument when calling that method.

In Listing 3-10, the stereotype annotations can have as a parameter the name of the resulting bean.

Listing 3-10. Declaring Spring Beans Using @Component

```
// HelloWorldMessageProvider.kt
package com.apress.prospring6.three.constructor

import com.apress.prospring6.two.decoupled.MessageProvider
import org.springframework.stereotype.Component

//simple bean without dependencies
@Component("provider")
class HelloWorldMessageProvider : MessageProvider {
    // some code omitted
}

// StandardOutMessageRenderer.kt
package com.apress.prospring6.three.setter;

import com.apress.prospring6.two.decoupled.MessageRenderer
import org.springframework.beans.factory.annotation.Autowired

//simple bean requiring a dependency
@Component("renderer")
class StandardOutMessageRenderer : MessageRenderer {
    override var messageProvider:MessageProvider? = null
        @Autowired set(value) { field = value }
    // some code omitted
}
```

By annotating a configuration class with @ComponentScan, when bootstrapping the ApplicationContext, Spring will seek out these classes, also called components, and instantiate the beans with the specified names. In Listing 3-11 you can see the simple HelloWorldConfiguration configuration class annotated with @ComponentScan.

Listing 3-11. Simple Spring Configuration Class with Component Scanning

```
package com.apress.prospring6.three.constructor

import org.springframework.context.annotation.ComponentScan

@Configuration
@ComponentScan
open class HelloWorldConfiguration {
}
```

The code to bootstrap a Spring environment using AnnotationConfigApplicationContext (see Listing 3-9) works with this class, too, with no additional changes.

The @ComponentScan annotation declares a scanning directive and may define specific packages to scan. When no package is configured, scanning occurs from the package of the class that declares this annotation, regardless of whether the class is public or package-private.

The class in Listing 3-11 tells Spring to look for bean definitions in package constructor and its subpackages. If we want to widen or restrict the scanning context, we can do so by declaring the @ComponentScan annotation with the basePackages attribute that allows the declaration of a package or a collection of packages where Spring will look for components.

For example:

- @ComponentScan(basePackages = "com.apress.prospring6") tells Spring to look for component classes in package com.apress.prospring6 and all its subpackages.

- @ComponentScan(basePackages = { "com.apress.prospring6.two", "com. apress.prospring6.three" }) tells Spring to look for component classes in package com.apress.prospring6.two and package com.apress.prospring6.three and all their subpackages.

ℹ️ Bean definitions on package-private classes are picked up by the @ComponentScan configuration that includes the package they are part of.

Component scanning is a time-consuming operation, and it is good programming practice to try to limit the places where Spring will look for bean definitions in the codebase. The @ComponentScan annotation provides other attributes beside basePackages to help build concise definitions of the scanning locations:

- basePackageClasses: A class or more can be configured; the package of each class specified will be scanned.

- includeFilters: Specifies which types are eligible for component scanning.

- excludeFilters: Specifies which types are not eligible for component scanning.

In real-life production applications, there might be legacy code, developed with older versions of Spring, or requirements might be of such a nature that require XML and configuration classes. Fortunately, XML and Java/Kotlin configuration can be mixed in more than one way. For example, a configuration class can import bean definitions from an XML file (or more) using @ImportResource, and the same bootstrapping using AnnotationConfigApplicationContext will work in this case as well. Other bean definitions from Java/Kotlin configuration classes can be imported using @Import.

So, Spring allows you to be really creative when defining your beans; you'll learn more about this in **Chapter 4**, which is focused solely on Spring application configuration.

Using Setter Injection

In the previous section, setter injection was used to configure the renderer bean, but since the focus was on the Spring configuration classes, some extra details are needed.

To configure setter injection, the @Autowired annotation must be put on every setter that is called by Spring to inject a dependency. Listing 3-12 shows the version of StandardOutMessageRenderer that is designed to support setter injection.

Listing 3-12. Declaring StandardOutMessageRenderer Beans Using @Component and Setter Injection

```
package com.apress.prospring6.three.setter

import org.springframework.beans.factory.annotation.Autowired
// other import statements omitted

@Component("renderer")
class StandardOutMessageRenderer : MessageRenderer {
    override var messageProvider:MessageProvider? = null
        @Autowired set(value) {
            println(" ~~ Injecting dependency using setter ~~")
            field = value
        }

    // other code omitted
}
```

To make sure that when executing the code the dependency is injected using the setter method. we added the println(" ~~ Injecting dependency using setter ~~") statement to the setter method.

The Java/Kotlin configuration class requires no changes; if @ComponentScan is configured correctly, the bean definitions are discovered regardless of the injection style used.

❗ Instead of @Autowired, you can use @Resource(name="provider") to achieve the same result. @Resource is one of the annotations in the JSR-250 ("Common Annotations for the Java Platform") standard that defines a common set of Java annotations for use on both JSE and JEE platforms. This annotation is currently part of the jakarta.annotation-api library. Different from @Autowired, the @Resource annotation supports the name parameter for more fine-grained DI requirements. Additionally, Spring supports use of the @Inject annotation introduced as part of JSR-299 ("Contexts and Dependency Injection for the Java EE Platform"), later moved to JSR-330 ("Dependency Injection for Java"). @Inject is equivalent in behavior to Spring's @Autowired annotation and currently is part of the jakarta.inject-api library.

The code to bootstrap a Spring application context to test that configuring a Spring bean using setter injection works as intended is the same as the code for the HelloWorldSpringAnnotated class.

ⓘ   In the project attached to this book, most class names containing a `main(..)` method to bootstrap a Spring application context are suffixed with Demo. The demo class for this section is named `SetterInjectionDemo` and all bean definitions and configuration are part of the `SetterInjectionDemo.java` file. This decision was made to keep all implementations in a single file to make it easy to find their locations within the project.

Using Constructor Injection

In the previous section a provider instance was injected into the `renderer` bean via a setter method. This works fine, because the @Autowired annotation by default enforces the injection of a dependency, and thus the Spring application cannot be started if there is a missing dependency. As you will see later in the book, there are cases when injecting a dependency via setter is not an option, because of the way Spring creates the beans: it first instantiates the constructor, then it invokes the setters to inject dependencies. If you want to make sure that a bean is not even created without its dependencies, you can do so by enforcing this earlier in the life cycle, right at the instantiation step, by declaring your dependency as an argument for the constructor, ergo designing your bean for *constructor injection.*

In our examples so far, creating a `renderer` if there is no provider makes no sense, so a better design for our `StandardOutMessageRenderer` class should involve a constructor with a `MessageProvider`, as shown in Listing 3-13.

Listing 3-13. `StandardOutMessageRenderer` Designed for Constructor Injection

```
package com.apress.prospring6.three.constructor
// import statements omitted

@Component("renderer")
class StandardOutMessageRenderer @Autowired constructor(
        override var messageProvider:MessageProvider?)
    : MessageRenderer {

    init {
        println(" ~~ Injecting dependency using constructor ~~")
    }
    // other code omitted
}
```

By implementing `MessageRenderer` like this, we've made it impossible to create an instance of `StandardOutMessageRenderer` without providing a value for the `messageProvider`. The @Autowired annotation is used to decorate the constructor, which tells Spring which constructor to use when instantiating this bean, in case there is more than one.

ⓘ   In Spring 4.x, it was decided that if a bean declares a single constructor that initializes all dependencies, the @Autowired annotation was redundant, so in the spirit of **convention over configuration**, the Spring IoC was modified to call the only constructor present to create the bean regardless of the presence/absence of the annotation. So, the `renderer` bean declared in Listing 3-13 is valid even if the @Autowired annotation is removed.

Since we mentioned that a class representing a bean definition can have more than one constructor, we present to you the ConstructorConfusion class in Listing 3-14.

Listing 3-14. ConstructorConfusion Class with Multiple Constructors

```kotlin
package com.apress.prospring6.three.constructor

import org.springframework.beans.factory.annotation.Autowired
import org.springframework.beans.factory.annotation.Value
import org.springframework.context.annotation.AnnotationConfigApplicationContext
import org.springframework.stereotype.Component

@Component
class ConstructorConfusion {
    private var someValue: String

    constructor(someValue: String) {
        println("ConstructorConfusion(String) called")
        this.someValue = someValue
    }

    @Autowired // this is what makes this work
    constructor(@Value("90") someValue: Int) {
        println("ConstructorConfusion(int) called")
        this.someValue = "Number: " + Integer.toString(someValue)
    }

    override fun toString(): String {
        return someValue
    }

    companion object {
        @JvmStatic
        fun main(args: Array<String>) {
            val ctx = AnnotationConfigApplicationContext()
            ctx.register(ConstructorConfusion::class.java)
            ctx.refresh()
            val cc = ctx.getBean(ConstructorConfusion::class.java)
            println("Does this work? $cc")
        }
    }
}
```

The ConstructorConfusion bean definition in Listing 3-14 is correct, because the second constructor is annotated with @Autowired. This tells Spring to use this constructor to instantiate this bean. Without that annotation, Spring cannot decide on its own which constructor to use, and running this class results in the following exception being thrown:

```
Caused by: org.springframework.beans.BeanInstantiationException:
    Failed to instantiate [com.apress.prospring6.three.constructor.ConstructorConfusion]:
    No default constructor found;
        nested exception is java.lang.NoSuchMethodException: com.apress.prospring6.three.
        constructor.ConstructorConfusion.<init>()
```

Notice the @Value annotation in the constructor annotated with @Autowired. This annotation is explained later in this chapter, but for now, in this simple example, know that it is necessary to inject a value for the constructor parameter, and that the constructor would not work without it.

For now, you can ignore that the ConstructorConfusion class has its own main(..) method used to do the following:

- Instantiate a simple, empty Spring application context of type AnnotationConfigApplicationContext

- that is then populated with the bean definition represented by the ConstructorConfusion class by calling ctx. register(ConstructorConfusion.class)

- and then the context is refreshed by calling refresh(), which re-creates all the beans according to the registered bean definitions.

Or you have already read all this and find it incredibly interesting that you can register bean definitions programmatically, without the need for a configuration class.

The example in Listing 3-14 also highlights that the @Autowired annotation can be applied to only one of the constructors within a class. If we apply the annotation to more than one constructor method, Spring will complain while bootstrapping ApplicationContext.

Another scenario that is interesting to introduce here is what happens if the dependency is not a bean. What if it is a simple object, such as a String? Let's tackle that by creating a configurable message provider. A configurable MessageProvider that allows the message to be defined externally is shown in Listing 3-15.

Listing 3-15. Configurable MessageProvider Implementation

package com.apress.prospring6.three.configurable

import org.springframework.beans.factory.annotation.Value
// import statements omitted

```
@Component("provider")
internal class ConfigurableMessageProvider(
        @Value("Configurable message") override var message: String) :
    MessageProvider {

    init {
        println("~~ Injecting '$message' value into constructor ~~")
        this.message = message
    }
}
```

By implementing MessageProvider like this, we've made it impossible to create an instance of ConfigurableMessageProvider without providing a value for the message. Notice the @Value annotation used to define the value to be injected into the constructor. This is how we inject values that are not beans into a Spring bean. Sadly, in this example the value is specified within the annotation declaration, so there is a necessary hard-coding, but using SpEL dynamic value injection is possible from other sources such as property files (more on this later in this chapter).

Using Field Injection

There is a third type of dependency injection supported in Spring called *field injection*. As the name indicates, the dependency is injected directly into the field, with no constructor or setter needed. This is done by annotating the class member with the @Autowired annotation. This might seem practical, because when the dependency is not needed outside the object it is part of, it relieves the developer of writing some code that is no longer used after the initial creation of the bean. In Listing 3-16, the bean of type NonSingletonDemo has a field of type Inspiration.

Listing 3-16. NonSingletonDemo Class Used to Show Field Injection

```
package com.apress.prospring6.three.field

import org.springframework.stereotype.Component
// import statements omitted

@Component("singer")
internal class Singer {
    @Autowired
    private val inspirationBean: Inspiration? = null

    fun sing() {
        println("... " + inspirationBean!!.lyric)
    }
}
```

The field is private, but the Spring IoC container does not really care about that; it uses reflection to populate the required dependency.

The Inspiration class code is shown in Listing 3-17 together with the class used to bootstrap a Spring application context; it is a simple bean with a String field.

Listing 3-17. Inspiration Class and Demo Class Used to Show How Field Injection Works

```
package com.apress.prospring6.three.field;
// import statements omitted

@Component
internal class Inspiration(
    @Value("For all my running, I can understand") lyric: String
) {
    var lyric = "I can keep the door cracked open, to let light through"

    init {
        this.lyric = lyric
    }
}

// demo class
object SingerFieldInjectionDemo {
    @JvmStatic
    fun main(args: Array<String>) {
        val ctx = AnnotationConfigApplicationContext()
        ctx.register(Singer::class.java, Inspiration::class.java)
        ctx.refresh()
        val singerBean = ctx.getBean(Singer::class.java)
        singerBean.sing()
    }
}
```

Finding one bean of type `Inspiration`, the Spring IoC container will inject that bean in the inspirationBean field of the `singer` bean. That is why when running the main class prints in the console *For all my running, I can understand.*

However, there are a few drawbacks, and this is why **using field injection is not recommended.** Here is the list of drawbacks:

- *A risk of violating the single responsibility principle*: Having more dependencies means more responsibilities for a class, which might lead to difficulty separating concerns at refactoring time. The situation when a class becomes bloated is easier to see when dependencies are set using constructors or setters but is quite well hidden when using field injection.

- *Dependency hiding*: The responsibility of injecting dependencies is passed to the container in Spring, but the class should clearly communicate the type of dependencies needed using a public interface, through methods or constructors. Using field injection, it can become unclear what type of dependency is really needed and if the dependency is mandatory or not. *(It's pretty similar to how some partners don't communicate their needs but expect you to magically read their minds and satisfy them.)*

- *Dependency on the Spring IoC*: Field injection introduces a dependency of the Spring container, as the `@Autowired` annotation is a Spring component; thus, the bean is no longer a POJO and cannot be instantiated independently. (Unless you use `@Resource` or `@Inject` and a different container, that is.)

- *Field injection cannot be used for final fields*: This type of field can only be initialized using constructor injection.

- *Difficulties writing tests*: Field injection introduces difficulties when writing tests because the dependencies must be injected manually.

However, it is practical to use @Autowired in instance variables *only* for @Configuration and @Test classes—for the latter primarily if integration testing where Spring is involved.

Using Injection Parameters

In previous examples, we briefly mentioned that other components and values can be injected into a bean by using both setter injection and constructor injection. Spring supports a myriad of options for injection parameters, allowing you to inject not only other components and simple values but also Java/Kotlin collections, externally defined properties, and even beans in another factory. Let's delve into this a little more.

Injecting Simple Values

Injecting simple values into your beans is easy. Spring supports a myriad of options for injection parameters, allowing you to inject not only other components and simple values but also collections, externally defined properties, and even beans in another factory. To do so, simply specify the value in the @Value annotation. By default, not only can the @Value annotation read String values, but it can also convert these values to any primitive or primitive wrapper class. The code snippet in Listing 3-18 shows a simple bean that has a variety of properties exposed for injection.

Listing 3-18. InjectSimpleDemo Class Used to Show Injecting Value in Properties of Various Types

```
package com.apress.prospring6.three.valinject

import org.springframework.beans.factory.annotation.Value
import org.springframework.context.annotation.AnnotationConfigApplicationContext
import org.springframework.stereotype.Component

@Component("injectSimple")
class InjectSimpleDemo {
    @Value("John Mayer")
    private val name: String? = null

    @Value("40")
    private val age = 0

    @Value("1.92")
    private val height = 0f

    @Value("false")
    private val developer = false
```

```
@Value("1241401112")
private val ageInSeconds: Long? = null
override fun toString(): String {
    return """
        Name: $name
        Age: $age
        Age in Seconds: $ageInSeconds
        Height: $height
        Is Developer?: $developer
    """.trimIndent()
}

companion object {
    @JvmStatic
    fun main(args: Array<String>) {
        val ctx = AnnotationConfigApplicationContext()
        ctx.register(InjectSimpleDemo::class.java)
        ctx.refresh()
        val simple = ctx.getBean("injectSimple") as InjectSimpleDemo
        println(simple)
    }
}
}
}
```

The @Value annotation can be used directly on fields as well, and is used like this in the InjectSimpleDemo class to keep things simple and avoid the boilerplate of setters code. If you run this class, the console output is as expected, shown in Listing 3-19.

Listing 3-19. Console Output Resulting When Running the Class in Listing 3-18

```
Name: John Mayer
Age: 39
Age in Seconds: 1241401112
Height: 1.92
Is Programmer?: false
```

Injecting Values Using SpEL

The example in Listing 3-18 shows the capabilities of automatic conversion that Spring has when injecting property values. However, the example is still quite basic since the values are hard-coded in the @Value annotation. This is where SpEL makes things interesting.

One powerful feature that was introduced in Spring 3 is the **Spring Expression Language (SpEL)**. SpEL enables you to evaluate an expression dynamically and then use it in Spring's ApplicationContext. You can use the result for injection into Spring beans. In this section, we look at how to use SpEL to inject properties from other beans, by using the example in the preceding section.

Suppose now we want to externalize the values to be injected into a Spring bean in a configuration class, as shown in Listing 3-20.

Listing 3-20. Spring Configuration Class Providing a Few Values As Fields

```
package com.apress.prospring6.three.valinject
// import statements omitted

@Component("injectSimpleConfig")
internal class InjectSimpleConfig {
    val name = "John Mayer"
    val age = 40
    val height = 1.92f
    val isDeveloper = false
    val ageInSeconds = 1241401112L
}
```

The first thing to do is to edit the @Value annotations and replace the hard-coded values with SpEL expressions referencing properties of this bean. The second thing to do is to add a bean of this type to the configuration. Both are shown in Listing 3-21.

Listing 3-21. @Value Annotations Customized to Use SpEL Expressions

```
package com.apress.prospring6.three.valinject
// import statements omitted

@Component("injectSimpleSpEL")
class InjectSimpleSpELDemo {
    @Value("#{injectSimpleConfig.name.toUpperCase()}")
    private val name: String? = null

    @Value("#{injectSimpleConfig.age + 1}")
    private val age = 0

    @Value("#{injectSimpleConfig.height}")
    private val height = 0f

    @Value("#{injectSimpleConfig.developer}")
    private val developer = false

    @Value("#{injectSimpleConfig.ageInSeconds}")
    private val ageInSeconds: Long? = null
    override fun toString(): String {
        return """
            Name: $name
            Age: $age
            Age in Seconds: $ageInSeconds
            Height: $height
            Is Developer?: $developer
            """.trimIndent()
    }
}
```

```
companion object {
    @JvmStatic
    fun main(args: Array<String>) {
        val ctx = AnnotationConfigApplicationContext()
        ctx.register(InjectSimpleConfig::class.java, InjectSimpleSpELDemo::class.java)
        ctx.refresh()
        val simple = ctx.getBean("injectSimpleSpEL") as InjectSimpleSpELDemo
        println(simple)
    }
}
}
}
```

Notice that we use the SpEL #{injectSimpleConfig.name} in referencing the property of the other bean. Notice also how there is no getter called, but the SpEL expression contains the bean and property name concatenated by a ".".(dot) and Spring knows exactly what to do. SpEL supports String manipulation and arithmetic operations as well, as shown by calling toUpperCase() on the name property before injection and by adding 1 to the value of the bean property before injection. If you run the main(..) method of the InjectSimpleSpELDemo class, the output depicted in Listing 3-22 should be printed in the console.

Listing 3-22. Console Output Resulting from Running the Class in Listing 3-21

```
Name: JOHN MAYER
Age: 41
Age in Seconds: 1241401112
Height: 1.92
Is Developer?: false
```

Since the toUpperCase() call was added to the name property, the output is almost identical to the example where values were hard-coded. Using SpEL, you can access any Spring-managed beans and properties and manipulate them for application use by Spring's support of sophisticated language features and syntax.

Injection and ApplicationContext Nesting

So far, the beans we have been injecting have been located in the same ApplicationContext (and hence the same BeanFactory) as the beans they are injected into. However, Spring supports a hierarchical structure for ApplicationContext so that one context (and hence the associating BeanFactory) is considered the parent of another. By allowing ApplicationContext instances to be nested, Spring allows you to split your configuration into different files, which is a godsend on larger projects with lots of beans.

When nesting ApplicationContext instances, Spring allows beans in what is considered the child context to reference beans in the parent context. In XML this was easy to do, because of the <ref/> tag, which could be configured to reference a bean in the parent context via its parent attribute. Using Java/Kotlin configuration and annotation, the task is a little more tedious but still doable. Let us show you the magic.

ApplicationContext nesting using AnnotationConfigApplicationContext is simple to understand. To nest one AnnotationConfigApplicationContext inside another, simply call the setParent() method in the child ApplicationContext as shown in Listing 3-23.

Listing 3-23. Nesting Application Contexts

```kotlin
package com.apress.prospring6.three.nesting
// import statements omitted

object ContextNestingDemo {
    @JvmStatic
    fun main(args: Array<String>) {
        val parentCtx = AnnotationConfigApplicationContext()
        parentCtx.register(ParentConfig::class.java)
        parentCtx.refresh()
        val childCtx = AnnotationConfigApplicationContext()
        childCtx.register(ChildConfig::class.java)
        childCtx.parent = parentCtx
        childCtx.refresh()
        val song1: Song = childCtx.getBean("song1") as Song
        val song2: Song = childCtx.getBean("song2") as Song
        val song3: Song = childCtx.getBean("song3") as Song
        println("from parent ctx: " + song1.title)
        println("from parent ctx: " + song2.title)
        println("from child ctx: " + song3.title)
    }
}
```

This method is inherited from the `org.springframework.context.support.`
`GenericApplicationContext` that is a superclass of `AnnotationConfigApplicationContext`. The
method is, however, declared higher in the hierarchy, in the `org.springframework.context.`
`ConfigurableApplicationContext` interface that provides facilities to configure an application context in
addition to the application context client methods in the `ApplicationContext` interface. The full hierarchy
that `AnnotationConfigApplicationContext` is part of is depicted in Figure 3-5.

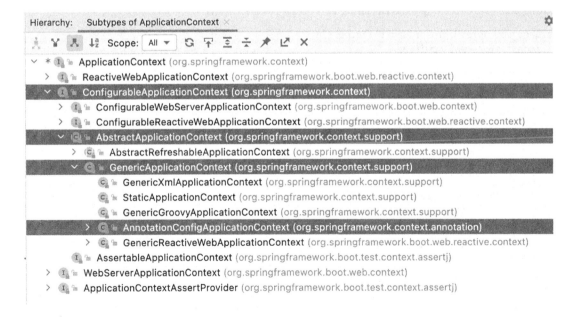

Figure 3-5. *AnnotationConfigApplicationContext hierarchy*

The context nesting is easy to set up, but accessing beans from the parent...not so much.

The Song class is just a very simple POJO with a field named `title`. To declare song title depending on the context, a class named `TitleProvider` is used. This class can be instantiated with various titles via a companion object builder method. This class is very simple as well. Both these classes are shown in Listing 3-24.

Listing 3-24. Song and `TitleProvider` Classes

```kotlin
package com.apress.prospring6.three.nesting

// Song.kt
class Song(val title: String?)

// TitleProvider.kt
class TitleProvider {
    var title:String? = "Gravity"

    companion object {
        fun instance(title: String?): TitleProvider {
            val childProvider = TitleProvider()
            if (title != null && title.isNotBlank())
                childProvider.title = title
            return childProvider
        }
    }
}
```

The `ParentConfig` class is simple and declares two `TitleProvider` beans named `parentProvider` and `childProvider` as shown in Listing 3-25.

Listing 3-25. `ParentConfig` Class Declaring Two `TitleProvider` Beans

```kotlin
package com.apress.prospring6.three.nesting
// import statements omitted

@Configuration
open class ParentConfig {
    @Bean
    open fun parentProvider(): TitleProvider {
        return TitleProvider.instance(null)
    }

    @Bean
    open fun childProvider(): TitleProvider {
        return TitleProvider.instance("Daughters")
    }
}
```

The ChildConfig class declares three Song beans, each of which has a title injected from a TitleProvider bean:

- song1 is injected with the title value provided by the bean named parentProvider; since there is a single bean named parentProvider in the parent context, which the child context inherits, the injected value is *Gravity*.

- song2 is injected with the title value provided the bean named childProvider declared in the parent context; since there is a bean named childProvider in the child context as well, to access the one from the parent context, some *coding acrobatics* are required (this is way easier using XML configuration):

  - To access the bean from the parent context, access to the current context is needed. This is done by implementing the ApplicationContextAware interface and declaring a property of type ApplicationContext that will be initialized by Spring with a reference to the current application context by calling the setApplicationContext(..) method.

  - Once we have a reference to the current context, we write a complicated SpEL expression designed to get a reference to the parent context, access the child-Provider, and get the title value, which is expected to be Daughters.

- song3 is injected with the title value provided the bean named childProvider; since there is a bean named childProvider in the current context, the injected value is *No Such Thing*.

The code is depicted in Listing 3-26.

Listing 3-26. Injecting Beans Properties from a Parent Context in Beans in a Child Context: Output

```
package com.apress.prospring6.three.nesting

import org.springframework.beans.BeansException
import org.springframework.context.ApplicationContextAware
// import statements omitted

@Configuration
open class ChildConfig : ApplicationContextAware {
    var applicationContext1: ApplicationContext? = null

    @Bean // overrides {@code childProvider} bean from parent context
    open fun childProvider(): TitleProvider {
        return TitleProvider.instance("No Such Thing")
    }

    @Bean
    open fun song1(@Value("#{parentProvider.title}") title: String?): Song {
        return Song(title)
    }
```

```
@Bean
open fun song2(
@Value("#{childConfig.applicationContext1.parent.getBean(\"childProvider\").title}")
title:String?): Song {
    return Song(title)
}

@Bean
open fun song3(@Value("#{childProvider.title}") title: String?): Song {
    return Song(title)
}

@Throws(BeansException::class)
override fun setApplicationContext(applicationContext: ApplicationContext) {
    this.applicationContext1 = applicationContext
}
}
```

The SpEL expression in the @Value annotation for bean song2 seems complicated, but it really isn't. Remember how we accessed beans in every demo class so far? This is exactly what this expression does, only instead of accessing the bean from the current context, it does so from its parent. Let us explain:

- The expression needs to start with childConfig because this is the name of the configuration bean. It was mentioned before that SpEL can access bean properties. The current application context is referenced by the applicationContext property of the bean childConfig.

- parent is a property of an ApplicationContext that references the parent context. If there is no parent, it is null, but in this example, we know that we have one.

- getBean("childProvider") is the typical method we've used before to obtain a reference to a bean using its name. In Kotlin code, a conversion to the appropriate type was needed, whereas SpEL figures it out on its own.

Listing 3-27 is the output from running the ContextNestingDemo class.

Listing 3-27. Injecting Beans Properties from a Parent Context in Beans in a Child Context

```
from parent ctx: Gravity
from parent ctx: No Such Thing
from child ctx: Daughters
```

As expected, the song1 and song2 beans both get a title value from beans in the parent ApplicationContext, whereas the song3 bean gets a title value from a bean in the child ApplicationContext.

Injecting Collections

Often your beans need access to collections of objects rather than just individual beans or values. Therefore, it should come as no surprise that Spring allows you to inject a collection of objects into one of your beans. In the previous edition of this book, lists, sets, maps, and properties values were configured using XML. Since this book is not focused on that, let's see how we can declare collections in using Java/Kotlin configuration. It's quite easy, really: just declare methods annotated with @Bean in a configuration class that returns List<E>, Set<E>, Properties, or Map<K,V>. This section covers only the List<E> type, but the sources for the book contain examples for all types.

For the next example, we'll make use of the Song class used in the previous section. The type CollectionConfig declares a List<Song> bean and is depicted in Listing 3-28.

Listing 3-28. Configuration Class Declaring a Bean of Type List<Song>

```kotlin
package com.apress.prospring6.three.collectioninject
// import statements omitted

@Configuration
internal open class CollectionConfig {
    @Bean
    open fun list(): List<Song> {
        return listOf(
            Song("Not the end"),
            Song("Rise Up")
        )
    }

    @Bean
    open fun set(): Set<Song> {
        return setOf(
            Song("Ordinary Day"),
            Song("Birds Fly")
        )
    }

    @Bean
    open fun map(): Map<String, Song> {
        return mapOf(
            "John Mayer" to Song("Gravity"),
            "Ben Barnes" to Song("11:11")
        )
    }

    @Bean
    open fun props(): Properties {
        val props = Properties()
        props["said.she"] = "Never Mine"
        props["said.he"] = "Cold and jaded"
        return props
    }

    @Bean
    open fun song1(): Song {
        return Song("Here's to hoping")
    }
```

```kotlin
    @Bean
    open fun song2(): Song {
        return Song("Wishing the best for you")
    }
}
```

The CollectionConfig class also declares two beans of type Song. The purpose of these beans will become obvious a bit further in this section.

The CollectingBean is a type for the bean where the list bean is injected and the values are printed by invoking the printCollections() method. The CollectionInjectionDemo class is where the main(..) method is declared containing the code to create the application context, get a reference to a CollectingBean bean, and invoking the printCollections() method to check that the list value was injected. The code Listing 3-29 shows both classes.

Listing 3-29. Demo Class for Testing Configuration Class Declaring a Bean of Type List<Song>

```kotlin
package com.apress.prospring6.three.collectioninject
// import statements omitted

object CollectionInjectionDemo {
    @JvmStatic
    fun main(args: Array<String>) {
        val ctx = AnnotationConfigApplicationContext()
        ctx.register(CollectionConfig::class.java, CollectingBean::class.java)
        ctx.refresh()
        val collectingBean = ctx.getBean(CollectingBean::class.java)
        collectingBean.printCollections()
    }
}

@Component
internal class CollectingBean {
    @Autowired
    @Qualifier("list")
    var songListResource:List<Song>? = null

    @Autowired
    var songList:List<Song>? = null

    @Autowired
    var songSet: Set<Song>? = null

    @Autowired
    @Qualifier("set")
    var songSetResource:Set<Song>? = null

    @Autowired
    var songMap: Map<String, Song>? = null

    @Autowired
    @Qualifier("map")
    var songMapResource:Map<String, Song>? = null
```

```kotlin
    @Autowired
    var props: Properties? = null
    fun printCollections() {
        println("-- list injected using @Autowired -- ")
        songList!!.forEach(Consumer<Song> { s: Song -> println(s.title) })
        println("""-- list injected using @Resource / @Autowired @Qualifier(\"list\") /
                @Inject @Named(\"list\") -- """)
        songListResource!!.forEach(Consumer<Song> { s: Song
            -> println(s.title) })
        println("-- set injected using @Autowired -- -- ")
        songSet!!.forEach(Consumer<Song> { s: Song -> println(s.title) })
        println("""-- set injected using @Resource / @Autowired @Qualifier(\"set\") /
                @Inject @Named(\"set\") -- """)
        songSetResource!!.forEach(Consumer<Song> { s: Song ->
            println(s.title) })
        println("-- map injected using  @Autowired -- ")
        songMap!!.forEach(BiConsumer<String, Song> { k: String, v: Song ->
            println(k + ": " + v.title) })
        println("""-- map injected using @Resource / @Autowired @Qualifier(\"map\") /
                @Inject @Named(\"map\")-- """)
        songMapResource!!.forEach(BiConsumer<String, Song> { k: String, v: Song ->
            println(k + ": " + v.title) })
        println("-- props injected with @Autowired -- ")
        props!!.forEach { k: Any, v: Any -> println("$k: $v") }
    }
}
```

The code looks simple enough, but when we run it, here's what is printed:

```
Here's to hoping
Wishing the best for you
```

Wait, what? Yup, the two extra Song beans have been added to a list and injected into the songList property, instead of the list bean, as we expected. What happened here? The behavior you are seeing is caused by the @Autowired annotation. The @Autowired annotation is semantically defined in a way that it always treats arrays, collections, and maps as sets of corresponding beans, with the target bean type derived from the declared collection value type. Our class has an attribute of type List<Song> and has the @Autowired annotation on it, thus Spring will try to inject all beans of type Song within the current ApplicationContext into this property, which will result in either the unexpected dependencies being injected or Spring throwing an exception if no bean of type Song was defined.

So, for collection type injection, we have to explicitly instruct Spring to perform injection by specifying the bean name, and this can be done by using the Spring @Qualifier annotation, the one in the org.springframework.beans.factory.annotation. This statement is necessary because there is a @Qualifier annotation in the Jakarta Inject library too, and it has a different purpose. This means annotating the songList dependency with @Autowired @Qualifier("list") ensures the expected behavior. However, there are three additional ways to do it:

- @Inject @Named("list"): Both annotations can be found in the jakarta.inject package. The @Inject annotation is the Jakarta equivalent of Spring's @Autowired and the @Named annotation is the equivalent of Spring's @Qualifier.

- @Resource(name="list"): This annotation, mentioned previously, can be found in the jakarta.annotation package and it is one of the preferred ways to do collection injection because using one annotation is better than using two of them.

- @Value("#{collectionConfig.list}"): Since it is preferable to keep it in the Spring domain, and add as little dependencies to your application as possible, this is actually the recommended way to inject collections, and there is no doubt what will be injected.

⚠️ The behavior described for injecting collections applies for Set and Map too, with the only difference being that in a Map Spring will inject {beanName,bean} key-value pairs.

Using Method Injection

Beside constructor and setter injection, another less frequently used DI feature that Spring provides is *Method Injection*. Spring's Method Injection capabilities come in two loosely related forms, Lookup Method Injection and Method Replacement. Lookup Method Injection provides another mechanism by which a bean can obtain one of its dependencies. Method Replacement allows you to replace the implementation of any method on a bean arbitrarily, without having to change the original source code. To provide these two features, Spring uses the dynamic bytecode enhancement capabilities of CGLIB. CGLIB is a powerful, high-performance, high-quality code-generation library. It can extend Java/Kotlin classes and implement interfaces at runtime. It is open source, and you can find the official repository at https://github.com/cglib/cglib.

Lookup Method Injection

Lookup Method Injection was added to Spring in version 1.1 to overcome the problems encountered when a bean depends on another bean with a different life cycle, specifically, when a singleton depends on a non-singleton. In this situation, both setter and constructor injection result in the singleton maintaining a single instance of what should be a non-singleton bean. In some cases, you will want to have the singleton bean obtain a new instance of the non-singleton every time it requires the bean in question.

Consider a scenario in which a LockOpener class provides the service of opening any locker. The LockOpener class relies on a KeyHelper class for opening the locker, which was injected into LockOpener. However, the design of the KeyHelper class involves some internal states that make it not suitable for reuse. Every time the openLock() method is called, a new KeyHelper instance is required. In this case, LockOpener will be a singleton. However, if we inject the KeyHelper class by using the normal mechanism, the same instance of the KeyHelper class (which was instantiated when Spring performed the injection the first time) will be reused. To make sure that a new instance of the KeyHelper instance is passed into the openLock() method every time it is invoked, we need to use Lookup Method Injection.

Typically, you can achieve this by having the singleton bean implement the ApplicationContextAware interface (we discuss this interface in **Chapter 4**). Then, using the ApplicationContext instance, the singleton bean can look up a new instance of the non-singleton dependency every time it needs it. Lookup Method Injection allows the singleton bean to declare that it requires a non-singleton dependency and that it will receive a new instance of the non-singleton bean each time it needs to interact with it, without needing to implement any Spring-specific interfaces.

Lookup Method Injection works by having your singleton declare a method, the lookup method, which returns an instance of the non-singleton bean. When you obtain a reference to the singleton in your application, you are actually receiving a reference to a dynamically created subclass on which Spring has implemented the lookup method. A typical implementation involves defining the lookup method, and thus the bean class, as abstract. This prevents any strange errors from creeping in when you forget to configure the Method Injection and you are working directly against the bean class with the empty method implementation instead of the Spring-enhanced subclass. This topic is quite complex and is best shown by example.

In this example, we create one non-singleton bean and two singleton beans that both implement the same interface. One of the singletons obtains an instance of the non-singleton bean by using "traditional" setter injection; the other uses Method Injection. The code sample in Listing 3-30 depicts the KeyHelper class, which in this example is the type of the non-singleton bean, which means instances of this type are created every time one is required to be injected as a dependency.

Listing 3-30. Non-Singleton Bean

```
package com.apress.prospring6.three.methodinject

import org.springframework.context.annotation.Scope
// import statements omitted

@Component("keyHelper")
@Scope("prototype")
class KeyHelper {
    fun open(){
    }
}
```

This class is decidedly unexciting, but it serves the purposes of this example perfectly. Next, in Listing 3-31 you can see the LockOpener interface, which is implemented by both of the singleton bean classes.

Listing 3-31. Singleton Bean Interface Type

```
package com.apress.prospring6.three.methodinject

interface LockOpener {
    fun createKeyOpener():KeyHelper?
    fun openLock()
}
```

This bean has two method: createKeyOpener() and openLock(). The sample application uses the createKeyOpener() method to get a reference to a KeyHelper instance and, in the case of the method lookup bean, to perform the actual method lookup. The openLock() method is a simple method that depends on the KeyHelper instance to do its processing. Listing 3-32 shows the StandardLockOpener class, which uses setter injection to obtain an instance of the KeyHelper class.

Listing 3-32. StandardLockOpener Class Configured Using Autowiring to Obtain a Dependency of Type
KeyHelper

```
package com.apress.prospring6.three.methodinject
// import statements omitted

@Component("standardLockOpener")
internal class StandardLockOpener : LockOpener {
    var keyOpener: KeyHelper? = null

    override fun createKeyOpener(): KeyHelper? {
        return keyOpener
    }

    @Autowired
    @Qualifier("keyHelper")
    fun setKeyHelper(keyHelper: KeyHelper?) {
        keyOpener = keyHelper
    }

    override fun openLock() {
        keyOpener!!.open()
    }
}
```

This code should all look familiar, but notice that the openLock() method uses the stored instance of
KeyHelper to complete its processing. In Listing 3-33, you can see the AbstractLockOpener class, which uses
Method Injection to obtain an instance of the KeyHelper class, configured using the org.springframework.
beans.factory.annotation.Lookup annotation.

Listing 3-33. AbstractLockOpener Class Configured Using Method Injection to Obtain a Dependency of
Type KeyHolder

```
package com.apress.prospring6.three.methodinject

import org.springframework.beans.factory.annotation.Lookup
// import statements omitted

@Component("abstractLockOpener")
internal abstract class AbstractLockOpener : LockOpener {
    @get:Lookup("keyHelper")
    abstract override fun createKeyOpener(): KeyHelper?

    override fun openLock() {
        myKeyOpener!!.open()
    }
}
```

Notice that the createKeyOpener() method is declared as abstract and that this method is used by
the openLock() method to obtain a KeyHelper instance. Populating an application context with the bean
definitions in this section might require writing more code than writing a simple configuration class, thus in
Listing 3-34 the configuration class is depicted.

Listing 3-34. The Kotlin Configuration Class for This Section

```kotlin
package com.apress.prospring6.three.methodinject
// import statements omitted


@Configuration
@ComponentScan
class LookupConfig
```

The configuration for the keyHelper and standardLockOpener beans should look familiar to you by now. For abstractLockOpener, you need to configure the lookup method by using the @Lookup annotation. This tells Spring which method on the bean it should override. This method must not accept any arguments, and the return type should be that of the bean you want to return from the method. In this case, the method should return a class of type KeyHelper, or its subclasses. The annotation attribute value tells Spring which bean the lookup method should return. Listing 3-35 shows the final piece of code for this example, which is the class containing the main() method used to run the example.

Listing 3-35. Main Class to Test Method Injection

```kotlin
package com.apress.prospring6.three.methodinject
import org.springframework.util.StopWatch
// import statements omitted

object MethodInjectionDemo {
    @JvmStatic
    fun main(args: Array<String>) {
        val ctx = AnnotationConfigApplicationContext(LookupConfig::class.java)
        val abstractLockOpener = ctx.getBean("abstractLockOpener", LockOpener::class.java)
        val standardLockOpener = ctx.getBean("standardLockOpener", LockOpener::class.java)
        displayInfo("abstractLockOpener", abstractLockOpener)
        displayInfo("standardLockOpener", standardLockOpener)
    }

    fun displayInfo(beanName: String, lockOpener: LockOpener) {
        val keyHelperOne = lockOpener.createKeyOpener()
        val keyHelperTwo = lockOpener.createKeyOpener()
        println("[" + beanName + "]: KeyHelper Instances the Same?  " +
            (keyHelperOne === keyHelperTwo))
        val stopWatch = StopWatch()
        stopWatch.start("lookupDemo")
        for (x in 0..100000 - 1) {
            val keyHelper = lockOpener.createKeyOpener()
            keyHelper!!.open()
        }
        stopWatch.stop()
        println("100000 gets took " + stopWatch.totalTimeMillis + " ms")
    }
}
```

In this code, you can see that the abstractLockOpener and standardLockOpener from the AnnotationConfigApplicationContext are retrieved and each reference is passed to the displayInfo() method. The instantiation of the abstract class is supported only when using Lookup Method Injection, in which Spring will use CGLIB to generate a subclass of the AbstractLockOpener class that overrides the method dynamically. The first part of the displayInfo() method creates two local variables of KeyHelper type and assigns them each a value by calling createKeyOpener() on the bean passed to it. Using these two variables, it writes a message to the console indicating whether the two references point to the same object. For the abstractLockOpener bean, a new instance of KeyHelper should be retrieved for each call to createKeyOpener(), so the references should not be the same.

For standardLockOpener, a single instance of Singer is passed to the bean by setter injection, and this instance is stored and returned for every call to getMyKeyOpener(), so the two references should be the same.

ℹ️   The StopWatch class used in the previous example is a utility class available with Spring. You'll find StopWatch very useful when you need to perform simple performance tests and when you are testing your applications.

The final part of the displayInfo() method runs a simple performance test to see which bean is faster. Clearly, standardLockOpener should be faster because it returns the same instance each time, but it is interesting to see the difference. We can now run the MethodInjectionDemo class for testing. Here is the output we received from this example:

```
[abstractLockOpener]: KeyHelper Instances the Same? false
100000 gets took 431 ms
[standardLockOpener]: KeyHelper Instances the Same? true
100000 gets took 1 ms
```

As you can see, the KeyHelper instances are, as expected, the same when we use standardLockOpener and different when we use abstractLockOpener. There is a noticeable performance difference when you use standardLockOpener, but that is to be expected.

Considerations for Lookup Method Injection

Lookup Method Injection is intended for use when you want to work with two beans of different life cycles. Avoid the temptation to use Lookup Method Injection when the beans share the same life cycle, especially if they are singletons. The output of running the previous example shows a noticeable difference in performance between using Method Injection to obtain new instances of a dependency and using standard DI to obtain a single instance of a dependency. Also, make sure you don't use Lookup Method Injection needlessly, even when you have beans of different life cycles.

Consider a situation in which you have three singletons that share a dependency in common. You want each singleton to have its own instance of the dependency, so you create the dependency as a non-singleton, but you are happy with each singleton using the same instance of the collaborator throughout its life. In this case, setter injection is the ideal solution; Lookup Method Injection just adds unnecessary overhead.

When you are using Lookup Method Injection, there are a few design guidelines that you should keep in mind when building your classes. In the earlier examples, we declared the lookup method in an interface. The only reason we did this was that we did not have to duplicate the displayInfo() method twice for two different bean types. As mentioned earlier, generally you do not need to pollute a business interface with unnecessary definitions that are used solely for IoC purposes. Another point is that although you don't have to make your lookup method abstract, doing so prevents you from forgetting to configure the lookup method and then using a blank implementation by accident.

Understanding Bean Naming

Spring supports quite a complex bean-naming structure that allows you the flexibility to handle many situations. Every bean must have at least one name that is unique within the containing `ApplicationContext`. Spring follows a simple resolution process to determine what name is used for the bean. When using XML configuration, if you give the `<bean>` tag an `id` attribute, the value of that attribute is used as the unique name within the application context.

When using Java/Kotlin configuration, unless explicitly configured, Spring generates bean names using a few strategies, which will be covered in this section. When retrieving beans from the application, bean names or bean types can be used, or both can be used. If multiple beans of the same type without ID or name are declared, Spring will throw an `org.springframework.beans.factory.NoSuchBeanDefinitionException` exception during `ApplicationContext` initialization. Using Java/Kotlin configuration, it is pretty difficult to cause collisions, but it might happen, so it is better to know what to expect.

Default Bean Naming Style for Beans Declared with @Component

For the purpose of this section, the configuration class enables component scanning for the `com.apress.prospring6.three.naming` package. We'll start by declaring a very simple bean, as shown in Listing 3-36.

Listing 3-36. The Simplest Bean Type

```
@Component
class SimpleBean { }
```

To figure out how Spring names the beans by default, we create an `ApplicationContext` based on a configuration that includes the `SimpleBean` class. This class is annotated with `@Component` and is discovered via component scanning. The `ApplicationContext` provides methods to retrieve references to the beans, but also to retrieve all the bean names in the context. In Listing 3-37, all the names of the beans in the context are printed in the console using a Logback logger.

Listing 3-37. Printing All Bean Names

```
package com.apress.prospring6.three.naming

import org.springframework.context.annotation.
    AnnotationConfigApplicationContext
import org.slf4j.Logger
import org.slf4j.LoggerFactory
// other import statements omitted

object BeanNamingDemo {
    private val logger: org.slf4j.Logger =
        org.slf4j.LoggerFactory.getLogger(BeanNamingDemo::class.java)
    @JvmStatic
    fun main(args: Array<String>) {
        val ctx = AnnotationConfigApplicationContext(BeanNamingCfg::class.java)
        ctx.beanDefinitionNames.forEach { beanName ->
            logger.debug(beanName)
        }
    }
}
```

```
@Configuration
@ComponentScan
internal open class BeanNamingCfg {
}

@Component
internal class SimpleBean
```

Part of the console output is depicted in Listing 3-38.

Listing 3-38. Console Log Showing All Bean Names in the Context: Output

```
DEBUG: BeanNamingDemo - org.springframework.context.annotation.
internalConfigurationAnnotationProcessor
DEBUG: BeanNamingDemo - org.springframework.context.annotation.
internalAutowiredAnnotationProcessor
DEBUG: BeanNamingDemo - org.springframework.context.annotation.
internalCommonAnnotationProcessor
DEBUG: BeanNamingDemo - org.springframework.context.event.internalEventListenerProcessor
DEBUG: BeanNamingDemo - org.springframework.context.event.internalEventListenerFactory
DEBUG: BeanNamingDemo - beanNamingCfg
DEBUG: BeanNamingDemo - simpleBean
```

In the list you can see a few bean names that start with `org.springframework`. These are what we call *infrastructure beans* and are internally used by Spring to process bean definitions and create beans. The beans that are not obviously Spring infrastructure beans are beans declared within the application configuration. In the output in Listing 3-38 there are two beans that should spark your interest:

- `beanNamingCfg`: This bean name is the same as the simple name of the configuration class `BeanNamingCfg`. The `@Configuration` annotation is annotated itself with `@Component`, and this means any configuration class is in essence a bean definition.

- `simpleBean`: This bean name is the same as the simple name of the bean class `SimpleBean`.

❗ As proven by the beanNamingCfg and simpleBean names, when bean names are not configured explicitly, Spring takes the simple name of the type declaring the bean, changes the first letter to lowercase, and uses the resulting value to name the bean.

Customizing Bean Naming Style

Before going further and explaining how beans declared with @Beans are named, we'll show you a neat trick. As in almost everything with Spring, if there is a default behavior, it can be customized. Thus, bean naming can be customized. The `@Configuration` annotation has an attribute named `nameGenerator`. The attribute value must be a class implementing `org.springframework.beans.factory.support.BeanNameGenerator` or extending any of the implementations provided by Spring. Listing 3-39 shows the `SimpleBeanNameGenerator` class and the `BeanNamingCfg`.

Listing 3-39. Console Log Showing All Bean Names in the Context

```
package com.apress.prospring6.three.generator

import org.springframework.beans.factory.config.BeanDefinition
import org.springframework.beans.factory.support.
      BeanDefinitionRegistry
import org.springframework.context.annotation.
      AnnotationBeanNameGenerator
import java.util.UUID
// other import statements omitted

@Configuration
@ComponentScan(nameGenerator = SimpleBeanNameGenerator::class)
internal open class BeanNamingCfg {
    @Bean
    open fun anotherSimpleBean(): SimpleBean {
        return SimpleBean()
    }
}

@Component
internal class SimpleBean

internal class SimpleBeanNameGenerator : AnnotationBeanNameGenerator() {
    override fun buildDefaultBeanName(definition: BeanDefinition, registry:
            BeanDefinitionRegistry): String {
        val beanName = definition.beanClassName
            .substring(definition.beanClassName.lastIndexOf(".") + 1).lowercase()
        val uid = UUID.randomUUID().toString().replace("-", "").substring(0, 8)
        return "$beanName-$uid"
    }
}
```

The org.springframework.context.annotation.AnnotationBeanNameGenerator class is the BeanNameGenerator implementation for bean classes annotated with the @Component annotation or with another annotation that is itself annotated with @Component. The SimpleBeanNameGenerator extends this class and overrides the buildDefaultBeanName(..) method to return a bean name composed from the lowercase simple class name concatenated with a unique identifier. When creating an application context and printing the bean names, the output looks pretty similar to that shown in Listing 3-40.

Listing 3-40. Console Log Showing All Bean Names in the Context

```
# infrastructure bean names omitted
DEBUG: BeanNameGerneratorDemo - beanNamingCfg
DEBUG: BeanNameGerneratorDemo - simplebean-07f01cdc
```

❗ The only thing to point out here is that the configuration class, although annotated with @Configuration, which is annotated itself with @Component, is not generated by the SimpleBeanNameGenerator class. This is because this class is not discovered through component scanning, since this is the class that enables component scanning with the custom bean generator that is processed by Spring before the generator is enabled.

Bean Naming Style for Beans Declared with @Bean

We mentioned previously that beans configured by methods annotated with @Bean are named as the methods that configure them. The easiest way to show this is to modify one of our previous examples and declare a SimpleBean in the BeanNamingCfg configuration class using the @Bean annotation. Listing 3-41 depicts the new configuration and the code to execute to list the bean names within the context.

Listing 3-41. Console Log Showing All Bean Names in the Context

```
package com.apress.prospring6.three.naming

import org.springframework.context.annotation.AnnotationConfigApplicationContext
import org.springframework.context.annotation.Bean
import org.springframework.context.annotation.ComponentScan
import org.springframework.context.annotation.Configuration
import org.springframework.stereotype.Component
import java.util.*
import java.util.function.Consumer

object BeanNamingDemo {
    private val logger: org.slf4j.Logger =
        org.slf4j.LoggerFactory.getLogger(BeanNamingDemo::class.java)
    @JvmStatic
    fun main(args: Array<String>) {
        val ctx = AnnotationConfigApplicationContext(BeanNamingCfg::class.java)
        ctx.beanDefinitionNames.forEach { beanName ->
            logger.debug(beanName)
        }
    }
}

@Configuration
@ComponentScan
internal open class BeanNamingCfg {
    @Bean
    open fun anotherSimpleBean(): SimpleBean {
        return SimpleBean()
    }
}
```

```
@Component
internal class SimpleBean
```

Running the code in Listing 3-41 produces the output shown in Listing 3-42.

Listing 3-42. Console Log Showing All Bean Names in the Context

```
# infrastructure bean names omitted
DEBUG: BeanNamingDemo - beanNamingCfg
DEBUG: BeanNamingDemo - simpleBean
DEBUG: BeanNamingDemo - anotherSimpleBean
```

As you can see, an entry named anotherSimpleBean is listed, which means that a SimpleBean was created and named as the method that created it.

Default naming of beans is practical only when one bean of a certain type is needed in the context of an application, but when this is not the case, explicitly naming the beans is the only option.

In the code in Listing 3-41, the two SimpleBean beans were configured through different methods, and thus the names were generated using different approaches. This means that retrieving a bean of type SimpleBean by calling ctx.getBean(SimpleBean.class) no longer works as intended, because that method expects one bean of type SimpleBean to be found. Calling that method will result in the following exception being thrown:

```
Exception in thread "main" org.springframework.beans.factory.
NoUniqueBeanDefinitionException:
No qualifying bean of type 'com.apress.prospring6.three.naming.SimpleBean' available:
    expected single matching bean but found 2: simpleBean,anotherSimpleBean
```

The exception message is pretty clear about what the issue is though.

If you need all the beans of a certain type from the application, there is a method for that, that is shown in Listing 3-43.

Listing 3-43. Code to List All SimpleBean Bean Names in the Context

```
val beans = ctx.getBeansOfType(SimpleBean::class.java)
beans.forEach{ (k, v) ->
    println(k)
}
```

The ctx.getBeansOfType(String.class) is used to obtain a map with all beans of type SimpleBean and their IDs that exist within ApplicationContext. The keys of the map are the bean IDs that are printed using the lambda expression in the previous code. With the configuration used so far in the section, this is the output:

```
simpleBean
anotherSimpleBean
```

Explicit Bean Naming

Configuring a bean explicitly is very easy to do. When the bean is declared with @Component, or any other stereotype annotation (@Service, @Repository, etc.), there is a default attribute named value that can be initialized with a value to be used as a name for the bean. Listing 3-44 shows a SimpleBean bean being configured with name simpleBeanOne.

Listing 3-44. Bean with Custom Name, Declared with @Component

```
@Component(value = "simpleBeanOne")
class SimpleBean { }
```

When an annotation attribute is declared to be default, this means when using the annotation, the name of the attribute can be skipped, so @Component(value = "simpleBeanOne") is equivalent to @Component("simpleBeanOne").

The @Bean annotation has a default attribute, named value as well, used for a similar purpose. It can be initialized with a value to be used as a name for the bean, but when an array of values is used, the first one in the array becomes the name and the rest become aliases. Listing 3-45 shows how to configure beans with aliases using @Bean, but also how to print the names and aliases for a bean.

Listing 3-45. Bean with Custom Name, Declared with @Bean

```
package com.apress.prospring6.three.explicit

import org.springframework.context.annotation.AnnotationConfigApplicationContext
import org.springframework.context.annotation.Bean
import org.springframework.context.annotation.ComponentScan
import org.springframework.context.annotation.Configuration
import org.springframework.stereotype.Component
import java.util.*

/**
 * Created by iuliana.cosmina on 09/03/2022
 */
object ExplicitBeanNamingDemo {
    private val logger: org.slf4j.Logger =
        org.slf4j.LoggerFactory.getLogger(ExplicitBeanNamingDemo::class.java)
    @JvmStatic
    fun main(args: Array<String>) {
        val ctx = AnnotationConfigApplicationContext(BeanNamingCfg::class.java)
        Arrays.stream(ctx.beanDefinitionNames).forEach { beanName: String? ->
            logger.debug(beanName)
        }
        val simpleBeans = ctx.getBeansOfType(SimpleBean::class.java)
        simpleBeans.forEach { (k: String?, v: SimpleBean?) ->
            val aliases = ctx.getAliases(k)
            if (aliases.isNotEmpty()) {
                logger.debug("Aliases for {} ", k)
                Arrays.stream(aliases).forEach { a: String? ->
                    logger.debug("\t {}", a)
                }
            }
```

```
        }
    }
}

@Configuration
@ComponentScan
internal open class BeanNamingCfg {
    // @Bean(name="simpleBeanTwo")
    // @Bean(value= "simpleBeanTwo")
    @Bean("simpleBeanTwo")
    open fun simpleBean2(): SimpleBean {
        return SimpleBean()
    }

    // @Bean(name= {"simpleBeanThree", "three", "numero_tres"})
    // @Bean(value= {"simpleBeanThree", "three", "numero_tres"})
    @Bean("simpleBeanThree", "three", "numero_tres")
    open fun simpleBean3(): SimpleBean {
        return SimpleBean()
    }
}

@Component("simpleBeanOne")
internal class SimpleBean
```

In the code snippet in Listing 3-45, all the possibilities to name a bean and specify aliases are covered; the annotations in the comments are equivalent to the annotation that is not commented. simpleBeanTwo doesn't have any aliases. simpleBeanThree has two of them. When the code snippet is run, the output in Listing 3-46 is produced.

Listing 3-46. Output Showing Bean Aliases

```
DEBUG: ExplicitBeanNamingDemo - simpleBeanTwo
DEBUG: ExplicitBeanNamingDemo - simpleBeanThree
DEBUG: ExplicitBeanNamingDemo - Aliases for simpleBeanThree
DEBUG: ExplicitBeanNamingDemo -       three
DEBUG: ExplicitBeanNamingDemo -       numero_tres
```

The @AliasFor Annotation

When it comes to aliases, in Spring 4.2 the @AliasFor annotation was introduced. This annotation is used to declare aliases for annotation attributes, and most Spring annotations make use of it. For example, the @Bean annotation has two attributes, name and value, which are declared as aliases for each other. The code snippet in Listing 3-47 is a snapshot of the @Bean annotation Java code and is taken from the official Spring GitHub repository. The code and documentation that are not relevant at the moment are omitted.

Listing 3-47. Code Snippet from the @Bean Annotation

```
package org.springframework.context.annotation;
import java.lang.annotation.Documented;
import java.lang.annotation.ElementType;
```

```
import java.lang.annotation.Retention;
import java.lang.annotation.RetentionPolicy;
import java.lang.annotation.Target;
import org.springframework.core.annotation.AliasFor;
// other import statements omitted

@Target({ElementType.METHOD, ElementType.ANNOTATION_TYPE})
@Retention(RetentionPolicy.RUNTIME)
@Documented
public @interface Bean {
    @AliasFor("name")
    String value() default {};

    @AliasFor("value")
    String name() default {};

// code omitted
}
```

This configuration using @AliasFor is what makes @Bean(name= {"simpleBeanThree", "three", "numero_tres"}) equivalent to @Bean(value= {"simpleBeanThree", "three", "numero_tres"}).

Something more interesting can be done with the @AliasFor annotation: aliases for meta-annotation attributes can be declared. In Listing 3-48 you can see an annotation named @Award that declares an attribute named prize and an annotation named @Trophy that is meta-annotated with @Award. This annotation declares an attribute that is an alias for the prize attribute in the @Award interface.

Listing 3-48. Usage of @AliasFor

```
package com.apress.prospring6.three.alias

// Award.kt
package com.apress.prospring6.three.alias

import java.lang.annotation.Documented
import java.lang.annotation.Retention
import java.lang.annotation.RetentionPolicy

@Target(AnnotationTarget.ANNOTATION_CLASS, AnnotationTarget.CLASS)
@Retention(RetentionPolicy.RUNTIME)
@Documented
annotation class Award(val prize: Array<String> = [])

// Trophy.kt
package com.apress.prospring6.three.alias

import org.springframework.core.annotation.AliasFor

@Award
annotation class Trophy(
    @get:AliasFor(annotation = Award::class, attribute = "value")
    val name: Array<String> = []
)
```

With these two annotations, a `Singer` class can be declared and annotated with `@Award` or `@Trophy`, as shown in Listing 3-49.

Listing 3-49. Singer Class Annotated with Alias Annotations

```
package com.apress.prospring6.three.alias

import org.springframework.stereotype.Component

@Component("johnMayer") //@Award(prize = {"grammy", "platinum disk"})
@Trophy(name = ["grammy", "platinum disk"])
class Singer {
    private val lyric = "I used to crave the sight of you"
    fun sing() {
        println(lyric)
    }
}
```

❗ Creating aliases for attributes of annotations using yet another annotation @AliasFor does have limitations. @AliasFor cannot be used on any stereotype annotations (@Component and its specializations). The reason is that the special handling of these value attributes was in place years before @AliasFor was invented. Consequently, because of backward-compatibility issues, it is simply not possible to use @AliasFor with such value attributes. When writing code to do just so (aliasing value attributes in stereotype annotations), no compile errors will be shown to you, and the code might even run, but any argument provided for the alias will be ignored. The same goes for the @Qualifier annotation.

Understanding Bean Instantiation Mode

Earlier in this chapter the term **singleton** was used to describe beans that are created only once within the context, and **non-singleton** was used to describe beans that are created every time they are requested from the context. By default, all beans in Spring are singletons. This means Spring maintains a single instance of the bean, all dependent objects use the same instance, and all calls to `ApplicationContext.getBean(..)` return the same instance. We demonstrated this in the previous section, where we were able to use identity comparison (`==`) rather than the `equals()` comparison to check whether the beans were the same.

The term *singleton* is used interchangeably in Java/Kotlin to refer to two distinct concepts: an object that has a single instance within the application, and the Singleton design pattern. We refer to the first concept as a singleton and to the Singleton pattern as Singleton. The Singleton design pattern was popularized in the seminal *Design Patterns: Elements of Reusable Object-Oriented Software*, by Erich Gamma et al. (Addison-Wesley, 1994). The problem arises when people confuse the need for singleton instances with the need to apply the *Singleton* pattern. Listing 3-50 shows a typical implementation of the Singleton pattern in Kotlin via *objects*.

Listing 3-50. Singleton Pattern in Kotlin

```
object Singleton {
}
```

This substantially differs from Java implementations, which require use of a somewhat clumsy construct using static fields and private constructors. The pattern achieves its goal of allowing you to maintain and access a single instance of a class throughout your application, but it does so at the expense of increased coupling. Your application code must always have explicit knowledge of the Singleton class in order to obtain the instance—completely removing the ability to code to interfaces.

In reality, the *Singleton* pattern is actually two patterns in one. The first, and desired, pattern involves maintenance of a single instance of an object. The second, and less desirable, is a pattern for object lookup that completely removes the possibility of using interfaces. Using the Singleton pattern also makes it difficult to swap out implementations arbitrarily because objects that require the Singleton instance access the Singleton object directly. This can cause all kinds of headaches when you are trying to unit test your application, because you are unable to replace the Singleton with a mock for testing purposes.

Fortunately, with Spring you can take advantage of the singleton instantiation model without having to work around the Singleton design pattern. All beans in Spring are, by default, created as singleton instances, and Spring uses the same instances to fulfill all requests for that bean. Of course, Spring is not just limited to the use of the Singleton instance; it can still create a new instance of the bean to satisfy every dependency and every call to getBean(). It does all of this without any impact on your application code, and for this reason, we like to refer to Spring as being **instantiation mode agnostic**. This is a powerful concept. If you start off with an object that is a singleton but then discover it is not really suited to multithread access, you can change it to a non-singleton (*prototype*) without affecting any of your application code.

❗ Although changing the instantiation mode of your bean won't affect your application code, it does cause some problems if you rely on Spring's life-cycle interfaces. We cover this in more detail in **Chapter 4**.

Changing the instantiation mode from singleton to non-singleton is simple. The configuration in Listing 3-51 depicts using @Scope with the scopeName attribute set to configure a bean as non-singleton.

Listing 3-51. Configure a Bean As Non-Singleton

```
@Component("nonSingleton")
@Scope(scopeName = "prototype")
class Singer(@Value("John Mayer") val name:String  = "unknown") {
}
```

As you can see, the only difference between this bean declaration and any of the declarations you have seen so far is that we add the scope attribute and set the value to prototype. Spring defaults the scope to the value singleton. The prototype scope instructs Spring to instantiate a new instance of the bean every time a bean instance is requested by the application. Listing 3-52 shows the effect this setting has on your application.

Listing 3-52. Accessing Non-Singleton Beans from the Context

```
package com.apress.prospring6.three.scope

import com.apress.prospring6.three.generator.BeanNameGerneratorDemo
import org.springframework.beans.factory.annotation.Value
import org.springframework.context.annotation.AnnotationConfigApplicationContext
import org.springframework.context.annotation.Scope
import org.springframework.stereotype.Component
```

```
@Component("nonSingleton")
@Scope(scopeName = "prototype")
internal class Singer(@Value("John Mayer") val name: String = "unknown") {

    override fun toString(): String {
        return "${super.toString()}, name=$name"
    }
}

object NonSingletonDemo {
    private val logger: org.slf4j.Logger =
        org.slf4j.LoggerFactory.getLogger(BeanNameGerneratorDemo::class.java)
    @JvmStatic
    fun main(args: Array<String>) {
        val ctx = AnnotationConfigApplicationContext()
        ctx.register(Singer::class.java)
        ctx.refresh()
        val singer1 = ctx.getBean("nonSingleton", Singer::class.java)
        val singer2 = ctx.getBean("nonSingleton", Singer::class.java)
        logger.info("Identity Equal?: " + (singer1 === singer2))
        logger.info("Value Equal:? " + (singer1 == singer2))
        logger.info(singer1.toString())
        logger.info(singer2.toString())
    }
}
```

Running this example gives you the output in Listing 3-53, which proves without a doubt that ctx.getBean("nonSingleton", Singer.class) returns two different instances.

Listing 3-53. Output of Code in Listing 3-52

```
INFO : NonSingletonDemo - Identity Equal?: false
INFO : NonSingletonDemo - Value Equal:? false
INFO : NonSingletonDemo - com.apress.prospring6.three.scope.Singer@6631f5ca[name=John Mayer]
INFO : NonSingletonDemo - com.apress.prospring6.three.scope.Singer@5ace1ed4[name=John Mayer]
```

You can see from this output that although the values of the two String objects are clearly equal, the identities are not, even though both instances were retrieved using the same bean name.

Choosing an Instantiation Mode

In most scenarios, it is quite easy to see which instantiation mode is suitable. Typically, you will find that singleton is the default mode for your beans. In general, singletons should be used in the following scenarios:

- *Shared object with no state*: You have an object that maintains no state and has many dependent objects. Because you do not need synchronization if there is no state, you do not need to create a new instance of the bean each time a dependent object needs to use it for some processing.

- *Shared object with read-only state*: This is similar to the previous point, but you have some read-only state. In this case, you still do not need synchronization, so creating an instance to satisfy each request for the bean is just adding overhead.

- *Shared object with shared state*: If you have a bean that has state that must be shared, singleton is the ideal choice. In this case, ensure that your synchronization for state writes is as granular as possible.

- *High-throughput objects with writable state*: If you have a bean that is used a great deal in your application, you may find that keeping a singleton and synchronizing all write access to the bean state allows for better performance than constantly creating hundreds of instances of the bean. When using this approach, try to keep the synchronization as granular as possible without sacrificing consistency. You will find that this approach is particularly useful when your application creates a large number of instances over a long period of time, when your shared object has only a small amount of writable state, or when the instantiation of a new instance is expensive.

You should consider using non-singletons in the following scenarios:

- *Objects with writable state*: If you have a bean that has a lot of writable state, you may find that the cost of synchronization is greater than the cost of creating a new instance to handle each request from a dependent object.

- *Objects with private state*: Some dependent objects need a bean that has private state so that they can conduct their processing separately from other objects that depend on that bean. In this case, singleton is clearly not suitable, and you should use non-singleton.

The main positive you gain from Spring's instantiation management is that your applications can immediately benefit from the lower memory usage associated with singletons, with very little effort on your part. Then, if you find that singleton mode does not meet the needs of your application, it is a trivial task to modify your configuration to use non-singleton mode.

Additional Bean Scopes

In addition to the singleton and prototype scopes, other scopes exist when defining a Spring bean for more specific purposes. You can also implement your own custom scope and register it in Spring's ApplicationContext. The following bean scopes are supported as of version 6:

- singleton: The default singleton scope. Only one object will be created per Spring IoC container.

- prototype: A new instance will be created by Spring when requested by the application.

- request: For web application use. When using Spring MVC for web applications, beans with request scope will be instantiated for every HTTP request and then destroyed when the request is completed.

- session: For web application use. When using Spring MVC for web applications, beans with session scope will be instantiated for every HTTP session and then destroyed when the session is over.

- application: Scopes a single bean definition to the life cycle of a ServletContext. The application scope is only valid in a Spring web application.

- thread: A new bean instance will be created by Spring when requested by a new thread, while for the same thread, the same bean instance will be returned. Note that this scope is not registered by default.

- custom: Custom bean scope that can be created by implementing the interface org. springframework.beans.factory.config.Scope and registering the custom scope in Spring's configuration (for XML, use the class org.springframework.beans. factory.config.CustomScopeConfigurer).

- websocket: Scopes a single bean definition to the life cycle of a WebSocket. The websocket scope is only valid in a Spring web application.

Resolving Dependencies

Spring is able to resolve dependencies by simply looking at your configuration files or annotations in your classes. Unfortunately, Spring is not aware of any dependencies that exist between beans in your code that are not specified in the configuration. For instance, take one bean, named johnMayer, of type Singer, which obtains an instance of another bean, called gopher, of type Guitar using ctx.getBean() and uses it when the johnMayer.sing() method is called. In this method, you get an instance of type Guitar by calling ctx. getBean("gopher"), without asking Spring to inject the dependency for you. In this case, Spring is unaware that johnMayer depends on gopher, and, as a result, it may instantiate the johnMayer bean before the gopher bean.

You can provide Spring with additional information about your bean dependencies by using the @DependsOn annotation. Listing 3-54 shows how the scenario for johnMayer and gopher beans would be configured.

Listing 3-54. Configuring Dependencies with @DependsOn

```
package com.apress.prospring6.three.dependson

import org.springframework.beans.BeansException
import org.springframework.context.ApplicationContext
import org.springframework.context.ApplicationContextAware
import org.springframework.context.annotation.AnnotationConfigApplicationContext
import org.springframework.context.annotation.DependsOn
import org.springframework.stereotype.Component

object DependsOnDemo {
    @JvmStatic
    fun main(args: Array<String>) {
        val ctx = AnnotationConfigApplicationContext()
        ctx.register(Singer::class.java, Guitar::class.java)
        ctx.refresh()
        val johnMayer = ctx.getBean("johnMayer", Singer::class.java)
        johnMayer.sing()
    }
}
```

```kotlin
@Component("gopher")
internal class Guitar {
    fun sing() {
        println("Cm Eb Fm Ab Bb")
    }
}

@DependsOn("gopher")
@Component("johnMayer")
internal class Singer : ApplicationContextAware {
    private var ctx: ApplicationContext? = null

    @Throws(BeansException::class)
    override fun setApplicationContext(applicationContext: ApplicationContext) {
        ctx = applicationContext
    }

    private var guitar: Guitar? = null

    fun sing() {
        guitar = ctx!!.getBean("gopher", Guitar::class.java)
        guitar!!.sing()
    }
}
```

In this configuration, we are declaring that bean johnMayer depends on bean gopher. Spring should take this into consideration when instantiating the beans and ensure that gopher is created before johnMayer. For the johnMayer bean, to retrieve the dependency on its own, it needs to access ApplicationContext. Thus, we also have to tell Spring to inject this reference, so when the johnMayer. sing() method will be called, it can be used to procure the gopher bean. This is done by making the Singer class implement the ApplicationContextAware interface. This is a Spring-specific interface that forces an implementation of a setter for an ApplicationContext object. It is automatically detected by the Spring IoC container, and the ApplicationContext that the bean is created in is injected into it. This is done after the constructor of the bean is called, so obviously using ApplicationContext in the constructor will lead to a NullPointerException.

When Listing 3-54 is run, the output will be as follows: Cm Eb Fm Ab Bb."

When developing your applications, avoid designing them to use this feature; instead, define your dependencies by means of setter and constructor injection contracts. However, if you are integrating Spring with legacy code, you may find that the dependencies defined in the code require you to provide extra information to the Spring Framework.

Autowiring Your Bean

Autowiring is the process of implicitly injecting beans into beans depending on them. Spring supports five modes for autowiring:

- byName: When using byName autowiring, Spring attempts to wire each property to a bean of the same name. So, if the target bean has a property named foo and a foo bean is defined in ApplicationContext, the foo bean is assigned to the foo property of the target.

- byType: When using byType autowiring, Spring attempts to wire each of the properties on the target bean by automatically using a bean of the same type in ApplicationContext.

- constructor: This functions just like byType autowiring, except that it uses constructors rather than setters to perform the injection. Spring attempts to match the greatest number of arguments it can in the constructor. So, if your bean has two constructors, one that accepts a String and one that accepts a String and an Integer, and you have both a String and an Integer bean in your ApplicationContext, Spring uses the two-argument constructor.

- default: Spring will choose between the constructor and byType modes automatically. If your bean has a default (no-arguments) constructor, Spring uses byType; otherwise, it uses constructor.

- no: No autowiring; this is the default.

Autowiring mode can be configured explicitly through metadata when using XML configuration, by specifying the value for the autowire attribute on the <bean/> element. Since this book does not cover XML, let's focus on annotation configuration.

Constructor Autowiring

When a dependency is provided using constructor injection, autowiring obviously is done through the constructor. If the class has more than one constructor, the constructor to be used is chosen based on a few conditions.

If none of the constructors is annotated with @Autowired, the most suitable will be used. If more than one is suitable, Spring just uses the no-argument constructor if there is one. If there is none, a BeanInstantiationException is thrown. Take a look at the sample in Listing 3-55.

Listing 3-55. Example Showing Autowiring by Type

```
package com.apress.prospring6.three.autowiring
import org.springframework.context.annotation.Lazy
// other import statements omitted

object AutowiringDemo {
    private val logger: Logger = LoggerFactory.getLogger(AutowiringDemo::class.java)
    @JvmStatic
    fun main(args: Array<String>) {
        val ctx = AnnotationConfigApplicationContext(AutowiringCfg::class.java)
        val target = ctx.getBean(Target::class.java)
        logger.info("Created target? {}", target != null)
        logger.info("Injected bar? {}", target.bar != null)
        logger.info("Injected fooOne? {}", if (target.fooOne != null) target.fooOne!!.id
        else "")
        logger.info("Injected fooTwo? {}", if (target.fooTwo != null) target.fooTwo!!.id
        else "")
    }
}
```

```kotlin
@Configuration
@ComponentScan
internal class AutowiringCfg

@Component
@Lazy
internal class Target {
    var fooOne: Foo? = null
    var fooTwo: Foo? = null
    var bar: Bar? = null

    constructor() {
        logger.info(" --> Target() called")
    }

    constructor(foo: Foo?) {
        fooOne = foo
        logger.info(" --> Target(Foo) called")
    }

    constructor(foo: Foo?, bar: Bar?) {
        fooOne = foo
        this.bar = bar
        logger.info(" --> Target(Foo, Bar) called")
    }

    companion object {
        private val logger: Logger = LoggerFactory.getLogger(Target::class.java)
    }
}

@Component
internal class Foo {
    var id = UUID.randomUUID().toString().replace("-", "").substring(0, 8)
}

@Component
internal class Bar
```

In this code, you can see that the Target class has three constructors:

- A no-argument constructor,

- A constructor that accepts a Foo instance

- A constructor that accepts a Foo instance and a Bar instance

Each of these constructors writes a message to console output when it is called. The main() method simply retrieves the Target bean declared in ApplicationContext, triggering the autowiring process. A few logging statements print details about the Target bean.

In addition to these constructors, the Target bean has three properties:

- Two of type Foo

- One of type Bar

Foo and Bar are simple classes. Every Foo object receives an unique ID when instantiated. The @Lazy annotation is used to inform Spring to instantiate the bean only when it is first requested, rather than at startup, so that we can output the result in the correct place in the testing program.

When running this code, the output in Listing 3-56 is printed, proving without a doubt that when Spring is not told what to do, it just goes straight for the no-argument constructor, which means none of the properties will be injected.

Listing 3-56. Example Showing Autowiring by Constructor when No Constructor Is Annotated with @Autowired

```
INFO : Target -  --> Target() called
INFO : AutowiringDemo - Created target? true
INFO : AutowiringDemo - Injected bar? false
INFO : AutowiringDemo - Injected fooOne?
INFO : AutowiringDemo - Injected fooTwo?
```

To change the behavior, just annotate any of the constructors with @Autowired. Since there are a Foo and Bar beans declared in the application, any of the other two constructors can be used to initialize Target.

If the no-argument constructor is deleted, the following exception is thrown.

```
Caused by: org.springframework.beans.BeanInstantiationException:
  Failed to instantiate [com.apress.prospring6.three.autowiring.Target]:
    No default constructor found;
      nested exception is java.lang.NoSuchMethodException:
        com.apress.prospring6.three.autowiring.Target.<init>()
```

The compiler allows you to annotate both of the remaining constructors with @Autowired, because the Kotlin compiler does not really care about what Spring allows or not, but running the code will confuse it and it won't be able to create the Target bean. It will throw a BeanCreationException and the following snippet shows the partial stacktrace, when the Target class has two annotated constructors.

```
Exception in thread "main" org.springframework.beans.factory.BeanCreationException: Error
creating bean with name 'target':
Invalid autowire-marked constructor: public com.apress.prospring6.three.autowiring.
Target(com.apress.prospring6.three.autowiring.
    Foo,com.apress.prospring6.three.autowiring.Bar).
    Found constructor with 'required' Autowired annotation already: public com.apress.
    prospring6.three.autowiring.Target(com.apress.prospring6.three.autowiring.Foo)
...
    at com.apress.prospring6.three.autowiring.AutowiringDemo.main(AutowiringDemo.java:51)
```

byType Autowiring

When there are no constructors declared, but there are setters annotated with @Autowired, Spring will use them and will identify the beans to be injected based on their type. Listing 3-57 shows a class named AnotherTarget that is pretty similar to the Target class, but the properties are injected using setters.

Listing 3-57. Example Showing Autowiring by Type Using Setters

```kotlin
object AutowiringDemo {
    private val logger = LoggerFactory.getLogger(AutowiringDemo::class.java)
    @JvmStatic
    fun main(args: Array<String>) {
        val ctx = AnnotationConfigApplicationContext(AutowiringCfg::class.java)
        val anotherTarget: AnotherTarget = ctx.getBean(AnotherTarget::class.java)
        logger.info("anotherTarget: Created anotherTarget? {}", anotherTarget != null)
        logger.info("anotherTarget: Injected bar? {}", anotherTarget.bar != null)
        logger.info(
            "anotherTarget: Injected fooOne? {}",
            if (anotherTarget.fooOne != null) anotherTarget.fooOne.id else ""
        )
        logger.info(
            "anotherTarget: Injected fooTwo? {}",
            if (anotherTarget.fooTwo != null) anotherTarget.fooTwo.id else ""
        )
    }
}


// some code from the previous example omitted

@Component
@Lazy
internal class AnotherTarget {
    var fooOne: Foo? = null
        @Autowired set(@Qualifier("foo") value) {
            logger.info(" --> AnotherTarget#setFooOne(Foo) called")
            field = value
        }

    var fooTwo: Foo? = null
        @Autowired set(@Qualifier("anotherFoo") value) {
            logger.info(" --> AnotherTarget#setFooTwo(Foo) called")
            field = value
        }

    var bar: Bar? = null
        @Autowired set(value) {
            logger.info(" --> AnotherTarget#setBar(Bar) called")
            field = value
        }
```

```
companion object {
    private val logger: org.slf4j.Logger =
        org.slf4j.LoggerFactory.getLogger(AnotherTarget::class.java)
}
}
```

When running this code, the output in Listing 3-58 is printed.

Listing 3-58. Example Showing Autowiring by Type when Setters Are Annotated with @Autowired

```
INFO : AnotherTarget -   --> AnotherTarget#setFooOne(Foo) called
INFO : AnotherTarget -   --> AnotherTarget#setFooTwo(Foo) called
INFO : AnotherTarget -   --> AnotherTarget#setBar(Bar) called
INFO : AutowiringDemo - anotherTarget: Created anotherTarget? true
INFO : AutowiringDemo - anotherTarget: Injected bar? true
INFO : AutowiringDemo - anotherTarget: Injected fooOne? a4eb2b71
INFO : AutowiringDemo - anotherTarget: Injected fooTwo? a4eb2b71
```

Spring injects dependencies by type when fields are directly annotated with @Autowired too, and since field injection is discouraged, the code won't be depicted in the book, but check out the com.apress. prospring6.three.autowiring.FieldTarget class in the project.

As you've seen so far, there is a single Foo bean declared and that bean is injected in both fooOne and fooTwo properties. If we declare another Foo bean, this will break the Target, the AnotherTarget and the FieldTarget beans definitions, and Spring won't be able to create them anymore, since dependencies are autowired by type and there are two dependencies of type Foo being required and Spring cannot figure out which of the two Foo beans are required where. Listing 3-59 shows the AutowiringCfg class being updated to declare a bean of type Foo.

Listing 3-59. AutowiringCfg Class Declaring a Bean of Type Foo

```
@Configuration
@ComponentScan
class AutowiringCfg {
    @Bean
    fun anotherFoo():Foo {
        return Foo()
    }
}
```

If you run the AutowiringDemo class, the following org.springframework.beans.factory. NoUniqueBeanDefinitionException exception will be thrown:

```
Caused by: org.springframework.beans.factory.NoUniqueBeanDefinitionException:
    No qualifying bean of type 'com.apress.prospring6.three.autowiring.Foo'
        available: expected single matching bean but found 2: foo,anotherFoo
```

To get Spring out of this pickle, the solution is to specify which bean we want injected where, which means switching from autowiring by type to autowiring by name.

byName Autowiring

Listing 3-60 shows the Target class with the constructors modified to receive specific beans as arguments. The @Qualifier annotation, previously used to inject collections, is what saves the day here as well.

Listing 3-60. Target Bean Class Configured Using Constructor Autowiring by Name

```
package com.apress.prospring6.three.autowiring
import org.springframework.beans.factory.annotation.Qualifier
// other import statements omitted
@Component
@Lazy
internal class Target {
    var fooOne: Foo? = null
    var fooTwo: Foo? = null
    var bar: Bar? = null

  @Autowired
    constructor(@Qualifier("foo") foo: Foo?) {
        fooOne = foo
        logger.info(" --> Target(Foo) called")
    }

  @Autowired
    constructor(@Qualifier("foo") foo: Foo?, bar: Bar?) {
        fooOne = foo
        this.bar = bar
        logger.info(" --> Target(Foo, Bar) called")
    }

    companion object {
        private val logger: Logger = LoggerFactory.getLogger(Target::class.java)
    }
}
```

Notice that the @Qualifier is placed on the argument, not on the constructor. If you use @Inject instead of @Autowired to inject dependencies, use @Named instead of @Qualifier. To fix the AnotherTarget class, the @Qualifier is placed on the setter arguments as shown in Listing 3-61.

Listing 3-61. AnotherTarget Bean Class Configured Using Setter Autowiring by Name

```
package com.apress.prospring6.three.autowiring;
import org.springframework.beans.factory.annotation.Qualifier;
// other import statements omitted

@Component
@Lazy
internal class AnotherTarget {
    var fooOne: Foo? = null
        @Autowired set(@Qualifier("foo") value) {
            logger.info(" --> AnotherTarget#setFooOne(Foo) called")
            field = value
        }
```

```
    var fooTwo: Foo? = null
        @Autowired set(@Qualifier("anotherFoo") value) {
            logger.info(" --> AnotherTarget#setFooTwo(Foo) called")
            field = value
        }

    var bar: Bar? = null
        @Autowired set(value) {
            logger.info(" --> AnotherTarget#setBar(Bar) called")
            field = value
        }

    companion object {
        private val logger: org.slf4j.Logger =
            org.slf4j.LoggerFactory.getLogger(AnotherTarget::class.java)
    }
}
```

Running the AutowiringDemo, accessing the AnotherTarget, and inspecting its dependencies prints the details in Listing 3-62, which makes it clear that there are two different Foo beans being injected.

Listing 3-62. Example Showing Autowiring by Type when Setters Are Annotated with @Autowired

```
INFO : AnotherTarget -   --> AnotherTarget#setFooOne(Foo) called
INFO : AnotherTarget -   --> AnotherTarget#setFooTwo(Foo) called
INFO : AnotherTarget -   --> AnotherTarget#setBar(Bar) called
INFO : AutowiringDemo - anotherTarget: Created anotherTarget? true
INFO : AutowiringDemo - anotherTarget: Injected bar? true
INFO : AutowiringDemo - anotherTarget: Injected fooOne? baa24632
INFO : AutowiringDemo - anotherTarget: Injected fooTwo? 0d74b352
```

As for the FieldTarget, things are even simpler; the @Qualifier annotation gets placed directly on the field being autowired, as shown in Listing 3-63.

Listing 3-63. FieldTarget Bean Class Configured Using Field Autowiring by Name

```
package com.apress.prospring6.three.autowiring
import org.springframework.beans.factory.annotation.Qualifier
// other import statements omitted

@Component
@Lazy
class FieldTarget {

    companion object {
        private val logger: org.slf4j.Logger =
            org.slf4j.LoggerFactory.getLogger(FieldTarget::class.java)
    }

    @Autowired @Qualifier("foo") var fooOne:Foo? = null
    @Autowired @Qualifier("anotherFoo") var fooTwo:Foo? = null
    @Autowired var bar:Bar? = null

}
```

Yet Another Pickle

When autowiring by type, things get complicated when bean types are related, and exceptions are thrown when you have more classes that implement the same interface and the property requiring to be autowired specifies the interface as the type, because Spring does not know which bean to inject. To create such a scenario, we'll transform Foo into an interface and declare two bean types implementing it, each with its bean declaration. The configuration is the default one with bean names generated by Spring, as shown in Listing 3-64.

Listing 3-64. Foo Implementation Classes and Configuration

```kotlin
package com.apress.prospring6.three.pickle
// other import statements omitted

internal interface Foo { // empty interface, used as a marker interface
}

internal class FooImplOne : Foo {
    var id = "one:" + UUID.randomUUID().toString().replace("-", "").substring(0, 8)
    override fun toString(): String {
        return super.toString() + ", id=" + id.toString()
    }
}

internal class FooImplTwo : Foo {
    var id = "two:" + UUID.randomUUID().toString().replace("-", "").substring(0, 8)
    override fun toString(): String {
        return super.toString() + ", id=" + id.toString()
    }
}

internal class Bar

@Configuration
@ComponentScan
internal class AutowiringCfg {
    @Bean
    fun fooImplOne(): Foo {
        return FooImplOne()
    }

    @Bean
    fun fooImplTwo(): Foo {
        return FooImplTwo()
    }

    @Bean
    fun bar(): Bar {
        return Bar()
    }
```

```
    @Bean
    fun trickyTarget(): TrickyTarget {
        return TrickyTarget()
    }
}

internal class TrickyTarget {
    var fooOne: Foo? = null
    var fooTwo: Foo? = null
    var bar: Bar? = null
}
```

The TrickyTarget code is pretty similar to the Target class, and when dependencies are injected by type as shown in Listing 3-64, Spring is unable to create this bean and a NoUniqueBeanDefinitionException is thrown:

```
Caused by: org.springframework.beans.factory.NoUniqueBeanDefinitionException:
No qualifying bean of type 'com.apress.prospring6.three.pickle.Foo'
available: expected single matching bean but found 2: fooImplOne,fooImplTwo
```

The console output is way longer, but the first lines in the previous output reveal the problem in quite a readable manner. When Spring does not know what bean to autowire, it throws an NoUniqueBeanDefinitionException with an explicit message. It tells you what beans were found but that it cannot choose which to use where. There are two ways to fix this problem.

The first way is to use the @Primary annotation in the bean definition that you want Spring to consider first for autowiring. This resolves the problem in a pretty weird way, because in both fooOne and fooTwo, the bean annotated with @Primary is injected. The configuration and resulting output is shown in Listing 3-65.

Listing 3-65. Configuration Using @Primary

```
package com.apress.prospring6.three.pickle
// import statements omitted
import org.springframework.context.annotation.Primary

@Configuration
@ComponentScan
class AutowiringCfg {

    @Bean @Primary
    fun fooImplOne(): Foo = FooImplOne()

    @Bean
    fun fooImplTwo(): Foo = FooImplTwo()

    @Bean
    fun bar(): Bar = Bar()

    @Bean
    fun trickyTarget(): TrickyTarget = TrickyTarget()
}
```

```
// Log for configuration using @Primary
INFO : TrickyTarget -  --> Property fooOne set
INFO : TrickyTarget -  --> Property fooTwo set
INFO : TrickyTarget -  --> Property bar set
INFO : PickleAutowiringDemo - target: Created target? true
INFO : PickleAutowiringDemo - target: Injected bar? true
INFO : PickleAutowiringDemo - target: Injected fooOne? com.apress.prospring6.three.pickle
.FooImplOne@2eea88a1[id=one:7ab78d36]
INFO : PickleAutowiringDemo - target: Injected fooTwo? com.apress.prospring6.three.pickle
.FooImplOne@2eea88a1[id=one:7ab78d36]
```

So, it's all back to normal, but still, using the @Primary is a solution only when there are just two bean-related types. If there are more, using it will not get rid of the NoUniqueBeanDefinitionException.

What will do the job is the second way, which will give you full control over which bean gets injected where, and this is to name your beans and configure them where to be injected using @Qualifier as shown in the previous section. Listing 3-66 shows the TrickyTarget class with setters configured with @Qualifier and the resulting output when the class PickleAutowiringDemo is run.

Listing 3-66. Configuration Using @Qualifier and Resulting Output

```
package com.apress.prospring6.three.pickle
// import statements omitted
import org.springframework.beans.factory.annotation.Qualifier

class TrickyTarget {
    companion object {
        private val logger: org.slf4j.Logger =
            org.slf4j.LoggerFactory.getLogger(FieldTarget::class.java)
    }

    var fooOne:Foo? = null
        @Autowired
        @Qualifier("fooImplOne")
        set(value) {
            field = value
            logger.info(" --> Property fooOne set")
        }

    var fooTwo:Foo? = null
        @Autowired
        @Qualifier("fooImplTwo")
        set(value) {
            field = value
            logger.info(" --> Property fooTwo set")
        }

    var bar:Bar? = null
        @Autowired
        set(value) {
            field = value
            logger.info(" --> Property bar set")
        }
```

```
constructor() {
    logger.info(" --> TrickyTarget() called");
}
}
```

```
// Log for configuration using @Qualifier
INFO : TrickyTarget -   --> TrickyTarget() called
INFO : TrickyTarget -   --> Property fooOne set
INFO : TrickyTarget -   --> Property fooTwo set
INFO : TrickyTarget -   --> Property bar set
INFO : PickleAutowiringDemo - target: Created target? true
INFO : PickleAutowiringDemo - target: Injected bar? true
INFO : PickleAutowiringDemo - target: Injected fooOne? com.apress.prospring6.three.pickle.
FooImplOne@7fd7a283[id=one:8efc8d31]
INFO : PickleAutowiringDemo - target: Injected fooTwo? com.apress.prospring6.three.pickle.
FooImplTwo@22f59fa[id=two:a5d9ed75]
```

When to Use Autowiring

When writing Spring applications, autowiring cannot be avoided; the whole idea behind Spring is that you can create your classes as you like and have Spring work for you. The question is not when you should use autowiring, but which type of autowiring is suitable for certain parts of your application. You may be tempted to use byType until you realize that you can have only one bean for each type in your ApplicationContext—a restriction that is problematic when you need to maintain beans with different configurations of the same type. The same argument applies to the use of constructor autowiring. In some cases, autowiring can save you time, but it does not really take that much extra effort to define your wiring explicitly, and you benefit from explicit semantics and full flexibility on property naming and on how many instances of the same type you manage.

Summary

In this chapter, we covered a lot of ground with both Spring Core and IoC in general. We showed you examples of the types of IoC and presented the pros and cons of using each mechanism in your applications. We looked at which IoC mechanisms Spring provides and when (and when not) to use each within your applications. While exploring IoC, we introduced the Spring BeanFactory, which is the core component for Spring's IoC capabilities, and then ApplicationContext, which extends BeanFactory and provides additional functionalities.

For ApplicationContext, we focused on AnnotationConfigApplicationContext, which allows external configuration of Spring by using annotation. We also discussed another method to declare DI requirements for ApplicationContext, by using Kotlin annotations.

This chapter also introduced you to the basics of Spring's IoC feature set including setter injection, constructor injection, Method Injection, autowiring, and bean inheritance. In the discussion of configuration, we demonstrated how you can configure your bean properties with a wide variety of values, including other beans.

This chapter only scratched the surface of Spring and Spring's IoC container. In the next chapter, you'll look at some IoC-related features specific to Spring, and you'll take a more detailed look at other functionality available in Spring Core.

CHAPTER 4

■ ■ ■

Advanced Spring Configuration and Spring Boot

In the previous chapter, we presented a detailed look at the concept of inversion of control (IoC) and how it fits into the Spring Framework. However, we have really only scratched the surface of what Spring Core can do. Spring provides a wide array of services that supplement and extend its basic IoC capabilities. In this chapter, you are going to explore these in detail. Specifically, you will be looking at the following:

- *Managing the bean life cycle*: So far, all the beans you have seen have been fairly simple and completely decoupled from the Spring container. In this chapter, we present some strategies you can employ to enable your beans to receive notifications from the Spring container at various points throughout their life cycles. You can do this either by implementing specific interfaces laid out by Spring, by specifying methods that Spring can call via reflection, or by using JavaBeans[1] life-cycle annotations.

- *Making your beans "Spring aware"*: In some cases, you want a bean to be able to interact with the `ApplicationContext` instance that configured it. For this reason, Spring offers two interfaces, `BeanNameAware` and `ApplicationContextAware` (introduced at the end of **Chapter 3**), that allow your bean to obtain its assigned name and reference its `ApplicationContext`, respectively. The section corresponding to this topic covers implementing these interfaces and gives some practical considerations for using them in your application.

- *Using FactoryBeans*: As its name implies, the `FactoryBean` interface is meant to be implemented by any bean that acts as a factory for other beans. The `FactoryBean` interface provides a mechanism by which you can easily integrate your own factories with the Spring `BeanFactory` interface.

- *Working with JavaBeans PropertyEditors*: The `PropertyEditor` interface is a standard interface provided in the `java.beans` package. `PropertyEditors` are used to convert property values to and from String representations. Spring uses `PropertyEditors` extensively, mainly to read values specified in the `BeanFactory` configuration and convert them into the correct types. In this chapter, we discuss the set of `PropertyEditors` supplied with Spring and how you can use them within your application. We also take a look at implementing custom `PropertyEditors`.

---

[1] `https://jcp.org/en/jsr/detail?id=250`

© Peter Späth, Iuliana Cosmina, Rob Harrop, Chris Schaefer 2023

P. Späth et al., *Pro Spring 6 with Kotlin*, https://doi.org/10.1007/978-1-4842-9557-1_4

- *Learning more about the Spring `ApplicationContext`*: As you know, `ApplicationContext` is an extension of `BeanFactory` intended for use in full applications. The `ApplicationContext` interface provides a useful set of additional functionalities, including internationalized message support, resource loading, and event publishing. In this chapter, we present a detailed look at the features in addition to IoC that `ApplicationContext` offers. We also jump ahead of ourselves a little to show you how `ApplicationContext` simplifies the use of Spring when you are building web applications.

- *Testing Spring applications*: **Chapter 3** explained how to build a Spring `ApplicationContext` and demonstrated that it is well constructed—beans were created as expected—by running a `main(..)` method. However, this is not the best way, because classes containing these methods are only compiled, not run, during the build, so any change in the bean declarations, or library upgrades that cause issues, might not become obvious until later in development. So, in this chapter we show how Spring Test contexts can be created to test Spring Applications.

- *Using Spring Boot*: Spring application configuration is made even more practical by using Spring Boot. This Spring project makes it easy to create stand-alone, production-grade, Spring-based applications that you can "just run."

- *Using configuration enhancements*: We present features that make application configuration easier, such as profile management, environment and property source abstraction, and so on. The section presenting those features shows how to use them to address specific configuration needs.

- *Using Groovy for configuration*: Spring 4.0 introduced the ability to configure bean definitions in the Groovy language, which, as you'll see, can be used as an alternative/supplement to the old XML and Java/Kotlin configuration styles.

Spring's Impact on Application Portability

Most of the features discussed in this chapter are specific to Spring and, in many cases, are not available in other IoC containers. Although many IoC containers offer life-cycle management functionality, they probably do so through a different set of interfaces than Spring. If the portability of your application between different IoC containers is truly important, you might want to avoid using some features that couple your application to Spring.

Remember, however, that by setting a constraint—meaning that your application is portable between IoC containers—you are losing out on the wealth of functionality Spring offers. Because you are likely to be making a strategic choice to use Spring, it makes sense that you use it to the best of its ability.

Be careful not to create a requirement for portability out of thin air. In many cases, the end users of your application do not care whether the application can run on three different IoC containers; they just want it to run. In our experience, it is often a mistake to try to build an application on the lowest common denominator of features available in your chosen technology. Doing so often sets your application at a disadvantage right from the get-go. However, if your application requires IoC container portability, do not see this as a drawback—it is a true requirement and, therefore, one your application should fulfill. In *Expert One-on-One: J2EE Development without EJB* (Wrox, 2004), Rod Johnson and Jürgen Höller describe these types of requirements as phantom requirements and provide a much more detailed discussion of them and how they can affect your project.

Although using these features may couple your application to the Spring Framework, in reality you are increasing the portability of your application in the wider scope. Consider that you are using a freely available, open source framework that has no particular vendor affiliation. An application built using

Spring's IoC container runs anywhere Java or Kotlin runs. For Java/Kotlin enterprise applications, Spring opens up new possibilities for portability. Spring provides many of the same capabilities as JEE and also provides classes to abstract and simplify many other aspects of JEE. In many cases, it is possible to build a web application using Spring that runs in a simple servlet container but with the same level of sophistication as an application targeted at a full-blown JEE application server. By coupling to Spring, you can increase your application's portability by replacing many features that either are vendor-specific or rely on vendor-specific configuration with equivalent features in Spring.

Bean Life-Cycle Management

An important part of any IoC container, Spring included, is that beans can be constructed in such a way that they receive notifications at certain points in their life cycle. This enables your beans to perform relevant processing at certain points throughout their life. In general, two life-cycle events are particularly relevant to a bean: *post-initialization* and *pre-destruction*.

 In the context of Spring, the *post-initialization* event is raised as soon as Spring finishes setting all the property values on the bean and finishes any dependency checks that you configured it to perform.

 The *pre-destruction* event is fired just before Spring destroys the bean instance.

However, for beans with prototype scope, the *pre-destruction* event will not be fired by Spring. The design of Spring is that the initialization life-cycle callback methods will be called on objects regardless of bean scope, while for beans with prototype scope, the destruction life-cycle callback methods will not be called.

Spring provides three mechanisms a bean can use to hook into each of these events and perform some additional processing:

- Interface-based mechanism

- Method-based mechanism

- Annotation-based mechanism

Using the interface-based mechanism, your bean implements an interface specific to the type of notification it wants to receive, and Spring notifies the bean via a callback method defined in the interface. For the method-based mechanism, Spring allows you to specify, in your `ApplicationContext` configuration, the name of a method to call when the bean is initialized and the name of a method to call when the bean is destroyed. For the annotation-based mechanism, you can use JSR-250 annotations to specify the method that Spring should call after construction or before destruction.

In the case of both events, the mechanisms achieve exactly the same goal. The interface-based mechanism is used extensively throughout Spring so that you don't have to remember to specify the initialization or destruction each time you use one of Spring's components. However, in your own beans, you may be better served using the method-based or annotation-based mechanism because your beans do not need to implement any Spring-specific interfaces. Although we stated that portability often isn't as important a requirement as many books lead you to believe, this does not mean you should sacrifice portability when a perfectly good alternative exists. That said, if you are coupling your application to Spring in other ways, using the interface-based method allows you to specify the callback once and then forget about it. If you are defining a lot of beans of the same type that need to take advantage of the life-cycle notifications, then using the interface-based mechanism can avoid the need for specifying the life-cycle callback methods for every bean in the bean configuration. Using JSR-250 annotations is a standard defined by the JCP and you are also not coupled to Spring's specific annotations. Just make sure that the IoC container you are running your application on supports the JSR-250 standard.

Overall, the choice of which mechanism you use for receiving life-cycle notifications depends on your application requirements. When using annotation-type configuration, just make sure you are using an IoC container that supports JSR-250. If you are not too concerned about portability or you are defining many beans of the same type that need the life-cycle notifications, using the interface-based mechanism is the best way to ensure that your beans always receive the notifications they are expecting. If you plan to use a bean across different Spring projects, you almost certainly want the functionality of that bean to be as self-contained as possible, so you should definitely use the interface-based mechanism.

Figure 4-1 shows a high-level overview of how Spring manages the life cycle of the beans within its container.

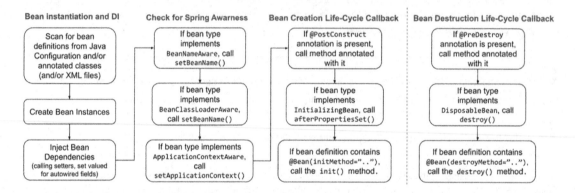

Figure 4-1. *Spring beans life cycle*

Hooking into Bean Creation

By being aware of when it is initialized, a bean can check whether all its required dependencies are satisfied. Although Spring can check dependencies for you, it is pretty much an all-or-nothing approach, and it doesn't offer any opportunities for applying additional logic to the dependency resolution procedure. Consider a bean that has four dependencies declared as setters, two of which are required and one of which has a suitable default in the event that no dependency is provided. Using an initialization callback, your bean can check for the dependencies it requires, throwing an exception or providing a default as needed.

A bean cannot perform these checks in its constructor because, at this point, Spring has not had an opportunity to provide values for the dependencies it can satisfy. The initialization callback in Spring is called after Spring finishes providing the dependencies that it can and performs any dependency checks that you ask of it.

You are not limited to using the initialization callback just to check dependencies; you can do anything you want in the callback, but it is most useful for the purpose we have described. In many cases, the initialization callback is also the place to trigger any actions that your bean must take automatically in response to its configuration. For instance, if you build a bean to run scheduled tasks, the initialization callback provides the ideal place to start the scheduler—after all, the configuration data is set on the bean.

❶   You will not have to write a bean to run scheduled tasks because this is something Spring can do automatically through its built-in scheduling feature or via integration with the Quartz scheduler. We cover this in more detail in **Chapter 12**.

Executing a Method When a Bean Is Created

As we mentioned previously, one way to receive the initialization callback is to designate a method on your bean as an initialization method and tell Spring to use this method as an initialization method. As discussed, this callback-based mechanism is useful when you have only a few beans of the same type or when you want to keep your application decoupled from Spring. Another reason for using this mechanism is to enable your Spring application to work with beans that were built previously or were provided by third-party vendors. Specifying a callback method is simply a case of specifying the name of the method as a value for the initMethod attribute in the @Bean annotation. This annotation is used to declare beans in Java/Kotlin configuration classes. Although Java/Kotlin configuration is covered a bit later in this chapter, the bean initialization part belongs here.

Code Listing 4-1 shows a basic bean with two dependencies.

Listing 4-1. Bean Type with Two Dependencies

```
package com.apress.prospring6.four.initmethod

import org.slf4j.LoggerFactory
import org.springframework.beans.factory.BeanCreationException
// other import statements omitted

class Singer {
    var name: String? = null
        set(value) {
            logger.info("Calling setName for bean of type {}.", Singer::class.java)
            field = value
        }

    var age = Int.MIN_VALUE
        set(value) {
            logger.info("Calling setAge for bean of type {}.", Singer::class.java)
            field = value
        }

    private fun init() {
        logger.info("Initializing bean")
        if (name == null) {
            logger.info("Using default name")
            name = DEFAULT_NAME
        }
        require(age != Int.MIN_VALUE) {

        "You must set the age property of any beans of type " + Singer::class.java }
    }
```

```kotlin
    override fun toString(): String {
        return "name=${name}, age=${name}"
    }

    companion object {
        private val logger = LoggerFactory.getLogger(Singer::class.java)
        private const val DEFAULT_NAME = "No Name"
    }
}

@Configuration
open class SingerConfiguration {
    @Bean(initMethod = "init")
    open fun singerOne(): Singer {
        val singer = Singer()
        singer.name = "John Mayer"
        singer.age = 43
        return singer
    }

    @Bean(initMethod = "init")
    open fun singerTwo(): Singer {
        val singer = Singer()
        singer.age = 42
        return singer
    }

    @Bean(initMethod = "init")
    open fun singerThree(): Singer {
        val singer = Singer()
        singer.name = "John Butler"
        return singer
    }
}

object InitMethodDemo {
    private val logger = LoggerFactory.getLogger(InitMethodDemo::class.java)
    @JvmStatic
    fun main(args: Array<String>) {
        val ctx = AnnotationConfigApplicationContext(SingerConfiguration::class.java)
        getBean("singerOne", ctx)
        getBean("singerTwo", ctx)
        getBean("singerThree", ctx)
    }

    fun getBean(beanName: String?, ctx: ApplicationContext): Singer? {
        return try {
            val bean = ctx.getBean(beanName) as Singer
            logger.info("Found: {}", bean)
            bean
        } catch (ex: BeanCreationException) {
```

```
        logger.error("An error occurred in bean configuration: " + ex.message)
        null
    }
  }
}
```

Notice that we have defined a method, init(), to act as the initialization callback. The init() method checks whether the name property has been set, and if it has not, it uses the default value stored in the DEFAULT_NAME constant. The init() method also checks whether the age property is set and throws IllegalArgumentException if it is not.

The main() method of the InitMethodDemo class attempts to obtain three beans from AnnotationConfigApplicationContext, all of type Singer, using its own getBean() method. Notice that in the getBean() method, if the bean is obtained successfully, its details are written to console output. If an exception is thrown in the init() method, as will occur in this case if the age property is not set, then Spring wraps that exception in BeanCreationException. The getBean() method catches these exceptions and writes a message to the console output informing us of the error, as well as returns a null value.

The code shown in Listing 4-2 extracts the ApplicationContext configuration that defines the beans used in Listing 4-1.

Listing 4-2. SingerConfiguration Configuring a Spring ApplicationContext with Three Singer Beans

```
@Configuration
open class SingerConfiguration {
    @Bean(initMethod = "init")
    open fun singerOne(): Singer {
        val singer = Singer()
        singer.name = "John Mayer"
        singer.age = 43
        return singer
    }

    @Bean(initMethod = "init")
    open fun singerTwo(): Singer {
        val singer = Singer()
        singer.age = 42
        return singer
    }

    @Bean(initMethod = "init")
    open fun singerThree(): Singer {
        val singer = Singer()
        singer.name = "John Butler"
        return singer
    }
}
```

As you can see, the @Bean annotation for each of the three beans has an initMethod attribute that tells Spring that it should invoke the init() method as soon as it finishes configuring the bean. The singerOne bean has values for both the name and age properties, so it passes through the init() method with absolutely no changes. The singerTwo bean has no value for the name property, meaning that in the init()

method, the name property is given the default value. Finally, the singerThree bean has no value for the age property. The logic defined in the init() method treats this as an error, so IllegalArgumentException is thrown.

Running the InitMethodDemo class yields the output in Listing 4-3.

Listing 4-3. Output Produced by Running InitMethodDemo

```
INFO : Singer - Calling setName for bean of type class com.apress.prospring6.four.
       initmethod.Singer.
INFO : Singer - Calling setAge for bean of type class com.apress.prospring6.four.
       initmethod.Singer.
INFO : Singer - Initializing bean
DEBUG: DefaultSingletonBeanRegistry - Creating shared instance of singleton bean 'singerTwo'
INFO : Singer - Calling setAge for bean of type class com.apress.prospring6.four.
       initmethod.Singer.
INFO : Singer - Initializing bean
INFO : Singer - Using default name
DEBUG: DefaultSingletonBeanRegistry - Creating shared instance of singleton bean
       'singerThree'
INFO : Singer - Calling setName for bean of type class com.apress.prospring6.four.
       initmethod.Singer.
INFO : Singer - Initializing bean
WARN : AbstractApplicationContext - Exception encountered during context initialization -
       cancelling refresh attempt: org.springframework.beans.factory.BeanCreationException:
       Error creating bean with name 'singerThree' defined in com.apress.prospring6.four.
       initmethod.SingerConfiguration: Invocation of init method failed; nested exception
       is java.lang.IllegalArgumentException: You must set the age property of any beans of
       type class com.apress.prospring6.four.initmethod.Singer
       Exception in thread "main" org.springframework.beans.factory.BeanCreationException:
       Error creating bean with name 'singerThree' defined in com.apress.prospring6.four.
       initmethod.SingerConfiguration: Invocation of init method failed; nested exception
       is java.lang.IllegalArgumentException: You must set the age property of any beans of
       type class com.apress.prospring6.four.initmethod.Singer
```

From this output, you can see that singerOne was configured correctly with the values that we specified in the configuration file. For singerTwo, the default value for the name property was used because no value was specified in the configuration. Finally, for singerThree, no bean instance was created since the init() method raised an error because of the lack of a value for the age property.

As you can see, using the initialization method is an ideal way to ensure that your beans are configured correctly. By using this mechanism, you can take full advantage of the benefits of IoC without losing any of the control you get from manually defining dependencies.

---

❶   The only constraint on your initialization method is that it cannot accept any arguments. You can define any return type, although it is ignored by Spring, and you can even use a static method, but the method must accept no arguments.

The benefits of this mechanism are negated when using a static initialization method, because you cannot access any of the bean's state to validate it. If your bean is using static state as a mechanism for saving memory and you are using a static initialization method to validate this state, then you should consider moving the static state to instance state and using a nonstatic initialization method. If you use Spring's singleton management capabilities, the end effect is the same, but you have a bean that is much simpler to test, and you also have the increased effect of being able to create multiple instances of the bean with their own state when necessary. Of course, in some instances, you need to use static state shared across multiple instances of a bean, in which case you can always use a static initialization method.

Implementing the `InitializingBean` Interface

The `InitializingBean` interface defined in Spring allows you to define inside your bean code for Spring to execute after it has finished configuring the bean. In the same way as when you are using an initialization method, this gives you the opportunity to check the bean configuration to ensure that it is valid, providing any default values along the way. The `InitializingBean` interface defines a single method, `afterPropertiesSet()`, that serves the same purpose as the `init()` method introduced in the previous section. Listing 4-4 shows a reimplementation of the previous example using the `InitializingBean` interface in place of the initialization method.

Listing 4-4. Singer Class Implementing InitializingBean

```
package com.apress.prospring6.four.intf

import org.springframework.beans.factory.InitializingBean
// other import statements omitted

class Singer : InitializingBean {
    var name: String? = null
        set(value) {
            logger.info("Calling setName for bean of type {}.", Singer::class.java)
            field = value
        }

    var age = Int.MIN_VALUE
        set(value) {
            logger.info("Calling setAge for bean of type {}.", Singer::class.java)
            field = value
        }

    @Throws(Exception::class)
    override fun afterPropertiesSet() {
        logger.info("Initializing bean using 'afterPropertiesSet()'")
        if (name == null) {
            logger.info("Using default name")
            name = DEFAULT_NAME
        }
        require(age != Int.MIN_VALUE) {
            "You must set the age property of any beans of type " + Singer::class.java }
    }

    override fun toString(): String {
        return "name=${name}, age=${name}"
    }
```

```kotlin
    companion object {
        private val logger = LoggerFactory.getLogger(Singer::class.java)
        private const val DEFAULT_NAME = "No Name"
    }
}

@Configuration
open class SingerConfiguration {
    @Bean
    open fun singerOne(): Singer {
        val singer = Singer()
        singer.name = "John Mayer"
        singer.age = 43
        return singer
    }

    @Bean
    open fun singerTwo(): Singer {
        val singer = Singer()
        singer.age = 42
        return singer
    }

    @Bean
    open fun singerThree(): Singer {
        val singer = Singer()
        singer.name = "John Butler"
        return singer
    }
}

object InitializingBeanDemo {
    private val logger = LoggerFactory.getLogger(InitializingBeanDemo::class.java)
    @JvmStatic
    fun main(args: Array<String>) {
        val ctx = AnnotationConfigApplicationContext(SingerConfiguration::class.java)
        getBean("singerOne", ctx)
        getBean("singerTwo", ctx)
        getBean("singerThree", ctx)
    }

    fun getBean(beanName: String?, ctx: ApplicationContext): Singer? {
        return try {
            val bean = ctx.getBean(beanName) as Singer
            logger.info("Found: {}", bean)
            bean
        } catch (ex: BeanCreationException) {
            logger.error("An error occured in bean configuration: " + ex.message)
            null
        }
    }
}
```

As you can see, not much in this example has changed. The only differences are that this class implements `InitializingBean` and that the initialization logic has moved into the `afterPropertiesSet()` method. The configuration no longer requires the `initMethod` attribute, and if you run the `InitializingBeanDemo` you will see an identical output.

Using the JSR-250 @PostConstruct Annotation

JSR-250 annotations were described in **Chapter 3** in connection to dependency autowiring using `@Resource`. This section shows you how to use the JSR-250 life-cycle annotation, `@PostConstruct`. Starting from Spring 2.5, JSR-250 annotations are also supported to specify the method that Spring should call if the corresponding annotation relating to the bean's life cycle exists in the class. Listing 4-5 shows the previous example written to make use of the `@PostConstruct` annotation.

Listing 4-5. Singer Class Implemented Using `@PostConstruct`

```
package com.apress.prospring6.four.jsr250;

import jakarta.annotation.PostConstruct;

class Singer {
    var name: String? = null
        set(value) {
            logger.info("Calling setName for bean of type {}.",
                com.apress.prospring6.four.intf.Singer::class.java)
            field = value
        }

    var age = Int.MIN_VALUE
        set(value) {
            logger.info("Calling setAge for bean of type {}.",
                com.apress.prospring6.four.intf.Singer::class.java)
            field = value
        }

    @PostConstruct
    @Throws(Exception::class)
    private fun postConstruct() {
        logger.info("Initializing bean using 'postConstruct()'")
        if (name == null) {
            logger.info("Using default name")
            name = DEFAULT_NAME
        }
        require(age != Int.MIN_VALUE) {
            "You must set the age property of any beans of type " + Singer::class.java }
    }

    override fun toString(): String {
        return "name=${name}, age=${name}"
    }
```

```
companion object {
    private val logger = LoggerFactory.getLogger(Singer::class.java)
    private const val DEFAULT_NAME = "No Name"
}
}
```

The program is the same as using the @Bean(initMethod=..) and InitializingBean approach; the @PostConstruct annotation is applied to the initialization method instead. The method is renamed to postConstruct in this scenario to make it even more obvious as to what the purpose of this method is. Note that you can name the method any way you want to.

ℹ The configuration and the class used to test this new `Singer` bean type are identical to those in the InitializingBean example in Listing 4-4, and so is the produced output, so it won't be repeated here, but feel free to execute the com.apress.prospring6.four.jsr250.PostConstructDemo class in the project for this book yourself to test this affirmation.

All three approaches have their benefits and drawbacks:

- Using an initialization method, you have the benefit of keeping your application decoupled from Spring, but you must remember to configure the initialization method for every bean that needs it.

- Using the InitializingBean interface, you have the benefit of being able to specify the initialization callback once for all instances of your bean class, but you have to couple your application to Spring to do so.

- Using annotations, you need to apply the annotation to the method and make sure that the IoC container supports JSR-250.

In the end, you should let the requirements of your application drive the decision about which approach to use. If portability is an issue, use the initialization or annotation method; otherwise, use the InitializingBean interface to reduce the amount of configuration your application needs and the chance of errors creeping into your application because of misconfiguration.

ℹ When configuring initialization with @Bean(initMethod=..) or @PostConstruct, there is the advantage of declaring the initialization method with a different access right. Initialization methods should be called only once by the Spring IoC, at bean creation time. Subsequent calls will lead to unexpected results or even failures. External additional calls can be prohibited by making the initialization method `private`. The Spring IoC will be able to call it via reflection, but any additional calls in the code won't be permitted.

Understanding Order of Resolution

All initialization mechanisms can be used on the same bean instance. In this case, Spring invokes the method annotated with @PostConstruct first and then afterPropertiesSet(), followed by the initialization method specified in the @Bean annotation. There is a technical reason for this order, and by following the path in Figure 4-1, you'll notice the following steps in the bean creation process:

1.   The constructor is called first to create the bean.

2.   The dependencies are injected (setters are called). If there are dependencies, the BeanPostProcessor infrastructure bean is consulted to call the setters. This is a Spring-specific infrastructure bean that performs bean modifications after they are created. The @Autowired annotation is registered by the AutowiredAnnotationBeanPostProcessor so this bean will call the setter methods found annotated with @Autowired.

3.   Now that the beans exist and the dependencies were provided, the pre-initialization BeanPostProcessor infrastructure beans are consulted to see whether they want to call anything from this bean. These are Spring-specific infrastructure beans that perform bean modifications after they are created. The @PostConstruct annotation is registered by the CommonAnnotationBeanPostProcessor bean, so this bean will call the method found annotated with @PostConstruct. This method is executed right after the bean has been constructed and before the class is put into service[2], before the actual initialization of the bean (before afterPropertiesSet and initMethod).

4.   The InitializingBean's afterPropertiesSet is executed right after the dependencies are injected. The afterPropertiesSet() method is invoked by a BeanFactory after it has set all the bean properties supplied and has satisfied BeanFactoryAware and ApplicationContextAware.

5.   The method specified by name in the initMethod attribute is executed last because this is the actual initialization method of the bean.

The AllInitMethodsDemo set of classes shown in code Listing 4-6 can be used to demonstrate all the previous affirmations.

Listing 4-6. AllInitMethodsDemo Example to Show Order of Initialization Methods

```
package com.apress.prospring6.four.all;
// import statement omitted

internal class Dependency
internal class MultiInit : InitializingBean {
    @set:Autowired
    var dependency: Dependency? = null
        set(dependency) {
            logger.info("2. Calling setDependency for bean of type {}.",
            MultiInit::class.java)
            field = dependency
        }

    init {
        logger.info("1. Calling constructor for bean of type {}.", MultiInit::class.java)
    }
```

---

[2] Check out this snippet from JEE official Javadoc: https://docs.oracle.com/javaee/7/api/javax/annotation/PostConstruct.html

```kotlin
    @PostConstruct
    @Throws(Exception::class)
    private fun postConstruct() {
        logger.info("3. Calling postConstruct() for bean of type {}.",
        MultiInit::class.java)
    }

    @Throws(Exception::class)
    override fun afterPropertiesSet() {
        logger.info("4. Calling afterPropertiesSet() for bean of type {}.",
        MultiInit::class.java)
    }

    @Throws(Exception::class)
    private fun initMe() {
        logger.info("5. Calling initMethod() for bean of type {}.", Bean::class)
    }

    companion object {
        private val logger = LoggerFactory.getLogger(MultiInit::class.java)
    }
}

@Configuration
internal open class MultiInitConfiguration {
    @Bean
    open fun dependency() = Dependency()

    @Bean(initMethod = "initMe")
    open fun multiInitBean() = MultiInit()
}

object AllInitMethodsDemo {
    @JvmStatic
    fun main(args: Array<String>) {
        AnnotationConfigApplicationContext(MultiInitConfiguration::class.java)
    }
}
```

When running the main(..) method in class AllInitMethodsDemo with DEBUG logs enabled for the org. springframework package, the output in Listing 4-7 is produced.

Listing 4-7. AllInitMethodsDemo Console Output

```
...
DEBUG: DefaultSingletonBeanRegistry - Creating shared instance of singleton bean 'org.
springframework.context.annotation.internalConfigurationAnnotationProcessor'
DEBUG: DefaultSingletonBeanRegistry - Creating shared instance of singleton bean 'org.
springframework.context.event.internalEventListenerProcessor'
DEBUG: DefaultSingletonBeanRegistry - Creating shared instance of singleton bean 'org.
springframework.context.event.internalEventListenerFactory'
```

```
DEBUG: DefaultSingletonBeanRegistry - Creating shared instance of singleton bean 'org.
springframework.context.annotation.internalAutowiredAnnotationProcessor'
DEBUG: DefaultSingletonBeanRegistry - Creating shared instance of singleton bean 'org.
springframework.context.annotation.internalCommonAnnotationProcessor'
DEBUG: DefaultSingletonBeanRegistry - Creating shared instance of singleton bean
'multiInitConfiguration'
DEBUG: DefaultSingletonBeanRegistry - Creating shared instance of singleton bean
'dependency'
DEBUG: DefaultSingletonBeanRegistry - Creating shared instance of singleton bean
'multiInitBean'
INFO : MultiInit - 1. Calling constructor for bean of type class com.apress.prospring6.four.
all.MultiInit.
INFO : MultiInit - 2. Calling setDependency for bean of type class com.apress.prospring6.
four.all.MultiInit.
INFO : MultiInit - 3. Calling postConstruct() for bean of type class com.apress.prospring6.
four.all.MultiInit.
INFO : MultiInit - 4. Calling afterPropertiesSet() for bean of type class com.apress.
prospring6.four.all.MultiInit.
INFO : MultiInit - 5. Calling initMethod() for bean of type class com.apress.prospring6.
four.all.MultiInit.
```

If you look at the detailed log of the Spring application, you might notice a few Spring-specific infrastructure beans. Their names hint to their type and responsibilities. For example, the org. springframework.context.annotation.internalCommonAnnotationProcessor bean is the CommonAnnotationBeanPostProcessor bean that provides support for the @PostConstruct annotation, and the org.springframework.context.annotation.internalAutowiredAnnotationProcessor bean is the AutowiredAnnotationBeanPostProcessor bean that provides support for the @Autowired annotation. If you want to identify other types of Spring-specific infrastructure beans using their names, take a look at the source code of the AnnotationConfigUtils[3].

Hooking into Bean Destruction

When using an ApplicationContext implementation that wraps the DefaultListableBeanFactory interface (such as AnnotationConfigApplicationContext, via the getDefaultListableBeanFactory() method), you can signal to BeanFactory that you want to destroy all singleton instances with a call to ConfigurableBeanFactory.destroySingletons(). Typically, you do this when your application shuts down, and it allows you to clean up any resources that your beans might be holding open, thus allowing your application to shut down gracefully. This callback also provides the perfect place to flush any data you are storing in memory to persistent storage and to allow your beans to end any long-running processes they may have started.

To allow your beans to receive notification that destroySingletons() has been called, you have three options, all similar to the mechanisms available for receiving an initialization callback. The destruction callback is often used in conjunction with the initialization callback. In many cases, you create and configure a resource in the initialization callback and then release the resource in the destruction callback.

---

[3] https://github.com/spring-projects/spring-framework/blob/main/spring-context/src/main/java/org/springframework/context/annotation/AnnotationConfigUtils.java

❶   The name of the method destroySingletons() gives a hint about an important detail. Spring only performs bean destruction for singleton beans. Beans with other scopes than singleton do not have their life cycle fully managed by Spring. For example, for prototype beans, the Spring container instantiates, configures, and otherwise assembles a prototype object, and hands it to the client, with no further record of that prototype instance.

Executing a Method When a Bean Is Destroyed

To designate a method to be called when a bean is destroyed, you simply specify the name of the method in the destroyMethod attribute of the bean's definition @Bean annotation. Spring calls it just before it destroys the singleton instance of the bean (Spring will not call this method for those beans with prototype scope). The code snippet in Listing 4-8 provides an example of using a destroy-method callback.

Listing 4-8. Example Showing How to Configure a Destroy Method Using the @Bean Annotation

```
package com.apress.prospring6.four.destroymethod;
// import statements omitted

internal class FileManager {
    private lateinit var file: Path

    init {
        logger.info("Creating bean of type {}", FileManager::class.java)
        try {
            file = Files.createFile(Path.of("sample"))
        } catch (e: IOException) {
            logger.error("Could not create file")
        }
    }

    @Throws(IOException::class)
    private fun destroyMethod() {
        logger.info(
            "Calling destroyMethod() on bean of type {}",
            FileManager::class.java
        )
        Files.deleteIfExists(file)
    }

    companion object {
        private val logger = LoggerFactory.getLogger(FileManager::class.java)
    }
}

@Configuration
internal open class DemoConfig {
    @Bean(destroyMethod = "destroyMethod")
```

```kotlin
    open fun fileManager(): FileManager {
        return FileManager()
    }
}

object DestroyMethodDemo {
    @JvmStatic
    fun main(args: Array<String>) {
        val ctx = AnnotationConfigApplicationContext(DemoConfig::class.java)
        ctx.close()
    }
}
```

Class `FileManager` defines a `destroyMethod()` method, in which the file that is created by its constructor gets deleted. The `main()` method retrieves a bean of type `FileManager` from the context and then invokes its `destroyMethod()` method (which will, in turn, invoke the `ConfigurableBeanFactory.destroySingletons()` method that was wrapped by the `ApplicationContext`), instructing Spring to destroy all the singletons managed by it. Both the constructor and the destroy method write a message to console output informing us that they have been called.

Implementing the `DisposableBean` Interface

As with initialization callbacks, Spring provides an interface, in this case `DisposableBean`, that can be implemented by your beans as a mechanism for receiving destruction callbacks. The `DisposableBean` interface defines a single method, `destroy()`, which is called just before the bean is destroyed. Using this mechanism is orthogonal to using the `InitializingBean` interface to receive initialization callbacks. Listing 4-9 shows a modified implementation of the `FileManager` class that implements the `DisposableBean` interface.

Listing 4-9. Example Showing How to Configure a Destroy Method Using the `DisposableBean` Interface

```kotlin
package com.apress.prospring6.four.intf;

import org.springframework.beans.factory.DisposableBean;
// other import statements omitted

internal class FileManager : DisposableBean {
    private lateinit var file: Path

    init {
        LOGGER.info("Creating bean of type {}", FileManager::class.java)
        try {
            file = Files.createFile(Path.of("sample"))
        } catch (e: IOException) {
            LOGGER.error("Could not create file")
        }
    }

    @Throws(Exception::class)
    override fun destroy() {
        LOGGER.info("Calling destroy() on bean of type {}", FileManager::class.java)
        Files.deleteIfExists(file)
    }
```

```
    companion object {
        private val LOGGER = LoggerFactory.getLogger(FileManager::class.java)
    }
}

@Configuration
internal open class DemoConfig {
    @Bean
    open fun fileManager() = FileManager()
}

object DisposableBeanDemo {
    @JvmStatic
    fun main(args: Array<String>) {
        val ctx = AnnotationConfigApplicationContext(DemoConfig::class.java)
        ctx.close()
    }
}
```

There is not much difference between the code that uses the callback method mechanism configured with @Bean(destroyMethod="..") and the code that uses the callback interface mechanism. The configuration is identical to that in the previous section, except for the missing (destroyMethod=".."), which is no longer necessary. The code to run the example is the same as well. Thus, we can skip showing these two implementations and jump to the next way of configuring a destroy method.

Using the JSR-250 @PreDestroy Annotation

The third way to define a method to be called before a bean is destroyed is to use the JSR-250 life-cycle @PreDestroy annotation, which is the inverse of the @PostConstruct annotation. Listing 4-10 shows a version of FileManager that uses @PreDestroy to perform destroy actions.

Listing 4-10. Example Showing How to Configure a Destroy Method Using the @PreDestroy Annotation

```
package com.apress.prospring6.four.jsr250;
import jakarta.annotation.PreDestroy;
// import statements omitted

class FileManager {
    private lateinit var file: Path

    init {
        LOGGER.info("Creating bean of type {}", FileManager::class.java)
        try {
            file = Files.createFile(Path.of("sample"))
        } catch (e: IOException) {
            LOGGER.error("Could not create file")
        }
    }

    @PreDestroy
    @Throws(IOException::class)
```

```kotlin
    private fun preDestroy() {
        LOGGER.info(
            "Calling preDestroy() on bean of type {}",
            FileManager::class.java
        )
        Files.deleteIfExists(file)
    }

    companion object {
        private val LOGGER = LoggerFactory.getLogger(FileManager::class.java)
    }
}

@Configuration
open class DemoConfig {
    @Bean
    open fun fileManager() = FileManager()
}

object PreDestroyDemo {
    @JvmStatic
    fun main(args: Array<String>) {
        val ctx = AnnotationConfigApplicationContext(DemoConfig::class.java)
        ctx.close()
    }
}
```

Running any of the examples declaring destroy callbacks results in a console log pretty similar to the one shown in Listing 4-11.

Listing 4-11. Log Sample Showing Bean Destruction

```
...
INFO : FileManager - Creating bean of type class com.apress.prospring6.four.*.FileManager
DEBUG: AbstractApplicationContext - Closing org.springframework.context.annotation.Annotatio
nConfigApplicationContext@79be0360, started on Fri Mar 25 12:05:49 GMT 2022
INFO : FileManager - Calling destroy()/destroyMethod()/preDestroy() on bean of type class
com.apress.prospring6.four.*.FileManager
```

The destruction callback is an ideal mechanism for ensuring that your applications shut down gracefully and do not leave resources open or in an inconsistent state. However, you still have to decide how to use the destruction method callback: using the @Bean(destroyMethod=".."), the DisposableBean interface, or the @PreDestroy annotation. Again, let the requirements of your application drive your decision in this respect; use the method callback where portability is an issue, and use the DisposableBean interface or a JSR-250 annotation to reduce the amount of configuration required.

Understanding Order of Resolution

As with the case of bean creation, you can use all mechanisms on the same bean instance for bean destruction. In this case, Spring invokes the method annotated with @PreDestroy first and then DisposableBean.destroy(), followed by your destroy method configured in your @Bean definition.

Using a Shutdown Hook

The only drawback of the destruction callbacks in Spring is that they are not fired automatically; you need to remember to call ctx.close() before your application is closed. When your application runs as a servlet, you can simply call destroy() in the servlet's destroy() method.

However, in a stand-alone application, things are not quite so simple, especially if you have multiple exit points out of your application. Fortunately, there is a solution. Java allows you to create a *shutdown hook*, which is a thread that is executed just before the application shuts down. This is the perfect way to invoke the destroy() method of your context (which was being extended by all concrete ApplicationContext implementations). The easiest way to take advantage of this mechanism is to use AbstractApplicationContext's registerShutdownHook() method. The method automatically instructs Spring to register a shutdown hook of the underlying JVM runtime. The bean declaration and configuration stay the same as before; the only thing that changes is the main method: the call of ctx. registerShutdownHook is added, and calls to ctx.destroy() or close() will be removed.

Running the code in Listing 4-12 produces the same output as the output displayed in Listing 4-11.

Listing 4-12. Registering Shutdown Hooks

```
package com.apress.prospring6.four.jsr250;
// import and some code omitted

object PreDestroyDemo {
    @JvmStatic
    fun main(args: Array<String>) {
        val ctx = AnnotationConfigApplicationContext(DemoConfig::class.java)
        ctx.registerShutdownHook()
    }
}
```

Making Your Beans "Spring Aware"

One of the biggest selling points of dependency injection over dependency lookup as a mechanism for achieving inversion of control is that your beans do not need to be aware of the implementation of the container that is managing them. To a bean that uses constructor or setter injection, the Spring container is the same as the container provided by Google Guice or PicoContainer. However, in certain circumstances, you may need a bean that is using dependency injection to obtain its dependencies so it can interact with the container for some other reason. An example of this may be a bean that automatically configures a shutdown hook for you, and thus it needs access to ApplicationContext. In other cases, a bean may want to know what its name is (that is, the bean name that was assigned within the current ApplicationContext) so it can perform some additional processing based on this name.

That said, this feature is really intended for internal Spring use. Giving the bean name some kind of business meaning is generally a bad idea and can lead to configuration problems as bean names have to be artificially manipulated to support their business meaning. However, we have found that being able to have a bean find out its name at runtime is really useful for logging. Say you have many beans of the same type running under different configurations. The bean name can be included in log messages to help you differentiate between the one that is generating errors and the ones that are working fine when something goes wrong.

Using the BeanNameAware Interface

The BeanNameAware interface, which can be implemented by a bean that wants to obtain its own name, has a single method: setBeanName(String). Spring calls the setBeanName() method after it has finished configuring your bean but before any life-cycle callbacks (initialization or destroy) are called (refer to Figure 4-1). In most cases, the implementation of the setBeanName() interface is just a single line that stores the value passed in by the container in a field for use later. Listing 4-13 shows a simple bean that obtains its name by using BeanNameAware and then later uses this bean name to print to the console.

Listing 4-13. BeanNameAware Sample Implementation

```kotlin
package com.apress.prospring6.four.aware

import org.springframework.beans.factory.BeanNameAware
// other imports omitted

internal class NamedSinger : BeanNameAware {
    private var name: String? = null

    /** @Implements [BeanNameAware.setBeanName]
     */
    override fun setBeanName(beanName: String) {
        name = beanName
    }

    fun sing() {
        logger.info("Singer $name - sing()")
    }

    companion object {
        private val logger = LoggerFactory.getLogger(NamedSinger::class.java)
    }
}

internal class FileManager {
    private var file: Path? = null

    init {
        logger.info("Creating bean of type {}", FileManager::class.java)
        try {
            file = Files.createFile(Path.of("sample"))
        } catch (e: IOException) {
            logger.error("Could not create file")
        }
    }

    @PreDestroy
    @Throws(IOException::class)
    private fun preDestroy() {
        logger.info(
```

```
            "Calling preDestroy() on bean of type {}",
            FileManager::class.java
        )
        file?.run{ Files.deleteIfExists(this) }
    }

    companion object {
        private val logger = LoggerFactory.getLogger(FileManager::class.java)
    }
}

internal class ShutdownHookBean : ApplicationContextAware {
    private val ctx: ApplicationContext? = null

    /** @Implements [ApplicationContextAware.setApplicationContext] }
     */
    @Throws(BeansException::class)
    override fun setApplicationContext(ctx: ApplicationContext) {
        if (ctx is GenericApplicationContext) {
            ctx.registerShutdownHook()
        }
    }
}
```

This implementation is fairly trivial. Remember that BeanNameAware.setBeanName() is called before the first instance of the bean is returned to your application via a call to ApplicationContext.getBean(), so there is no need to check whether the bean name is available in the sing() method. As you can see, no special configuration is required to take advantage of the BeanNameAware interface. In Listing 4-14, you can see a simple example configuration and application that retrieves the NamedSinger instance from ApplicationContext and then calls the sing() method.

Listing 4-14. BeanNameAware Example Usage

```
package com.apress.prospring6.four.aware
// other import statements omitted

@ComponentScan
internal class AwareConfig {
    @Bean
    fun johnMayer(): NamedSinger {
        return NamedSinger()
    }

    @Bean
    fun fileManager(): FileManager {
        return FileManager()
    }
```

```kotlin
    @Bean
    fun shutdownHookBean(): ShutdownHookBean {
        return ShutdownHookBean()
    }
}

object AwareDemo {
    @JvmStatic
    fun main(args: Array<String>) {
        val ctx = AnnotationConfigApplicationContext(AwareConfig::class.java)
        val singer = ctx.getBean(NamedSinger::class.java)
        singer.sing()

        // ctx.registerShutdownHook(); // no longer needed because of the ShutdownHookBean
    }
}
```

When run, this example generates a very simple output:

```
INFO : NamedSinger - Singer johnMayer - sing() ;
```

Notice the inclusion of the bean name in the log message for the call to the sing() method.

Using the BeanNameAware interface is really quite simple, and it is put to good use when you are improving the quality of your log messages. Avoid being tempted to give your bean names business meaning just because you can access them; by doing so, you are coupling your classes to Spring for a feature that brings negligible benefit. If your beans need some kind of name internally, have them implement an interface such as Nameable (which is specific to your application) with a method setName() or .name accessor and then give each bean a name by using dependency injection. This way, you can keep the names you use for configuration concise, and you won't need to manipulate your configuration unnecessarily to give your beans names with business meaning.

Using the ApplicationContextAware Interface

ApplicationContextAware was introduced at the end of **Chapter 3** to show how Spring can be used to deal with beans that require other beans to function that are not injected using constructors or setters in the configuration.

Using the ApplicationContextAware interface, it is possible for your beans to get a reference to the ApplicationContext instance that configured them. The main reason this interface was created is to allow a bean to access Spring's ApplicationContext in your application, for example, to acquire other Spring beans programmatically, using getBean(). You should, however, avoid this practice and use dependency injection to provide your beans with their collaborators. If you use the lookup-based getBean() approach to obtain dependencies when you can use dependency injection, you are adding unnecessary complexity to your beans and coupling them to the Spring Framework without good reason.

Of course, ApplicationContext isn't used just to look up beans; it performs a great many other tasks. As you saw previously, one of these tasks is to destroy all singletons, notifying each of them in turn before doing so. In the previous section, you saw how to create a shutdown hook to ensure that ApplicationContext is instructed to destroy all singletons before the application shuts down. By using the ApplicationContextAware interface, you can build a bean that can be configured in ApplicationContext to create and configure a shutdown hook bean automatically. Listing 4-15 shows the code for this bean.

Listing 4-15. ApplicationContextAware Implementation Example

```
package com.apress.prospring6.four.aware

import org.springframework.context.ApplicationContextAware
// other import statements omitted

internal class ShutdownHookBean : ApplicationContextAware {
    private val ctx: ApplicationContext? = null

    /** @Implements [ApplicationContextAware.setApplicationContext] }
     */
    @Throws(BeansException::class)
    override fun setApplicationContext(ctx: ApplicationContext) {
        if (ctx is GenericApplicationContext) {
            ctx.registerShutdownHook()
        }
    }
}
```

Most of this code should seem familiar to you by now. The ApplicationContextAware interface defines a single method, setApplicationContext(ApplicationContext), that Spring calls to pass your bean a reference to its ApplicationContext. In the previous code snippet, the ShutdownHookBean class checks whether ApplicationContext is of type GenericApplicationContext, meaning it supports the registerShutdownHook() method; if it does, it will register a shutdown hook to ApplicationContext. Listing 4-16 shows how to configure this bean to work with the FileManager bean introduced in the previous section.

Listing 4-16. ApplicationContextAware Bean Configuration and Code to Bootstrap the Spring Application Based on This Configuration

```
package com.apress.prospring6.four.aware
// import statements omitted

@ComponentScan
internal class AwareConfig {
    @Bean
    fun johnMayer(): NamedSinger {
        return NamedSinger()
    }

    @Bean
    fun fileManager(): FileManager {
        return FileManager()
    }

    @Bean
    fun shutdownHookBean(): ShutdownHookBean {
        return ShutdownHookBean()
    }
}
```

```
object AwareDemo {
    @JvmStatic
    fun main(args: Array<String>) {
        val ctx = AnnotationConfigApplicationContext(AwareConfig::class.java)
        val singer = ctx.getBean(NamedSinger::class.java)
        singer.sing()

        //ctx.registerShutdownHook(); // no longer needed because of the ShutdownHookBean
    }
}
```

Notice that no special configuration is required. The code to build a Spring application is simple too, as depicted by the new AwareDemo class. Calling ctx.registerShutdownHook() is no longer needed because this is done by the ShutdownHookBean. Running the previous example will generate a console output ending in

```
INFO : FileManager - Calling preDestroy() on bean of type class com.apress.prospring6.four.
aware.FileManager
```

Even without a call to ctx.registerShutdownHook() or ctx.close() that closes the application context removing the hooks, the preDestroy() method is called before the application shuts down, because the ShutdownHookBean.setApplicationContext(ApplicationContext ctx) method does shutdown hook registering.

Use of FactoryBeans

One of the problems that you will face when using Spring is how to create and then inject dependencies that cannot be created simply by using the constructor. To overcome this problem, Spring provides the FactoryBean interface that acts as an adapter for objects that cannot be created and managed using the standard Spring semantics. Typically, you use FactoryBeans to create beans that you cannot create by using the constructor, such as those you access through static factory methods, although this is not always the case. Simply put, a FactoryBean is a bean that acts as a factory for other beans. FactoryBeans are configured within your ApplicationContext like any normal bean, but when Spring uses the FactoryBean interface to satisfy a dependency or lookup request, it does not return FactoryBean; instead, it invokes the FactoryBean.getObject() method and returns the result of that invocation.

 Spring automatically calls the getObject() method—it is a bad practice to call that method manually.

The FactoryBean type is a generic type, declared as FactoryBean<T>, but because this type is mentioned numerous times in this chapter, we decided to skip the <T> everywhere unless it's really important to the context.

FactoryBeans are used to great effect in Spring; the most noticeable uses are the creation of transactional proxies, which we cover in **Chapter 9**, and the automatic retrieval of resources from a JNDI context. However, FactoryBeans are useful not just for building the internals of Spring; you'll find them really useful when you build your own applications because they allow you to manage many more resources by using IoC than would otherwise be available.

FactoryBean Example: The `MessageDigestFactoryBean`

Often the projects that we work on require some kind of cryptographic processing; typically, this involves generating a message digest or hash of a user's password to be stored in a database. In Kotlin, the MessageDigest class provides functionality for creating a digest of any arbitrary data. MessageDigest itself is abstract, and you obtain concrete implementations by calling MessageDigest.getInstance() and passing in the name of the digest algorithm you want to use. For instance, if we want to use the MD5 algorithm to create a digest, we use the following code to create the MessageDigest instance:

```
val md5 = MessageDigest.getInstance("MD5")
```

If we want to use Spring to manage the creation of the MessageDigest object, the best we can do without a FactoryBean is to have a property named algorithmName on our bean and then use an initialization callback to call MessageDigest.getInstance(). Using a FactoryBean, we can encapsulate this logic inside a bean. Then, any beans that require a MessageDigest instance can simply declare a property, messageDigest, and use the FactoryBean to obtain the instance. Listing 4-17 shows an implementation of FactoryBean that does this.

Listing 4-17. MessageDigestFactoryBean Implementation

```
package com.apress.prospring6.four.factory

import org.springframework.beans.factory.FactoryBean
import java.security.MessageDigest
// other import statements omitted

package com.apress.prospring6.four.factory

import org.springframework.beans.factory.FactoryBean
import org.springframework.beans.factory.InitializingBean
import java.security.MessageDigest

class MessageDigestFactoryBean : FactoryBean<MessageDigest?>, InitializingBean {
    var algorithmName = "MD5"
    private var messageDigest: MessageDigest? = null

    @Throws(Exception::class)
    /** @Implements [FactoryBean.getObject]
     */
    override fun getObject(): MessageDigest? {
        return messageDigest
    }

    /** @Implements [FactoryBean.getObjectType]
     */
```

```kotlin
    override fun getObjectType(): Class<MessageDigest> {
        return MessageDigest::class.java
    }

    /** @Implements [FactoryBean.isSingleton]
     */
    override fun isSingleton() = true

    @Throws(Exception::class)
    /** @Implements [InitializingBean.afterPropertiesSet]
     */
    override fun afterPropertiesSet() {
        messageDigest = MessageDigest.getInstance(algorithmName)
    }
}
```

Spring calls the getObject() method to retrieve the object created by the FactoryBean. This is the actual object that is passed to other beans that use the FactoryBean as a collaborator. MessageDigestFactoryBean passes a clone of the stored MessageDigest instance that is created in the InitializingBean.afterPropertiesSet() callback.

The getObjectType() method allows you to tell Spring what type of object your FactoryBean will return. This can be null if the return type is unknown in advance (for example, the FactoryBean creates different types of objects depending on the configuration, which will be determined only after the FactoryBean is initialized), but if you specify a type, Spring can use it for autowiring purposes. We return MessageDigest as our type (in this case, a class, but try to return an interface type and have the FactoryBean instantiate the concrete implementation class, unless necessary). The reason is that we do not know what concrete type will be returned (not that it matters, because all beans will define their dependencies by using MessageDigest anyway).

The isSingleton property allows you to inform Spring whether the FactoryBean is managing a singleton instance. Remember that by annotating the FactoryBean's definition with @Scope(scopeName = "singleton"), you tell Spring about the singleton status of the FactoryBean itself, not the objects it is returning. Now let's see how the FactoryBean is employed in an application. In Listing 4-18, you can see a simple bean that maintains two MessageDigest instances and then displays the digests of a message passed to its digest() method.

Listing 4-18. Simple Bean Maintaining Two MessageDigest Instances

```kotlin
package com.apress.prospring6.four.factory

import org.slf4j.LoggerFactory
import java.security.MessageDigest

class MessageDigester {
    var digest1: MessageDigest? = null
    var digest2: MessageDigest? = null

    fun digest(msg: String) {
        LOGGER.info("Using digest1")
        digest(msg, digest1)
        LOGGER.info("Using digest2")
        digest(msg, digest2)
    }
```

```kotlin
    private fun digest(msg: String, digest: MessageDigest?) {
        LOGGER.info("Using algorithm: " + digest!!.algorithm)
        digest.reset()
        val bytes = msg.toByteArray()
        val out = digest.digest(bytes)
        // we are printing the actual byte values
        LOGGER.info("Original Message: {} ", bytes)
        LOGGER.info("Encrypted Message: {} ", out)
    }

    companion object {
        private val LOGGER = LoggerFactory.getLogger(MessageDigester::class.java)
    }
}
```

Listing 4-19 shows an example configuration for two MessageDigestFactoryBean classes, one for the SHA1 algorithm and the other using the default (MD5) algorithm. The same listing also shows the FactoryBeanDemo class that retrieves the MessageDigester bean from the BeanFactory and creates the digest of a simple message.

Listing 4-19. Simple Configuration for MessageDigestFactoryBean and Code to Bootstrap a Spring Application to Test It

```kotlin
package com.apress.prospring6.four.factory
// import statements omitted

@Configuration
@ComponentScan
internal open class MessageDigestConfig {
    @Bean
    open fun shaDigest() =
        MessageDigestFactoryBean().apply {
            algorithmName = "SHA1"
        }

    @Bean
    open fun defaultDigest() = MessageDigestFactoryBean()

    @Bean
    @Throws(Exception::class)
    open fun digester() =
        MessageDigester().apply {
            digest1 = shaDigest().getObject()
            digest2 = defaultDigest().getObject()
        }
}

object FactoryBeanDemo {
    private val LOGGER = LoggerFactory.getLogger(FactoryBeanDemo::class.java)
    @JvmStatic
    fun main(args: Array<String>) {
        val ctx = AnnotationConfigApplicationContext(MessageDigestConfig::class.java)
```

```
        val digester = ctx.getBean(
            "digester",
            MessageDigester::class.java
        )
        digester.digest("Hello World!")
        ctx.close()
    }
}
```

As you can see, we not only have configured the two MessageDigestFactoryBean classes, but also have configured a MessageDigester, using the two MessageDigestFactoryBean classes, to provide values for the digest1 and digest2 properties. For the defaultDigest bean, since the algorithmName property was not specified, no injection will happen, and the default algorithm (MD5) that was coded in the class will be used. In Listing 4-20, you can see the console log produced by running the code in Listing 4-19.

Listing 4-20. Simple Message Digest Generated by the Application Configured by the MessageDigestConfig Class

```
INFO : MessageDigester - Using digest1
INFO : MessageDigester - Using algoritm: SHA1
INFO : MessageDigester - Original Message: [72, 101, 108, 108, 111, 32, 87, 111, 114, 108,
       100, 33]
INFO : MessageDigester - Encrypted Message: [46, -9, -67, -26, 8, -50, 84, 4, -23, 125, 95,
       4, 47, -107, -8, -97, 28, 35, 40, 113]
INFO : MessageDigester - Using digest2
INFO : MessageDigester - Using algoritm: MD5
INFO : MessageDigester - Original Message: [72, 101, 108, 108, 111, 32, 87, 111, 114, 108,
       100, 33]
INFO : MessageDigester - Encrypted Message: [-19, 7, 98, -121, 83, 46, -122, 54, 94, -124,
       30, -110, -65, -59, 13, -116]
```

We chose to print the numeric byte values instead of the messages as text to show the changes that encryption makes at the byte level. As you can see, the MessageDigest bean is provided with two MessageDigest implementations, SHA1 and MD5, even though no MessageDigest beans are configured in the BeanFactory. This is the FactoryBean at work.

FactoryBeans are the perfect solution when you are working with classes that cannot be created by using the constructor. If you work with objects that are created by using a factory method and you want to use these classes in a Spring application, create a FactoryBean to act as an adapter, allowing your classes to take full advantage of Spring's IoC capabilities.

ⓘ   The power of using FactoryBeans becomes obvious when XML configuration is used, since Spring automatically satisfies any references to a FactoryBean by the objects produced by that FactoryBean. This allows for the MessageDigester bean to be configured like this:

```
<beans ...>
    <bean id="shaDigest"
        class="com.apress.prospring6.ch4.MessageDigestFactoryBean"
        p:algorithmName="SHA1"/>
    <bean id="defaultDigest"
        class="com.apress.prospring6.ch4.MessageDigestFactoryBean"/>
```

```
    <bean id="digester"
        class="com.apress.prospring6.ch4.MessageDigester"
        p:digest1-ref="shaDigest"
        p:digest2-ref="defaultDigest"/>
</beans>
```

Accessing a FactoryBean Directly

Given that Spring automatically satisfies any references to a FactoryBean<T> by the objects produced by that FactoryBean, you may be wondering whether you can actually access the FactoryBean directly. The answer is *yes*. Accessing a FactoryBean is simple: you prefix the bean name with an ampersand in the call to getBean(), as shown in Listing 4-21.

Listing 4-21. Accessing a FactoryBean Directly

```
package com.apress.prospring6.four.factory
// import statements omitted

object FactoryBeanDemo {
    private val LOGGER = LoggerFactory.getLogger(FactoryBeanDemo::class.java)

    @JvmStatic
    fun main(args: Array<String>) {
        val ctx = AnnotationConfigApplicationContext(MessageDigestConfig::class.java)
        LOGGER.debug("-------------------------------------")
        val factoryBean = ctx.getBean("&shaDigest") as MessageDigestFactoryBean
        try {
            val shaDigest: MessageDigest = factoryBean.getObject()!!
            LOGGER.info("Explicit use digest bean: {}",
                                shaDigest.digest("Hello world".toByteArray()))
        } catch (ex: Exception) {
            LOGGER.error("Could not find MessageDigestFactoryBean ", ex)
        }
        ctx.close()
    }
}
```

This feature is used in a few places in the Spring code, but your application should really have no reason to use it. The FactoryBean is intended to be used as a piece of supporting infrastructure to allow you to use more of your application's classes in an IoC setting. Avoid accessing FactoryBean directly and invoking its getObject() manually, and let Spring do it for you; if you do this manually, you are making extra work for yourself and are unnecessarily coupling your application to a specific implementation detail that could quite easily change in the future.

JavaBeans `PropertyEditors`

If you are not entirely familiar with JavaBeans concepts, a `PropertyEditor` is an interface that converts a property's value to and from its native type representation into a `String`. Originally, this was conceived as a way to allow property values to be entered, as `String` values, into an editor and have them transformed into the correct type. However, because `PropertyEditor` implementations are inherently lightweight classes, they have found uses in many settings, including Spring.

Since a good portion of property values in a Spring-based application start life in the `BeanFactory` configuration file, they are essentially `Strings`. However, the property that these values are set on might not be `String`-typed. So, to save you from having to create a load of `String`-typed properties artificially, Spring allows you to define `PropertyEditor` beans to manage the conversion of `String`-based property values into the correct types. Figure 4-2 shows the full list of `PropertyEditor` implementations that are part of the Spring Framework, most of them being grouped in the `spring-beans` package; you can see this list with any smart Java editor, but in IntelliJ you can see all the implementations of a specific interface by opening its source code, selecting its name, and pressing Ctrl+H (macOS) or Ctrl+E (Windows).

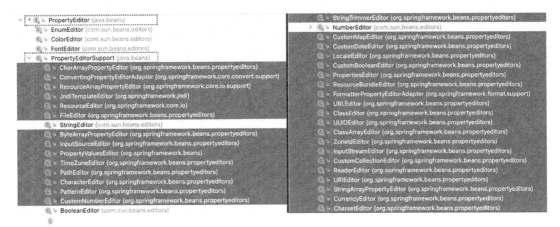

Figure 4-2. *Spring property editors*

The list in Figure 4-2 shows that the root of the hierarchy is the `java.beans.PropertyEditor` interface, but all Spring implementations actually extend the `java.beans.PropertyEditorSupport` class that provides support building a property editor. Or they delegate to an existing one, for example the `java.beans.StringEditor` that handles implicit conversion of `String` literals into property values to be injected in beans, that is preregistered with `BeanFactory`.

Using the Built-in `PropertyEditors`

Listing 4-22 shows a simple bean that declares 14 properties, one for each of the types supported by the built-in `PropertyEditor` implementations.

Listing 4-22. Bean with Types of All Property Types Supported by Default in Spring Applications

```
package com.apress.prospring6.four

import org.slf4j.LoggerFactory
import org.springframework.beans.PropertyEditorRegistrar
// other imports omitted
```

```
@Component
internal class ValuesHolder(stringList: List<String?>?) {
    var stringList: List<String>
    var inputStream: InputStream? = null

    init {
        this.stringList = java.util.List.of("Mayer", "Psihoza", "Mazikeen")
        try {
            inputStream = FileInputStream(
                System.getProperty("java.io.tmpdir")
                        + System.getProperty("file.separator")
                        + "test.txt"
            )
        } catch (e: FileNotFoundException) {
            e.printStackTrace() // we are not interested in the exception that much
        }
    }
}

@Component("builtInSample")
class DiverseValuesContainer {
    private var bytes // ByteArrayPropertyEditor
            : ByteArray? = null
    private var character //CharacterEditor
            : Char? = null
    private var cls // ClassEditor
            : Class<*>? = null
    private var trueOrFalse // CustomBooleanEditor
            : Boolean? = null
    private var stringList // CustomCollectionEditor
            : List<String>? = null
    private var date // CustomDateEditor
            : Date? = null
    private var floatValue // CustomNumberEditor
            : Float? = null
    private var file // FileEditor
            : File? = null
    private var stream // InputStreamEditor
            : InputStream? = null
    private var locale // LocaleEditor
            : Locale? = null
    private var pattern // PatternEditor
            : Pattern? = null
    private var properties // PropertiesEditor
            : Properties? = null
    private var trimString // StringTrimmerEditor
            : String? = null
    private var url // URLEditor
            : URL? = null
```

```kotlin
@Value("A")
fun setCharacter(character: Char?) {
    LOGGER.info("Setting character: {}", character)
    this.character = character
}

@Value("java.lang.String")
fun setCls(cls: Class<*>) {
    LOGGER.info("Setting class: {}", cls.name)
    this.cls = cls
}

@Value("#{systemProperties['java.io.tmpdir']}
            #{systemProperties['file.separator']}test.txt")
fun setFile(file: File) {
    LOGGER.info("Setting file: {}", file.absolutePath)
    this.file = file
}

@Value("en_US")
fun setLocale(locale: Locale) {
    LOGGER.info("Setting locale: {}", locale.displayName)
    this.locale = locale
}

@Value("name=Ben age=41")
fun setProperties(properties: Properties) {
    LOGGER.info("Loaded {}", properties.size.toString() + " properties")
    this.properties = properties
}

@Value("https://iuliana-cosmina.com")
fun setUrl(url: URL) {
    LOGGER.info("Setting URL: {}", url.toExternalForm())
    this.url = url
}

@Value("John Mayer")
fun setBytes(vararg bytes: Byte) {
    LOGGER.info("Setting bytes: {}", Arrays.toString(bytes))
    this.bytes = bytes
}

@Value("true")
fun setTrueOrFalse(trueOrFalse: Boolean?) {
    LOGGER.info("Setting Boolean: {}", trueOrFalse)
    this.trueOrFalse = trueOrFalse
}

@Value("#{valuesHolder.stringList}")
fun setStringList(stringList: List<String>?) {
```

```kotlin
        LOGGER.info("Setting stringList with: {}", stringList)
        this.stringList = stringList
    }

    @Value("20/08/1981")
    fun setDate(date: Date?) {
        LOGGER.info("Setting date: {}", date)
        this.date = date
    }

    @Value("123.45678")
    fun setFloatValue(floatValue: Float?) {
        LOGGER.info("Setting float value: {}", floatValue)
        this.floatValue = floatValue
    }

    @Value("#{valuesHolder.inputStream}")
    fun setStream(stream: InputStream?) {
        this.stream = stream
        LOGGER.info(
            "Setting stream & reading from it: {}",
            BufferedReader(InputStreamReader(stream))
                .lines().parallel().collect(Collectors.joining("\n"))
        )
    }

    @Value("a*b")
    fun setPattern(pattern: Pattern?) {
        LOGGER.info("Setting pattern: {}", pattern)
        this.pattern = pattern
    }

    @Value("    String need trimming    ")
    fun setTrimString(trimString: String?) {
        LOGGER.info("Setting trim string: {}", trimString)
        this.trimString = trimString
    }

    class CustomPropertyEditorRegistrar : PropertyEditorRegistrar {
        override fun registerCustomEditors(registry: PropertyEditorRegistry) {
            val dateFormatter = SimpleDateFormat("MM/dd/yyyy")
            registry.registerCustomEditor(
                Date::class.java,
                CustomDateEditor(dateFormatter, true)
            )
            registry.registerCustomEditor(String::class.java, StringTrimmerEditor(true))
        }
    }
}
```

```kotlin
    companion object {
        private val LOGGER = LoggerFactory.getLogger(DiverseValuesContainer::class.java)
        @Throws(Exception::class)
        @JvmStatic
        fun main(args: Array<String>) {
            val baseDir = File(System.getProperty("java.io.tmpdir"))
            val path = Files.createFile(Path.of(baseDir.absolutePath, "test.txt"))
            Files.writeString(path, "Hello World!")
            path.toFile().deleteOnExit()
            val ctx = AnnotationConfigApplicationContext()
            ctx.register(ValuesHolder::class.java, DiverseValuesContainer::class.java)
            ctx.refresh()
            ctx.close()
        }
    }
}
```

(remove the line break including spaces inside the @Value annotation parameter near setFile()) As you can see, although all the properties in the DiverseValuesContainer are not Strings, the values for the properties are specified as simple Strings. Also note that we registered the CustomDateEditor with the desired formatter, and StringTrimmerEditor, since those two editors were not registered by default in Spring by providing an implementation for org.springframework.beans.PropertyEditorRegistrar. Running this example yields the output shown in Listing 4-23.

Listing 4-23. Output Showing the Properties Being Injected with the Converted Values

```
INFO : DiverseValuesContainer - Loaded 1 properties
INFO : DiverseValuesContainer - Setting locale: English (United States)
INFO : DiverseValuesContainer - Setting date: Sun Aug 08 00:00:00 BST 1982
INFO : DiverseValuesContainer - Setting class: java.lang.String
INFO : DiverseValuesContainer - Setting file: /var/folders/gg/nm_
       cb2lx72q1lz7xwwdh7tnc0000gn/T/test.txt
INFO : DiverseValuesContainer - Setting URL: https://iuliana-cosmina.com
INFO : DiverseValuesContainer - Setting bytes: [74, 111, 104, 110, 32, 77, 97, 121, 101, 114]
INFO : DiverseValuesContainer - Setting stream & reading from it: Hello World!
INFO : DiverseValuesContainer - Setting pattern: a*b
INFO : DiverseValuesContainer - Setting character: A
INFO : DiverseValuesContainer - Setting Boolean: true
INFO : DiverseValuesContainer - Setting stringList with: [Mayer, Psihoza, Mazikeen]
INFO : DiverseValuesContainer - Setting float value: 123.45678
INFO : DiverseValuesContainer - Setting trim string:    String need trimming
```

As you can see, Spring has, using the built-in PropertyEditors, converted the String representations of the various properties to the correct types. Table 4-1 lists the most important built-in PropertyEditors available in Spring.

Table 4-1. *Spring* PropertyEditors

PropertyEditor	Description
ByteArrayPropertyEditor	Converts String values to their corresponding byte representations.
CharacterEditor	Populates a property of type Character from a String value.
ClassEditor	Converts from a fully qualified class name into a Class instance. When using this PropertyEditor, be careful not to include any extraneous spaces on either side of the class name when using GenericApplicationContext because this results in a ClassNotFoundException.
CustomBooleanEditor	Converts a string into a Kotlin Boolean type.
CustomCollectionEditor	Converts a source collection (e.g., represented by the valueHolder. stringList property SpEL expression) into the target Collection type.
CustomDateEditor	Converts a string representation of a date into a java.util.Date value. You need to register the CustomDateEditor implementation in Spring's ApplicationContext with the desired date format.
FileEditor	Converts a String file path into a File instance. Spring does not check whether the file exists.
InputStreamEditor	Converts a string representation of a resource (e.g., file resource using file:///D:/temp/test.txt or classpath:test.txt) into an input stream property.
LocaleEditor	Converts the String representation of a locale, such as en-GB, into a java. util.Locale instance.
PatternEditor	Converts a String into the JDK Pattern object, or the other way around.
PropertiesEditor	Converts a String in the format key1=value1 key2=value2 keyn=valuen into an instance of java.util.Properties with the corresponding properties configured.
StringTrimmerEditor	Performs trimming on the String values before injection. You need to explicitly register this editor.
URLEditor	Converts a String representation of a URL into an instance of java.net.URL.

This set of PropertyEditors provides a good base for working with Spring and makes configuring your application with common components such as files and URLs much simpler.

Creating a Custom PropertyEditor

Although the built-in PropertyEditor implementations cover most of the standard cases of property type conversion, there may come a time when you need to create your own PropertyEditor to support a class or a set of classes you are using in your application. Spring has full support for registering custom PropertyEditor implementations; the only downside is that the java.beans.PropertyEditor interface has a lot of methods, many of which are irrelevant to the task at hand, which is converting property types. Thankfully, starting with JDK 5 or newer the PropertyEditorSupport class can be used, which your own PropertyEditors can extend, leaving you to implement only a single method: setAsText().

Let's consider a simple example to see the implementation of a custom property editor in action. Suppose we have a FullName class with just two properties, firstName and lastName, defined as shown in code Listing 4-24.

Listing 4-24. NamePropertyEditor Class, to Be Used in Showing How to Build a Custom PropertyEditor

```
package com.apress.prospring6.four.custom

class FullName(val firstName: String, val lastName: String) {
    override fun toString(): String {
        return "firstName=${firstName}, lastName=${lastName}"
    }
}
```

To simplify the application configuration, let's develop a custom editor that converts a String with a space separator into the FullName class's first name and last name, respectively. Listing 4-25 depicts the custom property editor implementation.

Listing 4-25. FullName Class, to Be Used in Showing How to Build a Custom PropertyEditor

```
package com.apress.prospring6.four.custom

import java.beans.PropertyEditorSupport

class NamePropertyEditor : PropertyEditorSupport() {
    @Throws(IllegalArgumentException::class)
    override fun setAsText(text: String) {
        val name = text.split("\\s".toRegex()).dropLastWhile { it.isEmpty() }.toTypedArray()
        value = FullName(name[0], name[1])
    }
}
```

The implementation is simple. It extends JDK's PropertyEditorSupport class and implements the setAsText() method. In the method, we simply split the String into a string array with a space as the delimiter. Afterward, an instance of the FullName class is instantiated, passing in the String before the space character as the first name and passing the String after the space character as the last name. Finally, the converted value is returned by calling the setValue() method with the result. To use NamePropertyEditor in your application, you need to register the editor in Spring's ApplicationContext. Listing 4-26 shows an ApplicationContext configuration of a CustomEditorConfigurer and the NamePropertyEditor and the code to bootstrap a Spring application made of these beans.

Listing 4-26. Configuration and Bootstrap Code for a Spring Application Demonstrating a PropertyEditor

```
package com.apress.prospring6.four.custom

import org.slf4j.LoggerFactory
import org.springframework.beans.factory.annotation.Value
// other imports omitted
```

```
@Component
internal class Person {
    @set:Value("John Mayer")
    var name: FullName? = null
}


@Configuration
@ComponentScan
internal open class CustomPropertyEditorCfg {
    @Bean
    open fun customEditorConfigurer(): CustomEditorConfigurer {
        val cust = CustomEditorConfigurer()
        cust.setCustomEditors(mapOf(FullName::class.java to NamePropertyEditor::class.java))
        return cust
    }
}


object CustomPropertyEditorDemo {
    private val LOGGER = LoggerFactory.getLogger(CustomPropertyEditorDemo::class.java)
    @JvmStatic
    fun main(args: Array<String>) {
        AnnotationConfigApplicationContext(CustomPropertyEditorCfg::class.java).use { ctx ->
            val person = ctx.getBean(Person::class.java, "person")
            LOGGER.info("Person full name = {}", person.name)
        }
    }
}
```

You should notice two things in this configuration:

- Custom PropertyEditors get injected into the CustomEditorConfigurer bean by using the Map-typed customEditors property.

- Each entry in the Map represents a single PropertyEditor, with the entry key being the class for which the PropertyEditor is used. As you can see, the key for NamePropertyEditor is com.apress.prospring6.four.custom.FullName, which signifies that this is the class for which this implementation should be used.

Feel free to run the code in Listing 4-26 and the output should be a simple:

```
INFO : CustomPropertyEditorDemo - Person full name = com.apress.prospring6.four.custom.FullN
ame@5b38c1ec[firstName=John,lastName=Mayer]
```

This is the output from the toString() method implemented in the FullName class, and you can see that the first name and last name of the FullName object were correctly populated by Spring by using the configured NamePropertyEditor. Starting from version 3, Spring introduced the Type Conversion API and the Field Formatting Service Provider Interface (SPI), which provide a simpler and well-structured API to perform type conversion and field formatting. It's especially useful for web application development. Both the Type Conversion API and the Field Formatting SPI are discussed in detail in **Chapter 11**.

More Spring `ApplicationContext` Configuration

So far, although we are discussing Spring's `ApplicationContext`, most of the features that we have covered mainly surround the `BeanFactory` interface wrapped by `ApplicationContext`. In Spring, various implementations of the `BeanFactory` interface are responsible for bean instantiation, providing dependency injection and life-cycle support for beans managed by Spring. However, as stated earlier, being an extension of the `BeanFactory` interface, `ApplicationContext` provides other useful functionalities as well. The main function of `ApplicationContext` is to provide a much richer framework on which to build your applications.

`ApplicationContext` is much more aware of the beans (compared to `BeanFactory`) that you configure within it, and in the case of many of the Spring infrastructure classes and interfaces, such as `BeanFactoryPostProcessor`, it interacts with them on your behalf, reducing the amount of code you need to write in order to use Spring.

The biggest benefit of using `ApplicationContext` is that it allows you to configure and manage Spring and Spring-managed resources in a completely declarative way. This means that wherever possible, Spring provides support classes to load `ApplicationContext` into your application automatically, thus removing the need for you to write any code to access `ApplicationContext`. In practice, this feature is currently available only when you are building web applications with Spring, which allows you to initialize Spring's `ApplicationContext` in the web application deployment descriptor. When using a stand-alone application, you can also initialize Spring's `ApplicationContext` by simple coding, as you've been shown so far.

In addition to providing a model that is focused more on declarative configuration, `ApplicationContext` supports the following features:

- Internationalization

- Event publication

- Resource management and access

- Additional life-cycle interfaces

- Improved automatic configuration of infrastructure components

In the following sections, we discuss some of the most important features in `ApplicationContext` besides DI.

Internationalization

One area where Spring really excels is in support for internationalization (i18n). Using the `MessageSource` interface, your application can access String resources, called *messages*, stored in a variety of languages. For each language you want to support in your application, you maintain a list of messages that are keyed to correspond to messages in other languages. For instance, if you wanted to display "*The quick brown fox jumped over the lazy dog*" in English and in Ukrainian, you would create two messages, both keyed as `msg`; the one for English would read "*The quick brown fox jumped over the lazy dog*" and the one for Ukrainian would read "Те що Росія робить з Україною, є злочином."

Although you don't need to use `ApplicationContext` to use `MessageSource`, the `ApplicationContext` interface extends `MessageSource` and provides special support for loading messages and for making them available in your environment. The automatic loading of messages is available in any environment, but automatic access is provided only in certain Spring-managed scenarios, such as when you are using Spring's MVC framework to build a web application. Although any class can implement `ApplicationContextAware` and thus access the automatically loaded messages, we suggest a better solution later in this chapter, in the section "Using `MessageSource` in Stand-Alone Applications."

Internationalization with the `MessageSource`

Aside from ApplicationContext, Spring provides three MessageSource implementations:

- ResourceBundleMessageSource

- ReloadableResourceBundleMessageSource

- StaticMessageSource

The StaticMessageSource implementation should not be used in a production application because you can't configure it externally, and this is generally one of the main requirements when you are adding i18n capabilities to your application. ResourceBundleMessageSource loads messages by using a Kotlin ResourceBundle. ReloadableResourceBundleMessageSource is essentially the same, except it supports scheduled reloading of the underlying source files.

All three MessageSource implementations also implement another interface called HierarchicalMessageSource, which allows for many MessageSource instances to be nested. This is key to the way ApplicationContext works with MessageSource instances.

To take advantage of ApplicationContext's support for MessageSource, you must define a bean in your configuration of type MessageSource and with the name messageSource. ApplicationContext takes this MessageSource and nests it within itself, allowing you to access the messages by using ApplicationContext. This can be hard to visualize, so take a look at the example presented in Listing 4-27, which shows a simple application that accesses a set of messages for both the English and Ukrainian locales.

Listing 4-27. MessageSource Configuration Using Spring ApplicationContext

```
package com.apress.prospring6.four

import org.slf4j.LoggerFactory
import org.springframework.context.MessageSource
// other imports omitted

@Configuration
internal open class MessageSourceConfig {
    @Bean
    open fun messageSource(): MessageSource =
        ResourceBundleMessageSource().apply {
            setBasenames("labels")
        }
}

object MessageSourceDemo {
    private val LOGGER = LoggerFactory.getLogger(MessageSourceDemo::class.java)
    @JvmStatic
    fun main(args: Array<String>) {
        val ctx = AnnotationConfigApplicationContext(MessageSourceConfig::class.java)
        val english = Locale.ENGLISH
        val ukrainian = Locale.Builder().setLanguage("uk").setRegion("UA").build()
        LOGGER.info(ctx.getMessage("msg", null, english))
        LOGGER.info(ctx.getMessage("msg", null, ukrainian))
```

```
        LOGGER.info(ctx.getMessage("nameMsg",
            arrayOf<Any>("Iuliana", "Cosmina"), english))
        LOGGER.info(ctx.getMessage("nameMsg",
            arrayOf<Any>("Iuliana", "Cosmina"), ukrainian))
        ctx.close()
    }
}
```

Don't worry about the calls to getMessage() just yet; we will return to those shortly. For now, just know that they retrieve a keyed message for the specified locale.

In the MessageSourceConfig class we define a ResourceBundleMessageSource bean with the name messageSource as required by Spring. We configure it with a set of names to form the base of its file set. A Java ResourceBundle, which is used by ResourceBundleMessageSource, works on a set of properties files that are identified by base names. When looking for a message for a particular Locale, the ResourceBundle looks for a file that is named as a combination of the base name and the locale name. For instance, if the base name is foo and we are looking for a message in the en-GB (British English) locale, ResourceBundle looks for a file called foo_en_GB.properties.

For the previous example, the content of the properties files for English (labels_en.properties) and Ukrainian (labels_uk_UA.properties) is shown in Listing 4-28.

Listing 4-28. MessageSource Resource Files Content

```
#labels_en.properties
msg=Witnessing and not stopping evil is condoning it
nameMsg=My name is {0} {1}

#labels_de_DE.properties
msg=Бути свідком зла і не зупиняти його – це брати участь у цьому
nameMsg=Мене звати {0} {1}
```

These files are located in the resources directory and are added to the application classpath.

Now, this example just raises even more questions. What do those calls to getMessage() mean? Why did we use ApplicationContext.getMessage() rather than access the ResourceBundleMessageSource bean directly? We'll answer each of these questions in turn.

Using the getMessage() Method

The MessageSource interface defines three overloads for the getMessage() method. These are described in Table 4-2.

Table 4-2. *The Overloads for getMessage() in MessageSource*

Method Signature	Description
getMessage(String,Object[], Locale)	This is the standard getMessage() method. The String argument is the key of the message corresponding to the key in the properties file. In the previous Listing 4-27, the first call to getMessage() used msg as the key, and this corresponded to the following entry in the properties file for the en locale: msg=The quick brown fox jumped over the lazy dog. The Object[] array argument is used for replacements in the message. In the third call to getMessage(), we passed in an array of two Strings. The message keyed as nameMsg was My name is {0} {1}. The numbers in braces are placeholders, and each one is replaced with the corresponding entry in the argument array. The final argument, Locale, tells ResourceBundleMessageSource which properties file to look in. Even though the first and second calls to getMessage() in the example used the same key, they returned different messages that correspond to the Locale setting that was passed in to getMessage().
getMessage(String, Object[], String,Locale)	This overload works in the same way as getMessage(String,Object[], Locale), other than the second String argument, which allows us to pass in a default value in case a message for the supplied key is not available for the supplied Locale.
getMessage(MessageSourceRes olvable,Locale)	This overload is a special case. We discuss it in further detail in the upcoming section "The MessageSourceResolvable Interface."

Why Use ApplicationContext As a MessageSource?

To answer this question, we need to jump a little ahead of ourselves and look at the web application support in Spring. The answer, in general, is that you shouldn't use ApplicationContext as a MessageSource because doing so couples your bean to ApplicationContext unnecessarily (this is discussed in more detail in the next section). You should use ApplicationContext when you are building a web application by using Spring's MVC framework.

The core interface in Spring MVC is Controller. Unlike frameworks such as Struts that require you to implement your controllers by inheriting from a concrete class, Spring simply requires that you implement the Controller interface (or annotate your controller class with the @Controller annotation). Having said that, Spring provides a collection of useful base classes that you will use to implement your own controllers. Each of these base classes is a subclass (directly or indirectly) of the ApplicationObjectSupport class, which is a convenient superclass for any application objects that want to be aware of ApplicationContext. Remember that in a web application setting, ApplicationContext is loaded automatically.

ApplicationObjectSupport accesses this ApplicationContext, wraps it in a MessageSourceAccessor object, and makes that available to your controller via the protected getMessageSourceAccessor() method. MessageSourceAccessor provides a wide array of convenient methods for working with MessageSource instances. This form of autoinjection is quite beneficial; it removes the need for all of your controllers to expose a MessageSource property.

However, this is not the best reason for using ApplicationContext as a MessageSource in your web application. The main reason to use ApplicationContext rather than a manually defined MessageSource bean is that Spring does, where possible, expose ApplicationContext, as a MessageSource, to the view tier. This means when you are using Spring's JSP tag library, the <spring:message> tag automatically reads messages from ApplicationContext, and when you are using JSTL, the <fmt:message> tag does the same.

All of these benefits mean that it is better to use the `MessageSource` support in `ApplicationContext` when you are building a web application, rather than manage an instance of `MessageSource` separately. This is especially true when you consider that all you need to do to take advantage of this feature is to configure a `MessageSource` bean with the name `messageSource`.

Using `MessageSource` in Stand-Alone Applications

When you are using `MessageSource` in stand-alone applications, where Spring offers no additional support other than to nest the `MessageSource` bean automatically in `ApplicationContext`, it is best to make the `MessageSource` available by using dependency injection. You can opt to make your bean `ApplicationContextAware,` but doing so precludes its use in a `BeanFactory` context. Add to this that you complicate testing without any discernible benefit, and it is clear that you should stick to using dependency injection to access `MessageSource` objects in a stand-alone setting.

The `MessageSourceResolvable` Interface

You can use an object that implements `MessageSourceResolvable` in place of a key and a set of arguments when you are looking up a message from a `MessageSource`. This interface is most widely used in the Spring validation libraries to link `Error` objects to their internationalized error messages.

Application Events

Another feature of `ApplicationContext` not present in `BeanFactory` is the ability to publish and receive events by using `ApplicationContext` as a broker. In this section, you will take a look at its usage.

Using Application Events

An event is a class derived from `ApplicationEvent`, which itself derives from `java.util.EventObject`. Any bean can listen for events by implementing the `ApplicationListener<T>` interface; `ApplicationContext` automatically registers any bean that implements this interface as a listener when it is configured. Events are published using the `ApplicationEventPublisher.publishEvent()` method, so the publishing class must have knowledge of `ApplicationContext` (which extends the `ApplicationEventPublisher` interface). In a web application, this is simple because many of your classes are derived from Spring Framework classes that allow access to `ApplicationContext` through a protected method. In a stand-alone application, you can have your publishing bean implement `ApplicationContextAware` to enable it to publish events. Listing 4-29 shows an example of a basic event class.

Listing 4-29. Basic Spring `ApplicationEvent` Class

```
package com.apress.prospring6.four.events

import org.springframework.context.ApplicationEvent

class MessageEvent(source: Any, val message: String) : ApplicationEvent(source) {
    companion object {
        @JvmStatic
        private const val serialVersionUID = 1L
    }
}
```

This code is quite basic; the only point of note is that ApplicationEvent has a single constructor that accepts a reference to the source of the event. This is reflected in the constructor for MessageEvent. In Listing 4-30, you can see the code for the listener.

Listing 4-30. Basic Spring ApplicationListener Class

```
package com.apress.prospring6.four.events

import org.slf4j.LoggerFactory
import org.springframework.context.ApplicationListener
import org.springframework.stereotype.Component

@Component
class MessageEventListener : ApplicationListener<MessageEvent> {
    override fun onApplicationEvent(event: MessageEvent) {
        LOGGER.info("Received: {}", event.message)
    }

    companion object {
        private val LOGGER = LoggerFactory.getLogger(MessageEventListener::class.java)
    }
}
```

The ApplicationListener interface defines a single method, onApplicationEvent(..), that is called by Spring when an event is raised. MessageEventListener shows its interest only in events of type MessageEvent (or its subclasses) by implementing the strongly typed ApplicationListener interface. If a MessageEvent was received, it writes the message to stdout. Publishing events is simple; it is just a matter of creating an instance of the event class and passing it to the ApplicationEventPublisher.publishEvent() method, as shown in Listing 4-31.

Listing 4-31. Basic Spring ApplicationContextAware Class and Code to Test It

```
package com.apress.prospring6.four.events

import org.springframework.beans.BeansException
import org.springframework.context.annotation.*
// other imports omitted

@Configuration
@ComponentScan
internal open class EventsConfig

@Component
class Publisher : ApplicationContextAware {
    private var ctx: ApplicationContext? = null

    @Throws(BeansException::class)
    /** @Implements [ApplicationContextAware.setApplicationContext] }
     */
    override fun setApplicationContext(applicationContext: ApplicationContext) {
        ctx = applicationContext
    }
```

```kotlin
    fun publish(message: String?) {
        ctx!!.publishEvent(MessageEvent(this, message!!))
    }

    companion object {
        @JvmStatic
        fun main(args: Array<String>) {
            val ctx = AnnotationConfigApplicationContext(EventsConfig::class.java)
            val pub = ctx.getBean("publisher") as Publisher
            pub.publish("I send an SOS to the world... ")
            pub.publish("... I hope that someone gets my...")
            pub.publish("... Message in a bottle")
        }
    }
}
```

A code shortcut artifice was used here to keep things simple: the Publisher bean type contains the main(..) methods as well, which retrieves an instance of itself from ApplicationContext and then, using the publish() method, publishes two MessageEvent instances to ApplicationContext. The Publisher bean instance accesses the ApplicationContext instance by implementing ApplicationContextAware. The EventsConfig configuration class is empty and is just declared to enable component scanning within the package, so the Publisher and the MessageEventListener bean definitions are picked up.

Running this example results in the output shown in Listing 4-32, proving that the MessageEventListener reacts to the events published by the Publisher bean using the injected ApplicationContext.

Listing 4-32. Output Produced by Running the Code in Listing 4-31

```
INFO : MessageEventListener - Received: I send an SOS to the world...
INFO : MessageEventListener - Received: ... I hope that someone gets my...
INFO : MessageEventListener - Received: ... Message in a bottle
```

Considerations for Event Usage

In many cases in an application, certain components need to be notified of certain events. Often you do this by writing code to notify each component explicitly or by using a messaging technology such as JMS. The drawback of writing code to notify each component in turn is that you are coupling those components to the publisher, in many cases unnecessarily.

Consider a situation whereby you cache product details in your application to avoid trips to the database. Another component allows product details to be modified and persisted to the database. To avoid making the cache invalid, the update component explicitly notifies the cache that the user details have changed. In this example, the update component is coupled to a component that, really, has nothing to do with its business responsibility. A better solution would be to have the update component publish an event every time a product's details are modified and then have interested components, such as the cache, listen for that event. This has the benefit of keeping the components decoupled, which makes it simple to remove the cache if needed or to add another listener that is interested in knowing when a product's details change.

Using JMS in this case would be overkill because the process of invalidating the product's entry in the cache is quick and is not business critical. The use of the Spring event infrastructure adds very little overhead to your application.

Typically, we use events for reactionary logic that executes quickly and is not part of the main application logic. In the previous example, the invalidation of a product in cache happens in reaction to the updating of product details, it executes quickly (or it should), and it is not part of the main function of the application. For processes that are long-running and form part of the main business logic, it is recommended to use JMS or similar messaging systems such as RabbitMQ. The main benefits of using JMS are that it is more suited to long-running processes, and as the system grows, you can, if necessary, factor the JMS-driven processing of messages containing business information onto a separate machine.

Accessing Resources

Often an application needs to access a variety of resources in different forms. You might need to access some configuration data stored in a file in the file system, some image data stored in a JAR file on the classpath, or maybe some data on a server elsewhere. Spring provides a unified mechanism for accessing resources in a protocol-independent way. This means your application can access a file resource in the same way, whether it is stored in the file system, in the classpath, or on a remote server.

At the core of Spring's resource support is the `org.springframework.core.io.Resource` interface. The Resource interface defines ten self-explanatory methods:

- `contentLength()`
- `exists()`
- `getDescription()`
- `getFile()`
- `getFileName()`
- `getURI()`
- `getURL()`
- `isOpen()`
- `isReadable()`
- `lastModified()`

In addition to these ten methods, there is one that is not quite so self-explanatory: `createRelative()`. The `createRelative()` method creates a new Resource instance by using a path that is relative to the instance on which it is invoked. You can provide your own Resource implementations, although that is outside the scope of this chapter, but in most cases, you use one of the built-in implementations for accessing a file (the `FileSystemResource` class), a classpath (the `ClassPathResource` class), or URL resources (the `UrlResource` class). Internally, Spring uses another interface, `ResourceLoader`, and the default implementation, `DefaultResourceLoader`, to locate and create Resource instances. However, you generally won't interact with `DefaultResourceLoader`, instead using another `ResourceLoader` implementation, called `ApplicationContext`. Listing 4-33 depicts an application that accesses three resources by using `ApplicationContext`.

Listing 4-33. Application Sample Accessing Various Spring Resources

```
package com.apress.prospring6.four

import org.springframework.core.io.Resource
// other import statements omitted
```

```kotlin
object ResourceDemo {
    private val LOGGER = LoggerFactory.getLogger(ResourceDemo::class.java)
    @Throws(Exception::class)
    @JvmStatic
    fun main(args: Array<String>) {
        val ctx = AnnotationConfigApplicationContext()
        val baseDir = File(System.getProperty("java.io.tmpdir"))
        val filePath = Files.createFile(Path.of(baseDir.absolutePath, "test.txt"))
        Files.writeString(filePath, "Hello World!")
        filePath.toFile().deleteOnExit()
        val res1 = ctx.getResource("file://$filePath")
        displayInfo(res1)
        val res2 = ctx.getResource("classpath:test.txt")
        displayInfo(res2)
        val res3 = ctx.getResource("http://iuliana-cosmina.com")
        displayInfo(res3)
    }

    @Throws(Exception::class)
    private fun displayInfo(res: Resource) {
        LOGGER.info("Resource class: {}", res.javaClass)
        LOGGER.info("Resource URL content: {}",
            BufferedReader(InputStreamReader(res.url.content as InputStream)).lines().
            parallel()
                .collect(Collectors.joining("\n"))
        )
        LOGGER.info(" -------------")
    }
}
```

Notice that in each call to getResource(), we pass in a URI for each resource. You will recognize the common file: and http: protocols that we pass in for res1 and res3. The classpath: protocol we use for res2 is Spring-specific and indicates that ResourceLoader should look in the classpath for the resource.

Running this example results in the output depicted in Listing 4-34.

Listing 4-34. Output of Code in Listing 4-33

```
INFO : ResourceDemo - Resource class: class org.springframework.core.io.FileUrlResource
INFO : ResourceDemo - Resource URL content: Hello World!
INFO : ResourceDemo - -------------
INFO : ResourceDemo - Resource class: class org.springframework.core.io.ClassPathResource
INFO : ResourceDemo - Resource URL content: Hello World from the classpath!
INFO : ResourceDemo - -------------
INFO : ResourceDemo - Resource class: class org.springframework.core.io.UrlResource
INFO : ResourceDemo - Resource URL content: <html>
<center><h1>301 Moved Permanently</h1></center></body>
</html>
INFO : ResourceDemo - -------------
```

ℹ️   The reason you are getting the 301 Moved Permanently response when trying to access the
http://iuliana-cosmina.com site is because the site actually uses secure HTTP. To extract the actual
content of the main page, use ctx.getResource("https://iuliana-cosmina.com").

Notice that for both the file: and http: protocols, Spring returns a UrlResource instance. Spring
does include a FileSystemResource class, thus the DefaultResourceLoader does not use this class at all.
It's because Spring's default resource-loading strategy treats the URL and file as the same type of resource
with difference protocols (file: and http:). If an instance of FileSystemResource is required, use
FileSystemResourceLoader. Once a Resource instance is obtained, you are free to access the contents as
you see fit, using getFile(), getInputStream(), or getURL(). In some cases, such as when you are using the
http: protocol, the call to getFile() results in a FileNotFoundException. For this reason, we recommend
that you use getInputStream() to access resource contents because it is likely to function for all possible
resource types.

Advanced Java/Kotlin Configuration Classes

So far in the book Java/Kotlin configuration classes have been pretty basic. Let's proceed to more
configuration options. Considering the MessageRender and ConfigurableMessageProvider introduced in
Chapter 3, let's say we want to externalize the message into a properties file named message.properties.
The ConfigurableMessageProvider.message property is to be injected with a value read from this file by
using constructor injection. The content of message.properties is as follows:

```
message=Only hope can keep me together
```

Let's see the revised testing program, which loads the properties files by using the @PropertySource
annotation and then injects them into the message provider implementation. Listing 4-35 shows the
testing program, including the configuration class enriched with annotations on bean declarations and the
simplified bean types.

Listing 4-35. @PropertySource Usage Example

```kotlin
package com.apress.prospring6.four

import com.apress.prospring6.two.decoupled.MessageProvider
import com.apress.prospring6.two.decoupled.MessageRenderer
import org.springframework.core.env.Environment
// other import statements omitted

object PropertySourcesDemo {
    @JvmStatic
    fun main(args: Array<String>) {
        val ctx: ApplicationContext =
            AnnotationConfigApplicationContext(PropertySourcesCfg::class.java)
        val mr = ctx.getBean(
            "messageRenderer",
            MessageRenderer::class.java
        )
```

```kotlin
        mr.render()
    }
}

@Configuration
@PropertySource(value = ["classpath:message.properties"])
internal open class PropertySourcesCfg {
    @Autowired
    var env: Environment? = null
    @Bean
    @Lazy
    open fun messageProvider(): MessageProvider =
        ConfigurableMessageProvider(env!!.getProperty("message"))

    @Bean(name = ["messageRenderer"])
    @Scope(value = "prototype")
    @DependsOn(value = ["messageProvider"])
    open fun messageRenderer(): MessageRenderer =
        StandardOutMessageRenderer().apply {
            messageProvider = messageProvider()
        }
}

internal class ConfigurableMessageProvider(
    @param:Value("Configurable message")
    override val message: String
) :
    MessageProvider

internal class StandardOutMessageRenderer : MessageRenderer {
    override var messageProvider: MessageProvider? = null

    override fun render() {
        LOGGER.info(messageProvider!!.message)
    }

    companion object {
        private val LOGGER =
            LoggerFactory.getLogger(StandardOutMessageRenderer::class.java)
    }
}
```

Listing 4-35 introduces a few annotations that are explained in Table 4-3. Some of them have been used in **Chapter 3** already, but they were not explained at the time. Beans that are defined using a stereotype annotation like @Component, @Service, and others can be used in a Java configuration class, by enabling component scanning and autowiring them where needed. In the following Listing 4-36, we declare ConfigurableMessageProvider as a service bean.

Table 4-3. *Java Configuration Annotations Table*

Annotation	Description
@PropertySource	This annotation is used to load properties files into Spring's `ApplicationContext`, which accepts the location as the argument (more than one location can be provided).
@Lazy	This annotation instructs Spring to instantiate the bean only when requested. This annotation has a default `value` attribute that is `true` by default; thus, using `@Lazy(value=true)` is equivalent to using `@Lazy`.
@Scope	This annotation is used to define the bean scope, when the desired scope is other than singleton.
@DependsOn	This annotation tells Spring that a certain bean depends on some other beans, so Spring will make sure that those beans are instantiated first.
@Autowired	This annotation is used here on the env variable, which is of `Environment` type. This is the `Environment` abstraction feature that Spring provides. We discuss it later in this chapter.

An application can also have multiple configuration classes, which can be used to decouple configuration and organize beans by purpose (for example, one class can be dedicated to DAO beans declaration, another can be dedicated to the Service beans declaration, and so forth). To show this, we can modify the previous example and define the `ConfigurableMessageProvider` as a service and declare a configuration class named `ServiceConfig` declaring this bean type. The configuration class declaring the `MessageRenderer` bean will use `@Import` annotation to access the `MessageProvider` bean declared by the `ServiceConfig` class. Listing 4-36 shows these configuration classes.

Listing 4-36. @Import Usage Example

```
package com.apress.prospring6.four.multiple

import com.apress.prospring6.two.decoupled.MessageProvider
import com.apress.prospring6.two.decoupled.MessageRenderer
// other import statements omitted

@Service("provider")
internal class ConfigurableMessageProvider(
    // same code as in previous listings
}

internal class StandardOutMessageRenderer : MessageRenderer {
    // same code as in previous listings
}

@Configuration
@ComponentScan
internal open class ServiceConfig

@Configuration
@Import(ServiceConfig::class)
internal open class TheOtherConfig {
    @Autowired
    var provider: MessageProvider? = null
```

```kotlin
    @Bean(name = ["messageRenderer"])
    open fun messageRenderer(): MessageRenderer =
        StandardOutMessageRenderer().apply {
            messageProvider = provider
        }
}

object ImportDemo {
    @JvmStatic
    fun main(args: Array<String>) {
        val ctx: ApplicationContext =
            AnnotationConfigApplicationContext(TheOtherConfig::class.java)
        val mr = ctx.getBean(
            "messageRenderer",
            MessageRenderer::class.java
        )
        mr.render()
    }
}
```

In the main method in class ImportDemo, only the TheOtherConfig class is required when the application context is created, since this class imports all the bean definitions that are declared within or discovered via scanning by the ServiceConfig imported class.

Profiles

Another interesting feature that Spring provides is the concept of configuration profiles. Basically, a profile instructs Spring to configure only the ApplicationContext instance that was defined when the specified profile was active. In this section, we demonstrate how to use profiles in a simple program.

An Example of Using the Spring Profiles Feature

Let's say there is a service called FoodProviderService that is responsible for providing food to schools, including kindergarten and high school. The FoodProviderService interface has only one method called provideLunchSet(), which produces the lunch set to each student for the calling school. A lunch set is a list of Food objects, which is a simple class that has only a name attribute. Listing 4-37 shows the Food class.

Listing 4-37. Food Bean Type

```kotlin
package com.apress.prospring6.four.profile

class Food {
    var name: String? = null

    //constructor() {}
    constructor(name: String?) {
        this.name = name
    }
}
```

The FoodProviderService interface is depicted in Listing 4-38.

Listing 4-38. FoodProviderService Interface

```
package com.apress.prospring6.four.profile

interface FoodProviderService {
    fun provideLunchSet(): List<Food?>?
}
```

Now suppose that there are two providers for the lunch set, one for kindergarten and one for high school. The lunch set produced by them is different, although the service they provide is the same, that is, to provide lunch to pupils/students. So, now let's create two implementations of FoodProviderService, using the same name but putting them into different packages to identify their target school. The two classes are shown in Listing 4-39.

Listing 4-39. FoodProviderService Implementations

```
// chapter04/src/main/java/com/apress/prospring6/four/profile/
    kindergarten/FoodProviderServiceImpl.kt
package com.apress.prospring6.four.profile.kindergarten

import com.apress.prospring6.four.profile.Food
import com.apress.prospring6.four.profile.FoodProviderService

class FoodProviderServiceImpl : FoodProviderService {
    override fun provideLunchSet(): List<Food> {
        return listOf(Food("Milk"), Food("Biscuits"))
    }
}

// chapter04/src/main/java/com/apress/prospring6/four/profile/
    highschool/FoodProviderServiceImpl.java
package com.apress.prospring6.four.profile.highschool
// same imports as above

class FoodProviderServiceImpl : FoodProviderService {
    override fun provideLunchSet(): List<Food> {
        return listOf(Food("Coke"), Food("Hamburger"), Food("Fries"))
    }
}
```

From the previous listings, you can see that the two implementations provide the same FoodProviderService interface but produce different combinations of food in the lunch set. So, now suppose a kindergarten wants the provider to deliver the lunch set for their students; let's see how we can use Spring's profile configuration to achieve this. We will run through the Java/Kotlin configuration first. We will create two configuration classes, one for the kindergarten profile and the other for the high-school profile. Listing 4-40 depicts the two profile configurations.

Listing 4-40. Configuration Classes

```
package com.apress.prospring6.four.profile.highschool

import com.apress.prospring6.four.profile.FoodProviderService
import org.springframework.context.annotation.*

@Configuration
@Profile("highschool")
open class HighSchoolConfig {
    @Bean
    open fun foodProviderService(): FoodProviderService = FoodProviderServiceImpl()
}
```

```
package com.apress.prospring6.four.profile.kindergarten

import com.apress.prospring6.four.profile.FoodProviderService
import com.apress.prospring6.four.profile.highschool.FoodProviderServiceImpl
import org.springframework.context.annotation.*

@Configuration
@Profile("kindergarten")
open class KindergartenConfig {
    @Bean
    open fun foodProviderService(): FoodProviderService = FoodProviderServiceImpl()
}
```

In the two configuration classes, notice the @Profile annotation declared with "highschool" and "kindergarten" respectively. This annotation tells Spring that those beans in the file should be instantiated only when the specified profile is active. To activate the correct profile when using Spring's ApplicationContext in a stand-alone application, we need to provide the profile as a value for the spring. profiles.active JVM argument, set it on the created context, add the configuration classes, and then refresh the context. This will ensure that only the beans matching the configured profile will be added to the context. Listing 4-41 shows the code to do this and test the results by printing the items returned by the FoodProviderService.provideLunchSet() call.

Listing 4-41. FoodProviderService Testing

```
package com.apress.prospring6.four.profile
//import statements omitted

object ProfileDemo {
    private val LOGGER = LoggerFactory.getLogger(ProfileDemo::class.java)
    @JvmStatic
    fun main(args: Array<String>) {
        val profile = System.getProperty("spring.profiles.active")
        val ctx = AnnotationConfigApplicationContext()
        ctx.environment.setActiveProfiles(profile)
        //ctx.getEnvironment().setDefaultProfiles("kindergarten);
        ctx.register(HighSchoolConfig::class.java, KindergartenConfig::class.java)
        ctx.refresh()
        val foodProviderService = ctx.getBean(
```

```
        "foodProviderService",
        FoodProviderService::class.java
    )
    val lunchSet = foodProviderService.provideLunchSet()
    lunchSet!!.forEach(Consumer { food: Food? ->
        LOGGER.info(
            "Food: {}",
            food!!.name
        )
    })
    ctx.close()
  }
}
```

To provide the -Dspring.profiles.active="kindergarten" JVM argument when running the ProfileDemo class in IntelliJ IDEA, you need to customize the launcher as shown in Figure 4-3.

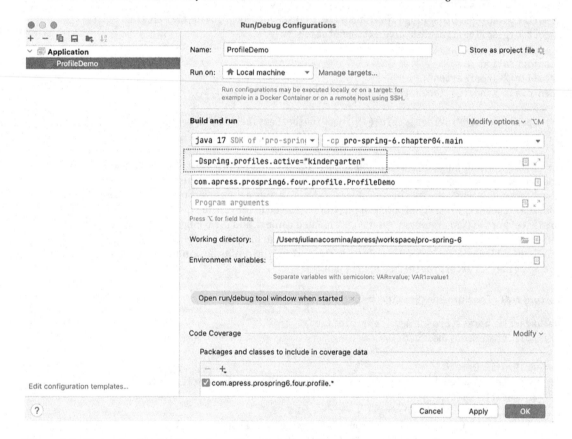

Figure 4-3. *Spring Application Launcher with activated profile*

You can provide the profile value in the same way when running a main class or executable JAR in the command line.

Running the ProfileDemo class with the JVM -Dspring.profiles.active="kindergarten" argument produces the following output:

```
DEBUG: AbstractEnvironment - Activating profiles [kindergarten]
INFO : ProfileDemo - Food: Coke
INFO : ProfileDemo - Food: Hamburger
INFO : ProfileDemo - Food: Fries
```

This is exactly what the implementation of the kindergarten provider will produce for the lunch set. Now change the profile argument from the previous listing to high school (-Dspring.profiles. active="highschool"), and the output will change to the following:

```
DEBUG: AbstractEnvironment - Activating profiles [highschool]
INFO : ProfileDemo - Food: Coke
INFO : ProfileDemo - Food: Hamburger
INFO : ProfileDemo - Food: Fries
```

The active profile was set programmatically in this example, by calling ctx.getEnvironment(). setActiveProfiles(".."), but this was required because of the way the context is created. The context is created empty and configuration is added after the profile is set. But the context can be created directly from the configuration classes, and if the JVM argument is provided, the profile is activated automatically. If no profile is specified, the application can still be functional by calling ctx.getEnvironment(). setDefaulltProfiles(".."), and providing as argument a list of profiles names to be activated by default.

Listing 4-42 shows the other way of configuring an application context using profiled configurations.

Listing 4-42. FoodProviderService Testing (Second Version)

```
package com.apress.prospring6.four.profile

import com.apress.prospring6.four.profile.highschool.HighSchoolConfig
import com.apress.prospring6.four.profile.kindergarten.KindergartenConfig
import org.slf4j.LoggerFactory
import org.springframework.context.annotation.AnnotationConfigApplicationContext

object AnotherProfileDemo {
    private val LOGGER = LoggerFactory.getLogger(AnotherProfileDemo::class.java)
    @JvmStatic
    fun main(args: Array<String>) {
        val ctx = AnnotationConfigApplicationContext(
            HighSchoolConfig::class.java,
            KindergartenConfig::class.java
        )
        val foodProviderService = ctx.getBean(
            "foodProviderService",
            FoodProviderService::class.java
        )
        val lunchSet = foodProviderService.provideLunchSet()!!
        lunchSet.forEach { food -> LOGGER.info("Food: {}", food!!.name) }
        ctx.close()
    }
}
```

Additionally, you can enable profiles by using the @ActiveProfiles annotation.

Considerations for Using Profiles

The profiles feature in Spring creates another way for developers to manage the application's running configuration, which used to be done in build tools (for example, Maven's profile support). Build tools rely on the arguments passed into the tool to pack the correct configuration/property files into the Java archive (JAR or WAR, depending on the application type) and then deploy to the target environment. Spring's profile feature lets you as an application developer define the profiles by yourself and activate them either programmatically or by passing in the JVM argument. By using Spring's profile support, you can now use the same application archive and deploy to all environments by passing in the correct profiles as an argument during JVM startup. For example, you can have applications with different profiles such as (dev, hibernate), (prd, jdbc), and so on, with each combination representing the running environment (development or production) and the data access library to use (Hibernate or JDBC). It brings application profile management into the programming side.

But this approach also has its drawbacks. For example, some may argue that putting all the configurations for different environments into application configuration files or Java/Kotlin classes and bundling them together will be error-prone if not handled carefully (for example, the administrator may forget to set the correct JVM argument in the application server environment). Packing files for all profiles together will also make the package a bit larger than usual. Again, let the application and configuration requirements drive you to select the approach that best fits your project.

Environment and PropertySource Abstraction

To set the active profile, a call to `ctx.getEnvironment()` or `ctx.environment` is necessary to provide access to Spring's `Environment` object. This is an abstraction layer that serves to encapsulate the environment of the running Spring application.

Besides the profile, other key pieces of information encapsulated by the `Environment` object are properties. Properties are used to store the application's underlying environment configuration, such as the location of the application folder, database connection information, and so on.

The `Environment` implementation performs a search over a set of `PropertySource` objects to look for property values. `PropertySource` abstraction features in Spring assist developers in accessing various configuration information from the running platform. Under the abstraction, all system properties, environment variables, and application properties are served by the `Environment` interface, which Spring populates when bootstrapping `ApplicationContext`. Listing 4-43 shows a simple example.

Listing 4-43. Using the Environment Interface

```kotlin
package com.apress.prospring6.four

import org.springframework.context.support.GenericApplicationContext
import org.springframework.core.env.ConfigurableEnvironment
import org.springframework.core.env.MapPropertySource
import org.springframework.core.env.MutablePropertySources
// other import statements omitted

class EnvironmentTest {
    @Test
    fun testPropertySourceOne() {
        val ctx = GenericApplicationContext()
        val env = ctx.environment
```

```
    val propertySources = env.propertySources
    val appMap: MutableMap<String, Any> = HashMap()
    appMap["user.home"] = "CUSTOM_USER_HOME"
    propertySources.addLast(MapPropertySource(
        "prospring6_MAP", appMap)) // notice the addLast
    LOGGER.info("-- Env Variables  from java.lang.System --")
    LOGGER.info("user.home: " + System.getProperty("user.home"))
    LOGGER.info("JAVA_HOME: " + System.getenv("JAVA_HOME"))
    LOGGER.info("-- Env Variables  from ConfigurableEnvironment --")
    LOGGER.info("user.home: " + env.getProperty("user.home"))
    LOGGER.info("JAVA_HOME: " + env.getProperty("JAVA_HOME"))
    ctx.close()
}

companion object {
    private val LOGGER = LoggerFactory.getLogger(EnvironmentTest::class.java)
}
}
```

In Listing 4-43, after the ApplicationContext initialization, we get a reference to the ConfigurableEnvironment interface, which extends Environment. Via this instance, a handle to MutablePropertySources (a default implementation of the PropertySources interface, which allows manipulation of the contained property sources) is obtained. Afterward, we construct a map, put the application properties into the map, and then construct a MapPropertySource class (a PropertySource subclass that reads keys and values from a Map instance) with the map. Finally, the MapPropertySource class is added to MutablePropertySources via the addLast() method. Running the program prints the output shown in Listing 4-44 in the console.

Listing 4-44. Values Extracted Using the Environment Interface

```
INFO : EnvironmentDemo - -- Env Variables  from java.lang.System --
INFO : EnvironmentDemo - user.home: /Users/iulianacosmina
INFO : EnvironmentDemo - JAVA_HOME: /Users/iulianacosmina/.sdkman/candidates/java/current

INFO : EnvironmentDemo - -- Env Variables  from ConfigurableEnvironment --
INFO : EnvironmentDemo - user.home: /Users/iulianacosmina
INFO : EnvironmentDemo - JAVA_HOME: /Users/iulianacosmina/.sdkman/candidates/java/current
```

For the first two lines, the JVM system property user.home and the environment variable JAVA_HOME are retrieved (as before using the JVM's System class). However, for the last two lines, you can see that all the system properties, environment variables, and application properties can be accessed via the Environment interface. You can see how the Environment abstraction can help you manage and access all the various properties within the application's running environment.

The Environment instance performs a search over a set of PropertySource objects. Spring accesses the properties in the following default order:

- System properties for the running JVM

- Environment variables

- Application-defined properties

The output shows that when defining the same application property named user.home, and adding it to the Environment interface via the MutablePropertySources class, the user.home value is still retrieved from the JVM properties, and the CUSTOM_USER_HOME is nowhere to be found. However, Spring allows you to control the order in which Environment retrieves the properties. Listing 4-45 shows the revised version of the code in Listing 4-43.

Listing 4-45. Using the Environment Interface (Part 2)

```kotlin
package com.apress.prospring6.four
// import statements omitted

class EnvironmentTest {
    @Test
    fun testPropertySourceTwo() {
        val ctx = GenericApplicationContext()
        val env = ctx.environment
        val propertySources = env.propertySources
        val appMap: MutableMap<String, Any> = HashMap()
        appMap["user.home"] = "CUSTOM_USER_HOME"
        propertySources.addFirst(MapPropertySource(
            "prospring6_MAP", appMap)) // notice the addFirst
        LOGGER.info("-- Env Variables  from java.lang.System --")
        LOGGER.info("user.home: " + System.getProperty("user.home"))
        LOGGER.info("JAVA_HOME: " + System.getenv("JAVA_HOME"))
        LOGGER.info("-- Env Variables  from ConfigurableEnvironment --")
        LOGGER.info("user.home: " + env.getProperty("user.home"))
        LOGGER.info("JAVA_HOME: " + env.getProperty("JAVA_HOME"))
        ctx.close()
    }
    ...
}
```

In Listing 4-45, notice the highlighted line. It declares an application property also called user.home, but this time is added as the first one to search for via the addFirst() method of the MutablePropertySources class. When you run the program, you will see the output shown in Listing 4-46.

Listing 4-46. Values Extracted Using the Environment Interface

```
INFO : EnvironmentTest - -- Env Variables  from java.lang.System --
INFO : EnvironmentTest - user.home: /Users/iulianacosmina
INFO : EnvironmentTest - JAVA_HOME: /Users/iulianacosmina/.sdkman/candidates/java/current

INFO : EnvironmentDemo - -- Env Variables  from ConfigurableEnvironment --
INFO : EnvironmentTest - user.home: CUSTOM_USER_HOME
INFO : EnvironmentTest - JAVA_HOME: /Users/iulianacosmina/.sdkman/candidates/java/current
```

The first two lines remain the same because we still use the getProperty() and getenv() methods of the JVM System class to retrieve them. However, when using the Environment interface, you will see that the user.home property we defined takes precedence since we defined it as the first one to search for property values.

In real life, you seldom need to interact directly with the Environment interface, but instead will use a property placeholder in the form of ${} (for example, ${application.home}) and inject the resolved value into Spring beans. Let's see this in action. Suppose we had a class to store all the application properties loaded from a property file. Listing 4-47 shows the AppProperty class and the contents of the application. properties file.

Listing 4-47. The AppProperty Bean Type

```
package com.apress.prospring6.four
// import statements omitted

internal class AppProperty {
    @set:Autowired
    var applicationHome: String? = null
        @Value("${application.home}") set(value) {
            field = value
        }

    @set:Autowired
    var userHome: String? = null
        @Value("${user.home}") set(value) {
            field = value
        }

    override fun toString(): String {
        return "applicationHome=${applicationHome}, userHome=${userHome}"
    }
}

// Contents of the application.properties file
application.home=application_home
user.home=/home/CUSTOM-USER-HOME
```

To add the contents of the application.properties file to Spring's application context, the @PropertySource annotation is required on the configuration class. This adds this file as a property source to the list of locations Environment is looking for properties in.

Listing 4-48 shows the configuration class, the test class, and the produced output of running the main(..) method.

Listing 4-48. Configuration Class for the AppProperty Bean, Test Class, and Console Output

```
package com.apress.prospring6.four

import org.springframework.context.annotation.PropertySource
// other import statements omitted

@Configuration
@PropertySource("classpath:application.properties")
@Configuration
@PropertySource("classpath:application.properties")
internal open class PropDemoConfig {
```

```
    @Autowired
    var environment: StandardEnvironment? = null

    @Bean
    open fun appProperty(): AppProperty {
        return AppProperty()
    }
}

object PropertySourceDemo {
    private val logger = LoggerFactory.getLogger(PropertySourceDemo::class.java)
    @JvmStatic
    fun main(args: Array<String>) {
        val ctx = AnnotationConfigApplicationContext(PropDemoConfig::class.java)
        val appProperty = ctx.getBean("appProperty", AppProperty::class.java)
        logger.info("Outcome: {}", appProperty)
    }
}

// output
INFO : PropertySourceDemo - Outcome: com.apress.prospring6.four.AppProperty@624ea235[
    applicationHome=application_home,
    userHome=/Users/iulianacosmina
]
```

So, what is going on with that output? Well, the application.home placeholder is properly resolved, while the user.home property is still retrieved from the JVM properties, as expected, because system properties take precedence over custom property sources. So, how do we instruct Spring that we want to consider our property source (the application.properties) as the one with the highest priority?

Unless you use XML configuration (check out the previous edition of the Java variant of this book) or manual explicit configuration as shown in Listing 4-45, you cannot, because the order is defined as previously stated: system properties, environment properties, then application-defined properties. If you really want to use Java/Kotlin configuration for your application and override the order of property sources, there is a way to do it—it is not clean, but it is possible.

First thing, let's start with the Environment hierarchy, displayed in Figure 4-4.

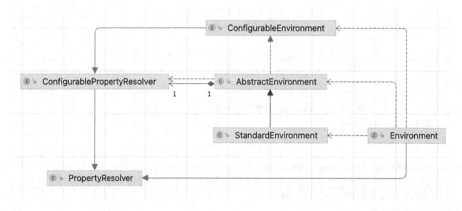

Figure 4-4. *IntelliJ IDEA Environment hierarchy*

Figure 4-4 depicts the family of Environment classes. In its center notice the StandardEnvironment class that is the type of the object created within the Spring context. StandardEnvironment implements the ConfigurableEnvironment interface, and this means we can manipulate this object and modify the priority of the locations where properties are read from.

Listing 4-49 shows the modified version of the PropDemoConfig class where the StandardEnvironment is autowired and an initialization method is declared to modify the property resource priority.

Listing 4-49. Configuration Class for the AppProperty Bean, with Customized Property Sources Locations

```
package com.apress.prospring6.four

import org.springframework.context.annotation.PropertySource
import org.springframework.core.env.StandardEnvironment
import org.springframework.core.io.support.ResourcePropertySource
// other import statements omitted

@Configuration
@PropertySource("classpath:application.properties")
internal open class PropDemoConfig {
    @Autowired
    var environment: StandardEnvironment? = null
    @PostConstruct
    open fun configPriority() {
        val rps = environment!!.propertySources.stream()
            .filter { ps: PropertySource<*>? -> ps is ResourcePropertySource }
            .findAny().orElse(null) as ResourcePropertySource
        environment!!.propertySources.addFirst(rps)
    }

    @Bean
    open fun appProperty(): AppProperty {
        return AppProperty()
    }
}
```

The ResourcePropertySource class loads a Properties object from a given Resource or resource (such as the classpath:application.properties used in this example). Since we know that a ConfigurableEnvironment interface keeps references to all its property sources in a MutablePropertySources class, all we have to do is access this object, identify the ResourcePropertySource, and add it back to the object by calling addFirst(..). It's the same thing we did in Listing 4-45, only instead of creating a new MapPropertySource, we used the existing ResourcePropertySource.

In practice, you might never need to do this, but in case you ever need to do some Spring code acrobatics like this, now you have a working sample. And if you execute the PropertySourceDemo class with this funky configuration, you will notice the output in Listing 4-50 confirms that the properties in the application.properties file took precedence over anything else.

Listing 4-50. Output Produced by Running the PropertySourceDemo with a Reprioritized Property Sources Location Configuration

```
INFO : PropertySourceDemo - Outcome: com.apress.prospring6.four.AppProperty@5340477f[
    applicationHome=application_home,
    userHome=/home/CUSTOM-USER-HOME
]
```

Testing Spring Applications

When developing applications for enterprise use, testing is an important way to ensure that the completed application performs as expected and fulfills all kinds of requirements (architectural, security, user requirements, and so on). Every time a change is made, you should ensure that the change doesn't impact the existing logic. Maintaining an ongoing build and test environment is critical for ensuring high-quality applications. Reproducible tests with high coverage for all your code allow you to deploy new applications, and changes to applications, with a high level of confidence. In an enterprise development environment, there are many kinds of testing that target each layer within an enterprise application, and each kind of testing has its own characteristics and requirements. In this section, we discuss the basic concepts involved in the testing of various application layers, especially in the testing of Spring-powered applications. We also cover the ways in which Spring makes implementing the test cases of various layers easier for developers.

This section introduces various kinds of testing and their purposes. It covers basic approaches to testing Spring applications, and in future chapters each code sample will be paired with a way to test it.

An *enterprise testing framework* refers to testing activities in the application's entire life cycle. In various phases, different testing activities are performed to verify that the functionalities of the application are working as expected, according to the defined business and technical requirements.

In each phase, different test cases are executed. Some are automated, while others are performed manually. In each case, the result is verified by the corresponding personnel (for example, business analysts, application users, and so on). Table 4-4 describes the characteristics and objectives of each type of testing, as well as common tools and libraries that are used for implementing the test cases.

Table 4-4. *Different Testing Categories Used in Practice*

Test Category	Description	Common Tools
Logic unit test	A logic unit test takes a single object and tests it by itself, without worrying about the role it plays in the surrounding system.	Unit test: JUnit, TestNG; Mock objects: Mockito, EasyMock
Integration unit test	An integration unit test focuses on testing the interaction between components in a "near real" environment. These tests exercise the interactions with the container (embedded database, web container, and so on).	Embedded database: H2; Database testing: DbUnit; In-memory web container: Jetty
Front-end unit test	A front-end unit test focuses on testing the user interface. The objective is to ensure that each user interface reacts to users' actions and produces output to users as expected.	Selenium, Cypress
Continuous build and code quality test	The application code base should be built on a regular basis to ensure that the code quality complies with the standard (for example, comments are all in place, no empty exception catch block, and so on). Also, test coverage should be as high as possible to ensure that all developed lines of codes are tested.	Code quality: PMD, Check-style, FindBugs, Sonar; Test coverage: Cobertura, EclEmma; Build tool: Gradle, Maven; Continuous build: Hudson, Jenkins

(continued)

Table 4-4. (*continued*)

Test Category	Description	Common Tools
System integration test	A system integration test verifies the accuracy of communication among all programs in the new system and between the new system and all external interfaces. The integration test must also prove that the new system performs according to the functional specifications and functions effectively in the operating environment without adversely affecting other systems.	IBM Rational Functional Tester, HP Unified Functional Testing
System quality test	A system quality test ensures that the developed application meets those nonfunctional requirements. Most of the time, this tests the performance of the application to ensure that the target requirements for concurrent users of the system and workload are met. Other nonfunctional requirements include security, high-availability features, and so on.	Apache JMeter, HP LoadRunner, Locust, K6
User acceptance test	A user acceptance test simulates the actual working conditions of the new system, including the user manuals and procedures. Extensive user involvement in this stage of testing provides the user with invaluable training in operating the new system. It also benefits the programmer or designer to see the user experience with the new programs. This joint involvement encourages the user and operations personnel to approve the system conversion.	IBM Rational TestManager, HP Quality Center

Now that the general testing academic details have been presented, let's get down to practice. Instead of presenting the full details and list of classes that the Spring Framework provides in the testing area, we cover the most commonly used patterns and the supporting interfaces and classes within the Spring TestContext Framework as we show how to implement the sample test cases in this chapter.

Using Spring Test Annotations

Before moving on to logic and integration tests, it's worth noting that Spring provides testing-specific annotations in addition to the standard annotations (such as `@Autowired` and `@Resource`). These annotations can be used in your logic unit tests, providing various functionality such as simplified context file loading, profiles, test execution timing, and much more. Table 4-5 outlines the annotations and their uses.

Table 4-5. *Spring Test Annotations*

Annotation	Description
@BootstrapWith	Class-level annotation used to determine how to bootstrap the Spring TestContext Framework.
@ContextConfiguration	Class-level annotation used to determine how to load and configure an ApplicationContext for integration tests. When using Junit 4, annotation test classes need to be annotated with @RunWith(SpringRunner.class). When using Junit Jupiter, test classes need to be annotated with @ExtendWith(SpringExtension.class).
@WebAppConfiguration	Class-level annotation used to indicate the ApplicationContext loaded should be a WebApplicationContext.
@ContextHierarchy	Class-level annotation used to define a hierarchy of ApplicationContexts for integration tests.
@DirtiesContext	Class- and method-level annotation used to indicate that the context has been modified or corrupted in some way during the execution of the test and should be closed and rebuilt for subsequent tests.
@ActiveProfiles	Class-level annotation indicating which bean profile should be active.
@TestPropertySource	Class-level annotation used to configure locations of properties files and inlined properties to be added to the Environment's set of PropertySources for an ApplicationContext for integration tests.
@DynamicPropertySource	Method-level annotation for integration tests that need to add properties with dynamic values to the Environment's set of PropertySources.
@TestExecutionListeners	Class-level annotation for configuring TestExecutionListeners that should be registered with the TestContextManager.
@RecordApplicationEvents	Class-level annotation used to Spring TestContext Framework to record all application events published in the ApplicationContext during the execution of a single test.
@Commit	Test-level annotation that is used to indicate that a test-managed transaction should be committed after the test method has completed.
@Rollback	Test-level annotation that is used to indicate whether a test-managed transaction should be rolled back< after the test method has completed. As expected, @Rollback(false) is equivalent to @Commit.
@BeforeTransaction	Method-level annotation indicating that the annotated method should be called before a transaction is started for test methods marked with the @Transactional annotation.

(*continued*)

Table 4-5. (*continued*)

Annotation	Description
@AfterTransaction	Method-level annotation indicating that the annotated method should be called after a transaction has ended for test methods marked with the @Transactional annotation.
@Sql	Class- and method-level annotation used to configure SQL scripts and statements to be executed against a given database during integration tests.
@SqlConfig	Class- and method-level annotation used to indicate how to parse and execute SQL scripts configured via the @Sql annotation.
@SqlMergeMode	Class- and method-level annotation used to indicate whether method-level @Sql declarations are merged with class-level @Sql declarations.
@SqlGroup	Container-level annotation that aggregates several @Sql annotations.
@IfProfileValue	Class- and method-level annotation used to indicate that the test method should be enabled for a specific set of environmental conditions.
@ProfileValueSourceConfiguration	Class-level annotation used to specify the ProfileValueSource used by @IfProfileValue. If this annotation is not declared on the test, SystemProfileValueSource is used as the default.
@Timed	Method-level annotation used to indicate that the test must finish in the specified time period.
@Repeat	Method-level annotation used to indicate that the annotated test method should be repeated the specified number of times.

Implementing Logic Unit Tests

As previously discussed, a logic unit test is the finest level of testing. The objective is to verify the behavior of an individual class, with all the class's dependencies being "mocked" with expected behavior. Considering the MessageRender and MessageProvider beans, testing the MessageRender bean in isolation, by injecting it with a mock MessageProvider bean, is a suitable example of unit testing. To help mock the behavior of the MessageProvider bean, we will show how to use Mockito[4], which is a popular mocking framework.

The Spring Framework provides first-class support for integration testing in the spring-test module. To provide a test context for the integration tests that will be created for this section, you will use the spring-test.jar library. This library contains valuable classes for integration testing with a Spring container. For the tests in this section, the spring-test, mockito-all, and junit-jupiter-engine are added to the configuration of the project.

Let's start small. Considering the MessageRender and MessageProvider beans, let's declare a test class that checks that the StandardOutMessageRenderer bean type works as intended, as in when render() is called, this invokes messageProvider.getMessage(). To perform this test we do not need a Spring ApplicationContext nor a MessageProvider; we just need a mock, a simple replacement. Listing 4-51 depicts the test class and the test method that need to be run to execute the test.

---

[4] https://site.mockito.org/

Listing 4-51. Unit Test for StandardOutMessageRenderer Using Mockito

```
package com.apress.prospring6.four

import com.apress.prospring6.two.decoupled.MessageProvider
import com.apress.prospring6.two.decoupled.MessageRenderer
import org.junit.jupiter.api.Test
import org.mockito.Mockito.mock
import org.mockito.Mockito.times
import org.mockito.Mockito.verify
import org.mockito.Mockito.`when` // when is a keyword in Kotlin!

class MessageRenderTest {
    @Test
    fun testStandardOutMessageRenderer() {
        val mockProvider: MessageProvider = mock(MessageProvider::class.java)
        `when`(mockProvider.message).thenReturn("test message")
        val messageRenderer: MessageRenderer = StandardOutMessageRenderer()
        messageRenderer.messageProvider = mockProvider
        messageRenderer.render()
        verify(mockProvider, times(1)).message
    }
}
```

The test method is annotated with the Junit Jupiter @Test annotation, which marks it as a test method.

The test method creates the context and checks the existence of the beans and the result of calling the render() method. Tests can be run in debug mode as well, and breakpoints can be used to pause execution to inspect objects for debugging purposes.

IntelliJ IDEA can run all the test methods within a test class, package, or module or a single method. Just right-click the component and there should be a Run option in the menu that is displayed. When you right-click the content of a test class, if you click outside any test method, the option will be to run all methods; when you right-click a method name or inside the method body, the Run option for the menu is specific to running that method. Figure 4-5 shows the IntelliJ IDEA menu that appears when a test method name is right-clicked (shown is the Java code, but it will work for Kotlin just the same).

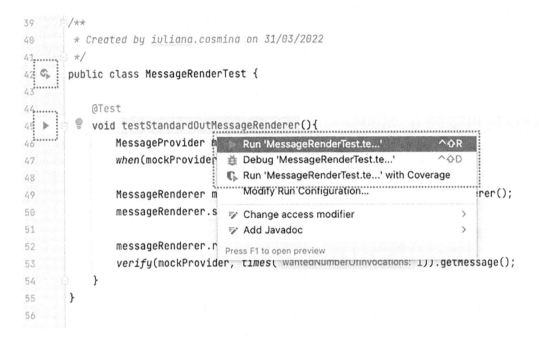

```
39      /**
40       * Created by iuliana.cosmina on 31/03/2022
41       */
42      public class MessageRenderTest {
43
44          @Test
45          void testStandardOutMessageRenderer(){
46              MessageProvider                Run 'MessageRenderTest.te...'        ^⇧R
47              when(mockProvider              Debug 'MessageRenderTest.te...'     ^⇧D
48                                             Run 'MessageRenderTest.te...' with Coverage
49              MessageRenderer m              Modify Run Configuration...              rer();
50              messageRenderer.s              Change access modifier            >
51                                             Add Javadoc                       >
52              messageRenderer.r         Press F1 to open preview
53              verify(mockProvider, times( wantedNumberOfInvocations: 1)).getMessage();
54          }
55      }
56
```

Figure 4-5. *IntelliJ IDEA options for running tests*

Figure 4-5 also shows two buttons to the left of the file. Clicking the button at the class level expands into a menu grouping options for running the test class. Clicking the button at the method level expands into a menu grouping options for running the test method. Feel free to experiment with those buttons and options a little to get used to them, then get back to reading the book.

The testStandardOutMessageRenderer() method verifies the behavior of the StandardOutMessageRenderer implementation in isolation. Its behavior cannot be influenced by anything else in the application; even its dependency on the MessageProvider instance is replaced with a mock implementation constructed by Mockito, with the perfect behavior configured by this line: when(mockProvider.getMessage()).thenReturn("test message").

The Mockito utility methods are quite practical, because they also make the test code very readable. The when(..) line configures the String value to be returned when the getMessage() method is called on this mock. How does this work? Well, Mockito implements the MessageProvider interface to create a mock object, and then creates a proxy to intercept calls to it. When we invoke the when(..) method, we are in fact recalling the last registered method call from that context and thenReturn() saves the return value for it. Anyway, Mockito is really useful for isolating components for unit testing, or for reducing the number of levels in an integration test to focus only on the bits that present interest.

ℹ️ In the company I've been working for the last three years, we rarely write unit tests, because integration tests cover the behavior the unit tests cover anyway. Lately, I've found myself agreeing to this more and more, because setting up the test context requires effort, and using the same context for multiple tests makes that effort worthwhile.

In this book, we will mostly use integration testing, but some unit tests will be covered here and there, just enough to make you comfortable with them and recognize them in the future. There is more than one option for mocking dependencies. JMock[5] is another library you can use, also EasyMock[6] and for writing checks, take a look at Hamcrest[7].

This being said, let's switch gears to integration testing.

Implementing an Integration Test

In this section, we will implement the integration test for the previous example. A configuration creating those beans and connecting them together is created. This configuration is used to create a test application context, and the test will check that the two beans are created correctly. To show how configurations can be aggregated for integration tests, the MessageProvider and MessageRenderer bean types have been declared in their own package with their own configuration class, as shown in Figure 4-6.

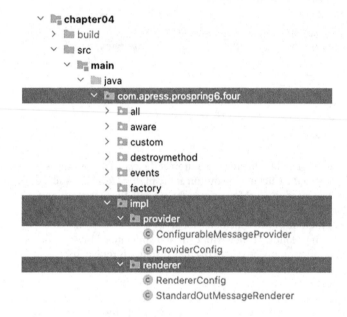

Figure 4-6. *Organizing beans with their own configuration*

Before introducing tests to create the ApplicationContext, we would have created a class with a main(..) method, but now that we know how to write a test, let's give it a try. Listing 4-52 shows a test method that tests the proper creation of an ApplicationContext containing the two beans.

---

[5] http://jmock.org
[6] https://easymock.org
[7] https://hamcrest.org

Listing 4-52. Integration Test for StandardOutMessageRenderer

```
package com.apress.prospring6.four

import com.apress.prospring6.four.impl.provider.ProviderConfig
// other imports omitted

class MessageRenderOneIT {
    @Test
    fun testConfig() {
        val ctx = AnnotationConfigApplicationContext(
            RendererConfig::class.java,
            ProviderConfig::class.java
        )
        val messageProvider = ctx.getBean(
            MessageProvider::class.java
        )
        val messageRenderer = ctx.getBean(
            MessageRenderer::class.java
        )
        Assertions.assertAll("messageTest",
            Executable { Assertions.assertNotNull(messageRenderer) },
            Executable { Assertions.assertNotNull(messageProvider) },
            Executable {
                Assertions.assertEquals(
                    messageProvider,
                    messageRenderer.messageProvider
                )
            }
        )
        messageRenderer.render()
    }
}
```

Compared to the initial approach of creating the ApplicationContext in a main method, there are three observations:

- In a test method, test utility methods can be used, in this case method assertAll(..) and other Junit Jupiter utility methods that were used to test our assumptions about the beans that were creates as part of the context.

- The render() method cannot be tested since it returns void; we can only check the console and look for the *Text Sample* text being printed, just as we did using a main(..) method.

- Tests are run when the project is built, which means configuration problems will be identified quickly.

The previous test method is a very simple way to move the logic from the main module to the test module. Also, this is not the efficient way to do it, because if we write more test methods in the same class, the context must be built for each method. Reusing a test context is possible in more than one way. Listing 4-53 shown the JUnit way.

Listing 4-53. Integration Test for StandardOutMessageRenderer with Shared Test Context (the JUnit Way)

```
package com.apress.prospring6.four

import com.apress.prospring6.four.impl.provider.ProviderConfig
// other import statements omitted

class MessageRenderTwoIT {
    @Test
    fun testProvider() {
        val messageProvider = ctx!!.getBean(
            MessageProvider::class.java
        )
        Assertions.assertNotNull(messageProvider)
    }

    @Test
    fun testRenderer() {
        val messageRenderer = ctx!!.getBean(
            MessageRenderer::class.java
        )
        Assertions.assertAll("messageTest",
            Executable { Assertions.assertNotNull(messageRenderer) },
            Executable { Assertions.assertNotNull(messageRenderer.messageProvider) }
        )
        messageRenderer.render()
    }

    companion object {
        var ctx: ApplicationContext? = null
        @BeforeAll @JvmStatic
        fun setUp() {
            ctx = AnnotationConfigApplicationContext(RendererConfig::class.java,
                ProviderConfig::class.java)
        }
    }
}
```

Sharing the test context among test methods the JUnit way is by declaring an ApplicationContext static reference and telling JUnit to call the setUp(..) method only once to initialize it by annotating it with @BeforeAll. This works for any other component that needs to be shared between the test methods.

⚠ The example in Listing 4-53 shows the test class written using annotations from Junit Jupiter, also known as Junit 5. An equivalent test can be written with JUnit 4. Check out the previous edition of the Java variant of this book if you are interested in using JUnit 4.

However, the best way, is the Spring way. The @ContextConfiguration annotation introduced in Table 4-5 is used to configure the configuration classes used to build the ApplicationContext, but to integrate the Spring test context with the Jupiter 5 programming model, the @ExtendWith annotation is also required together with the SpringExtension.class argument, because this is how we configure the extension for Spring. Listing 4-54 shows the code of this class.

Listing 4-54. Integration Test for StandardOutMessageRenderer with Shared Test Context (the Spring Way)

```
package com.apress.prospring6.four

import com.apress.prospring6.four.impl.provider.ProviderConfig
import com.apress.prospring6.four.impl.renderer.RendererConfig
// other imports omitted

//@ExtendWith(SpringExtension.class)
//@ContextConfiguration(classes = {RendererConfig.class, ProviderConfig.class})
@SpringJUnitConfig(classes = [RendererConfig::class, ProviderConfig::class])
class MessageRenderThreeIT {
    @Autowired
    var messageRenderer: MessageRenderer? = null

    @Autowired
    var messageProvider: MessageProvider? = null

    @Test
    fun testProvider() {
        Assertions.assertNotNull(messageProvider)
    }

    @Test
    fun testRenderer() {
        Assertions.assertAll("messageTest",
            Executable { Assertions.assertNotNull(messageRenderer) },
            Executable { Assertions.assertNotNull(messageRenderer!!.messageProvider) }
        )
        messageRenderer!!.render()
    }
}
```

Since the Spring ApplicationContext is integrated with the Jupiter programming model, we do not need to extract the beans from the context—we can just autowire them in the test class.

If you want to keep things simple, Junit Jupiter also provides the @SpringJUnitConfig annotation in the package org.springframework.test.context.junit.jupiter that replaces the @ExtendWith + @ContextConfiguration combination. Thus,

```
@ExtendWith(SpringExtension.class)
@ContextConfiguration(classes = {RendererConfig.class, ProviderConfig.class})
```

can be replaced with

```
@SpringJUnitConfig(classes = {RendererConfig.class, ProviderConfig.class})
```

Configuring Profile for Integration Testing

The bean definition profiles feature introduced in Spring 3.1 is useful for implementing a test case with the appropriate configuration of the testing components. Profiles are useful for other things as well. For example, if you are working on an application that integrates with an Amazon DynamoDB instance, you might not want to use that instance during development or during continuous integration builds, to avoid costs. So, you could configure a development profile that includes a connection bean that connects to a local DynamoDB container instead of the remote Amazon DynamoDB instance.

Are you still wondering why we need profiles when we could just isolate beans specific to a purpose in their own configuration files and just import those? Profiles are useful when, for some reason, you cannot do that, because you can annotate certain bean definitions with the @Profile(..) annotations and leave the rest of the bean definitions untouched.

For example, take a look at the configuration class in Listing 4-55; it declares a MessageRenderer bean that is not associated with a profile and a MessageProvider bean that is associated to a profile named dev.

Listing 4-55. Configuration Class with a Mean Associated to a Profile

```
package com.apress.prospring6.four.impl

import org.springframework.context.annotation.Profile
// other import statement omitted

@Configuration
open class AllConfig {
    @Profile("dev")
    @Bean
    open fun messageProvider():MessageProvider =
        ConfigurableMessageProvider("Text Sample")

    @Bean
    open fun messageRenderer():MessageRenderer =
        StandardOutMessageRenderer().apply {
            messageProvider = messageProvider()
        }
}
```

Not being associated to a profile means the MessageRenderer will be part of the context, regardless of the activated profile, which is what we are interested in, because this is the bean we are interested in testing.

To test this bean we need to provide a different MessageProvider dependency in the test context. We do this by declaring a new bean type named TestMessageProvider that implements MessageProvider but returns a different message. The implementation is basic, so it won't be shown here. Listing 4-56 shows the test configuration class declaring a bean definition associated to the test profile, the test class annotated with @ActiveProfiles("test") annotation to activate the test profile, and the test method that checks that the MessageRenderer was created as expected and the dependency injected is of type TestMessageProvider.

Listing 4-56. Test Configuration Class and profiled Test Class

```
package com.apress.prospring6.four

import org.springframework.context.annotation.Profile
import org.springframework.test.context.ActiveProfiles
import org.springframework.test.context.junit.jupiter.SpringJUnitConfig
```

```kotlin
// other import statements omitted

@Configuration
internal open class TestConfig {
    @Profile("test")
    @Bean
    open fun messageProvider(): MessageProvider {
        return TestMessageProvider("Test Message")
    }
}

@ActiveProfiles("test")
@SpringJUnitConfig(classes = [AllConfig::class, TestConfig::class])
class MessageRenderFourIT {
    @Autowired
    var messageRenderer: MessageRenderer? = null

    @Autowired
    var messageProvider: MessageProvider? = null

    @Test
    fun testConfig() {
        Assertions.assertAll("messageTest",
            Executable { Assertions.assertNotNull(messageRenderer) },
            Executable { Assertions.assertNotNull(messageProvider) },
            Executable { Assertions.assertTrue(messageProvider is TestMessageProvider) },
            Executable {
                Assertions.assertEquals(
                    messageProvider,
                    messageRenderer!!.messageProvider
                )
            }
        )
        messageRenderer!!.render()
    }
}
```

This is all that can be said at the moment about integration tests. As this book progresses and more complex applications are built, the tests will increase in complexity, and thus almost all annotations in Table 4-5 are going to be introduced and explained when needed.

Implementing a Front-End Unit Test

Another testing area of particular interest is testing the front-end behavior as a whole, upon the deployment of the web application to a web container like Apache Tomcat. The main reason is that even though we test every layer within the application, we still need to make sure that the views behave correctly with different actions from users. Automating front-end testing is important in saving time for developers and users when repeating the actions on the front end for a test case.

However, developing a test case for a front end is a challenging task, especially for those web applications with a lot of interactive, rich, and Ajax-based components.

Introducing Selenium

Selenium is a powerful and comprehensive tool and framework target for automating web-based front-end testing. The main feature is that by using Selenium, we can "drive" the browsers, simulating user interactions with the application, and perform verification of the view status.

Selenium supports common browsers including Firefox, Edge, and Chrome. In terms of languages, Selenium supports Java, C#, PHP, Perl, Ruby, and Python. Selenium is also designed with Ajax and rich Internet applications (RIAs) in mind, making automated testing of modern web applications possible.

If your application has a lot of front-end user interfaces and needs to run a large number of front-end tests, the `selenium-server` module provides built-in grid functionality that supports the execution of front-end tests among a group of computers.

The Selenium IDE is a Firefox plug-in that can help "record" user interactions with the web application. It also supports replay and exports the scripts into various formats that can help simplify the development of test cases.

Starting from version 2.0, Selenium integrates the WebDriver API, which addresses a number of limitations and provides an alternative, and simpler, programming interface. The result is a comprehensive object-oriented API that provides additional support for a larger number of browsers along with improved support for modern advanced web application testing problems.

Front-end web testing is a complex subject and beyond the scope of this book. From this brief overview, you can see how Selenium can help automate the user interaction with the web application front end with cross-browser compatibility. For more details, please refer to Selenium's online documentation[8].

Now that you have a basic idea of how to test Spring applications, let's switch gears to one of the most loved (and move hated by some) Spring projects: Groovy.

Configuration Using Groovy

Spring Framework 4.0 introduced the ability to configure bean definitions and `ApplicationContext` by using the Groovy language. This provides developers with another choice in configuration to either replace or supplement XML and/or annotation-based bean configuration. A Spring `ApplicationContext` can be created directly in a Groovy script or loaded from Java/Kotlin, both by way of the `GenericGroovyApplicationContext` class.

First let's dive into the details by showing how to create bean definitions from an external Groovy script and loading them from Kotlin. In previous sections and chapters, we introduced various bean classes, and to promote some code reusability, we will use in this example the `Singer` class shown in Listing 4-57.

Listing 4-57. Singer Class to Be Used in Groovy Examples

```
package com.apress.prospring6.four.groovy

class Singer {
    var name: String? = null
    var age = 0

    override fun toString(): String {
        return "name=${name}, age=${name}"
    }
}
```

---

[8] https://www.selenium.dev

As you can see, this is just a Kotlin class with a couple of properties describing a singer. We use this simple Kotlin class here to show that just because you configure your beans in Groovy doesn't mean your entire code base needs to be rewritten in Groovy. Not only that, but Kotlin classes can be imported from dependencies and used within Groovy scripts. Now, let's create the Groovy script (beans.groovy) that will be used to create the bean definition, as shown in Listing 4-58.

Listing 4-58. Singer Bean Groovy Definition

```
import com.apress.prospring6.four.groovy.Singer

beans {
    singer(Singer, name: 'John Mayer', age: 42)
}
```

This Groovy script starts with a top-level closure called beans, which provides bean definitions to Spring. First, we specify the bean name (singer), and then as arguments we provide the class type (Singer) followed by the property names and values that we would like to set. Next, let's create a simple test driver in Kotlin, loading bean definitions from the Groovy script, as shown in Listing 4-59.

Listing 4-59. Test Class to Test Groovy Beans

```
package com.apress.prospring6.four.groovy

import org.slf4j.LoggerFactory
import org.springframework.context.ApplicationContext
import org.springframework.context.support.GenericGroovyApplicationContext

object GroovyBeansFromJavaDemo {
    private val logger = LoggerFactory.getLogger(GroovyBeansFromJavaDemo::class.java)
    @JvmStatic
    fun main(args: Array<String>) {
        val context: ApplicationContext =
            GenericGroovyApplicationContext("classpath:spring/beans.groovy")
        val singer = context.getBean(
            "singer",
            Singer::class.java
        )
        logger.info("Singer bean: {}", singer)
    }
}
```

As you can see, the creation of ApplicationContext is carried out in typical fashion, but it's done by using the GenericGroovyApplicationContext class and providing your Groovy script that builds the bean definitions. Running GroovyBeansFromJavaDemo should print:

```
INFO : GroovyBeansFromJavaDemo - Singer bean: com.apress.prospring6.four.groovy.
Singer@272a179c[name=John Mayer,age=42]
```

---

❶   The only thing you must keep in mind when using Groovy bean definitions is that the `groovy-all` library must be on the project classpath. So, whatever build tool you are using, whether Maven or Gradle, make sure you mention it in your configuration file.

Now that you have seen how to load bean definitions from Kotlin via an external Groovy script, how can we go about creating the `ApplicationContext` and bean definitions from a Groovy script alone? There's not much to it, really, and the Groovy syntax is more simplistic than Java or Kotlin is, as shown in Listing 4-60.

Listing 4-60. Groovy Script to Declare Beans and Use Them

```
package com.apress.prospring6.four.groovy

import org.springframework.beans.factory.groovy.GroovyBeanDefinitionReader
import org.springframework.context.support.GenericApplicationContext

def ctx = new GenericApplicationContext()
def reader = new GroovyBeanDefinitionReader(ctx)

reader.beans {
    singer(Singer, name: 'John Mayer', age: 42)
}

ctx.refresh()
println ctx.getBean("singer")
```

When we run this sample, we get same output as before, only we don't get a log statement, since a logger is not used in this case, but a simple console output. This time we create an instance of a typical `GenericApplicationContext`, but use `GroovyBeanDefinitionReader`, which will be used to pass bean definitions to. Then, as in the previous Listing 4-59, we create a bean from our simple POJO, refresh `ApplicationContext`, and print the string representation of the `Singer` bean. It doesn't get any easier than that!

As you probably can tell, we are only scratching the surface of what can be done with the Groovy support in Spring. Since you have the full power of the Groovy language, you can do all sorts of interesting things when creating bean definitions. As you have full access to `ApplicationContext`, not only can you configure beans, but you can also work with profile support, property files, and so on. Just keep in mind, with great power comes great responsibility.

Using Spring Boot

Following this book so far has taught you more than one way to declare beans that make up a Spring application. But what if we tell you there is something even cooler than all that?

The Spring Boot project aims to simplify the getting-started experience of building an application by using Spring. Spring Boot takes the guesswork out of manually gathering dependencies and provides some of the most common features needed by most applications, such as metrics and health checks.

Spring Boot takes an "opinionated" approach to achieve the goal of developer simplification by way of providing starter projects for various types of applications that already contain the proper dependencies and versions, which means less time spent to get started. For those who may be looking to get away from XML completely, Spring Boot does not require any configuration to be written in XML.

In this example, we will create the traditional Hello World web application with a twist. You may be surprised to see the minimal amount of code required to do so as compared to your typical Java or Kotlin web application setup. Typically, we have started off examples by defining the dependencies you need to add to your project. Part of Spring Boot's simplification model is to prepare all the dependencies for you, and when using Maven, for example, you as the developer utilize a parent POM to obtain this functionality. When using Gradle, things become even simpler. There is no parent needed, except a Gradle plug-in and a starter dependency. If your project is simple enough, you can generate the full configuration using Spring Initializr, accessible at `https://start.spring.io`, download the basic structure and configuration form there, and start customizing it according to your needs. **Chapter 2** mentioned how powerful Spring Boot is. However, it can become a tough-to-manage beast without the proper understanding of Spring. Thankfully, you are reading this book, so you'll be fine.

Without further ado, let's get down to using Spring Boot!

As of the time this chapter is being written, Spring Boot version 3.0.0 has not been released yet. This is the reason why the project is currently configured to use version 3.0.0-M2. By the time this book is released the project will be updated with the official release version.

Each release of Spring Boot provides a curated list of dependencies it supports. The versions of the necessary libraries are selected so the API matches perfectly, and this is handled by Spring Boot. Therefore, the manual configuration of dependencies versions is not necessary. Upgrading Spring Boot will ensure that those dependencies are upgraded as well. With the previous configuration, a set of dependencies will be added to the project, each with the proper versions so that their API will be compatible. In a smart editor like IntelliJ IDEA, there is a Gradle (or Maven) Projects view, where you can expand each module and inspect the available tasks and dependencies, as shown in Figure 4-7.

The Spring Boot version in Figure 4-7 might be different in the project attached to the book, by the time the book is released. The reason behind this is that the code is written when Spring Boot 3 is still in development. So is Spring 6. The intention is to edit this book and update the image with the official version before publication, but in case we miss this image, just know that is all right as long as the code runs.

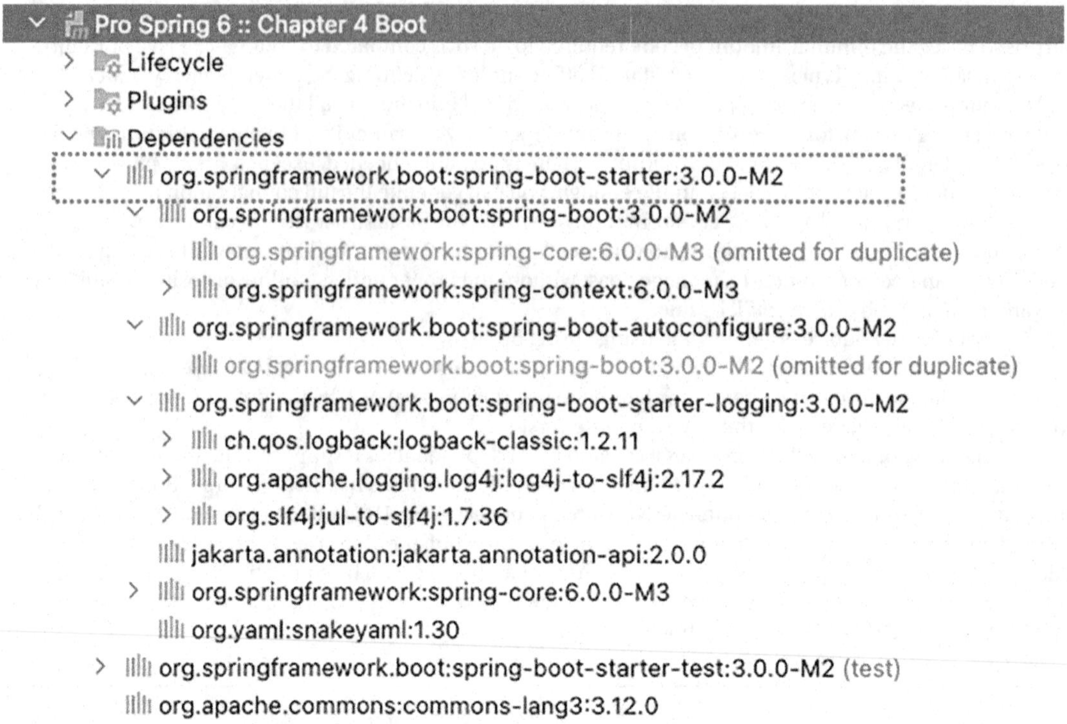
Pro Spring 6 :: Chapter 4 Boot
Lifecycle
Plugins
Dependencies
org.springframework.boot:spring-boot-starter:3.0.0-M2
org.springframework.boot:spring-boot:3.0.0-M2
org.springframework:spring-core:6.0.0-M3 (omitted for duplicate)
org.springframework:spring-context:6.0.0-M3
org.springframework.boot:spring-boot-autoconfigure:3.0.0-M2
org.springframework.boot:spring-boot:3.0.0-M2 (omitted for duplicate)
org.springframework.boot:spring-boot-starter-logging:3.0.0-M2
ch.qos.logback:logback-classic:1.2.11
org.apache.logging.log4j:log4j-to-slf4j:2.17.2
org.slf4j:jul-to-slf4j:1.7.36
jakarta.annotation:jakarta.annotation-api:2.0.0
org.springframework:spring-core:6.0.0-M3
org.yaml:snakeyaml:1.30
org.springframework.boot:spring-boot-starter-test:3.0.0-M2 (test)
org.apache.commons:commons-lang3:3.12.0

Figure 4-7. *Spring Boot starter library and dependencies*

The `chapter04-boot` project is very simple and declares a simple Spring boot starter dependency, the `spring-boot-starter` library. This dependency brings with it a set of Spring dependencies and their dependencies that make a strong foundation for building Spring application. The entry point of a Spring Boot project is the application class, the one annotated with `@SpringBootApplication`, in our case the `Chapter4application` class. When using Spring Initializr, this class is generated with an empty body for the `main(..)` method, but we like to complete that body with a few lines of code that list all the beans in the application context, as shown in Listing 4-61.

Listing 4-61. Spring Boot Application Class Modified to Show All Beans in the Application Context

```
package com.apress.prospring6.four.boot

import org.springframework.boot.SpringApplication
import org.springframework.boot.autoconfigure.SpringBootApplication
// other imports omitted

@SpringBootApplication(scanBasePackages = ["com.apress.prospring6.four.boot.runners"])
open class Chapter4Application {
    companion object {
        private val LOGGER =
            LoggerFactory.getLogger(Chapter4Application::class.java)
```

```
    @JvmStatic
    fun main(args: Array<String>) {
        val ctx = SpringApplication.run(arrayOf(Chapter4Application::class.java), args)
        assert(ctx != null)

        // listing all bean definition names
        // ctx.beanDefinitionNames.forEach(LOGGER::info)
        ctx.beanDefinitionNames.forEach(::println)
    }
  }
}
```

That is all. Really. The extra lines to check that a context was created and to list all the bean names in the context, is the bit we added. The only necessary statement to bootstrap a Spring application is SpringApplication.run(Chapter4Application.class, args).

The novelty here is the @SpringBootApplication annotation. This annotation is a top-level annotation designed to be used only at the class level. It is a convenience annotation that is equivalent to declaring the following three:

- @SpringBootConfiguration: This annotation indicates that this class provides configuration for a Spring Boot application. It is meta-annotated with @Configuration, which means this class can declare beans with @Bean.

- @EnableAutoConfiguration: This is a specific Spring Boot annotation from the package org.springframework.boot.autoconfigure that enables creating a default Spring ApplicationContext with all the infrastructure beans needed based on the project dependencies. @EnableAutoConfiguration works well with Spring-provided starter dependencies, but it is not directly tied to them, so other dependencies outside the starters can be used. For example, if there is a specific embedded server on the classpath, it will be used, unless there is another EmbeddedServletContainerFactory configuration in the project. This is a core element of the practicality of Spring Boot: it configures stable default infrastructure beans, but it is easy to customize as well.

- @ComponentScan: This annotation enables discovery of classes annotated with stereotype annotations. The attribute used to list the packages to scan used with @SpringBootApplication is basePackages. In version 1.3.0, another attribute was added to this annotation: basePackageClasses. This attribute provides a type-safe alternative to basePackages for specifying the packages to scan for annotated components. The package of each class specified will be scanned. By default @SpringBootApplication enables scanning for the package where the application class is declared and all packages under it.

If you ran the Chapter4Application call, you might have noticed that the number of infrastructure beans in the Spring Boot context is much higher than the number of beans in a simple Spring Classic application context. Being able to just declare your beans and run a Spring application comes with a cost: you avoid the work of setting up your context and allow Spring Boot to do it for you. The most basic Spring Boot application context is designed based on decisions of experienced developers who, after working with Spring for a long time, have identified the typical Spring components used in various Spring applications and baked that into default setups packed into the Spring Boot starter dependencies. There are multiple Spring Boot starter dependencies, and each of them is specific to the application being built: spring-boot-starter is used for the simplest Spring applications containing interoperating beans and writing logs;

181

spring-boot-starter-jpa is used for simple Spring applications that manage data stored in a database; spring-boot-starter-web is used to create a basic Spring web application; and so on. All these starter dependencies will be covered and explained in more detail in the applicable chapters in the book.

For now let's modify this Spring Boot application to add the MessageProvider and MessageRenderer beans that we've played with so far. The only things we have to do are as follows:

- Modify the configuration files to add a Maven/Gradle dependency on the chapter02 project where those two interfaces are declared.

- Copy the ConfigurableMessageProvider and StandardOutMessageRenderer classes into the chapter04-boot project and make sure they are annotated with @Component and @Autowired where necessary.

- Modify the Chapter4Application class to access the MessageRenderer and call render().

Listing 4-62 shows all these changes together, and the bean definitions have been added to the WithBeansApplication file, to keep all things in the same context close to each other. *(You will thank us when navigating the project!)*

Listing 4-62. Spring Boot Application Class with Developer Beans

```
package com.apress.prospring6.four.beans

import com.apress.prospring6.two.decoupled.MessageProvider
import com.apress.prospring6.two.decoupled.MessageRenderer

import org.springframework.boot.SpringApplication
import org.springframework.boot.autoconfigure.SpringBootApplication
// other import statements omitted

@Component("messageRenderer")
class StandardOutMessageRenderer : MessageRenderer {
    override var messageProvider: MessageProvider? = null
        @Autowired set(value) {
            field = value
        }

    override fun render() {
        logger.info(messageProvider!!.message)
    }

    companion object {
        private val logger: Logger =
            LoggerFactory.getLogger(StandardOutMessageRenderer::class.java)
    }
}

@Component
internal class ConfigurableMessageProvider(
    @Value(
```

```
        "Configurable message"
    ) override val message: String
) : MessageProvider

@SpringBootApplication
open class WithBeansApplication {
    companion object {
        private val logger: Logger =
            LoggerFactory.getLogger(WithBeansApplication::class.java)

        @JvmStatic
        fun main(args: Array<String>) {
            val ctx = SpringApplication.run(arrayOf(WithBeansApplication::class.java), args)
            val mr: MessageRenderer =
                ctx.getBean("messageRenderer", MessageRenderer::class.java)
            mr.render()
        }
    }
}
```

If you run the WithBeansApplication class and look at the console, you will also notice the Configurable message output being printed.

In this example we explicitly called the render() method on the MessageRenderer bean, but what if we did not have to? Spring Boot is the gift that keeps on giving, as you will discover reading this book, but we would like to introduce you right now to the org.springframework.boot.CommandLineRunner interface. This functional interface declares a single method named run() and is used to indicate that a bean should run—meaning the run() method is executed when it is contained within a Spring application. This means we can modify the StandardOutMessageRenderer class and make the run() method call render.

We can go even one step further. Since multiple CommandLineRunner beans can be defined within the same application context and can be ordered using the Ordered interface or @Order annotation, we can modify the ConfigurableMessageProvider as well to make it a CommandLineRunner, but in its run() method we make sure the message field is set with the command-line argument, thus making this implementation truly configurable.

Also, to make sure the two beans behave as expected, we use the @Order annotation on both, annotating ConfigurableMessageProvider with @Order(1) and MessageRenderer with @Order(2), to make sure they are initialized and run correctly. The new runner beans and configuration class are shown in Listing 4-63.

Listing 4-63. Spring Boot Application Class with Runner Beans

```
package com.apress.prospring6.four.boot.runners

import org.springframework.beans.factory.annotation.Autowired
// other import statements omitted

@Order(2)
@Component("messageRenderer")
internal class StandardOutMessageRenderer : MessageRenderer, CommandLineRunner {
    override var messageProvider: MessageProvider? = null
        @Autowired set(value) {
            field = value
        }
```

```kotlin
    override fun render() {
        logger.info(messageProvider!!.message)
    }

    @Throws(java.lang.Exception::class)
    override fun run(vararg args: String?) {
        render()
    }

    companion object {
        private val logger: Logger =
            LoggerFactory.getLogger(StandardOutMessageRenderer::class.java)
    }
}

@Order(1)
@Component
internal class ConfigurableMessageProvider(
    @param:Value("Configurable message")
     override var message: String
) : MessageProvider, CommandLineRunner {

    @Throws(java.lang.Exception::class)
    override fun run(vararg args: String) {
        if (args.size >= 1) {
            message = args[0]
        }
    }
}

@SpringBootApplication
open class WithRunnersApplication {
    companion object {
        @JvmStatic
        fun main(args: Array<String>) {
            SpringApplication.run(arrayOf(WithRunnersApplication::class.java), args)
        }
    }
}
```

When running the WithRunnersApplication, you will also notice the Configurable message output being printed. This happens because you probably ran it without providing any program arguments. To do that, open the launch configuration IntelliJ IDEA has created for this class and modify the Build and run section to include the Program arguments text box and introduce a value similar to the one shown in Figure 4-8.

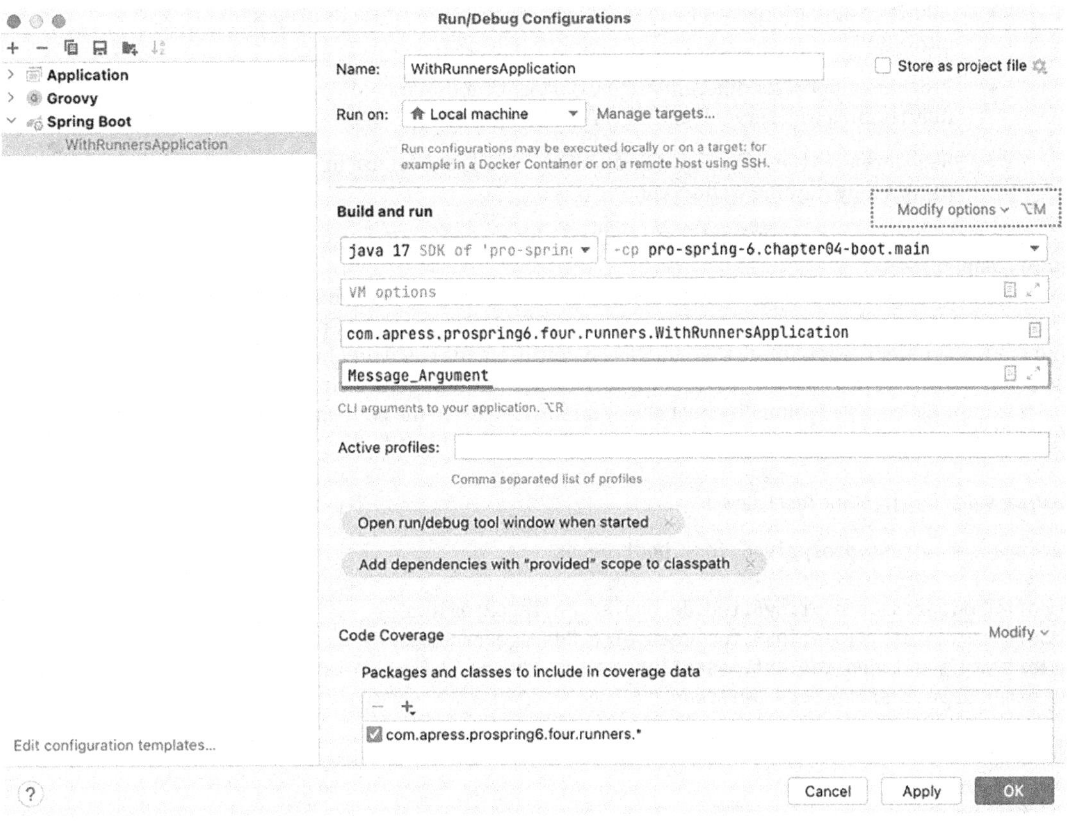

Figure 4-8. Spring Boot IntelliJ IDEA configuration window

If the Program arguments text box is not visible, add it from the Modify options menu (highlighted on the right in Figure 4-8).

If you run the code using the launcher, you will see the program argument you provided appearing in the console log.

`org.springframework.boot.ApplicationRunner` provides similar functionality but exposes the arguments as an instance of `ApplicationArguments` that provides additional arguments operations such as: returning the raw, unprocessed arguments by invoking `getSourceArgs()`, or returning the names of all arguments by invoking `getOptionNames()`, which is useful if you want to print some command-line suggestions, and so on.

The most useful Spring Boot starter library in our opinion is `spring-boot-starter-test`. When added to a project, it not only provides a cool set of classes for testing Spring Boot applications, but also brings in a rich set of testing libraries, so you don't have to add JUnit, mock, and so on, manually to your configuration.

Let's start with the basics. If the entry point of a Spring Boot application is the class annotated with `@SpringBootApplication`, the entry point of a Spring Boot test is the class annotated with `@SpringBootTest`. This annotation does the following things:

- Uses a default `SpringBootContextLoader` when no `ContextLoader` is defined, e.g., via `@ContextConfiguration(loader=..)`.

- Searches for a class annotated with `@SpringBootConfiguration` when nested @ `Configuration` is not used

- Allows custom properties to be specified for a test context via its properties attribute

- Provides support for different webEnvironment modes, including the ability to start a fully running web server listening on a random port

- Registers a TestRestTemplate and /or WebTestClient for use in web tests that are using a fully running web server

Some capabilities of @SpringBootTest won't be obvious now, but they will be when you start writing more complex tests.

Another thing you should know about @SpringBootTest is that it is annotated with @ExtendWith(SpringExtension.class) and thus by default integrates the Spring TestContext Framework into JUnit 5's Jupiter programming model. This obviously means you won't be able to write Junit 4 tests in a class annotated with @SpringBootTest, because the Junit 4 annotations won't be recognized.

Listing 4-64 shows a Spring Boot test class that runs its test in the context defined by the WithBeansApplication Spring Boot class.

Listing 4-64. Spring Boot Test Class

```
package com.apress.prospring6.four.boot.beans

import com.apress.prospring6.two.decoupled.MessageProvider
import com.apress.prospring6.two.decoupled.MessageRenderer
import org.junit.jupiter.api.Assertions.*
// other import statements omitted

@SpringBootTest
class BeansTest {
    @Autowired
    var context: ApplicationContext? = null

    @Autowired
    var messageRenderer: MessageRenderer? = null

    @Autowired
    var messageProvider: MessageProvider? = null

    @Test
    fun contextLoaded() {
        assertNotNull(context)
    }

    @Test
    fun rendererTest() {
        assertAll("messageTest",
            Executable { assertNotNull(messageRenderer) },
            Executable { assertNotNull(messageProvider) },
            Executable {
                assertEquals(
                    messageProvider,
                    messageRenderer!!.messageProvider
                )
```

```
        }
    )
    messageRenderer!!.render()
  }
}
```

If you noticed in Listing 4-64 that the WithBeansApplication class is not mentioned anywhere, you might be asking, *How does Spring Boot know to use that class?* Well, remember that @SpringBootTest searches for a class annotated with @SpringBootConfiguration. The search starts in the package where the test class is defined. So if the test class is defined in package com.apress.prospring6.four.beans, then Spring Boot looks for a configuration class in this package and, if it is not found, continues searching in the packages within it.

However, if you want to make it really obvious which Spring Boot configuration class is being used, you can use the classes attribute, such as

```
@SpringBootTest(classes = {WithBeansApplication.class})
```

This attribute can be used to add additional test configuration classes, to override beans with scoped variants. Also, @ActiveProfiles is supported on @SpringBootTest annotated classes too, and it is particularly useful when testing applications that involve database access, as we'll see from **Chapter 6** onward.

A Spring Boot test class is nothing but a test class, so running it does not require anything else than right-clicking in your editor and selecting Run or Debug, depending on your overall intentions.

💡 Since our technical reviewers insists, we will add this note: test classes and methods specifically can be run from the command line, using Maven or Gradle commands. This however is not relevant for this book, since the book is focused on the Spring Framework, so if you find yourself in need of doing that, the official documentation for the two build tools used to organize this project should suffice.

Summary

In this chapter, you saw a wide range of Spring-specific features that complement the core IoC capabilities. You saw how to hook into the life cycle of a bean and to make it aware of the Spring environment. We introduced FactoryBeans as a solution for IoC, enabling a wider set of classes. We also showed how you can use PropertyEditors to simplify application configuration and to remove the need for artificial String-typed properties. We showed you more than one way to define beans using annotations, Java/Kotlin configuration, and Groovy. Moreover, we finished with an in-depth look at some additional features offered by ApplicationContext, including i18n, event publication, and resource access.

We also covered features such as profiles support, and the environment and property source abstraction layer. Finally, we discussed various testing styles and testing Spring applications.

The icing on the cake was how to use Spring Boot to configure beans and boot up your application as soon as possible and with little effort.

So far, we have covered the main concepts of the Spring Framework and its features as a DI container, as well as other services that the core Spring Framework provides. In the next chapter and onward, we discuss using Spring in specific areas such as AOP, data access, transaction support, and web application support.

CHAPTER 5

■ ■ ■

Spring AOP

Besides dependency injection (DI), another core feature that the Spring Framework offers is support for aspect-oriented programming (AOP). AOP is often referred to as a tool for implementing crosscutting concerns. The term *crosscutting concerns* refers to logic in an application that cannot be decomposed from the rest of the application and may result in code duplication and tight coupling. By using AOP for modularizing individual pieces of logic, known as *concerns*, you can apply them to many parts of an application without duplicating the code or creating hard dependencies. Logging and security are typical examples of crosscutting concerns that are present in many applications. Consider an application that logs the start and end of every method for debugging purposes. You will probably refactor the logging code into a special class, but you still have to call methods on that class twice per method in your application in order to perform the logging. Using AOP, you can simply specify that you want the methods on your logging class to be invoked before and after each method call in your application.

It is important to understand that AOP complements object-oriented programming (OOP), rather than competing with it. OOP is very good at solving a wide variety of problems that we, as programmers, encounter. However, if you look at the logging example again, it is obvious to see where OOP is lacking when it comes to implementing crosscutting logic on a large scale. Using AOP on its own to develop an entire application is practically impossible, given that AOP functions on top of OOP. Likewise, although it is certainly possible to develop entire applications by using OOP, you can work smarter by employing AOP to solve certain problems that involve crosscutting logic.

The AOP framework is one of the core components of Spring, and important functionalities such as transactional data management and security would not be possible without it.

This chapter covers the following topics:

- *AOP basics*: Before discussing Spring's AOP implementation, we cover the basics of AOP as a technology. Most of the concepts covered in the "AOP Concepts" section are not specific to Spring and can be found in any AOP implementation. If you are already familiar with another AOP implementation, feel free to skip the "AOP Concepts" section.

- *Types of AOP*: There are two distinct types of AOP: static and dynamic. In static AOP, like that provided by AspectJ's[1] compile-time weaving mechanisms, the crosscutting logic is applied to your code at compile time, and you cannot change it without modifying the code and recompiling. With dynamic AOP, such as Spring AOP, crosscutting logic is applied dynamically at runtime. This allows you to make changes to the AOP configuration without having to recompile the application. These types of AOP are complementary, and, when used together, they form a powerful combination that you can use in your applications.

---

[1] https://www.eclipse.org/aspectj

© Peter Späth, Iuliana Cosmina, Rob Harrop, Chris Schaefer 2023
P. Späth et al., *Pro Spring 6 with Kotlin*, https://doi.org/10.1007/978-1-4842-9557-1_5

- *Spring AOP architecture*: Spring AOP is only a subset of the full AOP feature set found in other implementations such as AspectJ. In this chapter, we take a high-level look at which features are present in Spring, how they are implemented, and why some features are excluded from the Spring implementation.

- *Proxies in Spring AOP*: Proxies are a huge part of how Spring AOP works, and you must understand them to get the most out of Spring AOP. In this chapter, we look at the two kinds of proxy: the JDK dynamic proxy and the CGLIB proxy. We look at the different scenarios in which Spring uses each proxy, the performance of the two proxy types, and some simple guidelines to follow in your application to get the most from Spring AOP.

- *Using Spring AOP*: In this chapter, we present some practical examples of AOP usage. We start off with a detailed description of the AOP features that are available in Spring, complete with examples.

- *Advanced use of pointcuts*: We explore the `ComposablePointcut` and `ControlFlowPointcut` classes, introductions, and appropriate techniques you should employ when using pointcuts in your application.

- *AOP framework services*: The Spring Framework fully supports configuring AOP transparently and declaratively. We look at two ways (the `ProxyFactoryBean` class, and @AspectJ-style annotations) to inject declaratively defined AOP proxies into your application objects as collaborators, thus making your application completely unaware that it is working with advised objects.

- *Integrating AspectJ*: AspectJ is a fully featured AOP implementation. The main difference between AspectJ and Spring AOP is that AspectJ applies advice to target objects via weaving (either compile-time or load-time weaving), while Spring AOP is based on proxies. The feature set of AspectJ is much greater than that of Spring AOP, but it is much more complicated to use than Spring. AspectJ is a good solution when you find that Spring AOP lacks a feature you need.

AOP Concepts

As with most technologies, AOP comes with its own specific set of concepts and terms, and it's important to understand what they mean. The following are the core concepts of AOP:

- *Joinpoints*: A joinpoint is a well-defined point during the execution of your application. Typical examples of joinpoints include a call to a method, the method invocation itself, class initialization, and object instantiation. Joinpoints define the points in your application at which you can insert additional logic using AOP.

- *Advice*: The code that is executed at a particular joinpoint is the advice, defined by a method in your class. There are many types of advice, such as *before advice*, which executes before the joinpoint, and *after advice*, which executes after the joinpoint.

- *Pointcuts*: A pointcut is a collection of joinpoints that you use to define when advice should be executed. By creating pointcuts, you gain fine-grained control over how you apply advice to the components in your application. As mentioned previously, a typical joinpoint is a method invocation, or the collection of all method invocations in a particular class. Often you can compose pointcuts in complex relationships to further constrain when advice is executed.

- *Aspects*: An aspect is the combination of advice and pointcuts encapsulated in a class. This combination results in a definition of the logic that should be included in the application and where it should execute

- *Weaving*: This is the process of inserting aspects into the application code at the appropriate point. For compile-time AOP solutions, this weaving is generally done at build time. Likewise, for runtime AOP solutions, the weaving process is executed dynamically at runtime. AspectJ supports another weaving mechanism called *loadtime weaving (LTW)*, in which it intercepts the underlying JVM class loader and provides weaving to the bytecode when it is being loaded by the class loader.

- *Target*: An object whose execution flow is modified by an AOP process is referred to as the target object. Often you see the target object referred to as the *advised object*.

- *Introduction*: This is the process by which you can modify the structure of an object by introducing additional methods or fields to it. You can use introduction AOP to make any object implement a specific interface without needing the object's class to implement that interface explicitly.

Don't worry if you find these concepts confusing; this will all become clear when you see some examples. Also, be aware that you are shielded from many of these concepts in Spring AOP, and some are not relevant because of Spring's choice of implementation. We will discuss each of these features in the context of Spring as we progress through the chapter.

Types of AOP

As previously mentioned, there are two distinct types of AOP: static and dynamic. The difference between them is really the point at which the weaving process occurs and how this process is achieved.

Static AOP

In static AOP, the weaving process forms another step in the build process for an application. In JVM terms, you achieve the weaving process in a static AOP implementation by modifying the actual bytecode of your application, changing and extending the application code as necessary. This is a well-performing way of achieving the weaving process because the end result is just JVM bytecode, and you do not perform any special tricks at runtime to determine when advice should be executed. The drawback of this mechanism is that any modifications you make to the aspects, even if you simply want to add another joinpoint, require you to recompile the entire application. AspectJ's compile-time weaving is an excellent example of a static AOP implementation.

Dynamic AOP

Dynamic AOP implementations, such as Spring AOP, differ from static AOP implementations in that the weaving process is performed dynamically at runtime. How this is achieved is implementation-dependent, but as you will see, Spring's approach is to create proxies for all advised objects, allowing for advice to be invoked as required. The drawback of dynamic AOP is that, typically, it does not perform as well as static AOP, but the performance is steadily increasing. The major benefit of dynamic AOP implementations is the ease with which you can modify the entire aspect set of an application without needing to recompile the main application code.

Choosing an AOP Type

Choosing whether to use static or dynamic AOP is quite a hard decision. Both have their own benefits, and you are not restricted to using only one type. In general, static AOP implementations have been around longer and tend to have more feature-rich implementations, with a greater number of available joinpoints.

Typically, if performance is absolutely critical or you need an AOP feature that is not implemented in Spring, you will want to use AspectJ. In most other cases, Spring AOP is ideal. Keep in mind that many AOP-based solutions such as transaction management are already provided for you by Spring, so check the framework capabilities before rolling your own! As always, let the requirements of your application drive your choice of AOP implementation, and don't restrict yourself to a single implementation if a combination of technologies would better suit your application. In general, Spring AOP is less complex than AspectJ, so it tends to be an ideal first choice.

 You can't use AspectJ compile-time weaving with Kotlin. AspectJ doesn't understand Kotlin.

AOP in Spring

Spring's AOP implementation can be viewed as two logical parts. The first part is the AOP core, which provides fully decoupled, purely programmatic AOP functionality (also known as the Spring AOP API). The second part of the AOP implementation is the set of framework services that make AOP easier to use in your applications. On top of this, other components of Spring, such as the transaction manager and EJB helper classes, provide AOP-based services to simplify the development of your application.

The AOP Alliance

The AOP Alliance[2] is a joint effort among representatives of many open source AOP projects to define a standard set of interfaces for AOP implementations. Wherever applicable, Spring uses the AOP Alliance interfaces rather than defining its own. This allows you to reuse certain advice across multiple AOP implementations that support the AOP Alliance interfaces.

Spring AOP Architecture

Spring AOP is implemented in pure Java. There is no need for a special compilation process. The core architecture of Spring AOP is based on *proxies*. An advised instance of a class is the result of a *ProxyFactory* creating a proxy instance of that class with all the aspects woven into the proxy. *ProxyFactory* can be used *manually* in a purely programmatic approach to creating AOP proxies. For the most part, you don't need to use this in your application; instead, you can rely on the declarative AOP configuration mechanisms provided by Spring (the *ProxyFactoryBean* class, the aop namespace [when using XML], and @AspectJ-style annotations) to take advantage of declarative proxy creation. However, it is important to understand how proxy creation works, so this chapter aims to provide a very solid knowledge base.

---

[2] https://aopalliance.sourceforge.net

At runtime, Spring analyzes the crosscutting concerns defined for the beans in `ApplicationContext` and generates proxy beans (which wrap the underlying target bean) dynamically. Instead of calling the target bean directly, callers are injected with the proxied bean. The proxy bean then analyzes the running condition (that is, joinpoint, pointcut, or advice) and weaves in the appropriate advice accordingly. Figure 5-1 shows a high-level view of a Spring AOP proxy in action.

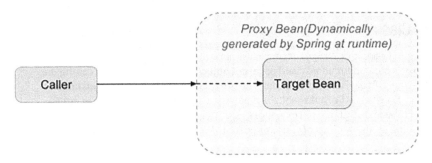

Figure 5-1. *Spring AOP proxy in action*

Internally, Spring has two proxy implementations:

- JDK dynamic proxies
- CGLIB proxies

By default, when the target object to be advised implements an interface, Spring will use a JVM dynamic proxy to create proxy instances of the target. However, when the advised target object doesn't implement an interface (for example, it's a concrete class), CGLIB will be used for proxy instance creation. One major reason is that the JVM dynamic proxy supports only the proxying of interfaces. We discuss proxies in detail in the section "Understanding Proxies."

Joinpoints in Spring

One of the more noticeable simplifications in Spring AOP is that it supports only one joinpoint type: **method invocation**. At first glance, this might seem like a severe limitation if you are familiar with other AOP implementations such as AspectJ, which supports many more joinpoints, but in fact this makes Spring more accessible.

The method invocation joinpoint is by far the most useful joinpoint available, and using it, you can achieve many of the tasks that make AOP useful in day-to-day programming. Remember that if you need to advise some code at a joinpoint other than a method invocation, you can always use Spring and AspectJ together.

Aspects in Spring

In Spring AOP, an aspect is represented by an instance of a class that implements the `Advisor` interface. Spring provides convenience `Advisor` implementations that you can reuse in your applications, thus removing the need for you to create custom `Advisor` implementations. There are two subinterfaces of `org.springframework.aop.Advisor`:

- `org.springframework.aop.PointcutAdvisor`
- `org.springframework.aop.IntroductionAdvisor`

The `PointcutAdvisor` interface is implemented by all `Advisor` implementations that use pointcuts to control the advice applied to joinpoints. In Spring, introductions are treated as special kinds of advice, and by using the `IntroductionAdvisor` interface, you can control those classes to which an introduction applies.

We discuss `PointcutAdvisor` implementations in detail in the upcoming section "Advisors and Pointcuts in Spring."

The `ProxyFactory` Class

The `org.springframework.aop.framework.ProxyFactory` class controls the weaving and proxy creation process in Spring AOP. A proxy is created for an **advised** or **target object**, which can be set by calling the `setTarget(..)` method. Internally, `ProxyFactory` delegates the proxy creation process to an instance of `org.springframework.aop.framework.DefaultAopProxyFactory`, which in turn delegates to either `org.springframework.aop.framework.CglibAopProxy` or `org.springframework.aop.framework.JdkDynamicAopProxy`, depending on the settings of your application. We discuss proxy creation in more detail later in this chapter.

❗ Starting with Spring 4, another implementation was added, `org.springframework.aop.framework.ObjenesisCglibAopProxy`, which extends `CglibAopProxy` to create proxy instances without invoking the constructor of the class. This is useful when a class has constructors with arguments, constructors with side effects, and constructors that throw exceptions.

The `ProxyFactory` class provides an implementation for the `addAdvice(Advice)` method (defined by the `org.springframework.aop.framework.Advised` interface) for cases where you want advice to apply to the invocation of all methods in a class, not just a selection. Internally, `addAdvice(..)` wraps the advice that you pass to it in an instance of `org.springframework.aop.support.DefaultPointcutAdvisor`, which is the standard implementation of `PointcutAdvisor`, and configures it with a pointcut that includes all methods by default. When you want more control over the `Advisor` that is created or when you want to add an introduction to the proxy, create the `org.springframework.aop.Advisor` yourself and use the `addAdvisor()` method of the `ProxyFactory`.

You can use the same `ProxyFactory` instance to create many proxies, each with different aspects. To help with this, `ProxyFactory` has `removeAdvice()` and `removeAdvisor()` methods, which allow you to remove any advice or advisors from the `ProxyFactory` that you previously passed to it. To check whether a `ProxyFactory` has particular advice attached to it, call `adviceIncluded()`, passing in the advice object for which you want to check.

Creating Advice in Spring

Spring supports six flavors of advice, described in Table 5-1.

Table 5-1. *Spring Advice Types*

Advice Name	Interface	Description
Before	org.springframework.aop. BeforeAdvice	Using before advice, you can perform custom processing before a joinpoint executes. A joinpoint in Spring is always a method invocation, which essentially allows you to perform preprocessing before the method executes. The before advice has full access to the target of the method invocation as well as the arguments passed to the method, but it has no control over the execution of the method itself. If the before advice throws an exception, further execution of the interceptor chain (as well as the target method) will be aborted, and the exception will propagate back up the interceptor chain.
After-returning	org.springframework.aop. AfterReturningAdvice	After-returning advice is executed after the method invocation at the joinpoint has finished executing and has returned a value. The after-returning advice has access to the target of the method invocation, the arguments passed to the method, and the return value. Because the method has already executed when the after-returning advice is invoked, it has no control over the method invocation at all. If the target method throws an exception, the after-returning advice will not be run, and the exception will be propagated up to the call stack as usual.
After(finally)	org.springframework.aop. AfterAdvice	After(finally) advice is executed no matter the result of the advised method. The advice is executed even when the advised method fails and an exception is thrown.
Throws	org.springframework.aop. ThrowsAdvice	Throws advice is executed after a method invocation returns, but only if that invocation threw an exception. It is possible for throws advice to catch only specific exceptions, and if you choose to do so, you can access the method that threw the exception, the arguments passed into the invocation, and the target of the invocation.
Around	org.aopalliance.intercept. MethodInterceptor	In Spring, around advice is modeled using the AOP Alliance standard of a method interceptor. Your advice is allowed to execute before and after the method invocation, and you can control the point at which the method invocation is allowed to proceed. You can choose to bypass the method altogether if you want, providing your own implementation of the logic.
Introduction	org.springframework.aop. IntroductionInterceptor	Spring models introductions as special types of interceptors. Using an introduction interceptor, you can specify the implementation for methods that are being introduced by the advice.

Interfaces for Advice

With regard to the `ProxyFactory` class, recall that advice is added to a proxy either directly, by using the `addAdvice(..)` method, or indirectly, by using an `Advisor` implementation with the `addAdvisor(..)` method. The main difference between advice and an advisor is that an advisor carries advice with the associated pointcut, which provides more fine-grained control on which joinpoints the advice will intercept.

With regard to advice, Spring has created a well-defined hierarchy for `Advice` interfaces. This hierarchy is based on the AOP Alliance interfaces and is shown in detail in Figure 5-2.

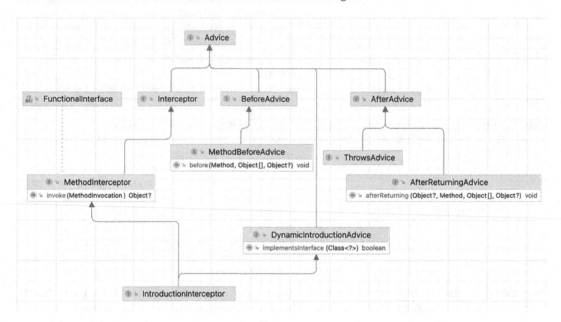

Figure 5-2. *Interfaces for Spring advice types as depicted in IntelliJ IDEA*

This kind of hierarchy has the benefit of not only being sound OO design but also enabling you to deal with advice types generically, such as by using a single `addAdvice(..)` method on the `ProxyFactory`, and you can add new advice types easily without having to modify the `ProxyFactory` class.

Creating Advice Programmatically

As mentioned earlier, *ProxyFactory* can be used *manually* in a purely programmatic approach to creating AOP proxies. An example is in order before switching to the declarative Spring way of doing it. All interfaces listed in Table 5-1 can be implemented to define advices for a desired target. Listing 5-1 shows three such implementations: a before advice, an after advice, and an around advice, each of them implementing the appropriate interfaces.

Listing 5-1. Three Types of Custom Advice

```
package com.apress.prospring6.five.manual

import org.aopalliance.intercept.MethodInterceptor
import org.aopalliance.intercept.MethodInvocation
import org.springframework.aop.AfterReturningAdvice
```

```kotlin
import org.springframework.aop.MethodBeforeAdvice
import org.springframework.util.StopWatch
import java.lang.reflect.Method
// other import statement omitted

internal class SimpleBeforeAdvice : MethodBeforeAdvice {
    @Throws(Throwable::class)
    override fun before(method: Method, args: Array<out Any>, @Nullable target: Any?) {
        LOGGER.info("Before: set up concert hall.")
    }

    companion object {
        private val LOGGER = LoggerFactory.getLogger(SimpleBeforeAdvice::class.java)
    }
}

internal class SimpleAfterAdvice : AfterReturningAdvice {
    @Throws(Throwable::class)
    override fun afterReturning(
        @Nullable returnValue: Any?,
        method: Method,
        args: Array<out Any>,
        @Nullable target: Any?
    ) {
        LOGGER.info("After: offer standing ovation.")
    }

    companion object {
        private val LOGGER = LoggerFactory.getLogger(SimpleAfterAdvice::class.java)
    }
}

internal class SimpleAroundAdvice : MethodInterceptor {
    @Throws(Throwable::class)
    override fun invoke(invocation: MethodInvocation): Any? {
        LOGGER.info("Around: starting timer")
        val sw = StopWatch()
        sw.start(invocation.method.name)
        val returnValue = invocation.proceed()
        sw.stop()
        LOGGER.info("Around: concert duration = {}", sw.totalTimeMillis)
        return returnValue
    }

    companion object {
        private val LOGGER = LoggerFactory.getLogger(SimpleAroundAdvice::class.java)
    }
}
```

SimpleBeforeAdvice, SimpleAfterAdvice, and SimpleAroundAdvice are designed to be used on instances of type Performance. SimpleBeforeAdvice and SimpleAfterAdvice just print log messages, to confirm that the advice was applied. SimpleAroundAdvice is a little bit more complex and uses a StopWatch instance to time the performance. The intercepted method is being called using Java Reflection.

Listing 5-2 depicts the Performance interface and the Concert implementation are depicted.

Listing 5-2. Types of Objects to Apply Advice On

```
// Performance.java
package com.apress.prospring6.five.manual

interface Performance {
    fun execute()
}

// Concert.java
package com.apress.prospring6.five.manual

import org.slf4j.LoggerFactory
import java.time.Duration

open class Concert : Performance {
    override fun execute() {
        LOGGER.info(" ... La la la la laaaa ...")
        try {
            Thread.sleep(Duration.ofMillis(2000).toMillis())
        } catch (_: InterruptedException) {
        }
    }

    companion object {
        private val LOGGER = LoggerFactory.getLogger(Concert::class.java)
    }
}
```

Adding open to all classes and methods (other than those with the override modifier) subject to manipulation or observation via AOP is extremely crucial if you want to use Spring + AOP + Kotlin. If you forget to add open, AOP might silently fail.

Putting advice instances and the target together is easy; we just need to instantiate the ProxyFactory class and set the target and the advice instances as depicted in Listing 5-3.

Listing 5-3. Example Showing Programmatically Creating and Applying Advice on a Target

```
package com.apress.prospring6.five.manual

import org.springframework.aop.framework.ProxyFactory
// other import statements omitted
```

```kotlin
object ManualAdviceDemo {
    @JvmStatic
    fun main(args: Array<String>) {
        val concert = Concert()
        val pf = ProxyFactory()
        with(pf){
            addAdvice(SimpleBeforeAdvice())
            addAdvice(SimpleAfterAdvice())
            addAdvice(SimpleAroundAdvice())
            setTarget(concert)
        }
        val proxy = pf.proxy as Performance
        proxy.execute()
    }
}
```

> ❗ The order of execution of the advice is determined by the advice type, not the order in which they are added to the `ProxyFactory` instance.

The `SimpleBeforeAdvice` prints a message, making sure the concert hall is set up before the concert. The `SimpleAroundAdvice` intercepts the `concert.execute()` method to start the timer before the method execution, to stop it and print the duration after the execution. The `SimpleAfterAdvice` prints a message, making sure there is a standing ovation after the concert.

Running the class in Listing 5-3 prints the log shown in Listing 5-4.

Listing 5-4. Console Output Produced by Executing the `ManualAdviceDemo` Class

```
> Task :chapter05:ManualAdviceDemo.main()
INFO : SimpleBeforeAdvice - Before: set up concert hall.
INFO : SimpleAroundAdvice - Around: starting timer
INFO : Concert -  ... La la la la laaaa ...
INFO : SimpleAroundAdvice - Around: concert duration = 2015
INFO : SimpleAfterAdvice - After: offer standing ovation.
```

The output from calling `execute()` on the proxy object is shown, and it includes the output of the before advice, the first message of the around advice, the actual message printed by the target object—the Concert object—the second message of the around advice, and the output of the after advice. The order of the messages demonstrates that the advices were applied where expected.

You can play around and write your own code samples implementing `org.springframework.aop.AfterAdvice` and `org.springframework.aop.ThrowsAdvice` or check out the examples in the project for this book. Because there is a lot of code duplication, they won't be covered here.

Applying advice this way is not really useful the best way is to declare your bean, and your advice bean and tell Spring how to do it. But before getting there some detailed conclusions about advice use are in order.

A Few Conclusions

Before advice is one of the most useful advice types available in Spring. This advice can modify the arguments passed to a method and can prevent the method from executing by raising an exception. This is most useful for secure implementations, where a before advice checks user credentials before allowing the method invocation to proceed.

After-returning advice is executed after the method invocation at the joinpoint returns. Given that the method has already executed, you can't change the arguments that are passed to it. Although you can read these arguments, you can't change the execution path, and you can't prevent the method from executing. These restrictions are expected; what might not be expected, however, is that **you cannot modify the return value in the after-returning advice**. When using after-returning advice, you are limited to adding processing. Although after-returning advice cannot modify the return value of a method invocation, it can throw an exception that can be sent up the stack instead of the return value.

Throws advice is similar to after-returning advice in that it executes after the joinpoint, which is always a method invocation, but throws advice executes only if the method throws an exception. Throws advice is also similar to after-returning advice in that it has little control over program execution. If you are using throws advice, you can't choose to ignore the exception that was raised and return a value for the method instead. **The only modification you can make to the program flow is to change the type of exception that is thrown.** This is quite a powerful concept and can make application development much simpler. Consider a situation where you have an API that throws an array of poorly defined exceptions. Using throws advice, you can advise all classes in that API and reclassify the exception hierarchy into something more manageable and descriptive. Of course, you can also use throws advice to provide centralized error logging across your application, thus reducing the amount of error-logging code that is spread across your application. After-throwing advice is useful in a variety of situations; it allows you to reclassify entire exception hierarchies as well as build centralized exception logging for your application. We have found that after-throwing advice is particularly useful when we are debugging a live application because it allows us to add extra logging code without needing to modify the application's code.

Around advice functions like a combination of before and after advice, with two differences:

- You can modify the return value.

- You can prevent the method from executing.

This means that by using around advice, you can essentially replace the entire implementation of a method with new code. Around advice in Spring is modeled as an interceptor using the `MethodInterceptor` interface as shown in the example in this section. There are many uses for around advice, and you will find that many features of Spring are created by using method interceptors, such as the remote proxy support and the transaction management features. Method interception is also a good mechanism for profiling the execution of your application, and the example shown, by timing the execution of the target method, does exactly that—records the duration this method takes to execute, enabling you to study the values to make a decision if the method should be optimized or not.

Choosing an Advice Type

In general, choosing an advice type is driven by the requirements of your application, but you should choose the most specific advice type for your need. That is to say, don't use around advice when before advice will do. In most cases, around advice can accomplish everything that the other three advice types can, but it may be overkill for what you are trying to achieve. By using the most specific type of advice, you are making the intention of your code clearer, and you are also reducing the possibility of errors. Consider an advice that counts method calls. When you are using before advice, all you need to code is the counter, but with around advice, you need to remember to invoke the method and return the value to the caller. These small things can allow spurious errors to creep into your application. By keeping the advice type as focused as possible, you reduce the scope for errors.

Advisors and Pointcuts in Spring

Thus far, all the examples you have seen have used the ProxyFactory class. This class provides a simple way of obtaining and configuring AOP proxy instances in custom user code. The ProxyFactory.addAdvice() method is used to configure advice for a proxy. This method delegates to addAdvisor() behind the scenes, creating an instance of org.springframework.aop.support.DefaultPointcutAdvisor and configuring it with a pointcut that points to all methods. In this way, the advice is deemed to apply to all methods on the target. In some cases, such as when you are using AOP for logging purposes, this may be desirable, but in other cases you may want to limit the methods to which the advice applies.

Of course, you could simply perform the checking in the advice itself that the method being advised is the correct one, but this approach has several drawbacks. First, hard-coding the list of acceptable methods into the advice reduces the advice's reusability. By using pointcuts, you can configure the methods to which an advice applies, without needing to put this code inside the advice; this clearly increases the reuse value of the advice. Other drawbacks with hard-coding the list of methods into the advice are performance related. To inspect the method being advised in the advice, you need to perform the check each time any method on the target is invoked. This clearly reduces the performance of your application. When you use pointcuts, the check is performed once for each method, and the results are cached for later use. The other performance-related drawback of not using pointcuts to restrict the list-advised methods is that Spring can make optimizations for unadvised methods when creating a proxy, which results in faster invocations on unadvised methods. These optimizations are covered in greater detail when we discuss proxies later in the chapter.

We strongly recommend that you avoid the temptation to hard-code method checks into your advice and instead use pointcuts wherever possible to govern the applicability of advice to methods on the target. That said, in some cases it is necessary to hard-code the checks into your advice. Consider the earlier example of the after-returning advice designed to catch weak keys generated by the KeyGenerator class. This kind of advice is closely coupled to the class it is advising, and it is wise to check inside the advice to ensure that it is applied to the correct type. We refer to this coupling between advice and target as *target affinity*. In general, you should use pointcuts when your advice has little or no target affinity. That is, it can apply to any type or a wide range of types. When your advice has strong target affinity, try to check that the advice is being used correctly in the advice itself; this helps reduce head-scratching errors when advice is misused. We also recommend you avoid advising methods needlessly. As you will see, this results in a noticeable drop in invocation speed that can have a large impact on the overall performance of your application.

The Pointcut Interface

Pointcuts in Spring are created by implementing the org.springframework.aop.Pointcut interface, which is shown in Listing 5-5 (full code is available on the GitHub Spring Framework repository[3]).

Listing 5-5. Spring Pointcut Interface

```
package org.springframework.aop;

public interface Pointcut {
    ClassFilter getClassFilter();

    MethodMatcher getMethodMatcher();

    // some non-relevant code missing
}
```

---

[3] https://github.com/spring-projects/spring-framework/blob/main/spring-aop/src/main/java/org/springframework/aop/Pointcut.java

As you can see from this code, the Pointcut interface defines two methods, getClassFilter() and getMethodMatcher(), which return instances of ClassFilter and MethodMatcher, respectively. Obviously, if you choose to implement the Pointcut interface, you will need to implement these methods. Thankfully, as you will see in the next section, this is usually unnecessary because Spring provides a selection of Pointcut implementations that cover most, if not all, of your use cases.

When determining whether a Pointcut applies to a particular method, Spring first checks to see whether the Pointcut interface applies to the method's class by using the ClassFilter instance returned by Pointcut.getClassFilter(). The ClassFilter functional interface is shown in Listing 5-6 (full code is available on the GitHub Spring Framework repository[4]).

Listing 5-6. Spring ClassFilter Interface

```
org.springframework.aop;

@FunctionalInterface
public interface ClassFilter {
    boolean matches(Class<?> clazz);
    // some non-relevant code missing
}
```

As you can see, the ClassFilter functional interface defines a single abstract method, matches(), that is passed an instance of Class that represents the class to be checked. As you have no doubt determined, the matches() method returns true if the pointcut applies to the class and returns false otherwise.

The MethodMatcher interface is more complex than the ClassFilter interface, as shown Listing 5-7 (full code is available on the GitHub Spring Framework repository[5]).

Listing 5-7. Spring MethodMatcher Interface

```
package org.springframework.aop;

import java.lang.reflect.Method

public interface MethodMatcher {

    boolean matches(Method method, Class<?> targetClass);
    boolean isRuntime();
    boolean matches(Method method, Class<?> targetClass, Object... args);
    // some non-relevant code missing
}
```

Spring supports two types of MethodMatcher, static and dynamic, which are determined by the return value of isRuntime(). Before using MethodMatcher, Spring calls isRuntime() to determine whether MethodMatcher is static, indicated by a return value of false, or dynamic, indicated by a return value of true.

---

[4] https://github.com/spring-projects/spring-framework/blob/main/spring-aop/src/main/java/org/springframework/aop/ClassFilter.java
[5] https://github.com/spring-projects/spring-framework/blob/main/spring-aop/src/main/java/org/springframework/aop/MethodMatcher.java

For a static pointcut, Spring calls the `matches(Method, Class<T>)` method of the `MethodMatcher` once for every method on the target, caching the return value for subsequent invocations of those methods. In this way, the check for method applicability is performed only once for each method, and subsequent invocations of a method do not result in an invocation of `matches()`.

With dynamic pointcuts, Spring still performs a static check by using `matches(Method, Class<T>)` the first time a method is invoked to determine the overall applicability of a method. However, in addition to this and provided that the static check returned `true`, Spring performs a further check for each invocation of a method by using the `matches(Method, Class<T>, Object[])` method. In this way, a dynamic `MethodMatcher` can determine whether a pointcut should apply based on a particular invocation of a method, not just on the method itself. For example, a pointcut needs to be applied only when the argument is an `Integer` with a value larger than 100. In this case, the `matches(Method,Class<T>, Object[])` method can be coded to perform further checking on the argument for each invocation.

Clearly, static pointcuts perform much better than dynamic pointcuts because they avoid the need for an additional check per invocation. Dynamic pointcuts provide a greater level of flexibility for deciding whether to apply advice. In general, we recommend you use static pointcuts wherever you can. However, in cases where your advice adds substantial overhead, it may be wise to avoid any unnecessary invocations of your advice by using a dynamic pointcut.

In general, you rarely create your own `Pointcut` implementations from scratch because Spring provides abstract base classes for both static and dynamic pointcuts. We will look at these base classes, along with other `Pointcut` implementations, over the next few sections.

Available `Pointcut` Implementations

As of version 4.0, Spring provides eight main implementations of the `Pointcut` interface: two abstract classes intended as convenience classes for creating static and dynamic pointcuts, and six concrete classes, one for each of the following:

- Composing multiple pointcuts together

- Handling control flow pointcuts

- Performing simple name-based matching

- Defining pointcuts using regular expressions

- Defining pointcuts using AspectJ expressions

- Defining pointcuts that look for specific annotations at the class or method level

Table 5-2 summarizes the main eight `Pointcut` interface implementations.

Table 5-2. *Summary of Spring* `Pointcut` *Implementations*

Implementation Class	Description
`org.springframework.aop.support.annotation.AnnotationMatchingPointcut`	This implementation looks for a specific Kotlin annotation on a class or method.
`org.springframework.aop.aspectj.AspectJExpressionPointcut`	This implementation uses an AspectJ weaver to evaluate a pointcut expression in AspectJ syntax.
`org.springframework.aop.support.ComposablePointcut`	The `ComposablePointcut` class is used to compose two or more pointcuts together with operations such as `union()` and `intersection()`.
`org.springframework.aop.support.ControlFlowPointcut`	`ControlFlowPointcut` is a special-case pointcut that matches all methods within the control flow of another method; that is, any method that is invoked either directly or indirectly as the result of another method being invoked.
`org.springframework.aop.support.DynamicMethodMatcherPointcut`	This implementation is intended as a base class for building dynamic pointcuts.
`org.springframework.aop.support.JdkRegexpMethodPointcut`	This implementation allows you to define pointcuts using JDK regular expression support.
`org.springframework.aop.support.NameMatchMethodPointcut`	Using `NameMatchMethodPointcut`, you can create a pointcut that performs simple matching against a list of method names.
`org.springframework.aop.support.StaticMethodMatcherPointcut`	The `StaticMethodMatcherPointcut` class is intended as a base for building static pointcuts.

Figure 5-3 shows the Pointcut Spring hierarchy.

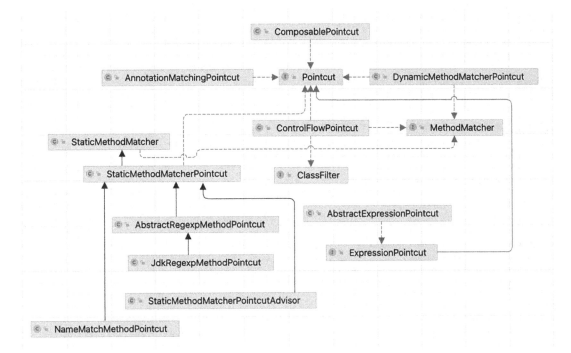

Figure 5-3. *Pointcut implementation classes represented as an UML diagram in IntelliJ IDEA*

Using DefaultPointcutAdvisor

Before you can use any Pointcut implementation, you must first create an instance of the Advisor interface, or more specifically a PointcutAdvisor interface. Remember from our earlier discussions that Advisor is Spring's representation of an aspect (see the earlier section "Aspects in Spring"), which is a coupling of advice and pointcuts that governs which methods should be advised and how they should be advised. Spring provides a number of implementations of PointcutAdvisor, but for now we will concern ourselves with just one, DefaultPointcutAdvisor. This is a simple PointcutAdvisor for associating a single Pointcut with a single Advice.

Using StaticMethodMatcherPointcut

In this section, we will create a simple static pointcut by extending the abstract StaticMethodMatcherPointcut class. Since the StaticMethodMatcherPointcut class extends the StaticMethodMatcher class (an abstract class too), which implements the MethodMatcher interface, you are required to implement the method matches(Method, Class<?>). The rest of the Pointcut implementation is handled automatically. Although this is the only method you are required to implement (when extending the StaticMethodMatcherPointcut class), you may want to override the getClassFilter() method as shown in the example Listing 5-8 to ensure that only methods of the correct type get advised.

For this example, we have two classes, GoodGuitarist and GreatGuitarist, with identical methods defined in both, which are implementations of the method in interface Singer. They are depicted together with the SimpleAroundAdvice designed to wrap around instances of these types.

Listing 5-8. Classes GoodGuitarist and GreatGuitarist to Be Used for Showing StaticMethodMatcherPointcut Usage

```kotlin
package com.apress.prospring6.two.common
// import statements omitted

package com.apress.prospring6.five.common

import org.slf4j.LoggerFactory

interface Singer {
    fun sing()
}

open class GoodGuitarist : Singer {
        override fun sing() {
                LOGGER.info("Head on your heart, arms around me")
        }

        companion object {
                private val LOGGER = LoggerFactory.getLogger(GoodGuitarist::class.java)
        }
}

open class GreatGuitarist : Singer {
        override fun sing() {
                LOGGER.info("You've got my soul in your hand")
        }

        companion object {
                private val LOGGER = LoggerFactory.getLogger(GreatGuitarist::class.java)
        }
}

class SimpleAroundAdvice : MethodInterceptor {
    @Throws(Throwable::class)
    override fun invoke(invocation: MethodInvocation): Any? {
        LOGGER.debug(">> Invoking " + invocation.method.name)
        val retVal = invocation.proceed()
        LOGGER.debug(">> Done")
        return retVal
    }

    companion object {
        private val LOGGER = LoggerFactory.getLogger(SimpleAroundAdvice::class.java)
    }
}
```

With this example, we want to be able to create a proxy of both classes by using the same DefaultPointcutAdvisor but have the advice apply only to the sing() method of the GoodGuitarist class.

To do this, we created the SimpleStaticPointcut class as shown in Listing 5-9, together with the class used to test it.

Listing 5-9. StaticMethodMatcherPointcut Implementation

```
package com.apress.prospring6.five.pointcut

import org.aopalliance.aop.Advice
import org.springframework.aop.Advisor
import org.springframework.aop.ClassFilter
import org.springframework.aop.Pointcut
import org.springframework.aop.framework.ProxyFactory
import org.springframework.aop.support.DefaultPointcutAdvisor
import org.springframework.aop.support.StaticMethodMatcherPointcut
import java.lang.reflect.Method;
// other static imports omitted

class SimpleStaticPointcut : StaticMethodMatcherPointcut() {
    override fun matches(method: Method, cls: Class<*>): Boolean {
        return "sing" == method.name
    }

    override fun getClassFilter(): ClassFilter {
        return ClassFilter { cls: Class<*> -> cls == GoodGuitarist::class.java }
    }
}

object StaticPointcutDemo {
    @JvmStatic
    fun main(args: Array<String>) {
        val johnMayer = GoodGuitarist()
        val ericClapton = GreatGuitarist()
        val proxyOne: Singer
        val proxyTwo: Singer
        val pc: Pointcut = SimpleStaticPointcut()
        val advice: Advice = SimpleAroundAdvice()
        val advisor: Advisor = DefaultPointcutAdvisor(pc, advice)
        var pf = ProxyFactory()
        pf.addAdvisor(advisor)
        pf.setTarget(johnMayer)
        proxyOne = pf.proxy as Singer
        pf = ProxyFactory()
        pf.addAdvisor(advisor)
        pf.setTarget(ericClapton)
        proxyTwo = pf.proxy as Singer
        proxyOne.sing()
        proxyTwo.sing()
    }
}
```

Notice that the getClassFilter() method was overridden to return a ClassFilter instance whose matches() method returns true only for the GoodGuitarist class. With this static pointcut, we are saying that only methods of the GoodGuitarist class will be matched, and furthermore, only the sing() method of that class is to be matched.

The main(..) method creates an instance of DefaultPointcutAdvisor by using the SimpleAroundAdvice and SimpleStaticPointcut classes. Also, because both classes (GoodGuitarist and GreatGuitarist) implement the same interface, you can see that the proxies can be created based on the interface, not on the concrete classes. Notice that the DefaultPointcutAdvisor instance is then used to create two proxies: one for an instance of GoodGuitarist and one for an instance of EricClapton. Finally, the sing() method is invoked on the two proxies. Running this example results in the output shown in Listing 5-10.

Listing 5-10. StaticMethodMatcherPointcut Example Output

```
DEBUG: SimpleAroundAdvice - >> Invoking sing
INFO : GoodGuitarist - Head on your heart, arms around me
DEBUG: SimpleAroundAdvice - >> Done

INFO : GreatGuitarist - You've got my soul in your hand
```

As you can see, the only method for which SimpleAroundAdvice was actually invoked was the sing() method for the GoodGuitarist class, exactly as expected. Restricting the methods to which advice applies is quite simple and, as you will see when we discuss proxy options, is key to getting the best performance out of your application.

Using DynamicMethodMatcherPointcut

Creating a dynamic pointcut is not much different from creating a static one, so for this example we will create a dynamic pointcut for the same classes we did previously, but we also need a method with arguments, to use this type of Pointcut. The easiest way to do this is to enrich the Singer interface with a default method, to not affect the other implementations. To match the context of this example, let's add a sing(String key) method that receives the value of the key for the singer to sing in. The implementation of the Singer interface is shown in Listing 5-11.

⚠️ Adding default implementations to interfaces has been introduced for compatibility reasons. We use it here for demonstration purposes only. Using default implementations is urgently discouraged in your code for any other use than writing frameworks or extending legacy code. Interfaces *describe* functionalities, whereas classes *implement* them.

Listing 5-11. Enriched Singer Interface

```
package com.apress.prospring6.five.common

import org.slf4j.Logger
import org.slf4j.LoggerFactory

interface Singer {
```

```
    fun sing()

    fun sing(key: String?) {
        LOGGER.info("Singing in the key of {}", key)
    }

    fun rest() {}

    companion object {
        val LOGGER = LoggerFactory.getLogger(Singer::class.java)
    }
}
```

Listing 5-12 shows the DynamicMethodMatcherPointcut implementation.

Listing 5-12. SimpleDynamicPointcut Implementation

```
package com.apress.prospring6.five.pointcut

import com.apress.prospring6.five.common.GoodGuitarist
import org.springframework.aop.ClassFilter
import org.springframework.aop.support.DynamicMethodMatcherPointcut
import java.lang.reflect.Method

internal class SimpleDynamicPointcut : DynamicMethodMatcherPointcut() {
    override fun getClassFilter(): ClassFilter {
        return ClassFilter { cls: Class<*> -> cls == GoodGuitarist::class.java }
    }

    override fun matches(method: Method, targetClass: Class<*>): Boolean {
        logger.debug("Static check for " + method.name)
        return "sing" == method.name
    }

    override fun matches(method: Method, targetClass: Class<*>, vararg args: Any):
            Boolean {
        logger.debug("Dynamic check for " + method.name)
        if (args.size == 0) {
            return false
        }
        val key = args[0] as String
        return key.equals("C", ignoreCase = true)
    }

    companion object {
        private val logger = LoggerFactory.getLogger(SimpleDynamicPointcut::class.java)
    }
}
```

As you can see from Listing 5-12, we override the getClassFilter() method in a similar manner as in the previous section. This removes the need to check the class in the method-matching methods, which is something that is especially important for the dynamic check. Although only the dynamic check is required, we implement the static check as well. The reason for this is that we know the sing() method (the one without arguments) will not be advised. Indicating this by using the static check, Spring never has to perform a dynamic check for this method. This is because when the static check method is implemented, Spring will first check against it, and if the checking result is not a match, Spring will stop doing any further dynamic checking. Moreover, the result of the static check will be cached for better performance. If the static check is not implemented, Spring performs a dynamic check each time the sing({key}) method is invoked.

As a recommended practice, perform the class checking in the getClassFilter() method, the method checking in the matches(Method, Class<?>) method, and the argument checking in the matches(Method,Class<?>, Object[]) method. This will make your pointcut much easier to understand and maintain, and performance will be better too.

In the matches(Method, Class<?>, Object[]) method, you can see that we return false if the value of the String argument passed to the sing({key}) method is not equal to "C"; otherwise, we return true. Note that in the dynamic check, we know that we are dealing with a method named sing because no other method makes it past the static check. In Listing 5-13, you can see the test class used to test this pointcut.

Listing 5-13. DynamicPointcutDemo Class to Test the Dynamic Pointcut

```kotlin
package com.apress.prospring6.five.pointcut
import org.springframework.aop.Advisor
import org.springframework.aop.framework.ProxyFactory
import org.springframework.aop.support.DefaultPointcutAdvisor
// other import statements omitted

object DynamicPointcutDemo {
    @JvmStatic
    fun main(args: Array<String>) {
        val target = GoodGuitarist()
        val advisor: Advisor = DefaultPointcutAdvisor(SimpleDynamicPointcut(),
            SimpleAroundAdvice())
        val pf = ProxyFactory()
        pf.setTarget(target)
        pf.addAdvisor(advisor)
        val proxy = pf.proxy as Singer
        proxy.sing("C")
        proxy.sing("c")
        proxy.sing("E")
        proxy.sing()
    }
}
```

Notice that we have used the same advice class as in the static pointcut example. However, in this example, only the first two calls to sing({key}) should be advised. The dynamic check prevents the third call to sing("E") from being advised, and the static check prevents the sing() method from being advised. Running this example yields the output in Listing 5-14.

Listing 5-14. DynamicPointcutDemo Output

```
DEBUG: SimpleDynamicPointcut - Static check for sing
DEBUG: SimpleDynamicPointcut - Static check for toString
DEBUG: SimpleDynamicPointcut - Static check for clone
DEBUG: SimpleDynamicPointcut - Static check for sing
DEBUG: SimpleDynamicPointcut - Static check for sing
```

```
DEBUG: SimpleDynamicPointcut - Dynamic check for sing
DEBUG: SimpleAroundAdvice - >> Invoking sing
INFO : Singer - Singing in the key of C
DEBUG: SimpleAroundAdvice - >> Done
DEBUG: SimpleDynamicPointcut - Dynamic check for sing
INFO : Singer - Singing in the key of E
DEBUG: SimpleDynamicPointcut - Static check for sing
DEBUG: SimpleDynamicPointcut - Dynamic check for sing
INFO : GoodGuitarist - Head on your heart, arms around me
```

As we expected, only the first two invocations of the sing({key}) method were advised. Notice that the sing() invocation is subject to a dynamic check, thanks to the static check that checks the method name. An interesting point to note here is that the sing({key}) method is subject to two static checks: one during the initial phase when all methods are checked, and another when it is first invoked. This is why the log contains so many Static check for sing entries.

■ As you can see, dynamic pointcuts offer a greater degree of flexibility than static pointcuts, but because of the additional runtime overhead they require, you should use a dynamic pointcut only when absolutely necessary.

Using Simple Name Matching

Often when creating a pointcut, we want to match based on just the name of the method, ignoring method signature and return type. In this case, you can avoid needing to create a subclass of StaticMethodMatcherPointcut and use NameMatchMethodPointcut (which is a subclass of StaticMethodMatcherPointcut) to match against a list of method names instead. When you are using NameMatchMethodPointcut, no consideration is given to the signature of the method, so if you have methods sing() and sing({key}), they are both matched for the name sing().

In Listing 5-15, you can see the GrammyGuitarist class, which is yet another implementation of Singer, because this Grammy award–winning singer sings using his voice, uses a guitar, and, being human, occasionally talks and rests during a performance.

Listing 5-15. GrammyGuitarist Implementation

```
package com.apress.prospring6.five.common

open class GrammyGuitarist : Singer {
    override fun sing() {
        LOGGER.info(
            """
                sing: Gravity is working against me
                And gravity wants to bring me down
                """.trimIndent()
        )
    }
```

```kotlin
    open fun sing(guitar: Guitar) {
        LOGGER.info("play: " + guitar.play())
    }

    open fun talk() {
        LOGGER.info("talk")
    }

    override fun rest() {
        LOGGER.info("zzz")
    }

    companion object {
        private val LOGGER = LoggerFactory.getLogger(GrammyGuitarist::class.java)
    }
}

open class Guitar {
    var brand = " Martin"

    open fun play(): String {
        return "G C G C Am D7"
    }
}
```

For this example, we want to match the sing(), sing(Guitar), and rest() methods by using NameMatchMethodPointcut. This translates to matching the names sing and rest. This is shown in Listing 5-16.

Listing 5-16. NamePointcutDemo Class, Used to Test NameMatchMethodPointcut

```kotlin
package com.apress.prospring6.five.pointcut

import org.springframework.aop.support.NameMatchMethodPointcut
// other import statements omitted

object NamePointcutDemo {
    @JvmStatic
    fun main(args: Array<String>) {
        val johnMayer = GrammyGuitarist()
        val pc = NameMatchMethodPointcut().apply {
            setMappedNames("sing","rest")
        }
        val advisor: Advisor = DefaultPointcutAdvisor(pc, SimpleAroundAdvice())
        val pf = ProxyFactory()
        pf.setTarget(johnMayer)
        pf.addAdvisor(advisor)
        val proxy = pf.proxy as GrammyGuitarist
        proxy.sing()
        proxy.sing(Guitar())
```

```
        proxy.rest()
        proxy.talk()
    }
}
```

There is no need to extend NameMatchMethodPointcut; you can simply create an instance of NameMatchMethodPointcut, and you are on your way. Notice that we have added two method names to the pointcut, sing and rest, using the setMappedNames(..) method. Running this example produces the output in Listing 5-17.

Listing 5-17. NamePointcutDemo Output

```
DEBUG: SimpleAroundAdvice - >> Invoking sing
INFO : GrammyGuitarist - sing: Gravity is working against me
And gravity wants to bring me down
DEBUG: SimpleAroundAdvice - >> Done

DEBUG: SimpleAroundAdvice - >> Invoking sing
INFO : GrammyGuitarist - play: G C G C Am D7
DEBUG: SimpleAroundAdvice - >> Done

DEBUG: SimpleAroundAdvice - >> Invoking rest
INFO : GrammyGuitarist - zzz
DEBUG: SimpleAroundAdvice - >> Done

INFO : GrammyGuitarist - talk
```

As expected, the sing(), sing(Guitar), and rest() methods are advised, thanks to the pointcut, but the talk() method is left unadvised.

For many of the Pointcut implementations, Spring also provides a convenience Advisor implementation that acts as the pointcut. For instance, instead of using NameMatchMethodPointcut coupled with DefaultPointcutAdvisor in the previous example, we could simply have used NameMatchMethodPointcutAdvisor, as shown in Listing 5-18.

Listing 5-18. NameMatchMethodPointcutAdvisor Usage Example

```
package com.apress.prospring6.five

import org.springframework.aop.support.NameMatchMethodPointcutAdvisor
// other import statements omitted

object NameMatchMethodPointcutAdvisorDemo {
    @JvmStatic
    fun main(args: Array<String>) {
        val johnMayer = GrammyGuitarist()
        val advisor = NameMatchMethodPointcutAdvisor(SimpleAroundAdvice()).apply {
            setMappedNames("sing", "rest")
        }
        val pf = ProxyFactory()
        pf.setTarget(johnMayer)
        pf.addAdvisor(advisor)
        val proxy = pf.proxy as GrammyGuitarist
```

```
            proxy.sing()
            proxy.sing(Guitar())
            proxy.rest()
            proxy.talk()
        }
    }
```

Notice that rather than creating an instance of NameMatchMethodPointcut, we configure the pointcut details on the instance of NameMatchMethodPointcutAdvisor by calling the setMappedNames(..) method and providing the method names as arguments. In this way, NameMatchMethodPointcutAdvisor is acting as both the advisor and the pointcut.

You can find full details of the different Advisor implementations by exploring the Javadoc for the org.springframework.aop.support package. There is no noticeable performance difference between the two approaches, and aside from there being slightly less code in the second example, there is very little difference in the actual coding approach. We prefer to stick with the first approach because we feel the intent is slightly clearer in the code. At the end of the day, the style you choose comes down to personal preference.

Creating Pointcuts with Regular Expressions

In the previous section, we discussed how to perform simple matching against a predefined list of methods. But what if you don't know all the method names in advance, and instead you know the pattern that the names follow? For instance, what if you want to match all methods whose names start with get? In this case, you can use the regular expression pointcut JdkRegexpMethodPointcut to match a method name based on a regular expression. Listing 5-19 depicts another Guitarist class, which contains three methods.

Listing 5-19. Guitarist Implementation

```
package com.apress.prospring6.five.common
// imports omitted

open class Guitarist : Singer {
    override fun sing() {
        LOGGER.info("Just keep me where the light is")
    }

    open fun sing2() {
        LOGGER.info("And wrap me in your arms")
    }

    override fun rest() {
        LOGGER.info("zzz...")
    }

    companion object {
        private val LOGGER = LoggerFactory.getLogger(Guitarist::class.java)
    }
}
```

Using a regular expression–based pointcut, we can match all methods in this class whose name starts with sing. This is shown in Listing 5-20.

Listing 5-20. Regex Pointcut Test Class

```
package com.apress.prospring6.five.pointcut

import org.springframework.aop.support.JdkRegexpMethodPointcut
// other import statements omitted

object RegexpPointcutDemo {
    @JvmStatic
    fun main(args: Array<String>) {
        val johnMayer = Guitarist()
        val pc = JdkRegexpMethodPointcut().apply {
            setPattern(".*sing.*")
        }
        val advisor: Advisor = DefaultPointcutAdvisor(pc, SimpleAroundAdvice())
        val pf = ProxyFactory()
        pf.setTarget(johnMayer)
        pf.addAdvisor(advisor)
        val proxy = pf.proxy as Guitarist
        proxy.sing()
        proxy.sing2()
        proxy.rest()
    }
}
```

Notice we do not need to create a class for the pointcut; instead, we just create an instance of JdkRegexpMethodPointcut and specify the pattern to match, and we are finished. The interesting thing to note is the pattern. When matching method names, Spring matches the fully qualified name of the method, so for sing1(), Spring is matching against com.apress.prospring6.five.common.Guitarist.sing1, which is why there's the leading .* in the pattern. This is a powerful concept because it allows you to match all methods within a given package, without needing to know exactly which classes are in that package and what the names of the methods are. Running this example yields the output shown in code Listing 5-21.

Listing 5-21. Regex Pointcut Test Class Output

```
DEBUG: SimpleAroundAdvice - >> Invoking sing
INFO : Guitarist - Just keep me where the light is
DEBUG: SimpleAroundAdvice - >> Done
DEBUG: SimpleAroundAdvice - >> Invoking sing2
INFO : Guitarist - And wrap me in your arms
DEBUG: SimpleAroundAdvice - >> Done
INFO : Guitarist - zzz...
```

As expected, only the sing() and sing2() methods have been advised because the rest() method does not match the regular expression pattern configured for the pointcut instance.

Creating Pointcuts with AspectJ Pointcut Expression

Besides JDK regular expressions, you can use AspectJ's pointcut expression language for pointcut declaration. Later in this chapter, you will see that when we declare the pointcut in a Java/Kotlin configuration, Spring defaults to using AspectJ's pointcut language. Moreover, when using Spring's @AspectJ annotation–style AOP support, you need to use AspectJ's pointcut language. So when declaring pointcuts by using expression language, using an AspectJ pointcut expression is the best way to go. Spring provides the class AspectJExpressionPointcut for defining pointcuts via AspectJ's expression language.

❗ To use AspectJ pointcut expressions with Spring, you need to include two AspectJ library files, aspectjrt.jar and aspectjweaver.jar, in your project's classpath. Check out chapter 5's build. gradle for the configuration.

Considering the previous implementation of the Guitarist class, the same functionality implemented with JDK regular expressions can be implemented using an AspectJ expression. The code for that is shown in code Listing 5-22.

Listing 5-22. AspectJ Regex Pointcut Test Class

```
package com.apress.prospring6.five.pointcut
import org.springframework.aop.aspectj.AspectJExpressionPointcut
// other import statements omitted

object AspectjexpPointcutDemo {
    @JvmStatic
    fun main(args: Array<String>) {
        val johnMayer = Guitarist()
        val pc = AspectJExpressionPointcut().apply {
            expression = "execution(* sing*(..))"
        }
        val advisor: Advisor = DefaultPointcutAdvisor(pc, SimpleAroundAdvice())
        val pf = ProxyFactory()
        pf.setTarget(johnMayer)
        pf.addAdvisor(advisor)
        val proxy = pf.proxy as Guitarist
        proxy.sing()
        proxy.sing2()
        proxy.rest()
    }
}
```

Note that we use the AspectJExpressionPointcut class' setExpression() method (via .expression = ...) to set the matching criteria. The expression execution(* sing*(..)) means that the advice should apply to the execution of any methods that start with sing, have any arguments, and return any types (yes, AspectJ is a lot more flexible and concise). Running the program will get the same result as the previous example using JDK regular expressions.

Creating Annotation Matching Pointcuts

If your application is annotation-based, you may want to use your own specified annotations for defining pointcuts—that is, apply the advice logic to all methods or types with specific annotations. Spring provides the class AnnotationMatchingPointcut for defining pointcuts using annotations. Again, let's reuse the previous example and see how to do it when using an annotation as a pointcut.

First we define an annotation called AdviceRequired, which is an annotation that we will use for declaring a pointcut. Listing 5-23 shows the annotation class and the modified AnnotatedGuitarist class that has the sing(Guitar) method annotated with it.

Listing 5-23. Custom Annotation to Be Used with an AnnotationMatchingPointcut and the Class Using It

```
package com.apress.prospring6.five.common

import org.springframework.aop.Advisor
// other import statements omitted

@Retention(AnnotationRetention.RUNTIME)
@Target(
    AnnotationTarget.ANNOTATION_CLASS,
    AnnotationTarget.CLASS,
    AnnotationTarget.FUNCTION,
    AnnotationTarget.PROPERTY_GETTER,
    AnnotationTarget.PROPERTY_SETTER
)
annotation class AdviceRequired
open class AnnotatedGuitarist : Singer {
    override fun sing() {}

    @AdviceRequired
    open fun sing(guitar: Guitar) {
        LOGGER.info("play: " + guitar.play())
    }

    companion object {
        private val LOGGER = LoggerFactory.getLogger(AnnotatedGuitarist::class.java)
    }
}
```

The interface AdviceRequired is declared as an annotation by using annotation class as the type, and the @Target annotation defines that the annotation can apply at either the type or method level. The class AnnotatedGuitarist class implements the Singer interface and adds its own sing(..) method that takes a Guitar argument and is annotated with @AdviceRequired.

The testing program is no different from what was presented before and is depicted in Listing 5-24 together with its output.

Listing 5-24. Testing Program for the AnnotationMatchingPointcut

```
package com.apress.prospring6.five

import com.apress.prospring6.five.common.AdviceRequired
import org.springframework.aop.support.annotation.AnnotationMatchingPointcut
// other import statements omitted

object AnnotationPointcutDemo {
    @JvmStatic
    fun main(args: Array<String>) {
        val johnMayer = AnnotatedGuitarist()
```

```
    val pc = AnnotationMatchingPointcut.forMethodAnnotation(
        AdviceRequired::class.java
    )
    val advisor: Advisor = DefaultPointcutAdvisor(pc, SimpleAroundAdvice())
    val pf = ProxyFactory()
    pf.setTarget(johnMayer)
    pf.addAdvisor(advisor)
    val proxy = pf.proxy as AnnotatedGuitarist
    proxy.sing(Guitar())
    proxy.rest()
  }
}

// output
DEBUG: SimpleAroundAdvice - >> Invoking sing
INFO : AnnotatedGuitarist - play: G C G C Am D7
DEBUG: SimpleAroundAdvice - >> Done
```

An instance of AnnotationMatchingPointcut is acquired by calling its static method forMethodAnnotation() and passing in the annotation type. This indicates that we want to apply the advice to all the methods annotated with the given annotation. It's also possible to specify annotations applied at the type level by calling the forClassAnnotation() method.

As you can see, since we annotated the sing(Guitar) method, only that method was advised.

Understanding Proxies

So far, we have taken only a cursory look at the proxies generated by ProxyFactory. We mentioned that two types of proxy are available in Spring: JDK proxies created by using the JDK Proxy class and CGLIB-based proxies created by using the CGLIB Enhancer class. You may be wondering exactly what the difference between the two proxies is and why Spring needs two types of proxy. In this section, we take a detailed look at the differences between the proxies.

The core goal of a proxy is to intercept method invocations and, where necessary, execute chains of advice that apply to a particular method. The management and invocation of advice is largely proxy independent and is managed by the Spring AOP framework. However, the proxy is responsible for intercepting calls to all methods and passing them as necessary to the AOP framework for the advice to be applied.

In addition to this core functionality, the proxy must support a set of additional features. It is possible to configure the proxy to expose itself via the AopContext class (which is an abstract class) so that you can retrieve the proxy and invoke advised methods on the proxy from the target object. The proxy is responsible for ensuring that when this option is enabled via ProxyFactory.setExposeProxy(), the proxy class is appropriately exposed. In addition, all proxy classes implement the Advised interface by default, which allows for, among other things, the advice chain to be changed after the proxy has been created. A proxy must also ensure that any methods that return this (that is, return the proxied target) do in fact return the proxy and not the target.

As you can see, a typical proxy has quite a lot of work to perform, and all of this logic is implemented in both the JDK and CGLIB proxies.

Using JDK Dynamic Proxies

JDK proxies are the most basic type of proxy available in Spring. Unlike the CGLIB proxy, the JDK proxy can generate proxies only of interfaces, not classes. In this way, any object you want to proxy must implement at least one interface, and the resulting proxy will be an object that implements that interface. Figure 5-4 shows an abstract schema of such a proxy.

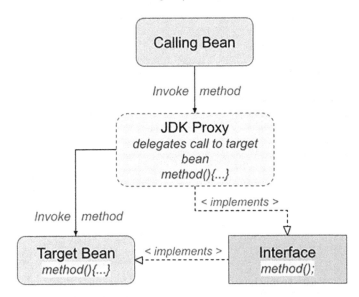

Figure 5-4. *JDK proxy abstract schema*

In general, it is good design to use interfaces for your classes, but it is not always possible, especially when you are working with third-party or legacy code. In this case, you must use the CGLIB proxy. When you are using the JDK proxy, all method calls are intercepted by the JVM and routed to the invoke() method of the proxy. This method then determines whether the method in question is advised (by the rules defined by the pointcut), and if so, it invokes the advice chain and then the method itself by using reflection. In addition to this, the invoke() method performs all the logic discussed in the previous section.

The JDK proxy makes no determination between methods that are advised and unadvised until it is in the invoke() method. This means that for unadvised methods on the proxy, the invoke() method is still called, all the checks are still performed, and the method is still invoked by using reflection. Obviously, this incurs runtime overhead each time the method is invoked, even though the proxy often performs no additional processing other than to invoke the unadvised method via reflection.

You can instruct ProxyFactory to use a JDK proxy by specifying the list of interfaces to proxy by using setInterfaces() (in the AdvisedSupport class that the ProxyFactory class extends indirectly).

Using CGLIB Proxies

With the JDK proxy, all decisions about how to handle a particular method invocation are handled at runtime each time the method is invoked. When you use CGLIB, CGLIB dynamically generates the bytecode for a new class on-the-fly for each proxy, reusing already generated classes wherever possible. The resulting proxy type in this case will be a subclass of the target object class. Figure 5-5 shows an abstract schema of such a proxy.

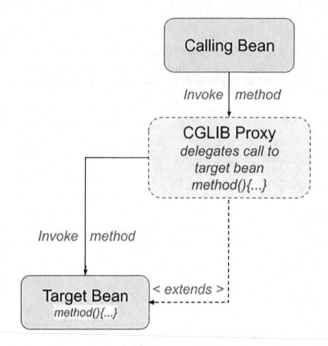

Figure 5-5. *CGLIB proxy abstract schema*

When a CGLIB proxy is first created, CGLIB asks Spring how it wants to handle each method. This means that many of the decisions that are performed in each call to invoke() on the JDK proxy are performed just once for the CGLIB proxy. Because CGLIB generates actual bytecode, there is also a lot more flexibility in the way you can handle methods. For instance, the CGLIB proxy generates the appropriate bytecode to invoke any unadvised methods directly, reducing the overhead introduced by the proxy. In addition, the CGLIB proxy determines whether it is possible for a method to return this; if not, it allows the method call to be invoked directly, again reducing the runtime overhead.

The CGLIB proxy also handles fixed-advice chains differently than the JDK proxy. A *fixed-advice chain* is one that you guarantee will not change after the proxy has been generated. By default, you are able to change the advisors and advice on a proxy even after it is created, although this is rarely a requirement. The CGLIB proxy handles fixed-advice chains in a particular way, reducing the runtime overhead for executing an advice chain.

---

❶ There are some limitations when working with CGLIB proxies:

1. For obvious reasons, GLIB proxies cannot be created for final classes (since they cannot be subclassed).

2. Since static members belong to a class, not to an instance, they cannot be proxied.

3. Private methods cannot be proxied either, since a subclass cannot access them.

Comparing Proxy Performance

So far, we've discussed only in loose terms the differences in implementation between the proxy types. In this section, we are going to run a simple test to compare the performance of the CGLIB proxy with the JDK proxy. For this purpose we need the simplest bean and its interface, with no-op methods and a no-op before advice.

The bean is named DefaultSimpleBean and implements the SimpleBean interface. It implements the two methods declared by the interface, aptly named advised() and unadvised(). These two methods are shown in Listing 5-25.

Listing 5-25. SimpleBean and Its Implementation

```kotlin
package com.apress.prospring6.five.performance

interface SimpleBean {
    fun advised()
    fun unadvised()
}

// DefaultSimpleBean.kt in the same package
open class DefaultSimpleBean : SimpleBean {
    override fun advised() {
        System.currentTimeMillis()
    }

    override fun unadvised() {
        System.currentTimeMillis()
    }
}
```

Listing 5-26 depicts the NoOpBeforeAdvice class, which is just simple before advice without any operation; this is needed to avoid polluting the output.

Listing 5-26. NoOpBeforeAdvice Implementation

```kotlin
package com.apress.prospring6.five.performance
// import statements omitted

class NoOpBeforeAdvice : MethodBeforeAdvice {
    @Throws(Throwable::class)
    override fun before(method: Method, args: Array<out Any>, @Nullable target: Any?) {
        // no-op
    }
}
```

Listing 5-27 shows the code used to test various types of proxies.

Listing 5-27. Various Types of Proxies

```kotlin
package com.apress.prospring6.five.performance

object ProxyPerfTestDemo {
    private val LOGGER = LoggerFactory.getLogger(ProxyPerfTestDemo::class.java)
    @JvmStatic
    fun main(args: Array<String>) {
        val target: SimpleBean = DefaultSimpleBean()
        val advisor = NameMatchMethodPointcutAdvisor(NoOpBeforeAdvice())
        advisor.setMappedName("advised")
        LOGGER.info("Starting tests ...")
        runCglibTests(advisor, target)
        runCglibFrozenTests(advisor, target)
        runJdkTests(advisor, target)
    }

    private fun runCglibTests(advisor: Advisor, target: SimpleBean) {
        val pf = ProxyFactory()
        pf.isProxyTargetClass = true
        pf.setTarget(target)
        pf.addAdvisor(advisor)
        val proxy = pf.proxy as SimpleBean
        val testResults = test(proxy)
        LOGGER.info(" --- CGLIB (Standard) Test results ---\n {} ", testResults)
    }

    private fun runCglibFrozenTests(advisor: Advisor, target: SimpleBean) {
        val pf = ProxyFactory()
        pf.isProxyTargetClass = true
        pf.setTarget(target)
        pf.addAdvisor(advisor)
        pf.isFrozen = true
        val proxy = pf.proxy as SimpleBean
        val testResults = test(proxy)
        LOGGER.info(" --- CGLIB (Frozen) Test results ---\n {} ", testResults)
    }

    private fun runJdkTests(advisor: Advisor, target: SimpleBean) {
        val pf = ProxyFactory()
        pf.setTarget(target)
        pf.addAdvisor(advisor)
        pf.setInterfaces(SimpleBean::class.java)
        val proxy = pf.proxy as SimpleBean
        val testResults = test(proxy)
        LOGGER.info(" --- JDK Test results ---\n {} ", testResults)
    }

    private fun test(bean: SimpleBean): TestResults {
        val testResults = TestResults()
        var before = System.currentTimeMillis()
        for (x in 0..499999) {
```

```
        bean.advised()
    }
    var after = System.currentTimeMillis()
    testResults.advisedMethodTime = after - before
    //-----
    before = System.currentTimeMillis()
    for (x in 0..499999) {
        bean.unadvised()
    }
    after = System.currentTimeMillis()
    testResults.unadvisedMethodTime = after - before
    //-----
    before = System.currentTimeMillis()
    for (x in 0..499999) {
        bean.equals(bean)
    }
    after = System.currentTimeMillis()
    testResults.equalsTime = after - before
    // ----
    before = System.currentTimeMillis()
    for (x in 0..499999) {
        bean.hashCode()
    }
    after = System.currentTimeMillis()
    testResults.hashCodeTime = after - before
    // -----
    val advised = bean as Advised
    before = System.currentTimeMillis()
    for (x in 0..499999) {
        advised.targetClass
    }
    after = System.currentTimeMillis()
    testResults.proxyTargetTime = after - before
    return testResults
    }
}
```

In this code, you can see that you are testing three kinds of proxies:

- A standard CGLIB proxy

- A CGLIB proxy with a frozen advice chain (that is, when a proxy is frozen by calling the setFrozen() method in the ProxyConfig class that ProxyFactory extends indirectly, CGLIB will perform further optimization; however, further advice change will not be allowed)

- A JDK proxy

For each proxy type, you run the following five test cases:

- *Advised method (test 1)*: This is a method that is advised. The advice type used in the test is before advice that performs no processing, so it reduces the effects of the advice on the performance tests.

- *Unadvised method (test 2)*: This is a method on the proxy that is unadvised. Often your proxy has many methods that are not advised. This test looks at how well unadvised methods perform for the different proxies.

- *The* equals() *method (test 3)*: This test looks at the overhead of invoking the equals() method. This is especially important when you use proxies as keys in a HashMap<K,V> or similar collection.

- *The* hashCode() *method (test 4)*: As with the equals() method, the hashCode() method is important when you are using HashMaps or similar collections.

- *Executing methods on the* Advised *interface (test 5)*: As we mentioned earlier, a proxy implements the Advised interface by default, allowing you to modify the proxy after creation and to query information about the proxy. This test looks at how fast methods on the Advised interface can be accessed using the different proxy types.

Table 5-3 shows the results of these tests.

Table 5-3. *Proxy Performance Test Results (in Milliseconds)*

Methods Being Tested	CGLIB (Standard)	CGLIB (Frozen)	JDK
advised()	126	73	159
unadvised()	127	28	96
equals()	20	16	122
hashCode()	28	20	33
Advised.getProxyTargetClass()	13	8	81

As you can see, the performance between standard CGLIB and JDK dynamic proxy for both advised() and unadvised() methods doesn't differ much. As always, these numbers will vary based on hardware and the JDK being used.

However, there is a noticeable difference when you are using a CGLIB proxy with a frozen advice chain. Similar figures apply to the equals() and hashCode() methods, which are noticeably faster when you are using the CGLIB proxy. For methods on the Advised interface, you will notice that they are also faster on the CGLIB frozen proxy. The reason for this is that Advised methods are handled early on in the intercept() method, so they avoid much of the logic that is required for other methods.

The TestResults class is a simple utility class with four properties, named after the method being tested. Saving the test results for each proxy type in an instance of this type is done for practical reasons, in an attempt to keep the code concise and readable. You can see this class in Listing 5-28.

Listing 5-28. TestResults Implementation

```
package com.apress.prospring6.five.performance
// import statements omitted

class TestResults {
    var advisedMethodTime: Long = 0
    var unadvisedMethodTime: Long = 0
    var equalsTime: Long = 0
    var hashCodeTime: Long = 0
    var proxyTargetTime: Long = 0
    override fun toString(): String {
```

```
        return ToStringBuilder(this)
            .append("advised", advisedMethodTime)
            .append("unadvised", unadvisedMethodTime)
            .append("equals ", equalsTime)
            .append("hashCode", hashCodeTime)
            .append("getProxyTargetClass ", proxyTargetTime)
            .toString()
    }

    companion object {
        private val LOGGER = LoggerFactory.getLogger(TestResults::class.java)
    }
}
```

Choosing a Proxy to Use

Deciding which proxy to use is typically easy. The CGLIB proxy can proxy both classes and interfaces, whereas JDK proxies can proxy only interfaces. In terms of performance, there is no significant difference between JDK and CGLIB standard mode (at least in running both advised and unadvised methods), unless you use CGLIB in frozen mode, in which case the advice chain can't be changed and CGLIB performs further optimization when in frozen mode. When proxying a class, the CGLIB proxy is the default choice because it is the only proxy capable of generating a proxy of a class. To use the CGLIB proxy when proxying an interface, you must set the value of the optimize flag in ProxyFactory to true by using the setOptimize() method.

Advanced Use of Pointcuts

Earlier in the chapter, we looked at the six basic Pointcut implementations Spring provides; for the most part, we have found that these meet the needs of our applications. However, sometimes you might need more flexibility when defining pointcuts. Spring provides two additional Pointcut implementations, ComposablePointcut and ControlFlowPointcut, which provide exactly the flexibility you need.

Using Control Flow Pointcuts

Spring control flow pointcuts, implemented by the ControlFlowPointcut class, are similar to the cflow construct available in many other AOP implementations, although they are not quite as powerful. Essentially, a control flow pointcut in Spring applies to all method calls below a given method or below all methods in a class. This is quite hard to visualize and is better explained using an example.

Listing 5-29 shows a SimpleBeforeAdvice class that writes out a message describing the method it is advising.

Listing 5-29. SimpleBeforeAdvice Implementation

```
package com.apress.prospring6.five.advanced

import org.springframework.aop.MethodBeforeAdvice
import java.lang.reflect.Method
// other import statements omitted
```

```kotlin
class SimpleBeforeAdvice : MethodBeforeAdvice {
    @Throws(Throwable::class)
    override fun before(method: Method, args: Array<out Any>, @Nullable target: Any?) {
        LOGGER.info("Before method: {}", method)
    }

    companion object {
        private val LOGGER = LoggerFactory.getLogger(SimpleBeforeAdvice::class.java)
    }
}
```

This advice class allows us to see which methods the ControlFlowPointcut applies to. The TestBean class is shown in Listing 5-30.

Listing 5-30. TestBean Implementation

```kotlin
package com.apress.prospring6.five.advanced
// import statements omitted

open class TestBean {
    open fun foo() {
        LOGGER.info("foo()")
    }

    companion object {
        private val LOGGER = LoggerFactory.getLogger(TestBean::class.java)
    }
}
```

You can see the simple foo() method that we want to advise. We have, however, a special requirement: we want to advise this method only when it is called from another, specific method. Listing 5-31 shows a simple driver program for this example.

Listing 5-31. ControlFlowDemo Implementation

```kotlin
package com.apress.prospring6.five.advanced

import org.springframework.aop.support.ControlFlowPointcut
// other import statements omitted

class ControlFlowDemo {
    fun run() {
        val target = TestBean()
        val pc: Pointcut = ControlFlowPointcut(ControlFlowDemo::class.java, "test")
        val advisor: Advisor = DefaultPointcutAdvisor(pc, SimpleBeforeAdvice())
        val pf = ProxyFactory()
        pf.setTarget(target)
        pf.addAdvisor(advisor)
        val proxy = pf.proxy as TestBean
        LOGGER.info("\tTrying normal invoke")
        proxy.foo()
        LOGGER.info("\tTrying under ControlFlowDemo.test()")
```

```
        test(proxy)
    }

    private fun test(bean: TestBean) {
        bean.foo()
    }

    companion object {
        private val LOGGER = LoggerFactory.getLogger(ControlFlowDemo::class.java)
        @JvmStatic
        fun main(args: Array<String>) {
            val ex = ControlFlowDemo()
            ex.run()
        }
    }
}
```

Notice that the advised proxy is assembled with ControlFlowPointcut, and then the foo() method is invoked twice, once directly from the run() method and once from the test() method.

Here is the line of particular interest:

```
val pc = ControlFlowPointcut(ControlFlowDemo.class, "test")
```

In this line, we are creating a ControlFlowPointcut instance for the test() method of the ControlFlowDemo class. Essentially, this says, "Pointcut all methods that are called from the ControlFlowExample.test() method." Note that "Pointcut all methods" in fact means "Pointcut all methods on the proxy object that is advised using the Advisor corresponding to this instance of ControlFlowPointcut." Running the code yields in the console the output shown in Listing 5-32.

Listing 5-32. ControlFlowDemo Console Output

```
INFO : ControlFlowDemo -    Trying normal invoke
INFO : TestBean - foo()
INFO : ControlFlowDemo -    Trying under ControlFlowDemo.test()
INFO : SimpleBeforeAdvice - Before method: public void com.apress.prospring6.five.advanced.
TestBean.foo()
INFO : TestBean - foo()
```

As you can see, when the sing() method is first invoked outside of the control flow of the test() method, it is unadvised. When it executes for a second time, this time inside the control flow of the test() method, the ControlFlowPointcut indicates that its associated advice applies to the method, and thus the method is advised. Note that if we had called another method from within the test() method, one that was not on the advised proxy, it would not have been advised.

Control flow pointcuts can be extremely useful, allowing you to advise an object selectively only when it is executed in the context of another. However, be aware that you take a substantial performance hit for using control flow pointcuts over other pointcuts.

Let's consider an example. Suppose we have a transaction processing system, which contains a TransactionService interface as well as an AccountService interface. We would like to apply after advice so that when the AccountService.updateBalance() method is called by TransactionService. reverseTransaction(), an e-mail notification is sent to the customer, after the account balance is updated. However, an e-mail will not be sent under any other circumstances. In this case, the control flow pointcut will be useful. Figure 5-6 shows the UML sequence diagram for this scenario.

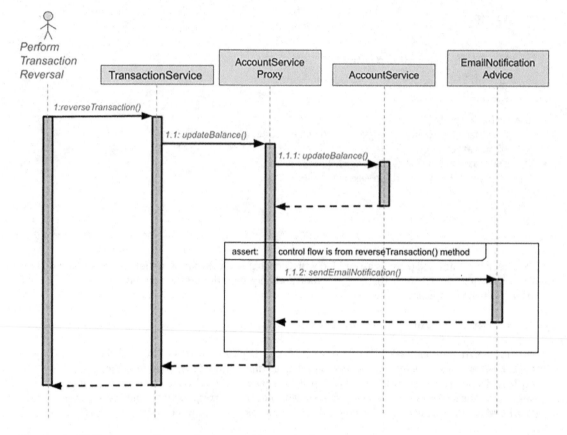

Figure 5-6. *UML sequence diagram for a control flow pointcut*

Using a Composable Pointcut

In previous pointcut examples, we used just a single pointcut for each Advisor. In most cases, this is usually enough, but in some cases, you may need to compose two or more pointcuts together to achieve the desired goal. Say you want to pointcut all getter and setter methods on a bean. You have a pointcut for getters and a pointcut for setters, but you don't have one for both. Of course, you could just create another pointcut with the new logic, but a better approach is to combine the two pointcuts into a single pointcut by using ComposablePointcut.

ComposablePointcut supports two methods: union() and intersection(). By default, ComposablePointcut is created with a ClassFilter that matches all classes and a MethodMatcher that matches all methods, although you can supply your own initial ClassFilter and MethodMatcher during construction. The union() and intersection() methods are both overloaded to accept ClassFilter and MethodMatcher arguments.

The ComposablePointcut.union() method can be called by passing in an instance of either the ClassFilter, MethodMatcher, or Pointcut interface. The result of a union operation is that ComposablePointcut will add an "or" condition into its call chain for matching with the joinpoints. It's the same for the ComposablePointcut.intersection() method, but this time an "and" condition will be added instead, which means that all ClassFilter, MethodMatcher, and Pointcut definitions within ComposablePointcut should be matched for applying an advice. You can imagine it as the WHERE clause in a SQL query, with the union() method like the "or" operator and the intersection() method like the "and" operator.

As with control flow pointcuts, this is quite difficult to visualize, and it is much easier to understand with an example. Listing 5-33 shows the GrammyGuitarist class used in a previous example with its four methods.

Listing 5-33. GrammyGuitarist Implementation

```kotlin
package com.apress.prospring6.five.common
// other import statements omitted

open class GrammyGuitarist : Singer {
    override fun sing() {
        LOGGER.info(
            """
                sing: Gravity is working against me
                And gravity wants to bring me down
                """.trimIndent()
        )
    }

    open fun sing(guitar: Guitar) {
        LOGGER.info("play: " + guitar.play())
    }

    open fun talk() {
        LOGGER.info("talk")
    }

    override fun rest() {
        LOGGER.info("zzz")
    }

    companion object {
        private val LOGGER = LoggerFactory.getLogger(GrammyGuitarist::class.java)
    }
}
```

With this example, we are going to generate three proxies by using the same ComposablePointcut instance, but each time, we are going to modify ComposablePointcut by using either the union() or intersection() method. Following this, we will invoke all three methods on the target bean proxy and look at which ones have been advised. Listing 5-34 depicts this.

Listing 5-34. Testing ComposablePointcut

```kotlin
package com.apress.prospring6.five

import org.springframework.aop.support.ComposablePointcut
import org.springframework.aop.support.StaticMethodMatcher
// other import statement omitted

object ComposablePointcutDemo {
    private val LOGGER = LoggerFactory.getLogger(ComposablePointcutDemo::class.java)
    @JvmStatic
    fun main(args: Array<String>) {
```

```kotlin
        val johnMayer = GrammyGuitarist()
        val pc = ComposablePointcut(ClassFilter.TRUE, SingMethodMatcher())
        LOGGER.info("Test 1 >> ")
        var proxy = getProxy(pc, johnMayer)
        testInvoke(proxy)
        LOGGER.info("Test 2 >> ")
        pc.union(TalkMethodMatcher())
        proxy = getProxy(pc, johnMayer)
        testInvoke(proxy)
        LOGGER.info("Test 3 >> ")
        pc.intersection(RestMethodMatcher())
        proxy = getProxy(pc, johnMayer)
        testInvoke(proxy)
    }

    private fun getProxy(pc: ComposablePointcut, target: GrammyGuitarist): GrammyGuitarist {
        val advisor: Advisor = DefaultPointcutAdvisor(pc, SimpleBeforeAdvice())
        val pf = ProxyFactory()
        pf.setTarget(target)
        pf.addAdvisor(advisor)
        return pf.proxy as GrammyGuitarist
    }

    private fun testInvoke(proxy: GrammyGuitarist) {
        proxy.sing()
        proxy.sing(Guitar())
        proxy.talk()
        proxy.rest()
    }
}

internal class SingMethodMatcher : StaticMethodMatcher() {
    override fun matches(method: Method, cls: Class<*>): Boolean {
        return method.name.startsWith("si")
    }
}

internal class TalkMethodMatcher : StaticMethodMatcher() {
    override fun matches(method: Method, cls: Class<*>): Boolean {
        return "talk" == method.name
    }
}

internal class RestMethodMatcher : StaticMethodMatcher() {
    override fun matches(method: Method, cls: Class<*>): Boolean {
        return method.name.endsWith("st")
    }
}
```

The first thing to notice in this example is the set of three private MethodMatcher implementations. SingMethodMatcher matches all methods that start with get. This is the default MethodMatcher that we use to assemble ComposablePointcut. Because of this, we expect that the first round of invocations on the GrammyGuitarist methods will result in only the sing() methods being advised.

TalkMethodMatcher matches all methods named talk, and it is combined with ComposablePointcut by using union() for the second round of invocations. At this point, we have a union of two MethodMatchers: one that matches all methods starting with si and one that matches all methods named talk. We now expect that all invocations during the second round will be advised. TalkMethodMatcher is very specific and matches only the talk() method. This MethodMatcher is combined with ComposablePointcut by using intersection() for the third round for invocations.

Because RestMethodMatcher is being composed by using intersection(), we expect none of the methods to be advised in the third round because there is no method that matches all the composed MethodMatchers.

Running the code in Listing 5-34 yields the console output shown in Listing 5-35.

Listing 5-35. ComposablePointcutDemo Output

```
INFO : ComposablePointcutDemo - Test 1 >>
INFO : SimpleBeforeAdvice - Before method: public void com.apress.prospring6.five.common.
GrammyGuitarist.sing()
INFO : GrammyGuitarist - sing: Gravity is working against me
And gravity wants to bring me down
INFO : SimpleBeforeAdvice - Before method: public void com.apress.prospring6.five.common.
GrammyGuitarist.sing(com.apress.prospring6.five.common.Guitar)
INFO : GrammyGuitarist - play: G C G C Am D7
INFO : GrammyGuitarist - talk
INFO : GrammyGuitarist - zzz
INFO : ComposablePointcutDemo - Test 2 >>
INFO : SimpleBeforeAdvice - Before method: public void com.apress.prospring6.five.common.
GrammyGuitarist.sing()
INFO : GrammyGuitarist - sing: Gravity is working against me
And gravity wants to bring me down
INFO : SimpleBeforeAdvice - Before method: public void com.apress.prospring6.five.common.
GrammyGuitarist.sing(com.apress.prospring6.five.common.Guitar)
INFO : GrammyGuitarist - play: G C G C Am D7
INFO : SimpleBeforeAdvice - Before method: public void com.apress.prospring6.five.common.
GrammyGuitarist.talk()
INFO : GrammyGuitarist - talk
INFO : GrammyGuitarist - zzz
INFO : ComposablePointcutDemo - Test 3 >>
INFO : GrammyGuitarist - sing: Gravity is working against me
And gravity wants to bring me down
INFO : GrammyGuitarist - play: G C G C Am D7
INFO : GrammyGuitarist - talk
INFO : GrammyGuitarist - zzz
```

Although this example demonstrated the use of MethodMatchers only in the composition process, it is just as simple to use ClassFilter when you are building the pointcut. Indeed, you can use a combination of MethodMatchers and ClassFilters when building your composite pointcut.

Composition and the `Pointcut` Interface

In the previous section, you saw how to create a composite pointcut by using multiple `MethodMatchers` and `ClassFilters`. You can also create composite pointcuts by using other objects that implement the `Pointcut` interface.

Another way to construct a composite pointcut is to use the `org.springframework.aop.support.Pointcuts` class. The class provides three static methods. The `intersection()` and `union()` methods both take two pointcuts as arguments to construct a composite pointcut. On the other hand, a `matches(Pointcut, Method, Class, Object[])` method is provided for performing a quick check on whether a pointcut matches with the provided method, class, and method arguments.

The `Pointcuts` class supports operations on only two pointcuts. So, if you need to combine `MethodMatcher` and `ClassFilter` with `Pointcut`, you need to use the `ComposablePointcut` class. However, when you need to combine just two pointcuts, the `Pointcuts` class will be more convenient.

Pointcut Summary

Spring offers a powerful set of `Pointcut` implementations that should meet most, if not all, of your application's requirements. Remember that if you can't find a pointcut to suit your needs, you can create your own implementation from scratch by implementing `Pointcut`, `MethodMatcher`, and `ClassFilter`.

You can use two patterns to combine pointcuts and advisors. The first pattern, the one we have used so far, involves having the `Pointcut` implementation decoupled from the advisor. In the code we have seen up to this point, we created instances of `Pointcut` implementations and then used the `DefaultPointcutAdvisor` implementation to add advice along with the `Pointcut` to the proxy.

The second option, one that is adopted by many of the examples in the Spring documentation, is to encapsulate the `Pointcut` inside your own `Advisor` implementation. This way, you have a class that implements both `Pointcut` and `PointcutAdvisor`, with the `PointcutAdvisor.getPointcut()` method simply returning this. This is an approach many classes, such as `StaticMethodMatcherPointcutAdvisor`, use in Spring. We find that the first approach is the most flexible, allowing you to use different `Pointcut` implementations with different `Advisor` implementations. However, the second approach is useful in situations where you are going to be using the same combination of `Pointcut` and `Advisor` in different parts of your application or, indeed, across many applications.

The second approach is useful when each `Advisor` must have a separate instance of a `Pointcut`; by making the `Advisor` responsible for creating the `Pointcut`, you can ensure that this is the case. If you recall the discussion on proxy performance from earlier in the chapter, you will remember that unadvised methods perform much better than methods that are advised. For this reason, you should ensure that, by using `Pointcuts`, you advise only the methods that are absolutely necessary. This way, you reduce the amount of unnecessary overhead added to your application by using AOP.

Getting Started with Introductions

Introductions are an important part of the AOP feature set available in Spring. By using introductions, you can introduce new functionality to an existing object dynamically. In Spring, you can introduce an implementation of any interface to an existing object. You may well be wondering exactly why this is useful. Why would you want to add functionality dynamically at runtime when you can simply add that functionality at development time? The answer to this question is easy: you add functionality dynamically when the functionality is crosscutting and is not easily implemented using traditional advice.

Introduction Basics

Spring treats introductions as a special type of advice, more specifically, as a special type of around advice. Because introductions apply solely at the class level, you cannot use pointcuts with introductions; semantically, the two don't match. An introduction adds new interface implementations to a class, and a pointcut defines which methods the advice applies to. You create an introduction by implementing the IntroductionInterceptor interface, which extends the MethodInterceptor and DynamicIntroductionAdvice interfaces.

Figure 5-7 shows this structure along with the methods of both interfaces, as depicted by the IntelliJ IDEA UML plug-in.

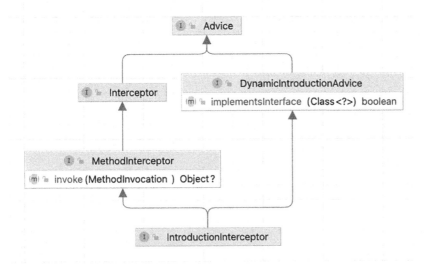

Figure 5-7. *UML sequence diagram for introductions*

As you can see, the MethodInterceptor interface defines an invoke() method. Using this method, you provide the implementation for the interfaces that you are introducing and perform interception for any additional methods as required. Implementing all methods for an interface inside a single method can prove troublesome, and it is likely to result in an awful lot of code that you will have to wade through just to decide which method to invoke. Thankfully, Spring provides a default implementation of IntroductionInterceptor, called DelegatingIntroductionInterceptor, which makes creating introductions much simpler. To build an introduction by using DelegatingIntroductionInterceptor, you create a class that both inherits from DelegatingIntroductionInterceptor and implements the interfaces you want to introduce. The DelegatingIntroductionInterceptor implementation then simply delegates all calls to introduced methods to the corresponding method on itself. Don't worry if this seems a little unclear; you will see an example of it in the next section.

Just as you need to use PointcutAdvisor when you are working with pointcut advice, you need to use IntroductionAdvisor to add introductions to a proxy. The default implementation of IntroductionAdvisor is DefaultIntroductionAdvisor, which should suffice for most, if not all, of your introduction needs. You should be aware that adding an introduction by using ProxyFactory.addAdvice() is not permitted and results in AopConfigException being thrown. Instead, you should use the addAdvisor() method and pass an instance of the IntroductionAdvisor interface.

When using standard advice—that is, not introductions—it is possible for the same advice instance to be used for many objects. The Spring documentation refers to this as the *per-class life cycle*, although you can use a single advice instance for many classes. For introductions, the introduction advice forms part of the state of the advised object, and as a result, you must have a distinct advice instance for every advised object. This is called the *per-instance life cycle*. Because you must ensure that each advised object has a distinct instance of the introduction, it is often preferable to create a subclass of DefaultIntroductionAdvisor that is responsible for creating the introduction advice. This way, you need to ensure only that a new instance of your advisor class is created for each object because it will automatically create a new instance of the introduction. For example, say you want to apply before advice to the setFirstName() method on all instances of the Contact class. Figure 5-8 shows the same advice that applies to all objects of the Contact type.

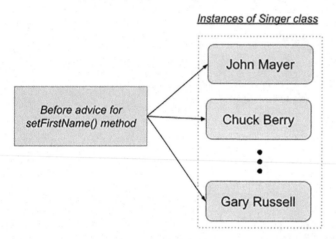

Figure 5-8. *Per-class life cycle of advice*

Now let's say you want to mix an introduction into all instances of the Contact class, and the introduction will carry information for each Contact instance (for example, an attribute isModified that indicates whether the specific instance was modified). In this case, the introduction will be created for each instance of Contact and tied to that specific instance, as shown in Figure 5-9.

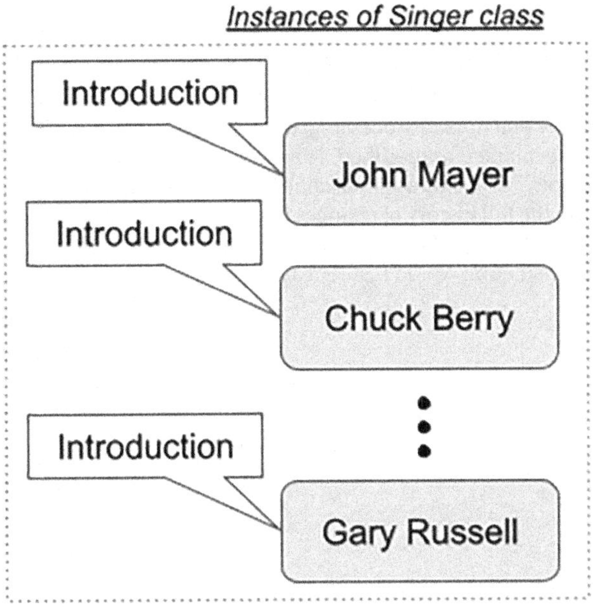

Instances of Singer class

Figure 5-9. *Per-instance introduction*

That covers the basics of introduction creation. We will now discuss how you can use introductions to solve the problem of object modification detection.

Object Modification Detection with Introductions

Object modification detection is a useful technique for many reasons. Typically, you apply modification detection to prevent unnecessary database access when you are persisting object data. If an object is passed to a method for modification but it comes back unmodified, there is little point in issuing an update statement to the database. Using a modification check in this way can really increase application throughput, especially when the database is already under a substantial load or is located on a remote network, making communication an expensive operation.

Unfortunately, this kind of functionality is difficult to implement by hand because it requires you to add it to every method that can modify object state to check whether the object state is actually being modified. When you consider all the null checks that have to be made and the checks to see whether the value is actually changing, you are looking at around eight lines of code per method. You could refactor this into a single method, but you still have to call this method every time you need to perform the check. Spread this across a typical application with many classes that require modification checks, and you have a disaster waiting to happen.

This is clearly a place where introductions will help. We don't want to have each class that requires modification checks inherit from some base implementation, losing its only chance for inheritance as a result, nor do we really want to be adding checking code to each and every state-changing method. Using introductions, we can provide a flexible solution to the modification detection problem without having to write a bunch of repetitive, error-prone code.

In this example, we are going to build a full modification check framework using introduction. The modification check logic is encapsulated by the IsModified interface, an implementation of which will be introduced into the appropriate objects, along with interception logic to perform modification checks automatically. For the purposes of this example, we use JavaBeans conventions, in that we consider a modification to be any call to an (implicit) setter method. Of course, we don't just treat all calls to a setter method as a modification; we check to see whether the value being passed to the setter is different from the one currently stored in the object. The only flaw with this solution is that setting an object back to its original state will still reflect a modification if any one of the values on the object has changed. For example, you have a Contact object with the firstName attribute. Let's say that during processing, the firstName attribute was changed from Peter to John. As a result, the object was marked as modified. However, it will still be marked as modified, even if the value is then changed back from John to its original value Peter in later processing.

One way to keep track of such changes is to store the full history of changes in the object's entire life cycle. However, the implementation would be nontrivial and for that reason our simple approach suffices for most requirements. Implementing the more complete solution would result in an overly complex example.

Using the IsModified Interface

Central to the modification check solution is the IsModified interface, which the fictional application uses to make intelligent decisions about object persistence. We do not cover how the application would use IsModified; instead, we focus on the implementation of the introduction. Listing 5-36 shows the IsModified interface.

Listing 5-36. The IsModified Interface

```kotlin
package com.apress.prospring6.five.introduction
```

```kotlin
interface IsModified {
    val isModified: Boolean
}
```

There's nothing special here—just a single val. Kotlin implicitly adds a method for that, isModified(), indicating whether an object has been modified.

Creating a Mixin

The next step is to create the code that implements IsModified and that is introduced to the objects; this is referred to as a *mixin*. As we mentioned earlier, it is much simpler to achieve this by subclassing DelegatingIntroductionInterceptor than to create one by directly implementing the IntroductionInterceptor interface. The mixin class, IsModifiedMixin, subclasses DelegatingIntroductionInterceptor and also implements the IsModified interface. This implementation is shown in Listing 5-37.

Listing 5-37. The IsModifiedMixin Class

```kotlin
package com.apress.prospring6.five.introduction
```

```kotlin
import java.lang.reflect.Method
import java.util.HashMap
import java.util.Map
import java.util.function.Predicate
import org.aopalliance.intercept.MethodInvocation
import org.springframework.aop.support.DelegatingIntroductionInterceptor
```

```kotlin
class IsModifiedMixin : DelegatingIntroductionInterceptor(), IsModified {
    override var isModified = false
        private set
    private val methodCache = mutableMapOf<Method, Method?>()
    private val isSetter =
        Predicate { invocation: MethodInvocation ->
            invocation.method.name.startsWith("set") && (invocation.arguments.size == 1)
        }

    @Throws(Throwable::class)
    override fun invoke(invocation: MethodInvocation): Any? {
        if (!isModified) {
            if (isSetter.test(invocation)) {
                val getter = getGetter(invocation.method)
                if (getter != null) {
                    val newVal = invocation.arguments[0]
                    val oldVal = getter.invoke(invocation.getThis())
                    isModified = if (newVal == null && oldVal == null) {
                        false
                    } else if (newVal == null || oldVal == null) {
                        true
                    } else {
                        newVal != oldVal
                    }
                }
            }
        }
        return super.invoke(invocation)
    }

    private fun getGetter(setter: Method): Method? {
        var getter = methodCache[setter]
        return getter ?:
            try {
                val getterName = setter.name.replaceFirst("set".toRegex(), "get")
                getter = setter.declaringClass.getMethod(getterName)
                synchronized(methodCache) { methodCache.put(setter, getter) }
                getter
            } catch (ex: NoSuchMethodException) {
                null
            }
    }

    companion object {
        @Serial
        private val serialVersionUID = 2L
    }
}
```

The first thing to notice here is the implementation of IsModified, which consists of the "modified" property. This example highlights why you must have one mixin instance per advised object—the mixin introduces not only methods to the object but also state. If you share a single instance of this mixin across many objects, then you are also sharing the state, which means all objects show as modified the first time a single object becomes modified.

You do not actually have to implement the invoke() method for a mixin, but in this case, doing so allows us to detect automatically when a modification occurs. We start by performing the check only if the object is still unmodified; we do not need to check for modifications once we know that the object has been modified. Next, we check to see whether the method is a setter, and if it is, we retrieve the corresponding getter method. Note that we cache the getter/setter pairs for quicker future retrieval. Finally, we compare the value returned by the getter with that passed to the setter to determine whether a modification has occurred. Notice that we check for the different possible combinations of null and set the modifications appropriately. It is important to remember that when you are using DelegatingIntroductionInterceptor, you must call super.invoke() when overriding invoke() because it is the DelegatingIntroductionInterceptor that dispatches the invocation to the correct location, either the advised object or the mixin itself.

You can implement as many interfaces as you like in your mixin, each of which is automatically introduced into the advised object.

Creating an Advisor

The next step is to create an Advisor to wrap the creation of the mixin class. This step is optional, but it does help to ensure that a new instance of the mixin is being used for each advised object. Listing 5-38 shows the IsModifiedAdvisor class.

Listing 5-38. The IsModifiedAdvisor Class

```
package com.apress.prospring6.five.introduction

import org.springframework.aop.support.DefaultIntroductionAdvisor

class IsModifiedAdvisor : DefaultIntroductionAdvisor(IsModifiedMixin()) {
    companion object {
        @JvmStatic private val serialVersionUID = 1L
    }
}
```

Notice that we have extended DefaultIntroductionAdvisor to create our IsModifiedAdvisor. The implementation of this advisor is trivial and self-explanatory.

Putting It All Together

Now that we have a mixin class and an Advisor class, we can test the modification check framework. The class that we are going to use is the Contact class that was mentioned earlier, which is part of a common package. This class is often used as a dependency for projects in this book for reasons of reusability. The contents of this class are shown in Listing 5-39.

Listing 5-39. The Contact Class

package com.apress.prospring6.five.introduction

```kotlin
open class Contact {
    open var name: String? = null
    open var phoneNumber: String? = null
    open var email: String? = null

    override fun toString(): String {
        return ToStringBuilder(this)
            .append("name", name)
            .append("phoneNumber", phoneNumber)
            .append("email", email)
            .toString()
    }
}
```

This bean has a set of properties, but only the name property gets used for testing the modification check mixin. Listing 5-40 shows how to assemble the advised proxy and then test the modification check code.

Listing 5-40. The IntroductionDemo Class

```kotlin
package com.apress.prospring6.five.introduction

import org.slf4j.LoggerFactory
import org.springframework.aop.IntroductionAdvisor
import org.springframework.aop.framework.ProxyFactory

object IntroductionDemo {
    private val LOGGER = LoggerFactory.getLogger(IntroductionDemo::class.java)
    @JvmStatic
    fun main(args: Array<String>) {
        val target = Contact().apply {
            name = "John Mayer"
        }
        val advisor: IntroductionAdvisor = IsModifiedAdvisor()
        val pf = ProxyFactory().apply {
            setTarget(target)
            addAdvisor(advisor)
            isOptimize = true
        }

        val o = pf.proxy
        val proxy = o as? Contact
        val proxyInterface = o as? IsModified

        LOGGER.info("Is Contact? => {} ", proxy is Contact)
        LOGGER.info("Is IsModified? => {} ", proxy is IsModified)
        LOGGER.info("Has been modified? => {} ", proxyInterface?.isModified)
        when(proxy){ is Contact ->   proxy.name = "John Mayer" }
        LOGGER.info("Has been modified? => {} ", proxyInterface?.isModified)
```

```
        when(proxy){ is Contact ->  proxy.name = "Ben Barnes" }
        LOGGER.info("Has been modified? => {} ", proxyInterface?.isModified)
    }
}
```

Notice that when we are creating the proxy, we set the optimize flag to true to force the use of the CGLIB proxy. The reason for this is that when you are using the JDK proxy to introduce a mixin, the resulting proxy will not be an instance of the object class (in this case Contact); the proxy implements only the mixin interfaces—it does not extend the original class. With the CGLIB proxy, the original class is extended by the proxy along with the mixin interfaces.

Notice in Listing 5-40 that we test first to see whether the proxy is an instance of Contact and then to see whether it is an instance of IsModified. Both tests return true when you are using the CGLIB proxy, but only the IsModified test returns true for the JDK proxy. Finally, we test the modification check code by first setting the name property to its current value and then to a new value, checking the value of the isModified flag each time. Running the example results in the output shown in Listing 5-41.

Listing 5-41. The IntroductionDemo Execution Output

```
INFO : IntroductionDemo - Is Contact? => true
INFO : IntroductionDemo - Is IsModified? => true
INFO : IntroductionDemo - Has been modified? => false
INFO : IntroductionDemo - Has been modified? => false
INFO : IntroductionDemo - Has been modified? => true
```

As expected, both instanceof tests return true. Notice that the first call to isModified(), before any modification occurred, returns false. The next call, after we set the value of name to the same value, also returns false. For the final call, however, after we set the value of name to a new value, the isModified() method returns true, indicating that the object has in fact been modified.

Introduction Summary

Introductions are one of the most powerful features of Spring AOP; they allow you not only to extend the functionality of existing methods but to extend the set of interfaces and object implementations dynamically. Using introductions is the perfect way to implement crosscutting logic that your application interacts with through well-defined interfaces. In general, this is the kind of logic that you want to apply declaratively rather than programmatically. By using IsModifiedMixin defined in this example and the framework services discussed in the next section, you can declaratively define which objects are capable of modification checks, without needing to modify the implementations of those objects.

Obviously, because introductions work via proxies, they add a certain amount of overhead. All methods on the proxy are considered advised since pointcuts cannot be used in conjunction with introductions. However, in the case of many of the services that you can implement by using introductions, such as the object modification check, this performance overhead is a small price to pay for the reduction in code required to implement the service, as well as the increase in stability and maintainability that comes from fully centralizing the service logic.

Framework Services for AOP

Up to now, we have had to write a lot of code to advise objects and generate the proxies for them. Although this in itself is not a huge problem, it does mean that all advice configuration is hard-coded into your application, removing some benefits of being able to advise a method implementation transparently. Thankfully, Spring provides additional framework services that allow you to create an advised proxy in your application configuration and then inject this proxy into a target bean just like any other dependencies.

Using the declarative approach to AOP configuration is preferable to the manual, programmatic mechanism. When you use the declarative mechanism, not only do you externalize the configuration of advice, but you also reduce the chance of coding errors. You can also take advantage of DI and AOP combined to enable AOP so that it can be used in a completely transparent environment.

Configuring AOP Declaratively

When using declarative configuration of Spring AOP, three options exist:

- *Using ProxyFactoryBean*: In Spring AOP, ProxyFactoryBean provides a declarative way to configure Spring's ApplicationContext (and hence the underlying BeanFactory) when creating AOP proxies based on defined Spring beans.

- *Using the Spring aop namespace*: Introduced in Spring 2.0, the aop namespace provides a simplified way (when compared to ProxyFactoryBean) to define aspects and their DI requirements in Spring applications. However, the aop namespace also uses ProxyFactoryBean behind the scenes. We do not show this option in this book since the focus is on using Java/Kotlin code-based configuration.

- *Using @AspectJ-style annotations*: The practical way to configure Spring AOP is to use @AspectJ-style annotations within your classes. Although the syntax it uses is based on AspectJ and you need to include some AspectJ libraries when using this option, Spring still uses the proxy mechanism (that is, creates proxied objects for the targets) when bootstrapping ApplicationContext.

Using ProxyFactoryBean

The ProxyFactoryBean class is an implementation of FactoryBean that allows you to specify a bean to target, and it provides a set of advice and advisors for that bean that are eventually merged into an AOP proxy. ProxyFactoryBean is used to apply interceptor logic to an existing target bean in such a way that when methods on that bean are invoked, the interceptors are executed before and after that method call. Because you can use both advisor and advice with ProxyFactoryBean, you can configure not only the advice declaratively but the pointcuts as well.

ProxyFactoryBean shares a common interface (the org.springframework.aop.framework. Advised interface) with ProxyFactory (both classes extend the org.springframework.aop.framework. AdvisedSupport class indirectly, which implements the Advised interface), and as a result, it exposes many of the same flags such as frozen, optimize, and exposeProxy. The values for these flags are passed directly to the underlying ProxyFactory, which allows you to configure the factory declaratively as well.

Using ProxyFactoryBean is simple. You define a bean that will be the target bean, and then using ProxyFactoryBean, you define the bean that your application will access, using the target bean as the proxy target. Where possible, define the target bean as an anonymous bean inside the proxy bean declaration. This prevents your application from accidentally accessing the unadvised bean. However, in some cases, such as the sample we are about to show you, you may want to create more than one proxy for the same bean, so you should use a normal top-level bean for this case.

For the following example, imagine this scenario: you have a singer working together with a documentarist to produce a documentary of a tour. In this case, Documentarist has a dependency on the Singer implementation. The Singer implementation that we will use here is the previously introduced GrammyGuitarist that has been shown twice before in this chapter, the last time in Listing 5-33. The Documentarist class that will basically tell the singer what to do while filming the documentary is shown in code Listing 5-42.

Listing 5-42. The Documentarist Class

```kotlin
package com.apress.prospring6.five.common

open class Documentarist {
    private var guitarist: GrammyGuitarist? = null
    open fun execute() {
        guitarist!!.sing()
        guitarist!!.talk()
    }

    open fun setDep(guitarist: GrammyGuitarist?) {
        this.guitarist = guitarist
    }
}
```

For this example, we are going to create two proxies for a single GrammySinger instance, both with the same basic advice shown in Listing 5-43.

Listing 5-43. The AuditAdvice Class

```kotlin
package com.apress.prospring6.five.common

import org.aspectj.lang.JoinPoint
import org.slf4j.Logger
import org.slf4j.LoggerFactory

class AuditAdvice : MethodBeforeAdvice {
    @Throws(Throwable::class)
    override fun before(method: Method, args: Array<out Any>, @Nullable target: Any?) {
        LOGGER.info("Executing {}", method)
    }

    companion object {
        private val LOGGER = LoggerFactory.getLogger(AuditAdvice::class.java)
    }
}
```

The first proxy will just advise the target by using the advice directly; thus, all methods will be advised. For the second proxy, we will configure AspectJExpressionPointcut and DefaultPointcutAdvisor so that only the sing() method of the GrammySinger class is advised. To test the advice, we will create two bean definitions of type Documentarist, each of which will be injected with a different proxy. Then we will invoke the execute() method on each of these beans and observe what happens when the advised methods on the dependency are invoked. Figure 5-10 shows the configuration for this example represented by the AopConfig class.

```
@Configuration
internal open class AopConfig : BeanFactoryAware {
    private var beanFactory: BeanFactory? = null

    @Throws(BeansException::class)                    @Bean
    override fun setBeanFactory(beanFactory: BeanFactory) {     open fun documentaristOne() = Documentarist().apply {
        this.beanFactory = beanFactory                     setDep(proxyOne()) }
    }
                                                      @Bean
    @Bean                                             open fun proxyTwo() = ProxyFactoryBean().apply {
    open fun johnMayer() = GrammyGuitarist()             isProxyTargetClass = true
                                                         setTarget(johnMayer())
    @Bean                                                setInterceptorNames("advisor")
    open fun advice(): Advice = AuditAdvice()            setBeanFactory(beanFactory!!)
                                                         isFrozen = true
    @Bean                                             }.`object` as GrammyGuitarist
    open fun proxyOne() = ProxyFactoryBean().apply {
        isProxyTargetClass = true                     @Bean
        setTarget(johnMayer())                        open fun documentaristTwo() = Documentarist().apply {
        setInterceptorNames("advice")                    setDep(proxyTwo()) }
        setBeanFactory(beanFactory!!)
        isFrozen = true                               @Bean
    }.`object` as GrammyGuitarist                     open fun advisor() = DefaultPointcutAdvisor().apply {
                                                         advice = advice()
                                                         pointcut = AspectJExpressionPointcut().apply {
                                                             expression = "execution(* sing*(..))" }
                                                      }
                                                  }
```

Figure 5-10. *Declarative AOP configuration*

Since the image might be unclear in print, Listing 5-44 shows the AopConfig class.

Listing 5-44. The AopConfig Configuration Class

```
package com.apress.prospring6.five
// import statements omitted

@Configuration
internal open class AopConfig : BeanFactoryAware {
    private var beanFactory: BeanFactory? = null

    @Throws(BeansException::class)
    override fun setBeanFactory(beanFactory: BeanFactory) {
        this.beanFactory = beanFactory
    }

    @Bean
    open fun johnMayer() = GrammyGuitarist()

    @Bean
    open fun advice(): Advice = AuditAdvice()
```

```kotlin
    @Bean
    open fun proxyOne() = ProxyFactoryBean().apply {
        isProxyTargetClass = true
        setTarget(johnMayer())
        setInterceptorNames("advice")
        setBeanFactory(beanFactory!!)
        isFrozen = true
    }.`object` as GrammyGuitarist

    @Bean
    open fun documentaristOne() = Documentarist().apply {
        setDep(proxyOne()) }

    @Bean
    open fun proxyTwo() = ProxyFactoryBean().apply {
        isProxyTargetClass = true
        setTarget(johnMayer())
        setInterceptorNames("advisor")
        setBeanFactory(beanFactory!!)
        isFrozen = true
    }.`object` as GrammyGuitarist

    @Bean
    open fun documentaristTwo() = Documentarist().apply {
        setDep(proxyTwo()) }

    @Bean
    open fun advisor() = DefaultPointcutAdvisor().apply {
        advice = advice()
        pointcut = AspectJExpressionPointcut().apply {
            expression = "execution(* sing*(..))" }
    }
}
```

We used an image to depict this configuration because it might look a little confusing and we wanted to make sure it is easy to see where each bean is injected. In the example, we are simply setting the properties that we set in code using Spring's DI capabilities. The only points of interest are that the pointcut is not declared as a bean, but as a simple POJO set on the advisor bean, since this is not meant to be shared, and we use the ProxyFactoryBean class to create proxies. The important point to realize when you are using ProxyFactoryBean is that the ProxyFactoryBean declaration is the one to expose to your application and the one to use when you are fulfilling dependencies. The underlying target bean declaration is not advised, so you should use this bean only when you want to bypass the AOP framework, although in general, your application should not be aware of the AOP framework and thus should not want to bypass it. For this reason, you should use anonymous beans wherever possible to avoid accidental access from the application.

Listing 5-45 shows a simple class that obtains the two Documentarist instances from ApplicationContext and then runs the execute() method for each one. In the same listing you can also see its output.

Listing 5-45. The Class Testing the ProxyFactoryBean Configuration

```
package com.apress.prospring6.five
// import statements omitted

object ProxyFactoryBeanDemo {
    @JvmStatic
    fun main(args: Array<String>) {
        val ctx = AnnotationConfigApplicationContext(
            AopConfig::class.java
        )
        val documentaristOne = ctx.getBean("documentaristOne",
            Documentarist::class.java)
        val documentaristTwo = ctx.getBean("documentaristTwo",
            Documentarist::class.java)
        println("Documentarist One >>")
        documentaristOne.execute()
        println("\nDocumentarist Two >> ")
        documentaristTwo.execute()
    }
}

// output
Documentarist One >>
INFO : AuditAdvice - Executing public void com.apress.prospring6.five.common.
GrammyGuitarist.sing()
INFO : GrammyGuitarist - sing: Gravity is working against me
And gravity wants to bring me down
INFO : AuditAdvice - Executing public void com.apress.prospring6.five.common.
GrammyGuitarist.talk()
INFO : GrammyGuitarist - talk

Documentarist Two >>
INFO : AuditAdvice - Executing public void com.apress.prospring6.five.common.
GrammyGuitarist.sing()
INFO : GrammyGuitarist - sing: Gravity is working against me
And gravity wants to bring me down
INFO : GrammyGuitarist - talk
```

As expected, both the sing() and talk() methods in the first proxy are advised because no pointcut was used in its configuration. For the second proxy, however, only the sing() method was advised because of the pointcut used in the configuration.

Using ProxyFactoryBean for Introductions

You can use the ProxyFactoryBean class not only to advise an object but also to introduce mixins to your objects. Remember from the earlier discussion on introductions that you must use an IntroductionAdvisor to add an introduction; you cannot add an introduction directly. The same rule applies when you are using ProxyFactoryBean with introductions. When you are using ProxyFactoryBean, it becomes much easier to configure your proxies if you created a custom Advisor for your mixin. Listing 5-46 shows a configuration snippet for the IsModifiedMixin introduction from earlier in the chapter.

Listing 5-46. The Class Testing the ProxyFactoryBean Configuration

```
package com.apress.prospring6.five

import org.springframework.aop.framework.ProxyFactoryBean
// other import statements omitted

@Configuration
internal open class IntroductionAopConfig {
    @Bean
    open fun guitarist(): Contact {
        val contact = Contact()
        contact.name = "John Mayer"
        return contact
    }

    @Bean
    open fun advisor(): IsModifiedAdvisor {
        return IsModifiedAdvisor()
    }

    @Bean
    open fun proxy(): Contact {
        val pfb = ProxyFactoryBean()
        pfb.isProxyTargetClass = true
        pfb.setTarget(guitarist())
        pfb.addAdvisor(advisor())
        pfb.isFrozen = true
        return pfb.getObject() as Contact
    }
}
```

Running this example you can see that the proxy effectively is obtained from ApplicationContext and no configuration is present in the application code.

Notice that there is no need to refer to the advisor bean by name to provide it as an argument to ProxyFactoryBean because addAdvisor(..) can be called directly and the advisor bean can be provided as the argument. This obviously simplifies the configuration.

ProxyFactoryBean Summary

When you use ProxyFactoryBean, you can configure AOP proxies that provide all the flexibility of the programmatic method without needing to couple your application to the AOP configuration. Unless you need to perform decisions at runtime as to how your proxies should be created, it is best to use the declarative method of proxy configuration over the programmatic method. Let's move on so you can see the most practical way for declarative Spring AOP.

Using @AspectJ-Style Annotations

When using Spring AOP with JDK 5 or newer, you can also use the @AspectJ-style annotations to declare your advice. However, as stated before, Spring still uses its own proxying mechanism for advising the target methods, not AspectJ's weaving mechanism.

In this section, we will go through how to implement the same aspects as the ones introduced at the beginning of the chapter by using @AspectJ-style annotations. AspectJ is a general-purpose aspect-oriented extension to Java born out of need to solve issues or concerns that are not well captured by traditional programming methodologies—in other words, crosscutting concerns. For the examples in this section, we will use annotations for other Spring beans as well, and we will use Java/Kotlin configuration classes.

Listing 5-47 depicts the GrammyGuitarist class with the bean being declared using annotations.

Listing 5-47. GrammyGuitarist Bean Declared Using the @Component Annotation

```
package com.apress.prospring6.five.annotated

import org.springframework.stereotype.Component
// other import statements missing

        LOGGER.info("sing: Wild blue, deeper than I ever knew")
    }

    open fun sing(guitar: Guitar) {
        LOGGER.info("play: " + guitar.play())
    }

    open fun talk() {
        LOGGER.info("talk")
    }

    override fun rest() {
        LOGGER.info("zzz")
    }

    companion object {
        private val LOGGER = LoggerFactory.getLogger(GrammyGuitarist::class.java)
    }
}
```

To make things more interesting, a NewDocumentarist class is introduced that calls sing(Guitar) as well. This class is shown in Listing 5-48.

Listing 5-48. NewDocumentarist Bean Declared Using the @Component Annotation

```
package com.apress.prospring6.five.annotated

import org.springframework.beans.factory.annotation.Autowired
import org.springframework.beans.factory.annotation.Qualifier
// other import statements omitted

@Component("documentarist")
open class NewDocumentarist {
```

```
    protected var guitarist: GrammyGuitarist? = null
        @Autowired
        @Qualifier("johnMayer")
        set(value) {
            field = value
        }

    open fun execute() {
        guitarist!!.sing()
        val guitar = Guitar()
        guitar.brand = "Gibson"
        guitarist!!.sing(guitar)
        guitarist!!.talk()
    }
}
```

Both classes are annotated with @Component to declare beans of these types. The annotation is also used to name the beans. In the NewDocumentarist class, the setter method of the property guitarist was annotated with @Autowired for automatic injection by Spring and with @Qualifier to configure the name of the bean that Spring should inject.

Now that we have the beans, let's start with a very simple before advice.

Declarative Before Advice with AspectJ Annotations

Using annotations, we don't always need to explicitly declare a Pointcut, since the AspectJ @Before annotation's default attribute can be configured with a pointcut expression representing where to bind the advice. Listing 5-49 shows the BeforeAdviceV1 class that declares the annotated advice.

Listing 5-49. BeforeAdviceV1 Class Declaring an Aspect Bean with a Single Before Advice

```
package com.apress.prospring6.five.advice

@Component
@Aspect
class BeforeAdviceV1 {
    @Before("execution(* com.apress.prospring6.five..sing*(com.apress.prospring6.five.
    common.Guitar))")
    fun simpleBeforeAdvice(joinPoint: JoinPoint) {
        val signature = joinPoint.signature as MethodSignature
        LOGGER.info(" > Executing: {} from {}", signature.name,
            signature.declaringTypeName)
    }

    companion object {
        private val LOGGER = LoggerFactory.getLogger(BeforeAdviceV1::class.java)
    }
}
```

ℹ️   Why the V1 suffix? Because there is more than one way to declare this advice and pointcut. In this section all classes declaring the same before advice in different ways are suffixed with a number that is also used as a suffix for the method testing the advice.

Notice how the advice class does not need to implement the `MethodBeforeAdvice`. Another thing to notice is the `@Aspect` annotation is used to declare that it's an aspect class. An aspect class groups together advice declarations, pointcuts, and other utility methods for declaring these.

The `@Before` annotation marks the `simpleBeforeAdvice(..)` method as a before advice and the expression provided as the value for its default attribute is a pointcut expression that means we want to advise all methods with the name starting with `sing`, and the classes are defined under the package `com.apress.prospring6.five` (including all the subpackages, which is what `..` means). Also, the `sing*` method should receive one argument with the `com.apress.prospring6.five.common.Guitar` type.

The before advice method accepts the joinpoint as an argument but not the method, object, and arguments. Actually, for the advice class, this argument is optional, so you can leave the method with no argument. However, if in the advice you need to access the information of the joinpoint being advised (in this case, we want to dump the information of the calling type and method name), then you need to define the acceptance of the argument. When the argument is defined for the method, Spring will automatically pass the joinpoint into the method for your processing. In this example, we use the `JoinPoint` to print the joinpoint details.

To test this advice we must design a Spring configuration class that discovers the `GrammyGuitarist` and `NewDocumentarist` and enables support for handling components marked with AspectJ's `@Aspect` annotation and others. To keep the code simple and the advices isolated for each scenario in this section, the aspect bean will be registered together with this configuration class in an empty `ApplicationContext`. This allows us to reuse this configuration class, and keep the testing snippets identical, the only difference being the aspect class added to the context.

The configuration class is shown in Listing 5-50.

Listing 5-50. AspectJ Spring Configuration Class

```
package com.apress.prospring6.five.annotated

import org.springframework.context.annotation.ComponentScan
import org.springframework.context.annotation.Configuration
import org.springframework.context.annotation.EnableAspectJAutoProxy

@ComponentScan
@Configuration
@EnableAspectJAutoProxy(proxyTargetClass = true)
open class AspectJAopConfig
```

Notice the `@EnableAspectJAutoProxy` annotation. This annotation enables support for handling components marked with AspectJ's `@Aspect` annotation and is designed to be used on classes annotated with `@Configuration`. It also has an attribute called `proxyTargetClass`. When set to `true` it indicates that subclass-based (CGLIB) proxies are to be created as opposed to standard Java/Kotlin interface-based proxies. In this example, CGLIB proxies are needed because even if `GrammyGuitarist` implements the `Singer` interface, and by default interface-based JDK dynamic proxies should be suitable, `NewDocumentarist` strictly requires the dependency to be of type `GrammyGuitarist` or an extension of it. So we need a proxy that extends `GrammyGuitarist`. Without the `proxyTargetClass = true` attribute when attempting to start a Spring application with this configuration, the following exception will be thrown:

Error creating bean with name 'documentarist': **Unsatisfied dependency expressed through method 'setGuitarist'** parameter 0; nested exception is org.springframework.beans.factory.BeanNotOfRequiredTypeException: Bean named 'johnMayer' is expected to be of type 'com.apress.prospring6.five.annotated.GrammyGuitarist' but was actually of type 'jdk.proxy3.$Proxy26'

A rule of thumb if at least one class in the configuration needs to be proxied by subclassing the proxyTargetClass=true, otherwise the application context won't be created correctly.

The class is also annotated with @ComponentScan that enables discovery of beans in the class where this class is (com.apress.prospring6.five.annotated) and its subpackages.

To test each type of advice introduced in this section, test methods are used, and grouped in the AnnotatedAdviceTest class shown in Listing 5-51.

Listing 5-51. AnnotatedAdviceTest Class Grouping All Annotated Aspect Tests and a Test Method Verifying the Before Advice Declared in Class BeforeAdviceV1

```
package com.apress.prospring6.five.annotated

import org.junit.jupiter.api.Test
import com.apress.prospring6.five.advice.BeforeAdviceV1
import org.springframework.context.annotation.AnnotationConfigApplicationContext

class AnnotatedAdviceTest {
    @Test
    fun testBeforeAdviceV1() {
        val ctx = AnnotationConfigApplicationContext()
        ctx.register(AspectJAopConfig::class.java, BeforeAdviceV1::class.java)
        ctx.refresh()
        Assertions.assertTrue(listOf(*ctx.beanDefinitionNames).contains("beforeAdviceV1"))
        val documentarist = ctx.getBean(
            "documentarist",
            NewDocumentarist::class.java
        )
        documentarist.execute()
        ctx.close()
    }
}
```

The testBeforeAdviceV1() method creates an ApplicationContext based on the AspectJAopConfig configuration class and adds the aspect bean declared by the BeforeAdviceV1 class to it. If the context can be created and the bean is found to be present, then the documentarist bean is retrieved and its execute() method is invoked. This will cause the proxy.sing() method to be called that includes the simpleBeforeAdvice. When all goes well, the test should pass and the produced console output should be as shown in Listing 5-52.

Listing 5-52. Console Output Produced by Running the testBeforeAdviceV1() Method

```
DEBUG: AbstractApplicationContext - Refreshing org.springframework.context.annotation.Annota
tionConfigApplicationContext@1046d517
...
DEBUG: ReflectiveAspectJAdvisorFactory - Found AspectJ method: public void com.apress.
prospring6.five.advice.BeforeAdviceV1.simpleBeforeAdvice(org.aspectj.lang.JoinPoint)
...
INFO : GrammyGuitarist - sing: Wild blue, deeper than I ever knew
INFO : BeforeAdviceV1 -  > Executing: sing from com.apress.prospring6.five.annotated.
GrammyGuitarist
INFO : GrammyGuitarist - play: G C G C Am D7
INFO : GrammyGuitarist - talk
DEBUG: AbstractApplicationContext - Closing org.springframework.context.annotation.Annotatio
nConfigApplicationContext@1046d517, started on ...
```

A few things were mentioned so far:

- In our example, we have a pointcut expression, but a pointcut can be declared separately from the advice, which is quite cool, since this means it can be reused.

- The before advice method accepts the joinpoint as an argument, but not the method, object, and arguments. However, the signature of this method is flexible, so we can add the argument value.

Listing 5-53 shows BeforeAdviceV2 has an advice declaration equivalent to BeforeAdviceV1, but the pointcut is separated from the advice declaration.

Listing 5-53. BeforeAdviceV2 Class Declaring an Aspect Bean with a Single Before Advice and a Pointcut

```kotlin
package com.apress.prospring6.five.advice

import org.aspectj.lang.annotation.Pointcut
// other import statements omitted

@Component
@Aspect
class BeforeAdviceV2 {
    @Pointcut("execution(* com.apress.prospring6.

            five..sing*(com.apress.prospring6.five.common.Guitar))")
    fun singExecution() {
    }

    @Before("singExecution()")
    fun simpleBeforeAdvice(joinPoint: JoinPoint) {
        val signature = joinPoint.signature as MethodSignature
        LOGGER.info(" > Executing: {} from {}", signature.name,
            signature.declaringTypeName)
    }
}
```

```
companion object {
    private val LOGGER = LoggerFactory.getLogger(BeforeAdviceV2::class.java)
}
}
```

(no line break and no spaces in the @Pointcut parameter) Notice how the expression is provided as a value for the `@Pointcut` default attribute and this annotation is used to decorate a different method than the advice. A call to this method is then used as an expression for the @Before annotation. The method annotated with @Pointcut must return void and can also have arguments, as shown a little bit later in this section.

The test method is 99% identical to the one shown in Listing 5-50, with the exception that the BeforeAdviceV1 gets replaced with the BeforeAdviceV2 type. The output is identical to that of the execution of testBeforeAdviceV1().

As previously mentioned, now that we have a pointcut, we can add another pointcut and compose them. The AspectJ pointcut expressions semantics are quite rich, and if you are interested you can check out the official documentation[6]. The second pointcut introduced in class BeforeAdviceV3 is used to declare that the bean used as a target should have a name that starts with john. This pointcut is composed with the singExecution() pointcut using an AND (&&) operation. This obviously ensures that all methods with the name starting with sing and the classes are defined under the package com.apress.prospring6.five (including all the subpackages, indicated by ..). Also, the sing* method should receive one argument with the com.apress.prospring6.five.common.Guitar type **AND** only the beans with names starting with john should be advised.

Listing 5-54 shows BeforeAdviceV3 which uses a before advice declaration that applies to a composed pointcut.

Listing 5-54. BeforeAdviceV3 Class Declaring an Aspect Bean with a Single Before Advice and Two Pointcuts That Are Composed

```
package com.apress.prospring6.five.advice
// import statements omitted

@Component
@Aspect
class BeforeAdviceV3 {
    @Pointcut("execution(* com.apress.prospring6.
        five..sing*(com.apress.prospring6.five.common.Guitar))")
    fun singExecution() {
    }

    @get:Pointcut("bean(john*)")
    val isJohn: Unit
        get() {}

    @Before("singExecution() && isJohn()")
    fun simpleBeforeAdvice(joinPoint: JoinPoint) {
        val signature = joinPoint.signature as MethodSignature
        LOGGER.info(" > Executing: {} from {}", signature.name,
            signature.declaringTypeName)
    }
```

---

[6] https://www.eclipse.org/aspectj/doc/released/progguide/semantics-pointcuts.html

```
        companion object {
            private val LOGGER = LoggerFactory.getLogger(BeforeAdviceV3::class.java)
        }
    }
```

(no line break and no spaces in the @Pointcut parameter) The test method is 99% identical to the one shown in Listing 5-50, with the exception that the BeforeAdviceV1 gets replaced with the BeforeAdviceV3 type. The output is identical to that of the execution of testBeforeAdviceV1(), since we only have one bean named johnMayer in the configuration.

As for the arguments, we can modify the advice to do some checks on the arguments of the method being advised, but this will require the modification of the pointcut identifying the method and the method it decorates, and also the signature of the advice. This version of this advice is depicted in Listing 5-55.

Listing 5-55. BeforeAdviceV4 Class Declaring an Aspect Bean with a Single Before Advice That Checks the Argument Value

```
package com.apress.prospring6.five.advice
// import statements omitted

@Component
@Aspect
class BeforeAdviceV4 {
    @Pointcut("execution(* com.apress.prospring6.
        five..sing*(com.apress.prospring6.five.common.Guitar))  && args(value)")
    fun singExecution(value: Guitar?) {
    }

    @get:Pointcut("bean(john*)")
    val isJohn: Unit
        get() {}

    @Before(value = "singExecution(guitar) && isJohn()", argNames = "joinPoint,guitar")
    fun simpleBeforeAdvice(joinPoint: JoinPoint, guitar: Guitar) {
        if (guitar.brand.equals("Gibson")) {
            val signature = joinPoint.signature as MethodSignature
            LOGGER.info(" > Executing: {} from {}", signature.name,
                signature.declaringTypeName)
        }
    }

    companion object {
        private val LOGGER = LoggerFactory.getLogger(BeforeAdviceV4::class.java)
    }
}
```

🔥 Notice that the pointcut expression includes the argument names, joinPoint and guitar, which means the advice method must have arguments with the names in the expression, using the same order as in the expression.

(no line break and no spaces in the @Pointcut parameter) The test method is 99% identical to the one shown in Listing 5-50, with the exception that the BeforeAdviceV1 gets replaced with the BeforeAdviceV4 type. The output is identical to that of the execution of testBeforeAdviceV1(), since we only have one bean named johnMayer in the configuration and this bean had a Guitar property with the brand set to Gibson. Feel free to modify the advice code and replace the guitar brand name and check how the advice output is no longer shown in the console when you run the test.

Declarative Around Advice with AspectJ annotations

Declaring an around advice is pretty similar, but there are a few differences. As expected, the annotation to declare the advice is @Around and the method signature includes a ProceedingJoinPoint since this type of advice has to have the possibility to call the target method.

Listing 5-56 depicts the class AroundAdviceV1 that declares a pointcut and an around advice. This version does not take parameters into account.

Listing 5-56. AroundAdviceV1 Class Declaring an Aspect Bean with a Single Around Advice That Wraps Around the Target Method

```
package com.apress.prospring6.five.advice

import org.aspectj.lang.ProceedingJoinPoint
import org.aspectj.lang.annotation.Around
// other import statements omitted

@Component
@Aspect
class AroundAdviceV1 {
    @Pointcut("execution(* com.apress.prospring6.
        five..sing*(com.apress.prospring6.five.common.Guitar))")
    fun singExecution() {
    }

    @Around("singExecution()")
    @Throws(Throwable::class)
    fun simpleAroundAdvice(pjp: ProceedingJoinPoint): Any {
        val signature = pjp.signature as MethodSignature
        LOGGER.info(" > Before Executing: {} from {}", signature.name,
            signature.declaringTypeName)
        val retVal = pjp.proceed()
        LOGGER.info(" > After Executing: {} from {}", signature.name,
            signature.declaringTypeName)
        return retVal
    }

    companion object {
        private val LOGGER = LoggerFactory.getLogger(AroundAdviceV1::class.java)
    }
}
```

(no line break and no spaces in the @Pointcut parameter) This advice does nothing else than print a message before and after invoking the target method. If a configuration is created from the AspectJAopConfig class and the AroundAdviceV1 and tested as shown previously in the section, the resulting output proves without a doubt that the advice method has executed as expected, since the message printed by the target method sing(Guitar) is wrapped between the messages printed by the simpleAfterAdvice as shown in Listing 5-57.

Listing 5-57. Console Output Produced by Testing the AroundAdviceV1 Aspect Class

```
INFO : GrammyGuitarist - sing: Wild blue, deeper than I ever knew
INFO : AroundAdviceV1 -  > Before Executing: sing from com.apress.prospring6.five.annotated.
GrammyGuitarist
INFO : GrammyGuitarist - play: G C G C Am D7
INFO : AroundAdviceV1 -  > After Executing: sing from com.apress.prospring6.five.annotated.
GrammyGuitarist
INFO : GrammyGuitarist - talk
```

Let's make things more interesting and introduce AroundAdviceV2, which also uses the argument of the target method; in this case, the Guitar.brand property value is added to the advice messages, as shown in Listing 5-58.

Listing 5-58. AroundAdviceV2 Class Declaring an Aspect Bean with a Single Around Advice That Wraps Around the Target Method

```
package com.apress.prospring6.five.advice
// other import statements omitted

@Component
@Aspect
class AroundAdviceV2 {
    @Pointcut("execution(* com.apress.prospring6.
        five..sing*(com.apress.prospring6.five.common.Guitar))  && args(value)")
    fun singExecution(value: Guitar?) {
    }

    @Around(value = "singExecution(guitar)", argNames = "pjp,guitar")
    @Throws(Throwable::class)
    fun simpleAroundAdvice(pjp: ProceedingJoinPoint, guitar: Guitar): Any {
        val signature = pjp.signature as MethodSignature
        LOGGER.info(
            " > Before Executing: {} from {} with argument {}",
            signature.name,
            signature.declaringTypeName,
            guitar.brand
        )
        val retVal = pjp.proceed()
        LOGGER.info(
            " > After Executing: {} from {} with argument {}",
            signature.name,
            signature.declaringTypeName,
            guitar.brand
        )
```

```
        return retVal
    }

    companion object {
        private val LOGGER = LoggerFactory.getLogger(AroundAdviceV2::class.java)
    }
}
```

(no line break and no spaces in the @Pointcut parameter) To underline how advice is being applied to all invocation, let's also extend the NewDocumentarist and change the brand of guitar our singer is playing. The new implementation is depicted in Listing 5-59.

Listing 5-59. CommandingDocumentarist Class

```
package com.apress.prospring6.five.annotated
// import statements omitted

@Component("commandingDocumentarist")
class CommandingDocumentarist : NewDocumentarist() {
    override fun execute() {
        guitarist!!.sing()
        val guitar = Guitar()
        guitar.brand = "Gibson"
        guitarist!!.sing(guitar)
        guitarist!!.sing(Guitar())
        guitarist!!.talk()
    }
}
```

When testing the new CommandingDocumentarist bean from a context created using the AspectJAopConfig, CommandingDocumentarist, and AroundAdviceV2 classes using a test method similar to what was shown so far, the output is as shown in Listing 5-60.

Listing 5-60. Output for Testing an AroundAdviceV2

```
INFO : GrammyGuitarist - sing: Wild blue, deeper than I ever knew

INFO : AroundAdviceV2 -  > Before Executing: sing from com.apress.prospring6.five.annotated.
GrammyGuitarist with argument Gibson
INFO : GrammyGuitarist - play: G C G C Am D7
INFO : AroundAdviceV2 -  > After Executing: sing from com.apress.prospring6.five.annotated.
GrammyGuitarist with argument Gibson

INFO : AroundAdviceV2 -  > Before Executing: sing from com.apress.prospring6.five.annotated.
GrammyGuitarist with argument  Martin
INFO : GrammyGuitarist - play: G C G C Am D7
INFO : AroundAdviceV2 -  > After Executing: sing from com.apress.prospring6.five.annotated.
GrammyGuitarist with argument  Martin

INFO : GrammyGuitarist - talk
```

You see that the around advice was applied to both invocations of the sing(Guitar) method, since applying the advice does not depend on the argument value.

Declarative After Advice with AspectJ Annotations

There are three AspectJ annotations for declaring after advice:

- @After declares advice that gets executed after the target method regardless if it returned normally or by an exception being thrown. This type of advice is typically used for releasing resources or sending notifications. Since the advice gets executed regardless of the target method, its behavior is similar to a try-catch statement.

- @AfterReturning declares advice that gets executed after the target method only if it returned normally.

- @AfterThrowing declares advice that gets executed after the target method only if it was returned by an exception being thrown.

To demonstrate how to configure each type of after advice, a new Singer implementation is needed. This implementation is named PretentiosGuitarist and it implements the sing(Guitar) method to throw an exception when the brand of the Guitar instance is "musicman". This class and the bean declaration are shown in Listing 5-61.

Listing 5-61. PretentiosGuitarist Class

```
package com.apress.prospring6.five.annotated
// import statements omitted

@Component("agustin")
open class PretentiosGuitarist : Singer {
    open fun sing(guitar: Guitar) {
        require(guitar.brand.lowercase() != "musicman") { "Unacceptable guitar!" }
        LOGGER.info("play: " + guitar.play())
    }

    override fun sing() {
        LOGGER.info("sing: solo tu puedes calmar el hambre de ti")
    }

    companion object {
        private val LOGGER = LoggerFactory.getLogger(PretentiosGuitarist::class.java)
    }
}
```

Let's start with the after advice. The AfterAdviceV1 class, the class that declares the after advice that intercepts the sing(Guitar) method, is shown in code Listing 5-62.

Listing 5-62. AfterAdviceV1 Class Declaring an Aspect Bean with a Single After Advice That Is Called after the Target Method

```
package com.apress.prospring6.five.advice

import org.aspectj.lang.annotation.After
// other import statements omitted

@Component
@Aspect
class AfterAdviceV1 {
    @Pointcut("execution(* com.apress.prospring6.
        five..PretentiosGuitarist.sing*(
        com.apress.prospring6.five.common.Guitar))  && args(value)")
    fun singExecution(value: Guitar?) {
    }

    @After(value = "singExecution(guitar) ", argNames = "joinPoint,guitar")
    fun simpleAfterAdvice(joinPoint: JoinPoint, guitar: Guitar) {
        val signature = joinPoint.signature as MethodSignature
        LOGGER.info(
            " > Executed: {} from {} with guitar {} ",
            signature.name,
            signature.declaringTypeName,
            guitar.brand
        )
    }

    companion object {
        private val LOGGER = LoggerFactory.getLogger(AfterAdviceV1::class.java)
    }
}
```

(no line break and no spaces in the @Pointcut parameter) Notice that the after advice has access to the argument of the target method and can make use of it, but it does not have access to the exception being thrown. Testing this advice requires a different approach: in the test method the proxy bean is accessed directly and the sing() method is invoked twice, once with a default Guitar instance and once with the same instance after the brand property was set to the name that causes the IllegalArgumentException to be thrown. The test method is shown in Listing 5-63.

Listing 5-63. Test Method for the AfterAdviceV1 Aspect

```
package com.apress.prospring6.five.annotated

import com.apress.prospring6.five.advice.AfterAdviceV1
import static org.junit.jupiter.api.Assertions.assertThrows
// other import statements omitted

class AnnotatedAdviceTest {
    @Test
    fun testAfterAdviceV1() {
        val ctx = AnnotationConfigApplicationContext()
```

```
    ctx.register(AspectJAopConfig::class.java, AfterAdviceV1::class.java)
    ctx.refresh()
    Assertions.assertTrue(listOf(*ctx.beanDefinitionNames).contains("afterAdviceV1"))
    val guitar = Guitar()
    val guitarist = ctx.getBean("agustin", PretentiosGuitarist::class.java)
    guitarist.sing(guitar)
    LOGGER.info("------------------")
    guitar.brand = "Musicman"
    Assertions.assertThrows(
        IllegalArgumentException::class.java,
        { guitarist.sing(guitar) }, "Unacceptable guitar!"
    )
    ctx.close()
}
companion object {
    private val LOGGER = LoggerFactory.getLogger(AnnotatedAdviceTest::class.java)
}
```

}

JUnit Jupiter provides a method named assertThrows(..) to test the assumption that the exception is thrown when calling sing(Guitar) the second time. Running the code generates in the console the output shown in Listing 5-64.

Listing 5-64. Output When Testing AfterAdviceV1

```
INFO : PretentiosGuitarist - play: G C G C Am D7
INFO : AfterAdviceV1 -  > Executed: sing from com.apress.prospring6.five.annotated.
PretentiosGuitarist with guitar  Martin
INFO : AnnotatedAdviceTest - ------------------
INFO : AfterAdviceV1 -  > Executed: sing from com.apress.prospring6.five.annotated.
PretentiosGuitarist with guitar Musicman
```

Notice that the advice is executed twice, but the stacktrace is nowhere to be seen. The reason for this is the assertThrows(..) method, but since the test passed we are sure the exception was thrown. If you have doubts, just comment the assertThrows(..) line, replace it with a call to sing(guitar), and rerun the test.

For the @AfterReturning the code stays mostly the same, the only thing being different is that the advice is annotated with @AfterReturning instead of @After and testing it will only cause > Executed: sing from com.apress.prospring6.five.annotated.PretentiosGuitarist with guitar Martin to be printed.

For the @AfterThrowing the code stays mostly the same, the only thing being different is that the advice is annotated with @AfterThrowing instead of @After and testing it will only cause > Executed: sing from com.apress.prospring6.five.annotated.PretentiosGuitarist with guitar Musicman to be printed.

One extra thing an @AfterThrowing advice can do, that the other two types of advice can't do is to intercept the exception thrown by the target method and replace it with a different exception type.

The AfterThrowingAdviceV2 aspect replaces the IllegalArgumentException thrown by the target method with an instance of RejectedInstrumentException, a very simple custom RuntimeException implementation. An after-throwing advice cannot prevent an exception being thrown by the target method, but it can replace the exception thrown by it. The AfterThrowingAdviceV2 code is shown in Listing 5-65.

Listing 5-65. AfterThrowingAdviceV2 Class Declaring an Aspect Bean with a Single @AfterThrowing Advice That Replaces the Target Method Exception

```
package com.apress.prospring6.five.advice

import com.apress.prospring6.five.common.RejectedInstrumentException
import org.aspectj.lang.annotation.AfterThrowing
// other import statements omitted

@Component
@Aspect
class AfterThrowingAdviceV2 {
    @Pointcut("execution(* com.apress.prospring6.
        five..PretentiosGuitarist.sing*(
        com.apress.prospring6.five.common.Guitar))  && args(value)")
    fun singExecution(value: Guitar?) {
    }

    @AfterThrowing(value = "singExecution(guitar) ", argNames = "joinPoint,guitar, ex",
    throwing = "ex")
    fun simpleAfterAdvice(joinPoint: JoinPoint, guitar: Guitar, ex:
    IllegalArgumentException) {
        val signature = joinPoint.signature as MethodSignature
        LOGGER.info(
            " > Executed: {} from {} with guitar {} ",
            signature.name,
            signature.declaringTypeName,
            guitar.brand
        )
        if (ex.message!!.contains("Unacceptable guitar!")) {
            throw RejectedInstrumentException(ex.message, ex)
        }
    }

    companion object {
        private val LOGGER = LoggerFactory.getLogger(AfterThrowingAdviceV2::class.java)
    }
}
```

(no line break and no spaces in the @Pointcut parameter) The introduction of the new exception type requires an updated test method that tests the assumption that the RejectedInstrumentException is thrown when invoking the sing(Guitar) method on the agustin bean. This test method is depicted in code Listing 5-66.

Listing 5-66. Test Method for the AfterThrowingAdviceV2 Aspect

```
package com.apress.prospring6.five.annotated

import com.apress.prospring6.five.advice.AfterThrowingAdviceV2
// other import statements omitted
```

```kotlin
class AnnotatedAdviceTest {
    @Test
    fun testAfterThrowingAdviceV2() {
        val ctx = AnnotationConfigApplicationContext()
        ctx.register(AspectJAopConfig::class.java, AfterThrowingAdviceV2::class.java)
        ctx.refresh()
        Assertions.assertTrue(listOf(*ctx.beanDefinitionNames).
            contains("afterThrowingAdviceV2"))
        val guitar = Guitar()
        val guitarist = ctx.getBean("agustin", PretentiosGuitarist::class.java)
        guitarist.sing(guitar)
        LOGGER.info("-------------------")
        guitar.brand = "Musicman"
        Assertions.assertThrows(
            RejectedInstrumentException::class.java,
            { guitarist.sing(guitar) }, "Unacceptable guitar!"
        )
        ctx.close()
    }

    companion object {
        private val LOGGER = LoggerFactory.getLogger(AnnotatedAdviceTest::class.java)
    }
}
```

The testAfterThrowingAdviceV2() test should pass and produce the output shown in Listing 5-67 in the console.

Listing 5-67. Output When Testing AfterThrowingAdviceV2

```
INFO : PretentiosGuitarist - play: G C G C Am D7
INFO : AfterAdviceV1 -  > Executed: sing from com.apress.prospring6.five.annotated.
PretentiosGuitarist with guitar  Martin
INFO : AnnotatedAdviceTest - -------------------
INFO : AfterAdviceV1 -  > Executed: sing from com.apress.prospring6.five.annotated.
PretentiosGuitarist with guitar Musicman
```

Declarative Introductions with AspectJ Annotations

Introductions were mentioned briefly when discussing proxies and we showed how code could be written to declare an aspect that decorates a target object with an interface and we also provided and implementation for that interface. Putting all of this together in an application was done using a ProxyFactory instance and ProxyFactoryBean. All was done programmatically at the time, but a declarative configuration is possible as well by using the AspectJ @DeclareParents annotation.

To demonstrate this, a new interface named Performer and its implementation named Dancer are introduced. They are both very simple and depicted in Listing 5-68.

Listing 5-68. Performer and Dancer Implementations

```
package com.apress.prospring6.five.common
// import statements omitted

interface Performer {
    fun perform()
}

class Dancer : Performer {
    override fun perform() {
        LOGGER.info(" Shake it to the left, shake it to the right!")
    }

    companion object {
        private val LOGGER = LoggerFactory.getLogger(Dancer::class.java)
    }
}
```

The @DeclareParents annotation is used to introduce the Performer interface for any bean of a type that implements Singer. Listing 5-69 shows the configuration of the AnnotatedIntroduction aspect.

Listing 5-69. AnnotatedIntroduction Class and Aspect Definition for Introduction

```
package com.apress.prospring6.five.annotated

import com.apress.prospring6.five.common.Dancer
import com.apress.prospring6.five.common.Performer
import org.aspectj.lang.annotation.DeclareParents
// other import statements omitted

@Component
@Aspect
object AnnotatedIntroduction {
    @DeclareParents(value = "com.apress.prospring6.five.common.Singer+",
        defaultImpl = Dancer::class)
    var performer: Performer? = null
}
```

The interface to be implemented is determined by the type of the annotated field, in this case Performer. The value attribute of @DeclareParents is used to tell Spring for what types the introduction must happen. Any bean of a matching type is wrapped in a proxy that implements the Performer interface and introduces the behavior described by the Dancer class.

Testing the introduction is easy: we just get the bean from the context and check its type via instanceof, then we convert it to Performer and invoke its perform() method. The testing method is depicted in Listing 5-70.

Listing 5-70. AnnotatedIntroduction Test Method

```
package com.apress.prospring6.five.annotated

import com.apress.prospring6.five.common.Performer
// other import statements omitted
```

```
class AnnotatedIntroductionTest {
    @Test
    fun testAnnotatedIntroduction() {
        val ctx = AnnotationConfigApplicationContext()
        ctx.register(AspectJAopConfig::class.java, AnnotatedIntroduction::class.java)
        ctx.refresh()
        Assertions.assertTrue(listOf(*ctx.beanDefinitionNames).
            contains("annotatedIntroduction"))
        val guitar = Guitar()
        val guitarist = ctx.getBean("agustin", PretentiosGuitarist::class.java)
        Assertions.assertTrue(guitarist is Singer)
        guitarist.sing(guitar)
        LOGGER.info("Proxy type: {} ", guitar.javaClass.name)
//        Assertions.assertTrue(guitarist is Performer)
//        val performer = guitarist as Performer
//        performer.perform()
        ctx.close()
    }

    companion object {
        private val LOGGER = LoggerFactory.getLogger(AnnotatedIntroductionTest::class.java)
    }
}
```

Running the test should pass and output from the target bean and the Dancer type should be present in the console log, as shown in Listing 5-71.

Listing 5-71. AnnotatedIntroduction Test Output

```
INFO : PretentiosGuitarist - play: G C G C Am D7
INFO : AnnotatedIntroductionTest - Proxy type: com.apress.prospring6.five.common.Guitar
INFO : Dancer -  Shake it to the left, shake it to the right!
```

Aspect Instantiation Models

> In Spring AOP, aspect classes cannot be the targets of advice from other aspects. The @Aspect annotation is also a marker interface, excluding the resulting beans from auto-proxying.

Since the @Aspect annotation is not sufficient for auto-detection in the classpath, aspect classes were registered as beans using @Component in the examples shown so far. They can be registered using @Bean as well. This means that each aspect class becomes a singleton bean in the Spring ApplicationContext.

To test this, we declare a BeforeAdviceV5 class that declares a single simple before advice, but we declare the default constructor to print the instantiation time of the object. The code of this aspect is almost identical to that of BeforeAdviceV2, the only extra thing being the constructor with the logging statement, so we won't list it here again. Listing 5-72 shows the method testing that the constructor of this aspect is called only once. The configuration declares two Singer beans: johnMayer and agustin.

Listing 5-72. BeforeAdviceV5 Test Method

```
package com.apress.prospring6.five.annotated

import com.apress.prospring6.five.advice.BeforeAdviceV5
// other import statements omitted

class AnnotatedAdviceTest {
    @Test
    fun testAfterThrowingAdviceV5() {
        val ctx = AnnotationConfigApplicationContext()
        ctx.register(AspectJAopConfig::class.java, BeforeAdviceV5::class.java)
        ctx.refresh()
        Assertions.assertTrue(listOf(*ctx.beanDefinitionNames).contains("beforeAdviceV5"))
        val johnMayer = ctx.getBean(
            "johnMayer",
            GrammyGuitarist::class.java
        )
        johnMayer.sing(Guitar())
        val pretentiousGuitarist = ctx.getBean(
            "agustin",
            PretentiosGuitarist::class.java
        )
        pretentiousGuitarist.sing(Guitar())
        ctx.close()
    }

    companion object {
        private val LOGGER = LoggerFactory.getLogger(AnnotatedAdviceTest::class.java)
    }
}
```

The test method retrieves these beans and calls sing(Guitar) on them. When looking in the console, we should see the BeforeAdviceV5 constructor message printed only once. Listing 5-73 shows the output of executing the test method in Listing 5-72.

Listing 5-73. BeforeAdviceV5 Test Method Output

```
INFO : BeforeAdviceV5 - BeforeAdviceV5 creation time: 2022-04-24T18:08:05.971660Z
...
INFO : BeforeAdviceV5 -  > Executing: sing from com.apress.prospring6.five.annotated.
GrammyGuitarist
INFO : GrammyGuitarist - play: G C G C Am D7
INFO : BeforeAdviceV5 -  > Executing: sing from com.apress.prospring6.five.annotated.
PretentiosGuitarist
INFO : PretentiosGuitarist - play: G C G C Am D7
```

The message is printed only once since the aspect class is annotated with @Component and the scope is not explicitly configured, so the resulting aspect is a singleton bean.

This leads to the conclusion that there is a way to do things differently. Consider a scenario where you need more than one aspect bean to be created, such as one per target. This is possible via configuration. The @Aspect annotation declares a single attribute that can be initialized with an AspectJ expression configuring how many aspect beans should be created and when.

> ❗ Of course, the Spring configuration must be modified to match, which means the aspect bean scope cannot be `singleton` anymore.

To create an aspect bean for each target bean, the @Aspect annotation should receive as a parameter a pertarget expression pointing at the type of the intended target beans, in this case Singer. BeforeAdviceV6 is depicted in code Listing 5-74.

Listing 5-74. BeforeAdviceV6 Aspect Class Declaring an Aspect for Each Singer Bean

```
package com.apress.prospring6.five.advice

import java.time.Instant
// other import statements omitted

@Component
@Scope("prototype")
@Aspect("pertarget(targetIdentifier())")
class BeforeAdviceV6 {
    init {
        LOGGER.info("BeforeAdviceV6 creation time: {}", Instant.now())
    }

    @Pointcut("target(com.apress.prospring6.five.common.Singer+))")
    fun targetIdentifier() {
    }

    @Pointcut("execution(* com.apress.prospring6.five..sing*(com.apress.prospring6.
        five.common.Guitar))")
    fun singExecution() {
    }

    @Before("singExecution()")
    fun simpleBeforeAdvice(joinPoint: JoinPoint) {
        val signature = joinPoint.signature as MethodSignature
        LOGGER.info(" > Executing: {} from {}", signature.name,
            signature.declaringTypeName)
    }

    companion object {
        private val LOGGER = LoggerFactory.getLogger(BeforeAdviceV6::class.java)
    }
}
```

(no line break and no spaces in the @Pointcut parameters) The method used for testing BeforeAdviceV6 is almost identical to the one for BeforeAdviceV5, the only difference being the number in the names, so the method won't be shown here. However, the output produced by it is interesting. The new aspect configuration causes an aspect to be created for each of the Singer beans in the configuration, and this is shown by the BeforeAdviceV6 constructor message being printed twice, with different date and time, as shown in Listing 5-75.

Listing 5-75. BeforeAdviceV6 Test Method Output

```
INFO : BeforeAdviceV6 - BeforeAdviceV5 creation time: 2022-04-24T18:34:23.037830Z
INFO : BeforeAdviceV6 -  > Executing: sing from com.apress.prospring6.five.annotated.
GrammyGuitarist
INFO : GrammyGuitarist - play: G C G C Am D7
INFO : BeforeAdviceV6 - BeforeAdviceV5 creation time: 2022-04-24T18:34:23.053335Z
INFO : BeforeAdviceV6 -  > Executing: sing from com.apress.prospring6.five.annotated.
PretentiosGuitarist
INFO : PretentiosGuitarist - play: G C G C Am D7
```

An alternative configuration involves the @Aspect annotation receiving as a parameter a perthis expression, pointing at the target method, in this case the sing(Guitar) method. The BeforeAdviceV7 aspect configuration is shown in Listing 5-76.

Listing 5-76. BeforeAdviceV7 Aspect Class Declaring an Aspect for Each Singer Bean

```kotlin
package com.apress.prospring6.five.advice;
// import statement omitted

@Component
@Scope("prototype")
@Aspect("perthis(singExecution())")
class BeforeAdviceV7 {
    init {
        LOGGER.info("BeforeAdviceV7 creation time: {}", Instant.now())
    }

    @Pointcut("execution(* com.apress.prospring6.
        five..sing*(com.apress.prospring6.five.common.Guitar))")
    fun singExecution() {
    }

    @Before("singExecution()")
    fun simpleBeforeAdvice(joinPoint: JoinPoint) {
        val signature = joinPoint.signature as MethodSignature
        LOGGER.info(" > Executing: {} from {}", signature.name,
            signature.declaringTypeName)
    }

    companion object {
        private val LOGGER = LoggerFactory.getLogger(BeforeAdviceV7::class.java)
    }
}
```

(no line break and no spaces in the @Pointcut parameter) The test method is almost identical, and the test output shows two aspect beans being created.

> ❗ So what is the difference between perthis(Pointcut) and pertarget(Pointcut)? The difference is represented by the object being examined when an advised joinpoint is reached. As you've noticed, pertarget specifies a type expression, which means a new aspect is to be instantiated for every new object that is the target of an advice-triggering joinpoint, while perthis specifies a method expression and, thus, a new aspect is to be instantiated for every new object referenced by this at the advice-triggering joinpoint.

You would rarely need to write your own aspects, since almost anything you might need when building a Spring application is already provided by Spring, but it is good to understand what happens under the hood and how Spring does its magic. And this is all that can be said about aspects with Spring, so let's see how you can work with aspects in a Spring Boot application.

Spring Boot AOP

Spring Boot provides a special AOP starter library, spring-boot-starter-aop, that removes the hassle of configuration, even if there is not much of it anyway. To use the library in a Spring Boot project, just create a Spring Boot project and add it as a dependency.

In Figure 5-11 you can see the set of libraries added as dependencies to the Spring Boot project.

```
∨ ᴀᵛ chapter05-boot
  > ᴛ Tasks
  ∨ ᴅᵢ Dependencies
    ∨ ᴅᵢ compileClasspath
        ⊪ org.aspectj:aspectjrt:1.9.9.1
        ⊪ org.aspectj:aspectjweaver:1.9.9.1
      > ⊪ org.jetbrains.kotlin:kotlin-stdlib-jdk8:1.8.10
      ∨ ⊪ org.springframework.boot:spring-boot-starter-aop:3.0.5
          ⊪ org.aspectj:aspectjweaver:1.9.9.1
          ⊪ org.springframework.boot:spring-boot-starter:3.0.5 (*)
          ⊪ org.springframework:spring-aop:6.0.7 (*)
```

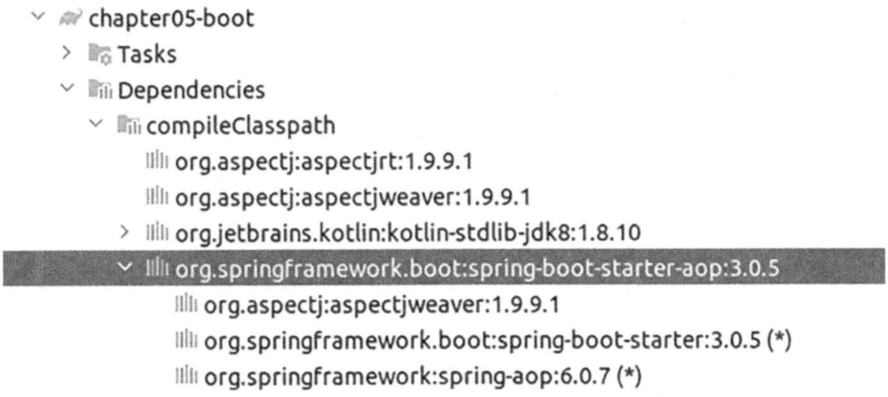

Figure 5-11. *Spring Boot AOP starter transitive dependencies as depicted in IntelliJ IDEA*

By adding this library to your project as a dependency, the @EnableAspectJAutoProxy(proxyTarget Class = true) annotation is no longer needed because the AOP Spring support is already enabled by default. The proxyTargetClass attribute does not have to be set anywhere either, because Spring Boot automatically detects what type of proxies you need.

Any of the aspects introduced in previous sections can be added to the Spring Boot project, and when proxies are used, you can watch the advice work as expected. But let's keep things simple. A GrammyGuitarist type is declared and its implementation is identical to the one used in the rest of the chapter, except that for the Spring Boot project, GrammyGuitarist does not implement the Singer interface. With these beans in the project, the Spring application can be configured using the class shown in Listing 5-77.

Listing 5-77. Spring Boot Chapter5Application Main Class

```
package com.apress.prospring6.five

import org.springframework.boot.SpringApplication
import org.springframework.boot.autoconfigure.SpringBootApplication

@SpringBootApplication
open class Chapter5Application {
    companion object {
        @JvmStatic
        fun main(args: Array<String>) {
            val ctx = SpringApplication.run(
                Chapter5Application::class.java, *args
            )!!

            // val documentarist:NewDocumentarist = ctx.getBean("documentarist",
            //          NewDocumentarist::class.java)
            documentarist.execute()
            ctx.close()
        }
    }
}
```

Simple, right? Also, the reason those two lines are commented is because the Chapter5Application class is used to only configure the Spring application. Since testing was mentioned in previous chapters, it only makes sense to test our application using a Spring Boot test class. Take a look at the Listing 5-78.

Listing 5-78. Spring Boot Chapter5ApplicationTest Main Class

```
package com.apress.prospring6.five

import org.springframework.boot.test.context.SpringBootTest
import static org.junit.jupiter.api.Assertions.*
// other imports omitted

@SpringBootTest
class Chapter5ApplicationTest {
    @Autowired
    var documentarist: NewDocumentarist? = null

    @Autowired
    var guitarist: GrammyGuitarist? = null

    @Test
    fun testDocumentarist() {
        Assertions.assertAll(
            Executable { Assertions.assertNotNull(documentarist!!.guitarist) },
            Executable { Assertions.assertNotNull(guitarist) },
            Executable {
                Assertions.assertTrue(
                    guitarist!!.javaClass.name.contains("SpringCGLIB")
```

```
            )
        }
    )
    documentarist!!.execute()
    }
}
```

The @SpringBootTest annotation ensures that the test context is populated with the beans declared in the Spring Boot configuration class, which means we can use @Autowired to access the beans in the test context.

When this test passes, this means the application context was created correctly. The two beans of type GrammyGuitarist and NewDocumentarist were created, and the GrammyGuitarist bean is a GCLIB proxy, since a JDK proxy is not suitable for it. This is because its type does not implement an interface.

This is all that can be said about AOP with Spring Boot; since Spring Boot provides no fancy, specialized components to simplify AOP with Spring because there is almost nothing to simplify.

Considerations for Declarative Spring AOP Configuration

Thus far we have shown you two ways to write your code using Spring AOP: using ProxyFactoryBean and using the @AspectJ-style annotations. XML AOP configuration is not the focus of this book, but its main advantage is that it makes easy to separate the configuration from your code. On the other hand, if your application is mainly annotation based, use the @AspectJ annotation. Again, let the requirements of your application drive the configuration approach, and make your best effort to be consistent.

Moreover, there are some other differences between the aop namespace and @AspectJ annotation approaches:

- The pointcut expression syntax has some minor differences (for example, in XML configuration, when using the aop namespace, you need to use and to aggregate conditions, but && in @AspectJ annotation).

- In XML configuration, the aop namespace approach supports only the singleton aspect instantiation model.

- In XML configuration, using the aop namespace, you can't "combine" multiple pointcut expressions. The example using @AspectJ showed that you can combine the two pointcut definitions (that is, singExecution(value) && isJohn()) in the before and around advice. When using the aop namespace and needing to create a new pointcut expression that combines the matching conditions, you need to use the ComposablePointcut class.

Summary

In this chapter, we covered a large number of AOP core concepts and looked at how these concepts translate into the Spring AOP implementation. We discussed the features that are (and are not) implemented in Spring AOP, and we pointed to AspectJ as an AOP solution for those features that Spring does not implement. We spent some time explaining the details of the advice types available in Spring, and you saw examples of the four types in action. We also looked at how you limit the methods to which advice applies by using pointcuts. In particular, we looked at the six basic pointcut implementations available with Spring. We also covered the details of how the AOP proxies are constructed, the different options, and what makes them different. We compared performance among three proxy types and highlighted some major differences and restrictions for choosing between a JDK proxy and a CGLIB proxy. We covered the advanced options for pointcutting, as well as how to extend the set of interfaces implemented by an object using introductions.

We also covered Spring Framework services to configure AOP declaratively, thus avoiding the need to hard-code AOP proxy construction logic into your code. We spent some time looking at how Spring and AspectJ are integrated to allow you to use the added power of AspectJ without losing any of the flexibility of Spring. That's certainly a lot of AOP!

In the next chapter, we move on to a completely different topic—how you can use Spring's JDBC support to radically simplify the creation of JDBC-based data access code.

CHAPTER 6

■ ■ ■

Spring Data Access with JDBC

By now you have seen how easy it is to build a fully Spring-managed application. You have a solid understanding of bean configuration and aspect-oriented programming (AOP). However, one part of the puzzle is missing: how do you get the data that drives the application?

Besides simple throwaway command-line utilities, almost every application needs to persist data to some sort of data store. The most usual and convenient data store is a database.

These are the top seven enterprise databases for 2023:

- *MariaDB*: One of the most popular databases for web applications(all WordPress blogs store their data in a MariaDB database).

- *Oracle Database*: The most widely used commercial relational database management system (especially in financial applications).

- *PostgreSQL*: A database management system written in C and used by businesses that deal with huge amounts of data.

- *Microsoft SQL Server*: Yet another favorite of financial companies, both on-premises and in the cloud.

- *MongoDB*: Most popular NoSQL database, a document-oriented database, available in the cloud as a service via self-healing clusters, known as MongoDB Atlas.

- *Redis*: A distributed in-memory key-value store, with great scalability.

- *Elasticsearch*: A full-text search engine based on Lucene.

Also, Oracle pushes seriously for the replacement of MariaDB with MySQL. If you are not working for a big company that can afford licenses for enterprise database or database cloud instances such as GCP Managed SQL instance or Amazon RDS or Aurora, you probably are using MariaDB, PostgreSQL, or other free database not listed here. MariaDB is generally more widely used for web application development, especially on the Linux platform; on the other side, PostgreSQL is friendlier to Oracle developers because its procedural language, PL/pgSQL, is very close to Oracle's PL/SQL language.

Even if you choose the fastest and most reliable database, you cannot afford to lose its speed and flexibility by using a poorly designed and implemented data access layer. Applications tend to use the data access layer very frequently; thus, any unnecessary bottlenecks in the data access code impact the entire application, no matter how well designed it is. This chapter is the first in a series of five that will show you

© Peter Späth, Iuliana Cosmina, Rob Harrop, Chris Schaefer 2023
P. Späth et al., *Pro Spring 6 with Kotlin*, https://doi.org/10.1007/978-1-4842-9557-1_6

how to work with SQL and NoSQL databases, how to manage transactions and how to use a persistence tool such as Hibernate. Specifically, we'll discuss the following:

- *Comparing traditional JDBC code and Spring JDBC support*: We explore how Spring simplifies the old-style JDBC code while keeping the same functionality. You will also see how Spring accesses the low-level JDBC API and how this low-level API is mapped into convenient classes such as JdbcTemplate.

- *Connecting to the database*: Even though we do not go into every little detail of database connection management, we do show you the fundamental differences between a simple Connection and a DataSource. Naturally, we discuss how Spring manages the data sources and which data sources you can use in your applications. Various libraries for connection pooling—the process through which connections are reused, rather than created every time a connection is requested—are also introduced.

- *Retrieving and mapping the data to Kotlin objects*: We show you how to retrieve data and then how to effectively map the selected data to Kotlin objects. You also learn that Spring JDBC is a viable alternative to object-relational mapping (ORM) tools (introduced in **Chapter 7**).

- *Inserting, updating, and deleting data*: We discuss how you can implement the insert, update, and delete operations by using Spring to execute these types of queries.

- *Testing JDBC code using an in-memory database*: We discuss approaches to testing JDBC code, explain why in-memory databases are suitable for testing, and introduce the @Sql* annotations family that provides support to write concise tests for your JDBC code. We also introduce you to a very practical library called Testcontainers that allows starting up and tearing down a Docker container within the life cycle of a test or test class.

- *Using Spring Boot JDBC*: We show how easy it is to configure distinct databases for production and test environments using the Spring Boot JDBC starter library.

Let's start with the simplest scenario involving databases: writing code to work with SQL databases and JDBC.

Sample Data Model for Example Code

Before proceeding with the discussion, we introduce a simple data model that is used for the examples throughout this chapter, as well as the next few chapters when discussing other data access techniques (we will expand the model accordingly to fulfill the needs of each topic as we go).

The model is a simple music database with two tables. The first one is the SINGER table, which stores a singer's information, and the other table is ALBUM, which stores details about the albums released by that singer. Each singer can have zero or more albums; in other words, it's a one-to-many relationship between SINGER and ALBUM. A singer's information includes their first and last names and date of birth. Figure 6-1 shows the entity-relationship (ER) diagram of the database.

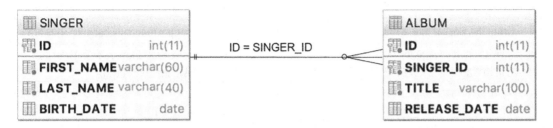

Figure 6-1. *Simple data model for the example code*

As you can see, both tables have an ID column that will be automatically assigned by the database during insertion. For the ALBUM table, there is a foreign-key relation to the SINGER table, which is linked by the column SINGER_ID with the primary key of the SINGER table (that is, the ID column).

ℹ️   In this chapter, we use the open source database MariaDB[1] to show interactions with a real database in some examples. MariaDB is a truly open source distribution of MySQL[2], released as a response to Oracle buying MySQL. The interesting thing you should be aware of is that MariaDB shows improved speed when compared to MySQL. In particular, MariaDB offers better performance when it comes to views and handling flash storage through its RocksDB[3] engine.

❗   This chapter, and probably the next ones in the data access series, requires you to have an instance of MariaDB available to use. We do not cover how to install MariaDB, but the chapter06 module has a CHAPTER06.adoc file instructing you how to start MariaDB in a Docker container. You can use another database of your choice, but you may need to modify the schema and function definitions. We also cover embedded database usage, which does not require a MariaDB database.

In case you want to install MariaDB locally, on the official site you can find very good tutorials on installing and configuring MariaDB. After you have downloaded MariaDB[4] and installed it, you can access it using the root account. Usually, when you develop an application, you need a new schema and user. For the code samples in this chapter, the schema is named musicdb, and the user to access it is named prospring6. The SQL code to execute to create them is located in docker-build/scripts/CreateTable.sql in the directory of the chapter06 project. The SQL code to execute to populate the tables is located in in docker-build/scripts/InsertData.sql in the directory of the chapter06 project.

---

[1] https://mariadb.com
[2] https://www.mysql.com
[3] https://rocksdb.org
[4] https://mariadb.com/kb/en/binary-packages

Using the Docker MariaDB container, you don't need to execute the scripts manually because they are automatically executed when the container is started. Follow the instructions in CHAPTER06.adoc if you are interested in this approach (and you should be, because containers are everywhere nowadays).

Following the instructions in the CHAPTER06.adoc should produce a MariaDB container named local-mariadb. If you use a smart editor(like IntelliJ IDEA, the editor recommended in this book), you can use the Database view to inspect your schema and tables. In Figure 6-2 you can see the contents of the musicdb schema as depicted in IntelliJ IDEA.

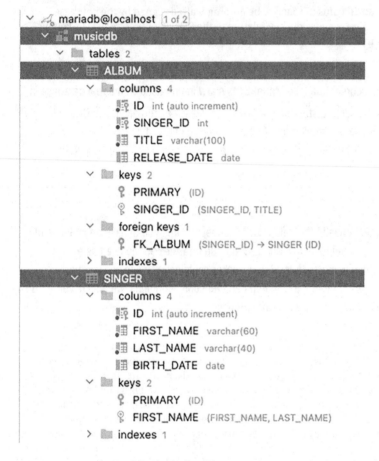

Figure 6-2. Contents of the musicdb schema

SQL tools are not available in the community edition of IntelliJ IDEA. You still can run all the code from this chapter even if you don't want to buy IntelliJ IDEA Ultimate. Just use any SQL admin client of your choice for investigating and maintaining DB instances. SQuirreL is an example for a powerful tool you can try (http://www.squirrelsql.org/).

As you can see, we have a one-to-many relationship between the SINGER and ALBUM tables and both have a primary key named ID. The foreign key linking records in ALBUM to parent records in SINGER is named SINGER_ID.

In later sections of this chapter, you will see examples of retrieving the data via JDBC from the database and directly mapping the result set into Kotlin objects (that is, POJOs). These classes that map to the records in tables are also called **pojos**. For the SINGER table, a Singer class is a pojo and instances of this class map to rows in the SINGER table.

In the *I Love Lucy* episode "Paris at Last," Lucy is rescued from arrest by an elaborate translation effort by her husband Ricky, two Paris policemen, and a third man who helps[5]. The episode basically shows Lucy getting in trouble and getting arrested by the French police. The two police officers cannot speak English, but one speaks both French and German; Ricky and Lucy cannot speak French, but Ricky speaks Spanish; and the third man speaks only German and Spanish. This leads to a chain of three translators between Lucy, who speaks only English, and the police chief, who speaks only French.

In a similar way, a Kotlin application and a database cannot communicate directly, so they need a translator, which in software is called a **driver**. In the *I Love Lucy* episode, they need three translators to get the job done. When it comes to Kotlin and most databases, we have the following options:

- We usually need one translator, the driver.

- We might use two, if we want to introduce a persistence layer such as Hibernate.

- We might use three, if we add Spring Data to easily map records to POJOs and handle transactions easily.

In this book, we show you how to do all three. Let's start with the basic one and define our POJOs. Listing 6-1 shows the Singer and Album classes that map to records in the SINGER and ALBUM tables, respectively.

Listing 6-1. POJOs for Working with the JDBC Driver

```kotlin
package com.apress.prospring6.six.plain.pojos

import java.io.Serializable
import java.time.LocalDate
import java.util.HashSet
import java.util.Set

// maps to table SINGER
class Singer() : Serializable {
    var id: Long? = null
    var firstName: String? = null
    var lastName: String? = null
    var birthDate: LocalDate? = null
    var albums: MutableSet<Album>? = null

    constructor(id: Long?, firstName: String?, lastName: String?, birthDate: LocalDate?,
            albums: MutableSet<Album>?) : this() {
        this.id = id
        this.firstName = firstName
        this.lastName = lastName
```

---

[5] https://youtu.be/Xle3I-5nfpI

```kotlin
            this.birthDate = birthDate
            this.albums = albums
    }

    fun addAlbum(album: Album): Boolean {
        if (albums == null) {
            albums = mutableSetOf(album)
            return true
        } else {
            if (albums!!.contains(album)) {
                return false
            }
        }
        albums!!.add(album)
        return true
    }

    override fun toString(): String {
        return "Singer[id=" + id +
                ",firstName=" + firstName +
                ",lastName=" + lastName +
                ",birthDate=" + birthDate +
                "]"
    }

    companion object {
        private const val serialVersionUID = 1L
    }
}
```

Let's start with a simple interface for SingerDao that encapsulates all the data access methods for Singer information. DAO is an acronym for *data access object,* and in the Spring world the term repository is used instead. The code is as shown in Listing 6-2.

Listing 6-2. SingerDao Interface

```kotlin
package com.apress.prospring6.six.plain.dao.pojos

import com.apress.prospring6.six.plain.dao.CoreDao
import com.apress.prospring6.six.plain.pojos.Singer

/**
 * Created by iuliana.cosmina on 03/05/2022
 */
interface SingerDao : CoreDao {
    fun findAll(): Set<Singer>
    fun findByFirstName(firstName: String): Set<Singer>
    fun findNameById(id: Long): String?
    fun findLastNameById(id: Long): String?
    fun findFirstNameById(id: Long): String?
    fun insert(singer: Singer): Singer?
    fun update(singer: Singer)
```

```
    fun delete(singerId: Long)
    fun findAllWithAlbums(): Set<Singer>
    fun insertWithAlbum(singer: Singer)
}
```

In the SingerDao interface, we define two finder methods and the insert(), update(), and delete() methods, respectively. They correspond to the CRUD terms (create, read, update, delete).

A Kotlin application needs a connection instance to communicate with the database and retrieve or send data. The CoreDao interface extended by SingerDao is a simple interface that groups methods related to connection management: getting a connection and closing a connection. This interface and the JDBC infrastructure are discussed later in the next section (and shown in Listing 6-4).

Finally, to facilitate testing, let's modify the logback.xml configuration file to turn the log level to DEBUG for all classes. At the DEBUG level, the application will output all the underlying SQL statements being fired to the database, so you know what exactly is going on; this is especially useful for troubleshooting SQL statement syntax errors. Listing 6-3 depicts the contents of the logback.xml file for the project containing the sources for the code from Chapter 6.

Listing 6-3. logback.xml Contents

```
<?xml version="1.0" encoding="UTF-8"?>
<configuration>

    <contextListener class="ch.qos.logback.classic.jul.LevelChangePropagator">
        <resetJUL>true</resetJUL>
    </contextListener>

    <appender name="console" class="ch.qos.logback.core.ConsoleAppender">
        <encoder>
            <pattern> %-5level: %class{0} - %msg%n</pattern>
        </encoder>
    </appender>

    <logger name="com.apress.prospring6.six" level="debug"/>

    <logger name="org.springframework" level="debug"/>

    <root level="info">
        <appender-ref ref="console" />
    </root>
</configuration>
```

Exploring the JDBC Infrastructure

JDBC provides a standard way for Java/Kotlin applications to access data stored in a database. The core of the JDBC infrastructure is a driver that is specific to each database; it is this driver that allows Kotlin code to access the database.

Once a driver is loaded, it registers itself with a java.sql.DriverManager class. This class manages a list of drivers and provides static methods for establishing connections to the database. The DriverManager's getConnection() method returns a driver-implemented java.sql.Connection interface. This interface allows you to run SQL statements against the database.

The JDBC framework is quite complex and well tested; however, with this complexity comes difficulty in development. The first level of complexity lies in making sure your code manages the connections to the database. A connection is a scarce resource and is very expensive to establish. Generally, the database creates a thread or spawns a child process for each connection. Also, the number of concurrent connections is usually limited, and an excessive number of open connections will slow down the database.

We will show you how Spring helps manage this complexity, but before we can proceed any further, we need to show you how to select, delete, and update data in pure JDBC.

As previously mentioned, a Kotlin application needs a connection instance to communicate with the database and retrieve or send data. The type for this instance is provided by the driver present on the project classpath. In our case the MariaDB driver was added to the classpath by declaring the `mariadb-java-client.jar` as a dependency in the Gradle configuration. Listing 6-4 shows the CoreDao code that contains two default methods, one for retrieving a connection and one for closing it, that are inherited by any type implementing this interface, directly or indirectly.

Listing 6-4. CoreDao Interface

```
package com.apress.prospring6.six.dao

import java.sql.Connection
import java.sql.DriverManager
import java.sql.SQLException

interface CoreDao {
    @get:Throws(SQLException::class)
    val connection: Connection?
        get() = DriverManager.getConnection(
            "jdbc:mariadb://localhost:3306/musicdb?useSSL=false",
            "prospring6", "prospring6"
        )

    @Throws(SQLException::class)
    fun closeConnection(connection: Connection?) {
        if (connection == null) {
            return
        }
        connection.close()
    }
}
```

🚫   Again, default implementations in interfaces are discouraged for other than legacy or framework code. We use it here for simplicity. Be careful when using this.

Keeping in mind what we already know about database connections, we will take the cautious and expensive (in terms of performance) approach of creating a connection for each statement. This greatly degrades the performance of Kotlin and adds extra stress to the database because a connection must be established for each query. However, if we kept a connection open, we could bring the database server to a halt.

As you can see, the reference type for the connection is the `java.sql.Connection` interface that is part of the JDK. Any JDBC driver that plays the role of a translator between a Kotlin application and a SQL database must have a class that implements this interface. The MariaDB implementation is `org.mariadb.jdbc.Connection`. To check that a driver is present on the classpath, most applications declare a `static` block that uses reflection to find the core driver class of that driver, an implementation of `java.sql.Driver`. Listing 6-5 shows the static block that does this for the MariaDB driver.

Listing 6-5. Static Block Used to Check the Presence of a JDBC Driver on the Classpath

```
package com.apress.prospring6.six.plain

import org.slf4j.Logger
import org.slf4j.LoggerFactory
// other import statements omitted

object PlainJdbcDemo {

    init {
        try {
            Class.forName("org.mariadb.jdbc.Driver")
        } catch (ex: ClassNotFoundException) {
            LOGGER.error("Problem loading DB Driver!", ex)
        }
    }
    // other code omitted
}
```

This code is far from complete, but it gives you an idea of the steps you need in order to manage a JDBC connection. This code does not even deal with connection pooling, which is a common technique for managing connections to the database more effectively. We do not discuss connection pooling at this point (connection pooling is discussed in the "Database Connections and DataSources" section later in this chapter); instead, the code snippet in Listing 6-6 shows an implementation of the `findAll()`, `insert()`, and `delete()` methods of the `SingerDao` interface using plain JDBC.

Listing 6-6. PlainSingerDao Implementation

```
package com.apress.prospring6.six.plain.dao.pojos

import java.sql.Connection
import java.sql.PreparedStatement
import java.sql.ResultSet
import java.sql.SQLException
import java.sql.Statement
// other import statements omitted

class PlainSingerDao : SingerDao {
    override fun findAll(): Set<Singer> {
        val result: MutableSet<Singer> = HashSet()
        try {
            connection.use { connection ->
                connection!!.prepareStatement(ALL_SELECT).use { statement ->
                    statement.executeQuery().use { resultSet ->
                        while (resultSet.next()) {
                            val singer = Singer().apply {
```

```kotlin
                                id = resultSet.getLong("id")
                                firstName = resultSet.getString("first_name")
                                lastName = resultSet.getString("last_name")
                                birthDate = resultSet.getDate("birth_date").toLocalDate()
                            }
                            result.add(singer)
                        }
                    }
                }
            }
        } catch (ex: SQLException) {
            LOGGER.error("Problem when executing SELECT!", ex)
        }
        return result
    }

    override fun insert(singer: Singer): Singer? {
        try {
            connection.use { connection ->
                val statement =
                    connection!!.prepareStatement(SIMPLE_INSERT,
                        Statement.RETURN_GENERATED_KEYS)
                statement.setString(1, singer.firstName)
                statement.setString(2, singer.lastName)
                statement.setDate(3, Date.valueOf(singer.birthDate))
                statement.execute()
                val generatedKeys = statement.generatedKeys
                if (generatedKeys.next()) {
                    singer.id = generatedKeys.getLong(1)
                }
                return singer
            }
        } catch (ex: SQLException) {
            LOGGER.error("Problem executing INSERT", ex)
        }
        return null
    }

    override fun delete(singerId: Long) {
        try {
            connection.use { connection ->
                connection!!.prepareStatement(SIMPLE_DELETE).use { statement ->
                    statement.setLong(1, singerId!!)
                    statement.execute()
                }
            }
        } catch (ex: SQLException) {
            LOGGER.error("Problem executing DELETE", ex)
        }
    }
```

```
// other methods omitted

    companion object {
        private val LOGGER = LoggerFactory.getLogger(PlainSingerDao::class.java)
    }
}
```

Notice the amount of code needed for each method. We always have to make sure the connection to the database can be used, and using it requires us to treat the checked SQLException that might be thrown. In earlier versions of Java when java.sql.Connection and other types needed to handle communication with the database, did not implement java.lang.AutoCloseable and there was no *try-with-resources* statement that code looked even uglier.

The class to test the methods in PlainSingerDao is shown in Listing 6-7.

Listing 6-7. PlainJdbcDemo Class That Tests Methods in PlainSingerDao

```
package com.apress.prospring6.six.plain
// import statements omitted

object PlainJdbcDemo {
    private val LOGGER = LoggerFactory.getLogger(PlainJdbcDemo::class.java)
    private val singerDao: SingerDao = PlainSingerDao()

    init {
        try {
            Class.forName("org.mariadb.jdbc.Driver")
        } catch (ex: ClassNotFoundException) {
            LOGGER.error("Problem loading DB Driver!", ex)
        }
    }

    @JvmStatic
    fun main(args: Array<String>) {
        LOGGER.info("Listing initial singer data:")
        listAllSingers()
        LOGGER.info("-------------")
        LOGGER.info("Insert a new singer")
        val singer = Singer()
        singer.firstName = "Ed"
        singer.lastName = "Sheeran"
        singer.birthDate = LocalDate.of(1991, 2, 17)
        singerDao.insert(singer)
        LOGGER.info("The singer has ID now: {}", singer.id)
        LOGGER.info("-------------")
        LOGGER.info("Listing singer data after new singer created:")
        listAllSingers()
        LOGGER.info("-------------")
        LOGGER.info("Deleting the previous created singer")
        singer.id?.run { singerDao.delete(this) }
        LOGGER.info("Listing singer data after new singer deleted:")
        listAllSingers()
    }
```

```kotlin
    private fun listAllSingers() {
        val singers = singerDao.findAll()
        for (singer in singers) {
            LOGGER.info(singer.toString())
        }
    }
}
```

The logger is used a lot in the example to print the contents of the database after each method is called. Running this program yields the result shown in Listing 6-8 (assuming you have a locally installed MariaDB database called musicdb that has a username and password set to prospring6 and the sample data was loaded).

Listing 6-8. PlainJdbcDemo Output

```
INFO : PlainJdbcDemo - Listing initial singer data:
INFO : PlainJdbcDemo - Singer[id=1,firstName=John,lastName=Mayer,birthDate=1977-10-16]
INFO : PlainJdbcDemo - Singer[id=2,firstName=Ben,lastName=Barnes,birthDate=1981-08-20]
INFO : PlainJdbcDemo - Singer[id=3,firstName=John,lastName=Butler,birthDate=1975-04-01]
INFO : PlainJdbcDemo - -------------
INFO : PlainJdbcDemo - Insert a new singer
INFO : PlainJdbcDemo - The singer has ID now: 19
INFO : PlainJdbcDemo - -------------
INFO : PlainJdbcDemo - Listing singer data after new singer created:
INFO : PlainJdbcDemo - Singer[id=1,firstName=John,lastName=Mayer,birthDate=1977-10-16]
INFO : PlainJdbcDemo - Singer[id=2,firstName=Ben,lastName=Barnes,birthDate=1981-08-20]
INFO : PlainJdbcDemo - Singer[id=3,firstName=John,lastName=Butler,birthDate=1975-04-01]
INFO : PlainJdbcDemo - Singer[id=19,firstName=Ed,lastName=Sheeran,birthDate=1996-08-11]
INFO : PlainJdbcDemo - -------------
INFO : PlainJdbcDemo - Deleting the previous created singer
INFO : PlainJdbcDemo - Listing singer data after new singer deleted:
INFO : PlainJdbcDemo - Singer[id=1,firstName=John,lastName=Mayer,birthDate=1977-10-16]
INFO : PlainJdbcDemo - Singer[id=2,firstName=Ben,lastName=Barnes,birthDate=1981-08-20]
INFO : PlainJdbcDemo - Singer[id=3,firstName=John,lastName=Butler,birthDate=1975-04-01]
```

As shown in the output, the first block of lines shows the initial data. The second block of lines shows that the new record was added. The final block of lines shows that the newly created singer *Ed Sheeran* was deleted.

As you can see in the previous code samples, a lot of code needs to be moved to a helper class or, even worse, duplicated in each DAO class. This is the main disadvantage of JDBC from the application programmer's point of view; you just do not have time to write repetitive code in every DAO class. Instead, you want to concentrate on writing code that actually does what you need the DAO class to do: select, update, and delete the data. The more helper code you need to write, the more checked exceptions you need to handle, and the more bugs you may introduce in your code. This is where a DAO framework and Spring come in. A framework eliminates the code that does not actually perform any custom logic and allows you to forget about all the housekeeping that needs to be performed. In addition, Spring's extensive JDBC support makes your life a lot easier.

ⓘ The plain JDBC code shown in this section can also be written using Kotlin data classes instead of POJOs. The project for this book contains code for this, but it won't be discussed in detail in the book since the focus of this book is Spring.

Spring JDBC Infrastructure

The code we discussed in the first part of the chapter is not very complex, but it is tedious, and because there is so much of it to write, the likelihood of coding errors is quite high. It is time to take a look at how Spring makes things easier and more elegant.

Overview and Used Packages

JDBC support in Spring is divided into the five packages detailed in Table 6-1; each handles different aspects of JDBC access.

Table 6-1. *Spring JDBC Packages*

Package	Description
org.springframework.jdbc.core	This package contains the foundations of JDBC classes in Spring. It includes the core JDBC class, JdbcTemplate, which simplifies programming database operations with JDBC. Several subpackages provide support of JDBC data access with more specific purposes (e.g., a JdbcTemplate class that supports named parameters) and related support classes as well.
org.springframework.jdbc.datasource	This package contains helper classes and DataSource implementations that you can use to run JDBC code outside a JEE container. Several subpackages provide support for embedded databases, database initialization, and various data source lookup mechanisms.
org.springframework.jdbc.object	This package contains classes that help convert the data returned from the database into objects or lists of objects. These objects and lists are plain Java/Kotlin objects and therefore are disconnected from the database.
org.springframework.jdbc.support	The most important class in this package is SQLException translation support. This allows Spring to recognize error codes used by the database and map them to higher-level exceptions.
org.springframework.jdbc.config	This package contains classes that support JDBC configuration within Spring's ApplicationContext. For example, it contains classes used to work with embedded databases.

Let's start the discussion of Spring JDBC support by looking at the lowest-level functionality. The first thing that you need to do before running SQL queries is to establish a connection to the database.

Database Connections and DataSources

You can use Spring to manage the database connection for you by providing a bean that implements javax. sql.DataSource. The difference between a DataSource and a Connection is that a DataSource provides and manages connections.

DriverManagerDataSource, in package org.springframework.jdbc.datasource, is the simplest implementation of a DataSource. By looking at the class name, you can guess that it simply calls DriverManager to obtain a connection. The fact that DriverManagerDataSource doesn't support database connection pooling makes this class unsuitable for anything other than testing. The configuration of DriverManagerDataSource is quite simple, as you can see in Listing 6-9; you just need to supply the driver class name, a connection URL, a username, and a password.

Listing 6-9. Contents of jdbc.Properties

```
driverClassName=org.mariadb.jdbc.Driver
url=jdbc:mariadb://localhost:3306/musicdb?useSSL=false
username=prospring6
password=prospring6
```

You most likely recognize the properties in the listing. They represent the values you normally pass to JDBC to obtain a Connection interface. The database connection information typically is stored in a properties file for easy maintenance and substitution in different deployment environments. The properties in jdbc.properties are injected by Spring into the properties in a Kotlin configuration class. Such a configuration class would look pretty much like the one shown in Listing 6-10.

Listing 6-10. Database Configuration Class

```kotlin
package com.apress.prospring6.six.config

import org.springframework.beans.factory.annotation.Value
import org.springframework.context.annotation.Bean
// more import statements omitted

@Configuration
@PropertySource("classpath:db/jdbc.properties")
open class SimpleDataSourceCfg {
    @Value("\${jdbc.driverClassName}")
    private val driverClassName: String? = null

    @Value("\${jdbc.url}")
    private val url: String? = null

    @Value("\${jdbc.username}")
    private val username: String? = null

    @Value("\${jdbc.password}")
    private val password: String? = null

    @Bean
    open fun dataSource(): DataSource? {
        return try {
            val dataSource = SimpleDriverDataSource()
```

```
            val driver = Class.forName(driverClassName) as Class<out Driver?>
            dataSource.setDriverClass(driver)
            dataSource.url = url
            dataSource.username = username
            dataSource.password = password
            dataSource
        } catch (e: Exception) {
            LOGGER.error("Simple DataSource bean cannot be created!", e)
            null
        }
    }

    companion object {
        private val LOGGER = LoggerFactory.getLogger(SimpleDataSourceCfg::class.java)
    }
}
```

Testing a configuration class like this is easy; just create an application context based on it and inspect the beans in it. Listing 6-11 shows a test class containing a method that checks the existence of the DataSource bean and uses it to execute a simple SQL check statement.

Listing 6-11. Test Class Checking the Validity of the SimpleDataSourceCfg Class

```
package com.apress.prospring6.six.plain
// import statements omitted

class DataSourceConfigTest {
    //@Disabled("needs MariaDB running, set up container, comment this to run")
    @Test
    @Throws(
        SQLException::class
    )
    fun testSimpleDataSource() {
        val ctx = AnnotationConfigApplicationContext(
            SimpleDataSourceCfg::class.java
        )
        val dataSource = ctx.getBean("dataSource", DataSource::class.java)
        Assertions.assertNotNull(dataSource)
        testDataSource(dataSource)
        ctx.close()
    }

    @Throws(SQLException::class)
    private fun testDataSource(dataSource: DataSource) {
        try {
            dataSource.connection.use { connection ->
                connection.prepareStatement("SELECT 1").use { statement ->
                    statement.executeQuery().use { resultSet ->
                        while (resultSet.next()) {
                            val mockVal = resultSet.getInt("1")
                            Assertions.assertEquals(1, mockVal)
                        }
```

```
                    }
                 }
              }
        } catch (e: Exception) {
            LOGGER.debug("Something unexpected happened.", e)
        }
    }

    companion object {
        private val LOGGER = LoggerFactory.getLogger(DataSourceConfigTest::class.java)
    }
}
```

A test class was used because it is more practical to reuse some of the code and also teaches you how to work with JUnit to quickly write tests for any piece of code you write. The testSimpleDataSource() method, is used to test the SimpleDataSourceCfg configuration class. After obtaining the DataSource bean from any configuration, the mock query SELECT 1 is used to test the connection to the MariaDB database.

In real-world applications, you can use the Apache Commons BasicDataSource[6] or a DataSource implemented by a JEE application server (for example, JBoss, WildFly, WebSphere, WebLogic, or GlassFish), which may further increase the performance of the application. You could use a DataSource in the plain JDBC code and get the same pooling benefits; however, in most cases, you would still need a central place to configure the DataSource. Spring, on the other hand, allows you to declare a dataSource bean and set the connection properties in the ApplicationContext definition files. The configuration example in Listing 6-12 demonstrates using an org.apache.commons.dbcp2.BasicDataSource implementation instead of SimpleDriverDataSource.

Listing 6-12. BasicDataSourceCfg Class

package com.apress.prospring6.six.config

import org.apache.commons.dbcp2.BasicDataSource
```
// other import statements omitted

@Configuration
@PropertySource("classpath:db/jdbc.properties")
open class BasicDataSourceCfg {
    // code omitted for duplication, same as in 6-10

    @Bean(destroyMethod = "close")
    open fun dataSource(): DataSource? {
        return try {
            val dataSource = BasicDataSource()
            dataSource.driverClassName = driverClassName
            dataSource.url = url
            dataSource.username = username
            dataSource.password = password
            dataSource
```

---

[6] https://commons.apache.org/proper/commons-dbcp

```
    } catch (e: Exception) {
        LOGGER.error("DBCP DataSource bean cannot be created!", e)
        null
    }
  }

  companion object {
      private val LOGGER = LoggerFactory.getLogger(BasicDataSourceCfg::class.java)
  }
}
```

This particular Spring-managed DataSource is implemented in `org.apache.commons.dbcp2.BasicDataSource`. The most important bit is that the bean type implements `javax.sql.DataSource`, and you can immediately start using it in your data access classes.

Another way to configure a dataSource bean is to use JNDI. If the application you are developing is going to run in a JEE container, you can take advantage of the container-managed connection pooling. To use a JNDI-based data source, you need to change the dataSource bean declaration, as shown in Listing 6-13.

Listing 6-13. JndiDataSourceCfg Class

```
package com.apress.prospring6.six.config

import org.springframework.jndi.JndiTemplate
// other import statements omitted

@Configuration
open class JndiDataSourceCfg {
    @Bean
    open fun dataSource(): DataSource? {
        return try {
            JndiTemplate().lookup("java:comp/env/jdbc/musicdb") as DataSource
        } catch (e: Exception) {
            LOGGER.error("JNDI DataSource bean cannot be created!", e)
            null
        }
    }

    companion object {
        private val LOGGER = LoggerFactory.getLogger(JndiDataSourceCfg::class.java)
    }
}
```

In this example the JndiTemplate gets used to obtain the data source by JNDI lookup. This is a very useful helper class that simplifies JNDI operations. It provides methods to look up and bind objects and allows implementations of the JndiCallback interface to perform any operation they like with a JNDI naming context provided.

As you can see, Spring allows you to configure the DataSource in almost any way you like, and it hides the actual implementation or location of the data source from the rest of the application's code. In other words, your DAO classes do not know and do not need to know where the DataSource points.

The connection management is also delegated to the dataSource bean, which in turn performs the management itself or uses the JEE container to do all the work.

Embedded Database Support

Starting from version 3.0, Spring also offers embedded database support, which automatically starts an embedded database and exposes it as a DataSource for the application. The embedded database support is extremely useful for local development or unit testing. Throughout the rest of the chapters covering data access, we use the embedded database to run the sample code, so your machine doesn't require a database to be installed in order to run the samples, but if you want a true developer experience, consider setting up a Docker container.

The configuration class in Listing 6-14 shows the minimal configuration required to set up an embedded H2 database in a Spring application context.

Listing 6-14. EmbeddedJdbcConfig Class

```
package com.apress.prospring6.six.config

import org.springframework.jdbc.datasource.embedded.EmbeddedDatabaseBuilder
import org.springframework.jdbc.datasource.embedded.EmbeddedDatabaseType
// other import statements omitted

@Configuration
open class EmbeddedJdbcConfig {
    @Bean
    open fun dataSource(): DataSource? {
        return try {
            val dbBuilder = EmbeddedDatabaseBuilder()
            dbBuilder.setType(EmbeddedDatabaseType.H2)
                .addScripts("classpath:h2/create-schema.sql",
                                "classpath:h2/test-data.sql").build()
        } catch (e: Exception) {
            LOGGER.error("Embedded DataSource bean cannot be created!", e)
            null
        }
    }

    companion object {
        private val LOGGER = LoggerFactory.getLogger(EmbeddedJdbcConfig::class.java)
    }
}
```

The EmbeddedDatabaseBuilder class uses the database creation and loading data scripts as arguments to create an instance of EmbeddedDatabase that implements DataSource.

❗   Note that the order of the scripts is important, and the file that contains Data Definition Language (DDL) should always appear first, followed by the file with Data Manipulation Language (DML). For the type attribute, we specify the type of embedded database to use. As of version 4.0, Spring supports HSQL (the default), H2, and DERBY.

Using DataSources in DAO Classes

The Data Access Object (DAO) pattern is used to separate low-level data accessing APIs or operations from high-level business services. The Data Access Object pattern requires the following components:

- *DAO interface*: This defines the standard operations to be performed on a model object (or objects).

- *DAO implementation*: This class provides a concrete implementation for the DAO interface. Typically, this uses a JDBC connection or data source to handle model object (or objects).

- *Model objects* (also called *data objects* or *entities*): These are simple POJOs mapping to table records.

Let's create a SingerDao interface to implement for the sample, as shown in Listing 6-15.

Listing 6-15. SingerDao Interface

```
interface SingerDao {
    fun findNameById(Long id:Long):String?
}
```

For the simple implementing class named JdbcSingerDao, first we will add a dataSource property. The reason we want to add the dataSource property to the implementation class rather than the interface should be quite obvious: the interface does not need to know how the data is going to be retrieved and updated. By adding DataSource mutator methods to the interface, in the best-case scenario this forces the implementations to declare the getter and setter stubs. Clearly, this is not a very good design practice. Take a look at the simple JdbcSingerDao class shown in Listing 6-16.

Listing 6-16. JdbcSingerDao Class

```
package com.apress.prospring6.six.plain
internal class JdbcSingerDao : SingerDao, InitializingBean {
    var dataSource: DataSource? = null

    @Throws(Exception::class)
    override fun afterPropertiesSet() {
        if (dataSource == null) {
            throw BeanCreationException("Must set dataSource on SingerDao")
        }
    }

    override fun findNameById(id: Long?): String {
        val result = ""
        try {
            dataSource!!.connection.use { connection ->
                connection.prepareStatement(FIND_NAME + id).use { statement ->
                    statement.executeQuery().use { resultSet ->
                        while (resultSet.next()) {
                            return resultSet.getString("first_name") + " " +
                                resultSet.getString("last_name")
                        }
                    }
                }
```

```
                }
            }
        } catch (ex: SQLException) {
            LOGGER.error("Problem when executing SELECT!", ex)
        }
        return result
    }

    companion object {
        private val LOGGER = LoggerFactory.getLogger(JdbcSingerDao::class.java)
    }
}
```

We can now instruct Spring to configure our singerDao bean by using the JdbcSingerDao implementation and set the dataSource property as shown in the SpringDatasourceCfg configuration class, shown in Listing 6-17. (Notice that we import the BasicDataSourceCfg class introduced in the previous section, to avoid duplicating code.)

Listing 6-17. SpringDatasourceCfg Configuration Class

```
package com.apress.prospring6.six.plain

import org.springframework.context.annotation.Configuration
import org.springframework.context.annotation.Import
import org.springframework.beans.factory.annotation.Autowired
import org.springframework.context.annotation.Bean
// other import statements omitted

@Import(BasicDataSourceCfg::class)
@Configuration
open class SpringDatasourceCfg {
    @Autowired
    var dataSource: DataSource? = null

    @Bean
    open fun singerDao(): SingerDao {
        val dao = JdbcSingerDao()
        dao.dataSource = dataSource
        return dao
    }
}
```

Spring now creates the singerDao bean by instantiating the JdbcSingerDao class with the dataSource property set to the dataSource bean. It is good practice to make sure that all required properties on a bean have been set. The easiest way to do this is to implement the InitializingBean interface and provide an implementation for the afterPropertiesSet() method. This way, we make sure that all required properties have been set on our JdbcSingerDao. For further discussion of bean initialization, refer to **Chapter 4**.

The code we have looked at so far uses Spring to manage the data source and introduces the SingerDao interface and its JDBC implementation. We also set the dataSource property on the JdbcSingerDao class in the Spring ApplicationContext file.

The SpringDatasourceCfg can be tested in the same way as BasicDataSourceCfg, but the test can also check the behavior of the findNameById(..) method. The test method is shown in Listing 6-18.

Listing 6-18. Testing the SpringDatasourceCfg Configuration Class

```kotlin
package com.apress.prospring6.six

import static org.junit.jupiter.api.Assertions.assertEquals
import static org.junit.jupiter.api.Assertions.assertNotNull
// other import statements omitted

class DataSourceConfigTest {

    //@Disabled("needs MariaDB running, set up container, comment this to run")
    @Test
    @Throws(
        SQLException::class
    )
    fun testSpringJdbc() {
        val ctx = AnnotationConfigApplicationContext(
            SpringDatasourceCfg::class.java
        )
        val dataSource = ctx.getBean("dataSource", DataSource::class.java)
        Assertions.assertNotNull(dataSource)
        testDataSource(dataSource)
        val singerDao = ctx.getBean(
            "singerDao",
            SingerDao::class.java
        )
        Assertions.assertEquals("John Mayer", singerDao.findNameById(1L))
        ctx.close()
    }

    // other code omitted for duplication

    companion object {
        private val LOGGER = LoggerFactory.getLogger(DataSourceConfigTest::class.java)
    }
}
```

Exception Handling

Spring advocates using runtime exceptions rather than checked exceptions, so we need a mechanism to translate the checked SQLException into a runtime Spring JDBC exception. Because Spring's SQL exceptions are runtime exceptions, they can be much more granular than checked exceptions. By definition, this is not a feature of runtime exceptions, but it is inconvenient to have to declare a long list of checked exceptions in the throws clause; hence, checked exceptions tend to be much more coarse-grained than their runtime equivalents.

💡 Kotlin handles exceptions more relaxed compared to Java. So concerning this we are already close to what Spring does.

Spring provides a default implementation of the SQLExceptionTranslator interface, which takes care of translating the generic SQL error codes into Spring JDBC exceptions. In most cases, this implementation is sufficient, but you can extend Spring's default implementation and set your new SQLExceptionTranslator implementation to be used in JdbcTemplate, as shown in Listing 6-19.

Listing 6-19. SQLExceptionTranslator Custom Implementation

```
package com.apress.prospring6.six

import org.springframework.dao.DataAccessException
import org.springframework.dao.DeadlockLoserDataAccessException
import org.springframework.jdbc.support.SQLErrorCodeSQLExceptionTranslator

import java.sql.SQLException

class MariaDBErrorCodesTranslator : SQLErrorCodeSQLExceptionTranslator() {
    override fun customTranslate(task: String, @Nullable sql: String?, sqlex: SQLException):
            DataAccessException? {
        return if (sqlex.errorCode == -12345) {
            CannotAcquireLockException(task, sqlex)
        } else null
    }
}
```

> ❶ At this point, it becomes clear that SQLErrorCodeSQLExceptionTranslator, a practical Spring-provided implementation of SQLExceptionTranslator, is part of the spring-jdbc.jar library, so this library needs to be added to the classpath. Yes, this is the section where we leave behind plain JDBC and we add Spring into the mix to make our development experience less of a headache when communicating with a database.

The org.springframework.dao.DataAccessException represents the Spring root of the hierarchy of runtime data access exceptions. Extensions of this class match specific data access exceptions and provide more information about the real cause of an exception when accessing a database. The full hierarchy is discussed later in the book.

To use the MariaDBErrorCodesTranslator we have to give up using the connection to communicate with the database directly and instead wrap the DataSource in Spring's JdbcTemplate as shown in Listing 6-20.

Listing 6-20. Introducing Spring's JdbcTemplate

```
package com.apress.prospring6.six.hybrid

import org.springframework.jdbc.core.JdbcTemplate
// other import statements omitted

internal class JdbcSingerDao : SingerDao, InitializingBean {
    private var jdbcTemplate: JdbcTemplate? = null
    var dataSource: DataSource? = null
```

```
    set(value) {
        field = value
        val errorTranslator = MariaDBErrorCodesTranslator().apply {
            setDataSource(value!!)
        }
        this.jdbcTemplate = JdbcTemplate().apply {
            dataSource = value
            exceptionTranslator = errorTranslator
        }
    }
}
// other code omitted

companion object {
    private val LOGGER = LoggerFactory.getLogger(JdbcSingerDao::class.java)
}
}
```

Having the custom SQL exception translator in place, Spring will invoke it upon SQL exceptions detected when executing SQL statements against the database, and custom exception translation will happen when the error code is -12345. For other errors, Spring will fall back to its default mechanism for exception translation. Obviously, nothing can stop you from creating SQLExceptionTranslator as a Spring-managed bean and using the JdbcTemplate bean in your DAO classes. Don't worry if you don't remember reading about the JdbcTemplate class; we are going to discuss it in more detail right now.

The JdbcTemplate Class

This class represents the core of Spring's JDBC support. It can execute all types of SQL statements. In the most simplistic view, you can classify the data definition and data manipulation statements. Data definition statements cover creating various database objects (tables, views, stored procedures, and so on). Data manipulation statements manipulate the data and can be classified as select and update statements. A select statement generally returns a set of rows; each row has the same set of columns. An update statement modifies the data in the database but does not return any results.

The JdbcTemplate class allows you to issue any type of SQL statement to the database and return any type of result. In this section, we will go through several common use cases for JDBC programming in Spring with the JdbcTemplate class.

Initializing JdbcTemplate in a DAO Class

Before discussing how to use JdbcTemplate, let's take a look at how to prepare JdbcTemplate for use in the DAO class. It's straightforward; most of the time you just need to construct the class by passing in the data source object (which should be injected by Spring into the DAO class). The last code snippet in the previous section in Listing 6-20 shows how to initialize the JdbcTemplate object. The general practice is to initialize JdbcTemplate within the same method/constructor where the data source object is injected by Spring. This ensures that JdbcTemplate will also be initialized and ready for use.

Once configured, JdbcTemplate is thread-safe. That means you can also choose to initialize a single instance of JdbcTemplate in Spring's configuration and have it injected into all DAO beans. A configuration like this is depicted in Listing 6-21.

Listing 6-21. JdbcTemplate Configured As a Bean

```
package com.apress.prospring6.six.template

import org.springframework.jdbc.core.JdbcTemplate
// other import statements omitted

@Import(BasicDataSourceCfg::class)
@Configuration
open class SpringJdbcTemplateCfg {
    @Autowired
    var dataSource: DataSource? = null

    @Bean
    open fun jdbcTemplate(): JdbcTemplate {
        return JdbcTemplate().apply {
            dataSource = this@SpringJdbcTemplateCfg.dataSource
        }
    }

    @Bean
    open fun singerDao(): SingerDao {
        return JdbcSingerDao().apply {
            setJdbcTemplate(jdbcTemplate())
        }
    }
}
```

Now that we have a JdbcTemplate bean, let's rewrite JdbcSingerDao to make use of it. Listing 6-22 makes it quite obvious that it is way easier to use the JdbcTemplate bean to communicate with the database, especially for retrieving a single value.

Listing 6-22. Using the JdbcTemplate Bean

```
package com.apress.prospring6.six.template

class JdbcSingerDao : SingerDao {
    private var jdbcTemplate: JdbcTemplate? = null
    fun setJdbcTemplate(jdbcTemplate: JdbcTemplate?) {
        this.jdbcTemplate = jdbcTemplate
    }

    override fun findNameById(id: Long): String {
        return jdbcTemplate!!.queryForObject(PARAMETRIZED_FIND_NAME,
            String::class.java, id)
    }
}
```

In Listing 6-22, we use the queryForObject(..) method of JdbcTemplate to retrieve the value of the first name in a record identified by its id. The first argument is the SQL string, and the last consists of the parameters to be passed to the SQL for parameter binding in varargs format. The second argument is the type to be returned, which is String in this case. Besides String, you can also query for other types such as Long and Int. Let's take a look at the outcome. Listing 6-23 shows the testing program. Again, a JUnit test class is used because this allows us to run test methods separately, and as tests are run when executing gradle build, we are also ensuring that our build remains stable.

Listing 6-23. Testing JdbcSingerDao That Uses the JdbcTemplate Bean

```
package com.apress.prospring6.six.template

import com.apress.prospring6.six.config.EmbeddedJdbcConfig
// other import statements omitted

class JdbcTemplateConfigTest {
    // @Disabled("needs MariaDB running, comment this to run")
    @Test
    fun testSpringJdbc() {
        val ctx = AnnotationConfigApplicationContext(
            SpringDatasurceCfg::class.java
        )
        val singerDao = ctx.getBean(
            "singerDao",
            SingerDao::class.java
        )
        Assertions.assertEquals("John Mayer", singerDao.findNameById(1L))
        ctx.close()
    }
}
```

When executing the test method testSpringJdbcWithH2Db(), we expect the *John Mayer* string to be returned by the singerDao.findNameById(1L) call, and we test this assumption using the assertTrue method. The test can be run with the original configuration class, the SpringJdbcTemplateCfg class, but this means the data source for this is MariaDB, and the test won't pass unless there is a MariaDB database installed and configured properly on the machine where the test is run. For this reason, the static class TestDbCfg was declared within the body of the test class, to inject an embedded database, instead of a real one. This test class is identical to the SpringJdbcTemplateCfg class, but instead of importing the BasicDataSourceCfg class, which configures an actual database, it imports the EmbeddedJdbcConfig class that configures an in-memory H2 database, which is more suitable for a test environment.

Of course, profiles could have been used for this example, but earlier in this chapter we hinted at the possibility to declare a static configuration class to be used in a test context, so we wanted to cover this scenario as well.

Using Named Parameters with NamedParameterJdbcTemplate

In previous examples, the SQL query used as an argument for the jdbcTemplate.queryForObject(..) method is declared using the normal placeholder (the ? character) as a query parameter, and the parameter values are passed using varargs:

```
select CONCAT(first_name , ' ' , last_name) from SINGER where id = ?
```

When using a normal placeholder, the order is important, and the order in which you put the parameters into the varargs must be the same as the order of the parameters in the query.

Some developers prefer to use named parameters to ensure that each parameter is being bound exactly as intended. In Spring, an extension of the JdbcTemplate class, NamedParameterJdbcTemplate (under the package org.springframework.jdbc.core.namedparam), provides support for this.

The initialization of NamedParameterJdbcTemplate is the same as JdbcTemplate, so we just need to declare a bean of type NamedParameterJdbcTemplate and inject it in the DAO class. In Listing 6-24, you can see the NamedTemplateDao equivalent of JdbcSingerDao that uses a NamedParameterJdbcTemplate.

Listing 6-24. NamedTemplateDao That Uses the NamedParameterJdbcTemplate Bean

```
package com.apress.prospring6.six.named

import org.springframework.jdbc.core.namedparam.NamedParameterJdbcTemplate
// other import statements omitted

internal class NamedTemplateDao : SingerDao {
    var namedTemplate: NamedParameterJdbcTemplate? = null

    override fun findNameById(id: Long?): String {
        return namedTemplate!!.queryForObject<String>(
            NAMED_FIND_NAME, mapOf<String, Long?>("singerId" to id),
            String::class.java
        )!!
    }
}
```

Instead of the ? placeholder, the named parameter (prefixed by a colon) is used instead: :singerId. Testing NamedTemplateDao is identical to testing JdbcSingerDao, so the code for this is omitted from the book, but it is part of the project.

Retrieving Domain Objects with RowMapper<T>

Examples using JdbcTemplate and related classes presented so far have been quite simple: a single value was returned by the query of a simple type, such as String. When the query returns multiple rows, that need to be converted in POJOs (like we did in the plain JDBC section), things get a little more complicated. However, Spring is here to help with its RowMapper<T> interface. As its name indicates, an instance of a type implementing RowMapper<T> is suitable only for row mapping to a single domain object. Spring's RowMapper<T> interface (in package org.springframework.jdbc.core) provides a simple way for you to perform mapping from a JDBC result set to POJOs or records. Let's see it in action by implementing the findAll() method of the SingerDao using the RowMapper<T> interface. In Listing 6-25, you can see the implementation of the findAll() method that returns a list of Singer records.

Listing 6-25. findAll() Using RowMapper<Singer>

```
package com.apress.prospring6.six.plain.records

import java.time.LocalDate
// in file Singer.kt
data class Singer( val id:Long?,
                   val firstName:String,
                   val lastName:String,
```

```kotlin
            val birthDate:LocalDate,
            val albums: MutableSet<Album>
)


// in file RowMapperCfg.kt
package com.apress.prospring6.six.rowmapper

import org.springframework.jdbc.core.RowMapper
// other imports statements omitted

interface SingerDao {
    fun findAll(): Set<Singer>
}

class RowMapperDao : SingerDao {
    var namedTemplate: NamedParameterJdbcTemplate? = null

    override fun findAll(): Set<Singer> {
        return namedTemplate!!.query(
            ALL_SELECT, SingerMapper()
        ).toSet()
    }

    class SingerMapper : RowMapper<Singer> {
        override
        fun  mapRow(rs:ResultSet, rowNum:Int):Singer {
            return Singer(rs.getLong("id"),
                    rs.getString("first_name"),
                    rs.getString("last_name"),
                    rs.getDate("birth_date").toLocalDate(),
                    mutableSetOf())
        }
    }
}
```

In Listing 6-25 we define an inner class named SingerMapper that implements the RowMapper<Singer>
interface. The class needs to provide the mapRow() implementation, which transforms the values in a specific
record of the ResultSet into the domain object you want. In this case records were used, because they exist,
and they are suitable for this example. Making it an inner class allows you to share the RowMapper<Singer>
among multiple finder methods in the same DAO class. If sharing the class is not necessary, SingerMapper
explicit implementation can be skipped altogether using lambda expressions; thus, the findAll() method
can be refactored as shown in Listing 6-26.

Listing 6-26. Using Lambdas to Avoid an Explicit Implementation of RowMapper<Singer>

```kotlin
package com.apress.prospring6.six.rowmapper
// other import statements omitted

class RowMapperDao : SingerDao {
    var namedTemplate: NamedParameterJdbcTemplate? = null
```

```kotlin
    override fun findAll(): Set<Singer> {
        return namedTemplate!!.query(
                ALL_SELECT
            ) { rs: ResultSet, rowNum: Int ->
                Singer(
                    rs.getLong("id"),
                    rs.getString("first_name"),
                    rs.getString("last_name"),
                    rs.getDate("birth_date").toLocalDate(),
                    mutableSetOf()
                )
            }.toSet()
    }
    // other code omitted
}
```

Testing the findAll() method is done in the same way everything has been tested so far. The configuration class that configures a MariaDB data source is named RowMapperCfg and is almost identical to previous classes using JdbcTemplate (or related implementations), so it won't be depicted here, but testing is always useful, so Listing 6-27 shows the test method and static test class for testing the findAll() method using an in-memory H2 database.

Listing 6-27. Method Testing findAll() and Output

```kotlin
package com.apress.prospring6.six.rowmapper

import org.junit.jupiter.api.Test
import static org.junit.jupiter.api.Assertions.assertEquals
// other import statements omitted

class JdbcNamedTemplateConfigTest {
    @Test
    fun testSpringJdbc() {
        val ctx = AnnotationConfigApplicationContext(
            TestDbCfg::class.java
        )
        val namedTemplate = ctx.getBean(
            "namedTemplate",
            NamedParameterJdbcTemplate::class.java
        )
        Assertions.assertNotNull(namedTemplate)
        val singerDao = ctx.getBean(
            "singerDao",
            SingerDao::class.java
        )
        Assertions.assertEquals("John Mayer", singerDao.findNameById(1L))
        ctx.close()
    }

    @Import(EmbeddedJdbcConfig::class)
    @Configuration
    open class TestDbCfg {
```

```kotlin
        @Autowired
        var dataSource: DataSource? = null

        @Bean
        open fun namedTemplate(): NamedParameterJdbcTemplate {
            return NamedParameterJdbcTemplate(dataSource)
        }

        @Bean
        open fun singerDao(): SingerDao {
            val dao = NamedTemplateDao()
            dao.namedTemplate = namedTemplate()
            return dao
        }
    }
}
```

```
# test method result
INFO : JdbcNamedTemplateConfigTest - Singer[id=1, firstName=John, lastName=Mayer,
birthDate=1977-10-16, albums=[]]
INFO : JdbcNamedTemplateConfigTest - Singer[id=2, firstName=Ben, lastName=Barnes,
birthDate=1981-08-20, albums=[]]
INFO : JdbcNamedTemplateConfigTest - Singer[id=3, firstName=John, lastName=Butler,
birthDate=1975-04-01, albums=[]]
```

The albums are not printed because the RowMapper<Singer> implementation does not actually set them on the returned Singer records. This is because they are not actually loaded from the database; for this we need a more complex query and something more powerful than RowMapper<Singer>.

Retrieving Nested Domain Objects with `ResultSetExtractor`

Let's proceed to a somewhat more complicated example, in which we need to retrieve the data from the parent (SINGER) and child (ALBUM) tables with a join and then transform the data back into the nested object (Set<Album> within Singer) accordingly.

For a more complicated scenario, we need to use the ResultSetExtractor<T> interface. To demonstrate its use, let's implement findAllWithAlbums() into the SingerDao interface. The method should populate the list of singers with their albums. Listing 6-28 shows the addition of the findAllWithAlbums() method to the interface and the implementation of the method using ResultSetExtractor<T>.

Listing 6-28. findAllWithAlbums() Using ResultSetExtractor<List<Singer>>

package com.apress.prospring6.six.rowmapper

import org.springframework.jdbc.core.ResultSetExtractor
// other import statements omitted

```kotlin
interface SingerDao {
    fun findAllWithAlbums(): Set<Singer>
}
```

```kotlin
class RowMapperDao : SingerDao {
    var namedTemplate: NamedParameterJdbcTemplate? = null

    override
    fun findAllWithAlbums():Set<Singer> {
        return namedTemplate!!.query(ALL_JOIN_SELECT,
            SingerWithAlbumsExtractor())!!.toSet()
    }

    class SingerWithAlbumsExtractor : ResultSetExtractor<Set<Singer>> {
        override
        fun extractData(rs:ResultSet):Set<Singer> {
            val map = mutableMapOf<Long, Singer>()
            while (rs.next()) {
                val id = rs.getLong("id")
                var singer = map[id];
                if (singer == null) {
                    singer = Singer(id,
                        rs.getString("first_name"),
                        rs.getString("last_name"),
                        rs.getDate("birth_date").toLocalDate(),
                        mutableSetOf())
                    map[id] = singer
                }

                val albumId = rs.getLong("album_id")
                if (albumId > 0) {
                    val album = Album(albumId,id,rs.getString("title"),
                        rs.getDate("release_date").toLocalDate()
                    );
                    singer.albums.add(album);
                }
            }
            return map.values.toSet()
        }
    }
}
```

The code looks quite like the RowMapper<T> sample, but this time we declare an inner class that implements ResultSetExtractor<T>. Then we implement the extractData(..) method to transform the result set into a list of Singer records accordingly. For the findAllWithDetail() method, the query uses a left join to join the two tables so that singers with no albums will also be retrieved. The result is a join of the two tables. Finally, we use the namedTemplate.query() method, passing in the query string and the result set extractor.

Of course, the SingerWithDetailExtractor inner class is not actually necessary because lambda expressions are an option. In Listing 6-29 you can see the findAllWithAlbums() version that makes use of lambda expressions.

Listing 6-29. `findAllWithAlbums()` Using Lambda Expressions

```kotlin
package com.apress.prospring6.six.rowmapper
// other import statements omitted

internal class RowMapperDao : SingerDao {
    var namedTemplate: NamedParameterJdbcTemplate? = null

    override fun findAllWithAlbums(): Set<Singer> {
        return namedTemplate!!.query<Set<Singer>>(
            ALL_JOIN_SELECT
        ) { rs: ResultSet ->
            val map: MutableMap<Long, Singer> =
                HashMap()
            var singer: Singer?
            while (rs.next()) {
                val id = rs.getLong("id")
                singer = map[id]
                if (singer == null) {
                    singer = Singer(
                        id, rs.getString("first_name"), rs.getString("last_name"),
                        rs.getDate("birth_date").toLocalDate(),
                        HashSet()
                    )
                    map[id] = singer
                }
                val albumId = rs.getLong("album_id")
                if (albumId > 0) {
                    val album =
                        Album(
                            albumId, id, rs.getString("title"),
                            rs.getDate("release_date").toLocalDate()
                        )
                    singer.albums.add(album)
                }
            }
            map.values.toSet()
        }!!
    }
}
```

Testing the `findAllWithAlbums()` method requires writing a method like the one depicted in Listing 6-27, the only thing being different this time is that the albums are part of the output as shown in Listing 6-30.

Listing 6-30. Method Testing `findAllWithAlbums()` Output

```
INFO : JdbcNamedTemplateConfigTest - Singer[id=1, firstName=John, lastName=Mayer,
birthDate=1977-10-16,
    albums=[Album[id=1, singerId=1, title=The Search For Everything, date=2017-01-20],
    Album[id=2, singerId=1, title=Battle Studies, date=2009-11-17]]]
```

```
INFO : JdbcNamedTemplateConfigTest - Singer[id=2, firstName=Ben, lastName=Barnes,
birthDate=1981-08-20,
    albums=[Album[id=3, singerId=2, title= 11:11 , date=2021-09-18]]]
INFO : JdbcNamedTemplateConfigTest - Singer[id=3, firstName=John, lastName=Butler,
birthDate=1975-04-01, albums=[]]
```

You can see the singers and their album details are listed accordingly. The data is based on the data population script that you can find in resources/h2/test-data.sql for each of the JDBC sample projects. So far, you have seen how to use JdbcTemplate to perform some common query operations. JdbcTemplate (and the NamedParameterJdbcTemplate class too) provides a number of overloading update() methods that support data update operations, including insert, update, delete, and so on. However, the update() method is quite self-explanatory, so we leave it as an exercise for you to explore. On the other side, as you will see in later sections, we will use the Spring-provided SqlUpdate class to perform data update operations.

Spring Classes That Model JDBC Operations

In the preceding section, you saw how JdbcTemplate and the related data mapper utility classes greatly simplify the programming model in developing data access logic with JDBC. Built on top of JdbcTemplate, Spring also provides a number of useful classes that model JDBC data operations and let developers maintain the query and transformation logic from ResultSet to domain objects in a more object-oriented fashion. Specifically, this section presents the following classes:

- MappingSqlQuery<T>: This abstract class allows you to wrap the query String together with the mapRow() method into a single class.

- SqlUpdate: This class allows you to wrap any SQL update statement into it. It also provides a lot of useful functions for you to bind SQL parameters, retrieve the RDBMS-generated key after a new record is inserted, and so on.

- BatchSqlUpdate: As its name indicates, this class allows you to perform batch update operations. For example, you can loop through a List object and have the BatchSqlUpdate queue up the records and submit the update statements for you in a batch. You can set the batch size and flush the operation at any time.

- SqlFunction<T>: This class allows you to call stored functions in the database with arguments and return types. Another class, StoredProcedure, also helps you to invoke stored procedures.

First let's take a look at how to set up the DAO implementation class by using annotations. Listing 6-31 shows the SingerRepo interface class with a complete listing of the data access services it provides.

Listing 6-31. SingerRepo Complete DAO Interface

```
package com.apress.prospring6.six.repo

import com.apress.prospring6.six.plain.records.Singer

import com.apress.prospring6.six.plain.records.Singer

interface SingerRepo {
    fun findAll(): List<Singer>
    fun findByFirstName(firstName: String): List<Singer>
```

```
    fun findNameById(id: Long): String?
    fun findLastNameById(id: Long): String?
    fun findFirstNameById(id: Long): String?
    fun findAllWithAlbums(): List<Singer>
    fun insert(singer: Singer)
    fun update(singer: Singer)
    fun delete(singerId: Long)
    fun insertWithAlbum(singer: Singer)
}
```

Chapter 3 introduced stereotype annotations, including @Repository, a specialization of the @Component annotation, that is designed to be used for beans handling database operations[7]. Listing 6-32 shows the initial declaration and injection of the data source property into a @Repository annotated DAO class using the JSR-250 annotation.

Listing 6-32. SingerJdbcRepo Class Implementing SingerRepo

```
package com.apress.prospring6.six.repo

import jakarta.annotation.Resource
import org.springframework.stereotype.Repository
// other import statements omitted

@Repository("singerRepo")
class SingerJdbcRepo : SingerRepo {
    @set:Autowired
    var dataSource: DataSource? = null
        set(dataSource) {
            field = dataSource ?: throw java.lang.IllegalArgumentException()
        }
...
}
```

In Listing 6-32, we use @Repository to declare the Spring bean with a name of singerRepo, and since the class contains data access code, @Repository also instructs Spring to perform database-specific SQL exceptions to the more application-friendly DataAccessException hierarchy in Spring.

The BasicDataSourceCfg configuration class, introduced earlier in the chapter, that declared a MariaDB poolable BasicDataSource bean works with this type of bean as well. You were instructed at the beginning of the chapter how to install and set up a MariaDB database and create the musicdb schema. Having the infrastructure in place, you can now proceed to writing the implementation of JDBC operations.

Querying Data by Using MappingSqlQuery<T>

Spring provides the MappingSqlQuery<T> abstract class for modeling query operations. Basically, we construct a MappingSqlQuery<T> class by using the data source and the query string. We then implement the mapRow() method to map each ResultSet record into the corresponding domain object. Let's begin by

---

[7] This indicates that the annotated class is a repository, originally defined by Eric Evans in *Domain-Driven Design* (Addison-Wesley Professional, 2003) as "a mechanism for encapsulating storage, retrieval, and search behavior which emulates a collection of objects."

creating the SelectAllSingers class (which represents the query operation for selecting all singers) that extends the MappingSqlQuery<T> abstract class. The SelectAllSingers class is shown in Listing 6-33.

Listing 6-33. SelectAllSingers Implementation

```
package com.apress.prospring6.six.repo

import com.apress.prospring6.six.plain.records.Singer
import org.springframework.jdbc.object.MappingSqlQuery
// other import statements omitted

class SelectAllSingers(dataSource: DataSource) :
        MappingSqlQuery<Singer?>(dataSource, ALL_SELECT) {
    @Throws(SQLException::class)
    override fun mapRow(rs: ResultSet, rowNum: Int): Singer {
        return Singer(
            rs.getLong("id"),
            rs.getString("first_name"),
            rs.getString("last_name"),
            rs.getDate("birth_date").toLocalDate(),
            mutableSetOf()
        )
    }
}
```

Within the SelectAllSingers class, the SQL for selecting all singers is declared. In the class constructor we provide the DataSource as well as the SQL statement. Moreover, the MappingSqlQuery<T>.mapRow() method is implemented to provide the mapping of the result set to the Singer record.

Having the SelectAllSingers class in place, we can implement the findAll() method in the SingerJdbcRepo class. Listing 6-34 depicts a section of the SingerJdbcRepo class.

Listing 6-34. SingerJdbcRepo.findAll() Implementation

```
package com.apress.prospring6.six.repo

// import statements omitted

@Repository("singerRepo")
class SingerJdbcRepo : SingerRepo {
    @set:Autowired
    var dataSource: DataSource? = null
        set(dataSource) {
            field = dataSource ?: throw java.lang.IllegalArgumentException()
            selectAllSingers = SelectAllSingers(dataSource)
        }
    private var selectAllSingers: SelectAllSingers? = null
  // other code omitted

    override fun findAll(): List<Singer> {
        return selectAllSingers!!.execute().requireNoNulls()
    }
```

```
// other code omitted

    companion object {
        private val LOGGER = LoggerFactory.getLogger(SingerJdbcRepo::class.java)
    }
}
```

In the set() accessor, upon the injection of the DataSource, an instance of the SelectAllSingers class is constructed. In the findAll() method, we simply invoke the execute() method, which is inherited from the SqlQuery<T> abstract class indirectly. That's all we need to do.

Figure 6-3 shows the full SelectAllSingers class hierarchy, with the SqlQuery<T> class shown in a red dotted rectangle to make its place in the hierarchy obvious.

Figure 6-3. *SelectAllSingers class hierarchy*

The findAll() method implemented this way can be run on the MariaDB database by creating an executable class that creates a Spring application context using the BasicDataSourceCfg class or can be tested against an embedded database in a test context.

Listing 6-35 depicts the RepoDemo class and its output.

Listing 6-35. RepoDemo Class and Its Output

```
package com.apress.prospring6.six.repo

import com.apress.prospring6.six.config.BasicDataSourceCfg
// other import statements omitted

object RepoDemo {
    private val LOGGER = LoggerFactory.getLogger(RepoDemo::class.java)
    @JvmStatic
    fun main(args: Array<String>) {
```

```
        val ctx = AnnotationConfigApplicationContext(
            BasicDataSourceCfg::class.java,
            SingerJdbcRepo::class.java
        )
        val singerRepo = ctx.getBean("singerRepo", SingerRepo::class.java)
        LOGGER.info("-------------------------")
        val singers = singerRepo.findAll()
        singers.forEach { singer -> LOGGER.info(singer.toString()) }
        ctx.close()
    }
}
```

```
# output
INFO : RepoDemo - Singer[id=1, firstName=John, lastName=Mayer, birthDate=1977-10-16,
albums=[]]
INFO : RepoDemo - Singer[id=2, firstName=Ben, lastName=Barnes, birthDate=1981-08-20,
albums=[]]
INFO : RepoDemo - Singer[id=3, firstName=John, lastName=Butler, birthDate=1975-04-01,
albums=[]]
```

Testing the method requires creating a test context based on the `EmbeddedJdbcConfig` class that we used earlier to declare an embedded in-memory H2 database (see Listing 6-14). The code from the `main()` method is almost identical to that in the test method, but it is depicted in Listing 6-36 to make obvious how easy it is to test Spring JDBC methods (so we can skip mentioning testing sometimes).

Listing 6-36. SingerJdbcRepo Test Method and Its Output

```
package com.apress.prospring6.six.repo

import com.apress.prospring6.six.config.EmbeddedJdbcConfig
// other import statements omitted

class RepoBeanTest {
    @Test
    fun testFindAllWithMappingSqlQuery() {
        val ctx = AnnotationConfigApplicationContext(
            EmbeddedJdbcConfig::class.java,
            SingerJdbcRepo::class.java
        )
        val singerRepo = ctx.getBean("singerRepo", SingerRepo::class.java)
        Assertions.assertNotNull(singerRepo)
        val singers = singerRepo.findAll()
        Assertions.assertEquals(3, singers.size)
        singers.forEach{ singer: Singer ->
            LOGGER.info(
                singer.toString()
            )
        }
        ctx.close()
    }
```

```kotlin
companion object {
    private val LOGGER = LoggerFactory.getLogger(RepoBeanTest::class.java)
}
}
```

```
# output
DEBUG: RdbmsOperation - SQL operation not compiled before execution - invoking compile
DEBUG: RdbmsOperation - RdbmsOperation with SQL [select * from SINGER] compiled
INFO : RepoBeanTest - Singer[id=1, firstName=John, lastName=Mayer, birthDate=1977-10-16,
albums=[]]
INFO : RepoBeanTest - Singer[id=2, firstName=Ben, lastName=Barnes, birthDate=1981-08-20,
albums=[]]
INFO : RepoBeanTest - Singer[id=3, firstName=John, lastName=Butler, birthDate=1975-04-01,
albums=[]]
```

If debug logging is enabled for org.springframework.jdbc, you can also see the query that was submitted by Spring.

The implementation for the findByFirstName() method is pretty similar to the implementation for findAll(), but it also involves a parameter. To keep things consistent, the SelectSingerByFirstName class is created for this operation and the code is depicted in Listing 6-37.

Listing 6-37. SelectSingerByFirstName Implementation

```kotlin
package com.apress.prospring6.six.repo

import com.apress.prospring6.six.plain.records.Singer
import org.springframework.jdbc.core.SqlParameter
import org.springframework.jdbc.object.MappingSqlQuery
// other import statements omitted

class SelectSingerByFirstName(dataSource: DataSource) :
        MappingSqlQuery<Singer?>(dataSource, FIND_BY_FIRST_NAME) {
    init {
        super.declareParameter(SqlParameter("first_name", Types.VARCHAR))
    }

    @Throws(SQLException::class)
    override fun mapRow(rs: ResultSet, rowNum: Int): Singer {
        return Singer(
            rs.getLong("id"), rs.getString("first_name"),
            rs.getString("last_name"),
            rs.getDate("birth_date").toLocalDate(),
            mutableSetOf()
        )
    }
}
```

The SelectSingerByFirstName class is similar to the SelectAllSingers class. One difference is that the SQL statement is different and carries a named parameter called first_name. Also, in the constructor method, the declareParameter() method is called (which is inherited from the org. springframework.jdbc.object.RdbmsOperation abstract class indirectly). Let's proceed to implement the findByFirstName(..) method in the SingerJdbcRepo class. The updated code is shown in Listing 6-38.

Listing 6-38. `SingerJdbcRepo.findByFirstName(..)` Implementation

package com.apress.prospring6.six.repo

```
// import statements omitted

@Repository("singerRepo")
class SingerJdbcRepo : SingerRepo {
    @set:Autowired
    var dataSource: DataSource? = null
        set(dataSource) {
            field = dataSource ?: throw java.lang.IllegalArgumentException()
            selectAllSingers = SelectAllSingers(dataSource)
            selectSingerByFirstName = SelectSingerByFirstName(dataSource)
            ...
        }
    private var selectAllSingers: SelectAllSingers? = null
    private var selectSingerByFirstName: SelectSingerByFirstName? = null
    ...

    override fun findAll(): List<Singer> {
        return selectAllSingers!!.execute().requireNoNulls()
    }

    override fun findByFirstName(firstName: String): List<Singer> {
        return selectSingerByFirstName!!.executeByNamedParam(
            mapOf( "first_name" to firstName)).toList().requireNoNulls()
    }
    ...

    companion object {
        private val LOGGER = LoggerFactory.getLogger(SingerJdbcRepo::class.java)
    }
}
```

Upon data source injection, an instance of SelectSingerByFirstName is constructed. Afterward, in the findByFirstName(..) method, a Map<K,V> is constructed with the named parameters and values. Finally, the executeByNamedParam(..) method (inherited from the SqlQuery<T> abstract class) is called. Testing this method requires a configuration class providing the database, and the EmbeddedJdbcConfig suits this purpose well. Listing 6-39 shows the test method and the output.

Listing 6-39. `SingerJdbcRepo.findByFirstName(..)` Test Method and Its Output

package com.apress.prospring6.six.repo

```
// import statements omitted

class RepoBeanTest {
    @Test
    fun testFindByNameWithMappingSqlQuery() {
        val ctx = AnnotationConfigApplicationContext(
            EmbeddedJdbcConfig::class.java,
```

```
            SingerJdbcRepo::class.java
        )
        val singerRepo = ctx.getBean("singerRepo", SingerRepo::class.java)
        Assertions.assertNotNull(singerRepo)
        val singers = singerRepo.findByFirstName("Ben")
        Assertions.assertEquals(1, singers.size)
        LOGGER.info("Result: {}", singers[0])
        ctx.close()
    }

    ...

    companion object {
        private val LOGGER = LoggerFactory.getLogger(RepoBeanTest::class.java)
    }
}
# output
DEBUG: RdbmsOperation - SQL operation not compiled before execution - invoking compile
DEBUG: RdbmsOperation - RdbmsOperation with SQL [select id, first_name, last_name, birth_
date from singer where first_name = :first_name] compiled
INFO : RepoBeanTest - Result: Singer[id=2, firstName=Ben, lastName=Barnes,
birthDate=1981-08-20, albums=[]]
```

Updating Data by Using SqlUpdate

For updating data, Spring provides the SqlUpdate class. Listing 6-40 shows the UpdateSinger class that extends the SqlUpdate class for update operations using Singer records.

Listing 6-40. SqlUpdate Extension to Update Singer Database Entries

```
package com.apress.prospring6.six.repo

import org.springframework.jdbc.core.SqlParameter
import org.springframework.jdbc.object.SqlUpdate
import java.sql.Types
// other import statements omitted

class UpdateSinger(dataSource: DataSource) : SqlUpdate(dataSource, UPDATE_SINGER) {
    init {
        super.declareParameter(SqlParameter("first_name", Types.VARCHAR))
        super.declareParameter(SqlParameter("last_name", Types.VARCHAR))
        super.declareParameter(SqlParameter("birth_date", Types.DATE))
        super.declareParameter(SqlParameter("id", Types.INTEGER))
    }
}
```

UpdateSinger is a customization of the SqlUpdate class with a custom query and the custom-named parameters. Listing 6-41 shows the implementation of the update() method in the SingerJdbcRepo class.

Listing 6-41. Using SqlUpdate in a Repo Class

```
package com.apress.prospring6.six.repo
// import statements omitted

@Repository("singerRepo")
class SingerJdbcRepo : SingerRepo {
    @set:Autowired
    var dataSource: DataSource? = null
        set(dataSource) {
            field = dataSource ?: throw java.lang.IllegalArgumentException()
            updateSinger = UpdateSinger(dataSource)
            ...
        }
    private var updateSinger: UpdateSinger? = null
    ...

    override fun update(singer: Singer) {
        updateSinger!!.updateByNamedParam(
            mapOf(
                "first_name" to singer.firstName,
                "last_name" to singer.lastName,
                "birth_date" to singer.birthDate,
                "id" to singer.id
            )
        )
        LOGGER.info("Existing singer updated with id: " + singer.id)
    }

    ...

    companion object {
        private val LOGGER = LoggerFactory.getLogger(SingerJdbcRepo::class.java)
    }
}
```

Upon data source injection, an instance of UpdateSinger is constructed. In the update() method, a Map<K,V> instance containing parameter names and their values is constructed from the passed-in Singer record, and then updateByNamedParam() is called to update the Singer database entry. Testing the operation is just as simple as the previous operations, and the test method (and output) is shown in Listing 6-42.

Listing 6-42. Method Used to Test the UpdateSinger Implementation and Its Output

```
@Test
fun testUpdateWithSqlUpdate() {
    val ctx = AnnotationConfigApplicationContext(
        EmbeddedJdbcConfig::class.java,
        SingerJdbcRepo::class.java
    )
    val singerRepo = ctx.getBean("singerRepo", SingerRepo::class.java)
    Assertions.assertNotNull(singerRepo)
    val singer = Singer(
```

```
        1L, "John Clayton", "Mayer",
        LocalDate.of(1977, 10, 16),
        mutableSetOf()
    )
    singerRepo.update(singer)
    val singers = singerRepo.findByFirstName("John Clayton")
    Assertions.assertEquals(1, singers.size)
    LOGGER.info("Result: {}", singers[0])
    ctx.close()
}

# output
DEBUG: RdbmsOperation - RdbmsOperation with SQL [update SINGER set first_name=:first_name,
last_name=:last_name, birth_date=:birth_date where id=:id] compiled
INFO : SingerJdbcRepo - Existing singer updated with id: 1
DEBUG: RdbmsOperation - RdbmsOperation with SQL [select id, first_name, last_name, birth_
date from SINGER where first_name = :first_name] compiled
INFO : RepoBeanTest - Result: Singer[id=1, firstName=John Clayton, lastName=Mayer,
birthDate=1977-10-16, albums=[]]
```

As you can see, we construct a Singer record with an existing ID and a new firstName and pass it to the update(..) method. The id field is used to identify the database records, and all other fields are used as new values for the matching columns.

Inserting Data and Retrieving the Generated Key

Inserting data is performed by extending SqlUpdate as well. The way we see it, inserting a new record is actually an update to the data in the table after all, right?

One interesting point is how the primary key is generated (which is typically the ID column). This value often is available only after the insert statement has completed; that's because, depending on the RDBMS type and configuration used, IDs do not get generated before an insert. Maybe the column ID is declared with the attribute AUTO_INCREMENT and is the primary key, and this value will be assigned by the RDBMS during the insert operation. If you are using Oracle, you will probably get a unique ID first from an Oracle sequence and then execute an insert statement with the query result.

In old versions of JDBC, generation of unique IDs is a bit tricky. For example, if we are using MariaDB, we need to execute the SQL select last_insert_id() function. For Microsoft SQL Server we execute select @@IDENTITY statements. Fortunately, starting from JDBC version 3.0, a new feature was added that allows the retrieval of an RDBMS-generated key in a unified fashion. In Listing 6-44 you can see the implementation of the insert() method, which also retrieves the generated key for the inserted contact record. It will work in most databases (if not all); just make sure you are using a JDBC driver that is compatible with JDBC 3.0 or newer.

We start by creating the InsertSinger class for the insert operation, which extends the SqlUpdate class. The code is shown in Listing 6-43.

Listing 6-43. SqlUpdate Extension to Insert a Singer Database Entry

```
package com.apress.prospring6.six.repo

import org.springframework.jdbc.object.SqlUpdate
import java.sql.Types
// more import statements omitted
```

```
class InsertSinger(dataSource: DataSource) :
        SqlUpdate(dataSource, INSERT_SINGER) {
    init {
        super.declareParameter(SqlParameter("first_name", Types.VARCHAR))
        super.declareParameter(SqlParameter("last_name", Types.VARCHAR))
        super.declareParameter(SqlParameter("birth_date", Types.DATE))
        super.setGeneratedKeysColumnNames("id")
        super.setReturnGeneratedKeys(true)
    }
}
```

The InsertSinger class is almost the same as the UpdateSinger class; we need to do just two more things. When constructing the InsertSinger class, we call the method SqlUpdate.setGeneratedKeysColumn Names() to declare the name of the ID column. The method SqlUpdate.setReturnGeneratedKeys() then instructs the underlying JDBC driver to retrieve the generated key. In Listing 6-44 you can see the implementation of the insert() method in the SingerJdbcRepo class.

Listing 6-44. Using SqlUpdate in a Repo Class to Insert a Singer Entry

```
package com.apress.prospring6.six.repo

import org.springframework.jdbc.support.GeneratedKeyHolder
import org.springframework.jdbc.support.KeyHolder
// other import statements missing

@Repository("singerRepo")
class SingerJdbcRepo : SingerRepo {
    @set:Autowired
    var dataSource: DataSource? = null
        set(dataSource) {
            field = dataSource ?: throw java.lang.IllegalArgumentException()
            insertSinger = InsertSinger(dataSource)
            ...
        }
    private var insertSinger: InsertSinger? = null
    ...

    override fun insert(singer: Singer) {
        val keyHolder: KeyHolder = GeneratedKeyHolder()
        insertSinger!!.updateByNamedParam(
            mapOf(
                "first_name" to singer.firstName,
                "last_name" to  singer.lastName,
                "birth_date" to singer.birthDate
            ), keyHolder
        )
        val generatedId = keyHolder.key!!.toLong()
        LOGGER.info("New singer  {} {} inserted with id {}  ",
            singer.firstName, singer.lastName, generatedId)
    }
```

```
// other code omitted

companion object {
    private val LOGGER = LoggerFactory.getLogger(SingerJdbcRepo::class.java)
}
}
```

Upon data source injection, an instance of InsertSinger is constructed. In the insert(..) method, we also use the SqlUpdate.updateByNamedParam() method. Additionally, we pass in an instance of KeyHolder to the method, which will have the generated ID stored in it. After the data is inserted, we can then retrieve the generated key from the KeyHolder. Testing the insert(..) method does not introduce anything new at this point, but just to confirm, the test method and its output are shown in Listing 6-45.

Listing 6-45. Method Used to Test the InsertSinger Implementation and Its Output

```
@Test
fun testInsertWithSqlUpdate() {
    val ctx = AnnotationConfigApplicationContext(
        EmbeddedJdbcConfig::class.java,
        SingerJdbcRepo::class.java
    )
    val singerRepo = ctx.getBean("singerRepo", SingerRepo::class.java)
    Assertions.assertNotNull(singerRepo)
    val singer = Singer(
        null, "Ed", "Sheeran",
        LocalDate.of(1991, 2, 17),
        mutableSetOf()
    )
    singerRepo.insert(singer)
    val singers = singerRepo.findByFirstName("Ed")
    Assertions.assertEquals(1, singers.size)
    LOGGER.info("Result: {}", singers[0])
    ctx.close()
}

# output
DEBUG: RdbmsOperation - RdbmsOperation with SQL [insert into singer (first_name, last_name,
birth_date) values (:first_name, :last_name, :birth_date)] compiled
INFO : SingerJdbcRepo - New singer  Ed Sheeran inserted with id 4
DEBUG: RdbmsOperation - RdbmsOperation with SQL [select id, first_name, last_name, birth_
date from SINGER where first_name = :first_name] compiled
INFO : RepoBeanTest - Result: Singer[id=4, firstName=Ed, lastName=Sheeran,
birthDate=1991-02-17, albums=[]]
```

Batching Operations with BatchSqlUpdate

For batch operations, we use the BatchSqlUpdate class. The new insertWithAlbum() method will insert both the singer and its released album into the database. To be able to insert the album record, we need to create the InsertSingerAlbum class, which is shown in Listing 6-46.

Listing 6-46. BatchSqlUpdate Extension to Insert a Singer with an album Collection in the Database

```
package com.apress.prospring6.six.repo

import org.springframework.jdbc.core.SqlParameter
import org.springframework.jdbc.object.BatchSqlUpdate
import java.sql.Types
// other import statements omitted

class InsertSingerAlbum(dataSource: DataSource) :
    BatchSqlUpdate(dataSource, INSERT_SINGER_ALBUM) {
    init {
        declareParameter(SqlParameter("singer_id", Types.INTEGER))
        declareParameter(SqlParameter("title", Types.VARCHAR))
        declareParameter(SqlParameter("release_date", Types.DATE))
        setBatchSize(BATCH_SIZE)
    }

    companion object {
        private const val BATCH_SIZE = 10
    }
}
```

Note that in the constructor, we call the BatchSqlUpdate.setBatchSize() method to set the batch size for the JDBC insert operation. In code Listing 6-47 shows the implementation of the insertWithAlbum() method in the SingerJdbcRepo class.

Listing 6-47. insertWithAlbum() Implementation Using the InsertSingerAlbum Class

```
package com.apress.prospring6.six.repo

import com.apress.prospring6.six.plain.records.Album
import com.apress.prospring6.six.plain.records.Singer
// other import statements omitted

@Repository("singerRepo")
class SingerJdbcRepo : SingerRepo {
    @set:Autowired
    var dataSource: DataSource? = null
        set(dataSource) {
            field = dataSource ?: throw java.lang.IllegalArgumentException()
            insertSinger = InsertSinger(dataSource)
            insertSingerAlbum = InsertSingerAlbum(dataSource)
            ...
        }
    private var insertSinger: InsertSinger? = null
    private var insertSingerAlbum: InsertSingerAlbum? = null
    ...

    override fun insertWithAlbum(singer: Singer) {
        val keyHolder = GeneratedKeyHolder()
        insertSinger!!.updateByNamedParam(
```

```kotlin
            mapOf(
                "first_name" to singer.firstName,
                "last_name" to singer.lastName,
                "birth_date" to singer.birthDate
            ), keyHolder
        )
        val newSingerId = keyHolder.key!!.toLong()
        LOGGER.info("New singer  {} {} inserted with id {}  ",
                singer.firstName, singer.lastName, newSingerId)
        val albums = singer.albums
        for (album in albums) {
            insertSingerAlbum!!.updateByNamedParam(
                mapOf(
                    "singer_id" to newSingerId,
                    "title" to album.title,
                    "release_date" to album.releaseDate
                )
            )
        }
        insertSingerAlbum!!.flush()
    }
    ...

    companion object {
        private val LOGGER = LoggerFactory.getLogger(SingerJdbcRepo::class.java)
    }
}
```

Each time the insertWithAlbum() method is called, a new instance of InsertSingerAlbum is constructed because the BatchSqlUpdate class is not thread safe. Then we use it just like SqlUpdate. The main difference is that the BatchSqlUpdate class will queue up the insert operations and submit them to the database in batch. Every time the number of records equals the batch size, Spring will execute a bulk insert operation to the database for the pending records. On the other hand, upon completion, we call the BatchSqlUpdate.flush() method to instruct Spring to flush all pending operations (that is, the insert operations being queued that still haven't reached the batch size yet). Finally, we loop through the list of Album objects in the Singer object and invoke the BatchSqlUpdate.updateByNamedParam() method. To facilitate testing, the insertWithAlbum() method is also implemented. As this implementation is pretty big, it can be reduced by making use of Java 8 lambda expressions and records of course, as shown in Listing 6-48.

Listing 6-48. findAllWithAlbum() Implementation Using a JdbcTemplate Instance

```kotlin
override fun findAllWithAlbums(): List<Singer> {
    val jdbcTemplate = JdbcTemplate(dataSource!!)
    val map: MutableMap<Long, Singer> = mutableMapOf()
    jdbcTemplate.query(FIND_SINGER_ALBUM) { rs ->
        while (rs.next()) {
            val singerID = rs.getLong("id")
            val singer = map.computeIfAbsent(singerID) { s: Long? ->
                Singer(
                    singerID,
                    rs.getString("first_name"),
```

```
                    rs.getString("last_name"),
                    rs.getDate("birth_date").toLocalDate(),
                    mutableSetOf()
                )
            }
            val albumID = rs.getLong("album_id")
            if (albumID > 0) {
                singer.albums.add(
                    Album(
                        albumID, singerID, rs.getString("title"),
                        rs.getDate("release_date").toLocalDate()
                    )
                )
            }
        }
    }
    return map.values.toList()
}
```

Testing this method does not present any special challenge. The test method and the output are shown in Listing 6-49.

Listing 6-49. Test Method insertWithAlbum() and findAllWithAlbum() and the Output

```
@Test
fun testInsertAlbumsWithBatchSqlUpdate() {
    val ctx = AnnotationConfigApplicationContext(
        EmbeddedJdbcConfig::class.java,
        SingerJdbcRepo::class.java
    )
    val singerRepo = ctx.getBean("singerRepo", SingerRepo::class.java)
    Assertions.assertNotNull(singerRepo)
    val singer = Singer(
        null, "BB", "King",
        LocalDate.of(1940, 9, 16),
        HashSet()
    )
    var album = Album(null, null, "My Kind of Blues", LocalDate.of(1961, 8, 18))
    singer.albums.add(album)
    album = Album(
        null, null, "A Heart Full of Blues",
        LocalDate.of(1962, 4, 20)
    )
    singer.albums.add(album)
    singerRepo.insertWithAlbum(singer)
    val singers = singerRepo.findAllWithAlbums()
    Assertions.assertEquals(4, singers.size)
    singers.forEach { s: Singer ->
        LOGGER.info(
            s.toString()
        )
    }
}
```

```
    ctx.close()
}

# output
DEBUG: RdbmsOperation - RdbmsOperation with SQL [insert into SINGER (first_name, last_name,
birth_date) values (:first_name, :last_name, :birth_date)] compiled
INFO : SingerJdbcRepo - New singer  BB King inserted with id 4

DEBUG: RdbmsOperation - RdbmsOperation with SQL [insert into ALBUM (singer_id, title,
release_date) values (:singer_id, :title, :release_date)] compiled

INFO : RepoBeanTest - Singer[id=1, firstName=John, lastName=Mayer, birthDate=1977-10-16,
albums=[Album[id=1, singerId=1, title=The Search For Everything, releaseDate=2017-01-20],
Album[id=2, singerId=1, title=Battle Studies, releaseDate=2009-11-17]]]
INFO : RepoBeanTest - Singer[id=2, firstName=Ben, lastName=Barnes, birthDate=1981-08-20,
albums=[Album[id=3, singerId=2, title= 11:11 , releaseDate=2021-09-18]]]
INFO : RepoBeanTest - Singer[id=3, firstName=John, lastName=Butler, birthDate=1975-04-01,
albums=[]]
INFO : RepoBeanTest - Singer[id=4, firstName=BB, lastName=King, birthDate=1940-09-16,
albums=[Album[id=4, singerId=4, title=My Kind of Blues, releaseDate=1961-08-18], Album[id=5,
singerId=4, title=A Heart Full of Blues, releaseDate=1962-04-20]]]
```

Calling Stored Functions by Using SqlFunction

Spring also provides classes to simplify the execution of stored procedures/functions using JDBC. In this
section, we show you how to execute a simple function by using the SqlFunction class. We show how to
use MariaDB for the database, create a stored function, and call it by using the SqlFunction<T> class. We're
assuming you have a MariaDB database with a schema called musicdb, with a username and password
both equaling prospring6 (the same as in the example in the section "Exploring the JDBC Infrastructure").
Let's create a stored function called getFirstNameById(..), which accepts the singer's ID and returns the
first name of the singer. Listing 6-50 shows the script to create the stored function in MariaDB (resources/
stored-function.sql). Run the script (one line) against the MariaDB database.

Listing 6-50. MariaDB Stored Function

```
CREATE FUNCTION IF NOT EXISTS getFirstNameById (in in_id INT) RETURNS VARCHAR(60) RETURN
(SELECT first_name FROM SINGER WHERE ID = in_id);
```

The stored function simply accepts the ID and returns the first name of the singer record with the
ID. Next we create a StoredFunctionFirstNameById class to represent the stored function operation, which
extends the SqlFunction<String> class. The generic type is the type of the result returned by the stored
function. You can see the content of the class in Listing 6-51.

Listing 6-51. StoredFunctionFirstNameById, Which Extends the SqlFunction<T> Class

```
package com.apress.prospring6.six.repo

import org.springframework.jdbc.object.SqlFunction
// other import statements omitted
```

```kotlin
class StoredFunctionFirstNameById(dataSource: DataSource) :
    SqlFunction<String?>(dataSource, SQL_CALL) {
    init {
        declareParameter(SqlParameter(Types.INTEGER))
        compile()
    }

    companion object {
        private const val SQL_CALL = "select getfirstnamebyid(?)"
    }
}
```

The SQL to call the stored function in MariaDB is very simple: `select getfirstnamebyid(?)`. Notice that it requires a parameter. Afterward, in the constructor, the parameter is declared, and we compile the operation. The class is now ready for use in the implementation class. Listing 6-52 shows the updated SingerJdbcRepo class to use the stored function.

Listing 6-52. SingerJdbcRepo Modified to Call a Stored Function

```kotlin
package com.apress.prospring6.six.repo
// import statements omitted

@Repository("singerRepo")
class SingerJdbcRepo : SingerRepo {
    @set:Autowired
    var dataSource: DataSource? = null
        set(dataSource) {
            field = dataSource ?: throw java.lang.IllegalArgumentException()
            storedFunctionFirstNameById = StoredFunctionFirstNameById(dataSource)
            ...
        }
    private var storedFunctionFirstNameById: StoredFunctionFirstNameById? = null
    ...

    override fun findFirstNameById(id: Long): String? {
        return storedFunctionFirstNameById!!.execute(id)[0]
    }

    ...

    companion object {
        private val LOGGER = LoggerFactory.getLogger(SingerJdbcRepo::class.java)
    }
}
```

Upon data source injection, an instance of `StoredFunctionFirstNameById` is constructed. Then in the `findFirstNameById()` method, its `execute()` method is called, passing in the contact ID. The method will return a list of `Strings`, and we need only the first one, because there should be only one record returned in the result set. Testing this functionality is not possible with H2, since the lightweight in-memory database does not have the concept of stored functions or procedures, so we'll test the method by invoking it in the `RepoDemo.main(..)` method. Listing 6-53 depicts the RepoDemo class and its output.

Listing 6-53. RepoDemo Class and Its Output

```
package com.apress.prospring6.six.repo
// import statements omitted

object RepoDemo {
    private val LOGGER = LoggerFactory.getLogger(RepoDemo::class.java)
    @JvmStatic
    fun main(args: Array<String>) {
        val ctx = AnnotationConfigApplicationContext(
            BasicDataSourceCfg::class.java,
            SingerJdbcRepo::class.java
        )
        val singerRepo = ctx.getBean("singerRepo", SingerRepo::class.java)
        LOGGER.info("-------------------------")
        val singers = singerRepo.findAll()
        singers.forEach { singer -> LOGGER.info(singer.toString()) }
        LOGGER.info("-------------------------")
        val firstName = singerRepo.findFirstNameById(2L)
        LOGGER.info("Retrieved {} ", firstName) // expect 'Ben'
        ctx.close()
    }
}
```

```
# output
INFO : RepoDemo - -------------------------
DEBUG: RdbmsOperation - RdbmsOperation with SQL [select * from SINGER] compiled
INFO : RepoDemo - Singer[id=1, firstName=John, lastName=Mayer, birthDate=1977-10-16, albums=[]]
INFO : RepoDemo - Singer[id=2, firstName=Ben, lastName=Barnes, birthDate=1981-08-20,
albums=[]]
INFO : RepoDemo - Singer[id=3, firstName=John, lastName=Butler, birthDate=1975-04-01,
albums=[]]
INFO : RepoDemo - -------------------------
DEBUG: RdbmsOperation - RdbmsOperation with SQL [select getfirstnamebyid(?)] compiled
INFO : RepoDemo - Retrieved Ben
```

You can see that the first name is retrieved correctly. What is presented here is just a simple sample to demonstrate the Spring JDBC module's function capabilities. Spring also provides other classes (for example, StoredProcedure) for you to invoke complex stored procedures that return complex data types. We recommend you refer to Spring's reference manual in case you need to access stored procedures using JDBC.

Spring Data Project: JDBC Extensions

In recent years, database technology has evolved so quickly with the rise of so many purpose-specific databases that, nowadays, an RDBMS is not the only choice for an application's back-end database. In response to this database technology evolution and the developer community's needs, Spring created the Spring Data project[8]. The major objective of the project is to provide useful extensions on top of Spring's core data access functionality to interact with databases other than traditional RDBMSs.

---

[8] https://spring.io/projects/spring-data

The Spring Data project comes with various extensions. One that we would like to introduce here is JDBC Extensions[9]. As its name implies, the extension provides some advanced features to facilitate the development of JDBC applications using Spring. The main features that JDBC Extensions provides are listed here:

- *QueryDSL support*: QueryDSL[10] is a domain-specific language that provides a framework for developing type-safe queries. Spring Data's JDBC Extensions provides QueryDslJdbcTemplate to facilitate the development of JDBC applications using QueryDSL instead of SQL statements.

- *Advanced support for Oracle Database*: The extension provides advanced features for Oracle Database users. On the database connection side, it supports Oracle-specific session settings, as well as Fast Connection Failover technology when working with Oracle RAC. It also provides classes that integrate with Oracle Advanced Queueing. On the data type side, it provides native support for Oracle's XML types, STRUCT and ARRAY, and so on.

If you are developing JDBC applications using Spring with Oracle Database, JDBC Extensions is really worth a look.

Spring JDBC Testing Annotations

In **Chapter 4**, you were introduced to a few testing annotations. Some of them were very obviously related to the data access context. @Sql, @SqlConfig, @SqlGroup, and @SqlMergeMode are part of the org.springframework.test.context.jdbc package and are suitable for testing pure Spring JDBC implementations. In this chapter all test methods were designed to build their own application context to keep the configuration obvious. All test methods that are using an in-memory database can be written to share the same test context and use these specialized annotations to customize it for each test method.

Let's start with @Sql. This annotation is used to annotate a test class or test method to configure SQL scripts and statements to be executed against a given database during integration tests. This annotation can be used with plain JDBC or with more complex applications that make use of persistence or transactions. @Sql can be used on a test class, and this means the statements or scripts configured with it will be applied to each test method in the class. Listing 6-54 shows a test class with a single test method for the findAll() method.

Listing 6-54. JdbcRepoTest Class Using @Sql* Annotations

```
package com.apress.prospring6.six.repo

import org.junit.jupiter.api.DisplayName
import org.junit.jupiter.api.Test
import org.springframework.jdbc.datasource.embedded.EmbeddedDatabaseBuilder
import org.springframework.jdbc.datasource.embedded.EmbeddedDatabaseType
import org.springframework.test.context.jdbc.Sql
import org.springframework.test.context.jdbc.SqlMergeMode
import org.springframework.test.context.junit.jupiter.SpringJUnitConfig
// other imports omitted
```

---

[9] https://spring.io/projects/spring-data-jdbc-ext
[10] https://querydsl.com

```kotlin
@SqlMergeMode(SqlMergeMode.MergeMode.MERGE)
@Sql("classpath:h2/drop-schema.sql", "classpath:h2/create-schema.sql")
@SpringJUnitConfig(classes = [EmptyEmbeddedJdbcConfig::class, SingerJdbcRepo::class])
class JdbcRepoTest {
    @Autowired
    var singerRepo: SingerRepo? = null

    @Test
    @DisplayName("should return all singers")
    @Sql(
        value = ["classpath:h2/test-data.sql"],
        config = SqlConfig(encoding = "utf-8", separator = ";", commentPrefix = "--")
    )
    fun testFindAllWithMappingSqlQuery() {
        val singers = singerRepo!!.findAll()
        Assertions.assertEquals(3, singers.size)
        singers.forEach(Consumer { singer: Singer ->
            LOGGER.info(
                singer.toString()
            )
        })
    }

    @Configuration
    open class EmptyEmbeddedJdbcConfig {
        @Bean
        open fun dataSource(): DataSource? {
            return try {
                val dbBuilder = EmbeddedDatabaseBuilder()
                dbBuilder.setType(EmbeddedDatabaseType.H2).setName("musicdb").build()
            } catch (e: Exception) {
                LOGGER.error("Embedded DataSource bean cannot be created!", e)
                null
            }
        }

        companion object {
            private val LOGGER =
                LoggerFactory.getLogger(EmptyEmbeddedJdbcConfig::class.java)
        }
    }

    companion object {
        private val LOGGER = LoggerFactory.getLogger(RepoBeanTest::class.java)
    }
}
```

The test `ApplicationContext` is created using the `@SpringJUnitJupiterConfig` annotation. This is a composed annotation that combines `@ExtendWith(SpringExtension.class)` from JUnit Jupiter with `@ContextConfiguration` from the Spring TestContext Framework. The `EmptyEmbeddedJdbcConfig` config class is an inner class declared in the test class body for practical reasons: it is small and is relevant only to this test class. The resulting test ApplicationContext contains beans that define a data source pointing to an empty in-memory H2 database named musicdb. Since the test class is targeting methods of the SingerJdbcRepo bean, this class is also added to the context.

The database schema with the SINGER and ALBUM is initialized by annotating the test class with this annotation: @Sql({ "classpath:h2/drop-schema.sql", "classpath:h2/create-schema.sql" }). These two scripts contain the SQL code to do exactly what their names suggest—drop and create the tables in the database schema.

Annotation @Sql(value = "classpath:h2/test-data.sql") is used to annotate the test method and is executed by default before the test method to prepare the database contents for the test. There would be no point in executing findAll() if there were no singers to be found, right?

This annotation is quite versatile and can be configured using @SqlConfigure to provide more details about the script being executed, such as encoding, which character is used as a statement separator and character used to prefix comments and many more. @Sql also provides an executionPhase attribute that is used to specify if the script or statements should be executed before or after the test method, which is useful for cleanup to avoid dirtying the context and preventing other tests from failing.

This means the annotation on the testFindAllWithMappingSqlQuery() test method can also be written as:

```
@Sql(value = "classpath:h2/test-data.sql",
    config = @SqlConfig(encoding = "utf-8", separator = ";", commentPrefix = "--"),
    executionPhase = Sql.ExecutionPhase.BEFORE_TEST_METHOD)
```

The @SqlMergeMode(SqlMergeMode.MergeMode.MERGE) annotation indicates that method-level @Sql declarations should be merged @Sql declarations, with class-level SQL scripts and statements executed before method-level scripts and statements. The other option is to use @SqlMergeMode(SqlMergeMode.MergeMode.OVERRIDE), which allows @Sql declaration annotations on methods to override the annotations at class level.

When @Sql annotations are used at class level, and @SqlMergeMode is not specified, the declarations configured by them are ignored, and this will almost definitely cause test failures.

As previously mentioned, @Sql can also specify statements, not only scripts. Listing 6-55 shows the testFindByNameWithMappingSqlQuery() method, used to check that the findByFirstName(..) method works as expected.

Listing 6-55. JdbcRepoTest.testFindByNameWithMappingSqlQuery() Test Method

```
package com.apress.prospring6.six.repo

import org.springframework.test.context.jdbc.SqlGroup
// other import statements omitted

@SqlMergeMode(SqlMergeMode.MergeMode.MERGE)
@Sql("classpath:h2/drop-schema.sql", "classpath:h2/create-schema.sql")
@SpringJUnitConfig(classes = [EmptyEmbeddedJdbcConfig::class, SingerJdbcRepo::class])
class JdbcRepoTest {
    @Autowired
    var singerRepo: SingerRepo? = null

    @Test
    @DisplayName("should return Chuck Berry")
    @SqlGroup(
        Sql(
```

```
            statements = arrayOf("insert into SINGER (first_name, last_name, birth_date)
            values ('Chuck', 'Berry', '1926-09-18')"),
            executionPhase = Sql.ExecutionPhase.BEFORE_TEST_METHOD
        ),
        Sql(
            statements = arrayOf("delete from  SINGER where first_name = 'Chuck'"),
            executionPhase = Sql.ExecutionPhase.AFTER_TEST_METHOD
        )
    )
    fun testFindByNameWithMappingSqlQuery() {
        val singers = singerRepo!!.findByFirstName("Chuck")
        Assertions.assertEquals(1, singers.size)
        LOGGER.info("Result: {}", singers[0])
    }

    ...

    companion object {
        private val LOGGER =
            LoggerFactory.getLogger(EmptyEmbeddedJdbcConfig::class.java)
    }
}

    companion object {
        private val LOGGER = LoggerFactory.getLogger(RepoBeanTest::class.java)
    }
}
```

Listing 6-55 shows how @Sql annotations can be grouped using the @SqlGroup annotation. Having multiple @Sql annotations on the same test method (or class) is allowed, but @SqlGroup is just a nicer way to group them to make it obvious that they are all relevant to the item they are set on.

For the same method, notice how the executionPhase attribute is used to insert the item targeted by the test method, by setting it to Sql.ExecutionPhase.BEFORE_TEST_METHOD for one of the @Sql annotations. For the other one, executionPhase is set to Sql.ExecutionPhase.AFTER_TEST_METHOD to delete the item from the database. This ensures that the test context is kept clean, and that the methods in the test class can be run in any order, and will still pass.

The @DisplayName annotation is a typical JUnit Jupiter annotation used to declare a custom display value for the annotated test class or test method. In an editor that supports JUnit 5, this can look very pretty, as shown in Figure 6-4.

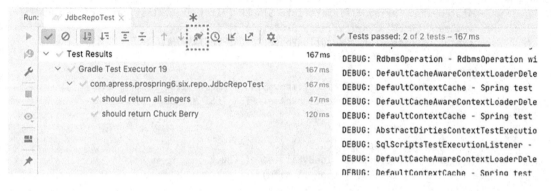

Figure 6-4. *Tests with pretty name*

In Figure 6-4, IntelliJ IDEA uses Gradle to run the tests, and by clicking the icon marked with a box and asterisk, a tab is opened in your browser showing the test results in HTML format. Notice that the display name is kept, which gives a lot of context for the assumptions checked by the test methods. The HTML format for the test results is shown in Figure 6-5.

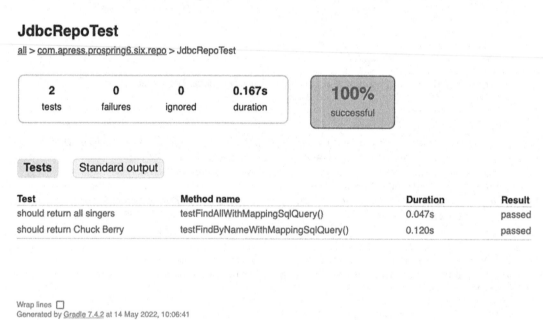

Figure 6-5. *HTML test results generated by Gradle*

The log level for the test can be configured to show more details. We recommend using `<logger name="com.apress.prospring6.six" level="debug"/>`. This way, queries, parameters, and results become visible. Also, you might see this exception being reported:

```
DEBUG: TestContextTransactionUtils - Caught exception while retrieving
PlatformTransactionManager for test context
    [
```

```
    DefaultTestContext@2320fa6f testClass = JdbcRepoTest, testInstance = com.apress.
    prospring6.six.repo.JdbcRepoTest@7c1e2a2d,
    testMethod = testFindByNameWithMappingSqlQuery@JdbcRepoTest,
    testException = [null],
    mergedContextConfiguration = [MergedContextConfiguration@7a560583 testClass =
    JdbcRepoTest, locations = '{}',
    classes = {
        'class com.apress.prospring6.six.repo.JdbcRepoTest$EmptyEmbeddedJdbcConfig, '
        'class com.apress.prospring6.six.repo.SingerJdbcRepo',
    },
    contextInitializerClasses = '[]',
    activeProfiles = '{}',
    propertySourceLocations = '{}',
    propertySourceProperties = '{}',
    contextCustomizers = set[[empty]],
    contextLoader = 'org.springframework.test.context.support.
    DelegatingSmartContextLoader',
    parent = [null]],
    attributes = map['org.springframework.test.context.event.
    ApplicationEventsTestExecutionListener.recordApplicationEvents' -> false]
]
org.springframework.beans.factory.NoSuchBeanDefinitionException: No bean named
'transactionManager' available
...
```

This exception shows that the @Sql* annotations family is suitable for applications using transactions as well (which will be covered in **Chapter 7**).

Introducing Testcontainers

As previously mentioned, testing stored functions and procedures is not possible with H2, since the lightweight in-memory database does not have these concepts. However, *not* testing the code written is not something that we want to encourage you to do. When in production, the code runs on an actual database; during daily builds, the tests could run a test database or a database in a container. Since preparing a test database might still be a costly operation, the most suitable alternative is to run the tests in a database in a container. To make this easy, the Testcontainers[11] library was invented.

Testcontainers is a Java library that supports JUnit tests, providing lightweight, throwaway instances of common databases, Selenium web browsers, or anything else that can run in a Docker container. Using this library, we can start a container using a lightweight MariaDB image and write a test for our stored function. This obviously requires Docker being installed on your computer. The good news is that you don't have to create the container manually, or run Docker commands, because Testcontainers provides all the components to do so from the code. These components integrate nicely with the JUnit Jupiter and Spring JDBC testing annotations introduced thus far.

The approach is similar to testing when using an embedded database, but instead of creating a DataSource bean using EmbeddedDatabaseBuilder, an org.testcontainers.containers. MariaDBContainer instance is used. The test configuration class is shown in Listing 6-56.

---

[11] https://www.testcontainers.org/

Listing 6-56. TestContainersConfig Using a MariaDBContainer

```kotlin
package com.apress.prospring6.six.repo

import org.testcontainers.containers.MariaDBContainer
// other import statements omitted

// annotations omitted
class StoredFunctionV1Test {
    @Autowired
    var singerRepo: SingerRepo? = null

    // test methods omitted for relevance

    @Configuration
    open class TestContainersConfig {
        var mariaDB: MariaDBContainer<*> = MariaDBContainer("mariadb:latest")

        @PostConstruct
        open fun initialize() {
            mariaDB.start()
        }

        @PreDestroy
        open fun tearDown() {
            mariaDB.stop()
        }

        @Bean
        open fun dataSource(): DataSource? {
            return try {
                val dataSource = BasicDataSource()
                dataSource.driverClassName = mariaDB.driverClassName
                dataSource.url = mariaDB.jdbcUrl
                dataSource.username = mariaDB.username
                dataSource.password = mariaDB.password
                dataSource
            } catch (e: Exception) {
                LOGGER.error("MariaDB TestContainers DataSource bean cannot be created!", e)
                null
            }
        }

        companion object {
            private val LOGGER = LoggerFactory.getLogger(TestContainersConfig::class.java)
        }
    }
}
```

Any code that might distract you from the Testcontainers central configuration was stripped away from the StoredFunctionV1TestTest class, the class where the TestContainersConfig is declared. It was declared inside the test class because this is the only place where it is used.

As you can see, the MariaDBContainer class provides all the properties necessary to create a DataSource bean. When instantiated, the MariaDBContainer constructor requires a single String argument representing the Docker container image and a tag representing the MariaDB version. To make sure the container is started gracefully, an initialize() method was added to the configuration annotated with @PostConstruct that calls mariaDB.start() to start the container. To make sure the container is stopped gracefully, a tearDown() method annotated with @PreDestroy that calls mariaDB.stop() was added to stop the container. These two methods are needed because the container is treated like a bean, and thus we must make sure that when the context is destroyed, the container is shut down gracefully and terminated as well.

Although this approach gets the job done, the recommended way is to rely on JUnit Jupiter life-cycle management to start and stop the container. This allows us to reuse the BasicDataSourceCfg configuration class. The practical part here is that the same DataSource bean declared in the BasicDataSourceCfg can be used, and since only the database location changes, the database is the same as the one declared for production, MariaDB. To make this work, we need to do the following three things:

- Declare our MariaDBContainer as a companion object field. Also we add the @Testcontainers annotation that is a JUnit Jupiter extension activating automatic startup and stop of containers used in a test case.

- Annotate the container field with @Container to let JUnit Jupiter know that this is the container instance we want managed. (Both @Testcontainers and this annotation are part of the junit-jupiter.jar Testcontainers library that is added to the classpath of the project.)

- Use @DynamicPropertySource on a method to register the container properties as configuration properties for the DataSource bean. This annotation was mentioned in **Chapter 4** and this test case is the first suitable place to use it in this book. It is used here to dynamically add properties to the Environment's set of PropertySources.

With this configuration the container is created and MariaDB is installed and started, but the schema, the data, and the stored function required for the tests are not there yet. The SQL scripts to do that still have to be configured using various @Sql* annotations. Listing 6-57 shows the full implementation of the StoredFunctionV2Test with the two methods: one testing the singerRepo.findAll() query and one testing the singerRepo.findFirstNameById(..) stored function.

Listing 6-57. StoredFunctionV2Test Using a MariaDBContainer to Test JDBC Methods On

```
package com.apress.prospring6.six.repo

import org.testcontainers.containers.MariaDBContainer
import org.testcontainers.junit.jupiter.Container
import org.testcontainers.junit.jupiter.Testcontainers

// import statements omitted

@Testcontainers
@SqlMergeMode(SqlMergeMode.MergeMode.MERGE)
@Sql("classpath:testcontainers/drop-schema.sql",
        "classpath:testcontainers/create-schema.sql") // This works
@SpringJUnitConfig(classes = [BasicDataSourceCfg::class, SingerJdbcRepo::class])
class StoredFunctionV2Test {
    @Autowired
    var singerRepo: SingerRepo? = null
```

```kotlin
@Test
fun testFindAllQuery() {
    val singers = singerRepo!!.findAll()
    Assertions.assertEquals(3, singers.size)
}

@Test
//@Sql({ "classpath:testcontainers/original-stored-function.sql" })
// This does not work!
// Testcontainers simply can't support all SQL dialects to 100%.
@Sql("classpath:testcontainers/stored-function.sql") // different SQL syntax
fun testStoredFunction() {
    val firstName = singerRepo!!.findFirstNameById(2L)
    Assertions.assertEquals("Ben", firstName)
}

companion object {
    @Container
    var mariaDB: MariaDBContainer<*> = MariaDBContainer("mariadb:latest")

    @DynamicPropertySource // this does the magic
    fun setUp(registry: DynamicPropertyRegistry) {
        with(registry) {
            add("jdbc.driverClassName") { mariaDB.driverClassName }
            add("jdbc.url") { mariaDB.jdbcUrl }
            add("jdbc.username") { mariaDB.username }
            add("jdbc.password") { mariaDB.password }
        }
    }
}
}
```

Using Testcontainers simplifies testing, but Testcontainers is not perfect, and simply can't support all SQL dialects to 100%. Sometimes perfectly valid SQL syntax is not recognized and some adjustements have to be made or files have to be copied onto the container and executed there. For example, the initial version of the getFirstNameById(..) stored function shown in Listing 6-50 caused the testStoredFunction() test method to fail, as shown in Figure 6-6.

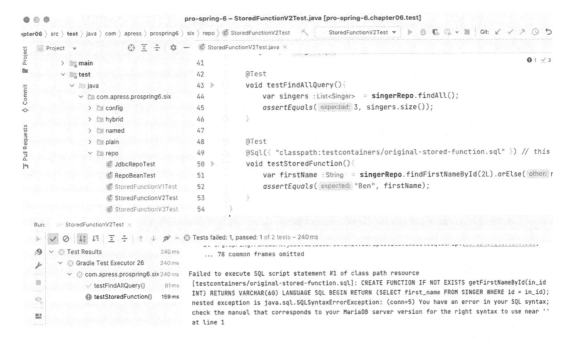

Figure 6-6. *Failing test using MariaDB test container*

To make StoredFunctionV1Test and StoredFunctionV2Test pass completely, the getFirstNameById(..) stored function declaration needs to be changed to the one in testcontainers/stored-function.sql that is depicted here:

```
CREATE FUNCTION getFirstNameById (in_id INT) RETURNS VARCHAR(60)
    RETURN (SELECT first_name FROM SINGER WHERE id = in_id);
```

However, when the right SQL changes can't be figured out, issues like these can be overcome by copying the SQL scripts onto the container and letting them be executed by Docker when creating the container. Of course, this means we no longer need the @Sql* annotations and the initialization() method is needed to copy the scripts onto the container and execute them. Listing 6-58 shows the full implementation of the StoredFunctionV3Test that actually works with the original SQL syntax of the stored function. A TestContainersConfig class is needed to declare the initialization() method.

Listing 6-58. GoodStoredFunctionTest Using a MariaDBContainer to Test JDBC Methods On

```
package com.apress.prospring6.six.repo

import org.testcontainers.ext.ScriptUtils
import org.testcontainers.jdbc.JdbcDatabaseDelegate
import org.testcontainers.shaded.com.google.common.io.Resources
import java.nio.charset.StandardCharsets
import javax.script.ScriptException
import java.io.IOException
// other import statements omitted


@Testcontainers
```

```kotlin
@SpringJUnitConfig(classes = [TestContainersConfig::class, SingerJdbcRepo::class])
class StoredFunctionV3Test {
    @Autowired
    var singerRepo: SingerRepo? = null

    @Test
    fun testFindAllQuery() {
        val singers = singerRepo!!.findAll()
        Assertions.assertEquals(3, singers.size)
    }

    @Test
    fun testStoredFunction() {
        val firstName = singerRepo!!.findFirstNameById(2L)
        Assertions.assertEquals("Ben", firstName)
    }

    @Configuration
    @Import(
        BasicDataSourceCfg::class
    )
    open class TestContainersConfig {
        @PostConstruct
        @Throws(ScriptException::class, IOException::class)
        open fun initialize() {
            val script1 =
                Resources.toString(Resources.getResource("testcontainers/create-schema.
                sql"), StandardCharsets.UTF_8)
            val script2 = Resources.toString(
                Resources.getResource("testcontainers/original-stored-function.sql"),
                StandardCharsets.UTF_8
            )
            mariaDB.start()
            ScriptUtils.executeDatabaseScript(
                JdbcDatabaseDelegate(mariaDB, ""),
                "schema.sql",
                script1,
                false,
                false,
                ScriptUtils.DEFAULT_COMMENT_PREFIX,
                ScriptUtils.DEFAULT_STATEMENT_SEPARATOR,
                "$$",
                "$$$"
            )
            ScriptUtils.executeDatabaseScript(
                JdbcDatabaseDelegate(mariaDB, ""),
                "schema.sql",
                script2,
                false,
                false,
                ScriptUtils.DEFAULT_COMMENT_PREFIX,
```

```
                ScriptUtils.DEFAULT_STATEMENT_SEPARATOR,
                "$$",
                "$$$"
            )
        }
    }

    companion object {
        @Container
        var mariaDB: MariaDBContainer<*> = MariaDBContainer("mariadb:latest")

        @DynamicPropertySource // this does the magic
        fun setUp(registry: DynamicPropertyRegistry) {
            with(registry) {
                add("jdbc.driverClassName") { mariaDB.driverClassName }
                add("jdbc.url") { mariaDB.jdbcUrl }
                add("jdbc.username") { mariaDB.username }
                add("jdbc.password") { mariaDB.password }
            }
        }
    }
}
```

Copying the files onto the container can be done in more than one way, but the only way we've found that works with the MariaDB image used for this example is the one depicted in Listing 6-58. The code it not the prettiest, but it gets the job done.

To add Testcontainers support to your project, you need to add the library specific to the type of container image you need. For this book, the `org.testcontainers:mariadb:1.17.2` library was added to the Gradle configuration.

To benefit from JUnit Jupiter's integration capabilities, provided by the `@Testcontainers` and the `@Container` annotations, the `org.testcontainers:junit-jupiter:1.17.2` library was added to the Gradle configuration.

There are other libraries available, and you can find them at the Maven Repository[12].

Considerations for Using JDBC

With the rich feature set Spring provides, you can see how Spring can make your life much easier when using JDBC to interact with the underlying RDBMS. However, there is still quite a lot of code you need to develop, especially when transforming the result set into the corresponding domain objects.

On top of JDBC, a lot of open source libraries have been developed to help close the gap between the relational data structure and Java's OO model. For example, iBATIS is a popular DataMapper framework that is also based on SQL mapping. iBATIS lets you map objects with stored procedures or queries to an XML

---

[12] https://mvnrepository.com/artifact/org.testcontainers

descriptor file. Like Spring, iBATIS provides a declarative way to query object mapping, greatly saving you the time it takes to maintain SQL queries that may be scattered around various DAO classes. There are also many other ORM frameworks that focus on the object model rather than the query. Popular ones include Hibernate, EclipseLink (also known as TopLink), and OpenJPA. All of them comply with the JCP's JPA specification.

In recent years, these ORM tools and mapping frameworks have become much more mature so that most developers will settle on one of them, instead of using JDBC directly. However, in cases where you need to have absolute control over the query that will be submitted to the database for performance purposes (for example, using a hierarchical query in Oracle), Spring JDBC is a viable option. And when using Spring, one great advantage is that you can mix and match different data access technologies. For example, you can use Hibernate as the main ORM and then JDBC as a supplement for some of the complex query logic or batch operations; you can mix and match them in a single business operation and then wrap them under the same database transaction. Spring will help you handle those situations easily.

Spring Boot JDBC

As we've already introduced Spring Boot for simple console applications, it is only logical to cover a Spring Boot starter library for JDBC in this book. It helps you remove boilerplate configurations and jump directly into implementation.

When `spring-boot-starter-jdbc` is added as a dependency to a project, a group of libraries is added to the classpath of the project. What is not added is a database driver. That decision must be taken by the developer. In this case, the `mysql-java-client` is added as a dependency just as for the non–Spring Boot project. In the same way, for running tests, the h2 library must be explicitly configured. The project that will be covered in this section is `chapter06-boot`. The autoconfigured libraries are depicted in Figure 6-7 in the IntelliJ IDEA Gradle Projects view.

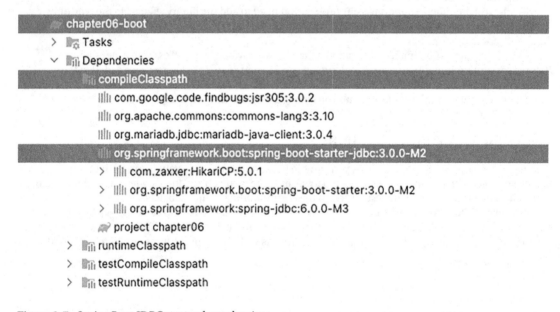

Figure 6-7. *Spring Boot JDBC starter dependencies*

The spring-boot-starter-jdbc library uses HikariCP[13] to configure the DataSource bean, which is a fast, reliable, and simple production-ready connection pool library. Thus, if there is no DataSource bean explicitly configured and there is an embedded database driver in the classpath, Spring Boot will automatically register the DataSource bean using in-memory database settings. Spring Boot also registers the following beans automatically:

- A JdbcTemplate bean
- A NamedParameterJdbcTemplate bean
- A PlatformTransactionManager (DataSourceTransactionManager) bean

The PlatformTransactionManager bean is not of interest at this time because it is covered in **Chapter 7**, but the first two are noteworthy because we previously configured them manually, and that is no longer needed.

Another interesting thing to note is that, to make sure the MariaDB data source is used when running the application and the H2 data source is used for tests, two application profiles are used: "dev" and "test".

Here are other things that might be interesting in that they reduce the amount of environment setup work:

- Spring Boot database connection details are configured in the application-{profileName}.properties/application-{profileName}.yaml file, which is located under src/main/resources. Listing 6-59 shows the configuration for the local containerized MariaDB database recommended in this chapter and the in-memory H2 configuration, used for tests.

Listing 6-59. MariaDB and H2 Database Connection Details for a Spring Boot Application

```
# application-dev.yaml
spring:
  datasource:
    driverClassName: org.mariadb.jdbc.Driver
    url: jdbc:mariadb://localhost:3306/musicdb?useSSL=false
    username: prospring6
    password: prospring6

# application-test.yaml
spring:
  datasource:
    url: "jdbc:h2:mem:mydb"
    username: "sa"
```

- Spring Boot looks for embedded database initialization files under src/main/resources. It expects to find a file named schema.sql that contains SQL DDL statements (for example, CREATE TABLE statements) and a file named data.sql that contains DML statements (for example, INSERT statements). It uses this file to initialize a database at boot time.
- The location and names for these files can be configured in the application.properties/application.yaml file, which is located under src/main/resources as well. A sample configuration file that would allow the Spring Boot application to use SQL files is shown in Listing 6-60.

---

[13] https://github.com/brettwooldridge/HikariCP

Listing 6-60. Database Initialization Spring Boot Configurations

```
# application-{profileName}.properties
spring.datasource.schema=db/schema.sql
spring.datasource.data=db/test-data.sql
```

```
# application-{profileName}.yml
spring:
    datasource:
        schema: db/schema.sql
        data: db/test-data.sql
```

- By default, Spring Boot initializes the database at boot time (unless already there), but this can be changed as well by adding the property `spring.datasource.initialize=false` to the `application-{profileName}.properties`/`application-{profileName}.yaml` file.

Aside from all that was mentioned, what is left to do with Spring Boot is to provide some domain classes and a DAO bean. As previously mentioned, Spring Boot automatically configures a `JdbcTemplate` bean, so we only need to create a simple `SingerJdbcRepo`. This bean gets injected automatically and we can hence use it to manage data. As for domain classes, the `Signer` and `Album` records introduced previously in the chapter suffice. Listing 6-61 shows a simple `SingerRepo` interface and `SingerJdbcRepo` implementing it.

Listing 6-61. Repository Interface And Implementation Via Spring Boot Configurations

```kotlin
// SingerDao.kt
package com.apress.prospring6.six.repo

import com.apress.prospring6.six.records.Singer
import java.util.stream.Stream

interface SingerRepo {
    fun findAll():Stream<Singer>
}
```

```java
// SingerJdbcRepo.java
package com.apress.prospring6.six.repo

import com.apress.prospring6.six.records.Singer
import org.springframework.jdbc.core.JdbcTemplate
import java.util.List
import java.util.stream.Stream
// other import statements omitted
open class SingerJdbcRepo : SingerRepo {
    private var jdbcTemplate: JdbcTemplate? = null
    private var storedFunctionFirstNameById: StoredFunctionFirstNameById? = null

    @Autowired
    open fun setJdbcTemplate(jdbcTemplate: JdbcTemplate) {
        this.jdbcTemplate = jdbcTemplate
```

```kotlin
        storedFunctionFirstNameById =
            StoredFunctionFirstNameById(jdbcTemplate.dataSource)
    }

    override fun findAll(): Stream<Singer> {
        return jdbcTemplate!!.queryForStream(
            ALL_SELECT
        ) { rs: ResultSet, rowNum: Int ->
            Singer(
                rs.getLong("id"),
                rs.getString("first_name"),
                rs.getString("last_name"),
                rs.getDate("birth_date"),
                mutableListOf()
            )
        }
    }

    override fun findFirstNameById(id: Long): String? {
        return storedFunctionFirstNameById!!.execute(id)[0]
    }

    internal class StoredFunctionFirstNameById(dataSource: DataSource?) :
        SqlFunction<String?>(dataSource!!, SQL_CALL) {
        init {
            declareParameter(SqlParameter(Types.INTEGER))
            compile()
        }

        companion object {
            private const val SQL_CALL = "select getfirstnamebyid(?)"
        }
    }

    companion object {
        const val ALL_SELECT = "select * from SINGER"
    }
}
```

Recall that the Spring Boot entry class is an executable class. The ApplicationContext created when running its main class can be used to retrieve the singerRepo bean and call the findAll() method. With the configuration of application-dev.yaml in Listing 6-59, the findAll() method will be executed on the MariaDB musicdb database SINGER table. The code for this class and its output when executed are shown in Listing 6-62.

Listing 6-62. Chapter6Application Spring Boot Main Class and Output Sample of Its Execution

```
package com.apress.prospring6.six

import org.springframework.boot.SpringApplication
import org.springframework.boot.autoconfigure.SpringBootApplication
//other import statements omitted

@SpringBootApplication
open class Chapter6Application {
    companion object {
        private val LOGGER = LoggerFactory.getLogger(Chapter6Application::class.java)
        @JvmStatic
        fun main(args: Array<String>) {
            System.setProperty(
                AbstractEnvironment.ACTIVE_PROFILES_PROPERTY_NAME, "dev")
            val ctx = SpringApplication.run(
                Chapter6Application::class.java, *args
            )
            val repo = ctx.getBean(
                SingerRepo::class.java
            )
            repo.findAll().forEach { singer -> LOGGER.info(singer.toString()) }
        }
    }
}
```

```
# output
INFO : StartupInfoLogger - Starting Chapter6Application using Java 17 on IulianasPrimary
       with PID 95259 ...
INFO : SpringApplication - The following 1 profile is active: "dev"
INFO : StartupInfoLogger - Started Chapter6Application in 2.027 seconds (JVM running
       for 3.023)
INFO : HikariDataSource - HikariPool-1 - Starting...
INFO : HikariPool - HikariPool-1 - Added connection org.mariadb.jdbc.
       Connection@2301b75  # (2)
INFO : HikariDataSource - HikariPool-1 - Start completed.
INFO : Chapter6Application - Singer[id=1, firstName=John, lastName=Mayer,
       birthDate=1977-10-16, albums=[]]
INFO : Chapter6Application - Singer[id=2, firstName=Ben, lastName=Barnes,
       birthDate=1981-08-20, albums=[]]
INFO : Chapter6Application - Singer[id=3, firstName=John, lastName=Butler,
       birthDate=1975-04-01, albums=[]]
INFO : HikariDataSource - HikariPool-1 - Shutdown initiated...
INFO : HikariDataSource - HikariPool-1 - Shutdown completed.
```

The line marked with (1) at the end sets the profile to be dev, which allows us to just run the class and get the expected behavior, instead of supplying the profile as a program argument. The line marked with (2) shows the connection type printed in the log. This makes it clear where the records are coming from.

A Spring Boot Test class can be easily written, and the embedded database is automatically created based on the configurations in Listing 6-59 (application-test.yaml), so all we are left to do is decorate the class and the test method with the @Sql* annotations introduced earlier in the chapter to make sure test data is available. Listing 6-63 shows this test class and the result of executing it.

Listing 6-63. Chapter6ApplicationTest Spring Boot Test Class and Output Sample of Its Execution

```
package com.apress.prospring6.six

import com.apress.prospring6.six.repo.SingerRepo
import org.springframework.boot.test.context.SpringBootTest
import org.springframework.test.context.jdbc.Sql
import org.springframework.test.context.jdbc.SqlConfig
import org.springframework.test.context.jdbc.SqlMergeMode
import org.springframework.test.context.ActiveProfiles
//other import statements omitted

@ActiveProfiles("test")
@SqlMergeMode(SqlMergeMode.MergeMode.MERGE)
@Sql("classpath:h2/drop-schema.sql", "classpath:h2/create-schema.sql")
@SpringBootTest(classes = [Chapter6Application::class])
open class Chapter6ApplicationTest {
    @Autowired
    var singerRepo: SingerRepo? = null

    @Test
    @DisplayName("should return all singers")
    @Sql(
        value = ["classpath:h2/test-data.sql"],
        config = SqlConfig(encoding = "utf-8", separator = ";", commentPrefix = "--"),
        executionPhase = Sql.ExecutionPhase.BEFORE_TEST_METHOD
    )
    open fun testFindAllWithJdbcTemplate() {
        val singers: List<Singer> = singerRepo!!.findAll().toList()
        Assertions.assertEquals(3, singers.size)
        singers.forEach{ singer: Singer ->
            LOGGER.info(
                singer.toString()
            )
        }
    }

    companion object {
        private val LOGGER = LoggerFactory.getLogger(Chapter6ApplicationTest::class.java)
    }
}

# output
 INFO : StartupInfoLogger - Starting Chapter6ApplicationTest using Java 17 on
        IulianasPrimary with PID 95805 ...
 INFO : SpringApplication - The following 1 profile is active: "test"
 INFO : HikariDataSource - HikariPool-1 - Starting...
 INFO : HikariPool - HikariPool-1 - Added connection conn0: url=jdbc:h2:mem:mydb user=SA
```

```
INFO : HikariDataSource - HikariPool-1 - Start completed.
INFO : Chapter6ApplicationTest - Singer[id=1, firstName=John, lastName=Mayer,
       birthDate=1977-10-16, albums=[]]
INFO : Chapter6ApplicationTest - Singer[id=2, firstName=Ben, lastName=Barnes,
       birthDate=1981-08-20, albums=[]]
INFO : Chapter6ApplicationTest - Singer[id=3, firstName=John, lastName=Butler,
       birthDate=1975-04-01, albums=[]]
INFO : HikariDataSource - HikariPool-1 - Shutdown initiated...
INFO : HikariDataSource - HikariPool-1 - Shutdown completed.
```

What about Testcontainers? Does it work with Spring Boot? The answer is *yes*, and the setup is even easier because it benefits a lot from the Spring Boot autoconfiguration. The approach to using Testcontainers in Spring Boot tests can be similar to what we did for Spring classic applications, but there is another way, that will result in a database instance per test class being created.

After adding the Testcontainers libraries mentioned previously in the chapter to the Spring Boot application classpath, the `spring.datasource.url` property can be set in the configuration file to `jdbc:tc:mariadb:10.7.4-focal:///testdb`. The `tc:` after the `jdbc:` prefix will make Testcontainers instantiate database instances without any code change. Hostname, port, and database name are ignored; you can set them to custom values or leave them as they are. The `///` are used to emphasize the unimportance of the `host:port` pair.

To keep test contexts separated, in the project we introduced the `testcontainers` profile with its corresponding `application-testcontainers.yaml` configuration file, depicted in Listing 6-64.

Listing 6-64. The Contents of the `application-testcontainers.yaml` Configuration File

```
spring:
  datasource:
    url: "jdbc:tc:mariadb:10.7.4-focal:///musicdb"

# Logging config
logging:
  pattern:
    console: " %-5level: %class{0} - %msg%n"
  level:
    root: INFO
    org.springframework.boot: DEBUG
    com.apress.prospring6.six: DEBUG
    org.testcontainers: DEBUG
```

Using this profile and configuration file, a Spring Boot test class is written that is almost identical to the one in Listing 6-63. The only differences are that the `testcontainers` profile is used and the scripts preparing the database for tests are MariaDB scripts. The test class is shown in Listing 6-65.

Listing 6-65. The Contents of the `Chapter6ApplicationV2Test` Configuration File

```
package com.apress.prospring6.six

import org.springframework.boot.test.context.SpringBootTest
import org.springframework.test.context.ActiveProfiles
import org.springframework.test.context.jdbc.Sql
import org.springframework.test.context.jdbc.SqlConfig
import org.testcontainers.junit.jupiter.Testcontainers
```

```
// other imports omitted

@ActiveProfiles("testcontainers")
/*@Sql(value = "classpath:testcontainers/create-schema.sql",
        config = @SqlConfig(encoding = "utf-8", separator = ";", commentPrefix = "--"),
        executionPhase = Sql.ExecutionPhase.BEFORE_TEST_METHOD)*/
@SpringBootTest(classes = [Chapter6Application::class])
class Chapter6ApplicationV2Test {
    @Autowired
    var singerRepo: SingerRepo? = null

    @Test
    @DisplayName("should return all singers")
    fun testFindAllWithJdbcTemplate() {
        val singers: List<Singer> = singerRepo!!.findAll()
            .toList()
        Assertions.assertEquals(3, singers.size)
        singers.forEach{ singer: Singer ->
            LOGGER.info(
                singer.toString()
            )
        }
    }

    @Test
    @DisplayName("find singer by name")
    @Sql("classpath:testcontainers/stored-function.sql")
    fun testStoredFunction() {
        val firstName = singerRepo!!.findFirstNameById(2L)
        Assertions.assertEquals("Ben", firstName)
    }

    companion object {
        private val LOGGER = LoggerFactory.getLogger(Chapter6ApplicationV2Test::class.java)
    }
}
```

Notice that there's no need to use @DynamicPropertySource to register dynamic properties for the spring.datasource.* property group. In the Chapter6ApplicationV2Test, the script to initialize the database was configured on the test class using a @Sql annotation, but the test script can be configured using the TC_INITSCRIPT variable inside the spring.datasource.url value.

So, in the application-testcontainers.yaml file, the spring.datasource.url property can be set to

jdbc:tc:mariadb:10.7.4-focal:///testdb?TC_INITSCRIPT=testcontainers/create-schema.sql

Also, the @Sql annotation can be removed from the Chapter6ApplicationV2Test class and the tests will still pass, because Testcontainers is looking for that initialization script on the classpath. You can also point to a location relative to the working directory, which will usually be the project root, using file:.

We encourage you to read more about Testcontainers; it provides a very practical way to write integration tests that run on a setup very similar to production and prove that the code being written will have the expected results in a production environment as well. In this book, whenever a database is needed for running tests, Testcontainers is recommended.

Summary

This chapter showed you how to use Spring to simplify JDBC programming. You learned how to connect to a database and perform selects, updates, deletes, and inserts, as well as call database stored functions. In production, using the `DataSource` bean or `JdbcTemplate` is rarely needed. This might be needed only if you have a very complex query, or a stored procedure or function to execute. Regardless, we covered `JdbcTemplate` and other Spring classes that are built on top of JdbcTemplate and that help you model various JDBC operations. We also showed how to use the new lambda expressions where appropriate. And because code is written by humans, and humans are not infallible, you were shown how to test your JDBC code in Spring Classic and Spring Boot applications.

In addition, Spring Boot JDBC was covered, because whatever helps you focus more on the implementation of the business logic of an application and less on the configurations is a great tool to know. In the next couple of chapters, we discuss how to use Spring with popular ORM technologies when developing data access logic and how to interact with NoSQL databases.

## CHAPTER 7

Spring with Hibernate

Chapter 6 introduced you to how to use JDBC drivers to communicate to SQL databases. However, even though Spring goes a long way toward simplifying JDBC development, you still have a lot of code to write. To avoid this and provide support for easier querying persistence frameworks were invented, such as MyBatis[1] and Hibernate[2]. jOOQ[3], one of the most recent libraries to emerge, is a database-mapping software library that generates Java code from your database and lets you build type-safe SQL queries through its fluent API. Some users have reported positive experiences when combining jOOQ with Hibernate, letting Hibernate do the tedious CRUD work, and jOOQ the complex querying and reporting through its sophisticated, yet intuitive query DSL. This chapter focuses mostly on Hibernate, one of the most commonly used object-relational mapping (ORM) libraries, but given its potential, jOOQ is introduced as well. In Chapter 6, working with Java/Kotlin and databases was compared to the *I Love Lucy* episode "Paris at Last," where three translators were needed to resolve a misunderstanding. JDBC was identified as the first translator, the driver, and in this chapter Hibernate, the persistence layer, is introduced as the second one.

If you have experience developing data access applications using EJB entity beans (prior to EJB 3.0), you may remember the painful process. Tedious configuration of mappings, transaction demarcation, and much boilerplate code in each bean to manage its life cycle greatly reduced productivity when developing enterprise Java or Kotlin applications. Just like Spring was developed to embrace POJO-based development and declarative configuration management rather than EJB's heavy and clumsy setup, the developer community realized that a simpler, lightweight, and POJO-based framework could ease the development of data access logic. Since then, many libraries have appeared; they are generally referred to as ORM libraries. The main objectives of an ORM library are to close the gap between the relational data structure in the relational database management system (RDBMS) and the object-oriented (OO) model in Java/Kotlin so that developers can focus on programming with the object model and at the same time easily perform actions related to persistence.

Among the many ORM libraries available in the open source community, Hibernate is one of the most successful. Its features, such as a POJO-based approach, ease of development, and support of sophisticated relationship definitions, have won the heart of the mainstream Java/Kotlin developer community.

Hibernate's popularity has also influenced the Java Community Process (JCP), which developed the Java Data Objects (JDO) specification as one of the standard ORM technologies in Java/Jakarta EE. Starting from EJB 3.0, the EJB entity bean was even replaced with the Java Persistence API (JPA). JPA has a lot of concepts that were influenced by popular ORM libraries such as Hibernate, TopLink, and JDO. The relationship between Hibernate and JPA is also very close. Gavin King, the founder of Hibernate, represented JBoss as one of the JCP expert group members in defining the JPA specification. Starting from version 3.2,

---

[1] https://mybatis.org/mybatis-3
[2] https://hibernate.org
[3] https://www.jooq.org

Hibernate provides an implementation of JPA. That means when you develop applications with Hibernate, you can choose to use either Hibernate's own API or the JPA API with Hibernate as the persistence service provider.

Having offered a brief history of Hibernate, this chapter will cover how to use Spring with Hibernate when developing data access logic. Hibernate is such an extensive ORM library that covering every aspect in just one chapter is simply not possible, and numerous books are dedicated to discussing Hibernate.

This chapter covers the basic ideas and main use cases of Hibernate in Spring. In particular, we discuss the following topics:

- *Configuring Hibernate SessionFactory*: The core concept of Hibernate revolves around the Session interface, which is managed by SessionFactory. We show you how to configure Hibernate's session factory to work in a Spring application.

- *Major concepts of ORMs using Hibernate*: We go through the major concepts of how to use Hibernate to map a POJO to the underlying relational database structure. We also discuss some commonly used relationships, including one-to-many and many-to-many.

- *Data operations*: We present examples of how to perform data operations (query, insert, update, delete) by using Hibernate in the Spring environment. When working with Hibernate, its Session interface is the main interface that you will interact with.

❗ When defining object-to-relational mappings, Hibernate supports two configuration styles. One is to configure the mapping information in XML files, and the other is to use Kotlin annotations within the entity classes (in the ORM or JPA world, a Kotlin class that is mapped to the underlying relational database structure is called an *entity class*). This chapter focuses on using the annotation approach for object-relational mapping. For the mapping annotation, we use the JPA standards (for example, under the jakarta.persistence package) because they are interchangeable with Hibernate's own annotations and will help you with future migrations to a JPA environment.

Sample Data Model for Example Code

Figure 7-1 shows the data model used in this chapter.

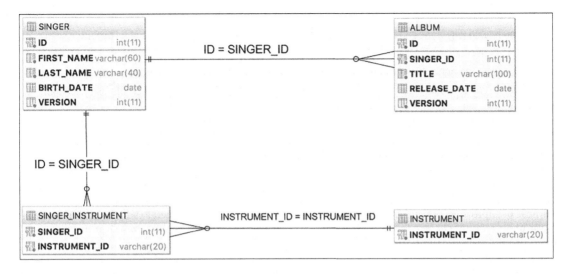

Figure 7-1. *Sample data model*

As shown in this data model, two new tables were added, namely, INSTRUMENT and SINGER_INSTRUMENT (the join table). SINGER_INSTRUMENT models the many-to-many relationships between the SINGER and INSTRUMENT tables. A VERSION column was added to the SINGER and ALBUM tables for optimistic locking, which will be discussed in detail later.

> ℹ In the examples in this chapter, we will use MariaDB in a Docker container manually built to simulate a local instance available on port 3306 for production-like code. The instructions for building the image and starting the container are provided in the project repository through the chapter07/CHAPTER07.adoc file. A Testcontainers MariaDB instance container is used for testing.

Configuring Hibernate's SessionFactory

As mentioned earlier in this chapter, the core concept of Hibernate is based on the org.hibernate.Session interface, which is obtained from org.hibernate.SessionFactory. Spring provides classes to support the configuration of Hibernate's session factory as a Spring bean with the desired properties. To use Hibernate, you must add the hibernate-core-jakarta library as a dependency to the project. To integrate it with Spring, spring-orm must be added as a dependency as well.

> ℹ As this chapter is being written, the most recent Hibernate version compatible with Spring ORM is 5.6.9.Final. Hibernate 6.1.0.Final has already been released, but Spring ORM does not currently support it.

❶ The reason why `hibernate-core-jakarta` is used as a dependency instead of `hibernate-core` is because of its dependency on Java Persistence API, which is part of the Java EE. Oracle made Java EE open source and gave the rights over it to the Eclipse Foundation, which was legally required to change the package name from `java`, as Oracle legally owns the Java brand now. So newer versions of Hibernate use package name `jakarta.*` instead of `javax.*`.

The Spring Hibernate configuration is built on top of a DataSource configuration, as introduced in **Chapter 6**. Apache DBCP2 was used to set up connection pooling, but in this chapter, to keep things interesting, we replaced this library with `hikariCP.jar`. The HikariCP[4] GitHub main page shows various benchmarks results proving this library to be the most efficient connection pooling library there is. With the purpose of improving performance and enriching the collection tools, we decided to add this dependency to the project for this chapter. From a configuration point of view, not much changes: the class that needs to be configured is named `HikariDataSource` instead of `BasicDataSource`, and it comes from the `com.zaxxer.hikari` package.

Listing 7-1 shows the new and improved `BasicDataSourceCfg` configuration class.

Listing 7-1. MariaDB DataSource Configuration Class

```
package com.apress.prospring6.seven.base.config

import com.zaxxer.hikari.HikariConfig
import com.zaxxer.hikari.HikariDataSource
import org.slf4j.Logger
import org.slf4j.LoggerFactory
import org.springframework.beans.factory.annotation.Value
import org.springframework.context.annotation.Bean
import org.springframework.context.annotation.Configuration
import org.springframework.context.annotation.Profile
import org.springframework.context.annotation.PropertySource

import javax.sql.DataSource

@Configuration
@PropertySource("classpath:db/jdbc.properties")
open class BasicDataSourceCfg {
    @Value("\${jdbc.driverClassName}")
    private val driverClassName: String? = null

    @Value("\${jdbc.url}")
    private val url: String? = null

    @Value("\${jdbc.username}")
    private val username: String? = null

    @Value("\${jdbc.password}")
    private val password: String? = null
```

---

[4] https://github.com/brettwooldridge/HikariCP

```kotlin
@Bean(destroyMethod = "close")
open fun dataSource(): DataSource? {
    return try {
        val hc = HikariConfig().apply {
            jdbcUrl = url
            driverClassName = this@BasicDataSourceCfg.driverClassName
            username = this@BasicDataSourceCfg.username
            password = this@BasicDataSourceCfg.password
        }
        val dataSource = HikariDataSource(hc)
        dataSource.maximumPoolSize = 25
        // 25 is a good enough data pool size, it is a database in a container after all
        dataSource
    } catch (e: Exception) {
        LOGGER.error("Hikari DataSource bean cannot be created!", e)
        null
    }
}

companion object {
    private val LOGGER = LoggerFactory.getLogger(BasicDataSourceCfg::class.java)
}
}
```

Since we are using Testcontainers, replacement of the production-like DataSource bean with a MariaDB test container can easily be done as it was shown in Chapter 6.

Listing 7-2 shows the HibernateConfig class that groups Hibernate-specific configurations.

Listing 7-2. HibernateConfig Configuration Class

```kotlin
package com.apress.prospring6.seven.base.config
import org.hibernate.cfg.Environment

import org.slf4j.Logger
import org.slf4j.LoggerFactory
import org.springframework.beans.factory.annotation.Autowired
import org.springframework.context.annotation.Bean
import org.springframework.context.annotation.ComponentScan
import org.springframework.context.annotation.Configuration
import org.springframework.context.annotation.Import
import org.springframework.orm.hibernate5.HibernateTransactionManager
import org.springframework.orm.hibernate5.LocalSessionFactoryBean
import org.springframework.transaction.PlatformTransactionManager
import org.springframework.transaction.annotation.EnableTransactionManagement

import javax.sql.DataSource
import java.util.Properties

@Import(BasicDataSourceCfg::class)
@Configuration
@ComponentScan(basePackages = ["com.apress.prospring6.seven.base"])
@EnableTransactionManagement
```

```kotlin
open class HibernateConfig {
    @Autowired
    var dataSource: DataSource? = null

    @Bean
    open fun hibernateProperties(): Properties {
        val hibernateProp = Properties()
        hibernateProp[Environment.HBM2DDL_AUTO] = "none"
        hibernateProp[Environment.FORMAT_SQL] = false
        hibernateProp[Environment.USE_SQL_COMMENTS] = false
        hibernateProp[Environment.SHOW_SQL] = false
        hibernateProp[Environment.MAX_FETCH_DEPTH] = 3
        hibernateProp[Environment.STATEMENT_BATCH_SIZE] = 10
        hibernateProp[Environment.STATEMENT_FETCH_SIZE] = 50
        return hibernateProp
    }

    @Bean
    open fun sessionFactory(): LocalSessionFactoryBean {
        val sessionFactory = LocalSessionFactoryBean()
        sessionFactory.setDataSource(dataSource!!)
        sessionFactory.setPackagesToScan("com.apress.prospring6.seven.base.entities")
        sessionFactory.hibernateProperties = hibernateProperties()
        return sessionFactory
    }

    @Bean
    open fun transactionManager(): PlatformTransactionManager {
        val transactionManager = HibernateTransactionManager()
        transactionManager.sessionFactory = sessionFactory().getObject()
        return transactionManager
    }

    companion object {
        private val LOGGER = LoggerFactory.getLogger(HibernateConfig::class.java)
    }
}
```

The Spring Hibernate configuration declares the following beans to support Hibernate's session factory:

- *dataSource*: This bean is imported from the BasicDataSourceCfg configuration class using the @Import annotation and injected into the HibernateConfig using autowiring.

- *transactionManager*: The Hibernate session factory requires a transaction manager for transactional data access. Spring provides a transaction manager specifically for Hibernate 5 declared in package org.springframework.orm. hibernate5.HibernateTransactionManager. The bean was declared with the transactionManager name. By default, when using XML configuration, Spring will look up the bean with the name transactionManager within its ApplicationContext whenever transaction management is required. Kotlin configuration is a little more flexible because the bean is being searched by its type, not by its name. We discuss transactions in detail in **Chapter 9**. In addition, the configuration class is annotated with @EnableTransactionManagement to support the declaration of transaction demarcation requirements using annotations (enables support for Spring's @Transactional).

- *Component scan*: The @ComponentScan annotation should be familiar to you from the previous chapters. We instruct Spring to scan the components under the package com.apress.prospring6.seven (not configured explicitly since this is the package the configuration class is declared in) to detect the beans annotated with @Repository, which contain methods for accessing data.

- *Hibernate SessionFactory*: The SessionFactory bean is the most important part. Within the bean, several properties are provided:

  - First, we need to inject the DataSource bean into the sessionFactory bean.

  - Second, we instruct Hibernate to scan for the domain objects under the package com.apress.prospring6.seven.entities.

  - Finally, the hibernateProperties bean provides configuration details for Hibernate. There are many configuration parameters, and we define only a few important properties that should be provided for every application. Table 7-1 lists the configuration properties for the Hibernate session factory in our example, the constants and their String values; you can find the other properties in interface org.hibernate.cfg.AvailableSettings, which is implemented by org.hibernate.cfg.Environment.

Table 7-1. Hibernate Properties

Property (Constant/Value)	Description
Environment.FORMAT_SQL/ hibernate.format_sql	Indicates whether SQL output in the log or console should be formatted. Default value is false.
Environment.USE_SQL_ COMMENTS/hibernate.use_ sql_comments	If set to true, Hibernate generates comments inside the SQL for easier debugging. Default value is false.
Environment.SHOW_SQL/ hibernate.show_sql	Indicates whether Hibernate should output the SQL queries to the logfile or console. You should enable this in a development environment, which can greatly help in the testing and troubleshooting process. Default value is false.
Environment.MAX_FETCH_ DEPTH/hibernate.max_ fetch_depth	Declares the "depth" for outer joins when the mapping objects have associations with other mapped objects. This setting prevents Hibernate from fetching too much data with a lot of nested associations. A commonly used value is 3. A value of 0 disables default outer join fetching.
Environment.STATEMENT_ BATCH_SIZE/hibernate. jdbc.batch_size	Instructs Hibernate on the number of update operations that should be grouped together into a batch. This is useful for performing batch job operations in Hibernate. Obviously, when we are doing a batch job updating hundreds of thousands of records, we want Hibernate to group the queries in batches, rather than submit the updates one by one. Recommended value is between 5 and 30.

(continued)

Table 7-1. (*continued*)

Property (Constant/Value)	Description
Environment.STATEMENT_ FETCH_SIZE/hibernate. jdbc.fetch_size	Specifies the number of records from the underlying JDBC ResultSet that Hibernate should use to retrieve the records from the database for each fetch. For example, a query was submitted to the database, and ResultSet contains 500 records. If the fetch size is 50, Hibernate will need to fetch 10 times to get all the data.
Environment.JTA_PLATFORM/ hibernate.transaction. jta.platform	This property, when present, should be set to a qualified class name representing an implementation of org.hibernate.engine. transaction.jta.platform.spi.JtaPlatform that defines how Hibernate interacts with JTA on a certain platform. If not present, Hibernate uses default org.hibernate.engine.transaction.jta. platform.internal.NoJtaPlatform, which means no transactions are used. In our configuration it is set to Spring's ConfigurableJtaPlatform implementation. Since this chapter does not focus on transactions, this property can be safely removed from the configuration.
Environment.HBM2DDL_AUTO/ hibernate.hbm2ddl.auto	Traditionally, the process of generating schema from entity mapping has been called HBM2DDL. This property can have any of the following values:
	* none tells Hibernate to do nothing with the existing schema.
	* create tells Hibernate to generate the schema matching the managed entity classes.
	* validate tells Hibernate to validate the schema; makes no changes to the database.
	* update tells Hibernate to update the schema, according to the changes made to the entity classes.
	* create-drop tells Hibernate to create the schema matching the managed entity classes and drop the schema when the SessionFactory is closed explicitly, typically when the application is stopped.

For a description of the full list of properties that Hibernate supports, please refer to Hibernate's ORM user guide[5], specifically Section 24.2.

ORM Mapping Using Hibernate Annotations

Having the configuration in place, the next step is to model the Kotlin POJO (or POKO, but we'll stick to the Java way in the book) entity classes and their mapping to the underlying relational data structure.

There are two approaches to the mapping. The first one is to design the object model and then generate the database scripts based on the object model. Configuring the Hibernate property hibernate. hbm2ddl.auto to create or create-drop takes care of this approach. However, this approach is not suitable for production environments, but rather for test environments that use in-memory databases, for which generating the tables based on Kotlin POJOs is not a costly operation.

---

[5] https://docs.jboss.org/hibernate/orm/5.6/userguide/html_single/Hibernate_User_ Guide.html#configurations-general

The second approach is to start with the data model (the tables) and then model the POJOs with the desired mappings. The latter approach is recommended for development and production environments, because it provides more control over the data model, which is useful in optimizing the performance of data access. Based on the data model, Figure 7-2 shows the corresponding object model class diagram.

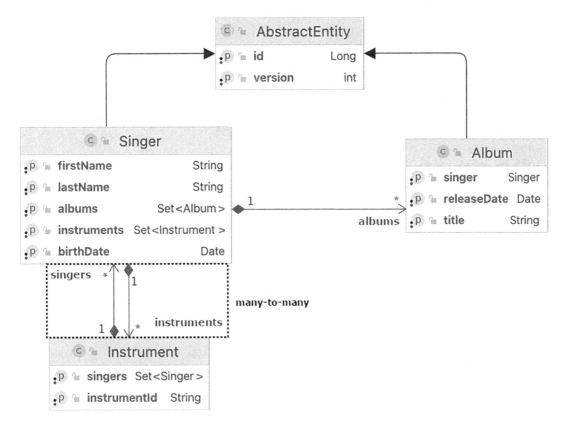

Figure 7-2. *Class diagram for the sample data model*

You can see there is a one-to-many relationship between Singer and Album, and there's a many-to-many relationship between the Singer and Instrument objects. The table that models the many-to-many relationship, SINGER_INSTRUMENT, is not mapped to a Kotlin class.

Notice also that Singer and Album have the id and version fields in common, and they are grouped into an abstract class named AbstractEntity to simplify the other entity classes. In production applications where auditing is usually set up, other fields that are part of this abstract class could be any of the following: createdAt, updatedAt, createdBy, updatedBy, and so on. The AbstractEntity class is annotated with the @ MappedSuperclass annotation that designates a class whose mapping information is applied to the entities that inherit from it.

Simple Mappings

Let's start by mapping the simple attributes of the class. Listing 7-3 shows the AbstractEntity class with the mapping information inherited by Singer and Album.

Listing 7-3. AbstractEntity Base Entity Class

```
package com.apress.prospring6.seven.base.entities

import jakarta.persistence.*
import java.io.Serializable
import java.util.*

@MappedSuperclass
abstract class AbstractEntity : Serializable {
    @get:Column(
        name = "ID"
    )
    @get:GeneratedValue(strategy = GenerationType.IDENTITY)
    @get:Id
    var id: Long? = null

    @get:Column(name = "VERSION")
    @get:Version
    var version = 0

    // equals & hashCode are very limited in scope in this scenario
    override fun equals(other: Any?): Boolean {
        if (this === other) return true
        if (other == null || javaClass != other.javaClass) return false
        val that = other as AbstractEntity
        return id == that.id
    }

    override fun hashCode(): Int {
        return Objects.hash(id)
    }

    companion object {
        private val serialVersionUID = 1L
    }
}
```

The AbstractEntity class does not map to any table, but annotations used in its configuration might be used in classes mapped to tables as well.

Listing 7-4 shows the Singer class with its mapping annotations.

Listing 7-4. Singer Entity Class

```
package com.apress.prospring6.seven.base.entities

import jakarta.persistence.Column
import jakarta.persistence.Entity
import jakarta.persistence.Table
// other import statements omitted
```

```kotlin
@Entity
@Table(name = "SINGER")
class Singer : AbstractEntity() {
        @get:Column(name = "FIRST_NAME")
        var firstName: String? = null

        @get:Column(name = "LAST_NAME")
        var lastName: String? = null

        @get:Column(name = "BIRTH_DATE")
        var birthDate: LocalDate? = null

        @get:OneToMany(
                mappedBy = "singer",
                cascade = [CascadeType.ALL],
                orphanRemoval = true
        )
        var albums: MutableSet<Album> = HashSet()

        @get:JoinTable(
                name = "SINGER_INSTRUMENT",
                joinColumns = [JoinColumn(name = "SINGER_ID")],
                inverseJoinColumns = [JoinColumn(name = "INSTRUMENT_ID")]
        )
        @get:ManyToMany
        var instruments: MutableSet<Instrument> = HashSet()

        fun addAlbum(album: Album): Boolean {
                album.singer = this
                return albums.add(album)
        }

        fun removeAlbum(album: Album) {
                albums.remove(album)
        }

        fun addInstrument(instrument: Instrument): Boolean {
                return instruments.add(instrument)
        }

        override fun toString(): String {
                return ("Singer - Id: " + id + ", First name: " + firstName
                                + ", Last name: " + lastName + ", Birthday: " + birthDate)
        }

        companion object {
                private val serialVersionUID = 2L
        }
}
```

First, we annotate the type with @Entity, which means that this is a mapped entity class. Also, a class annotated with @Entity must have a column annotated with @Id, this column representing the primary key of that table. The @Table annotation defines the table name in the database that this entity is being mapped to. For each mapped attribute, you annotate it with the @Column annotation, with the column names provided.

💡 Table and column names can be skipped if the type and attribute names are the same as the table and column names.

Here are a few highlights of this configuration:

- We annotate the id attribute with @Id. This means it is mapped to the primary key of the record. Hibernate will use it as the unique identifier when managing the contact entity instances within its session. Additionally, the @GeneratedValue annotation tells Hibernate how the id value was generated. The IDENTITY strategy means that the id value was generated by the back end during insert.

- We annotate the version attribute with @Version. This instructs Hibernate that we would like to use an optimistic locking mechanism, using the version attribute as a control. Every time Hibernate updates a record, it compares the version of the entity instance to that of the record in the database. If both versions are the same, it means that no one updated the data before, and Hibernate will update the data and increment the version column. However, if the version is not the same, it means that someone has updated the record before, and Hibernate will throw a StaleObjectStateException exception, which Spring will translate to HibernateOptimisticLockingFailureException. In this example we used an Int for version control. In addition to an integer, Hibernate supports using a timestamp. However, using an integer for version control is recommended since Hibernate will always increment the version number by 1 after each update. When using a timestamp, Hibernate will update the latest timestamp after each update. A timestamp is slightly less safe because two concurrent transactions may both load and update the same item in the same millisecond.

Another mapped object is Album, as shown in Listing 7-5.

Listing 7-5. Album Entity Class

```
package com.apress.prospring6.seven.base.entities

// import statements omitted

@Entity
@Table(name = "ALBUM")
class Album : AbstractEntity() {
        @get:Column
        var title: String? = null

        @get:Column(name = "RELEASE_DATE")
        var releaseDate: LocalDate? = null
```

```kotlin
    @get:JoinColumn(name = "SINGER_ID")
    @get:ManyToOne
    var singer: Singer? = null

    override fun equals(other: Any?): Boolean {
            if (this === other) return true
            if (other == null || javaClass != other.javaClass) return false
            if (!super.equals(other)) return false
            val album = other as Album
            return if (album.id != null && id != null) {
                    super.equals(other)
            } else title == album.title && releaseDate == album.releaseDate
    }

    override fun hashCode(): Int {
            return Objects.hash(super.hashCode(), title, releaseDate)
    }

    override fun toString(): String {
            return ("Album - Id: " + id + ", Singer id: " + (singer?.id?:"")
                            + ", Title: " + title + ", Release Date: " + releaseDate)
    }

    companion object {
            private val serialVersionUID = 3L
    }
}
```

The third entity class is named Instrument and maps to the INSTRUMENT table, a very simple table with a single column. This table was introduced just so that a many-to-many relationship is part of the code samples. This class is shown in Listing 7-6.

Listing 7-6. Instrument Entity Class

```kotlin
package com.apress.prospring6.seven.base.entities

// import statements omitted

@Entity
@Table(name = "INSTRUMENT")
class Instrument : Serializable {
        @get:Column(name = "INSTRUMENT_ID")
        @get:Id
        var instrumentId: String? = null

        @get:JoinTable(
                name = "SINGER_INSTRUMENT",
                joinColumns = [JoinColumn(name = "INSTRUMENT_ID")],
                inverseJoinColumns = [JoinColumn(name = "SINGER_ID")]
        )
```

```kotlin
    @get:ManyToMany
    var singers: MutableSet<Singer> = mutableSetOf()

    override fun toString(): String {
            return "Instrument :$instrumentId"
    }

    companion object {
            private val serialVersionUID = 4L
    }
}
```

One-to-Many Mappings

Hibernate has the capability to model many kinds of associations. The most common associations are one-to-many and many-to-many. In this chapter's source examples, each Singer has zero or more albums, so it's a one-to-many association (in ORM terms, the one-to-many association is used to model both zero-to-many and one-to-many relationships within the data structure). Listing 7-7 depicts the properties and the methods necessary to define the one-to-many relationship between the Singer and Album entities.

Listing 7-7. Singer and Album Code Snippets Used to Model One-to-Many and Many-to-One Relationships

```kotlin
package com.apress.prospring6.seven.base.entities

import jakarta.persistence.OneToMany
import jakarta.persistence.CascadeType
// other import statements omitted

// Singer.kt
class Singer : AbstractEntity() {
        ...
        @get:OneToMany(
                mappedBy = "singer",
                cascade = [CascadeType.ALL],
                orphanRemoval = true
        )
        var albums: MutableSet<Album> = mutableSetOf()
        ...
}

// Album.kt

import jakarta.persistence.ManyToOne
import jakarta.persistence.JoinColumn
// other import statements omitted

@Entity
@Table(name = "ALBUM")
class Album : AbstractEntity() {
        ...
```

```
@get:JoinColumn(name = "SINGER_ID")
@get:ManyToOne
var singer: Singer? = null
    ...
}
```

The getter method of the attribute albums is annotated with @OneToMany, which indicates the one-to-many relationship with the Album class. Several attributes are passed to the annotation. The mappedBy attribute indicates the property in the Album class that provides the association (that is, linked up by the foreign-key definition in the FK_ALBUM_SINGER table).

The cascade attribute set to CascadeType.ALL means that any operation done on the Singer record are propagated to albums linked to it. The orphanRemoval attribute means that after the albums set has been updated, the Album entries that no longer exist in the set should be deleted from the database.

The Singer class declares the one-to-many part of the relationship with Album. This means the Album entity must declare the many-to-one part of the relationship with Singer, and this is done using the @ManyToOne annotation. The @JoinColumn annotation associated with it is necessary to specify the underlying foreign-key column name.

Many-to-Many Mappings

Every singer can play zero or more instruments, and each instrument is also associated with zero or more singers, which means it's a many-to-many mapping. A many-to-many mapping requires a join table, which is SINGER_INSTRUMENT in this case. Listing 7-8 shows the code that needs to be added to the Singer class to implement this relationship.

Listing 7-8. Singer and Instrument Code Snippets Used to Model Many-to-Many Relationships

```
package com.apress.prospring6.seven.base.entities;

import jakarta.persistence.ManyToMany;
import jakarta.persistence.JoinTable;
import jakarta.persistence.JoinColumn;
// other import statements omitted

// Singer.kt
class Singer : AbstractEntity() {
        ...
        @get:JoinTable(
                name = "SINGER_INSTRUMENT",
                joinColumns = [JoinColumn(name = "SINGER_ID")],
                inverseJoinColumns = [JoinColumn(name = "INSTRUMENT_ID")]
        )
        @get:ManyToMany
        var instruments: MutableSet<Instrument> = mutableSetOf()
        ...
}
```

```kotlin
// Instrument.kt

import jakarta.persistence.ManyToMany
import jakarta.persistence.JoinColumn
// other import statements omitted

@Entity
@Table(name = "INSTRUMENT")
class Instrument : AbstractEntity() {
        ...
        @get:JoinTable(
                name = "SINGER_INSTRUMENT",
                joinColumns = [JoinColumn(name = "INSTRUMENT_ID")],
                inverseJoinColumns = [JoinColumn(name = "SINGER_ID")]
        )
        @get:ManyToMany
        var singers: MutableSet<Singer> = mutableSetOf()
          ...
}
```

The getter method of the attribute `instruments` in the `Singer` class is annotated with `@ManyToMany`. The `@JoinTable` annotation is used to indicate the underlying join table that Hibernate should look for. The name is the join table's name, `joinColumns` defines the column that is the foreign key to the `SINGER` table, and `inverseJoinColumns` defines the column that is the foreign key to the other side of the association (that is, the `INSTRUMENT` table). The code in the `Instrument` class is more or less the same as the code for `Singer`, but the `joinColumns` and `inverseJoinColumns` attributes are reversed to reflect the association.

The Hibernate Session Interface

In Hibernate, when interacting with the database, the main interface you need to deal with is the `Session` interface, which is obtained from an instance of `SessionFactory`. A `SessionFactory` instance is created and added to the application context and this is caused by configuring a `LocalSessionFactoryBean` as shown in the `HibernateConfig` class introduced earlier in the chapter (see Listing 7-2). This instance can then be autowired in repository classes and used to create a Hibernate `Session` used to communicate with the database. Listing 7-9 shows the `SingerDaoImpl` class that is used in the samples in this chapter and has the configured Hibernate `SessionFactory` injected into the class.

Listing 7-9. SingerDaoImpl Repository Class That Uses Hibernate's SessionFactory

```kotlin
package com.apress.prospring6.seven.base.dao

import com.apress.prospring6.seven.base.entities.Singer
import jakarta.annotation.Resource
import org.hibernate.SessionFactory
import org.slf4j.Logger
import org.slf4j.LoggerFactory
import org.springframework.stereotype.Repository
import org.springframework.transaction.annotation.Transactional
```

```kotlin
@Transactional
@Repository("singerDao")
class SingerDaoImpl(private val sessionFactory: SessionFactory) : SingerDao {
    ...
    companion object {
        private val LOGGER = LoggerFactory.getLogger(SingerDaoImpl::class.java)
        ...
    }
}
```

We declare the DAO class as a Spring bean by using the @Repository annotation, this integrates it into the Spring Context and exception translation where Spring's runtime DataAccessException family is enabled. The @Transactional annotation defines the transaction requirements that we discuss further in **Chapter 9**. The sessionFactory property is autowired by Spring using the constructor. The SingerDao interface is quite simple, with just three finder methods, one save(..) method, and one delete(..) method. The save(..) method performs both the insert and update operations. This interface is shown in Listing 7-10.

Listing 7-10. SingerDao Interface

```kotlin
package com.apress.prospring6.seven.base.dao

import com.apress.prospring6.seven.base.entities.Singer

interface SingerDao {
    fun findAll(): List<Singer>
    fun findAllWithAlbum(): List<Singer>
    fun findById(id: Long?): Singer?
    fun save(singer: Singer): Singer
    fun delete(singer: Singer)
    fun findAllDetails(firstName: String?, lastName: String?): Singer?
    fun findAllNamesByProjection(): Set<String>
    fun findFirstNameById(id: Long): String?
    fun findFirstNameByIdUsingProc(id: Long): String?
}
```

Querying Data by Using the Hibernate Query Language

Hibernate, together with other ORM tools such as JDO and JPA, is engineered around the object model. So, after the mappings are defined, we don't need to construct SQL to interact with the database. Instead, for Hibernate, we use the Hibernate Query Language (HQL) to define our queries. When interacting with the database, Hibernate will translate the queries into SQL statements on our behalf. When coding HQL queries, the syntax is quite like SQL. However, you need to think on the object side rather than database side. We will take you through several examples in the following sections.

Simple Querying with Lazy Fetching

Let's begin by implementing the findAll() method, which simply retrieves all the singers from the database. Listing 7-11 shows the updated code for this functionality.

Listing 7-11. SingerDaoImpl#findAll() Method

```
package com.apress.prospring6.seven.base.dao
// import statements omitted

@Transactional
@Repository("singerDao")
class SingerDaoImpl(private val sessionFactory: SessionFactory) : SingerDao {
    ...
  @Transactional(readOnly = true)
    override fun findAll(): List<Singer> {
        return sessionFactory.currentSession.createQuery(
            "from Singer s",
            Singer::class.java
        ).list()
    }
    ...
}
```

The accessor .currentSession gets hold of Hibernate's Session interface. Then, the Session. createQuery() method is called, passing in the HQL statement. The statement from Singer simply retrieves all singers from the database. An alternative syntax for the statement is select s from Singer s. The @Transactional(readOnly=true) annotation means we want the transaction to be set as read-only. Setting that attribute for read-only methods will result in better performance in some cases.

There are two ways to test the findAll() method: run the HibernateDemoV1 class, which will run this method on the MariaDB database available locally or in a container, or write a test method and execute it in the test context using a Testcontainers MariaDB data source. Listing 7-12 shows the contents of the HibernateDemoV1 class and the results of running the class.

Listing 7-12. HibernateDemoV1 Runnable Class and Its Output

```
package com.apress.prospring6.seven.base

import com.apress.prospring6.seven.base.config.HibernateConfig
import com.apress.prospring6.seven.base.dao.SingerDao
import org.slf4j.Logger
import org.slf4j.LoggerFactory
import org.springframework.context.annotation.AnnotationConfigApplicationContext

object HibernateDemoV1 {
    private val LOGGER = LoggerFactory.getLogger(HibernateDemoV1::class.java)
    @JvmStatic
    fun main(args: Array<String>) {
        val ctx = AnnotationConfigApplicationContext(
            HibernateConfig::class.java
        )

        val singerDao = ctx.getBean(
            SingerDao::class.java
        )
```

```
            LOGGER.info(" ---- Listing singer with id=2:")
            val singer = singerDao.findById(2L)
            LOGGER.info(singer.toString())

            // this works, but you have to recreate your container to run the other demo
            class ;)
            // singerDao.delete(singer);
            LOGGER.info(" ---- Listing singers:")
            singerDao.findAll().forEach{ s: Singer ->
                LOGGER.info(
                    s.toString()
                )
            }
            ctx.close()
        }
}

# output
---- Listing singers:
Singer - Id: 1, First name: John, Last name: Mayer, Birthday: 1977-10-16
Singer - Id: 3, First name: John, Last name: Butler, Birthday: 1975-04-01
Singer - Id: 2, First name: Eric, Last name: Clapton, Birthday: 1945-03-30
```

Although the singer records were retrieved, what about the albums and instruments? Let's modify the testing class to print the detailed information. In Listing 7-13, you can see the method singerDao.findAll() being replaced with singerDao.findAllWithAlbums() in the runnable HibernateDemoV2 class. The listing also shows the output printed when this class is executed.

Listing 7-13. HibernateDemoV2 Runnable Class and Its Output

```
// In SingerDao, use variant:
@Transactional(readOnly = true)
override fun findAllWithAlbum(): List<Singer> {
    return sessionFactory.currentSession.createQuery("from Singer s",
        Singer::class.java).list()
}

package com.apress.prospring6.seven.base
// import statements omitted

object HibernateDemoV2 {
    private val LOGGER = LoggerFactory.getLogger(HibernateDemoV2::class.java)
    @JvmStatic
    fun main(args: Array<String>) {
        val ctx = AnnotationConfigApplicationContext(
            HibernateConfig::class.java
        )
        val singerDao = ctx.getBean(
            SingerDao::class.java
        )
```

```
        LOGGER.info(" ---- Listing singer with id=2:")
        val singer = singerDao.findById(2L)
        LOGGER.info(singer.toString())

        // this works, but you have to recreate your container to run the other demo
        class ;)
        //singerDao.delete(singer);
        listSingersWithAlbum(singerDao.findAllWithAlbum())
        ctx.close()
    }

    private fun listSingersWithAlbum(singers: List<Singer>) {
        LOGGER.info(" ---- Listing singers with instruments:")
        singers.forEach{ s: Singer ->
            LOGGER.info(s.toString())
            s.albums.forEach{ a: Album ->
                LOGGER.info(
                    "\t" + a.toString()
                )
            }
            s.instruments.forEach{ i: Instrument ->
                LOGGER.info(
                    "\tInstrument: " + i.instrumentId
                )
            }
        }
    }
}
```

```
# output
INFO : HibernateDemoV2 - ---- Listing singers with instruments:
INFO : HibernateDemoV2 - Singer - Id: 1, First name: John, Last name: Mayer, Birthday:
1977-10-16
Exception in thread "main" org.hibernate.LazyInitializationException: failed to lazily
initialize a collection of role: com.apress.prospring6.seven.base.entities.Singer.albums,
could not initialize proxy - no Session
    at org.hibernate.collection.internal.AbstractPersistentCollection.throwLazy
    InitializationException(AbstractPersistentCollection.java:614)
    at org.hibernate.collection.internal.AbstractPersistentCollection.withTemporarySession
    IfNeeded(AbstractPersistentCollection.java:218)
    at org.hibernate.collection.internal.AbstractPersistentCollection.initialize(Abstract
    PersistentCollection.java:591)
    at org.hibernate.collection.internal.AbstractPersistentCollection.read(Abstract
    PersistentCollection.java:149)
    at org.hibernate.collection.internal.PersistentSet.iterator(PersistentSet.java:188)
    at java.base/java.lang.Iterable.forEach(Iterable.java:74)
    at com.apress.prospring6.seven.base.HibernateDemoV2.lambda$listSingersWithAlbum$2(
    HibernateDemoV2.java:62)
```

You will see Hibernate throw the `LazyInitializationException` when you try to access the associations because, by default, Hibernate will fetch the associations lazily. This means that Hibernate will not join the association tables (that is, `ALBUM` or `INSTRUMENT`) for records. The rationale behind this is for performance; as you can imagine, if a query is retrieving thousands of records and all the associations are retrieved, the massive amount of data transfer will degrade performance.

Querying with Associations Fetching

To have Hibernate fetch the data from associations, there are two options. The first is to declare the Java association with `fetch` mode `EAGER`: `@ManyToMany(fetch=FetchType.EAGER)`. This tells Hibernate to fetch the associated records in every query. However, as discussed, this will impact data retrieval performance. The second option is to instruct Hibernate to fetch the associated records in the query when required. If you use the `Criteria` query, you can call the function `Criteria.setFetchMode()` to instruct Hibernate to eagerly fetch the association. When using `NamedQuery`, you can use the fetch operator to instruct Hibernate to fetch the association eagerly.

Let's take a look at the implementation of the `findAllWithAlbum()` method, which will retrieve all singer information together with their albums and instruments. This example will use the `jakarta.persistence.NamedQuery` approach. `NamedQuery` can be externalized into an XML file or declared using an annotation on the entity class. In Listing 7-14 you can see the revised `Singer` entity class with the named query defined using annotations.

Listing 7-14. Singer Entity Class with `NamedQuery` Declaration Used in Method `SingerDaoImpl`. `findAllWithAlbum()`

```
package com.apress.prospring6.seven.base.entities;

import jakarta.persistence.NamedQueries
import jakarta.persistence.NamedQuery
// other import statements omitted

@Entity
@Table(name = "SINGER")
@NamedQueries({
    @NamedQuery(name="Singer.findAllWithAlbum",
        query="select distinct s from Singer s " +
                "left join fetch s.albums a " +
                "left join fetch s.instruments i")
})
public class Singer extends AbstractEntity {
 // content omitted
}
```

In Listing 7-14 we define a `NamedQuery` instance called `Singer.findAllWithAlbum`. Then we define the query in HQL. Pay attention to the `left join fetch` clause, which instructs Hibernate to fetch the association eagerly. We also need to use `select distinct`; otherwise, Hibernate will return duplicate objects (two Singer objects will be returned if a single singer has two albums associated with him).

The implementation of the `SingerDaoImpl.findAllWithAlbum()` method is shown in Listing 7-15.

Listing 7-15. SingerDaoImpl.findAllWithAlbum() Using the NamedQuery Instance Called Singer.
findAllWithAlbum, Declared in Listing 7-14

package *com.apress.prospring6.seven.base.dao*

```
// import statements omitted

@Transactional
@Repository("singerDao")
class SingerDaoImpl(private val sessionFactory: SessionFactory) : SingerDao {

    @Transactional(readOnly = true)
    override fun findAllWithAlbum(): List<Singer> {
        return sessionFactory.currentSession.createNamedQuery(
            "Singer.findAllWithAlbum", Singer::class.java
        ).list()
    }

    // other code omitted
}
```

This time, when running HibernateDemoV2, the Session.getNamedQuery() method is called, passing in the name of the NamedQuery instance, which now produces the expected output instead of throwing the LazyInitializationException. This output is shown in Listing 7-16.

Listing 7-16. Output of HibernateDemoV2 When SingerDaoImpl.findAllWithAlbum() Is Implemented Correctly

```
INFO : HibernateDemoV2 -  ---- Listing singers with instruments:
INFO : HibernateDemoV2 - Singer - Id: 1, First name: John, Last name: Mayer, Birthday:
        1977-10-16
INFO : HibernateDemoV2 -    Album - Id: 1, Singer id: 1, Title: The Search For Everything,
        Release Date: 2017-01-20
INFO : HibernateDemoV2 -    Album - Id: 2, Singer id: 1, Title: Battle Studies, Release
        Date: 2009-11-17
INFO : HibernateDemoV2 -        Instrument: Piano
INFO : HibernateDemoV2 -        Instrument: Guitar
INFO : HibernateDemoV2 - Singer - Id: 2, First name: Ben, Last name: Barnes, Birthday:
        1981-08-20
INFO : HibernateDemoV2 -    Album - Id: 3, Singer id: 2, Title:  11:11 , Release Date:
        2021-09-18
INFO : HibernateDemoV2 -        Instrument: Drums
INFO : HibernateDemoV2 -        Instrument: Piano
INFO : HibernateDemoV2 -        Instrument: Guitar
INFO : HibernateDemoV2 - Singer - Id: 3, First name: John, Last name: Butler, Birthday:
        1975-04-01
```

Now all the singers with details were retrieved correctly. Let's see another example with NamedQuery with parameters. This time, we will implement the findById() method that should fetch the associations as well. Listing 7-17 shows the Singer class with the new NamedQuery instance added.

Listing 7-17. Singer Entity Class with Two NamedQuery Instances

```
package com.apress.prospring6.seven.base.entities

import jakarta.persistence.NamedQueries
import jakarta.persistence.NamedQuery
// other import statements omitted

@Entity
@Table(name = "SINGER")
@NamedQueries(
        NamedQuery(
                name = "Singer.findById",
                query = """
                                select distinct s from Singer s
                                        left join fetch s.albums a
                                        left join fetch s.instruments i
                                        where s.id = :id
                                """
        ),
        NamedQuery(
                name = "Singer.findAllWithAlbum",
                query = """
                                select distinct s from Singer s
                                        left join fetch s.albums a
                                        left join fetch s.instruments i
                                """
        )
)
class Singer : AbstractEntity() {
 // content omitted
}
```

For the Singer.findById named query, we declare a named parameter: id. When this query is used, the parameter needs to be replaced with a concrete value. You can see the implementation of the SingerDaoImpl.findById() method in Listing 7-18.

Listing 7-18. SingerDaoImpl.findById() Method That Uses the Singer.findById NamedQuery Instance

```
package com.apress.prospring6.seven.base.dao
// import statements omitted

@Transactional
@Repository("singerDao")
class SingerDaoImpl(private val sessionFactory: SessionFactory) : SingerDao {
    @Transactional(readOnly = true)
    override fun findById(id: Long?): Singer? {
        return sessionFactory.currentSession.createNamedQuery(
            "Singer.findById",
```

```
            Singer::class.java
        ).setParameter("id", id).uniqueResult()
    }

    // other code omitted
}
```

The createNamedQuery(..) method returns an instance of a type that implements the org.hibernate. query.Query interface. For a Hibernate named query, the concrete type of the instance returned by this method is org.hibernate.query.internal.QueryImpl. This is a Hibernate internal type, as its package name makes it really obvious. In the same package there are also types specific to native and criteria queries, which are introduced a bit further in the chapter.

Providing the value for the id parameter is done by calling the setParameter(..) method on this instance. When the named query requires more than one parameter, their values can be provided by calling either method setParameterList() or setParameters(), which are part of the Query interface declaration.

Up to this point in the chapter, you have seen only how to test the repository class SingerDaoImpl methods by running an executable class. As previously mentioned, a Testcontainers MariaDB instance is used for testing in this chapter, so Listing 7-19 introduces the HibernateTest class that tests the two named queries introduced in the chapter, on a limited data set, that is part of the testcontainers/create-schema. sql script for this chapter.

Listing 7-19. HibernateTest Test Class Using a Testcontainers MariaDB Instance

```kotlin
package com.apress.prospring6.seven

import com.apress.prospring6.seven.base.config.HibernateConfig
import org.testcontainers.containers.MariaDBContainer
import org.testcontainers.junit.jupiter.Container
import org.testcontainers.junit.jupiter.Testcontainers
// other import statements omitted

@Testcontainers
@SqlMergeMode(SqlMergeMode.MergeMode.MERGE)
@Sql("classpath:testcontainers/drop-schema.sql",
        "classpath:testcontainers/create-schema.sql")
@SpringJUnitConfig(classes = [HibernateTest.TestContainersConfig::class])
class HibernateTest {
    @Autowired
    var singerDao: SingerDao? = null
    @Test
    @DisplayName("should return all singers")
    fun testFindAll() {
        val singers = singerDao!!.findAll()
        Assertions.assertEquals(3, singers.size)
        singers.forEach(Consumer { singer: Singer? ->
            LOGGER.info(
                singer.toString()
            )
        })
    }
```

```kotlin
@Test
@DisplayName("should return singer by id")
fun testFindById() {
    val singer = singerDao!!.findById(2L)
    Assertions.assertEquals("Ben", singer!!.firstName)
    LOGGER.info(singer.toString())
}
...

companion object {
    private val LOGGER = LoggerFactory.getLogger(HibernateTest::class.java)

    @Container
    var mariaDB: MariaDBContainer<*> = MariaDBContainer("mariadb:latest")

    @DynamicPropertySource // this does the magic
    @JvmStatic
    fun setUp(registry: DynamicPropertyRegistry) {
        registry.add("jdbc.driverClassName") { mariaDB.driverClassName }
        registry.add("jdbc.url") { mariaDB.jdbcUrl }
        registry.add("jdbc.username") { mariaDB.username }
        registry.add("jdbc.password") { mariaDB.password }
    }

    private fun listSingersWithAssociations(singers: List<Singer>) {
        LOGGER.info(" ---- Listing singers with instruments:")
        for (singer in singers) {
            LOGGER.info(singer.toString())
            for (album in singer.albums) {
                LOGGER.info("\t" + album.toString())
            }
            for (instrument in singer.instruments) {
                LOGGER.info("\tInstrument: " + instrument.instrumentId)
            }
        }
    }
}
}
```

One thing you might have noticed when Testcontainers was introduced in the Chapter 6, and that might be even more obvious now, is how practical it is to write tests using this library. For most cases, especially for small-scale, demonstrative applications like those in this book, the production-like Spring configuration can be reused without the need to introduce a different profile and extra configurations for testing contexts.

Inserting Data

Inserting data with Hibernate is simple as well, as is retrieving the database-generated primary key. When using pure JDBC in **Chapter 6**, we needed to explicitly declare that we wanted to retrieve the database-generated primary key, pass in the KeyHolder instance, and get the key back from it after executing the

INSERT statement. With Hibernate, none of those actions are required. Hibernate retrieves the generated key and populates the domain object after the insert operation. Listing 7-20 shows the implementation of the save(..) method using Hibernate's SessionFactory.

Listing 7-20. SingerDaoImpl.save(..) Method

```
package com.apress.prospring6.seven.base.dao
// import statements omitted

@Transactional
@Repository("singerDao")
class SingerDaoImpl(private val sessionFactory: SessionFactory) : SingerDao {

    // other code omitted

    @Transactional
    override fun save(singer: Singer): Singer {
        val session = sessionFactory.currentSession
        if (singer.id == null) {
            session.persist(singer)
        } else {
            session.merge(singer)
        }
        LOGGER.info("Singer saved with id: " + singer.id)
        return singer
    }
}
```

We added a logging statement to the implementation to print the singer.id field that is populated by Hibernate after the object is persisted. Recall that when we declared our Singer entity class, we declared it with a @OneToMany association to the Album class and a @ManyToMany association to the Instrument class. What do you think, will a Singer instance with the albums and instruments field populated be saved together with those associations? Let's test this assumption by creating a new method in the HibernateTest class, as shown in Listing 7-21.

Listing 7-21. HibernateTest.testInsert() Method

```
package com.apress.prospring6.seven
// import statements omitted

@Testcontainers
@SqlMergeMode(SqlMergeMode.MergeMode.MERGE)
@Sql("classpath:testcontainers/drop-schema.sql", "classpath:testcontainers/create-
schema.sql")
@SpringJUnitConfig(classes = [HibernateTest.TestContainersConfig::class])
class HibernateTest {
    @Autowired
    var singerDao: SingerDao? = null

    // other test methods omitted
```

```kotlin
@Test
@DisplayName("should insert a singer with associations")
@Sql(
    statements = [ // avoid dirtying up the test context
    "delete from ALBUM where SINGER_ID = (select ID from SINGER where FIRST_NAME = 'BB')",
    "delete from SINGER_INSTRUMENT where SINGER_ID = (select ID from SINGER where FIRST_
    NAME = 'BB')",
    "delete from SINGER where FIRST_NAME = 'BB'"],
    executionPhase = Sql.ExecutionPhase.AFTER_TEST_METHOD
)
fun testInsertSinger() {
    val singer = Singer()
    singer.firstName = "BB"
    singer.lastName = "King"
    singer.birthDate = LocalDate.of(1940, 8, 16)
    var album = Album()
    album.title = "My Kind of Blues"
    album.releaseDate = LocalDate.of(1961, 7, 18)
    singer.addAlbum(album)
    album = Album()
    album.title = "A Heart Full of Blues"
    album.releaseDate = LocalDate.of(1962, 3, 20)
    singer.addAlbum(album)
    singerDao!!.save(singer)
    Assertions.assertNotNull(singer.id)
    val singers = singerDao!!.findAllWithAlbum()
    Assertions.assertEquals(4, singers.size)
    listSingersWithAssociations(singers)
}


@Configuration
@Import(HibernateConfig::class)
open class TestContainersConfig {
    @Autowired
    var hibernateProperties: Properties? = null
    @PostConstruct
    open fun initialize() {
        hibernateProperties!![Environment.FORMAT_SQL] = true
        hibernateProperties!![Environment.USE_SQL_COMMENTS] = true
        hibernateProperties!![Environment.SHOW_SQL] = true
    }
}


    ...
fun listSingersWithAssociations(singers:List<Singer>) {
    LOGGER.info(" ---- Listing singers with instruments:")
    // code omitted for duplication
}
...
```

In the testInsertSinger() method a new singer record in the SINGER table with two child records in the ALBUM table get created and then the assumption that the insertion succeeds is tested. All singer instances and their associations are logged in the console too, to make it really obvious that the insertion succeeded.

To test the insert method in isolation, without dirtying the test context, a few SQL statements to do the cleanup after the test method is executed are configured using the @Sql annotation. Another thing that was done for this test context is to override the format_sql, use_sql_comments, and show_sql hibernate properties in a test configuration class and set them to true. This will cause all SQL queries generated by Hibernate to be printed in the log.

When executing the testInsertSinger() method, the test is expected to pass. All the data in the SINGER, ALBUM tables and the instruments associated with singer records get printed, together with the SQL queries used to select the data as shown in Listing 7-22.

Listing 7-22. HibernateTest.testInsert() Method Logs

```
...
INFO : Dialect - HHH000400: Using dialect: org.hibernate.dialect.MariaDB106Dialect
Hibernate:
    /* insert com.apress.prospring6.seven.base.entities.Singer
        */ insert
        into
            SINGER
            (VERSION, BIRTH_DATE, FIRST_NAME, LAST_NAME)
        values
            (?, ?, ?, ?)
Hibernate:
    /* insert com.apress.prospring6.seven.base.entities.Album
        */ insert
        into
            ALBUM
            (VERSION, RELEASE_DATE, SINGER_ID, title)
        values
            (?, ?, ?, ?)
Hibernate:
    /* insert com.apress.prospring6.seven.base.entities.Album
        */ insert
        into
            ALBUM
            (VERSION, RELEASE_DATE, SINGER_ID, title)
        values
            (?, ?, ?, ?)
INFO : SingerDaoImpl - Singer saved with id: 4
...
INFO : HibernateTest -  ---- Listing singers with instruments:
INFO : HibernateTest - Singer - Id: 1, First name: John, Last name: Mayer, Birthday:
1977-10-16
INFO : HibernateTest -  Album - Id: 2, Singer id: 1, Title: Battle Studies, Release Date:
2009-11-17
INFO : HibernateTest -  Album - Id: 1, Singer id: 1, Title: The Search For Everything,
Release Date: 2017-01-20
INFO : HibernateTest -  Instrument: Guitar
INFO : HibernateTest -  Instrument: Piano
```

```
INFO : HibernateTest - Singer - Id: 2, First name: Ben, Last name: Barnes, Birthday:
1981-08-20
INFO : HibernateTest -  Album - Id: 3, Singer id: 2, Title:  11:11 , Release Date:
2021-09-18
INFO : HibernateTest -  Instrument: Guitar
INFO : HibernateTest -  Instrument: Drums
INFO : HibernateTest -  Instrument: Piano
INFO : HibernateTest - Singer - Id: 4, First name: BB, Last name: King, Birthday: 1940-08-16
INFO : HibernateTest -  Album - Id: 4, Singer id: 4, Title: A Heart Full of Blues, Release
Date: 1962-03-20
INFO : HibernateTest -  Album - Id: 5, Singer id: 4, Title: My Kind of Blues, Release Date:
1961-07-18
INFO : HibernateTest - Singer - Id: 3, First name: John, Last name: Butler, Birthday:
1975-04-01
```

The logging configuration has been modified so that more detailed Hibernate information is printed. From the INFO log record, we can see that the ID of the newly saved contact was populated correctly. Hibernate will also show all the SQL statements being executed against the database, so you know what is happening behind the scenes.

Updating Data

Updating a record is as easy as inserting data. Suppose for the singer with an ID of 5 we want to update the first name and last name and remove one album. The testUpdate() method used to test the update operation is shown in Listing 7-23.

Listing 7-23. HibernateTest.testUpdate() Method

```
package com.apress.prospring6.seven

// import statements omitted

@Testcontainers
@SqlMergeMode(SqlMergeMode.MergeMode.MERGE)
@Sql("classpath:testcontainers/drop-schema.sql",
        "classpath:testcontainers/create-schema.sql")
@SpringJUnitConfig(classes = [HibernateTest.TestContainersConfig::class])
class HibernateTest {
    @Autowired
    var singerDao: SingerDao? = null

    ...
    @Test
    @SqlGroup(
        Sql(
            scripts = ["classpath:testcontainers/add-nina.sql"],
            executionPhase = Sql.ExecutionPhase.BEFORE_TEST_METHOD
        ),
```

```kotlin
        Sql(
            scripts = ["classpath:testcontainers/remove-nina.sql"],
            executionPhase = Sql.ExecutionPhase.AFTER_TEST_METHOD
        )
    )
    @DisplayName("should update a singer")
    fun testUpdate() {
        val singer = singerDao!!.findById(5L)
        //making sure such singer exists
        Assertions.assertNotNull(singer)
        //making sure we got expected singer
        Assertions.assertEquals("Simone", singer!!.lastName)
        //retrieve the album
        val album = singer.albums.stream().filter {
                a: Album -> a.title == "I Put a Spell on You" }
            .findFirst().orElse(null)
        Assertions.assertNotNull(album)
        singer.firstName = "Eunice Kathleen"
        singer.lastName = "Waymon"
        singer.removeAlbum(album)
        val version = singer.version
        singerDao!!.save(singer)
        val nina = singerDao!!.findById(5L)
        Assertions.assertEquals(version + 1, nina!!.version)

        // test the update
        listSingersWithAssociations(singerDao!!.findAllWithAlbum())
    }
    ...

    companion object {
        private val LOGGER = LoggerFactory.getLogger(HibernateTest::class.java)

        @Container
        var mariaDB: MariaDBContainer<*> = MariaDBContainer("mariadb:latest")

        @DynamicPropertySource // this does the magic
        @JvmStatic
        fun setUp(registry: DynamicPropertyRegistry) {
            registry.add("jdbc.driverClassName") { mariaDB.driverClassName }
            registry.add("jdbc.url") { mariaDB.jdbcUrl }
            registry.add("jdbc.username") { mariaDB.username }
            registry.add("jdbc.password") { mariaDB.password }
        }

        private fun listSingersWithAssociations(singers: List<Singer>) {
            LOGGER.info(" ---- Listing singers with instruments:")
            for (singer in singers) {
                LOGGER.info(singer.toString())
                for (album in singer.albums) {
                    LOGGER.info("\t" + album.toString())
                }
```

```
                for (instrument in singer.instruments) {
                    LOGGER.info("\tInstrument: " + instrument.instrumentId)
                }
            }
        }
    }
}
```

As shown in this test method, we first retrieve the record with an ID of 5. Next, we change the first name and last name. We then loop through the Album objects, retrieve the one with the title I *Put a Spell on You*, and remove it from the singer's albums property. Finally, we call the singerDao.save() method and check that the value of the version field of the saved record is incremented. When executed, this test method is expected to pass and print the output shown in Listing 7-24.

Listing 7-24. HibernateTest.testUpdate() Method Logs

```
Hibernate:
    /* update
        com.apress.prospring6.seven.base.entities.Singer */ update
            SINGER
        set
            VERSION=?,
            BIRTH_DATE=?,
            FIRST_NAME=?,
            LAST_NAME=?
        where
            ID=?
            and VERSION=?
Hibernate:
    /* delete com.apress.prospring6.seven.base.entities.Album */ delete
        from
            ALBUM
        where
            ID=?
            and VERSION=?
INFO : SingerDaoImpl - Singer saved with id: 5
INFO : HibernateTest -  ---- Listing singers with instruments:
...
INFO : HibernateTest - Singer - Id: 5, First name: Eunice Kathleen, Last name: Waymon,
        Birthday: 1933-02-21
INFO : HibernateTest -  Album - Id: 4, Singer id: 5, Title: Little Girl Blue, Release Date:
        1959-02-20
INFO : HibernateTest -  Album - Id: 5, Singer id: 5, Title: Forbidden Fruit, Release Date:
        1961-08-18
INFO : HibernateTest -  Instrument: Voice
INFO : HibernateTest -  Instrument: Piano
```

Note that the first name and last name are updated and the I *Put a Spell on You* album is removed. The album can be removed because of the orphanRemoval=true attribute we pass into the one-to-many association, which instructs Hibernate to remove all orphan records that exist in the database but are no longer found in the object when persisted.

Deleting Data

Deleting data is simple as well. Just call the `session.delete()` method and pass in the Singer object. Listing 7-25 shows the code for deletion.

Listing 7-25. `SingerDaoImpl.delete()` Method

```
package com.apress.prospring6.seven.base.dao
// import statements omitted

@Transactional
@Repository("singerDao")
class SingerDaoImpl(private val sessionFactory: SessionFactory) : SingerDao {

    @Transactional
    override fun delete(singer: Singer) {
        sessionFactory.currentSession.remove(singer)
        LOGGER.info("Singer deleted with id: " + singer.id)
    }
    ...

    companion object {
        private val LOGGER = LoggerFactory.getLogger(SingerDaoImpl::class.java)
    }
}
```

The delete operation will delete the singer record, together with all its associated information, including albums and instruments, as we defined `cascade=CascadeType.ALL` in the mapping. Listing 7-26 shows the code for testing the delete method, `testDelete()`.

Listing 7-26. `HibernateTest.testDelete()` Method

```
package com.apress.prospring6.seven
// import statements omitted

@Testcontainers
@SqlMergeMode(SqlMergeMode.MergeMode.MERGE)
@Sql("classpath:testcontainers/drop-schema.sql",
        "classpath:testcontainers/create-schema.sql")
@SpringJUnitConfig(classes = [HibernateTest.TestContainersConfig::class])
class HibernateTest {
    @Autowired
    var singerDao: SingerDao? = null

    @Test
    @Sql(scripts = ["classpath:testcontainers/add-chuck.sql"],
            executionPhase = Sql.ExecutionPhase.BEFORE_TEST_METHOD)
    @DisplayName("should delete a singer")
    fun testDelete() {
        val singer = singerDao!!.findById(6L)
        // making sure such singer exists
        Assertions.assertNotNull(singer)
```

```
        singerDao!!.delete(singer!!)
        listSingersWithAssociations(singerDao!!.findAllWithAlbum())
    }

    companion object {
        private val LOGGER = LoggerFactory.getLogger(HibernateTest::class.java)

        @Container
        var mariaDB: MariaDBContainer<*> = MariaDBContainer("mariadb:latest")

        @DynamicPropertySource // this does the magic
        @JvmStatic
        fun setUp(registry: DynamicPropertyRegistry) {
            registry.add("jdbc.driverClassName") { mariaDB.driverClassName }
            registry.add("jdbc.url") { mariaDB.jdbcUrl }
            registry.add("jdbc.username") { mariaDB.username }
            registry.add("jdbc.password") { mariaDB.password }
        }

        private fun listSingersWithAssociations(singers: List<Singer>) {
            ...
        }
    }
}
```

The testDelete() method retrieves the singer with an ID of 6 and then calls the singerDao.delete(..) method to delete the singer record from the database. Running the program will produce the output shown in Listing 7-27.

Listing 7-27. HibernateTest.testDelete() Method Output

```
Hibernate:
    /* delete com.apress.prospring6.seven.base.entities.Album */ delete
        from
            ALBUM
        where
            ID=?
            and VERSION=?
Hibernate:
    /* delete com.apress.prospring6.seven.base.entities.Singer */ delete
        from
            SINGER
        where
            ID=?
            and VERSION=?
INFO : SingerDaoImpl - Singer deleted with id: 6
INFO : HibernateTest -  ---- Listing singers with instruments:
INFO : HibernateTest - Singer - Id: 1, First name: John, Last name: Mayer, Birthday:
1977-10-16
INFO : HibernateTest -  Album - Id: 2, Singer id: 1, Title: Battle Studies, Release Date:
2009-11-17
```

```
INFO : HibernateTest -  Album - Id: 1, Singer id: 1, Title: The Search For Everything,
Release Date: 2017-01-20
INFO : HibernateTest -  Instrument: Piano
INFO : HibernateTest -  Instrument: Guitar
INFO : HibernateTest - Singer - Id: 2, First name: Ben, Last name: Barnes, Birthday:
1981-08-20
INFO : HibernateTest -  Album - Id: 3, Singer id: 2, Title: 11:11, Release Date: 2021-09-18
INFO : HibernateTest -  Instrument: Piano
INFO : HibernateTest -  Instrument: Guitar
INFO : HibernateTest -  Instrument: Drums
INFO : HibernateTest - Singer - Id: 3, First name: John, Last name: Butler, Birthday:
1975-04-01
```

You can see that the singer with an ID of 6 was deleted together with its child record in the ALBUM table.

Executing SQL Native Queries

HQL queries are easy to write, but writing complex queries that span across multiple tables and do complex calculations (like are often needed in financial domains) is difficult, if not impossible. More often than not, the generated SQL query would not be as efficient as a native query written by a SQL expert. For the examples in the project associated with this book, it is just as easy to write HQL queries as it is to write SQL native queries, but assuming you would need to execute a SQL native query, the Hibernate session allows native SQL query execution as well using the createNativeQuery(..) method. An example of using this method with a relatively complex query is shown in Listing 7-28.

Listing 7-28. SingerDaoImpl.findAllDetails() Method That Executed a Native SQL Query

```
package com.apress.prospring6.seven.base.dao
// import statements omitted

@Transactional
@Repository("singerDao")
class SingerDaoImpl(private val sessionFactory: SessionFactory) : SingerDao {
    @Transactional(readOnly = true)
    override fun findAllDetails(firstName: String?, lastName: String?): Singer? {
        val results = sessionFactory.currentSession
            .createNativeQuery<Tuple>(
                ALL_SELECT,
                Tuple::class.java
            )
            .setParameter("firstName", firstName)
            .setParameter("lastName", lastName)
            .list()
        val singer = Singer()
        for (item in results) {
            if (singer.firstName == null && singer.lastName == null) {
                singer.firstName = (item["FIRST_NAME"] as String)
                singer.lastName = (item["LAST_NAME"] as String)
            }
```

```kotlin
        val album = Album()
        album.title = (item["TITLE"] as String)
        album.releaseDate = ((item["RELEASE_DATE"] as Date).toLocalDate())
        singer.addAlbum(album)
        val instrument = Instrument()
        instrument.instrumentId = (item["INSTRUMENT_ID"] as String)
        singer.instruments.add(instrument)
    }
    return singer
}

companion object {
    private val LOGGER = LoggerFactory.getLogger(SingerDaoImpl::class.java)
    private val ALL_SELECT: String = """
        select distinct s.FIRST_NAME, s.LAST_NAME, a.TITLE, a.RELEASE_DATE,
                            i.INSTRUMENT_ID
        from SINGER s
        inner join ALBUM a on s.id = a.SINGER_ID
        inner join SINGER_INSTRUMENT si on s.ID = si.SINGER_ID
        inner join INSTRUMENT i on si.INSTRUMENT_ID = i.INSTRUMENT_ID
        where s.FIRST_NAME = :firstName and s.LAST_NAME= :lastName
        """
    }
}
```

When an ALL_SELECT SQL query uses named parameters, values for these parameters are provided by calling the setParameter(..) method that is called on the org.hibernate.query.NativeQuery instance returned by the createNativeQuery(..) call. For a Hibernate native SQL query, the concrete type of the instance returned by this method is org.hibernate.query.internal.NativeQueryImpl. Since we are executing a native query, we lose the benefit of automatic mapping of the database records to Kotlin entities, but it is worth it for the benefit of performance.

Concerning conciseness while accessing and manipulating data, jOOQ provides better support, but this will be shown later in the chapter, after showing the other interesting things that Hibernate can be used for.

Calling Stored Functions with Hibernate

Hibernate provides support for calling stored procedures and functions. This section demonstrates how to use Hibernate to call a simple stored function in a MariaDB database using Hibernate Session's createSQLQuery(..) method.

The function being called is the same introduced in Chapter 6. Its SQL creating code is depicted in a comment on the SingerDaoImpl.findFirstNameById(..) in Listing 7-29.

Listing 7-29. SingerDaoImpl.findFirstNameById() Method Using Hibernate Session to Call a Stored Function

```java
package com.apress.prospring6.seven.base.dao;
// import statements omitted

@Repository("singerDao")
public class SingerDaoImpl implements  SingerDao {
```

```
    /*
    CREATE FUNCTION IF NOT EXISTS
        getFirstNameById (in_id INT) RETURNS VARCHAR(60)
    RETURN (SELECT first_name FROM SINGER WHERE id = in_id);
    */
        @Transactional(readOnly = true)
        override fun findFirstNameById(id: Long): String? {
            val firstNameResult = AtomicReference<String>()
            sessionFactory.currentSession.doWork { connection: Connection ->
                connection.prepareCall(
                    "{ ? = call getfirstnamebyid(?) }"
                ).use { function ->
                    function.registerOutParameter(1, Types.VARCHAR)
                    function.setLong(2, id)
                    function.execute()
                    firstNameResult.set(function.getString(1))
                }
            }
            return firstNameResult.get()
        }
    // other methods omitted
}
```

The stored function simply accepts the ID and returns the first name of the singer record with the ID. The createSQLQuery(..) method takes a native SQL function call statement as an argument and returns an instance of org.hibernate.query.NativeQueryImpl. The function call requires an argument that is provided by calling the set*(..) method. There is a version of this method that sets parameters using their index and one that does the same using their name. This function is a simple one, thus the Hibernate code to call it is simple as well.

Configuring Hibernate to Generate Tables from Entities

In startup applications using Hibernate, it is common behavior to first write the entity classes and then generate the database tables based on their contents. Usually, a framework like Flyway[6] is added in the mix to manage different versions of the application's database schema reliably and easily, but that topic is beyond the scope of this book.

Generating the database schema from entity classes is done by using the Environment.HBM2DDL_AUTO/ hibernate.hbm2ddl.auto Hibernate property. When the application is started the first time, this property value is set to create; this will make Hibernate scan the entities and generate tables and keys (primary, foreign, unique) according to the relationships defined using JPA and Hibernate annotations.

If the entities are configured correctly and the resulting database objects are exactly as expected, the value of the property should be changed to update. This tells Hibernate to update the existing database with any changes performed later on entities and keep the original database and any data that has been inserted into it.

In production applications, it is practical to write integration tests that run on a pseudo-database that is discarded after all test cases are executed. Usually, the test database is an in-memory database and Hibernate is told to create the database and discard it after the execution of the tests by setting the Environment.HBM2DDL_AUTO value to create-drop. With the introduction of Testcontainers, this functionality is not necessary, but if, for some reason, you are prohibited from installing Docker on the

---

[6] https://flywaydb.org

machine where your tests are running, or the application is so small that Testcontainers is overkill, Hibernate and an embedded in-memory database can come to the rescue. You can find the full list of values for the hibernate.hbm2ddl.auto property in the Hibernate official documentation[7].

Listing 7-30 shows the Kotlin configuration class named HibernateTestConfig class. As you can see, Environment.HBM2DDL_AUTO/hibernate.hbm2ddl.auto is set to create-drop and an H2 embedded data source was set up.

Listing 7-30. HibernateTestConfig Configuration Class

```kotlin
package com.apress.prospring6.seven.config

import org.hibernate.SessionFactory
import org.hibernate.cfg.Environment
import org.springframework.jdbc.datasource.embedded.EmbeddedDatabaseBuilder
import org.springframework.jdbc.datasource.embedded.EmbeddedDatabaseType
import org.springframework.orm.hibernate5.HibernateTransactionManager
import org.springframework.orm.hibernate5.LocalSessionFactoryBuilder
import org.springframework.transaction.PlatformTransactionManager
// other import statements omitted

@Configuration
@ComponentScan(basePackages = ["com.apress.prospring6.seven.base"])
@EnableTransactionManagement
open class HibernateTestConfig {
    @Bean
    open fun dataSource(): DataSource? {
        return try {
            val dbBuilder = EmbeddedDatabaseBuilder()
            dbBuilder.setType(EmbeddedDatabaseType.H2).setName("testdb").build()
        } catch (e: Exception) {
            LOGGER.error("Embedded DataSource bean cannot be created!", e)
            null
        }
    }

    @Bean
    open fun hibernateProperties(): Properties {
        val hibernateProp = Properties()
        hibernateProp[Environment.DIALECT] = "org.hibernate.dialect.H2Dialect"
        hibernateProp[Environment.HBM2DDL_AUTO] = "create-drop"
        hibernateProp[Environment.FORMAT_SQL] = true
        hibernateProp[Environment.USE_SQL_COMMENTS] = true
        hibernateProp[Environment.HIGHLIGHT_SQL] = true
        hibernateProp[Environment.SHOW_SQL] = true
        hibernateProp[Environment.MAX_FETCH_DEPTH] = 3
        hibernateProp[Environment.STATEMENT_BATCH_SIZE] = 10
        hibernateProp[Environment.STATEMENT_FETCH_SIZE] = 50
        return hibernateProp
    }
```

---

[7] See Table 3-7 at https://docs.jboss.org/hibernate/orm/5.0/manual/en-US/html/ch03.html

```kotlin
@Bean
open fun sessionFactory(): SessionFactory {
    return LocalSessionFactoryBuilder(dataSource())
        .scanPackages("com.apress.prospring6.seven.base.entities")
        .addProperties(hibernateProperties())
        .buildSessionFactory()
}

@Bean
open fun transactionManager(): PlatformTransactionManager {
    return HibernateTransactionManager(sessionFactory())
}

companion object {
    private val LOGGER = LoggerFactory.getLogger(HibernateTestConfig::class.java)
}
}
```

Of course, even if the database schema is created, there is no data, so we cannot run any tests. One solution is to use the @Sql* annotation family to set it all up, as in **Chapter 6**. Another solution is to write ordered tests, where the first test inserts the data, the second queries it, the third updates it, and the last one deletes it. Doing it this way, we validate all CRUD operations in SingerDaoImpl. The H2HibernateTest class that uses the HibernateTestConfig to configure its test context is shown in Listing 7-31.

Listing 7-31. H2HibernateTest Test Class

```kotlin
package com.apress.prospring6.seven

import com.apress.prospring6.seven.config.HibernateTestConfig
import org.junit.jupiter.api.MethodOrderer
import org.junit.jupiter.api.Order
import org.junit.jupiter.api.TestMethodOrder
// other import statements omitted

@SpringJUnitConfig(classes = [HibernateTestConfig::class])
@TestMethodOrder(
    MethodOrderer.OrderAnnotation::class
)
class H2HibernateTest {
    @Autowired
    var singerDao: SingerDao? = null
    @Commit
    @Test
    @Order(1)
    @DisplayName("01. should insert a singer with albums")
    fun testInsert() {
        val singer = Singer()
        singer.firstName = "BB"
        singer.lastName = "King"
        singer.birthDate = LocalDate.of(1940, 8, 16)
        var album = Album()
        album.title = "My Kind of Blues"
```

```kotlin
        album.releaseDate = LocalDate.of(1961, 7, 18)
        singer.addAlbum(album)
        album = Album()
        album.title = "A Heart Full of Blues"
        album.releaseDate = LocalDate.of(1962, 3, 20)
        singer.addAlbum(album)
        val created = singerDao!!.save(singer)
        Assertions.assertNotNull(created.id)
    }

    @Test
    @Order(2)
    @DisplayName("02. should return all singers")
    fun testFindAll() {
        val singers = singerDao!!.findAll()
        Assertions.assertEquals(1, singers.size)
        singers.forEach(Consumer { singer: Singer? ->
            LOGGER.info(
                singer.toString()
            )
        })
    }

    @Test
    @Order(3)
    @DisplayName("03. should update a singer")
    fun testUpdate() {
        val singer = singerDao!!.findAll()[0]

        // making sure such singer exists
        Assertions.assertNotNull(singer)
        singer.firstName = "Riley B. "
        val version = singer.version
        singerDao!!.save(singer)
        val bb = singerDao!!.findById(singer.id)
        Assertions.assertEquals(version + 1, bb!!.version)
    }

    @Test
    @Order(4)
    @DisplayName("04. should delete a singer")
    fun testDelete() {
        val singer = singerDao!!.findAll()[0]
        // making sure such singer exists
        Assertions.assertNotNull(singer)
        singerDao!!.delete(singer)
        Assertions.assertEquals(0, singerDao!!.findAll().size)
    }

    companion object {
        private val LOGGER = LoggerFactory.getLogger(HibernateTest::class.java)
    }
}
```

Notice that the class is annotated with @TestMethodOrder(MethodOrderer.OrderAnnotation.class) and each test method is annotated with @Order({x}), where x represents the numeric order of the test method. The test methods are executed in ascending order, and if all goes well, they should all pass. This obviously introduces a certain dependency between the test methods, and if one fails, all the others that follow might fail too.

ℹ️ Using Hibernate Tools[8] it is possible to also generate entity classes *in Java* from an existing schema, but the resulting code is not always the best and might need adjustments.

Annotating Methods or Fields?

In the previous example, the entities had JPA annotations on their getters. In Kotlin, you can see that from the annotations looking like @get:Annotation. But JPA annotations can be used directly on the fields, which has a few advantages:

- Annotating entity fields does not enforce providing setters/getters. This is useful for the @Version annotated field and other audit scope fields, which should never be modified manually; only Hibernate should have access to them.

- Annotating fields allows to do extra processing in setters (for example, encrypting/calculating the value after loading it from the database). The problem with the property access is that the setters are also called when the object is loaded.

There are a lot of discussions on the Internet regarding which is better, annotating accessors or annotating entity fields. From a performance point of view, there isn't any difference. The decision is eventually up to the developer because there might be some valid cases when annotating accessors makes more sense. But keep in mind that in the database the state of the objects is actually saved, and the state of the object is defined by the values of its fields, not the values returned by accessors. This also means that an object can be accurately re-created from the database exactly the way it was persisted. So, in a way, setting the annotations on the getters can be seen as breaking encapsulation.

Listing 7-32 shows the AbstractEntity mapped class that was rewritten to annotate the fields common to all Hibernate entity classes in an application.

Listing 7-32. AbstractEntity Mapped Class with JPA Annotated Fields

```
package com.apress.prospring6.seven.crud.entities

import jakarta.persistence.*
import java.io.Serial
import java.io.Serializable

@MappedSuperclass
abstract class AbstractEntity : Serializable {
    companion object {
```

---

[8] https://github.com/hibernate/hibernate-tools

```
    @Serial
    private val serialVersionUID:Long = 1L
}

@Id
@GeneratedValue(strategy = GenerationType.IDENTITY)
@Column(updatable = false)
var id:Long

@Version
@Column(name = "VERSION")
var version:Int
}
```

Listing 7-33 shows the Singer entity class that was rewritten to have annotated fields.

Listing 7-33. Singer Entity Class with JPA Annotated Fields

```
package com.apress.prospring6.seven.crud.entities

import jakarta.persistence.*
// other import statements omitted

@Entity
@Table(name = "SINGER")
@NamedQueries(
        NamedQuery(
                name = "Singer.findById",
                query = """
                                select distinct s from Singer s
                                        left join fetch s.albums a
                                        left join fetch s.instruments i
                                        where s.id = :id
                                """
        ),
        NamedQuery(
                name = "Singer.findAllWithAlbum",
                query = """
                                select distinct s from Singer s
                                        left join fetch s.albums a
                                        left join fetch s.instruments i
                                """

        )
)
```

```kotlin
@NamedStoredProcedureQuery(
        name = "getFirstNameByIdProc",
        procedureName = "getFirstNameByIdProc",
        parameters = [StoredProcedureParameter(
                name = "in_id",
                type = Long::class,
                mode = ParameterMode.IN
        ), StoredProcedureParameter(name = "fn_res", type = String::class,
                                                mode = ParameterMode.OUT)]
)
class Singer : AbstractEntity() {
        @Column(name = "FIRST_NAME")
        var firstName: String? = null

        @Column(name = "LAST_NAME")
        var lastName: String? = null

        @Column(name = "BIRTH_DATE")
        var birthDate: LocalDate? = null

        @OneToMany(
                mappedBy = "singer",
                cascade = [CascadeType.ALL],
                orphanRemoval = true
        )
        var albums: MutableSet<Album> = HashSet()

        @JoinTable(
                name = "SINGER_INSTRUMENT",
                joinColumns = [JoinColumn(name = "SINGER_ID")],
                inverseJoinColumns = [JoinColumn(name = "INSTRUMENT_ID")]
        )
        @ManyToMany
        var instruments: MutableSet<Instrument> = mutableSetOf()
        ...
}
```

Considerations When Using Hibernate

As shown in the examples in this chapter, once all the object-to-relational mapping, associations, and queries are properly defined, Hibernate can provide an environment for you to focus on programming with the object model, rather than composing SQL statements for each operation. In the past few years, Hibernate has been evolving quickly and has been widely adopted by Java and Kotlin developers as the data access layer library, both in the open source community and in enterprises. However, there are some points you need to bear in mind:

- Because you don't have control over the generated SQL, you should be careful when defining the mappings, especially the associations and their fetching strategy.

- You should observe the SQL statements generated by Hibernate to verify that all perform as you expect.

- SQL is a highly expressive and type-safe language with a rich syntax, so writing SQL queries is not easy and syntax errors are a common occurrence.

- Understanding the internal mechanism of how Hibernate manages its session is important, especially in batch job operations. Hibernate will keep the managed objects in session and will flush and clear them regularly. Poorly designed data access logic may cause Hibernate to flush the session too frequently and greatly impact the performance (in our examples, we flushed it explicitly in the save(..) and delete(..) methods).

- If you want absolute control over the query, you can use a native query, as already shown in this chapter. More examples will be shown in the next chapter as well.

- The settings (batch size, fetch size, and so forth) play a significant role in tuning Hibernate's performance. You should define them in your session factory and adjust them while load testing your application to identify the optimal value.

After all, Hibernate, and its excellent JPA support that we discuss in **Chapter 8**, is a natural decision for Kotlin developers looking for an OO way to implement data access logic.

💡 If you are interested in harnessing the full power of Hibernate in a project, you should read Vlad Mihalcea's *High-Performance Java Persistence*[9].

Introducing jOOQ

jOOQ stands for Java Object Oriented Querying and is a light database-mapping software library written in Java that implements the active record pattern[10]. Its purpose is to be both relational and object-oriented by providing a domain-specific language to construct queries from classes generated from a database schema. jOOQ is SQL-centric and focused on the database. Its capabilities are incredible: it can generate POJO classes that map to database records and DAO classes too, and it supports quite an extensive number of databases[11].

🔥 jOOQ creates Java code, not Kotlin code. Since Kotlin seamlessly integrates with Java, you can still use jOOQ even if your application is written in Kotlin.

Also, jOOQ can be integrated with Hibernate: JPA can be kept for modifications, and jOOQ can be used to generate expensive SQL native queries that can be executed with JPA native queries. This section will show you how to use jOOQ to generate POJOs and DAOs and how to configure jOOQ in a Spring application to make use of them.

---

[9] https://vladmihalcea.com/books/high-performance-java-persistence
[10] https://en.wikipedia.org/wiki/Active_record_pattern
[11] https://www.jooq.org/doc/latest/manual/reference/supported-rdbms

🛈 As of jOOQ 3.15, the commercial edition is not published to Maven Central and is available only from the jOOQ website[12]. The distribution can be downloaded as a ZIP file, which contains scripts to publish the artifacts in a local repository (via mvn `install` or mvn `deploy`). Our recommendation is to run the `maven-install` script specific to your operating system. At the time of writing, version 3.16.7 is the most recent.

🖋 Since using jOOQ requires you to manually install it first on your computer, we created the project `chapter07-jooq`, which is not part of the full build for the book. To add it to the full build, remove the commented configuration snippet from the main `settings.gradle`.

Assuming you managed to install the jOOQ libraries in your local Maven repository, the next step is to add the necessary libraries to your Gradle configuration. Luckily for us, the `jooq-codegen.jar` file that needs to be used for code generation depends on the main `jooq.jar` and `jooq-meta.jar` that will be added to the project as its transitive dependencies.

Next, we need to generate the jOOQ classes. There is more than one way to do it:

- Programmatic way using the `org.jooq.codegen.GenerationTool` and XML configuration

- Programmatic way using the `org.jooq.codegen.GenerationTool` and explicit configuration in the Java code

- Using the `nu.studer.jooq` plug-in

In `chapter07-jooq`, the plug-ins are configured, which you can take a look at after cloning the repository. Listing 7-34 shows the `GenerateJOOQSources` class, an executable class that contains the two programmatic code-generation versions.

Listing 7-34. Programmatic jOOQ Code Generation Class

```
package com.apress.prospring6.seven.util

import org.jooq.codegen.GenerationTool
import org.jooq.meta.jaxb.Configuration
import org.jooq.meta.jaxb.Database
import org.jooq.meta.jaxb.Generate
import org.jooq.meta.jaxb.Generator
import org.jooq.meta.jaxb.Jdbc
import org.jooq.meta.jaxb.Target
// other import statements omitted
```

---

[12] https://www.jooq.org/download/versions

```kotlin
object GenerateJOOQSources {
    private val LOGGER = LoggerFactory.getLogger(GenerateJOOQSources::class.java)
    @Throws(Exception::class)
    @JvmStatic
    fun main(args: Array<String>) {
        if (args.size > 0) { // run with any argument to run this one
            // programmatic  version 1
            LOGGER.info("... Generating jOOQ using programmatic version 1 with XML
            configuration ...")
            val resource = GenerateJOOQSources::class.java.getResource("/jooq-config.xml")!!
            val jooqCfg = Paths.get(resource.toURI()).toFile()
            GenerationTool.generate(
                Files.readString(jooqCfg.toPath())
            )
        } else {
            // programmatic version 2
            LOGGER.info("... Generating jOOQ using programmatic version 2 with programmatic
            configuration ...")
            GenerationTool.generate(
                Configuration()
                    .withJdbc(
                        Jdbc()
                            .withDriver("org.mariadb.jdbc.Driver")
                            .withUrl("jdbc:mariadb://localhost:3306/musicdb")
                            .withUser("prospring6")
                            .withPassword("prospring6")
                    )
                    .withGenerator(
                        Generator()
                            .withDatabase(
                                Database()
                                    .withName("org.jooq.meta.mariadb.MariaDBDatabase")
                                    .withInputSchema("musicdb")
                                    .withIncludes(".*")
                            )
                            .withGenerate(
                                Generate()
                                    .withPojos(true)
                                    .withPojosToString(true)
                                    .withDaos(true)
                            )
                            .withTarget(
                                Target()
                                    .withPackageName("com.apress.prospring6.seven.jooq.
                                    generated")
                                    .withDirectory("./chapter07-jooq/src/main/generated")
                            )
                    )
            )
        }
    }
}
```

To run the second version, just execute the class with an argument, any argument. The jooq-config. xml file is located in the resources directory, and it contains the same information shown in the full programmatic version in version2, but in XML format.

Notice that the generated sources are saved in a directory named generated, saved at the same level with the kotlin directory, the one that Gradle knows contains the project sources. A small configuration is necessary for Gradle to tell them that the generated directory also contains sources for the project. Separating the generated sources from the concrete project sources is a good practice for clarity reasons and avoiding the risk of overriding concrete classes with generated ones in case of misconfiguration.

If the withDirectory property is not set, the generated sources are put into the target/generated-sources directory. For easy access and visibility, we decided to put them in a more obvious location.

Once the GenerateJOOQSources is executed, the generated directory should be populated with a lot of classes, as shown in Figure 7-3.

Figure 7-3. *Classes generated by jOOQ*

The reason there are so many classes in the generated directory is that the configuration shown in Listing 7-34 requested them through this snippet: `withPojos(true).withPojosToString(true).withDaos(true)`. There are a lot more possible options, all of which you can find in the official documentation. For the example in this book, we just configured for POJO classes to be generated for the tables in the MariaDB schema, `toString()` methods for them, for logging purposes, and DAO classes to manage data. The generated POJO classes look like the Hibernate entity classes but without the annotations. The classes under package `daos` look very similar to the DAO classes we've been writing so far, only the instances returned are of the types declared in the `pojos` package.

Now that we have the classes, let's use them. The first step is to configure jOOQ support in the Spring application, which is quite easy. At the core of jOOQ is a class named `org.jooq.DSLContext`. An instance of this class is the main entry point for client code to access jOOQ classes and functionality that are related to `org.jooq.Query` execution. To configure it properly, it needs a connection to the database and a few details regarding syntax being used when generating queries and other such little things. The most important piece is the database connection. Earlier this chapter presented the BasicDataSourceCfg configuration class that configures a MariaDB DataSource; this class can be reused, because the database connection can be retrieved from it. Listing 7-35 shows the JOOQConfig class that contains a single DSLContext declaration.

Listing 7-35. Spring Configuration Class to Enable Support for jOOQ

```kotlin
package com.apress.prospring6.seven.jooq.config

import org.jooq.DSLContext
import org.jooq.conf.RenderNameCase
import org.jooq.conf.RenderQuotedNames
import org.jooq.conf.Settings
import org.jooq.impl.DSL
import javax.sql.DataSource
import java.sql.SQLException
// other import statements omitted

@Configuration
open class JOOQConfig {
    @Autowired
    var dataSource: DataSource? = null

    @Bean
    open fun dslContext(): DSLContext? {
        try {
            return DSL.using(
                dataSource!!.connection,
                Settings()
                    .withRenderNameCase(RenderNameCase.UPPER)
                    .withRenderQuotedNames(RenderQuotedNames.NEVER)
                    .withRenderSchema(false)
                    .withRenderGroupConcatMaxLenSessionVariable(false)
            ) // needed because of this: https://blog.jooq.org/mysqls-allowmultiqueries-
              flag-with-jdbc-and-jooq/
        } catch (ex: SQLException) {
            LOGGER.error("Problem initializing jOOQ.DSLContext!", ex)
        }
        return null
    }

    companion object {
        private val LOGGER = LoggerFactory.getLogger(JOOQConfig::class.java)
    }
}
```

Notice how the BasicDataSourceCfg configuration class is not imported using @Import. This is because we want to keep the jOOQ configuration detached and only introduce it to the configuration when a context is created.

Now we'll use our new configuration class. The easiest way to keep the project compiling even when the generated classes are not there is to write tests. Another great thing about jOOQ is that it integrates nicely with Spring Test components and Testcontainers, which makes writing tests easier, too. We just had to copy the HibernateTest class and replace the test context annotation configuration and the body of each method, and, *voilà*, we had a class testing SQL native queries generated by jOOQ's DSLContext. Listing 7-36 shows a few test methods from the JOOQDslTest, because you don't have to use the jOOQ-generated DAOs if you don't want to.

Listing 7-36. Testing jOOQ's DSLContext

```kotlin
package com.apress.prospring6.seven

import com.apress.prospring6.seven.base.config.BasicDataSourceCfg
import com.apress.prospring6.seven.jooq.config.JOOQConfig
import com.apress.prospring6.seven.jooq.generated.tables.records.SingerRecord
import org.jooq.DSLContext
import com.apress.prospring6.seven.jooq.generated.tables.Singer.SINGER
// other import statements omitted

@Testcontainers
@SqlMergeMode(SqlMergeMode.MergeMode.MERGE)
@Sql("classpath:testcontainers/drop-schema.sql", "classpath:testcontainers/create-
schema.sql")
@SpringJUnitConfig(classes = [BasicDataSourceCfg::class, JOOQConfig::class])
class JOOQDslTest {
    @Autowired
    var dslContext: DSLContext? = null

    @Test
    @DisplayName("should return all singers")
    fun findAll() {
        val singers: Result<SingerRecord> = dslContext!!.selectFrom<SingerRecord>(SINGE
        R).fetch()
        Assertions.assertEquals(3, singers.size)
    }

    @Test
    @DisplayName("should return singer by id")
    fun testFindById() {
        val singerRecord: SingerRecord = dslContext!!.selectFrom<SingerRecord>(SINGER)
            .where(SINGER.ID.eq(2)).fetchOne()!!
        Assertions.assertNotNull(singerRecord)
        assertEquals("Ben", singerRecord.getFirstName())
    }

    ...

    companion object {
        private val LOGGER = LoggerFactory.getLogger(JOOQDslTest::class.java)

        @Container
        var mariaDB: MariaDBContainer<*> = MariaDBContainer("mariadb:latest")
```

```
        @DynamicPropertySource // this does the magic
        @JvmStatic
        fun setUp(registry: DynamicPropertyRegistry) {
            registry.add("jdbc.driverClassName") { mariaDB.driverClassName }
            registry.add("jdbc.url") { mariaDB.jdbcUrl }
            registry.add("jdbc.username") { mariaDB.username }
            registry.add("jdbc.password") { mariaDB.password }
        }
    }
}
```

Notice that the jOOQ syntax looks a lot like SQL. Also, if logging for org.jooq is configured to DEBUG, when the JOOQDslTest class is run, the generated SQL queries are dumped in the console, but also the results. A log sample is shown in Listing 7-37.

Listing 7-37. Log Snippets for the Execution of the JOOQDslTest Class

```
DEBUG: JooqLogger - Executing query       : select SINGER.ID, SINGER.VERSION, SINGER.
                                            FIRST_NAME, SINGER.LAST_NAME, SINGER.BIRTH_DATE
                                            from SINGER
DEBUG: JooqLogger - Fetched result        : +----+-------+----------+---------+----------+
DEBUG: JooqLogger -                        : |  ID|VERSION|FIRST_NAME|LAST_NAME|BIRTH_DATE|
DEBUG: JooqLogger -                        : +----+-------+----------+---------+----------+
DEBUG: JooqLogger -                        : |   1|      0|John      |Mayer    |1977-10-16|
DEBUG: JooqLogger -                        : |   2|      0|Ben       |Barnes   |1981-08-20|
DEBUG: JooqLogger -                        : |   3|      0|John      |Butler   |1975-04-01|
DEBUG: JooqLogger -                        : +----+-------+----------+---------+----------+
DEBUG: JooqLogger - Fetched row(s)         : 3
...
DEBUG: JooqLogger - Executing query       : select SINGER.ID, SINGER.VERSION, SINGER.FIRST_
                                            NAME, SINGER.LAST_NAME, SINGER.BIRTH_DATE from
                                            SINGER where SINGER.ID = ?
DEBUG: JooqLogger --> with bind values     : select SINGER.ID, SINGER.VERSION, SINGER.FIRST_
                                            NAME, SINGER.LAST_NAME, SINGER.BIRTH_DATE from
                                            SINGER where SINGER.ID = 2
DEBUG: JooqLogger - Fetched result        : +----+-------+----------+---------+----------+
DEBUG: JooqLogger -                        : |  ID|VERSION|FIRST_NAME|LAST_NAME|BIRTH_DATE|
DEBUG: JooqLogger -                        : +----+-------+----------+---------+----------+
DEBUG: JooqLogger -                        : |   2|      0|Ben       |Barnes   |1981-08-20|
DEBUG: JooqLogger -                        : +----+-------+----------+---------+----------+
DEBUG: JooqLogger - Fetched row(s)         : 1
```

Neat, right? What about retrieving singers with albums? This obviously requires a join. This can be done as well, but it requires a little manual work. The advantage is that we can design the classes to store the data and simplify them to hold only the necessary data. For example, we created a record named SingerWithAlbums that only contains the firstName, lastName, and List<AlbumRecord>. As the name indicates, AlbumRecord is also a record, and it only declares two fields, title and releaseDate. Listing 7-38 shows these two records and the test method loading the information using DSLContext.

Listing 7-38. jOOQ Way to Execute a Join Query

```
// ---------
// SingerWithAlbums.kt
data class SingerWithAlbums(val firstName:String,
                            val lastName:String,
                            val birthDate:LocalDate,
                            val albums:MutableList<AlbumRecord>)


// ---------
// AlbumRecord.kt
data class AlbumRecord ( val title:String, val releaseDate: LocalDate)


// ---------
// JOOQDslTest.java

import com.apress.prospring6.seven.base.config.BasicDataSourceCfg
import com.apress.prospring6.seven.jooq.config.JOOQConfig
import com.apress.prospring6.seven.jooq.generated.Tables.*
import com.apress.prospring6.seven.jooq.generated.tables.Singer
import com.apress.prospring6.seven.jooq.generated.tables.SingerInstrument
import com.apress.prospring6.seven.jooq.generated.tables.records.SingerRecord
import com.apress.prospring6.seven.jooq.records.AlbumRecord
import com.apress.prospring6.seven.jooq.records.SingerInstrumentRecord
import com.apress.prospring6.seven.jooq.records.SingerWithAlbums
import com.apress.prospring6.seven.jooq.records.SingerWithInstruments
import org.jooq.*
...


@Testcontainers
@SqlMergeMode(SqlMergeMode.MergeMode.MERGE)
@Sql("classpath:testcontainers/drop-schema.sql", "classpath:testcontainers/create-
schema.sql")
@SpringJUnitConfig(classes = [BasicDataSourceCfg::class, JOOQConfig::class])
class JOOQDslTest {
    ...
    @Test
    @DisplayName("should return all singers with albums as records")
    fun findAllWithAlbumsAsRecords() {
        val singerWithAlbums: List<SingerWithAlbums> =
            dslContext!!.select(
                SINGER.FIRST_NAME,
                SINGER.LAST_NAME,
                SINGER.BIRTH_DATE,
                DSL.multisetAgg<String?,LocalDate?>(ALBUM.TITLE, ALBUM.RELEASE_DATE)
                    .convertFrom<MutableList<AlbumRecord>>(
                        { r ->
                          r.map(
                                mapping { title:String, release:LocalDate ->
                                AlbumRecord(title, release)
                                }
```

```
                    )
                }
            )
        )
        .from(SINGER)
        .innerJoin(ALBUM).on(ALBUM.SINGER_ID.eq(SINGER.ID))
        .groupBy(SINGER.FIRST_NAME, SINGER.LAST_NAME, SINGER.BIRTH_DATE)
        .fetch(mapping{ firstName:String, lastName:String, birthDate:LocalDate,
                            albums:MutableList<AlbumRecord> ->
                SingerWithAlbums(firstName, lastName, birthDate, albums)
        })
    assertEquals(2, singerWithAlbums.size)
}
...
}
```

To make sure we only get the singers that have albums in the databases, we use the innerJoin(..) method. The multisetAgg(..) method is used to aggregate the column of an album into an AlbumRecord. Since we do not want duplicate entries, a groupBy(..) call is also necessary. As you might have noticed, the Kotlin code here looks a lot like its SQL equivalent as well, which makes it very easy to write and enables you to ensure that only the data you are interested in is extracted. The SINGER instance is of type com.apress. prospring6.seven.jooq.generated.tables.Singer that encapsulates all the metadata supporting writing jOOQ queries involving the SINGER table. The same goes for ALBUM and INSTRUMENT, which are not used in this example.

💡   A version of the generated classes is part of the repository, in case you are not interested in generating them yourself.

Listing 7-39 shows a snippet of the findAllWithAlbumsAsRecords() log, showing the generated query and the retrieved data.

Listing 7-39. findAllWithAlbumsAsRecords() Log Snippet Showing the jOOQ-Generated Query

```
DEBUG: JooqLogger - Executing query : select SINGER.FIRST_NAME, SINGER.LAST_NAME, SINGER.BIRTH_DATE,
JSON_MERGE_PRESERVE('[]', CONCAT('[', GROUP_CONCAT(JSON_ARRAY(ALBUM.TITLE, ALBUM.RELEASE_DATE)
separator ','), ']'))
from SINGER
join ALBUM on ALBUM.SINGER_ID = SINGER.ID
group by SINGER.FIRST_NAME, SINGER.LAST_NAME, SINGER.BIRTH_DATE
DEBUG: JooqLogger - Fetched result : +----------+---------+----------+------------------------------+
DEBUG: JooqLogger -            : |FIRST_NAME|LAST_NAME|BIRTH_DATE|multiset_agg                  |
DEBUG: JooqLogger -            : +----------+---------+----------+------------------------------+
DEBUG: JooqLogger -            : |Ben       |Barnes   |1981-08-20|[AlbumRecord[title=11:11,
                                                              releaseDate=..]]            |
DEBUG: JooqLogger -            : |John      |Mayer    |1977-10-16|[AlbumRecord[title=The Search
                                                              For .., r...                |
DEBUG: JooqLogger -            : +----------+---------+----------+------------------------------+
DEBUG: JooqLogger - Fetched row(s) : 2
```

In this example, because we wanted to keep our objects compact, we used some simplified records to represent singer and albums. Here is where Hibernate might meet jOOQ. Instead of mapping the jOOQ retrieved data to records, we could have mapped it to JPA entities.

Writing insert, update, and delete statements is just as easy; feel free to look at the examples provided with the book on your own, because now it's time to cover jOOQ DAO classes. The DAO classes generated by jOOQ are grouped under the daos package, and all of them extend org.jooq.impl.DAOImpl<R extends UpdatableRecord<R>, P, T>. This means that for the SINGER table, a class named SingerDao was created that extends DAOImpl<SingerRecord, com.apress.prospring6.seven.jooq.generated.tables.pojos. Singer, Integer>. This type of class is very similar in concept to the repository implementations generated by Spring Data, which will be introduced later in the book. The SingerRecord id gets generated by jOOQ and its purpose is to represent a singer instance holding a primary key that maps to a database record. This type of class is designed to be used internally by jOOQ, so you should never need to use one directly. The com. apress.prospring6.seven.jooq.generated.tables.pojos.Singer is a view on top of it that you can use in your code to interact with jOOQ DAO classes.

With the previous rather abstract way of looking at things in mind, let's see how we can test jOOQ DAO classes. Listing 7-40 shows two very simple test methods testing the SingerDao class.

Listing 7-40. JOOQDaoTest Class

```kotlin
package com.apress.prospring6.seven

import com.apress.prospring6.seven.base.config.BasicDataSourceCfg
import com.apress.prospring6.seven.jooq.config.JOOQConfig
import com.apress.prospring6.seven.jooq.generated.tables.daos.SingerDao
import org.jooq.DSLContext
// other import statements omitted

@Testcontainers
@SqlMergeMode(SqlMergeMode.MergeMode.MERGE)
@Sql("classpath:testcontainers/drop-schema.sql", "classpath:testcontainers/create-
schema.sql")
@SpringJUnitConfig(classes = [BasicDataSourceCfg::class, JOOQConfig::class])
class JOOQDaoTest {
    @Autowired
    var dslContext: DSLContext? = null

    @Test
    @DisplayName("should return all singers")
    fun findAll() {
        val dao = SingerDao(
            dslContext!!.configuration()
        )
        val singers = dao.findAll()
        Assertions.assertEquals(3, singers.size)
    }

    @Test
    @DisplayName("should return singer by id")
    fun testFindById() {
        val dao = SingerDao(
            dslContext!!.configuration()
        )
```

```kotlin
        val singer = dao.findById(2)
        Assertions.assertNotNull(singer)
        Assertions.assertEquals("Ben", singer!!.firstName)
    }

    @Test
    @SqlGroup(
        Sql(
            scripts = ["classpath:testcontainers/add-nina.sql"],
            executionPhase = Sql.ExecutionPhase.BEFORE_TEST_METHOD
        ),
        Sql(
            scripts = ["classpath:testcontainers/remove-nina.sql"],
            executionPhase = Sql.ExecutionPhase.AFTER_TEST_METHOD
        )
    )
    @DisplayName("should update a singer")
    fun testUpdate() {
        val dao = SingerDao(
            dslContext!!.configuration()
        )
        val nina = dao.findById(5)
        Assertions.assertNotNull(nina)
        nina!!.firstName = "Eunice Kathleen"
        nina.lastName = "Waymon"
        dao.update(nina)
        val updatedNina = dao.findById(5)
        Assertions.assertNotNull(updatedNina)
        Assertions.assertEquals("Eunice Kathleen", updatedNina!!.firstName)
        Assertions.assertEquals("Waymon", updatedNina.lastName)
    }

    companion object {
        @Container
        var mariaDB: MariaDBContainer<*> = MariaDBContainer("mariadb:latest")

        @DynamicPropertySource // this does the magic
        @JvmStatic
        fun setUp(registry: DynamicPropertyRegistry) {
            registry.add("jdbc.driverClassName") { mariaDB.driverClassName }
            registry.add("jdbc.url") { mariaDB.jdbcUrl }
            registry.add("jdbc.username") { mariaDB.username }
            registry.add("jdbc.password") { mariaDB.password }
        }
    }
}
```

Listing 7-41 depicts some snippets of the JOOQDaoTest execution log, showing the generated SQL queries and the data.

Listing 7-41. JOOQDaoTest Class Log Snippets

```
DEBUG: JooqLogger - Executing query    : select SINGER.ID, SINGER.VERSION, SINGER.
                                         FIRST_NAME, SINGER.LAST_NAME, SINGER.BIRTH_DATE
                                         from SINGER
DEBUG: JooqLogger - Fetched result     : +----+-------+----------+---------+----------+
DEBUG: JooqLogger -                    : |  ID|VERSION|FIRST_NAME|LAST_NAME|BIRTH_DATE|
DEBUG: JooqLogger -                    : +----+-------+----------+---------+----------+
DEBUG: JooqLogger -                    : |   1|      0|John      |Mayer    |1977-10-16|
DEBUG: JooqLogger -                    : |   2|      0|Ben       |Barnes   |1981-08-20|
DEBUG: JooqLogger -                    : |   3|      0|John      |Butler   |1975-04-01|
DEBUG: JooqLogger -                    : +----+-------+----------+---------+----------+
DEBUG: JooqLogger - Fetched row(s)     : 3
...
DEBUG: JooqLogger - Executing query    : select SINGER.ID, SINGER.VERSION, SINGER.FIRST_
                                         NAME, SINGER.LAST_NAME, SINGER.BIRTH_DATE from
                                         SINGER where SINGER.ID = ?
DEBUG: JooqLogger --> with bind values : select SINGER.ID, SINGER.VERSION, SINGER.FIRST_
                                         NAME, SINGER.LAST_NAME, SINGER.BIRTH_DATE from
                                         SINGER where SINGER.ID = 2
DEBUG: JooqLogger - Fetched result     : +----+-------+----------+---------+----------+
DEBUG: JooqLogger -                    : |  ID|VERSION|FIRST_NAME|LAST_NAME|BIRTH_DATE|
DEBUG: JooqLogger -                    : +----+-------+----------+---------+----------+
DEBUG: JooqLogger -                    : |   2|      0|Ben       |Barnes   |1981-08-20|
DEBUG: JooqLogger -                    : +----+-------+----------+---------+----------+
DEBUG: JooqLogger - Fetched row(s)     : 1
...
DEBUG: JooqLogger - Executing query    : select SINGER.ID, SINGER.VERSION, SINGER.FIRST_
                                         NAME, SINGER.LAST_NAME, SINGER.BIRTH_DATE from
                                         SINGER where SINGER.ID = ?
DEBUG: JooqLogger --> with bind values : select SINGER.ID, SINGER.VERSION, SINGER.FIRST_
                                         NAME, SINGER.LAST_NAME, SINGER.BIRTH_DATE from
                                         SINGER where SINGER.ID = 5
DEBUG: JooqLogger - Fetched result     : +----+-------+----------+---------+----------+
DEBUG: JooqLogger -                    : |  ID|VERSION|FIRST_NAME|LAST_NAME|BIRTH_DATE|
DEBUG: JooqLogger -                    : +----+-------+----------+---------+----------+
DEBUG: JooqLogger -                    : |   5|      0|Nina      |Simone   |1933-02-21|
DEBUG: JooqLogger -                    : +----+-------+----------+---------+----------+
DEBUG: JooqLogger - Fetched row(s)     : 1
DEBUG: JooqLogger - Executing query    : update SINGER set SINGER.VERSION = ?, SINGER.FIRST_
                                         NAME = ?, SINGER.LAST_NAME = ?, SINGER.BIRTH_DATE =
                                         ? where SINGER.ID = ?
DEBUG: JooqLogger --> with bind values : update SINGER set SINGER.VERSION = 0, SINGER.
                                         FIRST_NAME = 'Eunice Kathleen', SINGER.LAST_NAME
                                         = 'Waymon', SINGER.BIRTH_DATE = date '1933-02-21'
                                         where SINGER.ID = 5
DEBUG: JooqLogger - Affected row(s)    : 1
DEBUG: JooqLogger - Executing query    : select SINGER.ID, SINGER.VERSION, SINGER.FIRST_
                                         NAME, SINGER.LAST_NAME, SINGER.BIRTH_DATE from
                                         SINGER where SINGER.ID = ?
```

```
DEBUG: JooqLogger --> with bind values : select SINGER.ID, SINGER.VERSION, SINGER.FIRST_
                                          NAME, SINGER.LAST_NAME, SINGER.BIRTH_DATE from
                                          SINGER where SINGER.ID = 5
DEBUG: JooqLogger - Fetched result      : +----+-------+---------------+---------+----------+
DEBUG: JooqLogger -                     : |  ID|VERSION|FIRST_NAME     |LAST_NAME|BIRTH_DATE|
DEBUG: JooqLogger -                     : +----+-------+---------------+---------+----------+
DEBUG: JooqLogger -                     : |   5|      0|Eunice Kathleen|Waymon   |1933-02-21|
DEBUG: JooqLogger -                     : +----+-------+---------------+---------+----------+
DEBUG: JooqLogger - Fetched row(s)      : 1
```

The jOOQ-generated POJO classes map completely to the tables they model, which means that when using the DAO classes, we always work with a fully populated object. So if performance is an issue and you need only a small set of columns, using the DSLContext is the better approach.

This section showed you how to configure jOOQ in a Spring application and gave a few usage example to underline a few of the following benefits of using this framework:

- It allows the developer to think in terms of individual objects, rather than sets of objects.

- It saves you from writing SQL queries but allows you to write clear and concise Kotlin code representing the query logic.

- It generates very good, working SQL code, and the Java code provides type safety— there is no way to have a typo in your SQL query if you don't write the SQL query.

- It supports a large number of databases, so if you want to use a relational database in a project, there's a 99% chance you can use jOOQ too.

- It has very good integration with Spring.

Using the jOOQ framework also has a few disadvantages, of course, and this list is just a sampling of what was noticed while writing this section:

- You have to install jOOQ manually on you Maven repo, because it was pulled from Maven Central, starting with version3.16.6.

- Even if you don't have to write SQL queries, the Kotlin syntax for interacting with a database is a language itself. Luckily, the compiler helps here, so usually a compiling Kotlin code results in a valid SQL script.

- Currently there is some confusion regarding which version works with which JDK. For example, the community trial version was supposed to work with JDK 17+, but it didn't at the time of writing.

- Complex SQL queries will be represented by complex Kotlin queries, and traversing large object graphs can become very inefficient, so in the end it is the developer's responsibility to design the database schema properly.

This section was just meant to introduce you to jOOQ as a possible alternative for Hibernate. Its capabilities are very vast and covering them would require an entire book. If jOOQ looks interesting to you, you can advance your knowledge by reading more about it on its official page.

Spring Boot makes things even easier with jOOQ and Hibernate. Since the same library spring-boot-starter-data-jpa is used in **Chapter 8** and the code is pretty much the same as the code for classic non-Boot Spring application, we'll end this chapter here.

Summary

In this chapter, we first discussed the basic concepts of Hibernate and how to configure it within a Spring application. Then we covered common techniques for defining ORM mappings; associations; and how to use the HibernateTemplate class to perform various database operations. With regard to Hibernate, we covered only a small piece of its functionality and features. If you are interested in using Hibernate with Spring, we highly recommend you study Hibernate's standard documentation.

Also, numerous books discuss Hibernate in detail. We recommend *Beginning Hibernate 6* by Joseph Ottinger, Jeff Linwood, and Dave Minter (Apress, 2022)[13], as well as *Pro JPA 2* by Mike Keith and Merrick Schincariol (Apress, 2013)[14].

We also introduced you to jOOQ, a cool framework for generating SQL queries using Java code; jOOQ can be used either together with Hibernate or instead of Hibernate.

Chapter 8 will introduce you to JPA and how to use it when using Spring. Hibernate provides excellent support for JPA, and we will continue to use Hibernate as the persistence provider for the examples in Chapter 8. For query and update operations, JPA act likes Hibernate. We'll also discuss advanced topics including native and criteria query and how we can use Hibernate as well as its JPA support.

---

[13] https://link.springer.com/book/10.1007/978-1-4842-7337-1
[14] https://link.springer.com/book/10.1007/978-1-4302-4927-6

CHAPTER 8

■ ■ ■

Spring with JPA

In **Chapter 7**, we discussed how to use Hibernate with Spring when implementing data access logic with the ORM approach. We demonstrated how to configure Hibernates `SessionFactory` in Spring's configuration and how to use the Session interface for various data access operations. However, that is just one way Hibernate can be used. Another way of adopting Hibernate in a Spring application is to use Hibernate as a persistence provider of the standard Java Persistence API (JPA), now renamed to Jakarta Persistence API.

Hibernate's POJO mapping and its powerful query language (HQL) have gained great success and also influenced the development of data access technology standards in the Java world. After Hibernate, the Java Community Process members developed the Java Data Objects (JDO) standard and then JPA.

At the time of this writing JPA has reached version 3.1[1] and provides concepts that were standardized such as `PersistenceContext`, `EntityManager`, and the Java Persistence Query Language (JPQL). These standardizations provide a way for developers to switch between JPA persistence providers such as Hibernate, EclipseLink, Oracle TopLink, and Apache OpenJPA. As a result, most new JEE applications are adopting JPA as the data access layer.

Spring also provides excellent support for JPA. For example, the Spring container creates and manages an `EntityManager` instance, injecting it in the respective JPA components, based on a `EntityManagerFactoryBean` bean.

The Spring Data project also provides a subproject called Spring Data JPA, which provides advanced support for using JPA in Spring applications. The main features of the Spring Data JPA project include concepts of a repository and specification and support for the Query Domain-Specific Language (QueryDSL).

This chapter covers how to use JPA 3.1, recently outsourced by Oracle and thus renamed to Jakarta Persistence API[2], with Spring, using Hibernate as the underlying persistence provider. You will learn how to implement various database operations by using JPA's `EntityManager` interface and JPQL. Then you will see how Spring Data JPA can further help simplify JPA development. Finally, we present advanced topics related to ORM, including native queries and criteria queries.

Specifically, we discuss the following topics:

- *Core concepts of Jakarta Persistence API (JPA)*: We cover major concepts of JPA.

- *Configuring the JPA entity manager*: We discuss the types of `EntityManagerFactory` that Spring supports and how to configure the most commonly used one, `LocalContainerEntityManagerFactoryBean`.

- *Data operations*: We show how to implement basic database operations in JPA, which is much like the concepts when using Hibernate on its own.

- *Advanced query operations*: We discuss how to use native queries in JPA and the strongly typed Criteria API in JPA for more flexible query operations.

---

[1] https://jakarta.ee/specifications/persistence/3.1
[2] https://github.com/eclipse-ee4j/jpa-api

> ℹ️ Like Hibernate, JPA supports the definition of mappings either in XML or in Java/Kotlin annotations. This chapter focuses on the annotation type of mapping because its usage tends to be much more popular than the XML style.

Introducing JPA 3.1

Like other Java Specification Requests (JSRs), the objective of the JPA 2.1 specification as defined by JSR-338[3] is to standardize the ORM programming model in both the JSE and JEE environments. It defines a common set of concepts, annotations, interfaces, and other services that a JPA persistence provider should implement. When programming to the JPA standard, developers have the option of switching the underlying provider at will, just like switching to another JEE-compliant application server for applications developed on the JEE standards. Since Oracle is no longer in charge of JPA development, there will be no other JSRs for it in the future, but you can read about the latest releases on its Jakarta EE official site. The version used in this project is JPA version 3.1.

The core concept of JPA is the `EntityManager` interface, which comes from factories of the type `EntityManagerFactory`. The main job of `EntityManager` is to maintain a persistence context, in which all the entity instances managed by it will be stored. The configuration of `EntityManager` is defined as a *persistence unit*, and there can be more than one persistence unit in an application. If you are using Hibernate, you can think of the persistence context in the same way as the `Session` interface, while `EntityManagerFactory` is the same as `SessionFactory`. In Hibernate, the managed entities are stored in the session, which you can directly interact with via Hibernate's `SessionFactory` or `Session` interface. In JPA, however, you can't interact with the persistence context directly. Instead, you need to rely on `EntityManager` to do the work for you.

JPQL is similar to HQL, so if you have used HQL before, JPQL should be easy to pick up. However, in JPA 2, a strongly typed Criteria API was introduced, which relies on the mapped entities' metadata to construct the query. Given this, any errors will be discovered at compile time rather than runtime.

For a detailed discussion of JPA 2, we recommend the book *Pro JPA 2*[4] by Mike Keith and Merrick Schincariol (Apress, 2013).1 In this section, we discuss the basic concepts of JPA, the sample data model that will be used in this chapter, and how to configure Spring's *ApplicationContext* to support JPA.

Sample Data Model for Example Code

In this chapter, we use the same data model as used in **Chapter 7**. To get started, we will begin with the same database creation scripts used in Chapter 7. If you skipped Chapter 7, take a look at the data model presented in that chapter's "Sample Data Model for Example Code" section, which can help you understand the sample code in this chapter.

---

[3] https://jcp.org/aboutJava/communityprocess/final/jsr338/index.html
[4] https://link.springer.com/book/10.1007/978-1-4302-1957-6

Configuring JPA's `EntityManagerFactory`

As mentioned earlier in this chapter, to use JPA in Spring, we need to configure `EntityManagerFactory`, just like `SessionFactory` used in Hibernate. Spring supports three types of `EntityManagerFactory` configurations.

The first option uses the `LocalEntityManagerFactoryBean` class. It's the simplest one, which requires only the persistence unit name. However, since it doesn't support the injection of `DataSource` and hence isn't able to participate in global transactions, it's suitable only for simple development purposes.

The second option is for use in a JEE-compliant container, in which the application server bootstraps the JPA persistence unit based on the information in the deployment descriptors. This allows Spring to look up the entity manager via the JNDI JEE namespace. This obviously means that XML configuration is needed for this. The configuration snippet in Listing 8-1 depicts the element needed for looking up an entity manager via JNDI.

Listing 8-1. Spring XML Configuration Snippet Using JNDI JEE Namespace for Lookup

```
<beans ...>
    <jee:jndi-lookup id="prospring6Emf"
        jndi-name="persistence/prospring6PersistenceUnit"/>
</beans>
```

In the JPA specification, a persistence unit should be defined in the configuration file `META-INF/persistence.xml`. However, as of Spring 3.1, a new feature has been added that eliminates this need; we show you how to use it later in this chapter.

Luckily, there are various Kotlin configuration alternatives that can be used in a Spring `@Configuration` class. The configuration presented in Listing 8-2 is the most compact of them.

Listing 8-2. Spring Annotated Configuration Snippet Using JNDI JEE Namespace for Lookup

```
package com.apress.prospring6.eight.config

import org.springframework.context.annotation.Bean
import org.springframework.context.annotation.Configuration
import org.springframework.jdbc.datasource.lookup.JndiDataSourceLookup;
import javax.sql.DataSource

@Configuration
open class JndiDataSourceCfg {
    @Bean
    open fun dataSource(): DataSource {
        val dsLookup = JndiDataSourceLookup()
        dsLookup.isResourceRef = true
        return dsLookup.getDataSource("persistence/prospring6PersistenceUnit")
    }
}
```

The third option, which is the most common and is used in this chapter, is the `LocalContainerEntityManagerFactoryBean` class that supports the injection of `DataSource` and can participate in both local and global transactions. Listing 8-3 depicts the configuration snippet.

Listing 8-3. Spring Annotated Configuration Using LocalContainerEntityManagerFactoryBean

```kotlin
package com.apress.prospring6.eight.config

import org.hibernate.cfg.Environment
import org.hibernate.jpa.HibernatePersistenceProvider
// other import statements omitted

@Configuration
@PropertySource("classpath:db/jdbc.properties")
open class BasicDataSourceCfg {
    @Value("\${jdbc.driverClassName}")
    private val driverClassName: String? = null

    @Value("\${jdbc.url}")
    private val url: String? = null

    @Value("\${jdbc.username}")
    private val username: String? = null

    @Value("\${jdbc.password}")
    private val password: String? = null

    @Bean(destroyMethod = "close")
    open fun dataSource(): DataSource? {
        return try {
            val hc = HikariConfig().apply {
                jdbcUrl = url
                driverClassName = this@BasicDataSourceCfg.driverClassName
                username = this@BasicDataSourceCfg.username
                password = this@BasicDataSourceCfg.password
            }
            val dataSource = HikariDataSource(hc)
            dataSource.maximumPoolSize =
                25 // 25 is a good enough data pool size, it is a database in a container
                after all
            dataSource
        } catch (e: Exception) {
            LOGGER.error("Hikari DataSource bean cannot be created!", e)
            null
        }
    }

    companion object {
        private val LOGGER = LoggerFactory.getLogger(BasicDataSourceCfg::class.java)
    }
}
```

In this configuration, several beans are declared in order to be able to support the configuration of `LocalContainerEntityManagerFactoryBean` with Hibernate as the persistence provider. The purpose for each bean is described next:

- *Component scan*: The tag should be familiar to you. We instruct Spring to scan the components under the package `com.apress.prospring6.eight.service`.

- `dataSource`: This bean is injected and it is declared in a separate configuration class that contains only database-specific beans and properties (e.g., `BasicDataSourceCfg` introduced in **Chapter 7**).

- `transactionManager`: `EntityManagerFactory` requires a transaction manager for transactional data access. Spring provides a transaction manager specifically for JPA (`org.springframework.orm.jpa.JpaTransactionManager`). The bean is declared with an ID of `transactionManager` assigned. We discuss transactions in detail in **Chapter 9**. The `@EnableTransactionManagement` annotation is needed to support a declaration of the transaction demarcation requirements using annotations, but for now notice that this bean needs an `EntityManagerFactory` instance to be created that is provided by the `EntityManagerFactoryBean`, by calling `getObject();`.

- `JpaVendorAdapter`: This bean allows us to plug in vendor-specific behavior into Spring's `EntityManagerFactory` creators. In this case we are using Hibernate, and thus the type of the bean is `HibernateJpaVendorAdapter`.

- `EntityManagerFactoryBean`: This JPA bean is the most important part of this configuration. However, it is not part of it directly, but instead a `LocalContainerEntityManagerFactoryBean` bean is declared.

  - This bean needs the `DataSource` bean injected.

  - Second, we configure the property `jpaVendorAdapter` with the `HibernateJpaVendorAdapter` that is part of this configuration.

  - Third, although commented, it deserves a mention: calling the `setPersistenceProviderClass(..)` method sets the `PersistenceProvider` implementation class to use for creating the `EntityManagerFactory`. If not specified, the persistence provider will be taken from the `JpaVendorAdapter` (if any) or retrieved through scanning (as far as possible). This also means, when specified, the `JpaVendorAdapter` bean is no longer necessary.

  - Forth, we instruct the entity factory bean to scan for the domain objects with ORM annotations under the package `com.apress.prospring6.eight.entities` by setting the `packagesToScan` property to this value.

Note that this feature has been available only since Spring 3.1, at the same time with the introduction of support for domain class scanning, that allows to ditch the definition of the persistence unit from the `META-INF/persistence.xml` file.

  - Finally, the `jpaProperties` property provides configuration details for the Hibernate persistence provider. The configuration options are the same as some used in **Chapter 7**.

Using JPA Annotations for ORM Mapping

If you read **Chapter 7** you might have noticed that the annotations used to configure entity classes were JPA annotations. Hibernate used to have a set of its own, but when JPA was developed the team behind it decided to keep things simple and adopt the new specification. This is the reason why, if you take a look at the domain classes' source code in **Chapter 7**, you will see that same mapping annotations are used.

Once EntityManagerFactory has been properly configured, injecting it into your classes is simple. Let's start with a simple service class.

In a multilayered application, service classes depend on repository classes and service beans are the ones that are usually annotated with @Transactional, so that related repository calls can be grouped in the same transaction. Since the service classes in this project do nothing but call repository classes, we decided to combine the two, and thus a service class is annotated with @Repository and @Transactional.

The purpose of doing this is for simplicity, and except for academic purposes, you might never need to write code like this.

The @Transactional annotations are shown in the code of this chapter, because executing database operations outside of a transaction is not something you might ever want to do, unless you are using a database as a service (e.g., DynamoDB). Transactions are discussed in detail in **Chapter 9**.

The SingerService interface shown in Listing 8-4 declares the methods expected for the bean type to implement.

Listing 8-4. SingerService Interface

```
package com.apress.prospring6.eight.service

import com.apress.prospring6.eight.entities.Singer
import java.util.Optional
import java.util.stream.Stream

interface SingerService {
    fun findAll(): Stream<Singer>
    fun findAllWithAlbum(): Stream<Singer>
    fun findById(id: Long): Singer?
    fun save(singer: Singer)
    fun delete(singer: Singer)
    fun findAllByNativeQuery(): Stream<Singer>
    fun findFirstNameById(id: Long): String?
    fun findFirstNameByIdUsingProc(id: Long): String?
```

```kotlin
    companion object {
        const val ALL_SINGER_NATIVE_QUERY = "select ID, FIRST_NAME, LAST_NAME, BIRTH_DATE,
        VERSION from SINGER"
    }
}
```

The interface is very simple; it has just three finder methods, one save(..) method, and one delete(..) method. The save(..) method will serve both the insert and update operations. To keep things interesting and a little different, we've also changed the type returned by the methods from Set<T> to Stream<T>.

Listing 8-5 shows the code for the SingerServiceImpl class that implements the SingerService interface, which we will use as the sample for performing database operations using JPA.

Listing 8-5. SingerServiceImpl Bean Type

```kotlin
package com.apress.prospring6.eight.service

import jakarta.persistence.EntityManager
import jakarta.persistence.TypedQuery
import jakarta.persistence.PersistenceContext
// other import statements omitted

@Service("jpaSingerService")
@Repository
@Transactional
class SingerServiceImpl : SingerService {
    @PersistenceContext
    private val em: EntityManager? = null

    @Transactional(readOnly = true)
    override fun findAllWithAlbum(): Stream<Singer> {
        return em!!.createNamedQuery(
            Singer.FIND_ALL_WITH_ALBUM,
            Singer::class.java
        ).resultList.stream()
    }

    @Transactional(readOnly = true)
    override fun findAll(): Stream<Singer> {
        return em!!.createNamedQuery(
            Singer.FIND_ALL,
            Singer::class.java
        ).resultList.stream()
    }

    @Transactional(readOnly = true)
    override fun findById(id: Long): Singer? {
        val query = em!!.createNamedQuery(
            Singer.FIND_SINGER_BY_ID,
            Singer::class.java
        )
```

```kotlin
        query.setParameter("id", id)
        return try {
            query.singleResult
        } catch (nre: NoResultException) {
            null
        }
    }

    override fun save(singer: Singer) {
        if (singer.id == null) {
            LOGGER.info("Inserting new singer")
            em!!.persist(singer)
        } else {
            em!!.merge(singer)
            LOGGER.info("Updating existing singer")
        }
    }

    override fun delete(singer: Singer) {
        val mergedContact = em!!.merge(singer)
        em.remove(mergedContact)
        LOGGER.info("Singer with id: " + singer.id + " deleted successfully")
    }

    override fun findAllByNativeQuery(): Stream<Singer> {
        return em!!.createNativeQuery(SingerService.ALL_SINGER_NATIVE_QUERY,
            "singerResult")
            .resultList.stream() as Stream<Singer>
    }

    override fun findFirstNameById(id: Long): String {
        return em!!.createNamedQuery("Singer.getFirstNameById(?)")
            .setParameter(1, id).singleResult.toString()
    }

    override fun findFirstNameByIdUsingProc(id: Long): String {
        val query = em!!.createNamedStoredProcedureQuery("getFirstNameByIdProc")
        query.setParameter("in_id", 1L)
        query.execute()
        return query.getOutputParameterValue("fn_res") as String
    }

    companion object {
        private val LOGGER = LoggerFactory.getLogger(SingerServiceImpl::class.java)
    }
}
```

Several annotations are applied to the class:

- The @Service annotation is used to identify the class as being a Spring component that provides business services to another layer and assigns the Spring bean the name jpaSingerService.

- The @Repository annotation indicates that the class contains data access logic and instructs Spring to translate the vendor-specific exceptions to Spring's DataAccessException hierarchy.

- The @Transactional annotation is used for defining transaction requirements.

To inject EntityManager, we use the @PersistenceContext annotation, which is the standard JPA annotation for entity manager injection. It may be questionable as to why we're using the name @PersistenceContext to inject an entity manager, but if you consider that the persistence context itself is managed by EntityManager, the annotation naming makes perfect sense. If you have multiple persistence units in your application, you can also add the unitName attribute to the annotation to specify which persistence unit you want to be injected. Typically, a persistence unit represents an individual back-end DataSource.

Performing Database Operations with JPA

Executing queries and managing data with EntityManager is similar to using Hibernate's SessionFactory, the only difference being that there is no session involved.

The syntax for JPQL and HQL is so similar that all the HQL queries that we used in **Chapter 7** are reusable to implement the finder methods within the SingerService interface. To use JPA and Hibernate, the exact set of dependencies from Chapter 7 are required; the most important are spring-orm and hibernate-core-jakarta. The latter is the one that depends on Jakarta's persistence-api.jar and adds it to the classpath as a transitive dependency. Figure 8-1 shows the dependencies of this project in the Gradle View of IntelliJ IDEA.

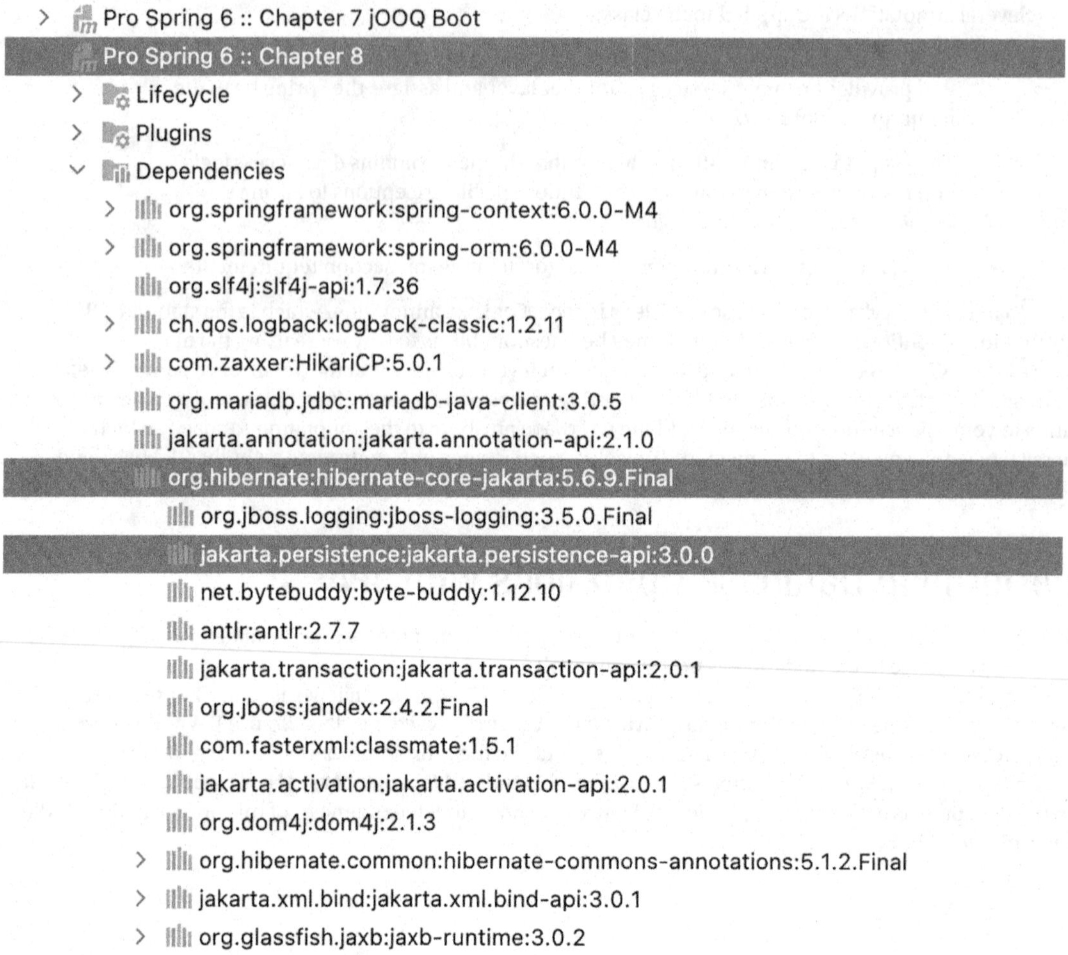

> 🗂 Pro Spring 6 :: Chapter 7 jOOQ Boot
  🗂 Pro Spring 6 :: Chapter 8
  > 📁 Lifecycle
  > 📁 Plugins
  ∨ 📁 Dependencies
    > ▥ org.springframework:spring-context:6.0.0-M4
    > ▥ org.springframework:spring-orm:6.0.0-M4
      ▥ org.slf4j:slf4j-api:1.7.36
    > ▥ ch.qos.logback:logback-classic:1.2.11
    > ▥ com.zaxxer:HikariCP:5.0.1
      ▥ org.mariadb.jdbc:mariadb-java-client:3.0.5
      ▥ jakarta.annotation:jakarta.annotation-api:2.1.0
      ▥ org.hibernate:hibernate-core-jakarta:5.6.9.Final
      ▥ org.jboss.logging:jboss-logging:3.5.0.Final
      ▥ jakarta.persistence:jakarta.persistence-api:3.0.0
      ▥ net.bytebuddy:byte-buddy:1.12.10
      ▥ antlr:antlr:2.7.7
      ▥ jakarta.transaction:jakarta.transaction-api:2.0.1
      ▥ org.jboss:jandex:2.4.2.Final
      ▥ com.fasterxml:classmate:1.5.1
      ▥ jakarta.activation:jakarta.activation-api:2.0.1
      ▥ org.dom4j:dom4j:2.1.3
    > ▥ org.hibernate.common:hibernate-commons-annotations:5.1.2.Final
    > ▥ jakarta.xml.bind:jakarta.xml.bind-api:3.0.1
    > ▥ org.glassfish.jaxb:jaxb-runtime:3.0.2

Figure 8-1. Spring with Hibernate JPA project dependencies

Using the Java Persistence Query Language to Query Data

Listing 8-6 recaps the important bits of code for the Singer domain object model class introduced **Chapter 7**. (The other classes won't be depicted.)

Listing 8-6. Singer Domain Object

```
package com.apress.prospring6.eight.entities

import jakarta.persistence.*
import java.io.Serial
// other import statements omitted

@Entity
@Table(name = "SINGER")
```

```
@NamedQueries(
        NamedQuery(name = Singer.FIND_ALL, query = "select s from Singer s"),
        NamedQuery(
                name = Singer.FIND_SINGER_BY_ID,
                query = """
                                select distinct s from Singer s
                                left join fetch s.albums a
                                        left join fetch s.instruments i
                                        where s.id = :id
                                """
                ),
        NamedQuery(
                name = Singer.FIND_ALL_WITH_ALBUM,
                query = """
                                select distinct s from Singer s
                                        left join fetch s.albums a
                                        left join fetch s.instruments i
                                """
        )
)
@SqlResultSetMapping(name = "singerResult",
    entities = [EntityResult(entityClass = Singer::class)])
@NamedNativeQueries(
        NamedNativeQuery(name = "Singer.getFirstNameById(?)",
                                        query = "select getfirstnamebyid(?)")
)
@NamedStoredProcedureQuery(
        name = "getFirstNameByIdProc",
        procedureName = "getFirstNameByIdProc",
        parameters = [StoredProcedureParameter(
                name = "in_id",
                type = Long::class,
                mode = ParameterMode.IN
        ), StoredProcedureParameter(name = "fn_res", type = String::class,
                                                mode = ParameterMode.OUT)]
)
class Singer : AbstractEntity() {
        @get:Column(name = "FIRST_NAME")
        var firstName: String? = null

        @get:Column(name = "LAST_NAME")
        var lastName: String? = null

        @get:Column(name = "BIRTH_DATE")
        var birthDate: LocalDate? = null

        @get:OneToMany(
                mappedBy = "singer",
                cascade = [CascadeType.ALL],
                orphanRemoval = true
        )
```

```kotlin
    var albums: MutableSet<Album> = mutableSetOf()

    @get:JoinTable(
            name = "SINGER_INSTRUMENT",
            joinColumns = [JoinColumn(name = "SINGER_ID")],
            inverseJoinColumns = [JoinColumn(name = "INSTRUMENT_ID")]
    )
    @get:ManyToMany
    var instruments: MutableSet<Instrument> = mutableSetOf()

    fun addAlbum(album: Album): Boolean {
            album.singer = this
            return albums.add(album)
    }

    fun removeAlbum(album: Album) {
            albums.remove(album)
    }

    fun addInstrument(instrument: Instrument): Boolean {
            return instruments.add(instrument)
    }

    override fun equals(other: Any?): Boolean {
            if (this === other) return true
            if (other == null || javaClass != other.javaClass) return false
            val singer = other as Singer
            return if (id != null) {
                    id == other.id
            } else firstName == singer.firstName && lastName == singer.lastName
    }

    override fun hashCode(): Int {
            return Objects.hash(firstName, lastName)
    }

    override fun toString(): String {
            return ("Singer - Id: " + id + ", First name: " + firstName
                            + ", Last name: " + lastName + ", Birthday: " + birthDate)
    }

    companion object {
            @Serial
            private val serialVersionUID = 2L
            const val FIND_ALL = "Singer.findAll"
            const val FIND_SINGER_BY_ID = "Singer.findById"
            const val FIND_ALL_WITH_ALBUM = "Singer.findAllWithAlbum"
    }
}
```

If you analyze the queries defined using @NamedQuery, you will see that there seems to be no difference between HQL and JPQL, at least not for the simple queries anyway. Now that we have entity classes and configuration, we can start implementing the methods to interact with the database. Let's begin by writing the findAll() method, which simply retrieves all the singers from the database. The method implementation is depicted in Listing 8-7.

Listing 8-7. findAll() Method Implemented Using EntityManager

```
package com.apress.prospring6.eight.service
// import statements omitted

@Service("jpaSingerService")
@Repository
@Transactional
class SingerServiceImpl : SingerService {
    @PersistenceContext
    private val em: EntityManager? = null

    @Transactional(readOnly = true)
    override fun findAll(): Stream<Singer> {
        return em!!.createNamedQuery(
            Singer.FIND_ALL,
            Singer::class.java
        ).resultList.stream()
    }

    ...

}
```

As shown in Listing 8-7, we use the EntityManager.createNamedQuery() method, passing in the name of the query and the expected return type. The method returns an instance of TypedQuery<X>. The accessor .resultList is then called to retrieve the singers, which are then returned as a stream. To test the implementation of the method, a test class is built that uses Testcontainers to spin up a MariaDB test container to run the queries on. The test method used to test SingerServiceImpl.findAll() and the Testcontainers setup are shown in Listing 8-8 (the latter will be omitted from future test samples).

Listing 8-8. Testing the findAll() Method

```
package com.apress.prospring6.eight

import org.testcontainers.containers.MariaDBContainer
import org.testcontainers.junit.jupiter.Container
import org.testcontainers.junit.jupiter.Testcontainers
import static org.junit.jupiter.api.Assertions.assertEquals
// other import statements omitted

@Testcontainers
@SqlMergeMode(SqlMergeMode.MergeMode.MERGE)
@Sql("classpath:testcontainers/drop-schema.sql", "classpath:testcontainers/create-
schema.sql")
@SpringJUnitConfig(classes = [SingerServiceTest.TestContainersConfig::class])
class SingerServiceTest {
```

```kotlin
    @Autowired
    @Qualifier("jpaSingerService")
    var singerService: SingerService? = null

    @Autowired
    var singerSummaryService: SingerSummaryService? = null

    @Test
    @DisplayName("should return all singers")
    fun testFindAll() {
        val singers: List<Singer> = singerService!!.findAll()!!
            .peek(
                Consumer { singer: Singer ->
                    LOGGER.info(
                        singer.toString()
                    )
                }).toList()
        Assertions.assertEquals(3, singers.size)
    }

    @Configuration
    @Import(JpaConfig::class)
    open class TestContainersConfig {
        @Autowired
        var jpaProperties: Properties? = null
        @PostConstruct
        open fun initialize() {
            jpaProperties!![Environment.FORMAT_SQL] = true
            jpaProperties!![Environment.USE_SQL_COMMENTS] = true
            jpaProperties!![Environment.SHOW_SQL] = true
        }
    }

    companion object {
        private val LOGGER = LoggerFactory.getLogger(SingerServiceTest::class.java)

        @Container
        var mariaDB: MariaDBContainer<*> = MariaDBContainer("mariadb:latest")

        @DynamicPropertySource // this does the magic
        @JvmStatic
        fun setUp(registry: DynamicPropertyRegistry) {
            registry.add("jdbc.driverClassName") { mariaDB.driverClassName }
            registry.add("jdbc.url") { mariaDB.jdbcUrl }
            registry.add("jdbc.username") { mariaDB.username }
            registry.add("jdbc.password") { mariaDB.password }
        }
    }
}
```

The TestContainersConfig class is introduced to override the Hibernate variables that control showing the generated SQL queries. If assertEquals() does not throw an exception (the test fails), running the testFindAll() test method produces the output shown in Listing 8-9.

Listing 8-9. Snippets of the Console Output When Running the testFindAll() Test Method

```
/* 1 */ DEBUG: LocalContainerEntityManagerFactoryBean - Building JPA container
EntityManagerFactory for persistence unit 'default'
DEBUG: LogHelper - PersistenceUnitInfo [
    name: default
    persistence provider classname: null
    classloader: jdk.internal.loader.ClassLoaders$AppClassLoader@5ffd2b27
    excludeUnlistedClasses: true
    JTA datasource: null
    Non JTA datasource: org.apache.tomcat.dbcp.dbcp2.BasicDataSource@40247d48
    Transaction type: RESOURCE_LOCAL
    PU root URL: file:/Users/iulianacosmina/apress/workspace/pro-spring-6/chapter08/build/
    classes/java/test/
    Shared Cache Mode: UNSPECIFIED
    Validation Mode: AUTO
    Jar files URLs []
    Managed classes names [
        com.apress.prospring6.eight.entities.AbstractEntity
        com.apress.prospring6.eight.entities.Album
        com.apress.prospring6.eight.entities.Instrument
        com.apress.prospring6.eight.entities.Singer]
    Mapping files names []
    Properties []
...
/* 2 */ DEBUG: JdbcEnvironmentInitiator - Database ->
        name : MariaDB
     version : 10.7.4-MariaDB-1:10.7.4+maria~focal
       major : 10
       minor : 7
...
/* 3 */ DEBUG: SqlStatementLogger - select singer0_.ID as id1_2_,
        singer0_.VERSION as version2_2_,
        singer0_.BIRTH_DATE as birth_da3_2_,
        singer0_.FIRST_NAME as first_na4_2_,
        singer0_.LAST_NAME as last_nam5_2_
    from SINGER singer0_
...
/* 4 */ INFO : SingerServiceTest - Singer - Id: 1, First name: John, Last name: Mayer,
Birthday: 1977-10-16
INFO : SingerServiceTest - Singer - Id: 2, First name: Ben, Last name: Barnes, Birthday:
1981-08-20
INFO : SingerServiceTest - Singer - Id: 3, First name: John, Last name: Butler, Birthday:
1975-04-01
```

This output consists of four different snippets:

- /* 1 */ is the EntityManager configuration used in this test context.

- /* 2 */ includes the properties of the container used to run the tests.

- /* 3 */ is the SQL native query generated for the Singer.findAll query.

- /* 4 */ shows the results returned by the execution of the Singer.findAll query.

❗ For associations, the JPA specification states that, by default, the persistence providers must fetch the association eagerly. However, for Hibernate's JPA implementation, the default fetching strategy is still lazy. So, when using Hibernate's JPA implementation, you don't need to explicitly define an association as lazy fetching. The default fetching strategy of Hibernate is different from the JPA specification.

Now let's implement the findAllWithAlbum() method, which will fetch the associated albums and instruments. The implementation is shown in Listing 8-10.

Listing 8-10. The findAllWithAlbum() Method

```
package com.apress.prospring6.eight.service
// all import statements omitted

/*
Annotation from Singer.java, to show the JQL query
@NamedQuery(name=Singer.FIND_ALL_WITH_ALBUM,
    query="select distinct s from Singer s " +
            "left join fetch s.albums a " +
            "left join fetch s.instruments i")
*/
@Service("jpaSingerService")
@Repository
@Transactional
class SingerServiceImpl : SingerService {
    @PersistenceContext
    private val em: EntityManager? = null

    @Transactional(readOnly = true)
    override fun findAllWithAlbum(): Stream<Singer> {
        return em!!.createNamedQuery(
            Singer.FIND_ALL_WITH_ALBUM,
            Singer::class.java
        ).resultList.stream()
    }
    ...
}
```

The findAllWithAlbum() method is the same as the findAll() method, but it uses a different named query with inner join fetch statements that are used to link records from different tables. The method used to test it and print the entries is shown in Listing 8-11.

Listing 8-11. Testing the findAllWithAlbum() Method

```
package com.apress.prospring6.eight
// all import statements omitted

// annotation omitted
class SingerServiceTest {
    @Autowired
    @Qualifier("jpaSingerService")
    var singerService: SingerService? = null

    @Autowired
    var singerSummaryService: SingerSummaryService? = null

    @Test
    @DisplayName("should return all singers with albums")
    fun testFindAllWithAlbum() {
        val singers: List<Singer> = singerService!!.findAllWithAlbum()!!
            .peek(
                Consumer { s: Singer ->
                    LOGGER.info(s.toString())
                    if (s.albums != null) {
                        s.albums.forEach(Consumer { a: Album ->
                            LOGGER.info(
                                "\tAlbum:$a"
                            )
                        })
                    }
                    if (s.instruments != null) {
                        s.instruments.forEach(Consumer { i: Instrument ->
                            LOGGER.info(
                                "\tInstrument: " + i.instrumentId
                            )
                        })
                    }
                }).toList()
        Assertions.assertEquals(3, singers.size)
    }
    ...
}
```

The JQL query is simple, but the generated SQL query is not so simple, as shown by the output of this method execution, depicted in Listing 8-12.

Listing 8-12. Snippets of the Console Output When Running the testFindAllWithAlbum() Test Method

```
DEBUG: SqlStatementLogger - select distinct singer0_.ID as id1_2_0_,
    albums1_.ID as id1_0_1_,
    instrument3_.INSTRUMENT_ID as instrume1_1_2_,
    singer0_.VERSION as version2_2_0_,
    singer0_.BIRTH_DATE as birth_da3_2_0_,
    singer0_.FIRST_NAME as first_na4_2_0_,
```

415

```
            singer0_.LAST_NAME as last_nam5_2_0_,
            albums1_.VERSION as version2_0_1_,
            albums1_.RELEASE_DATE as release_3_0_1_,
            albums1_.SINGER_ID as singer_i5_0_1_,
            albums1_.title as title4_0_1_,
            albums1_.SINGER_ID as singer_i5_0_0__,
            albums1_.ID as id1_0_0__,
            instrument2_.SINGER_ID as singer_i1_3_1__,
            instrument2_.INSTRUMENT_ID as instrume2_3_1__
        from SINGER singer0_
        left outer join ALBUM albums1_ on singer0_.ID=albums1_.SINGER_ID
        left outer join SINGER_INSTRUMENT instrument2_ on singer0_.ID=instrument2_.SINGER_ID
        left outer join INSTRUMENT instrument3_ on instrument2_.INSTRUMENT_ID=instrument3_.
        INSTRUMENT_ID
...
INFO : SingerServiceTest - Singer - Id: 1, First name: John, Last name: Mayer, Birthday:
        1977-10-16
INFO : SingerServiceTest -  Album:Album - Id: 1, Singer id: 1, Title: The Search For
        Everything, Release Date: 2017-01-20
INFO : SingerServiceTest -  Album:Album - Id: 2, Singer id: 1, Title: Battle Studies,
        Release Date: 2009-11-17
INFO : SingerServiceTest -  Instrument: Piano
INFO : SingerServiceTest -  Instrument: Guitar
INFO : SingerServiceTest - Singer - Id: 2, First name: Ben, Last name: Barnes, Birthday:
        1981-08-20
INFO : SingerServiceTest -  Album:Album - Id: 3, Singer id: 2, Title: 11:11, Release Date:
        2021-09-18
INFO : SingerServiceTest -  Instrument: Piano
INFO : SingerServiceTest -  Instrument: Drums
INFO : SingerServiceTest -  Instrument: Guitar
INFO : SingerServiceTest - Singer - Id: 3, First name: John, Last name: Butler, Birthday:
        1975-04-01
```

Now let's see the findById() method, which demonstrates how to use a named query with named parameters in JPA. The associations will be fetched as well. Listing 8-13 shows the implementation.

Listing 8-13. The findById() Method

```
package com.apress.prospring6.eight.service

import jakarta.persistence.NoResultException
// all import statements omitted

/*
Annotation from Singer.java, to show the JQL query
@NamedQuery(name=Singer.FIND_SINGER_BY_ID,
            query="""
                select distinct s from Singer s
                left join fetch s.albums a
                left join fetch s.instruments i
                where s.id = :id
                """)
```

```
*/
@Service("jpaSingerService")
@Repository
@Transactional
class SingerServiceImpl : SingerService {
    @PersistenceContext
    private val em: EntityManager? = null

    @Transactional(readOnly = true)
    override fun findById(id: Long): Singer? {
        val query = em!!.createNamedQuery(
            Singer.FIND_SINGER_BY_ID,
            Singer::class.java
        )
        query.setParameter("id", id)
        return try {
            query.singleResult
        } catch (nre: NoResultException) {
            null
        }
    }
    ...
}
```

EntityManager.createNamedQuery(java.lang.String name, java.lang.Class<T> resultClass) was called to get an instance of the TypedQuery<T> interface, which ensures that the result of the query must be of type Singer. Then the TypedQuery<T>.setParameter() method was used to set the values of the named parameters within the query and to invoke the .singleResult accessor, since the result should contain only a single Singer object with the specified ID. Testing it is very easy, and similar to what was done in **Chapter 7** for similar methods, so it won't be repeated here.

Querying with Untyped Results

In many cases, you want to submit a query to the database and manipulate the results at will, instead of storing them in a mapped entity class. After all, why use entity classes when you could use records, right? Also, records can be designed to store only a subset of columns, and thus this results in behavior identical to a projection query.

One typical example is a web-based report that lists only a certain number of columns across multiple tables. For example, say you have a web page that shows the singer information and their most recently released album title. The summary information contains the complete name of the singer and their most recently released album title. Singers without albums will not be listed. In this case, we can implement this use case with a query and then manually manipulate the ResultSet object.

Let's create a new class called SingerSummaryServiceImpl and name the method findAllAsRecord(). Listing 8-14 shows a typical implementation of the method and the SingerSummaryRecord record class.

417

Listing 8-14. The SingerSummaryServiceImpl.findAllAsRecord() Method

```
package com.apress.prospring6.eight.view

data class SingerSummaryRecord( val firstName:String,
                                val lastName:String,
                                val latestAlbum:String)


// ------------------------------
package com.apress.prospring6.eight.service

import com.apress.prospring6.eight.view.SingerSummary
import com.apress.prospring6.eight.view.SingerSummaryRecord
// other import statements

@Service("singerSummaryService")
@Repository
@Transactional(readOnly = true)
class SingerSummaryServiceImpl : SingerSummaryService {
    @PersistenceContext
    private val em: EntityManager? = null

    override fun findAllAsRecord(): Stream<SingerSummaryRecord> {
        // old style (Java)
        /* return
            em.createQuery(ALL_SINGER_SUMMARY_RECORD_JPQL_QUERY)
        .getResultList().stream().
            map(obj -> {
                Object[] values = (Object[]) obj;
                return new SingerSummaryRecord((String) values[0],(String) values[1],
                    (String) values[2]);
            });*/
        return em!!.createQuery(ALL_SINGER_SUMMARY_RECORD_JPQL_QUERY,
                Tuple::class.java).resultList.stream()
        .map{ tuple: Tuple ->
                SingerSummaryRecord(
                        tuple[0, String::class.java],
                        tuple[1, String::class.java],
                        tuple[2, String::class.java]
                )
        }
    }
}
```

SingerSummaryService is just the interface declaring the method to be implemented by
SingerSummaryServiceImpl.

As shown in Listing 8-14, we use the EntityManager.createQuery() method to create Query, passing in
the JPQL statement, and then get the result list. When we explicitly specify the columns to be selected within
JPQL, JPA will return an iterator, and each item within the iterator is an array of objects. We loop through the
iterator, and for each array object a SingerSummaryRecord instance is created. Each object array corresponds
to a record within the ResultSet object.

Listing 8-15 shows the testing method.

Listing 8-15. Testing the SingerSummaryServiceImpl.findAllAsRecord() Method

```
package com.apress.prospring6.eight
// import statements omitted

// annotations omitted
class SingerServiceTest {
    @Autowired
    @Qualifier("jpaSingerService")
    var singerService: SingerService? = null

    @Autowired
    var singerSummaryService: SingerSummaryService? = null

    @Test
    @DisplayName("should return all singers and their most recent album as records")
    fun testFindAllWithAlbumAsRecords() {
        val singers = singerSummaryService!!.findAllAsRecord()
            .peek({ s ->
                LOGGER.info(
                    s.toString()
                )
            }).toList()
        Assertions.assertEquals(2, singers.size)
    }

}
```

Executing this test method produces a similar output to that of other methods in this chapter, but the results are converted to String using the record toString() generated method, as shown in Listing 8-16.

Listing 8-16. Output Snippets Printed During Testing of the SingerSummaryServiceImpl. findAllAsRecord() Method

```
DEBUG: SqlStatementLogger - select singer0_.FIRST_NAME as col_0_0_,
    singer0_.LAST_NAME as col_1_0_,
    albums1_.title as col_2_0_ from SINGER singer0_
left outer join ALBUM albums1_ on singer0_.ID=albums1_.SINGER_ID
where
    albums1_.RELEASE_DATE=(select max(album2_.RELEASE_DATE) from ALBUM album2_
    where album2_.SINGER_ID=singer0_.ID)
...
INFO : SingerServiceTest - SingerSummaryRecord[firstName=John, lastName=Mayer,
    latestAlbum=The Search For Everything]
INFO : SingerServiceTest - SingerSummaryRecord[firstName=Ben, lastName=Barnes,
    latestAlbum=11:11]
```

In JPA, there is a more elegant solution than playing around with the ResultSet object array returned from the query, as discussed in the next section.

Querying for a Custom Result Type with a Constructor Expression

In JPA, when querying for a custom result like the one in the previous section, you can instruct JPA to directly construct a POJO from each record for you. This POJO is also called a *view* because it contains data from multiple tables. For the example in the previous section, a record called SingerSummaryRecord was created. For this example, a POJO called SingerSummary is used, which is equivalent to the record class. The SingerSummary class has the properties for each singer summary, with a constructor method that accepts all the properties. Using this class we can write a findAll() method and use a constructor expression within the query to instruct the JPA provider to map the ResultSet to the SingerSummary class. In Listing 8-17 you can see this method and the query it executes.

Listing 8-17. The SingerSummaryServiceImpl.findAll() Method

```
package com.apress.prospring6.eight.service
// all import statements omitted

/* select new com.apress.prospring6.eight.view.SingerSummary(
    s.firstName, s.lastName, a.title) from Singer s
left join s.albums a
where a.releaseDate=(select max(a2.releaseDate) from Album a2
                                where a2.singer.id = s.id)*/

@Service("singerSummaryService")
@Repository
@Transactional(readOnly = true)
class SingerSummaryServiceImpl : SingerSummaryService {
    @PersistenceContext
    private val em: EntityManager? = null

    override fun findAll(): Stream<SingerSummary> {
        return em!!.createQuery(
            ALL_SINGER_SUMMARY_JPQL_QUERY,
            SingerSummary::class.java
        ).resultList.stream()
    }

}
```

In the JPQL query, the "new" keyword is specified, together with the fully qualified name of the POJO class that will store the results and pass in the selected attributes as the constructor argument of each SingerSummary class. Finally, the SingerSummary class is passed into the createQuery() method to indicate the result type. Testing this method is no different than what we did for findAllAsRecord(), but the returned results are of type SingerSummary instead of SingerSummaryRecord, as you can see in Listing 8-18.

Listing 8-18. Testing the SingerSummaryServiceImpl.findAll() Method

```
package com.apress.prospring6.eight
// import statements omitted

// annotations omitted
class SingerServiceTest {
    @Autowired
```

```kotlin
    @Qualifier("jpaSingerService")
    var singerService: SingerService? = null

    @Autowired
    var singerSummaryService: SingerSummaryService? = null

  @Test
  @DisplayName("should return all singers and their most recent album as POJOs")
  fun testFindAllAsPojos() {
      val singers: List<SingerSummary> = singerSummaryService!!.findAll()
          .peek{ s: SingerSummary ->
              LOGGER.info(
                  s.toString()
              )
          }.toList()
      Assertions.assertEquals(2, singers.size)
  }

    // other methods and setup omitted
}
```

Executing this method produces the result in Listing 8-19.

Listing 8-19. Output Snippets Printed During Testing of the SingerSummaryServiceImpl. testFindAllAsPojos() Method

```
DEBUG: QueryTranslatorImpl - HQL: select new com.apress.prospring6.eight.view.
SingerSummary(s.firstName, s.lastName, a.title)
    from com.apress.prospring6.eight.entities.Singer s
    left join s.albums a where a.releaseDate=
        (select max(a2.releaseDate)
        from com.apress.prospring6.eight.entities.Album a2
        where a2.singer.id = s.id)
DEBUG: QueryTranslatorImpl - SQL: select singer0_.FIRST_NAME as col_0_0_,
    singer0_.LAST_NAME as col_1_0_,
    albums1_.title as col_2_0_ from SINGER singer0_
    left outer join ALBUM albums1_ on singer0_.ID=albums1_.SINGER_ID
    where albums1_.RELEASE_DATE=
        (select max(album2_.RELEASE_DATE)
        from ALBUM album2_
        where album2_.SINGER_ID=singer0_.ID)
...
INFO : SingerServiceTest - First name: John, Last Name: Mayer, Most Recent Album: The Search
        For Everything
INFO : SingerServiceTest - First name: Ben, Last Name: Barnes, Most Recent Album: 11:11
```

Notice that the JPQL query is represented in Kotlin by an org.hibernate.query.internal.QueryImpl instance, because Hibernate is the JPA provider for this application. Also notice in the native SQL generated query that there is no trace of the SingerSummary constructor.

Inserting Data

Inserting data by using JPA is simple. Like Hibernate, JPA also supports retrieving a database-generated primary key. Listing 8-20 shows the save(..) method.

Listing 8-20. The SingerServiceImpl.save(..) Method

```
package com.apress.prospring6.eight.service
// import statements omitted

@Service("jpaSingerService")
@Repository
@Transactional
class SingerServiceImpl : SingerService {
    @PersistenceContext
    private val em: EntityManager? = null

    override fun save(singer: Singer) {
        if (singer.id == null) {
            LOGGER.info("Inserting new singer")
            em!!.persist(singer)
        } else {
            em!!.merge(singer)
            LOGGER.info("Updating existing singer")
        }
    }
    ...
}
```

As shown here, the save(..) method first checks whether the object is a new entity instance, by checking the id value. If id is null (that is, not yet assigned), the object is a new entity instance, and the EntityManager.persist(..) method will be invoked. When calling the persist(..) method, EntityManager persists the entity and makes it a managed instance within the current persistence context. If the id value exists, then we're carrying out an update, and the EntityManager.merge(..) method will be called instead. When the merge(..) method is called, the EntityManager merges the state of the entity into the current persistence context.

Listing 8-21 shows the code to insert a new Singer record. It's all done in a test method because we want to test that the insert succeeds.

Listing 8-21. Testing the SingerServiceImpl.save(..) Method

```
package com.apress.prospring6.eight
// import statements omitted

// annotations omitted
class SingerServiceTest {
    @Autowired
    @Qualifier("jpaSingerService")
    var singerService: SingerService? = null

    @Autowired
    var singerSummaryService: SingerSummaryService? = null
```

```kotlin
@Test
@DisplayName("should insert a singer with associations")
@Sql(
    statements = [ // avoid dirtying up the test context
        "delete from ALBUM where SINGER_ID = (select ID from SINGER where FIRST_NAME =
        'BB')", "delete from SINGER_INSTRUMENT where SINGER_ID = (select ID from SINGER
        where FIRST_NAME = 'BB')", "delete from SINGER where FIRST_NAME = 'BB'"],
    executionPhase = Sql.ExecutionPhase.AFTER_TEST_METHOD
)
fun testInsert() {
    val singer = Singer()
    singer.firstName = "BB"
    singer.lastName = "King"
    singer.birthDate = LocalDate.of(1940, 8, 16)
    var album = Album()
    album.title = "My Kind of Blues"
    album.releaseDate = LocalDate.of(1961, 7, 18)
    singer.addAlbum(album)
    album = Album()
    album.title = "A Heart Full of Blues"
    album.releaseDate = LocalDate.of(1962, 3, 20)
    singer.addAlbum(album)
    singerService!!.save(singer)
    Assertions.assertNotNull(singer.id)
    val singers: List<Singer> = singerService!!.findAllWithAlbum()
        .peek
            { s: Singer ->
                LOGGER.info(s.toString())
                s.albums.forEach { a: Album ->
                    LOGGER.info(
                        "\tAlbum:$a"
                    )
                }
                s.instruments.forEach { i: Instrument ->
                    LOGGER.info(
                        "\tInstrument: " + i.instrumentId
                    )
                }
            }.toList()
    Assertions.assertEquals(4, singers.size)
}
...
}
```

As shown here, we create a new singer, add two albums, and save the object. The success of this operation is tested by verifying the size of the result set returned by the findAllWithAlbum() method.

The @Sql annotation is used to clean up the database to avoid accidentally failing other tests run on the initial test data set.

Updating Data

Updating data is as easy as inserting data, and as you've seen, a single method was created for the insert and update operation. There are two ways we can test an update operation: by updating the name or other properties of a singer record, or by removing related associations, such as an album. Listing 8-22 shows two ways to test the SingerServiceImpl.save(..) method for performing updates.

Listing 8-22. Testing the SingerServiceImpl.save(..) Method for Two Forms of the Update Operation

```
package com.apress.prospring6.eight;
// import statements omitted

// annotations omitted
@Testcontainers
@SqlMergeMode(SqlMergeMode.MergeMode.MERGE)
@Sql("classpath:testcontainers/drop-schema.sql", "classpath:testcontainers/create-
schema.sql")
@SpringJUnitConfig(classes = [SingerServiceTest.TestContainersConfig::class])
class SingerServiceTest {
    @Autowired
    @Qualifier("jpaSingerService")
    var singerService: SingerService? = null

    @Autowired
    var singerSummaryService: SingerSummaryService? = null

    @Test
    @SqlGroup(
        Sql(
            scripts = ["classpath:testcontainers/add-nina.sql"],
            executionPhase = Sql.ExecutionPhase.BEFORE_TEST_METHOD
        ),
        Sql(
            scripts = ["classpath:testcontainers/remove-nina.sql"],
            executionPhase = Sql.ExecutionPhase.AFTER_TEST_METHOD
        )
    )
    @DisplayName("should update a singer")
    fun testUpdate() {
        val singer = singerService!!.findById(5L)!!
        // making sure such singer exists
        Assertions.assertNotNull(singer)
        // making sure we got expected singer
        Assertions.assertEquals("Simone", singer.lastName)
        // retrieve the album
        val album = singer.albums.stream().filter { a: Album ->
                a.title == "I Put a Spell on You" }
            .findFirst().orElse(null)
        Assertions.assertNotNull(album)
        singer.firstName = "Eunice Kathleen"
        singer.lastName = "Waymon"
        singer.removeAlbum(album)
```

```
        val version = singer.version
        singerService!!.save(singer)
        val nina = singerService!!.findById(5L)!!
        Assertions.assertAll("nina was updated",
            Executable { Assertions.assertNotNull(nina) },
            Executable {
                Assertions.assertEquals(
                    version + 1,
                    nina.version
                )
            }
        )
    }


    @Test
    fun testUpdateAlbumSet() {
        val singer = singerService!!.findById(1L)!!
        // making sure such singer exists
        Assertions.assertNotNull(singer)
        // making sure we got expected record
        Assertions.assertEquals("Mayer", singer.lastName)
        // retrieve the album
        val album = singer.albums.stream().filter { a: Album ->
                a.title == "Battle Studies" }
            .findAny().orElse(null)
        singer.firstName = "John Clayton"
        singer.removeAlbum(album)
        singerService!!.save(singer)
        val singers: List<Singer> = singerService!!.findAllWithAlbum()
            .peek{ s: Singer ->
                    LOGGER.info(s.toString())
                    s.albums.forEach{ a: Album ->
                        LOGGER.info(
                            "\tAlbum:$a"
                        )
                    }
                    s.instruments.forEach{ i: Instrument ->
                        LOGGER.info(
                            "\tInstrument: " + i.instrumentId
                        )
                    }
                }.toList()
        Assertions.assertEquals(3, singers.size)
    }
    ...
}
```

In the testUpdate() method, we first retrieve the record with an ID of 5, and we change the first and last name. We call the SingerService.save(..) method and then retrieve the saved item from the database. The success of the update operation is confirmed by the incrementing of its version field.

In the testUpdateAlbumSet() method, we first retrieve the record with an ID of 1 and we change the first name. Then we loop through its Album associations and retrieve the one with title *Battle Studies* and remove it from the singer's albums property. Finally, we call the SingerService.save(..) method again. When you execute this method, you can check that the update operation succeeded by looking in the console log and checking that the *Battle Studies* album is not displayed.

❗ The album can be removed because of the orphanRemoval=true attribute that was defined in the one-to-many association, which instructs the JPA provider (Hibernate) to remove all orphan records that exist in the database but are no longer found in the object when persisted: @OneToMany(mappedBy = "singer", cascade=CascadeType.ALL, orphanRemoval=true).

Deleting Data

Deleting data is just as simple. Simply call the EntityManager.remove() method and pass in the Singer object. Listing 8-23 shows the updated code to delete a singer.

Listing 8-23. The SingerServiceImpl.delete(..) Method

```kotlin
package com.apress.prospring6.eight.service
// import statements omitted

@Service("jpaSingerService")
@Repository
@Transactional
class SingerServiceImpl : SingerService {
    @PersistenceContext
    private val em: EntityManager? = null

    override fun delete(singer: Singer) {
        val mergedContact = em!!.merge(singer)
        em.remove(mergedContact)
        LOGGER.info("Singer with id: " + singer.id + " deleted successfully")
    }
    ...
}
```

First the EntityManager.merge(..) method is invoked to merge the state of the entity into the current persistence context. The merge(..) method returns the managed entity instance. Then EntityManager. remove() is called, passing in the managed singer entity instance. The remove operation deletes the singer record, together with all its associated information, including albums and instruments, as we defined the cascade=CascadeType.ALL in the mapping. To test the delete operation, the testDelete() method can be used, which is depicted in Listing 8-24.

Listing 8-24. Testing the SingerServiceImpl.delete(..) Method

```kotlin
package com.apress.prospring6.eight
// import statements omitted

// annotations omitted
class SingerServiceTest {
    @Autowired
    @Qualifier("jpaSingerService")
    var singerService: SingerService? = null

    @Autowired
    var singerSummaryService: SingerSummaryService? = null

    @Test
    @Sql(scripts = ["classpath:testcontainers/add-chuck.sql"], executionPhase = Sql.
    ExecutionPhase.BEFORE_TEST_METHOD)
    @DisplayName("should delete a singer")
    fun testDelete() {
        val singer = singerService!!.findById(6L)!!
        // making sure such singer exists
        Assertions.assertNotNull(singer)
        singerService!!.delete(singer)
        val deleted = singerService!!.findById(6L)
        Assertions.assertTrue(deleted == null)
    }
    ...
}
```

Listing 8-24 retrieves the singer with an ID of 6 and then calls the delete(..) method to delete the singer information.

Using a Native Query

Having discussed performing trivial database operations by using JPA, now let's move on to some more advanced topics. Sometimes you may want to have absolute control over the query that will be submitted to the database. One example is using a hierarchical query in an Oracle database. This kind of query is database-specific and referred to as a *native query*.

JPA supports the execution of native queries; EntityManager will submit the query to the database as is, without any mapping or transformation performed. One main benefit of using JPA native queries is the mapping of ResultSet back to the ORM-mapped entity classes. The following two sections discuss how to use a native query to retrieve all singers and directly map ResultSet back to the Singer objects.

Using a Simple Native Query

To demonstrate how to use a native query, let's implement a new method to retrieve all the singers from the database. This method is shown in Listing 8-25.

Listing 8-25. The `SingerServiceImpl.findAllByNativeQuery(..)` Method

```
package com.apress.prospring6.eight.service
// import statements omitted

@Service("jpaSingerService")
@Repository
@Transactional
class SingerServiceImpl : SingerService {
    @PersistenceContext
    private val em: EntityManager? = null

    // select ID, FIRST_NAME, LAST_NAME, BIRTH_DATE, VERSION
  // from SINGER";
    override fun findAllByNativeQuery(): Stream<Singer> {
        return em!!.createNativeQuery(SingerService.ALL_SINGER_NATIVE_QUERY,
            "singerResult")
            .resultList.stream() as Stream<Singer>
    }
    ...
}
```

You can see that the native query is just a simple SQL statement to retrieve all the columns from the SINGER table. To create and execute the query, `EntityManager.createNativeQuery(..)` was first called, passing in the query string as well as the result type. The result type should be a mapped entity class (in this case the `Singer` class). The `createNativeQuery(..)` method returns a `Query` instance, which provides the `.resultList` accessor to get the result list. The JPA provider will execute the query and transform the ResultSet object into the entity instances, based on the JPA mappings defined in the entity class. Executing the previous method produces the same result as the `findAll()` method.

Native Querying with SQL ResultSet Mapping

Aside from the mapped domain object, you can pass in a String that indicates the name of a SQL ResultSet mapping. A SQL ResultSet mapping is defined at the entity class level by using the `@SqlResultSetMapping` annotation. A SQL ResultSet mapping can have one or more entity and column mappings. A SQL ResultSet mapping called `singerResult` is defined for the entity class, with the `entityClass` attribute in the Singer class itself. JPA supports more complex mapping for multiple entities and supports mapping down to column-level mapping.

After the SQL ResultSet mapping is defined, the `findAllByNativeQuery()` method can be invoked using the ResultSet mapping's name. Listing 8-26 shows the updated `findAllByNativeQuery()` method.

Listing 8-26. The `@SqlResultSetMapping` Mapping Results of the ALL_SINGER_NATIVE_QUERY Native Query

```
package com.apress.prospring6.eight.entities

import jakarta.persistence.EntityResult
import jakarta.persistence.SqlResultSetMapping
// other import statements omitted

@Entity
@Table(name = "SINGER")
```

```kotlin
@SqlResultSetMapping(
        name="singerResult",
        entities=@EntityResult(entityClass=Singer.class)
)
class Singer : AbstractEntity {
    // code omitted
}

// ---------------------
// other details omitted
class SingerServiceImpl : SingerService {

    override fun findAllByNativeQuery():Stream<Singer> {
        return em.createNativeQuery(ALL_SINGER_NATIVE_QUERY, "singerResult").resultList.
        stream() as Stream<Singer>
    }
    // other methods omitted
}
```

As you can see, JPA also provides strong support for executing native queries, with a flexible SQL ResultSet mapping facility provided.

Executing Stored Functions and Procedures

There is more than one way to configure support for SQL functions and procedures execution, but the easiest is to use native queries. To do so, write the SQL to declare your stored SQL function or procedure, use @NamedNativeQuery from the jakarta.persistence package to map its SQL invocation to a query name, and then use EntityManager.createNamedQuery(..) to create a native query and retrieve the result using getSingleResult() or .getResultList() or any other method available.

Listing 8-27 shows a very simple SQL stored function that returns the first name for a singer with a given id.

Listing 8-27. The getFirstNameById SQL Stored Function

```sql
CREATE FUNCTION IF NOT EXISTS getFirstNameById (in_id INT) RETURNS VARCHAR(60)
RETURN (SELECT first_name FROM SINGER WHERE id = in_id);
```

The getFirstNameById(..) stored function invocation can be mapped to a name using @NamedNativeQuery. This annotation can be included in @NamedNativeQueries when there is more than one native query declared for an entity type. These annotations are declared on the entity class, in this case the Singer class, as shown in Listing 8-28.

Listing 8-28. The getFirstNameById SQL Stored Function Invocation Being Mapped to Named Query Singer.getFirstNameById(?)

```kotlin
package com.apress.prospring6.eight.entities
// other class details omitted
import jakarta.persistence.NamedNativeQueries
import jakarta.persistence.NamedNativeQuery

@NamedNativeQueries({
```

```
        NamedNativeQuery(
                name = "Singer.getFirstNameById(?)",
                query = "select getfirstnamebyid(?)")
})
class Singer : AbstractEntity {
    // body omitted
}
```

The SQL stored function or procedure is nothing else than a native query, and thus it simply a native query and thus can be mapped to a named native query. The name is quite flexible, and in this scenario the chosen name is `Singer.getFirstNameById(?)` because it makes it quite obvious that the query is specific to `Singer` instances and that it requires a parameter.

Since the query is named, the `EntityManager.createNamedQuery(..)` method is used to create the query and retrieve the result, as shown in Listing 8-29.

Listing 8-29. Invoking a SQL Stored Function Using `EntityManager`

```
package com.apress.prospring6.eight.service
// other class details omitted

class SingerServiceImpl : SingerService {

    override fun findFirstNameById(id:Long):String {
        return em.createNamedQuery("Singer.getFirstNameById(?)")
                .setParameter(1, id).singleResult.toString();
    }
    ...

}
```

Testing this method is done by a method identical to the one introduced for testing SQL functions and procedures in **Chapter 7**.

The `jakarta.persistence` package includes an annotation named `@NamedStoredProcedureQueries` that is used to declare an array of SQL stored procedures, each of them configured using `@NamedStoredProcedureQuery`. When declared using these annotations, a stored function or procedure can be invoked from an `EntityManager` using the `createNamedStoredProcedureQuery(..)` method. Since these annotations are a bit misleading (their names imply that only SQL stored procedures are supported), we prefer to use named native queries instead.

Using the JPA Criteria API for a Criteria Query

Most applications provide a front end for users to search for information. Typically, many searchable fields are displayed, and the users enter information in only some of them and do the search. It's difficult to prepare many queries, with each possible combination of parameters that users may choose to enter. In this situation, the criteria API query feature comes to the rescue.

In JPA 2, one major new feature introduced was a strongly typed Criteria API query. In this new Criteria API, the criteria being passed into the query is based on the mapped entity classes' metamodel. As a result, each criteria specified is strongly typed, and errors will be discovered at compile time rather than runtime.

In the JPA Criteria API, an entity class metamodel is represented by the entity class name with a suffix of an underscore (_). For example, the metamodel class for the Singer entity class is `Singer_`. Listing 8-30 shows the `Singer_` class.

Listing 8-30. The Meta-Model for the Singer Entity

```
package com.apress.prospring6.eight.entities

import jakarta.persistence.metamodel.SetAttribute
import jakarta.persistence.metamodel.SingularAttribute
import jakarta.persistence.metamodel.StaticMetamodel
import java.time.LocalDate
import javax.annotation.processing.Generated

@Generated(value = arrayOf("org.hibernate.jpamodelgen.JPAMetaModelEntityProcessor"))
@StaticMetamodel(Singer::class)
object Singer_ : com.apress.prospring6.eight.entities.AbstractEntity_() {
        @Volatile
        var firstName: SingularAttribute<Singer, String>? = null

        @Volatile
        var lastName: SingularAttribute<Singer, String>? = null

        @Volatile
        var albums: SetAttribute<Singer, Album>? = null

        @Volatile
        var instruments: SetAttribute<Singer, Instrument>? = null

        @Volatile
        var birthDate: SingularAttribute<Singer, LocalDate>? = null
        const val FIRST_NAME = "firstName"
        const val LAST_NAME = "lastName"
        const val ALBUMS = "albums"
        const val INSTRUMENTS = "instruments"
        const val BIRTH_DATE = "birthDate"
}
```

The metamodel class is annotated with @StaticMetamodel, and the attribute is the mapped entity class. Within the class are the declaration of each attribute and its related types. It would be tedious to code and maintain those metamodel classes. However, tools can help generate those metamodel classes automatically based on the JPA mappings within the entity classes. The one provided by Hibernate is called Hibernate Metamodel Generator[5].

The way you go about generating your metamodel classes depends on what tools you are using to develop and build your project. We recommend reading the "Usage" section of the documentation[6] for specific details.

The required dependency for metamodel class generation is the hibernate-jpamodelgen library.

With the class generation strategy set up, let's define a query that accepts both the first name and last name for searching singers. For this we will add a method findByCriteriaQuery() in the SingerService interface and its implementation in SingerServiceImpl, as shown in Listing 8-31.

---

[5] https://hibernate.org/orm/tooling
[6] https://docs.jboss.org/hibernate/stable/jpamodelgen/reference/en-US/html_single

Listing 8-31. SingerServiceImpl.findByCriteriaQuery() Using JPA Criteria API

```kotlin
package com.apress.prospring6.eight.service

import com.apress.prospring6.eight.entities.Singer_
import org.apache.commons.lang3.StringUtils
import jakarta.persistence.criteria.CriteriaBuilder
import jakarta.persistence.criteria.CriteriaQuery
import jakarta.persistence.criteria.JoinType
import jakarta.persistence.criteria.Predicate
import jakarta.persistence.criteria.Root
// other import statements omitted

@Service("jpaSingerService")
@Repository
@Transactional
class SingerServiceImpl : SingerService {
        @PersistenceContext
        private val em: EntityManager? = null
        fun findByCriteriaQuery(firstName: String, lastName: String): Stream<Singer> {
                LOGGER.info("Finding singer for firstName: $firstName and lastName:
                $lastName")
                val cb: CriteriaBuilder = em!!.criteriaBuilder
                val criteriaQuery: CriteriaQuery<Singer> =
                        cb.createQuery(Singer::class.java)
                val singerRoot: Root<Singer> = criteriaQuery.from(Singer::class.java)
                singerRoot.fetch(Singer_.albums, JoinType.LEFT)
                singerRoot.fetch(Singer_.instruments, JoinType.LEFT)
                criteriaQuery.select(singerRoot).distinct(true)
                var criteria: Predicate = cb.conjunction()
                if (firstName.isNotBlank()) {
                        val firstNamePredicate: Predicate =
                                        cb.equal(singerRoot.get(Singer_.firstName), firstName)
                        criteria = cb.and(criteria, firstNamePredicate)
                }
                if (lastName.isNotBlank()) {
                        val lastNamePredicate: Predicate =
                                        cb.equal(singerRoot.get(Singer_.lastName), lastName)
                        criteria = cb.and(criteria, lastNamePredicate)
                }
                criteriaQuery.where(criteria)
                return em.createQuery(criteriaQuery).getResultList().stream()
        }
        // other methods and setup omitted
}
```

Let's break down the Criteria API usage.

- `EntityManager.criteriaBuilder` is called to retrieve an instance of `jakarta.persistence.criteria.CriteriaBuilder`.

- A typed query is created by calling `CriteriaBuilder.createQuery()` and passing in `Singer` as the result type. The resulting instance is of type `jakarta.persistence.criteria.CriteriaQueryImpl<Singer>` that implements `jakarta.persistence.criteria.CriteriaQuery<Singer>`.

- The two `Root<..>.fetch(..)` method calls enforce the eager fetching of the associations relating to `albums` and `instruments`. The `JoinType.LEFT` argument specifies an outer join. Calling the `Root<..>.fetch(..)` method with `JoinType.LEFT` as the second argument is equivalent to specifying the `left join fetch` join operation in JPQL.

- The `CriteriaQuery.select(..)` method is called and returns the root query object as the result type. The `distinct(..)` method called with argument `true` means that duplicate records should be eliminated.

- A `jakarta.persistence.criteria.Predicate` instance is obtained by calling the `CriteriaBuilder.conjunction()` method, which means that a conjunction of one or more restrictions is made. A `Predicate` can be a simple or compound predicate, and a predicate is a restriction that indicates the selection criteria defined by an expression.

- The firstName and lastName arguments are checked. For each `not null` argument, a new `Predicate` is constructed using the `CriteriaBuilder` instance (that is, the `CriteriaBuilder.and(..)` method). The method `equal()` is to specify an equal restriction, within which `Root<..>.get()` is called, passing in the corresponding attribute of the entity class metamodel to which the restriction applies. The constructed predicate is then "conjunct" with the existing predicate (stored by the variable criteria) by calling the `CriteriaBuilder.and()` method.

- The `Predicate` is constructed with all the criteria and restrictions and passed as the `where` clause to the query by calling the `CriteriaQuery.where(..)` method.

- Finally, `CriteriaQuery` is passed to `EntityManager`. `EntityManager` then constructs the query based on the `CriteriaQuery` value passed in, executes the query, and returns the result.

To test the criteria query operation, a new test method is added to the `SingerServiceTest` test class, as shown in Listing 8-32.

Listing 8-32. Testing the `SingerServiceImpl.findByCriteriaQuery()` Method

```
package com.apress.prospring6.eight
// import statements omitted

// annotations omitted
class SingerServiceTest {

    @Test
    fun testFindByCriteriaQuery(){
        val singers = singerService.findByCriteriaQuery("John", "Mayer").peek
        { s ->
```

```
            LOGGER.info(s.toString())
            s.albums.forEach{a ->
                LOGGER.info("\tAlbum:" + a.toString())}
            s.instruments.forEach{i ->
                LOGGER.info("\tInstrument: " + i.instrumentId)}
        }.toList()
        assertEquals(1, singers.size)
    }
    // other methods and setup omitted
}
```

The test is not that different from the previous tests in this chapter, nor is the output, as shown in Listing 8-33.

Listing 8-33. Console Output Snippets for the Execution of the testFindByCriteriaQuery() Test Method

```
INFO : SingerServiceImpl - Finding singer for firstName: John and lastName: Mayer
DEBUG: CriteriaQueryImpl - Rendered criteria query ->
    select distinct generatedAlias0 from Singer as generatedAlias0
    left join fetch generatedAlias0.albums as generatedAlias1
    left join fetch generatedAlias0.instruments as generatedAlias2
    where ( ( 1=1 )
        and ( generatedAlias0.firstName=:param0 ) )
        and ( generatedAlias0.lastName=:param1 )
...
DEBUG: QueryTranslatorImpl - parse() - HQL:
    select distinct generatedAlias0
    from com.apress.prospring6.eight.entities.Singer as generatedAlias0
    left join fetch generatedAlias0.albums as generatedAlias1
    left join fetch generatedAlias0.instruments as generatedAlias2
    where ( ( 1=1 )
        and ( generatedAlias0.firstName=:param0 ) )
        and ( generatedAlias0.lastName=:param1 )
...
DEBUG: QueryTranslatorImpl - SQL:
    select
        distinct singer0_.ID as id1_2_0_,
        albums1_.ID as id1_0_1_,
        instrument3_.INSTRUMENT_ID as instrume1_1_2_,
        singer0_.VERSION as version2_2_0_,
        singer0_.BIRTH_DATE as birth_da3_2_0_,
        singer0_.FIRST_NAME as first_na4_2_0_,
        singer0_.LAST_NAME as last_nam5_2_0_,
        albums1_.VERSION as version2_0_1_,
        albums1_.RELEASE_DATE as release_3_0_1_,
        albums1_.SINGER_ID as singer_i5_0_1_,
        albums1_.title as title4_0_1_,
        albums1_.SINGER_ID as singer_i5_0_0__,
        albums1_.ID as id1_0_0__,
        instrument2_.SINGER_ID as singer_i1_3_1__,
        instrument2_.INSTRUMENT_ID as instrume2_3_1__
    from SINGER singer0_
```

```
    left outer join ALBUM albums1_ on singer0_.ID=albums1_.SINGER_ID
    left outer join SINGER_INSTRUMENT instrument2_ on singer0_.ID=instrument2_.SINGER_ID
    left outer join INSTRUMENT instrument3_ on instrument2_.INSTRUMENT_ID=instrument3_.
INSTRUMENT_ID
    where 1=1
        and singer0_.FIRST_NAME=?
        and singer0_.LAST_NAME=?
...
INFO : SingerServiceTest - Singer - Id: 1, First name: John, Last name: Mayer, Birthday:
    1977-10-16
INFO : SingerServiceTest -  Album:Album - Id: 1, Singer id: 1, Title: The Search For
    Everything, Release Date: 2017-01-20
INFO : SingerServiceTest -  Album:Album - Id: 2, Singer id: 1, Title: Battle Studies,
    Release Date: 2009-11-17
INFO : SingerServiceTest -  Instrument: Guitar
INFO : SingerServiceTest -  Instrument: Piano
```

This output is loquacious, but it will show you exactly what is happening under the hood. It starts with a criteria query that gets transformed in HQL, which is then transformed in SQL, and finally executed on the database. This seems to be a little too much, right? Is the performance cost worth having strongly typed queries and having errors discovered at compile time rather than at runtime? It depends on the application profile and the query complexity. We already mentioned jOOQ in **Chapter 7**, which provides roughly the same benefits but without two levels of conversion and with a friendlier syntax.

Summary

In this chapter, we covered the basic concepts of JPA and how to configure JPA's EntityManagerFactory in Spring by using Hibernate as the persistence service provider. Then we discussed using JPA to perform basic database operations. Advanced topics included native queries and the strongly typed JPA Criteria API.

The purpose of this chapter was to introduce you to JPA's EntityManagerFactory, because from an architectural point of view, Hibernate's SessionFactory is an extension of it. Thus, the SessionFactory is also a JPA EntityManagerFactory, which means both contain the entity mapping metadata and allow you to create a Hibernate Session or an EntityManager.

However, the EntityManagerFactory is the standard implementation, and it is the same across all the implementations. This means that, although not very likely, if you would like to change your JPA provider, in this case Hibernate, to some other persistence implementation (e.g., Oracle TopLink), doing so is way easier when your code is not tied to your provider.

This being said, in **Chapter 9** we'll complete the whole picture of working with SQL databases in Spring by exploring transactions.

CHAPTER 9

Spring Transaction Management

Managing transactions is one of the most critical parts of building a reliable enterprise application. The most common type of transaction is a database operation. In a typical database update operation, a database transaction begins, data is updated, and then the transaction is committed or rolled back, depending on the result of the database operation. However, in many cases, depending on the application requirements and the back-end resources that the application needs to interact with (such as an RDBMS, message-oriented middleware, an ERP system, and so on), transaction management can be much more complicated.

In the early days of Java application development (after JDBC was created but before the JEE standard or an application framework like Spring was available), developers programmatically controlled and managed transactions within application code. When JEE and, more specifically, the EJB standard became available, developers were able to use container-managed transactions (CMTs) to manage transactions in a declarative way. But the complicated transaction declaration in the EJB deployment descriptor was difficult to maintain and introduced unnecessary complexity for transaction processing. Some developers favored having more control over the transaction and chose bean-managed transactions (BMTs) to manage transactions in a programmatic way. However, the complexity of programming with the Java Transaction API (JTA) also hindered developers' productivity.

As discussed in **Chapter 5**, transaction management is a crosscutting concern and should not be coded within the business logic. The most appropriate way to implement transaction management is to allow developers to define transaction requirements in a declarative way and have frameworks such as Spring, JEE, or AOP weave in the transaction processing logic on our behalf. In this chapter, we discuss how Spring helps simplify the implementation of transaction-processing logic. Spring provides support for both declarative and programmatic transaction management.

Spring offers excellent support for declarative transactions, which means you do not need to clutter your business logic with transaction management code. All you have to do is declare those methods (within classes or layers) that must participate in a transaction, together with the details of the transaction configuration, and Spring will take care of handling the transaction management. To be more specific, this chapter covers the following:

- *Spring transaction abstraction layer*: We discuss the base components of Spring transaction abstraction classes and explain how to use these classes to control the properties of the transactions.

- *Declarative transaction management*: We show you how to use Spring and just plain Kotlin objects to implement declarative transactional management. We offer examples for declarative transaction management using the XML configuration files as well as Kotlin annotations.

- *Programmatic transaction management*: Even though programmatic transaction management is not used very often, we explain how to use the Spring-provided TransactionTemplate class, which gives you full control over the transaction management code.

© Peter Späth, Iuliana Cosmina, Rob Harrop, Chris Schaefer 2023
P. Späth et al., *Pro Spring 6 with Kotlin*, https://doi.org/10.1007/978-1-4842-9557-1_9

Exploring the Spring Transaction Abstraction Layer

When developing your applications, no matter whether you choose to use Spring or not, you have to make a fundamental choice when using transactions about whether to use global transactions or local transactions. Local transactions are specific to a single transactional resource (a JDBC connection, for example), whereas global transactions are managed by the container and can span multiple transactional resources.

Transaction Types

Local transactions are easy to manage, and if all operations in your application need to interact with just one transactional resource (such as a JDBC transaction), using local transactions will be sufficient. However, if you are not using an application framework such as Spring, you have a lot of transaction management code to write, and if in the future the scope of the transaction needs to be extended across multiple transactional resources, you have to drop the local transaction management code and rewrite it to use global transactions.

In the Java world, global transactions are implemented with the JTA (Java/Jakarta Transaction API). In this scenario, a JTA-compatible transaction manager connects to multiple transactional resources via respective resource managers, which are capable of communicating with the transaction manager over the XA (Exchange Access) protocol (an open standard defining distributed transactions). The 2-Phase Commit (2PC) mechanism is used to ensure that all back-end data sources were updated or rolled back altogether. If either of the back-end resources fails, the entire transaction is rolled back, and hence the updates to all resources are rolled back too. The global transaction is an implementation of UserTransaction and normally needs to be sourced from JNDI. Since JNDI is specific to a server environment, this limits the potential reuse of application code. In the past there were some libraries that did not require a server, such as Atomikos[1], which was used in the previous edition the Java variant of this book but is not used in this chapter because the current version has not been adapted to the Jakarta Transaction API and thus is unusable with the most recent Spring version.

Figure 9-1 shows a high-level view of global transactions with JTA. As you can see, four main parties participate in a global transaction (also generally referred to as a *distributed transaction*). The first party is the back-end resource, such as an RDBMS, messaging middleware, an enterprise resource planning (ERP) system, and so on.

---

[1] https://www.atomikos.com

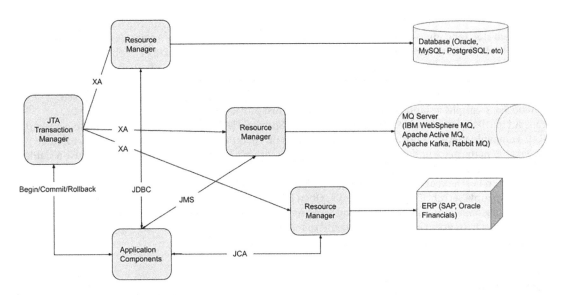

Figure 9-1. *Overview of global transactions with JTA*

The second party is the resource manager, which is generally provided by the back-end resource vendor and is responsible for interacting with the back-end resource. For example, when connecting to a MySQL database, we need to interact with the `MysqlXADataSource` class provided by MySQL's Java connector. Equivalent implementations exist for MariaDB as well. Other back-end resources (for example, MQ, ERP, and so on) provide their resource managers too.

The third party is the JTA transaction manager, which is responsible for managing, coordinating, and synchronizing the transaction status with all resource managers that are participating in the transaction. The previously mentioned XA protocol is used, which is an open standard widely used for distributed transaction processing. The JTA transaction manager also supports 2PC so that all changes will be committed together, and if any resource update fails, the entire transaction will be rolled back, resulting in none of the resources being updated. The entire mechanism was specified by the Java Transaction Service (JTS) specification.

The final component is the application. Either the application itself or the underlying container or Spring Framework that the application runs on manages the transaction (begin, commit, roll back a transaction, and so on). At the same time, the application interacts with the underlying back-end resources via various standards defined by JEE. As shown in Figure 9-1, the application connects to the RDBMS via JDBC, MQ via JMS, and an ERP system via Java EE Connector Architecture (JCA). JTA is supported by all full-blown JEE-compliant application servers (for example, JBoss, WebSphere, WebLogic, and GlassFish), within which the transaction is available via JNDI lookup. As for stand-alone applications or web containers (for example, Tomcat and Jetty), open source and commercial solutions exist that provide support for JTA/XA in those environments. The one favored by the Spring community used to be Atomikos, there was even a Spring Boot starter library for it. Unfortunately, the latest version of Atomikos when this chapter is being written (5.0.9) is not based on Jakarta JTA, which means building a Spring JTA application with the latest Spring version is not possible. The other alternative, Bitronix[2], is already archived on GitHub and no update has been done in the last 6 years. The last update on Java Open Transaction Manager (JOTM)[3] was done in 2009.

---

[2] `https://github.com/bitronix/btm`
[3] `https://jotm.ow2.org`

It looks like the interest in microservices, event-driven systems built using Apache Kafka, RabbitMQ, Azure Event Hub (and more), and the rise of DBaaS (database as a service) like Amazon's DynamoDB, MariaDB SkySQL where transactions are not particularly necessary, slowly making JTA obsolete. Of course, if you need to use global transactions, there is always the option to use an application EE server.

At the time of writing, Spring 6 JTA support with stand-alone implementations is unclear. Spring's components are based on Jakarta API, which means the stand-alone implementation must be based on it too. For example, a stand-alone implementation must provide an implementation for `jakarta.transaction.UserTransaction` to be compatible with Spring 6 JTA, and none of them do. Using a Jakarta EE 10–compatible server is not an option either. Jakarta EE 10[4] is the first major release of Jakarta EE since the "jakarta" namespace update, and a lot of application servers are not compatible with it, because a stable release is not yet available.

By the end of the year there might be compatible stand-alone implementations available, or Jakarta EE-10 compatible servers like Apache TomEE, Open Liberty, Eclipse Glassfish, and others[5]. If you are interested in global transactions with Spring 5 and Atomikos, feel free to check out *Pro Spring 5* and the sample project in its associated repofoonote:[https://github.com/Apress/pro-spring-5/tree/master/chapter09].

Implementations of the PlatformTransactionManager Interface

In Spring, the `PlatformTransactionManager` interface uses the `TransactionDefinition` and `TransactionStatus` interfaces to create and manage transactions. The concrete implementations of these interfaces must have detailed knowledge of the transaction manager.

Spring provides a rich set of implementations for the `PlatformTransactionManager` interface. Figure 9-2 shows a few of them.

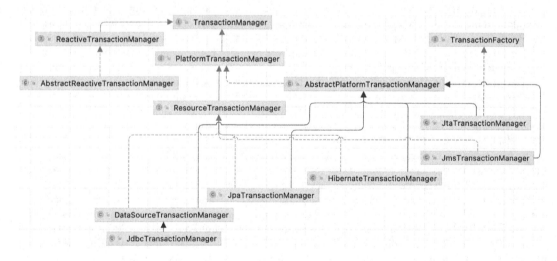

Figure 9-2. *PlatformTransactionManager implementations*

---

[4] https://eclipse-ee4j.github.io/jakartaee-platform/jakartaee10/JakartaEE10ReleasePlan
[5] https://jakarta.ee/compatibility

The DataSourceTransactionManager class, from package org.springframework.jdbc.datasource, is for generic JDBC connections. For the ORM side, there are a number of implementations, including JPA - the JpaTransactionManager class, and Hibernate 5 HibernateTransactionManager. There will probably be a new version for Hibernate 6 when Spring will include support for it. At the time when this book is being written, Spring does not yet support Hibernate 6, and the only HibernateTransactionManager available is the one from package org.springframework.orm.hibernate5. Since support for Hibernate 5 will probably not be dropped, expect a package named org.springframework.orm.hibernate6 to appear in Spring ORM 6.

For JMS, the implementations support JMS 2.0 through the JmsTransactionManager class. For JTA, the generic implementation class is JtaTransactionManager. For reactive servers, Spring provides AbstractReactiveTransactionManager, an abstract base class that implements Spring's standard reactive transaction workflow, serving as a basis for concrete platform transaction managers (like the R2dbcTransactionManager implementation for a single R2DBC ConnectionFactory).

Spring also provides several JTA transaction manager classes (not depicted here) that are specific to particular application servers. Those classes provide native support for WebSphere (the WebSphereUowTransactionManager class) and BEA WebLogic 9.0 and higher (the WebLogicJtaTransactionManager class).

ⓘ   JDO support was dropped in Spring 5, thus the JdoTransactionManager is missing from the class diagram in Figure 9-2. Starting with Spring 5, only Hibernate 5 is supported; implementations for Hibernate 3 and Hibernate 4 have been dropped. Support for JMS 1.1 was dropped in Spring 5. The CciLocalTransactionManager class that supports JEE, JCA, and the Common Client Interface (CCI) is currently deprecated.

Analyzing Transaction Properties

In this section, we discuss the transaction properties that Spring supports, focusing on interacting with RDBMS as the back-end resource.

Transactions have the four well-known ACID properties (atomicity, consistency, isolation, and durability), and it is up to the transactional resources to maintain these aspects of a transaction. You cannot control the atomicity, consistency, and durability of a transaction. However, you can control the transaction propagation and timeout, as well as configure whether the transaction should be read-only and specify the isolation level.

Spring encapsulates all these settings in a TransactionDefinition interface. This interface is used in the core interface of the transaction support in Spring, which is the PlatformTransactionManager interface, whose implementations perform transaction management on a specific platform, such as JDBC or JTA. The core method, PlatformTransactionManager.getTransaction(), takes a TransactionDefinition interface as an argument and returns a TransactionStatus interface. The TransactionStatus interface is used to control the transaction execution, more specifically to set the transaction result and to check whether the transaction is completed or whether it is a new transaction.

The TransactionDefinition Interface

As we mentioned earlier, the TransactionDefinition interface controls the properties of a transaction. Let's take a more detailed look at the TransactionDefinition interface[6], shown in Listing 9-1, and describe its methods.

Listing 9-1. Essential TransactionDefinition Source Code

```java
package org.springframework.transaction;

import org.springframework.lang.Nullable;

public interface TransactionDefinition {
    // Variable declarations and comments omitted

    default int getPropagationBehavior() {
        return PROPAGATION_REQUIRED; // 0
    }

    default int getIsolationLevel() {
        return ISOLATION_DEFAULT; // -1
    }

    default int getTimeout() {
        return TIMEOUT_DEFAULT; // -1
    }

    default boolean isReadOnly() {
        return false;
    }

    @Nullable
    default String getName() {
        return null;
    }

    // Return an unmodifiable {@code TransactionDefinition} with defaults.
    static TransactionDefinition withDefaults() {
        return StaticTransactionDefinition.INSTANCE;
    }
}
```

The simple and obvious methods of this interface are getTimeout(), which returns the time (in seconds) in which the transaction must complete, and isReadOnly(), which indicates whether the transaction is read-only. The transaction manager implementation can use this value to optimize the execution and check to make sure that the transaction is performing only read operations. The getName() method returns the name of the transaction.

---

[6] https://github.com/spring-projects/spring-framework/blob/main/spring-tx/src/main/java/org/springframework/transaction/TransactionDefinition.java

The other two methods, getPropagationBehavior() and getIsolationLevel(), need to be discussed in more detail. We begin with getIsolationLevel(), which controls what changes to the data other transactions see. Table 9-1 lists the transaction isolation levels you can use and explains which changes made in the current transaction other transactions can access. The isolation levels are represented as static values defined in the TransactionDefinition interface.

Table 9-1. *Transaction Isolation Levels*

Isolation Level	Description
ISOLATION_DEFAULT	Default isolation level of the underlying data store.
ISOLATION_READ_UNCOMMITTED	Lowest level of isolation; it is barely a transaction at all because it allows this transaction to see data modified by other uncommitted transactions.
ISOLATION_READ_COMMITTED	Default level in most databases; it ensures that other transactions are not able to read data that has not been committed by other transactions. However, the data that was read by one transaction can be updated by other transactions.
ISOLATION_REPEATABLE_READ	Stricter than ISOLATION_READ_COMMITTED; it ensures that once you select data, you can select at least the same set again. However, if other transactions insert new data, you can still select the newly inserted data.
ISOLATION_SERIALIZABLE	The most expensive and reliable isolation level; all transactions are treated as if they were executed one after another.

Choosing the appropriate isolation level is important for the consistency of the data, but making these choices can have a great impact on performance. The highest isolation level, ISOLATION_SERIALIZABLE, is particularly expensive to maintain.

The getPropagationBehavior() method specifies what happens to a transactional call, depending on whether there is an active transaction. Table 9-2 describes the values for this method. The propagation types are represented as static values defined in the TransactionDefinition interface.

Table 9-2. *Transaction Propagation Modes*

Propagation Mode	Value	Description
PROPAGATION_REQUIRED	0	Supports a transaction if one already exists. If there is no transaction, starts one. Default propagation mode in Spring.
PROPAGATION_SUPPORTS	1	Supports a current transaction; executes non-transactionally if no current transaction exists.
PROPAGATION_MANDATORY	2	Supports a current transaction; throws an exception if no current transaction exists.
PROPAGATION_REQUIRES_NEW	3	Creates a new transaction, suspending the current transaction if one exists.
PROPAGATION_NOT_SUPPORTED	4	Does not support execution with an active transaction. Always executes non-transactionally and suspends any existing transaction.
PROPAGATION_NEVER	5	Always executes non-transactionally even if an active transaction exists. Throws an exception if an active transaction exists.
PROPAGATION_NESTED	6	Runs in a nested transaction if an active transaction exists. If there is no active transaction, behaves as if PROPAGATION_REQUIRED is set.

The TransactionStatus Interface

The TransactionStatus interface[7] allows a transaction manager to control the transaction execution. The code can check whether the transaction is a new one or whether it is a read-only transaction, and it can initiate a rollback. The behavior described by the TransactionStatus interface is split between two interfaces: TransactionExecution, which declares basic transaction operations, and SavepointManager, which declares methods related to savepoints. All are shown in Listing 9-2.

Listing 9-2. Essential TransactionStatus Source Code

```java
// TransactionStatus.java
package org.springframework.transaction;

import java.io.Flushable;

public interface TransactionStatus extends TransactionExecution, SavepointManager,
Flushable {

    boolean hasSavepoint();

    @Override
    void flush();

}
// TransactionExecution.java
package org.springframework.transaction;

public interface TransactionExecution {
    boolean isNewTransaction();
    void setRollbackOnly();
    boolean isRollbackOnly();
    boolean isCompleted();
}

// SavepointManager.java
package org.springframework.transaction;

public interface SavepointManager {
    Object createSavepoint() throws TransactionException;
    void rollbackToSavepoint(Object savepoint) throws TransactionException;
    void releaseSavepoint(Object savepoint) throws TransactionException;
}
```

The methods in the TransactionExecution interface are fairly self-explanatory; the most notable one is setRollbackOnly(), which causes a rollback and ends the active transaction. The hasSavePoint() method from TransactionStatus returns whether the transaction internally carries a savepoint (that is, the transaction was created as a nested transaction based on a savepoint). The flush() method, also from TransactionStatus, flushes the underlying session to a data store if applicable (for example, when using

---

[7] https://github.com/spring-projects/spring-framework/blob/main/spring-tx/src/main/java/org/springframework/transaction/TransactionStatus.java

with Hibernate). The isCompleted() method from the TransactionExecution interface returns whether the transaction has ended (that is, committed or rolled back).

Sample Data Model and Infrastructure for Example Code

This section uses the same data model introduced in **Chapter 7**. There are two main tables, namely SINGER and ALBUM, that we have used throughout the chapters about data access. Feel free to set up the container as instructed in chapter09/README.adoc or ignore that altogether and just run the tests that are set up to use a MariaDB container set up by Testcontainers. JPA with Hibernate is used as the persistence layer for implementing data access logic.

The main project dependencies are Spring ORM and Hibernate. The Spring ORM library introduces the spring-tx transitive dependency that contains all the Spring components that provide transaction support.

Figure 9-3 shows the list of dependencies for the chapter09 project.

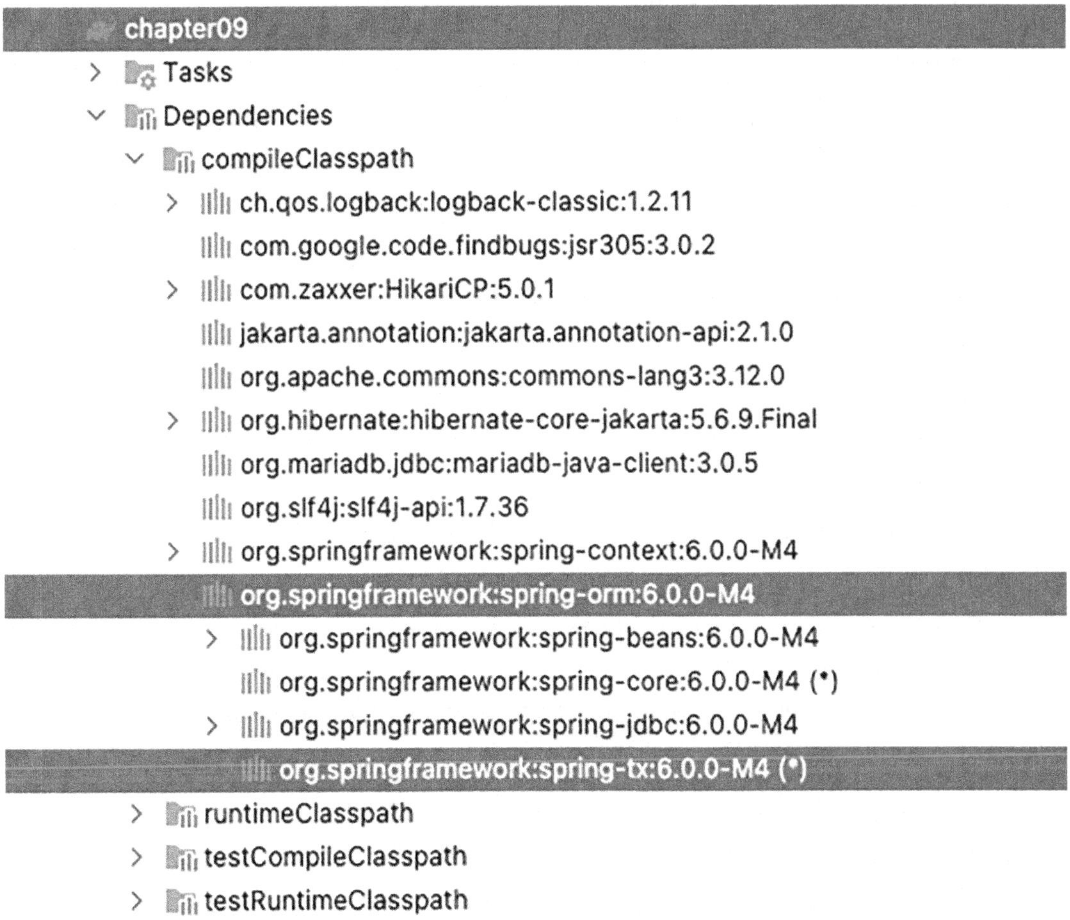

- chapter09
  - › Tasks
  - ⌄ Dependencies
    - ⌄ compileClasspath
      - › ch.qos.logback:logback-classic:1.2.11
      - com.google.code.findbugs:jsr305:3.0.2
      - › com.zaxxer:HikariCP:5.0.1
      - jakarta.annotation:jakarta.annotation-api:2.1.0
      - org.apache.commons:commons-lang3:3.12.0
      - › org.hibernate:hibernate-core-jakarta:5.6.9.Final
      - org.mariadb.jdbc:mariadb-java-client:3.0.5
      - org.slf4j:slf4j-api:1.7.36
      - › org.springframework:spring-context:6.0.0-M4
      - org.springframework:spring-orm:6.0.0-M4
        - › org.springframework:spring-beans:6.0.0-M4
        - org.springframework:spring-core:6.0.0-M4 (*)
        - › org.springframework:spring-jdbc:6.0.0-M4
      - org.springframework:spring-tx:6.0.0-M4 (*)
    - › runtimeClasspath
    - › testCompileClasspath
    - › testRuntimeClasspath

Figure 9-3. Project chapter09 dependencies as shown in the Gradle View

There are two main JPA entity classes, Singer and Album, that map to those tables that will be used in most examples in this chapter. These two classes should be familiar to you if you've read the previous data access chapters, but to keep things simple, their core parts are shown in Listing 9-3.

Listing 9-3. Singer and Album JPA Entity Classes

```kotlin
// Singer.kt
package com.apress.prospring6.nine.entities

import jakarta.persistence.*
// other import statements omitted

@Entity
@Table(name = "SINGER")
@NamedQueries(
        NamedQuery(name = Singer.FIND_ALL, query = "select s from Singer s"),
        NamedQuery(name = Singer.COUNT_ALL, query = "select count(s) from Singer s"),
        NamedQuery(
                name = Singer.FIND_BY_FIRST_AND_LAST_NAME,
                query = "select s from Singer s where s.firstName = :fn and
                s.lastName = :ln"
        )
)
class Singer : AbstractEntity() {
        @Column(name = "FIRST_NAME")
        var firstName: String? = null

        @Column(name = "LAST_NAME")
        var lastName: String? = null

        @Column(name = "BIRTH_DATE")
        var birthDate: LocalDate? = null

        @OneToMany(mappedBy = "singer")
        var albums: MutableSet<Album> = HashSet()

        @ManyToMany
        @JoinTable(
                name = "SINGER_INSTRUMENT",
                joinColumns = [JoinColumn(name = "SINGER_ID")],
                inverseJoinColumns = [JoinColumn(name = "INSTRUMENT_ID")]
        )
        var instruments: MutableSet<Instrument> = HashSet()

        fun addAlbum(album: Album): Boolean {
                album.singer = this
                return albums.add(album)
        }

        fun removeAlbum(album: Album) {
                albums.remove(album)
        }
```

```kotlin
        fun addInstrument(instrument: Instrument): Boolean {
                return instruments.add(instrument)
        }
...

        companion object {
                @Serial
                private val serialVersionUID = 2L
                const val FIND_ALL = "Singer.findAll"
                const val COUNT_ALL = "Singer.countAll"
                const val FIND_BY_FIRST_AND_LAST_NAME =
                             "Singer.findByFirstAndLastName"
        }
}

// -------------------------------------------------------
// Album.kt
package com.apress.prospring6.nine.entities

import jakarta.persistence.*
// other import statements omitted

@Entity
@Table(name = "ALBUM")
@NamedQueries(NamedQuery(name = Album.FIND_ALL, query = "select a from Album a where
a.singer= :singer"))
class Album : AbstractEntity() {
        @Column
        var title: String? = null

        @Column(name = "RELEASE_DATE")
        var releaseDate: LocalDate? = null

        @ManyToOne
        @JoinColumn(name = "SINGER_ID")
        var singer: Singer? = null

...

        companion object {
                @Serial
                private val serialVersionUID = 3L
                const val FIND_ALL = "Album.findAll"
        }
}
```

We use JPA with Hibernate as the persistence layer for implementing data access logic, which means the configuration will too be identical to the one in **Chapter 7**. Listing 9-4 shows only the piece of configuration that is relevant to transaction management.

Listing 9-4. Transaction Management Configuration Class

```
package com.apress.prospring6.nine.config

import org.springframework.orm.jpa.JpaTransactionManager
import org.springframework.orm.jpa.JpaVendorAdapter
import org.springframework.orm.jpa.LocalContainerEntityManagerFactoryBean
import org.springframework.orm.jpa.vendor.HibernateJpaVendorAdapter
import org.springframework.transaction.PlatformTransactionManager
import org.springframework.transaction.annotation.EnableTransactionManagement
// other import statements omitted

@Import(BasicDataSourceCfg::class)
@Configuration
@EnableTransactionManagement
@ComponentScan(basePackages = ["com.apress.prospring6.nine.repos", "com.apress.prospring6.
nine.services"])
open class TransactionCfg {
    @Autowired
    var dataSource: DataSource? = null

    @Bean
    open fun transactionManager(): PlatformTransactionManager {
        val transactionManager = JpaTransactionManager()
        transactionManager.entityManagerFactory = entityManagerFactory().getObject()
        return transactionManager
    }

    @Bean
    open fun jpaVendorAdapter(): JpaVendorAdapter {
        return HibernateJpaVendorAdapter()
    }

    @Bean
    open fun entityManagerFactory(): LocalContainerEntityManagerFactoryBean {
        val factory = LocalContainerEntityManagerFactoryBean()
        factory.setPersistenceProviderClass(HibernatePersistenceProvider::class.java)
        factory.setPackagesToScan("com.apress.prospring6.nine.entities")
        factory.dataSource = dataSource
        factory.setJpaProperties(jpaProperties())
        factory.jpaVendorAdapter = jpaVendorAdapter()
        return factory
    }

    @Bean
    open fun jpaProperties(): Properties {
        val jpaProps = Properties()
        jpaProps[Environment.HBM2DDL_AUTO] = "none"
        jpaProps[Environment.FORMAT_SQL] = false
```

```
        jpaProps[Environment.STATEMENT_BATCH_SIZE] = 30
        jpaProps[Environment.USE_SQL_COMMENTS] = false
        jpaProps[Environment.SHOW_SQL] = false
        return jpaProps
    }
}
```

Currently, using annotations is the most common way to define transaction requirements in Spring. The main benefit is that the transaction requirement together with the detail transaction properties (timeout, isolation level, propagation behavior, and so on) are defined within the code itself, which makes the application easier to trace and maintain. The configuration for the transactionManager bean, the core component ensuring those requirements are met, is done using Kotlin configuration. Because we are using JPA, our transactionManager is a JpaTransactionManager instance that implements Spring's standard transaction workflow in applications that use a single JPA EntityManagerFactory for transactional data access.

The @EnableTransactionManagement annotation is the one that completes this configuration, because it is responsible for enabling annotation-driven transaction capability. This annotation is used on Spring configuration classes to configure traditional, imperative transaction management or reactive transaction management. @EnableTransactionManagement is responsible for registering all infrastructure Spring beans that support transaction management, such as TransactionInterceptor and the proxy- or AspectJ-based advice that weaves the interceptor into the call stack when methods annotated with @Transactional are called.

There is no change in how the EntityManagerFactory bean is then configured.

With this configuration in place, any method interacting with the data layer can be annotated with @Transactional and the Spring IoC container will open a transaction before the method execution and close it right after.

Using Declarative Transactions

Configuring transactional behavior using annotations is referred to as *declarative* because the desired behavior is declared using annotations on the targeted methods. There is no code to be written to create, start, and end a transaction. The Spring transaction manager bean picks up the @Transactional annotations and wraps the method within the desired transactional behavior. This is done by using proxying, introduced in **Chapter 5**. The bean declaration annotated with @Transactional, or that contains methods annotated with @Transactional, is transformed at runtime into a bean that is wrapped into a proxy that injects transactional behavior for every targeted method.

Figure 9-4 shows what happens under the hood every time a method of a transactional bean is invoked.

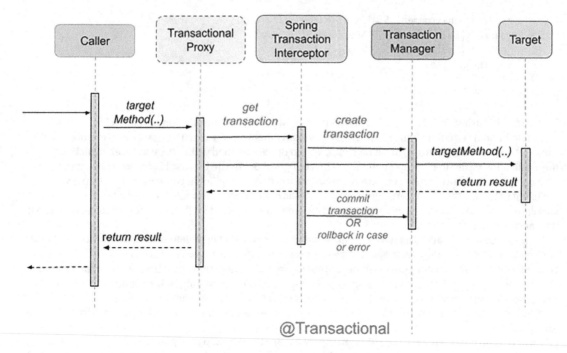

Figure 9-4. *Diagram showing how transactional behavior is injected in Spring*

In multilayered implementations, where service classes are calling repository classes to exchange data with the database, service methods are configured to be executed in transactions, providing the opportunity to provide atomic behavior for methods that involve multiple database operations. For this reason, in the examples in this section, the albums are not eagerly loaded for a singer, nor are they loaded through a named query, since they will be loaded through a repo method in the same method where singers are extracted as well, as shown in the AllServiceImpl class shown in Listing 9-5.

Listing 9-5. AllServiceImpl Method Showing Loading of Singers and Albums Through Repository Methods Executed in the Same Transaction

```
package com.apress.prospring6.nine.services

import org.springframework.stereotype.Service
import org.springframework.transaction.annotation.Transactional
// other import statements omitted

@Service
@Transactional
class AllServiceImpl(private val singerRepo: SingerRepo, private val albumRepo: AlbumRepo) :
    AllService {
    @Transactional(readOnly = true)
    override fun findAllWithAlbums(): Stream<Singer> {
        val singers = singerRepo.findAll()
        return singers.peek { s: Singer? ->
            s!!.albums = albumRepo.findBySinger(s)
                .collect(Collectors.toSet())
```

```kotlin
        }
    }

    @Transactional(readOnly = true)
    override fun findByIdWithAlbums(id: Long): Singer? {
        val singerOpt = singerRepo.findById(id)
        singerOpt?.run {
            albums = albumRepo.findBySinger(this)
                .collect(Collectors.toSet())
        }
        return singerOpt
    }

    @Transactional(propagation = Propagation.REQUIRES_NEW)
    override fun update(singer: Singer) {
        singerRepo.save(singer)
    }

    @Transactional(rollbackFor = [TitleTooLongException::class])
    @Throws(
        TitleTooLongException::class
    )
    override fun saveSingerWithAlbums(s: Singer, albums: Set<Album>) {
        val singer = singerRepo.save(s)
        albums.forEach{ a: Album ->
            a.singer = singer
        }
        albumRepo.save(albums)
    }

    @Transactional(readOnly = true, propagation = Propagation.SUPPORTS)
    override fun countSingers(): Long {
        return singerRepo.countAllSingers()
    }
}
```

When using annotation-based transaction management, the only annotation that we need to deal with is Spring's @Transactional. The @Transactional annotation can be applied at the class level, which means that, by default, Spring will ensure that a transaction is present before the execution of each method within the class. Starting with Spring 5, @Transactional is supported on interfaces and default methods in interfaces as well.

🛈   It is recommended to use Spring's @Transactional annotation only on non-private methods, since the transactional behavior is injected using AOP proxying.

💡   The implementation for the `SingerRepo` and `AlbumRepo` is not important for this chapter, but if you are curious, feel free to check the repository sources. Their methods are implemented using `EntityManager` as shown in **Chapter 8**.

The @Transactional annotation supports a number of attributes that you can provide to override the default behavior. Table 9-3 shows the available attributes, together with the default values and possible values.

Table 9-3. *Transaction Attributes*

Attribute Name	Default Value	Possible Values
propagation	Propagation.REQUIRED	Propagation.REQUIRED Propagation. SUPPORTS Propagation.MANDATORY Propagation.REQUIRES_NEW Propagation.NOT_SUPPORTED Propagation.NEVER Propagation.NESTED
isolation	Isolation.DEFAULT (default isolation level of the underlying resource)	Isolation.DEFAULT Isolation. READ_UNCOMMITTED Isolation.READ_ COMMITTED Isolation.REPEATABLE_READ Isolation.SERIALIZABLE
timeout	TransactionDefinition. TIMEOUT_DEFAULT (default transaction timeout in seconds of the underlying resource)	An integer value larger than zero; indicates the number in seconds for timeout
readOnly	false	{true, false}
rollbackFor	Exception classes for which the transaction will be rolled back	N/A
rollbackForClassName	Exception class names for which the transaction will be rolled back	N/A
noRollbackFor	Exception classes for which the transaction will not be rolled back	N/A
noRollbackForClassName	Exception class names for which the transaction will not be rolled back	N/A
value	" "	A qualifier value for the specified transaction; may be used to determine the target transaction manager, matching the qualifier value (or the bean name) of a specific transaction manager bean

As a result, based on Table 9-3, the @Transactional annotation without any attribute means that the transaction propagation mode is required, the isolation is the default isolation level of the underlying datastore, the timeout is the default timeout of the underlying transaction system, and the mode is read-write.

The @Transactional annotation can be applied at the method level as well, and this allows overriding of the transactional configuration at the class level. For example, use @Transactional(readOnly = true) if the transaction is effectively read-only in order to allow for corresponding optimizations at runtime. All attributes remain unchanged.

The readOnly flag configuration is just a hint for the underlying persistence system, and Hibernate is very good at taking hints, so don't use readOnly = true on a method designed to update an existing entry, for example, or you'll have to flush the changes explicitly.

Now that we have a service method, it is time to test it. Listing 9-6 shows the AllServiceTest class, which uses a MariaDB container managed by Testcontainers for database operations.

Listing 9-6. AllServiceTest Test Class

```
package com.apress.prospring6.nine
// import statements omitted

@Service
@Transactional
class AllServiceImpl(private val singerRepo: SingerRepo, private val albumRepo: AlbumRepo) :
    AllService {
    @Transactional(readOnly = true)
    override fun findAllWithAlbums(): Stream<Singer> {
        val singers = singerRepo.findAll()
        return singers.peek { s: Singer? ->
            s!!.albums = albumRepo.findBySinger(s)
                .collect(Collectors.toSet())
        }
    }

    @Transactional(readOnly = true)
    override fun findByIdWithAlbums(id: Long): Singer? {
        val singerOpt = singerRepo.findById(id)
        singerOpt?.run {
            albums = albumRepo.findBySinger(this)
                .collect(Collectors.toSet())
        }
        return singerOpt
    }

    @Transactional(propagation = Propagation.REQUIRES_NEW)
    override fun update(singer: Singer) {
        singerRepo.save(singer)
    }

    @Transactional(rollbackFor = [TitleTooLongException::class])
    @Throws(
        TitleTooLongException::class
    )
```

```
override fun saveSingerWithAlbums(s: Singer, albums: Set<Album>) {
    val singer = singerRepo.save(s)
    albums.forEach{ a: Album ->
        a.singer = singer
    }
    albumRepo.save(albums)
}

@Transactional(readOnly = true, propagation = Propagation.SUPPORTS)
override fun countSingers(): Long {
    return singerRepo.countAllSingers()
}
}
```

Testing methods designed to run in a transaction is no different from the testing done in the previous chapters, the only difference being the logging statements that you have to pay attention to. The focus in this chapter won't be on the SQL queries being generated, but on the transactions being used to execute those queries in. Take a look at the logging statements in Listing 9-7.

Listing 9-7. AllServiceTest.testFindAll() Execution Log Snippet Showing Transaction Management

```
DEBUG: AbstractPlatformTransactionManager - Creating new transaction with name
    [com.apress.prospring6.nine.services.AllServiceImpl.findAllWithAlbums]:
        PROPAGATION_REQUIRED,ISOLATION_DEFAULT,readOnly
DEBUG: JpaTransactionManager - Opened new EntityManager [SessionImpl(1958757239<open>)] for
    JPA transaction
DEBUG: DataSourceUtils - Setting JDBC Connection [HikariProxyConnection@282368256 wrapping
    org.mariadb.jdbc.Connection@7327a447] read-only
DEBUG: TransactionImpl - On TransactionImpl creation, JpaCompliance#isJpaTransactionComplia
    nceEnabled == false
DEBUG: TransactionImpl - begin
DEBUG: JpaTransactionManager - Exposing JPA transaction as JDBC [org.springframework.orm.
    jpa.vendor.HibernateJpaDialect$HibernateConnectionHandle@e645600]
TRACE: TransactionAspectSupport - Getting transaction for
    [com.apress.prospring6.nine.services.AllServiceImpl.findAllWithAlbums]
DEBUG: SqlStatementLogger - select singer0_.... from SINGER singer0_
...
DEBUG: TwoPhaseLoad - Done materializing entity [com.apress.prospring6.nine.entities.
    Singer#3]
TRACE: TransactionAspectSupport - Completing transaction for
    [com.apress.prospring6.nine.services.AllServiceImpl.findAllWithAlbums]
DEBUG: AbstractPlatformTransactionManager - Initiating transaction commit
DEBUG: JpaTransactionManager - Committing JPA transaction on EntityManager [SessionImpl
    (1958757239<open>)]
DEBUG: TransactionImpl - committing
DEBUG: DataSourceUtils - Resetting read-only flag of JDBC Connection
    [HikariProxyConnection@282368256 wrapping org.mariadb.jdbc.Connection@7327a447]
DEBUG: JpaTransactionManager - Closing JPA EntityManager [SessionImpl(1958757239<open>)]
    after transaction
DEBUG: SharedEntityManagerCreator$SharedEntityManagerInvocationHandler - Creating new
    EntityManager for shared EntityManager invocation
DEBUG: SqlStatementLogger - select album0_... from ALBUM album0_ where album0_.SINGER_ID=?
```

```
...
INFO : AbstractEntityManagerFactoryBean - Closing JPA EntityManagerFactory for persistence
       unit 'default'
...
INFO : AllServiceTest - Singer - Id: 1, First name: John, Last name: Mayer, Birthday:
       1977-10-16
INFO : AllServiceTest -      Album:Album - Id: 1, Singer id: 1, Title: The Search For
       Everything, Release Date: 2017-01-20
INFO : AllServiceTest -      Album:Album - Id: 2, Singer id: 1, Title: Battle Studies,
       Release Date: 2009-11-17
INFO : AllServiceTest - Singer - Id: 2, First name: Ben, Last name: Barnes, Birthday:
       1981-08-20
INFO : AllServiceTest -      Album:Album - Id: 3, Singer id: 2, Title: 11:11, Release Date:
       2021-09-1
INFO : AllServiceTest - Singer - Id: 3, First name: John, Last name: Butler, Birthday:
       1975-04-01
```

This log snippet contains relevant logging statements for classes in packages `org.springframework.orm.jpa` and `org.springframework.transaction`. The `JpaTransactionManager` handles the creation and commit operations of the transaction. Notice how before the execution of the `findAllWithAlbums()` method, Spring's `AbstractPlatformTransactionManager` (`JpaTransactionManager`'s superclass) creates a new transaction. Its name is equal to the fully qualified class name concatenated with the method name. Next to the transaction name are the transaction attributes: `PROPAGATION_REQUIRED,ISOLATION_DEFAULT,readOnly`. The transaction is represented by an instance of Hibernate's `TransactionImpl` from its internal package `org.hibernate.engine.transaction.internal`. This class implements (indirectly) the `jakarta.persistence.EntityTransaction` interface, which is used to control transactions on resource-local entity managers. The transaction is thus being obtained by the `EntityManager`, then the query is submitted, and upon completion and without any errors, the transaction is committed.

From the log you might think that the transaction is committed before the albums are retrieved from the database, but it is only logging timing. In fact, all queries are executed within the same transaction.

The next method we want to look at refers to the update operation. To check the result of an update operation, the `findById()` method is useful too. Listing 9-8 shows the implementation of the two methods.

Listing 9-8. `AllServiceImpl` in the Same Transaction

```kotlin
package com.apress.prospring6.nine.services
// import statements omitted

@Service
@Transactional
class AllServiceImpl(private val singerRepo: SingerRepo, private val albumRepo: AlbumRepo) :
AllService {

    @Transactional(readOnly = true)
    override fun findByIdWithAlbums(id: Long): Singer? {
        val singerOpt = singerRepo.findById(id)
        singerOpt?.run {
            albums = albumRepo.findBySinger(this)
                .collect(Collectors.toSet())
        }
        return singerOpt
    }
```

```
    @Transactional(propagation = Propagation.REQUIRES_NEW)
    override fun update(singer: Singer) {
        singerRepo.save(singer)
    }
    ...

}
```

The findByIdWithAlbums(..) method is also annotated with @Transactional(readOnly=true). Generally, the readOnly=true attribute should be applied to all finder methods. The main reason is that most persistence providers will perform a certain level of optimization on read-only transactions. For example, Hibernate will not maintain the snapshots of the managed instances retrieved from the database with read-only turned on.

In the AllServiceImpl.update(..) method, we simply invoke the SingerRepoIml.save(..) method and annotate the method with @Transactional(propagation = Propagation.REQUIRES_NEW). This means the class-level annotation is overridden and a new transaction is to be created and used to perform the update operation. The method to test the AllServiceImpl.update(..) operation first calls the findByIdWithAlbums(..) method to retrieve the record to be updated, as shown in Listing 9-9.

Listing 9-9. AllServiceTest Method Testing the AllServiceImpl.update(..) Method

```
package com.apress.prospring6.nine
// import statements omitted

@Testcontainers
@SqlMergeMode(SqlMergeMode.MergeMode.MERGE)
@Sql("classpath:testcontainers/drop-schema.sql", "classpath:testcontainers/create-
schema.sql")
@SpringJUnitConfig(classes = [AllServiceTest.TestContainersConfig::class])
class AllServiceTest : TestContainersBase() {
    @Autowired
    var service: AllService? = null

    @Test
    @SqlGroup(
        Sql(
            scripts = ["classpath:testcontainers/add-nina.sql"],
            executionPhase = Sql.ExecutionPhase.BEFORE_TEST_METHOD
        )
    )
    @DisplayName("should update a singer")
    fun testUpdate() {
        val singer = service!!.findByIdWithAlbums(5L)
        Assertions.assertNotNull(singer)

        // making sure we got expected singer
        Assertions.assertEquals("Simone", singer!!.lastName)
        singer.firstName = "Eunice Kathleen"
        singer.lastName = "Waymon"
        val version = singer.version
        service!!.update(singer)
        val nina = service!!.findByIdWithAlbums(5L)!!
```

```
            Assertions.assertEquals(version + 1, nina.version)
            Assertions.assertAll("nina was updated",
                Executable { Assertions.assertNotNull(nina) },
                Executable {
                    Assertions.assertEquals(
                        "Eunice Kathleen",
                        nina.firstName
                    )
                },
                Executable {
                    Assertions.assertEquals(
                        version + 1,
                        nina.version
                    )
                }
            )
        }
        ...
}
```

There are three things being updated for the singer instance: its firstName, lastName, and its album collection. This method is executed in its own transaction, separate from AllServiceImpl. findByIdWithAlbums(..), as it is revealed by the test execution log. The log in Listing 9-10 shows only the statements creating transactions relevant for the test method; the actual execution log is quite verbose and includes the transactions necessary to populate the database with the entries necessary for the test methods to be run.

Listing 9-10. AllServiceTest Method Testing the AllServiceImpl.update(..) Method Execution Log Snippet

```
DEBUG: AbstractPlatformTransactionManager - Creating new transaction with name
    [com.apress.prospring6.nine.services.AllServiceImpl.findByIdWithAlbums]:
        PROPAGATION_REQUIRED,ISOLATION_DEFAULT,readOnly
TRACE: TransactionAspectSupport - Getting transaction for
    [com.apress.prospring6.nine.services.AllServiceImpl.findByIdWithAlbums]
DEBUG: TransactionImpl - begin
...
TRACE: TransactionAspectSupport - Completing transaction for
    [com.apress.prospring6.nine.services.AllServiceImpl.findByIdWithAlbums]
....
DEBUG: AbstractPlatformTransactionManager - Creating new transaction with name
    [com.apress.prospring6.nine.services.AllServiceImpl.update]:
        PROPAGATION_REQUIRES_NEW,ISOLATION_DEFAULT
TRACE: TransactionAspectSupport - Getting transaction for
    [com.apress.prospring6.nine.services.AllServiceImpl.update]
DEBUG: TransactionImpl - begin
...
TRACE: TransactionAspectSupport - Completing transaction for
    [com.apress.prospring6.nine.services.AllServiceImpl.update]
...
DEBUG: AbstractPlatformTransactionManager - Creating new transaction with name
    [com.apress.prospring6.nine.services.AllServiceImpl.findByIdWithAlbums]:
```

```
        PROPAGATION_REQUIRED,ISOLATION_DEFAULT,readOnly
TRACE: TransactionAspectSupport - Getting transaction for
    [com.apress.prospring6.nine.services.AllServiceImpl.findByIdWithAlbums]
DEBUG: TransactionImpl - begin
...
TRACE: TransactionAspectSupport - Completing transaction for
    [com.apress.prospring6.nine.services.AllServiceImpl.findByIdWithAlbums]
....
```

Here's the fun part: because the update operation requires a non-read-only transaction, even without the @Transactional(propagation = Propagation.REQUIRES_NEW) configuration, the update operation would have been executed in its own newly created transaction anyway. The only thing important here is that creating this new transaction suspends the existing one, and thus the next time findByIdWithAlbums(..) is executed to retrieve the updated item from the database, it requires creating a new transaction, as shown by the last section of the log.

Let's design an example that shows an existing transaction being reused. Although pretty basic, a method returning the total number of singers in the database can be configured to run in an existing read-only transaction, since it does not modify the database. To make it execute in an existing transaction, the method is annotated with @Transactional(propagation = Propagation.SUPPORTS), as shown in Listing 9-11.

Listing 9-11. AllServiceImpl.countSingers(..) Method

```
package com.apress.prospring6.nine.services;
// import statements omitted

@Service
@Transactional
class AllServiceImpl(private val singerRepo: SingerRepo, private val albumRepo: AlbumRepo) :
    AllService {

    @Transactional(readOnly = true, propagation = Propagation.SUPPORTS)
    override fun countSingers(): Long {
        return singerRepo.countAllSingers()
    }
}
```

To make sure that this method is executed in an existing transaction, a test method can be written to compare the result of the AllServiceImpl.countSingers() method with the size of the collection returned by AllServiceImpl.findAllWithAlbums(), as shown in Listing 9-12.

Listing 9-12. AllServiceImplTest.testCount(..) Method

```
package com.apress.prospring6.nine
// import statements omitted

@Testcontainers
@SqlMergeMode(SqlMergeMode.MergeMode.MERGE)
@Sql("classpath:testcontainers/drop-schema.sql",
        "classpath:testcontainers/create-schema.sql")
@SpringJUnitConfig(classes = [AllServiceTest.TestContainersConfig::class])
class AllServiceTest : TestContainersBase() {
```

```kotlin
    @Autowired
    var service: AllService? = null

    @Test
    @DisplayName("should count singers")
    fun testCount() {
        val singers = service!!.findAllWithAlbums()
            .collect(Collectors.toSet())
        val count = service!!.countSingers()
        Assertions.assertEquals(count, singers.size.toLong())
    }
    ...
}
```

The expectation might be that a transaction is created to execute `service.findAllWithAlbums()` and this transaction is reused to execute `service.countSingers()`. The test execution log makes it pretty clear that a new transaction is not created for `service.countSingers()`, as shown in the log snippet in Listing 9-13.

Listing 9-13. `AllServiceTest` Method Testing the `AllServiceImpl.countSingers(..)` Method Execution Log Snippet

```
DEBUG: AbstractPlatformTransactionManager - Creating new transaction with name
    [com.apress.prospring6.nine.services.AllServiceImpl.findAllWithAlbums]:
        PROPAGATION_REQUIRED,ISOLATION_DEFAULT,readOnly
DEBUG: JpaTransactionManager - Opened new EntityManager [SessionImpl(1674995553<open>)] for
    JPA transaction
DEBUG: TransactionImpl - begin
TRACE: TransactionAspectSupport - Getting transaction for [com.apress.prospring6.nine.
    services.AllServiceImpl.findAllWithAlbums]
DEBUG: SqlStatementLogger - select singer0_.... from SINGER singer0_
...
TRACE: TransactionAspectSupport - Getting transaction for [com.apress.prospring6.nine.
    services.AllServiceImpl.countSingers]
DEBUG: EntityManagerFactoryUtils - Opening JPA EntityManager
DEBUG: SqlStatementLogger - select count(singer0_.ID) as col_0_0_ from SINGER singer0_
```

Notice that there is no log message saying `Creating new transaction with name[com.apress. prospring6.nine.services.AllServiceImpl.countSingers]`, and the reason is that no transaction is created to execute this method. Because of the transaction propagation mode being set to `PROPAGATION_SUPPORTS`, the method is executed within an existing transaction, or non-transactionally if none exists.

This section covered a few transaction configurations that you might find useful when writing transactional applications. For special cases, you may need to configure the timeout, isolation level, rollback (or not) for specific exceptions, and so on.

Configuring transactional behavior using annotations is practical since transactional behavior can be customized up to the method level. Just make sure to not mix up Spring's `@Transactional` with Jakarta's `@Transactional`, since Jakarta's version does not support as many options as Spring's version does.

Rolling Back Transactions

In database technologies, a *rollback* is an operation that returns the database to some previous state. Rollbacks are important for database integrity, because they restore a clean copy of the database even after erroneous operations are performed.

Table 9-3 in the preceding section lists four @Transactional attributes related to rollback behavior: rollbackFor, rollbackForClassName, noRollbackFor, and noRollbackForClassName. Their names are quite relevant towards the behavior they configure. Rollback is important for methods that perform more than one database operation within the same transaction. For example, let's assume we have a save(..) method that inserts a singer to the database, then retrieves the saved record to link it to a set of albums being saved to the database. Although not realistic, let's assume one of the albums cannot be saved, and we want to undo the entire process, an all-or-nothing approach.

By default, a transaction will be rolled back on RuntimeException and Error but not on checked exceptions (business exceptions). This means that if we try to insert an album twice, the transaction is automatically rolled back, since the exception thrown is of type jakarta.persistence. PersistenceException that is a subclass of RuntimeException.

However, if we introduce a limitation of 50 characters for the title length and throw a checked exception for a title longer than 50 characters, the transaction is not automatically rolled back. The rollback has to be explicitly configured using the rollbackFor attribute.

To test this, let's introduce the checked exception class shown in Listing 9-14.

Listing 9-14. TitleTooLongException Checked Exception Class

```
package com.apress.prospring6.nine.ex

class TitleTooLongException : Exception {
    constructor(message: String?) : super(message)
    constructor(message: String?, cause: Throwable?) : super(message, cause)

    companion object {
        @Serial
        private val serialVersionUID = 42L
    }
}
```

This exception is thrown by the save(..) method in the AlbumRepoImpl. Since we know we want to save a set of albums, we can also add a version of save(..) that takes a Set<Album> argument. This method can also be used to implement something that wasn't covered until this chapter: *batch writing*, the grouping of multiple save requests into one method call. The two methods are shown in Listing 9-15.

Listing 9-15. The Two Versions of the save(..) Methods That Throw TitleTooLongException Checked Exceptions

```
package com.apress.prospring6.nine.repos

import com.apress.prospring6.nine.ex.TitleTooLongException
// other import statements omitted

@Repository
class AlbumRepoImpl : AlbumRepo {
    @PersistenceContext
    private val em: EntityManager? = null
```

```kotlin
@Value("#{jpaProperties.get('hibernate.jdbc.batch_size')}")
private val batchSize = 0

@Throws(TitleTooLongException::class)
override fun save(albums: Set<Album>): Set<Album> {
    val savedAlbums: MutableSet<Album> = mutableSetOf()
    var i = 0
    for (a in albums) {
        savedAlbums.add(save(a))
        i++
        if (i % batchSize == 0) {
            // Flush a batch of inserts and release memory.
            em!!.flush()
            em.clear()
        }
    }
    return savedAlbums
}

@Throws(TitleTooLongException::class)
override fun save(album: Album): Album {
    if (50 < album.title!!.length) {
        throw TitleTooLongException("Title " + album.title + " too long!")
    }
    return if (album.id == null) {
        em!!.persist(album)
        album
    } else {
        em!!.merge(album)
    }
}
}
```

The save(Set<Album>) method is wrapped in a transaction together with the save(Singer) method in the AllServiceImpl class, in the saveSingerWithAlbums(..) method, as shown in Listing 9-16.

Listing 9-16. AllServiceImpl.saveSingerWithAlbums(..) Transactional Method

```kotlin
package com.apress.prospring6.nine.services

import com.apress.prospring6.nine.ex.TitleTooLongException
import org.springframework.transaction.annotation.Transactional
// other import statements omitted

@Service
@Transactional
class AllServiceImpl(private val singerRepo: SingerRepo, private val albumRepo: AlbumRepo) :
    AllService {
```

461

```
@Transactional(rollbackFor = [TitleTooLongException::class])
@Throws(
    TitleTooLongException::class
)
override fun saveSingerWithAlbums(s: Singer, albums: Set<Album>) {
    val singer = singerRepo.save(s)
    albums.forEach{ a: Album ->
        a.singer = singer
    }
    albumRepo.save(albums)
}
...

}
```

Since this is the method grouping multiple database operations together, the transaction in the context which it is executed in is rolled back, and any partial operation is reverted by default if a RuntimeException or a TitleTooLongException is thrown as configured by @Transactional(rollbackFor = [TitleTooLongException::class]).

To test this behavior we need two test methods. The test method in Listing 9-17 verifies the default rollback for any RuntimeException method. In this particular scenario, we are trying to insert the *Little Girl Blue* album, which already exists in the database, because it was inserted via the add-nina.sql test setup script.

Listing 9-17. Method Testing Transaction Rollback Caused by a RuntimeException Being Thrown

```
package com.apress.prospring6.nine

import jakarta.persistence.PersistenceException
// other import statements omitted

@Testcontainers
@SqlMergeMode(SqlMergeMode.MergeMode.MERGE)
@Sql("classpath:testcontainers/drop-schema.sql", "classpath:testcontainers/create-
schema.sql")
@SpringJUnitConfig(classes = [AllServiceTest.TestContainersConfig::class])
class AllServiceTest : TestContainersBase() {
    @Autowired
    var service: AllService? = null

    @Test
    @SqlGroup(
        Sql(
            scripts = ["classpath:testcontainers/add-nina.sql"],
            executionPhase = Sql.ExecutionPhase.BEFORE_TEST_METHOD
        )
    )
    @DisplayName("should perform a rollback because PersistenceException")
    fun testRollbackRuntimeUpdate() {
        // (1)
        val singer = service!!.findByIdWithAlbums(5L)
        Assertions.assertNotNull(singer)
        // (2)
```

```kotlin
        singer!!.firstName = "Eunice Kathleen"
        singer.lastName = "Waymon"
        val album = Album()
        album.title = "Little Girl Blue"
        album.releaseDate = LocalDate.of(1959, 2, 20)
        album.singer = singer
        // (3)
        val albums = mutableSetOf(album)
        // (4)
        Assertions.assertThrows(
            PersistenceException::class.java,
            { service!!.saveSingerWithAlbums(singer, albums) },
            "PersistenceException not thrown!"
        )
        // (5)
        val nina = service!!.findByIdWithAlbums(5L)!!
        Assertions.assertAll("nina was not updated",
            Executable { Assertions.assertNotNull(nina) },
            Executable {
                Assertions.assertNotEquals(
                    "Eunice Kathleen",
                    nina.firstName
                )
            },
            Executable {
                Assertions.assertNotEquals(
                    "Waymon",
                    nina.lastName
                )
            }
        )
    }
    ...

}
```

As indicated by the comments in Listing 9-17, the test method is made of five parts:

1. The singer is retrieved from the database by calling `service.findByIdWithAlbums(5L)`.

2. The singer's `firstName` and `lastName` are updated.

3. A set containing the *Little Girl Blue* album is created.

4. `service.saveSingerWithAlbums(singer, albums)` is called and the assumption that a `PersistenceException` gets thrown is tested. Calling this method triggers the rollback of the transaction in which this method is executed, thus the changed singer instance is reverted to its original state.

5. The singer is retrieved from the database by calling `service.findByIdWithAlbums(5L)` and the assumption about its first name and last name being unchanged is tested.

This test should pass because `PersistenceException` is a `RuntimeException` and, as mentioned previously, a transaction is by default rolled back for any `RuntimeException`. If you really want to be sure that the rollback happened, you can always check the log of the test method execution and look for messages mentioning the transaction rollback. Listing 9-18 shows log snippets printed in the console when the `testRollbackRuntimeUpdate()` method is executed mentioning the transaction being rolled back.

Listing 9-18. Logging Output

```
DEBUG: AbstractPlatformTransactionManager - Creating new transaction with name
    [com.apress.prospring6.nine.services.AllServiceImpl.saveSingerWithAlbums]:
    PROPAGATION_REQUIRED,ISOLATION_DEFAULT,
    -com.apress.prospring6.nine.ex.TitleTooLongException
DEBUG: TransactionImpl - begin
...
DEBUG: SqlStatementLogger - insert into ALBUM (VERSION, RELEASE_DATE, SINGER_ID, title)
        values (?, ?, ?, ?)
WARN : Slf4JLogger - Error: 1062-23000: Duplicate entry '5-Little Girl Blue' for key
        'SINGER_ID'
DEBUG: SqlExceptionHelper - could not execute statement [n/a]
        java.sql.SQLIntegrityConstraintViolationException:
        (conn=4) Duplicate entry '5-Little Girl Blue' for key 'SINGER_ID'
DEBUG: JdbcResourceLocalTransactionCoordinatorImpl$TransactionDriverControlImpl - JDBC
        transaction marked for rollback-only (exception provided for stack trace)
TRACE: TransactionAspectSupport - Completing transaction for
    [com.apress.prospring6.nine.services.AllServiceImpl.saveSingerWithAlbums]
    after exception:
    jakarta.persistence.PersistenceException:
        org.hibernate.exception.ConstraintViolationException: could not execute statement
DEBUG: AbstractPlatformTransactionManager - Initiating transaction rollback
DEBUG: JpaTransactionManager - Rolling back JPA transaction on EntityManager [SessionImpl
        (1299829127<open>)]
DEBUG: TransactionImpl - rolling back
```

Notice that the transaction is being rolled back and the cause is the `PersistenceException`, but also that the `TitleTooLongException` is mentioned in the description of the transaction being created to execute this method. This, of course, is the checked exception that we introduced and configured rollback for. To test that a rollback of the transaction is done, a different test must be written that causes this exception to be thrown. The test in Listing 9-19 sets a title for the album being inserted that is too long, causing the `TitleTooLongException` to be thrown.

Listing 9-19. Method Testing Transaction Rollback Caused by a `TitleTooLongException` (Checked) Being Thrown

```
package com.apress.prospring6.nine

import jakarta.persistence.PersistenceException
// other import statements omitted

@Testcontainers
@SqlMergeMode(SqlMergeMode.MergeMode.MERGE)
@Sql("classpath:testcontainers/drop-schema.sql", "classpath:testcontainers/create-schema.sql")
@SpringJUnitConfig(classes = [AllServiceTest.TestContainersConfig::class])
```

```kotlin
class AllServiceTest : TestContainersBase() {
    @Autowired
    var service: AllService? = null

    @Test
    @SqlGroup(
        Sql(
            scripts = ["classpath:testcontainers/add-nina.sql"],
            executionPhase = Sql.ExecutionPhase.BEFORE_TEST_METHOD
        )
    )
    @DisplayName("should perform a rollback because TitleTooLongException")
    fun testRollbackCheckedUpdate() {
        val singer = service!!.findByIdWithAlbums(5L)
        Assertions.assertNotNull(singer)
        singer!!.firstName = "Eunice Kathleen"
        singer.lastName = "Waymon"
        val album = Album()
        album.title = """
            Sit there and count your fingers
            What can you do?
            Old girl you're through
            Sit there, count your little fingers
            Unhappy little girl blue
            """
        album.releaseDate = LocalDate.of(1959, 2, 20)
        album.singer = singer
        val albums = mutableSetOf(album)
        Assertions.assertThrows(
            TitleTooLongException::class.java,
            { service!!.saveSingerWithAlbums(singer, albums) },
            "TitleTooLongException not thrown!"
        )
        val nina = service!!.findByIdWithAlbums(5L)!!
        Assertions.assertAll("nina was not updated",
            Executable { Assertions.assertNotNull(nina) },
            Executable {
                Assertions.assertNotEquals(
                    "Eunice Kathleen",
                    nina.firstName
                )
            },
            Executable {
                Assertions.assertNotEquals(
                    "Waymon",
                    nina.lastName
                )
            }
        )
    }
    ...
}
```

When this test method is executed, in the console log displays similar messages to the ones shown in Listing 9-18 mentioning the rollback.

The `rollbackFor` attribute can be configured with multiple values, and the exceptions that trigger a rollback must be of the configured type or their subclasses. If there is a need to restrict the rollback for an exact exception type, the `rollbackForClassName` attribute can be configured with an array of full checked exception class names.

The `noRollbackFor` attribute has a similar role to `rollbackFor`, but instead of configuring exception types for which rollback is triggered, it is used to configure checked exception types for which a rollback should not be triggered. The `noRollbackForClassName` attribute can be configured with an array of checked exception fully qualified class names for which rollback is not to be triggered.

❗ It is recommended to use `rollbackFor` and `noRollbackFor` in your configuration, instead of `rollbackForClassName` and `noRollbackForClassName`. Doing so keeps the configuration more concise and the context more relaxed, as they provide matching the exception type and its subclasses in a type-safe manner.

Using Programmatic Transactions

Another option is to control the transaction behavior programmatically. In this case, we have two options. The first one is to inject an instance of `PlatformTransactionManager` into the bean and interact with the transaction manager directly. Another option is to use the Spring-provided `TransactionTemplate` class, which simplifies your work a lot. In this section, we demonstrate using the `TransactionTemplate` class. To make it simple, in this section a new version of the `countSingers()` method is implemented for which the transactional behavior is provided using the `TransactionTemplate` bean. Listing 9-20 depicts the `ProgrammaticTransactionCfg` class, a configuration class introduced especially for demonstrating the use of programmatic transactions.

Listing 9-20. `ProgrammaticTransactionCfg` Configuration Class

```
package com.apress.prospring6.nine.config

import org.springframework.beans.factory.annotation.Autowired
import org.springframework.transaction.TransactionDefinition
import org.springframework.transaction.support.TransactionTemplate

@Import(BasicDataSourceCfg::class)
@Configuration
@ComponentScan(basePackages = ["com.apress.prospring6.nine.repos", "com.apress.prospring6.
nine.programmatic"])
open class ProgrammaticTransactionCfg {
    @Bean
    fun transactionTemplate(): TransactionTemplate {
        val tt = TransactionTemplate()
        tt.propagationBehavior = TransactionDefinition.PROPAGATION_REQUIRES_NEW
        tt.timeout = 30
        tt.transactionManager = transactionManager()
        return tt
```

```
    }

    @Autowired
    var dataSource: DataSource? = null

    @Bean
    open fun transactionManager(): PlatformTransactionManager {
        val transactionManager = JpaTransactionManager()
        transactionManager.entityManagerFactory = entityManagerFactory().getObject()
        return transactionManager
    }

    @Bean
    open fun jpaVendorAdapter(): JpaVendorAdapter {
        return HibernateJpaVendorAdapter()
    }

    @Bean
    open fun entityManagerFactory(): LocalContainerEntityManagerFactoryBean {
        val factory = LocalContainerEntityManagerFactoryBean()
        factory.setPersistenceProviderClass(HibernatePersistenceProvider::class.java)
        factory.setPackagesToScan("com.apress.prospring6.nine.entities")
        factory.dataSource = dataSource!!
        factory.setJpaProperties(jpaProperties())
        factory.jpaVendorAdapter = jpaVendorAdapter()
        return factory
    }

    @Bean
    open fun jpaProperties(): Properties {
        val jpaProps = Properties()
        jpaProps[Environment.HBM2DDL_AUTO] = "none"
        jpaProps[Environment.FORMAT_SQL] = false
        jpaProps[Environment.USE_SQL_COMMENTS] = false
        jpaProps[Environment.SHOW_SQL] = false
        return jpaProps
    }
}
```

A `TransactionTemplate` bean is defined, using the `org.springframework.transaction.support.`
`TransactionTemplate` class, with a few transaction attributes. The propagation mode is configured
to `PROPAGATION_REQUIRES_NEW` so that log messages about the transaction are easy to spot. The
`TransactionTemplate` adopts the same approach as other Spring templates, such as the `JdbcTemplate`
introduced in **Chapter 6**. Also, the `@EnableTransactionManagement` annotation is not needed since
transaction management is not now done explicitly. With this configuration, the implementation of the
`countSingers()` method changes to the one shown in Listing 9-21.

Listing 9-21. `ProgramaticServiceImpl` Class Containing `countSingers()` Method with Explicit Transaction Management

```
package com.apress.prospring6.nine.programmatic

import com.apress.prospring6.nine.repos.SingerRepo
import org.springframework.stereotype.Service
import org.springframework.transaction.support.TransactionTemplate

@Service
class ProgrammaticServiceImpl(
    private val singerRepo: SingerRepo,
    private val transactionTemplate: TransactionTemplate
) : ProgrammaticService {
    override fun countSingers(): Long {
        return transactionTemplate.execute {
                transactionStatus: TransactionStatus? ->
            singerRepo.countAllSingers() }?:0L
    }
}
```

A new class named `ProgramaticServiceImpl` is introduced to separate this transactional service from the ones configured with declarative transactions. The bean declared by this class requires a `SpringRepo` and a `TransactionTemplate` bean to be injected by Spring.

The `singerRepo.countAllSingers()` method is passed as an argument to the `TransactionTemplate.execute(..)` method and is wrapped in a declaration of an inner class that implements the `TransactionCallback<T>` interface. Then `doInTransaction()` is the method invoking the actual `singerRepo.countAllSingers()`. The logic runs within a transaction with the attributes as defined by the `transactionTemplate` bean. The reason you are not clearly seeing all of that in Listing 9-21 is that lambda expression are used. The code in Listing 9-16 is the unexpanded version of the method shown in Listing 9-22.

Listing 9-22. Expanded Version of the `countSingers()` Method

```
package org.springframework.transaction.support.TransactionCallback

override fun countSingers():Long {
    return transactionTemplate.execute(object : TransactionCallback<Long> {
        override fun doInTransaction( status:TransactionStatus ):Long {
            return singerRepo.countAllSingers();
        }
    })
}
```

Testing this method is not different than what we've shown so far, but what needs to be pointed out is what to look for in the execution log. Listing 9-23 shows the testing method, without all the setup needed for it and the most interesting lines in the execution log.

Listing 9-23. `countSingers()` Test Method and Execution Log Snippet

```
@Test
@DisplayName("should count singers")
```

```
fun testCount() {
    var count = service.countSingers()
    assertEquals(3, count )
}
```

```
//------ execution log ----
DEBUG: AbstractPlatformTransactionManager - Creating new transaction with name [null]:
       PROPAGATION_REQUIRES_NEW,ISOLATION_DEFAULT,timeout_30
DEBUG: TransactionImpl - begin
DEBUG: SqlStatementLogger - select count(singer0_.ID) as col_0_0_ from SINGER singer0_
...
DEBUG: AbstractPlatformTransactionManager - Initiating transaction commit
DEBUG: JpaTransactionManager - Committing JPA transaction on EntityManager
       [SessionImpl(981307724<open>)]
DEBUG: TransactionImpl - committing
DEBUG: JpaTransactionManager - Closing JPA EntityManager [SessionImpl(981307724<open>)]
       after transaction
```

The only thing to observe here is that since the transactionTemplate bean does not know any details about the method being executed in a transaction, it cannot name the transaction, so the transaction name is set to null, but the transaction attributes shown in the log are the ones configured for the transactionTemplate in the ProgrammaticTransactionCfg.

During your development career, you might never get to write code using TransactionTemplate (or its reactive counterpart, TransactionalOperator), simply because declarative transaction is much more practical, but in the improbable case you'd ever need it, now you know it exists and how to use it.

Considerations on Transaction Management

So, having discussed two ways for implementing transaction management, which one should you use? The declarative approach is recommended in all cases, and you should avoid implementing transaction management explicitly within your code as much as possible. Most of the time, when you find it necessary to code transaction control logic in the application, it is because of bad design, and in this case, you should consider refactoring your logic into manageable pieces and have the transaction requirements defined on those pieces declaratively.

There is another declarative way to configure transactional behavior in Spring, and that is by using AOP XML–style configuration. Since XML is not a focus of this book, you can check out the previous revision of the Java variant of this book if you are interested in this topic. For the declarative approach, using XML and using annotations both have their own pros and cons. Some developers prefer not to declare transaction requirements in code, while others prefer using annotations for easy maintenance, because you can see all the transaction requirement declarations within the code. Again, let the application requirements drive your decision, and once your team or company has standardized on the approach, stay consistent with the configuration style.

There is also a @Transactional annotation in the jakarta.transaction package. Spring supports this annotation as well, but it offers less configuration options than Spring's @Transactional does. So, when writing Spring applications, make sure you check the package the annotation is coming from.

Transactional Configuration with Spring Boot

Without adding Spring Data in the mix, a Spring Boot transactional application is pretty easy to configure, since the main dependency is `spring-boot-starter-jdbc` and to add transactional-specific components requires only adding `spring-orm` and `hibernate-core-jakarta` into the mix. The configuration for a Spring Boot transactional project that does not use Spring Data is shown in Figure 9-5.

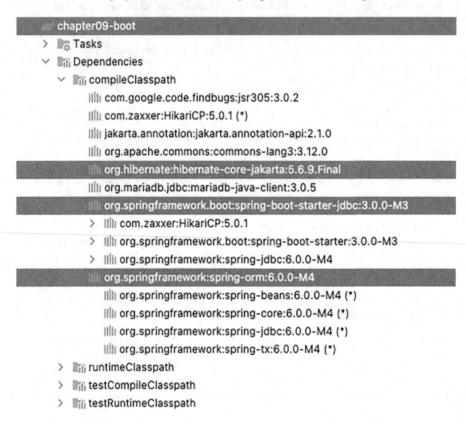

Figure 9-5. *Gradle View showing dependencies for the Spring Boot project*

Using Spring Boot allows a somewhat simplified configuration, since the `application.properties/application.yaml` files can be used to provide configuration using various Spring properties, instead of declaring Kotlin beans. As an example, take a look at the `application-dev.yaml` file contents in Listing 9-24.

Listing 9-24. `application-dev.yaml` Contents for the `chapter09-boot` Project

```
# datasource config
spring:
  datasource:
    driverClassName: org.mariadb.jdbc.Driver
    url: jdbc:mariadb://localhost:3306/musicdb?useSSL=false
    username: prospring6
    password: prospring6
    hikari:
```

```
      maximum-pool-size: 25
# JPA config
  jpa:
    generate-ddl: false
    properties:
      hibernate:
        jdbc:
          batch_size: 10
          fetch_size: 30
        max_fetch_depth: 3
        show-sql: true
        format-sql: false
        use_sql_comments: false
        hbm2ddl:
          auto: none


# Logging config
logging:
  pattern:
    console: "%-5level: %class{0} - %msg%n"
  level:
    root: INFO
    org.springframework.boot: INFO
    com.apress.prospring6.nine: INFO
```

The configuration is split into three sections: datasource, jpa, and logging. Properties with names starting with spring.datasource are set with values necessary for configuring a data source: connection URL, credentials, and connection pooling values. Properties with names starting with spring.jpa are set with values describing a persistence unit. You can easily recognize the Hibernate properties covered in **Chapter 7** and **Chapter 8**. Properties starting with logging are set with the typical value for logging configuration that in classic applications could be found in logback.xml files.

All this means that in a Spring Boot application there is no need for a configuration class to declare a data source bean, Spring will autoconfigure it based on the properties in the configuration file. The spring.jpa properties are used by Spring Boot to autoconfigure the persistence layer, a bean name jpaVendorAdapter of type HibernateJpaVendorAdapter is configured, including a bean named jpaVendorAdapter of type HibernateJpaVendorAdapter, a transactionManager bean of type JpaTransactionManager, and many more beans, including properties beans for Hibernate and JPA. The only thing Spring Boot does not configure is a bean of type LocalSessionFactoryBean, so that needs to be configured explicitly. Listing 9-25 shows the TransactionalConfig configuration that contains a single bean declaration of type LocalSessionFactoryBean.

Listing 9-25. TransactionalConfig Declaring a Bean of Type LocalSessionFactoryBean Using Beans Autoconfigured by Spring Boot

```
package com.apress.prospring6.nine.boot

import org.springframework.boot.context.properties.ConfigurationProperties
// other import statements omitted

@Configuration
@ComponentScan(basePackages = ["com.apress.prospring6.nine.boot.repos", "com.apress.
prospring6.nine.boot.services"])
```

```
@EnableTransactionManagement
open class TransactionalConfig {
    @Autowired
    var dataSource: DataSource? = null

    @Bean
    @ConfigurationProperties("spring.jpa.properties")
    open fun jpaProperties(): Properties {
        return Properties()
    }

    @Bean
    open fun sessionFactory(): LocalSessionFactoryBean {
        val sessionFactory = LocalSessionFactoryBean()
        sessionFactory.setDataSource(dataSource!!)
        sessionFactory.setPackagesToScan("com.apress.prospring6.nine.boot.entities")
        sessionFactory.hibernateProperties = jpaProperties()
        return sessionFactory
    }
}
```

Since the `LocalSessionFactoryBean` needs a data source, and needs the JPA properties to be configured, we need to access the JPA property values in the Spring Boot configuration file. This is done by configuring a bean of type `java.util.Properties` and annotating it with `@ConfigurationProperties("spring.jpa.properties")` to bind the properties declared in the Spring Boot configuration file to the `Properties` bean created by the method annotated with it.

And this is all that is needed to configure a Spring Boot transactional application. A Spring Boot test class can be created and the rollback tests can be added to it. When the test class is run, something peculiar happens, though—the test method in Listing 9-17, the one testing the rollback when a `RuntimeException` is thrown, fails. In the Gradle test page shown in Figure 9-6, it is quite obvious which test failed.

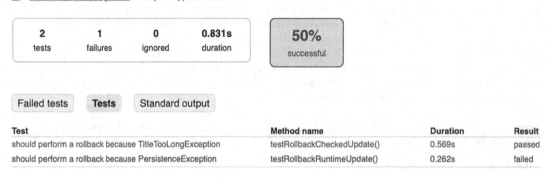

Figure 9-6. *Gradle test page showing a test failure*

If you look in the console log or click the test name, you will see this message:

```
org.opentest4j.AssertionFailedError:
PersistenceException not thrown!
    ==> Unexpected exception type thrown
        ==> expected: <jakarta.persistence.PersistenceException>
        but was: <org.springframework.dao.DataIntegrityViolationException>
```

So what is going on here? Why is there a different type of exception being thrown?

In **Chapter 6** you were introduced to the Spring hierarchy of runtime data access exceptions. Extensions of org.springframework.dao.DataAccessException (DataIntegrityViolationException is one of these extensions) match specific data access exceptions and provide more information about the real cause of an exception when accessing a database. They wrap around the exceptions thrown by all layers below Spring, and thus this is how the SQL checked exception java.sql.SQLIntegrityConstraintViolationException gets wrapped in a DataIntegrityViolationException instead of a PersistenceException. This happens in a Spring Boot application because Spring Boot autoconfigures a lot more beans than a developer might think to do; in this case Spring Boot autoconfigures an exception translator for the persistence layer, via its org.springframework.boot.autoconfigure.dao.PersistenceExceptionTranslationAutoConfiguration configuration class.

This means the test needs to be updated for the Spring Boot application to take this into account. The new test is shown in Listing 9-26.

Listing 9-26. The Spring Boot Version of the testRollbackRuntimeUpdate() Test Method

```
package com.apress.prospring6.nine;

import org.springframework.dao.DataIntegrityViolationException;
// other import statements omitted

@ActiveProfiles("test")
@SqlMergeMode(SqlMergeMode.MergeMode.MERGE)
@Sql("classpath:testcontainers/drop-schema.sql", "classpath:testcontainers/create-schema.sql")
@SpringBootTest(classes = [Chapter9Application::class])
open class Chapter9ApplicationTest {
    @Autowired
    var service: AllService? = null

    @Test
    @SqlGroup(
        Sql(
            scripts = ["classpath:testcontainers/add-nina.sql"],
            executionPhase = Sql.ExecutionPhase.BEFORE_TEST_METHOD
        ),
        Sql(
            scripts = ["classpath:testcontainers/remove-nina.sql"],
            executionPhase = Sql.ExecutionPhase.AFTER_TEST_METHOD
        )
    )
    @DisplayName("should perform a rollback because DataIntegrityViolationException")
    open fun testRollbackRuntimeUpdate() {
        val singer = service!!.findByIdWithAlbums(5L)
```

```kotlin
        Assertions.assertNotNull(singer)
        singer!!.firstName = "Eunice Kathleen"
        singer.lastName = "Waymon"
        val album = Album()
        album.title = "Little Girl Blue"
        album.releaseDate = LocalDate.of(1959, 2, 20)
        album.singer = singer
        val albums = mutableSetOf(album)
        Assertions.assertThrows(
            DataIntegrityViolationException::class.java,
            { service!!.saveSingerWithAlbums(singer, albums) },
            "PersistenceException not thrown!"
        )
        val nina = service!!.findByIdWithAlbums(5L)!!
        Assertions.assertAll("nina was not updated",
            Executable { Assertions.assertNotNull(nina) },
            Executable {
                Assertions.assertNotEquals(
                    "Eunice Kathleen",
                    nina.firstName
                )
            },
            Executable {
                Assertions.assertNotEquals(
                    "Waymon",
                    nina.lastName
                )
            }
        )
    }

    @Test
    @SqlGroup(
        Sql(
            scripts = ["classpath:testcontainers/add-nina.sql"],
            executionPhase = Sql.ExecutionPhase.BEFORE_TEST_METHOD
        ),
        Sql(
            scripts = ["classpath:testcontainers/remove-nina.sql"],
            executionPhase = Sql.ExecutionPhase.AFTER_TEST_METHOD
        )
    )
    @DisplayName("should perform a rollback because TitleTooLongException")
    open fun testRollbackCheckedUpdate() {
        val singer = service!!.findByIdWithAlbums(5L)
        Assertions.assertNotNull(singer)
        singer!!.firstName = "Eunice Kathleen"
        singer.lastName = "Waymon"
        val album = Album()
        album.title = """
            Sit there and count your fingers
```

```
        What can you do?
        Old girl you're through
        Sit there, count your little fingers
        Unhappy little girl blue
        """
    album.releaseDate = LocalDate.of(1959, 2, 20)
    album.singer = singer
    val albums = mutableSetOf(album)
    Assertions.assertThrows(
        TitleTooLongException::class.java,
        { service!!.saveSingerWithAlbums(singer, albums) },
        "TitleTooLongException not thrown!"
    )
    val nina = service!!.findByIdWithAlbums(5L)!!
    Assertions.assertAll("nina was not updated",
        Executable { Assertions.assertNotNull(nina) },
        Executable {
            Assertions.assertNotEquals(
                "Eunice Kathleen",
                nina.firstName
            )
        },
        Executable {
            Assertions.assertNotEquals(
                "Waymon",
                nina.lastName
            )
        }
    )
    }
}
```

This test method checks for the DataIntegrityViolationException being thrown when the bad update is being executed and thus this test passes. If you look in the execution log in the console, you will notice the same messages mentioning the transaction rollback that were printed for the test checking for the PersistenceException earlier in the chapter.

Transactional Tests

In **Chapter 4**, Table 4-5 listed and described the following test annotations that are relevant for transactional contexts:

- @Rollback

- @Commit

- @BeforeTransaction

- @AfterTransaction

The purpose of each is pretty obvious, thanks to their very relevant names. They are useful when writing transactional tests. Obviously, there is no need to annotate test methods with @Transactional when testing transactional services. You might want to do this to test your repositories in isolation. Although, with the introduction of Spring Data, testing repositories is not really necessary, as you will see in **Chapter 10**.

Test-managed transactions are not the same as the **Spring-managed transactions**, the ones managed by Spring in the application context (created to run methods annotated with @Transactional), or the same as **application-managed transactions**—those managed programmatically within the application.

The text context is based on the application context and thus Spring-managed and application-managed transactions will typically participate in test-managed transactions. This can be easily seen when running the test classes AllServiceTest and ProgramaticServiceTest introduced in previous sections. If you look in the execution log for the text Creating new transaction, you will notice that transactions are created for every test method. These transactions are the test-context transactions, and are created by default in a test context for the test methods. This might cause issues if some Spring-managed transactions are declared with a propagation mode other than REQUIRED or SUPPORTS.

Annotating a test method with @Transactional causes the test to be run within a transaction that will, by default, be automatically rolled back after completion of the test. Annotating a test class with @Transactional causes each test method within that class hierarchy to be run within a transaction. Propagation mode, rollback reasons, isolation, and so forth can be configured for test methods as well, when annotated with @Transactional.

The @Commit annotation is an alias for @Rollback(false), and they can both be used at the class level and method level. When used at the class level, the behavior applies to all test methods in the class. You can override the behavior at the class level, but try not to mix them, because the behavior of your tests might become unpredictable.

@BeforeTransaction and @AfterTransaction are the equivalents of @BeforeEach and @AfterEach for transactional methods. @BeforeTransaction indicates that the annotated method should be executed before a transaction is started for a test method configured to run within a transaction via Spring's @Transactional annotation. @AfterTransaction annotates a method that is executed after a transaction is ended for a test method annotated with Spring's @Transactional annotation. Starting with Spring 4.3, these two annotations can be used on interface default message as well.

This is all that can be said about Spring transactional applications at the moment. The information provided in this chapter should be enough to help you configure and work confidently with transactions in Spring applications.

Considerations on Transaction Management

So, having discussed the various ways for implementing transaction management, which one should you use? The declarative approach is recommended in all cases, and you should avoid implementing transaction management within your code as much as possible. Most of the time, when you find it necessary to code transaction control logic in the application, it is because of bad design, and in this case, you should consider refactoring your logic into manageable pieces and have the transaction requirements defined on those pieces declaratively.

For the declarative approach, using XML and using annotations both have their own pros and cons. Some developers prefer not to declare transaction requirements in code, while others prefer using annotations for easy maintenance, because you can see all the transaction requirement declarations within the code. Again, let the application requirements drive your decision, and once your team or company has standardized on the approach, stay consistent with the configuration style.

Summary

Transaction management is a key part of ensuring data integrity in almost any type of application. In this chapter, we discussed how to use Spring to manage transactions with almost no impact on your source code.

You were introduced to using annotations to configure declarative transactional behavior. You were also shown how to implement programmatic transactional behavior and how to test transactional services.

Local transactions are supported inside/outside a JEE application server, and only simple configuration is required to enable local transaction support in Spring. However, setting up a global transaction environment involves more work and greatly depends on which JTA provider and corresponding back-end resources your application needs to interact with. Also, the future seems to be all microservices running on serverless environments, where global transactions no longer really have a purpose.

Summary

CHAPTER 10

■ ■ ■

Spring Data with SQL and NoSQL Databases

Now that you've been introduced to multiple aspects of data access, such as connecting to the database, executing native queries with JDBC, mapping tables to entity classes to allow database records to be treated as objects in the Kotlin code, creating repository classes for data management using Hibernate sessions and `EntityManagerFactory`, and then executing multiple database operations in the same Spring-managed transaction, it is time to show you how to avoid writing all this code and let Spring do the job for you using the Spring Data.

The Spring Data JPA project is a subproject under the Spring Data umbrella project[1]. The main objective of the Spring Data project is to provide additional features for simplifying application development with various data sources. The Spring Data project contains multiple subprojects for interacting with SQL and NoSQL databases, both classic and reactive ones. It provides powerful repository and custom object-mapping abstractions, generation of repository queries based on configuration, support for transparent auditing, the possibility to extend repository code, and easy integration with Spring MVC controllers.

Spring Data provides a plethora of features designed to make data access easy, and this chapter focuses on a few aspects without going too much into detail, because that would require doubling the size of this book.

In this chapter we discuss the following:

- *Introducing Spring Data Java Persistence API (JPA)*: We discuss the Spring Data JPA project and demonstrate how it can help simplify the development of data access logic. Since JPA applies to SQL databases, MariaDB is used in the code samples.

- *Tracking entity changes and auditing*: In database update operations, it's a common requirement to keep track of the date an entity was created or last updated and who made the change. Also, for critical information such as a customer, a history table that stores each version of the entity is usually required. We discuss how Spring Data JPA and Hibernate Envers can help ease the development of such logic.

- *Spring Data for NoSQL databases*: We discuss what NoSQL databases are, why they are so interesting, what they are good for, and how accessing their data from a Spring application becomes easier with Spring Data. For the code samples, we use MongoDB.

- *Spring Data configuration with Spring Boot*: Spring Data makes things easier in Spring classic applications, but configuration becomes even easier in Spring Boot applications, since there is a special starter with a lot of auto-configuration options.

---

[1] `https://spring.io/projects/spring-data`

© Peter Späth, Iuliana Cosmina, Rob Harrop, Chris Schaefer 2023
P. Späth et al., *Pro Spring 6 with Kotlin*, https://doi.org/10.1007/978-1-4842-9557-1_10

In addition to introducing you too all these cool technologies, we will also show you how to test your repositories and services, using Testcontainers as a database access provider.

Introducing Spring Data JPA

Spring Data JPA eases development of applications that need to access JPA data sources. This obviously means Hibernate and Jakarta Persistence API components. The starting point in using Spring Data JPA is to add spring-data-jpa as a dependency to the project. Adding this dependency to your project results in all required Spring dependencies being added to the application classpath. The only thing left is to add Hibernate Core Jakarta to the configuration and override the jakarta.annotation-api when a different (more recent) version is desired. In Figure 10-1 you can see the list of dependencies for the chapter10 project, a Spring classic project using Spring Data JPA, as shown by the Gradle View in IntelliJ IDEA.

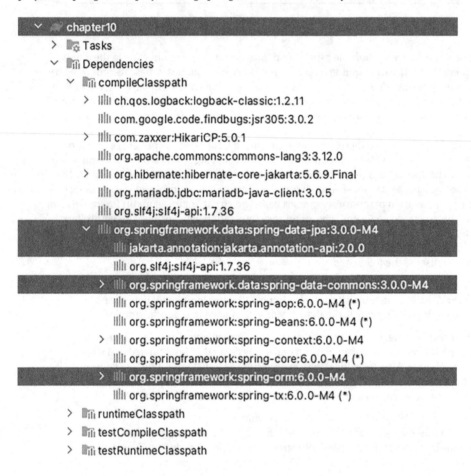

Figure 10-1. Gradle view showing dependencies for the chapter10 project

Using Spring Data JPA Repository Abstraction for Database Operations

In previous data access chapter repository classes (classes used to interact with the database) were created explicitly by the developer, and build around Hibernate components (Session, EntityManager) or Spring (JdbcTemplate). We had to explicitly configure them and inject them in the repository classes and then call their various methods to get the job done. The same applies for adding transactional behavior; if a repository needed to be transactional, we had to explicitly add the @Transactional annotation on the methods communicating with the database.

One of the main concepts of Spring Data and all its subprojects is the Repository abstraction, which belongs to the Spring Data Commons[2] project, one of the dependencies. In Spring Data JPA, the repository abstraction wraps the underlying JPA EntityManager and provides a simpler interface for JPA-based data access. What this means is that you do not have to write code using the EntityManager to access the data, unless you really have some custom query that Spring Data cannot generate for you based on your configurations.

The central interface within Spring Data is the org.springframework.data.repository. Repository<T,ID> interface, which is a marker interface (be sure not to mix it up with the @Repository stereotype annotation). Spring Data provides various extensions of the Repository<T, ID> interface; one of them is the org.springframework.data.repository.CrudRepository<T, ID> interface (which also belongs to the Spring Data Commons project), which we discuss in this section. Interfaces extending Repository<T, ID>, directly or by extending one of its subinterfaces, are called *domain repositories* because they replace the generic T with a concrete domain object type. These interfaces expose CRUD methods for managing domain objects.

Before explaining the CrudRepository<T, ID> interface and why it is important, take a look at Figure 10-2 that shows the Spring Repository<T, ID> interfaces hierarchy.

---

[2] https://github.com/spring-projects/spring-data-commons

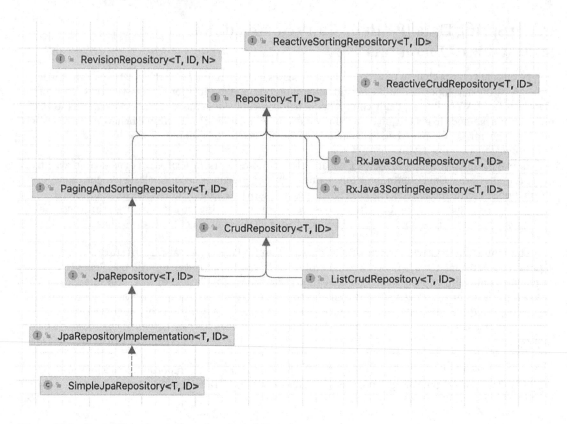

Figure 10-2. *Spring Data Repository interfaces hierarchy*

At this point you might be scratching your head and asking: *Hey, those are mostly interfaces, how are they supposed to do everything you mentioned previously?* Well, we are using Java 17 on this project, so technically, default methods might be an answer, but no. We are working with Spring, so the simplest answer is *proxying*. It will all become clear when you get to write some of your own repositories, but until then, let's go back to the CrudRepository<T, ID> interface.

The CrudRepository<T, ID> interface[3] provides a number of commonly used methods when handling data. Listing 10-1 shows a code snippet representing the interface declaration, which is extracted from Spring Data Commons project source code.

Listing 10-1. The CrudRepository<T, ID> Source Code

```
package org.springframework.data.repository;

import java.util.Optional;

@NoRepositoryBean
public interface CrudRepository<T, ID> extends Repository<T, ID> {
```

---

[3] https://github.com/spring-projects/spring-data-commons/blob/main/src/main/java/
org/springframework/data/repository/CrudRepository.java

```
<S extends T> S save(S entity);
<S extends T> Iterable<S> saveAll(Iterable<S> entities);

Optional<T> findById(ID id);
boolean existsById(ID id);
Iterable<T> findAll();
Iterable<T> findAllById(Iterable<ID> ids);

long count();

void deleteById(ID id);
void delete(T entity);
void deleteAllById(Iterable<? extends ID> ids);
void deleteAll(Iterable<? extends T> entities);
void deleteAll();
}
```

Looking at this interface, you might recognize method signatures that we've previously added to our repository interfaces and then implemented in the repository classes. The CrudRepository<T, ID> interface declares a complete set of methods you might expect a repository class to offer for data access. The names are self-explanatory and—don't panic—you do not have to provide the implementation for them! To put your mind at ease, let's take a look at an example.

The entity classes used in this chapter are the same as those that have been used in Chapters 6 through 9. Please review any of the previous chapters or take a peek at the code for the previous chapters if you need a reminder. If you've read the other chapters, entity classes like Singer and Album should be familiar to you by now.

Listing 10-2 depicts a classic repository interface named SingerRepository that declares just a few finder methods.

Listing 10-2. Classic SingerRepository Interface

package com.apress.prospring6.ten

import com.apress.prospring6.ten.entities.Singer

```
interface SingerRepository {
    fun findAll():List<Singer>
    fun findByFirstName(firstName:String):List<Singer>
    fun findByFirstNameAndLastName(firstName:String,
        lastName:String):List<Singer>
}
```

This interface can now be revised to transform it into a Spring Data domain repository interface by modifying it to extend CrudRepository<T, ID> as shown in Listing 10-3.

Listing 10-3. Spring Data Domain Repository SingerRepository Interface

```
package com.apress.prospring6.ten
// other import statements omitted

import org.springframework.data.repository.CrudRepository

interface SingerRepository : CrudRepository<Singer, Long> {
    fun findByFirstName(firstName:String)
        :Iterable<Singer>
    fun findByFirstNameAndLastName(firstName:String, lastName:String)
        :Iterable<Singer>
}
```

Notice that we just need to declare two methods in this interface, as the findAll() method is already provided by the CrudRepository<T, ID> interface. The SingerRepository interface extends the CrudRepository<T, ID> interface, passing in the entity class (Singer) and the ID type (Long).

One fancy aspect of Spring Data's Repository abstraction is that when you use the common naming convention of findBy{fieldName}, such as findByFirstName and findByFirstNameAndLastName do, you don't need to provide Spring Data JPA with the named query. Instead, at runtime, Spring Data JPA will "infer" and construct the query for you based on the method name and entity class replacing the generic type. For example, for the findByFirstName() method, Spring Data JPA will automatically prepare the query select s from Singer s where s.firstName = :firstName for you and set the named parameter firstName from the argument.

Now that we have declared our interface, we must create the configuration that will tell Spring Data where to find this interface. This is done by annotating the configuration class with @EnableJpaRepositories, as shown in Listing 10-4.

Listing 10-4. Spring Data JPA Configuration

```
package com.apress.prospring6.ten.config

import org.springframework.transaction.annotation.EnableTransactionManagement
import org.springframework.data.jpa.repository.config.EnableJpaRepositories
// other import statements omitted

@Import(BasicDataSourceCfg::class)
@Configuration
@EnableTransactionManagement
@ComponentScan(basePackages = ["com.apress.prospring6.ten"])
@EnableJpaRepositories("com.apress.prospring6.ten.repos")
open class DataJpaCfg {
    @Autowired
    var dataSource: DataSource? = null

    @Bean
    open fun transactionManager(): PlatformTransactionManager {
        val transactionManager = JpaTransactionManager()
        transactionManager.entityManagerFactory = entityManagerFactory().getObject()
        return transactionManager
    }
```

```
@Bean
open fun entityManagerFactory(): LocalContainerEntityManagerFactoryBean {
    return LocalContainerEntityManagerFactoryBean().apply {
        setPersistenceProviderClass(HibernatePersistenceProvider::class.java)
        setPackagesToScan("com.apress.prospring6.ten.entities")
        dataSource = this@DataJpaCfg.dataSource!!
        setJpaProperties(jpaProperties())
        jpaVendorAdapter = jpaVendorAdapter()
    }
}
...
}
```

The full configuration of this class and the BasicDataSourceCfg class have been covered repeatedly over the previous data access chapters (Chapters 6–9), and really, the only requirements to tell Spring where the repository interfaces are is @EnableJpaRepositories("com.apress.prospring6.ten.repos"). The @EnableJpaRepositories annotation is quite powerful, allowing you to specify multiple locations, in various ways, by declaring configuration attributes pretty similar to those of @ComponentScan. The default attribute is basePackages. Among the many other attributes, the namedQueriesLocation attribute is used to specify the location of a properties file containing named queries, the entityManagerFactoryRef attribute is used to specify the name of the EntityManager bean to use for creating queries, and the transactionManagerRef attribute is used to specify the name of the TransactionManager bean to create the repository instances.

So, how does this all work? Recall from **Chapter 5** that there are two types of proxies: JDK proxies, which implement the same interface as the target object, and class-based proxies, which extend the target object class. Spring Data JPA requires the repositories to be declared as interfaces extending Repository<T, ID> or one of its subinterfaces. By adding the @EnableJpaRepositories("com.apress.prospring6.ten.repos") configuration, we tell Spring to look in this package for these type of interfaces. For each of them, the Spring Data infrastructure components register the persistence technology-specific FactoryBean to create the appropriate proxies that handle invocations of the query methods.

So now that we have a Spring Data domain repository interface and a configuration telling Spring where it is, the next step is to create a transactional service to use our repository. The SingerServiceImpl class shown in Listing 10-5 just calls the SingerRepository instance methods.

Listing 10-5. SingerServiceImpl Class That Uses a Spring Data Repository Instance

package com.apress.prospring6.ten.service

```
import java.util.stream.Stream
import java.util.stream.StreamSupport
// other import statements omitted

@Service
@Transactional
class SingerServiceImpl(private val singerRepository: SingerRepository) : SingerService {
    @Transactional(readOnly = true)
    override fun findAll(): Stream<Singer> {
        return StreamSupport.stream(singerRepository.findAll().spliterator(),
            false)
    }
```

```kotlin
    @Transactional(readOnly = true)
    override fun findByFirstName(firstName: String): Stream<Singer> {
        return StreamSupport.stream(
            singerRepository.findByFirstName(firstName).spliterator(), false
        )
    }

    @Transactional(readOnly = true)
    override fun findByFirstNameAndLastName(firstName: String, lastName: String):
    Stream<Singer> {
        return StreamSupport.stream(
            singerRepository.findByFirstNameAndLastName(firstName, lastName).spliterator(),
            false
        )
    }

    @Transactional(propagation = Propagation.REQUIRES_NEW, label = ["modifying"])
    override fun updateFirstName(firstName: String, id: Long): Singer {
        singerRepository.findById(id).ifPresent { s: Singer? ->
            singerRepository.setFirstNameFor(
                firstName,
                id
            )
        }
        return singerRepository.findById(id).orElse(null)
    }

    @Transactional(readOnly = true)
    override fun findByLastName(lastName: String): Stream<SingerRepository.FullName> {
        return StreamSupport.stream(
            singerRepository.findByLastName(lastName).spliterator(), false
        )
    }
}
```

You can see that instead of EntityManager, we just need to inject the singerRepository instance, generated by Spring based on the SingerRepository interface, into the service class, and Spring Data JPA will do all the low-level work for us. In Listing 10-6, you can see a testing class, and by now you should already be familiar with its content.

Listing 10-6. SingerServiceTest Test Class

```kotlin
package com.apress.prospring6.ten
// import statements omitted

@Testcontainers
@SqlMergeMode(SqlMergeMode.MergeMode.MERGE)
@Sql("classpath:testcontainers/drop-schema.sql", "classpath:testcontainers/create-
schema.sql")
@SpringJUnitConfig(classes = [SingerServiceTest.TestContainersConfig::class])
```

```kotlin
open class SingerServiceTest : TestContainersBase() {
    @Autowired
    var singerService: SingerService? = null

    @Test
    fun testFindAll() {
        val singers: List<Singer> = singerService!!.findAll().peek{ s: Singer ->
                LOGGER.info(
                    s.toString()
                )
            }.toList()
        Assertions.assertEquals(3, singers.size)
    }

    @Test
    fun testFindByFirstName() {
        val singers: List<Singer> = singerService!!.findByFirstName("John")
            .peek{ s: Singer ->
                    LOGGER.info(
                        s.toString()
                    )
                }.toList()
        Assertions.assertEquals(2, singers.size)
    }

    @Test
    fun testFindByFirstNameAndLastName() {
        val singers: List<Singer> = singerService!!.findByFirstNameAndLastName(
                "John", "Mayer")
            .peek{ s: Singer ->
                LOGGER.info(
                    s.toString()
                )
            }.toList()
        Assertions.assertEquals(1, singers.size)
    }

    @Configuration
    @Import(DataJpaCfg::class)
    open class TestContainersConfig {
        @Autowired
        var jpaProperties: Properties? = null
        @PostConstruct
        open fun initialize() {
            jpaProperties!![Environment.FORMAT_SQL] = true
            jpaProperties!![Environment.USE_SQL_COMMENTS] = true
            jpaProperties!![Environment.SHOW_SQL] = true
            jpaProperties!![Environment.STATEMENT_BATCH_SIZE] = 30
        }
    }
}
```

```
    companion object {
        private val LOGGER = LoggerFactory.getLogger(SingerServiceTest::class.java)
    }
}
```

The test class is nothing special, and the Testcontainers MariaDB container configuration was isolated to the TestContainersBase class, to avoid repeating it here. When running this test class, all methods should pass, but as usual, let's crank up the log levels to TRACE for all Spring libraries and check out the execution log, which gives us a lot of information about what Spring is doing. Take a look at the log snippets in Listing 10-7.

Listing 10-7. SingerServiceTest Execution Log Snippets

```
DEBUG: RepositoryConfigurationDelegate - Scanning for JPA repositories in packages com.
apress.prospring6.ten.repos.
TRACE: ClassPathScanningCandidateComponentProvider - Scanning file [/../com/apress/
prospring6/ten/repos/SingerRepository.class]
DEBUG: ClassPathScanningCandidateComponentProvider - Identified candidate component class:
file [/../com/apress/prospring6/ten/repos/SingerRepository.class]
TRACE: RepositoryConfigurationDelegate - Spring Data JPA - Registering repository:
singerRepository
    - Interface: com.apress.prospring6.ten.repos.SingerRepository
    - Factory: org.springframework.data.jpa.repository.support.JpaRepositoryFactoryBean
INFO : RepositoryConfigurationDelegate - Finished Spring Data repository scanning in 37 ms.
Found 1 JPA repository interfaces.
...
DEBUG: RepositoryFactorySupport - Initializing repository instance for com.apress.
prospring6.ten.repos.SingerRepository...
...
DEBUG: RepositoryFactorySupport - Finished creation of repository instance for com.apress.
prospring6.ten.repos.SingerRepository.
...
TRACE: TransactionAspectSupport - Getting transaction for
    [com.apress.prospring6.ten.service.SingerServiceImpl.findAll]
TRACE: AbstractFallbackTransactionAttributeSource - Adding transactional method
    'org.springframework.data.jpa.repository.support.SimpleJpaRepository.findAll'
    with attribute: PROPAGATION_REQUIRED,ISOLATION_DEFAULT,readOnly
TRACE: TransactionAspectSupport - Getting transaction for
    [org.springframework.data.jpa.repository.support.SimpleJpaRepository.findAll]
```

Notice how the configured package com.apress.prospring6.ten.repos and its subpackages are scanned and the SingerRepository interface is identified as a candidate for creating a repository instance.

The peculiar thing about this log is that it seems as if a transaction is created for the repository instance method being called (line marked with <3>). So what is happening there? Well, the class backing up the proxy is org.springframework.data.jpa.repository.support.SimpleJpaRepository<T, ID>, and if you check out the Spring code[4], you will notice that this class is annotated with @Transactional(readOnly = true). This is where your transactions for the repository methods come from. They are needed because any JPA operation should be done in a transactional context; that way, in case of errors, a rollback will ensure

---

[4] https://github.com/spring-projects/spring-data-jpa/blob/main/spring-data-jpa/src/
main/java/org/springframework/data/jpa/repository/support/SimpleJpaRepository.java

the database is left in a good state. This obviously means that for service methods that just call a single repository method, an extra transaction is not needed. Even if configured, since the default propagation mode is PROPAGATION_REQUIRED, the service method will be executed within the same transaction as the repository method.

Before talking about more complex queries and how calling them is supported, let's talk about the JpaRepository<T, ID> interface.

Using JpaRepository

The JpaRepository<T, ID> interface is an even more advanced Spring interface than CrudRepository<T, ID> that can make creating custom repositories easier. The JpaRepository<T, ID> interface provides batch, paging, and sorting operations. Figure 10-3 shows the relationship between JpaRepository<T, ID> and the CrudRepository<T, ID> interface.

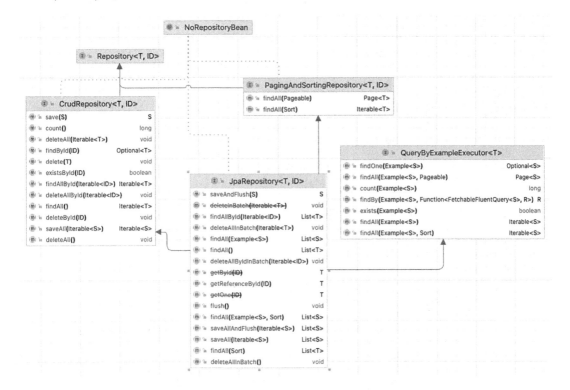

Figure 10-3. *Spring Data* JpaRepository<T, ID> *hierarchy*

Depending on the complexity of the application, you can choose to use CrudRepository<T, ID> or JpaRepository<T, ID>. As you can see from Figure 10-3, JpaRepository<T, ID> extends CrudRepository<T, ID> and thus provides all the same functionalities.

Spring Data JPA with Custom Queries

In complex applications, you might need custom queries that cannot be "inferred" by Spring.

Previous chapters introduced using named queries, declared on entity classes using the @NamedQuery annotation, as a way to provide support for query execution, whether with a Hibernate Session or EntityManager. Named queries are supported with Spring Data repositories, too. Spring Data tries to resolve a call to a method declared by the developer to a named query starting with the simple name of the configured domain class, followed by the method name, separated by a dot. This way of naming queries was used when working with a Hibernate Session or EntityManager too, just to make the transition practical. Named queries with Spring Data do have some limitations, however; for example, named parameters are not supported. As an example, consider a named query to select albums with a release date greater than 2010-01-01. Listing 10-8 presents the important code bits showing the named parameter query.

Listing 10-8. Album Entity with a Named Query

```kotlin
package com.apress.prospring6.ten.entities
import jakarta.persistence.NamedQuery
// other import statements omitted

@Entity
@Table(name = "ALBUM")
@NamedQuery(name = Album.FIND_WITH_RELEASE_DATE_GREATER_THAN, query = "select a from Album a
where a.releaseDate > ?1")
class Album : AbstractEntity() {
        @Column
        var title: String? = null

        @Column(name = "RELEASE_DATE")
        var releaseDate: LocalDate? = null

        @ManyToOne
        @JoinColumn(name = "SINGER_ID")
        var singer: Singer? = null

        override fun equals(other: Any?): Boolean {
                if (this === other) return true
                if (other == null || javaClass != other.javaClass) return false
                val album = other as Album
                return if (id != null) {
                        id == other.id
                } else title == album.title && releaseDate == album.releaseDate
        }

        override fun hashCode(): Int {
                return Objects.hash(title, releaseDate)
        }

        override fun toString(): String {
                return ("Album - Id: " + id + ", Singer id: " + (singer?.id?:"")
                                + ", Title: " + title + ", Release Date: " + releaseDate)
        }
}
```

```
companion object {
        @Serial
        private val serialVersionUID = 3L
        const val FIND_WITH_RELEASE_DATE_GREATER_THAN =
                    "Album.findWithReleaseDateGreaterThan"
    }
}
```

For cases requiring named parameters, the query must be defined explicitly using the @Query annotation. We'll use this annotation to search for all music albums containing The in their title. Listing 10-9 depicts the AlbumRepository interface.

Listing 10-9. AlbumRepository with Named Queries and @Query Methods

package com.apress.prospring6.ten.repos

import org.springframework.data.jpa.repository.Query
import org.springframework.data.repository.query.Param
// other import statements omitted

```
interface AlbumRepository : JpaRepository<Album?, Long?> {
    fun findBySinger(singer: Singer): Iterable<Album>
    fun findWithReleaseDateGreaterThan(rd: LocalDate): Iterable<Album>

    @Query("select a from Album a where a.title like %:title%")
    fun findByTitle(@Param("title") t: String): Iterable<Album>
}
```

Spring Data matches the findWithReleaseDateGreaterThan(..) method to the query named Album. findWithReleaseDateGreaterThan. The query for the findByTitle(..) method has a named parameter called title. When the name of the named parameter is the same as the name of the argument in the method annotated with @Query, the @Param annotation is not needed. If the method argument has a different name, the @Param annotation is needed to tell Spring that the value of this argument is to be injected in the named parameter in the query.

The AlbumServiceImpl service class is quite simple and only uses the albumRepository bean to call its methods, as shown in Listing 10-10.

Listing 10-10. AlbumServiceImpl Service Calling AlbumRepository Methods

package com.apress.prospring6.ten.service

import java.util.stream.Stream
import java.util.stream.StreamSupport
// other import statements omitted

```
@Service
@Transactional(readOnly = true)
class AlbumServiceImpl(private val albumRepository: AlbumRepository) :
    AlbumService {
    override fun findBySinger(singer: Singer): Stream<Album> {
        return StreamSupport.stream(albumRepository.findBySinger(singer).spliterator(),
            false)
    }
```

```kotlin
override fun findWithReleaseDateGreaterThan(rd: LocalDate): Stream<Album> {
    return StreamSupport.stream(
        albumRepository.findWithReleaseDateGreaterThan(rd).spliterator(),
        false
    )
}

override fun findByTitle(title: String): Stream<Album> {
    return StreamSupport.stream(albumRepository.findByTitle(title).spliterator(),
        false)
}
}
```

The findBySinger(..) query is an easy one, and Spring Data is able to resolve this one on its own. For this reason, the test class won't cover this one. Feel free to write the test for this one yourself. Listing 10-11 shows the test class for the two slightly complex queries.

Listing 10-11. AlbumServiceTest Class

```kotlin
package com.apress.prospring6.ten
// import statements omitted

@Testcontainers
@Sql("classpath:testcontainers/drop-schema.sql", "classpath:testcontainers/create-schema.sql")
@SpringJUnitConfig(classes = [AlbumServiceTest.TestContainersConfig::class])
class AlbumServiceTest : TestContainersBase() {
    @Autowired
    var albumService: AlbumService? = null

    @Test
    fun testFindWithReleaseDateGreaterThan() {
        val albums: List<Album> = albumService!!
            .findWithReleaseDateGreaterThan(LocalDate.of(2010, 1, 1))
            .peek{ s: Album ->
                LOGGER.info(
                    s.toString()
                )
            }.toList()
        Assertions.assertEquals(2, albums.size)
    }

    @Test
    fun testFindByTitle() {
        val albums: List<Album> = albumService!!
            .findByTitle("The")
            .peek{ s: Album ->
                LOGGER.info(
                    s.toString()
                )
            }.toList()
        Assertions.assertEquals(1, albums.size)
    }
```

```kotlin
@Configuration
@Import(DataJpaCfg::class)
open class TestContainersConfig {
    @Autowired
    var jpaProperties: Properties? = null
    @PostConstruct
    open fun initialize() {
        jpaProperties!![Environment.FORMAT_SQL] = true
        jpaProperties!![Environment.USE_SQL_COMMENTS] = true
        jpaProperties!![Environment.SHOW_SQL] = true
        jpaProperties!![Environment.STATEMENT_BATCH_SIZE] = 30
    }
}

companion object {
    private val LOGGER = LoggerFactory.getLogger(AlbumServiceTest::class.java)
}
}
```

Spring Data repositories are quite powerful and versatile. Methods annotated with @Query for example support sorting, by adding an org.springframework.data.domain.Sort parameter. Queries declared with the @Query annotations even support SpEL expressions.

The examples in this section only show queries that read data. Queries that modify data also need to be annotated, with @Modified. Just as an example, the SingerRepository is modified to add a query that changes the first name of a singer record based on its id. The method declaration is depicted in Listing 10-12.

Listing 10-12. @Modifying Annotated Spring Data Query Method

package com.apress.prospring6.ten.repos

import org.springframework.data.jpa.repository.Modifying;
```kotlin
// other import statements omitted

interface SingerRepository : CrudRepository<Singer, Long> {
    @Modifying
    fun findByFirstName(firstName: String): Iterable<Singer>

    @Modifying(clearAutomatically = true)
    @Query("update Singer s set s.firstName = ?1 where s.id = ?2")
    fun setFirstNameFor(firstName: String, id: Long): Int
    ...

}
```

The @Modifying annotation is designed to be used only together with the @Query annotation, and it makes no sense without it. If used on its own, it is just ignored by Spring Data.

The @Modifying annotation supports two attributes:

- flushAutomatically: When set to true (the default is false), it causes the underlying persistence context to be flushed *before* executing the modifying query.

- clearAutomatically: When set to true (the default is false), it causes the underlying persistence context to be flushed *after* executing the modifying query. This means the changed entities are persisted to the database, immediately after the execution of this method.

The reason setFirstNameFor(..) was annotated with @Modifying(clearAutomatically = true) is that in the service method, this method is invoked to perform an update, then the entity to be returned is retrieved from the database using the findById(id) repository method. Since changes get flushed at the end of a transaction, and we have no control over when that might be, the returned entity might not be the updated one.

To make things interesting, the service method calling setFirstNameFor(..) returns the updated instance, which we can test. The service method is shown in Listing 10-13.

Listing 10-13. Service Method Calling @Modified annotated Spring Data Query Method

```kotlin
package com.apress.prospring6.ten.service
// import statements omitted

@Service
@Transactional
class SingerServiceImpl(private val singerRepository: SingerRepository) : SingerService {
    @Transactional(readOnly = true)
    override fun findAll(): Stream<Singer> {
        return StreamSupport.stream(singerRepository.findAll().spliterator(),
            false)
    }

    @Transactional(propagation = Propagation.REQUIRES_NEW, label = ["modifying"])
    override fun updateFirstName(firstName: String, id: Long): Singer {
        singerRepository.findById(id).ifPresent { s: Singer? ->
            singerRepository.setFirstNameFor(
                firstName,
                id
            )
        }
        return singerRepository.findById(id).orElse(null)
    }
    ...
}
```

The test method is depicted in Listing 10-14.

Listing 10-14. Test Method for the Service Method Calling @Modified Annotated Spring Data Query Method

```
package com.apress.prospring6.ten

import org.springframework.test.annotation.Rollback;
// other import statements omitted

@Testcontainers
@SqlMergeMode(SqlMergeMode.MergeMode.MERGE)
@Sql("classpath:testcontainers/drop-schema.sql",
        "classpath:testcontainers/create-schema.sql")
@SpringJUnitConfig(classes = [SingerServiceTest.TestContainersConfig::class])
open class SingerServiceTest : TestContainersBase() {
    @Autowired
    var singerService: SingerService? = null

    @Rollback
    @Test
    @SqlGroup(
        Sql(
            scripts = ["classpath:testcontainers/add-nina.sql"],
            executionPhase = Sql.ExecutionPhase.BEFORE_TEST_METHOD
        )
    )
    @DisplayName("should update a singer's name")
    fun testUpdateFirstNameByQuery() {
        val nina = singerService!!.updateFirstName("Eunice Kathleen", 5L)
        Assertions.assertAll("nina was not updated",
            Executable { Assertions.assertNotNull(nina) },
            Executable {
                Assertions.assertEquals(
                    "Eunice Kathleen",
                    nina!!.firstName
                )
            }
        )
    }
    ...
}
```

ℹ️   Notice that instead of cleaning up the context by using a @Sql annotation and a delete script, the @Rollback annotation introduced in **Chapter 9** is used.

The @Modifying annotation works in the same way for conditional delete queries as well. There are more database operations that can be simplified with Spring Data JPA repositories. However, covering all of them is beyond the scope of this book. Feel free to research on your own in the official documentation[5].

---

[5] https://docs.spring.io/spring-data/data-jpa/docs/current/reference/html

Projection Queries

Chapters 7 and 8 already introduced the topic of projection queries, so this section shows only how to configure a projection query using Spring Data JPA.

To limit the result of a query to only a few fields, we need an interface that exposes accessor methods for the properties to be read. Spring supports quite a few interesting ways to declare projection interfaces, but for simplicity, in this example we'll just show an interface that exposes the first name and last name of a singer. The repository method and the interface are both shown in Listing 10-15.

Listing 10-15. Projection Interface and Repository Method

```
package com.apress.prospring6.ten.service
// import statements omitted

interface SingerService {
    fun findAll(): Stream<Singer>
    fun findByFirstName(firstName: String): Stream<Singer>
    fun findByFirstNameAndLastName(firstName: String, lastName: String): Stream<Singer>
    fun updateFirstName(firstName: String, id: Long): Singer
    fun findByLastName(lastName: String): Stream<SingerRepository.FullName>
}
// SingerRepository.kt
interface SingerRepository : CrudRepository<Singer, Long> {
    ...
    fun findByLastName(lastName: String): Iterable<FullName>

    interface FullName {
        val firstName: String
        val lastName: String
        // We can do that in Java, but for some reason not in Kotlin
        //val fullName: String
        //    get() = "$firstName $lastName"
    }
}
```

The service method does nothing other than call the findByLastName(..) method, and the test method just prints the results and tests the assumption that a single result is returned. Both are provided in the book repository, but they won't be listed here.

The only thing interesting to see is the actual type of the objects being returned by the repository method. Since the database results are modeled using the FullName interface, there must be an implementation generated by Spring, right? Well, not in the actual sense. A proxy is created, yet again, and that proxy implements the FullName interface, so calling the declared methods is forwarded to Spring Data infrastructure components responsible with storing and returning the actual values. This can be easily seen by setting a breakpoint in the test method and inspecting the contents of the returned collection using IntelliJ IDEA's evaluate expression at runtime feature. Just right-click the source code while the execution is paused, choose **Evaluate Expression** in the context menu, and insert singers.get(0). Notice the type of the object and, if you expand it, you will see the target objects and the interfaces implemented. It should look pretty similar to what is shown in Figure 10-4 (but note there is a small chance that some types might be renamed, moved, etc. by the time the final Spring Data JPA is released).

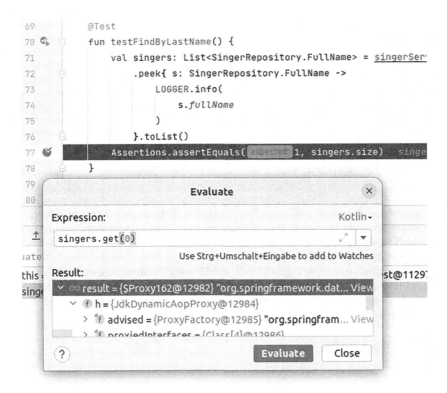

```
69        @Test
70        fun testFindByLastName() {
71            val singers: List<SingerRepository.FullName> = singerSer
72                .peek{ s: SingerRepository.FullName ->
73                    LOGGER.info(
74                        s.fullName
75                    )
76                }.toList()
77            Assertions.assertEquals( expected 1, singers.size)   singe
78        }
79
80
```

Evaluate

Expression: Kotlin▾

singers.get(0)

Use Strg+Umschalt+Eingabe to add to Watches

Result:

∨ ∞ result = {$Proxy162@12982} "org.springframework.dat... View

  ∨ f h = {JdkDynamicAopProxy@12984}

    > f advised = {ProxyFactory@12985} "org.springfram... View

    > f proxiedInterfaces = {Class[4]@12986}

(?)   Evaluate   Close

Figure 10-4. *Inspecting Spring Data instances*

Keeping Track of Changes on the Entity Class

In most applications, we need to keep track of basic audit activities for the business data being maintained by users. The audit information typically includes the user who created the data, the date it was created, the date it was last modified, and the user who last modified it.

The Spring Data JPA project provides this function in the form of a JPA entity listener, which helps you to keep track of the audit information automatically. To use the feature, until Spring 4, the entity class needed to implement the Auditable<U, ID, T extends TemporalAccessor> extends Persistable<ID> interface (belonging to Spring Data Commons)[6] or extend any class that implements this interface. Listing 10-16 shows the Auditable interface that was extracted from Spring Data's reference documentation.

Listing 10-16. The Auditable<U, ID, T extends TemporalAccessor> Interface

```
package org.springframework.data.domain;

import java.time.temporal.TemporalAccessor;
import java.util.Optional;
```

---

[6] https://github.com/spring-projects/spring-data-commons/blob/main/src/main/java/
org/springframework/data/domain/Auditable.java

```java
public interface Auditable<U, ID, T extends TemporalAccessor>
    extends Persistable<ID> {

    Optional<U> getCreatedBy();
    void setCreatedBy(U createdBy);
    Optional<T> getCreatedDate();
    void setCreatedDate(T creationDate);
    Optional<U> getLastModifiedBy();
    void setLastModifiedBy(U lastModifiedBy);
    Optional<T> getLastModifiedDate();
    void setLastModifiedDate(T lastModifiedDate);
}
```

As you can see from the definition of the Auditable<U, ID, T extends TemporalAccessor> interface, the date type columns are restricted to types extending java.time.temporal.TemporalAccessor. Starting with Spring 5, implementing Auditable<U, ID, T extends TemporalAccessor> is no longer necessary because everything can be replaced by annotations.

To show how this works, let's create a new table called SINGER_AUDIT in the database schema, which is based on the SINGER table, with four audit-related columns added. The columns record who created the entity, when the entity was created, the last user that edited the entity, and when. Listing 10-17 shows the table creation script (AuditSchema.sql).

Listing 10-17. The SINGER_AUDIT Table DDL

```sql
CREATE TABLE SINGER_AUDIT (
    ID INT NOT NULL AUTO_INCREMENT
    , FIRST_NAME VARCHAR(60) NOT NULL
    , LAST_NAME VARCHAR(40) NOT NULL
    , BIRTH_DATE DATE
    , VERSION INT NOT NULL DEFAULT 0
    , CREATED_BY VARCHAR(20)
    , CREATED_DATE TIMESTAMP
    , LAST_MODIFIED_BY VARCHAR(20)
    , LAST_MODIFIED_DATE TIMESTAMP
    , UNIQUE UQ_SINGER_AUDIT_1 (FIRST_NAME, LAST_NAME)
    , PRIMARY KEY (ID)
);
```

There are four audit-related columns. They correspond to @CreatedBy, @CreatedDate, @LastModifiedBy, and @LastModifiedDate annotations. They are part of the org.springframework.data. annotation package. Using these annotations, the type restriction for the date columns no longer applies. To keep things neatly organized, an @MappedSuperclass named AuditableEntity<U> is added to the project to group the audit fields together. This class is shown in Listing 10-18.

Listing 10-18. The AuditableEntity Abstract Class

```java
package com.apress.prospring6.ten.entities
import org.springframework.data.jpa.domain.support.AuditingEntityListener
import jakarta.persistence.EntityListeners
import org.springframework.data.annotation
```

```kotlin
// other import statements omitted

@Audited
@MappedSuperclass
@EntityListeners(AuditingEntityListener::class)
abstract class AuditableEntity<U> : Serializable {
        @CreatedDate
        @Column(name = "CREATED_DATE")
        protected var createdDate: LocalDateTime? = null

        @CreatedBy
        @Column(name = "CREATED_BY")
          var createdBy: String? = null

        @LastModifiedBy
        @Column(name = "LAST_MODIFIED_BY")
        var lastModifiedBy: String? = null

        @LastModifiedDate
        @Column(name = "LAST_MODIFIED_DATE")
        protected var lastModifiedDate: LocalDateTime? = null

        companion object {
                @Serial
                private val serialVersionUID = 8L
        }
}
```

The @Column annotations are applied on the auditing fields to map to the actual column in the table. The @EntityListeners(AuditingEntityListener.class) annotation registers AuditingEntityListener to be used for all entities extending this class in the persistent context.

💡 The @EntityListeners(AuditingEntityListener.class) annotation also replaces the need to declare an orm.xml configuration file, as indicated in the JPA specification. So, it is not necessary to add the following:

```xml
<?xml version="1.0" encoding="UTF-8" ?>
<entity-mappings ...>
    <description>JPA</description>
    <persistence-unit-metadata>
        <persistence-unit-defaults>
            <entity-listeners>
                <entity-listener
class="org.springframework...AuditingEntityListener" />
            </entity-listeners>
        </persistence-unit-defaults>
    </persistence-unit-metadata>
</entity-mappings>
```

Any class that needs auditing in our application should be declared to extend the AuditableEntity<U> class. So to map the SINGER_AUDIT table, the SingerAudit class depicted in Listing 10-19 needs to be written.

Listing 10-19. The SingerAudit Entity Class

```
package com.apress.prospring6.ten.entities
// import statements omitted

@Entity
@Audited
@Table(name = "SINGER_AUDIT")
class SingerAudit : AuditableEntity<SingerAudit>() {
    @Id
    @GeneratedValue(strategy = GenerationType.IDENTITY)
    @Column(name = "ID")
    val id: Long? = null

    @Version
    @Column(name = "VERSION")
    private val version = 0

    @Column(name = "FIRST_NAME")
    var firstName: String? = null

    @Column(name = "LAST_NAME")
    var lastName: String? = null

    @Column(name = "BIRTH_DATE")
    var birthDate: LocalDate? = null

    ...
}
```

To manage audited entities of type SingerAudit, a repository interface and a service class should be used. The SingerAuditRepository interface just extends CrudRepository<SingerAudit, Long>, which already declares all the methods that we are going to use for SingerAuditService, shown in Listing 10-20.

Listing 10-20. The SingerAuditService Interface

```
package com.apress.prospring6.ten.service
// import statements omitted

interface SingerAuditService {
    fun findAll(): Stream<SingerAudit>
    fun findById(id: Long): SingerAudit?
    fun save(singer: SingerAudit): SingerAudit
    fun findAuditByRevision(id: Long, revision: Int): SingerAudit?
    fun delete(id: Long)
}
```

The SingerAuditServiceImpl class that implements SingerAuditService does nothing more than call the SingerAuditRepository methods in a transactional context. Both are so simple they require no attention at this point. However, to tell Spring to take care of the automatic update of the audit fields, a little more configuration is needed: a configuration class must be annotated with EnableJpaAuditing and a bean that implements AuditorAware<T> must be configured, as shown in Listing 10-21.

Listing 10-21. The Spring Configuration Class for Enabling Automatic Auditing Support

```
package com.apress.prospring6.ten.config

import org.apache.commons.lang3.RandomStringUtils
import org.springframework.data.domain.AuditorAware
import org.springframework.data.jpa.repository.config.EnableJpaAuditing
// some import statements omitted

@EnableJpaAuditing
@Configuration
open class AuditCfg {
    @Bean
    open fun auditorProvider(): AuditorAware<String> {
        return AuditorAware<String> {
            Optional.of(
                "prospring6-" + RandomStringUtils.random(6, true,true)
            )
        }
    }
}
```

This is a very simple configuration. Here's the thing: in production-level applications, to populate the @CreatedBy and @LastModifiedBy annotated fields, the value is provided by a bean that interacts with Spring Security. In real situations, this should be an instance of user information, such as a User class that represents the logged-in user who is performing the data update action retrieved from the SecurityContextHolder. However, since that topic is quite advanced and is covered in **Chapter 17**, a bean of type AuditorAware<T> interface is used, passing in the type String. The lambda statement in Listing 10-21 can be expanded to the following:

```
object : AuditorAware<String> {
    override fun getCurrentAuditor():Optional<String> {
        return Optional.of("prospring6")
    }
}
```

In this anonymous implementation of AuditorAware<String>, the method getCurrentAuditor() is implemented. The value returned is *prospring6* concatenated with a randomly generated six-characters text. This will help generate different user values, so we can test that the @CreatedBy and @LastModifiedBy annotated fields values were set.

Now that the configuration and the implementation are in place, the next step is to test the code. Just to keep things limited to their own context, we added the AuditServiceTest class, which executes the three service methods in the SingerAuditServiceImpl class and checks the assumptions made about their effects. The test class and methods are shown in Listing 10-22.

Listing 10-22. The Class Used to Test the SingerAuditServiceImpl Class

```kotlin
package com.apress.prospring6.ten
// import statements omitted

@Testcontainers
@Sql("classpath:testcontainers/audit/drop-schema.sql", "classpath:testcontainers/audit/
create-schema.sql")
@SpringJUnitConfig(classes = [AuditServiceTest.TestContainersConfig::class])
class AuditServiceTest : TestContainersBase() {
    @Autowired
    var auditService: SingerAuditService? = null

    @BeforeEach
    fun setUp() {
        val singer = SingerAudit().apply {
            firstName = "BB"
            lastName = "King"
            birthDate = LocalDate.of(1940, 8, 16)
        }
        auditService!!.save(singer)
    }

    @Test
    fun testFindById() {
        val singer = auditService!!.findAll().findFirst().orElse(null)
        Assertions.assertAll("auditFindByIdTest",
            Executable { Assertions.assertNotNull(singer) },
            Executable {
                Assertions.assertNotNull(
                    singer.createdBy
                )
            },
            Executable {
                Assertions.assertNotNull(
                    singer.lastModifiedBy
                )
            }
        )
        LOGGER.info(">> created record: {} ", singer)
    }

    @Test
    fun testUpdate() {
        val singer = auditService!!.findAll().findFirst().orElse(null)
        Assertions.assertNotNull(singer)
        singer.firstName = "Riley B."
        val updated = auditService!!.save(singer)
        Assertions.assertAll("auditUpdateTest",
            Executable {
                Assertions.assertEquals(
                    "Riley B.",
```

```
                    updated.firstName
                )
        },
        Executable {
            Assertions.assertNotNull(
                updated.lastModifiedBy
            )
        },
        Executable {
            Assertions.assertNotEquals(
                updated.createdBy,
                updated.lastModifiedBy
            )
        }
    )
    LOGGER.info(">> updated record: {} ", updated)
}

@Configuration
@Import(
    DataJpaCfg::class,
    AuditCfg::class
)
open class TestContainersConfig {
    @Autowired
    var jpaProperties: Properties? = null
    @PostConstruct
    open fun initialize() {
        jpaProperties!![Environment.FORMAT_SQL] = true
        jpaProperties!![Environment.USE_SQL_COMMENTS] = true
        jpaProperties!![Environment.SHOW_SQL] = true
        jpaProperties!![Environment.STATEMENT_BATCH_SIZE] = 30
    }
}

companion object {
    private val LOGGER = LoggerFactory.getLogger(AuditServiceTest::class.java)
}
}
```

The test methods should pass, and check that the values for the audit fields are populated.

These test methods reveal something important: java.time.LocalDate is not a good type for the fields annotated with @CreatedDate and @LastModifiedDate for records designed to be edited more than once a day. For our examples, we used java.time.LocalDateTime to make it really obvious the records were changed.

JPA auditing support requires an additional library to be added to the classpath. Spring Data needs `spring-aspects` to create special proxies that intercept entity updates and add their own changes before the entities get persisted.

Keeping Entity Versions by Using Hibernate Envers

In an enterprise application, for business-critical data, it is always a requirement to keep a few versions of each entity. For example, in a customer relationship management (CRM) system, each time a customer record is inserted, updated, or deleted, the previous version should be kept in a history or auditing table to fulfill the company's auditing or other compliance requirements.

To accomplish this, there are two common options. The first one is to create database triggers that will clone the pre-update record into the history table before any update operations. The second is to develop the logic in the data access layer (for example, by using AOP). Both options have their drawbacks, however. The trigger approach is tied to the database platform, while implementing the logic manually is quite clumsy, might affect performance, and is very error-prone.

Hibernate Envers[7] (short for *entity versioning system*) is a Hibernate module specifically designed to automate the versioning of entities. In this section, we discuss how to use Envers to implement the versioning of the `SingerAudit` entity introduced in the previous section.

Hibernate Envers is not a feature of JPA. We introduce it here because we believe it's worthwhile to cover this after we have discussed some basic auditing features that you can use with Spring Data JPA.

Spring Data provides a module for Hibernate Envers named `spring-data-envers`. Module `spring-data-jpa` is a transitive dependency of the Spring Data Envers library. Figure 10-5 shows the dependencies of a Spring Data project using Hibernate Envers for versioning entities.

---

[7] `https://hibernate.org/orm/envers/`

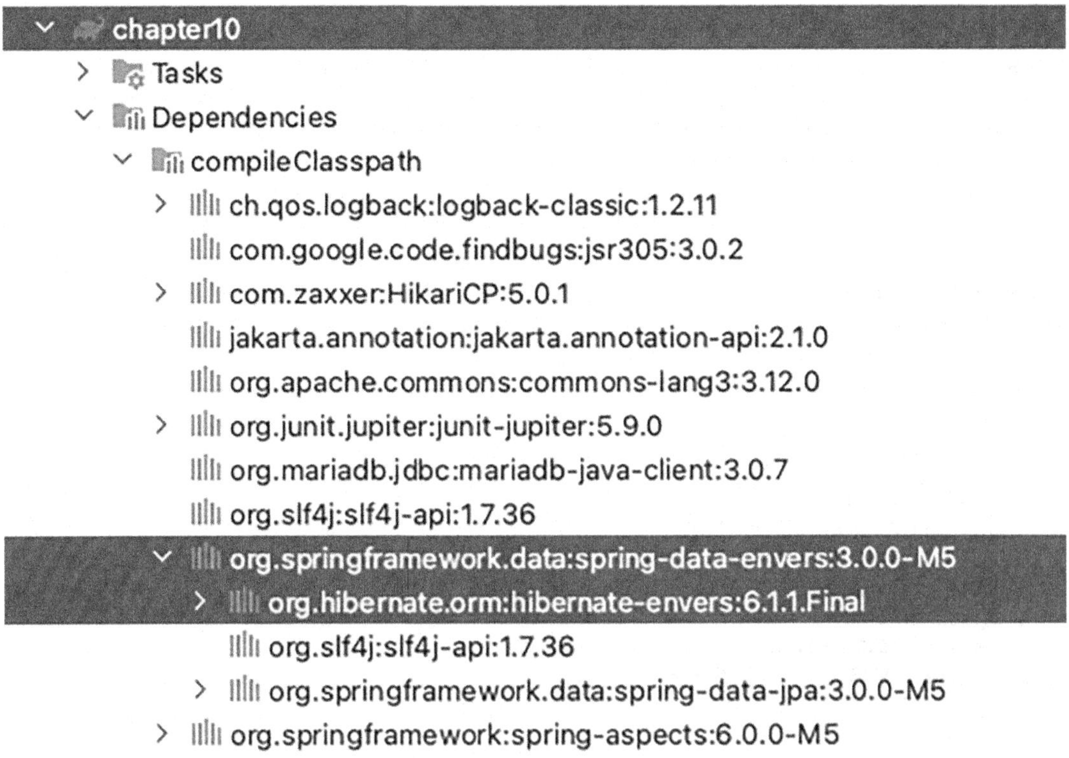

> ∨ 🔗 **chapter10**
>   > 🔧 Tasks
>   ∨ 🗄 Dependencies
>   ∨ 🗄 compileClasspath
>   > ∥∥∥ ch.qos.logback:logback-classic:1.2.11
>   ∥∥∥ com.google.code.findbugs:jsr305:3.0.2
>   > ∥∥∥ com.zaxxer:HikariCP:5.0.1
>   ∥∥∥ jakarta.annotation:jakarta.annotation-api:2.1.0
>   ∥∥∥ org.apache.commons:commons-lang3:3.12.0
>   > ∥∥∥ org.junit.jupiter:junit-jupiter:5.9.0
>   ∥∥∥ org.mariadb.jdbc:mariadb-java-client:3.0.7
>   ∥∥∥ org.slf4j:slf4j-api:1.7.36
>   ∨ ∥∥∥ org.springframework.data:spring-data-envers:3.0.0-M5
>   > ∥∥∥ org.hibernate.orm:hibernate-envers:6.1.1.Final
>   ∥∥∥ org.slf4j:slf4j-api:1.7.36
>   > ∥∥∥ org.springframework.data:spring-data-jpa:3.0.0-M5
>   > ∥∥∥ org.springframework:spring-aspects:6.0.0-M5

Figure 10-5. *Gradle View showing dependencies for the* chapter10 *Envers project*

Envers supports two auditing strategies, which are shown in Table 10-1.

Table 10-1. *Envers Auditing Strategies*

Auditing Strategy	Description
Default	Envers maintains a column for the revision of the record. Every time a record is inserted or updated, a new record will be inserted into the history table with the revision number retrieved from a database sequence or table.
Validity audit	This strategy stores both the start and end revisions of each history record. Every time a record is inserted or updated, a new record will be inserted into the history table with the start revision number. At the same time, the previous record will be updated with the end revision number. It's also possible to configure Envers to record the timestamp at which the end revision was updated into the previous history record.

In this section, we demonstrate the validity audit strategy. Although it will trigger more database updates, retrieving the history records becomes much faster. Because the end revision timestamp is also written to the history records, it will be easier to identify the snapshot of a record at a specific point in time when querying the data.

Adding Tables for Entity Versioning

To support entity versioning, we need to add a few tables. First, for each table that the entity (in this case, the SingerAudit entity class) will be versioning, we need to create the corresponding history table. For the versioning of records in the SINGER_AUDIT table, let's create a history table called SINGER_AUDIT_H. The code in Listing 10-23 shows the table creation script.

Listing 10-23. SQL Code Describing the Hibernate Audit Table for the SingerAudit Entity (AuditSchema.sql)

```
CREATE TABLE SINGER_AUDIT_H (
    ID INT NOT NULL AUTO_INCREMENT
    , FIRST_NAME VARCHAR(60) NOT NULL
    , LAST_NAME VARCHAR(40) NOT NULL
    , BIRTH_DATE DATE
    , VERSION INT NOT NULL DEFAULT 0
    , CREATED_BY VARCHAR(20)
    , CREATED_DATE TIMESTAMP
    , LAST_MODIFIED_BY VARCHAR(20)
    , LAST_MODIFIED_DATE TIMESTAMP
    , AUDIT_REVISION INT NOT NULL
    , ACTION_TYPE INT
    , AUDIT_REVISION_END INT
    , AUDIT_REVISION_END_TS TIMESTAMP
    , UNIQUE UQ_SINGER_AUDIT_H_1 (FIRST_NAME, LAST_NAME)
    , PRIMARY KEY (ID, AUDIT_REVISION)
);
```

To support the validity audit strategy, we need to add four columns for each history table, shown highlighted in Listing 10-23. Table 10-2 shows the columns and their purposes.

Table 10-2. History Columns

Column	Data Type	Description
AUDIT_REVISION	INT	The start revision of the history record
ACTION_TYPE	INT	The action type, with these possible values: 0 for add, 1 for modify, and 2 for delete
AUDIT_REVISION_END	INT	The end revision of the history record
AUDIT_REVISION_END_TS	TIMESTAMP	The timestamp at which the end revision was updated

Hibernate Envers requires another table for keeping track of the revision number and the timestamp at which each revision was created for insert, add, update, or delete operations. The table should be named REVINFO and a foreign key should be added to the SINGER_AUDIT_H table to link each audited record to its versions. Its schema is very simple and is shown in Listing 10-24.

Listing 10-24. SQL Code Describing the Hibernate Audit REVINFO Table (AuditSchema.sql)

```sql
CREATE TABLE REVINFO (
    REVTSTMP BIGINT NOT NULL
    , REV INT NOT NULL AUTO_INCREMENT
    , PRIMARY KEY (REVTSTMP, REV)
);

ALTER TABLE SINGER_AUDIT_H
    ADD CONSTRAINT SINGER_AUDIT_H_TO_REVISION
        FOREIGN KEY ( AUDIT_REVISION ) REFERENCES REVINFO( REV);
```

The REV column is for storing each revision number, which will be auto-incremented when a new history record is created. The REVTSTMP column stores the timestamp (in a number format) of when the revision was created.

Configuring EntityManagerFactory for Entity Versioning

Hibernate Envers is implemented in the form of EJB listeners. We can configure those listeners in the LocalContainerEntityManagerFactory bean by setting a set of specific Envers properties. The Kotlin configuration class is mostly identical to the one used so far for a transactional Spring application, the only difference being that the Envers properties are added to the Properties object set on the LocalContainerEntityManagerFactoryBean object by calling setJpaProperties(..). In Listing 10-25 you can see these properties.

Listing 10-25. Envers Properties to Be Set on the LocalContainerEntityManagerFactoryBean

```kotlin
package com.apress.prospring6.ten.config

import org.hibernate.envers.configuration.EnversSettings
import org.hibernate.cfg.Environment
// other import statements omitted

@Import(BasicDataSourceCfg::class)
@Configuration
@EnableTransactionManagement
@ComponentScan(basePackages = ["com.apress.prospring6.ten"])
@EnableJpaRepositories("com.apress.prospring6.ten.repos")
open class EnversConfig {
    @Autowired
    var dataSource: DataSource? = null

    @Bean
    open fun transactionManager(): PlatformTransactionManager {
        return JpaTransactionManager().apply {
            entityManagerFactory = entityManagerFactory().getObject()
        }
    }
}
```

```kotlin
@Bean
open fun jpaVendorAdapter(): JpaVendorAdapter {
    return HibernateJpaVendorAdapter()
}

@Bean
open fun entityManagerFactory(): LocalContainerEntityManagerFactoryBean {
    return LocalContainerEntityManagerFactoryBean().apply {
        setPersistenceProviderClass(HibernatePersistenceProvider::class.java)
        setPackagesToScan("com.apress.prospring6.ten.entities")
        dataSource = this@EnversConfig.dataSource!!
        setJpaProperties(jpaProperties())
        jpaVendorAdapter = jpaVendorAdapter()
    }
}

@Bean
open fun jpaProperties(): Properties {
    val jpaProps = Properties()
    jpaProps[Environment.HBM2DDL_AUTO] = "none"
    jpaProps[Environment.FORMAT_SQL] = false
    jpaProps[Environment.STATEMENT_BATCH_SIZE] = 30
    jpaProps[Environment.USE_SQL_COMMENTS] = false
    jpaProps[Environment.SHOW_SQL] = false

    //Properties for Hibernate Envers
    jpaProps[EnversSettings.AUDIT_TABLE_SUFFIX] = "_H"
    jpaProps[EnversSettings.REVISION_FIELD_NAME] = "AUDIT_REVISION"
    jpaProps[EnversSettings.REVISION_TYPE_FIELD_NAME] = "ACTION_TYPE"
    jpaProps[EnversSettings.AUDIT_STRATEGY] = ValidityAuditStrategy::class.java.name
    jpaProps[EnversSettings.AUDIT_STRATEGY_VALIDITY_END_REV_FIELD_NAME] = "AUDIT_
REVISION_END"
    jpaProps[EnversSettings.AUDIT_STRATEGY_VALIDITY_STORE_REVEND_TIMESTAMP] = "true"
    jpaProps[EnversSettings.AUDIT_STRATEGY_VALIDITY_REVEND_TIMESTAMP_FIELD_NAME] =
"AUDIT_REVISION_END_TS"
    return jpaProps
}
}
```

With this configuration, what happens under the hood is that audit event listeners (instances of types implementing org.hibernate.envers.event.spi.EnversListener) are attached to persistence events: add, insert, update, and delete. These listeners intercept the events post-insert, post-update, or post-delete and clone the pre-update snapshot of the entity class into the history table. The listeners are also attached to those association update events (pre-collection-update, pre-collection-remove, and pre-collection-recreate) for handling the update operations of the entity class's associations. Envers is capable of keeping the history of the entities within an association (for example *one-to-many* or *many-to-many*).

The properties are set in the configuration in Listing 10-25 and explained briefly in Table 10-3.

All constants are declared in the `org.hibernate.envers.configuration.EnversSettings` interface. The interface name is omitted in Table 10-3 because including it would make the table very difficult to fit on the printed page[8].

All property names in the second column start with `org.hibernate.envers`. Again, this prefix is omitted for purposes of fitting Table 10-3 on the printed page.

Table 10-3. *Envers Properties*

Constant	Property Name	Default Value	Description
AUDIT_TABLE_ SUFFIX	audit_table_ prefix	_AUD	The table name suffix for the versioned entity. For example, for the entity class SingerAudit, which is mapped to the SINGER_AUDIT table, Envers will keep the history in the table SINGER_AUDIT_H, since we defined the value _H for the property.
REVISION_FIELD_ NAME	revision_field_ name	REV	The history table's column for storing the revision number for each history record.
REVISION_TYPE_ FIELD_NAME	revision_type_ field_name	REVTYPE	The history table's column for storing the update action type.
AUDIT_STRATEGY	audit_strategy	org.hibernate. envers.strategy. DefaultAuditStrategy	The audit strategy to use for entity versioning.
AUDIT_STRATEGY_ VALIDITY_ END_ REV_FIELD_NAME	audit_strategy_ validity_ end_ rev_field_name	REVEND	The history table's column for storing the end revision number foreach history record. Required only when using the validity audit strategy.
AUDIT_STRATEGY_ VALIDITY_ STORE_REVEND_ TIMESTAMP	audit_strategy_ validity_ store_ revend_timestamp	false	Indicates whether to store the timestamp when the end revision number for each history record is updated. Required only when using the validity audit strategy.
AUDIT_STRATEGY_ VALIDITY_ REVEND_ TIMESTAMP_ FIELD_NAME	audit_strategy_ validity_ revend_ timestamp_field_ name	REVEND_TSTMP	The history table's column for storing the timestamp when the end revision number for each history record is updated. Required only when using the validity audit strategy and the previous property is set to true.

[8] https://docs.jboss.org/hibernate/orm/current/javadocs/org/hibernate/envers/configuration/EnversSettings.html

The default values in Table 10-3 are the ones used by Hibernate when configured to generate the database schema and no values are explicitly configured for these properties.

You can find the full list of Hibernate properties in the Hibernate official documentation[9].

Enabling Entity Versioning and History Retrieval

To enable versioning of an entity, just annotate the entity class with the @Audited annotation provided by Hibernate. This annotation can be used at the class level and then the changes on all entity fields are audited. If you want to escape certain fields from auditing, use the Hibernate Envers @NotAudited annotation on those fields. Listing 10-26 shows the SingerAudit class annotated with @Audited and the other Jakarta-specific annotations.

Listing 10-26. Entity Class Annotated with the Hibernate Envers @Audited Annotation

```
package com.apress.prospring6.ten.entities

import org.hibernate.envers.Audited
// other import statements omitted

@Entity
@Audited
@Table(name = "SINGER_AUDIT")
class SingerAudit : AuditableEntity<SingerAudit> {
    // body omitted
}
```

The entity class is annotated with @Audited, which Envers listeners will check for and perform versioning of the updated entities. By default, Envers will also try to keep a history of the associations; if you want to avoid this, use the @NotAudited annotation.

To retrieve the history records, Envers provides the org.hibernate.envers.AuditReader interface, which can be obtained from the AuditReaderFactory class. To do this, a new method called findAuditByRevision() is added to the SingerAuditService interface for retrieving the SingerAudit history records by audited record id and revision number. Listing 10-27 shows the SingerAuditServiceImpl implementation.

Listing 10-27. Service Method for Retrieving History Records by Revision

```
package com.apress.prospring6.ten.service

import jakarta.persistence.PersistenceContext
import org.hibernate.envers.AuditReaderFactory
```

---

[9] https://docs.jboss.org/hibernate/orm/current/userguide/html_single/Hibernate_User_Guide.html#envers-configuration

```kotlin
@Service("singerAuditService")
@Transactional
class SingerAuditServiceImpl(private val singerAuditRepository: SingerAuditRepository) :
SingerAuditService {
    @Transactional(readOnly = true)
    ...

  @PersistenceContext
  var entityManager:EntityManager? = null

    @Transactional(readOnly = true)
    override fun findAuditByRevision(id: Long, revision: Int): SingerAudit? {
        var auditReader = AuditReaderFactory.get(entityManager)
        return auditReader.find(SingerAudit::class.java, id, revision)
    }
}
```

The `SingerAuditServiceImpl` class must be modified, obviously, and the `EntityManager` must be injected into it so that the `AuditReaderFactory` can use it to create an `org.hibernate.envers.AuditReader` instance to read the audit records. This can easily be avoided by using custom implementations for Spring Data custom repositories, and since our focus is set on Spring, let's do that.

Custom Implementations for Spring Data Repositories

Spring Data provides default options for handling database records and creating query methods with little coding. However, there are cases when that is not enough, and the Envers example introduced here is a good example for that.

To add a custom method to the default functionality of a Spring Data repository, we need to define a fragment interface declaring the behavior we want to add. In our case, as depicted in Listing 10-28, the interface is named `CustomSingerAuditRepository` and declares a single method with the sole purpose of retrieving older versions of `SingerAudit` records using their `id` and revision number.

Listing 10-28. Fragment Interface Declaring a Method for Retrieving Versions of `SingerAudit` Records

package com.apress.prospring6.ten.repos.envers

import com.apress.prospring6.ten.entities.SingerAudit

```kotlin
interface CustomSingerAuditRepository {
    fun findAuditByIdAndRevision(id: Long, revision: Int): SingerAudit?
}
```

ℹ️   The Java code variant for the same interface lets this method return an `Optional<SingerAudit>`. In Kotlin you can avoid using optionals, thanks to its elaborated null-value handling.

CHAPTER 10 ■ SPRING DATA WITH SQL AND NOSQL DATABASES

Now that we have an interface, we need to provide an implementation. This is where the class CustomSingerAuditRepositoryImpl depicted in Listing 10-29 comes in.

Listing 10-29. Using the CustomSingerAuditRepository Interface

```
package com.apress.prospring6.ten.repos.envers

import com.apress.prospring6.ten.entities.SingerAudit
import jakarta.persistence.EntityManager
import jakarta.persistence.PersistenceContext
import org.hibernate.envers.AuditReaderFactory

class CustomSingerAuditRepositoryImpl : CustomSingerAuditRepository {
    @PersistenceContext
    private val entityManager: EntityManager? = null

    override fun findAuditByIdAndRevision(id: Long, revision: Int): SingerAudit? {
        val auditReader = AuditReaderFactory.get(entityManager)
        return auditReader.find(SingerAudit::class.java, id, revision)
    }
}
```

 Notice that we just moved the Envers-specific code from SingerAuditServiceImpl to this class.

To tell Spring Data that we want this method to be added to its default set of functionalities, we need to make the Spring Data repository for the SingerAudit entity extend the CustomSingerAuditRepository interface too, as depicted in Listing 10-30.

Listing 10-30. Implementation of the CustomSingerAuditRepository Interface

```
package com.apress.prospring6.ten.repos

import com.apress.prospring6.ten.entities.SingerAudit
import com.apress.prospring6.ten.repos.envers.CustomSingerAuditRepository
import org.springframework.data.jpa.repository.JpaRepository

interface SingerAuditRepository :
    JpaRepository<SingerAudit, Long>, CustomSingerAuditRepository
```

❗ The most important part of the class name that corresponds to the fragment interface is the Impl postfix. This is what allows Spring Data to identify where the implementation for that method is coming from and add it to its JPA repository proxies. After all, convention over configuration is one of the core values of the Spring Framework.

ⓘ   However, being easy to customize is also a Spring value, and thus if you want to name your custom repository implementation differently, you have to tell Spring about it. The customization is somewhat limited; you can only specify a different postfix to replace the default `Impl`, using `@EnableJpaRepositories(repositoryImplementationPostfix = "${custom-prefix})`, but it is better than nothing.

This means that now the `SingerAuditServiceImpl` class can be cleaned up of the Envers-specific code and the `findAuditByRevision(..)` method just invokes the `findAuditByIdAndRevision(..)` method provided by the Spring JPA `SingerAuditRepository`, as shown in Listing 10-31.

Listing 10-31. Adapting the `SingerAuditServiceImpl` class

package com.apress.prospring6.ten.service

```
@Service("singerAuditService")
@Transactional
class SingerAuditServiceImpl(private val singerAuditRepository: SingerAuditRepository) :
SingerAuditService {

    ...

    @Transactional(readOnly = true)
    override fun findAuditByRevision(id: Long, revision: Int): SingerAudit? {
        return singerAuditRepository.findAuditByIdAndRevision(id, revision)
    }
}
```

What is left is to test that this works. Writing a test method is not that difficult, but to make sure that our revisioning works, an update and a delete operation should be checked. The test class is shown in Listing 10-32.

Listing 10-32. Testing the Envers Auditing in a Spring Application

package com.apress.prospring6.ten
// import statements omitted

```
@Testcontainers
@Sql("classpath:testcontainers/audit/drop-schema.sql", "classpath:testcontainers/audit/
create-schema.sql")
@SpringJUnitConfig(classes = [EnversConfig::class, AuditCfg::class])
class EnversServiceTest : TestContainersBase() {
    @Autowired
    var auditService: SingerAuditService? = null

    @BeforeEach
    fun setUp() {
        val singer = SingerAudit()
        singer.firstName = "BB"
        singer.lastName = "King"
        singer.birthDate = LocalDate.of(1940, 8, 16)
        auditService!!.save(singer)
    }
```

```kotlin
@Test
fun testFindAuditByRevision() {
    // update to create new version
    val singer = auditService!!.findAll().findFirst().orElse(null)
    Assertions.assertNotNull(singer)
    singer.firstName = "Riley B."
    auditService!!.save(singer)
    val oldSinger = auditService!!.findAuditByRevision(singer.id!!, 1)
    Assertions.assertEquals("BB", oldSinger!!.firstName)
    LOGGER.info(">> old singer: {} ", oldSinger)
    val newSinger = auditService!!.findAuditByRevision(singer.id!!, 2)
    Assertions.assertEquals("Riley B.", newSinger!!.firstName)
    LOGGER.info(">> updated singer: {} ", newSinger)
}

@Test
fun testFindAuditAfterDeletion() {
    // delete record
    val singer = auditService!!.findAll().findFirst().orElse(null)!!
    auditService!!.delete(singer.id!!)

    // extract from audit
    val deletedSinger = auditService!!.findAuditByRevision(singer.id!!, 1)
    Assertions.assertEquals("BB", deletedSinger!!.firstName)
    LOGGER.info(">> deleted singer: {} ", deletedSinger)
}

companion object {
    private val LOGGER = LoggerFactory.getLogger(EnversServiceTest::class.java)
}
}
```

To get a glimpse of what is happening, you can try taking a look in the console log messages printed when the test method are executed. Unfortunately, at this point in the book, if we enable TRACE log for org.hibernate, the log becomes unreadable, but we can search and show the most important bits in Listing 10-33.

Listing 10-33. Envers Auditing Test Execution Log

```
TRACE: TransactionAspectSupport - Getting transaction for
    [com.apress.prospring6.ten.service.SingerAuditServiceImpl.save]
TRACE: AbstractEntityPersister - Updating entity:
    [com.apress.prospring6.ten.entities.SingerAudit#1]
...
DEBUG: SqlStatementLogger - insert into REVINFO (REVTSTMP) values (?)
TRACE: AbstractEntityPersister - Inserting entity:
    [com.apress.prospring6.ten.entities.SingerAudit_H#component[
        id,AUDIT_REVISION]{id=1, AUDIT_REVISION=org.hibernate.envers.DefaultRevisionEntity#1}]
DEBUG: SqlStatementLogger - insert into REVINFO (REVTSTMP) values (?)
```

```
TRACE: AbstractEntityPersister - Inserting entity:
    [com.apress.prospring6.ten.entities.SingerAudit_H#component[
        id,AUDIT_REVISION]{id=1, AUDIT_REVISION=org.hibernate.envers.
        DefaultRevisionEntity#2}]
...
TRACE: TransactionAspectSupport - Getting transaction for
    [com.apress.prospring6.ten.service.SingerAuditServiceImpl.findAuditByRevision]
DEBUG: QueryTranslatorImpl - parse() - HQL:
    select e__ from com.apress.prospring6.ten.entities.SingerAudit_H e__
    where e__.originalId.AUDIT_REVISION.id <= :revision
        and e__.ACTION_TYPE <> :_p0
        and e__.originalId.id = :_p1
        and (e__.AUDIT_REVISION_END.id > :revision or e__.AUDIT_REVISION_END is null)
TRACE: QueryParameters - Named parameters: {_p1=1, _p0=DEL, revision=1}
DEBUG: Loader - Result row: EntityKey[com.apress.prospring6.ten.entities.SingerAudit_
H#component[id,AUDIT_REVISION]{id=1, AUDIT_REVISION=org.hibernate.envers.
DefaultRevisionEntity#1}]
INFO : EnversServiceTest - >> old singer: com.apress.prospring6.ten.entities.
SingerAudit@20524816[
    id=1,version=0,firstName=BB,lastName=King,birthDate=1940-08-16,
    createdBy=prospring6-0e94fe,
    createdDate=2022-08-07T13:40:31,
    lastModifiedBy=prospring6-0e94fe,
    lastModifiedDate=2022-08-07T14:40:30
]
...
TRACE: QueryParameters - Named parameters: {_p1=1, _p0=DEL, revision=2}
DEBUG: Loader - Result row: EntityKey[com.apress.prospring6.ten.entities.SingerAudit_
H#component[id,AUDIT_REVISION]{id=1, AUDIT_REVISION=org.hibernate.envers.
DefaultRevisionEntity#2}]
INFO : EnversServiceTest - >> updated singer: com.apress.prospring6.ten.entities.
SingerAudit@6347f9cc[
    id=1,version=0,firstName=Riley B.,lastName=King,birthDate=1940-08-16,
    createdBy=prospring6-0e94fe,
    createdDate=2022-08-07T14:40:30,
    lastModifiedBy=prospring6-TJFUWY,
    lastModifiedDate=2022-08-07T14:40:31
]
...
```

Notice how every action on the SINGER_AUDIT table causes an entry to be created in REVINFO and SINGER_AUDIT_H. Then, when SingerAudit entries are extracted with a certain revision, they are extracted from the SINGER_AUDIT_H table. After the update operation, the SingerAudit's first name is changed to *Riley B.* As expected, when looking at the history, at revision 1, the first name is *BB*. At revision 2, the first name becomes *Riley B.* Also notice that the lastModifiedDate date and lastModifiedBy user of revision 2 reflect the updated date and time and a different username, generated by the *AuditAware<String>* bean.

Spring Boot Data JPA

Up to this point, we have configured everything explicitly, including entities, databases, repositories, and services. As you probably expect by now, there should be a Spring Boot starter artifact to make things easier. Spring Boot JDBC was introduced in **Chapter 9**, but it's capabilities truly shine in combination with Spring Data and there is a starter library for that called `spring-boot-starter-data-jpa`. Adding this library to a project classpath adds transitively all the dependencies necessary to a Spring transactional application: `hibernate-core` for persistence, `HikariCP` for connection pooling, `spring-data-jpa` for data access using Spring Data repository interfaces, and `spring-tx` for transaction management. The project dependencies are shown in Figure 10-6.

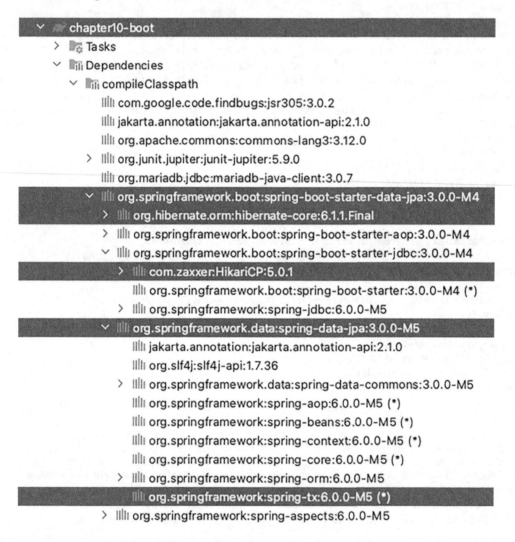

Figure 10-6. *Gradle View showing dependencies for the chapter10-boot project*

The Spring Boot Data JPA configuration has two parts: the main class annotated with @SpringBootApplication and the application-dev.yaml (or application-dev.properties) file. Of course, the -dev suffix is added because we are using an application profile named dev. This is a practical way to isolate bean declarations based on context.

For this project the application-dev.yaml file has the contents shown in Listing 10-34.

Listing 10-34. Spring Boot Data JPA Configuration yaml Configuration

```yaml
# datasource config
spring:
  datasource:
    driverClassName: org.mariadb.jdbc.Driver
    url: jdbc:mariadb://localhost:3306/musicdb?useSSL=false
    username: prospring6
    password: prospring6
    # HikariCP
    hikari:
      maximum-pool-size: 25
  # JPA config
  jpa:
    generate-ddl: false
    properties:
      hibernate:
        naming:
          physical-strategy:
        jdbc:
          batch_size: 10
          fetch_size: 30
        max_fetch_depth: 3
        show-sql: true
        format-sql: false
        use_sql_comments: false
        hbm2ddl:
          auto: none

# Logging config
logging:
  pattern:
    console: "%-5level: %class{0} - %msg%n"
  level:
    root: INFO
    org.springframework.boot: DEBUG
    com.apress.prospring6.ten.boot: INFO
    org.springframework.orm.jpa: TRACE
```

The configuration is split in three sections: datasource, jpa, and logging. Properties with names starting with spring.datasource are set with values necessary for configuring a data source: connection URL, credentials, and connection pooling values. Properties with names starting with spring.jpa are set with values describing a persistence unit. You can easily recognize the Hibernate properties covered in Chapters 7 and 8. Properties starting with logging are set with the typical value for logging configuration that in classic applications could be found in logback.xml files.

In a Spring Boot Data JPA application, the autoconfiguration mechanism takes care of declaring the necessary beans like dataSource, EntityManager, LocalSessionFactoryBean, TransactionManager, and so on, based on the properties in the configuration file, but we still have to configure a few things:

- *Location of the entity classes*: Since the LocalSessionFactoryBean is autoconfigured for us, the way to specify the packages where the entity classes are located is to use the @EntityScan annotation from the org.springframework.boot.autoconfigure. domain package.

- *Location of the Spring Data repository interfaces*: This is easily done by adding the @EnableJpaRepositories annotation to a class annotated with @Configuration, if there is one, or the @SpringBootApplication annotated class if there is not.

- *Transactional behavior*: This is easily done by adding the @EnableTransactionManagement annotation to a class annotated with @Configuration, if there is one, or the @SpringBootApplication annotated class if there is not.

Listing 10-35 shows the configuration for the project analyzed in this section.

Listing 10-35. Spring Boot Data JPA Annotation Configuration

```
package com.apress.prospring6.ten.boot

import com.apress.prospring6.ten.boot.service.SingerService
import org.slf4j.Logger
import org.slf4j.LoggerFactory
import org.springframework.boot.SpringApplication
import org.springframework.boot.autoconfigure.SpringBootApplication
import org.springframework.boot.autoconfigure.domain.EntityScan
import org.springframework.core.env.AbstractEnvironment
import org.springframework.data.jpa.repository.config.EnableJpaRepositories
import org.springframework.transaction.annotation.EnableTransactionManagement

@EntityScan(basePackages = ["com.apress.prospring6.ten.boot.entities"])
@EnableTransactionManagement
@EnableJpaRepositories("com.apress.prospring6.ten.boot.repos")
@SpringBootApplication
open class Chapter10Application {
    companion object {
        private val LOGGER = LoggerFactory.getLogger(Chapter10Application::class.java)

        @JvmStatic
        fun main(args: Array<String>) {
            System.setProperty(AbstractEnvironment.ACTIVE_PROFILES_PROPERTY_NAME,
                "dev")
            val ctx = SpringApplication.run(Chapter10Application::class.java, *args)
            val service = ctx.getBean(
                SingerService::class.java
            )
            LOGGER.info(" ---- Listing singers:")
            service.findAll().forEach { s -> LOGGER.info(s.toString()) }
        }
    }
}
```

As you can see, the Spring Boot main configuration class has a main(..) method. This makes this class executable, and running the code in this class's main(..) method ensures that the configuration is correct. However, running the class with the configuration shown so far ends with the following error:

```
Exception in thread "main" org.springframework.dao.InvalidDataAccessResourceUsageException:
JDBC exception executing SQL
[select s1_0.id,
       s1_0.birth_date,
       s1_0.first_name,
       s1_0.last_name,
       s1_0.version
    from singer s1_0
]; SQL [n/a]
...
Caused by: java.sql.SQLSyntaxErrorException: (conn=308) Table 'musicdb.singer' doesn't exist
    at org.mariadb.jdbc.export.ExceptionFactory.createException(ExceptionFactory.java:280)
    at org.mariadb.jdbc.export.ExceptionFactory.create(ExceptionFactory.java:368)
```

So, what is going on here? If the data source was configured correctly, why is the singer table not found? If you think the reason is that the table names are case-sensitive, you are somewhat right. Before explaining what is going on in this Spring Boot Data JPA application, let's talk about Hibernate naming strategies.

Hibernate uses two different naming strategies[10] to map names from the object model to the corresponding database names:

- ImplicitNamingStrategy: The proper logical name is determined from the domain model mapping, either from configuration annotations like @Column and @Table (as you've seen in previous chapters) or it can be determined by Hibernate using an implementation of org.hibernate.boot.model.naming.ImplicitNamingStrategy configured via the Environment.IMPLICIT_NAMING_STRATEGY / hibernate. implicit_naming_strategy property.

- PhysicalNamingStrategy: The proper logical name is determined by Hibernate using an implementation of org.hibernate.boot.model.naming. PhysicalNamingStrategy configured via the Environment.PHYSICAL_NAMING_ STRATEGY / hibernate.physical_naming_strategy property.

The purpose of these two strategies is to reduce the explicit configuration a developer has to provide.

Many organizations define rules around the naming of database objects (tables, columns, foreign keys, etc.). The idea of a PhysicalNamingStrategy is to help implement such naming rules without having to hard-code them into the mapping via explicit names.

Most companies have their own standards of naming things, this goes for database objects (tables, columns, foreign keys, etc.) as well. Some companies prefer to name database objects in uppercase letters, making it easier to discern between HQL and SQL native queries in code. We followed this approach for this book as well.

In a Spring Boot Data JPA application, the default strategy of determining database objects names is an implementation of PhysicalNamingStrategy named org.hibernate.boot.model.naming. CamelCaseToUnderscoresNamingStrategy that is provided by Hibernate. As its name indicates, the logical names are assumed to be in camel case and separated by underscores. This is the reason why the Singer entity class gets mapped to the singer table, and since MariaDB is installed on a Linux container, database objects names are case-sensitive, so SINGER is clearly not equal to singer.

---

[10] https://docs.jboss.org/hibernate/orm/current/userguide/html_single/Hibernate_ User_Guide.html#naming

The solution here is to provide our own PhysicalNamingStrategy bean, instructing Spring Boot how to determine the database object names. The PhysicalNamingStrategy interface declares five methods for each named database object[11]. The body of this interface is declared in Listing 10-36.

Listing 10-36. Hibernate's PhysicalNamingStrategy Interface

```
package org.hibernate.boot.model.naming;

import org.hibernate.Incubating;
import org.hibernate.engine.jdbc.env.spi.JdbcEnvironment;

@Incubating
public interface PhysicalNamingStrategy {

    Identifier toPhysicalCatalogName(Identifier logicalName, JdbcEnvironment
    jdbcEnvironment);

    Identifier toPhysicalSchemaName(Identifier logicalName, JdbcEnvironment
    jdbcEnvironment);

    Identifier toPhysicalTableName(Identifier logicalName, JdbcEnvironment jdbcEnvironment);

    Identifier toPhysicalSequenceName(Identifier logicalName, JdbcEnvironment
    jdbcEnvironment);

    Identifier toPhysicalColumnName(Identifier logicalName, JdbcEnvironment
    jdbcEnvironment);
}
```

ℹ The @Incubating annotation indicates something that is still being actively developed and therefore may change at a later time.

To make things simpler, we can extend the PhysicalNamingStrategyImpl class provided by Hibernate and override only the methods we are interested in. The HibernateCfg configuration class shown in Listing 10-37 declares a bean of an anonymous type extending PhysicalNamingStrategyImpl.

Listing 10-37. Custom PhysicalNamingStrategy Implementation

```
package com.apress.prospring6.ten.boot

import org.hibernate.boot.model.naming.Identifier
import org.hibernate.boot.model.naming.PhysicalNamingStrategyStandardImpl
import org.hibernate.engine.jdbc.env.spi.JdbcEnvironment
import org.springframework.context.annotation.Bean
import org.springframework.context.annotation.Configuration
```

---

[11] https://github.com/hibernate/hibernate-orm/blob/main/hibernate-core/src/main/java/org/hibernate/boot/model/naming/PhysicalNamingStrategy.java

```kotlin
@Configuration(proxyBeanMethods = false)
open class HibernateCfg {
    @Bean
    open fun caseSensitivePhysicalNamingStrategy(): PhysicalNamingStrategyStandardImpl {
        return object : PhysicalNamingStrategyStandardImpl() {
            override fun toPhysicalTableName(logicalName: Identifier,
                    context: JdbcEnvironment): Identifier {
                return apply(logicalName, context)!!
            }

            override fun toPhysicalColumnName(logicalName: Identifier,
                    context: JdbcEnvironment): Identifier {
                return apply(logicalName, context)!!
            }

            private fun apply(name: Identifier?, context: JdbcEnvironment): Identifier? {
                if (name == null) {
                    return null
                }
                val builder = StringBuilder(name.text.replace('.', '_'))
                var i = 1
                while (i < builder.length - 1) {
                    if (isUnderscoreRequired(builder[i - 1], builder[i], builder[i + 1])) {
                        builder.insert(i++, '_')
                    }
                    i++
                }
                return Identifier.toIdentifier(builder.toString().uppercase(Locale.
                getDefault()))
            }

            private fun isUnderscoreRequired(before: Char, current: Char, after: Char) =
                Character.isLowerCase(before) &&
                Character.isUpperCase(current) &&
                Character.isLowerCase(after)

        }
    }
}
```

The proxyBeanMethods attribute is set to false because methods annotated with @Bean in this class should not get proxied in order to enforce bean life-cycle behavior. The code used to determine the logical names for tables and columns is declared in the apply() method.

If you are executing the Chapter10Application class with this new configuration class, the execution successes and the expected output, the singer instances as string, is printed.

The repository data classes and service classes are the same as shown earlier in this chapter in the classic Spring application. The test methods are the same as well, the only difference being in the configuration of the test context. An application-test.yaml or application-test.propeties file is recommended, since the data source has to be replaced with a Testcontainers data source. The configuration file used in this section's example is shown in Listing 10-38.

Listing 10-38. Spring Boot Data JPA Test Configuration yaml Configuration

```yaml
spring:
  datasource:
    url: "jdbc:tc:mariadb:10.9-rc:///testdb?TC_INITSCRIPT=testcontainers/create-schema.sql"
  jpa:
    properties:
      hibernate:
        jdbc:
          batch_size: 10
          fetch_size: 30
        max_fetch_depth: 3
        show-sql: true
        format-sql: true
        use_sql_comments: true
        hbm2ddl:
          auto: none

# Logging config
logging:
  pattern:
    console: " %-5level: %class{0} - %msg%n"
  level:
    root: INFO
    org.springframework.boot: DEBUG
    com.apress.prospring6.ten.boot: DEBUG
    org.springframework.orm.jpa: TRACE
```

Notice that Hibernate-specific properties useful for debugging are set to `true` and the logging configuration is more detailed.

The Spring Boot test configuration class is annotated with `@SpringBootTest` and additional annotations required to set up a test context, as shown in Listing 10-39.

Listing 10-39. Spring Boot Data Test Class

```kotlin
package com.apress.prospring6.ten.boot

import org.springframework.boot.test.context.SpringBootTest
import org.springframework.test.context.ActiveProfiles
import org.springframework.test.context.jdbc.Sql
import org.springframework.test.context.jdbc.SqlMergeMode
import org.testcontainers.junit.jupiter.Testcontainers
// other import statements omitted

@ActiveProfiles("test")
@SqlMergeMode(SqlMergeMode.MergeMode.MERGE)
@Sql("classpath:testcontainers/drop-schema.sql", "classpath:testcontainers/create-
schema.sql")
@SpringBootTest(classes = [Chapter10Application::class])
class Chapter10ApplicationTest {
    @Autowired
    var singerService: SingerService? = null
```

```kotlin
    @Test
    fun testFindAll() {
        val singers = singerService!!.findAll().peek { s -> LOGGER.info(s.toString()) }
            .toList()
        Assertions.assertEquals(3, singers.size)
    }

    @Test
    fun testFindAllWithAlbums() {
        val singers = singerService!!.findAllWithAlbums()
            .peek { s ->
                LOGGER.info(s.toString())
                s.albums.forEach { a -> LOGGER.info("\t" + a.toString()) }
            }.toList()
        Assertions.assertEquals(3, singers.size)
    }

    companion object {
        private val LOGGER = LoggerFactory.getLogger(Chapter10Application::class.java)
    }
}
```

What tells Spring Boot to initialize the test context based on the configuration in application-test.yaml is the @ActiveProfiles("test") enabling the test context. The @SpringBootTest(classes = [Chapter10Application::class]) is explicitly configured to use the Chapter10Application configuration. This is not necessary when there is a single Spring Boot test class named exactly as the Spring Boot configuration class suffixed with Test, but throughout the book's examples, this form is used for a bit of extra clarity, to make it obvious where the configuration for the beans tested is coming from.

Considerations Using Spring Data JPA

Using Spring Data JPA's Repository abstraction can help simplify JPA application development. Spring Boot can simplify development even more, but customizing configurations might require a bit of learning. Referring again to the *I Love Lucy* episode "Paris at Last" introduced in **Chapter 6**, Spring Data JPA is the last translator in the chain. Its job is based on the translators before it, the JDBC driver, JPA, and Hibernate (and similar, like Oracle TopLink), and it is what makes writing Kotlin code to access data easiest, because it focuses on the business logic and hides the technical complexity and boilerplate code. All these technical layers together make it pretty easy and fast to implement the persistence layer. Spring Data JPA also comes with some simplicity for customizing transactional behavior. All these make this combo very popular, especially for big enterprise projects, because for smaller projects, they might be overkill. Plus, the more technologies you add in your project, the steeper the learning curve is for developers and the more failure points you add at the points where those are glued together.

Thus far this chapter has introduced the core concepts and interfaces of Spring Data JPA repositories. JPA is suitable when working with normalized, SQL databases. How about when working with nonstructured, non-strongly relational data that is not a good fit for a SQL database? Does Spring Data offer something for that? Of course! You can learn about that in the next section.

Spring Data with MongoDB[12]

Almost all data is relational in some way, and for years SQL databases that represented those relationship through concepts like foreign keys dominated the industry. Organizing your data to reduce duplication and storage costs, however, introduced delays when handling that data since relationships had to be taken into account. As the quantity of data grows, the quantity of metadata describing relationships grows too, and operations become slower. Relational databases are well suited to accomplish tasks that involve a lot of tables, that involve complex and huge queries, and in which transactional operations are crucial (ACID) and speed is not always a requirement. Other good uses cases are big cascade deletes and keeping relationships and data integrity.

In this new age of the Internet, speed is the most common requirement. SQL databases, although efficient in storing data and very precise and consistent in providing it when requested, are not suitable for Internet services, where speed is more important than data integrity. NoSQL databases are useful when your data isn't strongly structured, when data relations aren't deep, when you need to save data for a small amount of time (caching), or your queries aren't very complex. For example, eBay is using MongoDB, Amazon is using DynamoDB, a NoSQL database created to satisfy its own commercial needs, that is known to be the most suitable NoSQL database for shopping sites, as it is highly customizable, fast, and infinitely scalable in the Amazon cloud.

Thus, NoSQL databases appeared to satisfy this need for getting things quickly, even if not always consistent. For example, when you access the Amazon shopping site, you don't expect to get the most recent products immediately, but you will eventually get them. Also, being nonrelational, NoSQL databases have some data duplication, thus data integrity comes second to speed of retrieval.

Another thing you need to keep in mind is that relational databases are not a very good model of real systems. They force you to declare your full data structure before you even start writing the code to interact with them, and making changes later is tricky, which is a problem because in real life changes happen constantly. The main advantage of NoSQL is that, aside from a main identifier for every record, everything else is easily modifiable later. Amazon's DynamoDB is a step even further in that direction because, aside from the primary key, all other columns—named *attributes*—in a record can be different from record to record. This level of flexibility, unfortunately, means that writing a Spring Data library for working with DynamoDB is almost impossible.

Since NoSQL databases have become widely used, it is only suitable to add a section about how Spring can help interact with them. Spring provides quite a few data libraries for working with NoSQL databases, but our favorite is MongoDB[13], for which classic and reactive API is provided. Aside from that, there is support for Apache Cassandra[14] (an open source NoSQL database manageable to handle massive amounts of data, fast), Couchbase[15](a modern cloud database that offers the robust capabilities required for business-critical applications on a highly scalable and available platform), and Redis[16] (an open source, BSD licensed, in-memory data structure store, used as a database, cache, and message broker).

Recently, since it has become clear that fully nonrelational data does not exist, the NoSQL term is slowly changing meaning from "non-SQL" to "not only SQL." So, feel free to explore the NoSQL data realm, because you'll likely end up working with one of these databases.

---

[12] https://spring.io/projects/spring-data-mongodb
[13] https://www.mongodb.com
[14] https://cassandra.apache.org
[15] https://www.couchbase.com
[16] https://redis.io/

MongoDB Concepts

For this section, you can install MongoDB on your computer, but the recommended way is to use Docker and set up the container as recommended in the CHAPTER10-MONGO.adoc file present in the chapter10-mongo project. Of course, you can skip this step altogether and just run the tests that use a Testcontainers MongoDB container.

You must enter a paid program in order to use MongoDB for a commercial project. If you don't want to do that, use a more commercial-friendly licensed product such as Apache Cassandra. Usage patterns are similar, though. So reading and understanding the MongoDB part of this book will help in either way.

MongoDB is a document-oriented NoSQL database used for high-volume data storage. Instead of using tables and rows as in the traditional relational databases, MongoDB makes use of collections and documents. Documents in a collection do not have a fixed structure, like all rows in a table do.

Although we already mentioned what NoSQL databases are good for, to keep things consistent, the Singer class is mapped to a MongoDB collection named singers. This is done in Spring by annotating the Singer class with @Document, from package org.springframework.data.mongodb.core.mapping. This annotation is useful to configure the collection name to be different from the class name, since the MongoDB standard is to name collections with the plural of the type of documents in it.

The Singer class is shown in Listing 10-40.

Listing 10-40. Singer Class Configured As a MongoDB Document

```
package com.apress.prospring6.ten.document

import org.springframework.data.mongodb.core.index.Indexed
import org.springframework.data.mongodb.core.mapping.Document
import org.springframework.data.mongodb.core.mapping.MongoId

import java.time.LocalDate

@Document(collection = "singers")
class Singer {
    @MongoId
    var id: String? = null

    @Indexed
    var firstName: String? = null

    @Indexed
    var lastName: String? = null

    var birthDate: LocalDate? = null

    constructor() {}
    constructor(firstName: String?, lastName: String?, birthDate: LocalDate?) {
        this.firstName = firstName
        this.lastName = lastName
        this.birthDate = birthDate
    }
}
```

```kotlin
    override fun toString(): String {
        return "Singer{" +
                "id='" + id + '\'' +
                ", firstName='" + firstName + '\'' +
                ", lastName='" + lastName + '\'' +
                ", birthDate=" + birthDate +
                '}'
    }
}
```

MongoDB requires that all documents have an _id field. Using Spring Data, the field mapped to it is annotated with @Id or @MongoId from the org.springframework.data.mongodb.core.mapping. The @MongoId annotation is meta-annotated with @Id and, although used here to make it obvious that this class maps to a MongoDB document, it provides the possibility to configure the field type using @MongoId(). When annotated like this, Spring Data will attempt to convert the value to the declared type.

The @Indexed annotation tells the mapping framework to call createIndex(...) on that property of your document, making searches faster.

If the name of the field is required to be different in the document than the one in the Kotlin class, you can annotate it with the @Field annotation to configure the desired value.

In Spring, types are mapped to and from a MongoDB representation using a set of built-in converters. This is why we can declare the LocalDate birthDate field without any conversion annotation.

Now that we have a document, the next step is to create a repository for handling singer instances. The approach is similar to the one shown for Spring Data JPA. In Spring Data MongoDB, there is a MongoRepository<T, ID> interface that is an extension of CrudRepository<T, ID> from the org.springframework.data.repository package (there is also a reactive version, but more about that in **Chapter 20**), and that is the interface our SingerRepository interface must extend. The SingerRepository interface is shown in Listing 10-41.

Listing 10-41. SingerRepository MongoDB Data Repository Interface

```kotlin
package com.apress.prospring6.ten.repos

import com.apress.prospring6.ten.document.Singer
import org.springframework.data.mongodb.repository.MongoRepository
import org.springframework.data.mongodb.repository.Query
import org.springframework.data.repository.query.Param

import java.time.LocalDate

interface SingerRepository : MongoRepository<Singer, String> {
    fun findByFirstName(firstName: String): Iterable<Singer>

    @Query("{'firstName' : ?0, 'lastName' : ?1}")
    fun findByPositionedParams(fn: String, ln: String): Iterable<Singer>

    @Query("{'firstName' : :#{#fn}, 'lastName' : :#{#ln}}")
    fun findByNamedParams(
        @Param("fn") fn: String,
        @Param("ln") ln: String
    ): Iterable<Singer>
}
```

The SingerRepository interface introduced here contains two MongoDB custom queries. When writing MongoDB query expressions, parameters can be specified by position or they can be named, just like for SQL queries. The only difference is the query expression syntax; MongoDB queries are essentially JSON objects. The findByPositionedParams(..) method uses indexes that match the order of the parameters, the ?0 corresponds to the first argument in the method, and the value of the argument will be used instead of ?0. This means that developers must keep track of positions and not mix them up, because, although MongoDB will not fail, it won't return the expected result. However, query expressions are pretty simple, and thus this is the recommended approach.

It is possible to use named parameters as well, which are referenced via their names mixed with the @Param annotation and SpEL expressions. The expressions are more complex and verbose, but this approach is more flexible and there is no risk of mistakenly positioning the arguments. Use whichever option you are more comfortable with.

As we are already used to, a SingerService bean is used to invoke repository methods, and its implementation, being basic, it is not worth repeating here. What is important is the Spring configuration for connecting to a MongoDB instance and enabling Spring Data MongoDB repository support. The @Configuration class to be used looks as shown in Listing 10-42.

Listing 10-42. Mongo Configuration Bean Declaration

```
// File mongo.properties:
mongo.url=mongodb://localhost:27017/musicdb
mongo.db=musicdb
mongo.user=prospring6
mongo.password=prospring6
mongo.authSource=admin
```

```
package com.apress.prospring6.ten.config

import com.mongodb.client.MongoClients
import com.mongodb.client.MongoClient

@ComponentScan(basePackages = ["com.apress.prospring6.ten.service"])
@EnableMongoRepositories(basePackages = ["com.apress.prospring6.ten.repos"])
@Configuration
@PropertySource("classpath:mongo.properties")
// We can't use that, because for simplicity the docker mongo was not
// started as a replica set:
// @EnableTransactionManagement
open class MongoCfg : AbstractMongoClientConfiguration() {
    @Value("\${mongo.url}")
    private val url: String? = null

    @Value("\${mongo.db}")
    private val database: String? = null

    @Value("\${mongo.user}")
    private val user: String? = null

    @Value("\${mongo.password}")
    private val password: String? = null
```

```kotlin
@Value("\${mongo.authSource}")
private val authSource: String? = null

override fun getMappingBasePackages() =
    mutableSetOf("com.apress.prospring6.ten.document")

@Bean
open fun transactionManager(dbFactory: MongoDatabaseFactory?):
        MongoTransactionManager {
    return MongoTransactionManager(dbFactory!!)
}

override fun getDatabaseName(): String = database!!

override fun autoIndexCreation(): Boolean {
    return true
}

override fun mongoClientSettings(): MongoClientSettings {
    val builder = MongoClientSettings.builder()
    builder.applyConnectionString(ConnectionString(url!!))
        .credential(
            MongoCredential.createScramSha1Credential(
                user!!,
                authSource!!,
                password!!.toCharArray())))
    this.configureClientSettings(builder)
    return builder.build()
}
}
```

The `MongoClientSettings` builder is used to internally create a `MongoClient` instance based on the connection string and other parameters provided. Also check out the properties file in the resources collection of the sources bundle.

Enabling support for MongoDB Data repositories is done by annotating the configuration class with `@EnableMongoRepositories`. If no base package is configured, the infrastructure scans the package of the annotated configuration class.

One thing that needs to be mentioned here is that starting with MongoDB 4.0, transactions are supported as well. Transactions are built on top of `Sessions` and, consequently, require an active `com.mongodb.session.ClientSession`. If a transaction manager bean is not configured, transactions are disabled.

Spring provides the `MongoTransactionManager` class for MongoDB transaction management. The `MongoTransactionManager` class binds a `ClientSession` to the thread. `MongoTemplate` detects the session and operates on these resources, which are associated with the transaction accordingly. Since Spring Data MongoDB repositories are backed up by a `MongoTemplate` bean, their methods are executed in a transactional context.

As for the project dependencies, because all these classes have to come from somewhere, the main dependencies of the project are the `spring-data-mongodb` and `mongodb-driver-sync` libraries. The `mongodb-driver-sync` library is a wrapper around `mongodb-driver-core` to provide classic behavior when interacting with a MongoDB instance. There is also a wrapper providing reactive behavior in the `mongodb-driver-reactivestreams` library.

Figure 10-7 shows the dependencies for the chapter10-mongo project.

```
∨  🏀 chapter10-mongo
   >  🛠 Tasks
   ∨  🗄 Dependencies
      ∨  🗄 compileClasspath
         >  ⅢⅢ ch.qos.logback:logback-classic:1.2.11
            ⅢⅢ com.google.code.findbugs:jsr305:3.0.2
            ⅢⅢ jakarta.annotation:jakarta.annotation-api:2.1.0
            ⅢⅢ org.apache.commons:commons-lang3:3.12.0
         >  ⅢⅢ org.junit.jupiter:junit-jupiter:5.9.0
         ∨  ⅢⅢ org.mongodb:mongodb-driver-sync:4.7.1
               ⅢⅢ org.mongodb:bson:4.7.0-beta0
               ⅢⅢ org.mongodb:mongodb-driver-core:4.7.0-beta0 (*)
            ⅢⅢ org.slf4j:slf4j-api:1.7.36
         ∨  ⅢⅢ org.springframework.data:spring-data-mongodb:4.0.0-M5
            >  ⅢⅢ org.mongodb:mongodb-driver-core:4.7.0-beta0
               ⅢⅢ org.slf4j:slf4j-api:1.7.36
            >  ⅢⅢ org.springframework.data:spring-data-commons:3.0.0-M5
               ⅢⅢ org.springframework:spring-beans:6.0.0-M5 (*)
            >  ⅢⅢ org.springframework:spring-context:6.0.0-M5
               ⅢⅢ org.springframework:spring-core:6.0.0-M5 (*)
               ⅢⅢ org.springframework:spring-expression:6.0.0-M5 (*)
            >  ⅢⅢ org.springframework:spring-tx:6.0.0-M5
         >  ⅢⅢ org.springframework:spring-aspects:6.0.0-M5
```

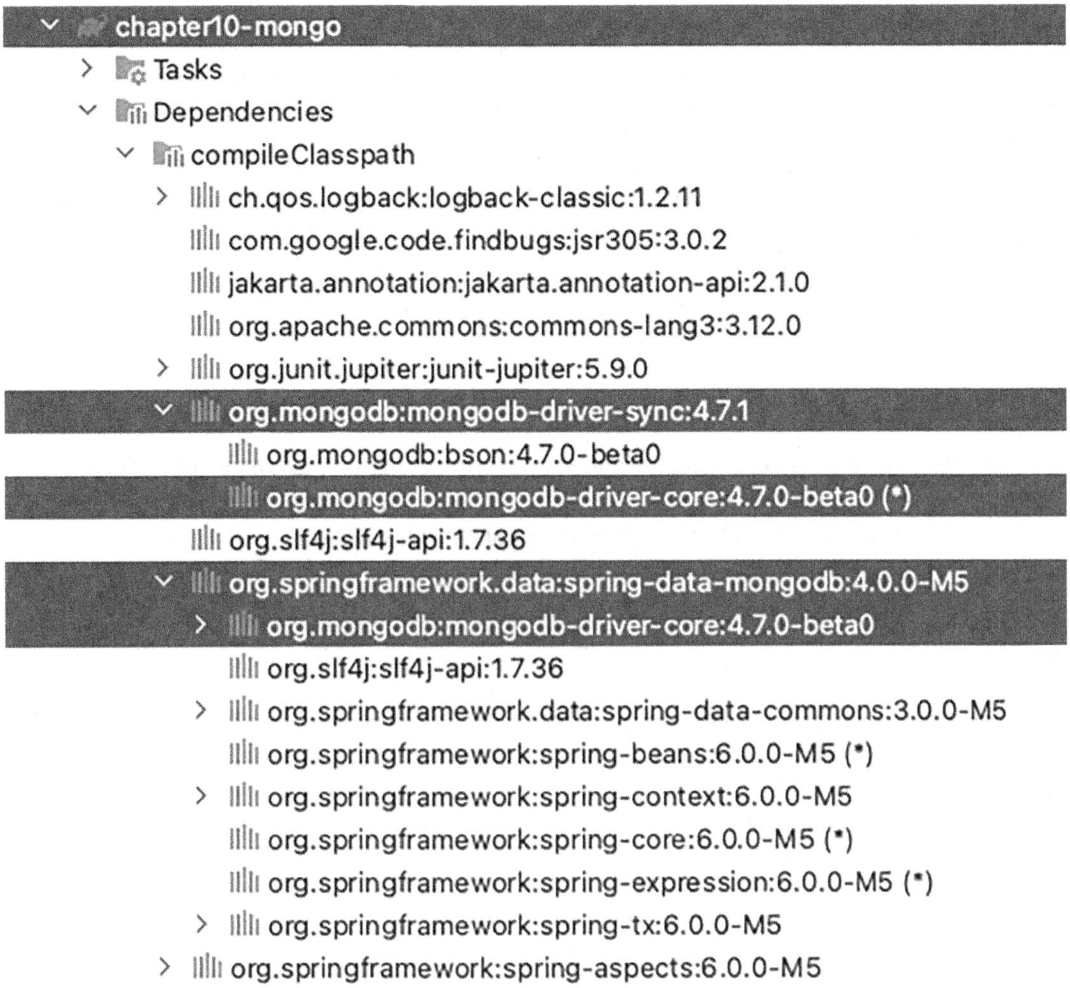

Figure 10-7. *Gradle View showing dependencies for the* chapter10-mongo *project*

Because of Spring Data consistency in its APIs, writing tests for a Spring Data Mongo application is no different from writing tests for a Spring Data JPA application.

If you are interested in working with Spring and MongoDB, the official documentation from Spring[17] and MongoDB[18] are rich and easy to follow. Also, feel free to give the Spring Boot MongoDB starter a try. A simple project is provided in the book repository.

---

[17] https://docs.spring.io/spring-data/data-mongo/docs/current/reference/html/#reference

[18] https://www.mongodb.com/docs/manual/reference/

Considerations Using Spring Data

Whether you are using Spring Data JPA or MongoDB or any other module for a specific database, Spring Data reduces the work you have to do by a lot. Add in Spring Boot, and even configuration work is reduced considerably. However, to harness Spring Data's true power, you must understand all its building blocks. This book is good for achieving that, because it slowly builds all the layers, showing you the effort that you will be spared by using all that Spring has to offer correctly.

Still, depending on the size and scope of the project, using Spring Data might be overkill, so take that into consideration before starting to write your application. It's like choosing a smartphone for your 83-year-old grandma who only needs to make and receive phone calls, and because she has arthritis, she might drop it a lot. So, it makes no sense to buy her an expensive, complex, fragile phone that provides a lot of functionalities that she will never use, when all her needs can be satisfied by a flip phone. So, consider the needs your project is trying to satisfy and choose the tools based on that.

Summary

Since this is the last chapter in the series of chapters covering data access, an overall summary is in order:

- JPA is a specification that defines an API   object-relational mappings and for managing persistent objects. It existed as part of JEE until Oracle decided to make it open source and donate it to Jakarta. This triggered a package rename from javax to jakarta.

- All JPA implementations like Hibernate and EclipseLink latest version have aligned to the new specification.

- Spring Data JPA adds a layer on top of JPA and uses all its features, like entity, association mapping, entity life-cycle management, and adds its own features, like the Spring Data no-code repositories.

- There are multiple Spring Data libraries, each designed to reduce boilerplate code when working with a particular database. Spring Data JPA is suitable for working with any relational database. For NoSQL databases, there are several libraries for MongoDB, CouchBase, Redis, etc.

- Transactional behavior is easy to configure by declaring a TransactionManager bean and annotating service classes and methods with Spring's @Transactional annotation. It is configured in the same way for relational databases and nonrelational databases, with only the type of the TransactionManager being different.

- Spring Data Boot starters reduce the effort you must expend to interact with a database by reducing the code necessary to be written to configure the application.

- Testcontainers is an amazing tool for testing Spring applications that require a database because it is easy to set up, allowing you to reuse most of the production-scoped configuration. This enables you to run integration tests in a test context as close to the production context as possible. Of course, it requires you to have Docker installed and access to the Internet, so that container images can be pulled when needed.

This concludes the data access chapter series.

CHAPTER 11

▩ ▩ ▩

Validation, Formatting, and Type Conversion

In an enterprise application, validation is critical. The purpose of validation is to verify that the data being processed fulfills all predefined business requirements as well as ensure the data integrity and usefulness in other layers of the application.

In application development, data validation is always mentioned alongside conversion and formatting. The reason is that the format of the source of data most likely is different from the format being used in the application. For example, in a web application, a user enters information in the web browser front end. When the user saves that data, it is sent to the server (after the local validation has completed). On the server side, a data-binding process is performed, in which the data from the HTTP request is extracted, converted, and bound to corresponding domain objects (for example, a user enters singer information in an HTML form that is then bound to a `Singer` object in the server), based on the formatting rules defined for each attribute (for example, the date format pattern is yyyy-MM-dd). When the data binding is complete, validation rules are applied to the domain object to check for any constraint violation. If everything runs fine, the data is persisted, and a success message is displayed to the user. Otherwise, validation error messages are populated and displayed to the user.

In the first part of this chapter, you will learn how Spring provides sophisticated support for type conversion, field formatting, and validation. Specifically, this chapter covers the following topics:

- *The Spring type conversion system and the Formatter service provider interface (SPI)*: We present the generic type conversion system and Formatter SPI. We cover how the new services can be used to replace the previous `PropertyEditor` support and how they convert between any Kotlin types.

- *Validation in Spring*: We discuss how Spring supports domain object validation. First, we provide a short introduction to Spring's own Validator interface. Then, we focus on the JSR-349 (Bean Validation) support.

Spring Type Conversion System

In Spring 3, a new type conversion system was introduced, providing a powerful way to convert between any Java types within Spring-powered applications. All classes are in the `org.springframework.core.convert` package. This section shows how this new service can perform the same functionality provided by the previous `PropertyEditor` support, as well as how it supports the conversion between any Kotlin types. We also demonstrate how to implement a custom type converter by using the Converter SPI.

© Peter Späth, Iuliana Cosmina, Rob Harrop, Chris Schaefer 2023
P. Späth et al., *Pro Spring 6 with Kotlin*, https://doi.org/10.1007/978-1-4842-9557-1_11

Conversion from a `String` Using `PropertyEditors`

Chapter 4 covered how Spring handles the conversion from a `String` in the properties files into the properties of POJOs by supporting `PropertyEditors`. Let's do a quick review here and then cover how Spring's Converter SPI (available since 3.0) provides a more powerful alternative.

Listing 11-1 shows a record named `Blogger`. We are using records (or *data classes* in Kotlin) because we know we do not intend to modify these beans in any way, nor do we need to proxy them. Also, using records also reduces the code we need to write.

Listing 11-1. The Blogger Record with Various Field Types

```
package com.apress.prospring6.eleven.domain

import java.net.URL
import java.time.LocalDate

data class Blogger (val firstName:String?, val lastName:String?, val birthDate:LocalDate,
                    val personalSite:URL)
```

For the `birthDate` attribute, the `java.time.LocalDate` type is used. In addition, there is a URL type field that indicates the blogger's personal web site, if applicable. Suppose we want to construct `Blogger` instances in Spring's `ApplicationContext`, with values stored either in Spring's configuration or in a properties file. To make things practical, the `AppConfig` class declares two `Blogger` beans: `awsBlogger`, which is created with property values injected using `@Value` annotations with hard-coded values, and `springBlogger`, which is created with property values injected using `@Value` annotations with values read from the `blogger.properties` configuration file. The properties file is configured using the `@PropertySource` annotation introduced in **Chapter 4**. The `AppConfig` class is shown in Listing 11-2, with the contents of the `blogger.properties` file presented in the first comment.

Listing 11-2. A Spring Configuration Class Declaring Two Blogger Beans

```
package com.apress.prospring6.eleven

import org.springframework.beans.factory.annotation.Value
import org.springframework.context.annotation.Bean
import org.springframework.context.annotation.Configuration
import org.springframework.context.annotation.PropertySource

import java.net.URL
import java.time.LocalDate

/*
springBlogger.firstName=Iuliana
springBlogger.lastName=Cosmina
springBlogger.birthDate=1983-08-16
springBlogger.personalSite=https://iuliana-cosmina.com
*/
@PropertySource("classpath:blogger.properties")
@Configuration
```

```kotlin
open class AppConfig {
    @Bean
    @Throws(Exception::class)
    open fun awsBlogger(
        @Value("Alex") firstName: String?,
        @Value("DeBrie") lastName: String?,
        @Value("https://www.alexdebrie.com/") personalSite: URL?,
        @Value("1980-01-02") birthDate: LocalDate?
    ): Blogger { // I really don't know when his birthday is ;)
        return Blogger(firstName!!, lastName!!, birthDate!!, personalSite!!)
    }

    @Bean
    @Throws(Exception::class)
    open fun springBlogger(
        @Value("\${springBlogger.firstName}") firstName: String?,
        @Value("\${springBlogger.lastName}") lastName: String?,
        @Value("\${springBlogger.personalSite}") personalSite: URL?,
        @Value("\${springBlogger.birthDate}") birthDate: LocalDate?
    ): Blogger {
        return Blogger(firstName!!, lastName!!, birthDate!!, personalSite!!)
    }
}
```

An attempt to create an application context based on the AppConfig class would fail with a stacktrace making it quite obvious that Spring cannot convert the text representations of calendar dates to java.time. LocalDate:

```
org.springframework.beans.factory.UnsatisfiedDependencyException:
    Error creating bean with name 'awsBlogger' defined in com.apress.prospring6.eleven.
    AppConfig:
        Unsatisfied dependency expressed through method 'awsBlogger' parameter 3:
        Failed to convert value of type 'java.lang.String' to required type 'java.time.
        LocalDate';
        Cannot convert value of type 'java.lang.String' to required type 'java.time.
        LocalDate':
            no matching editors or conversion strategy found
    at app//org.springframework.beans.factory.support.ConstructorResolver.createArgument
    Array(ConstructorResolver.java:774)
Caused by: java.lang.IllegalStateException:
    Cannot convert value of type 'java.lang.String' to required type 'java.time.LocalDate':
    no matching editors or conversion strategy found at
        org.springframework.beans.TypeConverterDelegate.convertIfNecessary(TypeConverterDel
        egate.java:262)
```

To fix this, we need to tell Spring how to do the conversion of text representations of calendar dates to java.time.LocalDate. We can do so by using an extension of PropertyEditorSupport like the LocalDatePropertyEditor shown in Listing 11-3.

Listing 11-3. LocalDatePropertyEditor Class

```
package com.apress.prospring6.eleven.property.editor

import java.beans.PropertyEditorSupport
import java.time.LocalDate
import java.time.format.DateTimeFormatter

class LocalDatePropertyEditor : PropertyEditorSupport() {
    private val dateFormat = DateTimeFormatter.ofPattern("yyyy-MM-dd")

    @Throws(IllegalArgumentException::class)
    override fun setAsText(text: String) {
        value = LocalDate.parse(text, dateFormat)
    }
}
```

A CustomEditorConfigurer bean needs to be part of the configuration to register our custom property editor: LocalDatePropertyEditor. The old-style approach, introduced in Spring 2, is to declare a PropertyEditorRegistrar bean that maps the LocalDatePropertyEditor instance to the correct type, in this case LocalDate. By the magic of lambda expressions, a bean of a custom type implementing PropertyEditorRegistrar can be created in a single line. Listing 11-4 shows the configuration class declaring all the necessary beans to enable the proper conversion of text representations to LocalDate.

Listing 11-4. PropertyEditorRegistrar Class

```
package com.apress.prospring6.eleven.property.editor

import org.springframework.beans.PropertyEditorRegistrar
import org.springframework.beans.factory.config.CustomEditorConfigurer

import java.time.LocalDate;
// other import statements omitted

@Configuration
open class CustomRegistrarCfg {
    @Bean
    open fun registrar(): PropertyEditorRegistrar {
        return PropertyEditorRegistrar { registry: PropertyEditorRegistry ->
            registry.registerCustomEditor(
                LocalDate::class.java, LocalDatePropertyEditor()
            )
        }
    }

    @Bean
    open fun customEditorConfigurer(): CustomEditorConfigurer {
        val cus = CustomEditorConfigurer()
        val registrars = arrayOfNulls<PropertyEditorRegistrar>(1)
        registrars[0] = registrar()
```

```
        cus.setPropertyEditorRegistrars(registrars)
        return cus
    }
}
```

To test this class, we simply need to build an application context based on the AppConfig and CustomRegistrarCfg classes and retrieve the two blogger beans and print their properties to the console. This can be done using a test method, as shown in Listing 11-5.

Listing 11-5. ConvertersTest Class and Method Used to Test the LocalDatePropertyEditor

package com.apress.prospring6.eleven

```
class ConvertersTest {
    @Test // the old way
    fun testCustomPropertyEditorRegistrar() {
        AnnotationConfigApplicationContext(
            AppConfig::class.java,
            CustomRegistrarCfg::class.java
        ).use { ctx ->
            val springBlogger = ctx.getBean("springBlogger", Blogger::class.java)
            LOGGER.info("SpringBlogger info: {}", springBlogger)
            val awsBlogger = ctx.getBean("awsBlogger", Blogger::class.java)
            LOGGER.info("AwsBlogger info: {}", awsBlogger)
        }
    }

    companion object {
        private val LOGGER = LoggerFactory.getLogger(ConvertersTest::class.java)
    }
}

// expected output
INFO ConvertersTest -
    SpringBlogger info: Blogger{ firstName='Iuliana',
                                lastName='Cosmina',
                                birthDate=1983-08-16,
                                personalSite=https://iuliana-cosmina.com}
INFO ConvertersTest -
    AwsBlogger info: Blogger{firstName='Alex',
                            lastName='DeBrie',
                            birthDate=1980-01-02,
                            personalSite=https://www.alexdebrie.com/}
```

When running this method, the context should be successfully created and the two beans retrieved from it and printed.

There is another version of this procedure that requires a single bean of type CustomEditorConfigurer that registers the custom property editor by mapping it to a certain type, and a PropertyEditorRegistrar is not necessary, as shown in the configuration class in Listing 11-6.

Listing 11-6. CustomEditorCfg Class

```
package com.apress.prospring6.eleven.property.editor

import org.springframework.beans.factory.config.CustomEditorConfigurer
// other imports statement omitted

@Configuration
open class CustomEditorCfg {
    @Bean
    open fun customEditorConfigurer(): CustomEditorConfigurer {
        val cus = CustomEditorConfigurer()
        cus.setCustomEditors(mapOf(LocalDate::class.java to
            LocalDatePropertyEditor::class.java))
        return cus
    }
}
```

This is the old way of doing it. The new way involves classes from the org.springframework.core. convert package and is discussed in the next section.

Introducing Spring Type Conversion

Spring 3.0 introduced a general type conversion system that resides under the package org. springframework.core.convert. In addition to providing an alternative to PropertyEditor support, the type conversion system can be configured to convert between any Kotlin types and POJOs (while PropertyEditor is focused on converting String representations in the properties file into Java/ Kotlin types).

Implementing a Custom Converter

To see the type conversion system in action, let's revisit the previous example and use the same Blogger class. Suppose this time we want to use the type conversion system to convert the date in String format into the blogger's birthDate property, which is of LocalDate type. To support the conversion, instead of creating a custom PropertyEditor, we create a custom converter by implementing the org.springframework. core.convert.converter.Converter<S,T> interface. The code snippet in Listing 11-7 shows the custom converter.

Listing 11-7. LocalDateConverter Implementation

```
package com.apress.prospring6.eleven.converter.bean

import org.springframework.core.convert.converter.Converter

import java.time.LocalDate
import java.time.format.DateTimeFormatter
```

```kotlin
class LocalDateConverter : Converter<String, LocalDate> {
    private val dateFormat = DateTimeFormatter.ofPattern("yyyy-MM-dd")
    override fun convert(source: String): LocalDate {
        return LocalDate.parse(source, dateFormat)
    }
}
```

We implement the interface `Converter<String, DateTime>`, which means the converter is responsible for converting a `String` (the source type S) to a `LocalDate` type (the target type T).

To use this converter instead of the `PropertyEditor`, we need to configure an instance of the `org.springframework.core.convert.ConversionService` interface in Spring's `ApplicationContext`. Listing 11-8 shows the Kotlin configuration class.

Listing 11-8. Kotlin Configuration Class for Using a Converter Implementation

```kotlin
package com.apress.prospring6.eleven.converter.bean

import org.springframework.context.support.ConversionServiceFactoryBean
// other import statements omitted

@Configuration
@ComponentScan
open class ConverterCfg {
    @Bean
    open fun conversionService(): ConversionServiceFactoryBean {
        val conversionServiceFactoryBean = ConversionServiceFactoryBean()
        val convs = mutableSetOf<Any>(
            LocalDateConverter())
        conversionServiceFactoryBean.setConverters(convs)
        conversionServiceFactoryBean.afterPropertiesSet()
        return conversionServiceFactoryBean
    }
}
```

Here we instruct Spring to use the type conversion system by declaring a `conversionService` bean with the class `ConversionServiceFactoryBean`. This type of bean groups multiple conversion services. If no conversion service bean is defined, Spring will use the `PropertyEditor`-based system.

By default, the type conversion service supports conversion between common types including strings, numbers, enums, collections, maps, and so on. In addition, the conversion from `Strings` to Java/Kotlin types within the `PropertyEditor`-based system is supported.

The testing method is almost identical to the one shown earlier in Listing 11-5, the only difference being that the `CustomRegistrarCfg` class is replaced with `ConverterCfg`.

Converting Between Arbitrary Types

The real strength of the type conversion system is the ability to convert between arbitrary types. Listing 11-9 introduces the record `SimpleBlogger` that only has two fields and the converter implementation that converts a `Blogger` instance to a `SimpleBlogger` instance.

Listing 11-9. SimpleBlogger Record and Converter

package com.apress.prospring6.eleven.domain

import com.apress.prospring6.eleven.Blogger
import org.springframework.core.convert.converter.Converter
import java.net.URL

```
data class SimpleBlogger (val fullName:String, val personalSite:URL) {
    class BloggerToSimpleBloggerConverter : Converter<Blogger, SimpleBlogger> {
        override fun convert(source:Blogger):SimpleBlogger =
            SimpleBlogger(source.firstName + " " + source.lastName, source.personalSite)
    }
}
```

To add this converter to the application context configuration, an instance of BloggerToSimpleBloggerConverter needs to be added to the converters set of the ConversionServiceFactoryBean as shown in Listing 11-10.

Listing 11-10. Registering SimpleBlogger Class and Converter

package com.apress.prospring6.eleven.converter.bean
// import statements omitted

```
@Configuration
@ComponentScan
open class ConverterCfg {
    @Bean
    open fun conversionService(): ConversionServiceFactoryBean {
        val conversionServiceFactoryBean = ConversionServiceFactoryBean()
        val convs = mutableSetOf<Any>(
            LocalDateConverter(),
            SimpleBlogger.BloggerToSimpleBloggerConverter())
        conversionServiceFactoryBean.setConverters(convs)
        conversionServiceFactoryBean.afterPropertiesSet()
        return conversionServiceFactoryBean
    }
}
```

To test this converter, we need to retrieve the converter bean from the context and convert one of our Blogger instances to a SimpleBlogger instance, as shown in Listing 11-11.

Listing 11-11. Conversion to SimpleBlogger

package com.apress.prospring6.eleven

import org.springframework.core.convert.ConversionService

```
class ConvertersTest {
```

```kotlin
    @Test
    fun testConvertingToSimpleBlogger() {
        AnnotationConfigApplicationContext(AppConfig::class.java,
                ConverterCfg::class.java).use { ctx ->
            val springBlogger = ctx.getBean("springBlogger", Blogger::class.java)
            LOGGER.info("SpringBlogger info: {}", springBlogger)
            val conversionService =
                ctx.getBean(
                    ConversionService::class.java
                )
            val simpleBlogger =
                conversionService.convert(springBlogger, SimpleBlogger::class.java)
            LOGGER.info("simpleBlogger info: {}", simpleBlogger)
        }
    }
    ...

    companion object {
        private val LOGGER = LoggerFactory.getLogger(ConvertersTest::class.java)
    }
}

// expected output
INFO ConvertersTest - SpringBlogger info:
    Blogger[firstName=Iuliana,
            lastName=Cosmina,
            birthDate=1983-08-16,
            personalSite=https://iuliana-cosmina.com]
INFO ConvertersTest - simpleBlogger info:   SimpleBlogger[fullName=Iuliana Cosmina,
        personalSite=https://iuliana-cosmina.com]
```

As you have probably noticed, the conversion from String to java.net.URL was done automatically for the personalSite field. This is because Spring registers out of the box a set of converters that handle the most common development use cases (e.g., from a string representing a list of items separated by commas to an Array, from a List to a Set, etc.).

With Spring's type conversion service, you can create custom converters easily and perform conversion at any layer within your application. One possible use case is that you have two systems with the same blogger information that you need to update. However, the database structure is different (for example, in system A has two field names, but system B has a single field, and so on). You can use the type conversion system to convert the objects before persisting to each individual system.

Starting with Spring 3.0, Spring MVC makes heavy use of the conversion service (as well as the Formatter SPI discussed in the next section). In the web application context configuration, a Java/Kotlin configuration class annotated with @EnableWebMvc (introduced in Spring 3.1) will automatically register all default converters (for example, StringToArrayConverter, StringToBooleanConverter, and StringToLocaleConverter, all residing under the org.springframework.core.convert.support package) and formatters (for example, CurrencyStyleFormatter, DateFormatter, and AbstractNumberFormatter, all residing under various subpackages within the org.springframework.format package). More details are covered in **Chapter 14**, when we discuss web application development in Spring.

Field Formatting in Spring

Besides the type conversion system, another great feature that Spring brings to developers is the Formatter SPI. As you might expect, this SPI can help configure the field-formatting aspects. In the Formatter SPI, the main interface for implementing a formatter is the org.springframework.format.Formatter<T> interface. Spring provides a few implementations of commonly used types, including CurrencyStyleFormatter, DateFormatter, AbstractNumberFormatter, and PercentStyleFormatter.

Implementing a Custom Formatter

Implementing a custom formatter is easy too. We will use the same Blogger record, but instead of using a converter, we'll implement a custom formatter for converting the LocalDate type of the birthDate attribute to and from a String. This involves extending Spring's org.springframework.format. support.FormattingConversionServiceFactoryBean class and providing our custom formatter. The FormattingConversionServiceFactoryBean class is a factory class that provides convenient access to the underlying FormattingConversionService class, which supports the type conversion system, as well as field formatting according to the formatting rules defined for each field type.

In Listing 11-12 you can see a custom class that extends the FormattingConversionServiceFactoryBean class, with a custom formatter defined for formatting Java's LocalDate type. Notice that the formatter is configurable with a date pattern.

Listing 11-12. ApplicationConversionServiceFactoryBean Implementation

```
package com.apress.prospring6.eleven.formatter.factory

import org.springframework.format.Formatter
import org.springframework.format.support.FormattingConversionServiceFactoryBean
// other import statements omitted

@Service("conversionService")
class ApplicationConversionServiceFactoryBean :
            FormattingConversionServiceFactoryBean() {
    private var dateTimeFormatter: DateTimeFormatter? = null

    @set:Autowired(required = false)
    var datePattern = DEFAULT_DATE_PATTERN

    private val formatters: MutableSet<Formatter<*>> = mutableSetOf()

    @PostConstruct
    fun init() {
        dateTimeFormatter = DateTimeFormatter.ofPattern(datePattern)
        formatters.add(getDateTimeFormatter())
        setFormatters(formatters)
    }

    private fun getDateTimeFormatter(): Formatter<LocalDate> {
        return object : Formatter<LocalDate> {
            @Throws(ParseException::class)
            override fun parse(source: String, locale: Locale): LocalDate {
                LOGGER.info("Parsing date string: $source")
```

540

```
                    return LocalDate.parse(source, dateTimeFormatter)
                }

                override fun print(source: LocalDate, locale: Locale): String {
                    LOGGER.info("Formatting datetime: $source")
                    return source.format(dateTimeFormatter)
                }
            }
        }

        companion object {
            private val LOGGER = LoggerFactory.getLogger(
                ApplicationConversionServiceFactoryBean::class.java
            )
            private const val DEFAULT_DATE_PATTERN = "yyyy-MM-dd"
        }
    }
```

In Listing 11-12, you can easily locate the custom formatter. It implements the Formatter<LocalDate>
interface and implements two methods defined by the interface. The parse(..) method parses the String
format into the LocalDate type (the locale was also passed for localization support), while the LOGGER.
info(..) method is to format a LocalDate instance into a String. The date pattern can be injected into the
bean (or the default will be yyyy-MM-dd). Also, in the init() method, the custom formatter is registered by
calling the setFormatters() method. You can add as many formatters as required.

Since ApplicationConversionServiceFactoryBean is configured as a bean, the simplest way to use
it is just to create an annotation context using the AppConfig class and this bean. Listing 11-13 shows a test
method creating this context and printing the two Blogger beans.

Listing 11-13. ApplicationConversionServiceFactoryBean Testing

package com.apress.prospring6.eleven
// import statements omitted

```
class FormattersTest {
    @Test
    fun testFormattingFactoryService() {
        AnnotationConfigApplicationContext(
            AppConfig::class.java,
            ApplicationConversionServiceFactoryBean::class.java
        ).use { ctx ->
            val springBlogger = ctx.getBean("springBlogger", Blogger::class.java)
            LOGGER.info("SpringBlogger info: {}", springBlogger)
            val awsBlogger = ctx.getBean("awsBlogger", Blogger::class.java)
            LOGGER.info("AwsBlogger info: {}", awsBlogger)
        }
    }

    companion object {
        private val LOGGER = LoggerFactory.getLogger(FormattersTest::class.java)
    }
}
```

The purpose of this test is to show that the application context is created correctly, and the two `Blogger` beans are too.

💡 This method might not look like a test because there are no assertion statements, but this method essentially tests the assumption that all beans in the configuration are configured correctly. If you run the Gradle build, a very nice web page with test results is generated for you. Figure 11-1 shows this page and the console execution log showing these tests passing.

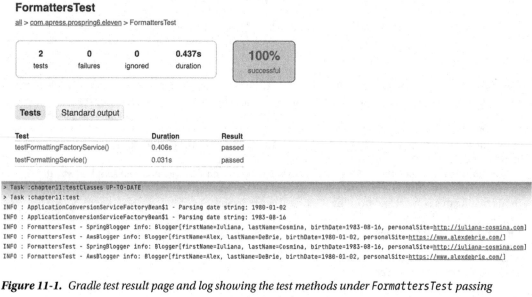

Figure 11-1. *Gradle test result page and log showing the test methods under FormattersTest passing*

The output of executing the `testFormattingFactoryService()`, proves that the responsibility of converting a text representation to a `LocalDate` was taken over by the `Formatter<LocalDate>` instance.

The `Formatter<T>` SPI is a composed interface, extending interfaces `Printer<T>` and `Parser<T>`. All three interfaces are part of the `org.springframework.format` package. Each of the methods implemented in the `Formatter<LocalDate>` shown in Listing 11-12 is provided by one of these interfaces. The three interfaces are shown in Listing 11-14.

Listing 11-14. Spring Formatting SPI Interfaces[1]

```
// ---- Formatter.java ----
package org.springframework.format;

public interface Formatter<T> extends Printer<T>, Parser<T> {
}
```

---

[1] https://github.com/spring-projects/spring-framework/tree/main/spring-context/src/main/java/org/springframework/format

```java
// ---- Printer.java ----
@FunctionalInterface
public interface Printer<T> {
    String print(T fieldValue, Locale locale);
}

// ---- Parser.java ----
import java.text.ParseException;
import java.util.Locale;

@FunctionalInterface
public interface Parser<T> {
    T parse(String clientValue, Locale locale) throws ParseException;
}
```

Every time you need a formatter, all you have to do is implement the Formatter<T> interface and parametrize it with the desired type and then add it to the Spring configuration either by using custom FormattingConversionServiceFactoryBean or by declaring a bean of type FormattingConversionService and adding the formatter instance to it. The easiest is to use the DefaultFormattingConversionService, an out-of-the-box specialization of FormattingConversionService configured by default with converters and formatters appropriate for most applications.

Listing 11-15 shows the FormattingServiceCfg that declares a bean named conversionService that is a DefaultFormattingConversionService to which the Formatter<LocalDate> implementation is added.

Listing 11-15. Configuration Class Using DefaultFormattingConversionService to Register a Custom Formatter

```kotlin
package com.apress.prospring6.eleven.formatter

import org.springframework.format.Formatter
import org.springframework.format.support.DefaultFormattingConversionService
import org.springframework.format.support.FormattingConversionService
// other import statements omitted

@Configuration
open class FormattingServiceCfg {
    @Bean
    open fun conversionService(): FormattingConversionService {
        val formattingConversionServiceBean = DefaultFormattingConversionService(true)
        formattingConversionServiceBean.addFormatter(localDateFormatter())
        return formattingConversionServiceBean
    }

    private fun localDateFormatter(): Formatter<LocalDate> {
        return object : Formatter<LocalDate> {
            @Throws(ParseException::class)
            override fun parse(source: String, locale: Locale): LocalDate {
                return LocalDate.parse(source, dateTimeFormatter)
            }
```

```kotlin
        override fun print(source: LocalDate, locale: Locale): String {
            return source.format(dateTimeFormatter)
        }

        protected val dateTimeFormatter: DateTimeFormatter
            get() = DateTimeFormatter.ofPattern("yyyy-MM-dd")
        }
    }
}
```

---

❶ When declaring a bean of type `FormattingConversionService` to customize the list of converters and formatters in your Spring application, make sure this bean is named `conversionService`, because Spring does not like it any other way. The same applies for a bean of type `ConversionServiceFactoryBean`, the convenient implementation to configure access to a `ConversionService` configured with converters appropriate for most environments.

---

❶ Notice that the `DefaultFormattingConversionService` constructor with a value of `true`. This value is assigned to the `registerDefaultFormatters` field and is necessary to enable the set of default formatters in the context. If set to `false` this bean will just enable the default set of converters.

Validation in Spring

Validation is a critical part of any application. Validation rules applied on domain objects ensure that all business data is well-structured and fulfills all the business definitions. The ideal case is that all validation rules are maintained in a centralized location, and the same set of rules are applied to the same type of data, no matter which source the data comes from (for example, from user input via a web application, from a remote application via web services, from a JMS message, or from a file).

When talking about validation, conversion and formatting are important too, because before a piece of data can be validated, it should be converted to the desired POJO according to the formatting rules defined for each type. For example, a user enters some information via a web application within a browser and then submits that data to a server. On the server side, if the web application was developed in Spring MVC, Spring will extract the data from the HTTP request and perform the conversion from a `String` to the desired type based on the formatting rule (for example, a `String` representing a date will be converted into a `LocalDate` field, with the formatting rule yyyy-MM-dd). The process is called *data binding*. When the data binding is complete and the domain object constructed, validation will then be applied to the object, and any errors will be returned and displayed to the user. If validation succeeds, the object will be persisted to the database.

Spring supports two main types of validation. The first one is provided by Spring. Validators are created by implementing the `org.springframework.validation.Validator` interface, depicted in Listing 11-16.

Listing 11-16. Spring's Validator Interface[2]

```
package org.springframework.validation;

public interface Validator {

    boolean supports(Class<?> clazz);
    void validate(Object target, Errors errors);

}
```

The other type of validation is via Spring's support of JSR-349 (Bean Validation)[3]. We present both types of validation in the following sections.

Using the Spring Validator Interface

Using Spring's Validator interface, we can develop some validation logic by creating a class to implement the interface. Let's see how it works. For the Blogger class that we've worked with so far, suppose the first name cannot be empty. To validate Blogger objects against this rule, a custom validator is needed. Listing 11-17 shows the BloggerValidator validator class.

Listing 11-17. Custom Validator for Blogger Class

```
package com.apress.prospring6.eleven.validator

import org.springframework.validation.Errors
import org.springframework.validation.ValidationUtils
import org.springframework.validation.Validator
// other import statements omitted

@Component("simpleBloggerValidator")
class SimpleBloggerValidator : Validator {
    override fun supports(clazz: Class<*>): Boolean {
        return Blogger::class.java == clazz
    }

    override fun validate(target: Any, errors: Errors) {
        ValidationUtils.rejectIfEmpty(errors, "firstName", "field.required")
    }
}
```

The validator class implements the Validator interface and implements two methods. The supports(..) method indicates whether validation of the passed-in class type is supported by the validator. The validate(..) method performs validation on the passed-in object. The result will be stored in an instance of the org.springframework.validation.Errors interface. In the validate(..)

---

[2] https://github.com/spring-projects/spring-framework/blob/main/spring-context/src/
main/java/org/springframework/validation/Validator.java
[3] https://beanvalidation.org/3.0

method, we perform a check only on the firstName attribute and use the convenient `ValidationUtils.`
`rejectIfEmpty(..)` method to ensure that the first name of the blogger is not empty. The last argument
is the error code, which can be used for looking up validation messages from resource bundles to display
localized error messages.

💡 To add this bean to a Spring application context, the annotation @ComponentScan(basePackages =
["com.apress.prospring6.eleven.validator"]) is required on an existing configuration class, and
when the application starts it will be automatically picked up. However, in our test methods, we avoid that
annotation to avoid test context pollution, and instead we build it explicitly from the application configuration
class AppConfig and any other validator bean class targeted by the test.

❗ Any external data entering a system needs to be validated, converted, and formatted to types that are
known. Converters, formatters, and validators are necessary components for applications that handle user-
provided data, like web applications with forms, or applications that import data from any third-party source.

Using Spring MVC for writing Spring applications is covered in **Chapter 14**. In this type of applications
is where the power of converters, formatters, and validators truly shines. Since we are not there yet,
application contexts in this chapter are created by direct instantiation, and the validator is invoked explicitly.
The `SimpleBloggerValidator` is tested in Listing 11-18.

Listing 11-18. Testing the Custom Validator for the Blogger Class

```
package com.apress.prospring6.eleven

import com.apress.prospring6.eleven.formatter.FormattingServiceCfg
import com.apress.prospring6.eleven.validator.BloggerValidator
import org.springframework.validation.BeanPropertyBindingResult
import org.springframework.validation.ValidationUtils
// other import statements omitted

class SpringValidatorTest {
    @Test
    @Throws(MalformedURLException::class)
    fun testSimpleBloggerValidator() {
        AnnotationConfigApplicationContext(
            AppConfig::class.java,
            FormattingServiceCfg::class.java,
            SimpleBloggerValidator::class.java
        ).use { ctx ->
            val blogger = Blogger("", "Pedala", LocalDate.of(2000, 1, 1),
                URL("https://none.co.uk"))
            val blogger2 =
                Blogger(null, "Pedala", LocalDate.of(2000, 1, 1), URL("https://none.co.uk"))
```

```
    val bloggerValidator =
        ctx.getBean(SimpleBloggerValidator::class.java)
    val result =
        BeanPropertyBindingResult(blogger, "blogger")
    ValidationUtils.invokeValidator(bloggerValidator, blogger, result)
    val errors = result.allErrors
    Assertions.assertEquals(1, errors.size)
    errors.forEach(Consumer { e: ObjectError ->
        LOGGER.info(
            "Object '{}' failed validation. Error code: {}",
            e.objectName,
            e.code
        )
    })
    // ---------------'null' passes the validation--------------------
    val result2 =
        BeanPropertyBindingResult(blogger2, "blogger2")
    ValidationUtils.invokeValidator(bloggerValidator, blogger2, result)
    val errors2 = result2.allErrors
    Assertions.assertEquals(0, errors2.size)
    }
}

companion object {
    private val LOGGER = LoggerFactory.getLogger(SpringValidatorTest::class.java)
}
}
```

In the test method in Listing 11-18, a Blogger object is constructed with the first name set to an empty String value. Then, the validator bean is retrieved from ApplicationContext. To store the validation result, an instance of the BeanPropertyBindingResult class is constructed using the object to be validated and a name for it, which is what the second argument is for. This might be useful for reporting the error to the next service in the chain, or for logging. To perform the validation, the ValidationUtils. invokeValidator() method is called, and then a normal assertion statement checks the number of error objects returned. Since the Blogger instance is created with no firstName, the validation fails and an error object with the field.required error code is created.

This example shows a very simple validation, just checking that a property of the object is empty, but the validate(..) method can be even more complex, testing more of the object properties against different rules.

⚠ A null value is not the same as an empty String value , so a Blogger object with a null first name will not fail the validation rule described by the SimpleBloggerValidator class.

For example, the version of BloggerValidator in Listing 11-19 checks if at least one of firstName or lastName is present and not null (the StringUtils.isEmpty(..) method makes sure of that), and the birthDate is after January 1, 1983.

Listing 11-19. Complex Validator Implementation for Blogger

```kotlin
package com.apress.prospring6.eleven.validator

import org.apache.commons.lang3.StringUtils
// import statements omitted

@Component("complexBloggerValidator")
class ComplexBloggerValidator : Validator {
    override fun supports(clazz: Class<*>): Boolean {
        return Blogger::class.java == clazz
    }

    override fun validate(target: Any, errors: Errors) {
        val b = target as Blogger
        if (StringUtils.isEmpty(b.firstName) && StringUtils.isEmpty(b.lastName)) {
            errors.rejectValue("firstName", "firstNameOrLastName.required")
            errors.rejectValue("lastName", "firstNameOrLastName.required")
        }
        if (b.birthDate.isBefore(LocalDate.of(1983, 1, 1))) {
            errors.rejectValue("birthDate", "birthDate.greaterThan1983")
        }
    }
}
```

Aside from this, the `Validator` interface can be implemented to validate complex objects by reusing validation logic for nested objects. To show this, a new class is introduced named `BloggerWithAddress` that models exactly what its name says: a blogger with an address. The address is modeled using a record, the blogger however is modeled with a class because this allows for a validation to be applicable to all the classes extending it. Listing 11-20 shows the `Address` record and the `BloggerWithAddress` class.

Listing 11-20. Complex `BloggerWithAddress` with a Nested Field of Type `Address`

```kotlin
// ---- Address.kt ----
package com.apress.prospring6.eleven.domain

data class Address(val city:String, val country:String)

// ---- BloggerWithAddress.kt ----
package com.apress.prospring6.eleven.domain

class BloggerWithAddress(
    var firstName: String?,
    var lastName: String,
    var birthDate: LocalDate,
    var personalSite: URL?,
    var address: Address
) {

    override fun toString(): String =
        "BloggerWithAddress{" +
                "firstName='" + firstName + '\'' +
```

```
                ", lastName='" + lastName + '\'' +
                ", birthDate=" + birthDate +
                ", personalSite=" + personalSite +
                ", address=" + address +
                '}'
}
```

Listing 11-21 shows the AddressValidator that verifies that both city and country fields are populated and that they contain only letters.

Listing 11-21. AddressValidator Class

```
package com.apress.prospring6.eleven.validator

import org.apache.commons.lang3.StringUtils
// other import statements omitted

@Component("addressValidator")
class AddressValidator : Validator {
    override fun supports(clazz: Class<*>): Boolean {
        return Address::class.java == clazz
    }

    override fun validate(target: Any, errors: Errors) {
        ValidationUtils.rejectIfEmpty(errors, "city", "city.empty")
        ValidationUtils.rejectIfEmpty(errors, "country", "country.empty")
        val address = target as Address
        if (!StringUtils.isAlpha(address.city)) {
            errors.rejectValue("city", "city.onlyLettersAllowed")
        }
        if (!StringUtils.isAlpha(address.country)) {
            ValidationUtils.rejectIfEmpty(errors, "country", "country.onlyLettersAllowed")
        }
    }
}
```

Listing 11-22 shows the BloggerWithAddressValidator validator that checks that fields address and personalSite are populated, that at least one of firstName and lastName is populated, and that the address is valid, using the AddressValidator.

Listing 11-22. BloggerWithAddressValidator Class

```
package com.apress.prospring6.eleven.validator
// import statements omitted

@Component("bloggerWithAddressValidator")
class BloggerWithAddressValidator(addressValidator: Validator) :
    Validator {
    private val addressValidator: Validator
```

```kotlin
    init {
        require(addressValidator.supports(Address::class.java)) {
            "The supplied [Validator] must " +
                    "support the validation of [Address] instances."
        }
        this.addressValidator = addressValidator
    }

    override fun supports(clazz: Class<*>): Boolean {
        return BloggerWithAddress::class.java.isAssignableFrom(clazz)
    }

    override fun validate(target: Any, errors: Errors) {
        ValidationUtils.rejectIfEmptyOrWhitespace(errors, "address", "address.required")
        ValidationUtils.rejectIfEmptyOrWhitespace(errors, "personalSite", "personalSite.
        required")
        val b = target as BloggerWithAddress
        if (StringUtils.isEmpty(b.firstName) && StringUtils.isEmpty(b.lastName)) {
            errors.rejectValue("firstName", "firstNameOrLastName.required")
            errors.rejectValue("lastName", "firstNameOrLastName.required")
        }
        try {
            errors.pushNestedPath("address")
            ValidationUtils.invokeValidator(addressValidator, b.address, errors)
        } finally {
            errors.popNestedPath()
        }
    }
}
```

Notice that the `BloggerWithAddressValidator` is a composed object that has a nested `AddressValidator` field. This field is used to validate the nested address field in a `BloggerWithAddress` instance. Notice the body of the `supports(..)` method. The `BloggerWithAddress::class.java. isAssignableFrom(clazz)` statement validates that the target object is either an instance of `BloggerWithAddress` or an instance of its superclass.

The two methods `pushNestedPath(..)` and `popNestedPath(..)` are used to generate nested error properties for the error messages. For example, when the current path is `blogger.`, a call to `pushNestedPath("address")` results in the path being changed to `blogger.address.`, which means the error properties are relative to this path. Then, a call to `popNestedPath()` results in the path reverting to `blogger.` again.

To test this implementation, we'll do the same as before: construct a Spring configuration using the `AddressValidator`, `BloggerWithAddressValidator`, and the existing `AppConfig` class. Then we'll create a `BloggerWithAddress` instance that fails the validation and check that our validator reports the existing error. The code is shown in Listing 11-23.

Listing 11-23. Testing the BloggerWithAddressValidator Class

package com.apress.prospring6.eleven
// import statements omitted

```
class SpringValidatorTest {

    @Test
    @Throws(MalformedURLException::class)
    fun testBloggerWithAddressValidator() {
        AnnotationConfigApplicationContext(
            AppConfig::class.java,
            FormattingServiceCfg::class.java,
            AddressValidator::class.java,
            BloggerWithAddressValidator::class.java
        ).use { ctx ->
            val address =
                Address("221B", "UK")
            val blogger =
                BloggerWithAddress(null, "Mazzie", LocalDate.of(1973, 1, 1), null, address)
            val bloggerValidator = ctx.getBean(
                BloggerWithAddressValidator::class.java
            )
            val result =
                BeanPropertyBindingResult(blogger, "blogger")
            ValidationUtils.invokeValidator(bloggerValidator, blogger, result)
            val errors = result.allErrors
            Assertions.assertEquals(2, errors.size)
            errors.forEach{ e: ObjectError ->
                LOGGER.info(
                    "Error Code: {}",
                    e.code
                )
            }
        }
    }
    ...
}
```

```
\\ expected output
DEBUG ValidationUtils - Validator found 2 errors
INFO SpringValidatorTest - Error Code: personalSite.required
INFO SpringValidatorTest - Error Code: city.onlyLettersAllowed
```

Two objects fail with the validation: the address has a city named 221B and the blogger has a null personalSite.

The examples in this section all print the error codes. Outputting messages that correspond to validation errors is a topic for **Chapter 14**. That's pretty much it for Spring validation. The next section covers Spring integration with Jakarta's Bean Validation API and Hibernate Validator.

Using JSR-349 Bean Validation

As of Spring 4, full support for JSR-349 (Bean Validation 3.0)[4] has been implemented. The Bean Validation API defines a set of constraints in the form of Java/Kotlin annotations (for example, @NotNull) under the package jakarta.validation.constraints that can be applied to the domain objects. In addition, custom validators (for example, class-level validators) can be developed and applied by using annotation.

Using the Bean Validation API frees you from coupling to a specific validation service provider. By using the Bean Validation API, you can use standard annotations and the API for implementing validation logic to your domain objects, without knowing the underlying validation service provider. For example, Hibernate Validator[5] is a JSR-349 reference implementation.

Spring provides seamless support for the Bean Validation API. The main features include support for JSR-349 standard annotations for defining validation constraints, custom validators, and configuration of JSR-349 validation within Spring's ApplicationContext. We'll go through these features one by one in the following sections.

Dependencies

For the following sections we need to add the hibernate-validator library to the chapter11 project's classpath. The current version specific to Jakarta 10 is 8.0.0.Final. Its transitive dependency is jakarta.validation-api version 3.0.2. We also need an implementation of jakarta.el.ExpressionFactory, because it provides an implementation for creating and evaluating Jakarta Expression Language expressions, thus we add the Glassfish jakarta.el version 5.0.0-M1 library too.

These dependencies are configured using Maven/Gradle and are shown in the IntelliJ IDEA Gradle View in Figure 11-2.

---

[4] https://beanvalidation.org/3.0
[5] https://hibernate.org/validator

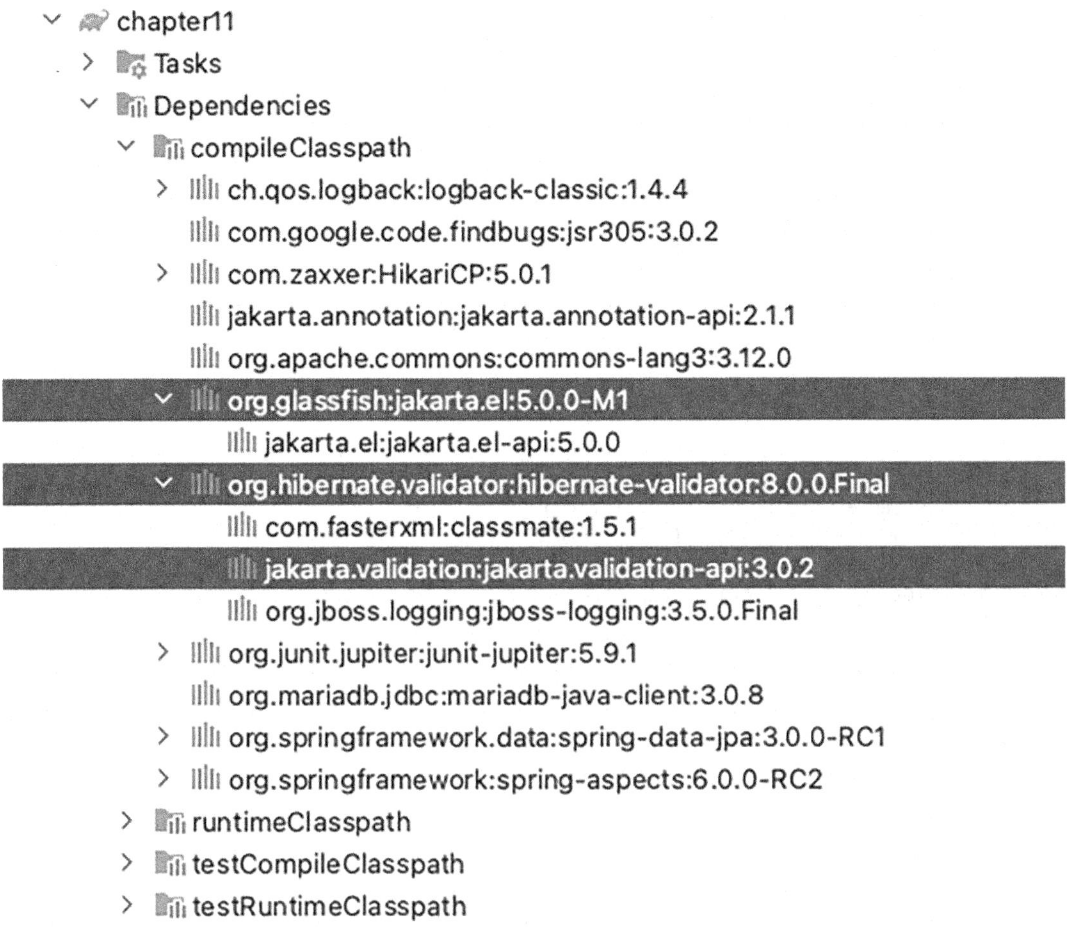

- ∨ 🐢 chapter11
  - ⟩ 🧰 Tasks
  - ∨ 🗂 Dependencies
    - ∨ 🗂 compileClasspath
      - ⟩ ‖‖‖ ch.qos.logback:logback-classic:1.4.4
      - ‖‖‖ com.google.code.findbugs:jsr305:3.0.2
      - ⟩ ‖‖‖ com.zaxxer:HikariCP:5.0.1
      - ‖‖‖ jakarta.annotation:jakarta.annotation-api:2.1.1
      - ‖‖‖ org.apache.commons:commons-lang3:3.12.0
      - ∨ ‖‖‖ org.glassfish:jakarta.el:5.0.0-M1
        - ‖‖‖ jakarta.el:jakarta.el-api:5.0.0
      - ∨ ‖‖‖ org.hibernate.validator:hibernate-validator:8.0.0.Final
        - ‖‖‖ com.fasterxml:classmate:1.5.1
      - ‖‖‖ jakarta.validation:jakarta.validation-api:3.0.2
        - ‖‖‖ org.jboss.logging:jboss-logging:3.5.0.Final
      - ⟩ ‖‖‖ org.junit.jupiter:junit-jupiter:5.9.1
      - ‖‖‖ org.mariadb.jdbc:mariadb-java-client:3.0.8
      - ⟩ ‖‖‖ org.springframework.data:spring-data-jpa:3.0.0-RC1
      - ⟩ ‖‖‖ org.springframework:spring-aspects:6.0.0-RC2
    - ⟩ 🗂 runtimeClasspath
    - ⟩ 🗂 testCompileClasspath
    - ⟩ 🗂 testRuntimeClasspath

Figure 11-2. *Gradle View showing dependencies for the* chapter11 *project*

Defining Validation Constraints on Domain Object Properties

For the next sections, the type targeted by validation is a variation of Singer that has two enum type fields used to set its genre and gender. The Singer class is shown in Listing 11-24 together with the two enum declarations.

Listing 11-24. The Enriched Singer Class

```
package com.apress.prospring6.eleven.domain

import jakarta.validation.constraints.NotNull
import jakarta.validation.constraints.Size
```

```kotlin
class Singer {
    @NotNull @Size(min = 2, max = 60) var firstName: String? = null
    var lastName: String? = null
    @NotNull var genre: Genre? = null
    var gender: Gender? = null
    val isCountrySinger: Boolean
        get() = genre == Genre.COUNTRY

    override fun toString(): String {
        return "Singer{" +
                "firstName='" + firstName + '\'' +
                ", lastName='" + lastName + '\'' +
                ", genre=" + genre +
                ", gender=" + gender +
                '}'
    }

    enum class Genre(private val code: String) {
        POP("P"), JAZZ("J"), BLUES("B"), COUNTRY("C");

        override fun toString() = this.code
    }

    enum class Gender(private val code: String) {
        MALE("M"), FEMALE("F"), UNSPECIFIED("U");

        override fun toString() = this.code
    }
}
```

Two constraints are applied to the firstName property: the @NotNull annotation, which indicates that the value should not be null, and the @Size annotation, which governs the length of the firstName property. The @NotNull constraint is applied to the genre property too. The genre property indicates the music genre a singer belongs to, while the gender property is not relevant for a musical career (or for any career), so it could be null.

Configuring Bean Validation Support in Spring

To configure support of the Bean Validation API in Spring's ApplicationContext, we define a bean of type org.springframework.validation.beanvalidation.LocalValidatorFactoryBean in Spring's configuration. Listing 11-25 depicts the configuration class.

Listing 11-25. Configuring Support for Jakarta Validation in a Spring Application

package com.apress.prospring6.eleven.validator

import org.springframework.validation.beanvalidation.LocalValidatorFactoryBean
// other import statements omitted

@Configuration
@ComponentScan

```
open class JakartaValidationCfg {
    @Bean
    open fun validator() = LocalValidatorFactoryBean()
}
```

The declaration of a LocalValidatorFactoryBean bean and enabling component scanning in the current package so the SingerValidationService bean is registered are all that is needed. Listing 11-26 shows SingerValidationService, a service class that provides a validation service for the Singer class.

Listing 11-26. SingerValidationService, a Validation Service for the Singer Class

package com.apress.prospring6.eleven.validator

```
// other import statements omitted
import jakarta.validation.ConstraintViolation
import jakarta.validation.Validator
import org.springframework.stereotype.Service

@Service("singerValidationService")
class SingerValidationService(private val validator: Validator) {
    fun validateSinger(singer: Singer): Set<ConstraintViolation<Singer>> {
        return validator.validate(singer)
    }
}
```

An instance of the jakarta.validation.Validator was injected.

💡   Note the difference from the Spring-provided Validator interface, which is org.springframework. validation.Validator. Using Jakarta Validator allows you to decouple the business logic from Spring if necessary.

Once the LocalValidatorFactoryBean is defined, you can inject any Validator bean anywhere in your application and use it. To perform validation on a POJO, the Validator.validate(..) method is called. The validation results will be returned as a Set of the ConstraintViolation<T> interface.

To test this configuration, we'll use the same approach as before, as shown in Listing 11-27.

Listing 11-27. Testing SingerValidationService

package com.apress.prospring6.eleven

```
import com.apress.prospring6.eleven.validator.JakartaValidationCfg
import com.apress.prospring6.eleven.validator.SingerValidationService
import akarta.validation.ConstraintViolation
// other import statements omitted

class JakartaValidationTest {
    @Test
    fun testSingerValidation() {
        AnnotationConfigApplicationContext(JakartaValidationCfg::class.java).use { ctx ->
```

```
            val singerBeanValidationService =
                ctx.getBean(
                    SingerValidationService::class.java
                )
            val singer = Singer()
            singer.firstName = "J"
            singer.lastName = "Mayer"
            singer.genre = null
            singer.gender = null
            val violations =
                singerBeanValidationService.validateSinger(singer)
            Assertions.assertEquals(4, violations.size)
            listViolations(violations)
        }
    }
    ...


    companion object {
        private val LOGGER = LoggerFactory.getLogger(JakartaValidationTest::class.java)
        private fun listViolations(violations: Set<ConstraintViolation<Singer>>) {
            violations.forEach{ violation: ConstraintViolation<Singer> ->
                LOGGER.info(
                    "Validation error for property: {} with value: {} with error
                    message: {}",
                    violation.propertyPath, violation.invalidValue, violation.message
                )
            }
        }
    }
}
// expected output
INFO : Version - HV000001: Hibernate Validator 8.0.0.Alpha1
...
INFO : JakartaValidationTest$Companion - Validation error for property: firstName with
value: J ...
INFO : JakartaValidationTest$Companion - Validation error for property: gender with value:
null ...
INFO : JakartaValidationTest$Companion - Validation error for property:  with value:
Singer{firstName='J', lastName='Mayer', genre=null, gender=null} with error message: Country
Singer should have gender and last name defined
INFO : JakartaValidationTest$Companion - Validation error for property: genre with value:
null ...
```

As shown in this listing, a Singer object is constructed with firstName and genre violating the constraints declared using annotations. The SingerValidationService.validateSinger(..) method is called, which in turn will invoke JSR-349 (Bean Validation 3.0). Running the program also prints in the console the rules that were violated and the values that were rejected. As you can see, there are four violations, and the messages are shown. In the output, you can see that Hibernate Validator had already constructed default validation error messages based on the annotation. You can also provide your own validation error message, which we demonstrate in the next section.

Creating a Custom Validator

Besides property-level validation, we can apply class-level validation. This applies when in the same class a field value depends on the value of another field; for example, age and dateOfBirth are related to each other, and an object is not valid if age is 15 and dateOfBirth is 1980-01-01. For the Singer class, for country singers, we want to make sure that the lastName and gender properties are not null (again, not that gender matters, but just for educational purposes). In this case, we can develop a custom validator to perform the check. In the Bean Validation API, developing a custom validator is a two-step process. First, create an Annotation type for the validator, as shown Listing 11-28. Second, develop the class that implements the validation logic.

Listing 11-28. Annotation for Custom Validator for Singer Instances

```
package com.apress.prospring6.eleven.validator

import jakarta.validation.Constraint
import jakarta.validation.Payload

import java.lang.annotation.*

@Retention(RetentionPolicy.RUNTIME)
@Target(AnnotationTarget.ANNOTATION_CLASS, AnnotationTarget.CLASS)
@Constraint(validatedBy = [CountrySingerValidator::class])
@Documented
annotation class CheckCountrySinger(
    val message: String = "Country Singer should have gender and last name defined",
    val groups: Array<KClass<*>> = [],
    val payload: Array<KClass<out Payload>> = []
)
```

The @Target(... AnnotationTarget.CLASS) annotation means that the annotation should be applied only at the class level. The @Constraint annotation indicates that it's a validator, and the validatedBy attribute specifies the class providing the validation logic. Within the body, three attributes are defined (in the form of a method), as follows:

- The message attribute defines the message (or error code) to return when the constraint is violated. A default message can also be provided in the annotation.

- The groups attribute specifies the validation group, if applicable. It's possible to assign validators to different groups and perform validation on a specific group.

- The payload attribute specifies additional payload objects (of the class implementing the jakarta.validation.Payload interface). It allows you to attach additional information to the constraint (for example, a payload object can indicate the severity of a constraint violation).

Listing 11-29 shows the CountrySingerValidator class that provides the validation logic.

Listing 11-29. CountrySingerValidator Class

```
package com.apress.prospring6.eleven.validator

import com.apress.prospring6.eleven.domain.Singer
import jakarta.validation.ConstraintValidator
import jakarta.validation.ConstraintValidatorContext
```

```kotlin
class CountrySingerValidator : ConstraintValidator<CheckCountrySinger?, Singer> {
    override fun initialize(constraintAnnotation: CheckCountrySinger?) {}
    override fun isValid(singer: Singer, context: ConstraintValidatorContext): Boolean {
        return (singer.genre == null || !singer.isCountrySinger ||
            singer.lastName != null) && singer.gender != null
    }
}
```

CountrySingerValidator implements the ConstraintValidator<CheckCountrySinger, Singer> interface, which means that the validator checks the @CheckCountrySinger annotation on the Singer classes. The isValid() method is implemented, and the underlying validation service provider (for example, Hibernate Validator) will pass the instance under validation to the method. In the method, we verify that if the singer is a country music singer, the lastName and gender properties should not be null. The result is a Boolean value that indicates the validation result.

To enable the validation, apply the @CheckCountrySinger annotation to the Singer class, as shown in Listing 11-30.

Listing 11-30. Annotated Singer Class

package com.apress.prospring6.eleven.domain

import com.apress.prospring6.eleven.validator.CheckCountrySinger

```kotlin
// other import statements omitted

@CheckCountrySinger
class Singer {
    ...
}
```

Notice that the class in Listing 11-29, CountrySingerValidator, is not declared as a bean. It is an implementation of jakarta.validation.ConstraintValidator and therefore is automatically detected by the SingerValidationService bean. To test the custom validation, another test method is needed, shown in Listing 11-31.

Listing 11-31. Testing Custom Validation

Package com.apress.prospring6.eleven
```kotlin
// import statements omitted

class JakartaValidationTest {

    @Test
    fun testCountrySingerValidation() {
        AnnotationConfigApplicationContext(JakartaValidationCfg::class.java).use { ctx ->
            val singerBeanValidationService =
                ctx.getBean(
                    SingerValidationService::class.java
                )
            val singer = Singer()
            singer.firstName = "John"
            singer.lastName = "Mayer"
```

```
            singer.genre = Singer.Genre.COUNTRY
            singer.gender = null
            val violations =
                singerBeanValidationService.validateSinger(singer)
            Assertions.assertEquals(2, violations.size)
            listViolations(violations)
        }
    }
    ...
}
```

```
// expected output
INFO : JakartaValidationTest$Companion - Validation error for property: gender with value:
null ...
INFO : JakartaValidationTest$Companion - Validation error for property:  with value:
Singer{firstName='John', lastName='Mayer', genre=C, gender=null} with error message: Country
Singer should have gender and last name defined
```

In the output, you can see that the value being checked (which is the Singer instance) violates the validation rule for country singers, because the gender property is null. Note also in the output that the property path is empty because this is a class-level validation error.

Using AssertTrue for Custom Validation

Besides implementing a custom validator, another way to apply custom validation using the Bean Validation API is to use the @AssertTrue annotation. To use this annotation for the Singer class, the @CheckCountrySinger annotation should be removed, the isCountrySinger() method should be annotated with @AssertTrue, and the validation logic from the CountrySingerValidator.isValid(..) method should be moved into this method as well. Since we want to keep the Singer class as it is, a duplicate SingerTwo is created with these changes and a validator for these types of instances named SingerTwoValidationService is added to the configuration.

In Listing 11-32 you can see the SingerTwo class containing the isCountrySinger() method. The SingerTwoValidationService is almost identical to SingerValidationService, the only difference being the domain object type it works on.

Listing 11-32. Using the @AssertTrue Annotation

package com.apress.prospring6.eleven.domain

import jakarta.validation.constraints.AssertTrue
```
// other import statements omitted

class SingerTwo() {
    @NotNull @Size(min = 2, max = 60) var firstName: String? = null
    var lastName: String? = null
    @NotNull var genre: Singer.Genre? = null
    @NotNull var gender: Singer.Gender? = null

    @AssertTrue(message =
        "ERROR! Individual customer should have gender and last name defined")
    fun isCountrySinger(): Boolean  = genre == null || (genre != Singer.Genre.COUNTRY ||
            (gender != null && lastName != null))
```

```
    override fun toString() = "Singer{" +
                "firstName='" + firstName + '\'' +
                ", lastName='" + lastName + '\'' +
                ", genre=" + genre +
                ", gender=" + gender +
                '}'
}
```

When invoking validation, the provider invokes the checking and makes sure that the result is true. JSR-349 also provides the @AssertFalse annotation to check for some condition that should be false. The test method in Listing 11-33 tests whether the validation rule introduced by the @AssertTrue annotation is violated.

Listing 11-33. Testing the @AssertTrue Annotation

```
package com.apress.prospring6.eleven
// import statements omitted

class JakartaValidationTest {

    @Test
    fun testCountrySingerTwoValidation() {
        AnnotationConfigApplicationContext(JakartaValidationCfg::class.java).use { ctx ->
            val singerBeanValidationService = ctx.getBean(
                SingerTwoValidationService::class.java
            )
            val singer = SingerTwo()
            singer.firstName = "John"
            singer.lastName = "Mayer"
            singer.genre = Singer.Genre.COUNTRY
            singer.gender = null

            val violations: Set<ConstraintViolation<SingerTwo>> =
                singerBeanValidationService.validateSinger(singer)
            Assertions.assertEquals(2, violations.size)
            violations.forEach{ violation: ConstraintViolation<SingerTwo> ->
                LOGGER.info(
                    "Validation error for property: {} with value: {} with error
                    message: {}",
                    violation.propertyPath, violation.invalidValue, violation.message
                )
            }
        }
    }
    ...
}
// expected output
INFO : JakartaValidationTest - Validation error for property: countrySinger
    with value: false
    with error message: ERROR! Individual customer should have gender and last name defined
```

Implementing validation this way makes it clear which rule was violated and allows a custom message to be configured. It also provides the advantage of keeping the code in the same scope. Some developers might say that the domain object is polluted with validation logic and recommend against this approach, but we like this approach for simple validation rules. When the code required to verify that some domain object becomes bigger than some other one, that is when a separate validator class is needed.

Deciding Which Validation API to Use

Having discussed Spring's own `Validator` interface and the Bean Validation API, which one should you use in your application? JSR-349 is definitely the way to go. The following are the major reasons:

- JSR-349 is a Jakarta EE standard and is broadly supported by many front-end/back-end frameworks (for example, Spring, JPA 3, Spring MVC, etc.).

- JSR-349 provides a standard validation API that hides the underlying provider, so you are not tied to a specific provider.

- Spring tightly integrates with JSR-349 starting with version 4. For example, in the Spring MVC web controller, you can annotate the argument in a method with the `@Valid` annotation (under the package `jakarta.validation`), and Spring will invoke JSR-349 validation automatically during the data-binding process. Moreover, in a Spring MVC web application context configuration, a simple annotation (`@EnableWebMvc`) configures Spring to automatically enable the Spring type conversion system and field formatting, as well as support of JSR-349 (Bean Validation).

- If you are using JPA 3, the provider will automatically perform JSR-349 validation to the entity before persisting, providing another layer of protection.

For detailed information about using JSR-349 (Bean Validation) with Hibernate Validator as the implementation provider, please refer to Hibernate Validator's documentation page.

Configuring Validation in a Spring Boot Application

As you can probably imagine by now, there is a Spring Boot starter library that adds all the necessary libraries to the project classpath, so you can start writing your validators right away. The library is named `spring-boot-starter-validation` and having it in the classpath also removes the necessity of explicitly declaring a `LocalValidatorFactoryBean`.

Figure 11-3 shows the collection of libraries added to the project classpath by Spring Boot.

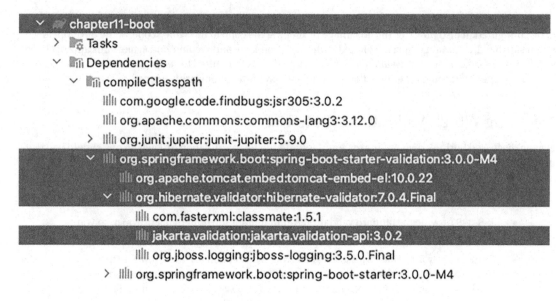

Figure 11-3. *Gradle View showing dependencies for the* chapter11-boot *project*

To test that the validation works, without any other explicit configuration, we copied the Singer object and the SingerValidationService into this project, next to the main class, the one annotated with @SpringBootApplication, and modified the main method to create a Singer instance and validate it using the SingerValidationService bean as we've done so far in the chapter.

Figure 11-4 shows the project content.

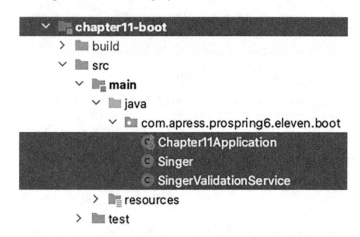

Figure 11-4. *Project view showing the contents of the* chapter11-boot *project*

The code to test our validation is in the body of the @SpringBootApplication class for simplicity reasons. What would be the point to have an empty main method anyway? You can see the code validating the Singer object in Listing 11-34.

Listing 11-34. Spring Boot main Method Validating a Singer Instance

```
package com.apress.prospring6.eleven.boot

import org.slf4j.Logger
import org.slf4j.LoggerFactory
import org.springframework.boot.SpringApplication
import org.springframework.boot.autoconfigure.SpringBootApplication
import org.springframework.core.env.AbstractEnvironment

@SpringBootApplication
open class Chapter11Application {
    companion object {
        private val LOGGER = LoggerFactory.getLogger(Chapter11Application::class.java)

        @JvmStatic
        fun main(args: Array<String>) {
            System.setProperty(AbstractEnvironment.ACTIVE_PROFILES_PROPERTY_NAME,
                "dev")
            val ctx = SpringApplication.run(
                Chapter11Application::class.java, *args
            )
            val singerBeanValidationService = ctx.getBean(
                SingerValidationService::class.java
            )
            val singer = Singer()
            singer.firstName = "J"
            singer.lastName = "Mayer"
            singer.genre = null
            singer.gender = null
            val violations = singerBeanValidationService.validateSinger(singer)
            if (violations.size != 2) {
                LOGGER.error("Unexpected number of violations: {}", violations.size)
            }
            violations.forEach { violation ->
                LOGGER.info(
                    "Validation error for property: {} with value: {} with error
                    message: {}",
                    violation.getPropertyPath(), violation.invalidValue, violation.message
                )
            }
        }
    }
}
```

Summary

In this chapter, we covered the Spring type conversion system as well as the field Formatter SPI. You saw how the new type conversion system can be used for arbitrary type conversion, in addition to the `PropertyEditors` support.

We also covered validation support in Spring, Spring's `Validator` interface, and the recommended JSR-349 (Bean Validation) support in Spring. We also introduced the Spring Boot Validation starter.

The gist of this chapter is simple: you can implement and configure conversion, formatting, and validation in multiple ways in a Spring application.

## CHAPTER 12

Task Scheduling

Task scheduling is a common feature in enterprise applications. Task scheduling is composed mainly of three parts:

- *The task*: The piece of business logic needed to run at a specific time or on a regular basis
- *The trigger*: Specifies the condition under which the task should be executed
- *The scheduler*: Executes the task based on the information from the trigger

Specifically, this chapter covers the following topics:

- *Task execution in Spring*: We briefly discuss Spring's `TaskExecutor` interface and how tasks are executed.
- *Task scheduling in Spring*: We discuss how Spring supports task scheduling, focusing on the `TaskScheduler` abstraction introduced in Spring 3. We also cover scheduling scenarios such as fixed-interval scheduling and `cron` expressions.
- *Asynchronous task execution*: We show how to use the `@Async` annotation in Spring to execute tasks asynchronously.

About Tasks

If you are a somewhat experienced developer, you are probably aware of the concept of execution threads. A Java/Kotlin application is described by code that the JVM can run on one or multiple threads, and one of the threads is the non-daemon thread that calls the `main(..)` method of a main class. In plain Java or Kotlin, the class to model an execution thread is `java.lang.Thread`. An execution thread can be created by extending this class and overriding its `run()` method. The resulting instance models an execution thread that must be started explicitly by invoking its `start()` method.

There exists another way to create threads, however, and this is by creating a class implementing `java.lang.Runnable`. This interface provides a common protocol for objects that need to execute code, including the `Thread` class. This means that `Runnable` instances can be created and passed to some components, called *executors*, that execute the code in the way they were configured: sequentially, in parallel, using threads provided by a thread pool, etc. In case it is not obvious what a task is, in a Kotlin application a *task* is any instance of type `Runnable`.

In Java or Kotlin, the `java.util.concurrent.Executor` interface represents the abstraction for asynchronous task execution. In Spring, there is an interface that extends this one and is basically identical, with the exception that it is annotated with `@FunctionalInterface` to mark it as a functional interface: `org.springframework.core.task.TaskExecutor`.

This interface is necessary for backward compatibility with JDK 1.4 in Spring 2.x.

Spring's TaskExecutor interface is depicted in Listing 12-1.

Listing 12-1. Spring's org.springframework.core.task.TaskExecutor Interface

```
package org.springframework.core.task;

import java.util.concurrent.Executor;

@FunctionalInterface
public interface TaskExecutor extends Executor {

    @Override
    void execute(Runnable task);
}
```

The interface has a single method, execute(Runnable task), that accepts a task for execution based on the semantics and configuration of the thread pool. Spring provides a few useful TaskExecutor implementations.

Task Executing in Java and Kotlin

In Java and Kotlin there are quite a few java.util.concurrent.Executor implementations. Thread pools provide the advantage of improved performance when executing a large number of asynchronous tasks, because they provide a way of bounding and managing the resources, including threads when executing a collection of tasks. ThreadPoolExecutor maintains basic statistics regarding the number of active and completed tasks, and one of our favorite implementations is to write a ThreadPoolMonitor class that implements java.lang.Runnable that prints those statistics.

This section introduces a hierarchy of classes that model various sorting algorithms, shown in Figure 12-1. These classes are suitable for creating sorting tasks that can be executed asynchronously by an executor.

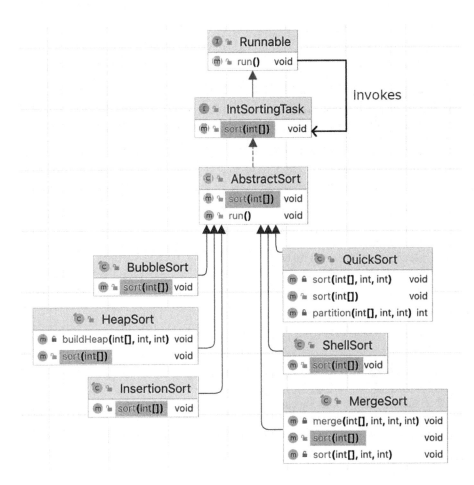

Figure 12-1. *Hierarchy of classes modeling various sorting algorithms*

The implementation of these sorting algorithms is not important for this chapter, but running them in parallel managed by a ThreadPoolExecutor class is.

All Java components specific to task executions can be found under the java.util.concurrent package. The ThreadPoolExecutor class is an implementation of ExecutorService that executes each submitted task using one of possibly several pooled threads, configured using Executors factory methods. The size of the thread pool and its maximum capacity are provided as arguments to its constructor. The tasks are provided as an implementation of BlockingQueue<Runnable>, which avoids the same task being submitted more than once for execution, by being thread-safe. It also supports operations that wait for the queue to become non-empty before retrieving an element, which allows for tasks to be added to this list after the execution of its contents began.

The ThreadPoolMonitor class is a custom extension of Thread written specifically for this section to print statistics for a running ThreadPoolExecutor, and its code is shown in Listing 12-2.

567

Listing 12-2. The ThreadPoolMonitor Monitor Class

```kotlin
package com.apress.prospring6.twelve.classic

import org.slf4j.Logger
import org.slf4j.LoggerFactory
import java.util.concurrent.ThreadPoolExecutor

class ThreadPoolMonitor : Runnable {
    var executor: ThreadPoolExecutor? = null
    protected var printInterval = 200

    override fun run() {
        try {
            while (executor!!.activeCount > 0) {
                monitorThreadPool()
                Thread.sleep(printInterval.toLong())
            }
        } catch (e: Exception) {
            LOGGER.error(e.message)
        }
    }

    private fun monitorThreadPool() {
        val strBuff = "CurrentPoolSize : " + executor!!.poolSize +
                " - CorePoolSize : " + executor!!.corePoolSize +
                " - MaximumPoolSize : " + executor!!.maximumPoolSize +
                " - ActiveTaskCount : " + executor!!.activeCount +
                " - CompletedTaskCount : " + executor!!.completedTaskCount +
                " - TotalTaskCount : " + executor!!.taskCount +
                " - isTerminated : " + executor!!.isTerminated
        LOGGER.debug(strBuff)
    }

    companion object {
        private val LOGGER = LoggerFactory.getLogger(ThreadPoolMonitor::class.java)
    }
}
```

Notice that ThreadPoolMonitor can be started as a thread executing independently from the sorting tasks managed by the ThreadPoolExecutor monitored by it.

Listing 12-3 shows the ClassicDemo class, which generates an array containing 100,000 elements with values between 0 and 500,000 that is handed over to be sorted in parallel by the tasks in Figure 12-1. These tasks are managed and executed by an instance of ThreadPoolExecutor, which is monitored by an instance of ThreadPoolMonitor.

Listing 12-3. The ClassicDemo Monitor Class

```
package com.apress.prospring6.twelve.classic

import java.util.List
import java.util.Random
import java.util.concurrent.LinkedBlockingQueue
import java.util.concurrent.ThreadPoolExecutor
import java.util.concurrent.TimeUnit

object ClassicDemo {
    // private static final Logger LOGGER = LoggerFactory.getLogger(ClassicDemo.class);
    @JvmStatic
    fun main(args: Array<String>) {
        val arr = Random().ints(100000, 0, 500000).toArray()
        // LOGGER.info("Starting Array: {} " , Arrays.toString(arr));

        val algsMonitor = ThreadPoolMonitor()
        val monitor = Thread(algsMonitor)

        val executor = ThreadPoolExecutor(2, 4, 0L, TimeUnit.MILLISECONDS,
            LinkedBlockingQueue())

        algsMonitor.executor = executor
        listOf(
            BubbleSort(arr),
            InsertionSort(arr),
            HeapSort(arr),
            MergeSort(arr),
            QuickSort(arr),
            ShellSort(arr)
        ).forEach(executor::execute)

        monitor.start()

        executor.shutdown()
        try {
            executor.awaitTermination(30, TimeUnit.MINUTES)
        } catch (e: InterruptedException) {
            throw RuntimeException(e)
        }
    }
}
```

The code has been split into six sections by using empty lines. Each section is responsible for the following:

- The first section creates the array. If you want to print it to check its values, feel free to un-comment the logging line.

- The second section creates the ThreadPoolMonitor instance (algsMonitor) and the Thread that will execute it (monitor).

- The third section creates ThreadPoolExecutor instance (executor). Notice that while initializing the ThreadPoolExecutor, we are keeping initial pool size as 2 and maximum pool size as 4.

- The fourth section configures the algsMonitor to monitor the executor, and then the tasks are created and submitted for execution.

- The fifth section starts the monitor thread.

- The final section shuts down the executor, causing the finish execution of all the submitted tasks and termination of the thread pool.

When the ClassicDemo class is executed, the log, shown in Listing 12-4, makes it obvious that tasks are being executed in parallel and that some complete faster than others... BubbleSort never had a chance in this competition, right?

Listing 12-4. The ClassicDemo Console Log

```
DEBUG: ThreadPoolMonitor - CurrentPoolSize : 2 - CorePoolSize : 2 - MaximumPoolSize :
4 - ActiveTaskCount : 2 - CompletedTaskCount : 0 - TotalTaskCount : 6 - isTerminated : false
INFO : AbstractSort - InsertionSort Sort Time: 0.8 seconds
DEBUG: ThreadPoolMonitor - MONITOR: [Sorting Algs Monitor] CurrentPoolSize :
2 - CorePoolSize : 2 - MaximumPoolSize : 4 - ActiveTaskCount : 2 - CompletedTaskCount :
1 - TotalTaskCount : 6 - isTerminated : false
INFO : AbstractSort - InsertionSort Sort Time: 0.847 seconds
INFO : AbstractSort - HeapSort Sort Time: 0.014 seconds
DEBUG: ThreadPoolMonitor - CurrentPoolSize : 2 - CorePoolSize : 2 - MaximumPoolSize :
4 - ActiveTaskCount : 2 - CompletedTaskCount : 2 - TotalTaskCount : 6 - isTerminated : false
INFO : AbstractSort - MergeSort Sort Time: 0.226 seconds
INFO : AbstractSort - QuickSort Sort Time: 0.011 seconds
INFO : AbstractSort - ShellSort Sort Time: 0.017 seconds
DEBUG: ThreadPoolMonitor - CurrentPoolSize : 1 - CorePoolSize : 2 - MaximumPoolSize :
4 - ActiveTaskCount : 1 - CompletedTaskCount : 5 - TotalTaskCount : 6 - isTerminated : false
...
DEBUG: ThreadPoolMonitor - CurrentPoolSize : 1 - CorePoolSize : 2 - MaximumPoolSize :
4 - ActiveTaskCount : 1 - CompletedTaskCount : 5 - TotalTaskCount : 6 - isTerminated : false
INFO : AbstractSort - BubbleSort Sort Time: 19.991 seconds
```

The log clearly shows the change in active, completed, and total completed tasks counts of the executor. For this example, the ThreadPoolExecutor was created by explicitly invoking the constructor, but a similar result could be obtained by calling the factory method Executors.newFixedThreadPool(6). There are other Kotlin extensions of the ExecutorService that allow more granular control over task execution, such as the ScheduledExecutorService, so feel free to take a deeper look. Next we'll turn to how Spring does task execution.

Task Executing in Spring

Spring's TaskExecutor interface was added in version 2.0. Similar to the JDK, out of the box, Spring provides a number of TaskExecutor implementations suited for different needs[1]. The most interesting are listed next:

- org.springframework.core.task.SyncTaskExecutor: Does not execute tasks asynchronously; invocation occurs in the calling thread.

- org.springframework.core.task.SimpleAsyncTaskExecutor: Creates new threads on each invocation; does not reuse existing threads.

- org.springframework.scheduling.concurrent.ConcurrentTaskExecutor: An adapter for a java.util.concurrent.Executor instance. Not usually used since there is a ThreadPoolTaskExecutor class, but it is useful if ThreadPoolTaskExecutor is not flexible enough.

- org.springframework.scheduling.concurrent.ThreadPoolTaskExecutor: TaskExecutor implementation providing the ability to configure ThreadPoolExecutor via bean properties and expose it as a Spring TaskExecutor.

- org.springframework.scheduling.quartz.SimpleThreadPoolTaskExecutor: Subclass of Quartz's SimpleThreadPool; used when you need to share a thread pool by both Quartz and non-Quartz components.

Each TaskExecutor implementation serves its own purpose, and all of them obviously have the same API. The only variation is in the configuration, when defining which TaskExecutor implementation you want to use and its properties, if any. Let's take a look at a simple example that prints out a number of random texts. The TaskExecutor implementation used is SimpleAsyncTaskExecutor. First let's create a bean class that holds the task execution logic, as shown in Listing 12-5.

Listing 12-5. The RandomStringPrinter Class

```
package com.apress.prospring6.twelve

// some import statements omitted
import org.springframework.core.task.TaskExecutor
import java.util.UUID

@Component
class RandomStringPrinter(private val taskExecutor: TaskExecutor) {
    fun executeTask() {
        for (i in 0..9) {
            taskExecutor.execute {
                LOGGER.info(
                    "{}: {}",
                    i,
                    UUID.randomUUID().toString().substring(0, 8)
                )
            }
        }
    }
}
```

---

[1] https://docs.spring.io/spring-framework/docs/current/javadoc-api/org/springframework/core/task/TaskExecutor.html

```
    companion object {
        private val LOGGER = LoggerFactory.getLogger(RandomStringPrinter::class.java)
    }
}
```

This class is just a regular bean that needs TaskExecutor to be injected as a dependency and defines a method executeTask(). The executeTask() method calls the execute method of the provided TaskExecutor by creating a new Runnable instance containing the logic we want to execute for this task. This might not be obvious here, as a lambda expression is used to create the Runnable instance. The configuration is quite simple; it is similar to the configuration depicted in the previous section. The only thing we have to take into account here is that we need to provide a declaration for a TaskExecutor bean, which needs to be injected in the RandomStringPrinter bean.

Listing 12-6 shows the configuration class and the demo class named SimpleAsyncTaskExecutorDemo.

Listing 12-6. The SimpleAsyncTaskExecutorDemo and AppConfig Monitor Classes

package com.apress.prospring6.twelve

```
// some import statements omitted
import org.springframework.scheduling.annotation.EnableAsync

@Configuration
@EnableAsync
internal open class AppConfig {
    @Bean
    open fun taskExecutor(): TaskExecutor {
        return SimpleAsyncTaskExecutor()
    }
}

object SimpleAsyncTaskExecutorDemo {
    @Throws(IOException::class)
    @JvmStatic
    fun main(args: Array<String>) {
        AnnotationConfigApplicationContext(
            AppConfig::class.java,
            RandomStringPrinter::class.java
        ).use { ctx ->
            val printer = ctx.getBean(RandomStringPrinter::class.java)
            printer.executeTask()
            System.`in`.read()
        }
    }
}
```

The most important bit in the class is the @EnableAsync annotation that enables Spring's asynchronous method execution capability, which means Spring will be searching for an associated thread pool definition, either a unique org.springframework.core.task.TaskExecutor bean in the context or an java.util.concurrent.Executor bean named taskExecutor otherwise. If none is found, a org.springframework.core.task.SimpleAsyncTaskExecutor will be used to process async method invocations.

When the `SimpleAsyncTaskExecutorDemo` class is run, the random strings are printed by each task in random order, since the tasks are executed asynchronously. This is obvious because each task has an associated number. Listing 12-7 shows sample output.

Listing 12-7. Log Sample Printed by the `SimpleAsyncTaskExecutorDemo` Class Execution

```
INFO : RandomStringPrinter - 6: 87548a56
INFO : RandomStringPrinter - 4: 019c9571
INFO : RandomStringPrinter - 3: a5cc57ef
INFO : RandomStringPrinter - 1: 8a6dc271
INFO : RandomStringPrinter - 5: 52fd6224
INFO : RandomStringPrinter - 8: 11810531
INFO : RandomStringPrinter - 2: 820b17a4
INFO : RandomStringPrinter - 7: 9e56cf1b
INFO : RandomStringPrinter - 0: eab9362a
INFO : RandomStringPrinter - 9: d24c2076
```

Task Scheduling in Spring

Executing tasks is clearly easy, but enterprise applications often need to do so in a more controlled manner, which means tasks must be scheduled. In many applications, various tasks (such as sending e-mail notifications to customers, running day-end jobs, doing data housekeeping, and updating data in batches) need to be scheduled to run on a regular basis, either in a fixed interval (for example, every hour) or at a specific schedule (for example, at 8 p.m. every night, from Monday to Friday).

There are many ways to trigger the execution of a task in a Spring application. One way is to trigger a job externally from a scheduling system that already exists in the application deployment environment. For example, many enterprises use commercial systems, such as Control-M or CA AutoSys, for scheduling tasks. If the application is running on a Linux/Unix platform, the crontab scheduler can be used. The job triggering can be done by sending a RESTful-WS request to the Spring application and having Spring's MVC controller trigger the task.

Another way is to use the task scheduling support in Spring. Spring provides three options in terms of task scheduling:

- *Support of JDK Timer*: Spring supports JDK's Timer object for task scheduling.

- *Integration with Quartz*: Quartz Job Scheduler[2] is a popular open source scheduling library.

- *Spring's own Spring TaskScheduler abstraction*: Spring 3 introduced the TaskScheduler abstraction, which provides a simple way to schedule tasks and supports most typical requirements.

This section focuses on using Spring's `TaskScheduler` abstraction for task scheduling, the consequence of which is that the project is quite simple and the only Spring dependency necessary is the `spring-context.jar` library.

---

[2] https://www.quartz-scheduler.org/

Introducing the Spring TaskScheduler Abstraction

Spring's TaskScheduler abstraction provides a variety of methods for scheduling tasks to run at some point in the future and has mainly three participants:

- *The Trigger interface*: The org.springframework.scheduling.Trigger interface provides support for defining the triggering mechanism. Spring provides two Trigger implementations. The CronTrigger class supports triggering based on a cron expression, while the PeriodicTrigger class supports triggering based on an initial delay and then a fixed interval.

- *The task*: The task is the piece of business logic that needs to be scheduled. In Spring, a task can be specified as a method within any Spring bean.

- *The TaskScheduler interface*: The org.springframework.scheduling. TaskScheduler interface provides support for task scheduling. Spring provides three implementation classes of the TaskScheduler interface. The ConcurrentTaskScheduler and ThreadPoolTaskScheduler classes (both under the package org.springframework.scheduling.concurrent) wrap the java. util.concurrent.ScheduledThreadPoolExecutor class. Both classes support task execution from a shared thread pool. The DefaultManagedTaskScheduler class (also in package org.springframework.scheduling.concurrent) is commonly used in a Jakarta EE environment.

Figure 12-2 shows the relationships between the Trigger interface, the TaskScheduler interface, and the task that implements the java.lang.Runnable interface.

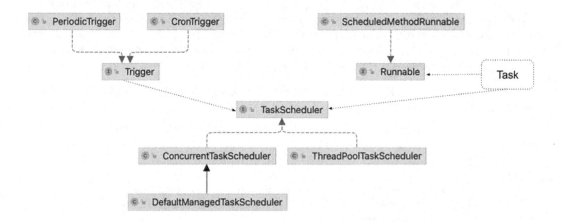

Figure 12-2. *Relationship between trigger, task, and scheduler*

Basically, task schedulers execute tasks based on a date, time, once, or repeatedly. Task executions are triggered by Trigger implementations, which provide granular control over the time tasks are executed, especially in relation to other task executions.

To schedule tasks by using Spring's TaskScheduler abstraction, a few annotations are necessary, which are demonstrated and described in the following section.

Exploring a Sample Task

To demonstrate task scheduling in Spring, let's implement a simple job first, namely, an application maintaining a database of car information. Listing 12-8 shows the Car class, which is implemented as a JPA entity class.

Listing 12-8. The Car Entity Class

```
package com.apress.prospring6.twelve.entities

import jakarta.persistence.*
import java.io.Serial
import java.io.Serializable
import java.time.LocalDate

@Entity
@Table(name = "CAR")
class Car : Serializable {
    @Id
    @GeneratedValue(strategy = GenerationType.IDENTITY)
    @Column(name = "ID")
    var id: Long? = null

    @Column(name = "LICENSE_PLATE")
    var licensePlate: String? = null

    @Column(name = "MANUFACTURER")
    var manufacturer: String? = null

    @Column(name = "MANUFACTURE_DATE")
    var manufactureDate: LocalDate? = null

    @Column(name = "AGE")
    var age = 0

    @Version
    var version = 0

    override fun toString(): String {
        return "Car{" +
                "id=" + id +
                ", licensePlate='" + licensePlate + '\'' +
                ", manufacturer='" + manufacturer + '\'' +
                ", manufactureDate=" + manufactureDate +
                ", age=" + age +
                ", version=" + version +
                '}'
    }
}
```

```
    companion object {
        @Serial
        private val serialVersionUID = 2L
    }
}
```

This entity class is used as a model for the CAR table generated by Hibernate. The configuration for the data access and services layers is provided by the BasicDataSourceCfg and JpaConfig classes, just like shown in the data access chapters. To tell Hibernate to create the table, the Environment.HBM2DDL_AUTO property is set to create-drop. To make sure there is some data to work with, a class named DBInitializer is introduced. Creating a bean of this type adds three Car records to the table. The DBInitializer class is shown in Listing 12-9.

Listing 12-9. DBInitializer Class That Populates the CAR Table

```
package com.apress.prospring6.twelve.config
// import statements omitted

@Service
class DBInitializer(private val carRepository: CarRepository) {
    @PostConstruct
    fun initDB() {
        LOGGER.info("Starting database initialization...")
        var car = Car().apply {
            licensePlate = "GRAVITY-0405"
            manufacturer = "Ford"
            manufactureDate = LocalDate.of(2006, 9, 12)
        }
        carRepository.save(car)
        car = Car().apply {
            licensePlate = "CLARITY-0432"
            manufacturer = "Toyota"
            manufactureDate = LocalDate.of(2003, 9, 9)
        }
        carRepository.save(car)
        car = Car().apply {
            licensePlate = "ROSIE-0402"
            manufacturer = "Toyota"
            manufactureDate = LocalDate.of(2017, 4, 16)
        }
        carRepository.save(car)
        car = Car().apply {
            licensePlate = "HUGO-0442"
            manufacturer = "Peugeot"
            manufactureDate = LocalDate.of(2014, 6, 1)
        }
        carRepository.save(car)
        car = Car().apply {
            licensePlate = "NESSIE-0842"
            manufacturer = "Ford"
            manufactureDate = LocalDate.of(2004, 8, 17)
        }
```

```
        carRepository.save(car)
        car = Car().apply {
            licensePlate = "CALEDONIA-1983"
            manufacturer = "Ford"
            manufactureDate = LocalDate.of(2001, 10, 2)
        }
        carRepository.save(car)
        LOGGER.info("Database initialization finished.")
    }

    companion object {
        private val LOGGER = LoggerFactory.getLogger(DBInitializer::class.java)
    }
}
```

The CarRepository bean injected in DBInitializer is a Spring Data typical repo, an interface extending CrudRepository<Car, Long>. The same bean is injected into the CarServiceImpl class depicted in Listing 12-10.

Listing 12-10. CarServiceImpl Class

package com.apress.prospring6.twelve.service

import org.springframework.scheduling.annotation.Scheduled
```
// import statements omitted

@Service("carService")
@Repository
@Transactional
class CarServiceImpl(private val carRepository: CarRepository) : CarService {
    override var isDone = false

    @Transactional(readOnly = true)
    override fun findAll(): Stream<Car> {
        return StreamSupport.stream(carRepository.findAll().spliterator(), false)
    }

    override fun save(car: Car): Car {
        return carRepository.save(car)
    }

    @Scheduled(fixedDelay = 10000)
    override fun updateCarAgeJob() {
        val cars = findAll()
        val currentDate = LocalDate.now()
        LOGGER.info("Car age update job started")
        check(System.nanoTime() % 5 != 0L) { "Task no " + Thread.currentThread().name +
            " is dead, dead dead..." }
        cars.forEach { car: Car ->
            val p = Period.between(car.manufactureDate, currentDate)
            val age = p.years
            car.age = age
```

```
            save(car)
            LOGGER.info("Car age update --> {}", car)
        }
        LOGGER.info("Car age update job completed successfully")
        isDone = true
    }

    companion object {
        private val LOGGER = LoggerFactory.getLogger(CarServiceImpl::class.java)
    }
}
```

The CarServiceImpl class contains three methods and one accessor, as shown here:

- findAll():Stream<Car>: Retrieves the information about all cars.

- save(Car car):Car: Persists an updated Car object:.

- updateCarAgeJob(): The job that needs to be run regularly to update the age of
  the car based on the manufacture date of the car and the current date. Notice
  the @Scheduled annotation, which configures for this method to be executed
  approximately every 10 seconds.

- isDone:boolean: A utility property designed to be used to know when the job ended,
  so the application can be shut down gracefully.

The only thing missing is the Spring application configuration that enables task scheduling. The
TaskSchedulingConfig class is shown in Listing 12-11.

Listing 12-11. TaskSchedulingConfig Class

```
package com.apress.prospring6.twelve.config

import org.springframework.context.annotation.ComponentScan
import org.springframework.context.annotation.Configuration
import org.springframework.scheduling.annotation.EnableScheduling

@Configuration
@ComponentScan(
    basePackages = ["com.apress.prospring6.twelve.spring"],
    excludeFilters = [ComponentScan.Filter(
        type = FilterType.ASSIGNABLE_TYPE,
        classes = [TaskSchedulingConfig2::class, TaskSchedulingConfig3::class,
                        TaskSchedulingConfig4::class]
    )]
)
@EnableScheduling
open class TaskSchedulingConfig
```

The @EnableScheduling annotation used on a @Configuration class enables detection of @Scheduled
annotations on any Spring-managed bean in the container or their methods. Methods annotated with
@Scheduled may even be declared directly within @Configuration classes, since configuration classes
are beans themselves. Since Spring 4.2, @Scheduled methods are supported on beans of any scope. This
annotation tells Spring to look for an associated scheduler definition: either a unique TaskScheduler bean in

the context or a TaskScheduler bean named taskScheduler or a ScheduledExecutorService bean. If none is found, a local single-threaded default scheduler will be created and used to execute scheduled tasks.

To schedule a specific method in a Spring bean, the method must be annotated with @Scheduled and pass in the scheduling requirements.

The testing program is shown in Listing 12-12.

Listing 12-12. CarTaskSchedulerDemo Class

```kotlin
package com.apress.prospring6.twelve
// import statements omitted

object CarTaskSchedulerDemo {
    private val LOGGER = LoggerFactory.getLogger(CarTaskSchedulerDemo::class.java)
    @Throws(IOException::class)
    @JvmStatic
    fun main(args: Array<String>) {
        initCtx(*args).use { ctx ->
            try {
                val taskScheduler =
                    ctx!!.getBean(ScheduledAnnotationBeanPostProcessor.
                        DEFAULT_TASK_SCHEDULER_BEAN_NAME)
                LOGGER.info(" >>>> 'taskScheduler' found: {}", taskScheduler.javaClass)
            } catch (nbd: NoSuchBeanDefinitionException) {
                LOGGER.debug("No 'taskScheduler' configured!")
            }
            try {
                val taskExecutor = ctx!!.getBean("taskExecutor")
                LOGGER.info(" >>>> 'taskExecutor' found: {}", taskExecutor.javaClass)
            } catch (nbd: NoSuchBeanDefinitionException) {
                LOGGER.debug("No 'taskExecutor' configured!")
            }
            System.`in`.read()
        }
    }

    private fun initCtx(vararg args: String): GenericApplicationContext? {
        if (args.isEmpty()) {
            return AnnotationConfigApplicationContext(TaskSchedulingConfig::class.java)
        } else if (args.size == 1) {
            if (args[0] == "1") {
                return AnnotationConfigApplicationContext(TaskSchedulingConfig::class.java)
            } else if (args[0] == "2") {
                return AnnotationConfigApplicationContext(TaskSchedulingConfig2::class.java)
            } else if (args[0] == "3") {
                return AnnotationConfigApplicationContext(TaskSchedulingConfig3::class.java)
            } else if (args[0] == "4") {
                return AnnotationConfigApplicationContext(TaskSchedulingConfig4::class.java)
            }
        }
        return null
    }
}
```

Since we want to check if we have a scheduler, we search for a scheduler bean named taskScheduler (this is the value of the DEFAULT_TASK_SCHEDULER_BEAN_NAME constant) in the demo code and print its class.

Scheduling tasks in Spring is implemented the same way as it is almost everywhere else, by proxying. The @EnableScheduling annotation adds a org.springframework.scheduling.annotation. ScheduledAnnotationBeanPostProcessor bean to the context that picks up methods annotated with @Scheduled. These methods are invoked by a TaskScheduler according to the fixedRate, fixedDelay, or cron expression configured via the @Scheduled annotation.

Since we need the main thread to continue its execution, so that we can see the updateCarAgeJob() method being executed repeatedly, the System.in.read() statement is used for waiting for the developer to press any key before exiting. The log printed in the console might look a lot like the one shown in Listing 12-13.

Listing 12-13. CarTaskSchedulerDemo Log

```
00:14:21.818 [main] INFO : ScheduledAnnotationBeanPostProcessor - No TaskScheduler/
ScheduledExecutorService bean found for scheduled processing
00:14:21.822 [main] DEBUG: CarTaskSchedulerDemo - No 'taskScheduler' configured!
00:14:21.900 [pool-1-thread-1] INFO : CarServiceImpl - Car age update job started
00:14:21.903 [pool-1-thread-1] INFO : CarServiceImpl - Car age update --> Car{id=1,
licensePlate='GRAVITY-0405', manufacturer='Ford', manufactureDate=2006-09-12, age=16,
version=0}
00:14:21.908 [pool-1-thread-1] INFO : CarServiceImpl - Car age update --> Car{id=2,
licensePlate='CLARITY-0432', manufacturer='Toyota', manufactureDate=2003-09-09, age=19,
version=0}
00:14:21.908 [pool-1-thread-1] INFO : CarServiceImpl - Car age update --> Car{id=3,
licensePlate='ROSIE-0402', manufacturer='Toyota', manufactureDate=2017-04-16, age=5,
version=0}
...
00:14:21.909 [pool-1-thread-1] INFO : CarServiceImpl - Car age update job completed
successfully
00:14:31.936 [pool-1-thread-1] INFO : CarServiceImpl - Car age update job started
00:14:31.936 [pool-1-thread-1] INFO : CarServiceImpl - Car age update --> Car{id=1,
licensePlate='GRAVITY-0405', manufacturer='Ford', manufactureDate=2006-09-12, age=16,
version=1}
00:14:31.937 [pool-1-thread-1] INFO : CarServiceImpl - Car age update --> Car{id=2,
licensePlate='CLARITY-0432', manufacturer='Toyota', manufactureDate=2003-09-09, age=19,
version=1}
00:14:31.937 [pool-1-thread-1] INFO : CarServiceImpl - Car age update --> Car{id=3,
licensePlate='ROSIE-0402', manufacturer='Toyota', manufactureDate=2017-04-16, age=5,
version=1}
00:14:31.938 [pool-1-thread-1] INFO : CarServiceImpl - Car age update job completed
successfully
...
```

The thread name is added to the log to make it obvious that the updateCarAgeJob() methods are executed in a thread pool, even if the default executor uses a single thread.

There are two ways to configure a task scheduler to be used: make the TaskSchedulingConfig class implement org.springframework.scheduling.annotation.SchedulingConfigurer and override the configureTasks(..) method to set up a custom task scheduler, or declare a task scheduler custom bean.

Listing 12-14 shows the TaskSchedulingConfig2 class that implements SchedulingConfigurer.

Listing 12-14. TaskSchedulingConfig2 Configuration Class

```
package com.apress.prospring6.twelve.spring.config

import org.springframework.context.annotation.FilterType
import org.springframework.scheduling.annotation.EnableScheduling
import org.springframework.scheduling.annotation.SchedulingConfigurer
import org.springframework.scheduling.concurrent.ThreadPoolTaskScheduler
import org.springframework.scheduling.config.ScheduledTaskRegistrar

import java.util.concurrent.Executor
import java.util.concurrent.ScheduledThreadPoolExecutor
// import statements omitted

@Configuration
@ComponentScan(
    basePackages = ["com.apress.prospring6.twelve.spring"],
    excludeFilters = [ComponentScan.Filter(
        type = FilterType.ASSIGNABLE_TYPE,
        classes = [TaskSchedulingConfig::class, TaskSchedulingConfig3::class,
                        TaskSchedulingConfig4::class]
    )]
)
@EnableScheduling
open class TaskSchedulingConfig2 : SchedulingConfigurer {
    override fun configureTasks(taskRegistrar: ScheduledTaskRegistrar) {
        taskRegistrar.setScheduler(taskExecutor())
    }

    @Bean(destroyMethod = "shutdown")
    open fun taskExecutor(): Executor {
        val tpts = ThreadPoolTaskScheduler()
        tpts.poolSize = 3
        tpts.threadNamePrefix = "tsc2-"
        tpts.setErrorHandler { }
        tpts.setRejectedExecutionHandler { r, executor -> }
        return tpts
    }

    companion object {
        private val LOGGER = LoggerFactory.getLogger(TaskSchedulingConfig2::class.java)
    }
}
```

The task scheduler is configured to name managed threads with the tsc2- to make it obvious that the tasks invoking updateCarAgeJob() are executed by it. Listing 12-12 already shows how to test this variant using an application argument "2".

When run, this version of the CarTaskSchedulerDemo produces the output shown in Listing 12-15.

Listing 12-15. CarTaskSchedulerDemo Log, Version 2

```
00:15:47.299 [main] DEBUG: CarTaskSchedulerDemo - No 'taskScheduler' configured!
00:15:47.299 [main] INFO : CarTaskSchedulerDemo -  >>>> 'taskExecutor' found: class
org.springframework.scheduling.concurrent.ThreadPoolTaskScheduler
00:15:47.375 [tsc2-1] INFO : CarServiceImpl - Car age update job started
00:15:47.378 [tsc2-1] INFO : CarServiceImpl - Car age update --> Car{id=1,
licensePlate='GRAVITY-0405', manufacturer='Ford', manufactureDate=2006-09-12, age=16,
version=0}
00:15:47.383 [tsc2-1] INFO : CarServiceImpl - Car age update --> Car{id=2,
licensePlate='CLARITY-0432', manufacturer='Toyota', manufactureDate=2003-09-09, age=19,
version=0}
00:15:47.383 [tsc2-1] INFO : CarServiceImpl - Car age update --> Car{id=3,
licensePlate='ROSIE-0402', manufacturer='Toyota', manufactureDate=2017-04-16, age=5,
version=0}
00:15:47.384 [tsc2-1] INFO : CarServiceImpl - Car age update job completed successfully
...
```

The reason you do not see more than one thread is because the tasks take so little time to execute there is no need to use another thread from the pool.

The other way to do the same thing is by declaring the task scheduler bean directly as shown in Listing 12-16.

Listing 12-16. TaskSchedulingConfig3 Configuration Class

```
package com.apress.prospring6.twelve.spring.config

@Configuration
@ComponentScan(
    basePackages = ["com.apress.prospring6.twelve.spring"],
    excludeFilters = [ComponentScan.Filter(
        type = FilterType.ASSIGNABLE_TYPE,
        classes = [TaskSchedulingConfig::class, TaskSchedulingConfig2::class,
                        TaskSchedulingConfig4::class]
    )]
)
@EnableScheduling
open class TaskSchedulingConfig3 {
    @Bean
    open fun taskScheduler(): TaskScheduler {
        val tpts = ThreadPoolTaskScheduler()
        tpts.poolSize = 3
        tpts.threadNamePrefix = "tsc3-"
        return tpts
    }
}
```

The test program for the TaskSchedulingConfig3 class is shown earlier in Listing 12-12 (use "3" as application argument), but the log presented in Listing 12-17 shows that the new task scheduler bean is used.

Listing 12-17. CarTaskSchedulerDemo Log, Version 3

```
00:16:32.485 [main] INFO : CarTaskSchedulerDemo -  >>>> 'taskScheduler' found: class
org.springframework.scheduling.concurrent.ThreadPoolTaskScheduler
00:16:32.558 [tsc3-1] INFO : CarServiceImpl - Car age update job started
00:16:32.560 [tsc3-1] INFO : CarServiceImpl - Car age update --> Car{id=1,
licensePlate='GRAVITY-0405', manufacturer='Ford', manufactureDate=2006-09-12, age=16,
version=0}
00:16:32.565 [tsc3-1] INFO : CarServiceImpl - Car age update --> Car{id=2,
licensePlate='CLARITY-0432', manufacturer='Toyota', manufactureDate=2003-09-09, age=19,
version=0}
00:16:32.565 [tsc3-1] INFO : CarServiceImpl - Car age update --> Car{id=3,
licensePlate='ROSIE-0402', manufacturer='Toyota', manufactureDate=2017-04-16, age=5,
version=0}
00:16:32.566 [tsc3-1] INFO : CarServiceImpl - Car age update job completed successfully
...
```

Asynchronous Task Execution in Spring

Since version 3.0, Spring also supports using annotations to execute a task asynchronously. To do this, you just need to annotate the method with @Async. This means the caller returns immediately while the actual execution happens in a task submitted to Spring TaskExecutor.

This being said, Listing 12-18 shows the AsyncServiceImpl class that defines two simple methods that are invoked by asynchronous tasks.

Listing 12-18. AsyncServiceImpl Bean Class

```
package com.apress.prospring6.twelve.spring.async

import java.util.concurrent.CompletableFuture
import java.util.concurrent.Future

import org.slf4j.Logger
import org.slf4j.LoggerFactory
import org.springframework.scheduling.annotation.Async

class AsyncServiceImpl : AsyncService {
    @Async
    override fun asyncTask() {
        LOGGER.info("Start execution of async. task")
        check(System.nanoTime() % 5 != 0L) { "Task no " + Thread.currentThread().name +
                " is dead, dead dead..." }
        try {
            Thread.sleep(10000)
        } catch (ex: Exception) {
            LOGGER.error("Task Interruption", ex)
        }
        LOGGER.info("Complete execution of async. task")
    }
```

```
    @Async
    override fun asyncWithReturn(name: String): Future<String>? {
        LOGGER.info("Start execution of async. task with return for {}", name)
        try {
            Thread.sleep(5000)
        } catch (ex: Exception) {
            LOGGER.error("Task Interruption", ex)
        }
        LOGGER.info("Complete execution of async. task with return for {}", name)
        return CompletableFuture.completedFuture("Hello: $name")
    }

    companion object {
        private val LOGGER = LoggerFactory.getLogger(AsyncServiceImpl::class.java)
    }
}
```

The AsyncService interface defines two methods that AsyncServiceImpl provides implementations for. The asyncTask() method is a simple task that logs information to the logger. The method asyncWithReturn() accepts a String argument and returns an instance of the java.util.concurrent. CompletableFuture<T> that can be used by the caller to retrieve the result of the execution later.

The @Async annotation is picked up by enabling Spring's asynchronous method execution capability, and that is done by annotating a Kotlin configuration class with @EnableAsync. Refining the configuration can be done by declaring the configuration class to implement org.springframework.scheduling. annotation.AsyncConfigurer.

Listing 12-19 shows the empty configuration class that enables asynchronous task execution.

Listing 12-19. AsyncConfig Bean Class

```
package com.apress.prospring6.twelve.spring.async;
// other import statements omitted
import org.springframework.scheduling.annotation.EnableAsync;

@Configuration
@EnableAsync
@ComponentScan
internal open class AsyncConfig {
    @Bean
    open fun asyncService(): AsyncService {
        return AsyncServiceImpl()
    }
}
```

ℹ️ The AsyncService bean was declared using @Bean, to avoid being picked up by the task scheduling configuration classes introduced previously and added into a context where it does not belong. This is a technical decision to avoid collision and log pollution, basically keeping the example scopes separate.

Testing this configuration requires explicit submission of tasks, especially since we need the results of the asyncWithReturn() invocation. The testing program is shown in Listing 12-20.

Listing 12-20. AsyncDemo Testing Class

```
package com.apress.prospring6.twelve.spring.async

import org.springframework.scheduling.annotation.EnableAsync
import java.util.concurrent.ExecutionException
// other import statements omitted

object AsyncDemo {
    private val LOGGER = LoggerFactory.getLogger(AsyncDemo::class.java)
    @Throws(IOException::class, ExecutionException::class, InterruptedException::class)
    @JvmStatic
    fun main(args: Array<String>) {
        AnnotationConfigApplicationContext(AsyncConfig::class.java).use { ctx ->
            val asyncService = ctx.getBean("asyncService", AsyncService::class.java)
            for (i in 0..4) {
                asyncService.asyncTask()
            }
            val result1 = asyncService.asyncWithReturn("John Mayer")
            val result2 = asyncService.asyncWithReturn("Eric Clapton")
            val result3 = asyncService.asyncWithReturn("BB King")
            Thread.sleep(6000)
            LOGGER.info(" >> Result1: " + result1!!.get())
            LOGGER.info(" >> Result2: " + result2!!.get())
            LOGGER.info(" >> Result3: " + result3!!.get())
            System.`in`.read()
        }
    }
}
```

The asyncTask() method is invoked five times and then asyncWithReturn() three times with different arguments and then we retrieve the result after sleeping for six seconds. Running the program produces the output shown in Listing 12-21.

Listing 12-21. AsyncDemo Log Sample

```
00:11:28.937 [main] INFO : AsyncExecutionAspectSupport - No task executor bean found for
async processing: no bean of type TaskExecutor and no bean named 'taskExecutor' either
00:11:28.944 [SimpleAsyncTaskExecutor-1] INFO : AsyncServiceImpl - Start execution of
async. task
00:11:28.944 [SimpleAsyncTaskExecutor-3] INFO : AsyncServiceImpl - Start execution of
async. task
00:11:28.944 [SimpleAsyncTaskExecutor-4] INFO : AsyncServiceImpl - Start execution of
async. task
00:11:28.944 [SimpleAsyncTaskExecutor-5] INFO : AsyncServiceImpl - Start execution of
async. task
00:11:28.944 [SimpleAsyncTaskExecutor-2] INFO : AsyncServiceImpl - Start execution of
async. task
```

```
00:11:28.945 [SimpleAsyncTaskExecutor-8] INFO : AsyncServiceImpl - Start execution of
async. task with return for BB King
00:11:28.945 [SimpleAsyncTaskExecutor-7] INFO : AsyncServiceImpl - Start execution of
async. task with return for Eric Clapton
00:11:28.945 [SimpleAsyncTaskExecutor-6] INFO : AsyncServiceImpl - Start execution of
async. task with return for John Mayer
00:11:33.951 [SimpleAsyncTaskExecutor-7] INFO : AsyncServiceImpl - Complete execution of
async. task with return for Eric Clapton
00:11:33.951 [SimpleAsyncTaskExecutor-6] INFO : AsyncServiceImpl - Complete execution of
async. task with return for John Mayer
00:11:33.951 [SimpleAsyncTaskExecutor-8] INFO : AsyncServiceImpl - Complete execution of
async. task with return for BB King
00:11:34.949 [main] INFO : AsyncDemo -  >> Result1: Hello: John Mayer
00:11:34.949 [main] INFO : AsyncDemo -  >> Result2: Hello: Eric Clapton
00:11:34.949 [main] INFO : AsyncDemo -  >> Result3: Hello: BB King
00:11:38.949 [SimpleAsyncTaskExecutor-5] INFO : AsyncServiceImpl - Complete execution of
async. task
00:11:38.949 [SimpleAsyncTaskExecutor-2] INFO : AsyncServiceImpl - Complete execution of
async. task
00:11:38.949 [SimpleAsyncTaskExecutor-3] INFO : AsyncServiceImpl - Complete execution of
async. task
00:11:38.949 [SimpleAsyncTaskExecutor-4] INFO : AsyncServiceImpl - Complete execution of
async. task
00:11:38.949 [SimpleAsyncTaskExecutor-1] INFO : AsyncServiceImpl - Complete execution of
async. task
```

From the output, you can see that all the calls were started at the same time. The three calls with return values complete first and are displayed on the console output. Finally, the five asyncTask() methods called are completed too.

Customizing this configuration is as simple as customizing the scheduled configuration—just make the configuration class implement AsyncConfigurer and override the getAsyncExecutor() method, as shown in Listing 12-22.

Listing 12-22. AsyncDemo with Custom Async Executor

```
package com.apress.prospring6.twelve.spring.async

import org.springframework.scheduling.annotation.AsyncConfigurer
import org.springframework.scheduling.concurrent.ThreadPoolTaskExecutor
// other import statements omitted

@Configuration
@EnableAsync
@ComponentScan
class AsyncConfig : AsyncConfigurer {
    override fun getAsyncExecutor(): Executor {
        val tpts = ThreadPoolTaskExecutor().apply {
            corePoolSize = 2
            maxPoolSize = 10
            threadNamePrefix = "tpte2-"
            queueCapacity = 5
        }
```

```
        tpts.initialize()
        return tpts
    }

    @Bean
    fun asyncService(): AsyncService {
        return AsyncServiceImpl()
    }
}
```

If more than one task executor is configured in the same application context, tasks can be assigned to a specific executor by using its name as a parameter for the @Async annotation, such as @Async("otherExecutor").

Both task executions and schedulers can be configured to handle situations in which tasks end with an exception being thrown using special exception handlers. As shown in Listing 12-23, the ThreadPoolTaskScheduler can be configured with an instance of org.springframework.util. ErrorHandler to handle errors that occur during asynchronous execution of tasks, and a task executor can be configured with an instance of type java.util.concurrent.RejectedExecutionHandler to handle rejected tasks.

Listing 12-23. TaskSchedulingConfig4 Example with an ErrorHandler and a RejectedExecutionHandler

```
package com.apress.prospring6.twelve.spring.config

import org.springframework.scheduling.annotation.EnableScheduling
import org.springframework.scheduling.concurrent.ThreadPoolTaskScheduler
import org.springframework.util.ErrorHandler

import java.util.concurrent.ConcurrentHashMap
import java.util.concurrent.RejectedExecutionHandler
import java.util.concurrent.ThreadPoolExecutor

/**
 * Created by iuliana on 29/10/2022
 */
@Configuration
@ComponentScan(
    basePackages = ["com.apress.prospring6.twelve.spring"],
    excludeFilters = [ComponentScan.Filter(
        type = FilterType.ASSIGNABLE_TYPE,
        classes = [TaskSchedulingConfig::class, TaskSchedulingConfig2::class,
        TaskSchedulingConfig3::class]
    )]
)
@EnableScheduling
open class TaskSchedulingConfig4 {
    @Bean
    open fun taskScheduler(): TaskScheduler {
        val tpts = ThreadPoolTaskScheduler()
        tpts.poolSize = 3
        tpts.threadNamePrefix = "tsc4-"
        tpts.setErrorHandler(LoggingErrorHandler("tsc4"))
```

```kotlin
        tpts.setRejectedExecutionHandler(RejectedTaskHandler())
        return tpts
    }
}

internal class LoggingErrorHandler(private val name: String) : ErrorHandler {
    override fun handleError(t: Throwable) {
        LOGGER.error(
            "[{}]: task failed because {}",
            name, t.message, t
        )
    }

    companion object {
        private val LOGGER = LoggerFactory.getLogger(LoggingErrorHandler::class.java)
    }
}

internal class RejectedTaskHandler : RejectedExecutionHandler {
    private val rejectedTasks: MutableMap<Runnable, Int> = ConcurrentHashMap()
    override fun rejectedExecution(r: Runnable, executor: ThreadPoolExecutor) {
        LOGGER.info(" >>  check for resubmission.")
        var submit = true
        if (rejectedTasks.containsKey(r)) {
            val submittedCnt = rejectedTasks[r]!!
            if (submittedCnt > 5) {
                submit = false
            } else {
                rejectedTasks[r] = rejectedTasks[r]!! + 1
            }
        } else {
            rejectedTasks[r] = 1
        }
        if (submit) {
            executor.execute(r)
        } else {
            LOGGER.error(">> Task {} cannot be re-submitted.", r.toString())
        }
    }

    companion object {
        private val LOGGER = LoggerFactory.getLogger(RejectedTaskHandler::class.java)
    }
}
```

The LoggingErrorHandler simply logs with the ERROR level the exception thrown by a task being processed. The RejectedTaskHandler resubmits a rejected task and keeps count of the number of resubmissions. If a task has been resubmitted more than five times, an exception is thrown and the task is not submitted anymore.

Listing 12-10 earlier in the chapter shows the CarServiceImpl throwing an IllegalStateException every time the internal time divides perfectly by 5. The stacktrace of this exception is shown in the console and the LoggingErrorHandler intercepts it and prints the task name, so we know which task failed.

There are two situations in which a task is rejected: when the task is submitted after shutdown() is invoked, and when the thread pool doesn't have any available threads for the task to execute in. For the first scenario, an implementation of RejectedExecutionHandler can only submit a notification or write a log with the details of the failed task. For the second scenario, an implementation like the one in RejectedTaskHandler tries to resubmit the task a few times back to the executor until a final rejection, if the task was still not executed. Unfortunately, this situation is difficult to reproduce with tasks that barely do anything, like the one in CarServiceImpl.

Feel free to run the examples in the chapter12 project and notice the exception handling specific to the TaskSchedulingConfig4 configuration.

Listing 12-20 shows the AsyncServiceImpl throwing an IllegalStateException every time the internal time divides perfectly by 5. For a Spring asynchronous task executor, a bean of type org.springframework. aop.interceptor.SimpleAsyncUncaughtExceptionHandler implements the org.springframework. aop.interceptor.AsyncUncaughtExceptionHandler that simply logs the exception. To override this behavior, we have to implement this interface and override the default one by implementing the getAsyncUncaughtExceptionHandler() method from the AsyncConfigurer interface.

Listing 12-24 shows the custom AsyncExceptionHandler class and the new asynchronous executor configuration.

Listing 12-24. Class Async2Demo with an AsyncExceptionHandler

```kotlin
package com.apress.prospring6.twelve.spring.async

import org.springframework.aop.interceptor.AsyncUncaughtExceptionHandler
// other import statements omitted

internal class AsyncExceptionHandler : AsyncUncaughtExceptionHandler {
    override fun handleUncaughtException(t: Throwable, method: Method, vararg obj: Any) {
        LOGGER.error("[{}]: task method '{}' failed because {}",
            Thread.currentThread(), method.name, t.message, t)
    }

    companion object {
        private val LOGGER = LoggerFactory.getLogger(AsyncExceptionHandler::class.java)
    }
}

@Configuration
@EnableAsync
@ComponentScan
internal open class Async2Config : AsyncConfigurer {
    override fun getAsyncExecutor(): Executor {
        val tpts = ThreadPoolTaskExecutor().apply {
            corePoolSize = 2
            maxPoolSize = 10
            threadNamePrefix = "tpte2-"
            queueCapacity = 5
        }
        tpts.initialize()
        return tpts
    }
}
```

```kotlin
    @Bean
    open fun asyncService(): AsyncService {
        return AsyncServiceImpl()
    }

    override fun getAsyncUncaughtExceptionHandler(): AsyncUncaughtExceptionHandler {
        return AsyncExceptionHandler()
    }
}

object Async2Demo {
    private val LOGGER = LoggerFactory.getLogger(AsyncDemo::class.java)
    @Throws(IOException::class, ExecutionException::class, InterruptedException::class)
    @JvmStatic
    fun main(args: Array<String>) {
        AnnotationConfigApplicationContext(Async2Config::class.java).use { ctx ->
            val asyncService = ctx.getBean("asyncService", AsyncService::class.java)
            for (i in 0..4) {
                asyncService.asyncTask()
            }
            val result1 = asyncService.asyncWithReturn("John Mayer")
            val result2 = asyncService.asyncWithReturn("Eric Clapton")
            val result3 = asyncService.asyncWithReturn("BB King")
            Thread.sleep(6000)
            LOGGER.info(" >> Result1: " + result1!!.get())
            LOGGER.info(" >> Result2: " + result2!!.get())
            LOGGER.info(" >> Result3: " + result3!!.get())
            System.`in`.read()
        }
    }
}
```

Again, feel free to run the examples in the chapter12 project and notice the exception handling specific to the Async2Config configuration.

Summary

In this chapter, we briefly covered Spring's TaskExecutor and common implementations. We also covered Spring's support for task scheduling. We focused on Spring's built-in TaskScheduler abstraction and demonstrated how to use it to fulfill task scheduling needs with a sample batch data update job. We also covered how Spring supports annotation for executing tasks asynchronously.

A Spring Boot section is not needed in this chapter because the scheduling and asynchronous execution of task annotations are part of the spring-context library and available with a basic Spring Boot configuration. Plus, configuring scheduled and asynchronous tasks is already as easy as it can be with Spring; there is not much Spring Boot could do to improve on this topic. If you are curious and want to convert the provided project to Spring Boot, you can find inspiration in previous chapters or in this brief tutorial: https://spring.io/guides/gs/scheduling-tasks.

Since the future seems to be serverless, there will be no servers to be up to run tasks at scheduled intervals. The current approach on cloud applications is to design microservices that run within containers that are scheduled for deployment (or to use scheduled lambdas in AWS, for example). In the next chapter we introduce Spring Remoting, which assists us for networking needs.

CHAPTER 13

Spring Remoting

Up to this point in the book, the projects have been relatively simple, insofar as they can be run on a single VM and the only component they exchange data with is a database, which can be local or remote. These types of applications are called *monolithic applications* and the type of communication involved is referred to as **inter-process communication.**

Most enterprise applications, however, are complex, composed of multiple parts, and communicate with other applications. Take, for example, a company selling products; when a customer places an order, an order-processing system processes that order and generates a transaction. During order processing, an inquiry is made to the inventory system to check whether the product is in stock. Upon order confirmation, a notification is sent to the fulfillment system to deliver the product to the customer. Finally, the information is sent to the accounting system, an invoice is generated, and the payment is processed.

This business process is not fulfilled by a single application, but by several applications working together. Some applications may be developed in-house, and others may be purchased from external vendors. Moreover, the applications may be running on different machines in different locations and implemented with different technologies and programming languages (for example, Java, .NET, or C++). Performing the handshaking between applications in order to build an efficient business process is always a critical task when designing and implementing an application. As a result, remoting support via various protocols and technologies is needed for an application to participate well in an enterprise environment.

In earlier times, communication between applications was achieved via *remoting* and *web services*. In remoting, the applications involved in the communication process may be located on the same computer or on two different computers either in the same network or in different networks. In remoting, both applications know about each other. A proxy of an application object is created on the other application, and this allows the execution of a foreign (remote) method to look like the invocation of a local method.

In the Java world, remoting support has existed since Java was first created. In the early days (Java 1.x), most remoting requirements were implemented by using traditional TCP sockets or Java Remote Method Invocation (RMI). After J2EE came on the scene, EJB and JMS became common choices for inter-application server communications.

The rapid evolution of XML and the Internet gave rise to remote support using XML over HTTP, also known as *web services*. This term includes any kind of remoting technology that sits on HTTP, including the Java API for XML-based RPC (JAX-RPC), the Java API for XML Web Services (JAXWS), and HTTP-based technologies (for example, Hessian[1] and Burlap[2]). Spring used to have its own HTTP-based remoting support, called the Spring HTTP Invoker. In the following years, to cope with the explosive growth of the Internet and more responsive web application requirements (for example, via Ajax), more lightweight and

---

[1] http://hessian.caucho.com/doc/hessian-overview.xtp
[2] http://hessian.caucho.com/doc/burlap.xtp

© Peter Späth, Iuliana Cosmina, Rob Harrop, Chris Schaefer 2023
P. Späth et al., *Pro Spring 6 with Kotlin*, https://doi.org/10.1007/978-1-4842-9557-1_13

efficient remoting support of applications has become critical for the success of an enterprise. Consequently, the Java API for RESTful Web Services (JAX-RS) was created and quickly gained popularity. Other protocols, such as Comet and HTML5 WebSocket, also attracted a lot of developers. Needless to say, remoting technologies keep evolving at a rapid pace.

Nowadays, the most popular application architecture style is *microservices*, small modules/elements that are independent of each other. At times, they are interdependent on other microservices or even a database. Breaking down applications into smaller elements brings scalability and efficiency to the structure. It also requires efficient communication between the services, which if not considered ahead of time can wreak havoc. Communication between the components of a microservices application is also referred to as **inter-service communication**.

The outright leader when choosing how services will communicate with each other tends to be *HTTP*. Communication via HTTP can be *synchronous*, which is when a service has to wait for another service to complete before it returns; this introduces a strong coupling of the two services. Communication via HTTP can also be *asynchronous*, which is when the service takes the request from the first service and immediately returns a URL. An alternative to HTTP is *gRPC*[3], a modern open source high-performance Remote Procedure Call (RPC) framework that can run in any environment. Unfortunately, there is no Spring module for working with gRPC.

The second communication pattern leveraged in microservices applications is *message-based communication*. The most popular protocol for this is Advanced Message Queuing Protocol (AMQP). Unlike HTTP, the services involved do not directly communicate with each other but instead interact via a message broker (Kafka, RabbitMQ, ActiveMQ, SNS, etc.).

Thus, the title of this chapter is somewhat misleading. Its content will cover a few ways to communicate between Spring applications remotely, but *Spring Remoting* is a term that is somewhat deprecated.

Communication Using HTTP

Using HTTP for communication obviously implies that the applications have to be web applications or expose some REST API to support those calls. To show how two Spring applications can communicate with each other via HTTP, a single application is used that models a person sending and receiving letters, as depicted in Figure 13-1. The application is started twice with different properties to model Evelyn and Tom, two pen pals sending letters to each other using POST requests and saving them into their own H2 database. The application instance representing Evelyn is started on port 8080, and the application representing Tom is started on port 8090.

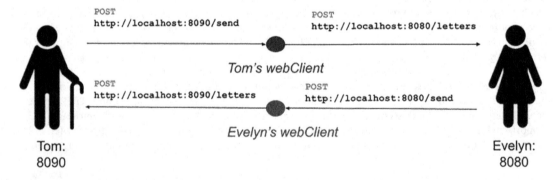

Figure 13-1. Abstract representation of the two pen pals' application instances

---

[3] https://grpc.io

To make Evelyn send a letter to Tom, a POST event is sent to `http://localhost:8080/send` with a body representing a letter. Internally, the `LetterSender` bean will make a POST call to Tom's exposed REST API at `http://localhost:8090/letters` using an instance of `webClient`.

ℹ️   To keep the discussion and examples simple in this chapter, maintaining secure communications between applications won't be a focus.

To make Tom send a letter to Evelyn, the same thing will be done, as already shown in Figure 13-1.

The `webClient` mentioned is an instance of Spring's `org.springframework.web.client.RestTemplate`, the web client class used to make REST calls in non-reactive applications. There is also an implementation for reactive applications, which is introduced in **Chapter 20**.

Introducing Spring Data REST

To keep things easy, only Spring Boot applications are used in this chapter. To keep things even simpler for the letter correspondence application over HTTP, Spring Data REST repositories are used. Spring Data REST takes the features of Spring HATEOAS (Hypermedia as the Engine of Application Stat) and Spring Data JPA and automatically combines them, allowing us to expose REST APIs to manage entities without declaring a controller to interact with the Spring Repository.

Figure 13-2 shows the dependencies needed for project `chapter13-sender-boot` to model the behavior we are interested in.

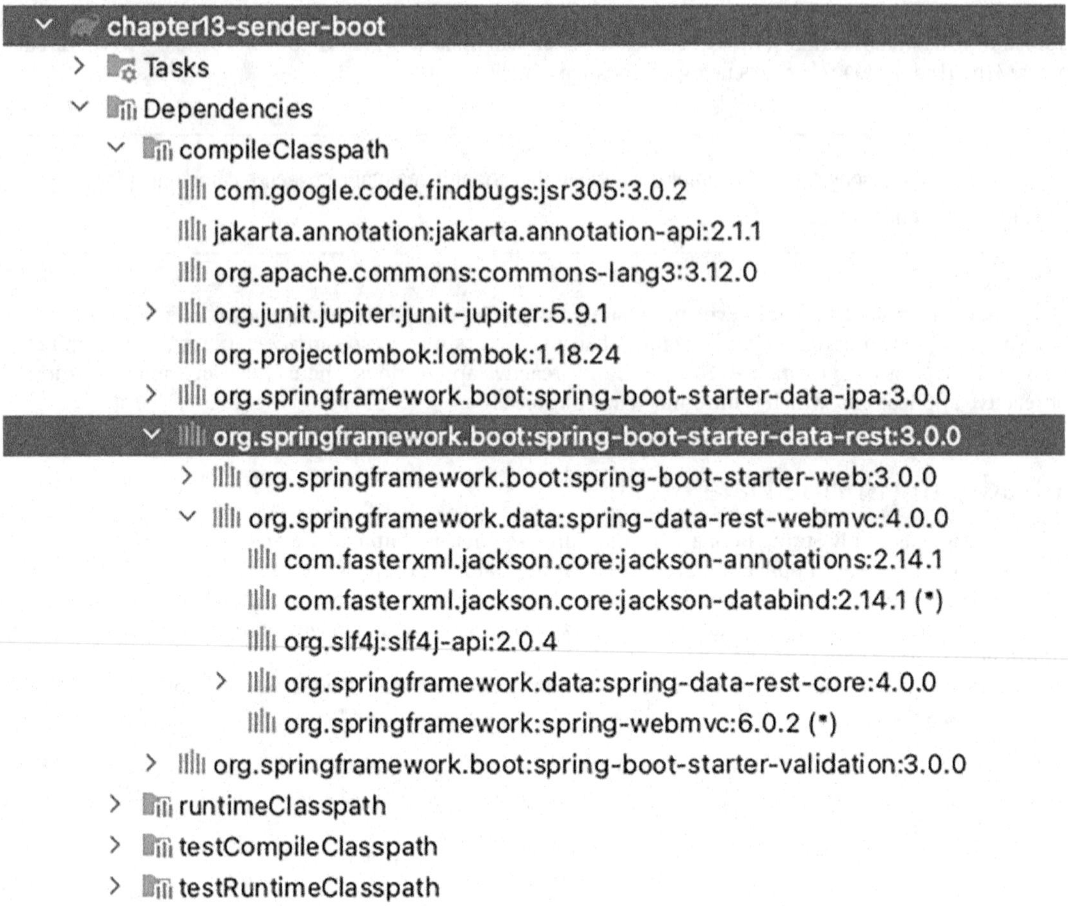

Figure 13-2. *Project* chapter13-sender-boot *dependencies*

Let's build the project step by step, starting with the entity class. The class that models a letter is shown in Listing 13-1.

Listing 13-1. The Letter Class

```
package com.apress.prospring6.thirteen

import jakarta.persistence.*

import java.io.Serial
import java.io.Serializable
import java.time.LocalDate
import jakarta.validation.constraints.NotEmpty
```

```kotlin
@Entity
class Letter() : Serializable {
    @Id
    @GeneratedValue(strategy = GenerationType.AUTO)
    var id: Long? = null

    @NotEmpty var title: String? = null
    var sender: String? = null
    var sentOn: LocalDate? = null

    @Enumerated(EnumType.STRING)
    var category = Category.MISC

    @NotEmpty var content: String? = null

    constructor(id: Long?, title: String?, sender: String?, sentOn: LocalDate?, category:
    Category, content: String?) : this() {
        this.id = id
        this.title = title
        this.sender = sender
        this.sentOn = sentOn
        this.category = category
        this.content = content
    }

    override fun hashCode() = content.hashCode() + 31*(
            category.hashCode() + 31*(
                    sentOn.hashCode() + 31*(
                            sender.hashCode() + 31*(
                                    title.hashCode() + 31*id.hashCode()))))

    override fun equals(other: Any?) =
        (other is Letter)
                && (other.id == id)
                && (other.title == title)
                && (other.sender == sender)
                && (other.sentOn == sentOn)
                && (other.category == category)
                && (other.content == content)

    companion object {
        @Serial
        private val serialVersionUID = 1L
    }
}
```

The Category enum is used to categorize letters based on tier scope. This enum has various values, and to ensure correct serialization and deserialization when letters are sent, CategorySerializer and CategoryDeserializer classes are declared as shown in Listing 13-2.

Listing 13-2. The Category Enum and Its CategorySerializer and CategoryDeserializer Classes

```kotlin
package com.apress.prospring6.thirteen

import com.fasterxml.jackson.core.JsonGenerator
import com.fasterxml.jackson.core.JsonParser
import com.fasterxml.jackson.databind.JsonDeserializer
import com.fasterxml.jackson.databind.JsonSerializer
// other import statements omitted

@JsonSerialize(using = Category.CategorySerializer::class)
@JsonDeserialize(using = Category.CategoryDeserializer::class)
enum class Category(val namex:String) {
    PERSONAL("Personal"),
    FORMAL("Formal"),
    MISC("Miscellaneous");

    class CategorySerializer : JsonSerializer<Category>() {
        @Throws(IOException::class)
        override fun serialize(enumValue: Category,
                gen: JsonGenerator, serializer: SerializerProvider) {
            gen.writeString(enumValue.namex)
        }
    }

    class CategoryDeserializer : JsonDeserializer<Category>() {
        @Throws(IOException::class, JsonProcessingException::class)
        override fun deserialize(parser: JsonParser, context
                  : DeserializationContext): Category? {
            val jsonValue = parser.text
            return eventOf(jsonValue)
        }
    }

    companion object {
        fun eventOf(value: String): Category? {
            val result = values().filter { m: Category ->
                m.namex.equals(value,ignoreCase = true)
            }.firstOrNull()
            return result
        }
    }
}
```

Now that we have the entity class in place, we can write the Spring Data REST Repository. This repository is just like a Spring Data Repository, either JpaRepository<T, ID>, CrudRepository<T, ID>, or PagingAndSortingRepository<T, ID>, but the class and its methods are decorated with special Spring Data REST annotations that tell Spring MVC (the topic of **Chapter 14**) to create RESTful endpoints for managing entities. The LetterRepository interface is shown in Listing 13-3.

Listing 13-3. The LetterRepository Spring Data REST Repository

```
package com.apress.prospring6.thirteen

import org.springframework.data.jpa.repository.JpaRepository
import org.springframework.data.repository.query.Param
import org.springframework.data.rest.core.annotation.RepositoryRestResource
import org.springframework.data.rest.core.annotation.RestResource

import java.time.LocalDate
import java.util.List

@RepositoryRestResource(
    collectionResourceRel = "mailbox",
    path = "letters",
    collectionResourceDescription = Description("Letters and Letter API")
)
interface LetterRepository : JpaRepository<Letter, Long> {
    @RestResource(path = "byCategory", rel = "customFindMethod")
    fun findByCategory(@Param("category") category: Category): List<Letter>
    fun findBySentOn(@Param("date") sentOn: LocalDate): List<Letter>

    @RestResource(exported = false)
    override fun deleteById(id: Long)
}
```

The @RepositoryRestResource annotation tells Spring MVC to create RESTful endpoints at /letters. This annotation is not necessary when the spring-boot-starter-data-rest is on the project classpath, but it is useful to customize the path all the management endpoints are relative to. The default root path for managing Letter instances is letters, the same one used in the example. When the http://localhost:8090/letters is accessed, a JSON construct similar to the one depicted in Listing 13-4 is shown.

Listing 13-4. The JSON Representation Returned When Accessing the http://localhost:8090/letters Endpoint

```
{
  "_embedded" : {
    "mailbox" : [ {
      "title" : "Salutations from England",
      "sender" : "Evelyn",
      "sentOn" : "2022-12-05",
      "category" : "Personal",
      "content" : "I would love to visit. Let's discuss dates.",
      "_links" : {
        "self" : {
          "href" : "http://localhost:8090/letters/1"
        },
        "letter" : {
          "href" : "http://localhost:8090/letters/1"
        }
      }
    } ]
  },
```

```
    "_links" : {
      "self" : {
        "href" : "http://localhost:8090/letters"
      },
      "profile" : {
        "href" : "http://localhost:8090/profile/letters"
      },
      "search" : {
        "href" : "http://localhost:8090/letters/search"
      }
    },
    "page" : {
      "size" : 20,
      "totalElements" : 2,
      "totalPages" : 1,
      "number" : 0
    }
  }
}
```

The collectionResourceRel declares the relative value to use when generating links to the collection resource. This means all Letter instances will be returned as part of the collection named mailbox that is a member of the JSON representation accessible at the URL http://localhost:8090/letters endpoint.

The @RestResource annotation tells Spring MVC what the value of the path of a resource is, and the value of the rel attribute will be in links. By executing a curl to http://localhost:8090/letters/search (or opening the URL in the browser), we can see our new methods listed with other resources, parameters names included, as shown in Listing 13-5.

Listing 13-5. The JSON Representation Returned When Accessing the http://localhost:8090/letters/search Endpoint

```
##  curl http://localhost:8090/letters/search
{
  "_links" : {
    "findBySentOn" : {
      "href" : "http://localhost:8090/letters/search/findBySentOn{?date}",
      "templated" : true
    },
    "customFindMethod" : {
      "href" : "http://localhost:8090/letters/search/byCategory{?category}",
      "templated" : true
    },
    "self" : {
      "href" : "http://localhost:8090/letters/search"
    }
  }
}
```

In Listing 13-3 the deleteById(..) method is annotated with @RestResource(exported = false). The exported attribute value decides if the resource is exported or not. In this example, the effect of this configuration is that no REST endpoint will be created for the deleteById(..) method. However, there are two links matching the two custom search methods declared in `LetterRepository` shown in Listing 13-3. The `{?category}` construct represents the request parameter name, thus the search by category request is actually similar to:

```
GET http://localhost:8090/letters/search/byCategory?category=PERSONAL
```

The purpose of the `LetterRepository` interface is to expose REST API endpoints to be invoked by a `RestTemplate` instance.

The next class to be analyzed is `LetterSenderController`. This class is a REST controller exposing a single POST handler used to trigger the sending letter operation on the current application. The handler method uses the `RestTemplate` bean to send a POST request to the other instance of the application representing letter destination. The `LetterSenderController` class is depicted in Listing 13-6.

Listing 13-6. The LetterSenderController Class

```kotlin
package com.apress.prospring6.thirteen

import org.springframework.beans.factory.annotation.Value
import org.springframework.http.HttpEntity
import org.springframework.http.HttpMethod
import org.springframework.http.MediaType
import org.springframework.web.bind.annotation.PostMapping
import org.springframework.web.bind.annotation.RequestBody
import org.springframework.web.bind.annotation.RestController
import org.springframework.web.client.RestTemplate
import java.time.LocalDate

@RestController
class LetterSenderController(
    private val webClient: RestTemplate,
    @param:Value("#{senderApplication.correspondentAddress}")
    private val correspondentAddress: String,
    @param:Value("#{senderApplication.sender}") private val sender: String
) {
    @PostMapping(path = ["send"], consumes = [MediaType.APPLICATION_JSON_VALUE])
    fun sendLetter(@RequestBody letter: Letter) {
        letter.sender = sender
        letter.sentOn = LocalDate.now()
        val request = HttpEntity(letter)
        webClient.exchange(
            "$correspondentAddress/letters", HttpMethod.POST, request,
            Letter::class.java
        )
    }

    companion object {
        val log = LoggerFactory.getLogger(LetterSenderController::class.java)
    }
}
```

Chapter 3 introduced stereotype annotations. The @RestController annotation is a convenience annotation that is itself annotated with @Controller and @ResponseBody. If @Controller is used to mark beans destined for web use, containing methods mapped to URLs, @RestController is used to mark beans destined for REST use, containing methods mapped to REST endpoints. Since neither Spring MVC support (**Chapter 14**) nor Spring REST support (**Chapter 15**) were introduced so far in the book, this explanation should suffice for now.

RestTemplate is a useful Spring class used to create synchronous clients to perform HTTP requests. It exposes a very simple set of methods used to set request content and headers and also exposes a simple template method API over underlying HTTP client libraries such as the JDK HttpURLConnection, Apache HttpComponents, and others. RestTemplate is typically used as a shared component; a single bean is declared in the application and injected wherever necessary. Starting with Spring version 5.0, this class is in maintenance mode, with only minor requests for changes and bugs to be accepted going forward. The recommendation is to use org.springframework.web.reactive.client.WebClient, which has a more modern API and supports sync, async, and streaming scenarios, but for non-reactive applications, the reactive WebClient is not suitable.

The LetterSenderController class configured with a sender (which is the name of the person sending the letter and its value) is injected from the main Spring Boot application class, referenced here using a SpEL expression: #{senderApplication.sender}. The same is valid for the person the letters are sent to, represented here by correspondentAddress, which is populated from a Spring Boot property as well. The values for these properties are read from the Spring Boot configuration file, the application.yaml file in this example. Its contents are shown in Listing 13-7.

Listing 13-7. The application.yaml File for the chapter13-sender-boot Project

```yaml
# Spring Boot application name
spring:
  application:
    name: chapter13-sender-app

# datasource config
  datasource:
    url: "jdbc:h2:mem:testdb"
    driverClassName: "org.h2.Driver"
    username: sa
    password: password

# jpa config
  jpa:
    database-platform: "org.hibernate.dialect.H2Dialect"
    hibernate:
      ddl-auto: create-drop
     # Uppercase Table Names
      naming:
        physical-strategy: org.hibernate.boot.model.naming.
        PhysicalNamingStrategyStandardImpl

# enabling the H2 web console
  h2:
    console:
      enabled: true
```

```
# application config
app:
  sender:
    name: "default"
  correspondent:
    address: "http://localhost:8090"

# server config
server:
  port: 8090
  compression:
    enabled: true
  address: 0.0.0.0

# logging config
logging:
  pattern:
    console: "%-5level: %class{0} - %msg%n"
  level:
    root: INFO
    org.springframework: DEBUG
    com.apress.prospring6.thirteen: INFO
```

This configuration is split into the following sections, some of which are already familiar to you if you've read the previous chapters:

- `# Spring Boot application name`: This section configures a value for the Spring ApplicationContext ID.

- `# datasource config`: This section configures the data source connection details; in this case the underlying database is an in-memory H2 database.

- `# jpa config`: This section configures the JPA details, such as: the dialect used to communicate with the database, whether the database should be created, and how the tables should be named; in this case, all table names are generated using uppercase letters.

- `# enabling the H2 web console`: As the section name indicates, to check if the application is doing the right thing, sometimes we might want to check the database and generated table. This property enables exposing the `/h2-console` endpoint that points to a web console for managing the H2 database (similar to phpMyAdmin[4], but way simpler). The login window and the console dashboard are shown in Figure 13-3.

---

[4] `https://www.phpmyadmin.net`

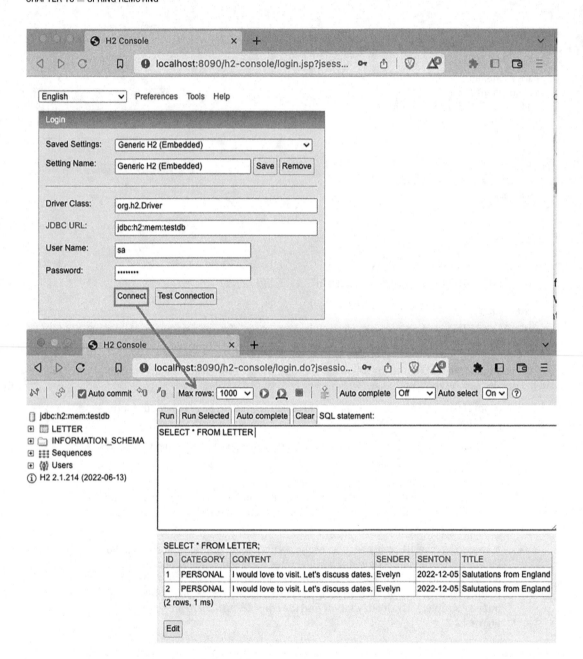

Figure 13-3. H2 Console login and dashboard

- # application config: This section configures the user sending the letters and the address to which the letters are being send. The default configuration is to configure an application where the letter sender and the correspondence address represent the same application.

- # server config: This section configures the URL where the application is available. Setting the address to 0.0.0.0 allows the application to be accessible on all network addresses associated with the computer the application runs in (e.g., http:// localhost:8090/letters, http://127.0.0.1:8090/letters, etc.).

- # logging config: This section configures the logging levels for packages and classes in the application.

Based on this configuration and a Spring Boot main class, an application that can communicate via HTTP with another one can be started. The Spring Boot main class is shown in Listing 13-8.

Listing 13-8. The Spring Boot Main Class for the chapter13-sender-boot Project

```
package com.apress.prospring6.thirteen

import org.springframework.boot.CommandLineRunner
// other import statements omitted

@SpringBootApplication
open class SenderApplication {
    @Value("\${app.sender.name}")
    var sender: String? = null

    @Value("\${app.correspondent.address}")
    var correspondentAddress: String? = null

    @Bean
    open fun restTemplate(): RestTemplate {
        return RestTemplate()
    }

    @Bean
    open fun initCmd(): CommandLineRunner {
        return CommandLineRunner { args: Array<String> ->
            log.info(
                " >>> Sender {}  ready to send letters to {} ",
                sender,
                correspondentAddress
            )
        }
    }

    companion object {
        val log = LoggerFactory.getLogger(SenderApplication::class.java)
        @JvmStatic
        fun main(args: Array<String>) {
            val ctx = SpringApplication.run(
                SenderApplication::class.java, *args
            )
        }
    }
}
```

The app.sender.name is read from the application.yaml file and injected into the sender property. The app.correspondent.address is read from the application.yaml file and injected into the correspondentAddress property. The SenderApplication configuration declares a bean named senderApplication, and the properties of this bean are injected in the LetterSenderController class using SpEL expressions as shown previously in Listing 13-6.

Now that all beans and configurations have been explained, let's start the two application instances, Tom and Evelyn, and start sending letters. To start two instances of the application, you can use IntelliJ IDEA launchers, but the easiest way is to build the application and start the applications using the generated JAR.

To build the project, go to the pro-spring-6/chapter13-sender-boot and run gradle clean build. The project is built and the executable is generated at chapter13-sender-boot/build/libs/chapter13-sender-boot-1.0-SNAPSHOT.jar.

To start the Tom application, open a terminal and run the command shown in Listing 13-9.

Listing 13-9. Starting the Tom Application

```
java -jar \
build/libs/chapter13-sender-boot-1.0-SNAPSHOT.jar \
--server.port=8090 \
--app.sender.name=Tom \
--app.correspondent.address=http://localhost:8080 # Evelyn's address
```

The application starts and the last two log entries printed should be as follows:

```
INFO: SenderApplication -  >>> Sender Tom  ready to send letters to http://localhost:8080
DEBUG: ApplicationAvailabilityBean - Application availability state ReadinessState changed
to ACCEPTING_TRAFFIC
```

The INFO log is printed by the CommandLineRunner bean.

To start the Evelyn application, open a terminal and run the command shown in Listing 13-10.

Listing 13-10. Starting the Evelyn Application

```
java -jar \
build/libs/chapter13-sender-boot-1.0-SNAPSHOT.jar \
--server.port=8080 \
--app.sender.name=Evelyn \
--app.correspondent.address=http://localhost:8090 # Tom's address
```

The application starts and the last two log entries printed should be as follows:

```
INFO : SenderApplication -  >>> Sender Evelyn  ready to send letters to http://
localhost:8090
DEBUG: ApplicationAvailabilityBean - Application availability state ReadinessState changed
to ACCEPTING_TRAFFIC
```

To make Tom send a letter to Evelyn, a POST request must be made to http://localhost:8090/send. The easiest way to do so is by executing the requests in the chapter13-sender-boot/src/test/resources/ Sender.http file, using the HTTPie[5] client embedded in IntelliJ IDEA.

---

[5] https://httpie.io

ℹ HTTPie is not included with the Community Edition of IntelliJ IDEA. However, you can achieve the same result using other HTTP clients like `curl`.

For example, the request to send a letter from Tom to Evelyn (one of the requests in the `Sender.http` file) is shown in Listing 13-11.

Listing 13-11. POST Request to Make Tom Send a Letter to Evelyn

```
### Tom sending letter to Evelyn
POST http://localhost:8090/send
Content-Type: application/json

{
  "title": "Salutations from Scotland",
  "category": "Personal",
  "content" : "Scotland is rather lovely this time of year. Would you like to visit?"
}

# Or, using curl
curl -X POST http://localhost:8090/send -H "Content-Type: application/json" -d
'{"title":"Salutations from Scotland","category":"Personal","content":"Scotland is rather
lovely this time of year. Would you like to visit?"}'
```

How do we know this worked? We look in Tom's log and look for the log entries that report that the restTemplate bean has performed the request. The log entries should look very similar to the ones shown in Listing 13-12.

Listing 13-12. Application Log Entries for Sending Requests Using a restTemplate Bean

```
DEBUG: LogFormatUtils - POST "/send", parameters={}
DEBUG: AbstractHandlerMapping - Mapped to com.apress.prospring6.thirteen.LetterSenderControl
ler#sendLetter(Letter)
DEBUG: CompositeLog - HTTP POST http://localhost:8080/letters
DEBUG: CompositeLog - Accept=[application/json, application/*+json]
DEBUG: CompositeLog - Writing [Letter(id=null, title=Salutations from Scotland,
sender=Tom, sentOn=2022-12-06, category=PERSONAL, content=Scotland is rather lovely this
time of year. Would you like to visit?)] with org.springframework.http.converter.json.
MappingJackson2HttpMessageConverter
DEBUG: CompositeLog - Response 201 CREATED
DEBUG: CompositeLog - Reading to [com.apress.prospring6.thirteen.Letter]
```

On the Evelyn application, you can see a matching log, depicted in Listing 13-13.

Listing 13-13. Application Log Entries for Receiving a POST Request

```
DEBUG: LogFormatUtils - POST "/letters", parameters={}
DEBUG: AbstractMessageConverterMethodProcessor - Using 'application/json', given
[application/json, application/*+json] and supported [application/hal+json, application/
json, application/prs.hal-forms+json]
```

```
DEBUG: LogFormatUtils - Writing [EntityModel { content: Letter(id=1, title=Salutations from
Scotland, sender=Tom, sentOn=2022-12-06, (truncated)...]
DEBUG: FrameworkServlet - Completed 201 CREATED
```

And to be really convinced, you can open http://localhost:8080/letters in a browser (or use the
GET request in the Sender.http file). The returned JSON representation for Evelyn should now have the
mailbox populated with the letter sent by Tom. The JSON representation is shown in Listing 13-14.

Listing 13-14. JSON Representation of Letter Resources for the Evelyn Application

```
### Root JSON representation of Evelyn's letters
GET http://localhost:8080/letters
Accept: application/json
###
{
  "_embedded" : {
    "mailbox" : [ {
      "title" : "Salutations from Scotland",
      "sender" : "Tom",
      "sentOn" : "2022-12-06",
      "category" : "Personal",
      "content" : "Scotland is rather lovely this time of year. Would you like to visit?",
      "_links" : {
        "self" : {
          "href" : "http://localhost:8080/letters/1"
        },
        "letter" : {
          "href" : "http://localhost:8080/letters/1"
        }
      }
    } ]
  },
  "_links" : {
    "self" : {
      "href" : "http://localhost:8080/letters"
    },
    "profile" : {
      "href" : "http://localhost:8080/profile/letters"
    },
    "search" : {
      "href" : "http://localhost:8080/letters/search"
    }
  },
  "page" : {
    "size" : 20,
    "totalElements" : 1,
    "totalPages" : 1,
    "number" : 0
  }
}
```

By default, RestTemplate registers all built-in message converters, depending on classpath checks that help to determine what optional conversion libraries are present. Since we have two copies of the same application communicating, they can both covert between Letter and its JSON representation and vice versa with no problem. You can also set the message converters to use explicitly if you need too.

However, RestTemplate can be used to communicate with any other application, written in any language, as long as the right converters are registered. For example, in Listing 13-15 a method is added to the LetterSenderController to perform a request to https://jsonplaceholder.typicode.com/users, an endpoint provided by a free fake API for testing and prototyping.

Listing 13-15. RestTemplate Being Used to Perform a GET to https://jsonplaceholder.typicode.com/users

```
package com.apress.prospring6.thirteen;
// other imports omitted

@RestController
class LetterSenderController(
    private val webClient: RestTemplate,
    @param:Value("#{senderApplication.correspondentAddress}")
    private val correspondentAddress: String,
    @param:Value("#{senderApplication.sender}") private val sender: String
) {
  ...
    @get:GetMapping(path = ["misc"], produces = [MediaType.APPLICATION_JSON_VALUE])
    val miscData: String
        get() {
            val response = webClient.getForObject(
                "https://jsonplaceholder.typicode.com/users",
                String::class.java
            )
            log.info("Random info from non-java application: {} ", response)
            return response!!
        }

    companion object {
        val log = LoggerFactory.getLogger(LetterSenderController::class.java)
    }

}
```

The returned result is an array of user objects in JSON representation. If the application had a User POJO definition matching the JSON representation, a converter would ensure a correct conversion.

The RestTemplate class used to submit the requests is quite versatile, but as previously mentioned, it is set to be deprecated. The future seems to be reactive, and WebClient and the new declarative HTTP interface are the replacements.

Starting with Spring 6 and Spring Boot 3, the Spring Framework supports proxying a remote HTTP service as a Java/Kotlin interface with annotated methods for HTTP exchanges, also called a *declarative HTTP interface*[6]. A declarative HTTP interface is an interface that helps reduce the boilerplate code, generates a proxy implementing this interface, and performs the exchanges at the framework level. This too will be covered in **Chapter 20**, because the focus of this chapter is on real remote communication.

Using JMS in Spring

Using message-oriented middleware, generally referred to as a message queue (MQ) server, is another popular way to support communication between applications. The main benefits of an MQ server are that it provides an asynchronous and loosely coupled way for application integration. In the Java/Kotlin world, JMS is the standard for connecting to an MQ server for sending or receiving messages. An MQ server maintains a list of queues and topics for which applications can connect to and send and receive messages to. The following is a brief description of the difference between a queue and a topic:

- *Queue*: A queue is used to support a point-to-point message exchange model. When a producer sends a message to a queue, the MQ server keeps the message within the queue and delivers it to one, and only one, consumer the next time the consumer connects.

- *Topic*: A topic is used to support the publish-subscribe model. Any number of clients can subscribe to the message within a topic. When a message arrives for that topic, the MQ server delivers it to all clients that have subscribed to the message. This model is particularly useful when you have multiple applications that will be interested in the same piece of information (for example, a news feed).

In JMS, a producer connects to an MQ server and sends a message to a queue or topic. A consumer also connects to the MQ server and listens to a queue or topics for messages of interest. In JMS 1.1, the API was unified, so the producer and consumer didn't need to deal with different APIs for interacting with queues and topics. As of Spring Framework 5, Spring's JMS package fully supports JMS 2.0 and requires the JMS 2.0 API to be present at runtime. Thus, a JMS 2.0–compatible provider is required. Starting with Spring 6, the JMS API specification used is the Jakarta Messaging API version 3.x, because the JMS API is one of the Java EE products that Oracle outsourced.

The previous edition of the Java variant of this book used a HornetMQ stand-alone server for sending messages, but the HornetMQ project has since then been decommissioned. This chapter demonstrates how to use Apache ActiveMQ Artemis[7], which has a Jakarta JMS–compatible version, and there is a Spring Boot starter for it, which will make things a lot easier.

The core of JMS communication in Spring is JmsTemplate, which simplifies creation and release of resources when sending and receiving synchronous messages. For convenience, JmsTemplate also exposes a basic request-reply operation that allows for sending a message and waiting for a response. JmsTemplate is similar to RestTemplate; they are both used in remote communication between applications, and they both expose practical APIs for developers to use. Instances of both types are thread-safe once configured, and thus a single JmsTemplate bean is necessary in an application, and it can be injected wherever necessary. There is one difference though: JmsTemplate is stateful, sort of, in that it maintains a reference to a ConnectionFactory, but this state is not conversational state.

---

[6] https://docs.spring.io/spring-framework/docs/current/reference/html/integration. html#rest-http-interface
[7] https://activemq.apache.org

Working with Apache ActiveMQ Artemis

Using Spring Boot makes development of JMS applications more practical since it autoconfigures a `jakarta.jms.ConnectionFactory` bean when it detects ActiveMQ Artemis is available on the classpath.

ActiveMQ Artemis can be used in a native mode, with the connection to the broker being provided by the Netty protocol. The `application.yaml` file can look like depicted in Listing 13-16.

Listing 13-16. `application.yaml` Configuration for an External ActiveMQ Artemis Server

```
spring:
    artemis:
        mode: native
        host: 0.0.0.0
        port: 61617
        user: prospring6
        password:prospring6
# or
spring:
    artemis:
        mode: native
        broker-url: tcp://${IP_ADDRESS}:61617
        user: prospring6
        password:prospring6
```

Starting with Spring Boot 3.x, properties `spring.artemis.host` and `spring.artemis.port` are marked as deprecated and the recommendation is to use `spring.artemis.broker-url`.

Installing ActiveMQ Artemis is not the focus of this book, so for the code samples, the embedded version is used. To use ActiveMQ Artemis embedded in a Spring Boot application, three things are necessary: `spring-boot-starter-artemis` on the classpath, `artemis-jakarta-server` on the classpath, and the Spring Boot embedded configuration. Figure 13-4 shows all the dependencies of the project specific to this section, `chapter13-artemis-boot`.

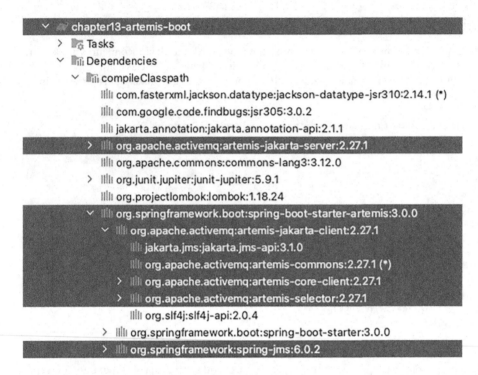

Figure 13-4. *Spring Boot Artemis JMS project dependencies*

The Spring Boot application configuration that uses an embedded ActiveMQ Artemis server is shown in Listing 13-17.

Listing 13-17. `application.yaml` Configuration for an Embedded ActiveMQ Artemis Server

```
spring:
  artemis:
    mode: embedded
    embedded:
      queues: prospring6
      enabled: true
```

Using Spring Boot is very practical, because there is no need to declare a `jakarta.jms.ConnectionFactory`; it is automatically set up. The `spring.artemis.embedded.queues` configures a comma-separated list of queues to create on startup. By default, Spring Boot configures a bean of type `org.springframework.jms.connection.CachingConnectionFactory`. This type is an extension of `org.springframework.jms.connection.SingleConnectionFactory`. This is a special class that ensures a single JMS connection is opened and shared between all objects needing to communicate with the JMS server. The `CachingConnectionFactory` adds caching behavior for message producers and consumers. Figure 13-5 shows the most common implementations of the `jakarta.jms.ConnectionFactory`.

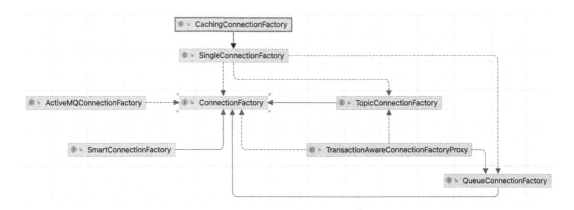

Figure 13-5. `jakarta.jms.ConnectionFactory` *hierarchy*

In the previous section we sent Letter instances between two applications, so in this section the same object will be sent to a JMQ queue by a Sender and read by a Receiver. Since Spring Boot is using an embedded Apache MQ Artemis server, we cannot start two applications and exchange messages between them. So, the functionality is simple and matches the schema depicted in Figure 13-6.

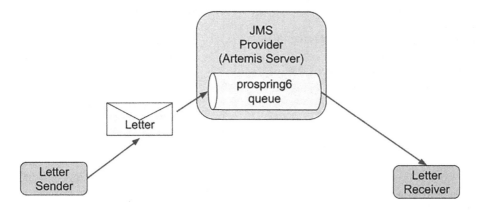

Figure 13-6. *Spring Boot JMS application abstract schema*

The Sender bean uses a JmsTemplate bean to send a Letter instance. The JmsTemplate bean is autoconfigured by Spring Boot too, so all we must do is inject it in the Sender bean declaration and use it. The Sender class and bean declaration is shown in Listing 13-18.

Listing 13-18. The JMS Producer, the Sender Class

package com.apress.prospring6.thirteen

import org.springframework.jms.core.JmsTemplate
`// other import statements omitted`

```
@Component
class Sender {
    private var jmsTemplate: JmsTemplate? = null
```

611

```kotlin
    constructor(jmsTemplate: JmsTemplate) {
        this.jmsTemplate = jmsTemplate
    }

    @PostConstruct
    fun init() {
        jmsTemplate!!.deliveryDelay = 2000L
    }

    @Value("\${spring.artemis.embedded.queues}")
    private val queueName: String? = null

    fun send(letter: Letter?) {
        log.info(" >> sending letter='{}'", letter)
        jmsTemplate!!.convertAndSend(queueName, letter)
    }
    companion object {
        val log = LoggerFactory.getLogger(Sender::class.java)
    }
}
```

Notice that the queue name is extracted from the Spring Boot configuration file using `@Value("${spring.artemis.embedded.queues}")`.

The Receiver is even simpler, as shown in Listing 13-19.

Listing 13-19. The JMS Consumer, the Receiver Class

package com.apress.prospring6.thirteen

import org.springframework.jms.annotation.JmsListener
```kotlin
// other import statements omitted

@Component
class Receiver {
    @JmsListener(destination = "\${spring.artemis.embedded.queues}")
    fun receive(letter: Letter?) {
        log.info(" >> received letter='{}'", letter)
    }
    companion object {
        val log = LoggerFactory.getLogger(Receiver::class.java)
    }
}
```

The most important thing in this bean declaration is the method annotated with `@JmsListener`. This annotation marks a method to be the target of a JMS message listener on the specified destination. This annotation can also specify a custom JMS `ConnectionFactory` using the `connectionFactory` attribute. Without it, it uses the default `ConnectionFactory` configured by Spring Boot.

Processing `@JmsListener` is the responsibility of a `org.springframework.jms.annotation.JmsListenerAnnotationBeanPostProcessor` bean that Spring Boot automatically configures. Without Spring Boot to configure this bean, the `@EnableJms` (from package `org.springframework.jms.annotation`) needs to be placed on a configuration class.

To test that letters sent by the Sender bean are received by the Receiver bean through the prospring6 queue, managed by the embedded Artemis server, we can write the program shown in Listing 13-20.

Listing 13-20. Program to Test JMS Message Handling

```
package com.apress.prospring6.thirteen

import java.util.UUID
// other impost statements omitted

@SpringBootApplication
open class ArtemisApplication {
    companion object {
        val log = LoggerFactory.getLogger(ArtemisApplication::class.java)
        @JvmStatic
        fun main(args: Array<String>) {
            try {
                SpringApplication.run(ArtemisApplication::class.java, *args).use { ctx ->
                    // Arrays.stream(ctx.getBeanDefinitionNames()).forEach(cn -> log.info("
                    // >>> {}: {}", cn, ctx.getBean(cn).getClass()));
                    val sender =
                        ctx.getBean(
                            Sender::class.java
                        )
                    for (i in 0..9) {
                        val letter =
                            Letter("Letter no. $i", "Test", LocalDate.now(),
                                UUID.randomUUID().toString())
                        sender.send(letter)
                    }
                    System.`in`.read()
                }
            } catch (e: IOException) {
                log.error("Problem reading keystrokes.")
            }
        }
    }
}
```

In Listing 13-20, the application context is created, and then the Sender bean is retrieved from the context and used to send ten Letter instances. The Receiver bean automatically reacts to Letter instances found in the queue and "consumes" them, which in this case this means they are just logged. When running this program, you might notice that it does not work as expected and the following message is printed in the console:

```
Exception in thread "main"
    org.springframework.jms.support.converter.MessageConversionException:
    Cannot convert object of type [com.apress.prospring6.thirteen.Letter] to JMS message.
    Supported message payloads are: String, byte array, Map<String,?>, Serializable object.
    at org.springframework.jms.support.converter.SimpleMessageConverter.toMessage(
    SimpleMessageConverter.java:79)
```

```
    at org.springframework.jms.core.JmsTemplate.lambda$convertAndSend$5(JmsTemplate.
    java:661)
    ...
    at com.apress.prospring6.thirteen.Sender.send(Sender.java:56)
    at com.apress.prospring6.thirteen.ArtemisApplication.main(ArtemisApplication.java:70)
```

So, what is the problem here? By default, as the message states, only a few types of messages can be written to the queue, and all of them are represented by types implementing jakarta.jms.Message, as shown in Figure 13-7.

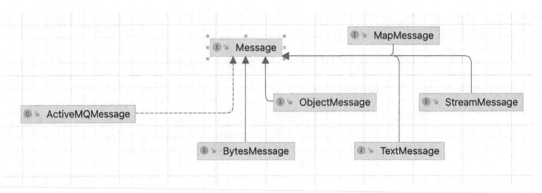

Figure 13-7. *Message Hierarchy*

ℹ   The `ActiveMQMessage` class is the message implementation that is part of the `active-server.jar` library, but it is not really necessary in a Spring application.

So, how do we add support for a different type? There is a hint in the error message: since there is no message converter, we need a message converter. The easiest way is to provide a converter that transforms a Letter to JSON text representation, so the Sender writes a jakarta.jms.TextMessage to the queue and transforms a JSON representation to a Letter so the Receiver can read it. And since we are working in a Spring context, the most suitable way is to declare a bean doing that, and because this is a Spring Boot application, the bean will be automatically used where needed. The JMS converter bean is shown in Listing 13-21, and it is configured using the Jackson library.

Listing 13-21. JMS Converter Bean

package com.apress.prospring6.thirteen

```
import com.fasterxml.jackson.databind.json.JsonMapper
import com.fasterxml.jackson.datatype.jsr310.JavaTimeModule
import org.springframework.jms.support.converter.MappingJackson2MessageConverter
import org.springframework.jms.support.converter.MessageConverter
import org.springframework.jms.support.converter.MessageType
// other import statements omitted
```

```kotlin
@SpringBootApplication
open class ArtemisApplication {
    @Bean
    open fun messageConverter(): MessageConverter {
        val mapper = JsonMapper().apply {
            registerModule(JavaTimeModule())
        }
        val converter = MappingJackson2MessageConverter().apply {
            setTargetType(MessageType.TEXT)
            setTypeIdPropertyName("_type")
            setObjectMapper(mapper)
        }
        return converter
    }
    // main method omitted
}
```

There are three lines in Listing 13-21 that are needed to configure the following:

- `converter.setTargetType(MessageType.TEXT)`: Specifies that the object should be marshalled to a `TextMessage` by being invoked with the `MessageType.TEXT` enum value. Other possible values are: `BYTES`, `MAP`, or `OBJECT`.

- `converter.setTypeIdPropertyName("_type")`: Specifies the name of the JMS message property that carries the type ID for the contained object. This property needs to be set to allow the conversion from an incoming message to a Java object.

- `mapper.registerModule(JavaTimeModule())`: This is needed because the `Letter` record contains a field named `sentOn` of type `java.time.LocalDate`

With this bean in the configuration, now the application behaves as it should. If we run the `main(..)` method and analyze the console, the log messages printed by the `Sender` before sending a `Letter` instance and the log messages printed by the `Receiver` after receiving a `Letter` instance are printed in the console. A sample log snippet is shown in Listing 13-22.

Listing 13-22. Spring Boot Console Log Snippet Showing JMS Messages Being Processed

```
INFO : ActiveMQServerLogger_impl - AMQ221007: Server is now live
INFO : ActiveMQServerLogger_impl - AMQ221001: Apache ActiveMQ Artemis Message Broker
version 2.27.1 [localhost, nodeID=62e0a32a-7a73-11ed-b408-3e5b0a7a3878]
...
INFO : Sender - >> sending letter='Letter[title=Letter no. 0, sender=Test,
sentOn=2022-12-12, content=95e3c388-37b5-499d-a720-c6b77b8cb99c]'
INFO : AuditLogger_impl - AMQ601267: User anonymous@invm:0 is creating a core session
on target resource ActiveMQServerImpl::name=localhost with parameters: [63310d25-7a73-
11ed-b408-3e5b0a7a3878, null, ****, 102400, RemotingConnectionImpl [ID=631dfa50-7a73-
11ed-b408-3e5b0a7a3878, clientID=null, nodeID=62e0a32a-7a73-11ed-b408-3e5b0a7a3878, tra
nsportConnection=InVMConnection [serverID=0, id=631dfa50-7a73-11ed-b408-3e5b0a7a3878]],
true, true, false, false, null, org.apache.activemq.artemis.core.protocol.core.impl.
CoreSessionCallback@4a09407d, true, {}]
...
```

```
INFO : Sender -  >> sending letter='Letter[title=Letter no. 1, sender=Test,
sentOn=2022-12-12, content=c9490fb3-49d3-4678-af76-a3c2fff3de21]'
•••
INFO : Receiver -  >> received letter='Letter[title=Letter no. 0, sender=Test,
sentOn=2022-12-12, content=95e3c388-37b5-499d-a720-c6b77b8cb99c]'
INFO : AuditLogger_impl - AMQ601759: User anonymous@invm:0 added acknowledgement of a
message from prospring6: CoreMessage[messageID=17,durable=true,userID=6337eaf6-7a73-
11ed-b408-3e5b0a7a3878,priority=4, timestamp=Mon Dec 12 23:19:12 GMT 2022,expiration=0,
durable=true, address=prospring6,size=588,properties=TypedProperties[__AMQ_
CID=63296c02-7a73-11ed-b408-3e5b0a7a3878,_type=com.apress.prospring6.thirteen.Letter,
_AMQ_SCHED_DELIVERY=1670887154279,_AMQ_ROUTING_TYPE=1]]@489572349 to transaction:
TransactionImpl [xid=null, txID=30, xid=null, state=ACTIVE, createTime=1670887154268(
Mon Dec 12 23:19:14 GMT 2022), timeoutSeconds=300, nr operations = 1]@16eb0e22
INFO : Receiver -  >> received letter='Letter[title=Letter no. 1, sender=Test,
sentOn=2022-12-12, content=c9490fb3-49d3-4678-af76-a3c2fff3de21]'
•••
```

Among the custom log messages confirming sending (producing) and receiving (consuming) of messages, there are Artemis-special logs. Since the server is an embedded one, each message is sent using an anonymous user, which is confirmed by the logs. As you can see from the logs, sending and receiving JMS messages is done in a JMS transaction, which Spring Boot manages by default.

More advanced behavior, like message consumption prioritization and handling errors, can be easily configured by customizing the Spring Boot configuration. Feel free to enrich your knowledge of Spring Boot JMS support by reading the official documentation[8].

Using Spring for Apache Kafka

In this section, we focus on the point-to-point style for using queues, which is a more commonly used pattern within a company, and not on any queueing technology. We are going to show you how to write Spring Boot applications using Apache Kafka[9].

In a world where the quantity of data to manage increases exponentially from year to year, and where making data accessible with lightning speed is essential for productivity, classical queuing technologies have difficulties adapting. Enter open source Apache Kafka, a distributed event streaming platform renowned for being used to build high-performance data pipelines, streaming analytics, data integration, and mission-critical applications by thousands of companies. Apache Kafka is known for its excellent performance, low latency, fault tolerance, and high throughput. It's capable of handling thousands of messages per second. So, of course, integrating with it was a priority for the Spring Team. The Spring for Apache Kafka (spring-kafka) project applies core Spring concepts to the development of Kafka-based messaging solutions.

ⓘ   Notice that the project is named *Spring for Apache Kafka*, not *Spring Kafka*, the reason being that the Apache Foundation wanted to avoid confusion regarding Kafka ownership. All open source Apache projects have their name prefixed with "Apache," and any project donated to the Apache Foundation gets renamed as such. For example, the Brooklyn orchestration server became Apache Brooklyn when it was donated to the Apache Foundation.

---

[8] https://docs.spring.io/spring-boot/docs/3.0.0/reference/htmlsingle/#messaging
[9] https://kafka.apache.org

As stated in the official documentation: "Apache Kafka is a distributed system consisting of servers and clients that communicate via a high-performance TCP network protocol. It can be deployed on bare-metal hardware, virtual machines, and containers in on-premises as well as cloud environments." For the example in this book, Apache Kafka is deployed on-premises in a Docker runtime.

The containers needed to run Apache Kafka locally are configured via a `docker-compose.yaml` file, and Docker Compose[10] is used to start up and shut down the containers. This configuration is provided by Bitnami[11], a library of installers or software packages for web applications and software stacks as well as virtual appliances. The full library is shared via GitHub and all container configurations are available here: `https://github.com/bitnami/containers`. The configuration necessary for the example in this book was downloaded from this repository[12]. The instructions to start the containers can be found in the `chapter13-kafka-boot/CHAPTER13-KAFKA-BOOT.adoc` document.

The reason why the term *containers* (plural) was used earlier is because two containers are needed. Here's the thing, in production environments, Apache Kafka is run as a cluster, and somebody must manage those instances. This is where Zookeeper comes in. Zookeeper is a software developed by Apache that acts as a centralized service and is used to maintain naming and configuration data and to provide flexible and robust synchronization within distributed systems. This means in a production environment you might see a setup like the one shown in Figure 13-8, where instances of Zookeeper coordinate with each other and each one of them is responsible for its own Apache Kafka server.

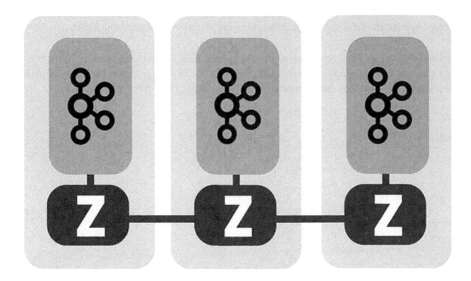

Figure 13-8. *Apache Kafka production setup*

In a production system, multiple instances of Zookeeper work together to manage Kafka data that is divided across multiple collections of nodes, and this is how Kafka achieves its high availability and consistency. In Figure 13-8 each gray rectangle is a node, the bubbles labeled with Z represent Zookeeper instances, and the black "grape" logos represent Apache Kafka instances. For a development Docker setup, though, one Zookeeper instance and one Apache Kafka instance is sufficient.

---

[10] `https://github.com/docker/compose`

[11] `https://bitnami.com`

[12] `https://github.com/bitnami/containers/blob/main/bitnami/kafka/docker-compose.yml`

Since we are using an Apache Kafka instance that is external to our application, we can write another application that can be started twice and simulate a communication between instances. As we did in the beginning of this chapter, an application will be started for Tom to send letter messages to Evelyn, and one for Evelyn to send letters to Tom. Tom and Evelyn have their own queues they receive messages on. Each application is a web application that will expose a single /kafka/send endpoint, and a POST method is used to trigger a message to be sent to the queue of the other person, as described in Figure 13-9.

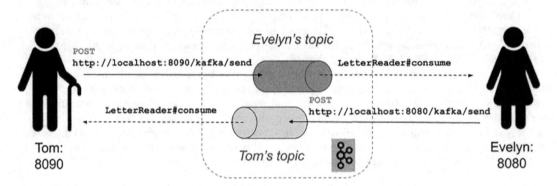

Figure 13-9. *Abstract representation of the two pen pals' application instances using Apache Kafka*

There is no Spring Boot starter for Apache Kafka, since you cannot start Kafka in embedded mode, but it is quite easy to create a Spring Boot web application, add spring-kafka as a dependency, and configure it using Spring properties. Figure 13-10 shows the dependencies of the chapter13-kafka-boot project.

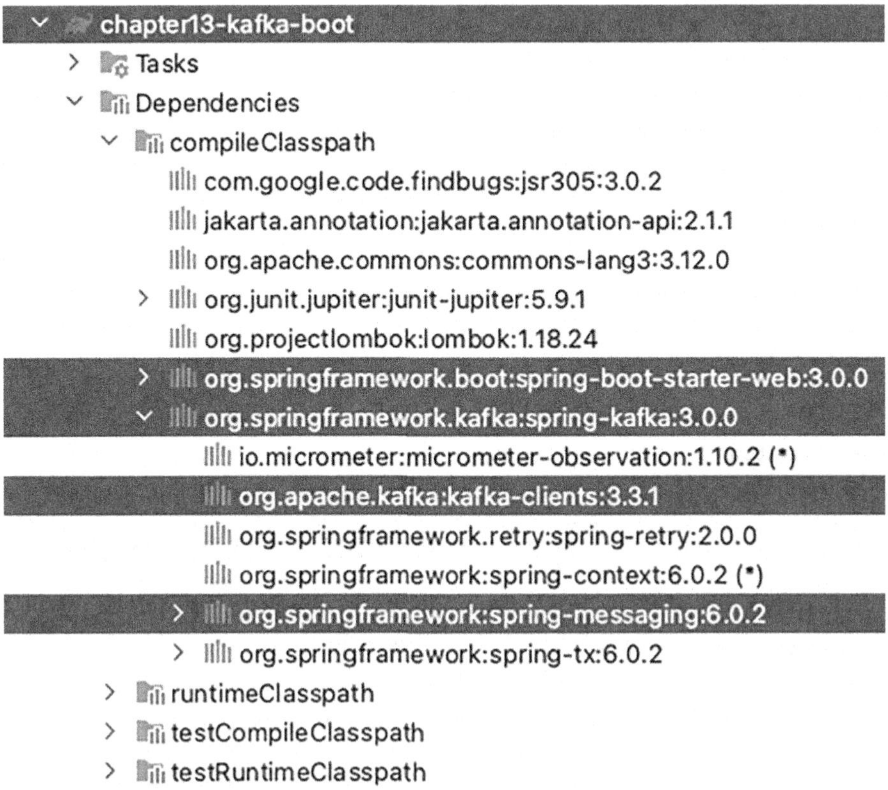

Figure 13-10. *Gradle configuration for a Spring Boot application using Apache Kafka*

Now that we have the desired behavior and the dependencies, let's see what we need to build this application. First we need to tell Spring Boot where Apache Kafka is running, so that its API can be called so that queues are created, and messages can be sent and received. In Listing 13-23 you can see the Spring Boot application configuration (the contents of the application.yaml file).

Listing 13-23. Spring Boot with Apache Kafka Application Configuration

```
# web config
server:
  port: 8090
  compression:
    enabled: true
  address: 0.0.0.0

# kafka config
spring:
  kafka:
    bootstrap-servers: localhost:9092
    consumer:
      group-id: letters-group-id
```

```yaml
# custom config
app:
  sending:
    topic:
      name: default  # topic where letters are sent
  receiving:
    topic:
      name: self # topic where letters are received

# logging config
logging:
  pattern:
    console: "%-5level: %class{0} - %msg%n"
  level:
    root: INFO
    org.springframework: DEBUG
    com.apress.prospring6.thirteen: INFO
```

The YAML configuration has been split in sections per scope, and the sections are explained in the following list:

- # web config: This section configures web application details, like the port, and if the application is exposed on all network IPs (0.0.0.0 means the application will be accessible at http://localhost:8090, http://127.0.0.1:8090, etc.).

- # kafka config: This section configures the location and port where the Apache Kafka cluster is available. The consumer.group-id is a Kafka abstraction that enables supporting both point-to-point and publish/subscribe messaging. This property can be used to group multiple consumers and customize the behavior per group, such as priority when consuming messages, parallelism, and so on.

- # custom config: Based on the values of these two properties, This section configures the topic where messages are sent (app.topic.sending.name) and the topic where messages are received (app.topic.receiving.name). The app.topic.receiving.name property also identifies the application: Tom or Evelyn.

- # logging config: This section configures log levels.

On the two topics, Letter record instances will be written. The record declaration is shown in Listing 13-24.

Listing 13-24. Letter Record Declaration

```kotlin
package com.apress.prospring6.thirteen

import com.fasterxml.jackson.annotation.JsonFormat
import com.fasterxml.jackson.annotation.JsonProperty

import java.time.LocalDate

data class Letter (@JsonProperty("title") val title:String,
                   @JsonProperty("sender") val sender:String,
                   @JsonFormat(shape = JsonFormat.Shape.STRING, pattern = "yyyy-MM-dd")
                   @JsonProperty("sentOn") val sentOn:LocalDate,
                   @JsonProperty("content") val content:String )
```

Since we do not plan to edit the received Letter instances, a Kotlin data class is suitable for this application.

The Apache Kafka cluster doesn't know what topics we need, so we have to configure them. It doesn't know what kind of object we plan to produce and consume from the topics, so we have to configure that as well. To keep it simple, we'll group all these configurations in a class named KafkaConfig, shown in Listing 13-25.

Listing 13-25. KafkaConfig Configuration Class

```kotlin
package com.apress.prospring6.thirteen

import org.apache.kafka.clients.admin.NewTopic
import org.apache.kafka.clients.consumer.ConsumerConfig
import org.apache.kafka.clients.producer.ProducerConfig
import org.apache.kafka.common.serialization.StringDeserializer
import org.apache.kafka.common.serialization.StringSerializer
import org.springframework.boot.autoconfigure.kafka.KafkaProperties
// some import statements omitted

@SuppressWarnings({"unchecked", "rawtypes"})
@Configuration
open class KafkaConfig() {
    @Autowired
    var kafkaProperties: KafkaProperties? = null

    @Value("#{kafkaApplication.sendingTopic}")
    var sendingTopicName: String? = null

    @Value("#{kafkaApplication.receivingTopic}")
    var receivingTopicName: String? = null

    constructor(kafkaProperties:KafkaProperties, sendingTopicName: String?,
    receivingTopicName: String?) : this() {
        this.kafkaProperties = kafkaProperties
        this.sendingTopicName = sendingTopicName
        this.receivingTopicName = receivingTopicName
    }

    @Bean // configs for the LetterSender
    open fun producerConfigs(): Map<String, Any> {
        val props: MutableMap<String, Any> = HashMap(
            kafkaProperties!!.buildProducerProperties()
        )
        props[ProducerConfig.KEY_SERIALIZER_CLASS_CONFIG] = StringSerializer::class.java
        props[ProducerConfig.VALUE_SERIALIZER_CLASS_CONFIG] = JsonSerializer::class.java
        return props
    }

    @Bean
    open fun producerFactory(): ProducerFactory<String, Any> {
        return DefaultKafkaProducerFactory(producerConfigs())
    }
```

```kotlin
@Bean
open fun kafkaTemplate(): KafkaTemplate<String, Any> {
    return KafkaTemplate(producerFactory())
}

@Bean // topic where Letters are sent
open fun sendingTopic(): NewTopic {
    return NewTopic(sendingTopicName, 1, 1.toShort())
}

@Bean // topic where to read letters from
open fun receivingTopic(): NewTopic {
    return NewTopic(receivingTopicName, 1, 1.toShort())
}

open fun consumerFactory(): ConsumerFactory<String, Any> {
    val jsonDeserializer = JsonDeserializer<Any>()
    jsonDeserializer.addTrustedPackages("*")
    return DefaultKafkaConsumerFactory(
        kafkaProperties!!.buildConsumerProperties(),
        StringDeserializer(),
        jsonDeserializer
    )
}

@Bean
open fun kafkaListenerContainerFactory(): ConcurrentKafkaListenerContainerFactory
<String, Any> {
    val factory = ConcurrentKafkaListenerContainerFactory<String, Any>()
    factory.consumerFactory = consumerFactory()
    return factory
}
}
```

In a Spring Boot application, all the Kafka-specific properties from the configuration are loaded into a KafkaProperties configuration bean. This bean is injected into the KafkaConfig class, so it can be extended with properties specific for a ProducerFactory<String,Any> or a ConsumerFactory<String, Any>—In this example we add serializers and deserializers, which are used to convert a Letter instance to a JSON representation before writing it to the topic, and vice versa when the message is consumed. Notice that the Letter type is not mentioned anywhere. The ProducerFactory only needs to know what to use to convert the message key and the message, because every message has to be identified uniquely by a unique key.

Before the application is started, the Apache Kafka cluster does not have any topics defined. A NewTopic bean is declared for each topic we need, which ensures a topic with the configured name is created if it doesn't already exist. A topic can be configured to be divided into multiple partitions and replicated across brokers. In our very simple example, both the number of partitions and the replication factor are set to 1.

The KafkaTemplate class is similar to JmsTemplate (and RestTemplate too), and a bean of this type is needed to execute high-level operations with Apache Kafka. The bean is thread-safe, and to produce messages the configured ProducerFactory<K, V> bean is used.

The ConsumerFactory<K, V> is needed to consume messages from a topic. For this simple scenario, we use Spring's DefaultKafkaConsumerFactory<K,V> implementation with a minimal configuration.

For messages to be consumed, they need to be picked up by a listener. To create one of those, beside the @KafkaListener attached to a consuming method, a ConcurrentKafkaListenerContainerFactory<K,V> is needed.

---

❶   The reason why none of the beans for producing and consuming messages are restricted to a certain type of message is that multiple types of messages can be written on the same queue, and read by different listeners, created by different ConcurrentKafkaListenerContainerFactory<K,V>.

Notice that Kafka properties are extracted from the Spring Boot configuration files and injected using @Value(value = "${spring.kafka.*}"), but custom properties like app.topic.sending.name need to first be declared as properties of the Spring Boot main configuration class and injected using SpEL.

The beans in this configuration must be injected in the beans used to produce and consume Letter instances. The class used to model a message producer is named LetterSender, because its responsibility is to send letters. The class is shown in Listing 13-26.

Listing 13-26. LetterSender Class and Bean Configuration

```kotlin
package com.apress.prospring6.thirteen

import org.springframework.beans.factory.annotation.Value
import org.springframework.kafka.core.KafkaTemplate
import org.springframework.stereotype.Service

@Service
class LetterSender {
    @Value("#{kafkaApplication.sendingTopic}")
    var sendingToTopicName: String? = null

    @Value("#{kafkaApplication.receivingTopic}")
    private val sender: String? = null // who is sending the letter
    private val kafkaTemplate: KafkaTemplate<String, Any>? = null

    // make application configurable
    fun send(letter: Letter) {
        log.info(">>>> [{}] Sending letter -> {}", sender, letter)
        kafkaTemplate!!.send(sendingToTopicName, UUID.randomUUID().toString(), letter)
    }

    companion object {
        val log = LoggerFactory.getLogger(LetterSender::class.java)
    }
}
```

The LetterSender bean needs the KafkaTemplate bean to send messages and the name of the topic the messages are sent to. There are multiple versions of the send(..) method, for example with parameters for choosing a partition and the time when the message was produced. There is also a version that returns a CompletableFuture<SendResult<K, V>>, which allows declaring a callback to be executed after the message is sent successfully.

kafkaApplication.receivingTopic is also the name of the application sending the messages and is injected in this bean for logging purposes.

The LetterSender bean is injected into the KafkaController, so sending a letter can be triggered via a POST request. The KafkaController class and bean configuration is shown in Listing 13-27.

Listing 13-27. KafkaController Class and Bean Configuration

```
package com.apress.prospring6.thirteen

import org.springframework.web.bind.annotation.*

@RestController
@RequestMapping(path = ["/kafka"])
class KafkaController {
    private var sender: LetterSender? = null

    constructor(sender:LetterSender) {
        this.sender = sender
    }

    @PostMapping(value = ["/send"])
    fun sendMessageToKafkaTopic(@RequestBody letter: Letter) {
        sender!!.send(letter)
    }
}
```

Now that you know how to send Letter instances to a topic, we'll demonstrate how you can consume them. The @KafkaListener was already mentioned, but where do we put it? On a method in a class called LetterReader, as shown in Listing 13-28.

Listing 13-28. LetterReader Class and Bean Configuration

```
package com.apress.prospring6.thirteen

import org.springframework.beans.factory.annotation.Value
import org.springframework.kafka.annotation.KafkaListener
import org.springframework.messaging.handler.annotation.Payload
import org.springframework.stereotype.Service

@Service
class LetterReader {
    @Value("#{kafkaApplication.receivingTopic}")
    private val receivingTopicName: String? = null // who is receiving the letter

    @KafkaListener(
        topics = ["#{kafkaApplication.receivingTopic}"],
        groupId = "\${spring.kafka.consumer.group-id}",
        clientIdPrefix = "json",
        containerFactory = "kafkaListenerContainerFactory"
    )
```

```kotlin
    fun consume(cr: ConsumerRecord<String?, Letter?>) {
        log.info("<<<< Receiving message at -> {}", cr.timestamp())
        log.info("<<<< Receiving message on topic -> {}", cr.topic())
        log.info("<<<< Receiving message on partition -> {}", cr.partition())
        log.info("<<<< Receiving message with headers -> {}", cr.headers())
        log.info("<<<< Receiving message with key -> {}", cr.key())
        log.info("<<<< Receiving message with value -> {}", cr.value())
    }

    companion object {
        val log = LoggerFactory.getLogger(LetterReader::class.java)
    }
}
```

The @KafkaListener annotation marks a method to be the target of a Kafka message listener. A listener needs to know the topics (yes, it can read messages from multiple topics) to read messages from, and this is configured using the topics attribute. If multiple groups are used and we want a listener to read messages only from a single group of topics, the groupId attribute is useful for that. And, since we want to make sure the message is converted correctly, we need to make sure the suitable listener is created, and this means specifying the suitable ConcurrentKafkaListenerContainerFactory<K,V> to use via the containerFactory method.

The consume(...) method can have various signatures, as long as Spring knows what to do with the message once consumed from the topic. The @Payload annotation from the org.springframework. messaging.handler.annotation package binds the body of a Kafka message to this method parameter and converts it to the appropriate type, in this case Letter. A different version of this method that consumes the entire messages as a ConsumerRecord<String, Letter> shows you how to run the two instances of the application.

The last class to examine is KafkaApplication, the main Spring Boot configuration class and runner, shown in Listing 13-29.

Listing 13-29. KafkaApplication Spring Boot Class

package com.apress.prospring6.thirteen;

```kotlin
@SpringBootApplication
open class KafkaApplication {
    @Value("\${app.sending.topic.name}")
    var sendingTopic: String? = null

    @Value("\${app.receiving.topic.name}")
    var receivingTopic: String? = null

    @Bean
    open fun initCmd(): CommandLineRunner {
        return CommandLineRunner { args: Array<String?>? ->
            log.info(
                " >>> Sender {}  ready to send letters to {} ",
                receivingTopic,
                sendingTopic
            )
        }
    }
}
```

```
    companion object {
        val log = LoggerFactory.getLogger(KafkaApplication::class.java)
        @JvmStatic
        fun main(args: Array<String>) {
            SpringApplication.run(KafkaApplication::class.java, *args)
        }
    }
}
```

Since this application is going to be started twice, once for Evelyn and once for Tom, a CommandLineRunner bean is created to show which application is running. The name of the topic where Letters are received is also the name of the application. As shown earlier in Figure 13-9, the application for Evelyn is started on port 8080, and the Tom application is started on 8090.

To start the two application instances, the way to go is either to configure different IntelliJ IDEA launchers or to build the application and start two instances using the JAR in different terminal windows using the commands shown in Listing 13-30.

Listing 13-30. Bash Commands to Start Two Instances of the Application

```
# starting Evelyn
java -jar build/libs/chapter13-kafka-boot-6.0-SNAPSHOT.jar --app.sending.topic.name=Tom
--app.receiving.topic.name=Evelyn --server.port=8080


# starting Tom
java -jar build/libs/chapter13-kafka-boot-6.0-SNAPSHOT.jar --app.sending.topic.name=Evelyn
--app.receiving.topic.name=Tom --server.port=8090
```

When we work on applications with multiple pieces, we like to have it all in separate IntelliJ terminals. As shown in Figure 13-11, there is a terminal where I run Docker Compose to start the Apache Kafka server, and another terminal with two windows where Evelyn and Tom can be seen running at the same time.

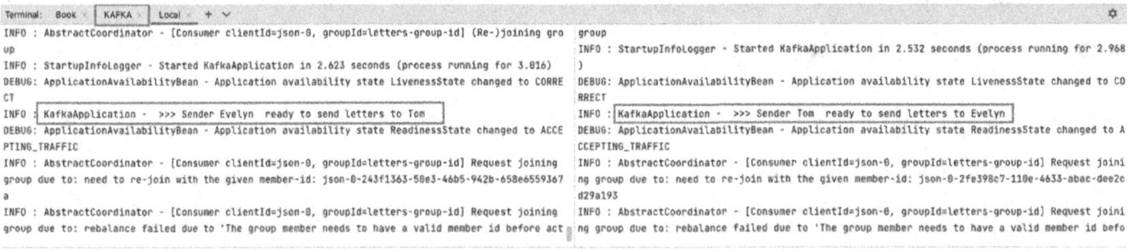

Figure 13-11. *IntelliJ IDEA terminals with Apache Kafka and two Spring Boot application instances running*

Requests can be made using curl [13] or Postman [14], or if you are using IntelliJ IDEA, you can use the HTTPie client. The request body to send a Letter from Evelyn to Tom, and vice versa, is shown in Listing 13-31.

---

[13] https://curl.se

[14] https://www.postman.com

Listing 13-31. POST Request for HTTPie to Send a Letter from the Two Application Instances to Each Other

```
### Evelyn sending letter message to Tom
POST http://localhost:8080/kafka/send
Content-Type: application/json

{
  "title": "To my Dear Friend",
  "sender": "HTTPIE",
  "sentOn" : "2022-12-04",
  "content" : "Haven't read anything written by you in a while. Miss you!"
}

### Tom sending letter message to Evelyn
POST http://localhost:8090/kafka/send
Content-Type: application/json

{
"title": "Miss you too",
"sender": "HTTPIE",
"sentOn" : "2022-12-05",
"content" : "Scotland is rather lovely this time of year. Would you like to visit?"
}
```

If you run the two requests, you will see both applications printing logs confirming the sending of a Letter and receiving one, as shown in Listing 13-32.

Listing 13-32. Evelyn Logs Confirming a Letter Is Sent and One Is Received

```
INFO : LetterSender - >>>> [Evelyn] Sending letter -> Letter[title=To my Dear Friend,
sender=HTTPIE, sentOn=2022-12-04, content=Haven't read anything written by you in a while.
Miss you!]
DEBUG: FrameworkServlet - Completed 200 OK
...
DEBUG: LogAccessor - Received: 1 records
INFO : LetterReader - <<<< [Evelyn] Reading letter ->
    Letter[
        title=Miss you too,
        sender=HTTPIE,
        sentOn=2022-12-05,
        content=Scotland is rather lovely this time of year. Would you like to visit?
    ]
```

The Tom application prints something similar.

It was mentioned previously that the method annotated with @KafkaListener can have a different signature, and all details of a message can be inspected, not only the body (payload). To achieve this, the method can be written as shown in Listing 13-33.

Listing 13-33. Evelyn Logs Confirming a Letter Is Sent and One Is Received

```
package com.apress.prospring6.thirteen

import org.apache.kafka.clients.consumer.ConsumerRecord
// other import statements omitted

@Service
class LetterReader {

    @KafkaListener(topics = ["#{kafkaApplication.receivingTopic}"],
            groupId = "${spring.kafka.consumer.group-id}",
            clientIdPrefix = "json",
            containerFactory = "kafkaListenerContainerFactory")
    fun consume(cr:ConsumerRecord<String, String>) {
        log.info("<<<< Receiving message at -> {}", cr.timestamp());
        log.info("<<<< Receiving message on topic -> {}", cr.topic());
        log.info("<<<< Receiving message on partition -> {}", cr.partition());
        log.info("<<<< Receiving message with headers -> {}", cr.headers());
        log.info("<<<< Receiving message with key -> {}", cr.key());
        log.info("<<<< Receiving message with value -> {}", cr.value());
    }

}
```

The ConsumerRecord<K, V> is part of the kafka-clients.jar library and, as you can see, it is a key/pair value mapping to the message identifier and payload, but also includes other useful information such as the topic name and partition number for where the message is received.

Listing 13-34 shows the output of this method when letters are being sent after this change.

Listing 13-34. Evelyn Logs Confirming a Letter Is Received As a ConsumerRecord<String, Letter>

```
INFO : LetterReader - <<<< Receiving message at -> 1671403710391
INFO : LetterReader - <<<< Receiving message on topic -> Evelyn
INFO : LetterReader - <<<< Receiving message on partition -> 0
INFO : LetterReader - <<<< Receiving message with headers -> RecordHeaders(headers = [],
isReadOnly = false)
INFO : LetterReader - <<<< Receiving message with key -> dcccbbe7-3b5f-4447-9c15-0272f45591a9
INFO : LetterReader - <<<< Receiving message with value ->
    Letter[
        title=Miss you too,
        sender=HTTPIE,
        sentOn=2022-12-05,
        content=Scotland is rather lovely this time of year. Would you like to visit?
    ]
```

Summary

In this chapter, we covered the most commonly used remoting techniques in Spring-based applications. For each scenario in this chapter, you've been shown how to send and receive messages. Communication between remote applications is a vast subject, and there are multiple technologies that can be used for this purpose. This chapter's purpose was to introduce you to the most common of them and give you an overall idea of how Spring applications can be designed to communicate with other applications, written with Spring or not.

Spring Boot was exclusively used for this chapter, as the focus was on the integration of Spring with each of the technologies, REST, JMS, and Apache Kafka.

In the next chapter, we discuss using Spring for writing web applications.

CHAPTER 14

Spring MVC

In an enterprise application, the presentation layer critically affects the users' level of acceptance of the application. The presentation layer is the front door into your application. It lets users perform business functions provided by the application, as well as presents a view of the information that is being maintained by the application. How the user interface performs greatly contributes to the success of the application. Because of the explosive growth of the Internet (especially these days), as well as the rise of different kinds of devices that people are using, developing an application's presentation layer is a challenging task.

The following are some major considerations when developing web applications:

- *Performance*: Performance is always the top requirement of a web application. If users choose a function or click a link and it takes a long time to execute (in the world of the Internet, three seconds is like a century!), users will definitely not be happy with the application.

- *User-friendliness*: The application should be easy to use and easy to navigate, with clear instructions that don't confuse the user.

- *Interactivity and richness*: The user interface should be highly interactive and responsive. In addition, the presentation should be rich in terms of visual presentation, such as charting, a dashboard type of interface, and so on.

- *Accessibility*: Nowadays, users require that the application is accessible from anywhere via any device. In the office, they will use their desktop to access the application. On the road, users will use various mobile devices (including laptops, tablets, and smartphones) to access the application.

Developing a web application to fulfill the previous requirements is not easy, but they are considered mandatory for business users. Fortunately, many new technologies and frameworks have been developed to address those needs. Many web application frameworks and libraries—such as Spring MVC (Spring Web Flow), Apache Struts, Tapestry, Faces (previously Java Server Faces), Google Web Toolkit (GWT), jQuery, React, and Dojo, to name a few—provide tools and rich component libraries that can help you develop highly interactive web front ends. Spring Web Flow[1] provides a Faces integration that lets you use the Faces UI Component Model with Spring Web Flow controllers. In addition, many frameworks provide tools or corresponding widget libraries targeting mobile devices such as smartphones and tablets. The rise of the HTML5[2] and CSS3[3] standards and the support of these latest standards by most web browsers and mobile device manufacturers also help ease the development of web applications that need to be available anywhere, from any device.

---

[1] https://spring.io/projects/spring-webflow
[2] https://en.wikipedia.org/wiki/HTML5
[3] https://developer.mozilla.org/en-US/docs/Web/CSS

In parallel with Spring MVC, starting with version 5.0, Spring Framework introduced a reactive-stack web framework named Spring WebFlux[4]. This stack will be covered succinctly in **Chapter 20**.

In terms of web application development, Spring provides comprehensive and intensive support. The Spring MVC module provides a solid infrastructure and Model View Controller (MVC) framework for web application development. When using Spring MVC, you can use various view technologies (for example, JSP or Velocity). In addition, Spring MVC integrates with many common web frameworks and toolkits (for example, Struts and GWT). Other Spring projects help address specific needs for web applications. For example, Spring MVC, when combined with the Spring Web Flow project and its Spring Faces module, provides comprehensive support for developing web applications with complex flows and for using Faces as the view technology. Simply speaking, there are many choices out there in terms of presentation layer development. This chapter focuses on Spring MVC and discusses how we can use the powerful features provided by Spring MVC to develop highly performing web applications.

Specifically, this chapter covers the following topics:

- *Spring MVC*: We discuss the main concepts of the MVC pattern and introduce Spring MVC. We present Spring MVC's core concepts, including its `WebApplicationContext` hierarchy and the request-handling life cycle.

- *i18n, locale, and theming*: Spring MVC provides comprehensive support for common web application requirements, including i18n (internationalization), locale, and theming. We discuss how to use Spring MVC to develop web applications that support those requirements.

- *View support*: The use of view technologies in Spring MVC is pluggable. In this chapter, we focus on using Thymeleaf as the view part of the web application, because it allows development of simple web pages without explicit use of JavaScript and other dynamic technologies. Anything else that you might want to use and that is supported by Spring, such as Groovy Markup Templates and JSPs, can be easily plugged in just with simple configuration changes.

- *File upload support*: Instead of integration with Apache Commons FileUpload, we discuss how to use Spring MVC with the Jakarta's Servlet 5.0 container's built-in multipart support for file upload.

Setting Up the Data and Lower Level Layers

A web application must provide access to manipulate data that is stored in a remote location, on a certain type of storage, usually a database. Up to this chapter, you were introduced to how to configure a Spring application to manage data using Spring Data Repositories and declare transactional beans to manage data within a transaction. These are the two data layers of an application; in this chapter you will be introduced to configuring the last layer of an application: the presentation layer, which is the web application or web console that the end user works with, unaware of which kind of application is going to perform the heavy lifting in the backend.

This chapter uses the same database structure used in previous chapters, but a new column, PHOTO, is added to the SINGER table. The new SINGER table creation script is shown in Listing 14-1.

---

[4] `https://docs.spring.io/spring-framework/docs/current/reference/html/web-reactive.html`

Listing 14-1. The Updated SINGER Table

```
CREATE TABLE SINGER (
                         ID INT NOT NULL AUTO_INCREMENT
    , VERSION INT NOT NULL DEFAULT 0
    , FIRST_NAME VARCHAR(60) NOT NULL
    , LAST_NAME VARCHAR(40) NOT NULL
    , BIRTH_DATE DATE
    , PHOTO LONGBLOB NULL
    , UNIQUE (FIRST_NAME, LAST_NAME)
    , PRIMARY KEY (ID)
);
```

The PHOTO column, of the binary large object (LONGBLOB) data type, will be used to store the photo of a singer using file upload. To create the database and the tables in it, a Docker container is needed. Creating the image for it and running it is described in the chapter14/CHAPTER14.adoc file that is part of the project for this chapter.

To manage SINGER records as Java objects, we use Singer instances. This class is configured as a Jakarta Persistence entity that is shown in Listing 14-2.

Listing 14-2. The Updated Singer Entity

```
package com.apress.prospring6.fourteen.entities

import jakarta.persistence.*
import jakarta.validation.*
import org.springframework.format.annotation.DateTimeFormat

@Entity
@Table(name = "SINGER")
class Singer : AbstractEntity() {
        @Column(name = "FIRST_NAME")
        var firstName: @NotEmpty @Size(min = 2, max = 30) String? = null

        @Column(name = "LAST_NAME")
        var lastName: @NotEmpty @Size(min = 2, max = 30) String? = null

        @DateTimeFormat(pattern = "yyyy-MM-dd")
        @Column(name = "BIRTH_DATE")
        var birthDate: LocalDate? = null

        @OneToMany(mappedBy = "singer")
        var albums: MutableSet<Album> = HashSet()

        @Basic(fetch = FetchType.LAZY)
        @Lob
        @Column(name = "PHOTO")
        lateinit var photo: ByteArray

        @ManyToMany
        @JoinTable(
                name = "SINGER_INSTRUMENT",
```

```kotlin
            joinColumns = [JoinColumn(name = "SINGER_ID")],
            inverseJoinColumns = [JoinColumn(name = "INSTRUMENT_ID")]
    )
    var instruments: MutableSet<Instrument> = mutableSetOf()

    fun addAlbum(album: Album): Boolean {
            album.singer = this
            return albums.add(album)
    }

    fun removeAlbum(album: Album) {
            albums.remove(album)
    }

    fun addInstrument(instrument: Instrument): Boolean {
            return instruments.add(instrument)
    }

    override fun equals(other: Any?): Boolean {
            if (this === other) return true
            if (other == null || javaClass != other.javaClass) return false
            val singer = other as Singer
            return if (id != null) {
                    id == other.id
            } else firstName == singer.firstName && lastName == singer.lastName
    }

    override fun hashCode(): Int {
            return Objects.hash(firstName, lastName)
    }

    override fun toString(): String {
            return ("Singer - Id: " + id + ", First name: " + firstName
                            + ", Last name: " + lastName + ", Birthday: " + birthDate)
    }

    companion object {
            @Serial
            private val serialVersionUID = 2L
    }
}
```

AbstractEntity is an abstract class containing fields common to all entity classes used in the application (id and version). Notice that most fields have validation annotations on them, which are useful to validate user-provided data. The @DateTimeFormat annotation is a Spring annotation that configures a field or method parameter that should be formatted as a date or time according to the format provided as an attribute.

ℹ️ The ALBUM and INSTRUMENT tables and the entities for them are part of the project, but there is enough ground to cover on Spring MVC by only working with `Singer` instances, so they won't be mentioned in this chapter.

For managing Singer instances, a simple Spring Data Repository interface is necessary, as shown in Listing 14-3.

Listing 14-3. The SingerRepo Interface

```
package com.apress.prospring6.fourteen.repos

import com.apress.prospring6.fourteen.entities.Singer
import org.springframework.data.jpa.repository.JpaRepository
import org.springframework.data.jpa.repository.Query
import org.springframework.data.repository.query.Param
import org.springframework.stereotype.Repository

import java.time.LocalDate

interface SingerRepo : JpaRepository<Singer, Long> {
    @Query("select s from Singer s where s.firstName=:fn")
    fun findByFirstName(@Param("fn") firstName: String): Iterable<Singer>

    @Query("select s from Singer s where s.firstName like %?1%")
    fun findByFirstNameLike(firstName: String): Iterable<Singer>

    @Query("select s from Singer s where s.lastName=:ln")
    fun findByLastName(@Param("ln") lastName: String): Iterable<Singer>

    @Query("select s from Singer s where s.lastName like %?1%")
    fun findByLastNameLike(lastName: String): Iterable<Singer>

    @Query("select s from Singer s where s.birthDate=:date")
    fun findByBirthDate(@Param("date") date: LocalDate): Iterable<Singer>
}
```

All the extra methods are invoked by the `SingerService` bean, to preform various operations with Singer instances. The `SingerService` interface declaring all the methods available in the implementation is shown in Listing 14-4.

Listing 14-4. The SingerService Interface

```
package com.apress.prospring6.fourteen.services

import com.apress.prospring6.fourteen.entities.Singer
import com.apress.prospring6.fourteen.problem.InvalidCriteriaException
import com.apress.prospring6.fourteen.util.CriteriaDto
import org.springframework.data.domain.Page
import org.springframework.data.domain.Pageable
```

```
import java.util.List

interface SingerService {
    fun findAll(): List<Singer>
    fun findById(id: Long): Singer
    fun save(singer: Singer): Singer
    fun delete(id: Long)
    fun findAllByPage(pageable: Pageable): Page<Singer>

    @Throws(InvalidCriteriaException::class)
    fun getByCriteriaDto(criteria: CriteriaDto): List<Singer>
}
```

The SingerServiceImpl class that implements SingerService is transactional and mostly wraps around SingerRepo methods, except for the getByCriteriaDto(..) method. This method is used to delegate to one of the customized find* methods in SingerRepo based on the CriteriaDto instance passed as an argument; its code will be shown later in the chapter when the context is more relevant.

The configuration for the first two layers is provided by two classes. The BasicDataSourceCfg class, introduced in **Chapter 8**, provides a way to interact with the MariaDB database. The TransactionCfg class, introduced in **Chapter 9**, provides the details for database operations to happen in a transactional environment. Feel free to review those two chapters if these two configuration classes that are part of the chapter-14 project look foreign.

Now that the two lower layers are set up, we are ready to start covering Spring MVC.

Introducing Spring MVC

Before moving on to implement the presentation layer, let's go through some major concepts of MVC as a pattern in web applications and how Spring MVC provides comprehensive support in this area.

In the following sections, we present these high-level concepts one by one. First, we give a brief introduction to MVC. Second, we present a high-level view of Spring MVC and its WebApplicationContext hierarchy. Finally, we discuss the request life cycle within Spring MVC.

Introducing MVC

MVC is a commonly used pattern in implementing the presentation layer of an application. The main principle of the MVC pattern is to define an architecture with clear responsibilities for different components. As its name implies, there are three participants within the MVC pattern:

- *Model*: A model represents the business data as well as the "state" of the application within the context of the user. For example, in an e-commerce website, the model usually includes the user profile information, shopping cart data, and order data if users purchase goods on the site.

- *View*: This presents the data to the user in the desired format, supports interaction with users, and supports client-side validation, i18n, styles, and so on.

- *Controller*: The controller handles requests for actions performed by users in the front end, interacting with the service layer, updating the model, and directing users to the appropriate view based on the result of execution.

Figure 14-1 illustrates a commonly used web application pattern, which can be treated as an enhancement to the traditional MVC pattern because of the introduction of Spring as a main component.

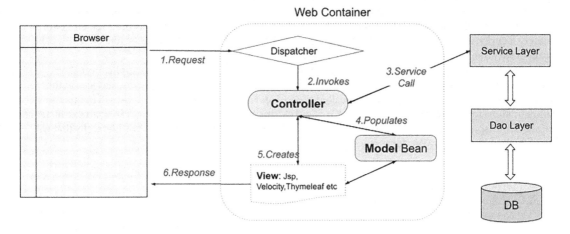

Figure 14-1. *The MVC pattern in a typical web application*

A normal view request is handled as follows:

1. *Request*: A request is submitted to the server. On the server side, most frameworks (for example, Spring MVC or Struts) have a dispatcher (in the form of a servlet) to handle the request.

2. *Invokes*: The dispatcher dispatches the request to the appropriate controller based on the HTTP request information and the web application configuration.

3. *Service call*: The controller interacts with the service layer.

4. *Model is populated*: The information obtained from the service layer is used by the controller to populate a model.

5. *View is created*: Based on the model, a view is created.

6. *Response*: The controller returns the corresponding view to the user.

Spring MVC Additions

In the Spring Framework, the Spring MVC module provides comprehensive support for the MVC pattern, with support for other features (for example, theming, i18n, validation, and type conversion and formatting) that ease the implementation of the presentation layer.

In the following sections, we discuss the main concepts of Spring MVC. Topics include Spring MVC's WebApplicationContext hierarchy, a typical request-handling life cycle, and configuration.

Spring MVC WebApplicationContext Hierarchy

In Spring MVC, DispatcherServlet is the central servlet that receives requests and dispatches them to the appropriate controllers. In a Spring MVC application, there can be any number of DispatcherServlet instances for various purposes (for example, handling user interface requests and RESTful-WS requests), and each `DispatcherServlet` instance has its own `WebApplicationContext` configuration, which defines the servlet-level characteristics, such as controllers supporting the servlet, handler mapping, view resolving, i18n, theming, validation, and type conversion and formatting.

Underneath the servlet-level `WebApplicationContext` configurations, Spring MVC maintains a root `WebApplicationContext`, which includes the application-level configurations such as the back-end data source, security, and service and persistence layer configuration. The root `WebApplicationContext` will be available to all servlet-level `WebApplicationContexts`.

Let's consider an example. Say we have two `DispatcherServlet` instances in an application. One servlet supports the user interface (called the *application servlet*), and the other provides services in the form of RESTful-WS to other applications (called the *RESTful servlet*). In Spring MVC, we will define the configurations for both the root `WebApplicationContext` instance and the `WebApplicationContext` instance for the two DispatcherServlet instances. Figure 14-2 shows the `WebApplicationContext` hierarchy that will be maintained by Spring MVC for this scenario.

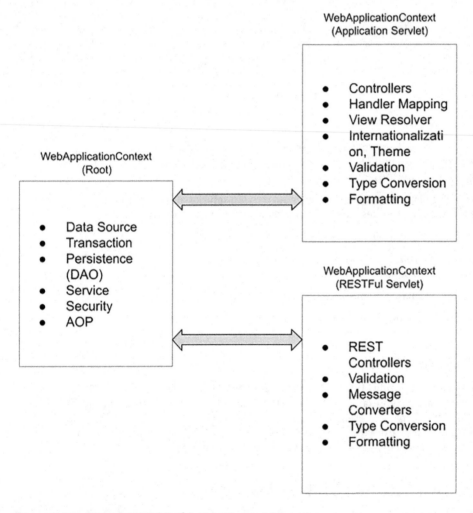

Figure 14-2. Spring MVC WebApplicationContext hierarchy

Spring MVC Request Life Cycle

Let's see how Spring MVC handles a request. Figure 14-3 shows the main components involved in handling a request in Spring MVC.

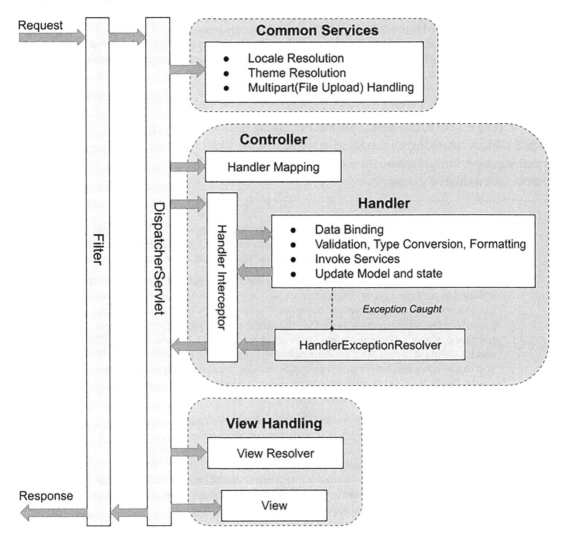

Figure 14-3. *Spring MVC Requests*

The main components and their purposes are as follows:

- *Filter*: The filter applies to every request. Several commonly used filters and their purposes are described in the next section.

- *Dispatcher servlet*: The servlet analyzes the requests and dispatches them to the appropriate controller for processing.1

- *Common services*: The common services will apply to every request to provide support, including i18n, theme, and file upload. Their configuration is defined in the DispatcherServlet's WebApplicationContext.

- *Handler mapping*: This maps incoming requests to handlers (a method within a Spring MVC controller class). Since Spring 2.5, in most situations the configuration is not required because Spring MVC will automatically register a HandlerMapping implementation out of the box that maps handlers based on HTTP paths expressed through the @RequestMapping annotation (and its extensions) at the type or method level within controller classes.

ℹ️ In Spring 2.5, DefaultAnnotationHandlerMapping was the default implementation. Starting with Spring 3.1, RequestMappingHandlerMapping has become the default implementation, which also supports request mapping to handlers defined without annotations, as long as the Spring conventions of naming controllers and methods are respected.

- *Handler interceptor*: In Spring MVC, you can register interceptors for the handlers for implementing common checking or logic. For example, a handler interceptor can check to ensure that the handlers can be invoked only during office hours.

- *Handler exception resolver*: In Spring MVC, the HandlerExceptionResolver interface (defined in package org.springframework.web.servlet) is designed to deal with unexpected exceptions thrown during request processing by handlers. By default, DispatcherServlet registers the DefaultHandlerExceptionResolver class (from package org.springframework.web.servlet.mvc.support). This resolver handles certain standard Spring MVC exceptions by setting a specific response status code. You can also implement your own exception handler by annotating a controller method with the @ExceptionHandler annotation and passing in the exception type as the attribute.

- *View Resolver*: Spring MVC's ViewResolver interface (from package org.springframework.web.servlet) supports view resolution based on a logical name returned by the controller. There are many implementation classes to support various view-resolving mechanisms. For example, the UrlBasedViewResolver class supports direct resolution of logical names to URLs. The ContentNegotiatingViewResolver class supports dynamic resolving of views depending on the media type supported by the client (such as XML, PDF, and JSON). There also exists a number of implementations to integrate with different view technologies, such as Thymeleaf[5] (ThymeleafViewResolver), FreeMarker[6] (FreeMarkerViewResolver), Velocity[7] (VelocityViewResolver), and JasperReports[8] (JasperReportsViewResolver).

These descriptions cover only a few commonly used handlers and resolvers. For a full description, please refer to the Spring Framework reference documentation and its Javadoc.

---

[5] https://www.thymeleaf.org
[6] https://freemarker.apache.org
[7] https://velocity.apache.org
[8] https://community.jaspersoft.com

Spring MVC Configuration

To enable Spring MVC within a web application, some initial configuration is required, especially for the web deployment descriptor web.xml. Since Spring 3.1, support has been available for code-based configuration within a Servlet 3.0 web container. This provides an alternative to the XML configuration required in the web deployment descriptor file (web.xml).

💡 If you are interested in using XML configuration, check out *Pro Spring 4*, the fourth edition of the Java variant of this book.

To configure Spring MVC support for web applications, we need to perform the following configurations for the web deployment descriptor:

- Configure the root WebApplicationContext
- Configure the servlet filters required by Spring MVC
- Configure the dispatcher servlets within the application

There are many ways to do this in Spring, but the easiest way is to extend AbstractAnnotationConfigDispatcherServletInitializer, a Spring utility class from the org.springframework.web.servlet.support, as shown in Listing 14-5.

Listing 14-5. Configuration Class for a Spring Web Application Context

```kotlin
package com.apress.prospring6.fourteen

import org.springframework.web.filter.CharacterEncodingFilter
import org.springframework.web.filter.HiddenHttpMethodFilter
import org.springframework.web.servlet.support.AbstractAnnotationConfigDispatcherServlet
Initializer

import jakarta.servlet.Filter
import java.nio.charset.StandardCharsets

class WebInitializer : AbstractAnnotationConfigDispatcherServletInitializer() {
    override fun getRootConfigClasses(): Array<Class<*>> {
        return arrayOf(BasicDataSourceCfg::class.java, TransactionCfg::class.java)
    }

    override fun getServletConfigClasses(): Array<Class<*>> {
        return arrayOf(WebConfig::class.java)
    }

    override fun getServletMappings(): Array<String> {
        return arrayOf("/")
    }

    override fun getServletFilters(): Array<Filter> {
        val cef = CharacterEncodingFilter().apply {
            encoding = StandardCharsets.UTF_8.name()
```

```
        setForceEncoding(true)
    }
    return arrayOf(HiddenHttpMethodFilter(), cef)
  }

}
```

The AbstractAnnotationConfigDispatcherServletInitializer class implements the org.
springframework.web.WebApplicationInitializer class. This interface needs to be implemented in
Servlet environments in order to configure the ServletContext programmatically. Spring provides more
than one implementation, as shown in Figure 14-4, depending on how complex the user customization
needs to be.

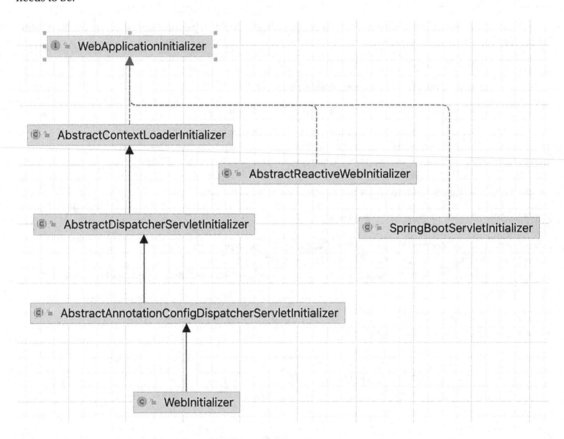

Figure 14-4. *Spring WebApplicationInitializer implementations*

In the previous example, the Spring class AbstractAnnotationConfigDispatcherServletInitializer
is used because it contains concrete implementations of methods needed for the configuration of Spring
web applications that use Kotlin-based Spring configuration.

All classes implementing the WebApplicationInitializer interface are automatically detected by the
org.springframework.web.SpringServletContainerInitializer class. Starting with Spring 6, this class
implements Servlet 3.0's jakarta.servlet.ServletContainerInitializer interface, which bootstraps
automatically in any Servlet 3.0 containers. As shown in Listing 14-5, the following methods were overridden
to plug in customized configurations:

- `getRootConfigClasses()`: A root application context of type `AnnotationConfigWebApplicationContext` will be created using the configuration classes returned by this method.

- `getServletConfigClasses()`: A web application context of type `AnnotationConfigWebApplicationContext` will be created using the configuration classes returned by this method.

- `getServletMappings()`: The `DispatcherServlet`'s mappings (context) are specified by the array of strings returned by this method.

- `getServletFilters()`: This method returns an array of implementations of `jakarta.servlet.Filter` that will be applied to every request.

Returning to the filters, Table 14-1 describes each of the filters in the array returned by `getServletFilters()`.

Table 14-1. *Commonly Used Spring MVC Servlet Filters*

Filter Class Full Name	Description
`org.springframework.web.filter.CharacterEncodingFilter`	This filter is used to specify the character encoding for the request.
`org.springframework.web.filter.HiddenHttpMethodFilter`	This filter provides support for HTTP methods other than GET and POST (for example, PUT).

▲ Although not needed here (and thus not used in the configuration), there is a filter implementation that should be mentioned: `org.springframework.orm.jpa.support.OpenEntityManagerInViewFilter`. This implementation binds a JPA `EntityManager` to the thread for the entire processing of the request. It is intended for the Open `EntityManager` in View pattern, allowing for lazy loading in web views despite the original transactions already being completed. Although practical, it is quite dangerous, as multiple requests might end up consuming all database-allowed open connections. Also, if the data set to load is big, the application might freeze. That is why developers prefer not to use it, instead having specific handlers called via Ajax requests to load the data in web-specific view objects (instead of entities).

Creating the First View in Spring MVC

Having the service layer and Spring MVC configuration in place, we can start to implement our first view. In this section, we will implement a simple view to display all singers that are saved in the SINGER table.

As mentioned at the beginning of chapter, Thymeleaf is used to design HTML pages. Thymeleaf is a modern server-side Java template engine for both web and stand-alone environments, and it integrates smoothly with Spring applications since it was created specifically for them. To integrate Thymeleaf with a Spring Web application, the Thymeleaf library needs to be on the classpath. And it is about time to list the dependencies of the chapter-14 project, which represents a Spring MVC application that is packed as a Web Application Archive (WAR) file and deployed on an Apache Tomcat 10[9] server.

---

[9] `https://tomcat.apache.org/download-10.cgi`

Figure 14-5 shows the dependencies of the chapter-14 project in the Gradle View.

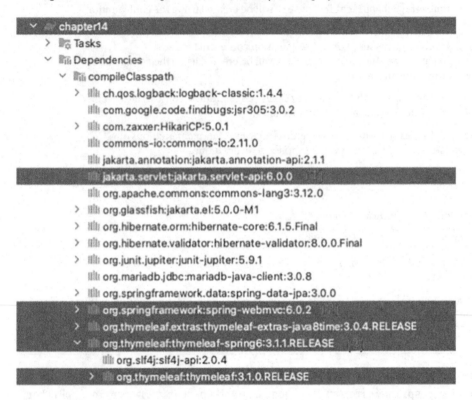

Figure 14-5. *Gradle View showing dependencies of the chapter-14 project*

The library marked with (1), jakarta.servlet-api library[10], is part of the Jakarta project and contains all the required interfaces, classes, and methods to develop a web application. To develop a Spring web application, we need to build on top of it. Version 6.0.0 of this library is suitable for a web application compatible with Apache Tomcat 10.

The library marked with (2), spring-webmvc, contains all the interfaces and classes used to develop a Spring Web application. Spring Web MVC is built on top of Servlet API and is part of the Spring Framework. Version 6.x is compatible with Jakarta EE 9.

The library marked with (3), thymeleaf-spring6, provides all interfaces and classes to integrate Thymeleaf with Spring.

Configuring DispatcherServlet

The next step is to configure DispatcherServlet. This is done by creating a configuration class that defines all infrastructure beans needed for a Spring web application. The Kotlin Config–based class for the chapter-14 project is depicted in Listing 14-6.

---

[10] https://projects.eclipse.org/projects/ee4j.servlet

Listing 14-6. Configuration Class for Spring's DispatcherServlet

```
package com.apress.prospring6.fourteen

import org.springframework.context.annotation.Description
import org.springframework.web.servlet.DispatcherServlet
import org.springframework.web.servlet.ViewResolver
import org.springframework.web.servlet.config.annotation.*
import org.thymeleaf.extras.java8time.dialect.Java8TimeDialect
import org.thymeleaf.spring6.SpringTemplateEngine
import org.thymeleaf.spring6.templateresolver.SpringResourceTemplateResolver
import org.thymeleaf.spring6.view.ThymeleafViewResolver
import org.thymeleaf.templatemode.TemplateMode

@Configuration
@EnableWebMvc
@ComponentScan(basePackages = ["com.apress.prospring6.fourteen"])
open class WebConfig : WebMvcConfigurer, ApplicationContextAware {
    private var applicationContext: ApplicationContext? = null

    @Throws(BeansException::class)
    override fun setApplicationContext(applicationContext: ApplicationContext) {
        this.applicationContext = applicationContext
    }

    @Bean
    open fun templateResolver() =
        SpringResourceTemplateResolver().apply {
            setApplicationContext(applicationContext!!)
            prefix = "/WEB-INF/views/"
            suffix = ".html"
            templateMode = TemplateMode.HTML
            isCacheable = false
        }

    @Bean
    @Description("Thymeleaf Template Engine")
    open fun templateEngine() = SpringTemplateEngine().apply {
            addDialect(Java8TimeDialect())
            setTemplateResolver(templateResolver())
            setTemplateEngineMessageSource(messageSource())
            enableSpringELCompiler = true
        }

    @Bean
    @Description("Thymeleaf View Resolver")
    open fun viewResolver() = ThymeleafViewResolver().apply {
            templateEngine = templateEngine()
            order = 1
        }
```

```kotlin
    // Declare our static resources. We added cache to the java config but it is not
        required.
    override fun addResourceHandlers(registry: ResourceHandlerRegistry) {
        super.addResourceHandlers(registry)
        registry.addResourceHandler("/images/**", "/styles/**")
            .addResourceLocations("/images/", "/styles/")
    }

    override fun configureDefaultServletHandling(configurer:
            DefaultServletHandlerConfigurer) {
        configurer.enable();
    }
    override fun addViewControllers(registry: ViewControllerRegistry) {
        registry.addRedirectViewController("/", "/home")
    }

}
```

The interface WebMvcConfigurer defines callback methods to customize the Kotlin-based configuration and Spring MVC gets enabled by using @EnableWebMvc. Although there can be more than one Kotlin-based configuration class in a Spring application, only one is allowed to be annotated with @EnableWebMvc. In Listing 14-6, you can observe that several methods are overridden to customize the configuration:

- addResourceHandlers(..): Adds handlers that are used to serve static resources such as images, JavaScript, and CSS files from specific locations under the web application root, the classpath, and others. In this customized implementation, any request with the URL containing resources will be treated by a special handler that bypasses all filters. The method defines the locations of the static resource files, which enables Spring MVC to handle the files within those folders efficiently. Within the tag, the location attribute defines the folders for the static resources. The WebMvcConfigurer.super.addResourceHandlers(registry) invocation indicates the root folder for the web application, which is by default /src/main/webapp. The resource handler path, /styles/**, defines the URL for mapping to CSS resources; as an example, for the URL http://localhost:8080/ch14/styles/standard. css, Spring MVC will retrieve the file standard.css from the folder /src/main/webapp/styles.

- configureDefaultServletHandling(..): Enables the mapping of DispatcherServlet to the web application's root context URL, while still allowing static resource requests to be handled by the container's default servlet.

- addViewControllers(..): Defines simple automated controllers preconfigured with the response status code and/or a view to render the response body. These views have no controller logic and are used to render a welcome page, perform simple site URL redirects, return a 404 status, and more. In Listing 14-6, we are using this method to perform a redirection to the home view, when the root (/) of the site is accessed, which basically turns the home page into a front page.

- viewResolver(..): Declares a view resolver of type ThymeleafViewResolver that matches symbolic view names to *.html templates under /WEB-INF/views. Thymeleaf is a templating tool, generating views per logical names by combining more fragments; this job is being performed by the

SpringResourceTemplateResolver bean declared in this configuration. The final view is a HTML page built by replacing Thymeleaf special constructs with HTML elements compiled together with Spring view data, and this is being taken care of by the SpringTemplateEngine.

Implementing Spring Controllers

The home view is simple and is the best example to introduce Spring controllers. *Spring controllers* are special beans annotated with the special stereotype annotation @Controller and its extensions like @RestController, covered in **Chapter 15**.

The HomeController class is depicted in Listing 14-7.

Listing 14-7. HomeController Class and Bean Declaration

```
package com.apress.prospring6.fourteen.controllers

import org.springframework.stereotype.Controller
import org.springframework.ui.Model
import org.springframework.web.bind.annotation.RequestMapping
import org.springframework.web.bind.annotation.RequestMethod

@Controller
class HomeController {
    @GetMapping(path = ["home"])
    fun home(model: Model): String {
        model.addAttribute("message", "Spring MVC ThymeleafExample!!")
        return "home"
    }
}
```

The annotation @Controller is applied to the class, indicating that it's a Spring MVC controller. The @RequestMapping annotation indicates the URL that will be handled by the method the annotation is placed on. The controller class is sometimes called a *handler*, because it handles requests, and the methods are called *handler methods*, because they handle requests too. Usually the handler methods handle requests that have a common root path declared using a @RequestMapping annotation at the class level; the controller class is just a way of grouping them together.

The @RequestMapping annotation placed on the home(..) method is mapped to the HTTP GET method via the method attribute. This means that any GET request to the URL /home will be handled by this method. Within the body of this method, "Spring MVC ThymeleafExample!!" is set as a value for the message property on the Model object. In the DispatcherServlet configuration, ThymeleafViewResolver is configured as the view resolver, with the file prefix /WEB-INF/views/ and the suffix .html. As a result, Spring MVC will pick up the file /WEB-INF/views/singers/home.html as the view and render it using the data in the Model object.

Implementing the View

The home.html Thymeleaf template is quite simple, as you can see in Listing 14-8

Listing 14-8. The Contents of the /WEB-INF/views/singers/home.html Thymeleaf View File

```
<!DOCTYPE HTML>
<html xmlns:th="http://www.thymeleaf.org">

    <head th:replace="~{templates/layout :: pageTitle('Singers Home Page')}"></head>

    <body>
        <div class="container">
            <header th:replace="~{templates/layout :: pageHeader}" ></header>

            <header th:replace="~{templates/layout :: pageMenu}" ></header>

            <section th:fragment="~{templates/layout :: pageContent}">
                <p th:text="Home Page" ></p>
                <p th:text="${message}" ></p>
            </section>

            <footer th:replace="~{templates/layout :: pageFooter}" ></footer>
        </div>
    </body>
</html>
```

This template should look pretty familiar to anyone who has seen HTML code. The only extra parts are all the elements prefixed with th:. The reason this template looks so simple is that the biggest parts are in a different template called a *layout*. This template contains the general layout of the site, and for each view, Thymeleaf replaces pieces of it with scoped ones. The general template of the site is located under chapter14/src/main/webapp/WEB-INF/views/templates/ and is named layout.html. Since the focus of this book is Spring, not Thymeleaf, and layout.html is quite big, it won't be shown here (feel free to check it out yourself in the boom project repo); only small Thymeleaf constructs are explained. The Thymeleaf constructs in Listing 14-8 are explained here:

- th:replace: Substitutes the <head> tag in the home.html template with the fragment from templates/layout.html, but substitutes the title with the one provided as a parameter for the custom function pageTitle(..).

- th:fragment: Substitutes the fragment from templates/layout.html with the fragment declared in the home.html. In this example the pageContent section declared in the templates/layout.html is a very simple generic one, so in each inheriting view it needs to be replaced with an appropriate one.

Testing the Home View

The view files are located under the WEB-INF directory located under the webapp directory that groups all the web resources. The internal structure of the project is the typical Maven one for a web project, and various plug-ins are configured for Gradle to build the project into a WAR file that can be deployed on an Apache Tomcat server. The structure of the project is displayed in Figure 14-6 (the .pom build file for Maven is not part of the Kotlin project sources, since we concentrate on Gradle).

648

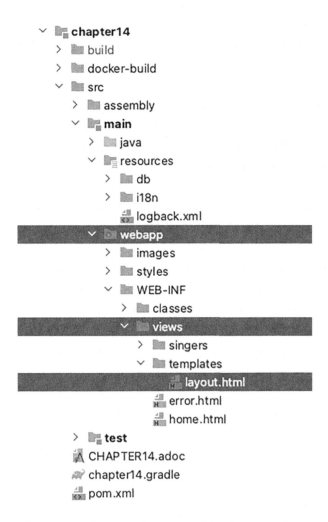

Figure 14-6. *The internal structure of* chapter-14 *project*

Testing the home.html view can be done in two ways:

- Write a Spring MVC test to test the mapping of the view and the population of the model.

- Build the project, deploy the resulting WAR file to a local Apache Tomcat, and check the home page.

Writing a test for a very simple view and controller is pretty simple. When the application context becomes more complex and more dependencies must be wired, it might be more complicated but not impossible. Listing 14-9 shows the test class and method that check the proper mapping of the /home path to the HomeController#home(..) method and the population of the model for the home.html view.

Listing 14-9. Testing the HomeController and the home.html View

```
package com.apress.prospring6.fourteen.controllers

import com.apress.prospring6.fourteen.WebConfig
import org.junit.jupiter.api.Test
import org.springframework.test.context.junit.jupiter.web.SpringJUnitWebConfig
import org.springframework.test.web.servlet.MockMvc
import org.springframework.test.web.servlet.request.MockMvcRequestBuilders
import org.springframework.test.web.servlet.setup.MockMvcBuilders
import org.springframework.web.context.WebApplicationContext

import org.hamcrest.Matchers.containsString
import org.springframework.test.web.servlet.result.MockMvcResultHandlers.print
import org.springframework.test.web.servlet.result.MockMvcResultMatchers.*

@SpringJUnitWebConfig(classes = [WebConfig::class])
class HomeControllerTest(wac: WebApplicationContext) {
    var mockMvc: MockMvc

    init {
        mockMvc = MockMvcBuilders.webAppContextSetup(wac).build()
    }

    @Test
    @Throws(Exception::class)
    fun testHome() {
        mockMvc.perform(MockMvcRequestBuilders.get("/home"))
            .andDo(MockMvcResultHandlers.print())
            .andExpect(MockMvcResultMatchers.status().isOk())
            .andExpect(MockMvcResultMatchers.view().name("home"))
            .andExpect(
                MockMvcResultMatchers.content()
                    .string(Matchers.containsString("Spring MVC ThymeleafExample!!"))
            )
    }
}
```

MockMvc is built on Servlet API mock implementations from the `spring-test` module and does not rely on a running container, but it still needs the `servlet-api` dependency. This is not an end-to-end test, and it works because the HomeController does not invoke a service and/or a repository.

The `MockMvcRequestBuilders.get(..)` method creates a MockHttpServletRequest instance that is configured with the parameters set for it to create a valid request. MockMvc performs the request on the context configured via the @SpringJUnitWebConfig annotation. This annotation is a special Spring Test annotation used to configure test context for Spring web applications. It is meta-annotated with @ExtendWith(SpringExtension.class) used to register the SpringExtension that integrates the Spring TestContext Framework into JUnit 5's Jupiter programming model.

It is also meta-annotated with @ContextConfiguration used to determine how to load and configure an ApplicationContext for integration tests. And it is meta-annotated with @WebAppConfiguration used to configure that a WebApplicationContext should be loaded for the test using a default for the path to the root of the web application.

The test checks all the important parts of a response:

- That the HTTP response code is the expected one through the .andExpect(status().isOk()) matcher

- That the logical view name is the expected one through the .andExpect(view(). name("home")) matcher

- That the attribute set on the Spring Model instance was added to the rendered view through the .andExpect(content().string(containsString("Spring MVC ThymeleafExample!!"))) matcher

The other method of checking that the home page is rendered correctly is by actually deploying the application. For this you have to do the following:

- Build the project, which generates the build/libs/chapter14-6.0-SNAPSHOT.war.

- Download and install Apache Tomcat 10.

 On Unix-based systems you might need to make all scripts under $TOMCAT_HOME/bin executable.

- Deploy the chapter14-6.0-SNAPSHOT.war, by using an IntelliJ IDEA Tomcat launcher.

To create an Apache Tomcat launcher, follow the instructions on the IntelliJ Official page[11].

You cannot create Tomcat launchers in the Community Edition of IntelliJ IDEA. However, you still can add custom deployment tasks to your build.gradle file.

In Figure 14-7 you can see that the Deployment tab is used to add the web artifact to the launcher. When added in exploded form, the launcher can be started in Debug mode and breakpoints from the code will pause the application to allow runtime debugging.

---

[11] https://www.jetbrains.com/help/idea/configuring-and-managing-application-server-integration.html

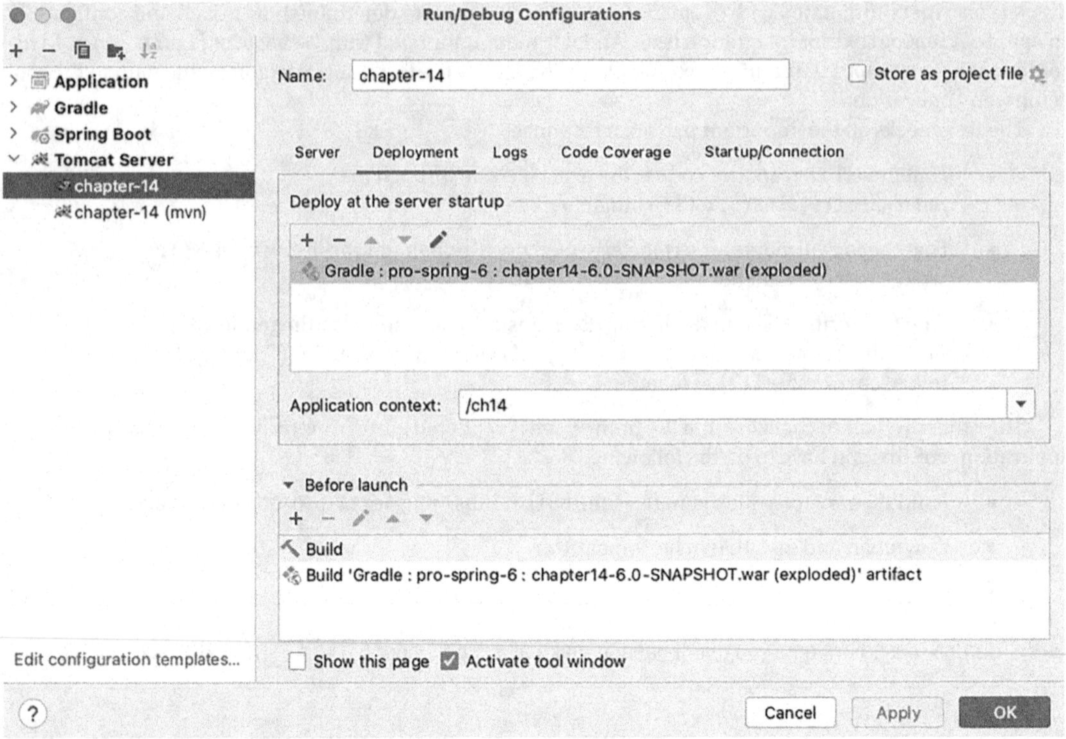

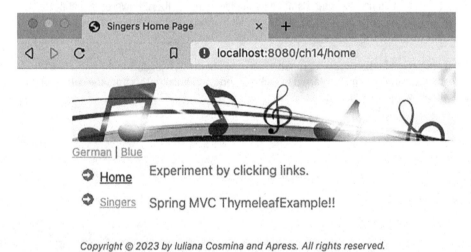

Figure 14-7. *IntelliJ IDEA launcher for the* chapter-14 *project*

Once a launcher is in place, you can start the application, and when the application is fully deployed, IntelliJ tries to open a web page with the http://localhost:8080/ch14/home location. If the page is loaded correctly, you should see a page that looks like the one shown in Figure 14-8.

Figure 14-8. *IntelliJ IDEA launcher for the* chapter-14 *project*

Now we have our first view working. In the upcoming sections, we will enrich the application with more views and enable support of i18n, themes, error handling, and so on.

Understanding the Spring MVC Project Structure

Before diving into the implementation of the various aspects of a web application, let's take a look at what the project structure in the sample web application developed in this chapter looks like.

Typically, in a web application, a lot of files are required to support various features. For example, there are a lot of static resource files, such as style sheets, JavaScript files, images, and component libraries. Then there are files that support presenting the interface in various languages. And, of course, there are the view pages that will be parsed and rendered by the web container, as well as the layout and definition files that will be used by the templating framework (for example, Thymeleaf) to provide a consistent look and feel of the application.

It's always good practice to store files that serve different purposes in a well-structured folder hierarchy to give you a clear picture of the various resources being used by the application and ease ongoing maintenance work.

The project structure was already introduced via Figure 14-6. Table 14-2 describes the folder structure of the web application that is developed in this chapter. Note that the structure presented here is not mandatory but is commonly used in the developer community for web application development.

Table 14-2. *Sample Web Project Folder Structure Description*

Folder Name	Purpose
images	Stores images used to style the site: logos, bullets, etc.
styles	Stores the style sheet files in supporting the CSS styles, look and feel for the site.
WEB-INF/classes	Stores property files for theme cookies configuration.
WEB-INF/views	Stores template files for creating views, in this case Thymeleaf templates.
resources/i18n	Stores files for supporting i18n. The file application*.properties stores the layout-related text (for example, page titles, field labels, and menu titles). The message*.properties file stores various messages (for example, success and error messages and validation messages). The sample will support both English (US) and German(DE). The i18n directory contains internationalization resources files. The files could have been placed under WEB-INF/i18n, but for easier migration to Spring Boot at the end of the chapter, it was placed under resources.

ⓘ   Sometimes there might also be a webapp/scripts directory containing generic JavaScript files necessary to make the pages dynamic. There might also be other directories specific to JavaScript frameworks used like jQuery[12] or jqgrid[13]. For the simple example in this chapter, no such files are needed.

---

[12] https://jquery.com
[13] http://www.trirand.com/blog

Most web files mentioned in Table 14-2 will not be shown here. Given that, we recommend you download a copy of the source code for this chapter and extract it to a temporary folder so that you can copy the files required into the project directly.

Enabling Internationalization (i18n)

When developing web applications, it's always good practice to enable i18n in the early stages. The main work is to externalize the user interface text and messages into properties files.

Even though you may not have i18n requirements on day one, it's good to externalize the language related settings so that it will be easier later when you need to support more languages.

With Spring MVC, enabling i18n is simple. First, externalize the language-related user interface settings into various properties files within the /resources/i18n folder, as described in Table 14-2. Because we will support both English (US) and German (DE), you will need two files. The global.properties file stores the settings for the default locale, which in this case is English (US). The global_de.properties file stores the settings in the German (DE) language.

Configuring i18n in the DispatcherServlet Configuration

Having the language files in place, the next step is to configure the DispatcherServlet instance's WebApplicationContext for i18n support. For this we need to declare a MessageSource bean in the WebConfig class introduced in Listing 14-6, inject it in the template resolver, and add request interceptors to replace all message codes in view templates with test representations in the configured language. The configuration modifications to support internationalization are depicted in Listing 14-10.

Listing 14-10. Adding Internationalization Configuration Class for Spring's DispatcherServlet

```
package com.apress.prospring6.fourteen

import org.springframework.context.MessageSource
import org.springframework.context.support.ReloadableResourceBundleMessageSource
import org.springframework.web.servlet.i18n.LocaleChangeInterceptor
import org.springframework.web.servlet.mvc.WebContentInterceptor
import org.springframework.web.servlet.config.annotation.InterceptorRegistry
import org.springframework.web.servlet.i18n.CookieLocaleResolver
// other import statements omitted

@Configuration
@EnableWebMvc
@ComponentScan(basePackages = ["com.apress.prospring6.fourteen"])
open class WebConfig : WebMvcConfigurer, ApplicationContextAware {
    private var applicationContext: ApplicationContext? = null

    @Bean
    @Description("Thymeleaf Template Engine")
    open fun templateEngine() = SpringTemplateEngine().apply {
            addDialect(Java8TimeDialect())
            setTemplateResolver(templateResolver())
            setTemplateEngineMessageSource(messageSource())
            enableSpringELCompiler = true
    }
```

```kotlin
override fun addInterceptors(registry: InterceptorRegistry) {
    with(registry){
        addInterceptor(localeChangeInterceptor()).addPathPatterns("/*")
        addInterceptor(themeChangeInterceptor())
        addInterceptor(webChangeInterceptor())
    }
}

@Bean
open fun messageSource(): MessageSource
    = ReloadableResourceBundleMessageSource().apply {
        setBasename("classpath:i18n/global")
        setDefaultEncoding(StandardCharsets.UTF_8.name())
        setUseCodeAsDefaultMessage(true)
        setFallbackToSystemLocale(true)
        // # -1 : never reload, 0 always reload
        // setCacheSeconds(0);
    }

@Bean
open fun localeChangeInterceptor() = LocaleChangeInterceptor().apply {
        paramName = "lang"
    }

@Bean
open fun localeResolver() = CookieLocaleResolver("locale").apply {
        setDefaultLocale(Locale.ENGLISH)
        setCookieMaxAge(Duration.ofHours(1))
    }
    ...
}
```

In this version of the configuration, the MessageSource bean is declared as a ReloadableResourceBundleMessageSource instance. The ReloadableResourceBundleMessageSource class implements the MessageSource interface, which loads the messages from the defined files (in this case, the global*.properties in the /resources/i18n folder) to support i18n.

Note the property fallbackToSystemLocale. This property instructs Spring MVC whether to fall back to the locale of the system that the application is running on when a special resource bundle for the client locale isn't found. The instance is configured using the location of the property files, classpath:i18n/global, which means they are expected to be on the application classpath, and thus under the resources directory at development time. The encoding is also configured, and in case a message code is used in the view files without a value configured for it in the resource files, the code is used as value.

A Spring MVC interceptor with class LocaleChangeInterceptor is defined, which intercepts all the requests to DispatcherServlet. The interceptor supports locale switching with a configurable request parameter. From the interceptor configuration, the URL parameter with the name lang is defined for changing the locale for the application and is customizable, so you can use a different one if you want.

Finally, a bean with the CookieLocaleResolver class is defined. This class supports the storage and retrieval of locale settings from the user browser's cookie.

Modifying Views for i18n Support

Now that internationalization support is configured, the view template files must be modified to support internationalization. The home.html view introduced previously does not have any elements needing internationalization, so to show how internationalization is supported in Thymeleaf templates, a snippet from the views/templates/layout.html file is shown in Listing 14-11.

Listing 14-11. views/templates/layout.html Snippet

```html
<!DOCTYPE HTML>
<html xmlns:th="http://www.thymeleaf.org"
    th:with="lang=${#locale.language}"
    th:lang="${lang}">

<head th:fragment="pageTitle(title)">
    <link rel="icon" type="image/png" th:href="@{/images/favicon.ico}">
    <link rel="stylesheet" type="text/css" th:href="@{/styles/bootstrap.min.css}">
    <meta http-equiv="Content-Type" content="text/html; charset=UTF-8" />
    <title th:text="${title}"> Layout Page </title>
    <link type="text/css" rel="stylesheet" th:href="@{/styles/general.css}" >
</head>

<body>
    <header th:fragment="pageHeader" class="page-header">
        <div class="row">
            <div class="col-lg-8 col-md-7 col-sm-6">
                <div class="banner"></div>
                <div class="themeLocal">
                    <span th:if="${#locale.language eq 'en'}">
                        <a th:href="@{/?lang=de}" th:text="#{locale.de}">DE</a>
                    </span>
                    <span th:unless="${#locale.language eq 'en'}">
                        <a th:href="@{/?lang=en}" th:text="#{locale.en}">EN</a>
                    </span>
                </div>
            </div>
        </div>
    </header>

    <section th:fragment="pageMenu">
        <!-- code omitted-->
    </section>

    <section th:fragment="pageContent">
        <div class="content">
            <p>Page Content</p>
        </div>
    </section>
```

```
<footer th:fragment="pageFooter">
    <div class="footer">
        <p th:text="#{footer.text}"></p>
    </div>
</footer>
</html>
```

The HTML lang attribute is used to identify the language of text content on the Web. The th:lang construct populates this attribute with the value of the lang parameter set by the LocaleChangeInterceptor on each request. Because we defined LocaleChangeInterceptor in DispatcherServlet's WebApplicationContext, Spring MVC stores the locale setting in your browser's cookie (with the name locale), and by default, the cookie is kept for the user session. If you want to persist the cookie for a longer time, in the CookieLocaleResolver bean definition, you can override the property cookieMaxAge, which is inherited from the class org.springframework.web.util.CookieGenerator, by calling setCookieMaxAge(...).

To switch to English (US), you can change the URL in your browser to reflect ?lang=en, and the page will switch back to English. Since the properties file named global_en.properties is not provided, Spring MVC falls back to use the default file global.properties, which stores the properties in the default language of the site, of English.

Locale-specific values will be accessed using the keys with the syntax #{key}, where key is the message key in the internationalization properties files.

Using Theming and Templating

Besides i18n, a web application requires an appropriate look and feel (for example, a business website needs a professional look and feel, while a social website needs a more vivid style), as well as a consistent layout so that users will not get confused while using the web application.

⚠️ Currently, the approach is to keep the website separate from the back end and create the website using evolved JavaScript frameworks like React[14] and TypeScript[15] that interact with a Spring REST Web application for data management and other high-level operations. This means, that the user interface will be mostly static. This is why the ThemeChangeInterceptor, ResourceBundleThemeSource, and CookieThemeResolver types that will be covered in this section are marked as deprecated in Spring 6.x, but no replacement is recommended.

Theming Support

Spring MVC provides comprehensive support for theming, and enabling it in web applications is easy. For this reason, we'll start with the Spring theming configurations, that need to be added to the WebConfig class, as shown in Listing 14-12.

---

[14] https://reactjs.org
[15] https://www.typescriptlang.org

Listing 14-12. WebConfig Theming Configuration

```
package com.apress.prospring6.fourteen

import org.springframework.ui.context.support.ResourceBundleThemeSource
import org.springframework.web.servlet.theme.CookieThemeResolver
import org.springframework.web.servlet.theme.ThemeChangeInterceptor
// other import statements omitted

@Configuration
@EnableWebMvc
@ComponentScan(basePackages = ["com.apress.prospring6.fourteen"])
open class WebConfig : WebMvcConfigurer, ApplicationContextAware {
    private var applicationContext: ApplicationContext? = null

    @Throws(BeansException::class)
    override fun setApplicationContext(applicationContext: ApplicationContext) {
        this.applicationContext = applicationContext
    }

    @Bean
    open fun themeSource() = ResourceBundleThemeSource()

    @Bean
    open fun themeChangeInterceptor() = ThemeChangeInterceptor().apply {
            paramName = "theme"
        }

    @Bean
    open fun themeResolver() = CookieThemeResolver().apply {
            defaultThemeName = "green"
            cookieMaxAge = 3600
            cookieName = "theme"
        }

    override fun addInterceptors(registry: InterceptorRegistry) {
        with(registry){
            addInterceptor(localeChangeInterceptor()).addPathPatterns("/*")
            addInterceptor(themeChangeInterceptor())
            addInterceptor(webChangeInterceptor())
        }
    }
    ...

}
```

The first bean, of type ResourceBundleThemeSource, is responsible for loading the ResourceBundle bean of the active theme. For example, if the active theme is called blue, the bean will look for the file blue. properties as the ResourceBundle bean of the theme. The property files for the two themes are located under WEB-INF/classes. The files are named blue.properties and green.properties and they match the blue and green theme. The content of the files is represented by the theme name as a property and other properties pointing to images and paths to CSS files specific to the team. For example, the content of the green.properties file is shown in Listing 14-13.

Listing 14-13. green.properties File Contents

```
css.style=/styles/decorator-green.css
banner.image=/images/banner-green.png
name=green
```

The new interceptor bean of type ThemeChangeInterceptor intercepts every request to add the theme parameter.

The bean of type CookieThemeResolver is used to resolve the active theme for users. The property defaultThemeName defines the default theme to use, which is the green theme. Note that as its name implies, the CookieThemeResolver class uses cookies to store the theme for the user. There is also a bean of type SessionThemeResolver that stores the *theme* attribute in a user's session, but in order to use it we would have to add security to our app, and we do not want to do that right now.

Now that theming is configured, there is not much change to be done. In the views/templates/layout. html file, we only need to add support for the theme parameter and add a menu option to change the theme, in the same way it was added for locale, as shown in Listing 14-14.

Listing 14-14. views/templates/layout.html Snippet

```html
<!DOCTYPE HTML>
<html xmlns:th="http://www.thymeleaf.org"
    th:with="lang=${#locale.language}, theme=${#themes.code('name')}"
    th:lang="${lang}"
    th:theme="${theme}">

<head th:fragment="pageTitle(title)">
    <link rel="icon" type="image/png" th:href="@{/images/favicon.ico}">
    <link rel="stylesheet" type="text/css" th:href="@{/styles/bootstrap.min.css}">
    <meta http-equiv="Content-Type" content="text/html; charset=UTF-8" />
    <title th:text="${title}"> Layout Page </title>
    <link type="text/css" rel="stylesheet" th:with="cssStyle=${#themes.code('css.style')}"
    th:href="@{(${cssStyle})}" >
    <link type="text/css" rel="stylesheet" th:href="@{/styles/general.css}" >
</head>

<body>
    <header th:fragment="pageHeader" class="page-header">
        <div class="row">
            <div class="col-lg-8 col-md-7 col-sm-6">
                <div class="banner"></div>
                <div class="themeLocal">
                    <span th:if="${#locale.language eq 'en'}">
                        <a th:href="@{/?lang=de}" th:text="#{locale.de}">DE</a>
                    </span>
                    <span th:unless="${#locale.language eq 'en'}">
                        <a th:href="@{/?lang=en}" th:text="#{locale.en}">EN</a>
                    </span> |
                    <span th:if="${#themes.code('name') eq 'green'}">
                        <a th:href="@{/?theme=blue}" th:text="#{theme.Blue}">BLUE</a>
                    </span>
```

```
                    <span th:unless="${#themes.code('name') eq 'green'}">
                        <a th:href="@{/?theme=green}" th:text="#{theme.Green}">GREEN</a>
                    </span>
                </div>
            </div>
        </div>
    </header>

    <section th:fragment="pageMenu">
        <!-- code omitted-->
    </section>

    <section th:fragment="pageContent">
        <div class="content">
            <p>Page Content</p>
        </div>
    </section>

    <footer th:fragment="pageFooter">
        <div class="footer">
            <p th:text="#{footer.text}"></p>
        </div>
    </footer>
</html>
```

Notice that in the <head> section the th:theme is added as an attribute. The value of this attribute is set by the ThemeChangeInterceptor bean. The #themes.code('css.style') construct is a context object used to retrieve the css.style property from the theme's ResourceBundle, which is the path to the style sheet file decorator-*.css. Its value is stored in the cssStyle variable using the th:with construct and then set as a value for the href attribute using th:href="@{(${cssStyle})}".

After rebuilding and redeploying the application to the server, open the browser and open http://localhost:8080/ch14 again, and you will see that the style defined in the green.css file was applied, since this is the theme configured to be the default in the ThemeChangeInterceptor bean declaration.

If you want, you can right-click the web page and analyze the HTML code that Thymeleaf produced for the home.html template.

Designing the Template Layout

The consistent structure of the site is already ensured by using the views/templates/layout.html file as a template, on which every view is based. To keep colors and element styling consistent and matching, a theme requires a combination of web design and Spring MVC configuration.

The common structure for all web pages has been presented as HTML already in Listing 14-11, but Figure 14-9 provides a more useful visual representation.

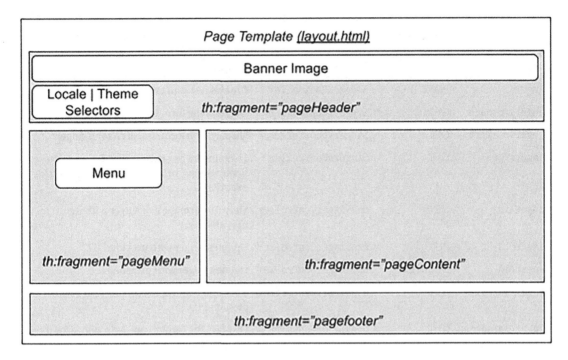

Figure 14-9. *Thymeleaf template with fragments*

The banner image and font color are part of the site theme, and thus when switching between blue and green theme, the banner and font color change too. Each view based on the layout.html can choose to replace some of their sections with fragments from it using the th:replace or they can declare their own fragments using th:fragment. Obviously, in most views the only things that are customized are the pageContent fragment and the page title that is part of the <head> element.

Implementing More Complex Views

Now we can proceed to implement the views that allow users to view the complete list of singers, view the details of a singer, edit existing singers, create new singers, or even delete them.

In the following sections, we discuss the mapping of URLs to the various views, as well as how the views are implemented. We also discuss how to enable JSR-349[16] validation support in Spring MVC for the edit view.

First, we need to design how the various URLs are to be mapped to the corresponding views. In Spring MVC, one of the best practices is to follow the RESTful-style URL for mapping views (wherever possible). Table 14-3 shows the URLs-to-views mapping, as well as the controller method name that will handle the action.

---

[16] https://beanvalidation.org/1.1

Table 14-3. *Sample Web Project Folder Structure Description*

URL	HTTP Method	Controller	Method Description
/singers	GET	SingersController	Lists all singers.
/singers	POST	SingersController	Creates new singer.
/singers/create	GET	SingersController	Displays the form to create a singer.
/singers/search	GET	SingersController	Displays the form to search for a singer.
/singers/go	GET	SingersController	Lists singers by criteria provided as request parameters: fieldName, fieldValue, and exactMatch.
/singer/id	GET	OneSingerController	Shows information of singer with the provided ID.
/singer/id	PUT	OneSingerController	Updates singer with provided ID.
/singer/id	DELETE	OneSingerController	Deletes singer with provided ID.
/singer/id/edit	GET	OneSingerController	Displays the form to edit the singer with the provided ID.
/singer/id/upload	GET	OneSingerController	Displays the form to upload a photo for the singer with the provided ID.
/singer/id/photo	GET	OneSingerController	Retrieves photo as a byte array for the singer with the provided ID.
/singer/id/photo	POST	OneSingerController	Submits user-provided image for singer with provided ID.

Implementing the List Singers View

To implement a view showing a set of data, we need three things:

- A mapping between the URL and the handler method
- A handler method to populate the model
- The view template, which we'll call list.html

As mentioned in Table 14-3, the request URL for showing a list of singers is /singers and the controller where the handler method is declared is the SingersController. There are two controllers in the project. The SingersController groups handles methods that do not affect a specific Singer instance identified by ID and all handled requests are grouped under the /singers path. The handler methods affecting a single Singer instance identified by ID are grouped under OneSingerController, and all handled requests are grouped under /singer/{id}.

Listing 14-15 shows the SingersController class and controller configuration and the handler method populating the model for the view showing the singers.

Listing 14-15. SingersController Controller and list(..) Method

```kotlin
package com.apress.prospring6.fourteen.controllers

import com.apress.prospring6.fourteen.services.SingerService
import org.springframework.context.MessageSource
import org.springframework.stereotype.Controller
import org.springframework.ui.Model
import org.springframework.web.bind.annotation.RequestMapping
// other import statements omitted

@Controller
@RequestMapping("/singers")
class SingersController(private val singerService: SingerService, private val messageSource:
MessageSource) {
    @GetMapping //@RequestMapping(method = RequestMethod.GET)
    fun list(uiModel: Model): String {
        var singers: List<Singer> = singerService.findAll().toMutableList()
        singers = singers.sortedBy ( Singer::id )
        uiModel.addAttribute("singers", singers)
        return "singers/list"
    }


    // --------------- create -------------------
    @GetMapping(value = ["/create"])
    fun showCreateForm(uiModel: Model): String {
        uiModel.addAttribute("singerForm", SingerForm())
        return "singers/create"
    }


    @PostMapping(consumes = [MediaType.MULTIPART_FORM_DATA_VALUE])
    @Throws(
        IOException::class
    )
    fun create(
        singerForm: @Valid SingerForm, bindingResult: BindingResult, uiModel: Model,
        httpServletRequest: HttpServletRequest,
        locale: Locale
    ): String {
        return if (bindingResult.hasErrors()) {
            uiModel.addAttribute("message", messageSource.getMessage("singer.save.fail",
            arrayOf(), locale))
            uiModel.addAttribute("singerForm", singerForm)
            "singers/create"
        } else {
            uiModel.asMap().clear()
            val s = Singer().apply {
                firstName = singerForm.firstName
                lastName = singerForm.lastName
                birthDate = singerForm.birthDate
            }
            // Process file upload
```

```
            if (!singerForm.file!!.isEmpty) {
                setPhoto(s, singerForm.file!!)
            }
            val created = singerService.save(s)
            "redirect:/singer/" + UrlUtil.encodeUrlPathSegment(
                created.id.toString(),
                httpServletRequest
            )
        }
    }


    // --------------- search -------------------
    @GetMapping(value = ["/search"])
    fun showSearchform(criteria: CriteriaDto?): String {
        return "singers/search"
    }


    @GetMapping(value = ["/go"])
    fun processSubmit(
        @ModelAttribute("criteriaDto") @Valid criteria: CriteriaDto,
        result: BindingResult, model: Model, locale: Locale
    ): String {
        return if (result.hasErrors()) {
            "singers/search"
        } else try {
            val singers: List<Singer> = singerService.getByCriteriaDto(criteria)
            if (singers.isEmpty()) {
                result.addError(
                    FieldError(
                        "criteriaDto",
                        "noResults",
                        messageSource.getMessage("NotEmpty.criteriaDto.noResults",
                        null, locale)
                    )
                )
                "singers/search"
            } else if (singers.size == 1) {
                "redirect:/singer/" + singers[0].id
            } else {
                model.addAttribute("singers", singers)
                "singers/list"
            }
        } catch (ice: InvalidCriteriaException) {
            result.addError(
                FieldError(
                    "criteriaDto", ice.fieldName,
                    messageSource.getMessage(ice.messageKey, null, locale)
                )
            )
```

```
        "singers/search"
    }
  }
}
```

The @RequestMapping annotation placed on the class indicates that all handler methods in this class either apply to the path provided as argument or to paths relative to that.

On the list(..) method, the @RequestMapping(method = RequestMethod.GET) applied to it indicates that the method is used to handle a GET request to the URL /singers. The Model object is populated with an attribute named singers and populated with the collection of singers returned by the singerService. findAll() invocation.

⚠ The findAll() method should never be used in production environments unless the size of the returned collection is manageable; otherwise, it might lead to serious performance problems.

The @GetMapping annotation is a meta-annotation replacing @RequestMapping(method = RequestMethod.GET). You can use it on handler methods to keep the code more readable.

The value returned by this method is "singers/list", which is the logical name of the view used to render the data in the model. This logical name is used by the ThymeleafViewResolver bean to identify the view template to use the HTML page that is returned as a response to the user request.

The views/singers/list.html template is shown in Listing 14-16.

Listing 14-16. views/singers/list.html Template Contents

```html
<!DOCTYPE HTML>
<html xmlns:th="http://www.thymeleaf.org">

  <head th:replace="~{templates/layout :: pageTitle('List Singers Page')}"></head>

  <body>
    <div class="container">
      <header th:replace="~{templates/layout :: pageHeader}" ></header>

      <header th:replace="~{templates/layout :: pageMenu}" ></header>

      <section th:fragment="~{templates/layout :: pageContent}">
        <div class="card border-success mb-3" style="max-width: 40rem;">
        <div class="card-header" th:text="#{singers.list.title}"/>
        <div class="card-body">
          <table th:if="${not #lists.isEmpty(singers)}" class="table table-hover">
            <thead>
            <tr>
              <th th:text="#{label.Singer.count}" class="table-success">COUNT</th>
              <th th:text="#{label.Singer.firstname}" class="table-
              success">FIRSTNAME</th>
              <th th:text="#{label.Singer.lastname}" class="table-success">LASTNAME</th>
            </tr>
            </thead>
            <tbody>
```

665

```
            <tr th:each="singer : ${singers}" >
              <td><a th:href="@{/singer/} + ${singer.id}" th:text="${singer.
                id}">ID</a></td>
              <td th:text="${singer.firstName}">...</td>
              <td th:text="${singer.lastName}">...</td>
            </tr>
          </tbody>
        </table>
      </div>
    </div>
  </section>

  <footer th:replace="~{templates/layout :: pageFooter}" ></footer>
  </div>
 </body>
</html>
```

Thymeleaf is pretty powerful and, in addition to its previously described capabilities, it supports arithmetic operations, comparators, and conditional expressions. For example, the th:if="${not #lists. isEmpty(singers)}" construct added as an attribute to the <table> element conditions the creation of the table based on the singer attribute value being a non-empty list. The th:each="singer : ${singers}" construct is used to iterate the values of the singers list. When set as an attribute for an HTML element, it will create a copy for each entry in the list. In this template, it creates a row in the table for each value of the singers list. Using the ${..} syntax, it creates a cell for each property of the objects in the list.

When opening http://localhost:8080/ch14/singers in the browser, an HTML table containing singers should be displayed in the page, and if you inspect the page source, you can see the HTML code generated by Thymeleaf. It should look like the code in Listing 14-17.

Listing 14-17. HTML Code Generated by Thymeleaf for the singers/list View

```
<table class="table table-hover">
  <thead>
    <tr>
      <th class="table-success">Cnt.</th>
      <th class="table-success">First Name</th>
      <th class="table-success">Last Name</th>
    </tr>
  </thead>
  <tbody>
    <tr >
      <td><a href="/ch14/singer/1">1</a></td>
      <td>John</td>
      <td>Mayer</td>
    </tr>
    <tr >
      <td><a href="/ch14/singer/2">2</a></td>
      <td>Ben</td>
      <td>Barnes</td>
    </tr>
    <!-- some rows omitted -->
  </tbody>
</table>
```

Implementing the Show Singer View

Implementing the show.html view to display the information for a singer is quite similar. Showing the information requires a GET request for all text information and another GET request to retrieve the photo as an array of bytes. The code for the two handling methods is shown in Listing 14-18.

Listing 14-18. OneSingerController Controller and show(..) and downloadPhoto(..) Methods

```kotlin
package com.apress.prospring6.fourteen.controllers

import org.springframework.http.MediaType
import org.springframework.web.bind.annotation.*
// other import statements omitted

@Controller
@RequestMapping("/singer/{id}")
class OneSingerController(private val singerService: SingerService, private val
messageSource: MessageSource) {
    @GetMapping
    fun showSingerData(@PathVariable("id") id: Long, uiModel: Model): String {
        val singer: Singer = singerService.findById(id)
        uiModel.addAttribute("singer", singer)
        return "singers/show"
    }
    ...

    @GetMapping("/photo")
    @ResponseBody
    fun downloadPhoto(@PathVariable("id") id: Long): ByteArray {
        val singer: Singer = singerService.findById(id)
        Companion.LOGGER.info("Downloading photo for id: {} with size: {}", singer.id,
        singer.photo.size)
        return singer.photo
    }
    ...

    companion object {
        private val LOGGER = LoggerFactory.getLogger(OneSingerController::class.java)

        @Throws(IOException::class)
        fun setPhoto(singer: Singer, file: MultipartFile) {
            val inputStream = file.inputStream
            val fileContent = IOUtils.toByteArray(inputStream)
            singer.photo = fileContent
        }
    }
}
```

The two methods are part of the OneSingerController, because both operations apply on a single Singer instance. All operations that apply to a Singer instance that exists in our system and thus has an id are grouped in this controller, and all operations are mapped to requests to URLs starting with /singer/{id}.

The code is easily readable, but some extra clarifications are needed regarding the annotations:

- The `@RequestMapping("/singer/{id}")` annotation declares the common URL path for all request URLs handled by methods in this controller. Since it is used at the type level, all method-level mappings inherit it, and additional method-level annotation URL paths are appended to it.

- The `@PathVariable("id")` annotation allows Spring to take the parameter from the URL path and inject it as a value to the id parameter that the `showSingerData(..)` method is invoked with. This annotation is itself configured with the name of the URL path variable for demonstration purposes, but when the URL path variable name is the same as the method parameter, this is not necessary. So in this scenario, `@PathVariable("id") Long id` is equivalent to `@PathVariable Long id`.

- The `@GetMapping(value = "/photo")` annotation is an equivalent to `@RequestMapping(value = "/photo", method = RequestMethod.GET)`. The value attribute in `@GetMapping` is an alias for the same attribute from `@RequestMapping`. In `@RequestMapping`, the value and path attributes are aliases for each other, and both are default attributes, which means all the following annotations are equivalent:

  - `@GetMapping(value = "/photo")`

  - `@GetMapping(path = "/photo")`

  - `@GetMapping("/photo")`

  - `@RequestMapping(value = "/photo", method = RequestMethod.GET)`

  - `@RequestMapping(path = "/photo", method = RequestMethod.GET)`

- The `@ResponseBody` annotation indicates that the returned value should be bound to the response body. This means that Spring is not looking for a view based on the returned value, but returns the value as it is.

The `downloadPhoto(..)` handler method is necessary because photos are saved in the database as an array of bytes, and to render them in HTML we need to provide this entire array of bytes as a source for an `<img>` element.

The fragment pageContent from the `show.html` view template is shown in Listing 14-19. (The rest of the template is inherited unchanged from `layout.html` and is omitted here to save book space.)

Listing 14-19. `views/singers/show.html` Template pageContent Fragment

```html
<section th:fragment="~{templates/layout :: pageContent}">
<div class="card border-info mb-3" style="max-width: 20rem;">
  <div class="card-header" th:text="#{singer.title}"/>
  <div class="card-body">
    <table>
      <tr>
        <th th:text="#{label.Singer.firstname}" >FN</th>
        <td th:text="${singer.firstName}" >FN</td>
      </tr>
      <tr>
        <th th:text="#{label.Singer.lastname}" >LN</th>
        <td th:text="${singer.lastName}" >LN</td>
      </tr>
```

```
<tr>
  <th th:text="#{label.Singer.birthDate}" >BD</th>
  <td th:text="${singer.birthDate}" >BD</td>
</tr>
<tr th:if="${singer.photo != null}">
  <td colspan="2">
    <img class="card-img-top" th:src="@{/singer/} + ${singer.id} + '/photo'">
  </td>
</tr>
<tr>
  <td colspan="2">
    <a th:href="@{/singer/} + ${singer.id} + '/edit'"
       th:text="#{command.edit}"
       class="btn-success">EDIT</a>
  </td>
  <td >
    <a th:href="@{/singer/} + ${singer.id} + '/upload'"
       th:text="#{command.update.photo}"
       class="btn-success">UPLOAD_PHOTO</a>
  </td>
</tr>
</table>
<div class="container col-lg-12">
  <form th:object="${singer}" th:action="@{/singer/} + ${singer.id}"
  th:method="delete"  class="col p-3">
    <input type="submit" th:value="#{command.delete}" id="deleteButton" class="btn
    btn-danger"/>
  </form>
</div>
</div>
</div>
</section>
```

To see the details of any singer, you can just click the link on the number in column Cnt. for that singer. Figure 14-10 shows the list of singers, pinpointing the links that cause the show view to be displayed.

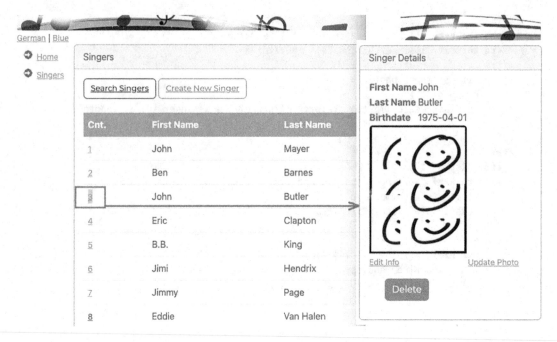

Figure 14-10. *List and show views*

The highlights of the show.html view template are as follows:

- In th:src="@{/singer/} + ${singer.id} + '/photo'", the @{...} Thymeleaf construct is used to build links relative to current page context. This means the value of the src attribute in the generated HTML becomes /ch14/singer/3/photo and the full source URL becomes http://localhost:8080/ch14/singer/3/photo that is mapped to the downloadPhoto(..) handler method.

- The same construct is used to generate the Edit Info and the Update Photo links. The Edit Info link opens a new page where the user can edit the singer's info. The Update Photo links opens a new page where the user can upload a new photo.

Handling a Delete Request

There is a form in the show.html template that is used to trigger a DELETE request for the singer being shown. The generated HTML is shown in Listing 14-20.

Listing 14-20. The Singer Delete Form

```
<form action="/ch14/singer/3" method="post" class="col p-3">
    <input type="hidden" name="_method" value="delete"/>
    <input type="submit" value="Delete" id="deleteButton" class="btn btn-danger"/>
</form>
```

Notice that in fact the form method is POST, but a hidden input was added to the form by Thymeleaf with the name _method and the value of delete. If it looks like this form input indicates the actual desired request method, it is because that is exactly what it is used for.

The explanation is simply that when it comes to the HTTP protocol, there are two main things people use it for: to retrieve data (GET) or to send data (POST). This means that methods like PUT and DELETE essentially do the same as POST—they are essentially *subcategories* of POST—and therefore no need exists to directly support more methods in HTML.

However, for practical reasons and readability, Thymeleaf allows declaration of forms with th:method="delete" or th:method="put" and does the heavy lifting of converting them to POST methods when the responses are generated. How does Spring deal with these requests, though? Or better stated, how should handling methods be mapped to these types of requests?

The answer is: in the same way as GET requests. After all, the @RequestMapping annotation can be configured for a specific HTTP method, and there are also the meta-annotations, @DeleteRequest and @PutRequest, equivalent to @RequestMapping (method = RequestMethod.DELETE) and @RequestMapping(method = RequestMethod.PUT).

Listing 14-21 shows the handler method for the request to delete a singer.

Listing 14-21. The Singer Delete Handler

```
package com.apress.prospring6.fourteen.controllers

import org.springframework.web.bind.annotation.DeleteMapping
// other import statements omitted

@Controller
@RequestMapping("/singer/{id}")
class OneSingerController(private val singerService: SingerService,
        private val messageSource: MessageSource) {

    // @RequestMapping(method = RequestMethod.DELETE)
    @DeleteMapping
    fun deleteSinger(@PathVariable("id") id: Long): String {
        singerService.findById(id)
        singerService.delete(id)
        return "redirect:/singers/list"
    }
    ...
}
```

One other thing is necessary, though: we need to tell Spring that we will have PUT and DELETE requests for the application, so that it knows to convert POST requests with _method hidden inputs to appropriate HTTP requests, so that they can be mapped to the suitable type of handlers. This is done by adding an instance of org.springframework.web.filter.HiddenHttpMethodFilter to the list of filters that modify requests before they are passed over to the DispatcherServlet. The modification is made in the WebInitializer class introduced earlier in Listing 14-5. At the time when this configuration was introduced, the getServletFilters() method was explained succinctly. The method is shown again in Listing 14-22.

Listing 14-22. The Configuration to Support PUT and DELETE Methods in a Spring Application

```
package com.apress.prospring6.fourteen

class WebInitializer : AbstractAnnotationConfigDispatcherServletInitializer {

    override fun getServletFilters(): Array<Filter> {
        val cef = CharacterEncodingFilter().apply {
```

```
            encoding = StandardCharsets.UTF_8.name()
            setForceEncoding(true)
        }
        return arrayOf(HiddenHttpMethodFilter(), cef)
    }

    // other methods omitted
}
```

⚠️ This piece of configuration is something that most developers forget when writing Spring Web applications, especially if this is not something that they do often. Who writes Spring Web applications from scratch often enough for these configurations to become routine, anyway?

Implementing the Edit Singer View

To edit a singer, we need a different type of view that not only shows data, but does so in components that are editable, and we also need a form to submit the edited data. For requests that submit data used to edit existing records on the server, the REST convention is to use a PUT to differentiate it from a normal POST request, for which the submitted data is used to create a new record.

The Edit Info link, introduced in the section "Implementing the Show Singer View," points to a page showing the singer details in editable fields. A GET request is submitted to the /singer/{id}/edit URL. Spring populates a model with the details of the Singer instance with the provided id and returns the singers/edit view logical name. The page contains a form that submits the edited data using a HTTP POST request to /singer/{id}.

The Thymeleaf fragment with the form design is shown in Listing 14-23.

Listing 14-23. The singers/edit.html Fragment Containing the Edit Singer Form

```html
<section th:fragment="~{templates/layout :: pageContent}">
<div class="content"> <!-- content -->
  <h4 th:text="#{command.edit} + ' ' + #{singer.title}">EDIT</h4>

  <div class="container col-lg-12">
    <form name="update_info" th:action="@{/singer/} + ${singer.id}" th:object="${singer}"
    th:method="put" class="col p-3">
      <input type="hidden" th:field="*{id}" />

      <div class="row mb-1">
        <label for="firstName" th:text="#{label.Singer.firstname} + ':'" class="col-sm-4
        form-label">FN:</label>
        <div class="col-sm-8">
          <input type="text" th:field="*{firstName}" class="form-control"/>
          <span th:if="${#fields.hasErrors('firstName')}" class="error" th:errors=
          "*{firstName}">MISSING FN</span>
        </div>
      </div>
```

```html
    <div class="row mb-1">
      <label for="lastName" th:text="#{label.Singer.lastname} + ':'" class=
      "col-sm-4  form-label">LN:</label>
      <div class="col-sm-8">
        <input type="text" th:field="*{lastName}" class="form-control"/>
        <span th:if="${#fields.hasErrors('lastName')}" class="error"
        th:errors="*{lastName}">MISSING LN</span>
      </div>
    </div>

      <div class="row mb-1">
        <label for="birthDate" th:text="#{label.Singer.birthDate} + ':'" class=
        "col-sm-4  form-label">BD:</label>
        <div class="col-sm-8">
          <input type="date" th:field="*{birthDate}" class="form-control datetimepicker-
          input" data-target="#datetimepicker1"/>
          <span th:if="${#fields.hasErrors('birthDate')}" class="error" th:errors="*{birth
          Date}">MISSING BD</span>
        </div>
      </div>

    <div class="form-group mb-1 align-items-end">
      <input type="submit" th:value="#{command.save}" id="saveButton" class="btn
      btn-primary"/>
    </div>
  </form>
  <p th:if="${message ne null}" th:text="${message}" class="error"></p>
  <div class="form-group mb-1 align-items-end">
    <a href="#" th:href="@{/singer/} + ${singer.id}" th:text="#{command.cancel}">
    CANCEL</a>
  </div>
  </div>
</div> <!-- content -->
</section>
```

The highlights in the edit.html template are as follows:

- th:object="${singer}": This construct is the model object; its properties are used to populate the fields.

- th:field="*{propName}": This construct is used to mark the form field, but also to populate them with properties of the singer object.

- th:if="${#fields.hasErrors('labelName')}": This construct is used to check if the data has any error. If yes the element containing it as attribute is displayed and the element is populated with an error message. The error message is displayed after the form was submitted, Spring performed the validation, the errors were added to the model and the response redirects back to the edit view with data and errors this time.

- th:if="${message ne null}": This construct tests if the message object is not null and displays the element containing it as an attribute. It is used in this case to add an additional message telling the user why the singer was not saved.

As mentioned in the previous section, DELETE and PUT methods are supported by Thymeleaf and Spring. Notice that the edit form has the attribute th:method="put", but if you look in the generated HTML, the form method is POST, but a hidden input was added to the form by Thymeleaf with the name of _method and the value of put. This input configures the actual desired request method, and Spring treats these POST requests as PUT requests thanks to the HiddenHttpMethodFilter previously mentioned in the "Handling a Delete Request" section.

Now that we have the view, let's see what the Spring code to display it and process the submitted data looks like. The code for the two handler methods is shown in Listing 14-24.

Listing 14-24. The Handler Methods for Showing the Edit View and Processing a PUT Request

```kotlin
package com.apress.prospring6.fourteen.controllers

import org.springframework.web.bind.annotation.PutMapping
// other import statements omitted

@Controller
@RequestMapping("/singer/{id}")
class OneSingerController(private val singerService: SingerService, private val
messageSource: MessageSource) {

    @GetMapping(path = ["/edit"])
    fun showEditForm(@PathVariable("id") id: Long, uiModel: Model): String {
        val singer: Singer = singerService.findById(id)
        uiModel.addAttribute("singer", singer)
        return "singers/edit"
    }

    @PutMapping
    fun updateSingerInfo(
        @Valid singer: Singer,
        bindingResult: BindingResult,
        uiModel: Model,
        locale: Locale
    ): String {
        return if (bindingResult.hasErrors()) {
            uiModel.addAttribute("message", messageSource.getMessage(
                "singer.save.fail", arrayOf(), locale))
            uiModel.addAttribute("singer", singer)
            "singers/edit"
        } else {
            uiModel.asMap().clear()
            val fromDb = singerService.findById(singer.id!!)
            fromDb.firstName = singer.firstName
            fromDb.lastName = singer.lastName
            fromDb.birthDate = singer.birthDate
            singerService.save(fromDb)
            "redirect:/singer/" + singer.id
        }
    }
    ...

}
```

Ignore the @Valid annotation and all the code related to error handling—that has its own section later in this chapter. One thing to notice in this code section is the introduction of the redirect: keyword. Prefixing a logical view name with "redirect:" tells Spring to use the logical view name as a redirect URL. In case of a successful edit operation, the redirection is to the page showing the singer details; in case of validation errors, the user is returned to the edit page and the errors are shown.

The edit form should look like the one depicted in Figure 14-11; otherwise something went wrong when deploying the project.

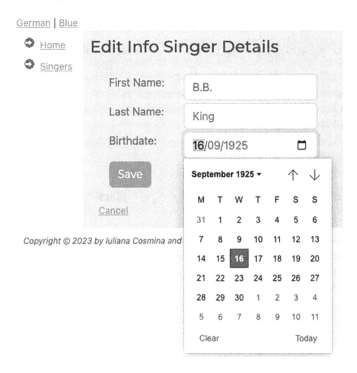

Figure 14-11. *The edit view*

Implementing the Create Singer View

Implementing the create singer view is much like implementing the edit view. To make things interesting, the create.html file contains a form that also includes a file chooser to upload a photo of the singer. Aside from that, the form is pretty much identical to the one in edit.html. The pageContent fragment containing the form for creating a singer is shown in Listing 14-25.

Listing 14-25. The singers/create.html Form

```
<section th:fragment="~{templates/layout :: pageContent}">
<div class="content">  <!-- content -->
  <h4 th:text="#{command.create} + ' ' + #{singer.new}">CREATE</h4>
  <div class="container col-lg-12">
    <form name="create_singer" th:action="@{/singers}" th:object="${singerForm}"
    th:method="post" class="col p-3" enctype="multipart/form-data">
      <div class="row mb-1">
```

675

```
<label for="firstName" th:text="#{label.Singer.firstname} + ':'" class="col-sm-4
form-label">FN:</label>
<div class="col-sm-8">
  <input type="text" th:field="*{firstName}" class="form-control"/>
  <span th:if="${#fields.hasErrors('firstName')}" class="error" th:errors=
  "*{firstName}">MISSING FN</span>
</div>
</div>


<div class="row mb-1">
  <label for="lastName" th:text="#{label.Singer.lastname} + ':'" class="col-
  sm-4  form-label">LN:</label>
  <div class="col-sm-8">
    <input type="text" th:field="*{lastName}" class="form-control"/>
    <span th:if="${#fields.hasErrors('lastName')}" class="error"
    th:errors="*{lastName}">MISSING LN</span>
  </div>
</div>


<div class="row mb-1">
  <label for="birthDate" th:text="#{label.Singer.birthDate} + ':'" class="col-
  sm-4  form-label">BD:</label>
  <div class="col-sm-8">
    <input type="date" th:field="*{birthDate}" class="form-control datetimepicker-
    input" data-target="#datetimepicker1"/>
    <span th:if="${#fields.hasErrors('birthDate')}" class="error" th:errors=
    "*{birthDate}">MISSING BD</span>
  </div>
</div>
<div class="row mb-1">
  <label for="file" th:text="#{label.Singer.photo} + ':'" class="col-sm-4  form-
  label">PH</label>
  <div class="col-sm-8">
    <input type="file" th:field="*{file}" name="file" id="file" class="form-control"/>
  </div>
</div>


<div class="form-group mb-1 align-items-end">
  <input type="submit" th:value="#{command.save}" id="saveButton" class="btn btn-
  primary"/>
</div>
</form>
<p th:if="${message ne null}" th:text="${message}" class="error"></p>
<div class="form-group mb-1 align-items-end">
  <a href="#" th:href="@{/singers}" th:text="#{command.cancel}"> CANCEL</a>
</div>
</div>
</div> <!-- content -->
</section>
```

Having a file chooser in the form means that an input field of type file is part of the form, which in turn means that the type of the form must be declared to be enctype="multipart/form-data". This is a special type used for forms that allows inclusion of entire files in the submitted data. The singer information has a field of LONGBLOB type to store a photo, which can be uploaded from the client. This where the data from the creation form should end up. But, user data that includes files needs special handling on the server side.

For a long time, the standard servlet specification didn't support file upload. As a result, Spring MVC worked with other libraries (the most common one being the Apache Commons FileUpload library[17]) to serve this purpose. Spring MVC has built-in support for Commons FileUpload. However, starting from Servlet 3.0, file upload has become a built-in feature of the web container. Apache Tomcat 7 supports Servlet 3.0, and Spring has also supported Servlet 3.0 file upload since version 3.1.

Supporting file upload is thus an easy feat to do in Spring web applications, especially when deploying applications to Apache Tomcat 10.

Let's start with the code for processing the submission data. Since creating a new singer is not an operation on an existing singer, the handler method is in SingersController. The code is shown in Listing 14-26.

Listing 14-26. The Handler Method for Processing Data Submitted by a Form for Creating a Singer Instance

```kotlin
package com.apress.prospring6.fourteen.controllers

import org.springframework.web.bind.annotation.PostMapping
import org.springframework.http.MediaType
import com.apress.prospring6.fourteen.util.SingerForm
import com.apress.prospring6.fourteen.controllers.OneSingerController.Companion.setPhoto
// other import statements omitted

@Controller
@RequestMapping("/singers")
class SingersController(private val singerService: SingerService, private val messageSource:
MessageSource) {

    // --------------- create -------------------
    @GetMapping(value = ["/create"])
    fun showCreateForm(uiModel: Model): String {
        uiModel.addAttribute("singerForm", SingerForm())
        return "singers/create"
    }

    @PostMapping(consumes = [MediaType.MULTIPART_FORM_DATA_VALUE])
    @Throws(
        IOException::class
    )
    fun create(
        singerForm: @Valid SingerForm, bindingResult: BindingResult, uiModel: Model,
        httpServletRequest: HttpServletRequest,
        locale: Locale
    ): String {
        return if (bindingResult.hasErrors()) {
```

---

[17] https://commons.apache.org/proper/commons-fileupload/

```
            uiModel.addAttribute("message", messageSource.getMessage(
                "singer.save.fail", arrayOf(), locale))
            uiModel.addAttribute("singerForm", singerForm)
            "singers/create"
    } else {
        uiModel.asMap().clear()
        val s = Singer().apply {
            firstName = singerForm.firstName
            lastName = singerForm.lastName
            birthDate = singerForm.birthDate
        }
        // Process file upload
        if (!singerForm.file!!.isEmpty) {
            setPhoto(s, singerForm.file!!)
        }
        val created = singerService.save(s)
        "redirect:/singer/" + UrlUtil.encodeUrlPathSegment(
            created.id.toString(),
            httpServletRequest
        )
    }
}
...
}
```

The contents on the form do not map appropriately to a Singer instance, because the photo field value will be mapped in the handler method to an org.springframework.web.multipart.MultipartFile, and thus the SingerForm type is needed.

⚠️ In complex applications, the entity types declared in the DAO layer are never used in controllers from the web layer. Usually view types are introduced that wrap around one or more entity types and expose only useful fields, hiding some details, such as sensitive data like identifiers and passwords and fields that are not relevant to the web context such as the version field.

SingerForm is a view type that declares only the fields necessary for creating a Singer instance for the web layer. The fields of this type are also decorated with validation annotations that match the ones declared on the Singer class for the corresponding fields.

The SingerForm is shown in Listing 14-27.

Listing 14-27. The SingerForm View Type

```
package com.apress.prospring6.fourteen.util

import jakarta.validation.constraints.NotNull
import jakarta.validation.constraints.Size
import org.springframework.format.annotation.DateTimeFormat
import org.springframework.web.multipart.MultipartFile

import java.time.LocalDate
```

```kotlin
class SingerForm {
    @NotEmpty(message = "{NotEmpty.singer.firstName}") @Size(
        min = 2,
        max = 30,
        message = "{Size.singer.firstName}"
    ) var  firstName:String? = null

    @NotEmpty(message = "{NotEmpty.singer.lastName}") @Size(
        min = 2,
        max = 30,
        message = "{Size.singer.lastName}"
    ) var lastName:String? = null

    @DateTimeFormat(pattern = "yyyy-MM-dd")
    var birthDate: LocalDate? = null

    var file: MultipartFile? = null
}
```

Spring MVC is smart enough to take the uploaded content, convert it to a `MultipartFile`, and use it as a value for the `file` field in `SingerForm`. From the `SingerForm` populated by Spring MVC, a `Singer` instance is created. The `setPhoto(..)` method is used to read the uploaded content as a byte array that can then be saved into the `LONGBLOB` photo column in the `SINGER` table.

But is this enough? It turns out that this is not enough, because the Spring `DispatcherServlet` needs to be configured to support file uploads. In a Servlet 3.0+ compatible web container with Spring MVC, configuring file upload support is a two-step process.

First, in the Java-based configuration class that defines everything needed to create the `DispatcherServlet` definition, we need to add a bean of type `StandardServletMultipartResolver`. This is a standard implementation of the `MultipartResolver` interface, based on the Servlet 3.0 `jakarta.servlet.http.Part` API. Listing 14-28 depicts the declaration of this bean that needs to be added to the `WebConfig` class.

Listing 14-28. The Spring Bean Necessary to Support File Uploading

```kotlin
package com.apress.prospring6.fourteen

import org.springframework.web.multipart.support.StandardServletMultipartResolver
// other import statements omitted

@Configuration
@EnableWebMvc
@ComponentScan(basePackages = ["com.apress.prospring6.fourteen"])
class WebConfig : WebMvcConfigurer, ApplicationContextAware {
    @Bean(name = [DispatcherServlet.MULTIPART_RESOLVER_BEAN_NAME])
    open fun multipartResolver() = StandardServletMultipartResolver()
    // other configuration code omitted
}
```

The second step is to enable MultiParsing in Servlet 3.0+ environments; this means that the `WebInitializer` implementation needs some changes. There is a method called `customizeRegistration(..)` that is defined in the `AbstractDispatcherServletInitializer` abstract class, which is the class extended by AbstractAnnotationConfigDispatcherServletInitializer. This method must be implemented to register an instance of jakarta.servlet.MultipartConfigElement. The configuration snippet that needs to be added in the WebInitializer class is shown in Listing 14-29.

Listing 14-29. Configuration For WebInitializer

```kotlin
package com.apress.prospring6.fourteen

import jakarta.servlet.MultipartConfigElement
import jakarta.servlet.ServletRegistration
// other import statements omitted

class WebInitializer : AbstractAnnotationConfigDispatcherServletInitializer() {
    override fun getServletFilters(): Array<Filter> {
        val cef = CharacterEncodingFilter().apply {
            encoding = StandardCharsets.UTF_8.name()
            setForceEncoding(true)
        }
        return arrayOf(HiddenHttpMethodFilter(), cef)
    }

    public override fun customizeRegistration(registration: ServletRegistration.Dynamic) {
        registration.setInitParameter("throwExceptionIfNoHandlerFound", "true")
        registration.setMultipartConfig(multipartConfigElement) // <=> <multipart-config>
        super.customizeRegistration(registration)
    }

    private val multipartConfigElement: MultipartConfigElement
        get() = MultipartConfigElement(null, MAX_FILE_SIZE, MAX_REQUEST_SIZE,
            FILE_SIZE_THRESHOLD)

    // other configuration code omitted

    companion object {
        private const val MAX_FILE_SIZE: Long = 5000000

        // Beyond that size spring will throw exception.
        private const val MAX_REQUEST_SIZE: Long = 5000000

        // Size threshold after which files will be written to disk
        private const val FILE_SIZE_THRESHOLD = 0
    }
}
```

The first parameter of MultipartConfigElement is a temporary location where files should be stored. The second parameter is the maximum file size allowed for upload, which is 5MB in this case. The third parameter represents the size of the request, which is also 5MB here. The last parameter represents the threshold after which files will be written to disk.

To test the file upload function, redeploy the application and add a new singer with a photo. Upon completion, you will be able to see the photo in the show view.

Enabling JSR-349 (Bean Validation)

This topic was reserved until now so that the focus could be on building the web pages and linking functionality to various buttons and links. Just as important as making sure user requests are processed correctly is making sure the data submitted by the user is correct. This is especially important for data being saved into the database, because invalid data can yield invalid results or, in some cases, even allow a hacker to break into your system(e.g., via SQL injection[18]).

Chapter 11 introduced you to validation, formatting, and type conversion, and mentioned that the true power of Spring beans declared for these purposes is most useful in web applications when handling user-provided data. Chapter 11 introduced you to Spring's support of JSR-349 (Bean Validation)[19] (now part of Jakarta libraries). Listing 14-27 introduced class SingerForm that declares a few fields that are initialized with user-provided data. The same validation annotations are present in the Singer class that is used to create Singer domain objects.

Listing 14-30 shows the SingerForm version with validation annotation with customized error message codes.

Listing 14-30. The SingerForm Type Necessary to Support File Uploading

```
package com.apress.prospring6.fourteen.util

import jakarta.validation.constraints.*
import org.springframework.web.multipart.MultipartFile
// other import statements omitted

class SingerForm {
    @NotEmpty @Size(
        min = 2,
        max = 30
    ) var firstName: String? = null
    @NotEmpty @Size(
        min = 2,
        max = 30
    ) var lastName: String? = null

    @DateTimeFormat(pattern = "yyyy-MM-dd")
    var birthDate: LocalDate? = null

    var file: MultipartFile? = null
}
```

The constraints are applied to their respective fields. Note that for the validation message, you specify a message key by using curly braces. This will cause the validation messages to be retrieved from ResourceBundle and hence support i18n. The @Size annotation is special because it is declared with a minimum value and maximum value; these values are injected from the code into the internationalization messages using the {*} syntax.

---

[18] https://www.w3schools.com/sql/sql_injection.asp
[19] https://beanvalidation.org/3.0

The error message codes are resolved by an org.springframework.validation.
MessageCodesResolver bean registered automatically by Spring when validation is configured. The default implementation used by Spring is org.springframework.validation.DefaultMessageCodesResolver. This type of bean creates two message codes based on the annotations used on fields to enforce constraints, based on the name of the type where used and based on field names. For example, for the firstName field in class SingerForm, for the @Size validation this bean will create message codes for, in the following order:

- Validation name + object name + field name ⇒ Size.singerForm.firstName

- Validation name + field name ⇒ Size.firstName

- Validation name + field type ⇒ Size.java.lang.String

- Validation name ⇒ Size

However, if neither of these message properties is declared, the default message is set to annotation full name + "message" ⇒ jakarta.validation.constraints.Size.message. For the singerForm object, these messages are not declared in our initial internationalization files, but the ones for the singer object are. They are shown in Listing 14-31.

Listing 14-31. Message Codes for Validation Errors for Object singer, Field firstName

```
NotEmpty.singer.firstName=Please insert First Name Value
Size.singer.firstName=Length must be between {2} and {1}
NotEmpty.singer.lastName=Please insert Last Name Value
Size.singer.lastName=Length must be between {2} and {1}
typeMismatch.birthDate=Invalid format, should be \'yyyy-mm-dd\'
```

There are two solutions here: add a copy of messages in Listing 14-28 and replace singer with singerForm or configure the annotation validations to use the existing set of messages, using the messages attribute. The SingerForm version with customized error messages is depicted in Listing 14-32.

Listing 14-32. SingerForm Version with Customized Error Messages

```
package com.apress.prospring6.fourteen.util
import jakarta.validation.constraints.*
// other import statements omitted

class SingerForm {
    @NotEmpty(message = "{NotEmpty.singer.firstName}") @Size(
        min = 2,
        max = 30,
        message = "{Size.singer.firstName}"
    ) var firstName: String? = null
    @NotEmpty(message = "{NotEmpty.singer.lastName}") @Size(
        min = 2,
        max = 30,
        message = "{Size.singer.lastName}"
    ) var lastName: String? = null

    @DateTimeFormat(pattern = "yyyy-MM-dd")
    var birthDate: LocalDate? = null

    var file: MultipartFile? = null
}
```

To enable JSR-349 validation during the web data binding process, we just need to apply the @Valid annotation to the SingerForm argument of the SingersController.create(..) method and to the Singer argument of the OneSingerController.updateSingerInfo(..) method. Listing 14-33 shows the signatures for both methods.

Listing 14-33. Controllers with Validation

```
package com.apress.prospring6.fourteen.controllers

import jakarta.validation.Valid
// other import statements omitted

@Controller
@RequestMapping("/singer/{id}")
class OneSingerController {

    @PutMapping
    fun updateSingerInfo(@Valid singer:Singer,
                    bindingResult:BindingResult,
                    uiModel:Model, locale:Locale):String {
        // method body omitted
    }

// other methods omitted
}

@Controller
@RequestMapping("/singers")
class SingersController {

    @PostMapping(consumes = MediaType.MULTIPART_FORM_DATA_VALUE)
    fun create(@Valid singerForm:SingerForm,
                        bindingResult:BindingResult, uiModel:Model,
                        httpServletRequest:HttpServletRequest,
                        locale:Locale):String {
        // method body omitted
    }
// other methods omitted
}
```

We also want the JSR-349 validation message to use the same ResourceBundle instance as for the views. To do this, we need to configure the validator in the DispatcherServlet configuration, in the WebConfig class, as shown in Listing 14-34.

Listing 14-34. Spring Validation Configuration

```
package com.apress.prospring6.fourteen

import org.springframework.validation.Validator
import org.springframework.validation.beanvalidation.LocalValidatorFactoryBean
// other import statements omitted
```

```kotlin
@Configuration
@EnableWebMvc
@ComponentScan(basePackages = ["com.apress.prospring6.fourteen"])
open class WebConfig : WebMvcConfigurer, ApplicationContextAware {
    private var applicationContext: ApplicationContext? = null

    @Throws(BeansException::class)
    override fun setApplicationContext(applicationContext: ApplicationContext) {
        this.applicationContext = applicationContext
    }

    @Bean
    open fun validator(): Validator = LocalValidatorFactoryBean().apply {
        setValidationMessageSource(messageSource())
    }

    override fun getValidator() = validator()

    @Bean
    open fun messageSource(): MessageSource
        = ReloadableResourceBundleMessageSource().apply {
            setBasename("classpath:i18n/global")
            setDefaultEncoding(StandardCharsets.UTF_8.name())
            setUseCodeAsDefaultMessage(true)
            setFallbackToSystemLocale(true)
            // # -1 : never reload, 0 always reload
            // setCacheSeconds(0);
        }
    ...
}
```

First, a validator bean is defined, with the class LocalValidatorFactoryBean, for JSR-349 support. Note that we set the validationMessageSource property to reference the MessageSource bean defined, which instructs the JSR-349 validator to look up the messages by the code from the MessageSource bean. Then the getValidator() method is implemented to return the validator bean we defined.

That's all; we can test the validation now. Bring up the create singer view and click the Save button without inserting any data. The returned page will now report multiple validation errors, as shown in Figure 14-12.

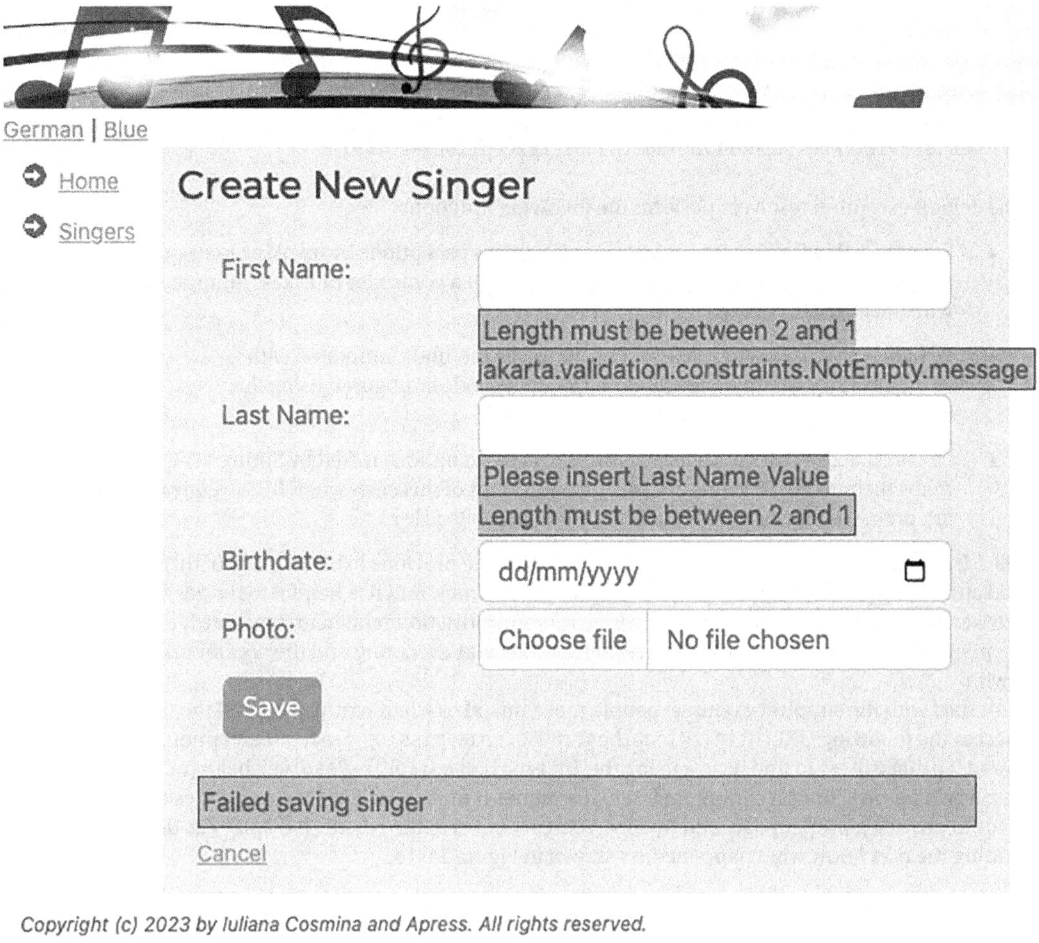

Figure 14-12. *View page with validation errors*

Switch to the German (DE) language and do the same thing. This time, the messages will be displayed in German.

The views are basically complete; all we need now is to handle potential errors.

Exception Handling

When handler methods are executed, things can go wrong. Some situations, like trying to access a URL that does not exist, might be expected, but others might not. In both scenarios, the activity has to be recorded and the end user has to be notified. Spring MVC catches and handles the exceptions using implementations of HandlerExceptionResolver. The typical way to treat an MVC exception is to prepare a model and select an error view. Multiple exception resolvers can be used and ordered in a chain to treat different types of exceptions in different ways. Spring MVC supports the default resolvers shown in Listing 14-35 (resolvers of these types are created automatically for you in a Spring web application), and they are declared in the DispatcherServlet.properties file that is packaged in the spring-webmvc.jar.

Listing 14-35. DispatcherServlet.properties Default Exception Resolvers

```
org.springframework.web.servlet.HandlerExceptionResolver=
    o.s.web.servlet.mvc.method.annotation.ExceptionHandlerExceptionResolver,\
    o.s.web.servlet.mvc.annotation.ResponseStatusExceptionResolver,\
    o.s.web.servlet.mvc.support.DefaultHandlerExceptionResolver
```

The default exception resolvers perform the following functions:

- ExceptionHandlerExceptionResolver: Resolves exceptions by invoking methods annotated with @ExceptionHandler found within a controller or a class annotated with @ControllerAdvice.

- ResponseStatusExceptionResolver: Resolves methods annotated with @ResponseStatus and maps them to the status code configured using this annotation.

- DefaultHandlerExceptionResolver: Resolves exceptions raised by Spring MVC and maps them to HTTP status codes. The equivalent of this class when REST requests are processed is class ResponseEntityExceptionHandler.

The SimpleMappingExceptionResolver class is not in the previous list, but beans of this type can be declared and configured to map exception classes to view names, and it is helpful to render error pages in a browser application. An exception resolver provides information related to the context in which the exception was thrown; that is, the handler method that was executing and the arguments that it was called with.

Let's start with the simplest example: people make mistakes when writing URLs all the time. Let's try to access the following URL: http://localhost:8080/ch14/missing. Since no exception handling is configured, Spring will try to find a view using the InternalResourceViewResolver bean (or whatever other view resolver is found). Since it cannot find one, it assumes it must be a static page and tries to render that. But it fails to provide a proper page, and Apache Tomcat comes to the rescue. It displays its default error page, letting the user know what happened, as shown in Figure 14-13.

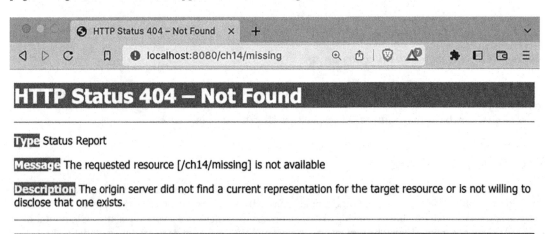

Figure 14-13. Apache Tomcat default error page for missing view

The default error message does a good job describing the problem, and it returns the proper HTTP status code for missing resources: 404. But still, it's not okay, because this looks like a technical exception or a development problem, and the recommended practice is to not let the end user know that. Also, there is no need to give so many details to the end user, because they should not be bothered with the internal problems an application has. So, what can be done? One rule of developing web applications is to keep the look and feel consistent, so instead of the Apache Tomcat page, we could display a customized error view. Out of the box, Spring MVC offers no default (fallback) error page when a view or a handler method is not found. It doesn't throw an exception either; it just forwards the responsibility of showing the appropriate message to the server. To override this behavior, we need to make the following changes to a Spring web application configuration.

First, customize the DispatcherServlet to throw org.springframework.web.servlet. NoHandlerFoundException when a handler method cannot be found. This is done by overriding the customizeRegistration(..) method from the AbstractDispatcherServletInitializer class in the WebInitializer class, as shown in Listing 14-36.

Listing 14-36. Customizing DispatcherServlet to Throw NoHandlerFoundException When Handlers Are Not Found

```kotlin
package com.apress.prospring6.fourteen

import jakarta.servlet.ServletRegistration
// other import methods omitted

class WebInitializer
    : AbstractAnnotationConfigDispatcherServletInitializer {

    override fun customizeRegistration(
            registration:ServletRegistration.Dynamic) {
        registration.setInitParameter(
            "throwExceptionIfNoHandlerFound", "true")
        super.customizeRegistration(registration)
    }

    // other config methods omitted
}
```

This configuration declares an initialization parameter named throwExceptionIfNoHandlerFound and sets it to "true", which causes the DispatcherServlet to throw an org.springframework.web.servlet. NoHandlerFoundException when a handler method cannot be found.

ℹ️ Note that adding this configuration does nothing if DefaultServletHttpRequestHandler is used, because requests will always be forwarded to it and a NoHandlerFoundException will never be thrown in that case. You can verify this by looking into the logs. If you see something similar to the following output snippet, you still have more steps to go:

```
DEBUG o.s.w.s.DispatcherServlet - GET "/ch14/missing", parameters={}
DEBUG o.s.w.s.h.SimpleUrlHandlerMapping - Mapped to org.springframework.web.servlet.
resource.DefaultServletHttpRequestHandler@763956dc
DEBUG o.s.w.s.DispatcherServlet - Completed 404 NOT_FOUND
```

So, if in your configuration you have the following:

```
override fun configureDefaultServletHandling(
        configurer:DefaultServletHandlerConfigurer) {
    configurer.enable()
}
```

Just remove this method and make do without DefaultServletHttpRequestHandler if you want NoHandlerFoundExceptions to be thrown.

But this does nothing without a bean of type HandlerExceptionResolver customized to do something else than simply tell the application server what to do. And this brings us to the next change. Next, an option is to implement the HandlerExceptionResolver interface or extend any of the classes that implement it and provide the desired implementation for the doResolveException(...) method that will return the desired view, as shown in Listing 14-37.

Listing 14-37. HandlerExceptionResolver Implementation

```
package com.example.problem

import org.springframework.http.HttpStatus
import org.springframework.web.servlet.ModelAndView
import org.springframework.web.servlet.NoHandlerFoundException
import org.springframework.web.servlet.handler.SimpleMappingExceptionResolver
import javax.servlet.http.HttpServletRequest
import javax.servlet.http.HttpServletResponse

class MissingExceptionResolver : SimpleMappingExceptionResolver() {
    override fun doResolveException(
        request: HttpServletRequest,
        response: HttpServletResponse, handler: Any, ex: Exception
    ): ModelAndView? {
        if (ex is NoHandlerFoundException) {
            val model = ModelAndView("error")
            model.addObject(
                "problem", "URL not supported : "
                        + request.requestURI
            )
            response.status = HttpStatus.NOT_FOUND.value()
            return model
        }
        return null
    }
}
```

ℹ️   Notice that for error handling the type ModelAndView is used. Since the exception handling method is not a normal handler method declared in a controller class, mapping its result to a view template is not possible. An object of this type is a holder for both Model and View objects in the web MVC framework, needed to return both a model and a view in a single object. This allows Spring MVC to customize the error view before being sent to the user with different error messages based on the exception thrown when a request is handled.

688

Here are a few details about a HandlerExceptionResolver implementation:

- It can return a ModelAndView that points to an error view, usually the same one for a related class of problems, or for the entire application.

- It can return an empty ModelAndView if the exception is handled within the resolver.

- It can return null if the exception remains unresolved, thus allowing other exception resolvers to try to handle it. If none of the exception resolvers can handle the exception, it is bubbled up to the Servlet container.

⚠ In Listing 14-37, note that the method returns an actual ModelAndView instance. HandlerExceptionResolve implementations are designed to make sure an exception is resolved to a view or allowed to bubble up to the Servlet container.

The next step is to declare a bean of this type with the lowest priority (highest precedence), so that every time something goes wrong within the application, this exception resolver will be used first.

The alternative to having multiple SimpleMappingExceptionResolver mapped to various types of exceptions is to declare different error handler methods and group all of them in a class annotated with @ControllerAdvice. This annotation is meta-annotated with @Component and this means a bean of this type will be created that will intercept any handler method exceptions annotated with @ExceptionHandler that have a handler method declared in the class annotated with it and render the corresponding error view. Listing 14-38, shows a class annotated with @ControllerAdvice.

Listing 14-38. GlobalExceptionHandler Implementation

```
package com.apress.prospring6.fourteen.problem

import jakarta.servlet.http.HttpServletRequest
import org.springframework.http.HttpStatus
import org.springframework.web.bind.annotation.ControllerAdvice
import org.springframework.web.bind.annotation.ExceptionHandler
import org.springframework.web.bind.annotation.ResponseStatus
import org.springframework.web.servlet.ModelAndView
import org.springframework.web.servlet.NoHandlerFoundException

@ControllerAdvice
class GlobalExceptionHandler {
    @ExceptionHandler(NotFoundException::class)
    @ResponseStatus(HttpStatus.NOT_FOUND)
    fun handle(ex: NotFoundException): ModelAndView {
        val mav = ModelAndView()
        mav.addObject("problem", ex.message)
        mav.viewName = "error"
        return mav
    }

    @ExceptionHandler(NoHandlerFoundException::class)
    @ResponseStatus(HttpStatus.NOT_FOUND)
    fun notFound(req: HttpServletRequest): ModelAndView {
```

```
        val mav = ModelAndView()
        mav.addObject("problem", "Not Supported " + req.requestURI)
        mav.viewName = "error"
        return mav
    }
}
```

To test that this exception handler works as expected, you could try accessing http://localhost:8080/ch14/singer/99 and http://localhost:8080/ch14/missing. Notice that there are different types of exceptions being thrown, which causes different error messages to be added to the error view model, as shown in Figure 14-14.

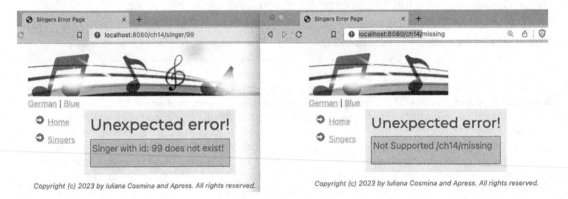

Figure 14-14. *Custom Error Messages*

You should view the error page with the proper exception message. Inspect the response contents and you will notice that although an error page is displayed, the HTTP status code is still 200. Since the user is trying to access a resource that does not exist, the HTTP status code should be 404. This can be done easily by annotating the exception handler method with @ResponseStatus(HttpStatus.NOT_FOUND), which was done in Listing 14-38.

And that's pretty much all your need to know when it comes to handling exceptions thrown by the handler methods.

Switching to Spring Boot

Switching to Spring Boot makes creating MVC applications simpler, because a Spring Boot application does not need an Apache Tomcat server. Also, the structure of the project is simpler and there is no need for special plug-ins to pack the application.

To create a full-blown Spring web application means that, beside the web layer and the view templating layer, you need a DAO layer and a service layer in place. This means you need the specific Boot starter library for persistence and transactions. If you've read this chapter up to this section, you know that you also need validation. The complete list of dependencies is shown in Figure 14-15.

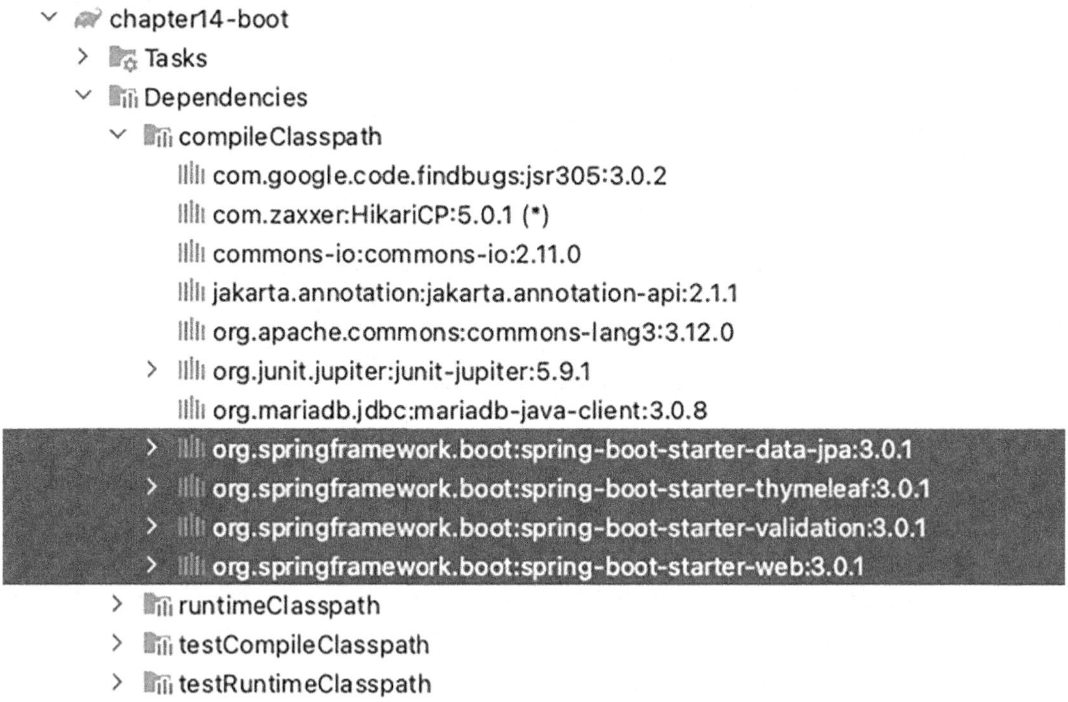

Figure 14-15. *Spring Boot web application dependencies*

The structure of the project must change as well, since all interface-related files and resource files can be placed under the resources directory. The internal structure of the project changes are shown in Figure 14-16. Ignore the pom.xml files, since we are using Gradle as a build tool.

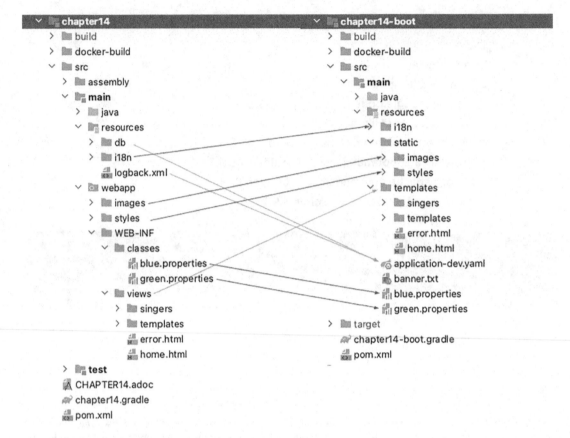

Figure 14-16. *Spring Boot web application project structure*

The orange arrows show the files that changed not only name but location as well. For example, the data source configuration files are no longer necessary, since their content is configured by using Spring Boot configuration properties. The logback.xml file is also no longer needed, because Logback configuration is done by using Spring Boot properties. And the views directory, containing the Thymeleaf templates, is renamed to templates, so instead of configuring Thymeleaf support using explicit bean configuration, Spring Boot out-of-the-box configurations can be used.

The blue.properties and green.properties files for theming configuration were moved from the classes directory to the root of the static folder to benefit of the default Spring Boot way of theming by using beans, because customizing them is a pain.

The next thing to analyze is the Spring Boot application-dev.yaml contents, shown in Listing 14-39.

Listing 14-39. Spring Boot Web Application Configuration

```
# web server configuration
server:
  port: 8081
  servlet:
    context-path: /
  compression:
    enabled: true
  address: 0.0.0.0
```

```yaml
# application configuration
spring:
  mvc:
    hiddenmethod:
      filter:
        enabled: true
  # internationalization configuration
  messages:
    basename: i18n/global
    encoding: UTF-8
    always-use-message-format: true
  # file upload configuration
  servlet:
    multipart:
      enabled: true
      max-file-size: 10MB
      max-request-size: 12MB
  # view resolver configuration
  thymeleaf:
    prefix: classpath:templates/
    suffix: .html
    mode: HTML
    cache: false
    check-template: false
    reactive:
      max-chunk-size: 8192
  # data source configuration
  datasource:
    driverClassName: org.mariadb.jdbc.Driver
    url: jdbc:mariadb://localhost:3306/musicdb?useSSL=false
    username: prospring6
    password: prospring6
    hikari:
      maximum-pool-size: 25
  jpa:
    generate-ddl: false
    properties:
      hibernate:
        jdbc:
          batch_size: 10
          fetch_size: 30
        max_fetch_depth: 3
        show-sql: true
        format-sql: false
        use_sql_comments: false
        hbm2ddl:
          auto: none

# Logging config
logging:
  pattern:
    console: "%-5level: %class{0} - %msg%n"
```

```
level:
  root: INFO
  org.springframework.boot: DEBUG
  com.apress.prospring6.fourteen: INFO
```

Each section of the configuration is prefixed by a comment revealing its scope. The following list further explains properties used in each section:

- `# web server configuration`: This section configures the URL where the application is available. Setting the address to `0.0.0.0` allows the application to be accessible on all network addresses associated with the computer the application runs in; for example, `http://localhost:8081/`, `http://127.0.0.1:8081/`, and so on.

- `# HTTP Method filter`: With `spring.mvc.hiddenmethod.filter.enabled` set to true, this section is the Spring Boot equivalent of configuring the filter for supporting PUT and DELETE HTTP methods.

- `# internationalization configuration`: This section configures the location, name, encoding, and so forth of the internationalization files.

- `# file upload configuration`: This section configures all components necessary to support file upload.

- `# view resolver configuration`: This section configures location, encoding, max size, and so forth for the Thymeleaf view templates. Spring Boot uses this configuration to configure a Thymeleaf Engine and Thymeleaf resolver bean.

- `# data source configuration`: This section groups all data source configurations, including persistence.

- `# Logging config`: This section configures logging.

The parts of the configuration that cannot be put in `application-dev.yaml` are placed into typical configuration classes, annotated with `@Configuration`.

💡 The HibernateCfg class is a workaround for a bug in Spring Data JPA with MariaDB, related to database objects naming. Without this class the repositories cannot be mapped to tables because Spring Boot looks for a table named `musicdb.singer` but doesn't find it, since the MariaDB Docker container was configured by declaring objects using uppercase letters. Since lowercasing the Docker SQL queries was a bit too much, there was an opportunity to introduce some advanced configuration example.

The HibernateCfg is shown in Listing 14-40.

Listing 14-40. HibernateCfg Class

```
package com.apress.prospring6.fourteen.boot

import org.hibernate.boot.model.naming.Identifier
import org.hibernate.boot.model.naming.PhysicalNamingStrategyStandardImpl
import org.hibernate.engine.jdbc.env.spi.JdbcEnvironment
```

```kotlin
import org.springframework.context.annotation.Bean
import org.springframework.context.annotation.Configuration

@Configuration(proxyBeanMethods = false)
open class HibernateCfg {
    @Bean
    open fun caseSensitivePhysicalNamingStrategy(): PhysicalNamingStrategyStandardImpl {
        return object : PhysicalNamingStrategyStandardImpl() {
            override fun toPhysicalTableName(logicalName: Identifier,
                    context: JdbcEnvironment): Identifier {
                return apply(logicalName, context)!!
            }

            override fun toPhysicalColumnName(logicalName: Identifier,
                    context: JdbcEnvironment): Identifier {
                return apply(logicalName, context)!!
            }

            private fun apply(name: Identifier?, context: JdbcEnvironment): Identifier? {
                if (name == null) {
                    return null
                }
                val builder = StringBuilder(name.text.replace('.', '_'))
                var i = 1
                while (i < builder.length - 1) {
                    if (isUnderscoreRequired(builder[i - 1], builder[i], builder[i + 1])) {
                        builder.insert(i++, '_')
                    }
                    i++
                }
                return Identifier.toIdentifier(builder.toString().uppercase(Locale.
                getDefault()))
            }

            private fun isUnderscoreRequired(before: Char, current: Char, after: Char):
            Boolean {
                return Character.isLowerCase(before) && Character.isUpperCase(current) &&
                    Character.isLowerCase(after)
            }
        }
    }
}
```

The PhysicalNamingStrategyStandardImpl class that is extended here is itself implementing PhysicalNamingStrategy, which is a pluggable strategy contract for applying physical naming rules for database object names. The @Configuration(proxyBeanMethods = false) configuration is used to exclude beans declared in this class from getting proxied to enforce bean life-cycle behavior. This means that any bean that is created by calling the caseSensitivePhysicalNamingStrategy() method will get a new copy of the PhysicalNamingStrategyStandardImpl bean.

The WebConfig class is a Spring Web configuration class extending WebMvcConfigurer and is necessary to configure the locale and theme interceptors and resolvers. They are not automatically configured by Spring Boot, so this job is left to the developer. The WebConfig class is shown in Listing 14-41.

Listing 14-41. WebConfig Class

package com.apress.prospring6.fourteen.boot

import java.util.Locale
// more import statements omitted

```
@Configuration
@ComponentScan(basePackages = ["com.apress.prospring6.fourteen.boot"])
open class WebConfig : WebMvcConfigurer {
    @Bean
    open fun localeChangeInterceptor() = LocaleChangeInterceptor().apply {
            paramName = "lang"
    }

    @Bean
    open fun themeChangeInterceptor() = ThemeChangeInterceptor().apply {
            paramName = "theme"
    }

    @Bean
    open fun localeResolver() = CookieLocaleResolver().apply {
            setDefaultLocale(Locale.ENGLISH)
            setCookieMaxAge(3600)
            setCookieName("locale")
    }

    @Bean
    open fun themeResolver() = CookieThemeResolver().apply {
            defaultThemeName = "green"
            cookieMaxAge = 3600
            cookieName = "theme"
    }

    @Bean
    open fun webChangeInterceptor() = WebContentInterceptor().apply {
            cacheSeconds = 0
            setSupportedMethods("GET", "POST", "PUT", "DELETE")
    }

    override fun addInterceptors(registry: InterceptorRegistry) {
        registry.addInterceptor(localeChangeInterceptor()).addPathPatterns("/*")
        registry.addInterceptor(themeChangeInterceptor())
        registry.addInterceptor(webChangeInterceptor())
    }
}
```

▲   Notice that this class is not annotated with @EnableWebMvc. It is not needed because Spring Boot configures the web application context. Using this annotation in a Spring Boot application will cause unpredictable behavior, if the application starts at all.

What is left is to tell Spring Boot where our entities and repository interfaces are and enable transactional support. These configurations are easily done via annotations placed on the Spring Boot main class, depicted in Listing 14-42.

Listing 14-42. Chapter14Application Class

```
package com.apress.prospring6.fourteen.boot

import org.springframework.boot.SpringApplication
import org.springframework.boot.autoconfigure.SpringBootApplication
import org.springframework.boot.autoconfigure.domain.EntityScan
import org.springframework.core.env.AbstractEnvironment
import org.springframework.data.jpa.repository.config.EnableJpaRepositories
import org.springframework.transaction.annotation.EnableTransactionManagement

import java.util.Arrays
import java.util.stream.Collectors

@EntityScan(basePackages = ["com.apress.prospring6.fourteen.boot.entities"])
@EnableTransactionManagement
@EnableJpaRepositories("com.apress.prospring6.fourteen.boot.repos")
@SpringBootApplication
open class Chapter14Application {
    companion object {
        @JvmStatic
        fun main(args: Array<String>) {
            System.setProperty(AbstractEnvironment.ACTIVE_PROFILES_PROPERTY_NAME, "dev")
            SpringApplication.run(Chapter14Application::class.java, *args)
        }
    }
}
```

The reason for declaring a profile named dev for running the application is so that the context can be slightly modified for running tests.

With the configuration described so far, running the Chapter14Application will start the same applications deployed on an Apache Tomcat server in previous sections.

Testing a Spring Boot Web Application

🛈   The Spring Boot testing procedure for web applications as described in the Java sister edition internally depends on the docker-machine project. Since development of this project is discontinued, the author of the Kotlin edition decided to abandon this section. A replacement is described at `https://spring.io/guides/gs/testing-web/`. Since just repeating the procedure elaborated there does not have much value, check it out if you want to conduct your own tests.

Summary

In this chapter, we covered many topics related to web development using Spring MVC. First, we discussed the high-level concepts of the MVC pattern. Then we covered Spring MVC's architecture, including its `WebApplicationContext` hierarchy, request-handling life cycle, and configuration.

Next you learned how to develop a sample singer management application using Spring MVC, with JSP as the view technology. During the course of developing the samples, we elaborated on different areas. Main topics included i18n, theming, and template support with Thymeleaf.

To integrate a Spring web application with a view technology, there needs to be at least a custom bean that implements Spring's `org.springframework.web.servlet.ViewResolver`. Thymeleaf is also a templating view technology, and thus its `ViewResolver` implementation relies on a `SpringTemplateEngine` and `SpringResourceTemplateResolver`.

And because Spring Boot is the prodigy feature of the Spring team, how to build a full-blown web application using it had to be covered. In the next chapter, we cover more features that Spring brings in terms of web application development by covering REST requests.

CHAPTER 15

■ ■ ■

Spring REST Support

Chapter 13 introduced communication over the HTTP protocol between two Spring web applications that exposed REST API. This chapter expands the subject by introducing you to RESTful web services, also referred to as RESTful-WS.

Nowadays, RESTful-WS is perhaps the most widely used technology for remote access, From remote service invocation via HTTP to supporting an Ajax-style interactive web front end, RESTful-WS is being adopted intensively, especially because of the rise of microservices. RESTful web services are popular for several reasons.

- *Easy to understand*: RESTful web services are designed around HTTP. The URL, together with the HTTP method, specifies the intention of the request. For example, the URL `http://somedomain.com/restful/customer/1` with an HTTP method of GET means that the client wants to retrieve the customer information, where the customer ID equals 1.

- *Lightweight*: RESTful is much more lightweight when compared to SOAP-based web services, which include a large amount of metadata to describe which service the client wants to invoke. For a RESTful request and response, it's simply an HTTP request and response, as with any other web application.

- *Firewall friendly*: Because RESTful web services are designed to be accessible via HTTP (or HTTPS), the application becomes much more firewall friendly and easily accessed by remote clients.

In this chapter, we present the basic concepts of RESTful-WS and Spring's support of RESTful-WS through its Spring MVC module.

Introducing RESTful Web Services

The REST in RESTful-WS is short for **RE**presentational **S**tate **T**ransfer, which is an architectural style. REST defines a set of architectural constraints that together describe a uniform interface for accessing resources. The main concepts of this uniform interface include the identification of resources and the manipulation of resources through representations.

For the identification of resources, a piece of information should be accessible via a uniform resource identifier (URI). For example, the URL `http://somedomain.com/api/singer/1` is a URI that often represents a resource, which is a piece of singer information with an identifier of 1. If the singer with an identifier of 1 does not exist, the client will probably get a 404 HTTP status code, just like a "page not found" error on a website. Another example, `http://somedomain.com/api/singers`, is a URI that might represent a resource that is a list of singer information. Those identifiable resources can be managed through various representations, as shown in Table 15-1.

Table 15-1. *Representations for Manipulating Resources*

HTTP Method	Description
GET	GET retrieves a representation of a resource.
HEAD	Identical to GET, without the response body. Typically used for getting a header.
POST	POST creates a new resource.
PUT	PUT updates a resource.
DELETE	DELETE deletes a resource.
OPTIONS	OPTIONS retrieves allowed HTTP methods.

For a detailed description of RESTful web services, we recommend *Ajax and REST Recipes: A Problem-Solution Approach by Christian Gross* (Apress, 2006).

Using Spring MVC to Expose RESTful Web Services

In this section, we show you how to use Spring MVC to expose the singer services as RESTful web services, as designed in the previous section. This sample builds upon the already introduced Singer class and the SingerRepo repository interface.

■ **INFO**   In the previous edition of the book, Castor[1] XML was used for serialization. In this edition, since the Castor library hasn't been maintained for a while, it was dropped in favor of Jackson[2].

The Jackson library is very capable and provides components for serializing objects to JSON and XML. Mapping Java properties to XML elements or JSON properties is easily done via annotations. Although Jackson annotations are named @Json*, they work as configurations for XML serialization too. Listing 15-1 shows the Singer class decorated with Jackson annotations.

Listing 15-1. The Updated Singer Class Decorated with Jackson Annotations

```
package com.apress.prospring6.fifteen.entities

import com.fasterxml.jackson.annotation.JsonFormat
import com.fasterxml.jackson.annotation.JsonIgnore
// other import statements omitted

@Entity
@Table(name = "SINGER")
class Singer {
        @JsonIgnore // do not serialize
        @Id
```

---

[1] https://castor.exolab.org/xml-framework.html
[2] https://github.com/FasterXML/jackson

```kotlin
@GeneratedValue(strategy = GenerationType.IDENTITY)
@Column(name = "ID")
var id: Long? = null

@JsonIgnore // do not serialize
@Version
@Column(name = "VERSION")
var version = 0

@Column(name = "FIRST_NAME")
var firstName: @NotEmpty @Size(min = 2, max = 30) String? = null

@Column(name = "LAST_NAME")
var lastName: @NotEmpty @Size(min = 2, max = 30) String? = null

@JsonFormat(pattern = "yyyy-MM-dd")
@DateTimeFormat(pattern = "yyyy-MM-dd")
@Column(name = "BIRTH_DATE")
var birthDate: LocalDate? = null

companion object {
        @Serial
        private val serialVersionUID = 2L
}

override fun equals(other: Any?): Boolean {
        if (this === other) return true
        if (javaClass != other?.javaClass) return false

        other as Singer

        if (id != other.id) return false
        if (firstName != other.firstName) return false
        if (lastName != other.lastName) return false
        return birthDate == other.birthDate
}

override fun hashCode(): Int {
        var result = id?.hashCode() ?: 0
        result = 31 * result + (firstName?.hashCode() ?: 0)
        result = 31 * result + (lastName?.hashCode() ?: 0)
        result = 31 * result + (birthDate?.hashCode() ?: 0)
        return result
}

override fun toString(): String {
        return "Singer(id=$id, version=$version, firstName=$firstName,
        lastName=$lastName, birthDate=$birthDate)"
}
}
```

By default, all Singer fields that Jackson knows how to serialize to text values are serialized. If not all fields should be serialized, such as the version field, the @JsonIgnore annotation is used to tell Jackson to skip those fields.

For complex types such as calendar dates, there are two options: use the @JsonFormat annotation configured with the pattern we want our date value converted to or extend com.fasterxml.jackson. databind.ser.std.StdSerializer.

Implementing `SingerController`

To keep things simple, we'll skip declaring a SingerService and write a SingerController that uses SingerRepo. The SingerController is displayed in Listing 15-2.

Listing 15-2. The SingerController Implementation

```
package com.apress.prospring6.fifteen.controllers

import org.springframework.stereotype.Controller
import org.springframework.web.bind.annotation.*
// other import statements omitted

@Controller
@ResponseBody
@RequestMapping(path = ["singer"])
class SingerController(private val singerRepo: SingerRepo) {
    @ResponseStatus(HttpStatus.OK) // @GetMapping(path={"/", ""})
    @RequestMapping(path = ["/", ""], method = [RequestMethod.GET])
    fun all(): List<Singer> {
        return singerRepo.findAll()
    }

    @ResponseStatus(HttpStatus.OK) //@GetMapping(path = "/{id}")
    @RequestMapping(path = ["/{id}"], method = [RequestMethod.GET])
    fun findSingerById(@PathVariable id: Long): Singer? {
        return singerRepo.findById(id).orElse(null)
    }

    @ResponseStatus(HttpStatus.CREATED) //@PostMapping(path="/")
    @RequestMapping(path = ["/"], method = [RequestMethod.POST])
    fun create(@RequestBody singer: Singer): Singer {
        LOGGER.info("Creating singer: {}", singer)
        val saved = singerRepo.save(singer)
        LOGGER.info("Singer created successfully with info: $saved")
        return singer
    }

    @ResponseStatus(HttpStatus.OK) //@PutMapping(value="/{id}")
    @RequestMapping(path = ["/{id}"], method = [RequestMethod.PUT])
    fun update(
        @RequestBody singer: Singer,
        @PathVariable id: Long
    ) { // if we enable validation we cannot provide a Singer with missing fields
        LOGGER.info("Updating singer: {}", singer)
```

```
        val fromDb = singerRepo.findById(id).orElseThrow { IllegalArgumentException("Singer
        does not exist!") }
        fromDb.firstName = singer.firstName
        fromDb.lastName= singer.lastName
        fromDb.birthDate = singer.birthDate
        singerRepo.save(fromDb)
        LOGGER.info("Singer updated successfully with info: $fromDb")
    }

    @ResponseStatus(HttpStatus.NO_CONTENT) //@DeleteMapping(value="/{id}")
    @RequestMapping(path = ["/{id}"], method = [RequestMethod.DELETE])
    fun delete(@PathVariable id: Long) {
        LOGGER.info("Deleting singer with id: {}", id)
        singerRepo.deleteById(id)
        LOGGER.info("Singer deleted successfully")
    }

    companion object {
        val LOGGER = LoggerFactory.getLogger(SingerController::class.java)
    }
}
```

The main points about the previous class are as follows:

- The class is annotated with @Controller, indicating that it's a Spring MVC controller.

- The class-level annotation @RequestMapping(value="/singer") indicates that this controller will be mapped to all URLs under the main web context. In this sample, all URLs under http://localhost:8080/singer will be handled by this controller.

- The SingerRepo is required for this controller to work.

- The @RequestMapping annotation for each method indicates the URL pattern and the corresponding HTTP method that it will be mapped to. For example, the all() method will be mapped to the http://localhost:8080/singer URL, with an HTTP GET method. For the update(..) method, it will be mapped to the URL http://localhost:8080/singer/1 with an HTTP PUT method.

- What is the difference between this controller and the ones introduced in **Chapter 14**? What makes a controller get used for REST requests? Two things: the @ResponseBody annotation being placed on each handler method and the fact that the handler methods do not return a logical view name. The @ResponseBody annotation indicates a method return value should be bound to the web response body, which is the fancy technical way to say that the value returned by the method is actually a web response. If annotating each method with @ResponseBody seems verbose, you can easily skip that by just using it once on the class, but this means no method in the controller is expected to return a view or a view name.

- For methods that accept path variables (for example, the findSingerById(..) method), the path variable is annotated with @PathVariable. This instructs Spring MVC to bind the path variable within the URL (for example, http://localhost:8080/singer/1) into the id argument of the findSingerById(..) method. Note that for the id argument, the type is Long, and Spring's type conversion system will automatically handle the conversion from String to Long for us.

- For the create(..) and update(..) methods, the Singer argument is annotated with @RequestBody. This instructs Spring to automatically bind the content within the HTTP request body into the Singer domain object. The conversion will be done by the declared instances of the HttpMessageConverter<Object> interface (under the package org.springframework.http.converter) for supporting formats, which will be discussed later in this chapter.

Spring version 4.3 introduced some customization of the @RequestMapping annotations that match basic HTTP methods. Table 15-2 lists the equivalence between the new annotations and old-style @RequestMapping.

Table 15-2. *Annotations for Mapping HTTP Method Requests onto Specific Handler Methods Introduced in Spring 4.3*

Annotation	Old-Style Equivalent
@GetMapping	@RequestMapping(method = RequestMethod.GET)
@PostMapping	@RequestMapping(method = RequestMethod.POST)
@PutMapping	@RequestMapping(method = RequestMethod.PUT)
@DeleteMapping	@RequestMapping(method = RequestMethod.DELETE)

There is also another stereotype annotation that was introduced in Spring 4.0 for REST controller classes, called @RestController. This annotation is declared in the org.springframework.web.bind. annotation as well and is meta-annotated with @Controller and @ResponseBody, which basically give it the power of both. Using this annotation, and the ones in Table 15-2, the SingerController class becomes less verbose, as shown in Listing 15-3.

Listing 15-3. The SingerController Implementation Using @RestController

```
package com.apress.prospring6.fifteen.controllers

import org.springframework.web.bind.annotation.RestController
// other import statements omitted

@RestController
@RequestMapping(path = ["singer"])
class SingerController(private val singerRepo: SingerRepo) {

    ...
}
```

For a Spring Web REST application, one that doesn't require specialized web views, there is no need for specialized view resolver beans. So, the configuration is a little simpler. The WebInitializer class, the one configuring the DispatcherServlet is pretty standard for Spring web applications and when no specialized views are used, the HiddenHttpMethodFilter is not needed. See Listing 15-4.

Listing 15-4. The WebInitializer Class

```
package com.apress.prospring6.fifteen

import jakarta.servlet.Filter
import org.springframework.web.filter.CharacterEncodingFilter
import org.springframework.web.filter.HiddenHttpMethodFilter
import org.springframework.web.servlet.support.AbstractAnnotationConfigDispatcherServlet
Initializer

import java.nio.charset.StandardCharsets

import java.nio.charset.StandardCharsets

class WebInitializer : AbstractAnnotationConfigDispatcherServletInitializer() {
    override fun getRootConfigClasses(): Array<Class<*>> {
        return arrayOf(BasicDataSourceCfg::class.java, TransactionCfg::class.java)
    }

    override fun getServletConfigClasses(): Array<Class<*>> {
        return arrayOf(WebConfig::class.java)
    }

    override fun getServletMappings(): Array<String> {
        return arrayOf("/")
    }

    override fun getServletFilters(): Array<Filter> {
        val cef = CharacterEncodingFilter()
        cef.encoding = StandardCharsets.UTF_8.name()
        cef.setForceEncoding(true)
        return arrayOf(HiddenHttpMethodFilter(), cef)
    }
}
```

The Spring MVC configuration class (WebConfig, shown in Listing 15-5) is simple as well, since usually a REST application does not require theming or internationalization.

Listing 15-5. The WebConfig Class

```
package com.apress.prospring6.fifteen

import org.springframework.web.servlet.config.annotation.EnableWebMvc
import org.springframework.web.servlet.config.annotation.WebMvcConfigurer
// other import statements omitted

@Configuration
@EnableWebMvc
@ComponentScan(basePackages = ["com.apress.prospring6.fifteen"])
open class WebConfig : WebMvcConfigurer {
```

```kotlin
    override fun addViewControllers(registry: ViewControllerRegistry) {
        registry.addRedirectViewController("/", "/home")
    }

    @Bean
    open fun validator(): Validator {
        return LocalValidatorFactoryBean()
    }

    override fun getValidator(): Validator {
        return validator()
    }
}
```

This configuration is minimal, and even in classic configuration, Spring MVC determines the requested media types from the request based on the Accept header.

You can configure the requested media type based on path extension, query parameters, by overriding the configureContentNegotiation(..) method in your WebConfig class[3], or by declaring different handler methods and using the produces attribute.

In order to override the default message converters created by Spring MVC, implement the configureMessageConverters() method. And if you want to add custom message converters to the set of default ones, override method extendMessageConverters()[4].

For this chapter, we don't need to do any of that, because the default message converters configured by Spring MVC are all that we need.

So, now that we've decided the Accept header is the one that a client must provide in the request to specify the format they want for the data, do we need to configure anything else to make this work? The answer is no, but we do need to add the suitable Jackson libraries to the classpath so that Spring MVC can use them.

The dependencies for the chapter15 project are shown in Figure 15-1.

---

[3] https://docs.spring.io/spring-framework/docs/current/reference/html/web.
html#mvc-config-content-negotiation
[4] https://docs.spring.io/spring-framework/docs/current/reference/html/web.
html#mvc-config-message-converters

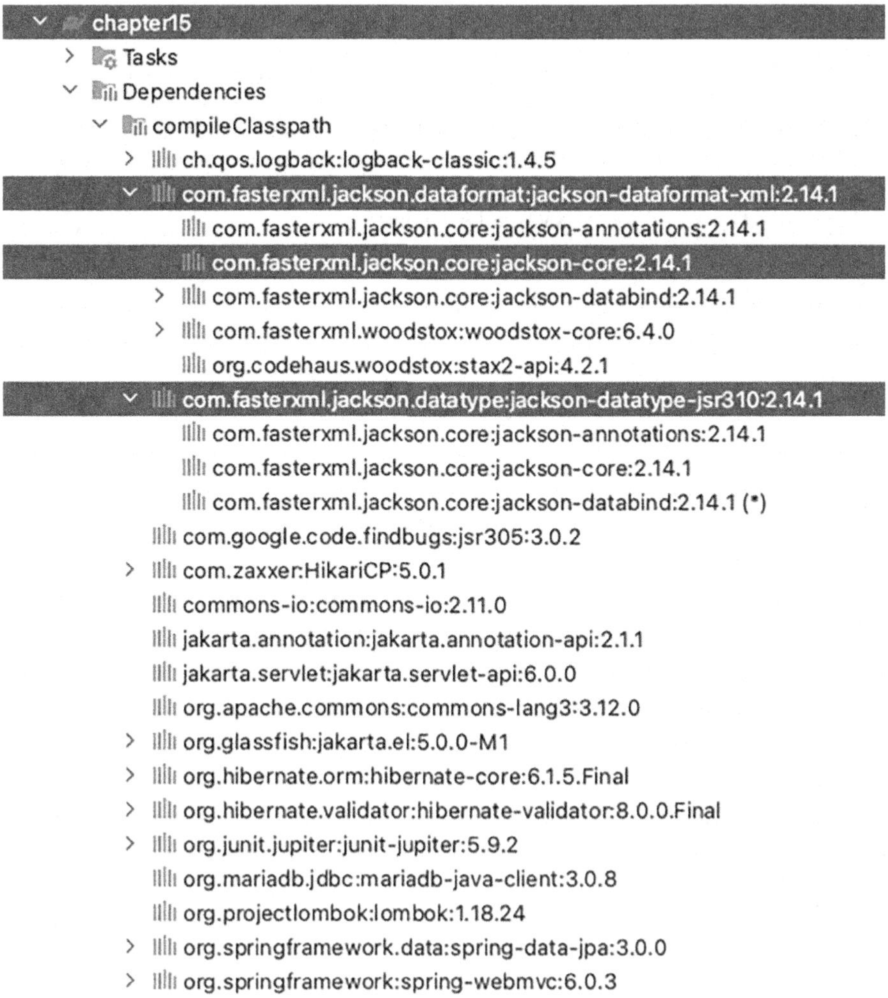

```
∨   chapter15
  >   Tasks
  ∨   Dependencies
    ∨   compileClasspath
      >   ch.qos.logback:logback-classic:1.4.5
      ∨   com.fasterxml.jackson.dataformat:jackson-dataformat-xml:2.14.1
            com.fasterxml.jackson.core:jackson-annotations:2.14.1
            com.fasterxml.jackson.core:jackson-core:2.14.1
        >   com.fasterxml.jackson.core:jackson-databind:2.14.1
        >   com.fasterxml.woodstox:woodstox-core:6.4.0
            org.codehaus.woodstox:stax2-api:4.2.1
      ∨   com.fasterxml.jackson.datatype:jackson-datatype-jsr310:2.14.1
            com.fasterxml.jackson.core:jackson-annotations:2.14.1
            com.fasterxml.jackson.core:jackson-core:2.14.1
            com.fasterxml.jackson.core:jackson-databind:2.14.1 (*)
          com.google.code.findbugs:jsr305:3.0.2
      >   com.zaxxer:HikariCP:5.0.1
          commons-io:commons-io:2.11.0
          jakarta.annotation:jakarta.annotation-api:2.1.1
          jakarta.servlet:jakarta.servlet-api:6.0.0
          org.apache.commons:commons-lang3:3.12.0
      >   org.glassfish:jakarta.el:5.0.0-M1
      >   org.hibernate.orm:hibernate-core:6.1.5.Final
      >   org.hibernate.validator:hibernate-validator:8.0.0.Final
      >   org.junit.jupiter:junit-jupiter:5.9.2
          org.mariadb.jdbc:mariadb-java-client:3.0.8
          org.projectlombok:lombok:1.18.24
      >   org.springframework.data:spring-data-jpa:3.0.0
      >   org.springframework:spring-webmvc:6.0.3
```

Figure 15-1. *Project chapter15 dependencies*

In Figure 15-1, three Jackson libraries are highlighted:

- jackson-dataformat-xml is needed for serialization to XML.

- jackson-core is the core Jackson library used for serialization to JSON and contains all the @Json* annotations.

- jackson-datatype-jsr310 is needed for serialization and formatting of Java 8 Date and Time types.

Now, the server-side service is complete. At this point, you can build the WAR file containing the web application and deploy it to an Apache Tomcat 10 instance or, if you are using IntelliJ IDEA, create an Apache Tomcat Launcher as shown in **Chapter 14**.

Testing the RESTful-WS Application

There are many ways to test a REST application. We can build a Java or Kotlin client, we can use HTTPie requests, or we can use curl[5], Postman[6], or any other application or CLI for making HTTP requests. Let's start with the simplest HTTPie, the IntelliJ IDEA HTTP client (IntelliJ IDEA Ultimate required). The request to retrieve all singers as XML and a snippet of the returned response are shown in Listing 15-6

Listing 15-6. HTTPie Request to Get All Singers As XML and Response

```
### Request
GET http://localhost:8080/ch15/singer/
Accept: application/xml

### Response
HTTP/1.1 200
Content-Type: application/xml;charset=UTF-8
Transfer-Encoding: chunked
Date: Tue, 17 Jan 2023 22:13:57 GMT
Keep-Alive: timeout=20
Connection: keep-alive

<List>
    <item>
        <firstName>John</firstName>
        <lastName>Mayer</lastName>
        <birthDate>1977-10-16</birthDate>
    </item>
    <item>
        <firstName>Ben</firstName>
        <lastName>Barnes</lastName>
        <birthDate>1981-08-20</birthDate>
    </item>
<!--  other elements omitted -->
</list>
```

This command sends an HTTP request to the server's RESTful web service; in this case, it invokes the all() method in SingerController to retrieve and return all singer information. Also, the Accept HTTP header value is set to application/xml, meaning that the client wants to receive data in XML format.

To get the data in JSON format, all we have to do is replace the Accept header value with application/json. And because curl was mentioned, Listing 15-7 shows the verbose (-v option) curl request for retrieving the data as JSON and a snippet of the response.

---

[5] https://curl.se
[6] https://www.postman.com

Listing 15-7. curl Request to Get All Singers As JSON and Response

```
### Request
curl -v -H "Accept: application/json" http://localhost:8080/ch15/singer/

### Response
*   Trying 127.0.0.1:8080...
* Connected to localhost (127.0.0.1) port 8080 (#0)
> GET /ch15/singer/ HTTP/1.1
> Host: localhost:8080
> User-Agent: curl/7.84.0
> Accept: application/json
>
* Mark bundle as not supporting multiuse
< HTTP/1.1 200
< Content-Type: application/json;charset=UTF-8
< Transfer-Encoding: chunked
< Date: Tue, 17 Jan 2023 22:22:54 GMT
<
* Connection #0 to host localhost left intact
[
    {
        "firstName":"John",
        "lastName":"Mayer",
        "birthDate":"1977-10-16"
    },
    {
        "firstName":"Ben",
        "lastName":"Barnes",
        "birthDate":"1981-08-20"
    }
# other JSON elements omitted
]
```

This command sends an HTTP request to the server's RESTful web service, and the same all() method in SingerController to retrieve and return all singer information. In this case, the -H option declares an HTTP header attribute, meaning that the client wants to receive data in JSON format.

Both HTTPie and curl make the same request, the only difference being the value of the Accept header. Changing the data format works because Spring MVC registers org.springframework.http.converter. HttpMessageConverter<T> implementations found on the classpath and uses them for content type resolution.

When Spring REST applications need to communicate with each other, for non-reactive applications a RestTemplate instance is used. **Chapter 13** introduced RestTemplate to test a Spring Boot application and the tests were designed to run in a Spring Boot test context. For this section, the application is configured in a classic way, without Spring Boot and packed as a *.war file that is deployed on an Apache Tomcat server. This means that the tests written for this application are separate from the application context. The application runs in Tomcat, and the test class shares only the classpath with the application, not the context, thus the test is equivalent to a client for the application.

Listing 15-8 shows the RestClientTest class that uses a RestTemplate instance to submit all type of HTTP requests to the application deployed on Tomcat.

Listing 15-8. RestClientTest Class Making Requests to ch15 Web Application Using RestTemplate

package com.apress.prospring6.fifteen

import org.springframework.web.client.RestTemplate
// other import statements omitted

```kotlin
class RestClientTest {
    val restTemplate = RestTemplate()

    @Test
    fun testFindAll() {
        LOGGER.info("--> Testing retrieve all singers")
        val singers = restTemplate.getForObject(
            URI_SINGER_ROOT,
            Array<Singer>::class.java
        )
        Assertions.assertTrue(singers!!.isNotEmpty())
        Arrays.stream(singers).forEach { s: Singer ->
            LOGGER.info(
                s.toString()
            )
        }
    }

    @Test
    fun testFindAllWithExecute() {
        LOGGER.info("--> Testing retrieve all singers")
        val singers = restTemplate.execute(
            URI_SINGER_ROOT, HttpMethod.GET,
            { request: ClientHttpRequest? ->
                LOGGER.debug(
                    "Request submitted ..."
                )
            },
            { response: ClientHttpResponse ->
                Assertions.assertEquals(
                    HttpStatus.OK,
                    response.statusCode
                )
                String(response.body.readAllBytes())
            }
        )
        LOGGER.info("Response: {}", singers)
    }

    @Test
    fun testFindById() {
        LOGGER.info("--> Testing retrieve a singer by id : 1")
        val singer = restTemplate.getForObject(
            URI_SINGER_WITH_ID,
            Singer::class.java, 1
```

```kotlin
    )
    Assertions.assertNotNull(singer)
    LOGGER.info(singer!!.toString())
}

@Test
fun testCreate() {
    LOGGER.info("--> Testing create singer")
    var singerNew = Singer().apply {
        firstName = "TEST"
        lastName = "Singer"
        birthDate = LocalDate.now()
    }
    singerNew = restTemplate.postForObject(
        URI_SINGER_ROOT, singerNew,
        Singer::class.java
    )!!
    LOGGER.info("Singer created successfully: $singerNew")
}

@Test
fun testDelete() {
    LOGGER.info("--> Testing delete singer by id : 57") // TODO check your database and
                                                        //      select an ID from there
    val initialCount = restTemplate.getForObject(
        URI_SINGER_ROOT,
        Array<Singer>::class.java
    )!!.size
    restTemplate.delete(URI_SINGER_WITH_ID, 57)
    val afterDeleteCount = restTemplate.getForObject(
        URI_SINGER_ROOT,
        Array<Singer>::class.java
    )!!.size
    Assertions.assertEquals(initialCount - afterDeleteCount, 1)
}

@Test
fun testUpdate() {
    LOGGER.info("--> Testing update singer by id : 1")
    val singer = restTemplate.getForObject(
        URI_SINGER_WITH_ID,
        Singer::class.java, 1
    )!!
    singer.firstName = "John"
    restTemplate.put(URI_SINGER_WITH_ID, singer, 1)
    LOGGER.info("Singer update successfully: $singer")
}

companion object {
    private const val URI_SINGER_ROOT =
        "http://localhost:8080/chapter15-1.0-SNAPSHOT/singer/"
    private const val URI_SINGER_WITH_ID =
```

711

```
        "http://localhost:8080/chapter15-1.0-SNAPSHOT/singer/{id}"
    val LOGGER = LoggerFactory.getLogger(RestClientTest::class.java)
  }
}
```

The RestClientTest class contains methods for testing all the URLs supported by the web application. Each method can be run individually in a smart editor such as IntelliJ IDEA. The URLs for accessing various operations are declared, which will be used in later samples. The RestTemplate instance is created and used in all test methods.

In the testFindAll() method, the RestTemplate#getForObject(..) method is called (which corresponds to the HTTP GET method), passing in the URL and the expected return type, which is the Singers[] class that contains the full list of singers.

Make sure the application server is running and the web application is exposed under context ch15. Running the testFindAll() test method, the test should pass and produce the output shown in Listing 15-9.

Listing 15-9. Console Log for Execution of RestClientTest#testFindAll()

```
11:33:06.970 [Test worker] INFO  c.a.p.f.RestClientTest - --> Testing retrieve all singers
11:33:07.002 [Test worker] DEBUG o.s.w.c.RestTemplate - HTTP GET http://localhost:8080/
ch15/singer/
11:33:07.018 [Test worker] DEBUG o.s.w.c.RestTemplate - Accept=[application/xml, text/xml,
application/json, application/*+xml, application/*+json]
11:33:07.090 [Test worker] DEBUG o.s.w.c.RestTemplate - Response 200 OK
11:33:07.096 [Test worker] DEBUG o.s.w.c.RestTemplate - Reading to [com.apress.prospring6.
fifteen.entities.Singer[]]
11:33:07.179 [Test worker] INFO  c.a.p.f.RestClientTest - Singer(id=null, version=0,
firstName=John, lastName=Mayer, birthDate=1977-10-16)
11:33:07.179 [Test worker] INFO  c.a.p.f.RestClientTest - Singer(id=null, version=0,
firstName=Ben, lastName=Barnes, birthDate=1981-08-20)
...
# the rest of the singers omitted
```

As you can see, the RestTemplate instance submits the request with Accept header values matching all converters found on the classpath, in this case application/xml, text/xml, application/json, application/xml, application/json, which guarantees a correct interpretation of the response and a successful conversion to the Java type provided as the argument, in this case an array of Singer. We cannot use List<Singer> as a type for the response to be converted to, because this type is generic and cannot be used as an argument.

The method getForObject(..), as its name makes it obvious, is useful for submitting GET requests. If you analyze the rest of the test methods, you can see that there are matching methods in RestTemplate for the rest of the HTTP methods: postForObject(..) for POST, put(..) for PUT, and delete(..) for DELETE. Aside from these, there are also the specialized execute(..) and exchange() sets of methods. The execute(..) method is suitable when a callback method (provided as an implementation for RequestCallback) must be executed right after the request is submitted, and since the type to convert the response body is not provided as an argument, a ResponseExtractor<T> can be provided to explicitly convert the body into the required type. There is more than one version of this method, including additional request parameters. Listing 15-10 shows how a test method equivalent to testFindAll(..) can be written using the execute(..) method.

Listing 15-10. Testing with template execute()

```
package com.apress.prospring6.fifteen

import org.springframework.web.client.RequestCallback
import org.springframework.web.client.ResponseExtractor
// other import statements omitted

class RestClientTest {

  @Test
    fun testFindAllWithExecute() {
        LOGGER.info("--> Testing retrieve all singers")
        val singers = restTemplate.execute<String>(URI_SINGER_ROOT, HttpMethod.GET,
            { request: ClientHttpRequest? ->
                LOGGER.debug(
                    "Request submitted ..."
                )
            },
            { response: ClientHttpResponse ->
                Assertions.assertEquals(HttpStatus.OK, response.statusCode)
                String(response.body.readAllBytes())
            }
            )
        LOGGER.info("Response: {}", singers)
    }
// other test methods omitted
}
```

Both RequestCallback[7] and ResponseExtractor<T>[8] are functional interfaces, which allows for their implementations to be declared inline using lambda expressions. The two functional interfaces are shown in Listing 15-11. Note that for Kotlin you usually don't need them—they are listed here just in case the need arises.

Listing 15-11. The RequestCallback and ResponseExtractor<T> Functional Interfaces

```
// comments omitted
package org.springframework.web.client

import java.io.IOException
import java.lang.reflect.Type

import org.springframework.http.client.ClientHttpRequest
```

---

[7] https://github.com/spring-projects/spring-framework/blob/main/spring-web/src/main/java/org/springframework/web/client/RequestCallback.java
[8] https://github.com/spring-projects/spring-framework/blob/main/spring-web/src/main/java/org/springframework/web/client/ResponseExtractor.java

```
@FunctionalInterface
interface RequestCallback {
    fun doWithRequest(request:ClientHttpRequest)
}
```

```
//-------------------------------
```

```
package org.springframework.web.client
```

```
import java.io.IOException
import java.lang.reflect.Type
```

```
import org.springframework.http.client.ClientHttpResponse
import org.springframework.lang.Nullable
```

```
@FunctionalInterface
interface ResponseExtractor<T> {
    @Nullable
    fun extractData(response:ClientHttpResponse) : T
}
```

The set of exchange(..) methods are the most general/capable methods provided by RestTemplate suitable when none of the other methods provides a complete enough parameter set to meet your needs. As its name reveals, the exchange(..) method is designed to do an exchange of information between the client and the application running on a server, and thus is most suitable for complex POST and PUT requests. Listing 15-12 shows the testCreate(..) version using exchange(..).

Listing 15-12. Using exchange() in Tests

```
package com.apress.prospring6.fifteen
```

```
import org.springframework.http.HttpEntity
import org.springframework.http.HttpMethod
// other import statements omitted
```

```
public class RestClientTest {

    @Test
    fun testCreateWithExchange() {
        LOGGER.info("--> Testing create singer")
        val singerNew = Singer().apply {
            firstName = "TEST2"
            lastName = "Singer2"
            birthDate = LocalDate.now()
        }
        val request = HttpEntity(singerNew)
        val created = restTemplate.exchange(
            URI_SINGER_ROOT, HttpMethod.POST, request,
            Singer::class.java
        )
        Assertions.assertEquals(HttpStatus.CREATED, created.statusCode)
        val singerCreated = created.body
```

```
        Assertions.assertNotNull(singerCreated)
        LOGGER.info("Singer created successfully: $singerCreated")
    }

// other test methods omitted
}
```

The `HttpEntity<T>` is powerful, as it can wrap together body and headers, making it also suitable for `RestTemplate#exchange(..)` to submit secured rest requests.

Testing with `RestTemplate` is simple, but the controller might need some work to make it more capable REST wise. What happens if the `Singer` instance we are trying to edit does not exist? What happens if we try to create a `Singer` instance with some name? What would the response be? Because all the handler methods were annotated with `@ResponseStatus` to configure the response status code to return when all goes well, but no error status code was configured anywhere, we'd run into trouble. For example, running the `testCreateWithExchange(..)` method now returns 500(`INTERNAL_SERVER_ERROR`) because the repository throws a `org.springframework.dao.DataIntegrityViolationException` that is not handled anywhere. And so, handling exceptions is necessary.

REST Exception Handling Using `ResponseEntity<T>`

The first thing we could do is treat an exception where it happens, and return the desired `HttpStatus` value explicitly via the `ResponseEntity<T>` type. This type is an extension of `org.springframework.http.HttpEntity<T>` that includes a `HttpStatusCode` status code. It can be used to wrap the result of a `RestTemplate` method invocation, but it can also be used as a return type in REST handler methods.

This being said, let's modify the `findSingerById(..)` handler method to return a `ResponseEntity<Singer>` that includes the `HttpStatus.OK` code when a singer with the provided id exists and return a `ResponseEntity<HttpStatus>` that includes the `HttpStatus.NOT_FOUND` code when a singer with the provided id cannot be found. Listing 15-13 shows this version of the method, which is part of a new REST controller class named `Singer2Controller`.

Listing 15-13. The `Singer2Controller#findSingerById(..)` Method That Returns a `ResponseEntity<T>`

```
package com.apress.prospring6.fifteen.controllers

import org.springframework.http.HttpStatus
import org.springframework.http.ResponseEntity
// other import statements omitted

@RestController
@RequestMapping(path = ["singer2"])
class Singer2Controller(private val singerRepo: SingerRepo) {
    @GetMapping(path = ["/{id}"])
    fun findSingerById(@PathVariable id: Long): ResponseEntity<Singer> {
        val fromDb: Optional<Singer> = singerRepo.findById(id)
        return fromDb
            .map { s: Singer ->
                ResponseEntity.ok().body(s)
            }
```

```
            .orElseGet {
                ResponseEntity.notFound()
                    .build()
            }
    }
    ...

}
```

Notice that now the @ResponseStatus(HttpStatus.OK) is no longer necessary, but also in case the id does not match an existing singer, an empty response is sent together in the HttpStatus.NOT_FOUND. The response is represented as a ResponseEntity<T> that contains a body and a successful 200(Ok) HTTP status code for a successful request, and only a 404(Not Found) HTTP status code for a failed request. The objects could also be created explicitly by invoking constructors, but ResponseEntity<T> provides builders for constructing requests specific to the most common HTTP status codes. Listing 15-14 shows the corresponding part.

Listing 15-14. The Singer2Controller#findSingerById(..) Method That Returns a ResponseEntity<T> Created Using Builders

```
fun findSingerById(@PathVariable id: Long): ResponseEntity<Singer> {
    val fromDb: Optional<Singer> = singerRepo.findById(id)
    return fromDb
        .map { s: Singer ->
            ResponseEntity.ok().body(s)
        }
        .orElseGet {
            ResponseEntity.notFound()
                .build()
        }
}
```

Since the response is a ResponseEntity<Singer>, to test this method two tests can be written using the RestTemplate#exchange(..) method, one positive, one negative. Listing 15-15 shows the two test methods.

Listing 15-15. Testing the Singer2Controller#findSingerById(..) Method

package com.apress.prospring6.fifteen

import org.springframework.web.client.HttpClientErrorException
import org.springframework.web.client.RestTemplate
import org.springframework.http.RequestEntity
// other import statements omitted

```
class RestClient2Test {
    var restTemplate = RestTemplate()

    @Test
    @Throws(URISyntaxException::class)
    fun testPositiveFindById() {
        val headers = HttpHeaders()
        headers.accept = listOf(MediaType.APPLICATION_JSON)
```

```kotlin
        val req = RequestEntity<HttpHeaders>(
            headers, HttpMethod.GET, URI(
                URI_SINGER2_ROOT + 1
            )
        )
        LOGGER.info("--> Testing retrieve a singer by id : 1")
        val response = restTemplate.exchange(
            req,
            Singer::class.java
        )
        Assertions.assertAll("findById",
            Executable {
                Assertions.assertEquals(
                    HttpStatus.OK,
                    response.statusCode
                )
            },
            Executable {
                Assertions.assertTrue(
                    Objects.requireNonNull(
                        response.headers[HttpHeaders.CONTENT_TYPE]
                    ).contains(MediaType.APPLICATION_JSON_UTF8_VALUE)
                )
            },
            Executable { Assertions.assertNotNull(response.body) },
            Executable {
                Assertions.assertEquals(
                    Singer::class.java,
                    response.body.javaClass
                )
            }
        )
    }

    @Test
    @Throws(URISyntaxException::class)
    fun testNegativeFindById() {
        LOGGER.info("--> Testing retrieve a singer by id : 99")
        val req = RequestEntity<HttpHeaders>(
            HttpMethod.GET, URI(
                URI_SINGER2_ROOT + 99
            )
        )
        Assertions.assertThrowsExactly(
            HttpClientErrorException.NotFound::class.java
        ) {
            restTemplate.exchange(
                req,
                HttpStatus::class.java
            )
        }
```

```
} // feel free to write the rest of the tests to test your understanding of the
exchange method

companion object {
    private const val URI_SINGER2_ROOT = "http://localhost:8080/ch15/singer2/"
    val LOGGER = LoggerFactory.getLogger(RestClientTest::class.java)
}
}
```

As mentioned previously, the RestTemplate#exchange(..) exchange methods are very powerful. In the testPositiveFindById() test method, the version of the method that requires a RequestEntity<T> and returns object type as arguments is invoked. The RequestEntity<T> type is an extension of HttpEntity<T> that exposes the HTTP method and the target URL. Just for fun, the requested resource representation is JSON, but RestTemplate is smart enough to convert it back to Singer so assertions can be run on the returned object.

In the testNegativeFindById() test method, notice that instead of inspecting a RequestEntity<T>, an assumption that an org.springframework.web.client.HttpClientErrorException.NotFound exception is thrown is checked. This is because under the hood an error handler receives and handles the response with the 404(Not Found) by throwing this type of exception. This kind of handling happens for other HTTP status codes corresponding to responses other than the successful one, and the exception types all extend org.springframework.web.client.HttpClientErrorException.

The rest of the methods in Singer2Controller are shown in Listing 15-16.

Listing 15-16. The Complete Singer2Controller

package com.apress.prospring6.fifteen.controllers
// import statements are omitted

```
@RestController
@RequestMapping(path = ["singer2"])
class Singer2Controller(private val singerRepo: SingerRepo) {
    @GetMapping(path = ["/", ""])
    fun all(): ResponseEntity<List<Singer>> {
        val singers = singerRepo.findAll()
        return if (singers.isEmpty()) {
            ResponseEntity.notFound().build()
        } else ResponseEntity.ok().body(singers)
    }

    @GetMapping(path = ["/{id}"])
    fun findSingerById(@PathVariable id: Long): ResponseEntity<Singer> {
        val fromDb: Optional<Singer> = singerRepo.findById(id)
        return fromDb
            .map { s: Singer ->
                ResponseEntity.ok().body(s)
            }
            .orElseGet {
                ResponseEntity.notFound()
                    .build()
            }
    }
```

```kotlin
@PostMapping(path = ["/"])
fun create(@RequestBody @Valid singer: Singer): ResponseEntity<Singer> {
    LOGGER.info("Creating singer: {}", singer)
    return try {
        val saved = singerRepo.save(singer)
        LOGGER.info("Singer created successfully with info: {}", saved)
        ResponseEntity<Singer>(saved, HttpStatus.CREATED)
    } catch (dive: DataIntegrityViolationException) {
        LOGGER.debug("Could not create singer.", dive)
        ResponseEntity.badRequest().build()
    }
}


@PutMapping(value = ["/{id}"])
fun update(@RequestBody @Valid singer: Singer, @PathVariable id: Long):
ResponseEntity<Any> {
    LOGGER.info("Updating singer: {}", singer)
    val fromDb: Optional<Singer> = singerRepo.findById(id)
    return fromDb
        .map<ResponseEntity<Any>> { s: Singer ->
            s.firstName = singer.firstName
            s.lastName = singer.lastName
            s.birthDate = singer.birthDate
            try {
                singerRepo.save(s)
                return@map ResponseEntity.ok().build<Any>()
            } catch (dive: DataIntegrityViolationException) {
                Companion.LOGGER.debug("Could not update singer.", dive)
                return@map ResponseEntity.badRequest().build<Any>()
            }
        }
        .orElseGet {
            ResponseEntity.notFound().build()
        }
}


@DeleteMapping(value = ["/{id}"])
fun delete(@PathVariable id: Long): ResponseEntity<Any> {
    LOGGER.info("Deleting singer with id: {}", id)
    val fromDb: Optional<Singer> = singerRepo.findById(id)
    return fromDb
        .map<ResponseEntity<Any>> { s: Singer? ->
            singerRepo.deleteById(id)
            ResponseEntity.noContent().build()
        }
        .orElseGet {
            ResponseEntity.notFound().build()
        }
}
```

```kotlin
    companion object {
        val LOGGER = LoggerFactory.getLogger(Singer2Controller::class.java)
    }
}
```

Looking at the full `Singer2Controller`, you might notice that there is a repetitive situation when a singer is not found in the database: a `ResponseEntity.notFound().build()` is built and returned. That leads to the same code being written quite a few times. Just to make the situation more dire, we've also returned this type of response when no singer is found in the database. So, can all this repetitive code be avoided? Of course, and you will learn how by reading the following section.

REST Exception Handling Using @RestControllerAdvice

To reduce the code that needs to be written, we can write a `SingerService` that wraps around the `SingerRepo` and throws an exception named `NotFoundException`, declared to extend `RuntimeException` because checked exceptions are annoying.

💡 Checked exceptions don't play a role in Kotlin. Exception mapping with the aim to generate helpful HTTP status codes still might be worthwhile to include in your code.

We inject a bean of this type in the controller and annotate this class with `@ResponseStatus(value= HttpStatus.NOT_FOUND)`, and *voila*, automatic mapping of this exception to the response status that is returned to the client. Listing 15-17 shows the `NotFoundException` class.

Listing 15-17. The `NotFoundException` REST-Specific Exception Class

```kotlin
package com.apress.prospring6.fifteen.problem

import org.springframework.http.HttpStatus
import org.springframework.web.bind.annotation.ResponseStatus

import java.io.Serial

@ResponseStatus(value = HttpStatus.NOT_FOUND, reason = "Requested item(s) not found")
class NotFoundException : RuntimeException {
    var objIdentifier: Long? = null

    constructor(cls: Class<*>) : super("table for " + cls.simpleName + " is empty")
    constructor(cls: Class<*>, id: Long) : super(cls.simpleName + " with id: " + id + " does
    not exist!")

    companion object {
        @Serial
        private val serialVersionUID = 2L
    }
}
```

Notice that an error message can be attached via the reason attribute, and it will be part of the response.

Listing 15-18 shows the SingerService implementation that throws this type of exception whenever some data cannot be found.

Listing 15-18. The SingerService Implementation Class

```
package com.apress.prospring6.fifteen.services

import com.apress.prospring6.fifteen.problem.NotFoundException
// other import statements omitted

@Transactional
@Service("singerService")
class SingerServiceImpl(private val singerRepo: SingerRepo) : SingerService {
    override fun findAll(): List<Singer> {
        val singers = singerRepo.findAll()
        if (singers.isEmpty()) {
            throw NotFoundException(Singer::class.java)
        }
        return singers
    }

    override fun findById(id: Long): Singer? {
        return singerRepo.findById(id).orElseThrow {
            NotFoundException(
                Singer::class.java, id
            )
        }
    }

    override fun save(singer: Singer): Singer {
        return singerRepo.save(singer)
    }

    override fun update(id: Long, singer: Singer): Singer {
        return singerRepo.findById(id)
            .map { s: Singer ->
                s.firstName = singer.firstName
                s.lastName = singer.lastName
                s.birthDate = singer.birthDate
                singerRepo.save(s)
            }
            .orElseThrow {
                NotFoundException(
                    Singer::class.java, id
                )
            }
    }

    override fun delete(id: Long) {
        val fromDb = singerRepo.findById(id)
        if (fromDb.isEmpty) {
```

```
            throw NotFoundException(
                Singer::class.java,
                id
            )
        }
        singerRepo.deleteById(id)
    }
}
```

Notice that most of the logic we previously had in the controller handler methods now has moved to this class. This means that we can write a new controller named Singer3Controller to use a bean of this type, and this controller is way more elegant and compact, as shown in Listing 15-19.

Listing 15-19. The Singer3Controller Class

```
package com.apress.prospring6.fifteen.controllers

import com.apress.prospring6.fifteen.services.SingerService
// other import statements omitted

@RestController
@RequestMapping(path = ["singer3"])
class Singer3Controller(private val singerService: SingerService) {
    @GetMapping(path = ["/", ""])
    fun all(): List<Singer> {
        return singerService.findAll()
    }

    @GetMapping(path = ["/{id}"])
    fun findSingerById(@PathVariable id: Long): Singer? {
        return singerService.findById(id)
    }

    @PostMapping(path = ["/"])
    @ResponseStatus(HttpStatus.CREATED)
    fun create(@RequestBody @Valid singer: Singer): Singer {
        LOGGER.info("Creating singer: $singer")
        return singerService.save(singer)
    }

    @PutMapping(value = ["/{id}"])
    fun update(@RequestBody @Valid singer: Singer, @PathVariable id: Long) {
        LOGGER.info("Updating singer: $singer")
        singerService.update(id, singer)
    }

    @ResponseStatus(HttpStatus.NO_CONTENT)
    @DeleteMapping(value = ["/{id}"])
    fun delete(@PathVariable id: Long) {
        LOGGER.info("Deleting singer with id: {}", id)
        singerService.delete(id)
    }
```

```
    companion object {
        val LOGGER = LoggerFactory.getLogger(Singer3Controller::class.java)
    }
}
```

To test that this exception causes a response with the 404(Not Found) HTTP status code, the job is done by the testNegativeFindById(..) introduced in Listing 15-15, but by sending the request "http://localhost:8080/ch15/singer3/99".

Having an exception annotated like this gets the job done, but our controller also throws a DataIntegrityViolationException that is not mapped to any HTTP status code. This type of exception is not part of our application, and thus cannot be annotated with @ResponseStatus.

For this type of exception, the solution is to write an exception handler class, annotate it with @RestControllerAdvice (the REST equivalent of @ControllerAdvice), and declare a method handler for the DataIntegrityViolationException, similar to what was done in **Chapter 14** for Spring web applications.

The RestErrorHandler class that is a global exception handler for REST requests is shown in Listing 15-20.

Listing 15-20. The RestErrorHandler Class

package com.apress.prospring6.fifteen.controllers

import org.springframework.dao.DataIntegrityViolationException
import org.springframework.http.HttpStatus
import org.springframework.http.ResponseEntity
import org.springframework.web.bind.annotation.ControllerAdvice
import org.springframework.web.bind.annotation.ExceptionHandler

```
@RestControllerAdvice
class RestErrorHandler {
    // in case you are not interested in annotating this class NotFoundException with
    // @ResponseStatus
    /*    @ExceptionHandler(NotFoundException::class)
    fun  handleNotFound(ex:NotFoundException):ResponseEntity<HttpStatus> {
        return ResponseEntity.notFound().build();
    }*/
    @ExceptionHandler(DataIntegrityViolationException::class)
    fun handleBadRequest(ex: DataIntegrityViolationException): ResponseEntity<Any?> {
        return ResponseEntity.badRequest().body(ex.message)
    }
}
```

How do we test that when a DataIntegrityViolationException happens we no longer have a 500(Internal Server Error)? Simple: we try to create a new Singer instance with an existing firstName and lastName, and since a combination of these two is declared to be the SINGER table unique key, the exception is thrown. The test is depicted in Listing 15-21.

Listing 15-21. The RestClient3Test#testNegativeCreate() Test Method

package com.apress.prospring6.fifteen

import org.springframework.web.client.HttpClientErrorException
import org.springframework.web.client.RestTemplate

```kotlin
// other import statements omitted

class RestClient3Test {
    var restTemplate = RestTemplate()

    @Test
    @Throws(URISyntaxException::class)
    fun testNegativeCreate() {
        LOGGER.info("--> Testing create singer")
        val singerNew = Singer()
        singerNew.firstName = "Ben"
        singerNew.lastName = "Barnes"
        singerNew.birthDate = LocalDate.now()
        val req = RequestEntity(
            singerNew, HttpMethod.POST, URI(
                URL_CREATE_SINGER
            )
        )
        Assertions.assertThrowsExactly(
            HttpClientErrorException.BadRequest::class.java
        ) {
            restTemplate.exchange(
                req,
                HttpStatus::class.java
            )
        }
    }
    ...
}
```

Notice that the type of exception being thrown by RestTemplate is HttpClientErrorException.
BadRequest, which is the type of exception matching the 400(Bad Request) HTTP status code.

This section about writing a Spring REST Web application must end here, because when it comes to REST APIs with Spring, the subject is quite vast. Check out the next section to see how easy it is to build a Spring REST Web application using Spring Boot.

RESTful-WS with Spring Boot

This section is included because Spring Boot makes everything easier to develop. The Singer entity, repository, service, exception, and exception handler classes are the same as before; there's no need to change anything. The same rule as for a classic Spring REST application applies: if we want XML and JSON serialization, we need to add the required Jackson libraries to the classpath. Figure 15-2 shows the chapter15-boot project dependencies.

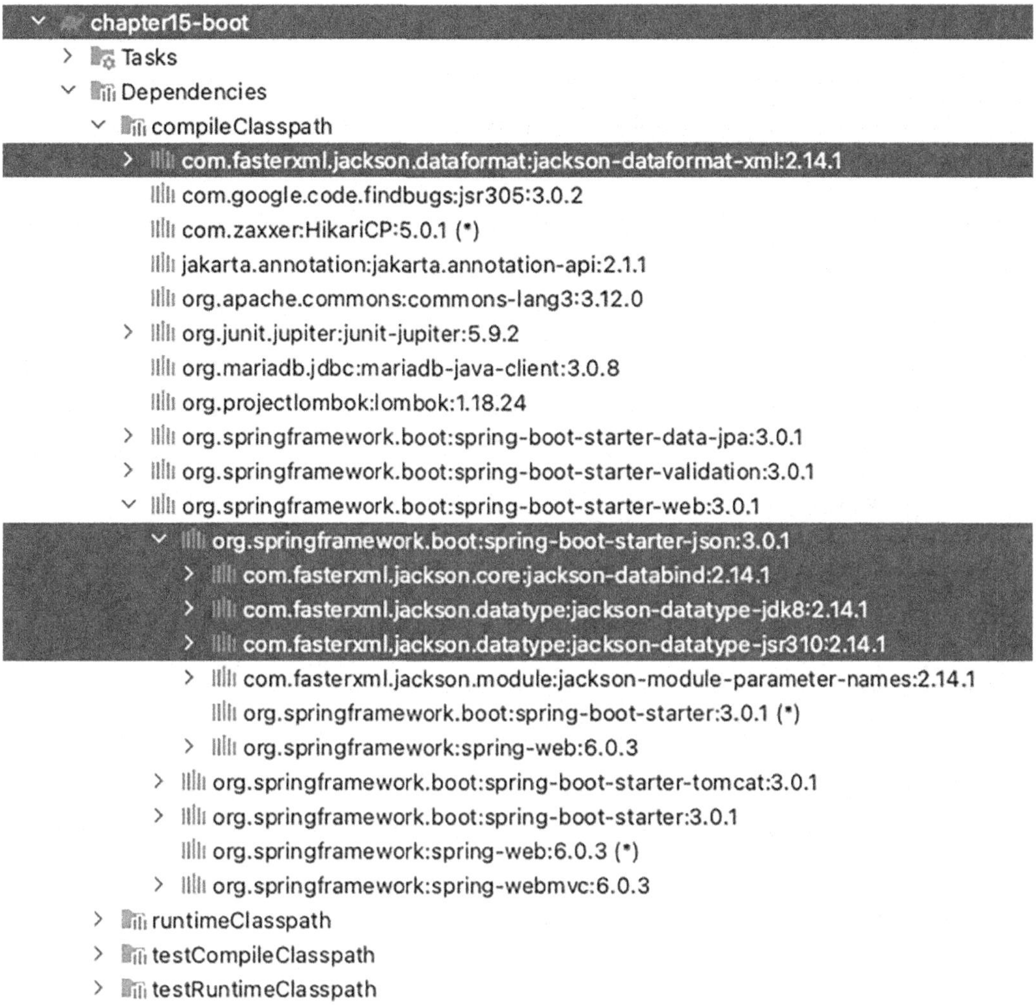

```
∨   chapter15-boot
    >   Tasks
    ∨   Dependencies
        ∨   compileClasspath
            >   com.fasterxml.jackson.dataformat:jackson-dataformat-xml:2.14.1
                com.google.code.findbugs:jsr305:3.0.2
                com.zaxxer:HikariCP:5.0.1 (*)
                jakarta.annotation:jakarta.annotation-api:2.1.1
                org.apache.commons:commons-lang3:3.12.0
            >   org.junit.jupiter:junit-jupiter:5.9.2
                org.mariadb.jdbc:mariadb-java-client:3.0.8
                org.projectlombok:lombok:1.18.24
            >   org.springframework.boot:spring-boot-starter-data-jpa:3.0.1
            >   org.springframework.boot:spring-boot-starter-validation:3.0.1
            ∨   org.springframework.boot:spring-boot-starter-web:3.0.1
                ∨   org.springframework.boot:spring-boot-starter-json:3.0.1
                    >   com.fasterxml.jackson.core:jackson-databind:2.14.1
                    >   com.fasterxml.jackson.datatype:jackson-datatype-jdk8:2.14.1
                    >   com.fasterxml.jackson.datatype:jackson-datatype-jsr310:2.14.1
                    >   com.fasterxml.jackson.module:jackson-module-parameter-names:2.14.1
                        org.springframework.boot:spring-boot-starter:3.0.1 (*)
                    >   org.springframework:spring-web:6.0.3
                >   org.springframework.boot:spring-boot-starter-tomcat:3.0.1
                >   org.springframework.boot:spring-boot-starter:3.0.1
                    org.springframework:spring-web:6.0.3 (*)
                >   org.springframework:spring-webmvc:6.0.3
        >   runtimeClasspath
        >   testCompileClasspath
        >   testRuntimeClasspath
```

Figure 15-2. *Project* chapter15-boot *dependencies*

Being a web application, the Spring Boot configuration is almost identical to the one introduced in **Chapter 14**, except the Thymeleaf section. Listing 15-22 shows the Spring Boot configuration contained by the application-dev.yaml.

Listing 15-22. The Spring Boot Configuration for the chapter15-boot Project

```
# web server config
server:
  port: 8081
  servlet:
    context-path: /
  compression:
    enabled: true # improves website performance by compressing response body
  address: 0.0.0.0
```

```
# datasource config
spring:
  datasource:
    driverClassName: org.mariadb.jdbc.Driver
    url: jdbc:mariadb://localhost:3306/musicdb?useSSL=false
    username: prospring6
    password: prospring6
    hikari:
      maximum-pool-size: 25
  jpa:
    generate-ddl: false
    properties:
      hibernate:
        jdbc:
          batch_size: 10
        show-sql: true
        format-sql: false
        use_sql_comments: false
        hbm2ddl:
          auto: none

# Logging config
logging:
  pattern:
    console: "%-5level: %class{0} - %msg%n"
  level:
    root: INFO
    org.springframework.boot: DEBUG
    com.apress.prospring6.fifteen: INFO
```

As usual, the dev profile is used to connect the application to an existing container. This allows for a test profile to spin up a container using Testcontainers.

Summary

In this chapter, we covered a few topics about creating Spring Restful web services and exposing them via Spring configuration. The types of configurations covered were the classic configuration, where the application is packed as a `*.war` and deployed to an Apache Tomcat 10 server, and configuration using Spring Boot. The REST APIs were consumed using `RestTemplate` and `TestRestTemplate`.

This chapter also covered various ways of writing handler methods for REST requests and exception handling. In the next chapter we talk about Spring Native Images, and some other useful supporting technologies.

CHAPTER 16

■ ■ ■

Spring Native and Other Goodies

In previous chapters, you saw how the Spring Framework can help Kotlin and Java developers create JEE applications. By using the Spring Framework's dependency injection (DI) mechanism and its integration with each layer (via libraries within the Spring Framework's own modules or via integration with third-party libraries), you can simplify implementing and maintaining business logic.

The Spring Framework has evolved a lot over the years, splitting into separate projects integrating with the latest technologies. Version 6 is truly rich in features and new projects. This chapter introduces you to three important new developments:

- *Spring Native Images*: Spring Boot 2.3.0 introduced the ability to package your app into a Docker image with Cloud Native Buildpacks (CNB). At the same time, Oracle was working on GraalVM[1], a high-performance JDK distribution written for Java and other JVM languages that promised incredible performance optimizations for individual languages and interoperability for polyglot applications. The goal was eventually to have compact, fast-starting applications that can be run, for example, in an AWS Lambda function. AWS Lambda functions are applications that are triggered on request, without the need for a server running all time. A Spring Boot application running on an AWS EC2 is an infrastructure as a service (IaaS), AWS Lambda is a platform as a service (PaaS). It helps you to run and execute your back-end code, only when needed. The Spring Native project provided support for compiling Spring applications to native executables using the GraalVM native-image compiler. This project is now retired, since it was experimental, and its result is the Spring Boot 3 official native support[2].

- *Spring for GraphQL*: GraphQL[3] is a query language for APIs and a runtime for fulfilling those queries with your existing data. For a long time, services have been communicating over HTTP using REST requests, handling information in various formats such a JSON, XML. and others. GraphQL adds the capability to easily declare which data you want retrieved without having to write complicated code to provide that data. Spring for GraphQL[4] provides support for Spring applications built on GraphQL Java. It is a joint collaboration between the GraphQL Java team and Spring engineering. In this chapter you will learn how to build a Spring Boot application capable of retrieving data efficiently in response to GraphQL queries.

---

[1] https://www.graalvm.org
[2] https://docs.spring.io/spring-boot/docs/current/reference/html/native-image.html
[3] https://graphql.org
[4] https://docs.spring.io/spring-graphql/docs/current/reference/html

P. Späth et al., *Pro Spring 6 with Kotlin*, https://doi.org/10.1007/978-1-4842-9557-1_16

- *Spring Kotlin applications*: Kotlin[5] is a cross-platform, statically typed, general-purpose, high-level programming language with type inference. Kotlin is designed to interoperate fully with Java, and the JVM version of Kotlin's standard library provides a more concise syntax, various types, and programming constructs. Some developers have described it as a cross between Scala and Java. The language has a great community supporting it, and it is developed by the team that produced the best Java editor, so it is no surprise its adoption was quick; its hype is well deserved. We use Kotlin throughout this book, so there's no need to discuss it further in this chapter.

Spring Native Images

A Spring Native image is a stand-alone executable that is created by processing a Spring application ahead of time using the GraalVM native-image compiler. Native images usually have a smaller memory footprint and start faster than their JVM counterparts. Also, you don't need a JVM to run them. In previous chapters the result of building a Spring project was an executable JAR containing all bytecode, a result of compiling all the Java and Spring code making up that project. To execute the JAR you need a JVM, provided by a JDK (or JRE, in the distant past before Java 9). Spring Native will produce an executable for the targeted system. A native executable is made of the following:

- *Substrate VM*: A virtual machine compiled and configured for the code that needs to be run on it. It is a replacement for a JVM. The process to create it is very similar to how jlink[6] is used to strip away from the JDK all modules that are not necessary for running an application, to assemble and optimize a set of modules and their dependencies into a custom runtime image.

- *DWARF info*: Information useful during debugging processes.

- *Initial heap*: Memory for the application to run.

- *Application compiled to native code*: In this case, a Spring Boot application and all its dependencies.

To keep things simple, this section leverages the Spring Boot ability to create Docker images to create a Docker image that contains the Spring native executable and run the application by starting up a container. This is easier since it doesn't require you to install GraalVM on your machine. Also, you obviously need Docker locally, because the Docker image that you will create needs to be added to an image catalog and then needs a runtime to run a container based on it.

So, what is *ahead-of-time (AOT) compilation* and how is it different from normal Java compilation? There are a few things that are worth mentioning:

- AOT compilation is a process that involves statically analyzing your application code from its *main* entry point.

- Code that cannot be reached when the native image is created is excluded from the executable. This obviously means that using Spring dynamic elements is out the window, along with the "automagic" that naive developers are so enthralled by. GraalVM must be told about reflection, resources, serialization, and dynamic proxies.

---

[5] https://kotlinlang.org
[6] https://docs.oracle.com/javase/9/tools/jlink.htm

- The application classpath is known at build time and does not change at runtime. This means there is no lazy class loading, and all the classes in the executables are loaded in memory on startup.

- There might be other limitations for Java and Kotlin applications that can only be discovered after more companies start using GraalVM. (For example, we've had some problems when building native images for macOS running Apple M1 architecture.)

So, the flexibility and dynamism of Spring Boot applications must be given up in exchange for a small memory footprint and a faster startup. This means profiles are not supported, and beans cannot be modified once created. Is this worth it? Time will tell.

When a Spring application is processed ahead of time, the following must happen for it to be transformed into a native executable:

- Java code is generated.

- Bytecode is generated for dynamic proxies.

- The following GraalVM JSON hint files are generated that describe how GraalVM should deal with things that it can't understand by directly inspecting the code:

  - Resource hints (`resource-config.json`)

  - Reflection hints (`reflect-config.json`)

  - Serialization hints (`serialization-config.json`)

  - Java proxy hints (`proxy-config.json`)

  - JNI hints (`jni-config.json`)

In a typical Spring application, a lot of reflection is required to inject beans into other beans. The Spring IoC container identifies `@Configuration` classes and bean definitions and creates a dependency tree to decide the order in which the beans are created, so that they can be injected. All this work is done when the application starts, also called *at runtime*. This obviously takes some time, as you've probably noticed if you've read the previous chapters and ran the code yourself.

In a Spring Native executable, Spring behaves differently. Configuration classes are no longer identified or parsed and bean definitions are not created at runtime; all this work is done at build time. The bean definitions are processed and converted into source code that is analyzed by the GraalVM compiler, so that the ones that are not reached (used) can be dropped. The generated code is seriously verbose, because without the power of Spring IoC, all that is left is very explicit code, injecting the right beans in the right places through classic Java and Kotlin code—direct assignment and explicit instantiation of the bean type. This obviously increases the build time, but that is not really a problem.

💡 Development can be done on a normal JVM for the developer's comfort and speed, and the production build can be isolated on a pipeline and run only when a release is necessary.

There are two main ways to build a Spring Boot native image application:

- Using Spring Boot support for Cloud Native Buildpacks (CNB)[7] to generate a lightweight container containing a native executable

- Using GraalVM Native Build Tools to generate a native executable

Spring Boot native support is a breeze, especially if you happen to use Gradle, which makes the configuration very concise because of the Gradle's Native Build Tools plug-in. The focus of this section, however, is not the code and techniques for writing a Spring application, but the configurations necessary to compile a Spring application into a native executable and run it using a Docker runtime.

The Spring Application

The Spring application that is compiled into a native executable in this section is a simple Spring Boot REST web application. It uses Spring Data JPA to retrieve data from a database running in a container on your local Docker instance (could be also remote if you have the resources). Figure 16-1 shows the Spring Boot variant of the simple project used in this section.

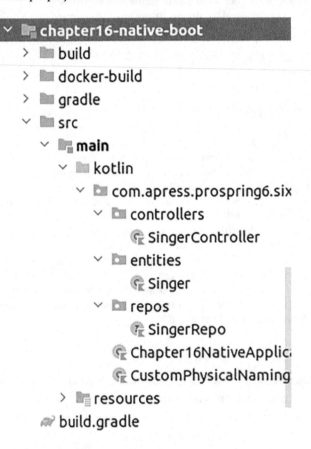

Figure 16-1. Project `chapter16-native-boot`

---

[7] https://buildpacks.io

All the classes should be familiar to you from previous chapters. The Singer class is a very simple entity class shown in Listing 16-1.

Listing 16-1. The Singer Entity Class

```kotlin
package com.apress.prospring6.sixteen.boot.entities

import jakarta.persistence.*
import org.springframework.format.annotation.DateTimeFormat
import jakarta.persistence.GenerationType.IDENTITY

@Entity
@Table(name = "SINGER")
class Singer {
    @Id
    @GeneratedValue(strategy = GenerationType.IDENTITY)
    @Column(name = "ID")
    var id: Long? = null

    @Version
    @Column(name = "VERSION")
    var version = 0

    @Column(name = "FIRST_NAME")
     val firstName: String? = null

    @Column(name = "LAST_NAME")
    val lastName: String? = null

    @DateTimeFormat(pattern = "yyyy-MM-dd")
    @Column(name = "BIRTH_DATE")
    val birthDate: LocalDate? = null

    companion object {
        @Serial
        private val serialVersionUID = 1L
    }

    override fun equals(other: Any?): Boolean {
        if (this === other) return true
        if (javaClass != other?.javaClass) return false

        other as Singer

        return id == other.id
    }

    override fun hashCode(): Int {
        return id?.hashCode() ?: 0
    }
}
```

To handle Singer instances, the SingerRepo interface is declared as extending JpaRepository<Singer, Long> as shown in Listing 16-2.

Listing 16-2. The SingerRepo Spring Data Interface Class

```
package com.apress.prospring6.sixteen.boot.repos

import com.apress.prospring6.sixteen.boot.entities.Singer
import org.springframework.data.jpa.repository.JpaRepository

interface SingerRepo : JpaRepository<Singer, Long> {
}
```

To keep things simple, the SingerController class requires an instance of SingerRepo to pass data back and forth via its handler methods (for simplicity, we are skipping the service layer). This class and bean declaration are shown in Listing 16-3.

Listing 16-3. The SingerController Class

```
package com.apress.prospring6.sixteen.boot.controllers

import org.springframework.web.bind.annotation.*
// other import statements omitted

@RestController
@RequestMapping(value = ["/singer"])
class SingerController(private val singerRepo: SingerRepo) {
    @GetMapping(path = ["/", ""])
    fun all(): List<Singer> {
        return singerRepo.findAll()
    }

    @GetMapping(path = ["/{id}"])
    fun findSingerById(@PathVariable id: Long): Singer? {
        return singerRepo.findById(id).orElse(null)
    }

    @PostMapping(path = ["/"])
    fun create(@RequestBody singer: Singer): Singer {
        LOGGER.info("Creating singer: {}", singer)
        return singerRepo.save(singer)
    }

    @PutMapping(value = ["/{id}"])
    fun update(@RequestBody singer: Singer, @PathVariable id: Long?): Singer {
        LOGGER.info("Updating singer: {}", singer)
        return singerRepo.save(singer)
    }
```

```kotlin
@DeleteMapping(value = ["/{id}"])
fun delete(@PathVariable id: Long) {
    LOGGER.info("Deleting singer with id: {}", id)
    singerRepo.deleteById(id)
}

companion object {
    val LOGGER = LoggerFactory.getLogger(SingerController::class.java)
}
}
```

The `CustomPhysicalNamingStrategy` bean is used to configure Spring Data to recognize database objects with names consisting of only of uppercase letters, and is out of scope for this section. The `Chapter16NativeApplication` class shown in Listing 16-4 is a basic Spring Boot configuration and main class, the entry point of this application.

Listing 16-4. The Chapter16NativeApplication Class

```kotlin
package com.apress.prospring6.sixteen.boot

import org.springframework.boot.SpringApplication
import org.springframework.boot.autoconfigure.SpringBootApplication
import org.springframework.boot.autoconfigure.domain.EntityScan
import org.springframework.data.jpa.repository.config.EnableJpaRepositories
import org.springframework.transaction.annotation.EnableTransactionManagement

@EntityScan(basePackages = ["com.apress.prospring6.sixteen.boot.entities"])
@EnableJpaRepositories("com.apress.prospring6.sixteen.boot.repos")
@EnableTransactionManagement
@SpringBootApplication
open class Chapter16NativeApplication {
    companion object {
        @JvmStatic
        fun main(args: Array<String>) {
            SpringApplication.run(Chapter16NativeApplication::class.java, *args)
        }
    }
}
```

As you can see, there is nothing in the code that needs to be modified for this application to be eligible to be compiled as a Spring Native executable. It is all in the configuration. So, let's look at the Gradle configuration first, because this is the smaller one. Listing 16-5 shows the Gradle configuration for the `chapter16-native-boot` project.

Listing 16-5. The Contents of the `build.gradle` File

```gradle
plugins {
    id 'org.jetbrains.kotlin.jvm' version '1.8.10'
    id 'org.springframework.boot' version '3.0.5'
    id 'org.graalvm.buildtools.native' version '0.9.22'
}
apply plugin: 'io.spring.dependency-management'
```

```
description 'Chapter 16 Boot:  Spring Native'
group = 'com.apress.prospring6'
version = '1.0-SNAPSHOT'

repositories {
    mavenCentral()
}

dependencies {
    runtimeOnly 'org.jetbrains.kotlin:kotlin-reflect:1.8.10'
    implementation 'org.springframework.boot:spring-boot-starter-web'
    implementation 'org.springframework.boot:spring-boot-starter-data-jpa'

    implementation "commons-io:commons-io:2.11.0"

    implementation "com.zaxxer:HikariCP:$hikariVersion"
    implementation "org.mariadb.jdbc:mariadb-java-client:$mariadbClientVersion"
}

tasks.named("bootBuildImage") {
    docker {
        buildpacks = [
                "gcr.io/paketo-buildpacks/graalvm",
                "gcr.io/paketo-buildpacks/java-native-image",
        ]
    }
    imageName = "prospring6-gradle-native:1.0"
}

bootJar {
    manifest {
        attributes 'Start-Class': 'com.apress.prospring6.sixteen.boot.
        Chapter16NativeApplication'
    }
}

// gradle bootBuildImage

test {
    useJUnitPlatform()
}

compileKotlin {
    kotlinOptions.jvmTarget = '1.8'
}

compileTestKotlin {
    kotlinOptions.jvmTarget = '1.8'
}
```

The most important part of this configuration is the GraalVM Native Image plug-in: `org.graalvm.buildtools.native`. The current version of this project is `0.9.22`. Because of its presence in the configuration, the Spring Boot Gradle plug-in adds AOT tasks to the project. Since IntelliJ IDEA is smart, it shows in the Gradle View all the tasks under their scope and the dependencies for AOT purposes. Figure 16-2 depicts the Gradle View, showing the AOT and Native task and dependency groups.

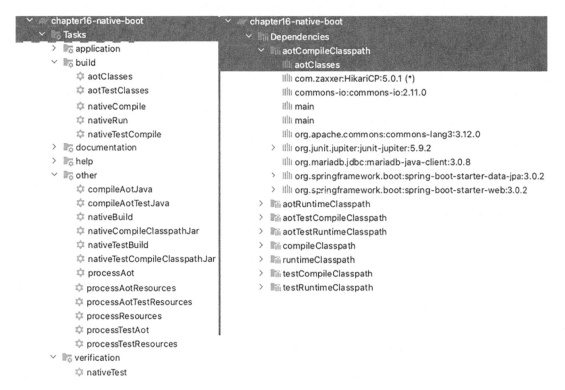

Figure 16-2. *AOT and Native task and dependency groups for project* `chapter16-native-boot`

Notice that in the `aotCompileClasspath` there is an item named `aotClasses`, which represents the static code generated for Spring configuration classes and bean definitions. The `main` probably represents the main entry point of the application, which is the main method in the `Chapter16NativeApplication` class.

Since Java 19 is configured for this project, we need to customize the Cloud Native Buildpacks used to create the executable. We do so by specifying an array with the two values shown in the configuration for the `buildpacks` property: `gcr.io/paketo-buildpacks/graalvm` and `gcr.io/paketo-buildpacks/java-native-image`. To easily recognize the resulting native image in the Docker dashboard, the `imageName` property is set to `prospring6-gradle-native:1.0`.

With this configuration, all that remains to do is to create the image by running `gradle bootBuildImage` in the terminal, in the chapter16-native-boot directory. The execution will take a long time, at least the first time. For this small project it took about 5 minutes, but this is because the Docker images the executable is based on need to be downloaded too. Listing 16-6 shows some snippets of this execution.

Listing 16-6. `gradle bootBuildImage` Execution Log Snippets

```
> Task :chapter16-native-boot:compileJava
...
> Task :chapter16-native-boot:processAot
...
>Task :chapter16-native-boot:compileAotJava
...
> Task :chapter16-native-boot:bootBuildImage
Building image 'docker.io/library/prospring6-gradle-native:1.0'

> Pulling builder image 'docker.io/paketobuildpacks/builder:tiny' ...
> Pulling run image 'docker.io/paketobuildpacks/run:tiny-cnb' ...
> Pulling buildpack image 'gcr.io/paketo-buildpacks/graalvm:latest' ...
> Pulling buildpack image 'gcr.io/paketo-buildpacks/java-native-image:latest' ...
> Executing lifecycle version v0.16.0

> Running creator
    [creator]     ===> ANALYZING
    [creator]     Previous image with name "docker.io/library/prospring6-gradle-native:1.0"
                  not found
    [creator]     ===> DETECTING
    [creator]     7 of 15 buildpacks participating
    [creator]     paketo-buildpacks/graalvm          7.10.0
...
    [creator]     ===> BUILDING
    [creator]     Paketo Buildpack for GraalVM 7.10.0
...
    [creator]        Build Configuration:
    [creator]         $BP_NATIVE_IMAGE                      true enable native image build
                      # other build specific variables
    [creator]        Native Image: Contributing to layer
    [creator]          Executing native-image  ... # classpath omitted
    [creator]        =================================================================
    [creator]        GraalVM Native Image: Generating '/layers/paketo-buildpacks_
                     native-image/native-image/com.apress.prospring6.sixteen.boot.
                     Chapter16NativeApplication' (static executable)...
    [creator]        =================================================================
    [creator]        [1/7] Initializing...
    [creator]        [2/7] Performing analysis...  [**********]          (138.0s @ 3.28GB)
    [creator]        [3/7] Building universe...                          (16.0s @ 3.34GB)
    [creator]        [4/7] Parsing methods...       [***]                (10.8s @ 3.47GB)
    [creator]        [6/7] Compiling methods...     [*******]            (75.3s @ 3.19GB)
    [creator]        [7/7] Creating image...                             (13.0s @ 2.88GB)
# listing packages, object types and  sizes omitted
...
    [creator]        20.4s (6.9% of total time) in 129 GCs | Peak RSS: 5.36GB | CPU load: 5.51
    [creator]        -----------------------------------------------------------------
    [creator]        Produced artifacts:
    [creator]        /layers/paketo-buildpacks_native-image/native-image/com.apress.prospring6.
                     sixteen.boot.Chapter16NativeApplication (executable)
```

```
[creator]        /layers/paketo-buildpacks_native-image/native-image/com.apress.prospring6.
                 sixteen.boot.Chapter16NativeApplication.build_artifacts.txt (txt)
[creator]        =====================================================
[creator]        Finished generating '/layers/paketo-buildpacks_native-image/native-image/
                 com.apress.prospring6.sixteen.boot.Chapter16NativeApplication' in 4m 53s.
[creator]        ===> EXPORTING
[creator]        Adding layer 'paketo-buildpacks/ca-certificates:helper'
[creator]        Adding layer 'buildpacksio/lifecycle:launch.sbom'
# layers to build the image
Successfully built image 'docker.io/library/prospring6-gradle-native:1.0'

BUILD SUCCESSFUL in 5m 36s
9 actionable tasks: 8 executed, 1 up-to-date
```

First, the compileJava task compiles the project, making sure all dependencies are provided and the project is functional. Then the processAot task generates the AOT Java code. Then the processAot task starts the application to check that it still works. Then the compileAotJava produces the **native bytecode**.

The results of all these tasks can be seen in the build/generated directory. This is where the AOT-generated Java code and the GraalVM JSON hint files are saved. The bytecode and native code are stored under build/classes/java/ directories grouped by their scope. Figure 16-3 shows these new directories and some contents.

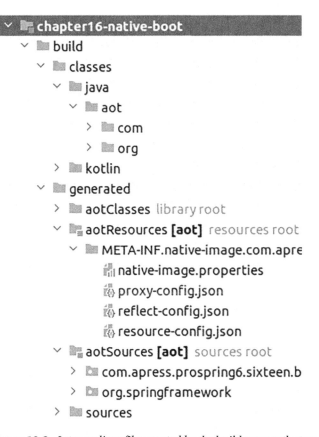

Figure 16-3. *Intermediary files created by the build process that produces a native image*

Finally, the bootBuildImage starts building the image for the native executable. First it downloads the base CND images, and then it builds the executable based on the GraalVM JDK 19.0.2, adding only bits and pieces necessary for the executable to run. In the end a static executable is produced, and then processed to compute the memory footprint and its storage requirements, which will determine these parameters for the Docker image.

If all these steps are successful, the Images tab of the Docker dashboard should list the recently produced prospring6-gradle-native:1.0 image, as shown in Figure 16-4.

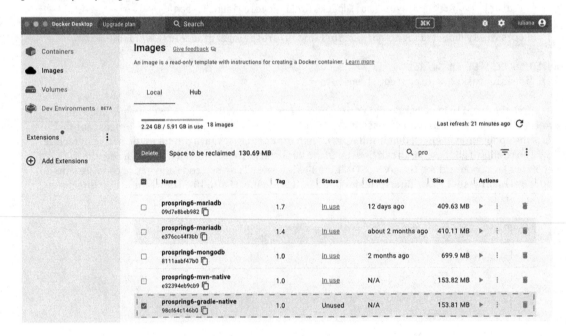

Figure 16-4. Docker dashboard showing the prospring6-gradle-native:1.0 image

Notice the size of the image. Clicking its name reveals details of the image, as shown in Figure 16-5, such as the layers, its contents, and its vulnerabilities (nothing to worry about necessarily, because any software has vulnerabilities; it only depends on how critical they are).

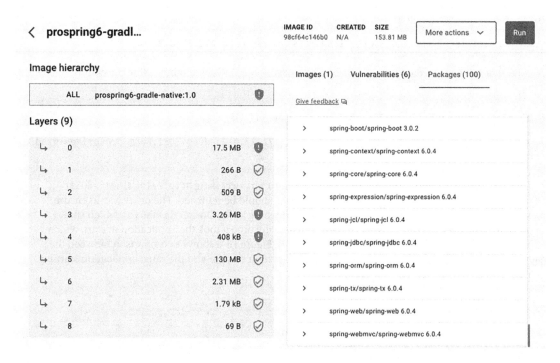

Figure 16-5. *Docker dashboard showing the details of the* `prospring6-gradle-native:1.0` *image*

To check if this image works, we should start a container based on it, but since we know our application needs a database, we need a way to tell it where to find it and how to connect to it. All these details are provided via program arguments that become environment variables for the container. Spring Boot applications can reference these variables in the configuration files. The `application.yaml` file data source configuration needs to be modified to pick up the values necessary for connecting to the database from environment variables. The configuration sample is depicted in Listing 16-7.

Listing 16-7. Spring Boot Configuration File That References Environment Variables

```
spring:
  datasource:
    driverClassName: org.mariadb.jdbc.Driver
    url: jdbc:mariadb://${DB_HOST:localhost}:${DB_PORT:3306}/${DB_
    SCHEMA:musicdb}?useSSL=false
    username: ${DB_USER:prospring6}
    password: ${DB_PASS:prospring6}
```

The `${VAR_NAME:default_value}` is used to provide a default value for a variable in case, when starting the application, the environment variable is neither set nor provided via the command line. All the variables in the configuration have default values. When running an application within a container that needs to connect to a database running in another container, the only variable we need an actual value for is the `DB_HOST`, because in a container `localhost` points to itself. To obtain the IP address of the container where the database is accessible, assuming the container is named `local-mariadb`, the command in Listing 16-8 gets the job done.

Listing 16-8. Command to Retrieve a Running Docker Container's IP Address

```
docker inspect local-mariadb | grep IPAddress  # assuming 172.17.0.2
```

Now that we have the database IP address, we can start our native container using the command in Listing 16-9.

Listing 16-9. Command to Start a Running Docker Container's IP

```
docker run --name prospring6-native -e DB_HOST=172.17.0.2 -d -p 8081:8081 prospring6-gradle-
native:1.0
```

To make sure the application started correctly, you can try accessing http://localhost:8081/ singers, and all Singer instances' JSON representations should be returned. The other way to ensure the application started correctly is to inspect the container log in the Docker dashboard, which shows not only the Spring Boot application startup log, but also the time it took the application to start, which is where one of the superpowers of native images shines. Figure 16-6 shows a comparison between the Chapter16NativeApplication being started on a local system on JVM and the same application starting from a native executable within a container.

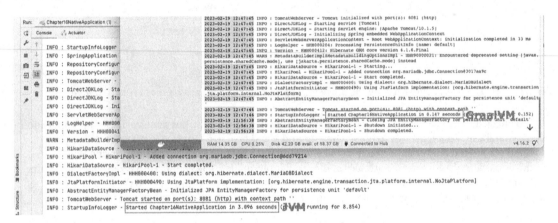

Figure 16-6. Startup times for a container based on the prospring6-gradle-native:1.0 image

The time dropped from 3 seconds to 0.147 second when the application was built into a native executable, so the startup time diminished by the factor of 20, and this is just for a small, very simple application. For applications doing more complex operations, the improvement might be even better.

To read more about native images and recommendations on how to better develop Spring applications such that they are easily built into native executables, read the official documentation, and keep an eye out for any talks on this subject at conferences. The technology, although out of the experimental phase, is still in an early phase and has a long way to go to become the industry default for Java applications, if that even happens at all.

Spring for GraphQL

GraphQL is a query language for APIs and a runtime for providing data according to those queries. GraphQL provides a complete and understandable description of the data in your API and allows the client to ask for some data and receive only what it asked for without writing complicated code to do so.

Consider the REST APIs built so far in this book. REST requests are mapped to URL paths such as `http://localhost:8081/singer/1`. A client sends an HTTP GET request and receives all the information about a `Singer` object that is saved in the database with id=1, in the SINGER table. If the client needs information about this singer that is held in other tables, different queries must be written, and they will be mapped to different URL paths. So, the client must do multiple requests. With GraphQL, the client doesn't have to change the URL for the request, just the schema used to specify the required data. In the end, GraphQL is just another alternative to established remote communications between applications such as REST, SOAP, or gRPC.

Facebook invented GraphQL because REST was not a solution to retrieve a graph of related information for a single request. Using REST, multiple back and forth communication would make the page load slowly and generate unacceptable flicker. We could describe GraphQL in a lot more depth, but for purposes of this discussion, we'll simply list its most important characteristics:

- GraphQL is schema based.

- GraphQL queries look a lot like JSON, but they are not JSON.

- GraphQL is heavily typed. The GraphQL schema language supports the scalar types of `String`, `Int`, `Float`, `Boolean`, and `ID`, so you can use these directly in the schema you pass to `buildSchema`.

- GraphQL is designed for developers.

- GraphQL is transport agnostic; it is mostly used over HTTP, but is not limited to it. For example, you can use it over TCP and over WebSockets.

- GraphQL queries are sent over using POST requests, as they are as big and as complex as necessary. They can specify data to be retrieved from different levels in a database by nesting the desired properties.

REST APIs are a collection of endpoints, whereas GraphQL APIs are focused on the data. This section is focused on writing a Spring Boot application with support for GraphQL. Core concepts of GraphQL are explained gradually as the need arises.

For this section we'll use a modified version of the database used so far in the book. The data managed by this application is stored in three tables, SINGER, AWARD, and INSTRUMENT, that are related as shown in Figure 16-7.

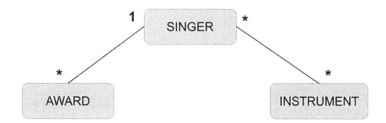

Figure 16-7. *Table relationships for project* `chapter16-graphql-boot`

For the code samples in this chapter, the tables are part of a schema that is named MUSICDB, and the user to access it is named prospring6. The SQL code to execute to create the schema can be found in the `chapter16-graphql-boot/docker-build/scripts/01_CreateTable.sql` file in the directory of the `chapter16-graphql-boot` project. The SQL code to execute to populate the tables can be found in in the `chapter16-graphql-boot/docker-build/scripts/02_InsertData.sql` file in the directory of the `chapter16-graphql-boot` project. These scripts are part of a Docker configuration used to build an image with the database needed for the examples.

Except for the `spring-boot-starter-graphql` dependency, all the dependencies are the same as for a Spring Boot web application backed up by a MariaDB database accessed through Spring Data repositories. Figure 16-8 shows the dependencies of the `chapter16-graphql-boot` project.

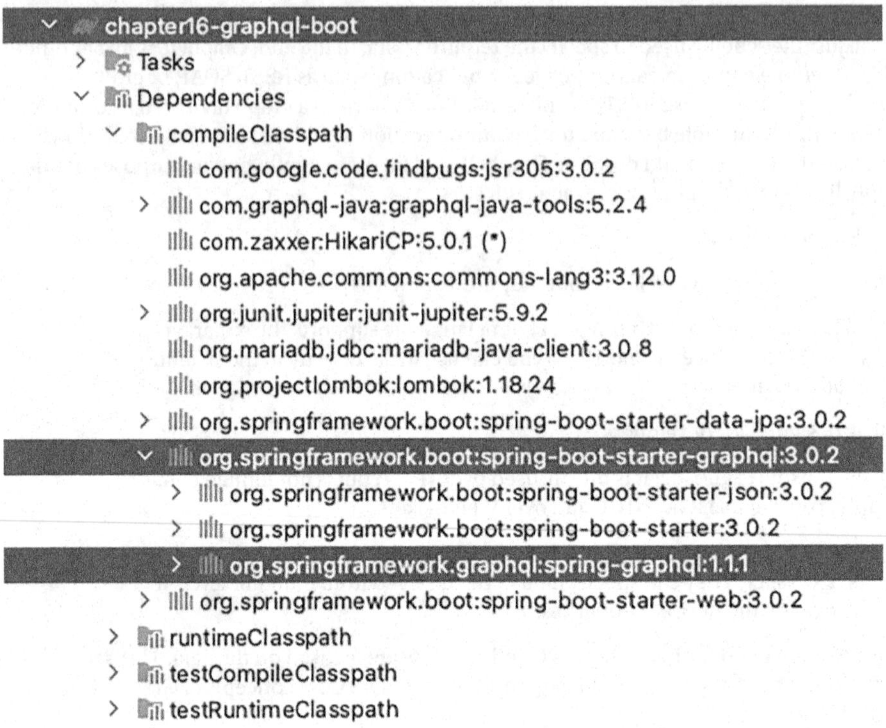

```
✓  chapter16-graphql-boot
   >  Tasks
   ✓  Dependencies
      ✓  compileClasspath
            com.google.code.findbugs:jsr305:3.0.2
         >  com.graphql-java:graphql-java-tools:5.2.4
            com.zaxxer:HikariCP:5.0.1 (*)
            org.apache.commons:commons-lang3:3.12.0
         >  org.junit.jupiter:junit-jupiter:5.9.2
            org.mariadb.jdbc:mariadb-java-client:3.0.8
            org.projectlombok:lombok:1.18.24
         >  org.springframework.boot:spring-boot-starter-data-jpa:3.0.2
         ✓  org.springframework.boot:spring-boot-starter-graphql:3.0.2
            >  org.springframework.boot:spring-boot-starter-json:3.0.2
            >  org.springframework.boot:spring-boot-starter:3.0.2
            >  org.springframework.graphql:spring-graphql:1.1.1
         >  org.springframework.boot:spring-boot-starter-web:3.0.2
      >  runtimeClasspath
      >  testCompileClasspath
      >  testRuntimeClasspath
```

Figure 16-8. *Dependencies for project* `chapter16-graphql-boot`

The `Singer` entity class is shown in Listing 16-10 and is no different than the entity classes introduced in the data access chapters.

Listing 16-10. The Singer Entity Class

```
package com.apress.prospring6.sixteen.boot.entities

import jakarta.persistence.*
// other import statements omitted

@Entity
@Table(name = "SINGER")
class Singer() : Serializable {

    @Id
    @GeneratedValue(strategy = GenerationType.IDENTITY)
    @Column(name = "ID")
    var id: Long? = null
```

```kotlin
    @Version
    @Column(name = "VERSION")
    var version = 0

    @Column(name = "FIRST_NAME")
    var firstName: String? = null

    @Column(name = "LAST_NAME")
    var lastName: String? = null

    @Column(name = "PSEUDONYM")
    var pseudonym: String? = null

    @Column(name = "GENRE")
    var genre: String? = null

    @DateTimeFormat(pattern = "yyyy-MM-dd")
    @Column(name = "BIRTH_DATE")
    var birthDate: LocalDate? = null

    @OneToMany(mappedBy = "singer")
    var awards: Set<Award>? = null

    @ManyToMany
    @JoinTable(
            name = "SINGER_INSTRUMENT",
            joinColumns = [JoinColumn(name = "SINGER_ID")],
            inverseJoinColumns = [JoinColumn(name = "INSTRUMENT_ID")]
    )
    var instruments: Set<Instrument>? = null

    // constructor, equals() and hashCode() omitted

    companion object {
            @Serial
            private val serialVersionUID = 1L
    }
}
```

Notice the @OneToMany relationship between the Singer and Award classes and the @ManytoMany relationship between Singer and Instrument. Both relationships are by default lazily initialized by the persistence provider runtime when first accessed. This is an important detail, as you will see later.

The Award entity class is shown in Listing 16-11.

Listing 16-11. The Award Entity Class

```kotlin
package com.apress.prospring6.sixteen.boot.entities;

import jakarta.persistence.*
// other import statements omitted
```

```kotlin
@Entity
@Table(name = "AWARD")
class Award : Serializable {
    @Id
    @GeneratedValue(strategy = GenerationType.IDENTITY)
    @Column(name = "ID")
    var id: Long? = null

    @Version
    @Column(name = "VERSION")
    var version = 0

    @ManyToOne
    @JoinColumn(name = "SINGER_ID")
    var singer: Singer? = null

    @Column(name = "YEAR")
    var year: Int? = null

    @Column(name = "TYPE")
    var category: String? = null

    @Column(name = "ITEM_NAME")
    var itemName: String? = null

    @Column(name = "AWARD_NAME")
    var awardName: String? = null

    companion object {
        @Serial
        private val serialVersionUID = 3L
    }

    override fun equals(other: Any?): Boolean {
        if (this === other) return true
        if (javaClass != other?.javaClass) return false

        other as Award

        return id == other.id
    }

    override fun hashCode(): Int {
        return id?.hashCode() ?: 0
    }

}
```

Notice the @ManyToOne relationship between Award and Singer. By default, the singer field is eagerly initialized by the persistence provider runtime when first accessed. The SINGER_ID column is actually a foreign key, making the singer record a parent of this award, so it makes sense that when an award is accessed, its parent should be accessible too.

The Instrument entity class is a very simple one, mapping to a table with a single column that is its primary key as well. It was introduced more as a dummy class to show a @ManyToMany relationship.

The Spring Data repository interfaces are the ones we are used to from Data Access chapters, simple extensions of JpaRepository. The repository interfaces are shown in Listing 16-12.

Listing 16-12. The Repository Interfaces

```
package com.apress.prospring6.sixteen.boot.entities
// import statements omitted

interface SingerRepo : JpaRepository<Singer, Long> { }

interface AwardRepo : JpaRepository<Award, Long>{ }

interface InstrumentRepo : JpaRepository<Instrument, String> {
}
```

For simplicity, we will not be using service beans, and we'll jump directly to implementing GraphQL controllers. Spring for GraphQL provides an annotation-based programming model where @Controller components use specific GraphQL annotations to decorate handler methods with flexible signatures, to fetch data for specific GraphQL fields. Let's consider the simplest example, querying for all the singers. Listing 16-13 shows a controller with a handler method for responding to a GraphQL query for retrieving all singers.

Listing 16-13. GraphQL Handler Method for Returning All Singers in the Singer Table

```
package com.apress.prospring6.sixteen.boot.controllers;

import org.springframework.graphql.data.method.annotation.QueryMapping
import org.springframework.stereotype.Controller

// other import statements omitted

@Controller
class SingerController(private val singerRepo:SingerRepo) {

    @QueryMapping
    fun  singers():Iterable<Singer>{
        return singerRepo.findAll()
    }

        // other handler methods omitted
}
```

The @Controller annotation is the same stereotype annotation introduced earlier in this book. It is automatically picked up by Spring Boot, which adds all org.springframework.graphql.execution. RuntimeWiringConfigurer beans to org.springframework.graphql.execution.GraphQlSource.Builder and enables support for annotated graphql.schema.DataFetcher instances.

The @QueryMapping annotation binds the method to a query, a GraphQL field under a Query type. @QueryMapping is a composed annotation that acts as a shortcut for @SchemaMapping with typeName="Query". It is a practical way to map controller methods to GraphQL queries. You can think of the @SchemaMapping as the @RequestMapping for GraphQL.

Now that we have a handler method, we need to configure the GraphQL schemas with objects, queries, and mutations definitions. These three terms are the core terms of GraphQL. As previously mentioned, GraphQL is statically typed, which means the server knows exactly the shape of every object you can query and any client can actually "introspect" the server and ask for the "schema." These types are declared in schema files located under resources/graphql and they map to all objects involved in GraphQL actions of any kind.

Listing 16-14 shows the schema for the Singer object and the singers query definition that are declared in resources/graphql/singer.graphqls.

Listing 16-14. GraphQL Schema for the Singer Type and singers Query

```
type Singer {
    id: ID!
    firstName: String!
    lastName: String!
    pseudonym: String
    genre: String
    birthDate: String
    awards: [Award]
    instruments: [Instrument]
}

type Query {
    singers: [Singer]
}
```

The schema describes what queries are possible and what fields you can get back for a certain type. If fields are supposed to be not null, in the declaration the type must be suffixed with ! (exclamation mark).

So, now that we have a schema, are we ready to submit GraphQL requests? Not yet, because we still need to configure the Spring Boot application to support GraphQL, as shown in Listing 16-15.

Listing 16-15. Spring Boot Application Configuration for GraphQL

```
server:
  port: 8081
  servlet:
    context-path: /
  compression:
    enabled: true
  address: 0.0.0.0

spring:
  graphql:
    graphiql:
      enabled: true
      path: graphiql
```

```
  datasource:
    driverClassName: org.mariadb.jdbc.Driver
    url: jdbc:mariadb://localhost:3307/musicdb?useSSL=false
    username: prospring6
    password: prospring6
    hikari:
      maximum-pool-size: 25
  jpa:
    generate-ddl: false
    properties:
      hibernate:
        naming:
          physical-strategy: com.apress.prospring6.sixteen.boot.CustomPhysicalNamingStrategy
        jdbc:
          batch_size: 10
          fetch_size: 30
        max_fetch_depth: 3
        hbm2ddl:
          auto: none
# logging configuration omitted
```

GraphQL queries can be sent to an application using a web interface named GraphiQL. This is a web console that can communicate with any GraphQL server and helps to consume and develop against a GraphQL API. It is included in the Spring Boot starter for GraphQL and is exposed by default at the /graphiql endpoint. In Listing 16-15, the same value is configured just to show that the property spring. graphql.graphiql.path can be used to customize the URL path where the web console is accessible. The endpoint is disabled by default, but it can be turned on by setting the spring.graphql.graphiql.enabled property to true. GraphiQL is a very practical tool to write and test queries, particularly during development and testing.

Now we are ready to start the application and write some queries. To access GraphiQL, open the http://localhost:8081/graphiql URL in the browser. As shown in Figure 16-9, this opens the GraphiQL web console, with an editor on the left where you can write queries and a panel on the right that displays the retrieved data.

Figure 16-9. *GraphiQL web console with a simple query*

The query in this image is simple; we can add more fields and even relationships. Figure 16-10 shows a GraphQL query that retrieves all the details for all the singers (not something you would ever need to do, but just know it is possible).

Figure 16-10. *GraphiQL web console with a nested query*

So this works, even though, as previously mentioned, the awards collection is lazily initialized. Also... how is GraphQL processing such queries? It would be interesting to see how many queries are executed on the table for retrieving that data—in short, how efficient it really is. To figure this out, let's enable SQL logging in the Spring Boot configuration by adding the property logging.level.sql=debug to the configuration.

If we send the same query and look in the console log, we can see the log in Listing 16-16.

Listing 16-16. Database Queries for a Nested GraphQL Query

```
DEBUG: SqlStatementLogger - select s1_0.ID,s1_0.BIRTH_DATE,s1_0.FIRST_NAME,s1_0.GENRE,s1_0.
LAST_NAME,s1_0.PSEUDONYM,s1_0.VERSION from SINGER s1_0
DEBUG: SqlStatementLogger - select a1_0.SINGER_ID,a1_0.ID,a1_0.AWARD_NAME,a1_0.TYPE,a1_0.
ITEM_NAME,a1_0.VERSION,a1_0.YEAR from AWARD a1_0 where a1_0.SINGER_ID=?
DEBUG: SqlStatementLogger - select a1_0.SINGER_ID,a1_0.ID,a1_0.AWARD_NAME,a1_0.TYPE,a1_0.
ITEM_NAME,a1_0.VERSION,a1_0.YEAR from AWARD a1_0 where a1_0.SINGER_ID=?
DEBUG: SqlStatementLogger - select a1_0.SINGER_ID,a1_0.ID,a1_0.AWARD_NAME,a1_0.TYPE,a1_0.
ITEM_NAME,a1_0.VERSION,a1_0.YEAR from AWARD a1_0 where a1_0.SINGER_ID=?
DEBUG: SqlStatementLogger - select a1_0.SINGER_ID,a1_0.ID,a1_0.AWARD_NAME,a1_0.TYPE,a1_0.
ITEM_NAME,a1_0.VERSION,a1_0.YEAR from AWARD a1_0 where a1_0.SINGER_ID=?
...
```

Two things are going on here:

- For every singer, an extra query is executed to extract the awards (N+1 complexity problem).

- This is possible because, by default, Spring Boot configures a Hibernate session to be open when a request for data is coming. This allows for lazy associations to be loaded, which improves developer productivity because it keeps things simple. There is no need for special queries with join statements. The bean providing this behavior is the OpenSessionInViewInterceptor[8].

The problem with the *session per request* transactional pattern is that it can become inefficient in production environments. This behavior can be disabled by adding the following property to the Spring Boot configuration: spring.jpa.open-in-view=false. This, however, does not go well with GraphQL nested queries when it tries to fetch lazy relationships.

What is the fix for this? We need to modify the GraphQL handler method and use Spring Data JPA Specification API methods to extract relationship data only when required. This obviously means we need to analyze the query sent by the client. There is more than one way to do this, but the easiest is to use the graphql.schema.DataFetchingEnvironment parameter inside the QueryResolver implementation. In methods annotated with @QueryMapping, Spring Boot automatically injects the value for this parameter and, depending on requested relations, we can build different queries. If you remember, we did have two relations, "awards" and "instruments". Listing 16-17 shows the improved singers(..) handler method.

Listing 16-17. The singers() Method

```
package com.apress.prospring6.sixteen.boot.controllers

import org.springframework.graphql.data.method.annotation.QueryMapping
import org.springframework.stereotype.Controller
import graphql.schema.DataFetchingEnvironment
import graphql.schema.DataFetchingFieldSelectionSet
import jakarta.persistence.criteria.Fetch
import jakarta.persistence.criteria.Join
import jakarta.persistence.criteria.JoinType
import org.springframework.data.jpa.domain.Specification
// other import statements omitted
```

---

[8] https://docs.spring.io/spring-framework/docs/current/javadoc-api/org/
springframework/orm/hibernate5/support/OpenSessionInViewInterceptor.html

```kotlin
@Controller
class SingerController(private val singerRepo: SingerRepo) {
    @QueryMapping
    fun singers(environment: DataFetchingEnvironment): Iterable<Singer> {
        val s = environment.selectionSet
        return if (s.contains("awards") && !s.contains("instruments"))
            singerRepo.findAll(fetchAwards())
        else if (s.contains("awards") && s.contains("instruments"))
            singerRepo.findAll(fetchAwards().and(fetchInstruments()))
        else if (!s.contains("awards") && s.contains("instruments"))
            singerRepo.findAll(fetchInstruments())
        else singerRepo.findAll()
    }

    private fun fetchAwards(): Specification<Singer?> {
        return Specification { root: Root<Singer?>, query: CriteriaQuery<*>?,
                                               builder: CriteriaBuilder? ->
            val f =
                root.fetch<Singer, Award>(
                    "awards",
                    JoinType.LEFT
                )
            val join =
                f as Join<Singer, Award>
            join.on
        }
    }

    private fun fetchInstruments(): Specification<Singer?> {
        return Specification { root: Root<Singer?>, query: CriteriaQuery<*>?,
                                               builder: CriteriaBuilder? ->
            val f =
                root.fetch<Singer, Instrument>(
                    "instruments",
                    JoinType.LEFT
                )
            val join =
                f as Join<Singer, Instrument>
            join.on
        }
    }
    // other methods omitted
}
```

The findAll(Specification<T> spec) method used to retrieve a list of Singer instances with some relationships loaded is provided by org.springframework.data.jpa.repository. JpaSpecificationExecutor<T>, so the SingerRepo must be modified to extend this interface too.

If we restart the application and send the query in Listing 16-18, we get the expected reply, and if we look in the console, we notice that a single query is executed.

Listing 16-18. GraphQL Query Requesting a One-to-Many Relationship

```
query {
  singers{
    firstName
    lastName
    pseudonym
    genre
    birthDate
    awards {
      awardName
      year
    }
  }
}
```

The query in the console log, is shown in Listing 16-19.

Listing 16-19. Query SQL Logged

```
select s1_0.ID,
       a1_0.SINGER_ID,
       a1_0.ID,a1_0.AWARD_NAME,
       a1_0.TYPE,
       a1_0.ITEM_NAME,
       a1_0.VERSION,a1_0.YEAR,
       s1_0.BIRTH_DATE,
       s1_0.FIRST_NAME,
       s1_0.GENRE,
       s1_0.LAST_NAME,
       s1_0.PSEUDONYM,
       s1_0.VERSION
from SINGER s1_0
    left join AWARD a1_0 on s1_0.ID=a1_0.SINGER_ID
```

What happens if we add the instruments relationship to the query as well? This is a many-to-many relationship that is modeled under the hood using two one-to-many relationships: one between SINGER and SINGER_INSTRUMENT and one between INSTRUMENT and SINGER_INSTRUMENT. Listing 16-20 shows the GraphQL query and the queries generated to extract the requested data.

Listing 16-20. GraphQL Query with a Many-to-Many Relationship

```
query {
  singers{
    firstName
    lastName
    pseudonym
    genre
    birthDate
    awards {
      awardName
      year
    }
```

```
    instruments {
      name
    }
  }
}
# Resulted queries
select s1_0.ID,
       a1_0.SINGER_ID,a1_0.ID,
       a1_0.AWARD_NAME,
       a1_0.TYPE,a1_0.ITEM_NAME,
       a1_0.VERSION,a1_0.YEAR,
       s1_0.BIRTH_DATE,
       s1_0.FIRST_NAME,
       s1_0.GENRE,
       i1_0.SINGER_ID,
       i1_1.INSTRUMENT_ID,
       s1_0.LAST_NAME,
       s1_0.PSEUDONYM,
       s1_0.VERSION
from SINGER s1_0
    left join AWARD a1_0 on s1_0.ID=a1_0.SINGER_ID
    left join (SINGER_INSTRUMENT i1_0 join INSTRUMENT i1_1 on i1_1.INSTRUMENT_ID=i1_0.
    INSTRUMENT_ID) on s1_0.ID=i1_0.SINGER_ID;

select s1_0.INSTRUMENT_ID,s1_1.ID,s1_1.BIRTH_DATE,s1_1.FIRST_NAME,s1_1.GENRE,s1_1.LAST_
NAME,s1_1.PSEUDONYM,s1_1.VERSION
from SINGER_INSTRUMENT s1_0
    join SINGER s1_1 on s1_1.ID=s1_0.SINGER_ID
    where s1_0.INSTRUMENT_ID=?;
select s1_0.INSTRUMENT_ID,s1_1.ID,s1_1.BIRTH_DATE,s1_1.FIRST_NAME,s1_1.GENRE,s1_1.LAST_
NAME,s1_1.PSEUDONYM,s1_1.VERSION
from SINGER_INSTRUMENT s1_0
    join SINGER s1_1 on s1_1.ID=s1_0.SINGER_ID
    where s1_0.INSTRUMENT_ID=?;
select s1_0.INSTRUMENT_ID,s1_1.ID,s1_1.BIRTH_DATE,s1_1.FIRST_NAME,s1_1.GENRE,s1_1.LAST_
NAME,s1_1.PSEUDONYM,s1_1.VERSION
from SINGER_INSTRUMENT s1_0
    join SINGER s1_1 on s1_1.ID=s1_0.SINGER_ID
    where s1_0.INSTRUMENT_ID=?;
select s1_0.INSTRUMENT_ID,s1_1.ID,s1_1.BIRTH_DATE,s1_1.FIRST_NAME,s1_1.GENRE,s1_1.LAST_
NAME,s1_1.PSEUDONYM,s1_1.VERSION
from SINGER_INSTRUMENT s1_0
    join SINGER s1_1 on s1_1.ID=s1_0.SINGER_ID
    where s1_0.INSTRUMENT_ID=?;
```

So, what happened? Well, JPA query generation is not that smart after all. If a SQL developer were to write a query to extract data from tables linked to each other via a many-to-many relationship like the one depicted in Listing 16-20, the query would look like the one shown in Listing 16-21.

Listing 16-21. SQL Query with a Many-to-Many Relationship

```
select
        s1_0.ID,a1_0.SINGER_ID,a1_0.ID,
        a1_0.AWARD_NAME,
        a1_0.YEAR,
        s1_0.BIRTH_DATE,
        s1_0.FIRST_NAME,
        s1_0.LAST_NAME,
        I.INSTRUMENT_ID
from SINGER s1_0
        left join AWARD a1_0 on s1_0.ID=a1_0.SINGER_ID
        left join SINGER_INSTRUMENT SI on s1_0.ID = SI.SINGER_ID
        left join INSTRUMENT I on I.INSTRUMENT_ID = SI.INSTRUMENT_ID;
```

Also, if you look carefully at the generated queries, you might notice that, regardless of the fields specified in your GraphQL queries, when the query is generated for the database, unless you explicitly write a SQL native query to specify the name of the columns you get data from, JPA will generate an SQL query that includes all columns. You might conclude from this example that GraphQL is not as efficient as advertised. Still, it was efficient enough to make Facebook the most widely used social network in the world.

Let's look at other GraphQL queries we can support. For example, if we want all the details for a singer with a specific ID, the query to write might look like the one depicted in Listing 16-22.

Listing 16-22. GraphQL Query for Retrieving Details for a Singer with id 1

```
query {
  singerById(id: 1){
    firstName
    lastName
    awards {
      awardName
      year
    }
    instruments{
      name
    }
  }
}
```

To support this query, we need to add the schema for it and the handler method. Also, this is a good opportunity to introduce the @Argument annotation. Listing 16-23 depicts the query schema and the handler method.

Listing 16-23. GraphQL Query Handler

```
type Query {
    singerById(id: ID!) : Singer
}
package com.apress.prospring6.sixteen.boot.controllers

import org.springframework.graphql.data.method.annotation.Argument
// other import statements omitted
```

```
@Controller
class SingerController {

    @QueryMapping
    fun singerById(@Argument id: Long, environment: DataFetchingEnvironment): Singer {
        var spec = byId(id)
        val s = environment.selectionSet
        if (s.contains("awards") && !s.contains("instruments"))
            spec = spec.and(fetchAwards())
        else if (s.contains("awards") && s.contains("instruments"))
            spec = spec.and(fetchAwards().and(fetchInstruments()))
        else if (!s.contains("awards") && s.contains("instruments")) spec =
            spec.and(fetchInstruments())
        return singerRepo.findOne(spec).orElse(null)
    }

// other methods omitted
}
```

The Spring GraphQL @Argument annotation binds a named GraphQL argument onto a method parameter. The same JPA Specification<Singer> instances are used to provide support for loading lazy relationships for individual singers as well.

Until now, we've only done data retrieval, so it is time to introduce how to support operations like creating a new Singer object and updating and deleting existing Singer objects. All these operations are supported through a concept, or type, called Mutation. Similar to a Query, a Mutation declares the schema for a create, update, or delete operation. GraphQL queries for these operations are mapped to handler methods annotated with @MutationMapping.

Listing 16-24 show the necessary mutations and the SingerInput type needed for create and update operations.

Listing 16-24. GraphQL Query for Retrieving Details for a Singer with id 1 (Declared in resources/ graphql/singer.graphqls)

```
type Mutation {
    updateSinger(id: ID!, singer: SingerInput): Singer!
    deleteSinger(id: ID!): ID!
}
input SingerInput {
    firstName: String!
    lastName: String!
    pseudonym: String
    genre: String
    birthDate: String
}
package com.apress.prospring6.sixteen.boot.controllers

import org.springframework.graphql.data.method.annotation.MutationMapping
// other import statements omitted

@Controller
class SingerController(private val singerRepo: SingerRepo) {
    @MutationMapping
```

```kotlin
fun newSinger(@Argument singer: SingerInput): Singer {
    val date: LocalDate = try {
        LocalDate.parse(singer.birthDate, DateTimeFormatter.ofPattern("yyyy-MM-dd"))
    } catch (e: DateTimeParseException) {
        throw IllegalArgumentException("Bade date format")
    }
    val newSinger = Singer(
        null, 0, singer.firstName, singer.lastName,
        singer.pseudonym, singer.genre, date, null, null
    )
    return singerRepo.save<Singer>(newSinger)
}


@MutationMapping
fun updateSinger(@Argument id: Long, @Argument singer: SingerInput): Singer {
    val fromDb: Singer = singerRepo.findById(id).orElseThrow{
        NotFoundException(
            Singer::class.java, id
        )
    }
    fromDb.firstName=singer.firstName
    fromDb.lastName=singer.lastName
    fromDb.pseudonym=singer.pseudonym
    fromDb.genre=singer.genre
    val date: LocalDate
    try {
        date = LocalDate.parse(singer.birthDate,
            DateTimeFormatter.ofPattern("yyyy-MM-dd"))
        fromDb.birthDate=date
    } catch (e: DateTimeParseException) {
        throw IllegalArgumentException("Bade date format")
    }
    return singerRepo.save(fromDb)
}


@MutationMapping
fun deleteSinger(@Argument id: Long): Long {
    singerRepo.findById(id).orElseThrow{
        NotFoundException(
            Singer::class.java, id
        )
    }
    singerRepo.deleteById(id)
    return id
}

data class SingerInput(
    val firstName: String,
    val lastName: String,
    val pseudonym: String,
    val genre: String,
```

```
        val birthDate: String
    )
    // other methods omitted
}
```

⚠️ In the current version of GraphQL, you cannot declare a query or mutation without a return type. A workaround is to return a typical value that represents a successful operation, such as a 0 (zero) or OK in the handler method, or just return null and declare a nullable type in the schema.

The GraphQL queries for creating, updating, and deleting a singer are shown in Listing 16-25.

Listing 16-25. GraphQL Query for Creating, Updating, and Deleting a Singer

```
# create singer
mutation {
  newSinger(singer: {
    firstName: "Lindsey"
    lastName: "Buckingham"
    pseudonym: "The Greatest"
    genre: "rock"
    birthDate: "1949-10-03"
  }) {
    id
    firstName
    lastName
  }
}

# update singer
mutation {
  updateSinger(id: 16, singer: {
    firstName: "Lindsey"
    lastName: "Buckingham"
    genre: "rock"
    birthDate: "1949-10-03"
  }) {
    id
    firstName
    lastName
  }
}

#delete singer
mutation {
  deleteSinger(id: 16)
}
```

Now that we've explored how to create Singer instances via GraphQL queries, what happens if we try to execute the query to create a singer twice? That is clearly not allowed, because singers are supposed to be unique in our database. Trying to create a singer with the same firstName and lastName causes a DataIntegrityViolationException to be thrown, which we can see the exception in the console log, but in GraphQL, the web console does not give a lot of details, as shown in Figure 16-11.

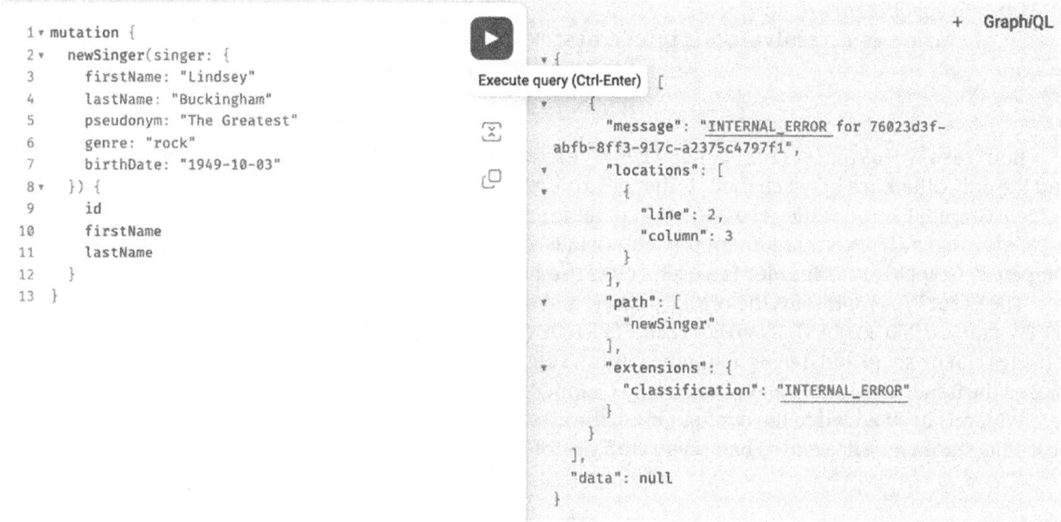

Figure 16-11. *GraphiQL web console showing an error when trying to execute the same mutation twice*

We know the server has a problem executing what we asked it to, but we do not know why. Obviously, proper exception handling is needed. When working with GraphQL, we handle errors by extending the org.springframework.graphql.execution.DataFetcherExceptionResolverAdapter class and overriding either the resolveToSingleError(..) method or resolveToMultipleErrors(..) method. Adding a bean of this type to the configuration provides a more concise way to represent data layer errors in the GraphQL response that is shown in the GraphiQL web console. Listing 16-26 shows a custom implementation of DataFetcherExceptionResolverAdapter.

Listing 16-26. Custom Implementation for DataFetcherExceptionResolverAdapter

```
package com.apress.prospring6.sixteen.boot.problem

import graphql.GraphQLError
...

@Component
class CustomExceptionResolver : DataFetcherExceptionResolverAdapter() {
    override fun resolveToSingleError(ex: Throwable, env: DataFetchingEnvironment):
    GraphQLError {
        return if (ex is DataIntegrityViolationException) {
            GraphqlErrorBuilder.newError()
                .errorType(ErrorType.BAD_REQUEST)
                .message("Cannot create duplicate entry:" + ex.cause!!.cause!!.message)
                .path(env.executionStepInfo.path)
```

```
            .location(env.field.sourceLocation)
            .build()
    } else super.resolveToSingleError(ex, env)
}

override fun resolveToMultipleErrors(ex: Throwable, env: DataFetchingEnvironment):
List<GraphQLError> {
    return super.resolveToMultipleErrors(ex, env)
}
}
```

Both resolveToSingleError(..) and resolveToMultipleErrors(..) have the same signature, and the only difference between them is that resolveToSingleError(..) resolves a thrown exception to a single GraphQL error, while resolveToMultipleErrors(..) does so to multiple GraphQL errors. The DataFetchingEnvironment argument provides details about the execution context in which the error happened. GraphqlErrorBuilder is a useful class used to build a GraphQL error.

The ErrorType represents the error category, and the values in this enum match the most common HTTP statuses: BAD_REQUEST, UNAUTHORIZED, FORBIDDEN, NOT_FOUND, and INTERNAL_ERROR. A customized message can be set to add details about the failure. The path is the name of the query or mutation that caused the issue. The location represents the GraphQL query lines that caused the error.

With this bean added to the configuration, the error becomes more readable, as shown in Figure 16-12, providing someone who sends a bad query with the information needed to correct it.

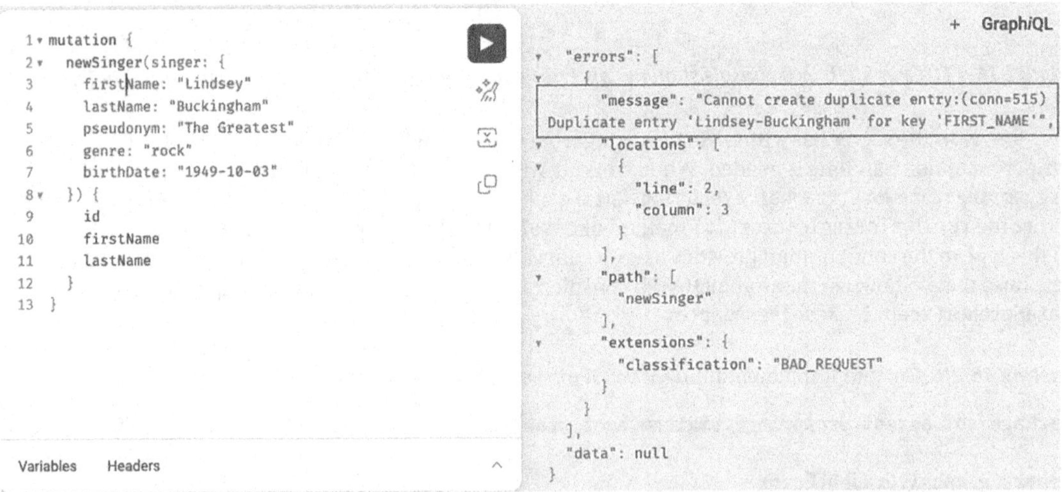

***Figure 16-12.** GraphiQL web console showing a customized error when trying to execute the same mutation twice*

Testing GraphQL controllers can be done as shown in previous chapters for web applications, using TestRestTemplate or MockMvc, or WebClient for a Spring Boot Reactive GraphQL application, by sending POST requests containing GraphQL queries in the body.

This section just touched on the basics on how to get started with building GraphQL APIs in Spring. If you would like to learn more about Spring support for GraphQL, feel free to check out the Spring for GraphQL official project page[9].

---

[9] https://spring.io/projects/spring-graphql

Summary

GraalVM native images are an evolving technology, and not all libraries provide support. Spring Native support was experimental until Spring Boot 3.

GraphQL's adoption by Spring is a clear sign that GraphQL is here to stay. There is one operation in GraphQL that was not covered in this chapter: *subscription.* Sometimes clients might want to receive updates from the server when data they care about changes. Subscription is the operation that provides this functionality. Another topic that was not touched upon is GraphQL on a reactive server like Netty. In a Spring Boot reactive application with GraphQL, testing is possible with `org.springframework.graphql.test.tester.GraphQlTester`[10].

---

[10] https://docs.spring.io/spring-graphql/docs/current/api/org/springframework/graphql/test/tester/GraphQlTester.html

Summary

CHAPTER 17

■ ■ ■

Securing Spring Web Applications

Chapter 14 explained how to build a Spring web application using classic, "manual"-style configuration and using Spring Boot with Thymeleaf. This chapter will take the application built in Chapter 14 and add a security layer that will declare which users are allowed to access various parts of the application. For example, only those users who logged into the application with a valid user ID can add a new singer or update existing singers. Other users, known as *anonymous users*, can only view singer information.

Spring Security[1] is the best choice for securing Spring-based applications. Spring Security provides authentication, authorization, and other security features for enterprise applications. Although mostly used in the presentation layer, Spring Security can help secure all layers within the application, including the service layer. In the following sections, we demonstrate how to use Spring Security to secure the singers application. For web applications, depending on the view technology used, there are tags that can be part of the view template to hide or show parts of the view based on the user rights.

Spring Security is a relatively complex framework that aims to make it easy for the developer to implement security in an application. Before being part of Spring, the project (started in late 2003) was named *Acegi Security*. The first Spring Security release was version 2.0.0 in April 2008.

When it comes to security in applications, there are two aspects that are important, and Spring Security can be used to configure both:

- *Authentication*: The process of proving that you are who you say you are. This means you submit your credentials to the application, and they are tested against a set of existing users, and if a match is found, you are given access to the application.

- *Authorization*: The process of granting an authenticated party permission to perform some particular actions. Spring Security is essentially a framework composed of intercepting rules for granting, or not granting, access to resources.

These two processes revolve a principal which refers to signifies a user, device, or system that could perform an action within the application, credentials that identification keys that a principal uses to confirm its identity (e.g., a username and password).

This chapter shows how to configure authorization and authentication with Spring Security version 6.x.

---

❶　You can find Spring Security's source code on GitHub at `https://github.com/spring-projects/spring-security/`.

---

[1] `https://docs.spring.io/spring-security/reference?`

© Peter Späth, Iuliana Cosmina, Rob Harrop, Chris Schaefer 2023
P. Späth et al., *Pro Spring 6 with Kotlin*, https://doi.org/10.1007/978-1-4842-9557-1_17

Configuring Spring Security - The Classic Way

This section shows how to secure the application built in **Chapter 14**. To add Spring Security to it, we obviously need to add a few libraries to the classpath. A minimal Spring Security configuration for a Spring web application typically looks similar to the one depicted in Figure 17-1.

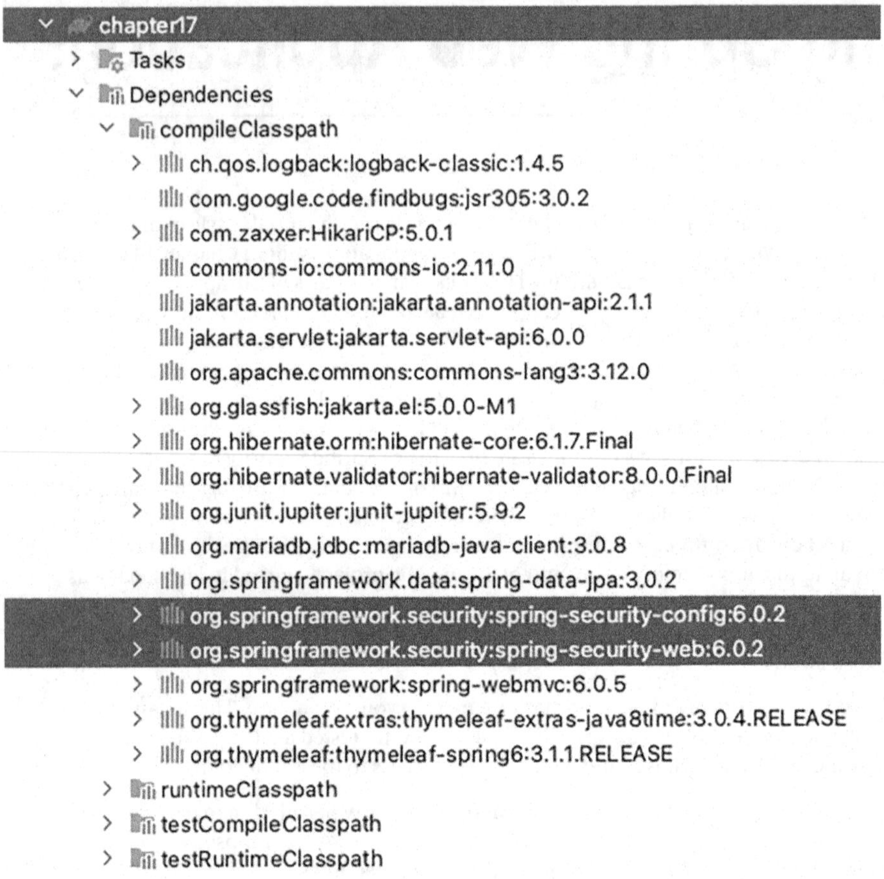

```
∨  chapter17
   >  Tasks
   ∨  Dependencies
      ∨  compileClasspath
         >  ch.qos.logback:logback-classic:1.4.5
            com.google.code.findbugs:jsr305:3.0.2
         >  com.zaxxer:HikariCP:5.0.1
            commons-io:commons-io:2.11.0
            jakarta.annotation:jakarta.annotation-api:2.1.1
            jakarta.servlet:jakarta.servlet-api:6.0.0
            org.apache.commons:commons-lang3:3.12.0
         >  org.glassfish:jakarta.el:5.0.0-M1
         >  org.hibernate.orm:hibernate-core:6.1.7.Final
         >  org.hibernate.validator:hibernate-validator:8.0.0.Final
         >  org.junit.jupiter:junit-jupiter:5.9.2
            org.mariadb.jdbc:mariadb-java-client:3.0.8
         >  org.springframework.data:spring-data-jpa:3.0.2
         >  org.springframework.security:spring-security-config:6.0.2
         >  org.springframework.security:spring-security-web:6.0.2
         >  org.springframework:spring-webmvc:6.0.5
         >  org.thymeleaf.extras:thymeleaf-extras-java8time:3.0.4.RELEASE
         >  org.thymeleaf:thymeleaf-spring6:3.1.1.RELEASE
      >  runtimeClasspath
      >  testCompileClasspath
      >  testRuntimeClasspath
```

Figure 17-1. *Project* chapter17 *dependencies*

The spring-security-config library contains Java/Kotlin configuration support. The spring-security-web library contains web security infrastructure code, such as various filters and other Servlet API dependencies.

The internals of Spring Security are complex, and the official documentation explains them very well and in detail. For the purpose of this book, the only thing you need to know is that once Spring Security is configured, all HTTP requests are intercepted by a Security Interceptor and access to resources is decided based on the user making the request. The Security Interceptor works with a preprocessing step and a postprocessing step. In the preprocessing step, it looks to see whether the requested resource is secured with some metadata information represented by an `org.springframework.security.access.ConfigAttribute`[2]. If it is not, the request is allowed to continue its way either to the requested URL or method. If the requested resource is secured, the Security Interceptor retrieves the `Authentication` object from the current `SecurityContext`. If necessary, the `Authentication` object will be authenticated against the configured `AuthenticationManager`.

Intercepting all requests to a web application requires a special servlet filter. The Spring Security filter that needs to be configured is named `springSecurityFilterChain` and, as its name makes obvious, it is not a single filter but a collection of filters that are chained together to protect the application URLs, validate submitted username and passwords, redirect to the login form, and so on. Spring Security provides ways to configure this filter and customize its various functions, to any depth necessary.

With the preceding details in mind, let's see how we can configure security support in a Spring web application with classic configuration.

💡 If you need to, please review **Chapter 14** at this point to re-familiarize yourself with the components of a Spring web application with classic configuration and how to pack up an application as a WAR file and deploy it to Apache Tomcat 10.

Figure 17-2 shows the configuration classes for a secured Spring web application with classic configuration.

---

[2] https://github.com/spring-projects/spring-security/blob/main/core/src/main/java/org/springframework/security/access/ConfigAttribute.java

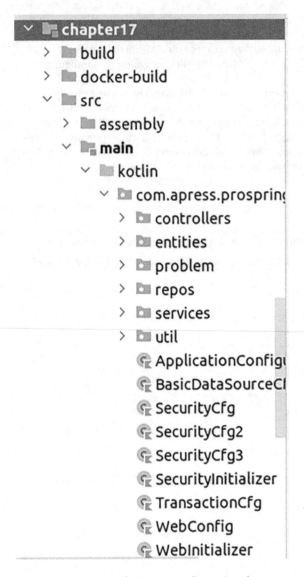

Figure 17-2. Project chapter17 configuration classes

One of the first things that we need to do is to make sure springSecurityFilterChain is the entry point to the application, registered with the highest precedence, to be the first filter in the chain, before any other registered jakarta.servlet.Filter. This is done by adding a class that implements org.springframework.web.WebApplicationInitializer to the application. In Figure 17-2 the class is named SecurityInitializer. Its implementation is shown in Listing 17-1.

Listing 17-1. The SecurityInitializer Class

```
package com.apress.prospring6.seventeen

import org.springframework.security.web.context.AbstractSecurityWebApplicationInitializer;
```

```kotlin
class SecurityInitializer : AbstractSecurityWebApplicationInitializer{
    override
    fun boolean enableHttpSessionEventPublisher() = true
}
```

Notice that the SecurityInitializer class does not implement WebApplicationInitializer directly, but by extending AbstractSecurityWebApplicationInitializer to benefit from the default implementation and reduce the work a developer must do.

💡   The enableHttpSessionEventPublisher() method is overridden to return true; by default it returns false, and we could have left it like that since this configuration is not really important for the rest of the chapter. This method should return true if session management has specified a maximum number of sessions, because in this case an org.springframework.security.web.session. HttpSession EventPublisher is added to the configuration to notify the session registry when a user logs out.

Now with the filter in place, let's give the filter the required components to do its job.

Notice that we haven't added any view template for the login page—with Spring Security, we don't have to. With a default configuration, a default very simple login page is included, and any request requiring authentication is redirected to it. So, we can jump directly to the Spring Security configuration. Listing 17-2 shows the SecurityCfg class, explanation of which follows the listing.

Listing 17-2. Basic Version of the SecurityCfg Class

```kotlin
package com.apress.prospring6.seventeen

import org.springframework.context.annotation.Configuration
import org.springframework.security.config.annotation.web.configuration.EnableWebSecurity

@Configuration
@EnableWebSecurity
open class SecurityCfg {
}
```

This is the simplest Spring Security configuration example possible. It sets up the securityFilterChain with a default configuration, so all requests are now blocked. If you deploy the project and try to access it at http://localhost:8080/ch17 (presuming you use Tomcat and the name of the WAR file is ch17.war), you are redirected to the login screen shown in Figure 17-3.

Figure 17-3. *Default login screen*

This is a very simple login page written in HTML with Bootstrap[3], with a form for submitting a username and password. You can inspect the source in your browser if you want to. If you try to introduce a username and password, you will be redirected to the same page, but with an error message added, as shown in Figure 17-4.

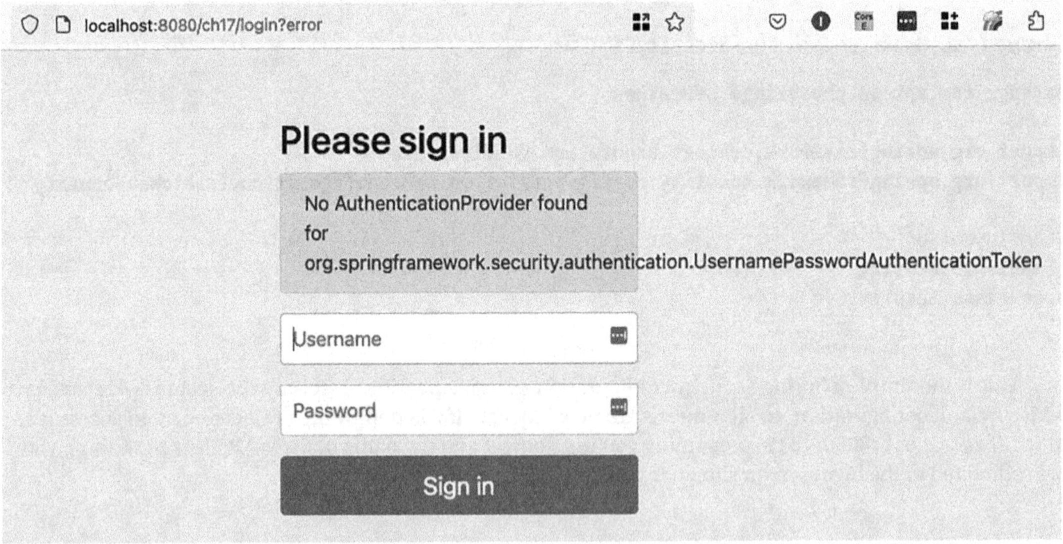

Figure 17-4. *Login screen with error message*

---

[3] https://getbootstrap.com/

What Spring is complaining about is that there is no AuthenticationProvider bean configured, and thus Spring does not know where to look for a username and a password to match the ones submitted so that your identity can be validated. To keep things as simple as possible as well, we'll configure a bean of type UserDetailsService to use in-memory authentication for demonstration purposes. It declares a single user named "john" with password "doe" and role "USER". The bean is shown in Listing 17-3.

Listing 17-3. The SecurityCfg Class

```
package com.apress.prospring6.seventeen

import org.springframework.security.core.userdetails.User
import org.springframework.security.core.userdetails.UserDetails
import org.springframework.security.core.userdetails.UserDetailsService
import org.springframework.security.provisioning.InMemoryUserDetailsManager
// some import statements omitted

@Configuration
@EnableWebSecurity
open class SecurityCfg {
    @Bean
    open fun userDetailsService(): UserDetailsService {
        UserDetails user = User.withDefaultPasswordEncoder()
                .username("john")
                .password("doe")
                .roles("USER")
                .build()
        return InMemoryUserDetailsManager(user)
    }
}
```

This configuration is compact, but it does a lot, a partial list of which follows:

- Blocks access to all application URLs

- Generates a login form

- Allows form-based authentication for a user named john with password doe

- Allows for a user to log out

- Prevents CSRF[4] attack

- Provides Session Fixation[5] protection

The UserDetailsService bean is a very simple one as well, and the User object is built with withDefaultPasswordEncoder(), which delegates to BCryptPasswordEncoder. If you want to build a demo application, and you need multiple users and roles, you can explicitly declare a BCryptPasswordEncoder bean and use it. Listing 17-4 shows you how.

---

[4] https://portswigger.net/web-security/csrf
[5] https://owasp.org/www-community/attacks/Session_fixation

Listing 17-4. The SecurityCfg with a BCryptPasswordEncoder Class

package com.apress.prospring6.seventeen

import org.springframework.security.crypto.bcrypt.BCryptPasswordEncoder
// some import statements omitted

```
@Configuration
@EnableWebSecurity
open class SecurityCfg {
    @Bean
    open fun encoder():PasswordEncoder  {
        return BCryptPasswordEncoder()
    }

    @Bean
    open fun userDetailsService(encoder:PasswordEncoder):
            UserDetailsService {
        val users  = User.builder().passwordEncoder(encoder::encode)
        val joe = users
                .username("john")
                .password("doe")
                .roles("USER")
                .build()
        val jane = users
                .username("jane")
                .password("doe")
                .roles("USER")
                .build()
        val admin = users
                .username("admin")
                .password("admin")
                .roles("ADMIN")
                .build()
        return InMemoryUserDetailsManager(jane, joe, admin)
    }
}
```

The class is annotated with the @EnableWebSecurity annotation to enable secured behavior in a Spring web application. This annotation exposes the SecurityFilterChain bean, so we can customize it. The configuration introduced so far does not show any of that. Every aspect of the SecurityFilterChain bean can be customized. Let's start small and add an explicit configuration for it that actually uses the defaults, just to have an idea of how it is done. Listing 17-5 introduces you to a custom SecurityFilterChain bean.

Listing 17-5. The SecurityCfg with a Simple SecurityFilterChain Class

package com.apress.prospring6.seventeen

import org.springframework.security.config.Customizer
import org.springframework.security.config.annotation.web.builders.HttpSecurity
import org.springframework.security.web.SecurityFilterChain
// some import statements omitted

```kotlin
@Configuration
@EnableWebSecurity
open class SecurityCfg {

    @Bean
    open fun securityFilterChain(http: HttpSecurity): SecurityFilterChain {
        http
            .authorizeHttpRequests{ authorize: AuthorizeHttpRequestsConfigurer<*>.
            AuthorizationManagerRequestMatcherRegistry ->
                authorize
                    .anyRequest().authenticated()
            }
            .logout(Customizer.withDefaults())
            .formLogin(Customizer.withDefaults())
            return http.build()
    }

    @Bean
    open fun encoder(): PasswordEncoder {
        return BCryptPasswordEncoder()
    }

    // more methods omitted
}
```

One by one, here is an explanation of all the important bits of this configuration:

- `HttpSecurity`: This object allows configuration of web-based security for specific HTTP requests. Spring injects an instance of this object, which can be further configured.

- `authorizeHttpRequests(...)`: This method provides support for customizing access to various resources to authenticated users. The syntax is builder specific and multiple rules can be connected to each other through `.and()` methods.

- `httpBasic(Customizer.withDefaults())`: This method is used to configure HTTP basic authentication for the application. The `withDefaults()` method returns an empty implementation of the `Customizer<T>` functional interface. This does not generate a login form, and authentication is enforced by the browser by blocking access to the application via a dialog box that allows the user to submit a username and password. Since it does not require a form, basic authentication is more suitable for REST requests. This method invocation is equivalent to `httpBasic()`.

- `formLogin(Customizer.withDefaults())`: This method is used to configure a login form. With an empty `Customizer<T>`, it obviously defaults to the generic out-of-the-box form, but a `Customizer<FormLoginConfigurer<?>>` can configure the path of the login page, and the names of the username and password form parameters. This method invocation is equivalent to `formLogin()`.

- `logout(Customizer.withDefaults())`: This method is used to configure logout support. This functionality is automatically enabled when configuring security using `@EnableWebSecurity`. This invocation, equivalent to `logout()`, is added to this configuration for teaching purposes.

Now that we have some defaults, let's customize some of them. Let's start with the hardest: let's add a custom default form. For this we need to create a Thymeleaf view template containing a simple authentication form. The base of this is the views/templates/layout.html template that declares sections for the header, menu, and footer, thus the authentication form will represent only the central part of the page, the pageContent section. The form is shown in Listing 17-6.

Listing 17-6. A Thymeleaf Authentication Form (views/auth.html)

```html
<!DOCTYPE HTML>
<html xmlns:th="http://www.thymeleaf.org">

    <head th:replace="~{templates/layout :: pageTitle('Login Page')}"></head>

    <body>
        <div class="container">
            <header th:replace="~{templates/layout :: pageHeader}" ></header>

            <header th:replace="~{templates/layout :: pageMenu}" ></header>

            <section th:fragment="~{templates/layout :: pageContent}">
                <div class="content">  <!-- content -->
                    <h5 th:text="#{command.login}">Log in</h5>
                    <div class="container col-lg-12">
                        <form th:action="@{/auth}" method="post">
                            <div class="row mb-1">
                                <input type="text" id="user" name="user"
                                        autofocus="autofocus" class="form-control"
                                        th:placeholder="#{label.username}" />
                            </div>
                            <div class="row mb-1">
                                <input type="password" id="pass" name="pass"
                                    class="form-control" th:placeholder="#{label.password}" />
                            </div>
                            <div class="form-group mb-1 align-items-end">
                                <input type="submit" th:value="#{command.signin}"
                                    id="loginButton" class="btn btn-dark"/>
                            </div>
                        </form>
                    </div>
                </div>
            </section>
            <footer th:replace="~{templates/layout :: pageFooter}" ></footer>
        </div>
    </body>
</html>
```

Intentionally, the URL for submitting the form is changed to /auth, the username and password fields are renamed to user and pass, and the file is named auth.html to provide as much configuration as possible.

To configure Spring Security to use this form as a login form, the .formLogin() invocation must be replaced with the configuration in Listing 17-7.

Listing 17-7. Spring Security Configuration with a Custom Form

```
.formLogin{ loginConfigurer -> loginConfigurer
      .loginPage("/auth")
      .loginProcessingUrl("/auth")
      .usernameParameter("user")
      .passwordParameter("pass")
      .defaultSuccessUrl("/home")
      .permitAll() }
.csrf().disable()
```

The name of each of these methods makes it very obvious as to which part of the configuration it covers:

- loginPage("/auth") configures the login form to be a view named auth. We can map this view name to the views/auth.html template, either via a @GetMapping handler method or by adding the mapping to the ViewControllerRegistry in the web configuration, as shown in Listing 17-8.

Listing 17-8. Mapping the /auth Path to the views/auth.html View File

package com.apress.prospring6.seventeen

import org.springframework.web.servlet.config.annotation.ViewControllerRegistry
```
// other import statements omitted

@Configuration
@EnableWebMvc
open class WebConfig : WebMvcConfigurer, ApplicationContextAware {
    override
    fun addViewControllers(registry:ViewControllerRegistry) {
        registry.addRedirectViewController("/", "/home")
        registry.addViewController("/auth").setViewName("auth")
    }

    // other bits of configuration omitted
}
```

- loginProcessingUrl("/auth") is needed to declare the /auth as the URL where the credentials are submitted, and is the one in the th:action="@{/auth}" Thymeleaf form declaration.

- defaultSuccessUrl("/home") is needed to redirect the user to the main page when the authentication succeeds. By default, the user is redirected to the root of the application, /, and in this example it is the same page we configured by this method too. The purpose of this is, of course, is to explicitly declare which method to use when you create your own configurations.

- csrf().disable() is needed to disable the generation of a CSRF token. As mentioned at the beginning of this section, by default CSRF protection is enabled, and to keep our form and the configuration simple, we decided to disable it.

ⓘ Spring Security 4 introduced the possibility of using CSRF tokens in Spring forms to prevent cross-site request forgery[6]. In this example, because we wanted to keep things simple, the usage of CSRF tokens was disabled by calling `csrf().disable()`. By default, a configuration without a CSRF element configuration is invalid, and any login request will direct you to a 403 error page stating the following:

```
Invalid CSRF Token 'null' was found on the request parameter'_csrf' or header
'X-CSRF-TOKEN'.
```

- `permitAll()` is needed to make sure unauthenticated users have access to the authentication form.

Now that we have a custom form, when we try to access the application at `http://localhost:8080/ch17` instead of the Spring Security default form, the custom form, we are redirected to the custom form, displaying the theme of the site, shown in Figure 17-5.

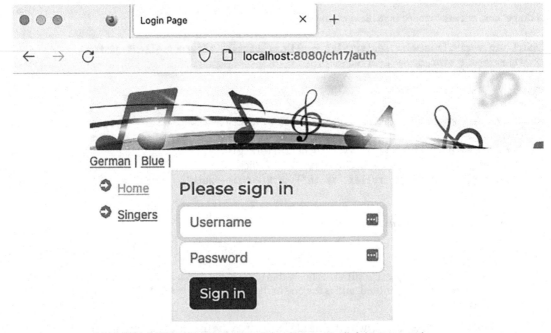

Figure 17-5. *Custom login form configured with Spring Security*

Each of the default configurations shown until now in this section will probably require small changes and adjustments in real applications. For example, the `authorizeHttpRequests(..)` method is used to set

---

[6] `https://en.wikipedia.org/wiki/Cross-site_request_forgery`

up authorization for specific URL paths. It can also be used to exclude some paths from this process like CSS and images, and we can add some extra cleanup steps, such as deleting authentication details from the browser cache or deleting some cookies. Listing 17-9 shows the full coding.

Listing 17-9. Customized Version of the SecurityFilterChain

```
package com.apress.prospring6.seventeen

import org.springframework.context.annotation.Bean
...

@Configuration
@EnableWebSecurity
open class SecurityCfg {
    @Bean
    @Throws(Exception::class)
    open fun securityFilterChain(http: HttpSecurity): SecurityFilterChain {
        http
            .authorizeHttpRequests{ authorize ->
                authorize
                    .requestMatchers("/styles/**", "/images/**").permitAll()
                    .anyRequest().authenticated()
            }
            .logout { httpSecurityLogoutConfigurer: LogoutConfigurer<HttpSecurity> ->
                httpSecurityLogoutConfigurer
                    .logoutUrl("/exit")
                    .permitAll()
                    .clearAuthentication(true)
            }
            .formLogin { loginConfigurer: FormLoginConfigurer<HttpSecurity> ->
                loginConfigurer
                    .loginPage("/auth")
                    .loginProcessingUrl("/auth")
                    .usernameParameter("user")
                    .passwordParameter("pass")
                    .defaultSuccessUrl("/home")
                    .permitAll()
            }
            .csrf().disable()
        return http.build()
    }

    @Bean
    open fun encoder(): PasswordEncoder {
        return BCryptPasswordEncoder()
    }

    @Bean
    open fun userDetailsService(encoder: PasswordEncoder): UserDetailsService {
        val users = User.builder().passwordEncoder(encoder::encode)
        val joe = users
```

```
                .username("john")
                .password("doe")
                .roles("USER")
                .build()
        val jane = users
                .username("jane")
                .password("doe")
                .roles("USER", "ADMIN")
                .build()
        val admin = users
                .username("admin")
                .password("admin")
                .roles("ADMIN")
                .build()
        return InMemoryUserDetailsManager(jane, joe, admin)
    }
}
```

Notice that the logout behavior has been configured as well, by providing a customizer as an argument for the `logout(..)` method; besides changing the logout URL from /logout to /exit, it also adds the `clearAuthentication(true)` call that tells Spring to clear the `Authentication` (default) when a user logs out.

Now that we have the full configuration, how do we tell Spring about it? To make sure it is used correctly, we need to add the `SecurityCfg` class to the collection of configuration classes that define our application context. In **Chapter 14** the `WebInitializer` class used to register a `DispatcherServlet` and use Java-based Spring configuration declares the root application as being configured via the `BasicDataSourceCfg` and `TransactionCfg` and the web application context as being configured by the `WebConfig` class. This configuration is shown in Listing 17-10.

Listing 17-10. Chapter 17 Web Application Configuration

```
package com.apress.prospring6.seventeen

import jakarta.servlet.Filter
...

@Configuration
@EnableWebMvc
open class WebConfig : WebMvcConfigurer, ApplicationContextAware {
    private var applicationContext: ApplicationContext? = null

    @Throws(BeansException::class)
    override fun setApplicationContext(applicationContext: ApplicationContext) {
        this.applicationContext = applicationContext
    }

    @Bean(name = [DispatcherServlet.MULTIPART_RESOLVER_BEAN_NAME])
    open fun multipartResolver(): StandardServletMultipartResolver {
        return StandardServletMultipartResolver()
    }
```

```kotlin
@Bean
open fun templateResolver() =
    SpringResourceTemplateResolver().apply {
        setApplicationContext(applicationContext!!)
        prefix = "/WEB-INF/views/"
        suffix = ".html"
        templateMode = TemplateMode.HTML
        isCacheable = false
    }

@Bean
@Description("Thymeleaf Template Engine")
open fun templateEngine() =
    SpringTemplateEngine().apply {
        addDialect(Java8TimeDialect())
        setTemplateResolver(templateResolver())
        setTemplateEngineMessageSource(messageSource())
        enableSpringELCompiler = true
    }

@Bean
@Description("Thymeleaf View Resolver")
open fun viewResolver(): ViewResolver =
    ThymeleafViewResolver().apply {
        templateEngine = templateEngine()
        order = 1
    }

@Bean
open fun themeSource() = ResourceBundleThemeSource()

@Bean
open fun validator(): Validator =
    LocalValidatorFactoryBean().apply {
        setValidationMessageSource(messageSource())
    }

override fun getValidator(): Validator = validator()

// Declare our static resources. I added cache to the java config but it is not
required.
override fun addResourceHandlers(registry: ResourceHandlerRegistry) {
    super.addResourceHandlers(registry)
    registry.addResourceHandler("/images/**", "/styles/**")
        .addResourceLocations("/images/", "/styles/")
}

override fun addViewControllers(registry: ViewControllerRegistry) {
    with(registry){
        addRedirectViewController("/", "/home")
```

```kotlin
                registry.addViewController("/auth").setViewName("auth")
        }
    }

    override fun addInterceptors(registry: InterceptorRegistry) {
        with(registry) {
            addInterceptor(localeChangeInterceptor()).addPathPatterns("/*")
            addInterceptor(themeChangeInterceptor())
            addInterceptor(webChangeInterceptor())
        }
    }

    @Bean
    open fun messageSource(): MessageSource =
        ReloadableResourceBundleMessageSource().apply {
            setBasename("classpath:i18n/global")
            setDefaultEncoding(StandardCharsets.UTF_8.name())
            setUseCodeAsDefaultMessage(true)
            setFallbackToSystemLocale(true)
            // # -1 : never reload, 0 always reload
            // setCacheSeconds(0);
        }

    @Bean
    open fun localeChangeInterceptor(): LocaleChangeInterceptor =
        LocaleChangeInterceptor().apply {
            paramName = "lang"
        }

    @Bean
    open fun themeChangeInterceptor() =
        ThemeChangeInterceptor().apply {
            paramName = "theme"
        }

    @Bean
    open fun localeResolver() =
        CookieLocaleResolver().apply {
            setDefaultLocale(Locale.ENGLISH)
            setCookieMaxAge(3600)
            setCookieName("locale")
        }

    @Bean
    open fun themeResolver() =
        CookieThemeResolver().apply {
            defaultThemeName = "green"
            cookieMaxAge = 3600
            cookieName = "theme"
        }
```

```kotlin
    @Bean
    open fun webChangeInterceptor() =
        WebContentInterceptor().apply {
            cacheSeconds = 0
            setSupportedMethods("GET", "POST", "PUT", "DELETE")
        }
}
```

When we know that security is implemented only for the web layer, we can add the SecurityCfg class to the web context. But there are situations when the security context spans through multiple layers, the most obvious examples being when the users accessing the application have their credentials stored in the database and when the service layer supports remote calls. In situations like these, a configuration class picking up all configuration is introduced and used to declare a single huge and all-powerful web application context. Listing 17-11 shows the ApplicationConfiguration class.

Listing 17-11. The ApplicationConfiguration Class

```kotlin
package com.apress.prospring6.seventeen

import org.springframework.context.annotation.ComponentScan
import org.springframework.context.annotation.Configuration

@Configuration
@ComponentScan
open class ApplicationConfiguration
```

The ApplicationConfiguration class is used as a single configuration entry point in the WebInitializer for the chapter17 project, shown in Listing 17-12.

Listing 17-12. The WebInitializer at Use

```kotlin
package com.apress.prospring6.seventeen
// import statements omitted

class WebInitializer : AbstractAnnotationConfigDispatcherServletInitializer() {
    override fun getRootConfigClasses() =
        arrayOf<Class<*>>()

    override fun getServletConfigClasses() =
        arrayOf<Class<*>>(ApplicationConfiguration::class.java)

    override fun getServletMappings() =
        arrayOf("/")

    override fun getServletFilters() =
        arrayOf(
            HiddenHttpMethodFilter(),
            CharacterEncodingFilter().apply {
                encoding = StandardCharsets.UTF_8.name()
                setForceEncoding(true)
            }
        )
```

```kotlin
    public override fun customizeRegistration(registration: ServletRegistration.Dynamic) {
        with(registration) {
            setInitParameter("throwExceptionIfNoHandlerFound", "true")
            setMultipartConfig(multipartConfigElement) // <=> <multipart-config>
        }
        super.customizeRegistration(registration)
    }

    private val multipartConfigElement = MultipartConfigElement(null, MAX_FILE_SIZE,
        MAX_REQUEST_SIZE, FILE_SIZE_THRESHOLD)

    companion object {
        private const val MAX_FILE_SIZE: Long = 5000000

        // Beyond that size spring will throw exception.
        private const val MAX_REQUEST_SIZE: Long = 5000000

        // Size threshold after which files will be written to disk
        private const val FILE_SIZE_THRESHOLD = 0
    }
}
```

With the configuration in place, what is left to do is tweak bits of the UI to provide some logout option displaying the logged-in user and so on. Since we are using Thymeleaf, this is quite easy to do, but it requires the thymeleaf-extras-springsecurity6 library to be added to the classpath. This library adds the Spring Security integration module to the application, which allows using Spring Security dialect constructs in the Thymeleaf templates. This means beside the attributes prefixed with th:, we can now use properties prefixed with sec: to access the security context and make decisions about how the view should look, such as for users with different roles.

Since we now have authenticated users, we can add the following to our layout template (views/templates/layout.html):

- A logout menu item

- A section where the name of the authenticated user is shown

These two modifications are shown in Listing 17-13.

Listing 17-13. Thymeleaf Security Constructs in views/templates/layout.html

```html
<!DOCTYPE HTML>
<html xmlns:th="http://www.thymeleaf.org" th:with="lang=${#locale.language},
theme=${#themes.code('name')}" th:lang="${lang}" th:theme="${theme}">
    <head th:fragment="pageTitle(title)">
        <!-- head contents omitted -->
    </head>
    <body>
        <header th:fragment="pageHeader" class="page-header">
            <div class="row">
                <div class="col-lg-8 col-md-7 col-sm-6">
                    <div class="banner"></div>
                    <div class="themeLocal">
                        <!-- theming links omitted -->
```

```
                <span sec:authorize="isAuthenticated()">
                    Authenticated: <em sec:authentication="name"></em>
                </span>
            </div>
        </div>
    </header>

    <section th:fragment="pageMenu">
        <div class="menu">
            <ul>
                <!-- other elements configuration omitted -->
                <li sec:authorize="isAuthenticated()">
                    <a th:href="@{/exit}" th:text="#{command.logout}">Sign Out</a>
                </li>
            </ul>
        </div>
    </section>

    <section th:fragment="pageContent">
        <div class="content">
            <p>Page Content</p>
        </div>
    </section>

    <footer th:fragment="pageFooter">
        <div class="footer">
            <p th:text="#{footer.text}"></p>
        </div>
    </footer>
</body>
</html>
```

❗ Most importantly, for the sec: attributes to be recognized, the SpringSecurityDialect must be registered with the SpringTemplateEngine bean in the WebConfig class, as shown in Listing 17-14.

Listing 17-14. Configuration Snippet to Register the SpringSecurityDialect with the SpringTemplateEngine

```
package com.apress.prospring6.seventeen;

import org.thymeleaf.extras.java8time.dialect.Java8TimeDialect;
import org.thymeleaf.extras.springsecurity6.dialect.SpringSecurityDialect;
import org.thymeleaf.spring6.SpringTemplateEngine;
// other import statements omitted
```

```kotlin
@Configuration
@EnableWebMvc
open class WebConfig : WebMvcConfigurer, ApplicationContextAware {
    private var applicationContext: ApplicationContext? = null

    @Bean
    @Description("Thymeleaf Template Engine")
    open fun templateEngine() =
        SpringTemplateEngine().apply {
            addDialect(Java8TimeDialect())
            setTemplateResolver(templateResolver())
            setTemplateEngineMessageSource(messageSource())
            addDialect(SpringSecurityDialect()) // this is needed to the sec: tags to be
            supported
            enableSpringELCompiler = true
        }

    // other configurations omitted
}
```

With this configuration in place, when a user has successfully logged into the application, the home page will show the user's name and the logout option, as shown in Figure 17-6.

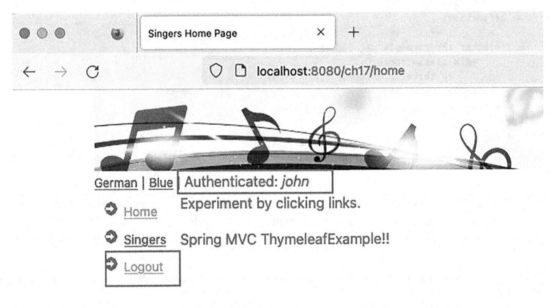

Figure 17-6. Home page shown to an authenticated user

In our configuration we have defined two roles, USER and ADMIN, but we are not using them for anything, because currently there is no configuration that is specific only to a certain role. Just to show how this can be done, let's allow only users with the ADMIN right to delete singers. This means we must do two things:

- Make sure the Delete button is not rendered for users that are not ADMIN

- Reject delete requests for users that are not ADMIN, by securing the controller method

Preventing the rendering of the Delete button is easily done by using a combination of Thymeleaf security constructs and SpEL expressions, as shown in Listing 17-15.

Listing 17-15. views/show.html Hiding the Delete Button for Non-Admin Users

```
<!DOCTYPE HTML>
<html xmlns:th="http://www.thymeleaf.org">

  <head th:replace="~{templates/layout :: pageTitle('Singer Page')}"></head>

  <body>
    <div class="container">
      <header th:replace="~{templates/layout :: pageHeader}" ></header>

      <header th:replace="~{templates/layout :: pageMenu}" ></header>

      <section th:fragment="~{templates/layout :: pageContent}">
          <!-- some elements omitted -->
          <div class="container col-lg-12">
            <form th:object="${singer}" th:action="@{/singer/} + ${singer.id}"
            th:method="delete"  class="col p-3">
              <input sec:authorize="hasRole('admin')"
                  type="submit" th:value="#{command.delete}"
                  id="deleteButton"
                  class="btn btn-danger"/>
            </form>
          </div>
        </div>net
      </div>
    </section>

      <footer th:replace="~{templates/layout :: pageFooter}" ></footer>
    </div>
  </body>
</html>
```

With this configuration, user john no longer can see the Delete button, while the admin user still can see it, as verified by Figure 17-7.

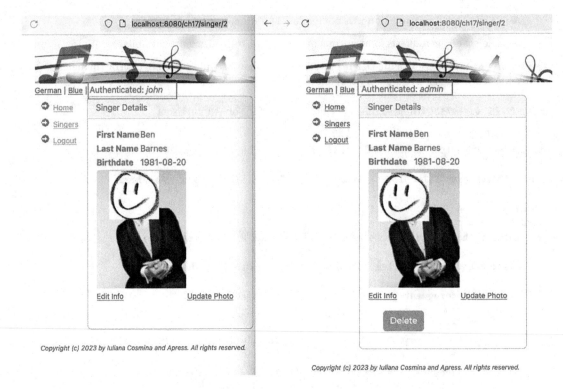

Figure 17-7. *Comparison of page display for user with role USER (left) and user with role ADMIN*

The Spring Security SpEL expression is quite versatile. The role name is not case sensitive, so hasRole('admin') is treated the same way as hasRole('ADMIN'). Also, if the role name does not have a ROLE_ prefix, it is added by default, such as hasRole('ROLE_ADMIN'). This makes it quite practical to configure authorization using SpEL expressions.

ℹ️   In Spring Security there are two ways to describe what a user can and cannot do. For each application user, *authorities* and *roles* are configured. Both roles and authorities are represented by a List<GrantedAuthority>, where the org.springframework.security.core.GrantedAuthority interface represents an authority granted to an Authentication object, thus a *permission*. A role is nothing else than a GrantedAuthority with names prefixed with ROLE_. Why are there two of ways? Because under the hood, Spring Security might be configured to treat roles differently than authorities. Authorities are fine-grained permissions targeting a specific action coupled sometimes with a specific data scope or context. For instance, Read, Write, and Manage can represent various levels of permissions to a given scope of information. On the other hand, roles are coarse-grained representations of a set of permissions. A ROLE_USER would only have Read or View authority, while a ROLE_ADMIN would have Read, Write, and Delete.

There is quite a long list of Spring Security SpEL expressions for configuring authorization, and their syntax and purpose are shown and described in Table 17-1.

Table 17-1. *Spring Security SpEL Expressions*

Expression	Description
hasRole(String role)	Returns true if the current principal has the specified role; e.g. hasRole('admin'). The role is not case sensitive, and if ROLE_ is not present, it is added by default. This behavior is customizable by modifying the defaultRolePrefix on DefaultWebSecurityExpressionHandler[7].
hasAnyRole(String... roles)	Returns true if the current principal has any of the specified roles; e.g., hasAnyRole('admin', 'manager').
hasAuthority(String authority)	Returns true if the current principal has the specified authority; e.g., hasAuthority('read').
hasAnyAuthority(String... authorities)	Returns true if the current principal has any of the specified authorities; e.g., hasAnyAuthority('read', 'write').
principal	Allows direct access to the principal object that represents the current user.
authentication	Allows direct access to the current Authentication object obtained from the SecurityContext.
isAnonymous()	Returns true if the current principal is an anonymous user.
isRememberMe()	Returns true if the current principal is a remember-me user.
isAuthenticated()	Returns true if the user is not anonymous.
isFullyAuthenticated()	Returns true if the user is not an anonymous and is not a remember-me user.
hasPermission(Object target, Object permission)	Returns true if the user has access to the provided target for the given permission; e.g., hasPermission(domainObject, 'read').
hasPermission(Object targetId, String targetType, Object permission)	Returns true if the user has access to the provided target, identified by its id and type, for the given permission; e.g., hasPermission (1, 'com.apress.Singer', 'read').

The hasRole('admin') Spring Security SpEL expression can be used to secure the delete handler method when provided as an attribute value to the @PreAuthorize annotation. This annotation and a few other annotations discussed later are part of the org.springframework.security.access.prepost package, which allows you to define security-specific actions before and after the execution of the annotated method. The @PreAuthorize annotation is configured with a method access-control expression that will be evaluated to decide whether a method invocation is allowed or not. Listing 17-16 shows the controller method annotated with @PreAuthorize.

---

[7] https://github.com/spring-projects/spring-security/blob/main/web/src/main/java/org/springframework/security/web/access/expression/DefaultWebSecurity ExpressionHandler.java

Listing 17-16. Secured Controller Method

```
package com.apress.prospring6.seventeen.controllers

import org.springframework.security.access.prepost.PreAuthorize
import org.springframework.stereotype.Controller
// other import statements omitted

@Controller
@RequestMapping("/singer/{id}")
open class OneSingerController(private val singerService: SingerService,
        private val messageSource: MessageSource) {

    ...
    @PreAuthorize("hasRole('ROLE_ADMIN')")
    @DeleteMapping
    open fun deleteSinger(@PathVariable("id") id: Long): String {
        singerService.findById(id)
        singerService.delete(id)
        return "redirect:/singers/list"
    }
    ...
}
```

In order to see this method not being executed for a user with a role different than admin, we have to temporarily remove sec:authorize="hasRole('ADMIN')" from the Delete button in views/singers/show. html. Since non-admin users are prohibited from executing this method, when clicking the Delete button, we are redirected to an Apache Tomcat default page for the 403(Forbidden) error. Since we want to redirect the user to the views/error.html, we need to add a method in the class annotated with @ControllerAdvice as shown in Listing 17-17.

Listing 17-17. Handler for an org.springframework.security.access.AccessDeniedException in a Spring Web Application

```
package com.apress.prospring6.seventeen.problem

import org.springframework.http.HttpStatus
import org.springframework.security.access.AccessDeniedException
// other import statements omitted

@ControllerAdvice
class GlobalExceptionHandler {
    ...
    @ExceptionHandler(AccessDeniedException::class)
    @ResponseStatus(HttpStatus.FORBIDDEN)
    fun forbidden(req: HttpServletRequest): ModelAndView {
        val mav = ModelAndView()
        mav.addObject("problem", "Method not allowed " + req.requestURI)
        mav.viewName = "error"
        return mav
    }
}
```

But wait! We also need to configure support for these types of annotations. The @EnableWebSecurity annotation only configures support for secured web requests, so to secure method invocations, we need to add the @EnableMethodSecurity annotation on the SecurityCfg class. The new configuration is shown in Listing 17-18.

Listing 17-18. SecurityCfg Configured to Support Secure Methods

```
package com.apress.prospring6.seventeen

import org.springframework.security.config.annotation.method.configuration.EnableMeth
odSecurity
// other import statements omitted

@Configuration
@EnableWebSecurity
@EnableMethodSecurity
open class SecurityCfg {
    // configuration beans omitted
}
```

With this configuration, when a non-admin user clicks the Delete button, the user is redirected to the page shown in Figure 17-8.

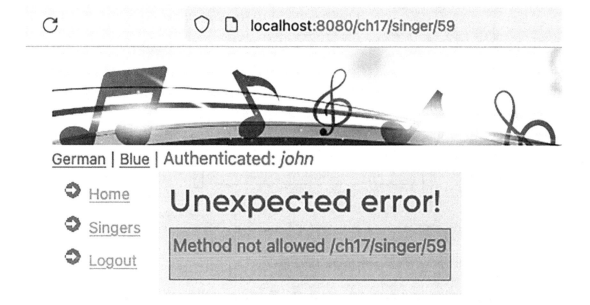

Figure 17-8. *Error page a non-admin user is redirected to after attempting to delete a singer record*

Securing methods is done via proxying. Security annotations are picked up and a proxy is created around the bean containing the annotated methods, to inject security checks where necessary.

As mentioned, the org.springframework.security.access.prepost package contains four annotations that support expression attributes to allow pre- and post-invocation authorization checks and also to support filtering of submitted collection arguments or return values: @PreAuthorize, @PreFilter, @PostAuthorize, and @PostFilter. By default, the support for these methods is enabled by the @EnableMethodSecurity annotation. But they can be disabled by configuring it like this: @EnableMethodSecurity(prePostEnabled= false).

To enable support for the @Secured annotation from package org.springframework.security.access.annotation, we configure @EnableMethodSecurity(secured = true). By default, the secured attribute is set to false.

Spring also provides support for Jakarta Annotations[8] (previously known as JSR-250 annotations). This library contains security annotations in the jakarta.annotation.security package that provide somewhat similar functionalities to the Spring Security annotations. However, they are standards-based annotations and allow simple role-based constraints to be applied, but they do not have the power of Spring Security's native annotations. The Jakarta Security annotations are @RolesAllowed, @DenyAll, @PermitAll, @RunAs, and @DeclareRoles. Support for these annotations is enabled by this configuration: @EnableMethodSecurity(jsr250Enabled=true); by default, jsr250Enabled is false.

Both approaches will lead to Spring Security wrapping the service class in a secure proxy. Figure 17-9 depicts the abstract schema of how a secured method executes and the components involved.

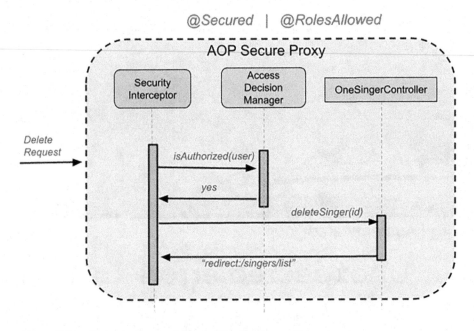

Figure 17-9. *Abstract schema of a secured method execution*

Feel free to read more about method security in the official documentation[9], since the subject is wider than the scope of this book.

---

[8] https://jakarta.ee/specifications/annotations/2.1
[9] https://docs.spring.io/spring-security/reference/servlet/authorization/method-security.html

JDBC Authentication

Thus far, you have been introduced to the quickest and easiest authentication mode, where the user credentials are stored in memory. For production applications, credentials are stored in relational databases, custom data stores, or LDAP. Since the application already stores the rest of the data in a database, it is very practical to add the necessary tables for storing credentials and groups. The focus of this section is JDBC authentication and storing authentication data in a MariaDB database.

Spring Security provides default queries for JDBC-based authentication, but for them to work, the tables must be created according to the Spring Security–provided schema. The schema is actually packed in the `spring-security-core.jar` that is the core Spring Security library and a dependency of `spring-security-config.jar`. The schema files are exposed as a classpath resource named `org/springframework/security/core/userdetails/jdbc/users.ddl`. The contents of this file are shown in Listing 17-19.

Listing 17-19. The Spring Security JDBC Schema[10]

```
create table users(
      username varchar(50) not null primary key,
      password varchar(500) not null,
      enabled boolean not null
);

create table authorities (
      username varchar(50) not null,
      authority varchar(50) not null,
      constraint fk_authorities_users foreign key(username) references users(username)
);

create unique index ix_auth_username on authorities (username,authority);
```

To create these tables, the contents of this file were added to the configuration for the `chapter17` project. There is more than one way to populate these tables, but Spring makes this easy as well, by providing a class named `UserDetailsManager` that extends `UserDetailsService` introduced in the previous section. A bean of this type, configured with a data source containing the Spring Security `users` and `authorities` tables as declared in Listing 17-19, is able to load credentials to facilitate the authentication process. The same class can also be used to initialize the tables. When starting a Spring Web–secured application for the first time, to easily populate the security tables, the `UserDetailsManager` bean can be configured as shown in Listing 17-20.

Listing 17-20. The Spring Security `UserDetailsManager` Configuration for Initializing Security Tables

```
package com.apress.prospring6.seventeen

import org.springframework.security.provisioning.JdbcUserDetailsManager
import org.springframework.security.provisioning.UserDetailsManager
// other import statements omitted
```

---

[10] https://github.com/spring-projects/spring-security/blob/main/core/src/main/resources/org/springframework/security/core/userdetails/jdbc/users.ddl

```
@Configuration
@EnableWebSecurity
@EnableMethodSecurity
open class SecurityCfg2 {
    ...
    @Bean
    open fun users(dataSource: DataSource): UserDetailsManager {
        val users = User.builder().passwordEncoder { rawPassword: String ->
            encoder().encode(
                rawPassword
            )
        }
        val joe = users
            .username("john")
            .password("doe")
            .roles("USER")
            .build()
        val jane = users
            .username("jane")
            .password("doe")
            .roles("USER", "ADMIN")
            .build()
        val admin = users
            .username("admin")
            .password("admin")
            .roles("ADMIN")
            .build()
        val manager = JdbcUserDetailsManager(dataSource)
        return with(manager) {
            createUser(joe)
            createUser(jane)
            createUser(admin)
            this
        }
    }
    // other configuration beans omitted
}
```

The next time the application is started with the same data source, the user creation can be removed, and the users created during the previous run will still be in our database and thus will work as expected. This reduces the Spring configuration to the one shown in Listing 17-21.

Listing 17-21. The Spring Security UserDetailsManager Configuration Without Initialization

```
package com.apress.prospring6.seventeen;
// import statements omitted

@Configuration
@EnableWebSecurity
@EnableMethodSecurity
open class SecurityCfg2 {
    @Bean
```

```kotlin
@Throws(Exception::class)
open fun securityFilterChain(http: HttpSecurity): SecurityFilterChain {
    // request configuration omitted
    return http.build()
}

@Bean
open fun encoder(): PasswordEncoder {
    return BCryptPasswordEncoder()
}

@Bean
open fun users(dataSource: DataSource): UserDetailsManager {
    return JdbcUserDetailsManager(dataSource)
}
}
```

So far, you've been introduced to the Spring Security in-memory and JDBC implementations of UserDetailsService. If for some reason you cannot use the Spring Security default schema, a custom implementation of UserDetailsService needs to be provided that is responsible for retrieving users and authorities based on user-provided data. An alternative is to configure an AuthenticationManagerBuilder bean, like shown in Listing 17-22.

Listing 17-22. The Spring Security AuthenticationManagerBuilder Configuration

```kotlin
package com.apress.prospring6.seventeen

import org.springframework.security.config.annotation.ObjectPostProcessor
import org.springframework.security.config.annotation.authentication.builders.Authenticatio
nManagerBuilder
// import statements omitted

@Configuration
@EnableWebSecurity
@EnableMethodSecurity
open class SecurityCfg3 {
    @Bean
    @Throws(Exception::class)
    open fun securityFilterChain(http: HttpSecurity): SecurityFilterChain {
        // request configuration omitted
        return http.build()
    }

    @Bean
    open fun encoder(): PasswordEncoder {
        return BCryptPasswordEncoder()
    }

    @Bean
    open fun authenticationManagerBuilder(
        objectPostProcessor: ObjectPostProcessor<Any>,
        dataSource: DataSource?
```

```
): AuthenticationManagerBuilder {
    val authenticationManagerBuilder =
        AuthenticationManagerBuilder(objectPostProcessor)
    val findUserQuery = """
                select username, password, enabled
                from users where username = ?
            """.trimIndent()
    val findRoles = """
                select username,authority from authorities
                where username = ?
            """.trimIndent()
    return try {
        authenticationManagerBuilder.jdbcAuthentication().dataSource(dataSource)
            .passwordEncoder(encoder())
            .usersByUsernameQuery(findUserQuery)
            .authoritiesByUsernameQuery(findRoles)
        authenticationManagerBuilder
    } catch (e: Exception) {
        throw RuntimeException("Could not initialize 'AuthenticationManagerBuilder'",e)
    }
}
}
```

Another shortcut was taken in Listing 17-22: the findUserQuery and findRoles are queries written for the Spring Security tables created previously, but this bean allows for users and authorities to be saved in tables with different names and different structures—as long as username, password, enabled, and authority columns exist, or the queries return them, the authentication process works as normal. For example, take a look at the alternative findUserQuery and findRoles in Listing 17-23, which are run on tables named staff and roles but rename the column to the one expected by the Spring Security AuthenticationManagerBuilder bean.

Listing 17-23. Alternative Queries for Retrieving Credentials

```
-- findUserQuery
    select staff_id as username,
    staff_credentials as password,
    active as enabled
    from staff  where staff_id = ?

-- findRoles
    select staff_id as username,
    role as authority
    from roles where staff_id = ?
```

Spring Security configuration is flexible, varied, and powerful, and you can even implement UserDetailsService to use Spring Data repositories for managing security data, or even use a NoSQL database as storage. It's really up to your development needs and your imagination; they are all just configurable beans after all.

Testing Secured Web Applications

Testing a secured Spring web application can be done in multiple ways as well. Integration tests for an application that gets deployed to Apache Tomcat require a lot of setup, so the easiest way is to use a web client that supports form authentication and use it to submit requests and test your assumptions. For this purpose, we chose REST Assured[11].

REST Assured provides a very simple API for validating REST services in Java. In Listing 17-24 you can see that three tests were written to cover the secured elements introduced in this section.

Listing 17-24. Testing Code

```kotlin
package com.apress.prospring6.seventeen.controllers

import io.restassured.RestAssured
import io.restassured.authentication.FormAuthConfig
import io.restassured.http.ContentType
import org.junit.jupiter.api.BeforeEach
import org.junit.jupiter.api.Test
import org.springframework.http.HttpStatus

import io.restassured.RestAssured.given
import org.junit.jupiter.api.Assertions.*
class SingerControllerTest {
    @BeforeEach
    fun setUp() {
        RestAssured.port = 8080
        RestAssured.baseURI = "http://localhost"
    }

    @Test
    fun johnShouldNotSeeTheDeleteButton() {
        val cfg = FormAuthConfig("/ch17/auth", "user", "pass")
            .withLoggingEnabled()
        val responseStr = RestAssured.given()
            .contentType(ContentType.URLENC)
            .auth().form("john", "doe", cfg)
            .`when`()["/ch17/singer/1"]
            .then()
            .assertThat().statusCode(HttpStatus.OK.value())
            .extract().body().asString()
        Assertions.assertAll(
            Executable {
                Assertions.assertTrue(
                    responseStr.contains(
                        "<div class=\"card-header\">Singer Details</div>"
                    )
                )
            },
```

---

[11] https://rest-assured.io

```kotlin
            Executable {
                Assertions.assertTrue(
                    responseStr.contains(
                        "<td>Mayer</td>"
                    )
                )
            },
            Executable {
                Assertions.assertFalse(
                    responseStr.contains(
                        "Delete"
                    )
                )
            }
        )
    }


    @Test
    fun johnShouldNotBeAllowedToDeleteSinger() {
        val cfg = FormAuthConfig("/ch17/auth", "user", "pass")
            .withLoggingEnabled()
        val responseStr = RestAssured.given()
            .contentType(ContentType.URLENC)
            .auth().form("john", "doe", cfg)
            .`when`().delete("/ch17/singer/1")
            .then()
            .assertThat().statusCode(HttpStatus.FORBIDDEN.value())
            .extract().body().asString()
    }


    @Test
    fun adminShouldSeeTheDeleteButton() {
        val cfg = FormAuthConfig("/ch17/auth", "user", "pass")
            .withLoggingEnabled()
        val responseStr = RestAssured.given()
            .contentType(ContentType.URLENC)
            .auth().form("admin", "admin", cfg)
            .`when`()["/ch17/singer/1"]
            .then()
            .assertThat().statusCode(HttpStatus.OK.value())
            .extract().body().asString()
        Assertions.assertAll(
            Executable {
                Assertions.assertTrue(
                    responseStr.contains(
                        "<div class=\"card-header\">Singer Details</div>"
                    )
                )
            },
            Executable {
                Assertions.assertTrue(
```

```
                    responseStr.contains(
                        "<td>Mayer</td>"
                    )
                )
            },
            Executable {
                Assertions.assertTrue(
                    responseStr.contains(
                        "Delete"
                    )
                )
            }
        )
    }
}
```

The `FormAuthConfig` object is configured to create a form authorization configuration with a predefined form action, username input tag, and password input tag. This object maps to the form in the `/views/auth.html` view template.

The `johnShouldNotSeeTheDeleteButton` test checks that user `john`, a non-admin user, is not able to see the Delete button, which proves that the Thymeleaf security element is behaving as desired. The `johnShouldNotBeAllowedToDeleteSinger` test checks that user `john` cannot submit a delete request. This proves that the `@PreAuthorize` annotation is configured correctly as well. The `adminShouldSeeTheDeleteButton` test checks that user `admin`, an admin user, can see the Delete button.

To wrap up this section, let's look at the security filters. As mentioned at the beginning of this section, the `securityFilterChain` is an entry point for a collection of security filters. If you want to make Spring show you the order of these filters being applied to your requests, simply configure TRACE logging for `org.springframework` in your `resources/logback.xml` file. This will print a lot of logging messages, but among them you should see a succession of logs similar to the ones in Listing 17-25.

Listing 17-25. Spring Security Filters Being Applied to the GET `/singers` Request

```
22:22:50.635 [http-nio-8080-exec-8] TRACE o.s.s.w.FilterChainProxy - Trying to match request
against DefaultSecurityFilterChain
[
    RequestMatcher=any request,
    Filters= [
        org.springframework.security.web.session.DisableEncodeUrlFilter@125ebc0d,
        org.springframework.security.web.context.request.async.WebAsyncManagerIntegration
        Filter@6525ad0,
        org.springframework.security.web.context.SecurityContextHolderFilter@3a7c81e1,
        org.springframework.security.web.header.HeaderWriterFilter@309cde68,
        org.springframework.security.web.authentication.logout.LogoutFilter@7111e25c,
        org.springframework.security.web.authentication.UsernamePasswordAuthentication
        Filter@5d008ea9,
        org.springframework.security.web.savedrequest.RequestCacheAwareFilter@202ba409,
        org.springframework.security.web.servletapi.SecurityContextHolderAwareRequest
        Filter@2d073dc4,
        org.springframework.security.web.authentication.AnonymousAuthentication
        Filter@77286aac,
        org.springframework.security.web.access.ExceptionTranslationFilter@2f8c1059,
        org.springframework.security.web.access.intercept.AuthorizationFilter@7fafe94a
```

```
    ]
] (1/1)
22:22:50.636  DEBUG o.s.s.w.FilterChainProxy - Securing GET /singers
22:22:50.636  TRACE o.s.s.w.FilterChainProxy - Invoking DisableEncodeUrlFilter (1/11)
22:22:50.636  TRACE o.s.s.w.FilterChainProxy - Invoking
WebAsyncManagerIntegrationFilter (2/11)
22:22:50.636  TRACE o.s.s.w.FilterChainProxy - Invoking SecurityContextHolderFilter (3/11)
22:22:50.636  TRACE o.s.s.w.FilterChainProxy - Invoking HeaderWriterFilter (4/11)
22:22:50.636  TRACE o.s.s.w.FilterChainProxy - Invoking LogoutFilter (5/11)
22:22:50.636  TRACE o.s.s.w.a.l.LogoutFilter - Did not match request to Or [Ant [pattern='/
exit', GET], Ant [pattern='/exit', POST], Ant [pattern='/exit', PUT], Ant [pattern='/exit',
DELETE]]
22:22:50.636  TRACE o.s.s.w.FilterChainProxy - Invoking
UsernamePasswordAuthenticationFilter (6/11)
22:22:50.636  TRACE o.s.s.w.a.UsernamePasswordAuthenticationFilter - Did not match request
to Ant [pattern='/auth', POST]
22:22:50.636  TRACE o.s.s.w.FilterChainProxy - Invoking RequestCacheAwareFilter (7/11)
22:22:50.636  TRACE o.s.s.w.s.HttpSessionRequestCache - matchingRequestParameterName is
required for getMatchingRequest to lookup a value, but not provided
22:22:50.636  TRACE o.s.s.w.FilterChainProxy - Invoking
SecurityContextHolderAwareRequestFilter (8/11)
22:22:50.636  TRACE o.s.s.w.FilterChainProxy - Invoking AnonymousAuthenticationFilter (9/11)
22:22:50.636  TRACE o.s.s.w.FilterChainProxy - Invoking ExceptionTranslationFilter (10/11)
22:22:50.636  TRACE o.s.s.w.FilterChainProxy - Invoking AuthorizationFilter (11/11)
...
```

The log snippet in Listing 17-25 shows a successful authenticated request of a user accessing something that user is authorized to access, which is why you can see all the filters being invoked to process the request.

💡 The first snippet of the log in Listing 17-25 shows all the types of the filters in the security chain. Feel free to inspect the code for each of them on GitHub[12].

As the name of the bean indicates, the filters are chained, and they are executed in a fixed order. The request object is passed from one filter to the next through the chain, just like an item on a conveyor belt in a factory goes through various machines. Some filters are critical, and if they find something wrong with the request, they throw an exception and the whole process stops; the rest of the filters are not applied to the request. Some of them are not critical, but they make changes to the request before sending it down the chain.

❗ The list of filters varies depending on what is configured in the application. For example, because we've disabled CSRF support, CsrfFilter does not appear in the list in Listing 17-25.

---

[12] https://github.com/spring-projects/spring-security/tree/main/web/src/main/java/org/springframework/security/web

For example, introducing a wrong username/password combination causes the UsernamePasswordAuthenticationFilter to throw a BadCredentialsException. This is the sixth filter in the chain, and this is where the process stops, so the five filters after it are not applied to the request because, as this filter makes clear, the request does not contain credentials recognized by the application, as shown in Listing 17-26.

Listing 17-26. Spring Security Filters Being Applied to the POST /auth Request with Wrong User and Password

```
22:34:23.027  DEBUG o.s.s.w.FilterChainProxy - Securing POST /auth
22:34:23.027  TRACE o.s.s.w.FilterChainProxy - Invoking DisableEncodeUrlFilter (1/11)
22:34:23.027  TRACE o.s.s.w.FilterChainProxy - Invoking
                                               WebAsyncManagerIntegrationFilter (2/11)
22:34:23.027  TRACE o.s.s.w.FilterChainProxy - Invoking SecurityContextHolderFilter (3/11)
22:34:23.027  TRACE o.s.s.w.FilterChainProxy - Invoking HeaderWriterFilter (4/11)
22:34:23.027  TRACE o.s.s.w.FilterChainProxy - Invoking LogoutFilter (5/11)
22:34:23.027  TRACE o.s.s.w.a.l.LogoutFilter - Did not match request to Or [Ant [pattern=
                                               '/exit', GET], Ant [pattern='/exit', POST],
                                               Ant [pattern='/exit', PUT], Ant [pattern=
                                               '/exit', DELETE]]
22:34:23.027  TRACE o.s.s.w.FilterChainProxy - Invoking
                                               UsernamePasswordAuthenticationFilter (6/11)
22:34:23.027  TRACE o.s.s.a.ProviderManager - Authenticating request with
                                               DaoAuthenticationProvider (1/1)
22:34:23.096  DEBUG o.s.s.a.d.DaoAuthenticationProvider - Failed to find user 'sfsfsf'
22:34:23.108  TRACE o.s.b.f.s.DefaultListableBeanFactory - Returning cached instance
                                               of singleton bean
                                               'delegatingApplicationListener'
22:34:23.108  TRACE o.s.s.w.a.UsernamePasswordAuthenticationFilter - Failed to process
                                               authentication request
org.springframework.security.authentication.BadCredentialsException: Bad credentials
.. // exception stacktrace omitted
22:34:23.108  TRACE o.s.s.w.a.UsernamePasswordAuthenticationFilter - Cleared
                                               SecurityContextHolder
22:34:23.108  TRACE o.s.s.w.a.UsernamePasswordAuthenticationFilter - Handling
                                               authentication failure
22:34:23.108  DEBUG o.s.s.w.s.HttpSessionEventPublisher - Publishing event: org.
springframework.security.web.session.HttpSessionCreatedEvent[source=org.apache.catalina.
session.StandardSessionFacade@587e2789]
22:34:23.108  DEBUG o.s.s.w.DefaultRedirectStrategy - Redirecting to /ch17/auth?error
```

As mentioned at the beginning of this section, each of the filters in the chain can be replaced with customized implementations. If you want to read more about Spring Security filter chain architecture and configuration, check out the official documentation[13].

---

[13] https://docs.spring.io/spring-security/reference/servlet/architecture.html

Configuring Spring Security: The Spring Boot Way

Securing a Spring Boot web application is easy too. Simply adding the `spring-boot-starter-security` dependency to the classpath adds default security configuration to your application. The Spring Security default configuration for a servlet-based Spring application is represented by the `SecurityAutoConfiguration` class from package `org.springframework.boot.autoconfigure.security.servlet`. By default, authentication gets enabled for the application and content negotiation is used to determine if basic or form login should be used. If the former is detected, a very simple default login form is generated.

Let's start with the basics: since we are reusing the UI from the non-Spring Boot project, we also need to add the `thymeleaf-extras-springsecurity6` library to the classpath. This makes the project classpath look like the one shown in Figure 17-10.

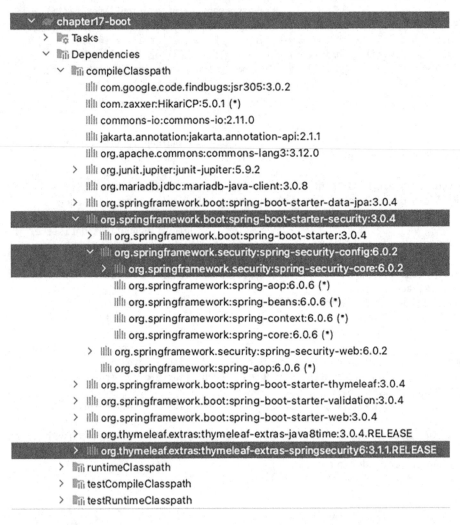

Figure 17-10. *chapter17-boot project dependencies in IntelliJ IDEA Gradle View*

The Spring Boot configuration file (chapter17-boot/src/main/resources/application-dev.yaml) is identical to the one covered in **Chapter 15**, but because the classpath contains the spring-boot-starter-security dependency, when starting the application and accessing it at http://localhost:8081, the default login form is shown. Without any specific security configuration, Spring Boot sets up in-memory authentication and generates a password for you that can be used with a user named user. The password is shown in the console log, as shown in Listing 17-27.

Listing 17-27. Spring Boot Default Generated Password for Spring Security Authentication

```
WARN : UserDetailsServiceAutoConfiguration -
Using generated security password: 82155279-ce4c-4670-9d86-4990370ea728

This generated password is for development use only. Your security configuration must be
updated before running your application in production.
```

As you can see, you are also warned that before production you must configure security properly. If you want to customize the default user and password, this is possible via the spring.security.user.username and spring.security.user.password properties. Listing 17-28 shows the YAML configuration to declare a user named john and password named doe. (Roles can also be configured.)

Listing 17-28. Spring Boot Default User Configuration for Spring Security Authentication (application-dev.yaml)

```
spring:
  security:
    user:
      name: john
      password: doe
      roles: user,admin
```

The limitation of this configuration is, of course, that you can have only one user, so the configuration with three users introduced in the previous section is not possible only with Spring Boot properties. When it comes to security, Spring Boot properties cannot help that much. So, unfortunately, the easiest way to do serious security handling in Spring Boot is to disable security autoconfiguration altogether and build our classes from scratch. To disable Spring Boot security autoconfiguration, we need to exclude the SecurityAutoConfiguration class from the application configuration. This can be done by customizing the @SpringBootApplication, as shown in Listing 17-29.

Listing 17-29. Excluding Spring Boot Default Security Configuration Class

```
package com.apress.prospring6.seventeen.boot

import org.springframework.boot.SpringApplication
import org.springframework.boot.autoconfigure.SpringBootApplication
import org.springframework.boot.autoconfigure.security.servlet.SecurityAutoConfiguration
import org.springframework.core.env.AbstractEnvironment

@SpringBootApplication(exclude = [ SecurityAutoConfiguration::class ])
//@SpringBootApplication
open class Chapter17Application {
    companion object {
        @JvmStatic
        fun main(args: Array<String>) {
```

```
        System.setProperty(AbstractEnvironment.ACTIVE_PROFILES_PROPERTY_NAME,
            "dev")
        SpringApplication.run(Chapter17Application::class.java, *args)
    }
  }
}
```

The exclusion also can be done via configuration of Spring Boot properties, as shown in Listing 17-30.

Listing 17-30. Disabling Spring Security Default Configuration in a Spring Boot Application (application-dev.yaml)

```
spring:
  autoconfigure:
    exclude: org.springframework.boot.autoconfigure.security.servlet.
    SecurityAutoConfiguration
```

With the default configuration removed, any of security configuration classes introduced in the previous section can be added to the application, and they get the job done just fine. As for testing, the REST Assured test class from the previous section works for the Spring Boot application too.

Of course, there are multiple ways to test secured applications, but the crux of the matter with web applications is the type of authentication used. Form-based authentication is tricky to mock, so you are better off just starting your application normally and then submitting some authenticated REST Assured requests and checking the assumption.

Summary

Application security is one of the most important aspects that needs to be incorporated when building an application designed to be used by the public over the Internet. Access to users' personal info must be restricted to validated parties; otherwise, there is a risk of identity theft that could destroy somebody's life. Leaked financial information could tear down global economies. Making it practical for developers to set up and maintain secure applications is something Spring Security shines at. This chapter has barely scratched the surface. If you want to read about Spring Security in depth and learn how to configure Spring Security with OAuth or JWT tokens, Apress published *Pro Spring Security for Spring 6 and Spring Boot 3* soon[14].

If you are interested in seeing more ways of configuring and testing Spring Security in classic and Spring Boot web applications, take a look at this repository: https://github.com/spring-projects/spring-security-samples.

---

[14] https://link.springer.com/book/10.1007/978-1-4842-5052-5

CHAPTER 18

Monitoring Spring Applications

A typical JEE application contains a number of layers and components, such as the presentation layer, service layer, persistence layer, and back-end data source. During the development stage, or after the application has been deployed to the quality assurance (QA) or production environment, we want to ensure that the application is in a healthy state without any potential problems or bottlenecks.

In a Java/Kotlin application, various areas may cause performance problems or overload server resources (such as CPU, memory, or I/O). Examples include inefficient Kotlin code, memory leaks (for example, code that keeps allocating new objects without releasing the reference and prevents the underlying JVM from freeing up the memory during the garbage collection process), miscalculated JVM parameters, miscalculated thread pool parameters, too generous data source configurations (for example, too many concurrent database connections allowed), improper database setup, and long-running SQL queries.

Consequently, we need to understand an application's runtime behavior and identify whether any potential bottlenecks or problems exist. In the Java/Kotlin world, a lot of tools can help monitor the detailed runtime behavior of JEE applications. Most of them are built on top of the Java Management Extensions (JMX) technology.

In this chapter, we present common techniques for monitoring Spring-based JEE applications. Specifically, this chapter covers the following topics:

- *Spring support of JMX*: We discuss Spring's comprehensive support of JMX and demonstrate how to expose Spring beans for monitoring with JMX tools. In this chapter, we show how to use the jvisualvm[1] as the application-monitoring tool.

- *Monitoring Hibernate statistics*: Hibernate (and many other frameworks) provides support classes and infrastructure for exposing the operational status and performance metrics using JMX. We show how to enable the JMX monitoring of those commonly used components in Spring-powered JEE applications.

- *Spring Boot JMX support*: Spring Boot provides a starter library for JMX support that comes with full default configuration out of the box. This library is called Actuator and is mainly used to expose operational information about the running application—health, metrics, info, dump, env, and so on. It uses HTTP endpoints or JMX beans to enable us to interact with it. Spring Boot Actuator is the focus of this chapter.

Remember that this chapter is not intended to be an introduction to JMX, and a basic understanding of JMX is assumed. For detailed information, please refer to Oracle's online resources[2].

---

[1] https://visualvm.github.io
[2] https://www.oracle.com/technical-resources/articles/javase/jmx.html

JMX Support in Spring

In JMX, the classes that are exposed for JMX monitoring and management are called *managed beans* (generally referred to as *MBeans*). The Spring Framework supports several mechanisms for exposing MBeans. This chapter focuses on exposing Spring beans (which were developed as simple POJOs) as MBeans for JMX monitoring.

In the following sections, we discuss the procedure for exposing a bean containing application-related statistics as an MBean for JMX monitoring. Topics include implementing the Spring bean, exposing the Spring bean as an MBean in Spring ApplicationContext, and using VisualVM to monitor the MBean.

Exporting a Spring Bean to JMX

As an example, we will use the REST sample from **Chapter 15**. Review that chapter for the sample application code or jump directly to the book's source companion, which provides the source code we will use to build upon.

Just for fun, let's expose some property values and some methods via JMX and declare them via an interface named AppStatistics as shown in Listing 18-1.

Listing 18-1. The AppStatistics Interface

```
package com.apress.prospring6.eighteen.audit

interface AppStatistics {
    val totalSingerCount: Int

    fun findJohn(): String?
    fun findSinger(firstName: String, lastName: String): String?
}
```

The implementation of the AppStatistics interface is a class named AppStatisticsImpl, and since this class is the one exposing attributes and operations via JMX, we need to add the proper annotations. The AppStatisticsImpl class is shown in Listing 18-2.

Listing 18-2. The AppStatisticsImpl Class

```
package com.apress.prospring6.eighteen.audit;
import org.springframework.jmx.export.annotation.*;
// other import statements omitted

@Component
@ManagedResource(description = "JMX managed resource", objectName = "jmxDemo:name=ProSpring
6SingerApp")
class AppStatisticsImpl(private val singerService: SingerService) : AppStatistics {

    @get:ManagedAttribute(description = "Number of singers in the application")
    override val totalSingerCount: Int
        get() = singerService.findAll().size

    @ManagedOperation
    override fun findJohn(): String? {
        val singers: List<Singer> = singerService.
```

```
            findByFirstNameAndLastName("John", "Mayer")
        return if (singers.isNotEmpty()) {
            (singers[0].firstName + " " + singers[0].lastName) + " " + singers[0].birthDate
        } else "not found"
    }


    @ManagedOperation(description = "Find Singer by first name and last name")
    @ManagedOperationParameters(
        ManagedOperationParameter(name = "firstName", description = "Singer's first name"),
        ManagedOperationParameter(name = "lastName", description = "Singer's last name")
    )
    override fun findSinger(firstName: String, lastName: String): String? {
        val singers: List<Singer> = singerService.
            findByFirstNameAndLastName(firstName, lastName)
        return if (singers.isNotEmpty()) {
            (singers[0].firstName + " " + singers[0].lastName) + " " + singers[0].birthDate
        } else "not found"
    }
}
```

In this example, the @ManagedResource annotation has an attribute called objectName, and its value represents the domain and name of the MBean. The @ManagedAttribute annotation is used to expose the given bean property as a JMX attribute. @ManagedOperation is used to expose a given method as a JMX operation. In this example, a few methods are defined to access database data and properties, such as the number of records in the SINGER table.

To expose the Spring bean as JMX, we need to add a configuration in Spring's ApplicationContext. This is done by annotating a configuration class with @EnableMBeanExport. This annotation enables the default exporting of all standard MBeans from the Spring context, as well as all @ManagedResource annotated beans. Basically, this annotation is what tells Spring to create an MBeanExporter bean with the name of mbeanExporter. To keep things neatly scoped, we add a new class named MonitoringCfg on which we add the @EnableMBeanExport annotation. This class is shown in Listing 18-3.

Listing 18-3. The MonitoringCfg Configuration Class

```
package com.apress.prospring6.eighteen

import org.springframework.context.annotation.Configuration
import org.springframework.context.annotation.EnableMBeanExport
import org.springframework.jmx.support.RegistrationPolicy

@EnableMBeanExport(registration = RegistrationPolicy.REPLACE_EXISTING)
@Configuration
open class MonitoringCfg {
    @Bean
    open fun sessionFactory(entityManagerFactory: EntityManagerFactory): SessionFactory {
        return entityManagerFactory.unwrap(SessionFactory::class.java)
    }
}
```

The @EnableMBeanExport annotation is responsible for registering Spring beans with a JMX MBean server (a server that implements JDK's javax.management.MBeanServer interface, which exists in most commonly used web and JEE containers, such as Apache Tomcat and WebSphere). When exposing a Spring bean as an MBean, Spring will attempt to locate a running `MBeanServer` instance within the server and register the MBean with it. We can control what happens when an MBean is registered with an `MBeanServer` instance. Spring's JMX support allows for three different registration behaviors when the registration process finds that an MBean has already been registered under the same `ObjectName`:

- `FAIL_ON_EXISTING`: The MBean is not registered and an `InstanceAlreadyExistsException` exception is thrown.

- `IGNORE_EXISTING`: The MBean is not registered. The existing MBean is unaffected, and no exception is thrown.

- `REPLACE_EXISTING`: The MBean is registered, overwriting the already registered MBean.

If not configured explicitly, the registration policy defaults to `FAIL_ON_EXISTING`.

With Apache Tomcat, an `MBeanServer` instance will be created automatically, so no additional configuration is required. By default, all public properties of the bean are exposed as attributes, and all public methods are exposed as operations.

Now the MBean is available for monitoring via JMX. Let's proceed to set up VisualVM and use its JMX client for monitoring purposes.

Using VisualVM for JMX Monitoring

VisualVM is a useful (free) tool that can help in monitoring Java and Kotlin applications in various aspects. It used to reside under the `bin` folder in the JDK installation folder, but since it was removed from more recent versions of the JDK, you can download a stand-alone version from the project website[3].

VisualVM uses a plug-in system to support various monitoring functions. To support monitoring MBeans of Java and Kotlin applications, we need to install the MBeans plug-in. To install the plug-in, follow these steps:

1. From VisualVM's menu, choose Tools ➤ Plug-ins to open the Plugins dialog shown in Figure 18-1.

2. Click the Available Plugins tab.

3. Click the Check for Newest button.

4. Select the plug-in `VisualVM-MBeans` and then click the Install button.

---

[3] `https://visualvm.github.io`

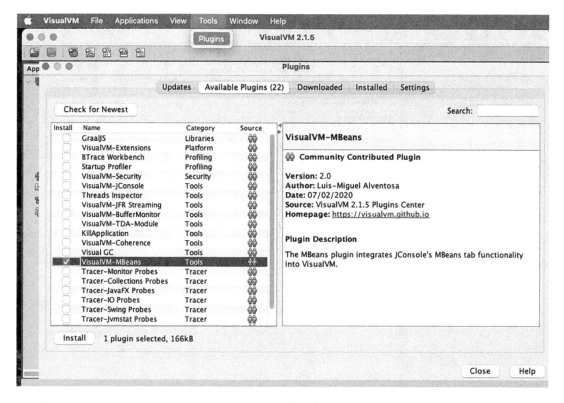

Figure 18-1. VisualVM-MBeans *plug-in selected for installation*

After completing the installation of the VisualVM-MBeans plug-in, verify that Apache Tomcat is up and that the sample application is running. Then, in VisualVM's Applications navigation pane, you should be able to see that the Tomcat process is running, as shown on the left in Figure 18-2. Double-click the Tomcat node in the Applications pane.

By default, VisualVM scans for the Java and Kotlin applications that are running on the JDK platform. Double-clicking the desired node brings up the monitoring screen. After the installation of the VisualVM-MBeans plug-in, the MBeans tab is available. Clicking this tab shows the available MBeans. You should see the node called jmxDemo. When you expand it, it will show the Prospring6SingerApp MBean that was exposed through the configuration in Listing 18-1.

On the Attributes tab to the right side, you will see that for the method that we implemented in the bean, an attribute named TotalSingerCount was automatically derived from the getTotalSingerCount() method. The value should be the same as the number of singers in the SINGER table, as shown in Figure 18-2.

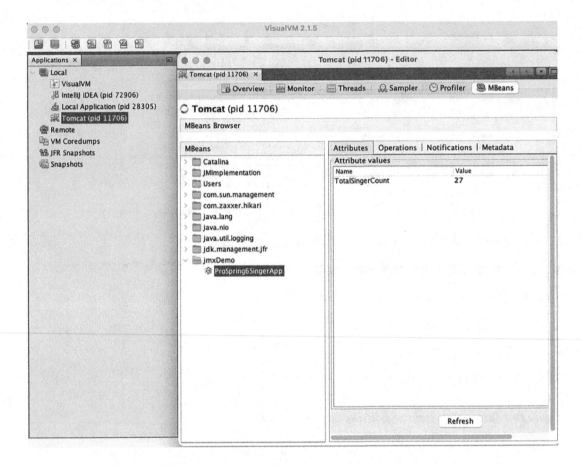

Figure 18-2. *The* Prospring6SingerApp *MBean exposed in VisualVM*

In a regular application, this number would change based on the number of singers added during the application runtime. To test how the MBean reflects the changes in the table, we can use a repeated test method to create a number of singers. Listing 18-4 shows the RestClientTest class containing a test method to create ten singers and a method to delete them.

Listing 18-4. The RestClientTest Class

```kotlin
package com.apress.prospring6.eighteen

import org.junit.jupiter.api.RepeatedTest
// other import statements omitted

class RestClientTest {
    var restTemplate = RestTemplate()
    @RepeatedTest(10)
    @Test
    fun testCreate() {
        LOGGER.info("--> Testing create singer")
        var singerNew = Singer().apply {
```

```
        firstName="TEST" + System.currentTimeMillis()
        lastName="Singer" + System.currentTimeMillis()
        birthDate=LocalDate.now()
    }
    singerNew = restTemplate.postForObject(
        URI_SINGER_ROOT, singerNew,
        Singer::class.java
    )!!
    LOGGER.info("Singer created successfully: $singerNew")
}

@Test
fun testDelete() {
    LOGGER.info("--> Deleting singers with id > 15")
    for (i in 16..99) {
        try {
            restTemplate.delete(URI_SINGER_WITH_ID, i)
        } catch (e: Exception) {
            // no need for this
        }
    }
}

companion object {
    private const val URI_SINGER_ROOT = "http://localhost:8080/chapter18-1.0-SNAPSHOT/
    singer/"
    private const val URI_SINGER_WITH_ID = "http://localhost:8080/chapter18-1.0-
    SNAPSHOT/singer/{id}"
    val LOGGER = LoggerFactory.getLogger(RestClientTest::class.java)
}
}
```

To see the MBean value change, run the testCreate() method and then click the Refresh button. You can also retrieve the current number of singers by going to the Operations tab and clicking the button labeled with the method name: getTotalSingerCount(). A pop-up with the operation return value is displayed, as shown in Figure 18-3.

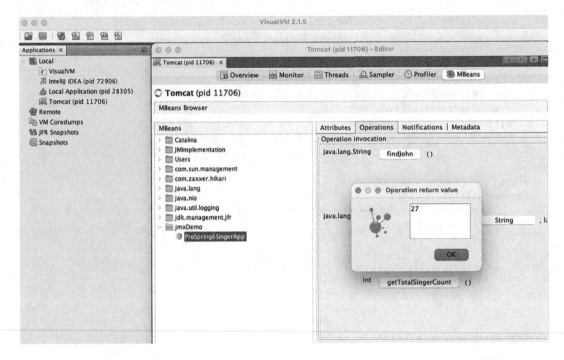

Figure 18-3. *Result of the MBean getTotalSingerCount() operation*

Feel free to try the other exposed operations: findJohn() and findSinger({"John", "Mayer"}).

Monitoring Hibernate Statistics

Hibernate also supports the maintenance and exposure of persistence-related metrics to JMX. To enable this, in the JPA configuration, we need to set a few Hibernate properties, as shown in Listing 18-5.

Listing 18-5. Hibernate Configuration with Statistics Enabled Class

```
package com.apress.prospring6.eighteen

import org.hibernate.cfg.Environment
// other import statements omitted

@Import(BasicDataSourceCfg::class)
@Configuration
@EnableJpaRepositories(basePackages = ["com.apress.prospring6.eighteen.repos"])
@EnableTransactionManagement
@ComponentScan(basePackages = ["com.apress.prospring6.eighteen.repos"])
open class TransactionCfg {
    @Autowired
    var dataSource: DataSource? = null

    @Bean
    open fun transactionManager(): PlatformTransactionManager {
```

```kotlin
        val transactionManager = JpaTransactionManager()
        transactionManager.entityManagerFactory = entityManagerFactory().getObject()
        return transactionManager
    }

    @Bean
    open fun jpaVendorAdapter(): JpaVendorAdapter {
        return HibernateJpaVendorAdapter()
    }

    @Bean
    open fun entityManagerFactory(): LocalContainerEntityManagerFactoryBean {
        val factory = LocalContainerEntityManagerFactoryBean()
        factory.setPersistenceProviderClass(HibernatePersistenceProvider::class.java)
        factory.setPackagesToScan("com.apress.prospring6.eighteen.entities")
        factory.dataSource = dataSource
        factory.setJpaProperties(jpaProperties())
        factory.jpaVendorAdapter = jpaVendorAdapter()
        return factory
    }

    @Bean
    open fun jpaProperties(): Properties {
        val jpaProps = Properties()
        jpaProps[Environment.HBM2DDL_AUTO] = "none"
        jpaProps[Environment.FORMAT_SQL] = false
        jpaProps[Environment.STATEMENT_BATCH_SIZE] = 30
        jpaProps[Environment.USE_SQL_COMMENTS] = false
        jpaProps["hibernate.jmx.enabled"] = true
        jpaProps["hibernate.jmx.usePlatformServer"] = true
        jpaProps[Environment.GENERATE_STATISTICS] = true
        return jpaProps
    }
}
```

The properties hibernate.jmx.enabled and hibernate.jmx.usePlatformServer are used to expose the Hibernate metrics via JMX. The property hibernate.generate_statistics instructs Hibernate to generate statistics for its JPA persistence provider, while the property hibernate.session_factory_name (Environment.SESSION_FACTORY_NAME) defines the name of the session factory required by the Hibernate statistics MBean.

Finally, we need to declare a Spring bean and configure it as an MBean to expose all the Hibernate statistics and metrics. Listing 18-6 shows a snippet of a class named CustomHibernateStatistics that exposes Hibernate statistics and metrics.

Listing 18-6. The MonitoringCfg Declaring an MBean to Expose Hibernate Statistics

```kotlin
package com.apress.prospring6.eighteen.audit

import org.hibernate.SessionFactory
import org.hibernate.stat.*
import org.springframework.jmx.export.annotation.*
// other import statements omitted
```

```
@Component
@ManagedResource(description = "JMX managed resource",
    objectName = "jmxDemo:name=ProSpring6SingerApp-hibernate")
class CustomHibernateStatistics(private val sessionFactory: SessionFactory) {
        private var stats: Statistics? = null
        @PostConstruct
        private fun init() {
                stats = sessionFactory.statistics
        }

        @ManagedOperation(description = "Get statistics for entity name")
        @ManagedOperationParameter(name = "entityName",
                description = "Full class name for the entity")
        fun getEntityStatistics(entityName: String): EntityStatistics {
                return stats!!.getEntityStatistics(entityName)
        }

        @ManagedOperation(description = "Get statistics for role")
        @ManagedOperationParameter(name = "role", description = "Role name")
        fun getCollectionStatistics(role: String): CollectionStatistics {
                return stats!!.getCollectionStatistics(role)
        }

        @ManagedOperation(description = "Get statistics for query")
        @ManagedOperationParameter(name = "hql", description = "Query name")
        fun getQueryStatistics(hql: String): QueryStatistics {
                return stats!!.getQueryStatistics(hql)
        }

        @get:ManagedAttribute
        val entityDeleteCount: Long
                get() = stats!!.entityDeleteCount

        @get:ManagedAttribute
        val entityInsertCount: Long
                get() = stats!!.entityInsertCount

        @get:ManagedAttribute
        val entityLoadCount: Long
                get() = stats!!.entityLoadCount

        // other methods/accessors omitted
}
```

Now that the Hibernate statistics are enabled and available via JMX, reload the application and refresh VisualVM; you will be able to see the Hibernate statistics MBean. Clicking the node displays the detail statistics on the right side. Note that for the information that is not of a Java/Kotlin primitive type (for example, a List), you can click in the field to expand it and show the content.

In VisualVM, you can see many other metrics, such as EntityNames, EntityInsertCount, Queries, PrepareStatementCount, and TransactionCount. Those metrics are useful for understanding the persistence behavior within your application and can assist you in troubleshooting and performance-tuning exercises.

If you run the `testCreate()` method again, you'll notice that the values change. Creating singers requires Hibernate to persist the instances, thus you will see the increases in the values of `TransactionCount`, `PrepareStatementCount`, and `EntityInsertCount` and a few others.

JMX with Spring Boot

Migrating the previous application to Spring Boot is easy, and the dependencies are provided and automatically configured. For JMX, no starter dependency is needed, but to enable JMX to expose MBeans, we need to add the `spring.jmx.enable=true` property to the configuration. To keep this application aligned to the previous section, we also add `spring.jmx.default-domain=jmxBootDemo` to change the domain name from bean to jmxBootDemo to identify easily the place where our MBeans are.

The application for this section is the same as the Spring Boot Web REST application from **Chapter 15**. With the `spring.jmx.enable=true` property added to the configuration the `org.springframework.boot.autoconfigure.jmx.JmxAutoConfiguration` class is added to the application that declares an MBeanServer with a bean ID of `mbeanServer` and exposes any of the beans that are annotated with Spring JMX annotations.

By default, Spring Boot will expose management endpoints as JMX MBeans under the `org.springframework.boot` domain. The `AppStatisticsImpl` class is identical to the one introduced in the previous section. And since Spring Boot exposes all JMX MBeans, if any of the libraries in the classpath contain them, they will be available under the `jmxDemo` domain. Now, if you open VisualVM and access the `Chapter18Application` node, you should see in the MBeans tab that the `jmxBootDemo` domain includes the `HikariDataSource` MBeans as shown in Figure 18-4.

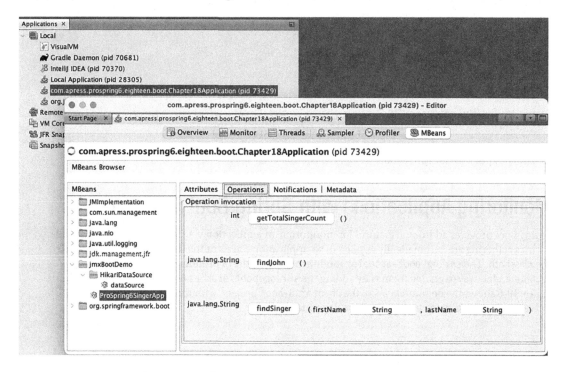

Figure 18-4. *Operations for the* `ProSpring6SingerApp` *MBean declared in the* `chapter18-boot` *project*

Notice that there is also an `org.springframework.boot` domain in the MBeans tab. There is not much under this domain, except management endpoints exposed as JMX beans. In a simple application such as this, there are not many attributes and operations available. You can inspect the values of the Spring Boot properties if you want, by invoking the `getProperty(..)` operation with the name of a property, such as `spring.jmx.enabled` as shown in Figure 18-5.

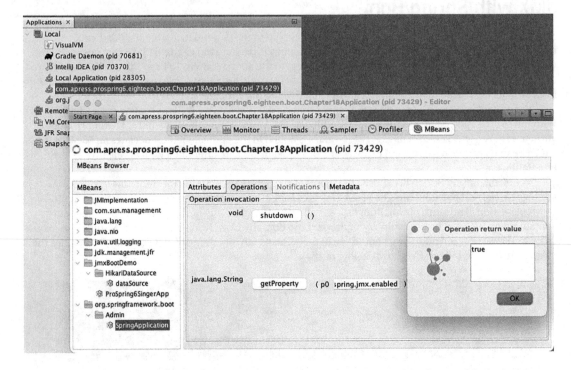

Figure 18-5. *Using `getProperty(..)` operation to inspect the value of the `spring.jmx.enabled` property*

It doesn't look like Spring Boot brings much extra to the table, but that changes when Spring Boot Actuator is added to the application.

Monitoring Applications with Spring Boot Actuator

Spring Boot provides additional features for monitoring an application via JMX. Auditing, health, and metrics gathering are automatically applied to an application once `spring-boot-actuator.jar` is on the classpath. The `spring-boot-actuator` module provides a list of production-ready features. The recommended way to enable them is by adding the `spring-boot-starter-actuator` to the classpath. Figure 18-6 shows the dependencies of the `chapter18-boot` project, with the `spring-boot-starter-actuator` expanded to see all the transitive dependencies.

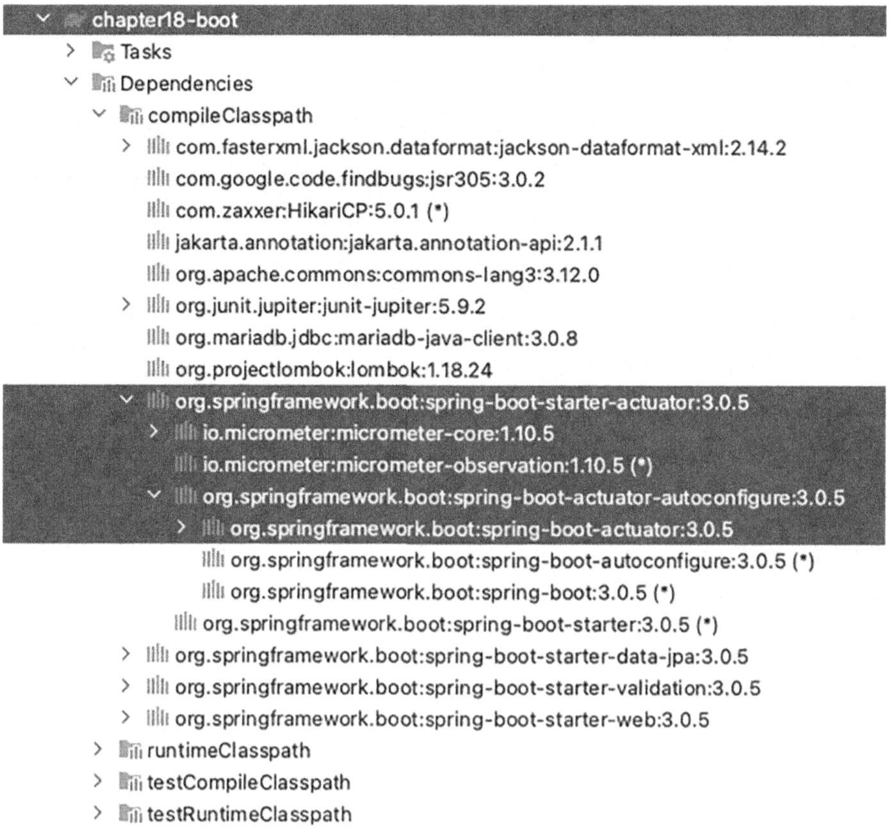

Figure 18-6. *Project chapter18-boot dependencies*

The Spring reference documentation defines an actuator as follows: "An actuator is a manufacturing term that refers to a mechanical device for moving or controlling something. Actuators can generate a large amount of motion from a small change[4]."

Spring Boot Actuator adds a collection of endpoints to an application that are used to monitor and interact with the application. Via configuration, we can expose these endpoints via JMX or HTTP and we can also decide if we want to expose all of them or only some of them. The configuration in Listing 18-7 is part of the application.yaml Spring Boot configuration file and enables exposing all Actuator endpoints over JMX under the jmxBootDemo domain.

Listing 18-7. Configuration to Expose All Actuator Endpoints over JMX Under the jmxBootDemo Domain

```
management:
  endpoints:
    jmx:
      domain: jmxBootDemo
      exposure:
        include: "*"
```

---

[4] https://docs.spring.io/spring-boot/docs/current/reference/html/actuator.html

With this configuration in place, when restarting the application and connecting VisualVM to it, a list of MBeans is added under the jmxBootDemo domain, grouped under the Endpoint node, as shown in Figure 18-7.

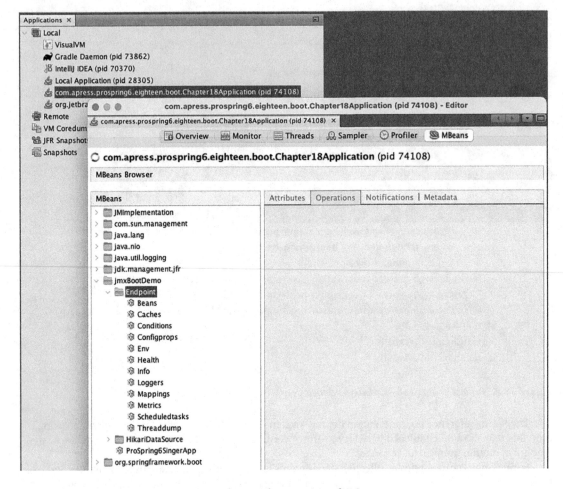

Figure 18-7. *Spring Boot Actuator JMX endpoints shown in VisualVM*

Table 18-1 lists the Spring Boot Actuator JMX endpoints and provides a short explanation of operations they expose.

Table 18-1. *Spring Boot Actuator JMX Endpoints*

Endpoint	Description
Beans	Operation beans() lists a complete list of all the Spring beans in your application.
Caches	Exposes operations to list and clear existing caches.
Conditions	Operation conditions() lists the conditions evaluated for the configuration of the Spring Boot application.
Configprops	Exposes operations to retrieve a collated list of configuration properties.
Env	Exposes operations to list properties from Spring's ConfigurableEnvironment.
Health	Operation health() lists application health information.
Info	Operation info() lists arbitrary application information.
Loggers	Exposes operations to show and modify the configuration of loggers in the application.
Mappings	Operation mappings() lists all @RequestMapping paths. This list includes the Actuator HTTP endpoints.
Metrics	Operation listNames() lists all metrics configured for the application.
Scheduledtasks	Operation scheduledTasks() lists all the scheduled tasks in the application.
Threaddump	Exposes operations to perform a thread dump.

If you've clicked and tried to invoke operations in the VisualVM UI you've probably realized the JMX endpoints are tedious to work with. The good news is that Spring Boot Actuator exposes these endpoints (and a few more) over HTTP as well, all grouped under the /actuator path by default. The path under which the endpoints are grouped and the port can be customized via configuration.

Listing 18-8 shows the configuration for exposing all Actuator endpoints over HTTP under path /monitoring and on port 9091.

Listing 18-8. Configuration to Expose All Actuator Endpoints over HTTP

```
management:
  endpoints:
    web:
      exposure:
        include: "*"
      base-path: /monitoring
  server:
    port: 9091
```

To check the result of this configuration, simply open http://localhost:9091/monitoring in a browser. The response format is JSON, and it contains a list of endpoints. Some of them match the JMX endpoints introduced previously, while others are endpoints specific to the Web. In a browser that displays JSON nicely, like Firefox, this page looks like the one depicted in Figure 18-8.

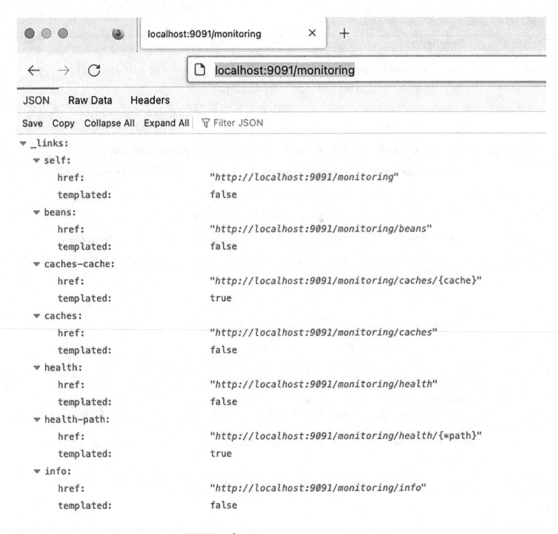

Figure 18-8. *Spring Boot Actuator HTTP endpoints*

For example, the /health endpoint exposes basic information about the application's health. By default, it just returns {"status":"UP"}—yes, really basic. To view more details, the property management. endpoint.health.show-details must be set to always in the Spring Boot configuration file application. yml or in the applications.properties file.

With this setting in place, details about the database used and its status are provided, along with details about the disk space. Listing 18-9 shows what we see on the /health page when we run the application locally.

Listing 18-9. /health Page Contents Sample

```
{
    "status":"UP",
    "components":{
        "db":{
```

```
            "status":"UP",
            "details":{
                "database":"MariaDB",
                "validationQuery":"isValid()"
            }
        },
        "diskSpace":{
            "status":"UP",
            "details":{
                "total":499963174912,
                "free":320641298432,
                "threshold":10485760,
                "path":"/workspace/pro-spring-6/.",
                "exists":true
            }
        },
        "ping":{
            "status":"UP"
        }
    }
}
```

Most endpoints are sensitive—they are not public by default—so if the application is secured, most information exposed by them will be omitted. The grouping of all endpoints under /actuator was introduced in Spring Boot 2.x. In the previous version, each available endpoint was exposed directly under the application context, so the /health endpoint was exposed under http://localhost:8081/health.

In this configuration the /actuator path was renamed to /monitoring via Spring Boot configuration. The same can be done for any of the endpoints; for example, via configuration we can rename the /health endpoint to /salud by setting the management.endpoints.web.path-mapping.health to this value.

If for security reasons we want these endpoints to be accessible only internally, we can configure the IP address by setting the management.server.address property to 127.0.0.1.

Another simple endpoint is the /info endpoint. This endpoint displays general information about the project that is being read from META-INF/build-info.properties (generated at build time) or Git files like git.properties (generated if there is a plug-in configured for this), or through any environment property under the info key. The information exposed by this endpoint can be configured using the Spring Boot configuration file. By default, as expected, accessing this endpoint displays the JSON equivalent of nothing, {}. Adding the properties shown in Listing 18-10 to the configuration file makes this endpoint a little more useful.

Listing 18-10. Spring Boot Configuration for the /info Endpoint

```
management:
  info:
    java:
      enabled: true # enable Java info
    env:
      enabled: true # enable environment info -  from 'application.yml' file

info:
  app:
    name: chapter18-boot
    description: "Pro Spring 6 - Chapter 18 :: Spring Actuator Application"
```

```
    version: 6.0-SNAPSHOT
  author: "Iuliana Cosmina"
```

When accessing the /info endpoint, the text in Listing 18-11 is returned.

Listing 18-11. Output of the /info Endpoint

```
{
    "app":{
        "name":"chapter18-boot",
        "description":"Pro Spring 6 - Chapter 18 :: Spring Actuator Application",
        "version":"6.0-SNAPSHOT"
    },
    "author":"Iuliana Cosmina",
    "build":{
        "artifact":"chapter18-boot",
        "name":"chapter18-boot",
        "time":"2023-03-25T00:32:55.002Z",
        "version":"6.0-SNAPSHOT",
        "group":"pro-spring-6"
    },
    "java":{
        "version":"19.0.1",
        "vendor":{
            "name":"Amazon.com Inc.",
            "version":"Corretto-19.0.1.10.1"
        },
        "runtime":{
            "name":"OpenJDK Runtime Environment",
            "version":"19.0.1+10-FR"
        },
        "jvm":{
            "name":"OpenJDK 64-Bit Server VM",
            "vendor":"Amazon.com Inc.",
            "version":"19.0.1+10-FR"
        }
    }
}
```

Other endpoints' contents can be customized as well, and not only through Spring Boot configuration properties, but also by implementing interfaces or extending specific classes from the org.springframework.boot.actuate package. For example, a custom implementation of org.springframework.boot.actuate.health.HealthIndicator can add additional information to the /health endpoint.

As expected, Spring Boot Actuator provides the option to create your own endpoints. This is done by annotating a bean with @Endpoint from the org.springframework.boot.actuate.endpoint.annotation package. Annotating its methods with @ReadOperation (handling GET requests), @WriteOperation (handling POST requests), and @DeleteOperation (handling DELETE requests) exposes them over JMX and HTTP both.

> ❗ In this book, some endpoints were mentioned to support filtering, because the data they display can be reduced by adding component names as suffixes to their URIs. Depending on the endpoint in question, those values can be bean names, fully qualified class names, property names, and so on. You might think of them as path variables, or filters, but the Spring team prefers to call them *tags*.

Spring Boot Actuator is really powerful and very customizable. To read more about it, check out the official documentation[5].

Using Spring Boot Actuator with Micrometer

Figure 18-6 (earlier in the chapter) shows the `spring-boot-starter-actuator` library with two transitive dependencies: `micrometer-core` and `micrometer-observation`. Micrometer[6] is an open source metrics facade that provides a vendor-neutral metrics collection API (the parent abstract implementation is `io.micrometer.core.instrument.MeterRegistry`[7]) and implementations for a variety of monitoring systems that were mentioned at the beginning of this chapter. It can be used with Spring Boot Actuator, but it is an independent platform, that can be used by itself.

If it's hard to wrap your head around Micrometer, think of SLF4J, which is a facade or abstraction for various logging frameworks. This means the developer can use the SLF4J to write log messages that will be gathered and written to the desired support by the framework configured by the application. In this book SLF4J is used together with Logback Classic, but we could easily swap Logback Classic with Log4j2 without any need of changes in the code. You could have the same for metrics starting with Spring Boot Actuator 2.x—Micrometer can be used to gather metrics and expose them in a format that any (almost) advanced monitoring system can interpret. Spring Boot 3 autoconfigures quite a long list of metrics out of the box. This list is returned by a GET request to the `http://0.0.0.0:9091/monitoring/metrics` endpoint (as configured in the previous section). Listing 18-12 lists the names of these metrics.

Listing 18-12. Spring Boot Metrics Listed by the `/metrics` Endpoint

```
{
    "names":[
        "application.ready.time",
        "application.started.time",
        "disk.free",
        "disk.total",
        "executor.active",
        "executor.completed",
        "executor.pool.core",
        "executor.pool.max",
        "executor.pool.size",
        "executor.queue.remaining",
        "executor.queued",
```

---

[5] https://docs.spring.io/spring-boot/docs/current/reference/html/actuator.html#actuator

[6] https://micrometer.io

[7] https://github.com/micrometer-metrics/micrometer/blob/main/micrometer-core/src/main/java/io/micrometer/core/instrument/MeterRegistry.java

```
        "hikaricp.connections",
        "hikaricp.connections.acquire",
        "hikaricp.connections.active",
        "hikaricp.connections.creation",
        "hikaricp.connections.idle",
        "hikaricp.connections.max",
        "hikaricp.connections.min",
        "hikaricp.connections.pending",
        "hikaricp.connections.timeout",
        "hikaricp.connections.usage",
        "jdbc.connections.active",
        "jdbc.connections.idle",
        "jdbc.connections.max",
        "jdbc.connections.min",
        "jvm.buffer.count",
        "jvm.buffer.memory.used",
        "jvm.buffer.total.capacity",
        "jvm.classes.loaded",
        "jvm.classes.unloaded",
        "jvm.compilation.time",
        "jvm.gc.live.data.size",
        "jvm.gc.max.data.size",
        "jvm.gc.memory.allocated",
        "jvm.gc.memory.promoted",
        "jvm.gc.overhead",
        "jvm.info",
        "jvm.memory.committed",
        "jvm.memory.max",
        "jvm.memory.usage.after.gc",
        "jvm.memory.used",
        "jvm.threads.daemon",
        "jvm.threads.live",
        "jvm.threads.peak",
        "jvm.threads.states",
        "logback.events",
        "process.cpu.usage",
        "process.files.max",
        "process.files.open",
        "process.start.time",
        "process.uptime",
        "system.cpu.count",
        "system.cpu.usage",
        "system.load.average.1m",
        "tomcat.sessions.active.current",
        "tomcat.sessions.active.max",
        "tomcat.sessions.alive.max",
        "tomcat.sessions.created",
        "tomcat.sessions.expired",
        "tomcat.sessions.rejected"
    ]
}
```

The metrics can be grouped in a few categories:

- Application times

- Uptime

- JVM—garbage collector activity, memory consumption, thread utilization, number of classes, etc. CPU usage

- Spring-specific components activity

- Cache activity

- Data source and HikariCP activity

- Tomcat usage

- Spring MVC and WebFlux request latencies (available only for Spring Boot MVC and WebFlux applications)

- Other custom components activity: `RestTemplate` latencies, file descriptor usage, event logging, RabbitMQ or ApacheMQ (if used) connection factories, etc.

So, when running the application generates a lot of data, what can we do with it? Well, we process it into reports and graphs that can be viewed with the naked eye, and that in turn can be used to predict future behavior. Micrometer cannot help with this, but there's a very easy-to-use tool that does the trick and integrates perfectly with Spring Boot Actuator and Micrometer: Prometheus[8]. Prometheus is an open source system-monitoring and alerting toolkit originally built at SoundCloud. It was released in 2012 and since then has become a stand-alone open source project with a big and active developer and user community.

To integrate our Spring Boot application with Prometheus, we need to add the `micrometer-registry-prometheus` dependency. After adding this dependency, it should appear in the IntelliJ IDEA Gradle View, together with its transitive dependencies, as depicted in Figure 18-9.

---

[8] `https://prometheus.io`

```
∨  ⟩ chapter18-boot
   >  ▦ Tasks
   ∨  ▦ Dependencies
      ∨  ▦ compileClasspath
         >  ▥ com.fasterxml.jackson.dataformat:jackson-dataformat-xml:2.14.2
            ▥ com.google.code.findbugs:jsr305:3.0.2
            ▥ com.zaxxer:HikariCP:5.0.1 (*)
         ∨  ▥ io.micrometer:micrometer-registry-prometheus:1.10.5
               ▥ io.micrometer:micrometer-core:1.10.5 (*)
            ∨  ▥ io.prometheus:simpleclient_common:0.16.0
               ∨  ▥ io.prometheus:simpleclient:0.16.0
                  >  ▥ io.prometheus:simpleclient_tracer_otel:0.16.0
                  >  ▥ io.prometheus:simpleclient_tracer_otel_agent:0.16.0
            ▥ jakarta.annotation:jakarta.annotation-api:2.1.1
            ▥ org.apache.commons:commons-lang3:3.12.0
         >  ▥ org.junit.jupiter:junit-jupiter:5.9.2
            ▥ org.mariadb.jdbc:mariadb-java-client:3.0.8
            ▥ org.projectlombok:lombok:1.18.24
         >  ▥ org.springframework.boot:spring-boot-starter-actuator:3.0.5
         >  ▥ org.springframework.boot:spring-boot-starter-data-jpa:3.0.5
         >  ▥ org.springframework.boot:spring-boot-starter-validation:3.0.5
         >  ▥ org.springframework.boot:spring-boot-starter-web:3.0.5
      >  ▦ runtimeClasspath                                    •
      >  ▦ testCompileClasspath
      >  ▦ testRuntimeClasspath
```

Figure 18-9. *Spring Boot Actuator and Prometheus application dependencies*

After adding the dependency and rebuilding the application, start the Spring Boot application by running the `Chapter18Application` main class. When opening the `http://localhost:9091/monitoring` URL, notice the prometheus endpoint with URL `http://localhost:9091/monitoring/prometheus`. This endpoint is provided by the `PrometheusScrapeEndpoint` class, from package `org.springframework.boot.actuate.metrics.export.prometheus` that is part of the Spring Boot Actuator project. This endpoint translates the metrics provided by Micrometer into a format that can be scraped by the Prometheus server. You can see a summary of the exposed metrics by accessing the Prometheus endpoint in Listing 18-13.

Listing 18-13. Snippet of Spring Boot Metrics Listed on the /prometheus Endpoint

```
# HELP hikaricp_connections_max Max connections
# TYPE hikaricp_connections_max gauge
hikaricp_connections_max{pool="HikariPool-1",} 25.0
# HELP jvm_threads_live_threads The current number of live threads including both daemon and
non-daemon threads
# TYPE jvm_threads_live_threads gauge
jvm_threads_live_threads 39.0
# HELP http_server_requests_seconds
# TYPE http_server_requests_seconds summary
```

```
http_server_requests_seconds_count{error="none",exception="none",method="GET",outcome=
"SUCCESS",status="200",uri="/singer/{id}",} 100.0
http_server_requests_seconds_sum{error="none",exception="none",method="GET",outcome=
"SUCCESS",status="200",uri="/singer/{id}",} 1.069158702
http_server_requests_seconds_count{error="none",exception="none",method="POST",outcome=
"SUCCESS",status="201",uri="/singer/",} 1000.0
http_server_requests_seconds_sum{error="none",exception="none",method="POST",outcome=
"SUCCESS",status="201",uri="/singer/",} 6.119599968
http_server_requests_seconds_count{error="none",exception="none",method="GET",outcome=
"SUCCESS",status="200",uri="/singer/",} 100.0
http_server_requests_seconds_sum{error="none",exception="none",method="GET",outcome=
"SUCCESS",status="200",uri="/singer/",} 1.052652658
...
```

The next step is to run Prometheus to plot the data. For this you need to install Prometheus as explained on the official page[9]. To keep things practical, we recommend to go the Docker route and run it in a container. In the chapter18-boot folder you will find a file named CHAPTER18-BOOT.adoc explaining how to set up Prometheus in a Docker container; these steps will be skipped here to avoid derailing the focus of the chapter.

Before starting the container, continue reading this section, because you need to tell Prometheus where the metrics are coming from via a configuration file.

The Prometheus configuration file is named prometheus.yaml. The name is not mandatory, but it does make its purpose obvious. According to the official documentation, we have to define a job that tells Prometheus how often to query the metrics and from where. The syntax is YAML and the most important properties are listed in Listing 18-14.

Listing 18-14. Prometheus Configuration

```
global:
  scrape_interval:     15s # By default, scrape targets every 15 seconds.

# Prometheus itself self-monitoring configuration
scrape_configs:
  - job_name: 'prometheus'

    # Override the global default and scrape targets from this job every 5 seconds.
    scrape_interval: 5s

    static_configs:
      - targets: ['0.0.0.0:9090']
  - job_name: 'chapter18-boot'
    metrics_path: '/monitoring/prometheus'
    # Override the global default and scrape targets from this job every 5 seconds.
    scrape_interval: 5s
```

---

[9] https://prometheus.io/docs/prometheus/latest/installation

```
static_configs:
    # When Prometheus is run in a Docker container the real IP within the network
    must be used
  - targets: ['192.168.0.6:9091']
```

Notice that for the chapter18-boot job, the metrics_path property is set to the Prometheus Actuator endpoint and targets is set to the IP address and port where the chapter18-boot application is running.

Before starting the Prometheus container, start the chapter18-boot application. By default, the Prometheus web console is available at http://localhost:9090. In the prometheus.yml file, the job named prometheus represents the configuration of the Prometheus application itself, and the configurations of this job can be customized to start Prometheus on a different IP and port.

The main page of the Prometheus web UI is pretty simplistic. The option of most interest for this discussion is Status ➤ Targets, highlighted in Figure 18-10.

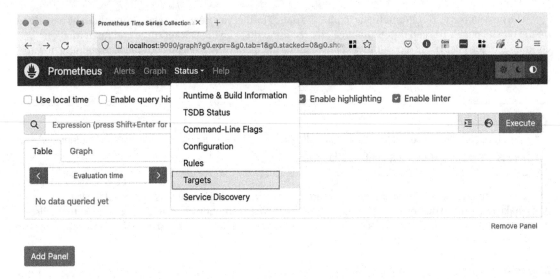

Figure 18-10. *Prometheus web UI*

Choosing the Targets menu item directs you to the page shown in Figure 18-11 confirming that chapter18-boot is UP and listing the job configurations and most recent time when the metrics were refreshed. If the text is DOWN and highlighted in red, either the application is not started or static_configs. targets was not set properly for the chapter18-boot job.

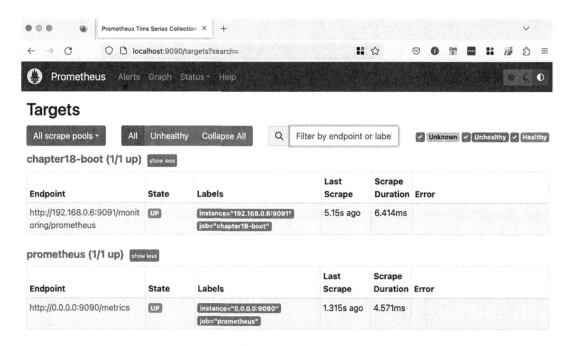

Figure 18-11. *Prometheus web UI showing* `chapter18-boot` *and Prometheus apps running*

If everything is okay, you can go back to the main page and select a metric. One of the most visible metrics is `system_cpu_usage`, so select that from the list of metrics and click the Execute button. The information is not really visible in the Graph tab until you reduce the interval for the metrics analysis by setting a sensible value, such as 15 or 30 minutes, in the first text field. The graph should be quite interesting, similar to what is depicted in Figure 18-12.

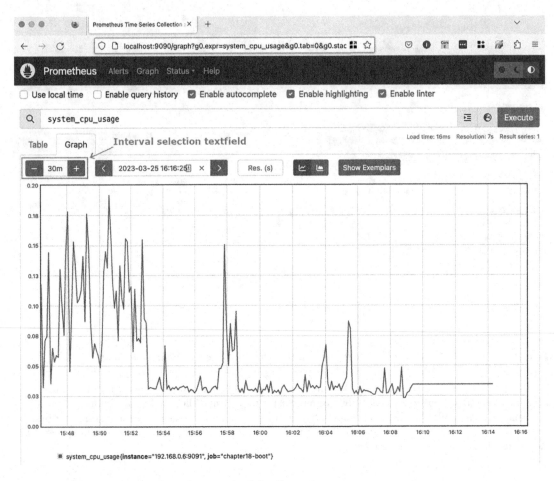

Figure 18-12. *Prometheus web UI showing graph for the* system_cpu_usage *metric*

As previously shown in Listing 18-13, several metrics related to the number of requests are available. To simulate a situation in which the server takes variable times to resolve requests, so that we can see the graph for the http_server_requests_seconds_count, we can modify the SingerController to introduce a different delay for each of the Singer instances returned when a GET request with the http://localhost:9091/singer/{id} URL is received. This is done by adding a Thread.sleep() in the handler method for this URI, that generates different delay times based on the record ID. The handler method is shown in Listing 18-15.

Listing 18-15. Custom Handler Method for Request Path /singer{id} with Various Delays

```
package com.apress.prospring6.eighteen.boot.controllers
// import statements omitted

@RestController
@RequestMapping(value = ["/singer"])
class SingerController(private val singerService: SingerService) {
    val LOGGER = LoggerFactory.getLogger(SingerController::class.java)
```

```kotlin
    @GetMapping(path = ["/{id}"])
    fun findSingerById(@PathVariable id: Long): Singer {
        val singer = singerService.findById(id)
        if (singer != null) {
            val msec = 10
            try {
                Thread.sleep(msec * id)
            } catch (e: InterruptedException) {
                e.printStackTrace()
            }
        }else{
            throw RuntimeException("Singer for ID=${id} does not exist")
        }
        return singer
    }
    // other methods and fields omitted
}
```

Now, in order to submit a lot of requests and produce a lot of data so that Prometheus has something to plot on the graph, the test class in Listing 18-16 has two very useful methods.

Listing 18-16. Test Class to Generate Metric Data

```kotlin
package com.apress.prospring6.eighteen.boot
// import statements omitted

class SingerControllerTest {
    private val restTemplate = RestTemplate()
    @RepeatedTest(50)
    fun testFindAll() {
        val singers = restTemplate.getForObject(
            BASE_URL,
            Array<Singer>::class.java
        )!!
        Assertions.assertTrue(singers.size >= 15)
    }


    @RepeatedTest(500)
    @Throws(URISyntaxException::class)
    fun testCreate() {
        val singerNew = Singer()
        singerNew.firstName = UUID.randomUUID().toString().substring(0, 8)
        singerNew.lastName = UUID.randomUUID().toString().substring(0, 8)
        singerNew.birthDate = LocalDate.now()
        val req = RequestEntity(
            singerNew, HttpMethod.POST, URI(
                BASE_URL
            )
        )
        val response = restTemplate.exchange(
            req,
            String::class.java
```

```kotlin
        )
        Assertions.assertEquals(HttpStatus.CREATED, response.statusCode)
    }

    @RepeatedTest(10)
    @Throws(URISyntaxException::class)
    fun testPositiveFindById() {
        val headers = HttpHeaders()
        headers.accept = List.of(MediaType.APPLICATION_JSON)
        for (i in 1..249) {
            val req = RequestEntity<HttpHeaders>(
                headers, HttpMethod.GET, URI(
                    BASE_URL + i
                )
            )
            val response = restTemplate.exchange(
                req,
                Singer::class.java
            )
            Assertions.assertAll("testPositiveFindById",
                Executable {
                    Assertions.assertEquals(
                        HttpStatus.OK,
                        response.statusCode
                    )
                },
                Executable {
                    Assertions.assertTrue(
                        Objects.requireNonNull(
                            response.headers[HttpHeaders.CONTENT_TYPE]
                        ).contains(MediaType.APPLICATION_JSON_VALUE)
                    )
                },
                Executable { Assertions.assertNotNull(response.body) },
                Executable {
                    Assertions.assertEquals(
                        Singer::class.java,
                        response.body.javaClass
                    )
                }
            )
        }
    }

    companion object {
        private const val BASE_URL = "http://localhost:8081/singer/"
    }
}
```

To get the expected result, run `testCreate()` first, and then run `testPositiveFindById()`. The second test will take a while to execute, but you can go to the Prometheus web UI and plot the graph for the `http_server_requests_seconds_count` metric and refresh the page from time to time to see the number of requests being handled growing over time.

Figure 18-13 shows the graph generated for this book. Notice how multiple request paths are grouped by color. Prometheus has two types of graphs, stacked and unstacked; the one in this image is the stacked type.

Figure 18-13. *Prometheus web UI showing graph for the* `http_server_requests_seconds_count` *metric*

Notice that the duration of a GET request to `/singer/` (shown in green at the bottom of the graph) never increases. Notice that the duration of the POST request to `/singer/` (shown in red) also increases as the table gets bigger. The duration of the GET request to `/singer/{id}` (shown in blue) is the one that shows the most increase, considering that is where the `Thread.sleep(..)` method is.

The Prometheus graphs are quite simple, and the default Micrometer metrics are basic too. In a production application, teams can define their own metrics depending on the services the application provides. For example, for a banking application, login failures coupled with certain originating IPs might reveal some type of hacking attempt, so a must-have metric is one that groups together failed logins and a class of IPs where requests are generated from.

The leading solution in visualizing metrics at the moment seems to be Grafana[10], and the good news is that it knows how to interpret Prometheus metrics. So, the Prometheus metrics can be forwarded to Grafana to plot some higher-definition graphs.

Summary

In this chapter, we covered the high-level topics of monitoring a Spring-powered JEE application. First, we discussed Spring's support of JMX, the standard in monitoring Java and Kotlin applications. We discussed implementing custom MBeans for exposing application-related information, as well as exposing statistics of common components such as Hibernate; and we showed how JMX can be used in a Spring Boot application.

Next, we showed the full power of Spring Boot Actuator in generating application metrics and how to plot those metrics using Prometheus. In the next chapter we talk about Spring's support for WebSockets.

---

[10] https://grafana.com

CHAPTER 19

■ ■ ■

Spring WebSocket Support

Traditionally, web applications have utilized the standard request/response HTTP functionality to provide communication between the client and server. As the Web has evolved, more interactive abilities have been required, some of which demand push/pull or real-time updates from the server. Over time, various methods have been implemented, such as continuous polling, long polling, and Comet. Each has its pros and cons, and the WebSocket protocol is an attempt to learn from those needs and deficiencies, creating a simpler and more robust way to build interactive applications. The HTML5 WebSocket specification defines an API that enables web pages to use the WebSocket protocol for two-way communication between browser and remote host.

This chapter presents a high-level overview of the WebSocket protocol, and the main functionality provided by the Spring Framework. Specifically, this chapter covers the following topics:

- *Introduction to WebSocket*: We provide a general introduction of the WebSocket protocol. This chapter is not intended to serve as a detailed reference of the WebSocket protocol but rather as a high-level overview[1].

- *Using WebSocket with Spring*: We dive into some details of using WebSocket with the Spring Framework; specifically, we cover using Spring's WebSocket API, utilizing SockJS as a fallback option for non-WebSocket-enabled browsers, and sending messages using Simple (or Streaming) Text-Oriented Message Protocol (STOMP) over SockJS/WebSocket.

Introducing WebSocket

WebSocket is a specification developed as part of the HTML5 initiative, allowing for a full-duplex single-socket connection in which messages can be sent between a client and a server. In the past, web applications requiring the functionality of real-time updates would poll a server-side component periodically to obtain this data, opening multiple connections or using long polling.

Using WebSocket for bidirectional communication avoids the need to perform HTTP polling for two-way communications between a client (for example, a web browser) and an HTTP server. The WebSocket protocol is meant to supersede all existing bidirectional communication methods utilizing HTTP for transport. The single-socket model of WebSocket results in a simpler solution, avoiding the need for multiple connections for each client and the corresponding overhead—for example, not needing to send an HTTP header with each message.

---

[1] https://www.rfc-editor.org/rfc/rfc6455

© Peter Späth, Iuliana Cosmina, Rob Harrop, Chris Schaefer 2023
P. Späth et al., *Pro Spring 6 with Kotlin*, https://doi.org/10.1007/978-1-4842-9557-1_19

WebSocket utilizes HTTP during its initial handshake, which in turn allows it to be used over standard HTTP (80) and HTTPS (443) ports. The WebSocket specification defines a `ws://` and a `wss://` scheme to indicate non-secure and secure connections, respectively. The WebSocket protocol has two parts: a handshake between the client and server and then data transfer. A WebSocket connection is established by making an upgrade request from HTTP to the WebSocket protocol during the initial handshake between the client and the server, over the same underlying TCP/IP connection. During the data transfer portion of the communication, both the client and server can send messages to each other simultaneously, opening the door to add more-robust real-time communication functionality to your applications.

Using WebSocket with Spring

As of version 4.1, the Spring Framework supports WebSocket-style messaging as well as STOMP as an application-level subprotocol. Within the framework, you can find support for WebSocket in the `spring-websocket` module, which is compatible with JSR-356 ("Java WebSocket")[2].

Application developers must also recognize that although WebSocket brings new and exciting opportunities, not all web browsers support the protocol. Given this, the application must continue to work for the user and utilize some sort of fallback technology to simulate the intended functionality as best as possible. To handle this case, the Spring Framework provides transparent fallback options via the SockJS protocol, which will we go into later in this chapter.

Unlike REST-based applications, where services are represented by different URLs, WebSocket uses a single URL to establish the initial handshake, and data flows over that same connection. This type of message-passing functionality is more along the lines of traditional messaging systems. As of Spring Framework 4, core message-based interfaces such as `Message` have been migrated from the Spring Integration project into a new module called `spring-messaging` to support WebSocket-style messaging applications.

When we refer to using STOMP as an application-level subprotocol, we are talking about the protocol that is transported via WebSocket. WebSocket itself is a low-level protocol that simply transforms bytes into messages. The application needs to understand what is being sent across the wire, which is where a subprotocol such as STOMP comes into play. During the initial handshake, the client and server can use the Sec-WebSocket-Protocol header to define what subprotocol to use. While the Spring Framework provides support for STOMP, WebSocket does not mandate anything specific.

Now that you have an understanding of what WebSocket is and the support Spring provides, you're likely wondering where you would want to use this technology. Given the single-socket nature of WebSocket and its ability to provide a continuous bidirectional data flow, WebSocket lends itself well to applications that have a high frequency of message passing and require low-latency communications. Applications that may be good candidates for WebSocket could include gaming, real-time group collaboration tools, messaging systems, time-sensitive pricing information such as financial updates, and so on. When designing your application with the consideration of using WebSocket, you must take into account both the frequency of messages and latency requirements. This will help determine whether to use WebSocket or, for example, HTTP long polling.

---

[2] `https://www.oracle.com/technical-resources/articles/java/jsr356.html`

Using the WebSocket API

As mentioned in the previous discussion, WebSocket simply transforms bytes into messages and transports them between client and server. Those messages still need to be understood by the application itself, which is where subprotocols such as STOMP come into play. If you want to work with the lower-level WebSocket API directly, the Spring Framework provides an API that you can interact with to do so. When working with Spring's WebSocket API, you would typically implement the WebSocketHandler interface or use convenience subclasses such as BinaryWebSocketHandler for handling binary messages, SockJsWebSocketHandler for SockJS messages, or TextWebSocketHandler for working with String-based messages. In this example, for simplicity we will use a TextWebSocketHandler to pass String-based messages via WebSocket. Let's start by taking a look at how we can receive and work with WebSocket messages at a low level, utilizing the Spring WebSocket API.

Obviously, we need to add to the classpath libraries that support WebSocket communication. Figure 19-1 shows the dependencies of a Spring web application that uses the WebSocket protocol to send messages to itself.

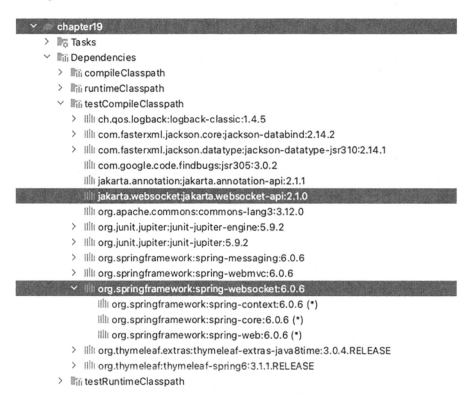

Figure 19-1. Project chapter19 dependencies

As you can see, the dependencies are typical for a Spring Web application, like the one introduced in **Chapter 14**. The Jakarta WebSocket API provides a platform-independent WebSocket protocol API to build bidirectional communications over the Web. The jakarta.websocket-api library contains the Jakarta WebSocket API for Server and Client (API only; it does not include an implementation). The spring-websocket library contains the Spring WebSocket API needed to write client- and server-side applications that handle WebSocket messages.

To send the messages and display them, a simple web page is created, named index.html. This page is built from a default Thymeleaf layout and contains static HTML and JavaScript that is used to communicate with the back-end WebSocket service. To handle the communication, we need to declare a special type that implements WebSocketHandler and a bean of that type. Figure 19-2 shows the hierarchy of types that implement org.springframework.web.socket.WebSocketHandler.

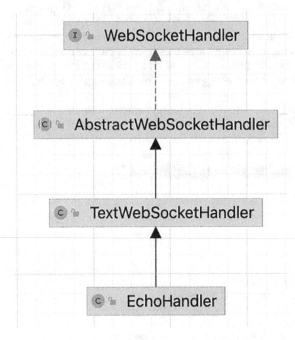

Figure 19-2. WebSocketHandler *implementations*

To keep things simple, and benefit from out-of-the-box Spring code, instead of implementing the WebSocketHandler directly, our EchoHandler class will instead extend the TextWebSocketHandler. This keeps our implementation concise, as the only method that needs to be implemented is handleTextMessage(..), as shown in Listing 19-1.

Listing 19-1. The EchoHandler Class

package com.apress.prospring6.nineteen

import org.springframework.web.socket.TextMessage
import org.springframework.web.socket.WebSocketSession
import org.springframework.web.socket.handler.TextWebSocketHandler

import java.io.IOException

```
class EchoHandler : TextWebSocketHandler() {
    @Throws(IOException::class)
    public override fun handleTextMessage(session: WebSocketSession,
            textMessage: TextMessage) {
        session.sendMessage(TextMessage(textMessage.payload))
    }
}
```

As you can see, this is a basic handler that takes the provided message and simply echoes it back to the client. The content of the received WebSocket message is contained in the getPayload() method.

Now that we have the type, we need to define a single handler mapping in this example, which receives requests at /echoHandler and uses the bean with the ID of echoHandler to receive a message and respond by echoing the provided message back to the client. To keep the WebSocket configuration separate from the MVC configuration, we introduce a class named WebSocketConfig that declares the mapping of the bean and enables support for communication using WebSocket, as shown in Listing 19-2.

Listing 19-2. The WebSocketConfig Configuration Class

```
package com.apress.prospring6.nineteen

import org.springframework.web.socket.config.annotation.EnableWebSocket
import org.springframework.web.socket.config.annotation.WebSocketConfigurer
import org.springframework.web.socket.config.annotation.WebSocketHandlerRegistry
// other import statements omitted

@Configuration
@EnableWebSocket
open class WebSocketConfig : WebSocketConfigurer {
    override fun registerWebSocketHandlers(registry: WebSocketHandlerRegistry) {
        registry.addHandler(echoHandler(), "/echoHandler")
    }

    @Bean
    open fun echoHandler(): EchoHandler {
        return EchoHandler()
    }
}
```

The @EnableWebSocket annotation enables support for processing WebSocket requests, while the WebSocketConfig configuration class implements Spring's WebSocketConfigurer interface that defines callback methods to configure the WebSocket request handling.

The Spring MVC configuration is nothing special (refer to **Chapter 14** if you need to jog your memory), but we do need to map the index.html page to the /index path. The controller is shown in Listing 19-3.

Listing 19-3. The IndexController Configuration Class

```
package com.apress.prospring6.nineteen

import jakarta.servlet.http.HttpServletRequest
import org.springframework.stereotype.Controller
import org.springframework.ui.Model
import org.springframework.web.bind.annotation.GetMapping

@Controller
open class IndexController {
    @GetMapping(path = ["index"])
    open fun index(model: Model, request: HttpServletRequest): String {
        val requestUrl = request.requestURL.toString()
        val webSocketAddress = requestUrl.replace("http", "ws").
            replace("index", "echoHandler")
```

```
        model.addAttribute("webSocket", webSocketAddress)
        return "index"
    }
}
```

The implementation is quite simple, but to keep the WebSocket handler URL dynamic and relative to the context path of the application, a little artifice is implemented that takes the URL of the initial request, which is `http://localhost:8080/ch19/index`, and uses it to produce the `ws://localhost:8080/ch19/echoHandler` value, which is added as the `webSocket` attribute to the `index` model.

That's pretty much all that is needed on the back end. Given that `EchoHandler` is a typical Spring bean, you can do anything you would in a normal Spring application, such as inject services, to carry out any functions this handler may need to do.

The `index.html` page is a very simple Thymeleaf view representing a simple front-end client where we can interact with the back-end WebSocket service. The front end is a simple HTML page with a bit of JavaScript that uses the browser's API to make the WebSocket connection; it also contains some jQuery[3] to handle button-click events and data display. I know jQuery is quite simple, but introducing a more complex JavaScript framework would be overkill for purposes of this discussion. The front-end application will have the ability to connect, disconnect, send a message, and display status updates to the screen. Listing 19-4 shows the code for the front-end client page (`views/index.html`).

Listing 19-4. The `views/index.html` View

```html
<html>

<head th:fragment="~{templates/layout :: pageTitle}">
    <title> WebSocket Tester </title>
    <script type="text/javascript" th:src="@{/js/jquery-3.6.4.min.js}"></script>
    <script type="text/javascript">
        let ping;
        let websocket;
        let supportsWebSockets = 'WebSocket' in window || 'MozWebSocket' in window;

        jQuery(function ($) {
            $("#connect").attr("disabled", true);
            if (supportsWebSockets) {
                console.log(">> webSocket protocol supported.")
                $("#connect").attr("disabled", false);
            }

            function writePing(message) {
                $('#pingOutput').append(message + '\n');
            }

            function writeMessage(message) {
                $('#messageOutput').append(message + '\n')
            }
```

---

[3] https://jquery.com

```javascript
$('#connect')
    .click(function doConnect() {
        websocket = new WebSocket($("#target").val());

        websocket.onopen = function (evt) {
            let badge= $("#badgeStatus");
            badge.text("Connected");
            badge.attr('class','badge bg-success');

            setInterval(function () {
                if (websocket !== "undefined") {
                    websocket.send("ping");
                }
            }, 3000);
        };

        websocket.onclose = function (evt) {
            let badge= $("#badgeStatus"); .
            badge.text("Disconnected");
            badge.attr('class','badge bg-light');
        };

        websocket.onmessage = function (evt) {
            if (evt.data === "ping") {
                writePing(evt.data);
            } else {
                writeMessage('ECHO: ' + evt.data);
            }
        };

        websocket.onerror = function (evt) {
            onError(writeStatus('ERROR:' + evt.data))
        };
    });

$('#disconnect')
    .click(function () {
        if (typeof websocket != 'undefined') {
            websocket.close();
            websocket = undefined;
        } else {
            alert("Not connected.");
        }
    });

$('#send')
    .click(function () {
        if (typeof websocket != 'undefined') {
            websocket.send($('#message').val());
        } else {
            alert("Not connected.");
```

```html
                    }
                });
            });
        </script>
    </head>

    <body>
    <div class="container">
        <header th:replace="~{templates/layout :: pageHeader}" ></header>

        <header th:replace="~{templates/layout :: pageMenu}" ></header>

        <section th:fragment="~{templates/layout :: pageContent}">
            <div class="card border-success mb-3" style="max-width: 40rem;">
                <div class="card-header">WebSocket Tester</div>
                <div class="row mb-1 m-sm-1">
                    <label for="target" th:text="Target" class="col-sm-4 form-label">FN:</label>
                    <div class="col-sm-8">
                        <input type="text" id="target" size="40" th:value="${webSocket}"
                        class="form-control"/>
                    </div>
                </div>
                <div class="row mb-1 m-sm-1">
                    <div class="col-sm-2"> <input type="submit" id="connect"  class="btn btn-
                    success" value="Connect"/></div>
                    <div class="col-sm-2"><input type="submit" id="disconnect"  class="btn btn-
                    danger" value="Disconnect"/></div>
                    <div class="col-sm-2"><span id="badgeStatus"></span></div>
                </div>
                <div class="row mb-1 m-sm-1">
                    <label for="message" th:text="Message" class="col-sm-4 form-
                    label">FN:</label>
                    <div class="col-sm-8">
                        <input type="text" id="message" value="" class="form-control"/>
                    </div>
                </div>
                <div class="row mb-1 m-sm-1">
                    <div class="col-sm-2"> <input type="submit" id="send"  value="Send"
                    class="btn btn-dark"/></div>
                </div>
                <div class="row mb-1 m-sm-1">
                    <label for="messageOutput" th:text="Echo" class="col-sm-4 form-
                    label">FN:</label>
                    <div class="col-sm-7">
                        <pre><textarea id="messageOutput" rows="5" cols="25" class="form-
                        control"></textarea></pre>
                    </div>
                </div>
                <div class="row mb-1 m-sm-1">
                    <label for="pingOutput" th:text="Ping" class="col-sm-4 form-
                    label">FN:</label>
                    <div class="col-sm-7">
```

```
            <pre><textarea id="pingOutput" rows="5" cols="25" class="form-
                control"></textarea></pre>
          </div>
        </div>
      </div>
    </section>

    <footer th:replace="~{templates/layout :: pageFooter}" ></footer>
    </div>
  </body>
</html>
```

The code snippet in Listing 19-4 provides a UI that allows us to call back into the WebSocket API and watch real-time results appear on the screen.

Build the project and deploy it into your web container whichever way you want, or use an IntelliJ IDEA Ultimate Tomcat launcher as instructed in **Chapter 14**. Then navigate to `http://localhost:8080/ch19/index` to bring up the UI. Click the Connect button and you will notice a Connected green badge next to the Connect and Disconnect buttons, as shown in Figure 19-3, and every three seconds a ping message will display in the Ping text area.

Go ahead and type a message in the Message text box and then click the Send button. This message will be sent to the back-end WebSocket service and displayed in the Echo box.

When you have finished sending messages, click the Disconnect button and you will notice that the green badge is replaced by a gray badge labeled Disconnected. You will not be able to send any further messages or disconnect again until you reconnect to the WebSocket service.

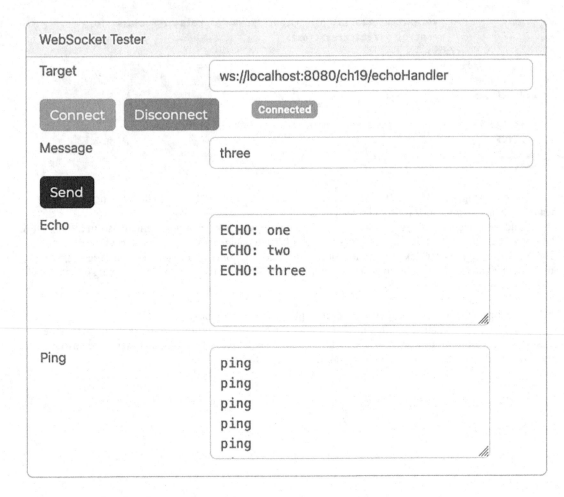

Figure 19-3. *WebSocket client page*

While this example utilizes the Spring abstraction on top of the low-level WebSocket API, you can clearly see the exciting possibilities this technology can bring to your applications. Now let's take a look at how to handle this functionality when the browser does not support WebSocket and a fallback option is required. The code in Listing 19-4 tests if WebSocket is not supported in the browser using the supportsWebSockets variable and disables the Connect button if it is not.

Using SockJS

Because not all browsers support WebSocket (e.g., this be the case for browsers on mobile devices) and applications still need to function correctly for end users, the Spring Framework provides a fallback option utilizing SockJS[4]. Using SockJS provides WebSocket-like behavior as close as possible during runtime without the need for changes to application-side code. The SockJS protocol is used on the client side via JavaScript libraries. The Spring Framework's spring-websocket library contains the relevant SockJS server-side components. When using SockJS to provide a seamless fallback option, the client will first send a GET request to the server by using a path of /info to obtain transport information from the server. SockJS will first try to use WebSocket, then HTTP streaming, and finally HTTP long polling as a last resort.

There is a simple modification to be made to support WebSocket communication using SockJS. First, we need to support asynchronous messaging, which is enabled in the configuration in Listing 19-5 using the @EnableAsync annotation.

Listing 19-5. Spring MVC Configuration for SockJS Asynchronous Configuration

```
package com.apress.prospring6.nineteen

import org.springframework.scheduling.annotation.EnableAsync
// other import statements omitted

@EnableAsync
@Configuration
@EnableWebMvc
@ComponentScan
open class WebConfig : WebMvcConfigurer, ApplicationContextAware {
    // other configuration omitted
}
```

The official Spring Javadoc states that the @EnableAsync annotation enables Spring's asynchronous method execution capability, thus enabling annotation-driven async processing for an entire Spring application context[5].

The second change must be done in WebSocketConfig to enable SockJS support for our handler, as shown in Listing 19-6.

Listing 19-6. Spring WebSocket for SockJS Configuration

```
package com.apress.prospring6.nineteen

import org.springframework.context.annotation.Bean
import org.springframework.context.annotation.Configuration
import org.springframework.web.socket.config.annotation.EnableWebSocket
import org.springframework.web.socket.config.annotation.WebSocketConfigurer
import org.springframework.web.socket.config.annotation.WebSocketHandlerRegistry
```

---

[4] https://github.com/sockjs
[5] https://docs.spring.io/spring-framework/docs/current/javadoc-api/org/springframework/scheduling/annotation/EnableAsync.html

```kotlin
@Configuration
@EnableWebSocket
open class WebSocketConfig : WebSocketConfigurer {
    override fun registerWebSocketHandlers(registry: WebSocketHandlerRegistry) {
        registry.addHandler(echoHandler(), "/echoHandler")
        registry.addHandler(echoHandler2(), "/sockjs/echoHandler").withSockJS()
    }

    @Bean
    open fun echoHandler(): EchoHandler {
        return EchoHandler()
    }

    @Bean
    open fun echoHandler2(): EchoHandler {
        return EchoHandler()
    }
}
```

Notice that another EchoHandler bean is declared and mapped to "/sockjs/echoHandler".

Next we will need to create an HTML page as we did in the WebSocket API sample, but this time utilizing SockJS to take care of the transport negotiation. The most notable differences are that we use the SockJS library rather than WebSocket directly and utilize a typical http:// scheme rather than ws:// to connect to the endpoint. To use SockJS, we need to add the corresponding JavaScript library to the HTML page, and instead of using a WebSocket for communication, we use a SockJS object. The HTML code is almost identical to that in views/index2.html, the only difference being that the JavaScript code to respond to handle the SockJS communication, as shown in Listing 19-7.

Listing 19-7. The JavaScript Code in views/index2.html View

```javascript
// <script type="text/javascript" th:src="@{/js/sockjs-1.6.1.min.js}"></script>
// <script type="text/javascript" th:src="@{/js/jquery-3.6.4.min.js}"></script>
let ping;
let websocket;

jQuery(function ($) {
    function writePing(message) {
        $('#pingOutput').append(message + '\n');
    }

    function writeMessage(message) {
        $('#messageOutput').append(message + '\n')
    }

    $('#connect')
        .click(function doConnect() {
            sockjs = new SockJS($("#target").val());

            sockjs.onopen = function (evt) {
                let badge= $("#badgeStatus");
                badge.text("Connected");
                badge.attr('class','badge bg-success');
```

```
            setInterval(function () {
                if (sockjs !== "undefined") {
                    sockjs.send("ping");
                }
            }, 3000);
        };

        sockjs.onclose = function (evt) {
            let badge= $("#badgeStatus");
            badge.text("Disconnected");
            badge.attr('class','badge bg-light');
        };

        sockjs.onmessage = function (evt) {
            if (evt.data === "ping") {
                writePing(evt.data);
            } else {
                writeMessage('ECHO: ' + evt.data);
            }
        };
    });

$('#disconnect')
    .click(function () {
        if (typeof sockjs != 'undefined') {
            sockjs.close();
            sockjs = undefined;
        } else {
            alert("Not connected.");
        }
    });

$('#send')
    .click(function () {
        if (typeof sockjs != 'undefined') {
            sockjs.send($('#message').val());
        } else {
            alert("Not connected.");
        }
    });
});
```

With the new SockJS code implemented, build and deploy the project to the container and navigate to the UI located at http://localhost:8080/ch19/index2, which has all the same features and functionality of the WebSocket example, as shown in Figure 19-4.

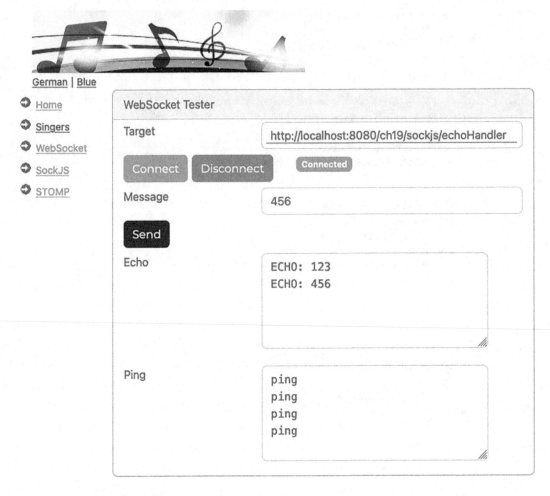

Figure 19-4. SockJS application page, after establishing a connection

To test the SockJS fallback functionality, try disabling WebSocket support in your browser. In Firefox, for example, navigate to the about:config page and then search for network.websocket.enabled. Toggle this setting to false, as shown in Figure 19-5, reload the sample UI, and reconnect.

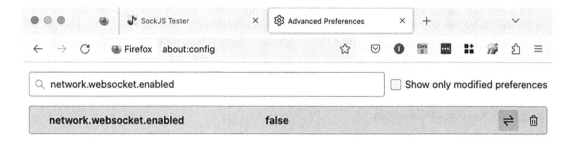

Figure 19-5. *Firefox about:config page*

Utilizing a tool such as Live HTTP Headers will allow you to inspect the traffic going from browser to server for verification purposes. After verifying the behavior, toggle the Firefox setting `network.websocket.enabled` back to `true`, reload the page, and reconnect. Watching the traffic via Live HTTP Headers will now show you the WebSocket handshake. In the simple example, everything should work just as with the WebSocket API.

Sending Messages with STOMP

When working with WebSocket, typically a subprotocol such as STOMP will be used as a common format between the client and the server so that both ends know what to expect and are able to react accordingly. STOMP is supported out of the box by the Spring Framework, and we will use this protocol in the sample.

STOMP (Simple Text-Oriented Messaging Protocol) is a simple, frame-based messaging protocol modeled on HTTP and can be used over any reliable bidirectional streaming network protocol such as WebSocket. STOMP has a standard protocol format; JavaScript client-side support exists for sending and receiving messages in a browser and, optionally, for plugging into traditional message brokers that support STOMP, such as RabbitMQ and ActiveMQ. Out of the box, the Spring Framework supports a simple broker that handles subscription requests and message broadcasting to connected clients in memory. In the STOMP example presented in this section, we will utilize the simple broker and leave the full-featured broker setup as an exercise for you[6].

 For a full description of the STOMP protocol, see the official website[7].

We will create a simple stock-ticker application that displays a few predefined stock symbols, their current price, and the timestamp upon price change. New stock symbols and starting prices can also be added through the UI. Any connecting clients (that is, other browser pages in tabs or totally new clients on other networks) will see the same data as they are subscribed to the message broadcasts. Every second, each stock price will be updated to a new random amount and the timestamp will be updated.

---

[6] https://docs.spring.io/spring-framework/docs/current/reference/html/web.html#websocket-stomp

[7] https://stomp.github.io/stomp-specification-1.2.html

To ensure that clients will be able to use the stock-ticker application even if their browser does not support WebSocket, we will utilize SockJS again to transparently handle any transport switching. Before diving into the code, it is worth noticing that STOMP messages support is provided by the spring-messaging library.

Let's first create the Stock domain object, which holds information about the stock such as its code and price, as shown in Listing 19-8.

Listing 19-8. The Stock Domain Object

```
package com.apress.prospring6.nineteen.stomp

import java.io.Serializable
import java.time.LocalDateTime
import java.time.format.DateTimeFormatter

class Stock() : Serializable {
    var code: String? = null
    var price = 0.0
    var date: LocalDateTime? = null

    constructor(code: String?, price: Double) : this() {
        this.code = code
        this.price = price
    }

    val dateFormatted: String
        get() = DateTimeFormatter.ofPattern(DATE_FORMAT).format(date)

    companion object {
        private const val serialVersionUID = 1L
        private const val DATE_FORMAT = "MMM dd yyyy HH:mm:ss"
    }
}
```

To handle requests for stock updates, a controller is needed. Listing 19-9 shows the StockController class.

Listing 19-9. The StockController Class

```
package com.apress.prospring6.nineteen.stomp

import org.springframework.messaging.handler.annotation.MessageMapping
import org.springframework.messaging.simp.SimpMessagingTemplate
import org.springframework.scheduling.TaskScheduler
// other import statements omitted

@Controller
open class StockController(
    private val taskScheduler: TaskScheduler,
    private val simpMessagingTemplate: SimpMessagingTemplate
) {
```

```kotlin
    private val stocks: MutableList<Stock> = ArrayList()
    private val random = Random(System.currentTimeMillis())

    @MessageMapping("/addStock")
    @Throws(Exception::class)
    open fun addStock(stock: Stock) {
        stocks.add(stock)
        broadcastUpdatedPrices()
    }

    private fun broadcastUpdatedPrices() {
        for (stock in stocks) {
            stock.price = stock.price + updatedStockPrice * stock.price
            stock.date = LocalDateTime.now()
        }
        simpMessagingTemplate.convertAndSend("/topic/price", stocks)
    }

    private val updatedStockPrice: Double
        get() {
            var priceChange = random.nextDouble() * 5.0
            if (random.nextInt(2) == 1) {
                priceChange = -priceChange
            }
            return priceChange / 100.0
        }

    @PostConstruct
    open fun broadcastTimePeriodically() {
        with(stocks){
            add(Stock("VMW", 1.00))
            add(Stock("EMC", 1.00))
            add(Stock("GOOG", 1.00))
            add(Stock("IBM", 1.00))
        }
        taskScheduler.scheduleAtFixedRate({ broadcastUpdatedPrices() },
            Duration.ofSeconds(2))
    }
}
```

The controller shows the following characteristics:

- The controller needs a task scheduler (**Chapter 12**) and a SimpMessagingTemplate to send stock prices updates every 2 seconds.

- The controller is initialized with a few predefined stock symbols in the list and their starting prices for demonstration purposes.

- The /addStock handler method allows the user to submit a Stock instance, which is added to the list of stocks, and then broadcasts the stocks to all subscribers.

- When broadcasting the stocks, we iterate through the list of Stock instances, updating the price for each, and then send them out to all subscribers of /topic/ price by using the wired SimpMessagingTemplate. The TaskExecutor instance broadcasts the updated list of stock prices to all subscribed clients by invoking the broadcastUpdatedPrices every 2 seconds.

With the controller in place, we now need an HTML UI to display stock information to clients. To make things easier, the views/index3.html view is written in Thymeleaf and inherits theme elements from the views/templates/layout.html template used in Chapters 14 and 17.

The HTML JavaScript code in the views/index3.html view is shown in Listing 19-10.

Listing 19-10. The StockController HTML Page

```
<html>
<head th:fragment="~{templates/layout :: pageTitle}">
    <!-- some head elements missing -->
    <script type="text/javascript" th:src="@{/js/sockjs-1.6.1.min.js}"></script>
    <script type="text/javascript" th:src="@{/js/stomp-1.7.1.min.js}"></script>
    <script type="text/javascript" th:src="@{/js/jquery-3.6.4.min.js}"></script>
    <script type="text/javascript">
        let stomp;

        function displayStockPrice(frame) {
            let stocks = JSON.parse(frame.body);

            $('#stock').empty();

            for (let i in stocks) {
                let stock = stocks[i];

                $('#stock').append(
                    $('<tr>').append(
                        $('<td>').html(stock.code),
                        $('<td>').html(stock.price.toFixed(2)),
                        $('<td>').html(stock.dateFormatted)
                    )
                );
            }
        }

        let connectCallback = function () {
            stomp.subscribe('/topic/price', displayStockPrice);
        };

        let errorCallback = function (error) {
            alert(error);
        };

        jQuery(function ($) {
            $("#addStockButton").attr("disabled", true);

            $('#connect')
```

```
                    .click(function doConnect() {
                        stomp = Stomp.over(new SockJS($("#target").val()));
                        stomp.connect("guest", "guest", connectCallback, errorCallback);
                        let badge=  $("#badgeStatus");
                        badge.text("Connected");
                        badge.attr('class','badge bg-success');
                        $("#addStockButton").attr('disabled', false);
                    });

                $('#disconnect')
                    .click(function () {
                        if (typeof stomp != 'undefined') {
                            stomp.disconnect();
                            stomp = undefined;
                            let badge=  $("#badgeStatus");
                            badge.text("Disconnected");
                            badge.attr('class','badge bg-light');
                            $("#addStockButton").attr('disabled', true);
                        } else {
                            alert("Not connected.");
                        }
                    });

                $('.addStockButton').click(function (e) {
                    e.preventDefault();
                    const stockStr = JSON.stringify({
                        'code': $('.addStock .code').val(),
                        'price': Number($('.addStock .price').val())
                    });
                    stomp.send('/app/addStock', {}, stockStr);
                    return false;
                });
            });
    </script>
</head>

<section th:fragment="~{templates/layout :: pageContent}">
    <div class="card border-success mb-3" style="max-width: 40rem; left:30px;">
        <div class="card-header">STOMP Tester</div>
        <div class="row mb-1 m-sm-1">
            <label for="target" th:text="Endpoint" class="col-sm-4 form-label">FN:</label>
            <div class="col-sm-8">
                <input type="text" id="target" size="40" th:value="${endpoint}" class="form-
                control"/>
            </div>
        </div>
        <div class="row mb-1 m-sm-1">
            <div class="col-sm-2"> <input type="submit" id="connect"  class="btn btn-
            success" value="Connect"/></div>
            <div class="col-sm-3"><input type="submit" id="disconnect"  class="btn btn-
            danger" value="Disconnect"/></div>
```

```
            <div class="col-sm-2"><span id="badgeStatus"></span></div>
        </div>
        <div class="row mb-1 m-sm-1">
            <div class="card border-warning mb-3" style="max-width: 35rem;">
                <div class="card-header">Stock Details</div>
                <div class="card-body">
                    <table class="table table-hover table-bordered">
                        <thead>
                        <tr>
                            <th scope="col">Code</th>
                            <th scope="col">Price</th>
                            <th scope="col">Time</th>
                        </tr>
                        </thead>
                        <tbody id="stock"></tbody>
                    </table>
                </div>
            </div>
        </div>

        <div class="row mb-1 m-sm-1 addStock">
            <label for="code" th:text="Code" class="col-sm-4 form-label">FN:</label>
            <div class="col-sm-8">
                <input type="text" id="code" value="" class="form-control code"/>
            </div>
        </div>
        <div class="row mb-1 m-sm-1 addStock">
            <label for="price2" th:text="Price" class="col-sm-4 form-label">FN:</label>
            <div class="col-sm-8">
                <input type="text" id="price2" value="" class="form-control price"/>
            </div>
        </div>
        <div class="row mb-1 m-sm-1 addStock">
            <div class="col-sm-2"><input type="submit" id="addStockButton" class="btn btn-
            danger addStockButton" value="Add Stock"/></div>
        </div>
    </div>
</section>
```

Similar to previous examples in this chapter, we have some HTML mixed in with JavaScript to update the display. The reason we combine HTML with JavaScript, although it is not respecting commonsense programming rules, is to keep the Spring MVC configuration as simple as possible; it also helps to make the page and the functions of its components easy to understand. We utilize jQuery to update HTML data, SockJS to provide transport selection, and the STOMP JavaScript library stomp.min.js for communication with the server. Data sent via STOMP messages is encoded in JSON format, which we extract on events. Upon a STOMP connection, we subscribe to /topic/price to receive stock-price updates.

The Java configuration for STOMP communication is represented by the StompConfig class shown in Listing 19-11.

Listing 19-11. The StompConfig Configuration Class

```
package com.apress.prospring6.nineteen

import org.springframework.context.annotation.Configuration
import org.springframework.scheduling.annotation.EnableAsync
import org.springframework.messaging.simp.config.MessageBrokerRegistry
import org.springframework.web.socket.config.annotation.EnableWebSocketMessageBroker
import org.springframework.web.socket.config.annotation.StompEndpointRegistry
import org.springframework.web.socket.config.annotation.WebSocketMessageBrokerConfigurer


@EnableAsync
@Configuration
@EnableWebSocketMessageBroker
open class StompConfig : WebSocketMessageBrokerConfigurer {
    override fun registerStompEndpoints(registry: StompEndpointRegistry) {
        registry.addEndpoint("/ws").withSockJS()
    }

    override fun configureMessageBroker(config: MessageBrokerRegistry) {
        config.setApplicationDestinationPrefixes("/app")
        config.enableSimpleBroker("/topic")
    }

    @Bean
    open fun taskExecutor(): TaskExecutor {
        return SimpleAsyncTaskExecutor()
    }
}
```

To enable Spring asynchronous calls and task execution, the configuration class must be annotated with @EnableAsync, and a bean of type org.springframework.core.task.TaskExecutor is needed to repeatedly broadcast stock information.

The @EnableWebSocketMessageBroker annotation on a configuration class enables broker-backed messaging over WebSocket using a higher-level messaging subprotocol. Notice the class implements the WebSocketMessageBrokerConfigurer interface that defines methods for configuring message handling with simple messaging protocols (e.g., STOMP) from WebSocket clients.

The registerStompEndpoints is implemented to register the /ws STOMP endpoints mapping. The http://localhost:8080/ch19/ws is used to initialize a SockJS instance that provides the support for STOMP communication. The configureMessageBroker is implemented to configure message broker options.

The applicationDestinationPrefixes property helps filter destinations targeting application annotated methods; this configuration sets the /app filter. This filter needs to prefix the URL path of the stock handler method, which is why Listing 19-10 includes the following:

```
stomp.send('/app/addStock', {}, stockStr)
```

The enableSimpleBroker("/topic") enables a simple message broker and configures one or more prefixes to filter destinations targeting the broker. In the StockController you see in the broadcastUpdatedPrices() method that stock data is published to the topic /topic/price as the destination, while in the index3.html you see the STOMP instance subscribing to this topic so that stock data can be retrieved.

When first accessing the page, there is no STOMP connection, thus the stock table is empty and the Add Stock button is disabled, as shown in Figure 19-6.

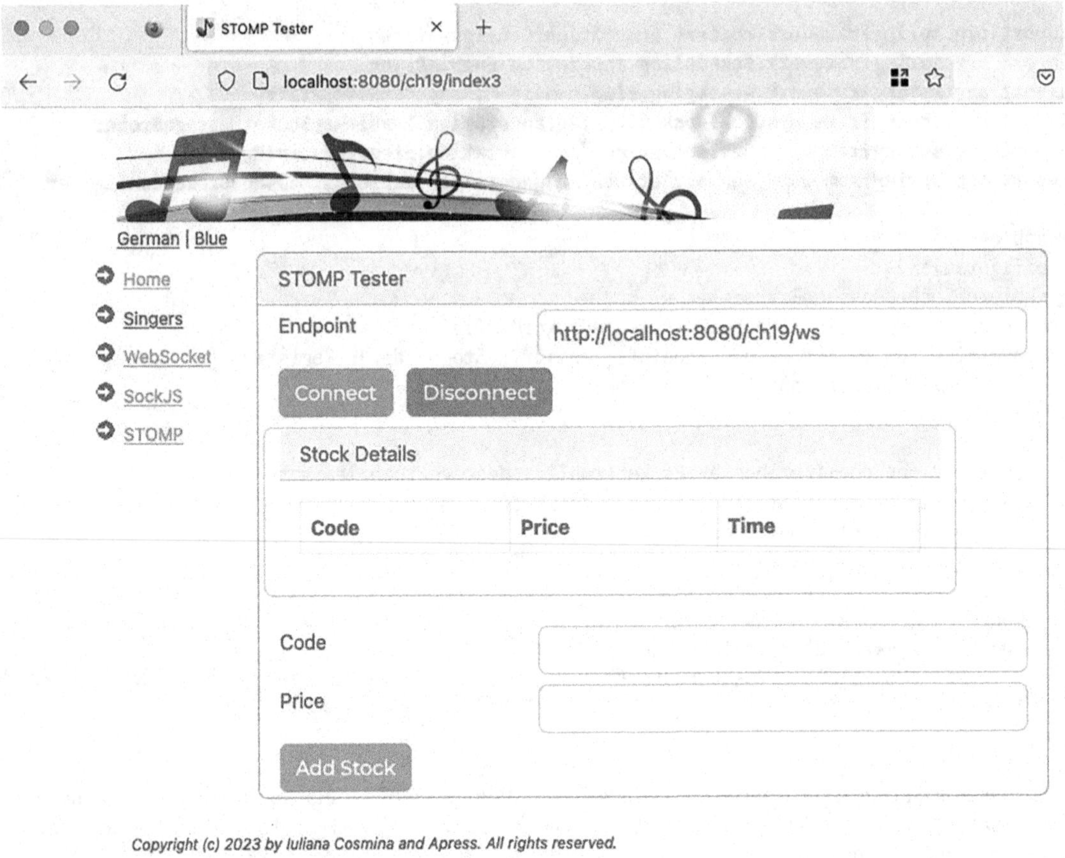

Figure 19-6. *STOMP application page, before establishing a connection*

After clicking the Connect button, the familiar green Connected badge appears, stock data is loaded in the table and refreshed every 2 seconds, and the Add Stock button is now enabled, which allows you to add your own stocks, as shown in Figure 19-7.

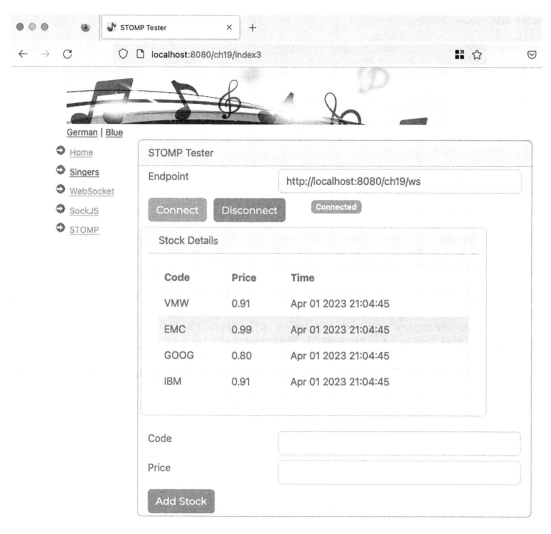

Figure 19-7. *STOMP application page, after establishing a connection*

Under the covers, a connection is established, and in the browser console we can see the browser subscribing to the topic/price queue and then information being received every 2 seconds. A snippet of the browser console log is shown in Listing 19-12.

Listing 19-12. Browser Console Log Snippet for STOMP Communication

```
Opening Web Socket...   stomp-1.7.1.min.js:8:1895
Web Socket Opened...    stomp-1.7.1.min.js:8:1895
>>> CONNECT
login:guest
passcode:guest
accept-version:1.1,1.0
```

```
heart-beat:10000,10000

<<< CONNECTED          stomp-1.7.1.min.js:8:1895
version:1.1
heart-beat:0,0

connected to server undefined stomp-1.7.1.min.js:8:1895
>>> SUBSCRIBE          stomp-1.7.1.min.js:8:1895
id:sub-0
destination:/topic/price

# this bit repeats every 2 seconds
<<< MESSAGE            stomp-1.7.1.min.js:8:1895
destination:/topic/price
content-type:application/json
subscription:sub-0
message-id:v41nbtcg-1338
content-length:593
```

```
[{"code":"VMW","price":0.8412643922671524,"date":[2023,4,1,22,34,0,818886000],"dateFormatted
":"Apr 01 2023 22:34:00"},{"code":"EMC","price":0.3389473652730331,"date":[2023,4,1,22,34,0
,818888000],"dateFormatted":"Apr 01 2023 22:34:00"},{"code":"GOOG","price":0.86116531147
55639,"date":[2023,4,1,22,34,0,818889000],"dateFormatted":"Apr 01 2023 22:34:00"},{"code":"
IBM","price":0.6431663274824831,"date":[2023,4,1,22,34,0,818889000],"dateFormatted":"Apr 01
2023 22:34:00"},{"code":"TSL001","price":1.1764953118520888E-4,"date":[2023,4,1,22,34,0,8188
90000],"dateFormatted":"Apr 01 2023 22:34:00"}]
```

```
...

>>> DISCONNECT         stomp-1.7.1.min.js:8:1895
```

Spring Boot Equivalent Application

Converting the preceding application to a Spring Boot application is fairly easy because there is a spring-boot-starter-websocket library. The dependencies for the chapter19-boot project are shown in Figure 19-8.

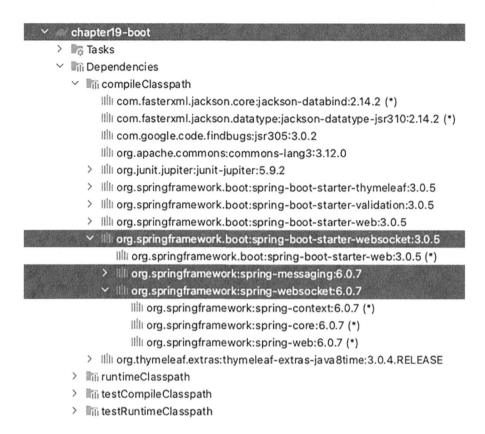

Figure 19-8. Project chapter19-boot dependencies

Because the user can choose to either use communication directly over WebSocket or use high-level protocols such as STOMP, configuration classes for the two situations are still required together with the @EnableWebSocket or @EnableWebSocketMessageBroker annotation. So, aside from a simplification in build configurations and the lack of a server to run the application in, Spring Boot does not reduce developers' work too much. For this reason, this chapter will not cover how to write a Spring Boot application for communication using WebSocket, since all the details have already been covered in **Chapter 14**, the web chapter, and in this chapter, for everything related to WebSocket. However, the chapter19-boot project is part of the sources for the book, so feel free to check it out.

Summary

In this chapter, we covered the general concepts of WebSocket. We discussed the Spring Framework's support for the low-level WebSocket API and then moved on to using SockJS as a fallback option to select the appropriate transport, depending on the client browser. Finally, we introduced STOMP as a WebSocket subprotocol for passing messages between the client and server. For all examples, Kotlin configuration classes were shown and explained.

In the next chapter, we will discuss how to build a Reactive Spring application and how WebSocket can be used for reactive communication.

CHAPTER 20

■ ■ ■

Reactive Spring

The previous chapters demonstrated how to build and run typical Kotlin web applications on an instance of Apache Tomcat server that was either external, for Spring classic configuration, or embedded, for Spring Boot Web applications. Whatever the case, the Spring `DispatcherServlet` was responsible for directing incoming HTTP requests to all the handlers declared in the application. But can an application like the ones we developed thus far be used in a real production environment? How many HTTP requests can `DispatcherServlet` handle at the same time? Can that number be increased? `DispatcherServlet` does not truly have a say in the number of requests it can handle. The servlet container defines that, which in our case is the Apache Tomcat server.

Apache Tomcat is a popular choice for building and maintaining dynamic websites and applications based on the Java software platform. The Java Servlet API enables a web server to handle dynamic Java-based (or Kotlin-based) web content using the HTTP protocol. This is known as the **request-response model**: the client makes a request, and the server prepares a response and sends it back to the client. It is unidirectional and controlled by the client, and the server does not care if the client can handle the response. For example, when you enter a Facebook chat window in your browser, if the server were to send all conversations you've had with that friend, the page not only would take a long time to load, but might crash the browser.

Over the years, many improvements have been made to the software and application development style to support a more efficient client-server interaction, but the one that is the focus of this chapter is **reactive communication**.

💡 If you want a more detailed explanation of how client-server communication evolved, from the initial request-response model to the reactive model, check out *Pro Spring MVC with WebFlux* (Apress, 2021)[1]; start with Chapter 9.

Efficient reactive communication can only occur between a reactive client and a reactive server, ergo between reactive applications. Compared to a classic request-response style, where the client and server exchange data in disconnected blobs of information, reactive communication implies continuous data flow between the client and the server.

Reactive applications are the solution when it comes to handling large amounts of data. Reactive applications are designed with resilience, responsiveness, and scalability as a priority. The Reactive Manifesto[2]

---

[1] https://link.springer.com/book/10.1007/978-1-4842-5666-4
[2] https://www.reactivemanifesto.org/

© Peter Späth, Iuliana Cosmina, Rob Harrop, Chris Schaefer 2023
P. Späth et al., *Pro Spring 6 with Kotlin*, https://doi.org/10.1007/978-1-4842-9557-1_20

describes the characteristics of reactive applications. The Reactive Streams API specification[3] provides a minimum set of interfaces that application components should implement so that applications can be considered reactive. Thus, the Reactive Streams API is an interoperability specification that ensures that reactive components integrate flawlessly and keep the operations non-blocking and asynchronous.

Four key terms describe reactive applications:

- *Responsive*: Fast and consistent response times are expected.

- *Resilient*: Failures are expected, and applications are designed to handle them and self-heal.

- *Elastic*: The application should be able to deal with high loads by scaling up its capabilities automatically and scaling down when no longer needed.

- *Message-driven*: Reactive communication should be asynchronous; components should be loosely coupled and communicate using messages. Additionally, back pressure is applied to prevent producers of messages from overwhelming consumers.

Reactive applications are supposed to be more flexible, loosely coupled, non-blocking, and scalable, but at the same time easier to develop, more malleable to change, and more tolerant of failure. Building reactive applications requires following the principles of the reactive programming paradigm.

Having read the preceding introduction, you might think that reactive applications are the pinnacle of software design evolution and that every application in the world should be redesigned to be a reactive one. That is not always true, unfortunately. Reactive applications don't always run faster than classic ones, and they come with their own sets of problems. As you will see in this chapter, reactive programming is quite different from imperative programming and requires a bit of a mind shift. The main benefits of reactive applications are that they are non-blocking, and they are able to scale an application with a small, fixed number of threads and lesser memory requirements while at the same time making the best use of the available processing power.

In this chapter, you will learn about reactive programming and how you can build fully reactive applications using Spring WebFlux.

Introduction to Reactive Programming in Spring

Reactive programming is a declarative programming paradigm that is based on the idea of asynchronous event processing and data streams, or as we like to describe it, functional programming with reactive streams. Reactive Streams is an initiative to provide a standard for asynchronous stream processing with non-blocking back pressure. It is extremely useful for solving problems that require complex coordination across thread boundaries.

Java introduced the Streams API in and lambda expressions in version 8, which was the first step toward reactive programming because reactive programming can also be defined as *functional programming with reactive streams*. Reactive streams were not available until Java 9. Unable to wait for JDK 9, which was released with a six-month delay, the Pivotal open source team, the same one that created Spring, built Spring WebFlux[4] using Project Reactor[5], their own reactive library.

---

[3] https://www.reactive-streams.org/
[4] https://docs.spring.io/spring-framework/docs/current/reference/html/web-reactive.html
[5] https://projectreactor.io

⚠ Kotlin has its own idea about the reactive programming paradigm. It is called *Coroutines* respectively *Kotlin Flow*. Since we want to line up with the Java sister edition of this book, we restrict the discussion to the "Spring with Java way" of reactive programming. Feel free to discover Coroutines and Flow using the official documentation channels.

Reactive Streams provide a common API for reactive programming in Java or Kotlin. It is composed of four simple interfaces that provide a standard for asynchronous stream processing with non-blocking back pressure. If you want to write a component that can integrate with other reactive components, you need to implement one of these interfaces. On an abstract level, the components and the relationships between them, as described in the Reactive Streams specification, look like the representation shown in Figure 20-1.

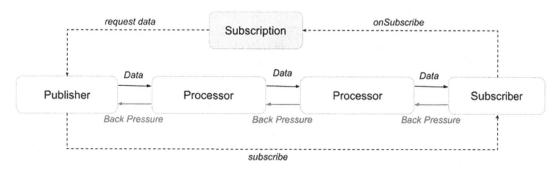

Figure 20-1. *Reactive Streams specification abstract representation*

If you think it looks a lot like the publisher/subscriber model with the bonus of back pressure, that's pretty much what it is. Data *flows* between components, each component processes it and passes it forward, and each component regulates the speed via back pressure. The most appropriate model in the real world is a factory conveyor belt. Let's go through the components in Figure 20-1.

- A **publisher** is a potentially infinite producer of data. In Java or Kotlin, a producer of data must implement `org.reactivestreams.Publisher<T>`. A publisher prepares and transfers the data to subscribers as individual messages. The publisher emits values on demand from the subscriber.

- A **subscriber** registers with the publisher to consume data. In Java or Kotlin, a data consumer must implement `org.reactivestreams.Subscriber<T>`. A subscriber receives messages from the publisher and processes them. It is a terminal operation in the Streams API.

- Upon subscribing, a **subscription** object is created to represent the one-to-one relationship between the publisher and the subscriber. This object requests data from the publisher and cancels the demand for data. In Java or Kotlin, a subscription class must implement `org.reactivestreams.Subscription`, and an object of this type can only be used once by a subscriber.

- A **processor** is a special component that has the same properties as a publisher and subscriber. In Java or Kotlin, a processor of data must implement org.reactivestreams.Processor<T,R>. Processors can be chained to form a stream-processing pipeline. A processor consumes data from the publisher/processor in front of it in the chain and emits data for the processor/subscriber after it in the chain to consume. The subscriber/processor applies back pressure to slow down the producer/processor when emitting data if it cannot consume it fast enough.

You can check out the code for these interfaces in your IDE or on GitHub[6].

⚠️ Most reactive implementations for the JVM were developed in parallel, so today we have RxJava[7], Akka Streams[8], Ratpack[9], Vert.x[10], and Project Reactor.

Code written with Reactive Streams looks similar to code written with non-Reactive Streams, but what happens under the hood is different. Reactive streams are **asynchronous**, but you do not have to write the logic of dealing with that. You need to declare what must happen when some value is emitted on a stream. The code you are writing is invoked when the stream emits an item asynchronously, independent of the main program flow. If there is more than one processor involved, each is executed on its own thread. Since your code runs asynchronously, you must be careful with the functions you are providing as arguments to your processor (transformer) methods. Make sure they are **pure functions**. Pure functions should only interact with the program through their arguments and return values. They return the same result for the same argument values, and they should never modify an object that requires synchronization, as this will probably cause unpredictable delay of the entire flow.

Project Reactor implements the Reactive Streams API to provide a non-blocking stable foundation with efficient demand management for reactive applications. It declares two main publisher implementations:

- reactor.core.publisher.Mono<T>: A reactive stream publisher representing zero or one element

- reactor.core.publisher.Flux<T>: A reactive stream publisher representing an asynchronous sequence of zero to infinity elements

Mono<T> and Flux<T> are similar to java.util.concurrent.Future<V>. They represent the result of an asynchronous computation. The difference between them is that Future<V> blocks the current thread until the computation completes when you try to get the result with the get() method. Mono<T> and Flux<T> both provide a family of block*() methods used to retrieve the value of an asynchronous computation that does not block the current thread.

To make it obvious how reactive programming looks different syntactically from imperative programming, let's consider the following scenario: given a list of singers, we want to find all with an age greater than 50, and we want to sum their ages. If the code is written in imperative style and for Java, it might look like the snippet shown in Listing 20-1.

---

[6] https://github.com/reactive-streams/reactive-streams-jvm/tree/master/api/src/main/java/org/reactivestreams
[7] https://github.com/ReactiveX/RxJava
[8] https://doc.akka.io/docs/akka/current/stream/index.html
[9] https://ratpack.io
[10] https://vertx.io

Listing 20-1. Java Imperative-Style Code to Process a List of Singers

```java
package com.apress.prospring6.twenty.boot;
// import statements omitted

public class SimpleProgrammingTest {
    List<Singer> singers = List.of(
            Singer.builder().firstName("John").lastName("Mayer").birthDate(LocalDate.
            of(1977, 10, 16)).build(),
            Singer.builder().firstName("B.B.").lastName("King").birthDate(LocalDate.of(1929,
            9, 16)).build(),
            Singer.builder().firstName("Peggy").lastName("Lee").birthDate(LocalDate.of(1920,
            5, 26)).build(),
            Singer.builder().firstName("Ella").lastName("Fitzgerald").birthDate(LocalDate.
            of(1917, 4, 25)).build()
    );

    Function<Singer, Pair<Singer, Integer>> computeAge = singer -> Pair.of(singer,Period.
    between(singer.getBirthDate(), LocalDate.now()).getYears());
    Predicate<Pair<Singer, Integer>> checkAge = pair -> pair.getRight() > 50;

    @Test
    void imperativePlay(){
        int agesum = 0;
        for (var s : singers) {
            var p = computeAge.apply(s);
            if (checkAge.test(p)) {
                agesum += p.getRight();
            }
        }
        assertEquals(300, agesum);
    }
}
```

Not pretty, right? Well, this is the type of code all Java developers used to write before the Stream API was introduced in Java 8. A set of instructions were listed one after the other for the JVM to execute. Additionally, using a Function<T,R> and a Predicate<T> is a bit of a cheat, considering those types did not exist before Java 8 either.

Using Kotlin and functional constructs, the same code can be written more declarative and more functional, as shown in Listing 20-2.

Listing 20-2. Declarative/Functional-Style Code Using Kotlin to Process a List of Singers

```kotlin
package com.apress.prospring6.twenty.boot

import org.junit.jupiter.api.Assertions.assertEquals
// import statements omitted

class SimpleProgrammingTest {
    var singers: List<Singer> = listOf(
        Singer().apply{firstName="John"; lastName = "Mayer";
            birthDate = LocalDate.of(1977, 10, 16)},
```

```
        Singer().apply{firstName="B.B."; lastName = "King";
            birthDate = LocalDate.of(1929, 9, 16)},
        Singer().apply{firstName="Peggy"; lastName = "Lee";
            birthDate = LocalDate.of(1920, 5, 26)},
        Singer().apply{firstName="Ella"; lastName = "Fitzgerald";
            birthDate = LocalDate.of(1917, 4, 25)}
    )
    var computeAge  = { singer: Singer ->
            Pair(
                singer,
                Period.between(singer.birthDate, LocalDate.now()).years
            )
    }
    var checkAge = { pair:Pair<Singer, Int> -> pair.second > 50 }

    @Test
    fun streamsPlay() {
        val agesum: Int = singers
            .map(computeAge)
            .filter(checkAge)
            .map{ obj:Pair<Singer, Int> -> obj.second }
            .reduce{ a: Int, b: Int -> Integer.sum(a, b) }
        Assertions.assertEquals(
            300,
            agesum
        )
    }
}
```

Declarative programming is more of a process of constantly defining what things are. Declarative programming focuses on *what* the program should achieve, while imperative programming focuses on *how* the program should achieve the result.

Transforming the code in Listing 20-2 to reactive code does not require much effort: we just replace Stream<T> with Flux<T> and make sure to declare a subscriber that does something with the result of the last processor in the chain (the reduce(..) function). The code is depicted in Listing 20-3.

Listing 20-3. Functional-Style Code Using Reactive Streams to Process a List of Singers

```
package com.apress.prospring6.twenty.boot

import reactor.core.publisher.BaseSubscriber
import reactor.core.publisher.Flux
// other import statements omitted

class SimpleProgrammingTest {
    var singers: List<Singer> = ...
    var computeAge  = { singer: Singer ->
            Pair(
                singer,
                Period.between(singer.birthDate, LocalDate.now()).years
            )
    }
```

```
        var checkAge = { pair:Pair<Singer, Int> -> pair.second > 50 }

        @Test
        fun reactivePlay() {
            Flux.fromIterable<Singer>(singers) // Flux<Singer>
                .map(computeAge) // Flux <Pair<Singer, Integer>>
                .filter(checkAge) // Flux <Pair<Singer, Integer>>
                .map{ obj -> obj.second } // Flux <Integer>
                .reduce(0,
                    { a: Int, b: Int ->
                        Integer.sum(
                            a,
                            b
                        )
                    })
                .subscribe(object : BaseSubscriber<Int>() {
                    override fun hookOnNext(agesum: Int) {
                        Assertions.assertEquals(
                            300,
                            agesum
                        )
                    }
                })
        }
}
```

The BaseSubscriber<T> abstract class is a simple base class for a Subscriber<T> implementation that lets the user perform a request(long) and cancel() on it directly. The hookOnNext(..) method is useful to attach behavior to the emitted value; in our case, this is the perfect place to check our assumption.

Now that you've been introduced to reactive programming with Project Reactor, let's switch gears and see how to write reactive applications using Spring WebFlux.

Introducing Spring WebFlux

Spring Web MVC is designed around the DispatcherServlet, which is the gateway that maps HTTP requests to handlers and is set up with theme configurations, internationalization, file upload, and view resolution. Spring MVC was built for the Servlet API and Servlet containers. This means that Spring MVC mostly uses blocking I/O and one thread per HTTP request. Supporting asynchronous processing of requests is possible but requires a larger thread pool, which in turn requires more resources and is difficult to scale.

Spring WebFlux is a reactive stack web framework that was added in Spring 5, and it is Spring's response to the rising issue of blocking I/O architecture. It can run on Servlet 3.1+ containers, but it can adapt to other native server APIs. The preferred server of choice is Netty[11], which is well established in the async, non-blocking space. Spring WebFlux is built with functional reactive programming in mind and allows for code to be written in declarative style. The two frameworks have a few elements in common and can even be used together. There is no reason for a handler method to not be able to return Flux<T> or Mono<T>, as will be shown soon in this chapter.

---

[11] https://netty.io

⚠ One thing to keep in mind when writing a reactive application is that every component of the application must be reactive; otherwise, the application will not truly be reactive, and the non-reactive component might become a bottleneck and break down the whole flow. For example, a three-tier application with the typical tiers, presentation, service, and database, will only be reactive if all three are reactive. Therefore, a reactive Spring WebFlux application must have reactive views, reactive controllers, reactive services, reactive repositories, and a reactive database (any SQL database that comes with a reactive driver, such as MongoDB, RethingDB, etc.). In addition, the client making calls to the application must be reactive too.

Before converting the singers application to a reactive one, let's review how Spring WebFlux works under the hood.

Reactive applications can be deployed on Servlet 3.1+ containers, such as Tomcat, Jetty, or Undertow. The trick here is to not use the `DispatcherServlet`. The `DispatcherServlet` is the central dispatcher for HTTP request handlers/controllers, and no matter how powerful it is, it is still a blocking component. This is where the new and improved Spring web components come to the rescue by introducing the `org.springframework.http.server.reactive.HttpHandler`[12]. This interface represents the lowest-level contract for reactive HTTP request handling, and Spring provides server adapters based on it for each supported server. Its code is shown in Listing 20-4.

Listing 20-4. HttpHandler Interface

```java
package org.springframework.http.server.reactive;

import reactor.core.publisher.Mono;
// other comments omitted
public interface HttpHandler {

    /**
     * Handle the given request and write to the response.
     * @param request current request
     * @param response current response
     * @return indicates completion of request handling
     */
    Mono<Void> handle(ServerHttpRequest request, ServerHttpResponse response);
}
```

Table 20-1 lists the servers supported by Spring WebFlux and the name of the adapter classes that represent the core of the non-blocking I/O to Reactive Streams bridge for each server.

---

[12] https://github.com/spring-projects/spring-framework/blob/main/spring-web/src/main/java/org/springframework/http/server/reactive/HttpHandler.java

Table 20-1. *HTTP Servers Supported by Spring WebFlux*

Server Name	Spring Adapter	Servlet API Used
Netty[13]	ReactorHttpHandlerAdapter	Netty API using the Reactor Netty library
Undertow[14]	UndertowHttpHandlerAdapter	Spring Web Undertow to Reactive Streams bridge
Tomcat[15]	TomcatHttpHandlerAdapter	Spring Web: Servlet 3.1 non-blocking I/O to Reactive Streams bridge
Jetty[16]	JettyHttpHandlerAdapter	Spring Web: Servlet 3.1 non-blocking I/O to Reactive Streams bridge

On top of HttpHandler, Spring provides the org.springframework.web.server.WebHandler[17] interface, which is a slightly higher-level contract describing all general-purpose server APIs with filter chain–style processing and exception handling. This interface is shown in Listing 20-5, and it seems to be pretty similar to HttpHandler.

Listing 20-5. WebHandler Interface

```
package org.springframework.web.server;

import reactor.core.publisher.Mono;

import org.springframework.web.server.adapter.HttpWebHandlerAdapter;
import org.springframework.web.server.adapter.WebHttpHandlerBuilder;

public interface WebHandler {
    /**
     * Handle the web server exchange.
     * @param exchange the current server exchange
     * @return {@code Mono<Void>} to indicate when request handling is complete
     */
    Mono<Void> handle(ServerWebExchange exchange);

}
```

Instead of using ServerRequest and ServerResponse objects in its handle(..) method, WebHandler uses an object of type ServerWebExchange, a specialized interface representing a contract for an HTTP request-response interaction that also exposes additional server-side processing-related properties and features such as request attributes. What does this mean for a Spring WebFlux configuration compared to a Spring Web MVC application?

---

[13] https://netty.io
[14] https://undertow.io
[15] https://tomcat.apache.org
[16] https://www.eclipse.org/jetty
[17] https://github.com/spring-projects/spring-framework/blob/main/spring-web/src/main/java/org/springframework/web/server/WebHandler.java

A Spring Web MVC application has an `org.springframework.web.servlet.DispatcherServlet` bean as the front controller intercepting all requests and matching them to handler methods. A Spring WebFlux application has an `org.springframework.web.reactive.DispatcherHandler` bean as a dispatcher for HTTP request handlers/controllers. `DispatcherHandler` is an implementation of `WebHandler` and `ApplicationContextAware` that gives it access to all the beans in the application configuration. It is the central `WebHandler` implementation and provides an algorithm for request processing performed by configurable components. It delegates to special beans to process requests and render appropriate responses, and their implementations are, as expected, non-blocking. Similar to the Spring MVC ecosystem, there is a `HandlerMapping` bean to map a request to a handler, a `HandlerAdapter` bean to invoke a handler, an `org.springframework.web.server.WebExceptionHandler` bean to handle exceptions, and a `HandlerResultHandler` bean to get the result from the handler and finalize the response, all of which are declared in the `org.springframework.web.reactive` package.

In the Spring typical way, for most cases, the configuration of the `DispatcherHandler` bean does not require code that describes it directly. To configure a Spring WebFlux application that will be run in a Servlet 3.1+ container, you need to do the following:

- Declare a Spring WebFlux configuration class and annotate it with `@Configuration` and `@EnableWebFlux`. The `@EnableWebFlux` annotation is part of the `org.springframework.web.reactive.config` package, and it enables the use of annotated controllers and functional endpoints.

- Extend the `org.springframework.web.server.adapter.AbstractReactiveWebInitializer` class and implement the `getConfigClasses()` method and inject your Spring WebFlux configuration class in it.

In a Spring Boot application, you do not need to do any of this. Just declare your controllers, your handler classes, and functional endpoints, and that is it. Because in this chapter the end game is to build a fully reactive application from the database to the presentation layer, the classic Spring configuration for a reactive application will not be shown. For a book that covers that configuration in detail, consult the previously referenced *Pro Spring MVC with WebFlux*[18].

Spring Boot Configuration for a Reactive Application

Let's start with the configuration. To build a reactive three-tier application, we need all layers to be represented by reactive components. This means the following:

- *The data access layer must be reactive*: This means that the database driver must be reactive and the persistence layer, if used, needs to be reactive too. The classic database JDBC drivers are not reactive, so in a reactive application, they represent a blocking I/O component that affects the behavior of the whole application. Therefore, there was a need for a SQL reactive driver, so R2DBC[19] was developed. The Reactive Relational Database Connectivity (R2DBC) project brings reactive programming APIs to relational databases, and a driver for MariaDB is available. For persistence, there is a Hibernate Reactive library[20], but its capabilities are limited, so we will not use it in this chapter.

- *The service layer must be reactive*: This is not that complicated; we just need to make sure the service classes only return `Flux<T>` and `Mono<T>` instances.

---

[18] https://link.springer.com/book/10.1007/978-1-4842-5666-4
[19] https://r2dbc.io
[20] https://hibernate.org/reactive

- *The web layer must be reactive*: This means controllers and handlers are reactive too, and thus only return `Flux<T>` and `Mono<T>` instances.

- *The presentation layer must be reactive*: This means that the view templates must be dynamic, so they can render the data as it arrives from the server. A combination of Thymeleaf[21] and jQuery[22] can handle reactive communication with a server well enough, but if you need a more advanced UI, React[23] and Angular[24] are a more appropriate choice.

Figure 20-2 shows the project dependencies.

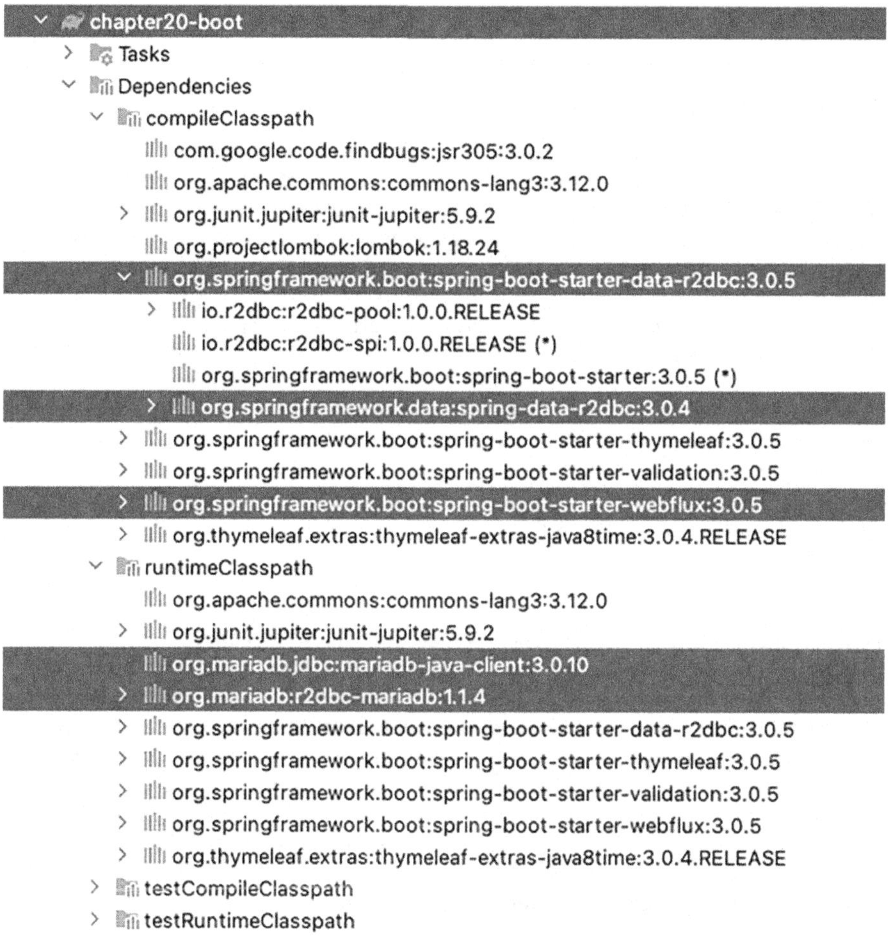

```
∨ 🐱 chapter20-boot
  > 🏴 Tasks
  ∨ 📚 Dependencies
    ∨ 📚 compileClasspath
        ⅲⅲ com.google.code.findbugs:jsr305:3.0.2
        ⅲⅲ org.apache.commons:commons-lang3:3.12.0
      > ⅲⅲ org.junit.jupiter:junit-jupiter:5.9.2
        ⅲⅲ org.projectlombok:lombok:1.18.24
      ∨ ⅲⅲ org.springframework.boot:spring-boot-starter-data-r2dbc:3.0.5
        > ⅲⅲ io.r2dbc:r2dbc-pool:1.0.0.RELEASE
          ⅲⅲ io.r2dbc:r2dbc-spi:1.0.0.RELEASE (*)
          ⅲⅲ org.springframework.boot:spring-boot-starter:3.0.5 (*)
        > ⅲⅲ org.springframework.data:spring-data-r2dbc:3.0.4
      > ⅲⅲ org.springframework.boot:spring-boot-starter-thymeleaf:3.0.5
      > ⅲⅲ org.springframework.boot:spring-boot-starter-validation:3.0.5
      > ⅲⅲ org.springframework.boot:spring-boot-starter-webflux:3.0.5
      > ⅲⅲ org.thymeleaf.extras:thymeleaf-extras-java8time:3.0.4.RELEASE
    ∨ 📚 runtimeClasspath
        ⅲⅲ org.apache.commons:commons-lang3:3.12.0
      > ⅲⅲ org.junit.jupiter:junit-jupiter:5.9.2
        ⅲⅲ org.mariadb.jdbc:mariadb-java-client:3.0.10
      > ⅲⅲ org.mariadb:r2dbc-mariadb:1.1.4
      > ⅲⅲ org.springframework.boot:spring-boot-starter-data-r2dbc:3.0.5
      > ⅲⅲ org.springframework.boot:spring-boot-starter-thymeleaf:3.0.5
      > ⅲⅲ org.springframework.boot:spring-boot-starter-validation:3.0.5
      > ⅲⅲ org.springframework.boot:spring-boot-starter-webflux:3.0.5
      > ⅲⅲ org.thymeleaf.extras:thymeleaf-extras-java8time:3.0.4.RELEASE
  > 📚 testCompileClasspath
  > 📚 testRuntimeClasspath
```

Figure 20-2. Project `chapter20-boot` dependencies

---

[21] https://www.thymeleaf.org
[22] https://jquery.com
[23] https://react.dev
[24] https://angular.io

The main dependency of `spring-boot-starter-data-r2dbc` is `spring-data-r2dbc`[25], which is part of the Spring Data family, and it makes it easy to implement reactive repositories. Spring Data R2DBC is quite simple: it does not offer caching, lazy loading, write-behind, or many other features of ORM frameworks, but it does offer object mapping, which is just enough to remove some boilerplate code, because converting database objects to Java objects can be a hassle.

The main dependency of `spring-boot-starter-webflux` is `spring-webflux`, which includes all Spring components that can be used to develop a reactive web application. The reactive-stack web framework, Spring WebFlux, was added to the Spring Framework in version 5, and it is non-blocking, supports Reactive Streams back pressure, and runs on such servers as Netty, Undertow, and Servlet containers. The Spring Boot WebFlux default configuration includes the Reactor Netty[26] server, which offers non-blocking and backpressure-ready TCP/HTTP/UDP/QUIC[27] clients and servers based on the Netty[28] framework.

Reactive Repository and Database

The database of choice for the project linked to this chapter is MariaDB. There is a stable R2DBC driver for MariaDB, so this will replace the blocking JDBC driver. The reactive driver provides non-blocking communication with the database, as expected, and authentication. Since using the driver is done under the hood by Spring Data, the only thing that lets a developer look at the code now is that a reactive driver is used in the configuration. The database connection URL no longer uses the `jdbc:` prefix but rather the r2dbc prefix.

Listing 20-6 shows the Spring Boot data source configuration properties in the `application.yaml` configuration file when a reactive driver is used.

Listing 20-6. Spring Boot Data Source Configuration with a Reactive Driver

```
spring:
  r2dbc:
    url: r2dbc:mariadb://localhost:3306/musicdb
    username: prospring6
    password: prospring6
```

Spring Data R2DBC provides a few useful classes, such as `R2dbcEntityTemplate` in the `org.springframework.data.r2dbc.core` package, which is the equivalent of `JdbcTemplate` for a reactive environment. It simplifies the use of Reactive R2DBC through entities and helps to avoid common errors. To perform database operations, `R2dbcEntityTemplate` delegates to a `DatabaseClient` (same package), which can also be used to run statements for mapped entities using the Criteria API. In this project, Spring Data repositories are used implicitly, thus there is no need to use any of these directly; just know that they exist and can be used if needed.

Spring Data reactive repositories are not that different from non-reactive repositories. They are just interfaces that provide a contract for the basic queries for an entity type: create, read, update, and delete. They can be expanded by adding (reactive version) `@Query` annotated methods and custom implementations if needed, as shown in **Chapter 10**.

---

[25] https://spring.io/projects/spring-data-r2dbc
[26] https://github.com/reactor/reactor-netty
[27] https://www.chromium.org/quic
[28] https://netty.io

Listing 20-7 shows the `SingerRepo` interface that extends the `ReactiveCrudRepository<T,ID>` Spring Data repository interface and adds its own reactive methods.

Listing 20-7. SingerRepo Reactive Repository Interface

```
package com.apress.prospring6.twenty.boot.repo

import com.apress.prospring6.twenty.boot.model.Singer
import org.springframework.data.r2dbc.repository.Query
...

interface SingerRepo : ReactiveCrudRepository<Singer, Long> {
    @Query("select * from singer where first_name=:fn and last_name=:ln")
    fun findByFirstNameAndLastName(@Param("fn") firstName: String,
        @Param("ln") lastName: String): Mono<Singer>

    @Query("select * from singer where first_name=:fn")
    fun findByFirstName(@Param("fn") firstName: String): Flux<Singer>

    @Query("select * from singer where last_name=:ln")
    fun findByLastName(@Param("ln") lastName: String): Flux<Singer>

    @Query("select * from singer where birth_date=:ln")
    fun findByBirthDate(@Param("bd") birthDate: LocalDate): Flux<Singer>
}
```

Note that some Spring Data components, such as the `@Param` annotation, can be used in a reactive context, and only those components interacting directly with the data flow need to be reactive. Spring Data now has two components: a reactive component in the `org.springframework.data.r2dbc.repository` package and a non-reactive component in the `org.springframework.data.jpa.repository.query` package.

The `ReactiveCrudRepository<T,ID>` interface used in this example is the reactive equivalent of `CrudRepository<T,ID>` introduced in **Chapter 10**, and its main characteristic is that it returns reactive types, so instead of data, we obtain a data reactive stream as a result that will emit the data when requested by a subscriber.

❗ Notice that to keep our repository fully reactive, all additional configured methods must return `Flux<T>` or `Mono<T>`.

When Spring Data reactive repositories are enriched with additional methods, via configuration as shown here, or by composing custom implementations via custom interfaces as shown in **Chapter 10**, you might want to test your repository. You can easily do so by using a combination of TestContainers, Junit 5, Spring Boot, and Project Reactor test libraries. *(Yeah, we know, it does not seem so easy when you need four libraries to get it done!)*

Figure 20-3 shows the test dependencies of the chapter20-boot project.

```
∨ 🐘 chapter20-boot
  > 📂 Tasks
  ∨ 🗂 Dependencies
    > 🗂 compileClasspath
    > 🗂 runtimeClasspath
    ∨ 🗂 testCompileClasspath
        ⅲ com.google.code.findbugs:jsr305:3.0.2
      > ⅲ io.projectreactor:reactor-test:3.5.4
        ⅲ org.apache.commons:commons-lang3:3.12.0
      > ⅲ org.junit.jupiter:junit-jupiter:5.9.2
        ⅲ org.mariadb.jdbc:mariadb-java-client:3.0.10
      > ⅲ org.mariadb:r2dbc-mariadb:1.1.4
      > ⅲ org.springframework.boot:spring-boot-starter-data-r2dbc:3.0.5
      > ⅲ org.springframework.boot:spring-boot-starter-test:3.0.5
      > ⅲ org.springframework.boot:spring-boot-starter-thymeleaf:3.0.5
      > ⅲ org.springframework.boot:spring-boot-starter-validation:3.0.5
      > ⅲ org.springframework.boot:spring-boot-starter-webflux:3.0.5
      > ⅲ org.testcontainers:junit-jupiter:1.17.6
      > ⅲ org.testcontainers:mariadb:1.17.6
      > ⅲ org.thymeleaf.extras:thymeleaf-extras-java8time:3.0.4.RELEASE
    > 🗂 testRuntimeClasspath
```

Figure 20-3. *Project* chapter20-boot *test dependencies*

To write the test, we need to do the following:

- Set up a MariaDB container, extract its properties, convert the connection URL to a reactive connection URL, and inject it into the Spring Boot Test context. This step is necessary so that Spring Boot can configure the R2DBC driver.

- Annotate the test class with @DataR2dbcTest to let Spring Boot know that the test context needed is one specific for a Reactive context, and we are only interested in Spring Data components.

- To check assertions on the data being manipulated reactively, we need to use Project Reactor's StepVerifier, which provides a declarative way of creating a verifiable script for an async Publisher sequence by expressing expectations about the events that will happen upon subscription.

- To control the order of the test methods being executed (we are keeping the test really simple here), mark methods with their execution step number and check assumptions. We use JUnit 5 annotations and static methods, which you should be familiar with at this point in the book.

Listing 20-8 shows the test class that checks the most important methods of the SingerRepo interface and uses all the libraries and components mentioned.

Listing 20-8. Reactive RepositoryTest Test Class

```kotlin
package com.apress.prospring6.twenty.boot

// Spring Boot imports
import org.springframework.boot.test.autoconfigure.data.r2dbc.DataR2dbcTest
import org.springframework.data.r2dbc.core.R2dbcEntityTemplate

// TestContainers imports
import org.testcontainers.containers.MariaDBContainer
import org.testcontainers.junit.jupiter.Container
import org.testcontainers.junit.jupiter.Testcontainers
import org.testcontainers.utility.MountableFile

// Project Reactor Test imports
import reactor.test.StepVerifier

// JUnit 5 import
import static org.junit.jupiter.api.Assertions.assertNotNull

// other import statements omitted

@DataR2dbcTest
@TestMethodOrder(MethodOrderer.OrderAnnotation::class)
class SingerRepoTest : ReactiveDbConfigTests() {
    @Autowired
    var singerRepo: SingerRepo? = null

    @Order(1)
    @Test
    fun testRepoExists() {
        Assertions.assertNotNull(singerRepo)
    }

    @Order(2)
    @Test
    fun testCount() {
        singerRepo!!.count()
            .log()
            .`as`<FirstStep<Long>> { publisher: Mono<Long> ->
                StepVerifier.create(
                    publisher
                )
            }
            .expectNextMatches { p: Long -> p == 4L }
            .verifyComplete()
    }

    @Order(3)
    @Test
    fun testFindByFistName() {
        singerRepo!!.findByFirstName("John")
```

```kotlin
            .log()
            .`as`<FirstStep<Singer>> { publisher: Flux<Singer> ->
                StepVerifier.create(
                    publisher
                )
            }
            .expectNextCount(2)
            .verifyComplete()
    }

    @Order(4)
    @Test
    fun testFindByFistNameAndLastName() {
        singerRepo!!.findByFirstNameAndLastName("John", "Mayer")
            .log()
            .`as`<FirstStep<Singer>> { publisher: Mono<Singer> ->
                StepVerifier.create(
                    publisher
                )
            }
            .expectNext(
                Singer().apply {
                    id = 1L
                    firstName = "John"
                    lastName = "Mayer"
                    birthDate = LocalDate.of(1977, 10, 16)
                }
            )
            .verifyComplete()
    }

    @Order(5)
    @Test
    fun testFindByFistNameAndLastNameNoResult() {
        singerRepo!!.findByFirstNameAndLastName("Gigi", "Pedala")
            .log()
            .`as`<FirstStep<Singer>> { publisher: Mono<Singer> ->
                StepVerifier.create(
                    publisher
                )
            }
            .expectNextCount(0)
            .verifyComplete()
    }

    @Order(6)
    @Test
    fun testCreateSinger() {
        singerRepo!!.save(
            Singer().apply {
                firstName = "Test"
```

```
                lastName ="Test"
                birthDate = LocalDate.now()
            }
        )
            .log()
            .`as`{ publisher: Mono<Singer> ->
                StepVerifier.create(
                    publisher
                )
            }
            .assertNext{ s ->
                Assertions.assertNotNull(s.id)
            }
            .verifyComplete()
    }

    @Order(7)
    @Test // negative test, lastName is null, which is not allowed
    fun testFailedCreateSinger() {
        singerRepo!!.save(
            Singer().apply {
                firstName = "Test"
                birthDate = LocalDate.now()
            }
        )
            .log()
            .`as`{ publisher: Mono<Singer> ->
                StepVerifier.create(
                    publisher
                )
            }
            .verifyError(TransientDataAccessResourceException::class.java)
    }

    @Order(8)
    @Test
    fun testDeleteSinger() {
        singerRepo!!.deleteById(4L)
            .log()
            .`as`<FirstStep<Void>> { publisher: Mono<Void> ->
                StepVerifier.create(
                    publisher
                )
            }
            .expectNextCount(0)
            .verifyComplete()
    }
}
```

Note that the test methods are written following the functional programming paradigm as well. Each statement declares the operation to be performed on the emitted data when it is emitted. The most important method here is verifyComplete(), which triggers the verification, expecting a completion signal as a terminal event.

The log() method was added to observe all Reactive Streams signals and trace them using a configured logging library, in this case Logback. When this test class is run, the tests should pass, and the console log, shown in Listing 20-9, might look verbose, but it makes it quite obvious that the SingerRepo and the R2DBC driver are indeed working together and communicating reactively.

Listing 20-9. Reactive Repository Test Class Console Log

```
INFO 14470 --- [    Test worker] c.a.p.twenty.boot.RepositoryTest        : Starting
RepositoryTest using Java 19.0.2 with PID 14470
INFO 14470 --- [    Test worker] .s.d.r.c.RepositoryConfigurationDelegate : Bootstrapping
Spring Data R2DBC repositories in DEFAULT mode.
INFO 14470 --- [    Test worker] .s.d.r.c.RepositoryConfigurationDelegate : Finished Spring
Data repository scanning in 130 ms. Found 1 R2DBC repository interfaces.
INFO 14470 --- [    Test worker] c.a.p.twenty.boot.RepositoryTest        : Started
RepositoryTest in 1.385 seconds (process running for 10.938)
INFO 14470 --- [    Test worker] reactor.Mono.UsingWhen.1                 :
onSubscribe(MonoUsingWhen.MonoUsingWhenSubscriber)
INFO 14470 --- [    Test worker] reactor.Mono.UsingWhen.1                 :
request(unbounded)
INFO 14470 --- [actor-tcp-nio-2] reactor.Mono.UsingWhen.1                 : onNext(4)
INFO 14470 --- [actor-tcp-nio-2] reactor.Mono.UsingWhen.1                 : onComplete()

INFO 14470 --- [    Test worker] reactor.Flux.UsingWhen.2                 :
onSubscribe(FluxUsingWhen.UsingWhenSubscriber)
INFO 14470 --- [    Test worker] reactor.Flux.UsingWhen.2                 :
request(unbounded)
INFO 14470 --- [actor-tcp-nio-2] reactor.Flux.UsingWhen.2                 :
onNext(Singer(id=3, firstName=John, lastName=Butler, birthDate=1975-04-01))
INFO 14470 --- [actor-tcp-nio-2] reactor.Flux.UsingWhen.2                 :
onNext(Singer(id=1, firstName=John, lastName=Mayer, birthDate=1977-10-16))
INFO 14470 --- [actor-tcp-nio-2] reactor.Flux.UsingWhen.2                 : onComplete()

INFO 14470 --- [    Test worker] reactor.Mono.Next.3                      :
onSubscribe(MonoNext.NextSubscriber)
INFO 14470 --- [    Test worker] reactor.Mono.Next.3                      :
request(unbounded)
INFO 14470 --- [actor-tcp-nio-2] reactor.Mono.Next.3                      :
onNext(Singer(id=1, firstName=John, lastName=Mayer, birthDate=1977-10-16))
INFO 14470 --- [actor-tcp-nio-2] reactor.Mono.Next.3                      : onComplete()

INFO 14470 --- [    Test worker] reactor.Mono.UsingWhen.4                 :
onSubscribe(MonoUsingWhen.MonoUsingWhenSubscriber)
INFO 14470 --- [    Test worker] reactor.Mono.UsingWhen.4                 :
request(unbounded)
INFO 14470 --- [actor-tcp-nio-2] reactor.Mono.UsingWhen.4                 :
onNext(Singer(id=5, firstName=Test, lastName=Test, birthDate=2023-04-15))
INFO 14470 --- [actor-tcp-nio-2] reactor.Mono.UsingWhen.4                 : onComplete()
```

```
INFO 14470 --- [    Test worker] reactor.Mono.UsingWhen.5            :
onSubscribe(MonoUsingWhen.MonoUsingWhenSubscriber)
INFO 14470 --- [    Test worker] reactor.Mono.UsingWhen.5            :
request(unbounded)
INFO 14470 --- [actor-tcp-nio-2] reactor.Mono.UsingWhen.5            : onComplete()
```

This console log shows the thread identifiers and makes it quite obvious that repository operations are executed on a different thread, as expected for a reactive component.

All of that is well and good, but can we check erroneous behavior? How can we check that a Singer object without a lastName cannot be saved in the table? Technically, this should never happen because we expect Spring validation to prevent such an object from being passed as an argument to the repository bean, but just as an example, let's do it. StepVerifier provides a few methods for that: the verifyError*() family allows a developer to check if an operation completed with an error and what the characteristics of that error are. For example, in Listing 20-10, we check that trying to save a Singer object without a lastName fails and a TransientDataAccessResourceException is thrown.

Listing 20-10. Check Failed Executions

```
import org.springframework.dao.TransientDataAccessResourceException
...


@Test // negative test, lastName is null, which is not allowed
fun testFailedCreateSinger() {
    singerRepo!!.save(
        Singer().apply {
            firstName = "Test"
            birthDate = LocalDate.now()
        }
    )
        .log()
        .`as`{ publisher: Mono<Singer> ->
            StepVerifier.create(
                publisher
            )
        }
        .verifyError(TransientDataAccessResourceException::class.java)
}
```

Now that we have a reactive data repository, we can use it to build a reactive service.

Reactive Services

A reactive service class is nothing special in this scenario; it just forwards returned objects from a reactive repository and replaces lower-level data processing exceptions with exceptions to service-level scoped exceptions. In a real implementation, a service method might apply more transformations to the data returned by the repository methods by adding its own processor functions, as shown in the beginning of this chapter.

Listing 20-11 shows the SingerService interface, the template for our reactive service.

Listing 20-11. SingerService Interface Describing the Template for a Reactive Service Class

```
package com.apress.prospring6.twenty.boot.service
// import statements omitted

interface SingerService {
    fun findAll(): Flux<Singer>
    fun findById(id: Long): Mono<Singer>
    fun findByFirstNameAndLastName(firstName: String, lastName: String): Mono<Singer>
    fun findByFirstName(firstName: String): Flux<Singer>
    fun findByCriteriaDto(criteria: CriteriaDto): Flux<Singer>
    fun save(singer: Singer): Mono<Singer>
    fun update(id: Long, updateData: Singer): Mono<Singer>
    fun delete(id: Long): Mono<Void>
}
```

Note that all methods return reactive types, which is what makes it truly a reactive service capable of interacting with a reactive repository and a reactive controller without hindering the data flow.

The SingerServiceImpl class, implementing this interface, is shown in Listing 20-12.

Listing 20-12. SingerServiceImpl Reactive Service Class and Bean Definition

```
package com.apress.prospring6.twenty.boot.service
// import statements omitted

import java.time.LocalDate
import java.time.format.DateTimeFormatter

@Transactional
@Service
open class SingerServiceImpl : SingerService {
    private val singerRepo: SingerRepo? = null

    override fun findAll(): Flux<Singer> {
        return singerRepo!!.findAll()
    }

    override fun findByCriteriaDto(criteria: SingerService.CriteriaDto): Flux<Singer> {
        val fieldName = SingerService.FieldGroup.getField(criteria.fieldName!!.uppercase())
        return when (fieldName) {
            SingerService.FieldGroup.FIRSTNAME -> if ("*" == criteria.fieldValue)
            singerRepo!!.findAll() else singerRepo!!.findByFirstName(
                criteria.fieldValue!!
            )

            SingerService.FieldGroup.LASTNAME -> if ("*" == criteria.fieldValue)
            singerRepo!!.findAll() else singerRepo!!.findByLastName(
                criteria.fieldValue!!
            )

            SingerService.FieldGroup.BIRTHDATE -> if ("*" == criteria.fieldValue)
            singerRepo!!.findAll() else singerRepo!!.findByBirthDate(
```

```kotlin
                LocalDate.parse(criteria.fieldValue!!, DateTimeFormatter.
                ofPattern("yyyy-MM-dd"))
            )
        }
    }

    override fun findByFirstNameAndLastName(firstName: String, lastName: String):
    Mono<Singer> {
        return singerRepo!!.findByFirstNameAndLastName(firstName, lastName)
    }

    override fun findById(id: Long): Mono<Singer> {
        return singerRepo!!.findById(id)
    }

    override fun findByFirstName(firstName: String): Flux<Singer> {
        return singerRepo!!.findByFirstName(firstName)
    }

    override fun save(singer: Singer): Mono<Singer> {
        return singerRepo!!.save(singer)
            .onErrorMap { error: Throwable ->
                SaveException(
                    "Could Not Save Singer $singer",
                    error
                )
            }
    }

    override fun update(id: Long, updateData: Singer): Mono<Singer> {
        return singerRepo!!.findById(id)
            .flatMap<Singer>{ original: Singer ->
                original.firstName = updateData.firstName
                original.lastName = updateData.lastName
                original.birthDate = updateData.birthDate
                singerRepo.save(original)
                    .onErrorMap { error: Throwable? ->
                        SaveException(
                            "Could Not Update Singer $updateData",
                            error
                        )
                    }
            }
    }

    override fun delete(id: Long): Mono<Void> {
        return singerRepo!!.deleteById(id)
    }
}
```

The SingerServiceImpl class is pretty simple, having little logic of its own, mostly surrounding the search function and the Singer object update.

SaveException is just a simple class extending RuntimeException that wraps around the Spring Data exceptions to provide more information about the context in which the exception was produced.

The other thing to note here is that this service is transactional. Therefore, how do transactions work in a reactive application? They work pretty much the same as in an imperative application, but the functionality is based on different components.

Transactions in a reactive application have the same purpose as in an imperative application: to group multiple database operations in a single multistep operation that succeeds only if all the steps do; otherwise, any successful steps prior to the failed step get rolled back. In Spring applications, iterative and reactive transaction management is enabled by a PlatformTransactionManager that manages transactions for transactional resources, and resources are marked as transactional by annotating them with Spring's @Transactional from package org.springframework.transaction.annotation. At a lower level, though, things are a bit different.

Transaction management needs to associate its transactional state with an execution. In imperative programming, this is typically java.lang.ThreadLocal storage, so the transactional state is bound to a Thread in which the Spring container started to execute the code. In a reactive application, this does not apply because reactive execution requires multiple threads. The solution was to introduce a reactive alternative to ThreadLocal storage and this Reactor's reactor.util.context.Context typed contexts allow binding contextual data to a particular execution, and for reactive programming, this is a Subscription object. Project Reactor's Context interface lets Spring bind the transaction state, along with all resources and synchronizations, to a particular Subscription. All reactive code that uses Project Reactor can now participate in reactive transactions.

Starting with Spring Framework 5.2 M2, Spring supports reactive transaction management through the ReactiveTransactionManager SPI. The org.springframework.transaction.ReactiveTransactionManager is a transaction management abstraction for reactive and non-blocking integrations that uses transactional resources. It is a foundation for reactive @Transactional methods that return Publisher<T> types and for programmatic transaction management that uses TransactionalOperator. Spring Data R2DBC provides the R2dbcTransactionManager in the org.springframework.r2dbc.connection package that implements ReactiveTransactionManager.

Figure 20-4 shows the imperative and reactive hierarchies of interfaces and classes of org.springframework.transaction.TransactionManager.

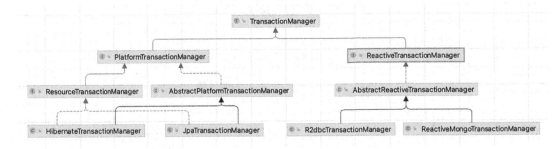

Figure 20-4. *TransactionManager imperative and reactive hierarchy, side by side*

In Figure 20-4, ReactiveMongoTransactionManager is included as well because the pro-spring-6 project has spring-data-mongodb in the classpath. This class is the reactive transaction manager for MongoDB and manages transactions so that code executed within a managed transaction participates in multi-document transactions.

The R2dbcTransactionManager wraps around a reactive connection to the database to perform its job, and this connection is provided by the R2DBC driver. In a Spring Boot application, the configuration is fairly simple, as shown in Listing 20-13.

Listing 20-13. Configuring an R2dbcTransactionManager

```
package com.apress.prospring6.twenty.boot

import io.r2dbc.spi.ConnectionFactory
import org.springframework.r2dbc.connection.R2dbcTransactionManager
import org.springframework.transaction.ReactiveTransactionManager
import org.springframework.transaction.annotation.EnableTransactionManagement
// other import statements omitted

@EnableTransactionManagement
@SpringBootApplication
open class Chapter20Application {
    @Bean
    open fun transactionManager(connectionFactory: ConnectionFactory):
    ReactiveTransactionManager {
        return R2dbcTransactionManager(connectionFactory)
    }

    companion object {
        val LOGGER = LoggerFactory.getLogger(Chapter20Application::class.java)
        @JvmStatic
        fun main(args: Array<String>) {
            System.setProperty(AbstractEnvironment.ACTIVE_PROFILES_PROPERTY_NAME,
                "dev")
            SpringApplication.run(Chapter20Application::class.java, *args)
        }
    }
}
```

Two things need to be clarified about the sample in Listing 20-13:

- The @EnableTransactionManagement annotation is needed to enable Spring's annotation-driven transaction management capability, meaning support for @Transactional annotations.

- The ConnectionFactory bean is not declared explicitly. Spring Boot creates this bean from the configuration in the application.yaml (or the equivalent application. properties) and injects it wherever needed, in this case in our reactive transaction management bean. (The Spring Boot configuration was already introduced in Listing 20-6.)

Although slightly repetitive, we can also write some tests for SingerServiceImpl. All we have to do is to add this bean to the test context. Listing 20-14 shows a few test methods for SingerServiceImpl.

Listing 20-14. Testing the SingerServiceImpl Reactive Service Class

```kotlin
package com.apress.prospring6.twenty.boot.service
// import statements omitted

@DataR2dbcTest
@TestMethodOrder(MethodOrderer.OrderAnnotation::class)
@Import(
    SingerServiceImpl::class
)
class SingerServiceTest : ReactiveDbConfigTests() {
    @Autowired
    var singerService: SingerService? = null

    @Order(2)
    @Test
    fun testFindAll() {
        singerService!!.findAll()
            .log()
            .`as`<FirstStep<Singer>> { publisher: Flux<Singer> ->
                StepVerifier.create(
                    publisher
                )
            }
            .expectNextCount(4)
            .verifyComplete()
    }

    @Order(3)
    @Test
    fun testFindById() {
        singerService!!.findById(1L)
            .log()
            .`as`<FirstStep<Singer>> { publisher: Mono<Singer> ->
                StepVerifier.create(
                    publisher
                )
            }
            .expectNextMatches { s: Singer -> "John" == s.firstName &&
                "Mayer" == s.lastName }
            .verifyComplete()
    }

    @Order(8)
    @Test
    fun testNoCreateSinger() {
        singerService!!.save(
            Singer().apply {
                firstName = "John"
                lastName = "Mayer"
                birthDate = LocalDate.now()
            }
```

```kotlin
    )
        .log()
        .`as`<FirstStep<Singer>> { publisher: Mono<Singer> ->
            StepVerifier.create(
                publisher
            )
        }
        .verifyError(SaveException::class.java)
}

@Order(9)
@Test
fun testUpdateSinger() {
    singerService!!.update(
        4L,
            Singer().apply {
                firstName = "Erik Patrick"
                lastName = "Clapton"
                birthDate = LocalDate.now()
            }
        )
        .log()
        .`as`<FirstStep<Singer>> { publisher: Mono<Singer> ->
            StepVerifier.create(
                publisher
            )
        }
        .expectNext(
            Singer().apply {
                id = 4L
                firstName = "Erik Patrick"
                lastName = "Clapton"
                birthDate = LocalDate.now()
            }
        )
        .verifyComplete()
}

@Order(10)
@Test
fun testUpdateSingerWithDuplicateData() {
    singerService!!.update(
        4L,
        Singer().apply {
            firstName = "John"
            lastName = "Mayer"
            birthDate = LocalDate.now()
        }
    )
        .log()
        .`as`<FirstStep<Singer>> { publisher: Mono<Singer> ->
```

```kotlin
                StepVerifier.create(
                    publisher
                )
            }
            .verifyError(SaveException::class.java)
    }

    @Order(11)
    @Test // negative test, lastName is null, which is not allowed
    fun testFailedCreateSinger() {
        singerService!!.update(
            4L,
            Singer().apply {
                firstName = "Test"
                birthDate = LocalDate.now()
            }
        )
            .log()
            .`as`<FirstStep<Singer>> { publisher: Mono<Singer> ->
                StepVerifier.create(
                    publisher
                )
            }
            .verifyError(SaveException::class.java)
    }

    @Order(12)
    @Test
    fun testDeleteSinger() {
        singerService!!.delete(4L)
            .log()
            .`as`<FirstStep<Void>> { publisher: Mono<Void> ->
                StepVerifier.create(
                    publisher
                )
            }
            .expectNextCount(0)
            .verifyComplete()
    }

// some test methods omitted
}
```

Listing 20-14 also shows the tests that check service-level exceptions being thrown instead of the Spring Data exceptions. The type of underlying exception is shown in the comments.

For all these situations, we chose to use onErrorMap(..) to transform the exception into something more useful. However, Project Reactor provides six methods to handle errors on its reactive types (Mono<T>, Flux<T>), which are listed and explained here:

- onErrorReturn(..): Declares a default value to be emitted in case an exception is thrown in the processor. This method does not hinder the data flow in any way; when processing a troublesome element, the default value is emitted, and the rest of the elements in the flow will be processed normally. There are three versions of this method:

  - One that takes as a parameter the value to be returned

  - One that takes as parameters the value to be returned and the type of exception for which the default value should be returned

  - One that takes as parameters the value to be returned and a predicate for the exception to match for the default value to be returned

- onErrorResume():Declares a default function to use to choose a fallback Publisher<T> in case an exception is thrown in the processor. It also comes with the same three flavors as described for onErrorReturn(..). For troublesome elements, the chosen Publisher<T> is used to emit a value, and the rest of the elements in the flow will be processed normally.

- onErrorContinue(..): Declares a consumer to be used in case an exception is thrown in the processor. This method also comes in three flavors, the same as described for onErrorReturn(..), but instead of returning a value, the consumer is executed. It processes the troublesome elements using the declared consumer and leaves the downstream chain as it is for good elements.

- doOnError(..): Consumes error and stops execution for further elements in the stream. It also comes in the same three flavors as described for onErrorReturn(..), but after the consumer is executed, the error is propagated and executed for further elements in the stream.

- onErrorMap(..): Casts one error into another and stops execution for further elements in the stream.

Since the test context does not have a transaction manager, tests are not transactional. Having a few service tests passing is proof that the reactive service layer works as well, so we can now continue the implementation by adding reactive controllers.

Reactive Controllers

As mentioned previously, a reactive controller is simply a controller that contains handler methods that return Flux<T> and Mono<T>. This makes sense for REST controllers because for a controller returning a logical view, name reactivity makes no sense truly, nor adds any benefits. That being said, take a look at Listing 20-15, which shows a REST controller for managing Singer instances.

Listing 20-15. The ReactiveSingerController Class

```
package com.apress.prospring6.twenty.boot.controller

import org.springframework.http.HttpStatus
import org.springframework.http.ResponseEntity
```

```kotlin
import reactor.core.publisher.Flux
import reactor.core.publisher.Mono
// other import statements omitted

@RestController
@RequestMapping(path = ["/reactive/singer"])
class ReactiveSingerController {
    lateinit var singerService: SingerService

    /* 1 */
    @GetMapping(path = ["", "/"])
    fun list(): Flux<Singer> {
        return singerService.findAll()
    }

    /* 3 */
    @GetMapping(path = ["/{id}"])
    fun findById(@PathVariable id: Long): Mono<ResponseEntity<Singer>> {
        return singerService.findById(id)
            .map { s -> ResponseEntity.ok().body(s) }
            .defaultIfEmpty(ResponseEntity.notFound().build())
    }

    /* 4 */
    @PostMapping
    @ResponseStatus(HttpStatus.CREATED)
    fun create(@RequestBody singer: Singer): Mono<Singer> {
        return singerService.save(singer)
    }

    /* 5 */
    @PutMapping("/{id}")
    fun updateById(@PathVariable id: Long, @RequestBody singer: Singer):
    Mono<ResponseEntity<Singer>> {
        return singerService.update(id, singer)
            .map { s -> ResponseEntity.ok().body(s) }
            .defaultIfEmpty(ResponseEntity.badRequest().build())
    }

    /* 2 */
    @DeleteMapping("/{id}")
    fun deleteById(@PathVariable id: Long): Mono<ResponseEntity<Void>> {
        return singerService.delete(id)
            .then(Mono.fromCallable {
                ResponseEntity.noContent().build<Void>()
            })
            .defaultIfEmpty(ResponseEntity.notFound().build())
    }
```

```
/* 6 */
@GetMapping(params = ["name"])
fun searchSingers(@RequestParam("name") name: String): Flux<Singer> {
    if (name.isBlank()) {
        throw IllegalArgumentException("Missing request parameter 'name'");
    }
    return singerService.findByFirstName(name)
}

/* 7 */
@GetMapping(params = ["fn", "ln"])
fun searchSinger(@RequestParam("fn") fn: String, @RequestParam("ln") ln: String):
Mono<Singer> {
    if (fn.isBlank()) {
        throw IllegalArgumentException("Missing request parameter 'fn'");
    }
    if (ln.isBlank()) {
        throw IllegalArgumentException("Missing request parameter 'ln'");
    }
    return singerService.findByFirstNameAndLastName(fn, ln)
}
}
```

Except for the returned types, which are necessary because the reactive SingerService is used, there is nothing special about this controller. When you start the application and test the reactive/singer endpoints using a client such as curl, Postman, or HttpIE or a browser (for the GET endpoints), you will notice that this controller does not behave in any way different from a non-reactive controller. This is because neither of these is a reactive client, but this academic example is too small and simple to actually notice anything.

 You can try to generate random data (a lot of it) to fill the SINGER table and then try to access the /reactive/singer endpoint to notice the data flow.

Therefore, there is not much that we can use this controller for right now, and that is okay. The reason this controller was introduced first is because the intention is to rewrite it using handler functions, one of the fancy features introduced by Spring WebFlow. You probably noticed in Listing 20-15 the comment with a number attached to each method. Those comments are included to make it easy to look up the handler function equivalent (in Listing 20-17).

Handler Classes and Functional Endpoints

A handler class is just a logical way of grouping handler functions. A handler function must implement the HandlerFunction[29] functional interface and provide an implementation for its handle(..) method that takes an org.springframework.web.reactive.function.server.ServerRequest argument and returns a Mono<org.springframework.web.reactive.function.server.ServerResponse>.

---

[29] https://github.com/spring-projects/spring-framework/blob/main/spring-webflux/src/main/java/org/springframework/web/reactive/function/server/HandlerFunction.java

Listing 20-16 shows its code.

Listing 20-16. The HandlerFunction Class

```
package org.springframework.web.reactive.function.server;

import reactor.core.publisher.Mono;

@FunctionalInterface
public interface HandlerFunction<T extends ServerResponse> {

    Mono<T> handle(ServerRequest request);

}
```

An implementation of HandlerFunction<T> represents a function that handles a request, and it can be mapped to the request path via a RouterFunction.

ℹ️ The version shown in Listing 20-16 is the reactive version, introduced as part of Spring WebFlux in version 5.0. The same goes for RouterFunction. In Spring MVC version 5.2, non-reactive versions were added in package org.springframework.web.servlet.function as a functional alternative to controllers. The syntax is more declarative and the request mapping is centralized in a single bean, making the configuration easier to read.

Let's make use of this new declarative syntax and write some code that declares handler functions instead of handler methods for requests. Listing 20-17 shows the SingerHandler class that groups all the handler functions analogous to the ones in the ReactiveSingerController class introduced in the previous section.

Listing 20-17. The SingerHandler Class

```
package com.apress.prospring6.twenty.boot.handler

import org.springframework.http.MediaType
import org.springframework.web.reactive.function.server.HandlerFunction
import org.springframework.web.reactive.function.server.ServerRequest
import org.springframework.web.reactive.function.server.ServerResponse
import java.net.URI
import org.springframework.web.reactive.function.server.ServerResponse.*
// other import statements omitted

@Component
class SingerHandler(private val singerService: SingerService) {
    /* 1 */
    var list: HandlerFunction<ServerResponse> = HandlerFunction<ServerResponse> {
    serverRequest: ServerRequest? ->
        ServerResponse.ok()
            .contentType(MediaType.APPLICATION_JSON)
            .body(singerService.findAll(), Singer::class.java)
    }
```

```kotlin
/* 2 */
var deleteById: HandlerFunction<ServerResponse> = HandlerFunction<ServerResponse> {
serverRequest: ServerRequest ->
    ServerResponse.noContent()
        .build(singerService.delete(serverRequest.pathVariable("id").toLong()))
}


/* 3 */
fun findById(serverRequest: ServerRequest): Mono<ServerResponse> {
    val id = serverRequest.pathVariable("id").toLong()
    return singerService.findById(id)
        .flatMap { singer ->
            ServerResponse.ok()
                .contentType(MediaType.APPLICATION_JSON).bodyValue(singer)
        }
        .switchIfEmpty(ServerResponse.notFound().build())
}


/* 4 */
fun create(serverRequest: ServerRequest): Mono<ServerResponse> {
    val singerMono = serverRequest.bodyToMono(
        Singer::class.java
    )
    return singerMono
        .flatMap<Any>(singerService::save)
        .log()
        .flatMap<ServerResponse> { s: Any ->
            ServerResponse.created(URI.create("/singer/" + (s as Singer).id))
                .contentType(MediaType.APPLICATION_JSON).bodyValue(s)
        }
    // .switchIfEmpty(status(HttpStatus.INTERNAL_SERVER_ERROR).build());
}


/* 5 */
fun updateById(serverRequest: ServerRequest): Mono<ServerResponse> {
    val id = serverRequest.pathVariable("id").toLong()
    return singerService.findById(id)
        .flatMap { fromDb ->
            serverRequest.bodyToMono<Singer>(Singer::class.java)
                .flatMap { s: Singer? ->
                    ServerResponse.ok()
                        .contentType(MediaType.APPLICATION_JSON)
                        .body(
                            singerService.update(id, s as Singer),
                            Singer::class.java
                        )
                }
        } // we switch to 400 because this is an invalid put request
        .switchIfEmpty(ServerResponse.badRequest().bodyValue("Failure to update
        singer!"))
    // we can put anything in the ServerResponse including an exception
```

```kotlin
    //) .switchIfEmpty(badRequest().bodyValue(new NotFoundException(String.class, id)));
}


/* 6 */
fun searchSingers(serverRequest: ServerRequest): Mono<ServerResponse> {
    val name = serverRequest.queryParam("name").orElse(null)
    return if (name.isBlank()) {
        // parameter is an empty string
        // return badRequest().bodyValue(new IllegalArgumentException("Missing request
        parameter 'name'"));
        ServerResponse.badRequest().bodyValue("Missing request parameter 'name'")
    } else ServerResponse.ok()
        .contentType(MediaType.APPLICATION_JSON).body(singerService.
        findByFirstName(name), Singer::class.java)
}


/* 7 */
fun searchSinger(serverRequest: ServerRequest): Mono<ServerResponse> {
    val fn = serverRequest.queryParam("fn").orElse(null)
    val ln = serverRequest.queryParam("ln").orElse(null)
    return if (fn == null || ln == null || fn.isBlank() || ln.isBlank()) {
        // one of {fn, ln} (or both) parameter is an empty string
        // return badRequest().bodyValue(new IllegalArgumentException("Missing request
        parameter, one of {fn, ln}"));
        ServerResponse.badRequest().bodyValue("Missing request parameter, one of
        {fn, ln}")
    } else singerService.findByFirstNameAndLastName(fn, ln)
        .flatMap { singer ->
            ServerResponse.ok()
                .contentType(MediaType.APPLICATION_JSON).bodyValue(singer)
        }
}


fun search(serverRequest: ServerRequest): Mono<ServerResponse> {
    val criteriaMono = serverRequest.bodyToMono(
        SingerService.CriteriaDto::class.java
    )
    return criteriaMono.log()
        .flatMap<SingerService.CriteriaDto?> { criteria: SingerService.CriteriaDto ->
            validate(
                criteria
            )
        }
        .flatMap { criteria: SingerService.CriteriaDto ->
            ServerResponse.ok()
                .contentType(MediaType.APPLICATION_JSON)
                .body(
                    singerService.findByCriteriaDto(criteria),
                    Singer::class.java
                )
        }
}
```

```kotlin
    private fun validate(criteria: SingerService.CriteriaDto): Mono<SingerService.
CriteriaDto?> {
        val validator = SingerService.CriteriaValidator()
        val errors = BeanPropertyBindingResult(criteria, "criteria")
        validator.validate(criteria, errors)
        if (errors.hasErrors()) {
            // throw new ServerWebInputException(errors.toString());
            throw MissingValueException.of(errors.allErrors)
        }
        return Mono.just(criteria)
    }

    fun searchView(request: ServerRequest?): Mono<ServerResponse> {
        return ServerResponse
            .ok()
            .contentType(MediaType.TEXT_HTML)
            .render("singers/search", SingerService.CriteriaDto())
    }
}
```

A bean of type SingerHandler is declared and is part of the Spring WebFlux application configuration, and its methods are used as handler functions for requests managing Singer instances.

The Listing 20-17 comments with numbers that mark the functions make it easy to identify the equivalent handler methods in ReactiveSingerController (Listing 20-15) but are also useful as pointers to explain the following particularities of each function:

1. list: A simple handler function that returns all the Singer objects instances retrieved by invoking singerService.findAll(). It is declared as a field of type HandlerFunction<ServerResponse> and it is a member of the SingerHandler class. It cannot be declared and initialized in the same line because of its dependency on singerService. To initialize this field, the singerService field must be initialized first. Since it is initialized in the constructor, the initialization of the list field is also part of the constructor. The initial ServerResponse. ok() sets the HTTP response status to 200 (OK), and it returns a reference to the internal BodyBuilder that allows for other methods to be chained to describe the request. The chain must end with one of the body*(..) methods that returns a Mono<ServerResponse>.

2. deleteById: A simple handler function that deletes a Singer instance with the ID matching the path variable. The path variable is extracted by calling serverRequest.pathVariable("id"). The ID argument represents the name of the path variable. The singerService.delete() method returns Mono<Void>, so Mono<ServerResponse> actually emits a response with an empty body and 204 (no content) status code set by ServerResponse.noContent().

3. findById: A handler function that returns a single Singer instance identified by the id path variable. The instance is retrieved by calling singerService. findById(..) that returns a Mono<Singer>. If this stream emits a value, this means a singer was found matching the path variable, and a response is created with the 200 (OK) status code and a body represented by the Singer instance as JSON. To access the Singer instance, emitted by the stream without blocking, the flatMap(..) function is used. If the stream does not emit a value, this means

a singer with the expected ID was not found, so an empty response is created with the status 404 (Not Found) by calling switchIfEmpty(ServerResponse.notFound().build()).

4. create: A handler function for creating a new Singer instance. The Singer instance is extracted from the request body. The request body is read as a Mono<Singer> by calling serverRequest.bodyToMono(String.class). The flatMap(singerService::save) stream emits a value when a successful save is executed, and the response is populated with a Location header pointing to the URL when the created resource can be accessed and the 201 (Created) response status gets returned. If the stream does not emit a value, this means the save operation failed, and there is an option to configure the desired response status by adding something such as.switchIfEmpty(status(HttpStatus.INTERNAL_SERVER_ERROR).build()) to this processing chain. However, we declared our SingerService to throw a SavingException when saving a Singer instance fails, and thus this no longer applies because the error handler will take care of it.

5. updateById: A handler function for updating a Singer instance. It is mentioned here just to point out that the switchIfEmpty(..) method can build a response with a custom body as well, not just a response status, and this method shows an example where the body is the "Failure to update singer!" text. The body can be any type of object, including the exception object being emitted by the singerService.update(..) method.

6. searchSingers: A handler function that handles a request with a parameter named name. Its value is extracted by calling serverRequest.queryParam("name").

Now that we have our handler functions, the next step is to map them to requests. This is done via a RouterFunction bean. This bean can be declared in any configuration class. The org.springframework.web.reactive.function.server.RouterFunction<T>[30] is a simple functional interface describing a function that routes incoming requests to HandlerFunction<T> instances. Its code is shown in Listing 20-18.

Listing 20-18. The RouterFunction Functional Interface

```
package org.springframework.web.reactive.function.server;
// import statements omitted

@FunctionalInterface
public interface RouterFunction<T extends ServerResponse> {

    Mono<HandlerFunction<T>> route(ServerRequest request);

    // default methods omitted
}
```

The route(..) method returns the handler function matching the request provided as an argument. If a handler function is not found, it returns an empty Mono<Void>. The RouterFunction<T> has a similar purpose as the @RequestMapping annotation in controller classes.

---

[30] https://github.com/spring-projects/spring-framework/blob/main/spring-webflux/src/main/java/org/springframework/web/reactive/function/server/RouterFunction.java

Composing a RouterFunction<T> for a Spring application is easy by using the builder methods in the org.springframework.web.reactive.function.server.RouterFunctions class. This class provides static methods for building simple and nested routing functions and can even transform a RouterFunction<T> into a HttpHandler, which makes the application run in a Servlet 3.1+ container. Before discussing routing functions any further, let's first see the configuration for handler functions in SingerHandler, shown in Listing 20-19.

Listing 20-19. The RoutesConfig Class Declaring the Routing Configuration Bean for the Handler Functions in SingerHandler

```
package com.apress.prospring6.twenty.boot

import org.springframework.web.reactive.function.server.RequestPredicates
import org.springframework.web.reactive.function.server.RouterFunction
import org.springframework.web.reactive.function.server.ServerResponse

import org.springframework.web.reactive.function.server.RequestPredicates.queryParam
import org.springframework.web.reactive.function.server.RouterFunctions.route

@Configuration
open class RoutesConfig {
    @Bean
    open fun staticRouter():RouterFunction<ServerResponse> {
        return resources("/images/**", ClassPathResource("static/images/"))
                .and(resources("/styles/**", ClassPathResource("static/styles/")))
                .and(resources("/js/**", ClassPathResource("static/js/")));
    }

    @Bean
    open fun singerRoutes( homeHandler:HomeHandler,
            singerHandler:SingerHandler):RouterFunction<ServerResponse> {
        return route()
                // returns home view template
                .GET("/", homeHandler::view)
                .GET("/home", homeHandler::view)
                .GET("/singers/search", singerHandler::searchView)
                .POST("/singers/go", singerHandler::search)
                // these need to be here, otherwise parameters will not be considered
                .GET("/handler/singer", queryParam("name", { _ -> true}),
                    singerHandler::searchSingers)
                .GET("/handler/singer", RequestPredicates.all()
                        .and(queryParam("fn", { _ -> true}))
                        .and(queryParam("ln", { _ -> true})), singerHandler::searchSinger)
                // requests with parameters always come first
                .GET("/handler/singer", singerHandler.list)
                .POST("/handler/singer", singerHandler::create)
                .GET("/handler/singer/{id}", singerHandler::findById)
                .PUT("/handler/singer/{id}", singerHandler::updateById)
                .DELETE("/handler/singer/{id}", singerHandler.deleteById)
                .filter { request, next ->
```

```
                LOGGER.info("Before handler invocation: {}", request.path())
                return@filter next.handle(request)
            }
        .build()
    }
    ...
    companion object {
        val LOGGER = LoggerFactory.getLogger(RoutesConfig::class.java)
    }
}
```

The singerRoutes bean is a router function used to route incoming requests to the handler functions declared in the SingerHandler bean introduced previously.

In Listing 20-19, each handler function corresponds to a handler function in SingerHandler. The route() method in RouterFunctionBuilder is further used to add router mappings via methods specific to HTTP methods, paths, and request parameters.

The following list discusses some of the lines:

- GET("/handler/singer", singerHandler.list): GET(..) is a static method from the abstract utility class org.springframework.web.reactive.function.server. RequestPredicates used here to create a route that maps GET requests to the / handler/singer URL with the singerHandler.list function.

- DELETE("/handler/singer/{id}", singerHandler.deleteById): DELETE(..) is a static method from the utility class RequestPredicates that creates a route that maps DELETE requests to the /handler/singer/{id} URL, where id is the name of the path variable to the singerHandler.deleteById function.

- GET("/handler/singer/{id}", singerHandler::findById): Maps GET requests to /handler/singer/{id} to singerHandler.findById.

- POST("/handler/singer", singerHandler::create): POST() is a static method from the utility class RequestPredicates that creates a route that maps POST requests to the /handler/singer URL to the singerHandler.create function.

- PUT("/handler/singer/{id}", singerHandler::updateById): PUT() is a static method from the utility class RequestPredicates that creates a route that maps PUT requests to the /handler/singer/{id} URL to the singerHandler.updateById function.

- GET("/handler/singer", queryParam("name", t -> true), singerHandler::searchSingers): Maps GET methods to the /handler/ singer?name=${val} to the singerHandler.searchSingers function. The parameters are declared via the RequestPredicates.queryParam(..) utility method, which basically returns a RequestPredicate that returns true if the parameter is part of the URL

The filter(..) statement declared a function that filters all requests. This statement in this example just prints a simple log, but it can be used to inspect any kind of cross-cutting concerns, such as logging, security, and so forth.

The build() method is called to construct the RouterFunction<ServerResponse> bean.

With this configuration in place, now we have a singer API available under /handler/singer URL. When you start the application and test the /handler/singer endpoints using a client like curl, Postman, or HTTPie or a browser (for the GET endpoints), you'll notice that all works well and the behavior is the same as the one implemented by the ReactiveSingerController.

❗ Routes for requests that have parameters need to be specified first in the builder, or at least before the routes based on the same path, but with no parameters. The request is checked against the existing routes of the router function in the order they were declared. Thus, a request to URL "/handler/singers?name=John" matches the first mapping to the "/handler/singers" found in the list. This is because the existence of the parameters is checked only after a route is found, since request parameters are optional and not part of the route. Therefore, a GET request to "/handler/singers" will first be matched against the first GET "/handler/singers" route, the existence of the name parameter is checked. If not found the conclusion is that this is not a match, and so the next GET "/handler/singers" in the list is checked for a match. But if neither fn nor ln parameters are found, thus this is not a match either, and so the next one in the list is checked. If this route has no parameters, the singerHandler.list finally gets invoked.

Reactive Error Handling

In the earlier "Reactive Services" section, we modified the save(..) and update(..) methods to emit exception messages of type SavingException. When a handler function or reactive handler method invokes one of these methods and the unexpected happens, the exception has to be handled. This allows developers to log the exception and save the context in which it was thrown and decide the HTTP status code. For reactive controllers, a class annotated with @RestControllerAdvice gets the job done, but for handler functions, we need something else, something more functional. We need a WebExceptionHandler bean. Fortunately, this bean works for reactive controllers too.

Spring Boot autoconfigures a default WebExceptionHandler bean of type DefaultErrorWebExceptionHandler. Figure 20-5 depicts the WebExceptionHandler hierarchy.

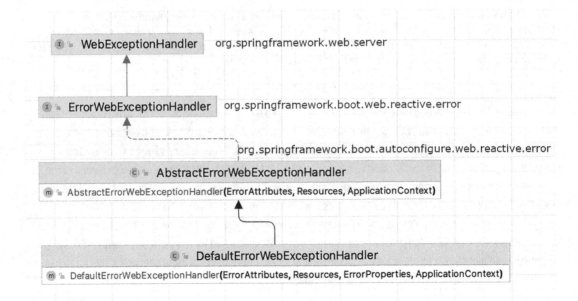

Figure 20-5. *WebExceptionHandler hierarchy*

The response returned by this bean is a generic JSON representation object that contains the 400(Bad Request) HTTP status code, the URI path, and an alphanumeric request identifier. If we want to customize the behavior, we need to declare our own WebExceptionHandler bean.

Listing 20-20 depicts a very simple version of the custom WebExceptionHandler bean that is added to the RoutingConfig class.

Listing 20-20. Custom WebExceptionHandler Bean

```
package com.apress.prospring6.twenty.boot

import org.springframework.web.server.WebExceptionHandler
// other import statements omitted

@Configuration
open class RoutesConfig {
    ...
    @Bean
    @Order(-2)
    open fun  exceptionHandler():WebExceptionHandler {
        return object : WebExceptionHandler {
            override fun handle(exchange: ServerWebExchange, ex: Throwable): Mono<Void> {
                when(ex) {
                    is SaveException -> {
                        LOGGER.debug("RouterConfig:: handling exception :: ", ex)
                        exchange.response.setStatusCode(HttpStatus.BAD_REQUEST)

                        // marks the response as complete and forbids writing to it
                        return exchange.response.setComplete()
                    }
```

```kotlin
                is IllegalArgumentException -> {
                    LOGGER.debug("RouterConfig:: handling exception :: " , ex)
                    exchange.response.setStatusCode(HttpStatus.BAD_REQUEST)

                    // marks the response as complete and forbids writing to it
                    return exchange.response.setComplete()
                }
                is MissingValueException -> {
                    exchange.response.setStatusCode(HttpStatus.BAD_REQUEST)
                    exchange.response.headers.add("Content-Type", "application/json")
                    try {
                        val message = JsonMapper().writeValueAsString(ex.fieldNames)
                        val buffer = exchange.response.
                            bufferFactory().wrap(message.toByteArray())
                        return exchange.response.writeWith(Flux.just(buffer))
                    } catch (_:JsonProcessingException) {
                    }
                }
            }
        }
        return Mono.error(ex)
        }
      }
    }
    companion object {
        val LOGGER = LoggerFactory.getLogger(RoutesConfig::class.java)
    }
}
```

Note that to ensure that our exception handler is used, we need to give it the highest priority by annotating it with @Order(-2); otherwise, Spring Boot will still use the default handler.

Testing Reactive Endpoints with WebTestClient

To test a reactive endpoint using an actual reactive client, we can use an instance of WebTestClient.

The WebClient API was introduced in Spring 5 to replace the existing RestTemplate client. In Spring 6, you can still use both to submit requests to a Spring application, with the WebClient being preferred for reactive applications since it is part of the spring-webflux package. WebClient can be used for synchronous or asynchronous HTTP requests with a functional fluent API that can integrate directly into your existing Spring configuration and the WebFlux reactive framework.

WebClient can only be used on top of an existing asynchronous HTTP client library. In the chapter20-boot project, this is Reactor Netty, but Jetty Reactive or Apache Reactive HTTP clients are just as good. WebClient can be used to make requests to other reactive services written in any language.

For testing reactive web applications, WebTestClient was introduced as well, as a counterpart for the WebClient used in production. WebTestClient uses WebClient internally to perform requests while also providing a fluent API to verify responses.

In this section we'll use a WebTestClient instance to submit some requests to the APIs built in the previous sections.

Let's start by testing the endpoints backed up by the ReactiveSingerController. Listing 20-21 shows the creation of a WebClient pointing at the root URL http://localhost:8081/reactive/singer and a test that checks that the expected number of records is returned.

Listing 20-21. Test Class Using a WebTestClient Instance

```
package com.apress.prospring6.twenty.boot.webclient

import org.springframework.test.web.reactive.server.WebTestClient
// other import statements omitted

class ReactiveSingerControllerTest {
    private val controllerClient = WebTestClient
        .bindToServer()
        .baseUrl("http://localhost:8081/reactive/singer")
        .build()

    ...
    @Test
    fun shouldReturnAFew() {
        controllerClient.get()
            .uri { uriBuilder: UriBuilder ->
                uriBuilder.queryParam(
                    "name",
                    "John"
                ).build()
            }
            .accept(MediaType.APPLICATION_JSON)
            .exchange()
            .expectStatus().isOk()
            .expectHeader().contentType(MediaType.APPLICATION_JSON)
            .expectBody()
            .jsonPath("$.length()").isEqualTo(2)
    }
    ...

    companion object {
        private val LOGGER = LoggerFactory.getLogger(SingerHandlerTest::class.java)
    }
}
```

There are a few things happening here:

- We create a WebTestClient instance by using the builder returned by WebTestClient.bindToServer(), and we set the base URL for this client to http://localhost:8081/reactive/singer. Obviously, this means that the application must be running for this test to work as intended.

- A GET request is sent to the configured base URL with the name parameter set to "John".

- To send the request, we call exchange().

- To check the result, we use the assertion methods available: expect*(..) to check statuses and headers and jsonPath(..).* to check assumption on the request body, especially when the body is in JSON format.

However, what is interesting to test is a negative scenario—for example, when we try to create another John Mayer, as shown in Listing 20-22.

Listing 20-22. Test Method for a Negative Scenario Using a WebTestClient

```
package com.apress.prospring6.twenty.boot.webclient

import org.springframework.test.web.reactive.server.WebTestClient
// other import statements omitted

class ReactiveSingerControllerTest {
    private val controllerClient = WebTestClient
        .bindToServer()
        .baseUrl("http://localhost:8081/reactive/singer")
        .build()

    ...
    @Test
    fun shouldFailToCreateJohnMayer() {
        controllerClient.post()
            .accept(MediaType.APPLICATION_JSON)
            .bodyValue(
                Singer().apply {
                    firstName = "John"
                    lastName = "Mayer"
                    birthDate = LocalDate.of(1977, 10, 16)
                }
            )
            .exchange()
            .expectStatus().is4xxClientError()
            .expectBody()
            .consumeWith { body: EntityExchangeResult<ByteArray?>? ->
                LOGGER.debug(
                    "body: {}",
                    body
                )
            }
    }
    ...
}
```

The shouldFailToCreateJohnMayer() test will pass, and no Singer instance will be created since there is already a singer with those names. The response HTTP code is 400, as proven by the response details printed in the console, shown in Listing 20-23. The response details include the object that failed validation.

Listing 20-23. Console Log for the shouldFailToCreateJohnMayer() Test

```
DEBUG c.a.p.t.b.w.SingerHandlerTest -- body:
> POST http://localhost:8081/reactive/singer
> accept-encoding: [gzip]
> user-agent: [ReactorNetty/1.1.5]
> host: [localhost:8081]
> WebTestClient-Request-Id: [1]
> Accept: [application/json]
```

```
> Content-Type: [application/json]
> Content-Length: [74]

{
    "id":null,
    "firstName":"John",
    "lastName":"Mayer",
    "birthDate":"1977-10-16"
}

< 400 BAD_REQUEST Bad Request
< content-length: [0]
```

The WebTestClient does not care what type of back-end component generates the response to the request that is sent, which means the tests written in this section pass if the base URL is replaced with http://localhost:8081/handler/singer and the requests are handled by functions in the SingerHandler class.

Reactive Web Layer

Migrating the web layer requires quite a few changes because rendering a view is quite difficult when you do not know how much data is actually being sent to be rendered. In the past, asynchronous JavaScript and XML (AJAX) was used to resolve this problem, but AJAX enables us to update pages only in response to user action on the page. It does not solve the problem of updates coming from the server. Since reactive communication involves data flowing in both directions, new web libraries were needed. There is more than one way to do so, but in this section, we cover the most common way to do so: by using **server-sent events**.

As a very simple example, let's create a page in the singer application to display the list of beans in the application context. In previous chapters, HomeController contained a single handler method that returned a simple String, and we will modify this method to return all the names of the beans in the application context as a Flux<String>.

Thymeleaf supports reactive views, and there is more than one way to populate the model with reactive data. To keep things quick and simple, we'll use the simplest way, in which we use a piece of JavaScript code to slowly populate the view with data coming as a flow. However, before that, we have to configure Thymeleaf for reactive support. Listing 20-24 shows this configuration class, which is a little verbose. Most property values set in it are already set by Spring Boot with their defaults, but the class is written like this to make it obvious what is customizable from a development point of view.

Listing 20-24. The Reactive Thymeleaf Configuration Class

```
package com.apress.prospring6.twenty.boot

import org.springframework.boot.autoconfigure.thymeleaf.ThymeleafProperties
import org.springframework.boot.context.properties.EnableConfigurationProperties
import org.springframework.web.reactive.config.ViewResolverRegistry
import org.springframework.web.reactive.config.WebFluxConfigurer
import org.thymeleaf.spring6.ISpringWebFluxTemplateEngine
import org.thymeleaf.spring6.view.reactive.ThymeleafReactiveViewResolver
// other import statements omitted

@Configuration
```

```
@EnableConfigurationProperties(ThymeleafProperties::class)
open class ReactiveThymeleafWebConfig(
            private val thymeleafTemplateEngine: ISpringWebFluxTemplateEngine) :
      WebFluxConfigurer {
      @Bean
      open fun thymeleafReactiveViewResolver() =
            ThymeleafReactiveViewResolver().apply {
                  templateEngine = thymeleafTemplateEngine
                  order = 1
            }

      override fun configureViewResolvers(registry: ViewResolverRegistry) {
            registry.viewResolver(thymeleafReactiveViewResolver())
      }

      @Bean
      open fun messageSource(): MessageSource =
            ResourceBundleMessageSource().apply {
                  setBasenames("i18n/global")
                  setDefaultEncoding("UTF-8")
            }

      override fun addFormatters(registry: FormatterRegistry) {
          registry.addFormatterForFieldAnnotation(
              DateTimeFormatAnnotationFormatterFactory())
      }
}
```

The template resolver bean that is responsible for resolving templates does not need to be reactive. Since the template resolver bean contains data from the application configuration, when using Spring Boot, it can be dropped altogether and replaced by annotating the configuration class with @EnableConfiguration Properties(ThymeleafProperties.class).

The template engine that uses the template resolver is reactive and is an implementation of ISpringWebFluxTemplateEngine. Therefore, SpringTemplateEngine, designed for integration with the Spring MVC type, must be replaced with SpringWebFluxTemplateEngine, an implementation of the ISpringWebFluxTemplateEngine interface, designed for integration with Spring WebFlux and execution of templates in a reactive-friendly way. Since the template engine requires a template resolver and nothing else, this bean declaration is skipped, Spring Boot is allowed to configure it, and we just inject it in our configuration.

The @EnableConfigurationProperties annotation enables support for Thymeleaf configuration properties. The ThymeleafProperties class is annotated with @ConfigurationProperties (prefix = "spring.thymeleaf"), which makes it a configuration bean for Thymeleaf properties. This means you can use application.yaml or application.properties to configure Thymeleaf. The properties are prefixed with spring.thymeleaf and allow you to configure the template resolver bean without writing additional code. The Spring Boot Thymeleaf configuration properties are depicted in Listing 20-25.

Listing 20-25. Spring Boot Thymeleaf Configuration

```
spring:
  thymeleaf:
    prefix: classpath:templates/
    suffix: .html
```

```
mode: HTML
cache: false
check-template: false
reactive:
  max-chunk-size: 8192
```

The ThymeleafReactiveViewResolver is an implementation of the org.springframework.web.reactive.result.view.ViewResolver interface, the Spring WebFlux view resolver interface. The responseMaxChunkSizeBytes is the one you should be interested in, because it defines the maximum size for the output org.springframework.core.io.buffer.DataBuffer instances produced by the Thymeleaf engine and passed to the server as output. This is important because if you have a lot of data being sent through a Flux<T>, you might want to render the view in chunks, bit by bit, instead of keeping a web page in a loading state, until the response is complete (especially because this is one of the main ideas of reactive communication).

Now, let's talk about our controller. Since HomeController needs to be annotated with @RestController, because its handler method returns a reactive stream of data, we need another way to return the logical view name. Surprisingly, we can use a handler function for this. First, let's look at HomeController, depicted in Listing 20-26.

Listing 20-26. The Reactive HomeController Class

```
package com.apress.prospring6.twenty.boot.controller
// import statements omitted

@RestController
class HomeController : ApplicationContextAware {
    private var ctx: ApplicationContext? = null

    @Throws(BeansException::class)
    override fun setApplicationContext(applicationContext: ApplicationContext) {
        ctx = applicationContext
    }

    @RequestMapping(
        value = ["/beans"],
        produces = [MediaType.TEXT_EVENT_STREAM_VALUE]
    )
    @ResponseBody
    fun getBeanNames(): Flux<String> {
        // The response payload for this request will be rendered in JSON get() {
        val beans = ctx!!.beanDefinitionNames.sorted()
        return Flux.fromIterable(beans).delayElements(java.time.Duration.ofMillis(200))
    }
}
```

Notice the MediaType.TEXT_EVENT_STREAM_VALUE, which is a constant with the text/event-stream. This is the MIME type specific to a simple stream of text data that the server sends to the client when a GET request is sent to this URL: http://localhost:8081/beans.

Messages in the event stream are separated by a pair of newline characters. A colon as the first character of a line is in essence a comment and is ignored.

When the application is started, you can test whether the method returns a flux of bean names by running a simple `curl` command. The command and a few events from the stream are shown in Listing 20-27.

Listing 20-27. Data Stream Returned by GET Request to `http://localhost:8081/beans`

```
> curl -H "Accept:text/event-stream" http://localhost:8081/beans
data:applicationAvailability

data:applicationTaskExecutor

data:chapter20Application

data:clientConnectorCustomizer

data:connectionFactory

data:data-r2dbc.repository-aot-processor#0
// the rest of the stream events omitted
```

Thymeleaf generates three types of server-sent events (SSEs):

- *Header*: The data is prefixed by `head:` or `{prefix_}head`. Used for a single event during the communication containing all the markup previous to the iterated data (if any). Example: *When you are reading a Facebook thread, the moment you open the page, all the comments that exist in the database, previous to the timestamp when you opened that page, should already be rendered in the page. There is no point to render them one by one. Thymeleaf supports this type of initializing event.*

- *Data message*: The data is prefixed by `message:` or `{prefix_}message`. Used for a series of events, one for each value produced by the data driver. Example: *When you are reading a Facebook thread, comments from other users that are being posted while you are viewing the page just appear in the comment section, one by one. Data from the comment would be sent to the client through an SSE of type message.*

- *Tail*: The data is prefixed by `tail:` or `{prefix_}tail`. Used for a single event during the communication containing all the markup following the iterated data (if any). Example: *Assuming Facebook had an option though which the user could choose to stop seeing new comments, an event of this type could be used to send all the comments exiting in the database with a timestamp value between the last displayed comment and the timestamp when the user chose to stop seeing new comments.*

❗ The `prefix` value cat be set via the `org.thymeleaf.spring6.context.webflux.ReactiveDataDriverContextVariable` constructor when a reactive stream is wrapped in it and the variable is added as an attribute to a Thymeleaf reactive view. The prefix is really useful when more than one SSE source is used on the same web page, because it helps separate the server-sent events in categories, so the data can be displayed in different parts of the page. This, however, is a complex scenario that we won't cover in this section.

The /beans URL is used as a source for a stream of SSEs. An EventSource instance is created using the URL, and it opens a persistent connection through which the server sends events in text/event-stream format. The connection remains open until closed by calling EventSource.close(). The events are marked as message events by Spring WebFlux, and an EventListener instance is set on the EventSource instance to intercept those events, extract the data, and add it to the HTML page.

The bean names stream was intentionally slowed down by calling the delayElements(Duration.ofMillis(200)) on the resulting Flux<String> to show the continuous communication. If you use Chrome or Firefox, when loading the page, you can see the events being sent by the server in the developer console. Just remove the comment from the console.log(event) statement from the body of the EventListener instance shown in the home.html template snippet (HTML and JavaScript) depicted in Listing 20-28.

Listing 20-28. Thymeleaf Template Snippet (from home.html) Used to Display the Bean Names Received As Server-Sent Events

```html
<section th:fragment="~{templates/layout :: pageContent}">
    <script type="text/javascript" th:inline="javascript">
        /*<![CDATA[*/
        $(window).on( "load", function() {
            renderBeans.start();
        });
        $(window).on( "onbeforeunload", function() {
            renderBeans.stop();
        });
        let renderBeans = {
            source: new EventSource(/*[[@{/beans}]]*/) ,
            start: function () {
                this.source.addEventListener("message", function (event) {
                    //console.log(event);
                    $("#beans").append('<li>'+ event.data +'</li>')
                });
                this.source.onerror = function () {
                    this.source.close();
                };
            },
            stop: function() {
                this.source.close();
            }
        };
        /*]]>*/
    </script>
    <div class="card border-success mb-3" style="max-width: 40rem; left:30px;">
        <div class="card-header"> Reactive Application Beans: </div>
        <div class="row mb-1 m-sm-1">
            <div class="scrollable">
                <ul id="beans">
                </ul>
            </div>
        </div>
    </div>
</section>
```

The /*[[@{|/beans|}]]*/ is a Thymeleaf link expression used to generate a URL relative to the application context. It looks weird, but all those symbols make sure that it is not interpreted like something else, and that it results in valid JavaScript code.

In Listing 20-28, the jQuery library is used to write the JavaScript code required to handle server-sent events. The SSEs are a server push technology enabling a client to receive automatic updates from a server via an HTTP connection. This means that the page is rendered, but the connection is kept open, so the server can send more data to the client. The server-sent events EventSource API is standardized as part of HTML5.

In Figure 20-6, the main page of the singers application is opened in Firefox, and you can see the stream of data being sent from the server in the developer console.

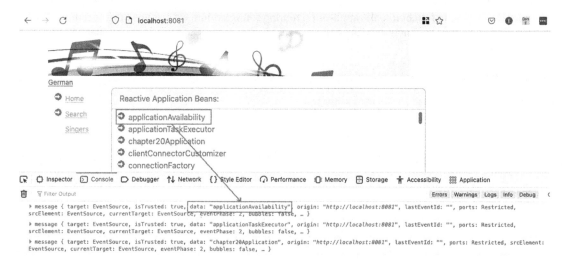

Figure 20-6. *Server-sent events displayed in Firefox's developer console*

There is one piece left that is missing: the mapping between the /home URL path and the home.html view. It was mentioned at the beginning of this section that this can be done by using a handler function and a routing function. Listing 20-29 shows the handler function for rendering the view template with the home name.

Listing 20-29. Handler Function for Mapping Returning a Logical View Name

```
package com.apress.prospring6.twenty.boot.handler

import org.springframework.http.MediaType
import org.springframework.stereotype.Component
import org.springframework.web.reactive.function.server.ServerRequest
import org.springframework.web.reactive.function.server.ServerResponse
import reactor.core.publisher.Mono

@Component
class HomeHandler {
    fun view(request: ServerRequest): Mono<ServerResponse> {
```

```
            return ServerResponse
                    .ok()
                    .contentType(MediaType.TEXT_HTML)
                    .render("home")
    }
}
```

The render(..) method has two versions. The one used in Listing 20-29 that just takes the logical view name as an argument is declared with var-args for the model attributes, in case there are any: render(String name, Object... modelAttributes). In the other version, the second argument is a Map<String, ?> representing the model used to render the template.

To add this handler function to the application routing configuration, we just need to inject the HomeHandler in the routing function bean configured in this chapter and add a GET(..) routing function, as shown in Listing 20-30.

Listing 20-30. Router Function Including the HomeHandler::view Handler Function

```
package com.apress.prospring6.twenty.boot
// import statements omitted

@Configuration
open class RoutesConfig {

    @Bean
    open fun singerRoutes( homeHandler:HomeHandler,
            singerHandler:SingerHandler):RouterFunction<ServerResponse> {
        return route()
                // returns home view template
                .GET("/", homeHandler::view)
                .GET("/home", homeHandler::view)
                .GET("/singers/search", singerHandler::searchView)
                .POST("/singers/go", singerHandler::search)
                // these need to be here, otherwise parameters will not be considered
                .GET("/handler/singer", queryParam("name", {_ -> true}),
                    singerHandler::searchSingers)
                .GET("/handler/singer", RequestPredicates.all()
                        .and(queryParam("fn", {_ -> true}))
                        .and(queryParam("ln", {_ -> true})), singerHandler::searchSinger)
                // requests with parameters always come first
                .GET("/handler/singer", singerHandler.list)
                .POST("/handler/singer", singerHandler::create)
                .GET("/handler/singer/{id}", singerHandler::findById)
                .PUT("/handler/singer/{id}", singerHandler::updateById)
                .DELETE("/handler/singer/{id}", singerHandler.deleteById)
                .filter { request, next ->
                    LOGGER.info("Before handler invocation: {}", request.path())
                    return@filter next.handle(request)
                }
            .build()
    }
    ...
}
```

Another interesting tidbit to know when writing Spring reactive web applications is that you can isolate the routing configuration for the static resources in a different routing function created with the `RouterFunctions.resources(..)` method. This method routes requests that match the given pattern to resources relative to the given root location, which is useful to skip the static resources from additional filtering that applies only to dynamic resources.

An example of `RouterFunction<ServerResponse>` for static resources is shown in Listing 20-31.

Listing 20-31. RouterFunction<ServerResponse> for Static Resources

```
package com.apress.prospring6.twenty.boot
import org.springframework.web.reactive.function.server.RouterFunction
import org.springframework.web.reactive.function.server.RouterFunctions.resources
// other import statements omitted

@Configuration
open class RoutesConfig {
    @Bean
    open fun staticRouter():RouterFunction<ServerResponse> {
        return resources("/images/**", ClassPathResource("static/images/"))
                .and(resources("/styles/**", ClassPathResource("static/styles/")))
                .and(resources("/js/**", ClassPathResource("static/js/")));
    }
    ...
}
```

Note that `RouterFunction<ServerResponse>` can be composed using the `and(.)` method. The resulting router function is a composed routing function that first invokes the first function, and then invokes the other function if this route has no result, and so on.

Handler Functions Validation

A functional endpoint can use Spring's validation facilities to apply validation to the request body. To explain how validation works, we'll add a criteria object that allows the user to specify the filter for a database query. This criteria object is used in the service to decide which query repo to execute.

The `CriteriaDto` class is added to the `SingerService` interface because it is only used in the context of this service and thus is very strongly related to it. Since we are working with data provided by the user, a validator class is needed as well. These two classes and the method skeleton for the service method using the `CriteriaDto` as an argument are shown in Listing 20-32.

Listing 20-32. CriteriaDto Object and CriteriaValidator Classes

```
package com.apress.prospring6.twenty.boot.service

import org.springframework.validation.Errors
import org.springframework.validation.ValidationUtils
import org.springframework.validation.Validator
// other import statements omitted

interface SingerService {
    fun findByCriteriaDto(criteria: CriteriaDto): Flux<Singer>
    ...
```

```kotlin
class CriteriaDto {
    var fieldName: String? = null
    var fieldValue: String? = null
}

class CriteriaValidator : Validator {
    override fun supports(clazz: Class<*>): Boolean {
        return CriteriaDto::class.java.isAssignableFrom(clazz)
    }

    override fun validate(target: Any, errors: Errors) {
        ValidationUtils.rejectIfEmpty(
            errors,
            "fieldName",
            "required",
            arrayOf<Any>("fieldName"),
            "Field Name is required!"
        )
        ValidationUtils.rejectIfEmpty(
            errors,
            "fieldValue",
            "required",
            arrayOf<Any>("fieldValue"),
            "Field Value is required!"
        )
    }
}

enum class FieldGroup {
    FIRSTNAME,
    LASTNAME,
    BIRTHDATE;

    companion object {
        fun getField(field: String): FieldGroup {
            return valueOf(field.uppercase(Locale.getDefault()))
        }
    }
}
}
```

Instances of this class are used to hold search criteria for a form object. For these instances to be valid, both fields must be present, and the validator checks these instances.

The FieldGroup enum is added to easily select the column based on which the filtering is done. Listing 20-33 shows the implementation of the findByCriteriaDto(..) method.

Listing 20-33. SingerServiceImpl#findByCriteriaDto(..) Implementation

package com.apress.prospring6.twenty.boot.service
// *import statements omitted*

```kotlin
@Transactional
@Service
open class SingerServiceImpl : SingerService {
    private val singerRepo: SingerRepo? = null
    ...
    override fun findByCriteriaDto(criteria: SingerService.CriteriaDto): Flux<Singer> {
        val fieldName = SingerService.FieldGroup.getField(criteria.fieldName!!.uppercase())
        return when (fieldName) {
            SingerService.FieldGroup.FIRSTNAME ->
                if ("*" == criteria.fieldValue) singerRepo!!.findAll()
                else singerRepo!!.findByFirstName(
                criteria.fieldValue!!
            )

            SingerService.FieldGroup.LASTNAME ->
                if ("*" == criteria.fieldValue) singerRepo!!.findAll()
                else singerRepo!!.findByLastName(
                criteria.fieldValue!!
            )

            SingerService.FieldGroup.BIRTHDATE ->
                if ("*" == criteria.fieldValue) singerRepo!!.findAll()
                else singerRepo!!.findByBirthDate(
                LocalDate.parse(criteria.fieldValue!!,
                    DateTimeFormatter.ofPattern("yyyy-MM-dd"))
            )
        }
    }
    ...
}
```

Just for fun, the possibility to select all the entries is added - just let the field value read *.

The findByCriteriaDto(..) method is invoked by a handler function in SingerHandler, which is shown in Listing 20-34.

Listing 20-34. Handler Function That Invokes the findByCriteriaDto(..) Service Method

package com.apress.prospring6.twenty.boot.handler

import org.springframework.validation.BeanPropertyBindingResult
// *import statements omitted*

```kotlin
@Component
class SingerHandler(private val singerService: SingerService) {
    ...
    fun search(serverRequest: ServerRequest): Mono<ServerResponse> {
```

```
        val criteriaMono = serverRequest.bodyToMono(
            SingerService.CriteriaDto::class.java
        )
        return criteriaMono.log()
            .flatMap<SingerService.CriteriaDto?> { criteria: SingerService.CriteriaDto ->
                validate(
                    criteria
                )
            }
            .flatMap { criteria: SingerService.CriteriaDto ->
                ServerResponse.ok()
                    .contentType(MediaType.APPLICATION_JSON)
                    .body(
                        singerService.findByCriteriaDto(criteria),
                        Singer::class.java
                    )
            }
    }

    private fun validate(criteria: SingerService.CriteriaDto):
            Mono<SingerService.CriteriaDto?> {
        val validator = SingerService.CriteriaValidator()
        val errors = BeanPropertyBindingResult(criteria, "criteria")
        validator.validate(criteria, errors)
        if (errors.hasErrors()) {
            // throw new ServerWebInputException(errors.toString());
            throw MissingValueException.of(errors.allErrors)
        }
        return Mono.just(criteria)
    }
    ...
}
```

Notice the validate(..) method, which is used as a processor in a reactive chain. For this simple example, the CriteriaValidator is instantiated in this method; in bigger applications where a validator is used in multiple handler function, you might want to declare it as a bean. If the validator. validate(criteria, errors) populates the errors object, a MissingValueException is created with the name of the fields that are missing and the error messages. The MissingValueException is a custom exception type, with a simple builder that allows converting the validation errors in representations that can be shown in the interface.

Listing 20-35 shows this custom exception type.

Listing 20-35. The MissingValueException Custom Exception Type

package com.apress.prospring6.twenty.boot.problem

import org.springframework.validation.FieldError
import org.springframework.validation.ObjectError
// some import statements omitted

```
class MissingValueException : RuntimeException {
        var fieldNames: Map<String, String> = mutableMapOf()
                private set

        constructor(message: String?, fieldNames: Map<String, String>) : super(message) {
                this.fieldNames = fieldNames
        }

        constructor(message: String?, cause: Throwable?, fieldNames: Map<String, String>) :
        super(message, cause) {
                this.fieldNames = fieldNames
        }

        companion object {
                fun of(errors: List<ObjectError>): MissingValueException {
                        val fields: List<String> = ArrayList()
                        val fieldNames = HashMap<String, String>()
                        errors.forEach(Consumer { err: ObjectError ->
                                fieldNames[(err as FieldError).field] = err.
                                getDefaultMessage()!!
                        })
                        return MissingValueException("Some values are missing!", fieldNames)
                }
        }
}
```

The next step is to also add a method in `SingerHandler` to render the search view, as shown in Listing 20-36.

Listing 20-36. The `SingerHandler.searchView()` Handler Function to Render the Thymeleaf Search View

```
package com.apress.prospring6.twenty.boot.handler
// import statements omitted

@Component
class SingerHandler(private val singerService: SingerService) {
    ...
    fun searchView(request: ServerRequest?): Mono<ServerResponse> {
        return ServerResponse
            .ok()
            .contentType(MediaType.TEXT_HTML)
            .render("singers/search", SingerService.CriteriaDto())
    }
}
```

Now, before designing the view template, we need to add the routing for the two new handler functions to the `singerRoutes` routing function introduced in Listing 20-19. We also need to add a new section in the `WebExceptionHandler` to handle the `MissingValueException`.

Listing 20-37 shows the minimal configuration of the `singerRoutes` routing function, with the two mappings and the new `WebExceptionHandler` bean that includes a block for handling the `MissingValueException`.

Listing 20-37. Minimal Configuration for a Routing Function

```kotlin
package com.apress.prospring6.twenty.boot
// import statements omitted

@Configuration
open class RoutesConfig {
    ...
    @Bean
    open fun singerRoutes( homeHandler:HomeHandler,
            singerHandler:SingerHandler):RouterFunction<ServerResponse> {
        return route()
                // returns home view template
                .GET("/", homeHandler::view)
                .GET("/home", homeHandler::view)
                .GET("/singers/search", singerHandler::searchView)
                .POST("/singers/go", singerHandler::search)
                // these need to be here, otherwise parameters will not be considered
                .GET("/handler/singer", queryParam("name", {_ -> true}),
                    singerHandler::searchSingers)
                .GET("/handler/singer", RequestPredicates.all()
                        .and(queryParam("fn", {_ -> true}))
                        .and(queryParam("ln", {_ -> true})), singerHandler::searchSinger)
                // requests with parameters always come first
                .GET("/handler/singer", singerHandler.list)
                .POST("/handler/singer", singerHandler::create)
                .GET("/handler/singer/{id}", singerHandler::findById)
                .PUT("/handler/singer/{id}", singerHandler::updateById)
                .DELETE("/handler/singer/{id}", singerHandler.deleteById)
                .filter { request, next ->
                    LOGGER.info("Before handler invocation: {}", request.path())
                    return@filter next.handle(request)
                }
            .build()
    }

    @Bean
    @Order(-2)
    open fun  exceptionHandler():WebExceptionHandler {
        return object : WebExceptionHandler {
            override fun handle(exchange: ServerWebExchange, ex: Throwable): Mono<Void> {
                when(ex) {
                    is SaveException -> {
                        LOGGER.debug("RouterConfig:: handling exception :: ", ex)
                        exchange.response.setStatusCode(HttpStatus.BAD_REQUEST)

                        // marks the response as complete and forbids writing to it
                        return exchange.response.setComplete()
                    }
```

```
            is IllegalArgumentException -> {
                LOGGER.debug("RouterConfig:: handling exception :: " , ex)
                exchange.response.setStatusCode(HttpStatus.BAD_REQUEST)

                // marks the response as complete and forbids writing to it
                return exchange.response.setComplete()
            }
            is MissingValueException -> {
                exchange.response.setStatusCode(HttpStatus.BAD_REQUEST)
                exchange.response.headers.add("Content-Type", "application/json")
                try {
                    val message = JsonMapper().writeValueAsString(ex.fieldNames)
                    val buffer = exchange.response.bufferFactory().
                        wrap(message.toByteArray())
                    return exchange.response.writeWith(Flux.just(buffer))
                } catch (_:JsonProcessingException) {
                }
            }
        }
        return Mono.error(ex)
    }
  }
}
    companion object {
        val LOGGER = LoggerFactory.getLogger(RoutesConfig::class.java)
    }
}
```

Now we have everything that we need but the view. The singers/search.html view needs to have a dynamic section where a table is built with the results of the search, a dynamic section that is displayed only when there are errors, and the JavaScript code that populates these elements.

The main section of the search.html view template is shown in Listing 20-38.

Listing 20-38. The Main Section of the singers/search.html View

```
<section th:fragment="~{templates/layout :: pageContent}">
    <div class="content">  <!-- content -->
        <h4 th:text="#{command.search} + ' ' + #{singer.title}">SEARCH</h4>

        <div class="container col-lg-12">
            <form action="#" th:action="@{/singers/go}" name="search"
            th:object="${criteriaDto}" method="post" class="col p-4" id="singerSearchForm">

                <div class="row mb-1">
                    <label for="fieldName" th:text="#{label.Criteria.fieldname} + ':'"
                    class="col-sm-4 form-label">FN:</label>
                    <div class="col-sm-8">
                        <select th:field="*{fieldName}" class="form-select">
                            <option th:value="firstName" th:text="#{label.Singer.
                            firstname}">FN</option>
                            <option th:value="lastName" th:text="#{label.Singer.
                            lastname}">LN</option>
```

909

```html
                <option th:value="birthDate" th:text="#{label.Singer.
                    birthDate}">BD</option>
            </select>
        </div>
    </div>

    <div class="row mb-1">
        <label for="fieldValue" th:text="#{label.Criteria.fieldvalue} + ':'"
        class="col-sm-4 form-label"></label>
        <div class="col-sm-8">
            <div>
                <input type="text" th:field="*{fieldValue}" class="form-
                control"/>
                <small th:text="#{label.dateFormat.accepted}" class="text-
                mutes">ACC</small></div>
        </div>
    </div>

    <div class="bs-component mb-1">
        <input type="submit" th:value="#{command.search}" id="searchButton"
        class="btn btn-dark"/>
        <div class="col-sm-8">
            <small id="errMessage"></small>
        </div>
    </div>
</form>
<script th:inline="javascript">
    /*<![CDATA[*/
    $( window ).on( "load", function() {
        $('#errMessage').hide();
        $('#singerSearchResults').hide();
    });
    function renderSearchResults(singers) {
        $('#errMessage').empty()
        $('#errMessage').hide();
        let content = '';
        let baseDetailUrl = /*[[@{/singers/}]]*/ '/singers';
        for (let i = 0; i < singers.length; i++) {
            content += '<tr>';
            content += '<td><a href="'+ baseDetailUrl + singers[i].
            id+'">'+singers[i].id+'</a></td>';
            content += '<td>'+singers[i].firstName+'</td>';
            content += '<td>'+singers[i].lastName+'</td>';
        }
        $('#singerSearchResults tbody').html(content);
        if(content !== '') {
            $('#singerSearchResults').show();
        } else {
            $('#singerSearchResults').hide();
        }
    }
```

```
$('#singerSearchForm').submit(function(evt){
    evt.preventDefault();
    let fieldName = $('#fieldName').val();
    let fieldValue = $('#fieldValue').val();
    let json = { "fieldName" : fieldName, "fieldValue" : fieldValue};

    $.ajax({
        url: $('#singerSearchForm')[0].action,
        type: 'POST',
        dataType: 'json',
        contentType: 'application/json',
        data: JSON.stringify(json),
        success: function(responseData) { renderSearchResults(respon
        seData);},
        error: function(e) {
            let jsonData = e.responseJSON;
            for(let i in jsonData) {
                let key = i;
                let val = jsonData[i];
                $('#errMessage').append("<p class=\"error\">"+ val +"</p>");
            }
            $('#errMessage').show();
        }
    });
})
/*]]>*/
</script>
<table id="singerSearchResults" class="table table-hover">
    <thead>
    <tr>
        <th th:text="#{label.Singer.count}" class="table-success">COUNT</th>
        <th th:text="#{label.Singer.firstname}" class="table-
        success">FIRSTNAME</th>
        <th th:text="#{label.Singer.lastname}" class="table-
        success">LASTNAME</th>
    </tr>
    </thead>
    <tbody>
        <th:block th:each="singer : ${singers}">
            <td><a th:href="@{/singer/} + ${singer.id}" th:text="${singer.
            id}">ID</a></td>
            <td th:text="${singer.firstName}">...</td>
            <td th:text="${singer.lastName}">...</td>
        </th:block>
    </tbody>
</table>
        </div>
    </div> <!-- content -->
</section>
```

The JavaScript code looks a lot like the code written to display the bean names, with the exception that this time column rows are being written and there is also an `error` section for the `$.ajax(..)` that is responsible for showing the validation error messages received from the server.

Figure 20-7 shows the Search Singer Details page with a validation error message being displayed after a request was sent without providing a value for the search.

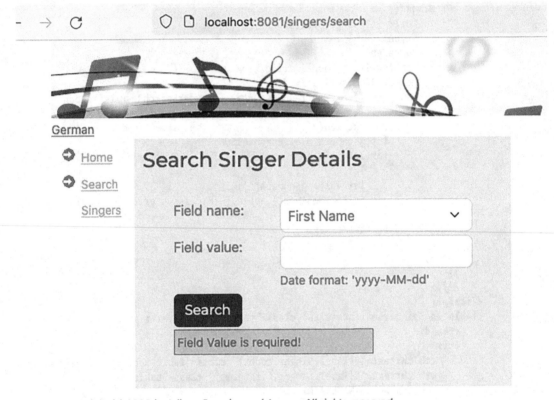

Figure 20-7. *Search Singer Details page with a validation error message*

Building Spring reactive applications is a vast subject, beyond the introductory scope of this chapter. If you are interested in building Spring reactive applications, take a look at the other resources referenced in this chapter and Josh Long's *Reactive Spring*, published on Leanpub and last updated in September 2022[31].

---

[31] https://leanpub.com/reactive-spring

Summary

This chapter gave you an insight into what is important when building a reactive Spring WebFlux application. We covered a few details regarding migrating multilayered applications to underline the fact that a reactive application is fully reactive only if all its components are reactive. To help you make the change from Spring Web MVC to WebFlux, we provided comparisons between configurations for the two technologies.

We also described using reactive controllers and handler functions. We then looked into testing reactive repositories and services and consuming reactive services using `WebTestClient` for testing purposes.

There are a few things to take away from this chapter. Spring WebFlux code is cleaner and more concise. Spring Boot provides so many components out of the box that it allows you to dedicate more time to development and spend less time on configuration. Error handling is easier to implement, and code is easier to read. However, not all components must be reactive. When all you have is a simple page to render to the user, there is no need to render it using a reactive component.

Index

■ B

U

V

W

X, Y

Z

Printed in the United States
by Baker & Taylor Publisher Services